THE BRITISH BOXING BOARD OF CONTROL

★ ★

BOXING YEARBOOK

★ ★ 2009 ★ ★

Edited by Barry J. Hugman

MAINSTREAM
PUBLISHING

EDINBURGH AND LONDON

First published in Great Britain in 2008 by
MAINSTREAM PUBLISHING COMPANY
(EDINBURGH) LTD
7 Albany Street
Edinburgh EH1 3UG

ISBN 9781845963255

A catalogue record for this book is available
from the British Library

Typeset and designed by
Typecast (Artwork & Design)

Printed in the UK by CPI William Clowes Beccles NR34 7TL

Contents

C000201913

TARA BOXING PROMOTIONS & MANAGEMENT

Doughty's Gym
Princess Road, Shaw, Oldham OL2 7AZ
Tel/Fax: 01706-845753 (Office)
Mobile: 07932-085865
Tel: 01706-846762 (Gym)

Trainers: JACK DOUGHTY & GARY FORD
Matchmaker: JOHN INGLE
MC: MICHAEL PASS / MIKE GOODALL

Acknowledgements

Now in its 25th year (the Silver Anniversary) this publication has always been very much a team effort, with many of the original members still participating, and I would like to thank all those who continue to help establish the *British Boxing Yearbook* as the '*Wisden*' of British boxing.

As in previous years, I am indebted to the BBBoC's General Secretary, Simon Block, along with Lynne Conway, Helen Oakley, Donna Streeter and Sarah Aldridge, for their help and support in placing information at my disposal and being of assistance when required. Simon's assistant, Robert Smith, who is also the Southern, Western and Welsh Area Secretary and a former pro fighter of note, was again extremely helpful, as were Dai Corp and John Carey.

On a business front, I would like to thank the BBBoC for their support and Bernard Hart, the Managing Director of the Lonsdale International Sporting Club, for his efforts in helping to organise the annual British Boxing Board of Control Awards Luncheon where the book will be officially launched. The Awards Luncheon or Dinner has been an ongoing function since 1984, when it was established as a vehicle to launch the first *Yearbook*. Following that, Bernard, ably backed up by Kymberley and Chas Taylor, helps to make sure that the standard remains top class. At the same time, I would like to thank all of those who advertised within these pages for their support.

Members of the *Yearbook* 'team' who wrote articles for this year's edition and who have recently been published, or are in the process of publishing their own books are: John Jarrett (having launched *Champ in the Corner: The Ray Arcel Story*, published by Tempus last year, John is currently working on a book about Mickey Walker, 'The Toy Bulldog'); Ralph Oates (as a boxing quiz book specialist, Ralph's latest book, *The Muhammad Ali Boxing Quiz Book*, is now on sale. He is also working on another book that will be titled *Aspects of Heavyweight Boxing*); Tracey Pollard (continues to work on a book about the life and times of Brian London, the former British heavyweight champion); Keith Robinson (has recently published *Lanky Bob: The Life, Times and Contemporaries of Bob Fitzsimmons*); Tony Gee (who has published the acclaimed *Up to Scratch* and is working on a book about the Scottish prize-ring); Bob Lonkhurst (the author of excellent biographies on Tommy Farr, Jack Petersen, Terry Spinks and Dave 'Boy' Green); and Wynford Jones (who has recently published *Benny's Boys: The Stable of Benny Jacobs*).

Once again, Wynford, a Class 'A' referee and a big supporter of boxing, came to my aid when travelling to the Board's offices on a regular basis in order to collate vital data required for this publication. Other members of the *Yearbook* 'team' are Bob Yalen, who has covered boxing with ABC across the world and looks after the 'World Title Bouts" section; Harold Alderman, an unsung hero who has spent over 40 years researching the early days of boxing through to modern times, Eric Armit, the Chairman of the Commonwealth Boxing Council and a leading authority on boxers' records throughout the world, is responsible for the 'A-Z of Current World Champions'; Derek O'Dell, a former amateur boxer and the former Chairman of Croydon EBA, produces the 'Obituaries" section; Edwin G. Hayman contributed the 'Unlikely British Champion' article; and Ray Caulfield, who is one of the leading lights of the London EBA and a driving force of the EBA movement as a whole, keeps the 'Directory of Ex-Boxers' Associations' up to date.

Regarding photographs, as in previous years many were produced by Les Clark (Les also puts together 'A Boxing Quiz with a Few Below the Belt' within these pages), who has possibly the largest library of both action shots and poses from British rings over the last 20 years or more. If anyone requires a copy of a photo that has appeared in the *Yearbook* credited to Les, or requires a list, he can be reached at 352 Trelawney Avenue, Langley, Berks SL3 7TS. Unfortunately, Les has been incapacitated recently with the loss of a leg, but bravely struggles on and is determined to get back at ringside as quickly as possible. We wish him well. With Les out of action towards the end of last year, Philip Sharkey came to the aid of the *Yearbook* when getting to as many shows as he could in the time left to make sure that the complement of illustrations was up to its normal standard. Philip also produced 'Glove Story', which reviews boxing books published during the season. Other photos were supplied by my good friend Larry Braysher, a well-known collector, who provided several illustrations for his article on Pedlar Palmer, as well as pictures for the 'Obituaries', 'World Champions Since Gloves' and several articles.

Also, additional input came from Michael Featherstone (who is always available to help out on birth/death details); Mrs Enza Jacoponi, the Secretary of the European Boxing Union (EBU Championship data covering the past 12 months); Simon Block (Commonwealth and British Championship data); Robert Smith, John Jarrett, Ken Morton and Les Potts (Area Championship data); Patrick Myler (Irish amateur boxing); Malcolm Collins (Welsh amateur boxing); Brian Donald (Scottish amateur boxing); Hannah McLafferty, Matthew Bozeat and Peter Foley (English Amateur Boxing). I must also make mention of John Sheppard, of BoxRec.Com, who kindly delivered the update for the 'Active British-Based Boxers: Career Records" section in the correct order for me to start my audit. John and his contributors also kept me informed of many old fighters who passed away during the season.

Almost last, but not least, my thanks go to Paul and Katy Bastin, who took over the typesetting from Jean Bastin, Paul's mother, who sadly passed away before work on the *Yearbook* got underway. As in previous years, my wife, Jennifer, looked after the proof reading. It goes without saying that without their input the book would not be the product it is.

EVANS-WATERMAN PROMOTIONS LTD
Licensed to the British Boxing Board of Control
88 WINDSOR ROAD, MAIDENHEAD, BERKS SL6 2DJ
Tel: 01628 623640   Fax: 01628 684633
Mobile: 07768 954643
e-mail: boxevans@yahoo.co.uk

CURRENT LIST

HEAVYWEIGHTS	Rounds			Rounds
Roman Greenberg	- 10 or 12	George Katsimpas	-	6 or 8 or 10
Michael Sprott	- 10 or 12	Danny Maka	-	4 or 6
Luke Simpkin	- 6 or 8	Gary Dawson	-	4 or 6
Ali Adams	- 4 or 6			
		LIGHT-MIDDLEWEIGHT		
CRUISERWEIGHT		Mark Douglas	-	4 or 6
Nick 'The Ox' Okoth	- 6 or 8			
		WELTERWEIGHT		
LIGHT-HEAVYWEIGHT		Patrick Doherty	-	4 or 6
Michael Banbula	- 4 or 6			
		LIGHT-WELTERWEIGHT		
SUPER-MIDDLEWEIGHT		Mark McCullough	-	6 or 8
Anthony Young	- 6 or 8			
		LIGHTWEIGHTS		
MIDDLEWEIGHTS		Shane Watson	-	6 or 8
Ozzy Adams	- 8 or 10	Ibrar Riyaz	-	4 or 6
Carl Drake	- 6 or 8 or 10			

WEST LONDON'S FINEST RISING STABLE
Trainers: Dave Laxen; Darren Whitman; Steve Bernath; Graham Stevenson; Les Southey
EVANS-WATERMAN PROMOTIONS LTD is a member of the P.B.P.A.

Introduction

by Barry J. Hugman

It gives me great pleasure to welcome you to the 25th edition of the *British Boxing Yearbook*. The format has not changed too much over the years, certainly not since the 1993 edition, as myself and the team continue to monitor and update the current goings on, while also continuing to research the past and pass on our findings.

Beginning with the modern era, once again we have decided to stay with the way we produce Active British Based-Boxers: Complete Records. The decision to have one alphabet, instead of separating champions, being taken on the grounds that because there are so many champions these days – British, Commonwealth, European, IBF, WBA, WBC, WBO, and more recently WBU, IBO, WBF, etc, etc, and a whole host of Inter-Continental and International titles – it would cause confusion rather than what was really intended. If you wish to quickly locate whether or not a boxer fought during the past season (1 July 2007 to 30 June 2008) then the Boxers' Record Index at the back of the book is the place to look. Also, as in the very first edition, we chart the promotions in Britain throughout the season, thus enabling one to refer to the exact venue within a boxer's record.

Regarding our records, if a fighter is counted out standing up we have continued to show it as a stoppage rather than that of a kayo or technical kayo, as in fights where the referee dispenses with the count. Thus fights are recorded as count outs (the count being tolled with the fighter still on the canvas), retirements (where a fighter is retired on his stool) and referee stopped contest. Of course, other types of decisions would take in draws, no contests, and no decisions. In these days of health and safety fears, more and more boxers are being counted out either standing up or when initially floored, especially when a referee feels that the man on the receiving end is unable to defend himself adequately or requires immediate medical attention. One of the reasons that we have yet to discriminate between cut-eye stoppages and other types of finishes, is because a fighter who is stopped because of cuts is often on his way to a defeat in the first place. Thus, if you want to get a true reflection on the fight it is probably better to consult the trade paper, *Boxing News*, rather than rely on a referee's decision to tell you all you want to know; the recorded result merely being a guide.

Continuing the trend, there are always new articles to match the old favourites. Regular features such as Home and Away with British Boxers (John Jarrett), World Title Bouts During the Season (Bob Yalen), A-Z of Current World Champions (Eric Armit), Directory of Ex-Boxers' Associations (Ray Caulfield), Obituaries (Derek O'Dell) and two regular quizzes (Ralph Oates and Les Clark), etc, being supported this year with interesting articles such as South Coast Saviour: An Appreciation of Jack Bishop (Bob Lonkhurst); Triumph over Tragedy: The legacy of Shannon's Gym (Tracey Pollard); The Unlikely British Champion (Edwin G. Hayman); Glove Story: A Review of British Boxing Books in 2007-2008 (Philip Sharkey); Malcolm Collins: A Man of Class (Ralph Oates); Dick Richardson: The Maesglas Marciano (Wynford Jones); Pedlar Palmer: The Box o' Tricks (Larry Braysher); Con O'Kelly: The First White Hope? (Keith R. Robinson); The Demise of the (Bareknuckle) Traditional Prize-ring in Britain: A Brief Look at some Pertinent Causes (Tony Gee).

Elsewhere, hopefully, you will find all you want to know about British Area, English, Celtic, British, Commonwealth, European and world title bouts that took place in 2007-2008, along with the amateur championships that were held in England, Scotland, Wales and Ireland, as well as being able to access details on champions from the past, both amateur and professional.

Historically, what was started several years ago under the heading of 'Early Gloved Championship Boxing', is still being researched for new material and we hope to present further offerings once we have something to share with you. Much of this earlier work was due to Harold Alderman painstakingly piecing together results for the pre-Lonsdale Belt and named-weight division period. There are still many who believe as gospel much of what was reported down the ages by 'respected' men such as Nat Fleischer, the owner of *The Ring* magazine and the *Ring Record Book*, and then copied by numerous historians who failed to grasp what the sport was really like before the First World War. Basically, boxing prior to the period in question was a shambles, following bare fists with an assortment of driving gloves, knuckle gloves, and two-ounce gloves, etc, until it arrived at what we recognise today. There were no commissions, with newspapermen becoming all-powerful by naming their own champions at all kinds of weights, and in much of America the sport was illegal, no-decision contests rescuing it from being abolished. If you thought today was dire, then boxing prior to that period was almost impossible in all divisions bar the heavyweights. Because travel was difficult and news travelled slowly, fighters were able to move from town to town proclaiming themselves to be the best and 'ringers' constantly prevailed. With today's research being aided by access to early newspapers, and the use of computers, it is becoming clear that men like Fleischer 'took' the best fighters of the day and then 'fitted' them into the named-weight divisions we now know so well. As not to confuse anybody any further we continue to list world champions from 1889 through to 1909 despite the weights for named weight divisions not being universally agreed to, apart from the heavyweights.

Abbreviations and Definitions used in the record sections of the Yearbook:
PTS (Points), CO (Count Out), RSC (Referee Stopped Contest), RTD (Retired), DIS (Disqualification), NC (No Contest), ND (No Decision).

British Boxing Board of Control Ltd: Structure

(Members of the Commonwealth Boxing Council and European Boxing Union)

PRESIDENT	Lord Brooks of Tremorfa DL
CHAIRMAN	Charles Giles
VICE CHAIRMAN	John Handelaar
GENERAL SECRETARY	Simon Block
ADMINISTRATIVE STEWARDS	Baroness Golding* John Rees QC Dave Roden Andrew Vanzie* John Williamson
REPRESENTATIVE STEWARDS	Geoff Boulter Bernard Connolly Martin Florey Ken Honniball Phil Lundgren Ron Pavett Fred Potter
STEWARDS OF APPEAL*	Robin Simpson QC Geoffrey Finn William Tudor John Robert Kidby Prof. Andrew Lees Timothy Langdale QC John Mathew QC Ian Mill QC Colin Ross-Munro QC Peter Richards FRCS Nicholas Valios QC
HONORARY STEWARDS*	Sir Henry Cooper OBE, KSG Mary Peters DBE Leonard Read QPM Bill Sheeran Billy Walker
HONORARY MEDICAL CONSULTANT*	Dr Roger C. Evans FRCP
HONORARY PARLIAMENTARY CONSULTANT*	Jimmy Wray MP Ian Stewart MP
LEGAL CONSULTANT	Michael Boyce DL
MARKETING CONSULTANT	Nicky Piper MBE
HEAD OFFICE	The Old Library Trinity Street Cardiff CF10 1BH Tel: 02920 367000 Fax: 02920 367019 E-mail: sblock@bbbofc.com Website: www.bbbofc.com

* Not directors of the company

AREA COUNCILS - AREA SECRETARIES

AREA NO 1 (SCOTLAND)
Brian McAllister
11 Woodside Crescent, Glasgow G3 7UL
Telephone 0141 3320392. Fax 0141 3312029
E-Mail bmacallister@mcallisters-ca.com

AREA NO 2 (NORTHERN IRELAND)
John Campbell
8 Mount Eden Park, Belfast, Northern Ireland BT9 6RA
Telephone 02890 299 652. Fax 02890 382 906
Mobile 07715 044061

AREA NO 3 (WALES)
Robert Smith
The Old Library, Trinity Street, Cardiff CF10 1BH
Telephone 02920 367000
Fax 02920 367019
E-Mail rsmith@bbbofc.com

AREA NO 4 (NORTHERN)
(Northumberland, Cumbria, Durham, Cleveland, Tyne and Wear, North Yorkshire [north of a line drawn from Whitby to Northallerton to Richmond, including these towns].)
John Jarrett
5 Beechwood Avenue, Gosforth, Newcastle upon Tyne NE3 5DH
Telephone/Fax 01912 856556
E-Mail John.jarrettl@tesco.net

AREA NO 5 (CENTRAL)
(North Yorkshire [with the exception of the part included in the Northern Area - see above], Lancashire, West and South Yorkshire, Greater Manchester, Merseyside and Cheshire, Isle of Man, North Humberside.)
Richard Jones
1 Churchfields, Croft, Warrington, Cheshire WA3 7JR
Telephone/Fax 01925 768132
E-Mail r.m.jones@mmu.ac.uk

AREA NO 6 (SOUTHERN)
(Bedfordshire, Berkshire, Buckinghamshire, Cambridgeshire, Channel Islands, Isle of Wight, Essex, Hampshire, Kent, Hertfordshire, Greater London, Norfolk, Suffolk, Oxfordshire, East and West Sussex.)
Robert W. Smith
The Old Library, Trinity Street, Cardiff CF10 1BH
Telephone 02920 367000. Fax: 02920 367019
E-Mail rsmith@bbbofc.com

AREA NO 7 (WESTERN)
(Cornwall, Devon, Somerset, Dorset, Wiltshire, Avon, Gloucestershire.)
Robert Smith
The Old Library, Trinity Street, Cardiff CF10 1BH
Telephone 02920 367000
Fax 02920 367019
E-Mail rsmith@bbbofc.com

AREA NO 8 (MIDLANDS)
(Derbyshire, Nottinghamshire, Lincolnshire, Salop, Staffordshire, Herefordshire and Worcestershire, Warwickshire, West Midlands, Leicestershire, South Humberside, Northamptonshire.)
Les Potts
1 Sunnyside Villas, Gnosall, Staffordshire
Telephone 01785 823641. Mobile 07973 533835
E-Mail lezpotts@hotmail.com

Foreword

by Simon Block *(General Secretary, British Boxing Board of Control)*

The 2007-2008 boxing season has been one of the most successful in the history of our sport here in Britain.

Despite losing a quartet of our world champions – Enzo Maccarinelli, Junior Witter, Gavin Rees and Clinton Woods – and with David Haye voluntarily having relinquished his WBC/WBA cruiserweight championship, with fewer world champions than this time last year the sport itself has been extremely buoyant.

What a year for Joe Calzaghe. His win over Mikkel Kessler in the early hours of Sunday, 4 November 2007 was one of the great British wins. Kessler proved to be a formidable world champion in his own right and the quality of his performance during the contest only serves to enhance Joe's status as one of world boxing's superstars at this time. His technically good, but less interesting win over the renowned Bernard Hopkins and, in between, his becoming the BBC 'Sports Personality of the Year' has also added to his reputation.

Carl Froch currently stands on the threshold of taking over Joe's old status as WBC world super-middleweight champion, while Ricky Hatton remains our most popular boxer. The British contingent virtually took over Las Vegas last December during his contest against Floyd Mayweather and although Ricky was unsuccessful his appeal did not diminish, achieving runner-up status to Joe in the BBC 'Sports Personality of the Year' award. In May of 2008 the highest gate in British boxing since 1942 was recorded when 57,000 people crammed in to the Manchester City Football Ground to see his successful come back contest against Juan Lazcano. Incredibly 49,000 of those tickets were sold in the first week. Alex Arthur has been elevated by the WBO from 'Interim' to full world championship status at super- featherweight and he deserves some high profile contests this season.

Ever the innovator, Barry Hearn turned to the past in reviving the old novice competition-type tournament in a brand new packaging when he and Sky Sport staged the 'Prizefighter Competition' on 11 April at York Hall, Bethnal Green. This proved to be a great success and has led to Sky allocating further resources from their budget for similar tournaments to take place later this year and into the next.

The middle part of this decade has been the most successful for about ten years but, as always, we must look over our shoulder to see where the stars of the future are coming from. In an otherwise very poor world heavyweight situation, David Haye surely has the potential to become a star in this division while Amir Khan continues to be the most exciting of our young prospects. Although I have never considered the amateur sport to be merely a breeding ground for future professionals, there will surely be, as night follows day, at least some of the Great Britain team that went to Beijing who turn professional and become the attractions of the future.

The quality of domestic British, Commonwealth and European championships, as well as English, Celtic and Area championships, remains extremely good and competitive, but I still believe it is a shame that all television companies insist on a title for their main event. When future star John Murray won the vacant British lightweight championship against Lee Meager in July, the contest of the night for me and most of the crowd was the one between my pal Nadeem Siddique, with whom I have

had a good relationship since he very kindly ferried me down one night from Glasgow to Sheffield, and Martin Gethin. Martin first impressed me when I saw him box in Las Vegas the night before Ricky's unsuccessful challenge to Mayweather. This really was a punch up of the old kind and would have been a worthy top of the bill for any tournament. It is a great pity that promoters are not able to make contests such as this, without a title, the main events. The very fact that there is now a 'stars" circuit in America and the interest generated by the possibility a few months ago of a match between Oscar de la Hoya against Manny Pacquiao demonstrates that it is matches that sell, not titles.

Finally, this will be my last Foreword in the *Yearbook* as I shall be retiring as General Secretary around the same time as publication. It has been a great pleasure and privilege for me to have been of service both to the British Boxing Board of Control and the sport of professional boxing these last 28 years and I hope, along the way, I have made my contribution. It will be my intention to continue as Honorary Secretary of the Commonwealth Boxing Council at least into the immediate future and I will always be proud to remain a Vice-President of both the Kent and Sussex Ex-Boxers' Associations, as well as being an Honorary Member of the London Ex-Boxers' Association. Boxing is the greatest of all sports and I am so pleased to have been able to play a small part outside the ropes and certainly more than I ever achieved inside.

Congratulations to Barry and the boys for producing the 'Silver Anniversary' edition of the *Yearbook* and, who knows, I might be asked to write a small piece for the 'Golden Anniversary' edition in 25 years hence.

British Boxing Board of Control Awards

Now in its 25th year, the BBBoC Awards Ceremony will be held in London later this year and will once again be co-hosted by the Lonsdale International Sporting Club's Bernard Hart. The winners of these prestigious statuettes, designed in the form of a boxer, are selected by a well-informed panel of judges who make a judgement on the season as a whole at an annual meeting.

British Boxer of the Year: The outstanding British Boxer at any weight. 1984: Barrry McGuigan. 1985: Barry McGuigan. 1986: Dennis Andries. 1987: Lloyd Honeyghan. 1988: Lloyd Honeyghan. 1989: Dennis Andries. 1990: Dennis Andries. 1991: Dave McAuley. 1992: Colin McMillan. 1993: Lennox Lewis. 1994: Steve Robinson. 1995: Nigel Benn. 1996: Prince Naseem Hamed. 1997: Robin Reid. 1998: Carl Thompson. 1999: Billy Schwer. 2000: Glenn Catley. 2001: Joe Calzaghe. 2002: Lennox Lewis. 2003: Ricky Hatton. 2004: Scott Harrison. 2005: Ricky Hatton. 2006: Joe Calzaghe. 2007: Ricky Hatton.

British Contest of the Year: Although a fight that took place in Europe won the 1984 Award, since that date, the Award, presented to both participants, has applied to the best all-action contest featuring a British boxer in a British ring. 1984: Jimmy Cable v Said Skouma. 1985: Barry McGuigan v Eusebio Pedroza. 1986: Mark Kaylor v Errol Christie. 1987: Dave McAuley v Fidel Bassa. 1988: Tom Collins v Mark Kaylor. 1989: Michael Watson v Nigel Benn. 1990: Orlando Canizales v Billy Hardy. 1991: Chris Eubank v Nigel Benn. 1992: Dennis Andries v Jeff Harding. 1993: Andy Till v Wally Swift Jnr. 1994: Steve Robinson v Paul Hodkinson. 1995: Steve Collins v Chris Eubank. 1996: P. J. Gallagher v Charles Shepherd. 1997: Spencer Oliver v Patrick Mullings. 1998: Carl Thompson v Chris Eubank. 1999: Shea Neary v Naas Scheepers. 2000: Simon Ramoni v Patrick Mullings. 2001: Colin Dunne v Billy Schwer. 2002: Ezra Sellers v Carl Thompson. 2003: David Barnes v Jimmy Vincent. 2004: Michael Gomez v Alex Arthur. 2005: Jamie Moore v Michael Jones. 2006: Kevin Anderson v Young Muttley. 2007: Jamie Moore v Matthew Macklin.

Overseas Boxer of the Year: For the best performance by an overseas boxer in a British ring. 1984: Buster Drayton. 1985: Don Curry. 1986: Azumah Nelson. 1987: Maurice Blocker. 1988: Fidel Bassa. 1989: Brian Mitchell. 1990: Mike McCallum. 1991: Donovan Boucher. 1992: Jeff Harding. 1993: Crisanto Espana. 1994: Juan Molina. 1995: Mike McCallum. 1996: Jacob Matlala. 1997: Ronald Wright. 1998: Tim Austin. 1999: Vitali Klitschko. 2000: Keith Holmes. 2001: Harry Simon. 2002: Jacob Matlala. 2003: Manuel Medina. 2004: In-Jin Chi. 2005: Joshua Okine. 2006: Tshifhiwa Munyai. 2007: Steve Molitor

Special Award: Covers a wide spectrum, and is an

appreciation for services to boxing. 1984: Doctor Adrian Whiteson. 1985: Harry Gibbs. 1986: Ray Clarke. 1987: Hon. Colin Moynihan. 1988: Tom Powell. 1989: Winston Burnett. 1990: Frank Bruno. 1991: Muhammad Ali. 1992: Doctor Oswald Ross. 1993: Phil Martin. 1994: Ron Olver. 1995: Gary Davidson. 1996: Reg Gutteridge and Harry Carpenter. 1997: Miguel Matthews and Pete Buckley. 1998: Mickey Duff and Tommy Miller. 1999: Jim Evans and Jack Lindsay. 2000: Henry Cooper. 2001: John Morris and Leonard 'Nipper' Read. 2002: Roy Francis and Richie Woodhall. 2003: Michael Watson. 2004: Dennie Mancini and Bob Paget. 2005: Barry McGuigan. 2006: Jack Bishop. 2007: James Cook MBE and Enzo Calzaghe.

Sportsmanship Award: This Award recognises boxers who set a fine example, both in and out of the ring. 1986: Frank Bruno. 1987: Terry Marsh. 1988: Pat Cowdell. 1989: Horace Notice. 1990: Rocky Kelly. 1991: Wally Swift Jnr. 1992: Duke McKenzie. 1993: Nicky Piper. 1994: Francis Ampofo. 1995: Paul Wesley. 1996: Frank Bruno. 1997: Lennox Lewis. 1998: Johnny Williams. 1999: Brian Coleman. 2000: Michael Ayers and Wayne Rigby. 2001: Billy Schwer. 2002: Mickey Cantwell. 2003: Francis Ampofo. 2004: Dale Robinson and Jason Booth. 2005: Ricky Hatton and Kostya Tszyu. 2006: Enzo Maccarinelli and Mark Hobson. 2007: Mark Thompson.

Ricky Hatton, the 2007 'British Boxer of the Year'

Mark Clifford

11

3 Bull Ring
Sedgley, Dudley
West Midlands, DY3 1RU

Telephone: (01902) 670007
Fax: (01902) 665195
Mobile: 07976 283 157

1st team Ltd

Paul (PJ) Rowson Promoter & Manager
Errol Johnson Promoter, Manager, Matchmaker & Trainer

HEAVYWEIGHT
Neil Perkins 3-0

CRUISERWEIGHT
Rob Norton (English Champion)

LIGHT-HEAVYWEIGHT
Jonjo Finnegan
Hastings Rasani

SUPER-MIDDLEWEIGHT
Matty Hough
Joe Skeldon

MIDDLEWEIGHT
Steven Bendall (English Champion)
Keiron Gray 2-0
Sam Horton 9-0

LIGHT-MIDDLEWEIGHT
Terry Adams
Jamie Ball 2-0
Russell Colley 2-0
Rob Kenney 7-0-1
Duane Parker 4-0
Marcus Portman

WELTERWEIGHT
Jimmy Beech
Steve Cooper
Stuart Elwell 10-3
Martin Gordon
Mark Lloyd (Midlands Area Champion) 11-1
Kevin McCauley 1-1
Young Mutley 25-3
Matt Seawright
Keith Sheen no bouts
Billy Smith

LIGHT-WELTERWEIGHT
Peter Buckley
Tristan Davies 10-1
Scott Evans 5-0
James Flinn 2-0
Dean Harrison 12-0
Rob Hunt 10-0
Chris Lewis no bouts
Jason Nesbitt
Karl Taylor

LIGHTWEIGHT
Martin Gethin 14-0-1
Steve Saville

SUPER-FEATHERWEIGHT
Steve Gethin
Tony Hanna (British Masters Champion)
Shaun Walton

FEATHERWEIGHT
Chris Male no bouts.
Lyndsey Scragg 6-0

FLYWEIGHT
James Mulhern 1-0
Delroy Spencer

1st Team's Trainer/Cornerman Bob Plant, who is also the proprietor of TKO (UK) Boxing Supplies. Tel: 0844 561 6609
Other Trainers/Cornermen: Paul Dykes, Jay Morris, Paul Gough and Shaun Cooper.
Cornerman: Wayne Downing

South Coast Saviour: An Appreciation of Jack Bishop

by Bob Lonkhurst

By its very nature boxing is without doubt one of the most fascinating and contentious of sports. It creates cult heroes, warriors, men of extreme courage and skill who, by the very nature of their trade, are a sport's writers dream.

Yet for boxing to survive there have always been lesser-known individuals who make massive contributions to keep alive a sport which a section of society would love to see banned. Invariably their commitment is brought about through a love of the sport and respect for the combatants. The publicity they receive for their efforts is generally minimal.

Jack Bishop cetainly falls into the latter category because, assisted originally by his good friend Johnny Chapman he has kept small-hall boxing alive in Southampton and Portsmouth for more than 20 years. Despite both being senior citizens, Jack is 85 years of age and Johnny 74, their level of enthusiasm would put many a youngster to shame.

Although both boxed with success in the services, they didn't meet until the mid-1980s when they were amongst a group of people who organized a function that raised £4,000 for a young Portsmouth boxer suffering from cancer. In order to send the lad to America for treatment a total of £15,000 was required and that amount was raised thanks to concerted efforts over the next seven months.

Having a lot in common, Bishop and Chapman became close friends. Jack was already established within professional boxing as a manager and promoter, and asked Johnny to help train his boxers. He agreed and after settling

Jack (left) as a young bugler and drummer in the Royal Marines

down applied for a British Boxing Board of Control trainer and seconds licence which was granted in February 1990.

Jack Bishop was born at Southsea Naval Maternity Home in May 1923. His mother, a Londoner, was in lodgings at Portsmouth whilst her husband, a career sailor, was in port. Shortly after Jack's birth, however, his father was posted to the East Indies for two and a half years so his mother took him to her home at Shadwell in east London, where they remained until Jack was nine. They then returned to Portsmouth, but whilst living in London Jack developed a cockney accent that soon became a source of amusement to some local boys who subjected him to bullying. The main offender, who lived almost opposite him, continuously ridiculed Jack over his accent and often gave him a thump around the head. "I was frightened to death of him", Jack recalled. "If I came out of my house and saw him in the street I would run straight back in again".

At the age of ten Jack joined the Naval Cadets and was attached to HMS Excellent based at Whale Island. He was only able to do so because his father was a serving sailor. To his horror when he got there he found that the bully from his street had also joined. "I would not have joined if I had known he would be there", he remarked.

At the time the whole group were training for the Southern Counties Cadet Corps boxing championships. Jack, the bully and a third lad all of the same age and weight were in the 'mosquito' class and had to box off to find a winner to represent HMS Excellent. Jack drew the bully, whom he comfortably outpointed over three rounds, and went forward to win his weight division against lads from Navy, Army and Air Force Cadets. His prize was a large bronze medal.

Even to this day Jack has a vivid memory of the events. "I remember it gave me immense satisfaction to know that I could fight", he remarked with a wry grin. "I never wanted to fight outside a boxing ring and would rather walk away from trouble, but to beat that lad was wonderful". Although he had no proper trainer Jack carried on boxing in the cadets against youngsters from other clubs and cadet corps. Most of the bouts took place at Whale Island, Portsmouth because the facilities were the finest in Southern England.

Jack left school at the age of 14 and after working as a page boy in a Plaza cinema for a few months he joined the Royal Marines as a Boy Bugler. He underwent six months training at Eastney Barracks where he had to learn to play three instruments, but found it difficult because he was not musically minded. At the completion of the training he passed his final exam whereupon he was permitted to wear the uniform and attaching drummer's cords.

Within a few weeks he was drafted to the original HMS Ark Royal and joined the ship at Birkenhead where it had recently been launched. This only occurred because his father was already a crew member and, in those days, a father could 'claim' a son and have him on the same ship. A reference to Jack and his father is made in the book Ark

Royal (page 24), published in 1956.

During 1939 whilst the Ark Royal was docked at Portsmouth, the Lord of the Admiralty, much to the annoyance of the government, gave a speech in which he said that war was imminent. Jack's father was due to leave the Navy the day that war broke out, but his services were retained. After hearing the speech he told Jack to leave the ship so that if it was shelled and sunk one of them would hopefully remain alive. Jack's mother knew nothing about what was said.

After explaining the situation to the Major of the Marines, Jack was sent back to Eastney Barracks just as the reserve fleet was being called up. He was drafted to HMS Colombo as a Bugler and sent to Scapa Flow in the Hebrides. By the time they arrived war had broken out and the night they set anchor the battleship HMS Royal Oak was torpedoed by a German submarine nearby. The most upsetting thing for Jack was that a boy he joined up with, who occupied the next bed to him throughout training, went down with it.

Jack first saw action in 1939 off Gibraltar and was involved in the Battle of Spartivento in the Mediterranean. Although he survived, war took its toll in that he sustained serious damage to his ears from the noise of intensive gunfire as he stood behind two turrets of six-inch piat guns for more than two hours. During the same battle he was blown off

Jack as a young amateur boxer

a ladder whilst climbing a rig and sustained a serious leg injury. On returning to Portsmouth he was taken to hospital where it was found the injury was so severe that he was medically discharged.

Determined to serve his country Jack re-enlisted into the Army, passing his medical A1 and being sent to Bournemouth Recruitment Centre as a Drill Instructor. He found it boring so when he saw a War Office memo asking for volunteers for airborne troops he applied and was accepted. After initial training he was attached to the 1st Airborne Division based at Salisbury Plain. Jack went on to serve throughout the war in airborne divisions and saw service in North Africa, Sicily, Italy, Holland, France and Belgium. He also flew with the American Air Force on secret missions to Yugoslavia to drop arms to the partisans. When the missions were over each American Serviceman was awarded a bronze flying cross for flying unarmed unescorted planes over enemy territory. They also received a $50 bonus, but all Jack got was an American breakfast of flapjacks and prunes.

Jack should have been discharged from the services once war was over because he was physically unfit. This, however, was deferred because he was an expert at 'bombing-up', a skill he acquired in the Airborne Division which was essential, particularly on the missions to Yugoslavia. It consisted of packing weapons and rations into torpedo-like tubes with parachutes attached and then fitted beneath the fuselage of aircraft in preparation for drops over designated areas.

There was an urgent need for a 'bombing-up' expert in Palestine and Jack was selected. When he got there, however, he failed a medical examination to establish his fitness for flying. "You are not going anywhere except home", the doctor told him.

Returning to the 1st Airborne Division, which by this time had moved to Lincoln, Jack subsequently received a medical discharge and was granted a pension. He gave up boxing because of eye trouble, but had taken part in about 160 contests, winning more than he lost. He was a southpaw and boxed at lightweight throughout his senior career, winning Naval Cadets and 1st Airborne Divisional championships.

He got married and set up home in Lincoln and a few years later was invited to train boxers at the Lincoln Pegasus, a Territorial Army boxing club, for the national championships in London. Jack did a great job, the club winning the team championship and Roy Sewards taking the individual light-heavyweight title. "I do not think it was too much to do with me", he remarked with typical modesty. "I think they just had a good batch of boxers to be honest".

It was a one-off job for Jack because several of the boxers turned professional. A couple of years later, however, he received a call from Ken Richardson, a professional manager from Retford, asking if he would train his stable of boxers. Bishop agreed and soon became successful, thus prompting a local newspaper to run an article about the rapid growth of professional boxing in Lincoln. "The man behind it is Jack Bishop, formerly trainer with Lincoln Pegasus ABC now disbanded", it stated. Ken Richardson told the press, "Jack knows the business and has his heart and soul in the sport. My advice to any lads in the Lincoln area wanting to box is to contact him".

One of the men Jack trained was former paratrooper, Roy Sewards, an exciting hit-or-be-hit fighter who built a reasonable record. Unfortunately, his recklessness caused him to suffer two stoppage defeats to Jack Bodell (cut eyes) and one to Jack Grant (cut eye) in challenges for the Midlands Area light-heavyweight title, and also three stoppages to Young John McCormack.

Jack moved to Fareham in the 1960s following the breakdown of his marriage. He severed all boxing connections and obtained employment for two years as a Chief Officer Steward on the Queen Mary, travelling between Southampton and New York. Then for 12 years he was manager of a coal company.

One evening during 1970, a trainer from Titchfield ABC called at Jack's house and explained that Charlie Cooper, a talented youngster at the club, was due to face ABA welterweight champion Terry Waller. He asked Jack to train him for the contest because nobody in the club had sufficient experience. Bishop agreed, but insisted that having worked with professionals it would be strictly a one-off.

Cooper and Bishop got on well, and although Charlie lost a close decision, a bond had already been formed. A few weeks later Charlie called at Jack's house saying he was thinking of turning professional. Charlie persuaded Jack to become his manager and trainer and became his first boxer in Hampshire.

Charlie, however, had nowhere to train, but after a conversation with his father, who owned a large plot of land at Marchwood, Jack managed to obtain a large hut from Chichester Council. It was part of an old army camp and needed to be dismantled, so he took one of his coal lorries, collected the hut and took it to Charlie's father who erected it on his land and turned it into a sizeable gym.

Cooper started his professional career brightly, winning his first 11 contests in just 14 months, including points victories over Des Rae and Pat Thomas. After a couple of years, however, he left Jack because he had been advised that he could do better in London. Not wishing to fall out with him Jack offered Charlie his contract back, whereupon the boxer approached Mickey Duff who asked why he had left Bishop. Charlie apparently said he could not get on with Bishop to which Duff remarked, "Well you certainly won't get on with me".

After another manager/trainer relationship broke down Charlie returned to Jack and admitted he should never have left him. Unfortunately, Charlie had by this time become less dedicated to boxing because he was already an ambitious young businessman who could make good money outside the ring. When he retired in 1978 following two defeats in Denmark he had a record of 15 victories and a draw from 27 contests. Although he lost on points to Kirkland Laing and stopped Roy Commosioung in an eliminator for the Southern Area light-middleweight title, he never reached his potential much to Jack's disappointment.

As soon as it became known that Bishop was training Charlie Cooper, he got plenty of other enquiries from ambitious local lads wanting to turn professional. He set up a gym in an old warehouse on the dockside and although the Council found out they let him continue. He worked hard to make a go of it and in 1973 Jan Magdziarz, Syd Paddock and Peter Brisland joined his camp, followed by David Fry, Kevin Paddock and Tony Mikulski. Most showed promise and Jack got them plenty of work at small halls around the country and in the plush Sporting Clubs in London.

As a trainer and manager Bishop has handled almost 100 boxers from the Southampton, Portsmouth and Gosport areas. Jan Magdziarz became his first champion when he won the Southern Area middleweight title in 1976. Gary Cooper, who turned professional with him in 1978, won the Southern Area light-middleweight championship in 1985 and the British title in 1988. Paul McCarthy became Southern Area middleweight champion in 1987 and his brother Steve took the Southern Area light-heavyweight title in November 1988, followed by the vacant British crown in October 1990.

By this time Bishop was firmly established as a promoter, having been granted a Board of Control licence in 1986. With a number of good young boxers under his wing he recognized the need for professional shows at Southampton. He then teamed up with his former heavyweight Syd Paddock and, as S & J Promotions, staged their first show at The Guildhall on 11 November 1986. It was the first professional promotion at the venue for a decade and featured local boxers Gary Cooper, Peter Bunting, Bobby Williams, Dean Turner and Clayon Stewart all from Jack's stable. It was a great value show, the type of which he still continues to stage more than 20 years later.

One of the most unsavory incidents Jack experienced at a boxing promotion occurred at one of his shows at The Guildhall on 21 September 1989. His boxer Steve McCarthy

Jack seen here with his first British champion, Gary Cooper

was fighting former British light-heavyweight champion Tony Wilson in a championship eliminator. Steve appeared to be winning the bout comfortably when in round three Wilson's mother scrambled into the ring and started hitting Steve with her stiletto-heeled shoe. McCarthy refused to continue and Wilson was declared the winner on a retirement. There was bedlam outside the ring, and whilst trying to get his boxer back to the dressing room, Jack was stabbed in the arm by a person believed to be a Wilson supporter. Justice was seen to be done, however, when Steve won the vacant British light-heavyweight title in October 1990, beating Serge Fame on points at Battersea. Although Steve continued boxing for some years he relinquished both of his titles.

In 1996 Danny Ruegg from Bournemouth became Western Area super-bantamweight champion and in December 2005 Jack's senior professional, Colin Kenna, won the Southern Area heavyweight title by knocking out Wayne Llewelyn in two rounds on a Bishop promotion at Portsmouth. Jack's most recent champion is Steve Ede from Gosport, who won the British Masters middleweight title on his promotion at Southampton in February 2007.

Despite his success as a promoter Jack went through a period of not staging a show between 1991 and 2001. He claims that he went from having 17 active professionals to just one because there was a sudden lack of local interest. That, however, has changed and he currently has a stable of ten professionals who train at his gym at the Old Cattle Market in the St Mary's district of Southampton with him and new assistant, Johnny Smith, an uncle of one of Jack's boxers, Lloyd Smith. Jack acquired the premises from the local council in the mid-1980s and has been there ever since.

Like Bishop, Johnny Chapman was an established boxer in the services, but at a higher level. Meticulous records and scrapbooks created by his father reveal that he had a total of 307 contests, of which he lost only 22. At his home in Portsmouth, a cabinet crammed with trophies are a testimony of his success. His wealth of experience has made him the perfect partner for Jack for so many years.

Chapman was born near Reading in June 1934. His father owned two farms, but when war was declared he volunteered for the Royal Air Force. Johnny went to live with his grandmother at Hartley Witney, where he went to school. Many of his lessons took place in air-raid shelters.

At the age of 12 he joined the Army Cadets and soon took up boxing. His first contest was at a summer camp in Dorset against a lad from another Cadet Corps, who he knocked out in the first round. Johnny was a big lad and by the time he was 15 he weighed 11 stone.

Two years later he started work at a Royal Air Force establishment factory at Farnborough and because of the nature of his work his call-up for National Service was deferred until he was 21. His passion for boxing grew and he trained wherever he could. He even sparred with Jack Gardner at Basingstoke in 1951 when Jack prepared for his fight with Bruce Woodcock.

Johnny developed rapidly and represented the RAF team with considerable success at venues throughout Southern England. At Ipswich he beat Nebraska Golden

Gloves champion, Paul Menard, an American airman, in two rounds. At the same venue he stopped American serviceman, Tommy Mottern, in the first round despite giving away four stones in weight (Mottern weighed 17 stone four pounds to Chapman's 13 stone four pounds). United States Forces champion Sammy 'Preacher' Williams was stopped at Norwich Lads Club and in 1954, representing Southern Counties against the Navy at Ramsgate, Chapman stopped Billy Baxter in the opening round.

Johnny was fighting and beating quality opposition and none came bigger than Irish docker, Danno Maher, who although only 5'10" tall weighed 22 stone. Chapman beat him comfortably on points at the National Stadium in Dublin and again two weeks later at Dundalk.

Although only 19, Chapman topped the bill on a big open-air show at Woking football ground on 6 June 1953 to celebrate the Coronation. His opponent was George Erasmus, a Staff Sergeant in the Commonwealth Coronation Forces, who was light-heavyweight champion of Rhodesia. He was a top class fighter, who stopped Johnny on a cut eye, and whilst in England represented Southern Counties at a number of shows.

Despite the occasional setback Chapman continued to progress. He was light-heavyweight champion of Hampshire in 1953, won three Southern Counties titles, at light-heavyweight in 1953 and heavyweight in '54 and '55. He was also Civil Service heavyweight champion in 1955, '56 and '57. After his third success he was presented with a replica of the trophy to keep. In 1955 he entered the London South West Divisional championships at Nine Elms Baths, Battersea. After three contests he lost in the final at 1am to Paul Dempsey (Battersea) on a third-round stoppage.

In September that year he started his deferred National

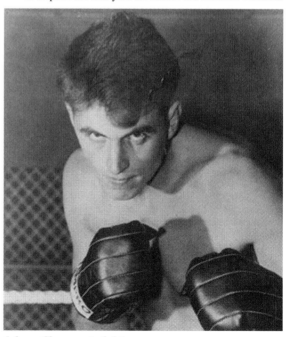

Johnny Chapman in fighting pose

Service and was sent to RAF Bridgnorth for his square bashing. Once it became known that he was a successful heavyweight boxer he was sent home to get his kit. Within a very short time he became a member of the RAF team, which was a great advantage because he received better food and other privileges.

Within a few weeks Chapman was transported daily to RAF Cosford to spar with Sergeant Bruce Wells, who was training to box the reigning European amateur middleweight champion Genadi Schatkov in the first ever ABA v Russia international. Wells, who had won European gold in 1953, was the top boxer in the RAF and it was a tremendous privilege for Johnny to spar with him. They formed a bond and are still friends today.

Chapman was creating a good impression in the ring and was picked to represent the RAF in matches in Denmark and Sweden on 11 and 13 January 1956. Against Sparta Club of Copenhagen he beat Goffsjaick Hansen on points in a 7-3 victory, but lost on a majority decision in Stockholm to Thorner Ahsman, later to become a good professional, in a 6-4 defeat.

On 4 February 1956, boxing for the RAF against Scotland at Dundee, Chapman beat John Fairley on points. Fellow team members included Bruce Wells, Johnny Kidd, Freddie Cross and Owen Reilly, whilst top names in the Scottish team were Chic Caldewood, John 'Cowboy' McCormack and Derry Treanor.

One day in 1956, the PTI at Bridgnorth ordered Chapman to spar with another boxer who was training for the RAF championships. Needle quickly developed between them and the action got extremely rough for a couple of rounds before Johnny ended matters with a heavy knockout. Having made his mark he was promptly entered for the Group championships which he won. After nine fights in just ten days he won the Command championships.

In March 1956 he captured the RAF heavyweight title at Stafford when he knocked out LAC Jim Thatcher (Middle Wallop) in the second round. That victory took Johnny into the Imperial Services championships at RAF Hullavington three weeks later. After receiving a bye in the semi-finals he outpointed Army champion, Sergeant Alf Bray, to become one of six RAF winners that night.

His success propelled Chapman into the semi-finals of the ABA championships at Wembley on 27 April 1956. Despite having won 24 of 26 contests that season he was knocked out in the third round by London champion, Dave Thomas (Polytechnic). The defeat by Thomas proved to be only a temporary set-back and Johnny remained a regular member of the RAF team. In September 1956, he was one of a group of 23 boxers selected to undergo special training at Uxbridge for the annual Britannia Shield competition, which the RAF staged with Allied Countries to commemorate the wartime alliances. Although Johnny looked certain to box in the competition he had to pull out through injury.

On 27 October 1956, a number of RAF boxing stars formed a guard of honour at St Johns Church, London Road, Hook, at the wedding of Johnny to his fiancée Eileen Frood. They included RAF and ISBA champion Bruce Wells, Owen Reilly, holder of ABA, ISBA and RAF titles, Britannia

Shield winner LAC Eddie West, and former ABA light-welterweight champion Frank McQuillan. One of the first people to send John a congratulatory telegram was Bootle heavyweight, Dave Rent, who had recently lost to the RAF champion on a disqualification at Mile End. Dave was in fact so upset with the decision that he quit amateur boxing, went to the USA and turned professional under Al Weill.

In 1957, Chapman again won the RAF heavyweight title when outpointing old foe LAC Jim Thatcher (Middle Wallop), who had replaced him in the Britannia Shield. Victory took him into the Imperial Services championships for the second successive year, but he was disqualified in the opening round of his semi-final against Sergeant Tommy Gibbons (Coldstream Guards). The referee ruled that Chapman was guilty of persistent holding, but most people thought the official was too hasty considering the importance of the bout. Gibbons went on to win the title, outpointing Leading Seaman James in the final.

After being demobbed from the RAF in October 1957, Johnny moved to Islington and got a job as a meat porter at Smithfield Market. By this time he had signed professional terms with Ted Walker, a boxing manager he had known for some time. He also recommended that RAF mates Johnny Kidd and Len Barrow did likewise, as the three had got to know each other by frequently boxing in the same representative teams and championships. They trained at Walker's gym at Fitzroy Square off Tottenham Court Road in London. It was a busy place, used regularly by Terry Downes, Yolande Pompey, Eddie Hearn and Ernie Fossey amongst others. Johnny sparred with most of them and with a reputation of being able to box and punch and having a good chin a successful professional career appeared on the cards.

His professional debut was at the National Sporting Club in London on 6 January 1958 against Jamaican-born Maxie Earle, who he stopped in four rounds. What seemed like the perfect start to a professional career, however, turned into disaster. At Manor Place Baths two weeks later against Jack da Costa (Barbados), Chapman looked well on the way to victory when he sustained a badly cut left eye (five stitches) and was stopped in round two. Then at Rotherham in April, Maxie Earle knocked him down three times in the opening round and the fight was stopped.

John's career then stuttered and he was outpointed by Johnny Smith, the father of Jack Bishop's current assistant, and drew with Bernie Jelley. He split with Ted Walker, after which he was trained by Solly Cantor. Victories over Tony Smith (disqualification), Bernie Jelley (points) and Cliff Purnell (disqualification) gave a glimmer of hope, but then disaster struck again, this time out of the ring.

A lover of cricket, Johnny played matches most weekends and was his team's wicket-keeper. During one game the ball flew through a batsman's legs and hit him on the temple knocking him out. When he came round in the dressing room everything was black and he could hear people asking if he was alright. He did not go to hospital and after a couple of pints with his mates assumed he was alright. As he had suffered temporary blindness, however, he eventually saw his doctor who confirmed that his vision was not good. He was advised to give up boxing because a blow around the left eye could cause him to lose his sight. He accepted the advice and has worn glasses ever since.

After working at Smithfield Market for several years Chapman set up his own wholesale meat business. He moved to Basingstoke and later set up a wholesale toys and fancy goods business supplying bingo halls and small shops. It was extremely successful, but in 1973 he fell foul of Customs and Excise over insufficient VAT payments and spent five years paying off what was owed.

This was a bad period in his life because he also went through a divorce. Johnny, however, was a grafter and determined to get back to the good times he moved to Portsmouth where he bought an old car and took up mini-cabbing. Within five years he was the Director of a company running 54 cabs. When he eventually sold out he went on the road as a sales rep, travelling all over the country. He also ran his own transport company with a number of heavy goods vehicles. A few years later he bought a café in Portsmouth, which did well, and he eventually had several others at different locations throughout the town. By this time he had remarried and he and his new wife worked seven days a week.

At the age of 60, Chapman sold his cafes and retired, but it was not long before he got bored. Having kept his HGV licence he went back to lorry driving, travelling throughout England and Scotland. By this time he was well established within professional boxing and because of his involvement with Jack Bishop knew people in most parts of the country with whom he could meet socially. In 1999, however, he was forced to give up work following an accident when a load of material fell off the back of a lorry. He sustained a serious leg injury that meant he could no longer drive a lorry. Since then he has devoted most of his time to boxing.

Jack Bishop and Johnny Chapman are two real old-stagers of British boxing. With a wealth of experience between them they are dedicated to their trade, which is essential for the well-being of the young boxers they handle. In 2006, the British Boxing Board of Control recognized Jack's personal commitment to the sport by presenting him with a special award for services to boxing. It was well deserved because apart from his high quality shows he has always had a great relationship with his boxers. He does not regard them as money-making machines for his benefit and always takes the blame for any defeat. Many of his former boxers have kept in touch with him, and the esteem in which he is held was typified in 2007, when he was very ill. Charlie Cooper got in touch and told him to get whatever treatment he needed no matter what the cost. Charlie insisted that he would pay for it.

Bishop is an honourable man, who is very proud of having been on active military service when he was 16. His bravery and commitment were rewarded by him being decorated with eight campaign medals. He was even involved in a number of special missions, which cannot be disclosed. Although he admits that the state of boxing generally does not compare to when he first held a licence he is quick to say that the present British Boxing Board of Control is the best he has served under in over 40 years.

Jack in the corner with Colin Kenna

Philip Sharkey

Triumph over Tragedy: The Legacy of Shannon's Gym

By Tracey Pollard

Bob (left) celebrates in the aftermath of another Wayne Rigby win

If ever a boxing gym has overcome adversity and tragedy and, not only survived but flourished, it is Shannon's Gym in Manchester. The successful professional gym that has produced several champions was in fact born out of tragedy. Today, popular trainer Bob Shannon guides professional boxers, frequently to titles, after following on from his father Bob senior who was a respected amateur coach.

Bob Shannon senior had started his own amateur boxing gym in the early '70s at Brookdale Park School in Newton Heath, Manchester. In 1974 he moved to the BDS on Whitworth Street and finally to the Seamens' Mission in Salford two years later. Bob's three sons, Anthony, Ian and Bobby, all boxed and Bobby was particularly talented, winning the Schoolboys' championships, National Boys' Club championships and reaching the Junior ABA semi-finals. Bobby and two of his young stablemates, Billy Graham and Phil Martin would later become three of the country's most successful professional trainers.

Sadly, in 1976 Bob senior, a mechanic, was killed in a tragic accident when a truck he was working on collapsed on top of him. When Bob junior opened his own gym in the basement of Crossley House in Openshaw he dedicated it to his dad and named it Shannon's Gym in his memory. The gym had quite a history in boxing with Bob fighting there himself as an amateur and Henry Cooper's Golden Gloves tournament having been held there. A generation earlier, respected professional trainer, Ken Daniels, also fought there as an amateur. Bob received a lot of good advice from Ken and also from one of the fighters he had trained, the late Phil Martin, who at that time had his own gym, the renowned Champs' Camp, which produced many champions.

Shannon's Gym was always a family affair, with Bob's wife, Jean, his son, Robert and daughter, Nicola, all involved. The fourth generation added the toughest little fighter of them all to the Shannon dynasty. Bob's grandson Robbie was born with a rare genetic disease, citrullinaemia. Bob's daughter Michelle had to feed him every two hours through a tube in his stomach and administer the drugs which were keeping him alive every four hours. She has devotedly endured years of near-sleepless nights that have seen little Robbie beat the odds. He has a healthy brother and sister but recently his new baby brother was born with the same condition.

Nicola trained the youngsters at Bob's gym and Robert worked alongside his dad. He had shown great promise as a boxer and his first fight was voted 'Fight of the Night' but he chose to join his dad in the corner instead and became the country's youngest licensed second. Father and son were a familiar sight in the corner with fighters like Wayne Rigby.

Wayne was always a dedicated and hard-working boxer. Even as an amateur he had impressed coaches with his determination and as a pro he would be in bed by 9pm and up at 4am to run before starting work. He was the perfect fighter to work with and Bob, who has a sergeant major style of training like his dad, joins his lads on punishing runs for miles around the local hills. On weeknights Wayne's sessions at the gym included gruelling pad work with Bob and ferocious sparring sessions with stablemate Gary Hibbert, who held the Central Area lightweight title that Wayne had held a few years earlier. In 1998 Wayne defeated Tanveer Ahmed for the vacant British Lightweight title, which he successfully defended against Matt Brown, stopping him in the eighth round. He lost the title to Bobby Vanzie in October '08 in the tenth round of their contest before stopping three of his next four opponents, the third being Dariusz Snarski for the IBO Inter-Continental lightweight title. This led to a challenge for the IBO title and two epic encounters with Michael Ayres.

The first of their sensational battles earned both fighters 'Sportsmanship' awards, Ayres winning when the referee stopped the fight in the tenth round. The return was equally exciting but this time went the distance with Ayres again emerging victorious. After the fight Bob said: "It was an honour and a privilege to be in Wayne's corner". Wayne bounced back with a step up to light-welterweight and a third-round stoppage over Keith Jones, followed by a points win over Antonio Ramirez for the vacant WBF title. He retained the title when he stopped Sedat Puskulla in the first round but when he dropped back to lightweight and was stopped by Colin Dunne in a challenge for the WBU title in 2002, it signalled the last few fights in the career of this true Manchester warrior.

It was in June '03 that the Shannon family were devastated by the tragic death of Robert, who was killed in a car crash, aged just 21, the same age Bob had been when his father died. Tributes poured in for the popular young man and his large funeral was attended by many members of the boxing fraternity. He was exceptionally close to his family and for Bob it seemed an impossible task to carry on the Shannon boxing legacy without his son by his side. For many months the future of Shannon's Gym hung in the balance as the fighters wondered if Bob would return. Fortunately, he eventually did.

Andy Morris, who used to visit Shannon's Gym twice a week to spar, won the ABA lightweight title in '02 and went on to become one of Shannon's successful professionals. Andy turned pro in '03 after winning a bronze medal in the Commonwealth Games in Manchester. He was still undefeated two years later when he captured the vacant English featherweight title with a points win over Rocky Dean. Six months later he became British featherweight champion when outscoring John Simpson on his Scottish doorstep for the title and successfully defended against Rendall Munroe in Edinburgh. However, when Andy put his belt on the line in a return with Simpson in December '06 he was unexpectedly stopped on a cut in the fifth round, many feeling the stoppage to be premature. Over the years Bob had developed a reputation as one of the best cutsmen in the country but he was not given the opportunity to work on Andy's cut. After dominating their first encounter and looking likely to do so again, he was stunned to be handed his first defeat. Having given an impressive career-best performance to claim the title, when the two met for a third time Simpson did the same. The rubber match was Andy's last fight to date and this time the referee stopped the contest in the seventh round without argument.

Namibian, Ali Nuumbembe was also a medallist in the 2002 Commonwealth Games, who then joined the professionals at Shannon's Gym. He won his first nine fights and then went from six rounds to his first title fight when he was offered the chance to fight for the vacant Namibian welterweight title. Facing a hostile crowd and the popular local champion back home in Namibia, Ali lost on a highly controversial decision that had the Namibian press calling for an investigation into the referee, who had a string of questionable decisions to explain. Back in England, Ali returned to winning form with victories over Lee Armstrong and Frannie Jones, followed by an ambitious contest with the British champion, David Barnes, for the vacant IBO Inter-Continental title. It was his first 12-round fight and he would be facing his first southpaw, a highly-rated, talented champion at very short notice. Undeniably the underdog, he was expected to lose but instead fought a very close draw. Barnes later joined Ali as a member of Shannon's stable.

Ali only suffered one defeat in his next six fights, to the then unrecognised talent of Ajose Olusegun, who stopped him in six rounds. One fight later he fought Kevin Anderson, the British and Commonwealth champion for the Commonwealth title and won on points. Following the fight Anderson decided to commute from Scotland to Manchester to train at Shannon's Gym, prompting Bob to hope that Ali would fight Floyd Mayweather next!

Sadly, Ali's father died later that year and he spent some time with his family in Namibia. When he returned he defended his title against Craig Watson. It was not his best performance and it needed to be against a talented boxer like Watson, who was best known as the man who decked Amir Khan as an amateur. Ali sustained a very bad cut that bled profusely and the fight was stopped in the ninth round. Unfortunately, Ali did not get to fight a rematch for the title as expected and, with few title options available to him, he decided to rejoin his family and girlfriend in Namibia, where he returned to service in the Namibian Army. He has since become the Namibian champion.

As for his former opponents, David Barnes dropped down to light-welterweight and became British champion for a second time, five years after winning the welterweight title. Although that was an achievement in itself, it was most unusual to do so at a lower weight and David joined a select group of champions at two weights that includes Bunny Johnson.

After losing his Commonwealth title to Ali, Kevin Anderson turned to Bob to help him prepare for his British title defence. He said: "I've come to Bob who turns out champions year after year. You never see a bad kid turned out by Bob. You know after ten minutes that he's the right man". Within ten minutes of the six-hour drive from his home in Scotland, Kevin was sparring with a former holder of his crown, David Barnes. That is not an easy spar on any day but just days later David stopped his opponent in 57 seconds! Next up, Kevin defended against the tough Eamonn Magee and floored him for the first time in his career before retaining his title on points. Unfortunately, he lost it the same way, on points to Kevin McIntyre in November '07. McIntyre, who had failed to take the title from Barnes in '03, dominated the fight but was unable to do the same in the rematch. Some thought that Anderson, clearly back on form, deserved a draw, if not the verdict.

When former undefeated, WBF European super-cruiserweight champion, Chris Bacon, decided to return to the game after a five-year absence, he turned to Bob. In the interim, Chris had excelled at judo, competing in the Olympics, and also had some success in the sport of cage fighting. The Australian-born, 37-year-old fighter spent eight weeks of hard training with Bob for a ring return that ended in two minutes and three seconds when he stopped Oneal Murray with a terrific right. His second fight was for the Central Area cruiserweight title against Tony Moran. It was a tough fight, with Chris getting knocked down for the first time in his career (in any of his careers!) but eventually overwhelming Moran in the seventh round. Chris was training for an English title challenge when he was forced to accept that at this stage of his life he was struggling to juggle business and family commitments along with his training and so, regretfully, he retired.

There is also a new generation of fighters at Shannon's Gym, including Johnny 'Rocco' Hussey and 2006 ABA welterweight champion, Denton Vassell, who remains unbeaten in the early stages of his professional career. They were recently joined by the former British Masters middleweight champion, Prince Arron.

Bob Shannon has overcome devastating personal tragedy to build up one of the country's top professional boxing gyms, which is a fitting tribute to his father and his beloved son and a proud legacy for his six grandchildren.

Dick Richardson: The Maesglas Marciano

by Wynford Jones

Dick Richardson was born in Newport on 1 June 1934 and coming from the Maesglas area of the town as it then was, the one-time milkman became known as the 'Maesglas Marciano' during a career which saw him compete not only with the best heavyweights in Britain but also the best from Europe and America.

As a youngster his preferred sport was rugby but in 1949 he won a Welsh Schoolboy title at 116lb and it was during his time in the Army, while completing his National Service, that his ring career took off. In one of his early contests he faced a certain Brian Harper for the first time and was beaten inside a couple of rounds in an Imperial Services tournament. They would meet again several years later on one of the most controversial nights of boxing ever staged in Wales.

While stationed at Farnborough in Hampshire Dick came under the wing of Johnny Lewis, a lightweight from Aberaeron, who, living in London, became a great favourite during his own boxing career at venues such as Manor Place Baths, where he was a big ticket seller. Johnny would train Dick throughout his professional career and they were to become life-long friends but, at the time they left the army, Johnny felt Dick would not have survived in lodgings so he and his wife Janet persuaded Dick to move into their home for a couple of years, thus ensuring that the impressionable young man was not overly tempted by the bright lights of the big city.

On 14 September 1954, just a fortnight after coming out of uniform, Dick was ready to make his professional debut,

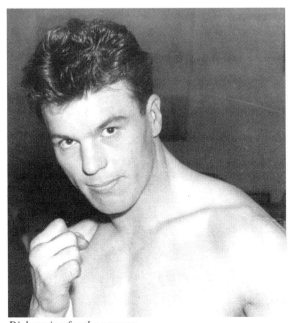

Dick posing for the camera

with Johnny having brought in Wally Lesley as manager. Wally was a shrewd businessman who would ensure that Dick earned well from his exploits in the ring. The third member of the team was Frank Duffett, as the cutsman. At the time, along with Danny Vary and Danny Holland, Frank was regarded as one of our top men in this capacity.

The venue for Dick's first assignment was Harringay Arena on a bill topped by Dai Dower against Hilaire Gaviano of France. Dick's opponent was fellow-debutant Jim Cooper, whose brother Henry was also having his first paid outing. While Henry knocked out Harry Painter in a round, Dick lost a disputed decision on points over six rounds, having put Jim Cooper down for two counts in the opening round but failing to take advantage of the situation. Although he allowed the Londoner to box from a distance to steal the verdict, Dave Phillips, writing in the South Wales Echo, saw Dick, standing at 6'2" and weighing over 14 stone, as a most promising prospect.

Dick's second contest ended in a draw but after this he put together a string of inside the distance wins. He was extremely busy during 1955, boxing no less than 14 times and in the process he avenged his defeat by Cooper when Jim was stopped in two rounds at Streatham Ice Rink. His only loss that year was a fifth-round disqualification to Hugh Ferns but he soon rediscovered his momentum and his contest against Peter Bates at the White City represented a genuine step up in class. Topping the bill was Don Cockell against Nino Valdes and there was plenty of Welsh interest on the bill, including Joe Erskine, Trevor Snell and Noel Trigg. With the rain lashing down, Dick's fight followed that of Cockell, who retired after three rounds, and their encounter saved the show. In complete contrast to what had gone before, Richardson and Bates, two of the hardest punchers in the country, simply slugged it out. Dick, weighing in at ten pounds lighter than Bates was on the receiving end for a time and was floored for a count of two by a left to the chin. The Gwent man was surprised by the ferocity of the attack but soon showed that he was able to repay with interest and he attacked with fierce body shots, finally flattening Bates for a count of nine by way of a perfect left to the jaw. Bates continued to take tremendous punishment to the head that completely closed his left eye. Dick tore in at the start of the third round and pummelled Bates around the ring and he wisely retired at the end of the round.

The winning streak continued for Dick and this led to a match with fellow-Welshman Joe Erskine at Cardiff on 7 March 1956. Dick was beaten on points over ten rounds by the masterful Erskine and Joe repeated his win when the pair met again at Porthcawl in 1959. Dick trained for the first Erskine fight at Aberystwyth and such was the level of interest in the town that a decision was made to promote Dick's next contest there. The opponent would be the German Gunther Nurnberg, who was stopped in three rounds, but Johnny Lewis insists the contest was a flop at the box office. The contest was staged at Park Avenue, home of Aberystwyth FC, and many of the locals, who have a reputation for being careful with money, opted to watch the fight from nearby Constitution Hill!

Promoter Jack Solomons was anxious to show the British public that Dick was not just another heavyweight but he was criticised in some quarters when he announced the match between Dick and Ezzard Charles to take place at the famous Harringay Arena on 2 October 1956. Charles, the former heavyweight champion of the world, had twice boxed Rocky Marciano, losing on points over 15 rounds in June 1954 and losing inside eight rounds in their September return. He was the first man to beat Joe Louis, the ageing 'Brown Bomber', in 14 years and paid the price for this with cool acceptance from the public. The names of Archie Moore and Jersey Joe Walcott figured prominently in the record of Charles so Solomon reckoned on him being the ideal opponent for Dick at this stage in his career.

The contest turned out to be the proverbial 'stinker'. Referee Frank Wilson cautioned Charles three times in the first round but the second round was even worse and after another interlude of grabbing and stumbling he ordered Charles to his corner and disqualified him. Charles insisted Dick was using his head all the time and that he was trying to push him off, while Dick was convinced that after landing a big left hook to the ribs, Charles just did not want to know! The contest showed that the former champion was clearly past his best but Dick did not really know how to handle him.

Dick was then matched with Nino Valdes, who was to prove a thorn in the flesh of British heavyweights. The contest took place on 4 December 1956 and Dave Phillips summed up the fight as follows in the South Wales Echo: "After eight torrid, horrid rounds of rough-house brawling and mauling, 22-year-old Dick Richardson, of Newport, mouth gashed, right eye closed by an outsize blue-black 'mouse' but still doggedly determined to slug it out to the bitter end, was forced to retire in his contest with world-ranked Nino Valdes, of Cuba, at Harringay Arena last night". During the contest Dick showed enormous courage, coupled with a huge will to win, and early in the encounter Valdes did not know how to cope with the wild swings and youthful enthusiasm of the Welshman. Right from the off Dick showed no respect for the Cuban's reputation but as the contest developed Valdes took advantage of the Welshman's tactic of trying to make it an inside fight. Valdes was beginning to land with sharp hooks and uppercuts, dropping Dick in the second round, and a vicious left-hook half closed Dick's right eye during the fourth round. By now, Dick was finding it difficult to cope with the ringwise Cuban and was reduced to jabbing and claiming his man, which together with headwork brought a caution from referee Andrew Smythe of Belfast. As Dick's aggression ebbed away Valdes was able to make his greater reach and weight count. During the seventh and eighth rounds he hammered Richardson unmercifully to the head, gashing his mouth, and at the bell manager Wally Lesley took one look at his man's puffed and blood-masked face before calling the referee over to indicate their retirement. Dick was almost in tears as he left the ring to a tremendous ovation, while Valdes was virtually ignored. Nino insisted that Dick was the best of the British heavyweights he had faced.

In 1957 he drew with Joe Bygraves for the Empire title in Cardiff. This was a close contest and it looked as

Dick and Ezzard Charles, the former world heavyweight champion, enjoy a joke or two before their disappointing contest in October 1956

The Welshman suffers defeat at the hands of the hard-hitting Nino Valdes

though Bygraves had taken enough after ten rounds, but his manager kept him in the fight and even though Dick won the last two rounds they came out all square on the card of referee Eugene Henderson, a result which Johnny Lewis still maintains was fair. The decision, which allowed Bygraves to retain his title, was not well received by the crowd of more than 20,000 but the contest never came up to championship standard. Dick enjoyed the physical advantages and jabbed superbly at times, but Bygraves was the more skilful of the two. Whilst Dick attacked furiously in the latter stages of the contest he lacked the skill to deal with Bygraves, who was weakening rapidly, and the final round saw both men punching away fiercely in the centre of the ring. Even though Dick had been deprived of a victory he finished the stronger of the two against a very experienced opponent.

Dick then went on to stop the German Hand Kalbfell in the fourth round of their contest at Coney Beach Arena, Porthcawl and this was a good performance bearing in mind that the latter had gone the distance with Archie Moore.

In October, he was matched with Willie Pastrano at Harringay Arena and the show was a sell-out two weeks beforehand. Pastrano back-pedalled for lengthy periods with Dick stalking continuously but the American used his brilliant left hand to repel the Welshman's attacks. The eighth was Dick's best round and the crowd were on their feet in the ninth round as he produced an all-out assault that he continued into the final round, but the maestro was rarely troubled and thoroughly deserved his victory.

In December Dick was back in the ring at Harringay, this time against Bob Baker, another American. Baker had enjoyed a distinguished career and had beaten many top-class opponents. Realistically, he had far too much experience for Dick and was able to ride punches and reply with ease. Dick was also 18 pounds lighter than his opponent and did not have the know-how to deal with Baker's leads. It was never an exciting contest but Baker showed his class with movement from the hips to sway out of range of Dick's attacks. He was, without doubt, the master but acknowledged the power of the Welshman's punching at the end.

The Welshman was certainly being thrown in against experienced men and in March 1958 he faced Cleveland Williams at the Empress Hall, Earls Court on a bill which featured Floyd Patterson with his sparring partner Dusty Rhodes. Referee Frank Wilson had warned Dick three times for butting and disqualified him in the fourth round, a decision that was booed for several minutes. Writing in the Western Mail, Alan Wood felt that Dick was well on top, having attacked Williams from the first bell. He showed little regard for the American's reputation and threw punches from all angles. Dick clearly had no fear of taking on top-ranking Americans and the victory for Williams was a hollow one. The defeat was a costly one for the Richardson camp as Cus D'Amato, the manager of Floyd Patterson, had agreed beforehand that if Dick emerged as the winner he should travel to America to challenge for the heavyweight championship of the world.

A return was set for Coney Beach Arena, Porthcawl in July. Williams and manager Bill Gore had arrived in Wales a couple of days before and had visited the fairground arena, with Williams signing autographs for Welsh fans. On 2 July, the day of the fight, Williams refused to leave his room at the Esplanade Hotel for the weigh-in. He then sent a message

Dick seen here giving some pointers to the young Billy Walker

asking to weigh-in at his hotel so Dick rushed across town and prepared to step on the scales. By now, Williams was refusing to leave his bed and was examined by Dr Jack Matthews, the former Wales and British Lions centre, who during the 1940s had created his own piece of boxing history by facing Rocky Marciano in a contest at RAF St Athan. Dr Matthews pronounced Williams fit to box and in all, he was examined by no less than four British Boxing Board of Control doctors. In the opinion of each he was fit to box, but after several changes of mind, Williams stayed in his hotel room. Promoter Sir Leslie Joseph and Board secretary Ted Waltham did everything they could to persuade Williams to box but manager Bill Gore was then left to explain his fighter's actions and almost unbelievably said: "Call it hoodoo or voodoo, he thought it would be bad for him to fight tonight". Williams would later claim that he had received a message from beyond. Initially, the Williams camp agreed a one-week postponement but the promoter's problem was rather more immediate in having to call off the show at just a few hours' notice with almost 12,000 tickets having been sold.

On 5 July, Williams did some light roadwork, but the next day both he and Gore flew back to America and Bob Baker was called in as a replacement. Baker's main concern was his money but he clearly felt that Williams did not relish facing Dick. This time, Dick came away with a win on points over ten rounds. Instead of trying to outbox Baker, he had now learned his lesson and stood his ground. Dick was much more effective in this mode and Baker, according to Johnny Lewis, acknowledged as much after the contest.

In September he was matched with Henry Cooper, again at Porthcawl, but Dick was stopped in the fifth round. After four rounds of mauling and brawling Dick cut loose in the fifth unleashing a right to Cooper's body and a left to the head. Cooper went down for a count of seven and when he rose, Dick went in to finish the job. He punched away wildly and Copper was close to being knocked out, but suddenly he caught Dick with a superb left to the jaw. Dick held on, but as the referee separated them he staggered back against the ropes. Cooper then picked his punches carefully and with Richardson sinking to the canvas, referee Ike Powell stopped the contest. Following this questions were raised regarding Dick's ability to finish a man off. The defeat was to prove costly yet again, with agreement having been reached for Dick, should he win, to travel to America to face Archie Moore with the purse, expenses and air-fares for four already finalised. He ended the year with a points win against Garvin Sawyer and boxed just three times during 1959.

After beating Bert Whitehurst and losing his return in June against Joe Erskine at Coney Beach, on 1 December, Dick faced another experienced American in Mike DeJohn at Wembley. DeJohn had appeared regularly on BBC Grandstand's Fight of the Week and was the brother of Johnny DeJohn, manager of Carmen Basilio, and a member of a famous fighting family. Uproar followed the decision of referee Bill Williams. There was a second or so of silence as the referee raised DeJohn's arm and then a storm of booing broke out. It was a rough, tough fight but several ringside reporters had Richardson winning by seven rounds to three. In the opinion of many, it was Dick's finest performance to

date as he outboxed and outfought the American, while being rarely troubled by his opponent. Promoter Jack Solomons promised a return contest as soon as possible and New York matchmaker Lou Burston commented: "Dick may not have won according to the referee, but he won in my opinion, quite easily". DeJohn himself couldn't believe that he had received an early Christmas present and said as much in Dick's dressing room after the fight.

Following the huge disappointment of this result, Dick was given the opportunity of facing Hans Kalbfell for the vacant European heavyweight title in Dortmund. Germany was not a happy hunting ground for British fighters but it proved exceptionally so for Dick, opening the door to some big purses. It was an uncompromising affair with George Whiting, writing in the Evening Standard describing Kalbfell's face at the end as "rather like a meringue that had been severely trodden on". Dick reduced the crowd to silence at the Westfalenhalle as the punches rammed into Kalbfell's face, but the strength of the German became a factor as Dick began to tire. The contest ended in the 13th round when Dick hammered Kalbfell to the floor but there was more than a little confusion in what followed. After Kalbfell rose at eight Dick stormed in for the finish but the bell rang and then there was uproar. The Richardson camp feared disqualification at this point but the referee made his way through the throng of people to raise Dick's hand in victory, insisting he had stopped the contest. Dick and his cornermen needed a police escort as they left the ring with missiles being thrown at them, but the new champion would need time for the cuts and bruises to heal.

Four months later Dick was back in action at Porthcawl for his return with Mike DeJohn, but once more there was to be controversy. The contest took place in atrocious weather conditions, with the seconds having to wear raincoats. Dick was down three times in the first round and the contest deteriorated, so much so that Dick was disqualified in the eighth round for a blatant butt. The Ring Magazine described the ensuing scenes as disgraceful, with Dick's supporters hurling chairs, bottles and rain-soaked newspapers into the ring. Referee Eugene Henderson had to be protected as he left the ring and later ten policemen were called in to escort him from his changing room to his hotel.

Dick's first defence of his European title was set for Porthcawl's Coney Beach Arena on 29 August 1960, and his opponent was to be Blackpool's Brian London. They had, of course, boxed as amateurs with Brian appearing under his family name of Harper, but this contest will always be remembered for the wrong reasons. The newspapers talked of 'Porthbrawl', and the tension of the evening spilled over into a full-scale riot after London was retired by his corner at the end of the eighth round. Brian's father Jack and his brother then became involved in a brawl with Dick's cornermen. Jack London and Johnny Lewis both ended up on the floor while Wally Lesley had to receive hospital treatment. The BBBoC's Ted Waltham announced that there would be an inquiry and a portion of London's purse was withheld pending the result.

Taking place on a windy evening, the preliminaries seemed to take an age, but when the first bell sounded

Richardson and London set about each other in tigerish fashion. London was the more aggressive of the two and his punches seemed to carry more effect. London looked to be getting the better of things in the second round but following two straight lefts and a left hook from Dick a swelling began to develop around his left eye. Despite that, near the end of the round the Blackpool man scored with a string of lefts. London continued to show the greater skill during the third round but just as the bell sounded, Dick landed a cracking left hook to the body and both men glared at each other as they returned to their corners. They pummelled each other in the fourth round but London's left hand was proving to be the significant factor and before the round ended he caught Dick with a big left as he came forward. They matched each other punch for punch in the fifth round but by now London held a clear lead and was beginning to exude confidence, so much so that in the sixth round he was almost inviting Richardson to do something. Dick replied in the seventh, catching London three times with his left but London came back to rock Dick with perhaps the best left hand of the fight. Blood now began to flow from London's left eye and he gestured frantically to referee Andrew Smythe as Dick warmed to his task. Johnny Lewis now urged Dick to try to take London out but as the bell sounded for round eight London rushed off his stool and made straight for Dick. After the referee promptly spoke to both men, they stormed forward again and London landed a big body shot as the referee separated them but by now they were shouting at each other. The crowd booed loudly as London went back to his corner at the end of the round and seconds later his cornermen signalled their man's retirement. London then left his stool and rushed towards Dick. Almost immediately the seconds became involved in a free for all and it took between 20 and 30 policemen to restore order. Dick was eventually cheered from the ring but London was jeered all the way back to his dressing room and needed the protection of several policemen. Amazingly, with the passage of time this contest is still a frequent topic of conversation.

In February 1961 Dick returned to Dortmund to defend his title against Hans Kalbfell and this time he came away with a win on points after 15 rounds. Both Wally Lesley and Johnny Lewis had urged Dick not to go for a knockout but to stick to his boxing in order to minimise the risk of disqualification and his jab was rarely out of Kalbfell's face as the plan worked superbly. He then faced Howard King at Wembley and lost a poor contest on points over ten rounds with King having brought Dick down to his level.

In February 1962 Dick was off to Germany again to defend his European title and this time his opponent was Karl Mildenberger, a southpaw who would go on to last into the 12th round against Muhammed Ali in a challenge for the heavyweight championship of the world in 1966. Mildenberger was a big favourite but Dick knocked him out in the first round, thus making it a hat-trick of successful visits to the Westfalenhalle. Early in the round it seemed that Dick might be outgunned but he caught Mildenberger with a big right hand and the contest was all over. Sadly, as on many occasions in Dick's career, victory was followed by yet another setback.

On 17 June 1962, Dick made the fourth defence of his title against former heavyweight champion of the world, Ingemar Johansson, at the Ullevi Stadium in Gothenburg. The European title had been a wonderful earner for Dick and he was to receive a purse of £40,000 for his night's work. George Whiting, of the Evening Standard, had expressed the view afterwards that Dick's only asset was his willingness to fight and had he remembered his limitations and gone slamming and banging into Johannson he might conceivably have come through his ordeal with less painful consequences. Dick absorbed a stream of left jabs from the Swede and in the eighth round Johannson showed the right hand with which he had captured the world title. A big right dumped Dick face-down in a neutral corner for a count of nine and a second right completed the job. After a reign of two years and three months the title was gone, but for Johannson there was only to be one more contest, that being a successful defence of his title against Brian London the following year in Stockholm.

Dick's final appearance in the ring came in March 1963 when he was knocked out by Henry Cooper in the fifth round of their contest at the Empire Pool, Wembley in what was Dick's only challenge for the British title. In his autobiography, Henry described Dick as one of the 'bully boys' of the ring and claims to have been butted in the early stages of their fight resulting in a split eyebrow. A fierce battle ensued with Henry once more establishing his superiority, his famed left hook proving decisive.

There is no doubt that Dick Richardson was a promoter's dream, attracting huge crowds to the major boxing venues, and such was his popularity at the box-office that more than a third of his contests were staged at open-air stadia, but after an eight-and-a-half-year career he left the ring with a record of 47 fights, which included 31 wins and two draws with 14 losses. Dick went on to run a butcher's business for many years but undertook a great deal of charity work and was involved for a time as a 'minder' for several show business personalities. He was always popular at meetings of various ex-boxer associations and there were innumerable heartfelt tributes when he succumbed to cancer on 14 July 1999. Johnny Lewis, now well into his '70s, still talks of Dick's honesty and immense loyalty. In Johnny's words: "Dick was a tearaway who became an absolute gentleman and he loved being invited to boxing functions with no thought of financial gain".

The fact that Dick's record contains a couple of defeats by disqualification suggests that perhaps his temperament was not all that it might have been and there was the occasional joker who said that Dick needed three gloves whenever he fought, the third being for his head! Controversy, it seems, was never far away and with a little luck he may have achieved much more, but his approach was uncompromising and his courage was beyond question. The heavyweight division was extremely competitive in Britain, Europe and America during the late '50s and early '60s, and with Dick standing out as arguably the most colourful character on the home front his army of supporters who packed out the venues at which he boxed were guaranteed excitement whenever he stepped through the ropes to ply his trade.

The Unlikely British Champion

by Edwin G. Hayman

Following a highly successful amateur career, when he became a junior, and four-times senior ABA champion, British Commonwealth gold, and Olympic and European bronze medallist, Pat Cowdell was expected to light up the featherweight division when he turned professional in 1977. A veritable star, he did so when winning the British and European titles and a magnificent Lord Lonsdale Belt outright in record time.

Pat Cowdell, from Warley, stepped into the Manchester ring on 24 May 1986 to defend his British super-featherweight title against locally-based Najib Daho. Although he had twice won vacant Central Area belts, Daho was fully expected to be outclassed, having lost 18 and drawn one of 48 bouts. Obviously a proficient boxer, Cowdell had not been defeated as featherweight champion, weight forcing him up a division. Pat had 32 victories and four losses on his record, two of them being inflicted by all-time great boxers, Salvador Sanchez (Mexico) and Azumah Nelson (Ghana), in world championship challenges. While the confrontation caused a certain amount of interest, Najib was a distinct underdog in boxing parlance. But, literally taking advantage of his great opportunity with both hands, Daho knocked Cowdell to the canvas four times to record a sensational win, via a knockout in the very first round. However unlikely, Najib was the British super-featherweight champion.

Born on 13 January 1959, in Morocco, North Africa, Abdul Najob Daho arrived in England when aged 15, to live in Manchester with his father, a master chef. Hardy and extremely streetwise he took to boxing, joining the local YMCA. During a short amateur career, Najib lost only to Eddie Copeland, the future (1979) ABA light-welterweight champion. This success prompted him to turn professional, in the lightweight division, when aged 18 years and four months. At Wolverhampton on 17 May 1977, Daho won his debut, stopping Kevin Sheehan in round two. A natural fighter, Najib lacked artistry and quickly discovered that amateur and professional boxing were worlds apart. Courage and strength would only take him so far. Dubbed 'The Casbah Kid', Daho fought ten times in his first year without the vest, losing five. A draw with Mick Bell was bettered six weeks later, but he needed to pace himself efficiently and use more guile. Not endowed skilfully, Najib was forced to expend too much energy, throwing too many punches in an effort to offset some opponents' superior boxing. Obviously this was exacting, especially when ineffective. Undaunted, 'The Casbah Kid' persevered, showing improvement as he gained experience. Given the opportunity to box for the vacant Central Area lightweight title, Daho, having his first ten rounder, outpointed Brian Snagg. At the end of 1979 his record was won 15, lost 11, with one draw, and he rated number 13 British lightweight.

Having been victorious in England, Scotland and Wales, Najib was excited at the prospect of his first continental match, but when tackling Dan M'Putu, in Dunkirk, France, he was

Najib Daho

outpointed by a heavier foe, whose strength prevailed.

The most famous boxer to cross gloves with Daho climbed into the ring with him in Mayfair on 15 May 1980. Scotland's Ken Buchanan became the only man to knockout 'The Casbah Kid', doing so in round seven. A former world and undefeated European and British lightweight champion, Ken also won outright a Lord Lonsdale Belt and is a Hall of Fame inductee. Najib suffered another set-back before the year ended, when Winston Spencer stopped him in round five, in Glasgow. Thus Spencer duplicated his 1977 win over Daho in Wolverhampton.

Najib did not box for a year and then, a return contest with conquerer Paul Chance resulted in another eight-round points defeat. At this career stage, Daho had only two more wins than losses, only to rise phoenix-like with an amazing revival. Thirteen victories from his next 16 contests elevated Najib to the top rung of the British super-featherweight ladder. His defeats were a ten-round stoppage by Arthur Mayisela, the South African light-welterweight title-holder; and two points losses to Scotland's Ian McLeod, one being an eliminator for the British lightweight championship. Held in Vosloorus, South Africa, the Mayisela bout was too ambitious, given the size and strength of the opposition, and when McLeod effectively blocked the route to lightweight honours Daho dropped down a division and challenged the super-featherweights.

Contesting the vacant Central Area 130lbs belt, Najib and Kevin Pritchard were thrilled when the bout was upgraded, to final eliminator status for the British title also. Successful on points, 'The Casbah Kid made history, as the first of his race to box for a championship of Great Britain. In warm-ups for this, he defeated Edward Lloyd (Wales), and African Sammy Meck, before simplifying his awesome task, producing a first-round kayo over Pat Cowdell. A magnificent scalp hung on the belt of Daho. Pat was his second and last count-out victim, whereas it was the second, and last, inside-the-distance loss for Cowdell.

The most prestigious combat for Najib was next on his agenda, a shot at the IBF world super-featherweight championship. Born in England, and raised in Australia, the holder, Barry Michael, had lost to 'The Casbah Kid' in 1979, a fact that gave Daho supreme confidence. However, on 23 August 1986 in Manchester, Michael, cleverly blending fighting and boxing skills, successfully defended his belt for the third time. Outpointed, the British champion gave his usual plucky performance, being far from disgraced.

Ten weeks later, Najib attempted to annex the European crown, in Kortrijk, Belgium. He trailed on points, when a badly lacerated mouth forced his retirement after five rounds. His antagonist, Jean-Marc Renard, had lost just three contests and was later on defeated in a WBA world title challenge.

Thirsting for revenge, Pat Cowdell was compelled to wait for their return bout, until first the mouth and then a knee that Daho had injured whilst training were healed. In addition, Najib, now overweight, took two undemanding matches, to aid peak fitness. He won these in two and four rounds respectively.

On 26 October 1987, Daho defended against the former titleholder in Ashton. Lightning did not strike the same place twice and Pat Cowdell regained the British championship, stopping Najib in round nine. Bereft of his cherished Lord Lonsdale Belt, the downcast 'Casbah Kid' was inactive for 12 months, before being uplifted by the offer of a final British eliminator versus Pat Doherty of Croydon, in Oldham. To his dismay, Daho was stopped in the ninth round again, this time due to cuts. Pat Doherty was champion of Ireland, qualifying because his parents were from Kilkenny. He moved up in weight, to the lightweight section, and won the Commonwealth belt from Murad 'Mo' Hussein (West Ham), also stopped on cuts. Pat had no qualms accepting a challenge from Najib and their second confrontation took place in Manchester on 31 May 1989. Back to his natural division poundage, Daho was in superb condition. Revenge was sweet as he stopped Pat Doherty in round 11. 'The Kid' was ecstatic.

In Oldham, on 17 October 1989, Canadian champion Johnny Kalbhenn fought tooth and nail in an attempt to dethrone the emperor. Sorely tested, Daho dug deep, battled back resolutely throughout and deservedly retained with a points decision. This was the last time Najib had a victorious arm raised. Defending once more, five months later, on 21 March 1990 in Preston, Daho lost his championship to Carl Crook, from Chorley. A stylist, Carl had height, reach, and age advantages over his opponent, and also punched more powerfully. He enhanced his career record to 21 wins, with one loss and one draw, when soundly outpointing Najib.

It was generally expected that the ex-champion would now announce his retirement from the sport. Nevertheless he did not. On 26 November 1990, a remarkable occurance amazed the boxing fraternity. At Bethnal Green, Najib Daho substituted at merely one week's notice to box for the vacant British Commonwealth super-featherweight title. Moreover, astonishingly he scaled only 127 pounds, three pounds under the division limit. This was the lightest Daho ever weighed professionally. His foe, Ghana's Thunder Aryeh, a former British Commonwealth featherweight champion,

won on points over a weakened shadow of 'The Casbah Kid'. Realistically, Najib had only a 'snowball's hell survival chance' of victory, boxing in such an injury-prone dehydrated condition. He did incredibly well to last the scheduled distance.

Daho returned to Preston to confront Carl Crook again, on 24 April 1991. Since their previous encounter, Carl had won and also successfully defended the British Championship. Both this and the Commonwealth title were at stake here and Najib, at lightweight, was at full strength once more. However, Daho was now a veteran in boxing terms and bearing in mind the result of their previous clash, Najib appeared to be an unlikely British champion. Skill overcame tenacity and Crook gradually overwhelmed his challenger. Daho would battle on, though courage alone is not enough, and his sensible chief second threw the towel into the ring in round ten. Carl thus won outright a Lord Lonsdale Belt in record time, whereas Najib gracefully retired from boxing, a qualified chef, aged 32 years and three months. From 60 contests as payee, he won 34, drew one and lost 25. Standing 5'5" tall, with his heaviest weight inside a boxing ring being 139 pounds, versus George McGurk, Najib Daho is forever in boxing records. Once a champion, always a champion, unlikely or not. He did his country, his family, and himself, proud, showing true grit, determination, and ringcraft.

It was indeed a sorrowful day when news of the death of Najib, in a Moroccan road accident, was announced on 29 August 1993. 'The Casbah Kid' was only 34 years, seven months old. RIP champ.

Point of interest

When Najib Daho (Morocco) won the British super-featherweight title on 24 May 1986, he became the 18th champion to be born outside the United Kingdom and Ireland, and the first from Morocco. As at the end of June 2008, there have been 30 men who fall into this catagory. They are:-

Antigua: Maurice Hope (L.Middle)
Barbados: Andy Straughn (Cruiser)
Curacao, DWI: Tom Collins (L.Heavy)
Ghana: Francis Ampofo (Fly), Tee Jay (Cruiser)
Guyana: Dennis Andries (L.Heavy), Howard Eastman (Middle)
Hungary: Joe Bugner (Heavy)
Jamaica: James Cook (S.Middle), Hughroy Currie (Heavy), Lloyd Honeyghan (Welter), Bunny Johnson (L.Heavy/Heavy), Kirkland Laing (Welter), Gary Mason (Heavy), Neville Meade (Heavy), Des Morrison (L.Welter), Henry Rhiney (Welter), Bruce Scott (Cruiser), Bunny Sterling (Middle)
Morocco: Najib Daho (S.Feather)
Nigeria: Tony Ekubia (L.Welter), Herbie Hide (Heavy), Peter Oboh (L.Heavy), James Oyebola (Heavy)
South Africa: Ben Foord (Heavy)
St Kitts: Roy Gumbs (Middle), Pat Thomas (Welter/L.Middle)
St Lucia: Sylvester Mittee (Welter)
Tunisia: Charlie Magri (Fly)
Zimbabwe: Ian Napa (Bantam)

Pedlar Palmer: The Box o' Tricks

by Larry Braysher

Can there be anything more disconcerting for a boxer than to throw a punch, only to discover that his opponent is no longer there and his earnest efforts are doing nothing more than causing a draught. For the opponents of 'Pedlar' Palmer this was very often an occupational hazard, as they discovered that his nickname 'the box o' tricks' had not been given lightly.

Palmer, who was born in Canning Town, East London on 19 November 1876 and christened Thomas, was one of those people who you could say was born to box. Not only did he have an abundance of natural talent but fighting was ingrained in him almost from birth. It was said that his mother could lick any woman in Plaistow, while his father standing six foot tall and weighing 14 stone was a bare-knuckle fighter of some repute and would have done better at the game had he been able to acquire a wealthy backer, something which was essential in those days. Still, he knew talent when he saw it and had great ambitions for young Tom. Being well known within his sport his father was acquainted with Charlie Mitchell and the great Jem Mace. As a result the youngster had the rare opportunity, for a seven-year-old, to spar with Mace and display his precocious gifts. At the conclusion, Mace declared that one day the boy would be a champion. Whether Mace was just being kind to the son of

An early pose of Thomas 'Pedlar' Palmer

a friend we will never know, but the boy's talent was special even at this stage and the old champion's prophecy did come true. Then, whilst waiting for his son to grow and develop, his father organised Tom and his brother Matt into a midget boxing act. They started touring the Music Halls and became a great favourite with audiences.

On reaching the age of 15 young Tom turned professional and was soon cutting a swathe through the local opposition. When his father had boxed, his other occupation had been that of a door-to-door peddler, and was known as Palmer the Peddler. So now that Tom was following in the family tradition, he too attracted the nickname but with a slight variation, and so 'Pedlar Palmer' was born.

Pedlar's style was all his own, the bobbing and swaying, ducking and dancing made him a very difficult person to pin down, let alone hit cleanly. He was unique in an age where aggression and gameness were the normal attributes most desired of a boxer. That is not to say Pedlar did not have grit when it was needed. In fact, in the later stages of his career, when his special skills began to desert him he showed enormous courage in the ring.

However now his star was rising and inevitably he came to the notice of the National Sporting Club, who in effect ran boxing as far as Great Britain was concerned. On 27 February 1893 he was matched there with Jim Collins, a bout he won comfortably enough, and it was noted at the club that he had put on a creditable show. Although his first appearance at boxing's headquarters had been a fairly minor contest, his next was definitely a step up in both position on the bill and class of opponent. This time he was to meet Walter Croot, one of the best bantam weights in the country. There were those present that night who thought that the youngster had taken on someone like Croot too early in his career and that for all his skills the other man's experience would be too much. But the 19-year-old Pedlar was supremely confident, and as it turned out this was not misplaced when he delivered a display that put him firmly on the fistic map and leapfrogged him over many of his contemporaries. In short, Croot could not lay a glove on him. He rattled home his own punches as the frustrated opponent often found himself punching thin air. Finally, the battered Croot was rescued in the 17th round when the fight was stopped.

Pedlar was now a firm favourite at the NSC and the powers that be knew that this young man with these superb skills could go on to be the first world champion nurtured by the club from the outset of his career. More consecutive wins followed and two years later he had acquired a 'backer', Alf Snelling, a bookmaker and NSC member, and also a fight with the 'Brilliant Brummie', Birmingham's Billy Plimmer for the English (British) bantamweight title and a purse of £1,500. Even more important was the fact that the victor of this match could also make a justified claim for the world crown. The black Canadian George Dixon had been the acknowledged world bantam champ, but increasing weight had seen him vacate the title and move up to featherweight. Now several claimants were jostling for the world title, including Plimmer, who had been campaigning with success in the United States. On the night though, Palmer was at his brilliant best and although Plimmer tried to stay with him, it was all too much and some indiscipline saw him disqualified in the 14th round and Palmer crowned English (British) champion.

Moreover, he had also gained recognition by many as a world champ except in America where Chicago's Jimmy Barry was still the main man. As if to give the Americans a glimpse of the opposition, Pedlar arranged a short trip there where he boxed an entertaining draw with the redoubtable George Dixon. Although his version of the noble art was not to every American's taste with his hit-and-not-be-hit style, the result of his fight against Dixon could not be denied and he returned home with his reputation enhanced.

Pedlar was at the top of his game now and the purse money he was attracting was very good indeed. However, his easy-going attitude, which was to cause him hardships in later life, was unfortunately being noted by friends and hangers-on alike. From one of his earlier bouts at the NSC he was paid a healthy £175, but by the following morning he had just £27 left, after a few hours' celebrations. Then there was the diamond encrusted belt presented to him by wealthy admirers. Naturally, he was immensely proud of the belt, but some 'friends' asked to borrow it and when it was belatedly returned the diamonds had been replaced with cut

glass. In later years when he used to recall the story Pedlar just shrugged his shoulders.

Despite the United States refusing to recognise Pedlar as the best man at his weight in the world, it was ironic therefore that this did not prevent a procession of top-class American fighters travelling across the Atlantic in an effort to relieve him of his crown. Johnny Murphy, Dave Sullivan and Billy Rotchford all came and attempted to wrest Pedlar's version of the world title from him, but they all left empty-handed. Even Billy Plimmer was given another chance and although this time he lasted a few rounds longer, he was stopped in the 17th. Then in 1899 came the opportunity Pedlar and his backers had been yearning for, a chance to get world recognition as king of the bantamweights. The Americans were now championing a fiery, two-fisted knockout specialist called Terry McGovern. The winner of a bout between these two could call himself champion with no arguments to the contrary. Pedlar and his team which included NSC stalwards Charles Blacklock and 'Peggy' Bettinson travelled to the United States for what was to be a landmark bout in Pedlar's career. Well, it was a landmark, but not in the way Pedlar hoped.

The two met at Tuckahoe, New York and had widespread publicity with special trains conveying some of the 10,000 people who had travelled to the fight. However, onlookers noted that whereas McGovern looked relaxed and unperturbed in his corner, Pedlar, normally supremely self-assured, looked somewhat tense and nervous. Almost from

Pedlar posing with 'Terrible' Terry McGovern, who flattened him in 75 seconds at Tuckahoe, New York on 12 September 1899

the first bell McGovern charged into Pedlar and although the Englishman tried all his tricks, punches that normally missed were catching him flush. Eventually he took a count of 'six' and the end was in sight. Suffering under a fusillade of punches he sank to the floor again, and referee George Siler counted to ten. He could have counted to 20 and it would not have made any difference. After two minutes and 32 seconds of action it was all over and McGovern was undisputed champion. Tragically, although the American became recognised as one of the great champions his personal life suffered. Plagued with psychiatric problems McGovern later spent several periods in institutions. In 1910 he collapsed and shortly afterwards died, aged only 38 years.

What about Pedlar? Well, naturally he was crestfallen, although he confessed that after being caught early in the round he could not remember much more. However, he had lost any claim to the world title, lost his unbeaten record and perhaps, more importantly, lost a degree of confidence. Pedlar's story was not done though and there were plenty more good days still to come, but in truth he was never quite the same fighter again.

Now back in 'Blighty', Pedlar had some rebuilding work to do to his career and what better way than to defend his British title against the up and coming Harry Ware. To the spectators at the NSC that night it was clear that although Pedlar did not box badly he still had a hangover from his McGovern experience. He received the points verdict after 15 rounds, but it was fair to say that a number of the audience felt that it should have gone the other way. Still it was a win and after such a close-run thing a return between the two was a natural.

Pedlar's free and easy lifestyle also extended to his training and as someone with so much natural talent he tended to look upon it as a bit of a chore. For the Ware return though he resolved to pull out all the stops and to train properly and under supervision. Joe Palmer was a relative of Pedlar's and he was a good quality professional athlete. He was also steeped in boxing, his uncle having met Pedlar's father for the Essex championship on Plaistow Marshes with bare knuckles many years before. Joe also went on to become a top-class boxing referee. Therefore, he was happy to undertake Pedlar's training and whisked him away from his East London haunts down to Hove in Sussex where they obtained the use of a private gym which was loaned to them.

However, Pedlar, who was normally a heavy smoker with a love of beer and a bet, found the monastic existence too hard to take. Joe had noticed that despite all the roadwork his charge was doing the weight loss seemed only a fraction of what he expected. His suspicions aroused, he had also noticed that on their daily runs there was one particular winding hill which Pedlar used to sprint up leaving Joe well behind and out of his sight for several minutes. On this occasion, Joe really gritted his teeth and caught up with Pedlar at the top of the hill much earlier than usual. As he came round the bend he was just in time to see the landlord of a nearby public house handing over a tankard of beer to the expectant Pedlar, all by prior arrangement.

Although this ruse had been rumbled there were still the cigarettes to contend with and Joe knew he could smell the smoke from Pedlar's bedroom. Of course he denied all knowledge and several searches by Joe proved fruitless. It was only when the trainer accidentally knocked a picture hanging on the wall that several cigarettes fell down from behind it. There were another couple of pictures hanging in the room, and sure enough when moved by Joe these too rained cigarettes. Joe subsequently discovered that a maid at the boarding house, who Pedlar had befriended, used to put them in place every day when the pair were out training. The final straw for Joe though, was finding Pedlar's room empty late one evening. Making enquiries he discovered that the miscreant had shinned down the drainpipe and found him propping up the bar, beer in hand, at a local pub. On this occasion Joe exploded and told Pedlar a few home truths and was determined to leave his relative without a trainer. However, after a plea for clemency from the contrite boxer there was no more of this particular 'box of tricks' from Pedlar. In fact, at the weigh-in for the contest Pedlar's weight was dead right. Nonetheless, it did not stop him from losing on points over 20 rounds to Ware, which also saw him lose his English (British) title. The fact that most people thought he looked a good winner on the night was of little consolation.

Despite his recent disappointments, Pedlar was lifted when the opportunity came for him to dispute the world bantamweight title again. McGovern had moved up in weight and a new American, Harry Harris, was on the scene claiming the title. Harris was also willing to travel to England and box Pedlar at the NSC over 15 rounds. At almost 5'8" in height, Harris was abnormally tall for his weight and although Pedlar had early success when he put his man down in the third round, the American came on stronger as the fight progressed. It became an uphill battle for Pedlar and although he stuck to his task, making it an excellent contest for onlookers, he visited the canvas four times and was a clear loser at the finish.

Despite that being his last chance of winning the world title, Pedlar kept himself busy. He was now losing the odd bout but was still good enough to beat the likes of Spike Robinson, Digger Stanley and win a rubber match with Harry Ware. Although money was coming in, it was still going out just as fast. Pedlar's former backer, Alf Snelling, had encouraged him to open a bank account to safeguard some of his cash. However, although he did, Pedlar never really understood the intricacies of finance. There was never any shortage of types ready to cadge a loan or handout, for which he readily used his cheques. Eventually he was called in to see his bank manager who tried to explain that he was overdrawn and had no money left in the account. Pedlar replied that there had to be a mistake and that there must be plenty of money left as he had all these cheques left in his book that still had to be used.

In 1904 Pedlar received an offer to box in South Africa. Albert Fleming, the son of the late John Fleming (an NSC founder member), was running the Wanderers Stadium in Johannesburg and he offered Pedlar a first-class ticket to come out and engage in three contests. It was a long way from home but it was a tempting offer and the proposed purse money sounded good. He also took into account that he was a married man with children to support. So after seeking some advice from his old friend Jack Hare, who had visited South Africa previously, he agreed to the trip and set sail from Southampton. Accompanying him was his brother Matt, who would train him and being no mean performer himself, maybe engage in a bout or two.

Pedlar's first bout was against the South African bantam champion Danny Hyman, an ex-patriot Englishman who had settled out there. It was too much of a step-up in class though for the local man and he was stopped in nine rounds. Next came a bout with their featherweight champion, Watty Austin, who had built up an unbeaten record. The bout was one for the purists with both men exhibiting some exceptional skills before the referee announced a draw after 20 rounds. A return for the two was an obvious conclusion and this time it would be for a purse of £500, winner take all. On the night, Pedlar's brother Matt took part in an earlier contest but was kayoed in five rounds. Pedlar had been visibly upset by the result and was considerably fired up when he entered the ring for his own bout. This time he won in a canter and ended the unbeaten run of the South African.

So Pedlar returned home with his reputation enhanced and well paid for his efforts. For Matt, his brother, the losing bout meant that the trip had not been a personal success though. Matt was as talented a boxer as Pedlar some said, but he did not have a strong constitution and tended to flag over longer distances. Some years later he died in a London hospital whilst still a relatively young man.

Pedlar was soon back in action on his return to England and following a points victory over Young Joseph he

The once famous Palmer had seen better years when this picture was taken

was rewarded with two chances at the English (British) featherweight title. First he dropped a points verdict to the very capable Ben Jordan, prior to the new star of the NSC, Joe Bowker, proving too young and strong before stopping him inside 12 rounds.

There were a few more bouts and Pedlar still won more than he lost, but little more than a year later he was virtually a retired boxer. Unfortunately, he did not get much chance to enjoy the new direction his life had taken and 'Lady Luck' deserted him once again when he was involved in an altercation with another passenger whilst travelling home on a train from Epsom Races. Apparently the man concerned was somewhat boisterous when he entered the carriage and this led to words between himself and Pedlar, which resulted in the ex-boxer striking the man. In one of those freak accidents that mercifully rarely occurs, the man died virtually instantly. Naturally, to kill a man in what was generally a minor fracas was devastating to Pedlar and something he could never have foerseen. He was charged with murder, later reduced to manslaughter, for which he received five years' penal servitude.

On his release from prison, Pedlar was 35 years old and although he did not kid himself that his best days in the ring were over it was the only way he knew to raise some urgently required funds. Thus a comeback was launched. It did not take him long to realise that although his ring skills were still evident for a few rounds his stamina had left him, and it must have been a sad sight to see the former champion doing all he could to avoid the rushes of much younger men. His last competitive bout was a curious affair at Hoxton Baths with Jim Driscoll, another former great now also well past his best. Pedlar, who had not boxed for some time, went down five times and stopped in four rounds.

Although now retired once and for all from the ring it did not mean a quieter existence for the old champion. He still loved a bet, being was a part-time bookmaker, and still appeared for the odd exhibition bout with old friends. Also his son Billy was a more than useful featherweight during the 1920s. Pedlar and his family became resident in Brighton and he was a regular sight around the town with his muffler and bowler hat set at a jaunty angle. However, there were still bad times ahead for him and in 1930 he appeared at Brighton Magistrates Court charged with Attempted Suicide. The court heard that he had become depressed and taken to drink following the recent loss of one of his daughters, when another family member came home to find him with his head in the oven with the gas on. The magistrates took a lenient view, however, when his wife spoke on his behalf and they bound him over for six months on the condition that he gave up drink.

Pedlar lived out the rest of his days in Brighton and it was 1949 before he died following a bout of pneumonia, aged 72 years. Pedlar had earned between £30,000 and £50,000 from boxing, an enormous amount of money then, none of which was left at the end. Forever the eternal optimist, with his Macawber-like 'something will turn up' attitude, Pedlar was a larger than life character and for those who knew him and saw him box he would never be forgotten. He would have been the first to say he had a good innings.

Con O'Kelly: The First White Hope?

by K R Robinson

After his comprehensive defeat of Jim Jeffries at Reno on 4 July 1910 Jack Johnson was grudgingly recognized as the world's first, undisputed, black heavyweight boxing champion. Jack London's provocative and racist call for a white man to wipe the golden smile from the face of 'Lil Arthur' led to hundreds of strong, young men throwing their hats into the professional ring. Carl Morris - the Salpula Giant – has, on the word of Nat Fleischer, long been accepted as the original White Hope. This is open to dispute.

George Cornelius O'Kelly, born at Dunmanway, County Cork on 4 March 1884, was an Irishman from head to toe – friendly, garrulous and with a touch of the blarney. After 18 months teacher training on leaving school, Con moved to England, where he eventually adopted Hull as his home town and joined the local police force in 1902. The police and fire services operated in unison and so he found himself a fire-fighter.

Con was a big man and naturally athletic so he joined the Hull Police Athletic Club where he swam, ran, hurdled and jumped to police championship standard. A colleague suggested that he try his hand at wrestling and, though he had some wrestling experience at home in Ireland, it now became his obsession. He threw himself into the study of his chosen sport and quickly became conversant with the basics of the various styles – Cumberland, Westmoreland, collar and elbow, Devon, Cornwall, Graeco-Roman and Jiu-Jitsu; indeed so adept did he become at the Japanese style that he was engaged as instructor to the police force, teaching the rudiments to most of his fellow coppers. Con made his first public appearance as a wrestler, lasting 15 minutes, against professional Tom McInerny at Hull Hippodrome in February 1907, winning £10 which he donated to charity. After failing to gain a fall against McInerny, Con next defeated Joe Carroll, the middleweight champion catch-as-catch-can wrestler of the world, for a silver cup. He entered the British Amateur Wrestling Championships in November 1907, winning the super-heavyweight title by defeating his four opponents in a total of 34 minutes.

During March 1908 Con was fighting a fire in a sawmill when a 20-foot brick wall collapsed on him and three others. Rushed to the Royal Infirmary, Con was badly cut and bruised and off work for a month but was soon back in the ring, although the loss of his British Championship to London policeman Edmund Barrett should not have been too much of a surprise.

London was the venue of the 1908 summer Olympics and Con was one of an eight-man team selected to represent the United Kingdom in the freestyle heavyweight competition. Only two 'foreign' wrestlers competed – Lee J. Talbott of the USA and Jacob Gundersen of Norway. Con beat Talbott in one minute, 20 seconds in the first round of the competition, while Harry Foskett fell after four minutes and five seconds in the quarter-finals and old rival Edmund Barrett was beaten on the two minute, 14 second mark in the semi-final.

O'Kelly faced Gundersen in the final: best of three falls. Jacob put up stubborn resistance for the first fall before succumbing after 13 minutes, 27 seconds. Con gained the second fall, and the gold medal, on the three minute, 35 second mark. It is popular to denigrate the early Olympic champions but little more could have been asked of O'Kelly than he achieved, beating both of the foreign competitors – Gundersen was said to be champion of Norway and Sweden - and reversing his previous defeat against Barrett.

Con returned to Hull for a hero's welcome. 12,000 people thronged the Paragon Station where he was greeted by the chiefs of the police and fire services. Con was hoisted onto the shoulders of six of his fireman pals and carried to a horse-drawn fire engine draped with Union flags, which took him off to the fire station for a grand reception.

As a young man of 22 with a wife and young son, Con was at a crossroads. Though he had been most careful to preserve his amateur status he was now beset by offers of personal stage appearances and professional matches. A devout Catholic, Con was considered a level-headed fellow with an engaging personality. This was well illustrated by his meeting with J. Frank Bradley, editor of the popular sporting paper Mirror of Life, who was in Hull to act as referee for a boxing competition. While dining in a local restaurant Bradley was informed that a young man wished to see him. Once ushered in Con introduced himself and enthralled the journalist with his account of his Olympic campaign and discussed his plans for the future. He had decided that this lay in professional wrestling and he expressed his ambition to face world's champion Frank Gotch and the Pole Stanislaus Zbyszko, both of whom he challenged through the pages of the Mirror of Life.

O'Kelly seen here on Police duty in 1908

Still a policeman, Con engaged in various charity events while awaiting developments. At the Palace Theatre, before the Mayoress of Hull, he threw Walter Colley, North of England heavyweight champion, and two of his pupils in 23 seconds! Two months later, at the Alexandra Theatre, Con undertook to throw six men within thirty minutes, a feat accomplished in three minutes and ten seconds, presided over by old prize-ring champion Jem Mace.

Though his challenges to Gotch and Zbyszko had come to nought Con was matched with Switzerland's John Lemm for the world heavyweight championship, £100 a-side and a percentage of the gate. Gotch and George Hackenschmidt were the leading heavyweights but could not come to terms. O'Kelly versus Lemm was an attempt to establish a champion whom the leading contenders would have to challenge. The match took place as a matinee at the Oxford Music Hall in London on 14 January 1909.

The music hall was packed with personalities - Arthur Bettinson of the National Sporting Club, Eugene Corri the leading boxing referee, Charlie Mitchell, Bob Fitzsimmons, Jimmy Britt and Gunner Moir, amongst others, witnessed an exciting contest. Con gained the first fall, due to an error of judgement on Lemm's part, in three minutes, 17 seconds. Lemm then equalled the score in five minutes, 52 seconds and gained the decider in two minutes, three seconds. Professional wrestling was going through a period of confusion and the National Sporting Club, along with a newly-created board of control, were attempting to establish an element of honesty and fairness within the sport. Praise was lavished on Lemm and O'Kelly and the quality and organization of the promotion. O'Kelly had been allowed to take leave from the police force to train for his encounter with Lemm but there was opposition within the Watch Committee to his pursuing a professional career as a sportsman while remaining a constable. The breaking-point came when Con was challenged by Jose Lavette, described as the Spanish champion. Con replied that as he was prevented from wrestling for money he was willing to meet Lavette in a private contest, best of three pin-falls. The Spaniard responded in terms questioning the Irishman's motives and pluck. Con immediately tendered his resignation from the police force and defeated Lavette in two straight falls in a public contest.

Con's achievements in the wrestling ring brought the sport well to the fore in the Hull area. The most popular and accessible form was 'forfeit matches' staged at music-halls and theatres. A well-known wrestler performed 'strongman' stunts, demonstrated holds, and wrestled exhibition matches with a partner much as a similarly ranked boxer would perform. The climax was a challenge to local wrestlers to last 15 minutes for a 'forfeit' of £5. When such an attraction appeared in Hull, Con was usually the target of the challenges; on occasions these were even printed on bills posted around the town.

John Lemm proved a big hit when he appeared in the city during March 1909. The Swiss and his manager were interviewed by a representative of the Hull Daily News after an evening performance at the Hippodrome in which he had seen off three local challengers. Lemm had a high opinion of O'Kelly and expressed his willingness to again meet the Irishman but believed that Con needed the extra experience of meeting men such as Pat Connolly and Jimmy Essen, the leading Irish and Scottish grapplers. O'Kelly came back to Hull from an engagement elsewhere with an immediate challenge to Lemm for a match for £250 a-side, three falls, catch-as-catch-can. He was, however, at pains to explain that he had interesting prospects – being in negotiation to meet Frank Gotch in Montreal in September and seriously considering an offer from Bob Fitzsimmons to make him a champion boxer.

The old heavyweight champion was at the tail end of his boxing career and appearing at the Oxford Music Hall as an actor, and he had been an interested spectator when Con wrestled Lemm. Fitz was an accepted expert on all matters concerning boxers and boxing and a greatly-respected former heavyweight champion. He rarely sponsored young fighters and his approach to Con was unique. "There is one Englishman today who I would back against the world if I had him in training for six months. That man is O'Kelly, of Hull, the policeman wrestler. He is my ideal boxer. I would undertake to make him the greatest boxer in the world. He ought to quit wrestling and put on the gloves right away, before he is a day older. O'Kelly stands 6'3", he is 47 inches round the chest, he has the right long arms and slender legs, and could be turned into a terrific fighting machine. There is not a man in training today who would not go under to O'Kelly. There is fame and fortune for him when he enters the ring".

O'Kelly was certainly an impressive figure. Prior to his match with Lemm, his personal statistics were published in the Sporting Life: Age 24 years. Height 6'2¾". Weight 15 stone eight pounds. Chest 51 inches. Waist 32½ inches. Biceps 16½ inchess. Thigh 26¾ inches. Neck 21½ inches. Calf 17 inches. Surely a neck size of 21½ inches required no special exercise. Indeed, on the few occasions when he was staggered or floored during his subsequent boxing career he was never in danger of being counted out. His immediate reaction to being stung was always to fight back. When fouled he would retaliate. Con was nothing if not competitive.

Con's first big wrestling match in Hull occurred on Saturday 15 May at the Boulevard Stadium. In the opposite corner was Andre Markovitch, the champion of Servia. Though outweighed by the far-more-experienced foreign champion, Con was taller and stronger and showed greatly improved technique, drawing praise in the widespread coverage in Yorkshire newspapers. Much of the credit for his improvement was laid at the door of Joe Carroll, his former opponent and now trainer. Con gained the first fall in 14 minutes, 27 seconds and the second in eight minutes, 12 seconds.

O'Kelly was back in Hull on 31 May for the first showing of Jimmy Essen at the Hippodrome. Con was known by the audience to be in the building and after Joe Carroll had failed in an attempt to stay 15 minutes with the Scotsman the cry went up for "O'Kelly". Con pushed his way to ringside where he was greeted warmly by Essen and he accepted the challenge of lasting 15 minutes for a tenner. The manager of the theatre, Mr Harry Dunford, intervened to explain that: "The house must be closed by law by 11 o'clock and there was no time for the match to take place tonight".

Con returned the following evening to relieve Essen of his £10. On two more occasions during Essen's stay at the Hippodrome, Con repeated the feat, much to Jimmy's dismay and increasing desperation. Each evening the theatre was packed to the ceiling and the electric atmosphere was increased by Essen's rough, tough tactics, but Con was undaunted by the wild Scotsman and was well able to last. Both men addressed the crowd, Essen declaring that O'Kelly was much too good for forfeit wrestling and he challenged him to a match to a finish. Con said he was ready as soon as Jimmy came up with the cash - the bout to be within three weeks.

Before negotiations could be resolved Lemm returned to the Hippodrome and offered to forfeit £10 if he could not pin the big Irishman in five minutes. A Mr Graham offered to increase the forfeit to £20 and the match was on. Lemm put up a titanic struggle but failed to save his forfeit. Lemm pleaded that the mat was too small but with it increased in size he could beat Con. O'Kelly expressed his willingness to wrestle every night for a tenner but Apollo, Lemm's manager, would not agree. As traditionally a forfeit lost was deducted from the loser's salary this was not unexpected. Con travelled to Middlesbrough the following evening and relieved Jimmy Essen of a further £20 by staying ten minutes. The next evening he repeated the feat, this time over 15 minutes. Agreement was reached for a match to a finish – the best of three pin-falls, catch-as-catch-can, for a purse of £300 and Essen's British heavyweight wrestling championship at the Boulevard on 3 July.

4,500 spectators packed the arena to witness the match. The Scotsman opened aggressively, gaining the first fall in 15 minutes and sending Con reeling and dazed back to his dressing-room for the ten minutes respite. The action resumed with Con none the worse; indeed Essen was kept on the defensive for most of the 34 minutes before Con gained the equalizing fall. The deciding session lasted 39 minutes before O'Kelly flattened Jim and pinned him. Con's ecstatic supporters carried him shoulder-high to his dressing-room - British heavyweight champion. Con had suffered a blackened left eye, caused by violent contact with the ring floor in the first session, which accounted for his unsteady condition after the first fall.

Con went back to the music-hall circuit in company with Joe Carroll but returned to Hull on 3 August when Carroll met Jiu-Jitsu champion Yukio Tani of Japan, attempting to stay 15 minutes for £5. Tani saved his forfeit in 11 minutes, 25 seconds. Joe pleaded for another chance and it was agreed that Yukio would forfeit £5 the following evening if Carroll could last five seconds longer. Con seconded his trainer who gained the forfeit. Anxious for action, O'Kelly promised to throw Tani and the other half-dozen members of his company for a forfeit. It was finally agreed that Con would attempt to stay 15 minutes against the Japanese for £20 the next evening, when Con took the money. Con had a weight advantage of six stones!

Con was in demand on the circuit but meaningful matches were hard to arrange. Busy as the wrestling scene was in Europe the centre of action was rapidly shifting to America. Hackenschmidt was playing hard to get and both Frank Gotch and Stanislaus Zbyszco had returned to the States. O'Kelly had been so successful with his music-hall appearances and forfeit matches that he could easily afford his passage across the pond. He starred for a week at the Hippodrome at Hull from 11 October, taking on two opponents each evening in forfeit matches and only losing his fiver when Yorkshire heavyweight champion Baldwin stayed ten minutes without being thrown. In company with Joe Carroll, Con left Liverpool aboard the SS Carmania on 26 October bound for the States. A crowd of admirers saw him off with a rousing rendition of 'Has Anybody Here Seen Kelly'. He settled in Boston - a city with a large Irish population - but had hardly had time to draw breath when Lemm, Essen and Pat Connolly all arrived determined to meet Gotch for the championship.

Con's first Stateside bout was in New York; a city said to have an Irish population greater than the Auld Sod. Though the Irish were a fiercely proud and tight-knit community, factional rivalry was only just below the surface. When Pat Connolly of County Galway and Con O'Kelly of County Cork were matched at the Grand Central Palace for the heavyweight championship of Ireland and the promise of a match with Gotch for the winner, trouble seemed guaranteed.

The two men faced each other on 22 November before an excited and partisan crowd of a couple of thousand. Reports vary but the gist of the matter was that two highly-trained athletes lost their cool in their efforts to prevail. Connolly, the smaller man by more than 40lb, took his opponent by surprise and attacked from the start. Taken aback, O'Kelly sought refuge on the canvas, much to the annoyance of the crowd. What happened next is confused. Either the reeling O'Kelly butted his opponent in the face or Connolly gouged O'Kelly's eye. Both men now resorted to punching in retaliation. Referee Tom Jenkins parted the pair and made them shake hands before restarting the contest. Within seconds fists were again flying and blood flowing. Jenkins warned the two men that any further infringements of the rules would bring disqualification - a warning reinforced by Captain Langtry of the 25th Police Precinct, who had entered the ring.

Shortly after another restart Connolly, known as the 'Galway Tiger', was back on top, sending Con twice flying into the ropes, then slamming him to the mat with crotch holds followed by two further visits from waist holds. After 25 minutes both men were staggering groggily around the ring exchanging wild swings. True to his word Jenkins sent the pair back to their dressing-rooms. After what was described as the worst wrestling bout ever held in New York City, the crowd left the arena all rivalry forgotten; indeed they declared that neither of the contestants was an Irishman - and the Irish heavyweight championship remained vacant.

Con's American campaign had gotten off to a disastrous start and in 29 minutes his New York prospects had been reduced to nil. Nothing daunted, Con returned to Boston where he was matched with another new arrival, Austrian

Joseph Schubert, at the Columbia on 8 December. The Boston Post summed up the match: "The sons of Old Erin were on hand in large numbers at the Columbia last night to see Con O'Kelly, their new idol, in action, and the pity of it Con was not made to extend himself for Schubert, his opponent, was far too light a man to give the Irishman a battle. Con had everything his own way and made the Austrian look a novice. The Irish giant got his man on the mat for his first fall in about three minutes; the second session went about eight minutes with the son of Old Erin coming out on top. It was a good bout while it lasted, but the sporting fans failed to get a good line on the Irishman's abilities as a grappler".

Con cast his eyes south to St Louis where Jim Jeffries and his Athletic Combination – including Frank Gotch – were in the middle of a 13-week tour, playing to sell-out houses. After almost six years in retirement, Jeff had been pressurized into returning to the ring to try and regain the heavyweight championship for the white race from Jack Johnson. Once his tour was over Jeff intended to set up a training-camp in California to prepare for his comeback. Having gained an introduction to Jeff, Con proved himself an instant hit with the old champion who suggested to his manager Sam Berger, former 1904 Olympic heavyweight boxing champion, that the giant Irishman would be a great asset in maintaining morale at his camp on the coast. "He'd be a great man to jolly everyone along, and besides that he looks to me as if he'd make a corking good fighter", Jeffries told Berger. Con was pretty cute when it came to public relations - he happily gave interviews to the press, was always eager to address the crowd from the ring and maintained correspondence with his home-town newspaper, the Hull Daily News. A letter from Con was published on 5 January 1910 announcing that he had just taken $500 off Gotch by resisting the world champion for 15 minutes in a forfeit match. O'Kelly enclosed a cartoon from the St Louis Republic which mocked Gotch's frustration. The Irishman was brim-full of confidence, declaring his willingness to wrestle Gotch, Zbyszco or Dr B.F. Roller but he acknowledged that everyone wanted to face the champion. He had two matches lined up and if he won both he intended to return home.

After the Gotch handicap match Berger approached Con with an offer to join Jeffries' combination. Con agreed but explained that he could not commit to joining Jeff's training-camp as he wanted to satisfy himself that he could be a first-class wrestler. If not he would join Jeff on the west coast. Next stop after St Louis was Milwaukee where Con stayed 15 minutes with Roller. Chicago followed, where he threw Jim McCormick in nine minutes, 22 seconds and Jim Lauria of Kansas City in eight minutes, 42 seconds. On 8 January, still in Chicago, Con beat Otto Speck with a first fall in six minutes, 20 seconds and a second in four minutes, ten seconds, appearing second on the bill to top-notcher Charles Kid Cutler. Con was obviously in very good form and his homecoming was delayed. Still in Chicago, on 14 January he beat Walter Willoughby, gaining two straight falls in 19 minutes, 20 seconds and ten minutes, 30 seconds.

On 25 January Con again wrote to the Hull Daily News." I am in great shape, and so is Jim Jeffries. The latter finishes

his tour in three weeks... On 1 April he enters into serious training for his fight with Johnson, and by July it is expected he will be in splendid condition. I shall come back a finished boxer".

One wonders what had caused O'Kelly to have a change of mind and decide to become a boxer. Perhaps he figured that there were just too many contenders for Gotch's championship. (Con was a great admirer of Gotch; maybe he didn't fancy his chances!), or did Jeffries convince him that Fitz was right and he had a golden future with gloves?

Interviewed by Ed Smith of the Chicago Evening American in mid-March, Con told Smith that he was training hard with a view to contesting the British heavyweight boxing championship next winter. He was taking daily lessons from Tom Ryan and was very hopeful of some day being heavyweight champion of the world. Tommy Ryan, a former world welter and middleweight champion, soon emerged as Con's manager and trainer. Bob Fitzsimmons had returned to Australia to have what was to be the final major contest of his career against Bill Lang and so was not available to look after his 'discovery'. Ryan, who was credited with moulding Jeffries into a top-class fighter and masterminding his championship winning victory over Fitz, would probably have been the trainer of choice for any big heavyweight. Relations between Ryan and Jeffries had sometimes been fraught over the years but Jeff may have recommended his old trainer.

The views of Jeff and Fitz would be enough to persuade most people that Con was a good investment but Tommy was not like most people: he was a highly opinionated individual who knew exactly what he wanted. "All I want to know about this fellow (O'Kelly) is whether he is game or not. He's big enough, if he's only good enough. He has a lot of natural talent for boxing, and the main thing I like about him is that he hasn't a bad habit to begin with. Usually when I take hold of a fighter and start to work with him I discover that he has a lot of bad tricks that he has picked up himself or obtained from others. It is a difficult task to break a man of these tricks. It is sometimes impossible, for I have noticed that a man may forget them while he is in training, but as soon as he gets into a real fight he resorts right back to them again. O'Kelly is loose and free in his action, that is a great point in his favour. There is no tied-up action, not a muscle bound in any way I can discover. I figured that perhaps the wrestling game might have tied him, but it hasn't. You see Con is a natural athlete. He never got any of his muscle from the gymnasium apparatus. What he possesses is his by his own right of natural culture. O'Kelly is bred to be game, but you never can tell. Still he looks awfully good to me right now, and stands his gruelling and his instructions like a real promising bit of championship material. I'm going along with him". Tommy took 'The Irish Harp', as Con was dubbed by the press, north to the Pastime Gym in Syracuse, where he was put through his paces. Ryan was delighted with him, saying: "I tell you, and I know, in gameness, speed and strength this young fellow promises to have it on Jeffries, and his chances of fighting to the top is 100 per-cent better than I thought Jeffries' were when I first started training the Californian. You know why? He's a smart fellow. He wants to learn, and being just naturally bright, he picks things up easily. You can make fighters, all kinds of them, but if they're blockheads you can't shape their heads for them. This fellow has the head."

Johnson was not taking Jeffries' challenge lightly; he approached Ryan to act as his trainer for the forthcoming battle. Tommy, with Con in tow, visited Jack in Chicago to discuss terms; he was quite clear as to the terms required. "I intend to have a talk with Johnson tomorrow morning about training him for this fight. You remember we talked over this proposition before, but we never reached agreement. I will have an understanding with him tomorrow, and if he agrees to listen to my dictates. I will start him in training at once".

There never was a chance that Jack would agree to Ryan's terms as he explained in his autobiography. "In my training periods I never maintained a particular chief trainer. I never left it to my trainers to devise methods nor did I look to them for instructions. I had worked out my own system which I believe surpasses all others, and my trainers and others were directed to follow to the letter". Rumour was that Ryan feared that if he trained a winning Johnson his life and reputation would be at risk, so he declined to come to terms. This was just a rumour. Come April, Tommy considered that Con was ready for his first outing and negro Joe Kid Cotton, a protege of Joe Choynski, was lined up. Cotton, who had sparred Johnson and Choynski, argued that any fighter who could stand up before the champion for six fast rounds must be a better man than the ordinary run of fighters. But the match faded as Cotton joined Johnson's camp and Choynski joined Jeff as joint trainer with Jim Corbett.

Though the Cotton match had fallen through Tommy and Con were still working out in Chicago and were there when Johnson departed for the west coast. After Jeff's defeat, Con was asked what made him think that he had the beating of the black champ. "Well I'll tell you. I feel it. Down in me heart there is something that tells me that I'm the one to bring the championship back where it belongs. I felt it when I left Chicago and shook hands with Johnson just before he started out for the West. I have felt it ever since and in three short years t'will be Con O'Kelly, the white man, and not Jack Johnson, the coloured man, who'll have the belt. You don't believe it now, but I'm really anxious to get at that fellow. Tommy says wait, and of course he's right, but I want to be the first to best him, and I want him to be as good as he is now. Sure it's now that I feel that I'm able to beat him. A couple of years from now they'll say I couldn't beat him in his prime. But I'm telling you now that I'm to be the champion, and 'tis over him I'll get it from".

Johnson was well aware of Con's ambitions. When interviewed after his great victory over Jeff on the fourth of July, as to his next opponent, Jack declared: "Langford I do not think much of, Burns I have whipped once before, Ketchel is too easy, and I do not think that (Con) O'Kelly would have a chance".

Con's first opponent as a boxer was the Pole, Con Cominsky, at Sioux City on 17 June 1910. Cominsky, who was put away in three rounds, claimed a win over Kid Cotton. Next in line was Al Williams of Pittsburg on 15 August. Under the management of Jimmy Dime, Williams

had racked up seven or eight wins, all by knockout, and threatened to give Con a tough time. The hall was packed in anticipation. Con started nervously and Williams showed his greater experience early on, but the Irishman's greater strength began to tell in the clinches. Con displayed commendable skills in ducking and blocking, though Williams lacked nothing in endeavour. Both were landing solid punches but Con seemed to have the edge in power. Al touched down late in the fifth but fought back well. The sixth was even. Con came on strongly in the seventh when they engaged in some fierce rallies, each emerging with facial damage. Con rushed Williams over the ropes in the eighth, and received a warning from the referee before trapping Al in a corner where the bout ended with Al being kayoed by a hard right swing to the jaw.

Black fighter Billy Edwards of Pittsburg was next up on 19 August, in the open air at Watertown near Syracuse. Billy was promised $100 by a local sport if he beat the 'Harp'. Edwards started off well, sending Con staggering back to his corner at the end of the first round. Con came out fresh and smiling for the second and concentrated on his opponent's body. By the third O'Kelly was fully recovered from his first-round beating and continued his body attack that had Edwards wincing. Billy was landing his jab to the head. The fourth was evenly fought but the Pittsburg man seemed to be weakening. Ryan was concerned at Con's reckless approach in the fifth and called out to him to calm down. Con seemed content to take Edwards' jabs in order to get at his body in the next and Billy was visibly shaken at the end of the round. Edwards adopted a defensive jabbing stance in the seventh but shipped steady punishment and had to hang on to survive. The pair exchanged lefts and rights at the start of the last but Billy's punches were weak and Con forced him back on the defensive. O'Kelly swung heavy blows to head and body but failed to find a finisher. Most agreed that Billy had been well beaten.

Joe Coyne of Pittsburg was then stopped in three at the Lenox AC, Utica. Con won well, again showing good defensive work in blocking and ducking. Brave but out-gunned, Buck Smith of Philadelphia, another Jimmy Dime fighter, was then knocked out in the eighth of a ten-round bout at Oswego.

Ryan was delighted with Con's progress - he was strong and game and was fast developing the skills to match his punching power. The pair were keeping a keen eye on the heavyweight situation in England and Con was confident that he could make headway on the home front. Con wrote to the Hull Daily News, expecting to return home on 20 November. "I'm ready to meet any of the half dozen or so claimants to the (British) title, Iron Hague, Jewey Smith, PO Curran, Bombardier Billy Wells, Sergeant Sunshine, Ben Taylor, Gunner Hewitt or anyone else in England can be accommodated first come first served. I want to start at the bottom and work myself up to the top if I can, and if I cannot do it, then I ought to quit the boxing game and shall not want to be a champion. I expect to find plenty of the English heavyweights only too willing to try conclusions with me. At least I hope so, as it will give me just the right sort of experience I am looking for prior to my return to America".

Ryan was convinced that O'Kelly was ready for an improvement in opposition, as Con recorded on 5 November: "I am faced with a tough proposition, as I am fixed up with Marvin Hart, who, as everyone interested in boxing knows, can boast of having beaten Jack Johnson, the present holder of the championship of the world. Hart it was on Jeffries' retirement, who succeeded to the title. I am having a sort of stiff trial before then, however, being due to meet a very clever coloured boxer, who enjoys a big reputation out here".

That man was Jeff Madden of Boston. The bout at New Bedford was over ten rounds, two rounds of which proved, if Ryan still entertained any doubts, that Con was game. The Syracuse Post-Standard reported: "Jeff Madden is one of the cleverest boxers doing business today....Yet with the exception of the ninth round, when the game Madden found O'Kelly's jaw with a right swing, and followed it with a series of vicious uppercuts, O'Kelly was entitled to every round. That ninth round was a wonder. It started with O'Kelly repeating a trick he had worked several times and rendering Madden groggy. Then suddenly the Boston man came back. He landed his right flush on the giant's jaw. O'Kelly reeled. While the crowd yelled like madmen, Madden fought his hardest to put the big man out. Con fought back desperately. They fought like fiends for ten seconds beyond the bell, when their seconds jumped through the ropes and hauled them to their chairs. This was the crucial time. O'Kelly was dazed when he took to his chair. Within a minute of rest his brain was cleared. He came out for the tenth with Madden, as before, on the aggressive, O'Kelly kept his head. He stalled and blocked and dodged with beautiful precision, and all the time he was smashing rights and lefts into Madden's body and terribly disfigured face. When the bell rang Madden had not landed a blow. He staggered to his corner, the recipient of a great ovation for his gameness, while O'Kelly, with not a mark of the battle on his face, vaulted over the ropes as lightly as a boy, as fresh as when he started". If these two rounds proved O'Kelly's gameness the previous eight showed vast improvement in his blocking, parrying and left-hand work generally; indeed, he didn't use his right to any effect until the fifth. Like so many projected matches, the one with Hart failed to be brought off and Marvin fought his last battle, losing to Carl Morris in three rounds on 20 December.

On 1 November Con was billed to face a veteran in the shape of Hank Griffin of Los Angeles at the Lenox AC at Utica. Hank, now in his 40th year, had been a magnificent fighter in his day: his showings against Jack Johnson - a win over 20 rounds, one draw over 15 and two over 20 - are now legendary. Hank was one of the few opponents who had gained the champion's respect. Johnson stated in his book: "In summing up my fights, throughout my career, there were none, even in the championship bouts, which were harder than those with Griffin, and I believe that the greatest punishment I ever received in the ring was at the hands of Griffin".

Old as Griffin was a victory over him would be an achievement for a six-fight novice. For six rounds Hank boxed superbly, out-boxing and out-pointing Con, but in the seventh O'Kelly caught Griffin with a right to the jaw, a right to the face and a hard left to the body. The last was the most significant blow of the fight, convincing Hank that he wanted to take none similar and he back-peddled for the rest of the bout – apart from being knocked through the ropes in the last round. The general consensus however was that Hank had nicked it. Griffin was full of praise for the Irishman, saying: "O'Kelly isn't a boxer, he's a fighter and I have never seen any man with only six months' experience make a better showing than he did tonight. He kept forcing me in the latter part of the fight and I simply had to give ground. Those body punches hurt a mighty lot more than they seemed to the spectators, and they had me about all in. Take it from me, that fellow is a comer, and another year of experience will make him a wonder". Hank was emphatic that he didn't want a second helping of the 'Harp', but Ryan could be pretty persuasive and a return was arranged for the Central City AC on 28 November. After a tame first round, Con caught Griffin with a hard right under his arm as Hank raised his fist to protect his jaw. Obviously hurt, Griffin survived through to the middle of the fourth round when his second threw in the sponge, unseen by Con who continued his attack. Hank's second, Ralph Calloway, tried to stem the flow of leather assisted by two policemen who joined the fray! Once order was restored Griffin explained that his shoulder was dislocated, a diagnosis confirmed by two physicians. The 'real' Hank Griffin, operating his own hotel and gym at Ann Arbor, Michigan, protested that he had been retired since 1904 and had not faced O'Kelly at either Utica or Central City. 'Young' Hank Griffin was managed by Billy Gibson, a canny operator who later looked after Benny Leonard and Gene Tunney. Whether Ryan was aware of the ringer is a moot point but Con was undoubtedly innocent of involvement.

A return with Jeff Madden was arranged for New Bedford on 2 January. The closeness of the previous encounter promised fireworks but the crowd of 3,000 were disappointed. Madden outgeneraled and outpointed Con, whose only success was to floor Jeff for a count of five in the ninth. Referee Patsey Downey declared a draw, as prearranged if both fighters were on their feet at the final bell. More significant than the 'loss' was a right-hand chop from Madden that caught Con above the left eye, causing a bad cut which provided a ready target for Jeff's accurate right handers.

For a boxing virgin Con had been matched against some pretty tough cookies. Every contest promised a slugfest – a fact not lost on fight fans who packed the halls when O'Kelly was billed. Fellow 'White Hopes' were conspicuously missing from his record - not that matches were not mooted. Joe Choynski, subsequent to training Jeffries, had selected a 'Hope' in the person of Miles McLeod. Hailing from Missouri, McLeod was an impressive 6'6" tall and 270lb in weight. Jim Corbett also backed the giant. Challenges flew and Ryan agreed terms with Joe – accepting a date – for a match with Con. Con must have relished the chance of eliminating a potential rival but it was not to be; indeed there is no record of McLeod ever having a fight.

The heavyweight scene at home was still mired in

confusion. The champion, Iron Hague, having had a bad run of losses and struggling to regain form. The rising star Bombardier Billy Wells was a polished boxer and formidable puncher who was to become England's first heavyweight hero of the modern boxing era, unrivalled in popularity and public esteem until the advent of Henry Cooper 50 years later. Ryan entered into negotiation with Charles Mathieson, the National Sporting Club's agent in New York, in late 1910, for a bout between Con and Wells scheduled for Derby week in 1911.

Con was pencilled in to top the bill at the Onondaga AC, Syracuse on 17 January against Al Kubiak, a native of Bamberg, Germany, who had been raised in Grand Rapids, Michigan. Al had started well in 1907, not losing for two years until faced with the erratic Sandy Ferguson of Boston who kayoed him in four rounds. Kubiak won a newspaper decision over Joe Jeannette shortly after, which seemed to embolden his management. Al was matched with Sam Langford, Jeannette, Sam McVea and Morris Harris, all of whom gained quick victories. Kubiak was withdrawn from facing Con due to a management mix-up. Al's suggested replacement was Carl Morris, who refused the job because he said he could earn $12,000 a fight in Oklahoma. No offer was made from Oklahoma for Con to face their home-State boy. Tommy Ryan voiced the opinion that all the 'White Hopes' were afraid to meet his man.

Con's opponent on the 17 January was finally agreed to be Dan Porky Flynn of Boston. Flynn was to become a very knowledgeable journeyman; a skilled and crafty operative who knew how to look after himself. He did not punch hard enough to worry the top flight but could hurt their pride when in form. In January 1911 Flynn was young and ambitious, taking the first five rounds off his slow-starting opponent. Ryan's coaching was taking effect: Con's attack was not so bull-like as before and his defensive work continued to improve, though Porky was able to keep up a regular tattoo on his previously damaged left eye. Flynn did not escape injury, being badly marked around his eyes, and Con's body attack took its toll. Spectators agreed that Flynn and O'Kelly had served up the best boxing exhibition seen in years. So evenly fought was the bout that both men had his supporters and a draw seemed the fairest decision. Even the press failed to agree. It was probably Con himself who insisted on a further bout with Jeff Madden, which took place again at New Bedford on 23 January and was scheduled for 15 rounds. Con appeared with a plaster stuck over his damaged eye, which was soon dislodged by Jeff and the blood flowed. Early in the fourth Madden was brought to the canvas by a heavy right to the jaw. After taking an eight count Jeff rushed at Con, who connected with a body punch that sent him back to the floor and provoked his corner to throw in the sponge. A maddened Madden attacked his seconds before referee Downey intervened. The crowd was none too happy with the ending and there were calls of 'fix'.

What proved to be the final bout of Con's US campaign took place at the Onondaga Club at Syracuse on 1 March against Jim Barry of Montana. On his night Barry was a pretty good fighter. When Sam Fitzpatrick, Jack Johnson's sacked manager, returned from Australia after Johnson's title

victory over Tommy Burns he was questioned as to which white fighter might have a chance against 'Lil Arthur'. Apart from Jeffries, Sam reasoned that Jim Barry was the leading white boxer but he really did not have a chance. Jim's record boasted wins over Gunboat Smith, Sandy Ferguson, Jim Stewart and Tony Ross, and draws with Ross, Fireman Jim Flynn and Sam Langford. This final encounter is significant as Jim was one of the few white fighters happy to share a ring with the great black fighters of the day – Langford, Jeannette and McVea. Barry didn't often win, nor draw for that matter, but he put up a fight and deserved respect for his courage. Unfortunately, Con caught him on a good night! Reports of the bout are pretty sketchy. The pair sparred for six rounds, then Barry opened up and outclassed the 'Harp' in every aspect of the game; indeed the general opinion was that had he chosen Jim could have ended it at any time. Con was a groggy and sadly battered man at the end of the ten rounds.

It could be argued that Con had come a long way in nine months. Without any previous boxing experience he had fought himself into a position as a leading 'White Hope'. McLeod, Kubiak and Morris had all avoided a match. His performance against Flynn was perhaps his best – in a 12 or 15-rounder he would surely have won – and against Barry he faced the most experienced man of his campaign when probably not in the best of condition. The New York Times reported that O'Kelly's weight had dropped to 200lb and he was suffering from sciatica. The damage to his eye inflicted by Madden did not help and after being away from his wife and young son for 18 months Con could be forgiven for being homesick.

Con's home-town supporters afforded him a big welcome when he arrived back in Hull on 28 March. He'd been a very active competitor both as wrestler and boxer in the States and it was thought that his sojourn in the land of the mighty dollar had left him financially secure. He took over as landlord of the Grapes public house in Hull during 1912 and is said to have owned other property in the city.

Con didn't return to the ring until 10 March 1913. Why he had taken so long a break is a matter of conjecture. The recurring eye damage, an operation on his nose or a contractual dispute with Ryan, who had originally proposed accompanying Con back to England with middleweight Howard Morrow, would have all played a part.

England's resident 'White Hope', Bombardier Billy Wells, was matched to challenge Jack Johnson for the world title in October 1911, but the bout was prevented by a moral minority in Parliament and the pulpit. Fears were raised that the bout could provoke race riots, as had happened after Johnson's victory over Jeffries, though Johnson had proved a popular attraction in the music-halls and large crowds cheered him when he appeared in court to argue in favour of the bout. Another underlying fear was that a Johnson victory might undermine the authority of the military in the colonies and encourage racial unrest. In his first comeback bout Con knocked out Gunner McFadden of Plymouth in two rounds at the National Sporting Club in Covent Garden. He received a big ovation on entering the ring, but when the bout was over the cheers were for his opponent. Con

O'Kelly with his young son, who boxed professionally as Young Con O'Kelly from 1924 to 1938, winning 50 of 74 contests

started by jabbing over the head of his crouching, ducking adversary but soon found his range and a right cross and left hook put the Gunner down for a nine count. The big Irishman stood over his opponent, which delayed the count and allowed McFadden to survive the round. Con landed several body blows, a right to the chin and another to the body put McFadden down for the full count.

O'Kelly had done all that could have been asked of him but the smaller, older man got the members' sympathy. After so long out of the ring Con was probably rusty. In America he had been served up a steady diet of tough customers but was not overmatched. Jim Barry had had a good night against him and had gone on to gain wins over Gunboat Smith and Bill Lang in the following 12 months. Back home different attitudes seemed to apply.

Con's next opponent was Battling Jim Johnson, a native of Danville, Virginia. Jim was quite as big as Con, as strong as an ox and almost impervious to punishment. He did not rate with the other leading black contenders – Langford, Jeannette or McVea – but was not far short. He had good wins over fellow black fighters Black Bill (Claude Brooks), Bill Tate and Morris Harris and a 15-round draw with McVea. His record against British fighters showed wins over Ben Taylor, Jewey Smith, Denis Haugh and Tom Cowler. On the debit side he had a loss (and a win) against the obscure American Alf Langford, a loss over 20 to South African Fred Storbeck and an 18-round loss to McVea. The general opinion was that Johnson was too hard a nut to crack.

The bout took place at the Liverpool Stadium on 3 April before a large audience of sportsmen gathered on the eve of the Grand National. The pair got to work without delay at the first bell, engaging in heavy in-fighting. Con scored to the ribs, then Jim with an uppercut to the head that was answered by a left to the nose, and they then exchanged heavy head punches for an even round.

Con opened the second with a hard jab to the nose. Some fierce work ensued which culminated in Con being brought to his knees by a right hook. Upon his rising a right swing caught the Irishman over the ear and he suffered three head punches without return. Battling Jim took the round. Con started the third trying for a kayo but Johnson avoided his swings by fractions. Jim retaliated with a huge body punch that made Con hang on. The Battler sailed in and forced Con onto the defensive. Con used the ring to his advantage but went unsteadily to his corner at the end of the round. Jim seemed to be taken by surprise in the fourth when caught by a facer and he was almost sent over the ropes. He counter-attacked and seemed to have greater sting in his punches. Con went to the floor though the punch was disputed. Johnson took the round. Con was caught and staggered early in the next, his returns being ably avoided by Jim. Again they exchanged heavy body blows until a swing to the point sent Johnson reeling into the ropes. They were cheered to the echo at the end of an even round. The sixth was fought on even terms, blow for blow, each intent on scoring a knockout. Con had the best of the seventh, twice staggering Johnson. Con again had the best of the next but had to use the ring late in the session after Jim landed two hard lefts to the face. Jim scored two knockdowns in the ninth. The first from a left to the jaw and the second from a right; each being a six count. Con's left eye was closing and he was glad to hear the bell. Johnson rained punches on his game opponent in the tenth. Con turned to his corner as if to retire and Jim left the ring. Con's seconds pushed him back out to finish the round and Johnson was brought back before Con was retired in his corner by Dr O'Connell, the doctor in attendance.

None could now question Con's gameness but the Hull Daily News correspondent put forward the suggestion that Con in future should draw the colour line. Con was now managed by Silas Alger of Plymouth who, upon Con's request to accept an offer of a return with Johnson at Bordeaux, is said to have replied "no, cut out the coloured men".

Notwithstanding Alger's dictum, Con was back in the ring on 28 April at Hull to face Australian black veteran Cyclone Billy Warren, in a scrambling affair which ended in Warren's disqualification in the fourth. Fellow Irishman Dennis Haugh was of sterner stuff but, vastly outweighed, was kayoed in the third round on 12 May at St James' Hall, Newcastle. Perhaps somewhat embarrassed by his recent performances Con addressed the audience, telling a little of his history and experiences in America and his hope that he should soon regain his best form and prove to be the champion heavyweight of Britain.

O'Kelly made his debut in the west country at the Old Cosmo Gym, Plymouth on 30 May against Bombardier Legassick, who was really a light-heavyweight and as such stood little chance against the huge O'Kelly. The Bombardier showed great courage and won over the fans by taking an aggressive role, until caught by a couple of Con's swings and counted out before the end of the first. Frenchman Gustave Marthuin faced Con at the Cosmo on 13

June. Outweighed, outreached and by no means in the best of condition Marthuin survived the full 15 rounds that the tame affair lasted. Gustave hustled his way inside to nullify Con's height and reach advantages and landed to the body and the head without causing the big man much inconvenience. The reporter from Boxing voiced his opinion that Con's muscles were in need of loosening up. Con was next matched against Gunner Rawles in Dublin during August 1913, with the winner to meet Bombardier Wells, but the bout was not brought off.

Con disappeared from the boxing scene for nine months, returning to Hull on 10 April 1914 to face veteran Ben Taylor, the 'Woolwich Infant'. At the turn of the century Ben had been considered a real prospect but he lacked dedication and by 1914 he was just a 'name' opponent. Con started fast, flooring Ben for eight in the first and finishing him in the second. Gunner McMurray also fell in two on 11 May and Harry Smith of South Africa retired after five on 8 June, both at Hull. Next came Petty Officer Smales, who was kayoed in two at Grimsby on 15 June. Con was now considered to be improving and worthy of a more competitive match. Gunner James Moir, the former English heavyweight champion, was selected to face him at Hull on 29 June. Moir was at the end of a career in which he divided his time between boxing and wrestling, having spent much of his time as an exhibition partner to George Hackenschmidt. He was a hard puncher and could pull off an upset, as he did in knocking out Bombardier Billy Wells in three rounds in 1911. Moir was a known quantity but he withdrew, suffering from gastritis, a week before the contest.

American 'White Hope' Tom Kennedy was substituted. This was definitely a case of the replacement being superior to the original. A better-than-average boxer, though not a hard puncher, Kennedy had fought most of the leading 'Hopes' – Al Palzer, Carl Morris, Jim Stewart, Frank Moran, Bombardier Billy Wells, Jim Savage, Battling Levinsky and Jim Coffey – usually holding his own but losing inside the distance to Palzer, Wells and Savage. The pair shaped up at 9.40. The first round was very low-key. Kennedy landed two light lefts to the face. O'Kelly missed with a swinging right to the head but landed a left to the body. Early in the second Con landed a hard right to the jaw of Kennedy, who was dazed and stalled cleverly to evade O'Kelly's wild follow-up. Had he steadied himself Con might have stopped the American. Kennedy then fell to the floor, holding himself in apparent pain from a body shot, but soon got to his feet when the referee told him to box on. The remainder of the round degenerated into a scramble, though Tom is said to have landed three suspiciously low blows that may have provoked the fireworks of the third. O'Kelly swung wildly in what was to prove to be the last round while Kennedy landed short hooks to the head at close quarters. Con retaliated with a blatant head-butt that brought about his disqualification.

Before his home crowd of three thousand supporters Con was disgraced, leaving the ring to boos and catcalls while Kennedy was cheered enthusiastically when declared the winner. The general opinion was that O'Kelly had 'fouled out' in the face of a beating It was a difficult conclusion to justify given that Con had taken little punishment and it was

Kennedy who had gone to the canvas claiming a low blow in the second. Furthermore, some report Tom landing three low blows in the same round for which he was warned by the referee. There is some suspicion that the wily Kennedy was up to no good on the referee's blindside just prior to the offending butt.

Some questioned Con's aptitude for the game but intended to suspend judgment until he had fulfilled his next scheduled bout against Bandsman Dick Rice at Leeds in August. However, this was not to be, for two weeks later Con was back in Plymouth to face Petty Officer Matthew Curran. Nutty Curran, as the tar was known, was a broth of a boy from County Clare and was a perfect contradiction, winning and losing many bouts on fouls, while winning and losing often on knockouts. He was erratic, colourful, and an exciting attraction in Plymouth where most of his contests took place. After beating Iron Hague in February 1910 and Bill Lang on a foul in January 1911, Nutty reigned as unofficial British and Empire champion for a period, though he was ignored by the NSC when they selected those who would contest the newly inaugurated heavyweight Lonsdale Belt in April 1911. Curran had knockout victories over Hague, Jem Roche, Jewey Smith, Jack Burns, Gunner Moir and Harry Smith. He was certainly a threat to the 'Harp'.

The Mirror of Life covered the bout, which was over 20 three-minute rounds for a purse of £200 (£125 to the winner) and a side stake of £20. The report stated: "There was very little done in the initial round, Curran walking around the ring for the most part with O'Kelly slowly following him. Curran tried a rush now and again but was met with a left to the face. There was a lot of holding at the opening of the second round, with the Hull man the chief offender. Curran in the third round landed two telling lefts to the face and body. In the clinches O'Kelly employed a downward right to the ear. During the fourth round Curran had slightly the better of the exchanges. At the opening of the fifth round O'Kelly sent his right to the body with great force, but the blow apparently had no effect. Con played for the stomach in the sixth round and now and then shook Curran with his left. The PO turned aside O'Kelly's deliveries and smashed left and right to the face. A straight right to the jaw sent 'Nutty' to the boards for a count of five in the seventh meeting and when he resumed he rushed O'Kelly to the ropes. The latter sent out right and lefts in his endeavour to finish the bout, and at the end of the session Curran was again on the boards. In the eighth round, after some infighting, Curran leant on the ropes, complaining that he had been hit low. The referee made no comment, and O'Kelly went over to finish his man. After landing several blows to which Curran made no retaliation the latter's seconds threw up the towel. Though Curran was a 'winning' fighter - easily discouraged and prone to lapses in concentration when pitted against tough opposition – he was a known quantity and Con's victory did no harm to his reputation.

Two weeks later Con was back at Hull where he defeated Frank McGuiness in one round, this being Frank's second one-round loss in three days. What was to prove to be Con's final contest took place at Belfast when he stopped Harry Smith again, this time in eight rounds, on 5 August – the day after the First World War was declared.

Con O'Kelly's boxing career falls naturally into two parts - his beginnings in America and his years in England. Under the tutelage of Tommy Ryan he was well trained and well conditioned, and ringside reports consistently commented on his improving defensive skills. His advantages in height and weight could so easily have worked against him had he not been guided by Ryan, who had created Jim Jeffries from the same raw material. O'Kelly was the physical equal of Jeffries and possessed of the same natural athleticism as the Boilermaker. Con was intelligently matched with opponents who would be able to test him but were not liable to collapse under his initial assault.

Back home in England it is most noticeable that Con was a beginner again. In contrast to his experience in America, aside from his good-class opponents - Johnson, Kennedy and Curran – he fought men who had little to teach him and had little resistance to his punching power. Few of his opponents could match him physically, though one must admit that the heavyweight talent in Britain lacked the size and quality of that in the States. His loss to Johnson was predictable after almost two years out of the ring. The substitution of the ringwise Kennedy for the rough-and-tumble Moir did Con no favours. His win over Curran was his best home win.

Bob Fitzsimmons had spent some time in Britain - November 1908 to June 1909. He went to the fights, sparred 'Iron' Hague, the English heavyweight champion, and visited gyms. Asked to comment on our heavyweights he did not mince his words. "English heavyweights are third rate compared with pugilists in the States. The noble art is a lost art in England. Your fighting men do not take their business seriously. They do not train as they ought to train. When I was in the fighting business I left off smoking and drinking for years at a stretch, ran and walked miles every day, ate only the plainest and best muscle building food, slept like a top eight hours a night, and got up in the morning a new-made man. The result was that I felt so fit that it was impossible for me to imagine that any man alive could beat me or tire me. A fight is half won when a man enters the ring confident of winning...Footwork is even more important than fist work...English heavyweights are slow. They can hit hard, no doubt, but a trained man can get out of the way of their lunges. Of sidestepping they know nothing. In a word they lack science".

Con launched his boxing career with the enthusiastic backing of Fitz and Ryan. He had all the qualities his boosters valued - teetotal, non-smoking, strong, game, durable, with unbounded confidence in his abilities and a desperation to learn. The effectiveness of the schooling he received from Ryan is beyond doubt as from being a complete novice he advanced to the position of being a respected fighter, avoided by other developing 'White Hopes' and a sure draw at the box office in only nine months. After his return from the States, Con failed to progress and the suspicion must be that he was not being trained correctly. The only trainer mentioned during this period of his career was Fred Drummond - a third-rate heavy fighting out of Lambeth. As a wrestler Con was trained by Joe Carroll, a world champion renowned for his skills. Tommy Ryan was from the same school. Why didn't O'Kelly follow this same course by employing a top-rate trainer after his return home? Admittedly there were few such boxing trainers in the UK but there was big money awaiting a winning British heavyweight. Con was intelligent enough to appreciate what was at stake. Perhaps he was badly advised. Silas Alger was at base a manager and promoter, not a trainer.

Once having returned to Hull and to the bosom of his family, Con could not be blamed if he was reluctant to go back to the States. However, his chances of a world-title challenge against Jack Johnson certainly improved from June 1913 when the champion established residence in France.

Possession of the British championship was the pre-requisite to challenging Johnson. After the Curran fight there were again moves to match O'Kelly against the Bombardier at the Club, but the declaration of war closed the National for the foreseeable future and only they could promote a championship challenge and award the Lonsdale Belt to the winner. Con's career was essentially no further forward now than when he had returned from the US in 1911. Indeed, his progress had already been hampered by two long periods of inactivity. Con was a very ambitious man and made no secret of his aim to win the British championship and then the world championship. However, he was happily married, financially secure, and was not dependent on boxing for his livelihood. Without the possibility of a championship challenge against Jack Johnson boxing's original 'White Hope' retired.

The Demise of the (Bareknuckle) Traditional Prize-ring in Britain: A Brief Look at some Pertinent Causes

by Tony Gee

During the majority of the 18th century and a considerable proportion of the 19th, what can be termed the traditional prize-ring formed a distinct part of Britain's sporting scene, albeit subject to significant geographical variations. Despite bareknuckle fighting being deemed illegal for most of this period, some of its exponents (pugilists were inevitably drawn from the lower classes of society) could boast of being associated with nobility and gentry; others were featured in literature and art; and all leading combatants, to a greater or lesser extent, earned celebrity status (as well as, at least for a short time, a degree of financial prosperity). What, therefore, led to the sport's downfall and ultimate demise?

Whilst there may be a temptation to attribute the death of the prize-ring to any one of a number of causes, it actually appears as though a combination of factors were responsible for bringing about its disappearance. Arguably one of the most telling of these was the emergence of a society which placed increasing emphasis on humanitarianism, moral improvement, and respectability. As the historian G M Trevelyan noted, men could hardly be permitted to fight in the bareknuckle arena when it was forbidden for animals to be set upon one another. Clearly, as observed by W Russel Gray, when writing in the *Journal of Popular Culture* on the sport's decline (although, it should perhaps be said, not always accurately), in an "age of reform, and the Victorian era undeniably was that, prize fighting was an inevitable target". It is fair to say that the bareknuckle ring had flourished in comparatively more callous and less sensitive times, and obviously in a more restrained and (outwardly at least) virtuous and decorous age, and one in which there was growing social concern, it would always be facing a losing battle for survival.

Interestingly, as Richard Holt wrote in *Sport and the British*, it was not just pressure from the likes of "well-organised groups of evangelicals and business men" with which traditional sports ("especially those which involved fighting") now had to contend; in addition to such reformers' active opposition, there was seemingly a gradual change in popular taste amongst a section of the working classes themselves (who no longer countenanced entertainments that they had previously favoured). It appears as though the two were not completely unlinked. Pamela Horn, for instance, when discussing the decline of cockfighting, dogfighting, and bull- and badger-baiting in *Pleasures & Pastimes in Victorian Britain*, credited the "teachings of evangelical religion and new approaches to discipline promoted by industrial capitalism" with turning many people against these traditional sports. The result, she implied, was the gradual emergence of an "artisan sub-culture which rejected such rowdy amusements and preferred to patronize the new commercial recreations on offer, such as railway excursions and the music hall". (Some evidence of this shift in taste amongst the aspiring working class can be found in the Victorian press. In 1851, for instance, it was claimed that the

working men of Birmingham and the manufacturing area to its north were formerly notorious for the "brutality of their sports", including pugilism, but that there had been a "vast improvement" in their interests and manners, although there still existed a fondness for traditional amusements among the uneducated sector.)

Of course, the progressively dire position in which prize-fighting eventually found itself was not helped by the unacceptable conduct, and especially the levels of dishonesty and laziness, of a seemingly increasing number of its participants. Their behaviour led to the situation which Pendragon (the respected fistic authority, Henry Sampson) later noted in his invaluable book on the bareknuckle sport's downfall, namely that the "oracles of the ring" were regularly "denouncing malefactors and threatening to withdraw their protection from the prize-ring". (The writer implied that by 'oracles' he was referring to the sporting press of the time, of which *Bell's Life in London and Sporting Chronicle* had long been the definitive voice of pugilism.) Such examples in *Bell's Life* included one in 1863 when the newspaper warned that, unless the state of affairs improved, it would make every effort to abolish a "sport which, as at present carried on, cannot be defended on any ground whatever".

By 1869, at least according to an article on the decline of the prize-ring which appeared in *Tinsleys' Magazine* (an illustrated monthly publication containing both non-fiction and fictional stories), the bareknuckle pugilist had "converted his noble science into a mere ignoble system of swindling". Rather than demonstrate his strength and science in the fistic arena, the magazine declared, he instead endeavoured through the "sale of colours and other devices, and by an understanding with his partner and the police, to enrich himself, while depriving his expectant patrons of an edifying spectacle of endurance and ferocity". Pendragon, writing from first-hand knowledge, seems to have concurred with *Tinsleys'* accusations, remarking that, with regard to "shams and swindles", for every determined and hard-fought battle "any one who cares to look through the columns of the sporting journals will find a dozen 'disgraceful exhibitions', 'fiascos', [or] 'tedious travesties'". Moreover, a retrospect of prize-fighting in the *Illustrated Sporting and Theatrical News* in the same year as the *Tinsleys' Magazine* article asserted that the fistic "fraternity" had for a considerable time "done everything in their power to disgust both patrons and backers". It concluded by stating its "firm belief that pugilists, and pugilists alone, are to blame for the present state of the prizering; and that were it possible for the men to behave themselves respectably - as professionals at other games have to do - the ring might again flourish".

In addition, it would appear that crowd behaviour scarcely helped matters, as one gentleman's late 19th-century description of the experience of attending contests during the prize-ring's final years seems to indicate. In *Thoughts Upon Sport*, Harry R Sargent maintained that owing to the actions of "howling ruffians maddened with the most brutal excitement", for a long period there had seldom been a "conclusion of a prize-fight brought off with fair play". Indeed, Pendragon went as far to opine that there would have been a future for the sport had it not been for the complete breakdown of order accompanying bareknuckle affairs. He cited robbery, as well as rampage and rioting. It was no doubt scant compensation that, as claimed in the *Sporting Life* in 1864 by a supporter of the prize-ring, should gentlemen be "relieved of any superfluous jewellery, it is done in a professional manner, and the victims are treated with no unnecessary violence". Such problems relating to the conduct of both the combatants themselves and the mob, it should be emphasized, were hardly new. However, the degree of degradation, inside and outside the ropes, when combined with a comparative lack of first-rate pugilists (apart from a few quality lighter men) capable of performances of sufficient calibre as to excite interest from disillusioned followers, certainly did little to aid the sport's cause.

The second half of the 1860s saw the occurrence of three events which were ultimately responsible for the final nails being driven into the prize-ring's coffin. These were the introduction of new legislation prohibiting railway companies in the United Kingdom from providing special trains for prize-ring excursions, as well as banning them from stopping ordinary trains between stations to "accommodate any parties attending a prize fight"; the first warrant issued by a Home Secretary for the apprehension

of pugilists for having intended to commit a breach of the peace; and the framing of the Marquess of Queensberry's rules for gloved bouts.

Penalizing railway companies for furnishing the means of transportation to prize-fights was, in fact, not an original idea (prosecution having been suggested, for instance, in a letter to *The Times* in 1856). Section 21 of 'The Regulation of Railways Act, 1868' now made companies liable to fines of between £200 and £500 for such actions. (*Bell's Life in London* reported that the clause was proposed by Sir C O'Loghlen during a debate on the Bill in the House of Commons and, although a Mr Clay argued against it, opining that the "knife would be introduced when we got rid of prize fighting", it was agreed to without the need for a division.) As a result the ability of fistic parties to successfully evade the forces of law and order was considerably hampered; in his 1925 autobiography, the noted referee Bernard John Angle went so far as to assert that a "mortal blow" had been dealt to the prize-ring. Soon after the Act was passed, the then Manchester-domiciled fighter Harry Allen became the first would-be combatant apprehended as a result of a Home Secretary's warrant. (The arrest of his scheduled opponent for the championship of England, Joe Goss, followed shortly afterwards.) The *Illustrated Sporting and Theatrical News*, reporting the legal proceedings which prevented the match, felt that the warrant was an "innovation which bids fair to be the death-blow to pugilism". (The previously referred to retrospect of prize-fighting in the same publication the

Harry Allen, an experienced pugilist and contender for the championship of England, who in August 1868 had the dubious distinction of being the first would-be combatant apprehended as a result of a Home Secretary's warrant

next year explained that prior to the thwarting of the Allen/ Goss contest, "warrants which had been granted for the apprehension of bellicose pugilists only took effect in the counties in which they were issued, and the steps taken by the Home Secretary completely paralysed those who had formerly set the police at defiance".) It does however seem to have been the gradual acceptance for professional purposes of the rules of the (then 8th but now considered 9th) Marquess of Queensberry that can be said to have had the most valid claim for eventually sounding the death-knell of an activity which was, without doubt, amongst the most colourful of those that make up Britain's rich and dramatic sporting history.

Careful analysis of the circumstances surrounding the demise of the prize-ring has not only highlighted the significance of all the above factors but also clearly emphasized that it certainly did not disappear overnight. Whilst some were apparently ready to embrace the gloved approach, others appeared to agree with *Tinsleys' Magazine* that there "is a certain makebelieve in the glove-business which quite unfits it for comparison with the real thing". (This was a sentiment that was repeated, for example, later in *Fencing, Boxing, Wrestling*, The Badminton Library of Sports and Pastimes, E B Michell considering all but bareknuckle fights "mere travesties of the original".) Interestingly, men too young to remember or not even born in 1860 when Tom Sayers clashed with the American John C Heenan in what was the prize-ring's last great event on British soil, still seemingly felt compelled to test themselves with the 'raw'uns'. As a result there were, for instance (as I have found during relatively recent extensive research), more bareknuckle contests, albeit predominantly minor ones, taking place in Britain during the last two decades of the 19th century (and even occasionally in the first decade of the 20th) than is perhaps realised.

In fact in 1881 the then Home Secretary, Sir William Harcourt, thought it necessary to dispatch notices to the chairmen of quarter sessions desiring them, so *The Sportsman* and the *Sporting Chronicle* reported, to devote "special attention to cases of breach of the peace, or what the right hon. gentleman regards as the recent 'epidemic of prize fighting'". The situation that Harcourt perceived as an epidemic is probably not that surprising, given that in 1887 the *Sporting Life* was still seeing gloved bouts as a mere learning experience for bareknuckle combat, declaring that anybody "standing on the very lowest rung of the ladder of common sense should be aware that boxing with the mittens is intended as a preliminary to using the raw material". Indeed, even in modern times, with the traditional prize-ring very much part of Britain's sporting past, organized bareknuckle affairs do nevertheless take place. (An article in *The Independent* in 1998 highlighted their continuance, for instance, "amongst a small and intransigent sector of the travelling nation in Ireland and Britain who, even though semi-urbanised, are fighting a rearguard action against assimiliation".)

The author would like to thank Dr Kasia Boddy for kindly proofreading this article.

Malcolm Collins: A Man Of Class

by Ralph Oates

If I were to mention the 'Fab Four' you would be excused for thinking that I was talking about the phenomenal pop group of the '60s, The Beatles – John, Paul, George and Ringo, who rocked the world with their music. However, prior to these highly successful musicians from Liverpool, there was another group who could easily be described as the 'Fab Four', who duly made their respective mark, not in the world of music but in the world of boxing. The fighters themselves were the most talented men to put the gloves on during the period they fought. Indeed, it would not be an exaggeration to say that in the 1950s Britain had four of the most gifted amateur boxers in the featherweight division. These home-grown fighters were more than able to match, if not defeat, any of the opponents in the world at their weight at that given time and hence not be out of their league in any shape or form when put to the test in major international bouts.

Dave Charnley, Dick McTaggart, Tommy Nicholls and Malcolm Collins were the magical names who operated in our amateur rings at the time. These fighters were competitive and would often meet each other in bouts that more than thrilled the fans. Class, pride and honour went hand in hand with these boxers; they wanted to be the best and to do so they faced each other at the first opportunity. There was no way any of the four would want to avoid each other and to reach any kind of championship status they had to meet and beat their rivals to reach the top. In each case their respective records are first class. Quality is a word which comes to mind when looking at each in turn. Yet is that really such a surprise, since each learned their trade the hard way, the traditional way, boxing good men and taking no shortcuts. Hence they added to their fistic education as they progressed.

Dave Charnley won the ABA title at feather in 1954 and also a bronze medal at the Empire games which took place in Vancouver, Canada the same year, before going on in the professional ranks to capture the British (winning a Lonsdale Belt outright), European and British Empire lightweight titles. Along the way, Dave fought class fighters like Carlos Ortiz, Emile Griffith, Brian Curvis, Willie Toweel, Paul Armstead, Maurice Cullen, Sammy McCarthy, Don Jordan, Peter Waterman, Lennie Matthews, Kenny Lane and Bunny Grant, etc. Charnley also challenged twice for the world crown against American champion Joe Brown. In 1959 he retired in round five due to an eye injury at the Sam Houston Coliseum, Houston before duly fighting his way back into contention to earn a well-deserved second crack at the championship which came in 1961. This time the venue was in England and once again the challenge was against the still reigning champion 'Old Bones' Brown at Earls Court. On this occasion Charnley lost a 15-round points decision. However, many considered him unlucky not to have had his hand raised in victory after a close fought contest. Dave had his last pro bout in 1964, thus ending his paid career with a record of 61 contests, winning 48, losing 12, with just the one draw.

Then we have Scot, Dick McTaggart, another boxing master who won many honours during his amateur career, amongst them the ABA lightweight crown in 1956, 1958 and 1960. He also won the gold medal in the Olympic Games that were held in Melbourne, Australia in 1956. Not only that but the fighter from Dundee was awarded the Val Barker trophy for best stylist at these games – quite an outstanding accomplishment to say the least. Dick also won the bronze medal in the 1960 Games, which took place in Rome, Italy and if that was not enough he won the European title in Belgrade, Yugoslavia in 1961. In 1962 McTaggart won a silver medal in the Empire games which were held in Perth, Australia, going on from here to add to his trophy collection by winning the ABA light-welterweight title in 1963 and 1965.

Tommy Nicholls was another whose boxing was always considered to be in the class 'A' category. Tommy also claimed his share of titles in the amateur ranks, winning the ABA bantamweight title in 1951 and 1952. Moving up in weight, Tommy took the ABA featherweight crown in 1955, to go with the European title which he won in Berlin, West Germany that very same year. Then came a second ABA featherweight crown in 1956, plus a silver medal at the Australian 1956 Olympic Games in Melbourne.

Last but by no means least is Malcolm Collins. To say that Collins could punch and box a bit would be an

Malcolm in fighting pose

understatement to say the least. Malcolm had consummate ring skills, coupled with the kind of punching power which could take a man out for the full count once the blow had found its designated target, hence making any points decision unnecessary. Make no mistake, when boxing this man no opponent could afford a lapse in concentration – not for one single moment. This made Collins a very dangerous opponent to face in the ring. During his career Malcolm won a number of titles (all will be revealed in the question and answer section which follows). However, there is no doubt that Collins ranks with the very best of amateurs that Britain has produced over the years. On behalf of the Yearbook I contacted Malcolm to ask about his time in the unpaid ranks, and his opinions about the sport in general.

(Ralph Oates) In which year were you born?

(Malcolm Collin) I was born in 1935.

(RO) Where were you born?

(MC) In Cardiff, South Wales.

(RO) How old were you when you started to box?

(MC) I was 12 years of age.

(RO) Have any other members of your family ever boxed?

(MC) No, I was the first one to take to the ring.

(RO) What made you take up boxing?

(MC) Bullying at school. The sport gave me both the confidence and the ability to be able to repel those who took pleasure in bullying. It is often said, and it is true, that if you stand up to a bully and give him a little of his own medicine back he will think twice about it in the future.

(RO) Which club did you box for?

(MC) Melingriffith.

(RO) Who was your trainer at the club?

(MC) Ernie Hurford. Ernie was a very good man who knew the sport; he also trained Joe Erskine when he was a professional. Joe, of course, was a classy boxer who won the British and British Empire heavyweight titles in the paid ranks and crossed gloves with the likes of Henry Cooper (five times), Johnny Williams, Dick Richardson, Nino Valdes, Joe Bygraves, Ingemar Johannson, Brian London, Willie Pastrano, Karl Mildenberger, Billy Walker, George Chuvalo, Johnny Prescott and Jack Bodell. That is quite a line-up in a career which saw Joe take part in 54 contests, winning 45, losing eight, with one draw. That is some record when you consider who he fought.

(RO) Approximately how many amateur bouts did you have?

(MC) I had 250.

(RO) Can you remember how many you actually won?

(MC) Yes, I can. I won 242.

(RO) In which weight division did you box?

(MC) Featherweight.

(RO) Which titles did you win in the amateur ranks?

(MC) Schoolboy (twice), Youth (twice), Army Cadets (three times), Senior WABA (five times), ABA (twice) in 1957 and 1958. I also represented Great Britain and the RAF, winning the silver medal at the Empire Games, now Commonwealth, in 1954 and 1958.

(RO) I understand you had a record number of first-round victories. How many exactly?

(MC) That is right. I won all my Welsh titles by means of a first-round knockout, a record of 31 all together.

(RO) You fought Dave Charnley, Dick McTaggart and Tommy Nicholls during your stint in the unpaid ranks.

(MC) That is correct, I did. I outpointed McTaggart in a Wales v RAF encounter and Nicholls (twice) in an ABA semi-final and a Wales v England meeting, losing only to Charnley on a close points decision in the ABA quarter-final.

(RO) Can you remember the occasion when you really started to make your mark in the amateur ranks?

(MC) I think fans started to notice me when I boxed the highly-favoured Freddy Woodman, a London Divisional champion who had fought and beaten some very good men. He was 24 and I was 17 years of age. I had never boxed in a four-round contest before, so the odds were very much against me pulling off a win that night at Manor Place Baths against such an experienced and well-schooled fighter. The smart money would have been on Freddy. However, I put him down for a count of nine in round two, and went on to win on points.

(RO) Another notable fighter who you defeated was Fred Teidt of Ireland.

(MC) Yes, Fred was another fine fighter, who was good enough to win the welterweight silver medal at the 1956 Olympic Games, losing to Nicolai Linca of Romania. He also won bronze in the European Championships that took place in Prague, Czechoslovakia during 1957. When fighting Fred in a Wales v Ireland match I gave away a stone in weight.

(RO) In which stance did you box?

(MC) Southpaw.

(RO) Many fighters do not like boxing southpaws. How did you feel about meeting them in combat?

(MC) It really made no difference to me at all. I fought Charnley, McTaggart and Nicholls, who all were southpaws. You have to be able to cope with all styles in boxing.

(RO) Who was your most difficult opponent in the amateur ranks?

(MC) I would have to say Dick McTaggart, as we were both counter-punchers. When we fought it was a good contest, with us both not only attempting to outpunch but to also out-think each other.

(RO) It is very obvious from your record that you were a puncher. Many punchers often develop problems with their hands, at some stage. Did you get any problems?

(MC) Well, I broke bones in my hands on three occasions. I was in fact seriously considering retirement when a new rule was introduced which allowed bandages to be worn. This of course helped me to avoid any further damage to my hands.

(RO) What would you say was your proudest moment in boxing?

(MC) Carrying the flag in the 1958 Commonwealth Games (then Empire) in my home city, Cardiff. That really made me feel very proud, a moment to savour and long remember. I reached the finals, losing on points to Wally Taylor of Australia.

(RO) At the same Games fellow Welshman Howard Winstone won gold at bantamweight. Howard, of course, went on to win the (WBC) world, British and European

featherweight titles in the professional ranks.

(MC) Yes, he did. Howard was a good boxer who deserved the successes that came his way.

(RO) This of course was the second time that you had won a silver medal at the Empire Games.

(MC) Yes. The first occasion was in 1954 in Canada and I lost in the finals to a very good boxer in Len Leisching of South Africa.

(RO) Why did you not turn professional?

(MC) To be honest, I did not need the money since I had a very good job at the time. So the desire to punch for pay was not there and that I feel is vital if you are to succeed in the professionals.

(RO) In which year did you retire from boxing?

(MC) I decided to retire in 1958.

(RO) Do you believe that boxing instils discipline and respect to those who participate in the sport?

(MC) Yes I do. By the very nature of the sport discipline and respect is a vital element which a fighter really must learn if he is to succeed at any level.

(RO) How do you feel about female involvement in the sport?

(MC) I know of course we have in Britain Jane Couch and Cathy Brown to name just two, who have flown the flag for a few years now with some degree of success and in America, of course, Muhammed Ali's daughter Laila Ali has kept women's boxing in the headlines, while Germany's Regina Halmich has also been very successful. However, I am not too happy about it, to be truthful. (Must be my age).

(RO) Who is your favourite old-time fighter?

(MC) Muhammed Ali. The man did it all, winning a gold medal at light-heavyweight at the 1960 Olympic Games which were held in Rome, Italy. To win gold, Ali, who was then of course Cassius Clay, defeated an extremely difficult opponent in the shape of Poland's experienced Zbigniew Pietrzykowski, a talented southpaw who knew his way around the ring. Then, of course, in the professional ranks he became the first man to win the world heavyweight title on three occasions. You have to admire his determination along with his obvious boxing skills.

(RO) How do you feel about title fights being held over the duration of 12 rounds rather than 15?

(MC) In my opinion it makes very little difference. If the fighter has trained properly for the contest he should be able to meet the requirements which the sport and the fight at the time demands.

(RO) How do you feel boxers compare today with past fighters with regard to their skill and technique in both the

Malcolm (left) on his way to a points win over future Olympic champion, Dick McTaggart

Malcolm (right) storms to another first-round win

amateur and professional ranks.

(MC) Every sport has improved over the years. It really is very hard to compare like for like. There is no benchmark, as in running, to measure the past champions with today's men. Each period in history produced champions who were good at their given time.

(RO) Who is your favourite modern-day fighter?

(MC) Southpaw Joe Calzaghe. By any standards his performance in both the amateur and professional rings has been outstanding. His record speaks for itself, a point which was more than confirmed when he put his WBO super-middleweight title on the line against WBA and WBC holder Mikkel Kessler of Denmark, winning a 12-round points decision during 2007 to become the undisputed world champion. This took his undefeated record to 44 with the added addition of now having participated in 22 world championship bouts. Both Kessler and Calzaghe put on a fine performance of boxing on the night, that proved they were class men. Calzaghe also, let us not forget, had an excellent amateur pedigree, winning ABA titles in three different weight divisions, welterweight (1991), light-middleweight (1992) and middleweight (1993). That is a remarkable feat.

(RO) Which is your favourite weight division?

(MC) Featherweight. They are fast reactionaries and in my day, the likes of McTaggart, Charnley, Nicholls and myself were southpaws and featherweights. The division has also produced many world champions in the pro ranks who can be considered great, like George Dixon, Willie Pep, Sandy Saddler, Vicente Saldivar, Eusebio Pedroza and many more.

(RO) Who, in your opinion, was the best professional heavyweight champion in the history of the sport?

(MC) Muhammed Ali. This fighter always seemed to do the impossible, being able not only to box but also take a punch. Take a look at the names on his record, such as Sonny Liston, Floyd Patterson, Joe Frazier, Ken Norton, George Foreman, Jerry Quarry, Jimmy Ellis, Karl Mildenberger, Zora Folley, Earnie Shavers, Henry Cooper, Ernie Terrell, Larry Holmes, Leon Spinks and many other quality fighters. Ali fought the best in his era; there is no mistake about that. Everyone was given a chance when this man was at the top.

(RO) Which is your favourite world heavyweight title fight?

(MC) Must be the 'Rumble in the Jungle'. I refer, of course, to the Ali-Foreman contest that took place in Zaire on 30 October 1974. Ali really looked up against it. Foreman was a thunderous puncher who was undefeated in 40 bouts, with 37 of his wins coming inside the scheduled distance. He was clearly a formidable opponent who looked unbeatable at the time. Yet Ali, who many felt was past his best, turned on his magic to knock out Foreman in eight rounds and regain the crown for a second time. This was a magnificent moment in boxing, with the sport proving once again that in the square ring nothing is certain.

(RO) How do you feel about fighters who continue to box on even when middle-aged?

(MC) At the end of the day it really is their decision; only the fighter knows if he should continue or not.

(RO) What changes, if any, would you like to see made in both the amateur and professional side of the sport?

(MC) I would like to see the amateurs go back to boxing three-minute rounds. On the professional side I would like to see some referees stepping in more quickly when a boxer is taking too much punishment.

(RO) Out of all boxers in recent years who would you say was an excellent role model for the sport?

(MC) Muhammed Ali. I know he had his critics but he overcame many obstacles both inside and outside of the ring during his career, showing courage, dignity, and strength of character along the way. Many lesser men would surely have gone under when faced with the enormous pressures and problems that he had to endure. Ali had a true fighting heart.

(RO) What annoys you in the sport, both amateur and professional?

(MC) Poor refereeing decisions.

(RO) How do you feel about the vast number of world governing bodies in the sport at the moment?

(MC) In my opinion there should only be one world titleholder at any weight. A world champion should be exactly that, a world champion; the very best at his weight. It is foolish when you consider that at any given poundage you can have four men (WBC, WBA, IBF, WBO) or more calling themselves a world champion. It really devalues the worth of the term 'world champion'. How many people can name the various champions today. Even the keen fans of the sport have trouble knowing their names and that is not good for the game. Every effort should be made to get back to the one world champion per division set-up. This, I think, would be a sensible step.

(RO) How do you feel about there being so many weight divisions in the sport today?

(MC) I am okay with this, since it helps many fighters to fit into a division that is right for their weight.

(RO) What would you say to those who would like to ban boxing?

(MC) I would say to them: consider what you are saying and look at the positives which come from the sport. Let us not also forget that amateur boxing is entirely different to the professionals. Amateur boxing is still a sport, whereas professional boxing is more inclined to be a business.

(RO) There have been a number of films made about boxing over the years. Do you have a favourite?

(MC) No, I cannot say that I have.

(RO) What was the best advice you were given when boxing?

(MC) Keep cool under pressure.

(RO) Do you favour the advice given from the corner to a boxer between the rounds?

(MC) Some can of course be of help, yet too much advice can be non-productive. Boxers can only do what they can do during the course of a fight and it is often difficult to carry out much of the instructions and advice given in the heat of battle.

(RO) Looking at the domestic scene at the moment, who do you tip for the top in the amateur and professional ranks?

(MC) Wales have quite a number of talented boxers at amateur level coming through. I cannot comment too much

Malcolm seen here with his trophy cabinet

on the professional side, since the amateurs are my main interest.

(RO) How long have you been married?

(MC) 51 years (I always lose on points to my wife Margaret).

(RO) Do you discuss boxing much at home?

(MC) No, I cannot say that I do.

(RO) Do you have a hobby?

(MC) Yes, underwater swimming which I find very enjoyable.

(RO) What advice would you give to anyone embarking on a career in boxing?

(MC) Put the time into your training, there are no shortcuts.

(RO) Looking back at your career, would you do anything differently if you had your time over?

(MC) Yes, I would have deferred my National Service and then possibly I could have gone to the Olympics in 1956. However, I made my choice and trained as a PTI in the RAF.

(RO) Clearly, you feel you might have obtained a medal at the said games.

(MC) It's always difficult to predict when competing with the best from each country, but I feel I would have been in with a good chance. The gold medal winner at my weight was Vladimir Safronov from Russia, who defeated Tommy Nicholls in the final.

(RO) What are your ambitions for the future?

(MC) To write about amateur boxers. Many articles are written about boxers when they become champions. I like to write about small club shows and often smile to myself when a youngster becomes a champion and I have written about his ability long before. It really gives me a great sense of satisfaction and pride.

Speaking to Malcolm it is very clear that he still loves boxing and enjoys the amateur side of the sport in which he is still very much involved, in a writing capacity. Today, he is both a father and a grandfather, and is a most contented man. It is a great shame that he did not go to the Olympic Games in 1956 for the reason given, since with his ability it is very possible that he may well have brought home a medal of some kind. We will never know for sure, since destiny directed Malcolm away from his chosen route to a different path, so we can only speculate on the kind of successes this fine fighter might have aspired to at the Games. We can also take this a stage further and wonder just how well Malcolm would have done had he decided to join the paid ranks. With his obvious talent he would have been a major player, of that I have little doubt. A British, European, British Empire or even a world crown might have been his in due course, or even a showdown with Howard Winstone. This would have been a fight worth watching, with all tickets being sold at record pace and a natural for Wales. Who would have won? Now, that is a question which needs a great deal of thought, but that is boxing. Yet today Malcolm can look back and feel very proud of his vast achievements in the ring and they were indeed truly vast. Over the years Wales has produced a number of magnificent boxers, men who fought not only with skill but with fire and passion. Malcolm Collins is a class act, who sits comfortably on that roll of honour. Indeed, Malcolm was a credit to both Welsh and British boxing and is still so today. On behalf of the Yearbook I wish Malcolm, his wife Margaret and family, the very best for the future.

Glove Story: A Review of British Boxing Books in 2007-2008

by Philip Sharkey

With so many books on British boxing and boxers published this year I sincerely hope I have not missed any out, apologies if I have. Let us begin with a story that starts with an original British Boxing Board of Control licence holder and the founder of Scotland's most famous boxing family.

A BOXING DYNASTY: THE TOMMY GILMOUR STORY starts way back with Tommy junior's grandfather Jim representing Great Britain at the 1920 Olympics in Belgium. He was outpointed by a Norwegian at the Games but on his return home he went on to forge a career as a boxer, promoter and bookmaker, laying the foundations of a dynasty that has now reached its fourth generation. Jim, fondly known as the 'Auld Yin', toughened himself up working in the shipyards of Govan where his boxing skills and reputation served him well in the unregulated gambling world, although it seems that it was his computer like brain, working out the odds, that gave the Gilmours a head start out of the poverty of pre-war Glasgow. Jim, one of the founding licence holders of the BBBoC, promoted in Scotland through the depression era (no mean feat when work and spare cash was in short supply), by which time his son Tommy senior had learned the ropes, going on to manage and promote Scottish greats, Jake Kilrain, Charlie Hill, Bert Gilroy, Jimmy Croll, John Smillie, British and Empire champion Jackie Brown and Tommy Junior's favourites, Chic Calderwood and Peter Keenan. It would have been a big surprise if Tommy junior had not gone into the boxing business; he was already holding the round cards on his father's promotions from the age of nine! Tommy Gilmour junior's book starts with the nail-biting account of negotiating and finally promoting Pat Clinton's world title fight with Isidro Perez. Tommy spills the beans on his father's falling out with Peter Keenan, the tragic Chic Calderwood, and traces his own career as Scotland's most successful promoter/manager. Tommy finishes by telling us his son Christopher looks set to continue the family boxing business and, by incredible coincidence, he is promoting in partnership with Bert Gilroy's grandson. GILROY WAS HERE: A biography about Bert Gilroy was published in 2006 so just misses my reviews, but it is available from www.bertgilroy.com. Tommy senior and Bert worked together over 60 years ago! It is a book that is as much a history of Scottish boxing as it is a history of the Gilmour clan. Now on to a tough wee man Tommy promoted.

JOHN DAVISON: LITTLE MAN, BIG HEART - I WENT FROM WHEELER DEALER TO WORLD CHAMPION BOXER - THIS IS MY TRUE STORY. The popular Tynesider John 'Dava' Davison was a late starter at the game and was already 25 when he had his first amateur bout. However, within 12 months he reached the ABA finals, knocking out two England reps in the first round of their respective bouts. They were Colin Lynch and the England captain, multi titled Paul 'Hoko' Hodkinson, who would later go on to become British European and WBC world champion. After being overlooked for the 1988 Olympics, John was about to hang up his gloves when local promoter Tommy Conroy talked him into turning pro, thus beginning a five-year roller-coaster ride. John's book gives a gritty account of working class life on a tough Newcastle estate, and growing up during Margaret Thatcher's tenure as Prime Minister at a time when the North East's proud industrial heritage went through a sad decline. John tells it as he fought, tough and uncompromising, but with sprinkles of Geordie humour, especially with his tales of antiques and car boot sales.

One of the boxers profiled in Wynford Jones fine book, BENNY'S BOYS: THE STABLE OF BENNY JACOBS is Ronnie Rush, who trained John Davison's nemesis, Steve Robinson. And boy did Benny have some talented fighters! Joe Erskine, Darkie Hughes, Phil Edwards, Harry Carroll and Lennie 'The Lion' Williams. He also started the careers of Kelvin Smart and the tragic Rudi Pika before ill health saw him hand their contracts over to Mickey Duff, at the time Britain's most powerful promoter. Wynford, a BBBoC referee since 1977 and president of the Welsh Ex Boxers Association, tells the story of Benny and his stable of boxers, including the aforementioned, along with men such as Teddy Best, Aryee Jackson, Redvers Sangoe, Ron 'Ponty' Davies, Gordon Blakey, Tanos Lambrianides, Terry Crimmins and Dennis Pleace. Also included are the records of another 14 of his lads. Benny was quite a character, but the respect and love his fighters had for him was evident at his funeral, held at the Synagogue, Penylan Gardens, Cardiff. All his surviving boxers turned up and not one had a bad word to say about him. It is a lovingly assembled book that keeps alive the memory of one of boxing's lesser known, but much respected characters. Wynford's book can be bought by post: 3 Sycamore Close, Aberdare, Wales CF44 8YD.

THE BIG IF: THE LIFE AND DEATH OF JOHNNY OWEN by Rick Broadbent not only tells the story of Welsh hero Johnny Owen, but mirrors the upbringing and career of Mexican world bantamweight champion Lupe Pintor, the man in the opposite corner that fateful night in September 1980. Although both were from humble beginnings, for all the love and support Johnny had from his family, Lupe knew only beatings and abuse. As stated earlier, the book charts Johnny's rise through the amateur ranks, turning pro, and winning British, Commonwealth and European titles that put him in the world's top-ten, and therefore eligible for a shot at the champion. We are also told of Pintor's rough ride to becoming world champion. While we presume the writer's depiction of the two gladiators parallel lives will end on that upsetting night, we move forward 25 years to the unveiling of a statue to Johnny in his hometown of Merthyr when Johnny's father Dick meets for the first time since that terrible night, special guest Lupe Pintor. An astonishing bond between two proud men is forged and although neither speaks the same language, tears, sorrow, forgiveness and hope is the language understood by both at such an emotional time. It is a sad but inspirational story. To invite a lad who had just stopped your son in an amateur contest to your home for tea as the Owen family did might seem unusual to those who do not understand the great camaraderie boxing cultivates, but that is how Johnny became great friends with former British, European and world flyweight champion Charlie Magri.

Charlie's autobiography CHAMPAGNE CHARLIE (edited by James Mc'Donnell) explodes a few myths. For a start Charlie is not really a Charlie, and neither is he a cockney! He first became interested in boxing through his life-long pal Jimmy Batten and loved the fact that it was a one-on-one sport, unlike his football team where he often found himself substituted. He quickly rose through the amateur ranks under the astute guidance of Arbour Youths' Jimmy Graham and ABA titles, England vests and eventually Olympic selection followed. Surprisingly, Charlie was beaten by the host countries Ian Clyde. Maybe this was an omen for his pro career, because every time Charlie was about to reach the peak, fate knocked him back. Charlie turned pro with Terry Lawless and won the British flyweight title in only his third fight. He was given a Lonsdale Belt to keep as there were no other worthy challengers! This meant looking to the continent, where he won the European title, and taking on the top Mexican and South American eight-stone men. With world titles slightly scarcer than today, Charlie had to wait his turn and suffered a shock defeat to a Mexican import that placed him at the back of an ever-growing queue. As we find out, Charlie is made of sterner stuff and eventually fought his way to world title glory on an emotional night in Wembley, when stopping Eleoncio Mercedes in the seventh round. His boxing career exposed him to the harsh realities of the pro game, of which he talks honestly and openly. Charlie was ruthless in the ring but outside very much a quiet, humble man and this comes across in many of the great reminiscences he recalls in his life story.

Billy Walker, the 'Blond Bomber', may never have won a title but his charisma made him as popular as Charlie, his handsome looks custom-made for television and his story is told in WHEN THE GLOVES CAME OFF: THE POWERFUL PERSONAL STORY OF BRITAIN'S PLAYBOY BOXER BILLY WALKER. Robin McGibbon not only covers the good times of the young, fit heavyweight with the world at his feet but also recounts the depths of despair Billy suffered in losing his wife to cancer. As boxing fans of a certain age will never forget, Billy made his name on prime-time television as part of the GB amateur team that destroyed the Yanks, Billy knocking out Cornelius Perry in the final fight of the evening at heavyweight. With his ex-boxer brother George as his manager he was the hottest property in boxing and the astute George made sure they

Charlie Magri (left), Britain's former world flyweight champion, seen here with his publisher, Cass Pennant   Philip Sharkey

earned 'top dollar' when Billy turned pro. Billy is very revealing, writing candidly about his life and loves in and out of the ring. He only fought for titles twice, but headlined and sold out shows from the start. How pro boxing has changed with television companies thinking every fight they broadcast has to be for a title, however obscure, for the public to be interested in watching.

Although he won a version of the world heavyweight title, beating Jimmy Thunder in New Zealand, Sheffield's Johnny Nelson had the worst possible start as a pro as documented in A HARD ROAD TO GLORY: JOHNNY NELSON. Johnny lost his first three fights and when the chance of glory was within his grasp he blew it on prime-time live television when fighting so cautiously even his mother gave him a verbal bashing! That was a draw against Carlos De Leon, but two years later he had clawed his way back to fight James Warring for the title, this time in the USA. After 12 negative rounds he lost on points in what was generally recognised as another stinker. Instead of thinking he had gone as far as he could, Johnny, with the unending support and faith of mentor Brendan Ingle, took his show on the road and for the next ten years and 21 bouts remained unbeaten, winning and retiring as undefeated WBO cruiserweight king and generally respected as the best man on the planet in that division. As if that is not enough of a story, Johnny pulls no punches talking about his fall outs with former close friends, Naseem Hamed, Herol Graham, and Glyn Rhodes, and run ins with gangsters and a kidnap plot!

Kidnap plots and gangsters form a large part of former Southern Area and WBU super-cruiserweight champion Dominic Negus life, his story being told in OUT OF THE SHADOWS: THE TRUE STORY OF DOMINIC NEGUS with Ivan Sage. It seems we see more of Dominic on television these days, as he provides security at many boxing shows and can be seen unobtrusively walking the main event boxer to the ring. Dominic did hit the big time in his own right when he fought Olympic gold medal winner and unbeaten hot prospect Audley Harrison live on the BBC. Audley, at 6'6"and 18 stone, had considerable advantages over a blown-up cruiser so it was no surprise Dominic did not take kindly to being hit when he was down. In fact, he was so incensed he jumped up and flew at Audley head-first! Showing a cool head referee Ian John-Lewis calmed things down and eventually Dominic lost on points, famously claiming in the post-fight interview that "my old mum hits harder than that". We can see from that incident that the 'Milky Bar Kid' was no respecter of reputations and this led to many difficult situations in his private life, where his boxing skills stood him in good stead. Thankfully, Dominic has realised that things had to change and he is now keeping to the straight and narrow, using the book to make some apologies to the people he has hurt both physically and emotionally.

From the 'Milky Bar Kid' to a British champion, who during his boxing career really was a milkman. ANDY TILL: BLOOD SWEAT TEARS...AND FEARS charts the life of the popular Lonsdale Belt winner and European title challenger. Andy is as blunt and forceful in his autobiography as he was between the ropes. The youngest of nine children, money was scarce, but it seems love and affection from his parents was non-existent. Following his brother to Northolt ABC, his natural strength and determination saw him reach the junior ABA finals three years running and then losing in the ABA senior final. He turned pro with local promoter/manager Harry Holland, staying with him throughout his boxing career. Interestingly, he was matched tough from the start. For instance, his second bout was against Graham Jenner, who was 5-2 at the time. Sparring in Harry's gym with the likes of Gary Hobbs and Rocky Kelly, Till feared no man! Following the traditional route, the Southern Area title was won, leading to securing a Lonsdale Belt outright, before an unsuccessful challenge for Laurent Boudouani's European title. Set out in 12 'rounds'(chapters) the one-minute rest in-between gives his friends and old opponents a page or two to add their views. The likes of Harry Holland, Sally Bloomfield, widow of Andy's trainer John, and old opponent WO Wilson all take time to recall their friendship and respect for him and his achievements in the ring. He really did have a 'lotta bottle' !

By coincidence, Andy's former manager and promoter Harry Holland has also written his memoirs and what an exciting life he has led. HARRY HOLLAND: A MAN OF MANY PARTS. Printer tells us that he was a van boy, car salesman, bouncer, boxer, music promoter, hairdresser, male model, male escort, debt collector, actor... What next. In his astonishingly frank book, Harry tells us of his colourful life in and out of the boxing ring. As a young boxing fan I always knew a Harry Holland Promotion would be a great night of boxing. He had such an exciting stable, Rocky Kelly, Andy Till, Serg Fame, James Cook and Trevor Smith. Harry later promoted Nigel Benn and was, of course, involved with promoting Audley Harrison whilst working as his cutsman. His career as a promoter started in the music business and his book tells of good times with Shakin Stevens, Mungo Jerry and Gene Vincent, along with occasional run-ins with the local Hells Angels just to keep him on his toes! Harry is now a regular face on East Enders, working on his stall or having a cup of tea in the café, probably thinking of writing the follow up.

Melanie Lloyd's long awaited second book: SWEET FIGHTING MAN 2 was launched to great acclaim in London's Piccadilly Circus, courtesy of the Lonsdale International Sporting Club, with many of her subjects turning up to chat and sign books. I feel the success of her books is in the mix of contenders and champions stretching back to the 1940s that she interviews. From Teddy Lewis to active pros Jane Couch, Tony Booth and Michael Sprott, Melanie lets her subjects talk freely about their boxing careers and generally tell their life-stories straight from the heart. Maybe because she is a woman, the boxers drop their guard a little so they open up more, but I believe it is her compassion and respect that has led the Sweet Fighting Men [and woman] to feel they can trust her with their memories.

From left to right: Harold Alderman, Reg Gutteridge and Ken Sellick are seen here with Melanie Lloyd at the launch of her eagerly awaited Sweet Fighting Man 2 publication. Harold and Melanie are both contributers to the Yearbook Philip Sharkey

George Cooper, Teddy Lewis, BF Williams (now an A grade referee), Michael Sprott, Mark Rowe, Jane Couch, Ivor 'The Engine' Jones, Tony Booth and Colin Jones, all tell of life's ups and downs, with an introduction from Sylvester Mitee and a last word from James Cook MBE. As Melanie says herself, "books last forever and boxing is a short career. One of the many things that keep me passionately driven as a boxing writer is the knowledge that, by writing books about boxers, I feel that I am in some way immortalising my subjects". Melanie will personally sign her book when you order through her website: www.sweetfightingman.com or by post with a cheque for £12.99 to Melanie Lloyd, Studio 22, 61 Victoria Road, Surbiton, Surrey.

The final three books are by fighters all still active and with more big fights to come, which is why some might view Amir Khan, Ricky Hatton and Joe Calzaghe as cashing in on their current popularity, (and who can blame them) rather than waiting until they retire and then writing a considered overview of their respective boxing careers and how they settled into 'civilian' life outside the ring. That said they are all interesting reads.

A BOY FROM BOLTON: MY STORY tells of Amir Khan's ambition to become Britain's youngest world champion, but with this book he must surely hold the record as the youngest British boxer to write his life story! The book ends after his win against Colin Bain on 8 July 2006 and includes his pro record up until then. It also lists his complete amateur record,

which is something other books often lack. He talks with great maturity about the dreadful London bombings and the issues facing young Muslims in Britain today, as well as his charity work and his family, including cousin Saj Mahmood, an England test cricketer.

Written before the biggest fight of his career against Floyd Mayweather, THE HITMAN MY STORY ends after Ricky Hatton's fight with Luis Colazzo. It has good statistics at the back and reminds us that Billy Graham always knew he had a special kid in his gym, bearing in mind that Ricky was sparring the likes of Paul Burke, Andy Holligan and Ensley Bingham, all hard-punching pro champions, when he was just 16.

NO ORDINARY JOE suffers the same drawback as it only goes up to Joe Calzaghe's fight with Peter Manfredo in April 2007. Like Manfredo, Joe has always been trained by his father and the book has some humorous stories about father-son relationships, like the time Enzo made Joe walk two miles to a weigh-in as he did not want to pay the parking fee! But Enzo must be getting the best from his son, as Joe was a triple ABA champion and is still undefeated as a professional. The book's opening chapter describes the night of his career-defining fight with then unbeaten Jeff 'Left Hook' Lacy, but of course he has gone on to defeat top-rated Mikkel Kessler and, travelling to the fight capital of the world, Bernard Hopkins in Las Vegas. So it seems that Joe, Ricky and Amir had better keep their pen and paper at the ready!

Home and Away with British Boxers, 2007-2008

by John Jarrett

JULY

They say there is good stuff in little bundles. Ian Napa is living proof of that. After narrow defeats in five championship contests in a ten-year professional career, this little fellow (one of the smallest fighters at 5'1") finally got his hands on some serious hardware; a Lonsdale Belt.

At the Robin Park Arena in Wigan, Napa put it all together to take a unanimous decision from former champion Jason Booth and claim the vacant British bantamweight title. It was also sweet revenge as Booth had thwarted Ian's bid for the British and Commonwealth flyweight titles almost seven years previously. Napa's better boxing and a strong finish got him home in front, taking his pro log to 14-6.

Those International titles are still going around. And they are always vacant, so everybody gets a shot at being a champion. Heywood light-middleweight Mark Thompson jumped at the chance to go for the WBC version against South African Vincent Vuma on the Wigan show and almost pulled it off. Mark started well but was floored in the fourth round before fighting back to dump Vuma in the fifth with a body shot. But Mark came up short in round eight when a left to the body had him on the deck again. He beat the count but was under fire when it was stopped, his first defeat in a dozen bouts. At 26, Mark will be back.

Fight number 13 proved unlucky for Amir Khan's opponent, not for the Bolton Olympian, as he took the Commonwealth lightweight championship off Scot Willie Limond in a thriller at London's O2 Arena. But for a while in the sixth round it looked as though the old superstition might prevail. It had been a cracker for five rounds with the champion holding his own against the favourite, getting home with several rights to the head that sounded alarm bells in the Khan corner. Out for round six and Willie caught Amir a big right to the head, followed up with more leather and a clubbing left, and Khan was on the deck. We had wondered about this moment, but we need not have worried. Amir was back on his feet and back in the fight, a big question answered. He could take a punch! Limond was unable to cash in and after a punishing eighth round he was unable to continue, being pulled out by his corner with a suspected broken jaw. Amir Khan, in his 13th professional fight, had won his first major championship and at 20, was still on course for the big one.

On the same show, Nicky Cook went for the big one, fighting Steve Luevano for the vacant WBO featherweight title. The Londoner gave it his best shot but was out of his depth as the Californian southpaw proved to be a class act, decking Cook four times before knocking him out in the 11th round. The 27-year-old from Dagenham suffered his first defeat after going 27-0 in a nine-year pro career that saw him take British, Commonwealth and European titles. Seven months earlier, Nicky had been primed to challenge then-champion Scott Harrison for this belt, only for the troubled titleholder to pull out with just days to go, leaving a somewhat deflated Cook to box an eight-rounder with Harry Ramogoadi. Nicky might have beaten Harrison. On his big night he could not beat Luevano.

Heavyweight fights can be sensational. They can also be soporific. Unfortunately for the customers at London's O2 Arena, the Commonwealth title defence by Matt Skelton against former victim Michael Sprott was a 12-round bore-snore that drew derisive comments from the crowd. Skelton had won their first fight by a late knockout but Sprott was still there at the final bell. By that time nobody cared who had won, they were just glad it was over! For the record, Skelton retained his title on a majority decision, taking his log to 21-1, 19 inside.

One week later, Frank Warren staged another mammoth bill, in Cardiff this time, with big puncher Enzo Maccarinelli putting his WBO cruiserweight title on the line against Wayne Braithwaite, from Guyana via New York. This time Enzo could not detonate the big bombs although he did deck the former WBC champion in round five. But if the big man from Swansea could not knock his man out, he certainly shut him out to fully earn the unanimous decision and keep alive his dream fight with London rival David Haye.

Alex Arthur does not take his coat off these days unless there is a title on the line. Fifteen of his previous 16 fights had been for one strap or another and this one at the Cardiff Indoor Arena against Koba Gogoladze was no exception. The boys were fighting for the interim WBO super-featherweight belt while champion-proper Joan Guzman struggled with his weight problem. At 29, the Edinburgh man had won all but one of his 24 pro fights, (18 inside) and his record was impressive; former undefeated British, Commonwealth, European, WBO Inter-Continental, WBA Inter-Continental and IBF Inter-Continental super-feather-weight champion.

David Haye is seen here with BBBoC Chairman, Charles Giles
Philip Sharkey

59

What more do they want? Well, the Scot added this trinket to his collection with a bloody victory over a tough awkward opponent. A clash of heads in the fourth round left Alex with cuts over and under his right eye and he put his foot to the floor, fearful of a stoppage. Gogoladze survived an eighth-round knockdown but had nothing left in round ten when it was stopped. Arthur looked a mess but he looked a winner, remaining on course for the crown.

Unfancied Gavin Rees upset Souleymane M'Baye by unanimous decision to win the WBA light-welterweight title, joining Ricky Hatton (IBO) and Junior Witter (WBC) as leaders of the ten-stone club. It was not the Frenchman's night, but it most certainly was a wonderful evening for the little Welsh underdog. He can bite!

The order of things was confirmed as Young Muttley was taught a lesson by the teacher. British light-welterweight champion Colin Lynes, an assistant school teacher in his day job, captured the vacant European title with a comprehensive defeat of the crowd favourite in the little Civic Hall at Wolverhampton. The man from Essex tamed the puncher and in round eight closed the show. A big right to the temple brought up a lump and brought Muttley down. He beat the count but was in trouble immediately when a left hook flattened him and the third man waved it off.

Irish middleweights John Duddy and Andy Lee added to their win records. Former amateur star Duddy came home in triumph after clocking up 20 straight wins in America, thrilling the Dublin crowd with a tenth-round stoppage over former Italian light-middleweight champion Alessio Furlan. John outboxed the visitor all the way and outpunched him in the final round, dropping him twice before it was called off. Andy Lee had an easy ride in Cologne on a Wladimir Klitschko bill, knocking out Austrian Thomas Hengstberger inside two rounds.

It all went pear-shaped for British super-featherweight champion Carl Johanneson at the Barnsley Metrodome as European champion Leva Kirakosyan retained his title with an emphatic fourth-round stoppage. The Armenian had stopped Carl inside a round previously and this time confirmed his superiority in brutal fashion with four knockdowns. London light-middleweight Anthony Small looked to be on his way to victory in his Commonwealth title challenge to brave Welshman Bradley Pryce on the O2 bill. But the champion pressed on resolutely as Small went through his flashy repertoire, finally getting home with some big shots to bring the referee's intervention in round seven.

AUGUST

The Point arena in Dublin's dockland was due for demolition as part of a major redevelopment plan for the area, but the work started sooner rather than later. On a warm summer evening, a Spanish wrecking crew moved in and levelled Irish icon Bernard Dunne while many of the six thousand fans were still looking for their seats. They billed Kiko Martinez as 'La Sensacion' and in just 86 seconds he did just what it said on the tin. Kiko's jackhammer fists devastated Mr Dunne almost before he could get his hands up and referee Terry O'Connor had to stop it before the fans thought Bernard was part of the canvas. He had been

down there three times already! So Senor Kiko Martinez was indeed 'The Sensation'. Going off his record you had to respect his power with 13 early nights in 16 undefeated fights. But his record showed his opposition to be somewhat less that top-drawer and it was the first time out of his comfort zone for the 21-year-old Alicante resident. How would he stand up with six thousand Irishmen baying for his blood? The Martinez camp were less than happy over the appointment of four British officials for the contest but the EBU dismissed their objections. As it turned out, Senor Martinez, like old Sam Langford many years ago, brought his own judge and jury in his two nutmeg-brown fists. They delivered a crushing verdict. The stunning victory brought Martinez the European super-bantamweight championship Dunne had defended twice since winning the belt ten months earlier. Bernard went into the ring a 1-4 betting favourite to retain his title and extend his unbeaten record to 25-0. One bookmaker was said to have given Kiko's manager Alberto Gonzales odds of 66-1 for a £10,000 wager that Martinez would win in the first round, a gamble that would have netted Senor Gonzales a tidy £666,000! The fight? There was no fight - just four punches. Three knockdowns; a right then a left hook, down – another right and another count – one more right-hand bomb and Dunne was done for, Mr O'Connor has seen enough, and it was all over in record time. The King is dead, long live the King!

On the Dublin bill in what would be the first British title fight to be held in the Republic of Ireland, Portsmouth puncher Tony Oakey retained his light-heavyweight championship against Belfast southpaw Brian Magee via a paper-thin majority draw decision, which did not sit well with the fans. It was Magee's better boxing against Oakey's busy workrate with Tony scraping home by a whisker. So where does that leave Dean Francis? The Commonwealth champion had thrown down a challenge to the winner for a double title showdown. But there was no winner! "Both Oakey and Magee have said they would fight me", said the Basingstoke man. "I just want them to know I'm ready".

Andy Lee, the Limerick southpaw who started his pro career in the United States, came home with an unbeaten 10-0 pro log and top trainer Emanuel Steward in his corner. It was all too much for Belfast middleweight Ciaran Healy, who pulled out after four rounds. Birmingham middleweight Matthew Macklin had Ricky Hatton in his corner for his fight with Darren Rhodes. Macklin managed quite well on his own and a right hand put the Leeds boy down and out in round four as Matthew took his record to 19-2.

Mr Hatton was also feeling quite pleased with himself as his mega-fight with Floyd Mayweather was announced for a December date at the MGM Grand in Las Vegas. Ricky's rabid fans were already scrambling for tickets since it was announced that only 3,900 would be available for British consumption. Hatton's last fight in Vegas had drawn a massive ten thousand followers to the Nevada desert oasis.

SEPTEMBER

Junior Witter finally delivered the fight he always promised us with a brilliant performance against Vivian Harris, outboxing and outpunching the Brooklyn-based Guyanese for six rounds before knocking him out in the seventh with a perfect left hook to retain his WBC light-welterweight title. The fight, at the Dome in Witter's adopted hometown of Doncaster, brought together two men who could box and punch at world level. Harris was a former WBA champion, as was Witter, and brought a 28-2-1 pro log to the ring with 18 stoppages. The Bradford native, a switch-hitter of the Ingle breed, had not lost in six years, his only defeat in a 38-fight career, with two draws. Harris was four years younger than Witter and four inches taller, but Junior was the better puncher and that proved the deciding factor as his dream fight with Ricky Hatton suddenly became viable again. It was not until round four that Harris got into the fight but he was suddenly stunned by a left-right, then shoved to the floor. When he got up, Witter left hooked him to the deck again and he did not look happy going to his stool. Junior strangely let Harris back into things in the fifth and sixth but closed the show in dramatic fashion in round seven with as good a left hook as you could wish for. Thus did Junior Witter become a major player in the light-welterweight division.

Now thirty-five and coming back after a year out (elbow surgery), Clinton Woods had no time to lose if he was to get his hands on a couple of big money fights. At the Hallam FM Arena in Sheffield, the IBF light-heavyweight champion punched himself back into condition with a decision over former foe Julio Gonzalez. A former WBO champion, the Mexican is a hard man to beat, only three losses in 44 fights and never stopped, yet Woods almost brought it off in a terrific 11th round. Gonzalez survived to finish on his feet but Clinton won't be looking for him again.

It looked like journey's end for 36-year-old Howard Eastman as the Battersea Bomber failed to explode when defending his British middleweight championship against Birmingham's Wayne Elcock at the Coventry Skydome. Elcock was a comfortable winner, the first British boxer to beat Eastman, and he was delighted with his victory, already talking of a crack at the European title. It was thought that Eastman's big punch would be a factor but Wayne was rarely troubled by the man who had stopped 35 of his 42 victims (4 defeats) in a 13-year pro career. Although the challenger was 33, he was comparatively fresh with only 20 fights under his belt (17-2-1) and this made the difference. Wayne was in tremendous condition and he finished strong to put the issue beyond doubt.

The ring action was red hot at the Kirkcaldy Ice Rink as Darlington's unfancied Franny Jones fought out of his skin in a bold bid to take the British welterweight title off Kevin Anderson. But it was a fight too far for Jones even if he did make it into the final round before the referee decided enough was enough. Franny was exhausted and unable to fight back as the Scot launched his final assault to seal victory. But the cheers at the end were as much for the gallant challenger as for the champion.

Two hands are better than one. Bristol bantamweight Lee Haskins will vouch for that after surrendering his challenge to British champion Ian Napa following seven rounds of a good fight at the York Hall. Lee had won the first three rounds but the champion was coming on strong

Kevin Mitchell (left) seen battering the 39-year-old Edison Torres to defeat inside three rounds at York Hall last January Philip Sharkey

when manager Chris Sanigar pulled Haskins out, Lee having injured the muscles in his right arm.

The Cinderella story came to a sad end when 35-year-old Buster Keeton lost his British cruiserweight title to Mark Hobson, the fight at the Hallam FM Arena in Sheffield being stopped in round four with the veteran starting to unravel after shipping some big punches from the former champion.

The rubber match between British featherweight champion John Simpson and Andy Morris left no doubts as to who was the better man. In the seventh round, Simpson stunned his man with a terrific right, then followed him to the ropes where a sustained attack dropped Andy on his face and brought the referee's intervention. There was no way back for the former champion this time. Possibly the better boxer of the two, Morris had beaten Simpson on points in their first meeting only to lose the return with a badly cut eye. But Simpson had the power this night in Mayfair and next morning he was taking the belt back to Greenock.

Hull veteran Tony Booth failed to regain the British Masters cruiserweight title he held in 2000 when Neil Simpson beat him over ten rounds at the local Civic Hall in a fight that was competitive all the way…At the Preston Guild Hall, WBU welterweight champion Michael Jennings made all the right moves in winning an eight rounds decision over Russian tough guy Vladimir Khodokovski in an excellent warm-up for his coming title defence against Ross Minter.

Welsh plasterer Scott Gammer put his gloves away after losing a ten rounds decision to big John McDermott on the Sheffield show. Bowing out with a record of 18-2-1, the former British heavyweight champion had nothing left in this eliminator for the title he held for five months (2006-2007) as McDermott moved to 23-3.

They call Germany's WBA flyweight champion Susianna Kentikian 'Killer Queen' and on a Friday night in Dusseldorf Shanee Martin found out why. The hard way. The 25-year-old from Colchester was unable to use her height advantage to keep the champion away and was brought down in round three, the referee stopping it, giving the 'Killer Queen' her 18th straight victory, 14 inside. This 20-year-old girl is clearly not one to take liberties with.

OCTOBER

Amir Khan is a physical marvel! How he keeps a welterweight body inside a lightweight frame beats the hell out of me, but he did it again at the Nottingham Arena when he retained his Commonwealth title against the game challenge of Stoke's Scott Lawton, the referee calling it off in round four. Coming out for the first, Amir forgot his gumshield and had to return to the corner for it. The champion did not forget how Willie Limond had dropped him in his previous outing and boxed accordingly, keeping a tight guard until he was happy to open up in the fourth with a furious attack that brought things to an end. In taking his pro log to 14-0 (11) Khan was still on track for a world title.

Michael Gomez always talked a good fight and he usually walked the walk, winning 34 of his 41 fights, 24 inside. He gave Alex Arthur his only defeat and won a Lonsdale Belt outright in his first reign as British super-featherweight champion, but he was 30 now and showing wear and tear. He still figured he could take Carl Johanneson's title when they clashed at the Doncaster Dome. Carl's last outing saw him badly beaten inside four rounds by European champion Leva Kirakosyan and he knew he had to win this one, saying, "I think this could be the end for the loser".

Well the fans were the winners as these two savaged each other for six rounds before Father Time and tough fights caught up with the Manchester Irishman. Johanneson outboxed and finally outpunched Gomez in the sixth, dropping him with two solid rights. Michael beat the count but was under fire again when the referee stopped it. Gomez protested but he was through for the night and Carl had a Lonsdale Belt to take home for keeps.

The York Hall was buzzing as British lightweight champion Jon Thaxton put his title on the line for the second time and dared Scot Dave Stewart to come and get it. Stewart went for it and got away to a fine start, shrugging off a first-round cut on his forehead to give the champion a tough night of it before his superior strength and fitness prevailed. Dave had a rough 11th and had nothing left in the final session. Bleeding from a nasty cut over the right eye, the result of an eighth-round clash of heads, Stewart took a knee twice before the referee called it off. A brave Scot!

The ring announcer at Jack Doughty's Shaw promotion thought he had it tough pronouncing the names of Choi Tseveenpurev and Abdul Tebazalwa. Then the bell rang and things really got tough, especially for Abdul, as the Mongol warrior went on the warpath, setting up a relentless attack

that decked the challenger in the sixth and took him to a split decision in this third defence of his WBF featherweight title. At 36, this guy just gets better!

English light-middleweight champion Andrew Facey was after Jamie Moore's British title when they clashed at the Robin Park Centre in Wigan. Jamie knew what he was up against, having been floored before stopping the Sheffield man almost four years ago. He stopped him this time but not before his awkward opponent had given him fits prior to Jamie dropping him in round nine and finishing the job in the 11th.

A record of eight fights, even if they were all wins, is hardly adequate preparation for a so-called world title fight, as West Ham featherweight Matthew Marsh learned to his cost when challenging WBU champion Derry Matthews at the York Hall. The Liverpool man gradually took control and when Referee Dave Parris ended it in round 11, Marsh had nothing left.

A chronic left elbow injury brought a summary ending to the career and the reign of Commonwealth super-bantamweight champion Isaac 'Argy' Ward at the Peterlee Leisure Centre where Ghana's Anyetei Laryea proved too big a hurdle for the Darlington man, who was retired by his corner after four painful rounds. One interested ringsider looking for a crack at the winner was Rendall Munroe, who had just won the English title at the weight when he forced Marc Callaghan to retire after six rounds in the same ring. The Leicester man had too much of everything and Callaghan was never at the races.

The promoters of former French amateur champion Giovanni Kopogo picked a patsy for his professional debut at the Tower Hotel in Wapping. Daniel Thorpe had lost 64 of his 89 fights and had just passed his 30th birthday. Get him on the phone! The Sheffield man turned up as promised, then spoiled everything by blasting Kopogo out of the picture halfway through round two. Mon Dieu! Leicester's Concepcion brothers were in action on the same night. If you wanted to see Martin fight Bradley Pryce for the Commonwealth light-middleweight title you went along to the Nottingham Arena, but you would have been disappointed as Martin was finished inside three rounds with the Welshman retaining his title. You should have gone to the Leicester Sporting Club show to see Kevin rack up his seventh straight win against southpaw David Kirk, points, six rounds.

They could match John Duddy with Wee Willie Winkie at the National Stadium and the Dublin fans would still pack the place out. They actually had a job getting an opponent with eight possibles turning the fight down for whatever reasons. However, before they got to Duddy, Manchester's Prince Arron said show me the money and the fight was on. But not for very long. The unbeaten Irish star ended what was a mismatch in round two. Aberdeen's Lee McAllister had the hometown fans roaring as he forced a ninth-round retirement (perforated eardrum) over Glasgow's Craig Docherty to win the vacant WBF lightweight championship. Docherty was ticked off for using his head and his forearm, while McAllister made do with just his fists. They were enough.

Anthony Small (left) won the Southern Area light-middleweight title when he stopped Takaloo in the seventh round last January   Philip Sharkey

NOVEMBER

On my left, Joe Calzaghe, WBO super-middleweight champion, undefeated in 43 contests – on my right, Martin Kessler, WBC and WBA super-middleweight champion, undefeated in 39 contests. Twelve rounds for all the marbles at the vast Millennium Stadium in Cardiff, a tremendous crowd of close on 50,000 holding its breath. Ring the bell! It was the fight the Welshman wanted above all else and Frank Warren, his promoter, had brought it right to his doorstep. Up to you, Joe. Well, he did not let us down, outboxing and outpunching the Dane throughout an excellent contest that enthralled the huge crowd and entertained a US television audience eager to see what this fellow Calzaghe was all about. They saw that Joe was all about skill, fitness, dedication, strength, determination, everything that makes a super-champ. They also saw a guy whose vocabulary does not include the word defeat and at the end of 12 rounds they saw the finest super-middleweight fighter in the world, bar none!

The Calzaghe gym had another big winner this night as WBO cruiserweight champion Enzo Maccarinelli sunk Mohamed Azzaoui with a devastating body shot in round four and the cry went up for a fight with David Haye. A week later, David Haye came home from Paris with the WBA and WBC cruiserweight belts strapped firmly around

his muscular middle after a sensational scrap with Jean-Marc Mormeck that saw both men on the deck. The Frenchman took an early lead in a way that belied his 35 years and in round four smashed his challenger to the floor. There was no doubting that Haye was in trouble. Although he beat the count he was still unsteady and Mormeck tagged him again before the bell. It was round six before David began his drive to the finishing line. He reached it in the seventh, terrific punches bringing the champion down on his face. Mormeck got up, but it was over for him and the referee called finis. Now they could get these two big punchers together, Haye v Maccarinelli. Mouths were watering…

Two years after losing to Martin Power in a challenge for the British bantamweight championship in a fine contest at the York Hall, Ian Napa reversed the order of things. This time the little man from Hackney was the champion, having picked up the vacant title with a unanimous decision over former conqueror Jason Booth, and this time Ian was the master, taking a one-sided decision in a thrilling scrap. Napa, one of the smallest men in the professional ring, has a big heart and a big engine, and both kept him going as Power struggled to repeat his former triumph over the Zimbabwe-born Londoner. Martin gave it his best shot but at the final bell Napa still had his title and his eyes on bigger things.

Another fighter with his sights set on world honours is Nottingham's British super-middleweight champion Carl Froch. In front of his hometown fans, the man they call 'The Cobra' took challenger Robin Reid apart and the former WBC world champion was pulled out by his corner after five rounds. Now 36 and 14 years into a professional career that saw him win Olympic Bronze and the WBC championship, Reid's future was all behind him. Froch, coming back from knee surgery that kept him idle for eight months, was soon in charge of the Runcorn veteran and after two trips to the canvas Reid failed to some up for the sixth round, claiming a shoulder injury. It was Carl's fourth British title defence and once again he was looking for Joe Calzaghe.

There was a shock on the Nottingham bill for British super-bantamweight champion Esham Pickering as he was outboxed over eight rounds by Pontefract southpaw Sean Hughes. If the champion figured he was in for an easy ride he received a rude awakening as Hughes dominated the action to possibly earn himself a rematch with the title on the line. Sean had been stopped in a previous challenge for this title against Michael Hunter.

Paisley postman Kevin McIntyre delivered the goods to the Magnum Centre in Irvine where he turned in a brilliant performance to outbox and outpunch British welter-weight champion Kevin Anderson, robbing his fellow Scot of the Lonsdale Belt he would have taken home for good had he won. But there was no way Anderson was coming back after being decked in the first and second rounds. First class delivery!

Barnet middleweight Darren Barker got his hands on the vacant Commonwealth title when he shut out Australian Ben Crampton over 12 one-sided rounds at York Hall, taking his pro log to 16-0. The man from Down Under, billed as 'Bazooka', was firing blank shells as he tried to preserve his unbeaten record but he was never there and finished up with

20-1-1 stats.

North East fighters were in good form, although English light-welterweight champion Nigel Wright had to settle for a share of the points after ten rounds with old rival Lenny Daws on the York Hall bill. The County Durham southpaw had beaten Daws twice, once in the amateurs, and many thought he won this one…Sunderland heavy-weight David Dolan scored four knockdowns inside three rounds to stop Hull veteran Tony Booth… Darlington big man Chris Burton made the trip to Tooting where he retained his unbeaten record (9-0) with a good points win over Franklin Egobi, while Hartlepool stablemate Craig Denton took the nod over Eder Kurti… Johnny Harrison's fans almost took the roof off the Plymouth Guildhall when he punched out a decision victory over Gatis Skuja for the vacant International Masters light-middleweight title, climbing off the floor to triumph.

DECEMBER

The Manchester faithful followed Ricky Hatton to Las Vegas in their thousands and he did not let them down as he battled Floyd Mayweather Jnr for his WBC welterweight championship at the MGM Grand Arena. The Hitman had won all 43 of his professional fights, but he didn't win this one. On this world stage, Floyd was the star and Ricky had to be happy with the chief supporting role. His dream of super-stardom ended in the tenth round after he had been smashed to the canvas for two counts to bring about the timely intervention of Referee Joe Cortez. Hatton had fought out of his skin in the early rounds, throwing everything at the American, but 'Pretty Boy' Floyd was on song this night and he trumped every move made by the 'Manchester Hitman', exploding in the tenth round with a brilliant left hook that sent Ricky flying across the ring into a corner post before landing on his back. He beat the count but was still shaky and a further two left hooks and a right sent him into the ropes before hitting the floor. It was all over. "He is the best, the pound-for-pound best", said Hatton afterwards. "I certainly know now he can fight".

Hatton did win in Las Vegas on the big night, but brother Matthew gave the family a winning start earlier in the evening when he tossed a beating into tough Puerto Rican Frankie Santos, taking every one of their eight rounds. It was actually a good weekend for the Brits. The night before the big one, at the MGM Conference Centre, six of our boxers were in action with wins for Manchester's unbeaten John Murray over Mexican Miguel Manguia; Edinburgh middleweight Craig McEwan made it 9-0 over Alfredo Contreras; Wolverhampton light-welter Martin Gethin stopped Fabian Luque; Wolverhampton light-welter Dean Harrison stopped Ramon Guevara; former British lightweight champion Lee Meager was held to a draw by Mexican Jose Gonzalez. The only loser was London middleweight Jimmy Campbell, who was stopped inside 80 seconds by Richard Pierson. Campbell, who is based in Indianapolis, was now 10-2.

Meanwhile, back in Bolton, Amir Khan was celebrating his 21st birthday with a one-round blowout of Graham Earl's candle to retain his Commonwealth lightweight title for the second time. The Luton man was a former Commonwealth and WBU champion at the weight but he had no answer for Khan's blistering attack. Earl was dropped with a left hook and a left-right. Up on rubber legs, he was under fire immediately when the referee jumped in to end it with just 72 seconds on the clock. It was a sensational victory for the former Olympian, his 15th, 12 inside schedule.

On the same bill, Dean Francis retained his Commonwealth light-heavyweight title, taking a unanimous decision over Ghana's Michael Gbenga. The challenger had stopped 15 of 16 victims but the only time he hurt Francis was in round eight when a solid right shook the Englishman. Francis finished well, taking his pro log to 29-2, 23 early.

Edinburgh's Alex Arthur must be wondering why he has not fought for a world title. He has won everything else. At the Meadowbank Sports Centre, the local favourite put his interim WBO super-featherweight championship on the line against Steve Foster and there were a few rocky moments before his hand was raised for the 26th time against one defeat. Foster climbed off the deck in round nine and two rounds later shocked the champion with a big right hand that dropped him with a thud. But Alex has a good chin and he was still there at the final bell to take the unanimous decision. Young Foster may well emulate his father one day and become a champ!

Over in Belfast it was a big test for middleweight favourite John Duddy as he met European champion and former world title challenger, Howard Eastman. A 6,000 sellout King's Hall cheered him to a narrow victory over ten rounds, spoiling Howard's 37th birthday and taking his unbeaten record to 23-0. In Dublin a week later, another Irish favourite in Andy Lee displayed what he had learned in American gyms working with legend Emanuel Steward as he forced a retirement after six rounds over Jason McKay. Officially, Belfast's McKay claimed a right shoulder injury but he was on a hiding to nothing as Lee decked him in round two and took his unbeaten record to 14-0, 11 inside. Victory gave Andy the vacant Irish super-middleweight belt. Duddy v Lee one day? Why not.

Stepping up a grade from his British middleweight championship win over Howard Eastman, Birmingham's Wayne Elcock travelled to Switzerland to challenge Arthur Abraham for his IBF title in Basle. Wayne did well for a few rounds before the unbeaten champion unleashed his big guns in round five, a heavy right sending Elcock halfway through the ropes before a thudding left hook left him defenceless and it was all over.

British heavyweight champion Danny Williams looked on his way to victory over IBF Inter-Continental champion Oleg Platov in a battle of big punchers, but a nasty cut over Platov's left eye brought a stoppage in round three and since four rounds had not been completed, the fight was declared a no contest. Danny was gutted!

Wigan was the place to be when four title fights drew the fans in. Gary Woolcombe picked up the vacant British light-middleweight belt with a bloody victory over Marcus Portman who was retired by his corner after eight rounds…Manchester southpaw Craig Watson relieved Ali Nuumbembe of the Commonwealth welterweight crown when a bad cut to Ali's left eyebrow brought an eighth-round stoppage...Jason Booth was another stoppage winner when contesting the vacant Commonwealth bantamweight title, Matthew Edmonds being saved by the referee in the ninth round...And the new British super-flyweight title was bestowed upon Chris Edwards via a split decision over Jamie McDonnell.

JANUARY

If Commonwealth heavyweight champion Matt Skelton thought WBA champion Ruslan Chagaev an easy mark after illness and injury had kept him idle for nine months, he received a rude shock as the Uzbek southpaw quickly shed the rust and retained his title with a unanimous decision in Dusseldorf. Chagaev hadn't lost in 24 fights (1 draw) and he did not lose this one. Skelton is strong, takes a good shot, and gives it everything. Unfortunately it was not enough this evening and it is not enough to take him any higher up the world rankings in a division sadly lacking in star quality. At 41, it is doubtful if Matt will get another chance at the world title, even the fragmented one. Yet he remained hopeful, telling reporters, "Another title shot might come along. I'm disappointed. I did not want to say I fought for a world title. That wasn't enough. I wanted to win it". On the undercard, Manchester lightweight Anthony Crolla took his pro log to 7-0 with five inside wins, but he isn't going to learn anything by knocking over novices like Tomasz Kwiecien, who had won one of his three fights. The Pole was sent crashing to the floor twice before the knockout ended his misery in round five of a contest that never should have happened.

Another fighter who could quite well have figured he was in the wrong business was Finland's Juho Tolppola. He found himself fighting Colin Lynes for the Hornchurch man's European light-welterweight title at the Goresbrook Leisure Centre in Dagenham and apart from the second round made little or no contribution to the proceedings. To be fair, he was a replacement for Italy's Gianluca Branco and he had a decent record of 20-3-1. But Lynes is one of our better champions and he outboxed and outpunched the visitor throughout the 12 rounds to take the unanimous decision. Colin, now 31-3, was looking for bigger fights. He deserves them. Lynes had won the title when his stablemate Ted Bami was forced to relinquish due to injury that kept him out of the ring for ten months. The Brixton man was back in an eight rounder on the Dagenham bill to take a decision from Frenchman Nicolas Guisset, but if he was thinking of chasing his old title he had some ten pounds to shed.

Chingford southpaw Michael Lomax, a former ABA champion, finished his six rounds with Glasgow's Craig Dickson covered in blood, the result of a clash of heads that saw Lomax take 16 stitches. The injury occurred in the dying seconds of the fight so Lomax made it to the bell and took the decision over the one-time Commonwealth title challenger. Close one!

The WBF belt around the somewhat ample middle of Polish heavyweight Albert Sosnowski marks him as a world champion and he has a record to back it up, statistically at any rate; 42-1 with 25 inside wins. But his ten rounds with Colin Kenna marked him as, at best, a third division champion. A

household name, but only in his own household, Albert won over ten rounds but it was a lousy fight.

Two months after shocking British super-bantamweight champion Esham Pickering in a non-title eight rounder, Pontefract's Sean Hughes was rewarded with a shot at the title at the Meadowside Leisure Centre in Burton. Sean had won the first one on points and he was winning this one, for two rounds anyway, his southpaw style proving troublesome to the champion. By the third round, however, Pickering had solved the puzzle and in round four he started landing his harder punches and Hughes was on the deck. He beat the count but was floored again and happy to hear the bell. The Yorkshireman came back strong over the next few rounds and it was shaping up to a helluva fight, but in round nine Esham put some big punches together and Hughes was all in when referee Howard Foster called it off at the 48-second mark of the round.

Bouncing back from a Commonwealth title defeat by Bradley Pryce, Anthony Small regrouped and went after the vacant Southern Area light-middleweight championship, meeting Takaloo at the York Hall. The Margate man was a former WBU welterweight champion, but at 32 with a 25-6 pro log, he was starting to look his age. Small is one of those fighters you either love or hate to see. He is flashy and cocky and takes liberties but he is also gifted and he can punch when he puts his mind to it. He did in the third round, decking Takaloo and cutting him on the left eye. Small floored him again in round four and in the seventh the 26-year-old Deptford boxer dropped the curtain on his show. Takaloo, face bloodied, was sent to the canvas once again by a right to the head. He got up but was all through and the

Martin Rogan (left) won Barry Hearn's Prizefighter competition last April when eliminating Alex Ibbs, David Ferguson and David Dolan. He is seen here against Ferguson   Philip Sharkey

referee called a halt to the fight, possibly ending Takaloo's career as a pro fighter.

Another young fighter to impress was Kevin Mitchell, slated to defend his Commonwealth super-featherweight title against Carl Johanneson. But Carl pulled out injured, and when Ghana's Thomas Aryeetey failed the medical, Mitchell had to settle for a veteran Venezuelan, Edison Torres, ten rounds or less. It proved to be less as the 39-year-old Torres quickly found young Mr Mitchell to be too good in all departments. Kevin's left hook was working well and in the third round Torres was sent reeling into the ropes, defence shot to hell. It was stopped and Mitchell moved to 25-0 with 18 inside. At 23, Mitchell is capable of bigger things. Younger brother Vinny made it a family double but he had to climb off the canvas after taking a big right hand in the first of a four-rounds lightweight bout against Crawley's Robin Deakin. Putting that behind him, Vinny took the points decision to notch up his third win as a pro.

FEBRUARY

Going 12 rounds for the first time in his 16-fight pro career, Amir Khan ticked all the boxes when retaining his Commonwealth lightweight championship against Australia's Gairy St Clair at the ExCel Arena in London. The Guyanese-born St Clair was a former IBF super-featherweight titleholder and had acquitted himself well against such fighters as Diego Corrales and Vivian Harris, but he didn't win a round against Bolton's former Olympic silver medallist. Khan impressed with his maturity, his control of the contest from first bell to last, his excellent condition and stamina, and an overall superb performance that keeps him on track for the world championship that surely awaits him in the not too distant future.

Michael Jennings is handsome, an excellent boxer, a solid puncher, and although the WBU welterweight champion he deserves better than that after a fine 32-1 pro record. That aside, he retained his title against the brave challenge of Ross Minter on the big London bill, referee Mickey Vann stopping it in the ninth round as the towel came in from Minter's corner. Crawley's Minter, watched from ringside by anxious father Alan, gave it his best shot but found the champion a class act. Ross was outboxed and outpunched, almost dropped in the first, decked at the end of round four, again in the ninth, and when he got up it was over. Coming back from nine months out following a knockout by American Freddy Curiel, Minter suffered a perforated eardrum, a scalp wound and a bloody nose. It was his third defeat in 21 fights.

Dagenham's former undefeated British, Commonwealth and European featherweight champion Nicky Cook had a walk in the park against ancient Bulgarian Kirkor Kirkorov, who was floored three times for a second-round stoppage.

Paisley postman Kevin McIntyre delivered a second victory over former champion Kevin Anderson as he retained the British welterweight title he had taken from the Buckhaven man in an upset five months previously. Second time around, at Glasgow's Kelvin Hall, Anderson was

better and southpaw McIntyre not as good, but he was good enough to take a unanimous decision from the three officials and keep the belt and take his pro log to 26-5.

With his noisy supporters threatening to take the roof off the Peterlee Leisure Centre, English light-welterweight champion Nigel Wright made a gallant effort to dent the undefeated 21-0 record of London-based Nigerian Ajose Olusegun and take his Commonwealth title. However, after 12 good rounds and three facial cuts, Nigel was still the English champion and Olusegun was looking for a world title shot. Nigel's self-confessed habit of switching off during a fight may well have cost him the victory. He is aware of the problem and commented afterwards, "I don't know why I didn't up it in the middle. I just switched off". It was the Wright thing, but it wasn't the right thing to do in a championship fight!

Eleven months after suffering his first pro defeat in a challenge for the vacant IBF super-bantamweight title, Hartlepool's Michael Hunter stepped out against tough Syrian Youssef Al Hamidi over six rounds in what would prove to be his last fight. The former British, Commonwealth and European super-bantamweight, and WBF champion, found the going tough before coming out with the decision and a cut by his left eye. Michael would later announce his retirement with a commendable 28-1-1 record. "It's just not there anymore", he said. A lad who may well replace Hunter in the affections of North East fans is Middlesbrough featherweight Paul Truscott, who took his record to 10-0 with a hard eight rounds against Frenchman Samir Kasmi.

Irish middleweights John Duddy and Andy Lee added to their win records at some cost, to Duddy anyway. With a Madison Square Garden date lined up for a shot at world champion Kelly Pavlik, John struggled to take a majority ten rounds decision from unknown Canadian Walid Smichet, coming out with five facial cuts, the worst one over the left eye that took 22 stitches. Promoter Bob Arum was not happy with what he saw from ringside and scrapped the Pavlik fight. Duddy took his unbeaten slate to 24-0 with a strong finish and the luck of the Irish. Andy Lee could well get the Pavlik title shot ahead of Duddy if his form against Argentinian Alejandro Gustavo Falliga was anything to go by. Fighting in Limerick where he grew up, the Detroit-based Lee did not put a glove wrong in stopping his man in round five after four knockdowns. "Andy is the best middleweight in the world just now", said a delighted trainer/manager Emanuel Steward, "title or no title".

At York Hall, British light-heavyweight champion Tony Oakey retained his title in no uncertain fashion when he knocked out former conqueror Peter Haymer in the ninth round. Haymer enjoyed height and reach advantages but he couldn't stop the forward march of the puncher from Portsmouth, who moved to 25-2-1 and was hoping for a European title shot. York Hall fans can't complain. Three weeks later they had another title fight with Commonwealth middleweight champion Darren Barker racking up an impressive win over Steven Bendall. The Coventry southpaw survived the shock of a first-round knockdown to reach the seventh but a clash of heads left him bleeding heavily from a cut over the right eye and his challenge was over. The undefeated champion moved to 17-0 and looked around for British titleholder Wayne Elcock…Sheffield's Lee Noble popped down to Crawley to beat local favourite Anthony Young in a ten rounds thriller for the British Masters middleweight title.

MARCH

All the world loves a puncher, especially a heavyweight puncher, which means that David Haye is headed for Millionaire's Row. He is a good bet to crack the jackpot in Las Vegas without going anywhere near the roulette tables. His ace in the hole is in his gloved fists and any of the top heavyweights will be pushing their luck getting in the ring with the South Londoner. He is a winner! The eagerly anticipated showdown with Enzo Maccarinelli, no mean banger himself with 21 inside wins in his 28-1 pro log, drew 20,000 fans to London's O2 Arena for a fight that would put the seal on Haye's future up at heavyweight, although on this night they were fighting for cruiserweight supremacy. Enzo's WBO belt was on the line along with David's WBC and WBA straps. The fight started at 2.25am to accommodate US television and ended at 2.04 of the second round to save the big Welshman from taking any more of David's Haye-makers, pun intended. In that second round, a Maccarinelli punch started blood from Haye's left eye and David knew it was time to close the show. Smashing blows drove Enzo back into a corner where he was pounded to the canvas. He got up but staggered back into the corner and when referee John Keane completed the mandatory eight count he rightly decreed that Maccarinelli's bid for the triple crown be aborted. Haye had unified the cruiserweight championships and was already looking to the heavyweight horizon where the sun was already rising.

The main event not withstanding, the fight of the night had to be the gruelling battle at super-featherweight between British champion Carl Johanneson and Commonwealth titleholder Kevin Mitchell. It was won by the Dagenham boy in the ninth round, the fight being stopped as Carl got up from a knockdown only to be swamped in a leather storm that brought the referee's intervention. The 23-year-old Mitchell came of age in this fight. After a brilliant start by Kevin, the man from Leeds was already bleeding from his nose and his right eye. Then Carl came on from the third, pounding the body. By round six he was in charge and Mitchell touched down from a sizzling right. It was ruled a slip but it was still a big round for Johanneson and it was looking as though the older, more experienced man would win the day. Well, young Mister Mitchell had other ideas. Coming out for round nine he banged in the left jab and Carl's mouth poured blood. Now he was looking shop worn and a terrific left hook brought him down on the canvas. He got to his feet but was met by a barrage of hooks, rights, and uppercuts. Although trying to cover up too many got through and the third man had seen enough. At 2.29 of the ninth round, Kevin Mitchell was a dual champion, still undefeated after 26 professional fights. Yes, the boy can fight.

Leicester bin-man Rendall Munroe deals with rubbish through the day and puts out the quality stuff at night, inside the boxing ring. The English super-bantamweight champion was reaching for the stars in Nottingham against unbeaten Spaniard Kiko Martinez, the European titleholder who had blitzed Bernard Dunne inside 86 seconds. Munroe was made of sturdier stock and after 12 rounds came out with the majority decision and the European title. On the same bill at the Harvey Hadden Complex, local favourite Jason Booth made the first defence of his Commonwealth bantamweight title with a unanimous decision over Ghanian Lante Addy, taking his record to 29-5.

Dropping down in weight rather than the conventional stepping up, former British welterweight champion David Barnes outboxed and outpunched Ted Bami to take the vacant British light-welterweight title on a unanimous decision in Manchester. "This shows I'm not finished", said a jubilant Barnes. "I want to be a world champion".

As Britain's first ever super-flyweight champion, Chris Edwards made the first ever defence of this title and blew it, losing a unanimous decision to young (22) Andy Bell at Barnsley. The Doncaster lad used height and reach advantages plus a third-round knockdown to take the title but Edwards fought him all the way in a gruelling match. This could go on again.

There was a rare old battle in Glasgow when local hard man Willie Limond beat Coatbridge warrior Martin Watson over 12 pulsating rounds to win the IBO Inter-Continental lightweight title. This was an X-certificate fight that tested both men as the action swung one way then the other before Limond finished like a train over the last three rounds to take the title.

Plans for Irish middleweights John Duddy and/or Andy Lee getting a crack at world champ Kelly Pavlik were shelved after first Duddy struggled to win his last fight, coming out with his face a bloody mask, and then Lee suffered his first pro defeat when the referee stopped his fight with Brian Vera at Uncasville, Connecticut, in round seven. Lee was ahead on the cards but a bad cut on his right eyelid put him out of the fight and in hospital for a 17-stitch repair job. Luck of the Irish?

A couple of weeks after Enzo Maccarinelli was blown away by David Haye, Enzo Calzaghe's gym dropped another of its world titles when Gavin Rees lost his WBA light-welterweight championship to Andreas Kotelnik, the fight being stopped with just 26 seconds left of the final round. The German-based Ukrainian was the better all-round fighter and Gavin was trailing going into the last three minutes. Kotelnik set up a big attack and Gavin Rees had his first pro defeat after going 27-0. The little Welshman had been looking for Amir Khan but now it was Kotelnik calling out Ricky Hatton…After losing to Howard Daley, Hull's 38-year-old Tony Booth promised to quit after his next fight. With stats of 50-105-9, it was probably a good idea.

APRIL

Joe Calzaghe's big gamble in Las Vegas paid off handsomely at the Thomas and Mack Centre where the 36-year-old Welshman hit the jackpot, taking a split decision over Bernard Hopkins to retain his undefeated record of 45 victories and book his place in boxing's Hall of Fame as

Matthew Marsh (right) took the fight to Esham Pickering to become the eighth British super-bantam champion at the end of 12 rounds last June   Philip Sharkey

possibly Britain's greatest ever fighter. In fact, make that one of the world's greatest ever fighters! This meeting of two top men was unfortunately not a great fight. Calzaghe himself said afterwards that he was not happy with his performance, even though it was a winning one. He did win it, albeit on a split decision, by outpunching Hopkins all through the 12 rounds. And he had to get off the floor to do it, a knockdown in the very first round stunning the thousands of British fans in the arena more than it did Joe, who quickly jumped to his feet and never looked back. The Philadelphia hard man attempted to gain points with his acting when his fists could not do it, claiming injury in rounds ten and 11 before the referee told him to get on with the job. The job title was light-heavyweight champion of the world with the prestigious Ring Magazine belt on the line and Calzaghe became the first man to hold both this and the Ring's super-middleweight belt. If Joe was a good winner then Hopkins was a bad loser, claiming he was robbed and refusing to give his conqueror any credit. "I don't think Calzaghe won", he told the press. "He got the victory. That's all". At the end of the day, Bernard, that is all that counts in your business. Calzaghe's super-middleweight stablemate Nathan Cleverly chalked up a good win when receiving a unanimous decision over North Carolina's Antonio Baker over eight rounds on the undercard, taking his unbeaten record to 12-0. It was an impressive debut, the judges giving Nathan every round.

Audley Harrison is pushing 37 and it is beginning to look as though the Olympic gold medal he won in 2000 may be the only worthwhile thing on his CV when he finally walks away from boxing. He did win the meaningless WBF heavyweight title a few years back but the odds are lengthening against him winning any serious hardware. On the Calzaghe card Harrison stopped Jason Barnett in five rounds, his first outing since Michael Sprott handed him a devastating knockout in November 2007. The clock is ticking...

Seven days before the Vegas show, a possible big fight for Joe Calzaghe went out the window as Clinton Woods took his IBF light-heavyweight title to Tampa and went home empty-handed after Florida southpaw Antonio Tarver outboxed and outfought the Sheffield man over 12 one-sided rounds. Calzaghe v Woods would have packed Cardiff's Millennium Stadium. That's the fight business for you! In the same ring, British heavyweight champion Danny Williams dumped Marcus McGhee in the first round, but the man from Little Rock got up and finished the course. Danny disappointed in taking the decision over a fighter he should have blown away inside a couple of rounds.

The second coming of Ryan Rhodes took place at York Hall in Bethnal Green when the Sheffield light-middleweight regained the British championship he first won 11 years previously, dropping Gary Woolcombe in the sixth round before lowering the boom in round nine with a big right hand. At 31, with career stats of 39-4, Ryan looks good for a few more years at the top.

On another night at York Hall, British lightweight champion Jonathan Thaxton found the gap between domestic level and a European championship too big to bridge, and although he was retired by his corner after five rounds with a badly cut right eye, the Norwich man had been running second to the titleholder Yuri Romanov throughout.

Commonwealth lightweight champion Amir Khan took his unbeaten run to 17 when he stopped Dane Martin Kristjansen in the seventh round at the Bolton Arena. The local idol risked disqualification when he landed punches after Kristjansen had dropped to a knee, but drew only a warning from referee Mickey Vann before felling his man twice more for the finish. The contest was for the vacant WBO Inter-Continental title and an eliminator for the main belt. Amir won but ringside opinion said he 'Khan' do better. No doubt he will!

Liverpool's Derry Matthews had won the WBU featherweight title and was still undefeated in 20 fights when he agreed to share the ring with a Mongolian warrior, Choi Tseveenpurev. It was a decision he would regret as Choi stormed to a fifth-round knockout after decking Derry four times.

Another WBU champion, welterweight Michael Jennings, was brilliant in a non-title bout against Georgie Ungiadze who was stopped in round seven. The Georgian was Michael's 33rd victim, against one defeat. A class act!

Barry Hearn's Prizefighter promotion at York Hall saw eight heavyweights box each other for a top prize of £25,000 and a cup. The tournament, a runaway success, was won by Belfast big man Martin Rogan, who powered his way to victories over Alex Ibbs, David Ferguson and David Dolan in the final, all contests over three rounds. Dolan was favourite going into the competition and beat Darren Morgan and Paul Butlin before giving Rogan a helluva fight and taking his first pro defeat in ten contests. Disappointed, David had to be content with second prize of £10,000. The other beaten warriors were Billy Bessey and Colin Kenna.

Dublin's former European super-bantamweight champion Bernard Dunne got back on the winning trail following his stunning one-round kayo by Kiko Martinez, beating Felix Machado over ten rounds at Mayo and taking his pro log to 25-1.

MAY

Last month it was the Calzaghe-Woods non-fight, this month it was the fight that never was, Junior Witter v Ricky Hatton. To keep that one alive, Witter had to retain his WBC light-welterweight title against the little-known American Timothy Bradley in the Nottingham ring. The man from California was undefeated in 21 fights with 11 inside wins, but you could still get 6 to 1 if you fancied a bet. A good bet as it turned out. Witter was dumped on the canvas in round six and blew his championship on a split decision, with many thinking Bradley an easier winner. The 34-year-old switch-hitting Yorkshireman had everything going for him with the world looking on via television, here and in the States. Hatton had suffered his first defeat, being knocked out by Floyd Mayweather, maybe now Junior could get the

fight he wanted more than any other. But when he walked out of the Trent FM Arena that night, Junior Witter was an ex-champ and nobody was talking Witter-Hatton.

A fortnight later, everybody was talking Ricky Hatton. With a hometown crowd estimated at 57,000 packed into Manchester City's ground, local hero Hatton lit up the night sky as he hammered out a 12-rounds decision over Mexican-American Juan Lazcano to retain his IBO light-welterweight title and Ring Magazine belt, keeping his name in the frame for more big fights down the line. At 29, with his record now 44-1, Ricky had once again whipped himself into fantastic shape and was a unanimous winner, even if he had to survive a couple of rocky moments in rounds eight and ten. What was equally fantastic about this fight was the fact that the City of Manchester Stadium was sold out within a day of tickets going on sale, something that amazed Ricky's American co-promoter, 'Golden Boy' Oscar De La Hoya. "Nobody else can do what Ricky Hatton did tonight, fill up a stadium like that", he told reporters. Ricky Hatton lives on!

Leicester bin-man Rendall Munroe delivered once again at the Harvey Haddon Sports complex in Nottingham where he retained his European super-bantamweight title against Salem Bouaita, forcing the French veteran to retire after seven rounds. This fellow just gets better and better, taking his pro log to 15-1, but he modestly shunned talk of a possible world title shot, saying, "I know I'm not quite ready for that yet". Well, maybe one day, son.

On the same bill, British bantamweight champion Ian Napa retained his title for the third time as he turned back the challenge of Belfast's Colin Moffett and took the Lonsdale Belt home for keeps. Moffett was unable to make full use of his height and reach advantages as the little champion forced his way inside to come out with the unanimous decision and call out the European champion.

Just turned 22, Paul Truscott gave himself a belated birthday present at the Eston Sports Academy where he beat Osumano Akaba for the vacant Commonwealth featherweight title, giving Middlesbrough its first champion since Cornelius Carr won the British super-middleweight title in 1994. The better boxer, Paul fought when he had to and punched his way to the unanimous decision, still unbeaten at 11-0.

European light-welterweight champion Colin Lynes left his title in the Ruffini Sports Palace in Turin when former champion Gianluca Branco won a close split decision to take the belt. The Hornchurch man started like a train and floored the Italian in the second round and many figured he did enough to win. But a close decision in Italy? Forget it! On the same bill, Belfast featherweight Martin Lindsay beat fellow Brit Marc Callaghan by unanimous decision, while Midlands heavyweight Paul Butlin took a fight too far when stepping in with former European champion Paolo Vidoz. Having taken the fight at a day's notice, Butlin was down and out in the second round.

It is doubtful whether British heavyweight champion Danny Williams will even go back to Spain for a holiday after what happened to him in his fight with Konstantin Airich in Bilbao. The unbeaten German had won nine of his ten fights, eight inside the distance, and he hurt Danny several times with his big punches before the Brixton 34-year-old made his own blows tell. But there was a problem with the referee, Alfredo Garcia Perez, who gave an amateurish performance, which was not surprising really as he was an amateur! A low blow in the second cost Williams two points and he was allowed to fight with one of his hand bandages unravelling before the referee himself wrapped it around Danny's glove before it became loose again. Knocked back to the ropes in the third and counted over, Danny finally tugged his loose bandage away himself before slipping to the canvas after hitting Airich and being counted over again. Following these episodes, Williams started taking charge in the fifth and dropped his man to the canvas. He did it again in round six and Airich was in real trouble when the bell rang. At 1.21 of the round! Rung by the promoter! When Williams again forced the action in round seven, the towel came in from the other corner and Danny's nightmare fight was over.

I do not think Nottingham's Carl Froch knew just who he would be fighting when he entered the ring on the Witter-Bradley bill after Dennis Inkin withdrew - twice; Alejandro Berrio would not sign the contract; Rubin Williams was denied permission to leave America. The guy Carl eventually took out his frustrations on was undefeated Pole Albert Rybacki and to quote the immortal Joe Jacobs, Albert "shoulda stood in bed". Froch hit him with everything but the stool and Rybacki was running a poor second when the referee ended it in round four.

JUNE

The old glove game received an injection of new blood this month as three new British champions were crowned - Paul Appleby, Kell Brook, and Matthew Marsh. The all-Scottish clash for the British featherweight title in Glasgow between champion John Simpson and his undefeated challenger Paul Appleby was a cracker from the opening bell and the narrow decision making the baby-faced Appleby the new champion could have gone the other way for some observers. However, the 20-year-old South Queensferry boy, taking part in only his 12th fight against a seasoned champion, convinced the men that matter, the three judges, that he was worthy of the unanimous decision and the Lonsdale Belt that went with it. This kid will just get better.

So will 22-year old Kell Brook who captured the vacant British welterweight championship with a seventh-round stoppage of Welshman Barrie Jones at York Hall. The Sheffield boy took his unbeaten tally to 17-0 as he broke down the southpaw's resistance with heavy, accurate shots and Jones was a well-beaten man at the finish.

A couple of weeks later York Hall was again the scene of a changing of the guard, as West Ham's Matthew Marsh hammered the British super-bantamweight title loose from the grasp of 40-fight veteran Esham Pickering, taking a unanimous decision and his pro log to 10-1. The Newark man had seen better days and at 32 was left to consider his future in the game.

Sunderland's 24-year old lightweight Paul 'The

Although Darren McDermott (left) is on the attack in this shot, Wayne Elcock held on to his British middleweight title when his opponent was stopped in the second round with a bad cut following a clash of heads
Philip Sharkey

Mackem' Holborn scored a personal goal at the city's Stadium of Light when he took a torrid ten rounder from Sheffield's Dwayne Hill to pick up the vacant International Masters title. The local southpaw survived two cuts over his left eye to take his record to 8-1-1 and will be the better for this fight.

For his 31st birthday, Michael Gomez went to the National Indoor Arena in Birmingham and ten thousand people turned up to help him celebrate. Unfortunately for him, there was one guy there determined to spoil the party. Amir Khan brought his Commonwealth lightweight championship belt along and he was fiercely determined to take it home to Bolton with him afterwards. The 21-one year old champion bounced the Manchester man on his backside in the opening round to set the crowd roaring and they never stopped. They roared louder in a sensational second round when Gomez brought Khan to a knee with a clubbing left to the head. Amir was straight up and back in the fight to punish Michael and make him pay dearly. The fourth round was a nightmare for Gomez, who by this time was cut over the left eye and reeling from Khan's blazing fists, before the end came in the fifth as another leather storm swept Gomez off his feet and it was stopped a few punches later. "He's classy, got heart, and his hand speed is tremendous", said Gomez afterwards. "That's what beat me. No excuses, the kid's good". But not yet good enough to go for a world title, according to Frank Warren, Amir's promoter. "He needs the right schooling and a couple more fights under his belt". But not too many like this one, Frank could have added.

In a supporting fight, Commonwealth light-middleweight champion Bradley Pryce had no trouble retaining his title with a sixth-round stoppage over Marcus Portman after the West Bromwich man had taken a count, while Coventry southpaw Steven Bendall upset the odds when he outpointed Liverpool's Paul Smith to take the English middle-weight title and keep his career alive at 29-4.

It was Friday the 13th and somebody was going to be unlucky when the dust settled in the British and Commonwealth light-heavyweight championship fight down in Portsmouth. Commonwealth titleholder Dean Francis tossed his strap into the pot with Tony Oakey's British belt, winner taking all. First round and Francis was off to a flyer, his left hand stunning the local hero and cutting his left eye. Then Oakey clicked into gear and he was on top, rocking Francis and cutting his left eye, winning the sessions. It was round six before the Basingstoke man got behind his punches again and he won the seventh. Round nine saw the end, a terrific left hook spreading Oakey on the canvas and although he beat the count he could not beat Francis, the fight being stopped at 2.47 of the round.

When Gary Lockett was matched with world middleweight champion Kelly Pavlik in Atlantic City, my first thought was that it was a bridge too far. And so it proved, with the world middleweight champion being too big, too strong, and too good for game Gary, who was floored three times and out of there inside three rounds. At 26, Kelly has 30 inside wins in an undefeated run of 34 fights and is good.

Wayne Elcock was still the British middleweight champion after 50 seconds of round two when the referee intervened with challenger Darren McDermott horribly cut following a clash of heads. This one must go on again when McDermott mends… It took Birmingham featherweight Anthony Hanna 100 fights to become an overnight success as the veteran took the vacant British Masters title with a last-minute stoppage over Scottish champion Furhan Rafiq in Glasgow… In Wigan, Former ABA champion Craig Lyon made a winning debut with a decision over veteran Delroy Spencer. The St Helen's bantamweight is the son of amateur legend John Lyon and loser Spencer tipped him to go right to the top! Watch this space.

Facts and Figures, 2007-2008

There were 665 (650 in 2006-2007) British-based boxers who were active between 1 July 2007 and 30 June 2008, spread over 203 (205 in 2006-2007) promotions held in Britain, not including the Republic of Ireland, during the same period. Those who were either already holding licenses or had been re-licensed amounted to 505, while there were 142 (168 in 2006-2007) new professionals, plus ten non-nationals who began their careers elsewhere, and eight women.

Unbeaten During Season (Minimum Qualification: 6 Contests)
8: Ricky Burns. 7: Kevin Concepcion, Martin Murray, Muhsen Nasser (1 draw). 6: Jack Arnfield, Billy Boyle, Amir Khan, Charles Paul King, Paul McCloskey.

Longest Unbeaten Sequence (Minimum Qualification: 10 Contests)
45: Joe Calzaghe. 27: Roman Greenberg, Kevin Mitchell. 24: John Murray, Albert Sosnowski. 23: Carl Froch, Ajose Olusegun. 22: Nadeem Siddique. 19: Lee McAllister. 18: Amir Khan, Muhsen Nasser (1 draw). 17: Darren Barker, Kell Brook, John Fewkes. 16: Paul McCloskey. 14: Steve McGuire (1 draw). 13: Martin Gethin (1 draw), Alex Matvienko (2 draws), Danny Reynolds (1 draw). 12: Paul Appleby, Nathan Cleverly, Kevin Concepcion, Gareth Couch, Dean Harrison, Patrick Hyland, Martin Lindsay, Andrew Murray, Kreshnik Qato. 11: Akaash Bhatia, Stuart Brookes, Paul Burns (3 draws), Chris Burton, Danny Butler, David Haye, Gary McArthur, Mark Moran (1 draw), JJ Ojuederie (1 draw), Nicki Smedley, Paul Truscott. 10: Adnan Amar, Alex Arthur, Rob Hunt, Charles Paul King, Ricky Owen, Martin Rogan, Brian Rose (1 draw).

Most Wins During Season (Minimum Qualification: 6 Contests)
8: Ricky Burns. 7: Kevin Concepcion, Martin Murray. 6: Jack Arnfield, Billy Boyle, Jamie Cox, David Dolan, John Donnelly, Amir Khan, Charles Paul King, Paul McCloskey, Muhsen Nasser.

Most Contests During Season (Minimum Qualification: 10 Contests)
22: Billy Smith. 20: Peter Dunn. 19: Paul Royston. 17: Delroy Spencer. 16: Kristian Laight. 15: Steve Cooper. 14: Duncan Cottier, Johnny Greaves, Shaun Walton. 13: Carl Allen. 14: Ernie Smith. 12: Jamie Ambler, Michael Banbula, Baz Carey, Leonard Lothian. 11: Karl Taylor, Lance Verallo. 10: James Tucker.

Most Contests During Career (Minimum Qualification: 50 Contests)

291: Pete Buckley. 164: Tony Booth. 148: Ernie Smith. 133: Karl Taylor. 125: Paul Bonson. 113: Peter Dunn. 100: Anthony Hanna. 95: Daniel Thorpe. 94: Carl Allen. 85: David Kirk. 84: Billy Smith. 83: Jason Nesbitt. 81: Delroy Spencer. 63: Chris Woollas. 60: Kristian Laight, Mark Phillips. 59: David Kehoe. 58: Simeon Cover. 57: Hastings Rasani. 51: Baz Carey. 50: Steve Gethin, Matt Scriven.

Stop Press: Results for July/August 2008 (British-Based Boxers' Results Only)

Everton Park Sports Centre, Liverpool – 4 July (Promoter: Matchroom)

David Barnes w pts 12 Barry Morrison (British L.Welterweight Title Defence), Ted Bami w rsc 7 Stuart Elwell, David Dolan w co 4 Elvecio Sobral, John Donnelly w pts 6 Faycal Messaoudene, Scott Quigg w rsc 2 Angelo Villano, Steve Williams w pts 4 Karl Taylor, Rhys Roberts w pts 4 Delroy Spencer, Joe Smyth w pts 4 Paul Bonson.

Ankara, Turkey 4 July

Herbie Hide w pts 12 Nuri Seferi (WBC International Cruiserweight Title Defence), Ondrejs Pala w pts 6 Henry Akinwande.

Dublin, Ireland – 5 July

Jamie Moore w rtd 3 Ciaran Healy (All-Ireland L.Middleweight Title Challenge), Paul Hyland w pts 10 Marc Callaghan (Vacant All-Ireland S.Bantamweight Title), Patrick Hyland w pts 8 Geoffrey Munika,

Leon, Spain – 5 July

Gennady Martirosyan w pts 8 Steve Conway.

Robin Park Centre, Wigan – 11 July (Promoter: Hennessy)

John Murray w rsc 5 Lee Meager (Vacant British Lightweight Title), Martin Gethin w rsc 7 Nadeem Siddique, Brian Magee w rsc 4 Simeon Cover, Steve O'Meara w pts 4 Billy Smith, Steve Saville w rsc 4 Mark Bett, Darren Askew w pts 4 Graham Fearn, Khurram Hussain w pts 4 Paddy Pollock, Ali Shah w pts 4 Pete Buckley.

Dublin, Ireland – 12 July

Jim Rock w co 7 Jonjo Finnegan (Vacant All-Ireland L.Heavyweight Title), Andrew Murray w pts 10 Peter McDonagh (Vacant All-Ireland Lightweight Title), Darren Corbett w pts 6 Remigijus Ziausys, Eugene Heagney w pts 4 Kemal Plavci.

Leisure Centre, Newport – 12 July (J. Sanigar)

Jamie Arthur w co 2 Dai Davies (Welsh S.Featherweight Title Challenge), Paul Samuels w rsc 4 Mark Nilsen, Matthew Edmonds w pts 6 Ayittey Mettle, Rob Turley w pts 6 Geoffrey Munika, Lee Selby w pts 6 Sid Razak, Justyn Hugh w pts 6 Pawel Trebinski.

Goresbrook Leisure Centre, Dagenham – 18 July (Promoter: Maloney)

Danny Williams w pts 12 John McDermott (British Heavyweight Title Defence), Ajose Olusegun w pts 6 Mihaita Mutu, Akaash Bhatia w rsc 3 John Vanemmenis, Scott Belshaw w pts 6 Daniel Peret, Gary Sykes w pts 6 Harry Ramogoadi, Chas Symonds w rsc 3 Alexander Spitjo, Tony Bellew w pts 4 Ayittey Powers, Sean Hughes w pts 4 Delroy Spencer, Scott Woolford w pts 4 Jimmy Beech, Gavin Tait w pts 4 Billy Smith.

Chekhov, Russia – 19 July

Dimitri Pirog w pts 10 Geard Ajetovic

University Arena, Limerick, Ireland – 19 July

Paul McCloskey w pts 10 Nigel Wright, Jason McKay w rsc 3 Marcin Piatkowski, Stephen Haughian w pts 8 Giuseppe Langella, John O'Donnell w rsc 5 Sorget Volodin.

Olympia, Liverpool – 19 July (Promoter: Greaves)

Derry Matthews w pts 8 John Gicheru, Mike Stafford w pts 4 Paul Bonson, John Watson w rtd 4 Ali Wyatt, Joe McNally w pts 6 James Tucker, Stephen Burke w pts 4 Baz Carey, Rhys Roberts w pts 4 Sid Razak, Scott Quigg w rsc 1 Peter Allen, Paul Edwards w pts 4 Robert Palmer, Amir Unsworth w pts 4 Senol Dervis, Joey Ainscough w pts 4 Robert Burton.

Civic Hall, Wolverhampton – 24 July (Promoter: Rowson)

Young Muttley w pts 6 Sergejs Savrinovics, Martin Gordon drew 4 Chris Thompson, Neil Perkins w pts 4 Howard Daley, James Mulhearn w pts 4 David Keogan, Joe Skeldon w rsc 6 Jason Smith, Scott Evans w pts 4 Pete Buckley, Jamie Ball w pts 4 Peter Dunn, Kevin McCauley w pts 4 Steve Cooper.

Rainton Meadows Arena – 25 July (Promoter: Jeffries)

Michael Banbula w pts 6 John Robinson, Chris Mullen w rtd 2 Matt Seawright, Bob Ajisafe w pts 4 Jamie Norkett, Mark Dawes w pts 6 Kark Taylor.

Rochester, New York, USA – 31 July

DeMarcus Corley w pts 8 Ashley Theophane.

The Colosseum, Watford – 1 August (Promoter: Feld)

Jamie Ambler w disq 1 Ojay Abrahams, Joey Vegas w rsc 7 JJ Ojuederie, Daley Ojuederie w rsc 4 Anthony Young, Matt Legg w rsc 2 Howard Daley, Ashley Sexton w pts 4 David Keogan, Joe Smythe w rsc 4 Lee Kellett, Caine Brodie w pts 4 Jamie Norkett, Saud Hafiz w rsc 3 Amir Nadi.

Edmonton, Alberta, Canada – 15 August

Darren Barker w pts 10 Larry Sharpe.

Altlanta, Georgia, USA – 29 August

Cedric Boswell w rsc 2 Roman Greenberg

Berlin, Germany – 30 August

Francesco Pianeta w rsc 8 Scott Gammer

Having launched 'The Champ in the Corner: The Ray Arcel story' last year, John Jarrett is currently working on a biography of Mickey Walker, 'The Toy Bulldog', and his equally colourful manager Doc Kearns. Sure to be another good read, it is set against a backdrop of the roaring '20s.

Diary of British Boxing Tournaments, 2007-2008

Tournaments are listed by date, town, venue and names promoter, as licensed by the BBBoC, and cover the period 1 July 2007 to 30 June 2008.

Code: SC = Sporting Club

Date	Town	Venue	Promoters
01.07.07	Colchester	Hippodrome Nightclub	Burns
06.07.07	Wigan	Robin Park Centre	Maloney
13.07.07	Barnsley	The Metrodome	Maloney
13.07.07	Birmingham	Holiday Inn	Purchase
14.07.07	Greenwich	O2 Arena	Warren
15.07.07	Hartlepool	Mayfair Suite	Garside
20.07.07	Wolverhampton	Civic Hall	Hearn
21.07.07	Cardiff	International Arena	Warren
22.07.07	Mansfield	Debdale Lane Sports Ground	Scriven
27.07.07	Houghton le Spring	Rainton Meadows Arena	Dunn
11.08.07	Liverpool	Olympia	Dixon
07.08.07	Doncaster	Dome Leisure Centre	Hennessy
07.09.07	Mayfair	Grosvenor House Hotel	Warren
08.09.07	Sutton in Ashfield	Leisure Centre	Calow
10.09.07	Glasgow	Radisson Hotel	Gilmour
14.09.07	Kirkcaldy	Ice Rink	Hearn
15.09.07	Birmingham	International Convention Centre	Rowson
15.09.07	Paisley	Linwood Leisure Centre	Braveheart
15.09.07	Bristol	Marriott Hotel	M & J Promotions
16.09.07	Southampton	Guildhall	Bishop
16.09.07	Sheffield	Don Valley Stadium	Rhodes
16.09.07	Derby	Heritage Hotel	Mitchell
21.09.07	Bethnal Green	York Hall	Maloney
21.09.07	Peterborough	East of England Showground	Sanders
21.09.07	Burton	Meadowside Leisure Centre	Rowson
22.09.07	Coventry	Leofric Hotel	Coventry SC
22.09.07	Wigan	Robin Park Centre	Wood
23.09.07	Longford	Thistle Hotel	Carman
23.09.07	Hartlepool	Mayfair Suite	Garside
25.09.07	Hull	City Hall	Hull & District SC
28.09.07	Birmingham	Holiday Inn Hotel	Purchase
28.09.07	Coventry	Skydome	Cowdell
28.09.07	Preston	Guildhall	Dixon
29.09.07	Sheffield	Hallam FM Arena	Hobson (Fight Academy)
04.10.07	Piccadilly	Café Royal	Helliet
05.10.07	Bethnal Green	York Hall	Hennessy
05.10.07	Sunderland	Tavistock Roker Hotel	Conroy
05.10.07	Newport	Leisure Centre	J & C Sanigar
06.10.07	Leicester	Aylestone Leisure Centre	Carpenter
06.10.07	Nottingham	Trent FM Arena	Warren
06.10.07	Aberdeen	Beach Ballroom	Ingle
07.10.07	Shaw	Tara Leisure Centre	Doughty
08.10.07	Birmingham	Burlington Hotel	Cowdell
08.10.07	Glasgow	Radisson Hotel	Gilmour
09.10.07	Tower Hamlets	Guoman Tower Hotel	Fearon
12.10.07	Leeds	Royal Armouries Museum	Wood
12.10.07	Peterlee	Leisure Centre	Hearn
13.10.07	Bethnal Green	York Hall	Warren
13.10.07	Newark	Showgrounds	Greaves
13.10.07	Belfast	Park Avenue Hotel	Wilton
13.10.07	Barnsley	Metrodome	Coldwell

19.10.07	Doncaster	Dome Leisure Centre	Maloney
19.10.07	Motherwell	Dalziel Park Hotel	Gilmour
19.10.07	Mayfair	Millennium Hotel	Feld
21.10.07	Swansea	Brangwyn Hall	Hodges
25.10.07	Wolverhampton	Civic Hall	Rowson
26.10.07	Wigan	Robin Park Centre	Maloney
26.10.06	Glasgow	SeeWoo Chinese Restaurant	Morrison
26.10.07	Birmingham	Burlington Hotel	Cowdell
31.10.07	Queensway	Royal Lancaster Hotel	Evans/Waterman
02.11.07	Irvine	Magnum Centre	Hearn
03.11.07	Derby	East Midlands Hilton Hotel	Mitchell
03.11.07	Cardiff	Millennium Stadium	Warren
05.11.07	Glasgow	Radisson Hotel	Gilmour
09.11.07	Nottingham	Trent FM Arena	Hennessy
09.11.07	Plymouth	Guildhall	J & C Sanigar
10.11.07	Portsmouth	Mountbatten Centre	Bishop
10.11.07	Stalybridge	Copley Sports Centre	Hobson (DVSA Promotions)
14.11.07	Bethnal Green	York Hall	Hennessy
15.11.07	Leeds	Elland Road Conference & Exhibition Centre	Bateson
17.11.07	Stoke	King's Hall	Carney
17.11.07	Glasgow	Bellahouston Leisure Centre	Braveheart
18.11.07	Birmingham	Rojac Building	Pegg
18.11.07	Tooting	Leisure Centre	Baker
23.11.07	Rotherham	Hellaby Hall Hotel	Hobson (Fight Academy)
23.11.07	Sheffield	Grosvenor Hotel	Rhodes
23.11.07	Houghton le Spring	Rainton Meadows Arena	Dunn
24.11.07	Clydebank	Playdome	C. Gilmour
25.11.07	Colchester	Hippdrome Nightclub	Burns
25.11.07	Colne	Municipal Hall	Wood
28.11.07	Walsall	Bank's Stadium	Rowson/Johnson
28.11.07	Piccadilly	Café Royal	Helliet
29.11.07	Bradford	Hilton Hotel	Garber
30.11.07	Newham	Leisure Centre	Maloney
30.11.07	Hull	KC Sports Arena	Hull & District SC
01.12.07	Liverpool	Olympia	Dixon
01.12.07	Bethnal Green	York Hall	Feld
01.12.07	Coventry	Leofric Hotel	Coventry SC
01.12.07	Nottingham	Victoria Leisure Centre	Scriven
01.12.07	Telford	Oakengates Theatre	Rowson
01.12.07	Chigwell	Prince Regent Hotel	Burns
02.12.07	Oldham	Sports Centre	Jones
02.12.07	Bristol	Marriott Hotel	M & J Promotions
03.12.07	Manchester	Piccadilly Hotel	Dixon
05.12.07	Sheffield	Don Valley Stadium	Coldwell
06.12.07	Sunderland	Tavistock Roker Hotel	Conroy
08.12.07	Bolton	The Arena	Warren
08.12.07	Wigan	Robin Park Centre	Maloney
08.12.07	Belfast	King's Hall	Peters
09.12.07	Glasgow	Thistle Hotel	Morrison
10.12.07	Cleethorpes	Beachcomber Club	Frater
10.12.07	Leicester	Ramada Jarvis Hotel	Griffin
10.12.07	Peterborough	Holiday Inn Hotel	Pauly
10.12.07	Birmingham	Holiday Inn Hotel	Cowdell
15.12.07	Edinburgh	Meadowbank Sports Centre	Warren
23.12.07	Bolton	De Vere White's Hotel	Wood
12.01.08	Bethnal Green	York Hall	Warren
18.01.08	Burton	Meadowside Leisure Centre	Hennessy
21.01.08	Glasgow	Radisson Hotel	Gilmour
25.01.08	Dagenham	Goresbrook Leisure Centre	Hearn

25.01.08	Birmingham	Holiday Inn Hotel	Pegg
31.01.08	Piccadilly	Café Royal	Helliet
01.02.08	Bethnal Green	York Hall	Maloney
02.02.08	Canning Town	ExCel Arena	Warren
03.02.08	Bristol	Marriott Hotel	M & J Promotions
08.02.08	Peterlee	Leisure Centre	Hearn
15.02.08	Sunderland	Tavistock Roker Hotel	Conroy
15.02.08	Sheffield	Don Valley Stadium	Rhodes
16.02.08	Blackpool	Tower Circus	Wood
16.02.08	Leicester	Aylestone Leisure Centre	Carpenter
18.02.08	Glasgow	Radisson Hotel	Gilmour
21.02.08	Leeds	Elland Road Conference & Exhibition Centre	Bateson
22.02.08	Bethnal Green	York Hall	Hennessy
22.02.08	Motherwell	Dalziel Park Hotel	Rea
23.02.08	Liverpool	Olympia	Dixon
23.02.08	Newark	Grove Leisure Centre	Greaves
23.02.08	Crawley	K2 Leisure Centre	Feld
25.02.08	Birmingham	Burlington Hotel	Cowdell
28.02.08	Wolverhampton	Civic Hall	Rowson/Johnson
29.02.08	Glasgow	Kelvin Hall	Hearn
29.02.08	Plymouth	Guildhall	J & C Sanigar
01.03.08	Stoke	Kings Hall	Carney
01.03.08	Coventry	Leofric Hotel	Coventry SC
02.03.08	Portsmouth	Mountbatten Centre	Bishop
07.03.08	Nottingham	Harvey Hadden Leisure Centre	Maloney
08.03.08	Greenwich	O2 Arena	Warren
14.03.08	Manchester	George Carnall Leisure Centre	Hearn
14.03.08	Glasgow	Thistle Hotel	Morrison
14.03.08	Manchester	Old Trafford Suite	Jones
16.03.08	Sheffield	Sheffield United's Forsyth Academy	Coldwell
16.03.08	Liverpool	Everton Park Sports Centre	Wood
17.03.08	Glasgow	Radisson Hotel	Gilmour
20.03.08	South Shields	Temple Park Sports Centre	Conroy
22.03.08	Sheffield	Don Valley Stadium	Hobson (Fight Academy)
22.03.08	Cardiff	International Arena	Warren
28.03.08	Barnsley	Metrodome	Maloney
28.03.08	Piccadilly	Café Royal	Evans/Waterman
29.03.08	Aberdeen	Beach Ballroom	Ingle
29.03.08	Glasgow	Scottish Exhibition Centre	Braveheart
30.03.08	Colne	Municipal Hall	Wood
30.03.08	Port Talbot	Afan Lido	Hodges
04.04.08	Bethnal Green	York Hall	Hennessy
05.04.08	Bolton	Arena	Warren
05.04.08	Newport	Leisure Centre	C & J Sanigar
10.04.08	Piccadilly	Café Royal	Helliet
11.04.08	Bethnal Green	York Hall	Hearn
13.04.08	Edgbaston	Tower Ballroom	Pegg
18.04.08	Bethnal Green	York Hall	Maloney
18.04.08	Houghton le Spring	Rainton Meadows Arena	Jeffries
20.04.08	Shaw	Tara Leisure Centre	Doughty
24.04.08	Piccadilly	Café Royal	Helliet
26.04.08	Wigan	Robin Park Centre	Wood
26.04.08	Darlington	Northgate ASE Club	Johnson
28.04.08	Glasgow	Radisson Hotel	Gilmour
30.04.08	Wolverhampton	Civic Hall	Rowson/Johnson
01.05.08	Piccadilly	Café Royal	Evans/Waterman
02.05.08	Bristol	Marriott Hotel	M & J Promotions
02.05.08	Nottingham	Harvey Hadden Leisure Centre	Maloney
09.05.08	Middlesbrough	Eston Sports Academy	Hearn

10.05.08	Notingham	Trent FM Arena	Hennessy
12.05.08	Birmingham	Burlington Hotel	Cowdell
15.05.08	Sunderland	Tavistock Roker Hotel	Conroy
16.05.08	Motherwell	Concert Hall	C. Gilmour
16.05.08	Burton	Meadowside Leisure Centre	Rowson/Johnson
16.05.08	Bloomsbury	Royal National Hotel	Feld
17.05.08	Sheffield	Bramall Lane Platinum Suite	Coldwell
17.05.08	Stoke	King's Hall	Carney
17.05.08	Glasgow	Thistle Hotel	Morrison
23.05.08	Wigan	Robin Park Centre	Wood
24.05.08	Cardiff	St David's Hall	Connaughton
24.05.08	Manchester	City of Manchester Stadium	Hatton/Maloney
25.05.08	Hartlepool	Mayfair Suite	Garside
30.05.08	Birmingham	Holiday Inn Hotel	Pegg
31.05.08	Belfast	Shorts Sports & Social Club	Wilton
31.05.08	Newark	Grove Leisure Centre	Greaves
05.06.08	Leeds	Elland Road Conference & Leisure Centre	Bateson
06.06.08	Glasgow	Kelvin Hall	Hearn/Gilmour
06.06.08	Stoke	Trentham Gardens	Carney
07.06.08	Wigan	Robin Park Centre	Dixon
09.06.08	Glasgow	Radisson Hotel	Gilmour
13.06.08	Portsmouth	Mountbatten Centre	Maloney
13.06.08	Sunderland	Stadium of Light	Conroy
14.06.08	Bethnal Green	York Hall	Warren
15.06.08	St Helens	Sutton Sports Centre	Wood
15.06.08	Bethnal Green	York Hall	Carter
20.06.08	Wolverhampton	Civic Hall	Rowson/Johnson
20.06.08	Plymouth	Guildhall	C & J Sanigar
21.06.08	Sheffield	Don Valley Stadium	Hobson (Fight Academy)
21.06.08	Birmingham	National Indoor Arena	Warren
21.06.08	Hull	KC Sports Arena	Greaves
22.06.08	Derby	University	Mitchell
27.06.08	Bethnal Green	York Hall	Hennessy
28.06.08	Leicester	Aylestone Leisure Centre	Carpenter

Active British-Based Boxers: Career Records

Shows the complete record for all British-based boxers who have been active between 1 July 2007 and 30 June 2008. Names in brackets are real names, where they differ from ring names, and the first place name given is the boxer's domicile. The given weight class for each boxer is based on the weights made for their last three contests and boxers are either shown as being self-managed or with a named manager, the information being supplied by the BBBoC shortly before going to press. Also included are foreign-born fighters who made their pro debuts in Britain, along with others like Shinny Bayaar (Mongolia), Franklin Egobi (Nigeria), Yassine El Maachi (Morocco), Ruben Groenewald (South Africa), Ayitey Powers (Ghana), Hastings Rasani (Zimbabwe), Sergei Rozhakmens (Latvia), Albert Sosnowski (Poland), Alex Stoda (Estonia) and Choi Tseveenpurev (Mongolia), who, although starting their careers elsewhere, now hold BBBoC licenses. Former champions, such as Herbie Hide and Neil Sinclair, who continue their careers elsewhere, are also included.

Ali Adams
Hammersmith. *Born* Baghdad, Iraq, 1 November, 1980
Heavyweight. *Ht* 6'4"
Manager D. Powell

19.10.07	Tony Booth W PTS 4 Mayfair
01.12.07	Radcliffe Green L CO 4 Bethnal Green
16.05.08	Gareth Hearns L PTS 4 Holborn

Career: 3 contests, won 1, lost 2.

Ali Adams   Philip Sharkey

Terry Adams
Birmingham. *Born* Birmingham, 1 November, 1978
L.Middleweight. *Ht* 5'8½"
Manager E. Johnson

19.02.04	Neil Addis W CO 2 Dudley
15.04.04	Geraint Harvey W PTS 6 Dudley
08.07.04	Geraint Harvey W RSC 6 Birmingham
15.10.04	Jamie Coyle L RSC 5 Glasgow
13.02.05	Michael Lomax L RSC 1 Brentwood
07.04.05	Keith Jones W PTS 6 Birmingham
24.07.05	Gavin Smith W PTS 6 Sheffield
30.09.05	Matt Galer L PTS 10 Burton
	(Vacant Midlands Area L.Middleweight Title)
24.02.06	Gatis Skuja DREW 4 Birmingham
05.03.06	Danny Goode L PTS 8 Southampton
30.03.06	Cello Renda L PTS 4 Peterborough
06.05.06	Ernie Smith W PTS 6 Birmingham
28.05.06	Danny Reynolds L RSC 1 Wakefield
06.10.06	Mark Lloyd L RSC 7 Wolverhampton
	(Vacant British Masters L.Middleweight Title)
11.12.06	Davey Jones L PTS 6 Cleethorpes
02.12.07	Danny Butler L PTS 10 Bristol
	(Vacant British Masters L.Middleweight Title)
01.02.08	Scott Woolford L PTS 4 Bethnal Green
23.02.08	Jay Morris L RSC 2 Crawley
23.05.08	Jack Arnfield L RSC 3 Wigan

Career: 19 contests, won 6, drew 1, lost 12.

Terry Adams   Philip Sharkey

Ade Adebolu
Llandeilo. *Born* Hackney, 15 January, 1988
Welterweight. *Ht* 5'7"
Manager D.H. Davies

01.12.07	John Watson L RSC 4 Liverpool
06.06.08	Scott Miller L RSC 2 Stoke

Career: 2 contests, lost 2.

Usman Ahmed
Derby. *Born* Derby, 21 November, 1981
Flyweight. *Ht* 5'6"
Manager M.Shinfield

30.09.06	Chris Edwards L PTS 6 Stoke
11.12.06	Delroy Spencer DREW 6 Cleethorpes
03.03.07	Gary Sheil W PTS 6 Alfreton
16.09.07	Gary Sheil W PTS 6 Derby

Career: 4 contests, won 2, drew 1, lost 1.

Joey Ainscough
Liverpool. *Born* Liverpool, 16 August, 1979
L.Heavyweight. *Ht* 6'0"
Manager D. Hobson

27.11.99	Mark Dawson W PTS 4 Liverpool
05.02.00	Hussain Osman L PTS 4 Bethnal Green
25.03.00	Chris Crook W PTS 4 Liverpool
06.05.07	Mark Phillips W PTS 6 Altrincham
11.08.07	Ernie Smith W PTS 6 Liverpool
03.12.07	Paulie Silva L PTS 10 Manchester
	(Vacant Central Area S.Middleweight Title)
23.02.08	Mark Nilsen W PTS 4 Liverpool

Career: 7 contests, won 5, lost 2.

Geard Ajetovic
Liverpool. *Born* Beocin, Yugoslavia, 28 February, 1981
S.Middleweight. *Ht* 5'8½"
Manager Self

19.04.03	Ojay Abrahams W PTS 4 Liverpool
17.05.03	Jason Samuels W PTS 4 Liverpool
26.09.03	Gary Beardsley W RSC 3 Reading
07.11.03	Joel Ani W RTD 1 Sheffield
06.02.04	Tomas da Silva W RSC 4 Sheffield
12.05.04	Dmitry Donetskiy W PTS 6 Reading
10.12.04	Conroy McIntosh W PTS 6 Sheffield
21.01.05	Dmitry Yanushevich W RSC 4 Brentford
24.07.05	Conroy McIntosh W PTS 6 Sheffield
14.10.05	Jason Collins W RSC 6 Huddersfield
26.11.05	Magid Ben Driss W PTS 8 Sheffield
18.03.06	Christophe Canclaux L PTS 8 Monte Carlo, Monaco
13.05.06	Manoocha Salari W RSC 4 Sheffield
27.04.07	Patrick J. Maxwell DREW 6 Wembley
29.05.07	Robert Roselia W PTS 10 Pont Audemer, France
13.07.07	Patrick J. Maxwell W RSC 3 Barnsley
14.11.07	Joey Vegas W RSC 4 Bethnal Green
08.02.08	Francis Cheka W PTS 8 Peterlee
27.06.08	Daniel Geale L PTS 12 Sydney, Australia
	(Vacant IBO Middleweight Title)

Career: 19 contests, won 16, drew 1, lost 2.

Bob Ajisafe
Darlington. *Born* Nottingham, 13 April, 1985
L.Heavyweight. *Ht* 6'2¼"
Manager M. Marsden

18.11.07	Tom Owens W RSC 2 Birmingham
22.02.08	Victor Smith W PTS 4 Bethnal Green
26.04.08	Jamie Norkett W PTS 4 Darlington
09.05.08	Yanko Pavlov W PTS 4 Middlesbrough

Career: 4 contests, won 4.

Bob Ajisafe   Philip Sharkey

Youssef Al Hamidi

Dewsbury. *Born* Syria, 16 December, 1977
Lightweight. *Ht* 5'5"
Manager C. Aston

05.10.06	Paul Holborn L PTS 6 Sunderland
28.10.06	Dwayne Hill W RSC 3 Sheffield
17.11.06	Akaash Bhatia L PTS 4 Bethnal Green
03.12.06	Paul Halpin W PTS 4 Bethnal Green
26.01.07	Clifford Smith DREW 4 Dagenham
09.03.07	Lee Cook L PTS 6 Dagenham
24.06.07	Michael Gomez L RTD 3 Wigan
03.11.07	Ricky Burns L PTS 6 Cardiff
25.11.07	Carl Allen W PTS 6 Colne
15.12.07	John Simpson L PTS 8 Edinburgh
08.02.08	Michael Hunter L PTS 6 Peterlee
20.03.08	George Watson L PTS 6 South Shields
05.04.08	Anthony Crolla W PTS 8 Bolton
10.05.08	John Murray L PTS 8 Nottingham
17.05.08	Scott Lawton L PTS 6 Stoke

Career: 15 contests, won 4, drew 1, lost 10

Youssef Al Hamidi   Philip Sharkey

Nasser Al Harbi

Birmingham. *Born* Birmingham, 20 June,
1989
Middleweight. *Ht* 5'11¼"
Manager R. Woodhall

13.04.08	Ernie Smith W PTS 4 Edgbaston
30.05.08	Paul Royston W PTS 6 Birmingham

Career: 2 contests, won 2.

Najah Ali

London. *Born* Baghdad, Iraq, 9 May, 1980
Flyweight. *Ht* 5'2¼"
Manager D. Powell

15.06.08	David Keogan W RSC 1 Bethnal Green

Career: 1 contest, won 1.

Carl Allen   Philip Sharkey

Carl Allen

Wolverhampton. *Born* Wolverhampton, 20
November, 1969
L.Welterweight. Former Undefeated
Midlands Area S. Bantamweight Champion.
Ht 5'7¼"
Manager Self

26.11.95	Gary Jenkinson W PTS 6 Birmingham
29.11.95	Jason Squire L PTS 6 Solihull
17.01.96	Andy Robinson L PTS 6 Solihull
13.02.96	Ervine Blake W RSC 5 Wolverhampton
21.02.96	Ady Benton L PTS 6 Batley
29.02.96	Chris Jickells W PTS 6 Scunthorpe
27.03.96	Jason Squire DREW 6 Whitwick
26.04.96	Paul Griffin L RSC 3 Cardiff
30.05.96	Roger Brotherhood W RSC 5 Lincoln
26.09.96	Matthew Harris W PTS 10 Walsall
	(Midlands Area S. Bantamweight Title Challenge)
07.10.96	Emmanuel Clottey L RTD 3 Lewisham
21.11.96	Miguel Matthews W PTS 8 Solihull
30.11.96	Floyd Havard L RTD 3 Tylorstown
29.01.97	Pete Buckley W PTS 8 Stoke
11.02.97	David Morris DREW 8 Wolverhampton
28.02.97	Ian McLeod L RTD 3 Kilmarnock
21.05.97	David Burke L PTS 4 Liverpool
30.06.97	Duke McKenzie L PTS 8 Bethnal Green
12.09.97	Brian Carr L PTS 8 Glasgow
04.10.97	Sergei Devakov L PTS 6 Muswell Hill
03.12.97	Chris Lyons W PTS 8 Stoke
21.05.98	Roy Rutherford L PTS 6 Solihull
09.06.98	Scott Harrison L RSC 6 Hull
30.11.98	Gary Hibbert L PTS 4 Manchester
09.12.98	Chris Jickells W RSC 3 Stoke
04.02.99	Mat Zegan L PTS 4 Lewisham

17.03.99	Craig Spacie W PTS 8 Stoke
08.05.99	Phillip Ndou L RSC 2 Bethnal Green
14.06.99	Pete Buckley W PTS 6 Birmingham
22.06.99	David Lowry L PTS 4 Ipswich
11.10.99	Lee Williamson L PTS 6 Birmingham
19.10.99	Tontcho Tontchev L CO 2 Bethnal Green
20.12.99	Nicky Cook L CO 3 Bethnal Green
08.02.00	Lee Williamson W PTS 8 Wolverhampton
29.02.00	Bradley Pryce L PTS 4 Widnes
28.03.00	Lee Williamson W PTS 8 Wolverhampton
16.05.00	Bradley Pryce L RSC 3 Warrington
24.06.00	Michael Gomez L CO 2 Glasgow
10.10.00	Steve Hanley W PTS 8 Brierley Hill
05.02.01	Lee Meager DREW 6 Hull
12.03.01	Pete Buckley W PTS 6 Birmingham
27.03.01	Pete Buckley W PTS 8 Brierley Hill
15.09.01	Esham Pickering L PTS 6 Derby
17.11.01	Steve Conway L PTS 8 Dewsbury
08.12.01	Esham Pickering L PTS 8 Chesterfield
07.02.02	Mark Bowen L PTS 6 Stoke
20.04.02	Esham Pickering L PTS 6 Derby
21.07.02	Eddie Nevins L PTS 4 Salford
07.09.02	Colin Toohey DREW 6 Liverpool
26.10.02	Dazzo Williams W RSC 2 Maesteg
02.12.02	Esham Pickering L PTS 6 Leicester
28.01.03	Lee Meager L PTS 8 Nottingham
09.05.03	Jeff Thomas DREW 6 Doncaster
08.11.03	Baz Carey W RSC 2 Coventry
28.11.03	Carl Greaves L PTS 4 Derby
28.02.04	Michael Kelly L PTS 4 Bridgend
03.04.04	Andy Morris L PTS 4 Manchester
16.04.04	Dave Stewart L PTS 6 Bradford
17.06.04	Scott Lawton L PTS 10 Sheffield
	(Vacant Midlands Area Lightweight Title)
03.09.04	Gavin Rees L PTS 6 Newport
22.10.04	Craig Johnson L PTS 6 Mansfield
12.11.04	Billy Corcoran L RSC 5 Wembley
13.12.04	Jonathan Thaxton L RSC 1 Birmingham
05.03.05	Ryan Barrett L PTS 4 Dagenham
15.05.05	Scott Lawton L PTS 6 Sheffield
18.06.05	Joe McCluskey L PTS 6 Coventry
16.09.05	Stefy Bull L PTS 10 Doncaster
	(Vacant WBF Inter-Continental Lightweight Title)
13.11.05	Carl Johanneson L RTD 2 Leeds
17.02.06	Dwayne Hill L PTS 6 Sheffield
25.02.06	Damian Owen L PTS 6 Bristol
10.03.06	Martin Gethin L PTS 4 Walsall
25.03.06	Haider Ali DREW 4 Burton
21.05.06	Andrew Murray L PTS 4 Bethnal Green
01.06.06	Tristan Davies L PTS 6 Birmingham
22.09.06	Ben Jones L PTS 4 Bethnal Green
13.10.06	Stefy Bull L PTS 6 Doncaster
10.11.06	Tristan Davies L PTS 10 Telford
	(Vacant Midlands Area Lightweight Title)
09.02.07	Henry Castle L RSC 4 Leeds
20.04.07	Martin Gethin DREW 6 Dudley
27.05.07	Femi Fehintola L PTS 6 Bradford
16.06.07	Garry Buckland L PTS 6 Newport
15.07.07	Mark Dawes L PTS 6 Hartlepool
15.09.07	Billy Smith L PTS 10 Birmingham
	(Vacant Midlands Area L.Welterweight Title)
17.11.07	Scott Lawton L PTS 6 Stoke
25.11.07	Youssef Al Hamidi L PTS 6 Colne
08.12.07	Gary Sykes L PTS 6 Wigan

25.01.08 Martin Gethin L PTS 6 Dagenham
15.02.08 Dwayne Hill L PTS 6 Sheffield
23.02.08 Amir Unsworth L PTS 4 Newark
14.03.08 Steve Bell L PTS 6 Manchester
10.05.08 Dave Ryan L PTS 4 Nottingham
06.06.08 Chris Goodwin L PTS 4 Stoke
15.06.08 Rick Godding L PTS 6 St Helens
22.06.08 Dave Ryan L PTS 8 Derby
Career: 94 contests, won 18, drew 7, lost 69.

Peter Allen
Birkenhead. *Born* Birkenhead, 13 August, 1978
Lightweight. *Ht* 5'5½"
Manager Self

30.04.98 Sean Grant L PTS 6 Pentre Halkyn
21.06.98 Garry Burrell W PTS 6 Liverpool
20.09.98 Simon Chambers L PTS 6 Sheffield
16.11.98 Stevie Kane W PTS 6 Glasgow
07.12.98 Simon Chambers L PTS 6 Bradford
28.02.99 Amjid Mahmood L PTS 6 Shaw
12.03.99 Marc Callaghan L PTS 4 Bethnal Green
15.09.99 Steve Brook L PTS 6 Harrogate
07.10.99 Nicky Wilders L PTS 6 Sunderland
18.10.99 Mark Hudson L PTS 6 Bradford
15.11.99 Craig Docherty L RSC 1 Glasgow
09.12.01 Jeff Thomas L PTS 6 Blackpool
01.03.02 Andrew Ferrans L PTS 8 Irvine
15.03.02 Ricky Burns L PTS 6 Glasgow
17.04.02 Andrew Smith W PTS 6 Stoke
24.06.02 Tasawar Khan L PTS 6 Bradford
14.09.02 Carl Greaves L PTS 6 Newark
08.10.02 Andrew Ferrans L PTS 8 Glasgow
21.10.02 Tony McPake L PTS 6 Glasgow
17.11.02 Choi Tseveenpurev L RSC 4 Shaw
16.02.03 Darryn Walton L PTS 6 Salford
31.05.03 Mally McIver L PTS 6 Barnsley
29.08.03 Steve Mullin L PTS 6 Liverpool
25.04.04 Craig Johnson L PTS 6 Nottingham
08.05.04 Michael Graydon L PTS 6 Bristol
30.05.04 Willie Valentine W PTS 4 Dublin
10.09.04 Steve Mullin L PTS 4 Liverpool
05.11.04 Damian Owen L RSC 1 Hereford
04.03.05 Isaac Ward DREW 6 Hartlepool
10.04.05 Lloyd Otte L PTS 6 Brentwood
30.04.05 Eddie Nevins W PTS 6 Wigan
25.09.05 Carl Johanneson L RTD 9 Leeds
         (Vacant Central Area S.Featherweight Title)
16.06.06 David Appleby DREW 4 Liverpool
21.07.06 Chris Pacy L RSC 2 Altrincham
24.09.06 Henry Castle L RSC 6 Southampton
07.03.08 Barrington Brown L PTS 4 Nottingham
28.03.08 Gary Sykes L PTS 6 Barnsley
18.04.08 Akaash Bhatia L PTS 6 Bethnal Green
Career: 38 contests, won 5, drew 2, lost 31.

Sherman Alleyne
Bedford. *Born* London, 3 October, 1976
Middleweight. *Ht* 5'5"
Manager J. Feld

24.09.06 Greg Barton L RSC 3 Bethnal Green
17.03.07 Max Maxwell L PTS 6 Birmingham
15.04.07 Jon Musgrave L PTS 6 Barnsley
26.04.07 Prince Arron L PTS 6 Manchester
01.06.07 Rocky Muscas W PTS 6 Peterborough
21.07.07 Kerry Hope L PTS 6 Cardiff
07.09.07 Denton Vassell L RSC 1 Mayfair
19.10.07 Danny Goode L PTS 4 Mayfair
02.03.08 Steve Ede L PTS 6 Portsmouth
22.03.08 Stuart Brookes L PTS 6 Sheffield
16.05.08 Gokhan Kazaz L PTS 4 Holborn
Career: 11 contests, won 1, lost 10.

Sherman Alleyne   Les Clark

Wayne Alwan Arab
Hackney. *Born* Zimbabwe, 28 February, 1982
Middleweight. *Ht* 5'10"
Manager M. Helliet

01.02.07 Peter Dunn W PTS 6 Piccadilly
04.10.07 Peter Dunn W PTS 6 Piccadilly
28.11.07 Mark Phillips W PTS 4 Piccadilly
10.04.08 Steve Cooper W PTS 6 Piccadilly
Career: 4 contests, won 4.

Adnan Amar
Nottingham. *Born* Nottingham, 17 February, 1983
English Welterweight Champion. Former Undefeated Midlands Area Welterweight Champion. Former Undefeated British Masters L.Middleweight Champion.
Ht 5'9½"
Manager J. Ingle

11.06.01 Steve Hanley W PTS 4 Nottingham
13.11.01 Duncan Armstrong W PTS 6 Leeds
21.10.02 Jason Gonzales W PTS 6 Cleethorpes
23.02.03 Arv Mittoo W PTS 6 Shrewsbury
16.03.03 Gareth Wiltshaw W PTS 6 Nottingham
16.04.03 Dave Cotterill W PTS 4 Nottingham
28.04.03 Ernie Smith W PTS 6 Cleethorpes
12.05.03 Pedro Thompson W RSC 4 Birmingham
08.06.03 David Kirk W PTS 6 Nottingham
06.09.03 Chris Duggan W PTS 4 Aberdeen
23.02.04 Wayne Shepherd W RSC 5 Nottingham
10.05.04 Ernie Smith W PTS 6 Birmingham
04.06.04 Dean Hickman L RSC 8 Dudley
         (Vacant Midlands Area L.Welterweight Title)
29.10.04 Daniel Thorpe W PTS 4 Worksop
25.06.05 Ernie Smith W PTS 6 Melton Mowbray
28.01.06 Ben Hudson W PTS 4 Nottingham
27.02.06 Simon Sherrington W RSC 6 Birmingham
         (Vacant British Masters L.Middleweight Title)
23.03.07 Ben Hudson W PTS 4 Nottingham
06.10.07 Ernie Smith W PTS 4 Nottingham

09.11.07 Darren Gethin W RSC 10 Nottingham
         (Midlands Area Welterweight Title Challenge)
18.01.08 Ian MacKillop W RSC 3 Burton
12.04.08 Artur Jashkul W RSC 6 Castlebar,
10.05.08 Mark Lloyd W PTS 10 Nottingham
         (Vacant English Welterweight Title)
Career: 23 contests, won 22, lost 1.

Jamie Ambler
Aberystwyth. *Born* Aberystwyth, 16 January 1985
L.Heavyweight. *Ht* 6'2½"
Manager N. Hodges

12.11.05 Liam Stinchcombe W RTD 3 Bristol
12.12.05 Jason Welborn L RSC 1 Birmingham
10.02.06 Jon Harrison L PTS 4 Plymouth
07.04.06 Danny Goode L PTS 4 Longford
21.04.06 Scott Jordan L PTS 4 Belfast
16.09.06 Jonjo Finnegan L PTS 6 Burton
24.09.06 Paul Morby L PTS 4 Southampton
03.11.06 Kenny Davidson W PTS 6 Glasgow
10.12.06 Stuart Brookes L RSC 1 Sheffield
16.02.07 Shon Davies L PTS 6 Merthyr Tydfil
26.03.07 Ricky Strike W CO 6 Glasgow
07.04.07 Kerry Hope L PTS 6 Cardiff
22.09.07 Martin Murray L PTS 6 Wigan
06.10.07 Tony Bellew L RSC 2 Nottingham
28.11.07 Matthew Hough DREW 4 Walsall
08.12.07 Alex Matvienko L PTS 4 Wigan
23.12.07 Nigel Travis W PTS 6 Bolton
03.02.08 Robert Boardman L PTS 6 Bristol
15.02.08 Jezz Wilson L PTS 6 Sheffield
29.02.08 Steve McGuire L PTS 6 Glasgow
30.03.08 David Gentles L PTS 6 Port Talbot
13.04.08 Joe Rea L PTS 4 Edgbaston
02.05.08 Danny Butler L CO 2 Bristol
27.06.08 Dwayne Lewis L RSC 2 Bethnal Green
Career: 24 contests, won 4, drew 1, lost 19.

Jamie Ambler   Les Clark

James Ancliff
Fettercairn. *Born* Perth, 26 February, 1984
Featherweight. *Ht* 5'5"
Manager A. Morrison/F. Warren

22.04.06 Mickey Coveney L PTS 6 Glasgow

28.10.06 John Baguley W PTS 6 Aberdeen
10.12.06 Neil Marston W PTS 6 Glasgow
26.05.07 John Baguley W PTS 6 Aberdeen
01.12.07 Mark Bett DREW 6 Liverpool
09.12.07 Michael Crossan W RSC 1 Glasgow
14.03.08 Buster Dennis L RSC 3 Glasgow
17.05.08 Cristian Nicolae W PTS 6 Glasgow
Career: 8 contests, won 5, drew 1, lost 2.

Kenny Anderson

Edinburgh. *Born* 5 January, 1983
L.Heavyweight. *Ht* 5'11½"
Manager Barry Hughes

14.10.06 Nick Okoth W RSC 4 Manchester
07.04.07 Jorge Gomez W RSC 3 Cardiff
21.07.07 Dean Walker W RSC 2 Cardiff
17.11.07 Shon Davies W RSC 3 Glasgow
15.12.07 Simeon Cover W CO 6 Edinburgh
29.03.08 Dean Walker W RTD 4 Glasgow
Career: 6 contests, won 6.

Kevin Anderson

Buckhaven. *Born* Kirkcaldy, 26 April, 1980
Former British & Commonwealth
Welterweight Champion. Former
Undefeated Celtic Welterweight Champion.
Ht 5'8¾"
Manager T. Gilmour

12.04.03 Paul McIlwaine W RSC 2 Bethnal Green
19.04.03 Piotr Bartnicki W RSC 2 Liverpool
17.05.03 Georges Dujardin W RSC 1 Liverpool
05.07.03 Mohamed Bourhis W CO 2 Brentwood
06.09.03 Sergei Starkov W PTS 6 Huddersfield
01.11.03 Alban Mothie W PTS 8 Glasgow
14.02.04 Andrei Napolskikh W PTS 8 Nottingham
13.03.04 Lance Hall W RSC 1 Huddersfield
22.04.04 Dmitri Yanushevich W RSC 2 Glasgow
27.05.04 Danny Moir W RSC 1 Huddersfield
15.10.04 Stephane Benito W RSC 6 Glasgow
26.11.04 Tagir Rzaev W PTS 6 Altrincham
31.01.05 Glenn McClarnon W RSC 4 Glasgow
(Vacant Celtic Welterweight Title)
11.06.05 Vladimir Borovski W PTS 10 Kirkcaldy
30.09.05 Joshua Okine W PTS 12 Kirkcaldy
(Commonwealth Welterweight Title Challenge)
17.03.06 Craig Dickson W RSC 7 Kirkcaldy
(Commonwealth Welterweight Title Defence)
01.06.06 Young Muttley W RSC 10 Birmingham
(British Welterweight Title Challenge. Commonwealth Welterweight Title Defence)
10.11.06 Anthony Guillet W PTS 8 Hartlepool
16.02.07 Ali Nuumbembe L PTS 12 Kirkcaldy
(Commonwealth Welterweight Title Defence)
11.05.07 Eamonn Magee W PTS 12 Motherwell
(British Welterweight Title Defence)
14.09.07 Franny Jones W RSC 12 Kirkcaldy
(British Welterweight Title Defence)
02.11.07 Kevin McIntyre L PTS 12 Irvine
(British Welterweight Title Defence)
29.02.08 Kevin McIntyre L PTS 12 Glasgow
(British Welterweight Title Challenge)
Career: 23 contests, won 20, lost 3.

Rod Anderton

Nottingham. *Born* Nottingham, 17 August, 1978
International Masters L.Heavyweight Champion. *Ht* 5'11¾"
Manager M. Shinfield

22.04.05 Michael Pinnock W PTS 6 Barnsley
18.06.05 Nicki Taylor W RSC 4 Barnsley
02.09.05 Paul Billington W RTD 1 Derby
08.12.05 Gary Thompson W PTS 6 Derby
28.01.06 Nick Okoth W PTS 4 Nottingham
14.05.06 Ojay Abrahams W PTS 6 Derby
06.10.06 Richard Turba L RSC 2 Mansfield
24.11.06 Phillip Callaghan W RSC 4 Nottingham
03.03.07 Michael Monaghan L PTS 10 Alfreton
(Vacant Midlands Area L.Heavyweight Title)
23.03.07 Phillip Callaghan DREW 4 Nottingham
13.07.07 Carl Wild W PTS 4 Barnsley
21.09.07 Dean Walker W PTS 6 Burton
07.03.08 Mark Nilsen W PTS 4 Nottingham
16.05.08 Hamed Jamali W PTS 10 Burton
(Vacant International Masters L.Heavyweight Title)
Career: 14 contests, won 11, drew 1, lost 2.

Rod Anderton   Les Clark

John Anthony

Doncaster. *Born* Doncaster, 16 October, 1974
Cruiserweight. *Ht* 5'11½"
Manager D. Coldwell

22.04.05 Gary Thompson W PTS 4 Barnsley
18.06.05 Lee Mountford W RSC 5 Barnsley
04.11.05 Sandy Robb L PTS 6 Glasgow
12.02.06 Lee Kellett W RSC 1 Manchester
03.06.06 Andrew Lowe L PTS 6 Chigwell
01.10.06 Clint Johnson W PTS 6 Rotherham
02.03.07 Andrew Young W RSC 1 Irvine
17.03.07 Alexander Alexeev L RSC 5 Stuttgart, Germany
15.04.07 JJ Ojuederie L PTS 6 Barnsley
27.04.07 Tony Salam L PTS 4 Wembley
18.05.07 Micky Steeds L PTS 6 Canning Town
31.10.07 Vadim Usenko L PTS 6 Bayswater
09.11.07 Kelly Oliver W RSC 5 Nottingham
01.12.07 Neil Simpson L PTS 4 Coventry
23.02.08 Santander Silgado L RSC 2 Halle, Germany
Career: 15 contests, won 6, lost 9.

Liam Anthony

Derby. *Born* Derby, 5 March, 1985
L.Middleweight. *Ht* 5'10"
Manager M. Shinfield

28.06.08 Billy Smith W PTS 6 Leicester
Career: 1 contest, won 1.

Adil Anwar

Leeds. *Born* Leeds, 6 July, 1987
L.Welterweight. *Ht* 5'9¾"
Manager M. Bateson

14.06.07 Craig Tomes W PTS 6 Leeds
15.11.07 Graeme Higginson L PTS 6 Leeds
21.02.08 Steve Cooper W PTS 6 Leeds
05.06.08 Scott Sandmann W RSC 1 Leeds
Career: 4 contests, won 3, lost 1.

Paul Appleby

Edinburgh. *Born* Edinburgh, 22 July, 1987
British Featherweight Champion. *Ht* 5'9"
Manager T. Gilmour

23.01.06 Graeme Higginson W RTD 3 Glasgow
17.03.06 Ian Reid W RSC 3 Kirkcaldy
28.04.06 Andy Davis W RSC 1 Hartlepool
01.06.06 Graeme Higginson W RSC 2 Birmingham
22.09.06 Mickey Coveney W PTS 6 Bethnal Green
15.12.06 Rakhim Mingaleev W PTS 4 Bethnal Green
16.02.07 Buster Dennis W PTS 8 Kirkcaldy
11.05.07 Istvan Nagy W RSC 5 Motherwell
12.10.07 Riaz Durgahed W RSC 3 Peterlee
02.11.07 Ben Odamattey W RSC 6 Irvine
29.02.08 Ferenc Szabo W RSC 3 Glasgow
06.06.08 John Simpson W PTS 12 Glasgow
(British Featherweight Title Challenge)
Career: 12 contests, won 12.

Callum Archer

Birmingham. *Born* Solihull, 14 September, 1989
Welterweight. *Ht* 5'9¼"
Manager P. Lynch

12.05.08 Russell Pearce DREW 6 Birmingham
Career: 1 contest, drew 1.

Jack Arnfield

Blackpool. *Born* Buxton, 22 May, 1989
L.Middleweight. *Ht* 6'2¼"
Manager S. Wood
26.10.07 Lewis Byrne W RSC 1 Wigan
25.11.07 Lance Verallo W RSC 4 Colne
08.12.07 Ben Hudson W PTS 4 Wigan
16.02.08 David Kirk W PTS 6 Blackpool
30.03.08 Billy Smith W PTS 6 Colne
23.05.08 Terry Adams W RSC 3 Wigan
Career: 6 contests, won 6.

Dean Arnold

Wednesbury. *Born* Sandwell, 10 March, 1990
L.Welterweight. *Ht* 5'7¼"
Manager E. Johnson

12.05.08 Kristian Laight W PTS 6 Birmingham
Career: 1 contest, won 1.

Paul Appleby   Les Clark

Prince Arron

Droylsden. *Born* Crumpsall, 27 December, 1987
Former Undefeated British Masters Middleweight Champion. *Ht* 6'3"
Manager W. Barker

28.04.06	Tommy Jones W PTS 6 Manchester	
18.06.06	Karl Taylor W PTS 6 Manchester	
10.07.06	Geraint Harvey W PTS 6 Manchester	
11.09.06	Martin Marshall W PTS 6 Manchester	
21.10.06	Anthony Small L RSC 2 Southwark	
23.11.06	Rocky Muscas W PTS 6 Manchester	
03.12.06	Danny Reynolds L PTS 6 Wakefield	
18.02.07	George Katsimpas W PTS 8 Bethnal Green	
26.04.07	Sherman Alleyne W PTS 6 Manchester	
29.06.07	Cello Renda W PTS 10 Manchester	
	(Vacant British Masters Middleweight Title)	
22.09.07	Olufemi Moses W PTS 6 Coventry	
12.10.07	Martin Marshall W PTS 4 Peterlee	
20.10.07	John Duddy L RSC 2 Dublin	

Career: 13 contests, won 10, lost 3.

Alex Arthur

Edinburgh. *Born* Edinburgh, 26 June, 1978
WBO Featherweight Champion. Former Undefeated British, Commonwealth, European, WBO Inter-Continental, WBA Inter-Continental & IBF Inter-Continental S.Featherweight Champion. Former British S.Featherweight Champion. *Ht* 5'9"
Manager F. Warren

25.11.00	Richmond Asante W RSC 1 Manchester	
10.02.01	Eddie Nevins W RSC 1 Widnes	
26.03.01	Woody Greenaway W RTD 2 Wembley	
28.04.01	Dafydd Carlin W PTS 4 Cardiff	
21.07.01	Rakhim Mingaleev W PTS 4 Sheffield	
15.09.01	Dimitri Gorodetsky W RSC 1 Manchester	
27.10.01	Alexei Slyautchin W RSC 1 Manchester	
17.11.01	Laszlo Bognar W RSC 3 Glasgow	
19.01.02	Vladimir Borov W RSC 2 Bethnal Green	
11.03.02	Dariusz Snarski W RSC 10 Glasgow	
	(Vacant IBF Inter-Continental S.Featherweight Title)	
08.06.02	Nikolai Eremeev W RTD 5 Renfrew	
	(Vacant WBO Inter-Continental S.Featherweight Title)	
17.08.02	Pavel Potipko W CO 1 Cardiff	
19.10.02	Steve Conway W CO 4 Renfrew	
	(Vacant British S. Featherweight Title)	
14.12.02	Carl Greaves W RSC 6 Newcastle	
	(British S.Featherweight Title Defence)	
22.03.03	Patrick Malinga W RSC 6 Renfrew	
	(Vacant WBA Inter-Continental S.Featherweight Title)	
12.07.03	Willie Limond W RSC 8 Renfrew	
	(British S.Featherweight Title Defence)	
25.10.03	Michael Gomez L RSC 5 Edinburgh	
	(British S.Featherweight Title Defence)	
27.03.04	Michael Kizza W CO 1 Edinburgh	
	(Vacant IBF Inter-Continental S.Featherweight Title)	
22.10.04	Eric Odumasi W RSC 6 Edinburgh	
	(IBF Inter-Continental S.Featherweight Title Defence)	
03.12.04	Nazareno Ruiz W PTS 12 Edinburgh	
	(IBF Inter-Continental S.Featherweight Title Defence)	
08.04.05	Craig Docherty W CO 9 Edinburgh	
	(Vacant British S.Featherweight Title. Commonwealth S.Featherweight Title Challenge)	
23.07.75	Boris Sinitsin W PTS 12 Edinburgh	
	(European S.Featherweight Title Challenge)	
18.02.06	Ricky Burns W PTS 12 Edinburgh	
	(British, Commonwealth & European S.Featherweight Title Defences)	
29.04.06	Sergey Gulyakevich W TD 7 Edinburgh	
	(European S.Featherweight Title Defence)	
04.11.06	Sergio Palomo W RSC 5 Glasgow	
	(European S.Featherweight Title Defence)	
21.07.07	Koba Gogoladze W RSC 10 Cardiff	
	(Vacant WBO Interim S.Featherweight Title)	
15.12.07	Steve Foster W PTS 12 Edinburgh	
	(WBO Interim S.Featherweight Title Defence)	

Career: 27 contests, won 26, lost 1.

Jamie Arthur

Cwmbran. *Born* Aberdeen, 17 December, 1979
S.Featherweight. *Ht* 5'9¼"
Manager C. Sanigar

22.03.03	Daniel Thorpe W PTS 4 Renfrew	
28.06.03	James Gorman W PTS 4 Cardiff	
13.09.03	Dave Hinds W RTD 1 Newport	
11.10.03	Dafydd Carlin W RSC 4 Portsmouth	
15.11.03	Andrei Mircea W RSC 3 Bayreuth, Germany	
06.12.03	Jus Wallie W PTS 4 Cardiff	
27.03.04	Karl Taylor W PTS 4 Edinburgh	
03.07.04	Frederic Bonifai W PTS 6 Newport	
03.09.04	Buster Dennis W PTS 6 Newport	
21.01.05	Haider Ali L RSC 3 Bridgend	
23.07.05	Harry Ramogoadi L RSC 5 Edinburgh	
05.04.08	Ayittey Mettle W PTS 6 Newport	

Career: 12 contests, won 10, lost 2.

Ryan Ashworth

Scarborough. *Born* Stockton, 20 March, 1984
Middleweight. *Ht* 5'8¼"
Manager Self

05.12.05	Omar Gumati W PTS 6 Leeds	
24.02.06	Jak Hibbert L PTS 6 Scarborough	
09.05.06	Peter Dunn W PTS 6 Leeds	
13.04.07	Alex Matvienko DREW 4 Altrincham	
26.10.07	Brett Flournoy L PTS 6 Wigan	
29.11.07	Muhsen Nasser L PTS 4 Bradford	
18.04.08	Paul Royston W PTS 6 Houghton le Spring	
25.05.08	Steve Cooper W PTS 6 Hartlepool	
13.06.08	Shaun Farmer W CO 3 Sunderland	

Career: 9 contests, won 5, drew 1, lost 3.

Ryan Ashworth   Les Clark

Darren Askew

Manchester. *Born* Whiehaven, 15 November, 1984
Welterweight. *Ht* 5'9¼"
Manager J. Pennington

07.10.07	Pete Buckley W PTS 6 Shaw	
10.11.07	Amir Nadi W PTS 6 Stalybridge	
23.11.07	Joe Elfidh L PTS 6 Rotherham	
20.04.08	Kristian Laight W PTS 6 Shaw	

Career: 4 contests, won 3, lost 1.

John Baguley

Sheffield. *Born* Rotherham, 13 March, 1988
Lightweight. *Ht* 5'9"
Manager J. Ingle

13.10.06	Wez Miller W PTS 4 Doncaster
28.10.06	James Ancliff L PTS 6 Aberdeen
07.11.06	Matthew Martin Lewis L PTS 6 Leeds
01.12.06	Deniss Sirjatovs W PTS 4 Doncaster
17.12.06	James Brown W PTS 6 Bolton
09.02.07	Stuart McFadyen L PTS 4 Leeds
27.04.07	Chris Hooper W RSC 1 Hull
26.05.07	James Ancliff L PTS 6 Aberdeen
10.06.07	Henry Jones W RSC 4 Neath
01.07.07	Tom Glover L PTS 10 Colchester
	(Vacant British Masters Lightweight Title)
15.07.07	James McElvaney L PTS 6 Hartlepool
22.09.07	Mark Moran L PTS 4 Wigan
05.11.07	Furhan Rafiq W PTS 6 Glasgow
17.11.07	Kevin Buckley L PTS 6 Stoke
23.02.08	Danny Stewart W RSC 2 Crawley
08.03.08	Vinny Mitchell L PTS 4 Greenwich
22.03.08	Femi Fehintola L PTS 6 Sheffield
07.06.08	John Watson L PTS 4 Wigan

Career: 18 contests, won 7, lost 11.

Ian Bailey

Slough. *Born* Taplow, 18 April, 1984
S.Bantamweight. *Ht* 5'4¼"
Manager J. Eames

15.06.08	Delroy Spencer W PTS 6 Bethnal Green

Career: 1 contest, won 1.

Ian Bailey   Philip Sharkey

Mariusz Bak

Brentford. *Born* Poland, 23 June, 1980
Lightweight. *Ht* 5'8½"
Manager J. Rooney

12.10.07	James McElvaney L PTS 4 Peterlee

Career: 1 contest, lost 1.

Jamie Ball

Coseley. *Born* Wordsley, 5 July, 1984
Middleweight. *Ht* 5'10¾"
Manager P. Rowson

20.06.08	Paul Royston W PTS 4 Wolverhampton

Career: 1 contest, won 1.

Jamie Ball   Philip Sharkey

Ted Bami (Minsende)

Brixton. *Born* Zaire, 2 March, 1978
Former Undefeated European
L.Welterweight Champion. Former WBF
L.Welterweight Champion. *Ht* 5'7"
Manager Self

26.09.98	Des Sowden W RSC 1 Southwark
11.02.99	Gary Reid W RSC 2 Dudley
10.03.00	David Kehoe W PTS 4 Bethnal Green
08.09.00	Jacek Bielski L RSC 4 Hammersmith
29.03.01	Keith Jones W PTS 4 Hammersmith
05.05.01	Francis Barrett W PTS 6 Edmonton
31.07.01	Lance Crosby W PTS 6 Bethnal Green
19.03.02	Michael Smyth W CO 4 Slough
23.06.02	Keith Jones W RSC 4 Southwark
17.08.02	Bradley Pryce W RSC 6 Cardiff
26.10.02	Adam Zadworny W PTS 4 Maesteg
07.12.02	Sergei Starkov W PTS 4 Brentwood
08.03.03	Andrei Devyataykin W RSC 1 Bethnal Green
12.04.03	Laszlo Herczeg W RSC 9 Bethnal Green
	(Vacant WBF L.Welterweight Title)
26.07.03	Samuel Malinga L RSC 3 Plymouth
	(WBF L.Welterweight Title Defence)
09.10.03	Zoltan Surman W RSC 3 Bristol
31.01.04	Jozsef Matolcsi W PTS 6 Bethnal Green
08.05.04	Viktor Baranov W RSC 2 Dagenham
08.10.04	Rafal Jackiewicz W PTS 8 Brentwood
13.02.05	Ricardo Daniel Silva W CO 2 Brentwood
21.10.05	Silence Saheed W PTS 6 Bethnal Green
24.02.06	Maurycy Gojko W CO 4 Dagenham
22.09.06	Giuseppe Lauri W PTS 12 Bethnal Green
	(Vacant European L.Welterweight Title)
30.03.07	Giuseppe Lauri W PTS 12 Crawley
	(European L.Welterweight Title Defence)
25.01.08	Nicolas Guisset W PTS 8 Dagenham
14.03.08	David Barnes L PTS 12 Manchester
	(Vacant British L.Welterweight Title)

Career: 26 contests, won 23, lost 3.

Ted Bami   Les Clark

Michael Banbula

Staines. *Born* Poland, 26 December, 1980
L.Heavyweight. *Ht* 5'11¼"
Manager Self

30.04.05	Gareth Lawrence L PTS 6 Dagenham
14.05.05	Tommy Tolan L PTS 4 Dublin
02.06.05	Cello Renda DREW 6 Peterborough
01.07.05	Gareth Lawrence L PTS 4 Fulham
16.07.05	Daniel Cadman L PTS 6 Chigwell
06.10.05	Danny McIntosh L PTS 6 Longford
22.10.05	Neil Tidman L PTS 6 Coventry
19.11.05	Danny Tombs L RSC 2 Southwark
21.09.07	Dwayne Lewis L PTS 4 Bethnal Green
28.09.07	Carl Dilks L PTS 6 Preston
09.10.07	Jack Morris W PTS 6 Tower Hamlets
18.11.07	Leon Senior L PTS 4 Tooting
01.12.07	Richard Horton L PTS 4 Bethnal Green
16.02.08	Kevin Concepcion L PTS 6 Leicester
02.03.08	Danny Couzens L PTS 6 Portsmouth
16.03.08	Martin Murray L PTS 6 Liverpool
28.03.08	James Tucker W PTS 4 Piccadilly
04.04.08	Victor Smith W PTS 4 Bethnal Green
01.05.08	Pawel Trebinski L PTS 6 Piccadilly
14.06.08	Tommy Saunders L RSC 1 Bethnal Green

Career: 20 contests, won 3, drew 1, lost 16.

Michael Banbula Philip Sharkey

Darren Barker

Barnet. *Born* Harrow, 19 May, 1982
Commonwealth Middleweight Champion.
Former Undefeated Southern Area
Middleweight Champion. *Ht* 6'0½"
Manager A. Sims

24.09.04	Howard Clarke W PTS 6 Nottingham
12.11.04	David White W RSC 2 Wembley
26.03.05	Leigh Wicks W RTD 4 Hackney
10.04.05	Andrei Sherel W RSC 3 Brentwood
09.07.05	Ernie Smith W PTS 6 Nottingham
16.07.05	Dean Walker W PTS 6 Chigwell
02.12.05	John-Paul Temple W RSC 6 Nottingham
20.01.06	Richard Mazurek W PTS 8 Bethnal Green
17.02.06	Louis Mimoune W RSC 2 Bethanl Green
12.05.06	Danny Thornton W RSC 6 Bethnal Green
12.07.06	Conroy McIntosh W RSC 7 Bethnal Green
15.09.06	Hussain Osman W PTS 10 Muswell Hill
	(Vacant Southern Area Middleweight Title)
24.11.06	Ojay Abrahams W RTD 1 Nottingham
08.12.06	Paul Samuels W RSC 1 Dagenham
05.10.07	Greg Barton W RSC 3 Bethnal Green
14.11.07	Ben Crampton W PTS 12 Bethnal Green
	(Vacant Commonwealth Middleweight Title)
22.02.08	Steven Bendall W RSC 7 Bethnal Green
	(Commonwealth Middleweight Title Defence)

Career: 17 contests, won 17.

James Barker

Droylsden. *Born* Salford, 17 July, 1985
Welterweight. *Ht* 5'9"
Manager W. Barker

23.02.07	Ali Hussain W PTS 6 Manchester
06.10.07	Muhsen Nasser L RSC 1 Aberdeen

Career: 2 contests, won 1, lost 1.

David Barnes (Smith)

Manchester. *Born* Manchester, 16 January, 1981
British L. Welterweight Champion.
Former Undefeated British Welterweight
Champion. *Ht* 5'8½"
Manager J. Trickett

07.07.01	Trevor Smith W RSC 2 Manchester
15.09.01	Karl Taylor W PTS 4 Manchester
27.10.01	Mark Sawyers W RSC 2 Manchester
15.12.01	James Paisley W RTD 2 Wembley
09.02.02	David Kirk W RTD 1 Manchester
04.05.02	David Baptiste W CO 3 Bethnal Green
01.06.02	Dimitri Protkunas W RSC 1 Manchester
28.09.02	Sergei Starkov W PTS 6 Manchester
12.10.02	Rusian Ashirov W PTS 6 Bethnal Green
14.12.02	Rozalin Nasibulin W RSC 3 Newcastle
18.01.03	Brice Faradji W PTS 6 Preston
05.04.03	Viktor Fesetchko W PTS 8 Manchester
17.07.03	Jimmy Vincent W PTS 12 Dagenham
	(Vacant British Welterweight Title)
13.12.03	Kevin McIntyre W RTD 8 Manchester
	(British Welterweight Title Defence)
03.04.04	Glenn McClarnon W PTS 12 Manchester
	(British Welterweight Title Defence)
12.11.04	James Hare W RSC 6 Halifax
	(British Welterweight Title Defence)
28.01.05	Juho Tolppola W PTS 10 Renfrew
22.04.05	Ali Nuumbembe DREW 12 Barnsley
	(Vacant WBO Inter-Continental Welterweight Title)
04.06.05	Joshua Okine L RSC 12 Manchester
	(Commonwealth Welterweight Title Challenge)
28.01.06	Fabrice Colombel W RSC 4 Nottingham
04.03.06	Silence Saheed W PTS 4 Manchester
10.12.06	Vadzim Astapuk W PTS 6 Sheffield
03.05.07	Jay Morris W RSC 1 Sheffield
02.11.07	Arek Malek W PTS 6 Irvine
14.03.08	Ted Bami W PTS 12 Manchester
	(Vacant British L.Welterweight Title)

Career: 25 contests, won 23, drew 1, lost 1.

Darren Barker Les Clark

Matthew Barney

Southampton. *Born* Fareham, 25 June, 1974
Cruiserweight. Former Undefeated WBU
L.Heavyweight Champion. Former
Undefeated British, IBO Inter-Continental,
Southern Area & British Masters
S.Middleweight Champion. *Ht* 5'10¾"
Manager J. Feld

04.06.98   Adam Cale W PTS 6 Barking
23.07.98   Adam Cale W PTS 6 Barking
02.10.98   Dennis Doyley W PTS 4 Cheshunt
22.10.98   Kevin Burton W PTS 6 Barking
07.12.98   Freddie Yemofio W PTS 4 Acton
17.03.99   Simon Andrews W RTD 4 Kensington
09.05.99   Gareth Hogg W PTS 4 Bracknell
20.05.99   Bobby Banghar W RSC 5 Kensington
      (British Masters S. Middleweight
      Final)
05.06.99   Paul Bowen DREW 10 Cardiff
      (Southern Area S. Middleweight Title
      Challenge)
20.08.99   Adam Cale W PTS 4 Bloomsbury
05.10.99   Delroy Leslie L PTS 10 Bloomsbury
      (Vacant Southern Area Middleweight
      Title)
15.04.00   Mark Dawson W PTS 6 Bethnal Green
06.05.00   Jason Hart W PTS 10 Southwark
      (Vacant Southern Area S. Middleweight
      Title)
30.09.00   Neil Linford L PTS 10 Peterborough
      (Elim. British S. Middleweight Title)
02.02.01   Darren Covill W PTS 6 Portsmouth
16.03.01   Matt Mowatt W RSC 1 Portsmouth
      (British Masters S. Middleweight Title
      Defence)
14.07.01   Robert Milewics W PTS 8 Wembley
20.10.01   Jon Penn W RSC 4 Portsmouth
26.01.02   Hussain Osman L RTD 9 Dagenham
      (Vacant IBO Inter-Continental
      S.Middleweight Title. Southern Area
      S.Middleweight Title Defence)
08.04.02   Hussain Osman W PTS 12
      Southampton
      (IBO Inter-Continental & Southern
      Area S. Middleweight Title Challenges)
22.09.02   Paul Owen W CO 7 Southwark
      (Vacant British Masters S.Middleweight
      Title)
20.10.02   Chris Nembhard W PTS 10 Southwark
      (Southern Area S. Middleweight Title
      Defence)
29.03.03   Dean Francis W PTS 12 Wembley
      (Vacant British S.Middleweight Title)
01.08.03   Charles Adamu L PTS 12 Bethnal
      Green
      (Vacant Commonwealth
      S.Middleweight Title)
11.10.03   Tony Oakey W PTS 12 Portsmouth
      (WBU L.Heavyweight Title Challenge)
10.09.04   Simeon Cover W PTS 4 Wembley
26.03.05   Thomas Ulrich L PTS 12 Riesa,
      Germany
      (European L.Heavyweight Title
      Challenge)
09.07.05   Carl Froch L PTS 12 Nottingham
      (British & Commonwealth
      S.Middleweight Title Challenges)
01.12.06   Varuzhan Davtyan W PTS 4 Tower Hill
23.02.07   Ayitey Powers W PTS 6 Peterborough
23.02.08   Kim Jenssen W PTS 6 Crawley
16.05.08   Ayitey Powers W PTS 6 Holborn
Career: 32 contests, won 25, drew 1, lost 6.

Ryan Barrett

Thamesmead. *Born* London, 27 December,
1982
Former Undefeated British Masters
Featherweight Champion. *Ht* 5'10"
Manager S. Barrett

13.06.02   Gareth Wiltshaw W PTS 4 Leicester
      Square
06.09.02   Jason Gonzales W PTS 4 Bethnal
      Green
12.12.02   Martin Turner W RSC 1 Leicester
      Square
08.03.03   David Vaughan DREW 4 Bethnal
      Green
04.10.03   Dafydd Carlin L PTS 4 Belfast
01.05.04   Marty Kayes W RSC 2 Gravesend
19.06.04   Kristian Laight W PTS 4 Muswell Hill
16.10.04   Daniel Thorpe W PTS 4 Dagenham
19.12.04   James Paisley W DIS 5 Bethnal Green
21.01.05   Peter McDonagh W PTS 8 Brentford
05.03.05   Carl Allen W PTS 4 Dagenham
23.03.05   Pete Buckley W PTS 6 Leicester
      Square
20.06.05   Anthony Christopher W RSC 1
      Longford
01.04.06   Martin Watson L PTS 10 Bethnal
      Green
      (Elim. British Lightweight Title)
23.07.06   Baz Carey W PTS 6 Dagenham
02.09.06   Amir Khan L RSC 1 Bolton
21.10.06   Steve Gethin W PTS 6 Southwark
03.12.06   Riaz Durgahed W PTS 6 Bethnal Green
18.02.07   Jamie McKeever W PTS 10 Bethnal
      Green
      (Vacant British Masters Featherweight
      Title)
08.06.07   John Simpson L CO 5 Mayfair
      (British Featherweight Title Challenge)
18.04.08   Henry Castle L RSC 3 Bethnal Green
Career: 21 contests, won 15, drew 1, lost 5.

Ryan Barrett   Philip Sharkey

(Alex) Sandy Bartlett

Inverness. *Born* Dingwall, 20 April, 1976
S.Featherweight. *Ht* 5'7"
Manager T. Gilmour

15.03.04   Marty Kayes W PTS 6 Glasgow
19.04.04   Abdul Mougharbel L PTS 6 Glasgow
11.10.04   Abdul Mougharbel W PTS 6 Glasgow
05.11.04   Ricky Owen L RSC 2 Hereford
19.09.05   Neil Marston W PTS 6 Glasgow
04.11.05   Craig Bromley L RSC 2 Glasgow
20.02.06   Kevin Townsley L PTS 4 Glasgow
25.03.06   John Bothwell L RSC 2 Irvine
02.12.06   Brian Murphy W RSC 5 Clydebank
02.03.07   Furhan Rafiq L PTS 6 Irvine
28.09.07   Scott Quigg L RSC 3 Preston
18.02.08   Furhan Rafiq L RSC 10 Glasgow
      (Vacant Scottish Area Featherweight
      Title)
Career: 12 contests, won 4, lost 8.

Greg Barton   Les Clark

Greg Barton

Southend. *Born* , Rochford, 4 April, 1982
Middleweight. *Ht* 5'11½"
Manager J. Eames/J. Feld

26.02.06   Leon Owen L RSC 1 Dagenham
24.09.06   Sherman Alleyne W RSC 3 Bethnal
      Green
15.12.06   Scott Jordan L PTS 4 Bethnal Green
18.02.07   Eder Kurti W PTS 4 Bethnal Green
08.06.07   Anthony Young L PTS 4 Mayfair
05.10.07   Darren Barker L RSC 3 Bethnal Green
01.12.07   Ernie Smith W PTS 4 Bethnal Green
Career: 7 contests, won 3, lost 4.

(Shinebayer) Shinny Bayaar (Sukhbaatar)

Carlisle. *Born* Mongolia, 27 August, 1977
Bantamweight. *Ht* 5'5½"
Manager J. Doughty

25.02.00   Yura Dima DREW 10 Erdene,
      Mongolia
28.06.00   Manny Melchor L PTS 12 Manila,
      Philippines
      (WBC International M.Flyweight Title
      Challenge)
10.10.01   Damien Dunnion L PTS 8 Stoke
09.12.01   Delroy Spencer W PTS 4 Shaw
17.11.02   Anthony Hanna W PTS 6 Shaw
20.03.03   Sunkanmi Ogunbiyi L PTS 4
      Queensway
08.06.03   Darren Cleary W RSC 2 Shaw
19.10.03   Delroy Spencer W PTS 6 Shaw
21.02.04   Reidar Walstad W RSC 1 Cardiff
31.10.04   Delroy Spencer W PTS 6 Shaw
11.12.04   Martin Power L PTS 10 Canning Town
20.11.05   Abdul Mougharbel W PTS 4 Shaw

02.04.06 Delroy Spencer W PTS 6 Shaw
15.09.06 Andrew Kooner W RSC 3 Muswell
          Hill
11.03.07 Pete Buckley W PTS 6 Shaw
20.04.08 Sumaila Badu W RSC 2 Shaw
Career: 16 contests, won 11, drew 1, lost 4.

Jimmy Beech
Walsall. *Born* Walsall, 19 January, 1979
Welterweight. *Ht* 5'7¼"
Manager E. Johnson

23.06.99 Ike Halls W RTD 2 West Bromwich
03.09.99 Tom Wood W PTS 6 West Bromwich
07.04.00 Willie Limond L RSC 2 Glasgow
28.01.01 Lenny Hodgkins W PTS 6
          Wolverhampton
16.11.01 Pete Buckley W PTS 6 West Bromwich
23.11.01 Henry Castle L PTS 4 Bethnal Green
07.02.02 Dave Cotterill W PTS 6 Stoke
25.02.02 Mickey Bowden W PTS 4 Slough
09.03.02 Tony Mulholland L PTS 6 Manchester
05.05.02 James Rooney W RSC 5 Hartlepool
25.05.02 Henry Castle L PTS 4 Portsmouth
07.09.02 Ricky Eccleston W RSC 3 Liverpool
28.09.02 Michael Gomez L RSC 4 Manchester
14.12.02 Gavin Rees L PTS 4 Newcastle
22.03.03 Willie Limond L CO 4 Renfrew
28.04.03 Tony McPake L PTS 6 Nottingham
27.05.03 Billy Corcoran W PTS 6 Dagenham
26.09.03 Dave Stewart L RTD 2 Reading
14.11.03 Scott Lawton L RSC 5 Bethnal Green
24.01.04 Steve Murray L RSC 4 Wembley
28.01.05 Martin Watson L PTS 4 Renfrew
26.02.05 Scott Haywood L PTS 6 Burton
11.03.05 Stefy Bull L PTS 4 Doncaster
08.05.05 Carl Johanneson L CO 2 Bradford
30.03.08 Shaun Horsfall L PTS 6 Colne
10.04.08 Peter Dunn W PTS 6 Piccadilly
20.04.08 Muhsen Nasser L PTS 6 Shaw
17.05.08 Scott Miller L RTD 2 Stoke
Career: 28 contests, won 10, lost 18.

Andy Bell (Langley)
Nottingham. *Born* Doncaster, 16 July, 1985
British S.Flyweight Champion. Former
Undefeated English S.Flyweight Champion.
Former Undefeated Midlands Area &
British Masters Bantamweight Champion.
Ht 5'8"
Manager M. Scriven

22.10.04 Steve Gethin W RSC 5 Mansfield
10.12.04 Dean Ward W PTS 6 Mansfield
06.03.05 Abdul Mougharbel W PTS 4 Mansfield
24.04.05 Wayne Bloy L PTS 4 Askern
13.05.06 Steve Gethin L RSC 2 Sutton in
          Ashfield
06.10.06 Shaun Walton W PTS 6 Mansfield
01.12.06 Jamie McDonnell L RSC 3 Doncaster
01.04.07 Neil Marston W RSC 8 Shrewsbury
          (*Vacant Midlands Area Bantamweight*
          Title)
19.05.07 Delroy Spencer W PTS 4 Nottingham
17.06.07 Mo Khaled W PTS 10 Mansfield
          (*Vacant British Masters Bantamweight*
          Title)
22.07.07 Delroy Spencer W PTS 6 Mansfield
07.09.07 Robert Nelson W RSC 7 Doncaster
          (*Vacant English S.Flyweight Title*)
01.12.07 Wayne Bloy W PTS 10 Nottingham
          (*English S.Flyweight Title Defence*)
28.03.08 Chris Edwards W PTS 12 Barnsley
          (*British S.Flyweight Title Challenge*)
Career: 14 contests, won 11, lost 3.

Billy Bell
South Shields, *Born* Westminster, 13 May,
1986
Featherweight. *Ht* 5'6"
Manager M. Gates

20.03.08 Duane Cumberbatch W PTS 6 South
          Shields
18.04.08 Dean Mills L PTS 6 Houghton le
          Spring
13.06.08 Tony McQuade W PTS 6 Sunderland
Career: 3 contests, won 2, lost 1.

Steve Bell
Manchester. *Born* Manchester, 11 June,
1975
Central Area S.Featherweight Champion.
Ht 5'10"
Manager F. Warren

08.05.03 Jus Wallie DREW 4 Widnes
27.09.03 Jaz Virdee W RSC 1 Manchester
13.12.03 Fred Janes W PTS 4 Manchester
03.04.04 Pete Buckley W PTS 4 Manchester
22.05.04 Haider Ali W PTS 6 Widnes
01.10.04 Daniel Thorpe W PTS 6 Manchester
11.02.05 Henry Janes W RTD 3 Manchester
03.06.05 Buster Dennis DREW 6 Manchester
04.03.06 Pete Buckley W PTS 4 Manchester
01.04.06 Jason Nesbitt W PTS 6 Bethnal Green
02.09.06 Daniel Thorpe W RTD 4 Bolton
28.10.06 Steve Gethin W RTD 5 Bethnal Green
10.03.07 Jamie McKeever W RSC 7 Liverpool
          (*Vacant Central Area S.Featherweight*
          Title)
31.05.07 Rom Krauklis W PTS 6 Manchester
06.10.07 Femi Fehintola L PTS 10 Nottingham
          (*Vacant English S.Featherweight Title*)
14.03.08 Carl Allen W PTS 6 Manchester
05.04.08 Baz Carey W PTS 6 Bolton
Career: 17 contests, won 14, drew 2, lost 1.

Tony Bellew
Liverpool. *Born* Liverpool, 30 November,
1982
L.Heavyweight. *Ht* 6'2½"
Manager F. Warren

06.10.07 Jamie Ambler W RSC 2 Nottingham
03.11.07 Adam Wilcox W RSC 3 Cardiff
08.12.07 Wayne Brooks W CO 3 Bolton
05.04.08 Paul Bonson W PTS 4 Bolton
Career: 4 contests, won 4.

Scott Belshaw
Lisburn N.Ireland. *Born* Aghalee, N.Ireland,
8 July, 1985
Heavyweight. *Ht* 6'7¼"
Manager F. Maloney/A. Wilton

07.10.06 Lee Webb W RSC 1 Belfast
11.11.06 Anatoliy Kusenko W RSC 1 Dublin
25.11.06 Alexander Subin W RSC 2 Belfast
26.01.07 Makhmud Otazhanov W RSC 2
          Dagenham
09.03.07 Paul King W PTS 4 Dagenham
30.06.07 Chris Woollas W CO 1 Belfast
26.01.08 Aleksandre Borhovs W RSC 3 Cork
07.03.08 Daniel Peret L PTS 6 Nottingham
31.05.08 Edgar Kalnars W RSC 4 Belfast
Career: 9 contests, won 8, lost 1.

Scott Belshaw   Les Clark

Steven Bendall
Coventry. *Born* Coventry, 1 December,
1973
English Middleweight Champion. Former
Undefeated IBO Inter-Continental &WBU
Inter-Continental Middleweight Champion.
Ht 6'0"
Manager Self

15.05.97 Dennis Doyley W RSC 2 Reading
13.09.97 Gary Reyniers W PTS 4 Millwall
27.02.99 Israel Khumalo W PTS 4 Oldham
02.07.99 Darren Covill W RTD 3 Bristol
24.09.99 Sean Pritchard W PTS 6 Merthyr
03.12.99 Ian Toby W PTS 6 Peterborough
07.04.00 Des Sowden W RSC 3 Bristol
02.06.00 Simon Andrews W RSC 5 Ashford
08.09.00 Jason Barker W PTS 6 Bristol
03.11.00 Eddie Haley W RSC 1 Ebbw Vale
01.12.00 Peter Mitchell W PTS 8 Peterborough
22.08.01 Bert Bado W RSC 1 Hammanskraal,
          South Africa
29.09.01 Alan Gilbert W RTD 3 Southwark
08.12.01 Jason Collins W PTS 12 Dagenham
          (*Vacant WBU Inter-Continental*
          Middleweight Title)
02.03.02 Ahmet Dottouev W RTD 4 Brakpan,
          South Africa
          (*WBU Inter-Continental Middleweight*
          Title Defence)
26.04.02 Viktor Fesetchko W RSC 10 Coventry
          (*Vacant IBO Inter-Continental*
          Middleweight Title)
13.07.02 Phillip Bystrikov W RSC 5 Coventry
06.09.02 Tomas da Silva W RSC 8 Bethnal
          Green
24.01.03 Lee Blundell W RSC 2 Sheffield
          (*IBO Inter-Continental Middleweight*
          Title Defence)
26.04.03 Mike Algoet W PTS 12 Brentford
          (*IBO Inter-Continental Middleweight*
          Title Defence)
14.11.03 Kreshnik Qato W PTS 8 Bethnal Green
17.09.04 Scott Dann L RSC 6 Plymouth
          (*Vacant British Middleweight Title*)
18.06.05 Ismael Kerzazi W PTS 8 Coventry
22.10.05 Magid Ben Driss W PTS 6 Coventry
15.12.05 Donovan Smillie W RSC 5 Coventry
          (*English Middleweight Title Challenge*)

22.04.06	Sebastian Sylvester L RSC 3 Mannheim, Germany	
	(European Middleweight Title Challenge)	
07.10.06	Conroy McIntosh W PTS 6 Weston super Mare	
01.12.06	Wayne Elcock L RSC 8 Birmingham	
	(English Middleweight Title Defence)	
20.07.07	Davey Jones W RTD 2 Wolverhampton	
28.09.07	Andrzej Butowicz W RSC 8 Coventry	
28.11.07	Alexander Matviechuk W PTS 6 Walsall	
22.02.08	Darren Barker L RSC 7 Bethnal Green	
	(Commonwealth Middleweight Title Challenge)	
21.06.08	Paul Smith W PTS 10 Birmingham	
	(English Middleweight Title Challenge)	

Career: 33 contests, won 29, lost 4.

Steven Bendall   Philip Sharkey

Billy Bessey   Philip Sharkey

Billy Bessey
Portsmouth. *Born* Portsmouth, 8 January, 1974
Heavyweight. *Ht* 6'1¼"
Manager J. Bishop

01.10.00	Paul Fiske W PTS 6 Hartlepool
26.02.01	Mark Hobson L PTS 4 Nottingham
06.05.01	Luke Simpkin W PTS 6 Hartlepool
04.06.01	Gary Williams W PTS 4 Hartlepool
21.11.04	Ebrima Secka W PTS 6 Bracknell
06.02.05	Paul King L PTS 6 Southampton
18.03.05	Martin Rogan L PTS 4 Belfast
04.12.05	Dave Clarke W PTS 6 Portsmouth
16.09.07	Luke Simpkin L CO 6 Southampton
10.11.07	Prince George Akrong W PTS 6 Portsmouth
02.12.07	Howard Daley W PTS 6 Oldham
02.03.08	Paul Bonson L PTS 6 Portsmouth
11.04.08	Dave Ferguson L PTS 3 Bethnal Green

Career: 13 contests, won 7, lost 6.

Mark Bett
Larkhall. *Born* Lanark, 30 September, 1982
Welterweight. *Ht* 5'7"
Manager A. Morrison

22.04.06	Marco Cittadini DREW 6 Glasgow
27.05.06	Colin Bain DREW 6 Glasgow
21.10.06	Marco Cittadini W PTS 6 Glasgow
10.12.06	Colin Bain L PTS 6 Glasgow
16.02.07	Ali Hussain DREW 6 Sunderland
16.03.07	Ali Hussain W RSC 3 Glasgow
24.06.07	Davey Watson L RTD 5 Sunderland
11.08.07	Amir Unsworth L RSC 4 Liverpool
06.10.07	Adam Kelly W RTD 3 Aberdeen
26.10.07	Paddy Pollock DREW 6 Glasgow
01.12.07	James Ancliff DREW 6 Liverpool
09.12.07	Gary McMillan L RSC 1 Glasgow
14.03.08	David Kehoe W PTS 6 Glasgow
29.03.08	Adam Kelly L PTS 6 Aberdeen
16.05.08	Charles Paul King L PTS 6 Motherwell
09.06.08	Matt Seawright W RSC 5 Glasgow

Career: 16 contests, won 5, drew 5, lost 6.

Akaash Bhatia
Harrow. *Born* Loughborough, 1 May, 1983
S.Featherweight. *Ht* 5'7"
Manager F. Maloney

30.05.06	Kristian Laight W PTS 4 Bethnal Green
29.06.06	Nikita Lukin W PTS 4 Bethnal Green
06.10.06	Rakhim Mingaleev W PTS 4 Bethnal Green
17.11.06	Youssef Al Hamidi W PTS 4 Bethnal Green
26.01.07	Sergii Tertii W RSC 2 Dagenham
27.04.07	Dai Davies W PTS 4 Wembley
13.07.07	Steve Gethin W RSC 5 Barnsley
21.09.07	Frederic Gosset W PTS 6 Bethnal Green
30.11.07	Riaz Durgahed W PTS 6 Newham
01.02.08	Wladimir Borov W PTS 8 Bethnal Green
18.04.08	Peter Allen W PTS 6 Bethnal Green

Career: 11 contests, won 11.

Willie Bilan
Fife. *Born* Kirkcaldy, 17 April, 1986
Welterweight. *Ht* 5'11¼"
Manager T. Gilmour

23.10.06	Steve Cooper W PTS 6 Glasgow
16.02.07	David Kehoe W RSC 1 Kirkcaldy
11.05.07	Steve Anning W PTS 4 Motherwell
14.09.07	Alexander Spitjo L CO 1 Kirkcaldy

Career: 4 contests, won 3, lost 1.

(Joe John) JJ Bird
Peterborough. *Born* Peterborough, 9 September, 1986
Middleweight. *Ht* 6'1½"
Manager G. De'Roux/D. Powell

23.02.07	Frank Celebi W PTS 4 Peterborough
01.06.07	Duncan Cottier W PTS 4 Peterborough
21.09.07	Lance Verallo W PTS 6 Peterborough
10.11.07	Paul Morby L PTS 6 Portsmouth
02.12.07	Tommy Heffron DREW 6 Oldham
27.06.08	David Walker W PTS 4 Bethnal Green

Career: 6 contests, won 4, drew 1, lost 1.

Chris Black
Coatbridge. *Born* Bellshill, 19 November, 1979
Middleweight. *Ht* 5'7½"
Manager T. Gilmour

22.10.04	Brian Coleman W PTS 4 Edinburgh
12.12.04	Jak Hibbert W RSC 2 Glasgow
28.01.05	Geraint Harvey W PTS 4 Renfrew
01.04.05	Tony Randell W PTS 6 Glasgow
17.06.05	Ciaran Healy DREW 4 Glasgow
22.04.06	Barrie Lee L PTS 10 Glasgow
	(Scottish L.Middleweight Title Challenge)
28.10.06	Tyan Booth L PTS 6 Aberdeen
19.10.07	Shaun Farmer W CO 1 Motherwell
24.11.07	Tyan Booth W PTS 6 Clydebank
22.02.08	Tony Randell W PTS 6 Motherwell
16.05.08	Darren Gethin W PTS 6 Motherwell

Career: 11 contests, won 8, drew 1, lost 2.

Wayne Bloy
Grimsby. *Born* Grimsby, 30 November, 1982
Bantamweight. *Ht* 5'5"
Manager C. Greaves

14.06.04	Neil Read DREW 6 Cleethorpes
20.09.04	Gary Ford W PTS 6 Cleethorpes
24.04.05	Andy Bell W PTS 4 Askern
23.05.05	Neil Marston W PTS 6 Cleethorpes
24.02.06	Abdul Mougharbel W PTS 6 Scarborough
13.10.06	Jamie McDonnell L PTS 4 Doncaster
23.02.07	Jamie McDonnell L RSC 3 Doncaster
	(Vacant English Bantamweight Title)
08.09.07	Delroy Spencer W PTS 4 Sutton in Ashfield
01.12.07	Andy Bell L PTS 10 Nottingham
	(English S.Flyweight Title Challenge)

Career: 9 contests, won 5, drew 1, lost 3.

Robert Boardman
Bristol. *Born* London, 9 September, 1987
L.Heavyweight. *Ht* 5'10"
Manager T. Gilmour

02.06.07	Mark Phillips W PTS 6 Bristol
02.12.07	Adam Wilcox W PTS 4 Bristol
03.02.08	Jamie Ambler W PTS 6 Bristol

Career: 3 contests, won 3.

Steve Bodger
Blackburn. *Born* Hannover, Germany, 29 August, 1981
Heavyweight. *Ht* 6'3¼"
Manager T. Schofield

15.05.08	Danny Hughes L PTS 6 Sunderland

Career: 1 contest, lost 1

Paul Bonson

Featherstone. *Born* Castleford, 18 October, 1971
Cruiserweight. Former Central Area L.Heavyweight Champion. *Ht* 5'10¼"
Manager Self

04.10.96	Michael Pinnock W PTS 6 Wakefield
14.11.96	Michael Pinnock DREW 6 Sheffield
22.12.96	Pele Lawrence DREW 6 Salford
20.04.97	Shamus Casey W PTS 6 Leeds
26.06.97	Andy Manning L PTS 6 Sheffield
19.09.97	Mike Gormley W PTS 6 Salford
03.10.97	Rudi Marcussen L PTS 4 Copenhagen, Denmark
03.12.97	Alex Mason DREW 6 Stoke
14.12.97	Willie Quinn L RSC 4 Glasgow
15.01.98	Alex Mason L PTS 6 Solihull
13.02.98	Peter Mason L PTS 4 Seaham
23.02.98	Martin McDonough W PTS 6 Windsor
07.03.98	Michael Bowen L PTS 6 Reading
14.03.98	Alain Simon L PTS 6 Pont Saint Maxence, France
08.04.98	Tim Brown DREW 4 Liverpool
21.05.98	Mark Hobson L PTS 6 Bradford
21.06.98	Kenny Rainford L PTS 6 Liverpool
01.09.98	Roberto Dominguez L PTS 8 Vigo, Spain
23.10.98	Rob Galloway W PTS 6 Wakefield
16.11.98	Chris P. Bacon L PTS 8 Glasgow
11.12.98	Robert Zlotkowski L PTS 4 Prestwick
20.12.98	Glenn Williams L PTS 6 Leeds
24.04.99	Kenny Gayle DREW 4 Peterborough
29.05.99	Dave Johnson L PTS 6 South Shields
19.06.99	Sebastiaan Rothmann L PTS 8 Dublin
12.07.99	Jim Twite L PTS 4 Coventry
07.08.99	Juan Perez Nelongo L PTS 8 Tenerife, Spain
11.09.99	Mark Hobson L PTS 4 Sheffield
02.10.99	Enzo Maccarinelli L PTS 4 Cardiff
16.10.99	Robert Zlotkowski L PTS 6 Bethnal Green
27.10.99	Peter McCormack W PTS 6 Birmingham
04.12.99	Glenn Williams W PTS 4 Manchester
11.12.99	Chris Davies L PTS 4 Merthyr Tydfil
05.02.00	Paul Maskell L PTS 4 Bethnal Green
11.03.00	Tony Dodson L PTS 4 Kensington
26.03.00	Wayne Buck L PTS 8 Nottingham
29.04.00	Cathal O'Grady L PTS 4 Wembley
13.05.00	Mark Hobson L PTS 4 Barnsley
25.06.00	Andy Manning W PTS 10 Wakefield *(Vacant Central Area L.Heavyweight Title)*
08.09.00	Robert Milewicz L PTS 4 Hammersmith
21.10.00	Jon Penn L PTS 6 Sheffield
12.11.00	Glenn Williams L PTS 10 Manchester *(Central Area L.Heavyweight Title Defence)*
24.11.00	Alex Mason L PTS 6 Darlington
09.12.00	Mark Baker L PTS 6 Southwark
23.01.01	Calvin Stonestreet W PTS 4 Crawley
03.02.01	Tony Dodson L PTS 4 Manchester
18.02.01	Butch Lesley L PTS 6 Southwark
13.03.01	Konstantin Schvets L PTS 6 Plymouth
07.04.01	Rob Hayes-Scott L PTS 4 Wembley
26.04.01	Mike White L PTS 6 Gateshead
17.05.01	Clint Johnson W PTS 6 Leeds
24.05.01	Sven Hamer L PTS 4 Kensington
04.06.01	Joe Gillon DREW 6 Glasgow
11.06.01	Darren Chubbs L PTS 4 Nottingham
21.06.01	Michael Pinnock W PTS 6 Sheffield
27.07.01	Clinton Woods L PTS 6 Sheffield
09.09.01	Eamonn Glennon W PTS 6 Hartlepool
28.09.01	Elvis Michailenko L PTS 6 Millwall
13.11.01	Tony Moran W PTS 6 Leeds
23.11.01	Elvis Michailenko L PTS 6 Bethnal Green
06.12.01	Shaun Bowes W RSC 5 Sunderland
16.12.01	Tommy Eastwood L PTS 4 Southwark
26.01.02	Dominic Negus L PTS 4 Bethnal Green
10.02.02	Butch Lesley L PTS 4 Southwark
25.02.02	Roman Greenberg L PTS 6 Slough
15.03.02	Michael Thompson L PTS 6 Spennymoor
22.03.02	Mark Smallwood L PTS 6 Coventry
19.04.02	Michael Thompson L PTS 6 Darlington
11.05.02	Mark Brookes L PTS 4 Chesterfield
15.06.02	Peter Haymer L PTS 4 Tottenham
23.06.02	Scott Lansdowne W PTS 6 Southwark
13.07.02	Jason Brewster W PTS 6 Wolverhampton
27.07.02	Albert Sosnowski L PTS 4 Nottingham
08.09.02	Varuzhan Davtyan L PTS 4 Wolverhampton
22.09.02	Neil Linford L PTS 6 Southwark
29.09.02	Tony Dowling L PTS 6 Shrewsbury
12.10.02	Andrew Lowe L PTS 4 Bethnal Green
25.10.02	Carl Froch L PTS 6 Bethnal Green
30.11.02	Robert Norton L PTS 6 Coventry
14.12.02	Nathan King W PTS 4 Newcastle
18.01.03	Enzo Maccarinelli L PTS 4 Preston
08.02.03	Steven Spartacus L PTS 6 Norwich
05.03.03	Marcus Lee W PTS 4 Bethnal Green
18.03.03	Mark Krence L PTS 4 Reading
28.03.03	Eric Teymour L PTS 6 Millwall
19.04.03	Tony Moran L PTS 4 Liverpool
12.05.03	Colin Kenna L PTS 6 Southampton
10.06.03	Lee Swaby L PTS 4 Sheffield
26.09.03	Garry Delaney L PTS 6 Reading
06.10.03	Pinky Burton L PTS 6 Barnsley
07.11.03	Carl Thompson L PTS 6 Sheffield
14.11.03	Tony Booth L PTS 6 Hull
01.12.03	David Ingleby W PTS 6 Leeds
20.02.04	Colin Kenna L PTS 6 Southampton
13.03.04	Neil Dawson L PTS 4 Huddersfield
16.04.04	John Keeton L PTS 4 Bradford
01.05.04	Carl Wright L PTS 6 Coventry
26.11.04	Tony Booth L PTS 6 Hull
06.12.04	Robert Norton L CO 6 Leicester *(Vacant British Masters Cruiserweight Title)*
06.02.05	Ovill McKenzie L PTS 4 Southampton
30.04.05	Tony Moran L PTS 6 Wigan
14.05.05	John Keeton L PTS 4 Aberdeen
18.06.05	Neil Simpson L PTS 6 Coventry
09.07.05	Dean Francis L PTS 6 Bristol
24.07.05	Toks Owoh L PTS 4 Leicester Square
03.09.05	Sam Sexton L PTS 6 Norwich
23.09.05	Gyorgy Hidvegi L PTS 4 Manchester
07.10.05	Junior MacDonald L PTS 4 Bethnal Green
20.11.05	Darren Stubbs L PTS 6 Shaw
10.12.05	Bruce Scott L PTS 4 Canning Town
24.02.06	Gyorgy Hidvegi DREW 8 Dagenham
05.03.06	Amer Khan L PTS 6 Sheffield
23.03.06	Ovill McKenzie L PTS 6 The Strand
30.03.06	Ovill McKenzie L RSC 3 Bloomsbury
06.05.06	Billy McClung L PTS 6 Irvine
09.06.06	Dean Cockburn L PTS 6 Doncaster
26.01.08	Jonathan O'Brien L PTS 4 Cork
02.03.08	Billy Bessey W PTS 6 Portsmouth
16.03.08	Paul Keir L PTS 4 Liverpool
05.04.08	Tony Bellew L PTS 4 Bolton
18.04.08	Micky Steeds L PTS 8 Bethnal Green
30.04.08	Neil Perkins L PTS 6 Wolverhampton
23.05.08	Scott Mitchell L PTS 6 Wigan
07.06.08	Mike Stafford L PTS 4 Wigan
21.06.08	Mark Krence L PTS 4 Sheffield

Career: 125 contests, won 20, drew 7, lost 98.

Paul Bonson　　　　Philip Sharkey

Jason Booth

Nottingham. *Born* Nottingham, 7 November, 1977
Commonwealth Bantamweight Champion. Former IBO S.Flyweight Champion. Former Undefeated British Flyweight Champion. Former Undefeated Commonwealth Flyweight Champion.
Ht 5'4"
Manager J. Gill/T. Harris

13.06.96	Darren Noble W RSC 3 Sheffield
24.10.96	Marty Chestnut W PTS 6 Lincoln
27.11.96	Jason Thomas W PTS 4 Swansea
18.01.97	David Coldwell W PTS 4 Swadlincote
07.03.97	Pete Buckley W PTS 6 Northampton
20.03.97	Danny Lawson W RSC 3 Newark
10.05.97	Anthony Hanna W PTS 6 Nottingham
19.05.97	Chris Lyons W PTS 6 Cleethorpes
31.10.97	Mark Reynolds W PTS 6 Ilkeston
31.01.98	Anthony Hanna W PTS 6 Edmonton
20.03.98	Louis Veitch W CO 2 Ilkeston *(Elim. British Flyweight Title)*
09.06.98	Dimitar Alipiev W RSC 2 Hull
17.10.98	Graham McGrath W RSC 4 Manchester
07.12.98	Louis Veitch W RSC 5 Cleethorpes
08.05.99	David Guerault L PTS 12 Grande Synthe, France *(European Flyweight Title Challenge)*
12.07.99	Mark Reynolds W RSC 3 Coventry
16.10.99	Keith Knox W RSC 10 Belfast *(British &Commonwealth Flyweight Title Challenges)*
22.01.00	Abie Mnisi W PTS 12 Birmingham *(Commonwealth Flyweight Title Defence)*
01.07.00	John Barnes W PTS 6 Manchester
13.11.00	Ian Napa W PTS 12 Bethnal Green *(British & Commonwealth Flyweight Title Defences)*
26.02.01	Nokuthula Tshabangu W CO 2 Nottingham *(Commonwealth Flyweight Title Defence)*
30.06.01	Alexander Mahmutov L PTS 12 Madrid, Spain *(European Flyweight Title Challenge)*

23.02.02	Jason Thomas W PTS 6 Nottingham
01.06.02	Mimoun Chent L TD 8 Le Havre, France
	(Vacant European Flyweight Title)
16.11.02	Kakhar Sabitov W RSC 6 Nottingham
28.04.03	Lindi Memani W PTS 8 Nottingham
20.09.03	Lunga Ntontela W PTS 12 Nottingham
	(IBO S.Flyweight Title Challenge)
13.03.04	Dale Robinson W PTS 12 Huddersfield
	(IBO S.Flyweight Title Defence)
17.12.04	Damaen Kelly L PTS 12 Huddersfield
	(IBO S.Flyweight Title Defence)
03.11.06	Abdul Mougharbel W PTS 6 Barnsley
09.02.07	Jamil Hussain W PTS 6 Leeds
06.07.07	Ian Napa L PTS 12 Wigan
	(Vacant British Bantamweight Title)
08.12.07	Matthew Edmonds W RSC 9 Wigan
	(Vacant Commonwealth Bantamweight Title)
07.03.08	Lante Addy W PTS 12 Nottingham
	(Commonwealth Bantamweight Title Defence)
13.06.08	Dai Davies W PTS 6 Portsmouth

Career: 35 contests, won 30, lost 5.

Tony Booth

Hull. *Born* Hull, 30 January, 1970
Heavyweight. Former Undefeated British
Masters L.Heavyweight Champion. Former
Undefeated British Masters & Central Area
Cruiserweight Champion. *Ht* 5'11½"
Manager Self

08.03.90	Paul Lynch L PTS 6 Watford
11.04.90	Mick Duncan W PTS 6 Dewsbury
26.04.90	Colin Manners W PTS 6 Halifax
16.05.90	Tommy Warde W PTS 6 Hull
05.06.90	Gary Dyson W PTS 6 Liverpool
05.09.90	Shaun McCrory L PTS 6 Stoke
08.10.90	Bullit Andrews W RSC 3 Cleethorpes
23.01.91	Darron Griffiths DREW 6 Stoke
06.02.91	Shaun McCrory L PTS 6 Liverpool
06.03.91	Billy Brough L PTS 6 Glasgow
18.03.91	Billy Brough W PTS 6 Glasgow
28.03.91	Neville Brown L PTS 6 Alfreton
17.05.91	Glenn Campbell L RSC 2 Bury
	(Central Area S. Middleweight Title Challenge)
25.07.91	Paul Murray W PTS 6 Dudley
01.08.91	Nick Manners DREW 8 Dewsbury
11.09.91	Jim Peters L PTS 8 Hammersmith
28.10.91	Eddie Smulders L RSC 6 Arnhem, Holland
09.12.91	Steve Lewsam L PTS 8 Cleethorpes
30.01.92	Serg Fame W PTS 6 Southampton
12.02.92	Tenko Ernie W RSC 4 Wembley
05.03.92	John Beckles W RSC 6 Battersea
26.03.92	Dave Owens L PTS 6 Hull
08.04.92	Michael Gale L PTS 8 Leeds
13.05.92	Phil Soundy W PTS 6 Kensington
02.06.92	Eddie Smulders L RSC 1 Rotterdam, Holland
18.07.92	Maurice Core L PTS 6 Manchester
07.09.92	James Cook L PTS 8 Bethnal Green
30.10.92	Roy Richie DREW 6 Istrees, France
18.11.92	Tony Wilson DREW 8 Solihull
25.12.92	Francis Wanyama L PTS 6 Izegem, Belgium
09.02.93	Tony Wilson W PTS 8 Wolverhampton
01.05.93	Ralf Rocchigiani DREW 8 Berlin, Germany
03.06.93	Victor Cordoba L PTS 8 Marseille, France

23.06.93	Tony Behan W PTS 6 Gorleston
01.07.93	Michael Gale L PTS 8 York
17.09.93	Ole Klemetsen L PTS 8 Copenhagen, Denmark
07.10.93	Denzil Browne DREW 8 York
02.11.93	James Cook L PTS 8 Southwark
12.11.93	Carlos Christie W PTS 6 Hull
28.01.94	Francis Wanyama L RSC 2 Waregem, Belgium
	(Vacant Commonwealth Cruiserweight Title)
26.03.94	Torsten May L PTS 6 Dortmund, Germany
21.07.94	Mark Prince L RSC 3 Battersea
24.09.94	Johnny Held L PTS 8 Rotterdam, Holland
07.10.94	Dirk Wallyn L PTS 6 Waregem, Belgium
27.10.94	Dean Francis L CO 1 Bayswater
23.01.95	Jan Lefeber L PTS 8 Rotterdam, Holland
07.03.95	John Foreman L PTS 6 Edgbaston
27.04.95	Art Stacey W PTS 10 Hull
	(Vacant Central Area Cruiserweight Title)
04.06.95	Montell Griffin L RSC 2 Bethnal Green
06.07.95	Nigel Rafferty W RSC 7 Hull
22.07.95	Mark Prince L RSC 2 Millwall
06.09.95	Leif Keiski L PTS 8 Helsinki, Finland
25.09.95	Neil Simpson W PTS 8 Cleethorpes
06.10.95	Don Diego Poeder L RSC 2 Waregem, Belgium
11.11.95	Bruce Scott L RSC 3 Halifax
16.12.95	John Marceta L RSC 2 Cardiff
20.01.96	Johnny Nelson L RSC 2 Mansfield
15.03.96	Slick Miller W PTS 6 Hull
27.03.96	Neil Simpson L PTS 6 Whitwick
17.05.96	Mark Richardson W RSC 2 Hull
13.07.96	Bruce Scott L PTS 8 Bethnal Green
03.09.96	Paul Douglas L PTS 4 Belfast
14.09.96	Kelly Oliver L RSC 2 Sheffield
06.11.96	MartinJolley W PTS 4 Hull
22.11.96	Slick Miller W RSC 5 Hull
11.12.96	Crawford Ashley L RSC 1 Southwark
18.01.97	Kelly Oliver L RSC 4 Swadlincote
27.02.97	Kevin Morton L PTS 6 Hull
25.03.97	Nigel Rafferty DREW 8 Wolverhampton
04.04.97	John Wilson L PTS 6 Glasgow
16.04.97	Robert Norton L RSC 4 Bethnal Green
15.05.97	Phill Day W PTS 4 Reading
11.09.97	Steve Bristow L PTS 4 Widnes
22.09.97	Martin Langtry W PTS 6 Cleethorpes
04.10.97	Bruce Scott W PTS 8 Muswell Hill
28.11.97	Martin Jolley W PTS 6 Hull
15.12.97	Nigel Rafferty W PTS 6 Cleethorpes
06.03.98	Peter Mason W RSC 3 Hull
09.06.98	Crawford Ashley L RSC 6 Hull
	(British L. Heavyweight Title Challenge. Vacant Commonwealth L. Heavyweight Title)
18.07.98	Omar Sheika W PTS 8 Sheffield
26.09.98	Toks Owoh L PTS 6 Norwich
29.10.98	Nigel Rafferty W PTS 8 Bayswater
14.12.98	Sven Hamer W PTS 6 Cleethorpes
05.01.99	Ali Saidi W RSC 4 Epernay, France
17.05.99	Darren Ashton W PTS 6 Cleethorpes
12.07.99	Neil Simpson L PTS 10 Coventry
	(Elim. British L. Heavyweight Title)
27.09.99	Adam Cale W PTS 6 Cleethorpes
16.10.99	Cathal O'Grady L CO 4 Belfast
18.01.00	Michael Sprott L PTS 6 Mansfield
12.02.00	Thomas Hansvoll L PTS 6 Sheffield
29.02.00	John Keeton L RSC 2 Widnes

09.04.00	Greg Scott-Briggs W PTS 10 Alfreton
	(Vacant British Masters L. Heavyweight Title)
15.05.00	Michael Pinnock W PTS 6 Cleethorpes
19.06.00	Toks Owoh L RSC 3 Burton
08.09.00	Dominic Negus W PTS 6 Bristol
30.09.00	Robert Norton L RSC 3 Peterborough
31.10.00	Firat Aslan L RSC 2 Hammersmith
11.12.00	Mark Krence L PTS 6 Sheffield
05.02.01	Denzil Browne L RSC 5 Hull
	(Vacant Central Area Cruiserweight Title)
01.04.01	Kenny Gayle DREW 4 Southwark
10.04.01	Mark Baker L PTS 4 Wembley
16.06.01	Butch Lesley L RSC 3 Dagenham
09.09.01	Tommy Eastwood L PTS 4 Southwark
22.09.01	Peter Haymer L PTS 4 Bethnal Green
15.10.01	Colin Kenna L PTS 6 Southampton
01.11.01	Terry Morrill W RSC 7 Hull
24.11.01	Matt Legg L PTS 4 Bethnal Green
16.12.01	Blue Stevens L PTS 4 Southwark
19.01.02	John McDermott L RSC 1 Bethnal Green
20.04.02	Enzo Maccarinelli L PTS 4 Cardiff
28.04.02	Scott Lansdowne W RSC 4 Southwark
10.05.02	Paul Buttery L PTS 4 Preston
23.06.02	Neil Linford L RSC 5 Southwark
03.08.02	Mark Krence L PTS 4 Derby
17.08.02	Enzo Maccarinelli L RTD 2 Cardiff
23.09.02	Slick Miller W PTS 6 Cleethorpes
05.10.02	Phill Day W PTS 4 Coventry
19.10.02	James Zikic L PTS 4 Norwich
27.10.02	Hughie Doherty L PTS 4 Southwark
21.11.02	Jamie Warters W PTS 8 Hull
28.11.02	Roman Greenberg L PTS 4 Finchley
08.12.02	David Haye L RTD 2 Bethnal Green
30.01.03	Mohammed Benguesmia L RTD 4 Algiers, Algeria
05.04.03	Jason Callum L PTS 6 Coventry
17.05.03	Tony Moran L PTS 6 Liverpool
26.07.03	Kelly Oliver L PTS 4 Plymouth
26.09.03	Radcliffe Green W PTS 6 Millwall
14.11.03	Paul Bonson W PTS 6 Hull
14.02.04	Oneal Murray W PTS 8 Holborn
01.05.04	Elvis Michailenko L RTD 4 Gravesend
15.08.04	Bash Ali L RSC 4 Lagos, Nigeria
	(WBF Cruiserweight Title Challenge)
26.11.04	Paul Bonson W PTS 6 Hull
11.12.04	Hovik Keuchkerian L CO 1 Madrid, Spain
05.03.05	Junior MacDonald L PTS 4 Southwark
15.04.05	Johny Jensen L PTS 6 Copenhagen, Denmark
04.06.05	Martin Rogan L RSC 2 Manchester
24.07.05	Coleman Barrett L PTS 4 Leicester Square
10.09.05	Darren Morgan L PTS 4 Cardiff
24.09.05	Carl Wright L PTS 4 Coventry
06.10.05	Tommy Eastwood L PTS 4 Longford
25.11.05	Dave Clarke DREW 6 Hull
26.02.06	Ovill McKenzie L PTS 4 Dagenham
05.03.06	Jon Ibbotson L PTS 4 Sheffield
30.03.06	Ervis Jegeni L RSC 1 Piccadilly
13.05.06	Paul Souter L PTS 4 Bethnal Green
26.05.06	Lee Mountford W PTS 6 Hull
12.07.06	Ervis Jegeni L PTS 4 Bethnal Green
23.07.06	Tommy Eastwood L PTS 4 Dagenham
24.09.06	Mervyn Langdale W RSC 1 Southampton
09.10.06	Oneal Murray W PTS 4 Bedworth
21.10.06	Danny Tombs W PTS 4 Southwark
03.11.06	Leigh Alliss L PTS 4 Bristol
03.12.06	JJ Ojuederie L PTS 4 Bethnal Green
23.02.07	Billy Wilson W RSC 5 Doncaster

07.04.07	Derek Chisora L PTS 4 Cardiff
21.04.07	Paulie Silva L PTS 6 Manchester
18.05.07	Troy Ross L RSC 2 Canning Town
13.07.07	Tom Owens L PTS 4 Birmingham
25.09.07	Neil Simpson L PTS 10 Hull
	(Vacant British Masters Cruiserweight
	Title)
19.10.07	Ali Adams L PTS 4 Mayfair
09.11.07	Ben Harding L PTS 4 Plymouth
23.11.07	David Dolan L RSC 3 Houghton le
	Spring
01.03.08	Neil Simpson L PTS 4 Coventry
14.03.08	Howard Daley L RTD 2 Manchester

Career: 164 contests, won 50, drew 9, lost 105.

Tony Booth   Philip Sharkey

Tyan Booth

Sheffield. *Born* Nottingham, 20 March, 1983
Welterweight. *Ht* 6'2½"
Manager J. Ingle

29.10.05	Jimi Hendricks W PTS 6 Aberdeen
08.11.05	Jimi Hendricks W PTS 6 Leeds
27.02.06	Jason Welborn W CO 4 Birmingham
06.05.06	Richard Turba W PTS 6 Blackpool
17.05.06	Alexis Callero LPTS 6 Lanzarote,
	Canary Islands, Spain
22.09.06	George Hillyard W PTS 6 Bethnal
	Green
13.10.06	Karl David W PTS 6 Aberavon
28.10.06	Chris Black W PTS 6 Aberdeen
24.11.06	Peter Dunn W PTS 4 Nottingham
02.12.06	Nathan Graham W PTS 6 Southwark
23.03.07	Darren Gethin L RSC 10 Nottingham
	(Vacant Midlands Area Welterweight
	Title)
24.11.07	Chris Black L PTS 6 Clydebank
03.12.07	Matthew Hall L PTS 8 Manchester
29.03.08	Colin McNeil W CO 1 Aberdeen
28.06.08	Kevin Concepcion L PTS 10 Leicester
	(Vacant British Masters Middleweight
	Title)

Career: 15 contests, won 10, lost 5.

John Bothwell

Ballieston. *Born* Glasgow, 8 August, 1981
Featherweight. *Ht* 5'5"
Manager T. Gilmour

17.10.03	Marty Kayes W PTS 6 Glasgow
30.10.03	Colin Moffett DREW 4 Belfast

07.12.03	Ian Reid W PTS 6 Glasgow
06.03.04	Fred Janes DREW 4 Renfrew
08.04.04	Chris Hooper L CO 2 Peterborough
28.05.04	Jason Nesbitt L RSC 3 Glasgow
01.04.05	Michael Crossan L PTS 6 Glasgow
20.05.05	Buster Dennis L RTD 4 Glasgow
14.10.05	Paul Griffin L RSC 1 Dublin
25.03.06	Sandy Bartlett W RSC 2 Irvine
05.06.06	Neil Marston W PTS 6 Glasgow
20.11.06	Jimmy Gilhaney L RSC 1 Glasgow
	(Vacant Scottish Area Featherweight
	Title)
10.09.07	Shaun Walton L PTS 6 Glasgow

Career: 13 contests, won 4, drew 2, lost 7.

Billy Boyle

Sheffield. *Born* Sheffield, 8 July, 1976
Cruiserweight. *Ht* 5'11½"
Manager G. Rhodes

20.04.07	David Ingleby W PTS 4 Sheffield
02.06.07	John Smith W RSC 3 Bristol
16.09.07	James Swindells W RSC 4 Sheffield
19.10.07	Lee Mountford W PTS 6 Doncaster
23.11.07	Clint Johnson W RSC 2 Sheffield
15.02.08	Nick Okoth W PTS 4 Sheffield
28.03.08	Mark Nilsen W RTD 1 Barnsley
21.06.08	Paul Davis W CO 5 Sheffield

Career: 8 contests, won 8.

Ryan Brawley

Irvine. *Born* Irvine, 2 February, 1986
Lightweight. *Ht* 5'10½"
Manager T. Gilmour

19.09.05	Pete Buckley W PTS 6 Glasgow
14.10.05	Lance Verallo W PTS 6 Motherwell
20.02.06	Gavin Deacon W PTS 4 Glasgow
25.03.06	Chris Long W PTS 8 Irvine
06.05.06	Dariusz Snarski W PTS 6 Irvine
28.04.07	Rom Krauklis W PTS 8 Clydebank
11.05.07	Zsolt Jonas W PTS 6 Motherwell
02.11.07	George Watson W PTS 6 Irvine
06.06.08	Jamie McKeever W RSC 7 Glasgow

Career: 9 contests, won 9.

Gordon Brennan

Dunfermline. *Born* Dunfermline, 1 August, 1982
L.Heavyweight. *Ht* 5'11"
Manager T. Gilmour

31.03.06	Jimi Hendricks W PTS 6 Inverurie
11.11.06	Tyrone Wright L PTS 6 Sutton in
	Ashfield
16.02.07	Simon Wood W PTS 4 Kirkcaldy
11.05.07	Leon Owen W PTS 4 Motherwell
14.09.07	Nick Okoth L PTS 4 Kirkcaldy

Career: 5 contests, won 3, lost 2.

Jimmy Briggs

Plymouth. *Born* Fareham, 17 December, 1987
Welterweight. *Ht* 5'8¼"
Manager N. Christian

09.11.07	Ben Wakeham L PTS 6 Plymouth
02.03.08	Lloyd Smith W PTS 6 Portsmouth
05.04.08	Jamie Way L PTS 6 Newport
20.06.08	Bheki Moyo W PTS 6 Plymouth

Career: 4 contests, won 2, lost 2.

Don Broadhurst

Birmingham. *Born* Birmingham, 2 February, 1984
Bantamweight. *Ht* 5'2½"
Manager F. Warren

02.09.06	Delroy Spencer W PTS 4 Bolton
18.11.06	Kemal Plavci W PTS 4 Newport
17.02.07	Ravil Mukhamadiarov W PTS 4
	Wembley
07.04.07	Delroy Spencer W PTS 4 Cardiff
21.07.07	Kakha Toklikishvili W PTS 4 Cardiff
06.10.07	Gary Sheil W PTS 6 Nottingham
08.12.07	Kakhaber Avetisian W RSC 3 Bolton
21.06.08	Alain Bonnel W PTS 6 Birmingham

Career: 8 contests, won 8.

Caine Brodie

London. *Born* Rinteln, Germany, 8 April, 1982
L.Heavyweight. *Ht* 5'11¼"
Manager J. Rooney

08.12.07	Andrei Tolstihs W PTS 4 Belfast

Career: 1 contest, won 1.

Kurt Bromberg

Leeds. *Born* Leeds, 16 January, 1985
Middleweight. *Ht* 5'11¼"
Manager M. Bateson

21.02.08	Jason Smith W PTS 6 Leeds
05.06.08	Gavin Brook W PTS 6 Leeds

Career: 2 contests, won 2.

Gavin Brook

Plymouth. *Born* Plymouth, 24 November, 1984
Middleweight. *Ht* 5'9¼"
Manager N. Christian

05.04.08	James Evans DREW 6 Newport
02.05.08	Kevin Hammond L RTD 1 Nottingham
05.06.08	Kurt Bromberg L PTS 6 Leeds

Career: 3 contests, drew 1, lost 2.

(Ezekiel) Kell Brook

Sheffield. *Born* Sheffield, 3 May, 1986
British Welterweight Champion. *Ht* 5'9"
Manager F. Warren

17.09.04	Pete Buckley W PTS 6 Sheffield
29.10.04	Andy Cosnett W CO 1 Worksop
09.11.04	Lee Williamson W RSC 2 Leeds
10.12.04	Brian Coleman W RSC 1 Sheffield
19.12.04	Karl Taylor W PTS 6 Bolton
04.03.05	Lea Handley W PTS 6 Rotherham
15.05.05	Ernie Smith W PTS 6 Sheffield
09.07.05	Jonathan Whiteman W RSC 2
	Nottingham
10.09.05	Ernie Smith W PTS 4 Cardiff
29.04.06	Ernie Smith W PTS 6 Edinburgh
01.06.06	Geraint Harvey W RSC 3 Barnsley
14.10.06	Duncan Cottier W RSC 3 Manchester
09.12.06	David Kirk W RSC 1 Canning Town
07.04.07	Karl David W RSC 3 Cardiff
06.10.07	Alex Stoda W PTS 6 Nottingham
22.03.08	Darren Gethin W RTD 3 Cardiff
14.06.08	Barrie Jones W RSC 7 Bethnal Green
	(Vacant British Welterweight Title)

Career: 17 contests, won 17.

Scott Brookes

Mexborough. *Born* Rotherham, 16
November, 1987
Cruiserweight. *Ht* 6'2"
Manager D. Hobson

06.10.06 Nicki Taylor W PTS 6 Mexborough
03.05.07 David Ingleby W PTS 6 Sheffield
29.09.07 Hastings Rasani W PTS 4 Sheffield
23.11.07 Carl Wild W PTS 4 Rotherham
Career: 4 contests, won 4.

Stuart Brookes

Mexborough. *Born* Mexborough, 31
August, 1982
Middleweight. Former Undefeated British
Masters L.Middleweight Champion.
Ht 5'9"
Manager Self

15.05.05 Geraint Harvey W PTS 6 Sheffield
24.07.05 Tony Randell W PTS 6 Sheffield
09.09.05 Tony Randell W RSC 3 Sheffield
26.11.05 Howard Clarke W PTS 6 Sheffield
05.03.06 Magic Kidem W RSC 1 Sheffield
06.10.06 Eder Kurti W PTS 6 Mexborough
10.12.06 Jamie Ambler W RSC 1 Sheffield
03.05.07 Lee Noble W PTS 10 Sheffield
    (Vacant British Masters L.Middleweight
    Title)
23.06.07 Taronze Washington W PTS 6 Las
    Vegas, Nevada, USA
23.11.07 Manoocha Salari W PTS 6 Rotherham
22.03.08 Sherman Alleyne W PTS 6 Sheffield
Career: 11 contests, won 11.

Wayne Brooks

Cardiff. *Born* Cardiff, 13 October, 1986
Cruiserweight. *Ht* 6'1"
Manager B. Coleman

13.10.06 Marko Doknic W RSC 3 Aberavon
15.12.06 Simon Wood W RSC 1 Bethnal Green
02.03.07 Nick Okoth DREW 4 Neath
10.06.07 Danny Couzens W PTS 4 Neath
08.12.07 Tony Bellew L CO 3 Bolton
30.03.08 Shon Davies L RSC 7 Port Talbot
    (Vacant Welsh Area L.Heavyweight
    Title)
Career: 6 contests, won 3, drew 1, lost 2.

Darren Broomhall

Alfreton. *Born* Chesterfield, 13 May, 1982
S.Featherweight. *Ht* 6'0¼"
Manager M. Scriven

10.12.04 Craig Bromley W PTS 6 Mansfield
24.04.05 Steve Gethin L CO 5 Derby
18.06.05 Rendall Munroe L RSC 3 Barnsley
22.07.07 Jonathan Whiteman W PTS 6
    Mansfield
08.10.07 Martin Gethin L RSC 3 Birmingham
23.02.08 John Watson L CO 1 Liverpool
Career: 6 contests, won 2, lost 4.

Chris Brophy

Swansea. *Born* Preston, 28 January, 1979
L.Middleweight. *Ht* 5'10"
Manager Self

29.10.03 Aidan Mooney L RSC 5 Leicester
    Square

30.11.03 Casey Brooke W PTS 6 Swansea
21.12.03 Gary O'Connor L PTS 6 Bolton
21.02.04 Tony Doherty L RSC 2 Cardiff
02.04.04 Tommy Marshall DREW 6 Plymouth
26.04.04 Scott Haywood L RSC 5 Cleethorpes
05.06.04 Ashley Theophane L RSC 3 Bethnal
    Green
17.09.04 Tommy Marshall W PTS 6 Plymouth
21.11.04 Jay Morris L RSC 1 Bracknell
31.01.05 George McIlroy L RSC 6 Glasgow
16.09.05 Garry Buckland L PTS 4 Plymouth
24.10.05 Mike Reid L RSC 2 Glasgow
26.02.06 Freddie Luke L PTS 4 Dagenham
11.03.06 Stephen Burke L PTS 4 Newport
08.09.06 Dee Mitchell L RSC 2 Birmingham
03.12.06 Danny Butler L PTS 4 Bristol
16.02.07 Barrie Jones L PTS 4 Merthyr Tydfil
24.02.07 Jimmy Doherty L PTS 6 Stoke
18.03.07 Chris Long DREW 6 Bristol
07.06.07 Patrick Doherty L CO 4 Kensington
15.09.07 Lewis Byrne L CO 5 Bristol
21.10.07 James Lilley L PTS 4 Swansea
02.12.07 Steve Cooper W PTS 6 Bristol
18.02.08 Stuart Elwell L PTS 6 Glasgow
14.03.08 Jonathan Hussey L RSC 6 Manchester
31.05.08 Andrew Alan Lowe L RSC 4 Newark
Career: 26 contests, won 3, drew 2, lost 21.

Nathan Brough

Liverpool. *Born* Liverpool, 18 May, 1984
Welterweight. *Ht* 6'0"
Manager T. Gilmour

08.06.07 Billy Smith W PTS 4 Motherwell
14.09.07 Alex Stoda W DIS 2 Kirkcaldy
01.12.07 Baz Carey W RSC 3 Liverpool
14.03.08 Leonard Lothian W PTS 6 Manchester
09.05.08 Arek Malek W PTS 6 Middlesbrough
Career: 5 contests, won 5.

Barrington Brown

Nottingham. *Born* Nottingham, 11 May,
1982
S.Featherweight. *Ht* 5'7"
Manager J. Gill/T. Harris

06.03.05 Paddy Folan W RSC 6 Shaw
30.09.05 Craig Morgan L PTS 6 Carmarthen
09.10.05 Vinesh Rungea W PTS 6 Hammersmith
18.02.06 Mick Abbott W PTS 6 Stoke
24.04.06 Kevin Townsley L PTS 6 Glasgow
30.05.06 Lloyd Otte W RSC 1 Bethnal Green
30.09.06 Gary Davis DREW 6 Stoke
03.11.06 Danny Wallace L PTS 4 Barnsley
07.03.08 Peter Allen W PTS 4 Nottingham
02.05.08 Dean Mills DREW 4 Nottingham
Career: 10 contests, won 5, drew 2, lost 3.

Paul Brown

Plymouth. *Born* Plymouth, 29 October,
1978
Middleweight. *Ht* 6'0¼"
Manager N. Christian

09.11.07 Jason Smith W PTS 6 Plymouth
29.02.08 Kenroy Lambert W RSC 6 Plymouth
02.05.08 Ollie Newham L RSC 4 Nottingham
Career: 3 contests, won 2, lost 1.

Garry Buckland

Cardiff. *Born* Cardiff, 12 June 1986
Celtic Lightweight Champion. Former

Undefeated Welsh L.Welterweight
Champion. *Ht* 5'7"
Manager B. Powell

05.03.05 Warren Dunkley W PTS 4 Dagenham
24.07.05 Danny Gwilym W RSC 2 Leicester
    Square
16.09.05 Chris Brophy W PTS 4 Plymouth
17.11.05 Bheki Moyo W RSC 3 Bristol
10.02.06 Anthony Christopher W RSC 4
    Plymouth
07.04.06 Judex Meemea W RSC 5 Bristol
14.07.06 Ubadel Soto W PTS 4 Alicante, Spain
15.09.06 Karl Taylor W PTS 6 Newport
10.11.06 Judex Meemea W PTS 6 Newport
03.03.07 Stuart Phillips W PTS 10 Newport
    (Vacant Welsh Area L.Welterweight
    Title)
16.06.07 Carl Allen W PTS 6 Newport
05.10.07 Martin Watson W PTS 10 Newport
    (Celtic Lightweight Title Challenge)
07.03.08 Alexander Spitjo W RSC 3 Nottingham
05.04.08 Ali Wyatt W PTS 6 Newport
13.06.08 Ben Murphy L PTS 6 Portsmouth
Career: 15 contests, won 14, lost 1.

Kevin Buckley

Chester. *Born* Chester, 20 April, 1986
Lightweight. *Ht* 5'7½"
Manager S. Goodwin

03.03.07 Shaun Walton W PTS 6 Burton
20.04.07 Pete Buckley W PTS 4 Dudley
20.07.07 Tony McQuade W PTS 4
    Wolverhampton
17.11.07 John Baguley W PTS 6 Stoke
01.03.08 Dwayne Hill W PTS 6 Stoke
Career: 5 contests, won 5.

Pete Buckley

Birmingham. *Born* Birmingham, 9 March,
1969
Welterweight. Former Undefeated Midlands
Area S. Featherweight Champion. Former
Midlands Area S. Bantamweight Champion.
Ht 5'8"
Manager Self

04.10.89 Alan Baldwin DREW 6 Stafford
10.10.89 Ronnie Stephenson L PTS 6
    Wolverhampton
30.10.89 Robert Braddock W PTS 6 Birmingham
14.11.89 Neil Leitch W PTS 6 Evesham
22.11.89 Peter Judson W PTS 6 Stafford
11.12.89 Stevie Woods W PTS 6 Bradford
21.12.89 Wayne Taylor W PTS 6 Kings Heath
10.01.90 John O'Meara W PTS 6 Kensington
19.02.90 Ian McGirr L PTS 6 Birmingham
27.02.90 Miguel Matthews DREW 6 Evesham
14.03.90 Ronnie Stephenson DREW 6 Stoke
04.04.90 Ronnie Stephenson L PTS 8 Stafford
23.04.90 Ronnie Stephenson W PTS 6
    Birmingham
30.04.90 Chris Clarkson L PTS 8 Mayfair
17.05.90 Johnny Bredahl L PTS 6 Aars,
    Denmark
04.06.90 Ronnie Stephenson W PTS 8
    Birmingham
28.06.90 Robert Braddock W RSC 5
    Birmingham
01.10.90 Miguel Matthews W PTS 8 Cleethorpes
09.10.90 Miguel Matthews L PTS 8
    Wolverhampton
17.10.90 Tony Smith W PTS 6 Stoke

29.10.90	Miguel Matthews W PTS 8 Birmingham
21.11.90	Drew Docherty L PTS 8 Solihull
10.12.90	Neil Leitch W PTS 8 Birmingham
10.01.91	Duke McKenzie L RSC 5 Wandsworth
18.02.91	Jamie McBride L PTS 8 Glasgow
04.03.91	Brian Robb W RSC 7 Birmingham
26.03.91	Neil Leitch DREW 8 Wolverhampton
01.05.91	Mark Geraghty W PTS 8 Solihull
05.06.91	Brian Robb W PTS 10 Wolverhampton
	(Vacant Midlands Area S. Featherweight Title)
09.09.91	Mike Deveney L PTS 8 Glasgow
24.09.91	Mark Bates W RTD 5 Basildon
29.10.91	John Armour L PTS 6 Kensington
14.11.91	Mike Deveney L PTS 6 Edinburgh
28.11.91	Craig Dermody L PTS 6 Liverpool
19.12.91	Craig Dermody L PTS 6 Oldham
18.01.92	Alan McKay DREW 8 Kensington
20.02.92	Brian Robb W RSC 10 Oakengates
	(Midlands Area S. Featherweight Title Defence)
27.04.92	Drew Docherty L PTS 8 Glasgow
15.05.92	Ruben Condori L PTS 10 Augsburg, Germany
29.05.92	Donnie Hood L PTS 8 Glasgow
07.09.92	Duke McKenzie L RTD 3 Bethnal Green
12.11.92	Prince Naseem Hamed L PTS 6 Liverpool
19.02.93	Harald Geier L PTS 12 Vienna, Austria
	(Vacant WBA Penta-Continental S. Bantamweight Title)
26.04.93	Bradley Stone L PTS 8 Lewisham
18.06.93	Eamonn McAuley L PTS 6 Belfast
01.07.93	Tony Silkstone L PTS 8 York
06.10.93	Jonjo Irwin L PTS 8 Solihull
25.10.93	Drew Docherty L PTS 8 Glasgow
06.11.93	Michael Alldis L PTS 8 Bethnal Green
30.11.93	Barry Jones L PTS 4 Cardiff
19.12.93	Shaun Anderson L PTS 6 Glasgow
22.01.94	Barry Jones L PTS 6 Cardiff
29.01.94	Prince Naseem Hamed L RSC 4 Cardiff
10.03.94	Tony Falcone L PTS 4 Bristol
29.03.94	Conn McMullen W PTS 6 Bethnal Green
05.04.94	Mark Bowers L PTS 6 Bethnal Green
13.04.94	James Murray L PTS 6 Glasgow
06.05.94	Paul Lloyd L RTD 4 Liverpool
03.08.94	Greg Upton L PTS 6 Bristol
26.09.94	John Sillo L PTS 6 Liverpool
05.10.94	Matthew Harris L PTS 6 Wolverhampton
07.11.94	Marlon Ward L PTS 4 Piccadilly
23.11.94	Justin Murphy L PTS 4 Piccadilly
29.11.94	Neil Swain L PTS 4 Cardiff
13.12.94	Michael Brodie L PTS 6 Potters Bar
20.12.94	Michael Alldis L PTS 8 Bethnal Green
10.02.95	Matthew Harris W RSC 6 Birmingham
	(Midlands Area S. Bantamweight Title Challenge)
23.02.95	Paul Ingle L PTS 8 Southwark
20.04.95	John Sillo L PTS 6 Liverpool
27.04.95	Paul Ingle L PTS 8 Bethnal Green
09.05.95	Ady Lewis L PTS 4 Basildon
23.05.95	Spencer Oliver L PTS 4 Potters Bar
01.07.95	Dean Pithie L PTS 4 Kensington
21.09.95	Patrick Mullings L PTS 6 Battersea
29.09.95	Marlon Ward L PTS 4 Bethnal Green
25.10.95	Matthew Harris L PTS 10 Telford
	(Midlands Area S. Bantamweight Title Defence)
08.11.95	Vince Feeney L PTS 8 Bethnal Green
28.11.95	Barry Jones L PTS 6 Cardiff
15.12.95	Patrick Mullings L PTS 4 Bethnal Green
05.02.96	Patrick Mullings L PTS 8 Bexleyheath
09.03.96	Paul Griffin L PTS 4 Millstreet
21.03.96	Colin McMillan L RSC 3 Southwark
14.05.96	Venkatesan Deverajan L PTS 4 Dagenham
29.06.96	Matt Brown W RSC 1 Erith
03.09.96	Vince Feeney L PTS 4 Bethnal Green
28.09.96	Fabrice Benichou L PTS 8 Barking
09.10.96	Gary Marston DREW 8 Stoke
06.11.96	Neil Swain L PTS 4 Tylorstown
29.11.96	Alston Buchanan L PTS 8 Glasgow
22.12.96	Brian Carr L PTS 6 Glasgow
11.01.97	Scott Harrison L PTS 4 Bethnal Green
29.01.97	Carl Allen L PTS 8 Stoke
12.02.97	Ronnie McPhee L PTS 6 Glasgow
25.02.97	Dean Pithie L PTS 4 Sheffield
07.03.97	Jason Booth L PTS 6 Northampton
20.03.97	Thomas Bradley W PTS 6 Newark
08.04.97	Sergei Devakov L PTS 6 Bethnal Green
25.04.97	Matthew Harris L PTS 6 Cleethorpes
08.05.97	Gregorio Medina L RTD 2 Mansfield
13.06.97	Mike Deveney L PTS 6 Paisley
19.07.97	Richard Evatt L PTS 4 Wembley
30.08.97	Michael Brodie L PTS 8 Cheshunt
06.10.97	Brendan Bryce W PTS 6 Piccadilly
20.10.97	Kelton McKenzie L PTS 6 Leicester
20.11.97	Ervine Blake L PTS 8 Solihull
06.12.97	Danny Adams L PTS 4 Wembley
13.12.97	Gary Thornhill L PTS 6 Sheffield
31.01.98	Scott Harrison L PTS 4 Edmonton
05.03.98	Steve Conway L PTS 6 Leeds
18.03.98	Ervine Blake L PTS 8 Stoke
26.03.98	Graham McGrath W RTD 4 Solihull
11.04.98	Salim Medjkoune L PTS 6 Southwark
18.04.98	Tony Mulholland L PTS 4 Manchester
27.04.98	Alston Buchanan L PTS 8 Glasgow
11.05.98	Jason Squire W RTD 2 Leicester
21.05.98	Lee Armstrong L PTS 6 Bradford
06.06.98	Tony Mulholland L PTS 6 Liverpool
14.06.98	Lee Armstrong L PTS 6 Shaw
21.07.98	David Burke L PTS 6 Widnes
05.09.98	Michael Gomez L PTS 6 Telford
17.09.98	Brian Carr L PTS 6 Glasgow
03.10.98	Justin Murphy L PTS 6 Crawley
05.12.98	Lehlohonolo Ledwaba L PTS 8 Bristol
19.12.98	Acelino Freitas L RTD 3 Liverpool
09.02.99	Chris Jickells L PTS 6 Wolverhampton
16.02.99	Franny Hogg L PTS 6 Leeds
26.02.99	Richard Evatt L RSC 5 Coventry
17.04.99	Martin O'Malley L RSC 3 Dublin
29.05.99	Richie Wenton L PTS 6 Halifax
14.06.99	Carl Allen L PTS 6 Birmingham
26.06.99	Paul Halpin L PTS 4 Millwall
15.07.99	Salim Medjkoune L PTS 6 Peterborough
07.08.99	Steve Murray L PTS 6 Dagenham
12.09.99	Kevin Gerowski L PTS 6 Nottingham
20.09.99	Mat Zegan L PTS 6 Peterborough
02.10.99	Jason Cook L PTS 4 Cardiff
09.10.99	Brian Carr L PTS 6 Manchester
19.10.99	Gary Steadman L PTS 4 Bethnal Green
27.10.99	Miguel Matthews W PTS 8 Birmingham
20.11.99	Carl Greaves L PTS 10 Grantham
	(British Masters S. Featherweight Title Challenge)
11.12.99	Gary Thornhill L PTS 6 Liverpool
29.01.00	Bradley Pryce L PTS 4 Manchester
19.02.00	Gavin Rees L PTS 4 Dagenham
29.02.00	Tony Mulholland L PTS 4 Widnes
20.03.00	Carl Greaves L PTS 4 Mansfield
27.03.00	James Rooney L PTS 4 Barnsley
08.04.00	Delroy Pryce L PTS 4 Bethnal Green
17.04.00	Franny Hogg L PTS 4 Glasgow
11.05.00	Craig Spacie L PTS 4 Newark
25.05.00	Jimmy Phelan DREW 6 Hull
19.06.00	Delroy Pryce L PTS 4 Burton
01.07.00	Richard Evatt L PTS 4 Manchester
16.09.00	Lee Meager L PTS 4 Bethnal Green
23.09.00	Gavin Rees L PTS 4 Bethnal Green
02.10.00	Brian Carr L PTS 4 Glasgow
14.10.00	Gareth Jordan L PTS 4 Wembley
13.11.00	Kevin Lear L PTS 6 Bethnal Green
24.11.00	Lee Williamson L PTS 6 Hull
09.12.00	Leo O'Reilly L PTS 4 Southwark
15.01.01	Eddie Nevins L PTS 4 Manchester
23.01.01	David Burke L PTS 4 Crawley
31.01.01	Tony Montana L PTS 6 Piccadilly
19.02.01	Kevin England W PTS 6 Glasgow
12.03.01	Carl Allen L PTS 6 Birmingham
19.03.01	Duncan Armstrong L PTS 6 Glasgow
27.03.01	Carl Allen L PTS 8 Brierley Hill
05.05.01	Danny Hunt L PTS 4 Edmonton
09.06.01	Gary Thornhill L PTS 4 Bethnal Green
21.07.01	Scott Miller L PTS 4 Sheffield
28.07.01	Kevin Lear L PTS 4 Wembley
25.09.01	Ricky Eccleston L PTS 4 Liverpool
07.10.01	Nigel Senior L PTS 6 Wolverhampton
31.10.01	Woody Greenaway L PTS 6 Birmingham
16.11.01	Jimmy Beech L PTS 6 West Bromwich
01.12.01	Chill John L PTS 4 Bethnal Green
09.12.01	Nigel Senior W PTS 6 Shaw
26.01.02	Scott Lawton L PTS 4 Bethnal Green
09.02.02	Sam Gorman L PTS 6 Coventry
23.02.02	Alex Moon L PTS 4 Nottingham
04.03.02	Leo Turner L PTS 6 Bradford
11.03.02	Martin Watson L PTS 4 Glasgow
26.04.02	Scott Lawton L PTS 6 Coventry
10.05.02	Lee Meager L PTS 6 Bethnal Green
08.06.02	Bradley Pryce L RSC 1 Renfrew
20.07.02	Jeff Thomas L PTS 4 Blackpool
23.08.02	Ben Hudson DREW 4 Bethnal Green
06.09.02	Dave Stewart L PTS 6 Bethnal Green
14.09.02	Peter McDonagh L PTS 4 Bethnal Green
20.10.02	James Paisley L PTS 4 Southwark
12.11.02	Martin Hardcastle DREW 6 Leeds
29.11.02	Daniel Thorpe L PTS 6 Hull
09.12.02	Nicky Leech L PTS 6 Nottingham
16.12.02	Joel Viney L PTS 6 Cleethorpes
28.01.03	Billy Corcoran L PTS 6 Nottingham
08.02.03	Colin Toohey L PTS 6 Liverpool
15.02.03	Terry Fletcher L PTS 4 Wembley
22.02.03	Dean Lambert L PTS 4 Huddersfield
05.03.03	Billy Corcoran L PTS 6 Bethnal Green
18.03.03	Nathan Ward L PTS 4 Reading
05.04.03	Baz Carey L PTS 4 Manchester
15.05.03	Mike Harrington W PTS 4 Clevedon
27.05.03	Dave Stewart L PTS 4 Dagenham
07.06.03	Rimell Taylor DREW 6 Coventry
12.07.03	George Telfer L PTS 4 Renfrew
22.07.03	Chas Symonds L PTS 6 Bethnal Green
01.08.03	Jas Malik W PTS 4 Bethnal Green
06.09.03	John Murray L PTS 4 Huddersfield
13.09.03	Isaac Ward L PTS 6 Wakefield
25.09.03	Gary Woolcombe L PTS 6 Bethnal Green
06.10.03	Scott Haywood L PTS 6 Barnsley
20.10.03	Joel Viney W PTS 6 Bradford
29.10.03	David Kehoe L PTS 6 Leicester Square
07.11.03	Femi Fehintola L PTS 6 Sheffield
14.11.03	Dave Stewart L PTS 4 Bethnal Green
21.11.03	Henry Castle L PTS 4 Millwall
28.11.03	Lee Meager L PTS 4 Derby
13.12.03	Derry Matthews L PTS 4 Manchester

21.12.03   Daniel Thorpe L PTS 6 Bolton
16.01.04   Nadeem Siddique L PTS 4 Bradford
16.02.04   Scott Haywood L PTS 6 Scunthorpe
29.02.04   Gary O'Connor L PTS 6 Shaw
03.04.04   Steve Bell L PTS 4 Manchester
16.04.04   Isaac Ward L PTS 6 Hartlepool
23.04.04   Colin Bain L PTS 6 Glasgow
06.05.04   Amir Ali L PTS 4 Barnsley
13.05.04   Lee Beavis L PTS 4 Bethnal Green
04.06.04   Tristan Davies L PTS 6 Dudley
03.07.04   Barrie Jones L PTS 4 Newport
03.09.04   Stefy Bull L PTS 6 Doncaster
10.09.04   Tiger Matthews L PTS 4 Liverpool
17.09.04   Kell Brook L PTS 6 Sheffield
24.09.04   Ceri Hall L PTS 6 Dublin
11.10.04   Darren Johnstone L PTS 6 Glasgow
22.10.04   Jonathan Whiteman L PTS 6 Mansfield
29.10.04   Colin Bain L PTS 4 Renfrew
09.11.04   Tom Hogan L PTS 6 Leeds
21.11.04   Chris McDonagh L PTS 4 Bracknell
10.12.04   Craig Johnson L PTS 6 Mansfield
17.12.04   Steve Mullin L PTS 4 Liverpool
12.02.05   Jay Morris L PTS 6 Portsmouth
21.02.05   Stuart Green L PTS 6 Glasgow
05.03.05   Paul Buckley L PTS 6 Southwark
23.03.05   Ryan Barrett L PTS 6 Leicester Square
09.04.05   Nadeem Siddique L PTS 6 Bradford
25.04.05   Jimmy Gilhaney L PTS 6 Glasgow
14.05.05   James Gorman L PTS 6 Dublin
27.05.05   Alan Temple L PTS 4 Spennymoor
04.06.05   Patrick Hyland L PTS 4 Dublin
25.06.05   Sean Hughes DREW 6 Wakefield
24.07.05   Scott Lawton L PTS 6 Sheffield
03.09.05   Jackson Williams L PTS 6 Norwich
19.09.05   Ryan Brawley L PTS 6 Glasgow
14.10.05   Jimmy Gilhaney L PTS 6 Motherwell
23.11.05   Shane Watson L PTS 6 Mayfair
02.12.05   Billy Corcoran L PTS 4 Nottingham
14.12.05   Stephen Burke L PTS 4 Blackpool
23.01.06   David Appleby L PTS 6 Glasgow
02.02.06   Michael Grant L PTS 4 Holborn
18.02.06   Jimmy Doherty L PTS 6 Stoke
04.03.06   Steve Bell L PTS 4 Manchester
13.03.06   Gary McArthur L PTS 6 Glasgow
25.03.06   Brian Murphy L PTS 6 Irvine
02.04.06   Barry Downes L PTS 6 Shaw
13.04.06   Paul Newby L PTS 6 Leeds
28.04.06   Gary O'Connor L PTS 6 Manchester
06.05.06   Ian Clyde L PTS 6 Stoke
20.05.06   Stephen Haughian L PTS 4 Belfast
09.06.06   Wez Miller L PTS 6 Doncaster
18.06.06   James Brown L PTS 6 Manchester
29.06.06   Rob Hunt L PTS 6 Dudley
10.07.06   Calvin White L PTS 6 Manchester
09.09.06   Stuart Green L PTS 8 Inverurie
18.09.06   Stuart Green L PTS 6 Glasgow
29.09.06   Mitch Prince L PTS 6 Motherwell
03.11.06   Mitch Prince L PTS 6 Glasgow
12.11.06   Danny Harding L PTS 6 Manchester
24.11.06   Adam Kelly L PTS 6 Hull
06.12.06   Daniel Thorpe L PTS 6 Rotherham
19.02.07   Mark Hastie L PTS 6 Glasgow
03.03.07   Wayne Downing L PTS 4 Burton
11.03.07   Shinny Bayaar L PTS 6 Shaw
26.03.07   Charles Paul King L PTS 6 Glasgow
20.04.07   Kevin Buckley L PTS 4 Dudley
28.04.07   Furhan Rafiq L PTS 6 Clydebank
03.06.07   Andrew Ward L PTS 4 Barnsley
24.06.07   Jon Kays L PTS 6 Wigan
23.09.07   Shane Watson L PTS 6 Longford
07.10.07   Darren Askew L PTS 6 Shaw
17.11.07   Chris Goodwin L PTS 4 Stoke
28.11.07   Kim Poulsen L PTS 6 Piccadilly
10.12.07   Leonard Lothian L PTS 6 Leicester
Career: 291 contests, won 31, drew 11, lost 249.

Pete Buckley   Philip Sharkey

(Andrew) Stefy Bull (Bullcroft)

Doncaster. *Born* Doncaster, 10 May, 1977
Central Area Lightweight Champion.
Former Undefeated WBF Inter-Continental
Lightweight Champion. Former Undefeated
Central Area Featherweight Champion.
Ht 5'10"
Manager J. Rushton

30.06.95   Andy Roberts W PTS 4 Doncaster
11.10.95   Michael Edwards W PTS 6 Stoke
18.10.95   Alan Hagan W RSC 1 Batley
28.11.95   Kevin Sheil W PTS 6 Wolverhampton
26.01.96   Robert Grubb W PTS 6 Doncaster
12.09.96   Benny Jones W PTS 6 Doncaster
15.10.96   Kevin Sheil DREW 6 Wolverhampton
24.10.96   Graham McGrath W PTS 6
     Birmingham
17.12.96   Robert Braddock W RSC 4 Doncaster
     (Vacant Central Area Featherweight
     Title)
10.07.97   Carl Greaves W PTS 6 Doncaster
11.10.97   Dean Pithie L RSC 11 Sheffield
     (Vacant WBO Inter-Continental
     S. Featherweight Title)
19.03.98   Chris Lyons W RSC 4 Doncaster
08.04.98   Alex Moon L RSC 3 Liverpool
31.07.99   Jason Dee L RSC 4 Carlisle
09.05.03   Joel Viney W RTD 3 Doncaster
02.06.03   Jason Nesbitt W PTS 6 Cleethorpes
05.09.03   Dave Hinds W PTS 6 Doncaster
20.02.04   Anthony Christopher W PTS 6
     Doncaster
07.05.04   Daniel Thorpe W PTS 10 Doncaster
     (Central Area Lightweight Title
     Challenge)
03.09.04   Pete Buckley W PTS 6 Doncaster
29.10.04   Haroon Din W RSC 2 Doncaster
     (Central Area Lightweight Title
     Defence)
04.02.05   Gwyn Wale W PTS 10 Doncaster
     (Central Area Lightweight Title
     Defence)
11.03.05   Jimmy Beech W PTS 4 Doncaster
20.05.05   Billy Smith W PTS 6 Doncaster
16.09.05   Carl Allen W PTS 10 Doncaster

     (Vacant WBF Inter-Continental
     Lightweight Title)
02.12.05   David Kehoe W PTS 6 Doncaster
03.03.06   Baz Carey W PTS 10 Doncaster
     (WBF Inter-Continental Lightweight
     Title Defence)
09.06.06   Scott Lawton L RSC 8 Doncaster
     (Vacant English Lightweight Title)
13.10.06   Carl Allen W PTS 6 Doncaster
07.04.07   Amir Khan L RSC 3 Cardiff
19.10.07   Kristian Laight W PTS 4 Doncaster
Career: 31 contests, won 25, drew 1, lost 5.

Robert Bunford

Llanelli. *Born* Carmarthen, 28 May, 1982
Featherweight. *Ht* 5'6"
Manager D. Davies

03.11.06   Ross Burkinshaw L CO 1 Barnsley
03.12.06   Robert Nelson L PTS 4 Wakefield
26.01.07   Kris Hughes L PTS 6 Glasgow
15.09.07   Stephen Russell L PTS 6 Paisley
Career: 4 contests, lost 4.

Stephen Burke

Liverpool. *Born* Liverpool, 18 March, 1979
Welterweight. *Ht* 5'8"
Manager Self

13.05.05   Imad Khamis W RSC 3 Liverpool
14.12.05   Pete Buckley W PTS 4 Blackpool
11.03.06   Chris Brophy W PTS 4 Newport
02.09.06   Billy Smith W PTS 4 Bolton
10.03.07   Daniel Thorpe W PTS 4 Liverpool
11.08.07   Craig Tomes W RSC 1 Liverpool
01.12.07   Billy Smith W PTS 6 Liverpool
Career: 7 contests, won 7.

Ross Burkinshaw

Sheffield. *Born* Sheffield, 10 August, 1986
Bantamweight. *Ht* 5'8"
Manager G. Rhodes

03.11.06   Robert Bunford W CO 1 Barnsley
09.02.07   Delroy Spencer W PTS 4 Leeds
13.07.07   Iordan Vasilev W CO 3 Barnsley
16.09.07   Faycal Messaoudene W PTS 4
     Sheffield
19.10.07   Shaun Doherty DREW 6 Doncaster
15.02.08   Abdul Mougharbel L RSC 2 Sheffield
Career: 6 contests, won 4, drew 1, lost 1.

Paul Burns

Uddingston. *Born* Rutherglen, 5 January, 1983
International Masters Welterweight
Champion. *Ht* 6'2"
Manager T. Gilmour

06.06.05   Terry Carruthers DREW 6 Glasgow
14.10.05   Surinder Sekhon W PTS 6 Motherwell
21.11.05   Malik Khan W RTD 2 Glasgow
13.03.06   David Kehoe W PTS 6 Glasgow
29.09.06   Peter Dunn W PTS 6 Motherwell
20.11.06   Steve Cooper DREW 6 Glasgow
28.04.07   Danny Gwilym W PTS 6 Clydebank
10.09.07   Steve Cooper W PTS 6 Glasgow
21.01.08   Andrew Butlin DREW 6 Glasgow
22.02.08   Matt Scriven W PTS 6 Motherwell
16.05.08   Gavin Tait W PTS 10 Motherwell
     (Vacant International Masters
     Welterweight Title)
Career: 11 contests, won 8, drew 3.

Ricky Burns

Coatbridge. *Born* Bellshill, 13 April, 1983
International Masters S.Featherweight
Champion. *Ht* 5'10"
Manager F. Warren/A. Morrison

20.10.01	Woody Greenaway W PTS 4 Glasgow
15.03.02	Peter Allen W PTS 4 Glasgow
08.06.02	Gary Harrison W RSC 1 Renfrew
06.09.02	Ernie Smith W PTS 6 Glasgow
19.10.02	Neil Murray W RSC 2 Renfrew
08.12.02	No No Junior W PTS 4 Glasgow
08.10.04	Daniel Thorpe W PTS 6 Glasgow
29.10.04	Jeff Thomas W PTS 4 Renfrew
12.12.04	Colin Bain W PTS 6 Glasgow
25.02.05	Graham Earl W PTS 8 Wembley
08.04.05	Buster Dennis W PTS 6 Edinburgh
17.06.05	Haider Ali W PTS 8 Glasgow
23.07.05	Alan Temple W PTS 4 Edinburgh
18.02.06	Alex Arthur L PTS 12 Edinburgh
	(British, Commonwealth & European S.Featherweight Title Challenges)
01.04.06	Adolph Avadja W RSC 5 Bethnal Green
04.11.06	Wladimir Borov W PTS 8 Glasgow
09.02.07	Carl Johanneson L PTS 12 Leeds
	(British S.Featherweight Title Challenge)
15.09.07	Ernie Smith W PTS 6 Paisley
13.10.07	Frederic Bonifai W RSC 5 Bethnal Green
26.10.07	Ben Odamattey W PTS 8 Glasgow
03.11.07	Youssef Al Hamidi W PTS 6 Cardiff
15.12.07	Billy Smith W PTS 6 Edinburgh
22.02.08	Silence Saheed W RSC 3 Motherwell
22.03.08	Billy Smith W PTS 4 Cardiff
17.05.08	Gheorghe Ghiompirica W PTS 10 Glasgow
	(Vacant International Masters S.Featherweight Title)

Career: 25 contests, won 23, lost 2.

Chris Burton

Darlington. *Born* Darlington, 27 February, 1981
Heavyweight. *Ht* 6'5"
Manager Self

02.06.05	David Ingleby W RSC 3 Yarm
03.03.06	Istvan Kecskes W PTS 4 Hartlepool
28.04.06	Istvan Kecskes W PTS 4 Hartlepool
23.06.06	Simon Goodwin W RSC 3 Blackpool
30.09.06	Istvan Kecskes W RSC 5 Middlesbrough
05.12.06	Paul Butlin W RSC 4 Wolverhampton
28.01.07	Chris Woollas W RSC 3 Yarm
06.05.07	Paul King W PTS 4 Darlington
18.11.07	Franklin Egobi W PTS 6 Tooting
08.02.08	Mathew Ellis W RTD 2 Peterlee
09.05.08	Lee Swaby W PTS 8 Middlesbrough

Career: 11 contests, won 11.

Robert Burton

Barnsley. *Born* Barnsley, 1 April, 1971
L.Heavyweight. Former Central Area
L.Middleweight Champion. Former Central
Area Welterweight Champion. *Ht* 5'9"
Manager Self

05.02.01	Gavin Pearson W RSC 3 Bradford
23.02.01	Scott Millar W CO 5 Irvine
20.03.01	Peter Dunn W PTS 6 Leeds
08.05.01	Arv Mittoo W PTS 4 Barnsley
10.06.01	Martyn Bailey DREW 6 Ellesmere Port
08.10.01	Gavin Pearson W RSC 2 Barnsley
16.11.01	Martyn Bailey DREW 4 Preston
24.11.01	Peter Dunn L PTS 6 Wakefield
28.01.02	Peter Dunn W RSC 8 Barnsley
	(Vacant Central Area Welterweight Title)
23.08.02	David Walker L RSC 2 Bethnal Green
19.10.02	John Humphrey L RTD 4 Norwich
09.02.03	Donovan Smillie L PTS 6 Bradford
24.03.03	Andy Halder L PTS 6 Barnsley
31.05.03	David Keir W RSC 9 Barnsley
	(Central Area Welterweight Title Defence)
01.11.03	Scott Dixon L PTS 6 Glasgow
08.12.03	Jed Tytler W PTS 6 Barnsley
10.02.04	Paul Lomax W PTS 6 Barnsley
06.05.04	Matthew Hatton L PTS 10 Barnsley
	(Central Area Welterweight Title Defence)
08.06.04	Lee Murtagh W CO 3 Sheffield
	(Vacant Central Area L.Middleweight Title)
12.11.04	Matthew Hatton L PTS 10 Halifax
	(Central Area L.Middleweight Title Defence)
11.02.05	Paul Smith L CO 1 Manchester
22.04.05	John Marshall L RTD 4 Barnsley
23.07.05	Craig Lynch L PTS 4 Edinburgh
30.09.05	Jonjo Finnegan DREW 4 Burton
22.10.05	Richard Mazurek W PTS 6 Coventry
25.11.05	Matthew Hough L PTS 4 Walsall
12.12.05	Cello Renda L CO 1 Peterborough
11.03.06	Matthew Hall L CO 1 Newport
13.04.06	Donovan Smillie DREW 6 Leeds
29.04.06	Craig Lynch L PTS 4 Edinburgh
01.06.06	Ryan Rowlinson W PTS 4 Barnsley
22.06.06	Jon Ibbotson DREW 6 Sheffield
15.09.06	Daniel Cadman L RSC 5 Muswell Hill
20.10.06	Jon Ibbotson L CO 2 Sheffield
24.11.06	Ricardo Samms L PTS 4 Nottingham
03.12.06	Darren Rhodes L PTS 6 Wakefield
16.03.07	Danny McIntosh L PTS 4 Norwich
15.04.07	Dean Walker W PTS 6 Barnsley
21.09.07	Adie Whitmore L PTS 6 Burton
25.05.08	Craig Denton L RSC 3 Hartlepool

Career: 40 contests, won 13, drew 5, lost 22.

Danny Butler

Bristol. *Born* Bristol, 10 November, 1987
British Masters L.Middleweight Champion.
Ht 5'10½"
Manager T. Woodward

25.02.06	Magic Kidem W PTS 6 Bristol
07.04.06	Tommy Jones W PTS 4 Bristol
21.05.06	Martin Sweeney W PTS 6 Bristol
03.12.06	Chris Brophy W PTS 4 Bristol
24.02.07	Rocky Chakir W PTS 6 Bristol
18.03.07	Pawel Jas W PTS 6 Bristol
01.06.07	Surinder Sekhon W PTS 6 Birmingham
15.09.07	Carl Drake W PTS 6 Bristol
02.12.07	Terry Adams W PTS 10 Bristol
	(Vacant British Masters L.Middleweight Title)
03.02.08	Dave Wakefield W RTD 7 Bristol
	(British Masters L.Middleweight Title Defence)
02.05.08	Jamie Ambler W CO 2 Bristol
	(British Masters L.Middleweight Title Defence)

Career: 11 contests, won 11.

Andrew Butlin

Huddersfield. *Born* Huddersfield, 31
January, 1982
Middleweight. *Ht* 5'10"
Manager Self

12.11.04	Martin Concepcion L RSC 1 Halifax
22.02.07	Steve Cooper W PTS 6 Leeds
14.04.07	Rocky Muscas W PTS 6 Wakefield
21.01.08	Paul Burns DREW 6 Glasgow
22.02.08	David Walker L PTS 6 Bethnal Green
16.03.08	Ben Hudson W PTS 6 Sheffield
24.04.08	Duncan Cottier W PTS 6 Piccadilly
06.06.08	Jamie Coyle L RTD 3 Glasgow

Career: 8 contests, won 4, drew 1, lost 3.

Andrew Butlin   Philip Sharkey

Paul Butlin

Oakham. *Born* Oakham, 16 March, 1976
Heavyweight. *Ht* 6'1½"
Manager Self

05.10.02	Dave Clarke W PTS 4 Coventry
16.11.02	Gary Williams W RSC 1 Coventry
09.12.02	Slick Miller W PTS 6 Nottingham
08.03.03	Dave Clarke W PTS 6 Coventry
19.04.03	Paul Buttery L RSC 3 Liverpool
27.04.04	Ebrima Secka W PTS 6 Leeds
26.09.04	Lee Mountford W PTS 6 Stoke
06.12.04	David Ingleby W CO 5 Leicester
30.04.05	David Ingleby L PTS 6 Coventry
25.06.05	Mal Rice W PTS 4 Melton Mowbray
22.10.05	Jason Callum W PTS 4 Coventry
18.03.06	David Ingleby W PTS 6 Coventry
05.12.06	Chris Burton L RSC 4 Wolverhampton
03.03.07	Luke Simpkin W PTS 4 Burton
12.01.08	Derek Chisora L PTS 4 Bethnal Green
29.02.08	Sebastian Koeber L PTS 6 Alsterdorf, Germany
11.04.08	David Dolan L PTS 3 Bethnal Green
11.04.08	Colin Kenna W RSC 2 Bethnal Green
16.05.08	Paolo Vidoz L CO 2 Turin, Italy

Career: 19 contests, won 12, lost 7.

Lewis Byrne

Cambridge. *Born* Gravesend, 28 December, 1984
L.Middleweight. *Ht* 5'11¼"
Manager D. Currivan

16.06.07	Robbie James L PTS 4 Newport
15.09.07	Chris Brophy W CO 5 Bristol
05.10.07	Jamie Way L PTS 4 Newport
26.10.07	Jack Arnfield L RSC 1 Wigan
01.12.07	Brett Flournoy L RSC 2 Liverpool

Career: 5 contests, won 1, lost 4.

Marc Callaghan   Philip Sharkey

Marc Callaghan

Barking. *Born* Barking, 13 November, 1977
Former English S.Bantamweight
Champion. Former Undefeated Southern
Area S.Bantamweight Champion. *Ht* 5'6"
Manager Self

08.09.98	Kevin Sheil W PTS 4 Bethnal Green
31.10.98	Nicky Wilders W RSC 1 Southend
12.01.99	Nicky Wilders W RTD 2 Bethnal Green
12.03.99	Peter Allen W PTS 4 Bethnal Green
25.05.99	Simon Chambers L RSC 1 Mayfair
16.10.99	Nigel Leake W PTS 4 Bethnal Green
20.12.99	Marc Smith W PTS 4 Bethnal Green
05.02.00	Steve Brook W RSC 2 Bethnal Green
01.04.00	John Barnes W PTS 4 Bethnal Green
19.08.00	Anthony Hanna W PTS 4 Brentwood
09.10.00	Jamie McKeever L PTS 6 Liverpool
04.11.00	Nigel Senior W RSC 4 Bethnal Green
03.03.01	Anthony Hanna W PTS 6 Wembley
26.05.01	Roy Rutherford L RSC 3 Bethnal Green
01.12.01	Nigel Senior L CO 1 Bethnal Green
26.01.02	Richmond Asante W PTS 4 Dagenham
18.03.02	Michael Hunter DREW 6 Crawley
11.05.02	Andrew Ferrans W PTS 6 Dagenham
21.09.02	Steve Gethin W PTS 6 Brentwood
07.12.02	Stevie Quinn L PTS 4 Brentwood
08.03.03	Dazzo Williams L PTS 8 Bethnal Green
05.07.03	Mark Payne L PTS 6 Brentwood
08.05.04	Baz Carey W PTS 6 Dagenham
27.05.04	Steve Gethin W PTS 6 Huddersfield
20.09.04	John Simpson L PTS 8 Glasgow
19.11.04	Michael Hunter L RSC 10 Hartlepool
	(British S.Bantamweight Title Challenge)
16.06.05	Ian Napa W PTS 10 Dagenham
	(Vacant Southern Area S.Bantamweight Title)

18.11.05	Jackson Asiku L RSC 1 Dagenham
	(Vacant Commonwealth Featherweight Title)
03.03.06	Sean Hughes W PTS 10 Hartlepool
	(Vacant English S.Bantamweight Title)
15.12.06	Dariusz Snarski W PTS 4 Bethnal Green
16.03.07	Esham Pickering L PTS 12 Norwich
	(Vacant British S.Bantamweight Title)
12.10.07	Rendall Munroe L RTD 6 Peterlee
	(English S.Bantamweight Title Defence)
16.05.08	Martin Lindsay L PTS 8 Turin, Italy
Career: 33 contests, won 19, drew 1, lost 13.

Phillip Callaghan   Les Clark

Phillip Callaghan

Leeds. *Born* Leeds, 16 May, 1973
L.Heavyweight. *Ht* 5'11"
Manager Self

15.10.06	Paul Davis L RSC 4 Norwich
24.11.06	Rod Anderton L RSC 4 Nottingham
23.02.07	Lee Jones L PTS 4 Birmingham
23.03.07	Rod Anderton DREW 4 Nottingham
20.04.07	Carl Wild L RSC 1 Sheffield
25.09.07	Phil Goodwin L PTS 6 Hull
26.10.07	Martin Murray L RSC 1 Wigan
25.01.08	Eddie McIntosh L PTS 4 Birmingham
Career: 8 contests, drew 1, lost 7.

Joe Calzaghe

Newbridge. *Born* Hammersmith, 23 March, 1972
WBO & WBA S.Middleweight Champion.
Former Undefeated WBC, British & IBF
S.Middleweight Champion. *Ht* 5'11"
Manager Self

01.10.93	Paul Hanlon W RSC 1 Cardiff
10.11.93	Stinger Mason W RSC 1 Watford
16.12.93	Spencer Alton W RSC 2 Newport
22.01.94	Martin Rosamond W RSC 1 Cardiff

01.03.94	Darren Littlewood W RSC 1 Dudley
04.06.94	Karl Barwise W RSC 1 Cardiff
01.10.94	Mark Dawson W RSC 1 Cardiff
30.11.94	Trevor Ambrose W RSC 2 Wolverhampton
14.02.95	Frank Minton W CO 1 Bethnal Green
22.02.95	Bobbi Joe Edwards W PTS 8 Telford
19.05.95	Robert Curry W RSC 1 Southwark
08.07.95	Tyrone Jackson W RSC 4 York
30.09.95	Nick Manners W RSC 4 Basildon
28.10.95	Stephen Wilson W RSC 8 Kensington
	(Vacant British S. Middleweight Title)
13.02.96	Guy Stanford W RSC 1 Cardiff
13.03.96	Anthony Brooks W RSC 2 Wembley
20.04.96	Mark Delaney W RSC 5 Brentwood
	(British S. Middleweight Title Defence)
04.05.96	Warren Stowe W RTD 2 Dagenham
15.05.96	Pat Lawlor W RSC 2 Cardiff
21.01.97	Carlos Christie W CO 2 Bristol
22.03.97	Tyler Hughes W CO 1 Wythenshawe
05.06.97	Luciano Torres W RSC 3 Bristol
11.10.97	Chris Eubank W PTS 12 Sheffield
	(Vacant WBO S. Middleweight Title)
24.01.98	Branco Sobot W RSC 3 Cardiff
	(WBO S. Middleweight Title Defence)
25.04.98	Juan Carlos Gimenez W RTD 9 Cardiff
	(WBO S. Middleweight Title Defence)
13.02.99	Robin Reid W PTS 12 Newcastle
	(WBO S. Middleweight Title Defence)
05.06.99	Rick Thornberry W PTS 12 Cardiff
	(WBO S. Middleweight Title Defence)
29.01.00	David Starie W PTS 12 Manchester
	(WBO S. Middleweight Title Defence)
12.08.00	Omar Sheika W RSC 5 Wembley
	(WBO S.Middleweight Title Defence)
16.12.00	Richie Woodhall W RSC 10 Sheffield
	(WBO S. Middleweight Title Defence)
28.04.01	Mario Veit W RSC 1 Cardiff
	(WBO S. Middleweight Title Defence)
13.10.01	Will McIntyre W RSC 4 Copenhagen, Denmark
	(WBO S. Middleweight Title Defence)
20.04.02	Charles Brewer W PTS 12 Cardiff
	(WBO S. Middleweight Title Defence)
17.08.02	Miguel Jimenez W PTS 12 Cardiff
	(WBO S. Middleweight Title Defence)
14.12.02	Tocker Pudwill W RSC 2 Newcastle
	(WBO S. Middleweight Title Defence)
28.06.03	Byron Mitchell W RSC 2 Cardiff
	(WBO S.Middleweight Title Defence)
21.02.04	Mger Mkrtchian W RSC 7 Cardiff
	(WBO S.Middleweight Title Defence)
22.10.04	Kabary Salem W PTS 12 Edinburgh
	(WBO S.Middleweight Title Defence)
07.05.05	Mario Veit W RSC 6 Braunschweig, Germany
	(WBO S.Middleweight Title Defence)
10.09.05	Evans Ashira W PTS 12 Cardiff *(WBO S.Middleweight Title Defence)*
04.03.06	Jeff Lacy W PTS 12 Manchester *(IBF S.Middleweight Title Challenge. BO S.Middleweight Title Defence)*
14.10.06	Sakio Bika W PTS 12 Manchester *(IBF& WBO S.Middleweight Title Defences)*
07.04.07	Peter Manfredo W RSC 3 Cardiff *(WBO S.Middleweight Title Defence)*
03.11.07	Mikkel Kessler W PTS 12 Cardiff *(WBA & WBC S.Middleweight Title Challenge. WBO S.Middleweight Title Defence)*
19.04.08	Bernard Hopkins W PTS 12 Las Vegas, Nevada, USA
Career: 45 contests, won 45.

Joe Calzaghe   Philip Sharkey

Drew Campbell

Colchester. *Born* Elgin, 30 September, 1980
L.Middleweight. *Ht* 5'9¼"
Manager T. Sims

22.09.07	Kevin Concepcion L PTS 4 Coventry
25.11.07	Rocky Muscus W PTS 6 Colchester
02.12.07	Lee Noble L PTS 6 Oldham
23.02.08	Joe McNally L PTS 4 Liverpool
22.03.08	Gavin Smith L PTS 6 Sheffield
26.04.08	Alex Matvienko L RSC 4 Wigan
20.06.08	Rob Kenney L PTS 4 Wolverhampton

Career: 7 contests, won 1, lost 6.

Drew Campbell   Philip Sharkey

Peter Cannon

Bradford. *Born* Bradford, 20 January, 1981
S.Middleweight. *Ht* 6'1"
Manager C. Aston

20.04.07	Jezz Wilson L RSC 5 Sheffield
29.11.07	Tony Stones DREW 6 Bradford

Career: 2 contests, drew 1, lost 1.

(Barry) Baz Carey

Coventry. *Born* Coventry, 11 March, 1971
L.Welterweight. *Ht* 5'4½"
Manager P. Carpenter

19.12.01	J.J. Moore L PTS 4 Coventry
18.01.02	J.J. Moore DREW 4 Coventry
25.02.02	Chris McDonagh L PTS 6 Slough
19.03.02	Ilias Miah W PTS 6 Slough
21.09.02	Jackson Williams L PTS 6 Norwich
10.10.02	Dean Scott W RSC 2 Stoke
19.10.02	Lee McAllister L PTS 4 Renfrew
21.11.02	Chris Hooper L RTD 3 Hull
22.03.03	Dave Hinds W PTS 6 Coventry
05.04.03	Pete Buckley W PTS 4 Manchester
12.05.03	Matthew Marshall L PTS 6 Southampton
07.06.03	Joel Viney W PTS 6 Coventry
26.07.03	Andrew Ferrans DREW 4 Plymouth
13.09.03	Paul McIlwaine W RTD 2 Coventry
12.10.03	Daniel Thorpe DREW 6 Sheffield
08.11.03	Carl Allen L RSC 2 Coventry
15.03.04	Andrew Ferrans L PTS 10 Glasgow *(Vacant British Masters S.Featherweight Title)*
17.04.04	Michael Kelly L PTS 4 Belfast
26.04.04	Rendall Munroe L PTS 6 Cleethorpes
08.05.04	Marc Callaghan L PTS 6 Dagenham
06.11.04	Daniel Thorpe L PTS 6 Coventry
20.11.04	Dave Hinds W RSC 4 Coventry
17.12.04	Kristian Laight W PTS 6 Coventry
30.04.05	Billy Smith W PTS 6 Coventry
26.05.05	Daniel Thorpe L PTS 6 Mayfair
10.09.05	Amir Khan L PTS 4 Cardiff
24.09.05	Billy Smith NC 5 Coventry
03.12.05	Billy Smith W PTS 6 Coventry
14.12.05	Jeff Thomas W PTS 6 Blackpool
03.03.06	Stefy Bull L PTS 10 Doncaster *(WBF Inter-Continental Lightweight Title Challenge)*
06.05.06	Scott Lawton L PTS 10 Stoke *(Midlands Area Lightweight Title Challenge)*
01.06.06	Martin Gethin L PTS 4 Birmingham

23.07.06	Ryan Barrett L PTS 6 Dagenham
09.10.06	Kristian Laight DREW 6 Bedworth
04.11.06	Barry Hughes L PTS 4 Glasgow
05.12.06	Dean Harrison L PTS 4 Wolverhampton
09.02.07	Chris Pacy L PTS 4 Leeds
23.02.07	Lewis Smith L PTS 6 Manchester
24.03.07	Billy Smith L PTS 10 Coventry *(Vacant Midlands Area L.Welterweight Title)*
13.10.07	Paul Newby L PTS 6 Barnsley
03.11.07	Dave Ryan L PTS 6 Derby
01.12.07	Nathan Brough L RSC 3 Liverpool
22.02.08	Jamie Spence L PTS 4 Bethnal Green
16.03.08	John Watson L PTS 4 Liverpool
29.03.08	Michael Gomez L PTS 6 Glasgow
05.04.08	Steve Bell L PTS 6 Bolton
30.04.08	Rob Hunt L PTS 6 Wolverhampton
17.05.08	Chris Goodwin L PTS 4 Stoke
31.05.08	Amir Unsworth L PTS 4 Newark
20.06.08	Steve Saville L PTS 4 Wolverhampton
27.06.08	Gareth Couch L PTS 4 Bethnal Green

Career: 51 contests, won 11, drew 4, lost 35, no contest 1.

Baz Carey   Philip Sharkey

Kris Carslaw

Paisley. *Born* Paisley, 1 September, 1984
L.Middleweight. *Ht* 5'9¼"
Manager Barry Hughes

15.09.07	Surinder Sekhon W PTS 4 Paisley
17.11.07	David Kehoe W PTS 4 Glasgow
15.12.07	Paul Royston W PTS 4 Edinburgh
29.03.08	Dave Wakefield W PTS 4 Glasgow

Career: 4 contests, won 4.

Henry Castle

Salisbury. *Born* Southampton, 7 February, 1979
Lightweight. *Ht* 5'6¾"
Manager R. Davies/F. Maloney

29.01.01	Jason Nesbitt W CO 6 Peterborough
26.03.01	Eddie Nevins W RSC 2 Peterborough
23.11.01	Jimmy Beech W PTS 4 Bethnal Green
11.03.02	David Lowry W RSC 1 Glasgow
20.04.02	Jason Nesbitt W PTS 4 Cardiff
25.05.02	Jimmy Beech W PTS 4 Portsmouth
17.08.02	Joel Viney W RSC 1 Cardiff
23.11.02	John Mackay L RTD 8 Derby
29.03.03	Jus Wallie L RSC 2 Portsmouth
25.09.03	Mark Alexander W PTS 6 Bethnal Green

95

21.11.03 Pete Buckley W PTS 4 Millwall
20.02.04 Daleboy Rees W RSC 4 Bethnal Green
26.06.05 Karl Taylor W PTS 6 Southampton
04.12.05 Gareth Couch L PTS 6 Portsmouth
24.09.06 Peter Allen W RSC 6 Southampton
03.12.06 Wladimir Borov W RSC 4 Bethnal Green
09.02.07 Carl Allen W RSC 4 Leeds
09.03.07 Ian Wilson L RSC 5 Dagenham
30.11.07 Kevin O'Hara W PTS 8 Newham
01.02.08 Frederic Gosset W PTS 6 Bethnal Green
18.04.08 Ryan Barrett W RSC 3 Bethnal Green
13.06.08 Lee Cook W RSC 5 Portsmouth
Career: 22 contests, won 18, lost 4.

Brock Cato
Dolgellau. *Born* Wrexham, 19 August, 1987
Welterweight. *Ht* 5'10¼"
Manager N. Hodges

30.03.08 Gary Cooper W RSC 2 Port Talbot
02.05.08 Lance Verallo W PTS 6 Bristol
Career: 2 contests, won 2.

(Yuvuzer) Rocky Chakir (Cakir)
Bristol. *Born* Trabzon, Turkey, 12 April, 1982
L.Middleweight. *Ht* 5'7¼"
Manager C. Sanigar

03.11.06 Pawel Jas W PTS 6 Bristol
10.11.06 Steve Anning L PTS 6 Newport
03.12.06 Chris Long L PTS 6 Bristol
24.02.07 Danny Butler L PTS 6 Bristol
23.09.07 Paul Porter W RSC 1 Longford
01.12.07 Lester Walsh W PTS 6 Coventry
25.02.08 Richard Mazurek W RSC 2 Birmingham
24.05.08 Jamie Way L PTS 6 Cardiff
Career: 8 contests, won 4, lost 4.

Rocky Chakir   Les Clark

Danny Chamberlain
Chelmsford. *Born* Watford, 6 March, 1982
L.Welterweight. *Ht* 5'11¼"
Manager R. Clark

15.06.08 Karl Taylor W PTS 6 Bethnal Green
Career: 1 contest, won 1

Danny Chamberlain   Philip Sharkey

Derek Chisora
Finchley. *Born* Zimbabwe, 29 December, 1983
Heavyweight. Ht. 6' 1¼"
Manager F. Warren

17.02.07 Istvan Kecskes W RSC 2 Wembley
07.04.07 Tony Booth W PTS 4 Cardiff
13.10.07 Darren Morgan W PTS 4 Bethnal Green
12.01.08 Paul Butlin W PTS 4 Bethnal Green
14.06.08 Sam Sexton W RSC 6 Bethnal Green
Career: 5 contests, won 5.

Charlie Chiverton
Mansfield. *Born* Mansfield, 2 May, 1988
S.Middleweight. *Ht* 5'10"
Manager M. Scriven

22.07.07 Ricky Strike W RSC 1 Mansfield
13.10.07 Davey Jones W PTS 4 Newark
Career: 2 contests, won 2.

Karl Chiverton   Les Clark

Karl Chiverton
Mansfield. *Born* Sutton in Ashfield, 1 March, 1986
Middleweight. *Ht* 5'9¾"
Manager M. Shinfield

18.09.04 Karl Taylor W PTS 6 Newark
10.12.04 Cafu Santos L RSC 4 Mansfield
13.05.06 Mark Wall W PTS 6 Sutton in Ashfield
16.09.06 Tony Randell W PTS 6 Burton
11.11.06 Ernie Smith W PTS 6 Sutton in Ashfield
19.05.07 Peter Dunn W PTS 4 Nottingham
22.07.07 Lance Verallo W PTS 6 Mansfield
26.10.07 Peter Dunn W PTS 6 Birmingham
10.12.07 Sean McKervey W PTS 6 Birmingham
28.03.08 Martin Sweeney W PTS 4 Barnsley
Career: 10 contests, won 9, lost 1.

Marco Cittadini
Glasgow. *Born* Glasgow, 12 September, 1977
L.Welterweight. *Ht* 5'7¾"
Manager R. Bannan

17.06.05 Barrie Jones L RSC 2 Glasgow
22.04.06 Mark Bett DREW 6 Glasgow
21.10.06 Mark Bett L PTS 6 Glasgow
15.09.07 Leonard Lothian DREW 6 Paisley
17.11.07 Daniel Thorpe W PTS 4 Glasgow
Career: 5 contests, won 1, drew 2, lost 2.

Nathan Cleverly
Cefn Forest. *Born* Caerphilly, 17 February, 1987
L.Heavyweight. *Ht* 6'1½"
Manager E. Calzaghe

23.07.05 Ernie Smith W PTS 4 Edinburgh
10.09.05 Darren Gethin W PTS 4 Cardiff
04.12.05 Lance Hall W RSC 3 Telford
04.03.06 Jon Foster W PTS 4 Manchester
01.06.06 Brendan Halford W PTS 4 Barnsley
08.07.06 Mark Phillips W PTS 4 Cardiff
14.10.06 Tony Quigley W RSC 5 Manchester
18.11.06 Varuzhan Davtyan W PTS 4 Newport
07.04.07 Nick Okoth W PTS 8 Cardiff
21.07.07 Ayitey Powers W CO 6 Cardiff
03.11.07 Joey Vegas W PTS 8 Cardiff
19.04.08 Antonio Baker W PTS 8 Las Vegas, Nevada, USA
Career: 12 contests, won 12.

Russ Colley   Philip Sharkey

Russ Colley
Wolverhampton. *Born* Wolverhampton, 9
December, 1983
L.Middleweight. *Ht* 5'9¼"
Manager E. Johnson

| 30.04.08 | Peter Dunn W PTS 4 Wolverhampton |
| 20.06.08 | Ricky Strike W PTS 4 Wolverhampton |

Career: 2 contests, won 2.

Charlie Collins
Bermondsey. *Born* Aldershot, 11 April, 1986
Welterweight. *Ht* 6'0"
Manager B. Baker

18.11.07 Byron Vince L RSC 3 Tooting
Career: 1 contest, lost 1.

Richard Collins
Brierley Hill. *Born* Wordsley, 29 November, 1985
L.Heavyweight. *Ht* 6'3"
Manager D. Powell

24.02.07 Justin Jones DREW 6 Stoke
28.06.07 Mark Phillips W PTS 4 Dudley
25.10.07 Dave Pearson W RSC 3 Wolverhampton
21.06.08 James Tucker W PTS 4 Birmingham
Career: 4 contests, won 3, drew 1.

Kevin Concepcion
Leicester. *Born* Leicester, 22 February, 1980
British Masters Middleweight Champion. *Ht* 5'10¾"
Manager P. Carpenter

23.09.06 Ben Hudson W PTS 6 Coventry
09.10.06 Ryan Rowlinson W PTS 6 Bedworth
02.12.06 Rocky Muscas W PTS 6 Coventry
24.03.07 Davey Jones W RSC 1 Coventry
13.05.07 Mark Phillips W PTS 6 Birmingham
22.09.07 Drew Campbell W PTS 4 Coventry
06.10.07 David Kirk W PTS 6 Leicester
01.12.07 Darren Rhodes W RSC 5 Coventry
16.02.08 Michael Banbula W PTS 6 Leicester
28.03.08 Darren Rhodes W CO 4 Barnsley
02.05.08 Billy Smith W PTS 6 Nottingham
28.06.08 Tyan Booth W PTS 10 Leicester
  (Vacant British Masters Middleweight Title)
Career: 12 contests, won 12.

Martin Concepcion
Leicester. *Born* Leicester, 11 August, 1981
Middleweight. *Ht* 5'9"
Manager F. Warren

06.12.03 Danny Gwilym W RSC 2 Cardiff
07.02.04 Jed Tytler W RSC 2 Bethnal Green
27.03.04 Joel Ani W RTD 3 Edinburgh
05.06.04 William Webster W RSC 1 Bethnal Green
30.07.04 Brian Coleman W RSC 1 Bethnal Green
10.09.04 Rob MacDonald W RSC 2 Bethnal Green
12.11.04 Andrew Butlin W RSC 1 Halifax
03.12.04 David Kirk W PTS 4 Edinburgh

11.12.04 Bertrand Souleyras W RSC 1 Canning Town
25.02.05 Craig Lynch W PTS 6 Wembley
03.06.05 Ernie Smith W PTS 4 Manchester
16.07.05 Ivor Bonavic L RSC 2 Bolton
28.01.06 Manoocha Salari L RSC 2 Nottingham
14.10.06 Thomas McDonagh L PTS 6 Manchester
30.03.07 Alfonso Gomez L RSC 7 Newcastle
14.07.07 Matthew Hall W RSC 1 Greenwich
06.10.07 Bradley Pryce L RSC 3 Nottingham
  (Commonwealth L.Middleweight Title Challenge)
21.06.08 Dee Mitchell W PTS 4 Birmingham
Career: 18 contests, won 13, lost 5.

Danny Connors
Chesterfield. *Born* Peterborough, 13 May, 1988
L.Middleweight. *Ht* 6'0"
Manager S. Calow

08.09.07 Paul Royston W PTS 4 Sutton in Ashfield
Career: 1 contest, won 1.

Steve Conway
Dewsbury. *Born* Hartlepool, 6 October, 1977
L.Middleweight. Former IBO L.Middleweight Champion. *Ht* 5'8"
Manager Self

21.02.96 Robert Grubb W PTS 6 Batley
24.04.96 Ervine Blake W PTS 6 Solihull
20.05.96 Chris Lyons W PTS 6 Cleethorpes
30.05.96 Ram Singh W PTS 6 Lincoln
03.02.97 Jason Squire W PTS 6 Leicester
11.04.97 Marc Smith W PTS 4 Barnsley
22.09.97 Arv Mittoo W PTS 6 Cleethorpes
09.10.97 Arv Mittoo W PTS 6 Leeds
01.11.97 Brian Carr L PTS 6 Glasgow
14.11.97 Brendan Bryce W PTS 6 Mere
04.12.97 Kid McAuley W RSC 5 Doncaster
15.12.97 Nicky Wilders W PTS 6 Cleethorpes
05.03.98 Pete Buckley W PTS 6 Leeds
25.04.98 Dean Phillips W PTS 6 Cardiff
09.05.98 Gary Flear W PTS 4 Sheffield
18.05.98 Brian Coleman W PTS 6 Cleethorpes
05.09.98 Benny Jones W PTS 4 Telford
19.12.98 Gary Thornhill L RSC 9 Liverpool
  (WBO Inter-Continental S. Featherweight Title Challenge)
04.06.99 Brian Coleman W PTS 6 Hull
27.09.99 Brian Coleman W PTS 6 Leeds
27.02.00 Chris Price W RTD 3 Leeds
21.03.00 Pedro Miranda L RSC 3 Telde, Gran Canaria
15.07.00 Arv Mittoo W PTS 6 Norwich
20.10.00 Junior Witter L RTD 4 Belfast
25.02.01 Ram Singh W RSC 2 Derby
02.06.01 Jimmy Phelan W PTS 4 Wakefield
18.08.01 Keith Jones W PTS 8 Dewsbury
17.11.01 Carl Allen W PTS 8 Dewsbury
27.04.02 Steve Robinson W PTS 8 Huddersfield
05.10.02 Rakheem Mingaleev W RSC 4 Huddersfield
19.10.02 Alex Arthur L CO 4 Renfrew
  (Vacant British S. Featherweight Title)
05.07.03 Dariusz Snarski W RSC 4 Brentwood
05.10.03 Brian Coleman W PTS 6 Bradford
06.11.03 Yuri Romanov L PTS 8 Dagenham
23.11.03 Gareth Wiltshaw W RSC 5 Rotherham
16.04.04 Norman Dhalie W CO 3 Hartlepool
23.10.04 Ernie Smith W PTS 6 Wakefield

25.09.05 Lee Williamson W PTS 6 Leeds
02.12.05 Mihaly Kotai W PTS 10 Nottingham
03.03.06 Mihaly Kotai W PTS 12 Hartlepool
  (IBO L.Middleweight Title Challenge)
03.06.06 Attila Kovacs L PTS 12 Szolnok, Hungary
  (IBO L.Middleweight Title Defence)
15.12.06 Grzegorz Proksa L PTS 6 Bethnal Green
10.11.07 Christophe Canclaux L RSC 3 Paris, France
Career: 43 contests, won 34, lost 9.

Lee Cook
Morden. *Born* London, 26 June, 1981
Lightweight. *Ht* 5'8"
Manager Self

24.09.04 Jus Wallie W RSC 2 Bethnal Green
26.11.04 Willie Valentine W PTS 4 Bethnal Green
05.03.05 Billy Smith W PTS 4 Southwark
29.04.05 Eddie Anderson W RSC 2 Southwark
20.05.05 Ian Reid W PTS 4 Southwark
04.11.05 Buster Dennis DREW 4 Bethnal Green
11.02.06 David Kehoe W RTD 2 Bethnal Green
02.04.06 Rakhim Mingaleev W PTS 4 Bethnal Green
09.03.07 Youssef Al Hamidi W PTS 6 Dagenham
15.06.07 Rom Krauklis W PTS 4 Crystal Palace
13.06.08 Henry Castle L RSC 5 Portsmouth
Career: 11 contests, won 9, drew 1, lost 1.

Nicky Cook   Philip Sharkey

Nicky Cook
Dagenham. *Born* Stepney, 13 September, 1979
Featherweight. Former Undefeated British, European & Commonwealth Featherweight Champion. Former Undefeated WBF Inter-Continental S. Featherweight Champion. *Ht* 5'6½"
Manager Self

11.12.98 Sean Grant W CO 1 Cheshunt
26.02.99 Graham McGrath W CO 2 Coventry
27.04.99 Vasil Paskelev W CO 1 Bethnal Green
25.05.99 Wilson Acuna W PTS 4 Mayfair
12.07.99 Igor Sakhatarov W PTS 4 Coventry
20.08.99 Vlado Varhegyi W PTS 4 Bloomsbury
27.11.99 John Barnes W PTS 6 Liverpool
20.12.99 Carl Allen W CO 3 Bethnal Green
10.03.00 Chris Jickells W RSC 1 Bethnal Green
27.05.00 Anthony Hanna W PTS 6 Mayfair
16.06.00 Salem Bouaita W PTS 6 Bloomsbury
04.11.00 Vladimir Borov W RSC 1 Bethnal
  Green
08.12.00 Rakhim Mingaleev W PTS 8 Crystal
  Palace
19.05.01 Foudil Madani W RSC 1 Wembley
28.11.01 Woody Greenaway W RSC 3 Bethnal
  Green
19.12.01 Marcelo Ackermann W RSC 3
  Coventry
  *(Vacant WBF Inter-Continental
  S.Featherweight Title)*
20.04.02 Jackie Gunguluza W RTD 4 Wembley
  *(WBF Inter-Continental
  S.Featherweight Title Defence)*
10.07.02 Andrei Devyataykin W PTS 8
  Wembley
05.10.02 Gary Thornhill W RSC 7 Liverpool
  *(WBF Inter-Continental
  S.Featherweight Title Defence)*
08.02.03 Mishek Kondwani W RSC 12
  Brentford
  *(Vacant Commonwealth Featherweight
  Title)*
31.05.03 David Kiilu W CO 2 Bethnal Green
  *(Commonwealth Featherweight Title
  Defence)*
24.10.03 Anyetei Laryea W PTS 12 Bethnal
  Green
  (Commonwealth Featherweight Title)
20.03.04 Cyril Thomas W CO 9 Wembley
  *(European Featherweight Title
  Challenge)*
08.10.04 Johny Begue W PTS 12 Brentwood
  *(European Featherweight Title
  Defence)*
16.06.05 Dazzo Williams W CO 2 Dagenham
  *(European &Commonwealth
  Featherweight Title Defences. British
  Featherweight Title Challenge)*
24.02.06 Yuri Voronin W PTS 12 Dagenham
  *(European Featherweight Title
  Defence)*
09.12.06 Harry Ramogoadi W PTS 8 Canning
  Town
14.07.07 Steven Luevano L CO 11 Greenwich
  (Vacant WBO Featherweight Title)
02.02.08 Kirkor Kirkorov W RSC 2 Canning
  Town
Career: 29 contests, won 28, lost 1.

Gary Cooper

Bargoed. *Born* Cardiff, 5 November, 1988
Middleweight. *Ht* 5'9¼"
Manager D. Gardiner

01.12.07 Mick Jenno L PTS 4 Liverpool
30.03.08 Brock Cato L RSC 2 Port Talbot
Career: 2 contests, lost 2.

Steve Cooper

Worcester. *Born* Worcester, 19 November,
1977
L.Middleweight. *Ht* 5'8½"
Manager E. Johnson

09.12.02 Darren Goode W CO 3 Birmingham
16.09.06 Dale Miles L PTS 6 Burton
29.09.06 Mark Hastie L PTS 6 Motherwell
09.10.06 Sean McKervey DREW 6 Birmingham
23.10.06 Willie Bilan L PTS 6 Glasgow
07.11.06 Tommy Broadbent L PTS 6 Leeds
20.11.06 Paul Burns DREW 6 Glasgow
11.12.06 Sean McKervey L PTS 6 Birmingham
22.02.07 Andrew Butlin L PTS 6 Leeds
03.03.07 Steve Anning L PTS 6 Newport
10.03.07 Denton Vassell L RSC 2 Liverpool
28.04.07 Andrew Alan Lowe L PTS 6 Newark
12.05.07 Jimmy Doherty L PTS 6 Stoke
25.05.07 Eamonn Goodbrand L PTS 6 Glasgow
03.06.07 Paul Royston W PTS 6 Barnsley
16.06.07 Jamie Way L PTS 6 Newport
10.09.07 Paul Burns L PTS 6 Glasgow
22.09.07 Sean McKervey L PTS 6 Coventry
05.10.07 Robbie James L PTS 6 Newport
13.10.07 Jon Musgrave L PTS 6 Barnsley
21.10.07 Russell Pearce L PTS 4 Swansea
02.12.07 Chris Brophy L PTS 6 Bristol
23.12.07 Chris Johnson L RSC 4 Bolton
31.01.08 Chris Thompson W RSC 2 Piccadilly
21.02.08 Adil Anwar L PTS 6 Leeds
01.03.08 Danny Coyle L PTS 6 Coventry
17.03.08 Steve Williams L PTS 6 Glasgow
10.04.08 Wayne Alwan Arab L PTS 6 Piccadilly
16.05.08 Simon Ivekich DREW 6 Burton
25.05.08 Ryan Ashworth L PTS 6 Hartlepool
15.06.08 Pat McAleese L RSC 4 Bethnal Green
Career: 31 contests, won 3, drew 3, lost 25.

Eddie Corcoran

Neasden. *Born* Manchester, 5 October, 1985
L.Welterweight. *Ht* 5'11½"
Manager J. Eames/F. Warren

09.12.06 David Kehoe W RSC 3 Canning Town
17.02.07 Karl Taylor W PTS 4 Wembley
13.10.07 Billy Smith W PTS 4 Bethnal Green
08.03.08 Johnny Greaves W PTS 4 Greenwich
14.06.08 Dave Wakefield W PTS 6 Bethnal
  Green
Career: 5 contests, won 5.

Dennis Corpe

Nottingham. *Born* Nottingham, 6 May, 1976
L.Middleweight. *Ht* 5'9¾"
Manager M. Scriven

22.10.04 Joe Mitchell L PTS 6 Mansfield
16.09.05 Mark Lloyd L PTS 6 Telford
01.10.05 Tiger Matthews L PTS 4 Wigan
19.05.07 Wayne Downing W PTS 4 Nottingham
20.07.07 Wayne Downing W RSC 3
  Wolverhampton
Career: 5 contests, won 2, lost 3.

Thomas Costello

Chelmsley Wood. *Born* Birmingham, 9
January, 1989
L.Middleweight. *Ht* 5'11"
Manager R. Woodhall

29.04.07 Deniss Sirjatovs W RSC 1 Birmingham
13.07.07 Jason Nesbitt W PTS 4 Birmingham
18.11.07 Duncan Cottier W PTS 4 Birmingham
02.02.08 David Kehoe W RSC 2 Canning Town
05.04.08 David Kirk W PTS 4 Bolton
21.06.08 Duncan Cottier W PTS 4 Birmingham
Career: 6 contests, won 6.

Duncan Cottier   Philip Sharkey

Duncan Cottier

Woodford. *Born* Isleworth, 10 October,
1977
Welterweight. *Ht* 5'7½"
Manager Self

05.03.05 Geraint Harvey W PTS 4 Dagenham
10.04.05 John O'Donnell L PTS 4 Brentwood
28.04.05 Stuart Phillips DREW 4 Clydach
13.05.05 David Burke L PTS 6 Liverpool
20.05.05 Colin McNeil L PTS 6 Glasgow
16.06.05 Robert Lloyd-Taylor L RSC 1 Mayfair
30.10.05 Aaron Balmer L PTS 4 Bethnal Green
19.11.05 Ashley Theophane L PTS 6 Southwark
04.12.05 Shane Watson L PTS 4 Portsmouth
19.12.05 Gilbert Eastman L RTD 3 Longford
28.01.06 Stephen Haughian L PTS 4 Dublin
18.02.06 Paul McCloskey L PTS 6 Edinburgh
26.02.06 Nathan Graham L PTS 4 Dagenham
05.03.06 Jay Morris W RSC 2 Southampton
30.03.06 Jamal Morrison DREW 4 Bloomsbury
06.04.06 Ben Hudson W PTS 4 Piccadilly
22.04.06 Paddy Pollock L PTS 6 Glasgow
12.05.06 John O'Donnell L RTD 3 Bethnal
  Green
08.07.06 Ross Minter L PTS 6 Cardiff
24.09.06 Jay Morris L PTS 4 Southampton
14.10.06 Kell Brook L RSC 3 Manchester
23.11.06 Lewis Smith L PTS 6 Manchester
02.12.06 Joe McCluskey L PTS 6 Coventry
09.12.06 Denton Vassell L PTS 4 Canning Town
17.02.07 Grant Skehill L PTS 4 Wembley
25.02.07 Danny Goode L PTS 6 Southampton
16.03.07 Eamonn Goodbrand L PTS 6 Glasgow
25.03.07 Scott Jordan L PTS 6 Dublin
15.04.07 Curtis Woodhouse L PTS 4 Barnsley
26.04.07 Olufemi Moses L PTS 4 Manchester
11.05.07 Tibor Dudas L PTS 4 Motherwell
01.06.07 JJ Bird L PTS 4 Peterborough
16.06.07 Lee Purdy L PTS 4 Chigwell
28.09.07 Max Maxwell L PTS 6 Birmingham
05.10.07 Peter McDonagh L PTS 4 Bethnal
  Green

13.10.07 Jamie Cox L PTS 4 Bethnal Green
10.11.07 Paul Dyer L PTS 6 Portsmouth
18.11.07 Thomas Costello L PTS 4 Birmingham
08.12.07 Willie Thompson L PTS 4 Belfast
12.01.08 Sam Webb L PTS 4 Bethnal Green
14.03.08 Gary McMillan L PTS 6 Glasgow
28.03.08 Paul Porter DREW 6 Piccadilly
04.04.08 Daniel Herdman L PTS 4 Bethnal Green
24.04.08 Andrew Butlin L PTS 6 Piccadilly
17.05.08 Paddy Pollock L PTS 6 Glasgow
14.06.08 Grant Skehill L PTS 4 Bethnal Green
21.06.08 Thomas Costello L PTS 4 Birmingham
Career: 47 contests, won 3, drew 3, lost 41.

Gareth Couch

High Wycombe. *Born* High Wycombe, 11 September, 1982
L.Welterweight. *Ht* 5'7½"
Manager Self

19.12.04 Oscar Milkitas W PTS 6 Bethnal Green
23.03.05 Ian Reid W RSC 6 Leicester Square
16.06.05 David Pereira W PTS 4 Mayfair
01.07.05 Silence Saheed W PTS 4 Fulham
23.11.05 Kyle Taylor W PTS 6 Mayfair
04.12.05 Henry Castle W PTS 6 Portsmouth
18.03.06 Martino Ciano W PTS 6 Monte Carlo, Monaco
18.10.06 Daniel Thorpe W PTS 4 Bayswater
04.11.06 Tony Jourda W PTS 6 Monte Carlo, Monaco
07.06.07 Rom Krauklis W PTS 8 Kensington
04.04.08 Tom Glover W PTS 6 Bethnal Green
27.06.08 Baz Carey W PTS 4 Bethnal Green
Career: 12 contests, won 12.

Gareth Couch   Philip Sharkey

Jane Couch

Fleetwood. *Born* Fleetwood, 12 August, 1968
L.Welterweight. Former Undefeated Womens IBF Welterweight Champion. Former Undefeated Womens BF Welterweight Champion. Former Undefeated Womens IBF Lightweight Champion. Former Womens BF L.Welterweight Champion. *Ht* 5'7"
Manager T. Woodward

30.10.94 Kalpna Shah W RSC 2 Wigan
29.01.95 Fosteres Joseph W PTS 6 Fleetwood
18.04.95 Jane Johnson W RSC 4 Fleetwood
01.07.95 Julia Shirley W PTS 6 Fleetwood
24.05.96 Sandra Geiger W PTS 10 Copenhagen, Denmark
  (Womens IBF Welterweight Title Challenge)
01.03.97 Andrea Deshong W RSC 7 New Orleans, Louisiana, USA
  (Womens IBF Welterweight Title Defence)
24.08.97 Leah Mellinger W PTS 10 Ledyard, Connecticut, USA
  (Womens IBF Welterweight Title Defence)
24.10.97 Dora Webber L PTS 6 Lula, Mississippi, USA
10.01.98 Dora Webber L PTS 10 Atlantic City, New Jersey, USA
  (Vacant Womens BF L.Welterweight Title)
25.11.98 Simone Lukic W RSC 2 Streatham
20.02.99 Marisch Sjauw W PTS 10 Thornaby
  (Womens IBF Welterweight Title Defence. Vacant Womens BF Welterweight Title)
01.04.99 Heike Noller W PTS 8 Birmingham
31.10.99 Sharon Anyos W PTS 10 Raynes Park
  (Vacant Womens IBF Lightweight Title)
09.03.00 Michelle Straus W RSC 3 Bethnal Green
01.07.00 Galina Gumliska W RSC 6 Southwark
  (Womens IBF Lightweight Title Defence)
19.08.00 Liz Mueller L PTS 6 Mashantucket, Connecticut, USA
16.06.01 Viktoria Oleynikov W PTS 4 Wembley
31.07.01 Shakurah Witherspoon W PTS 4 Montego Bay, Jamaica
16.12.01 Tzanka Karova W RSC 3 Bristol
21.06.02 Sumya Anani L RSC 4 Waco, Texas, USA
  (Vacant Womens IBA L.Welterweight Title)
03.08.02 Borislava Goranova W PTS 6 Blackpool
08.12.02 Borislava Goranova W PTS 10 Bristol
  (Vacant Womens BF L.Welterweight Title)
26.02.03 Borislava Goranova W RSC 7 Bristol
15.05.03 Larisa Berezenko W PTS 8 Clevedon
21.06.03 Lucia Rijker L PTS 8 Los Angeles, California, USA
21.09.03 Brenda Bell-Drexel W PTS 10 Bristol
21.12.03 Brenda Bell-Drexel W PTS 8 Bristol
29.02.04 Borislava Goranova W PTS 6 Bristol
03.04.04 Nathalie Toro L PTS 10 Vise, Belgium
  (Vacant Womens European L.Welterweight Title)

12.06.04 Jaime Clampitt W PTS 10 Mashantucket, Connecticut, USA
  (Womens BF L.Welterweight Title Defence)
02.12.04 Larisa Berezenko W PTS 6 Bristol
21.07.05 Jessica Rakoczy L RSC 6 Lemoore, California, USA
  (Vacant Womens WBC Lightweight Title. Womens IBA Lightweight Title Challenge)
12.11.05 Oksana Chernikova W PTS 6 Bristol
05.12.05 Myriam Lamare L RSC 3 Paris, France
  (Vacant Womens IBF L.Welterweight Title)
25.02.06 Galina Gumliiska W RSC 3 Bristol
06.05.06 Viktoria Oleynik W PTS 6 Birmingham
23.09.06 Holly Holm L PTS 10 Albuquerque, New Mexico, USA
  (Womens IBA L.Welterweight Title Challenge)
20.06.07 Jaime Clampitt L PTS 10 Mashantucket, Connecticut, USA
  (Vacant Womens IBF L.Welterweight Title)
08.12.07 Anne Sophie Mathis L RSC 2 Le Cannet, France
Career: 39 contests, won 28, lost 11.

Danny Couzens

Titchfield. *Born* Portsmouth, 29 August, 1984
Cruiserweight. *Ht* 6'0¾"
Manager J. Bishop

24.09.06 Csaba Andras L PTS 6 Southampton
10.06.07 Wayne Brooks L PTS 4 Neath
10.11.07 Shpetim Hoti W PTS 6 Portsmouth
02.03.08 Michael Banbula W PTS 6 Portsmouth
Career: 4 contests, won 2, lost 2.

Simeon Cover

Worksop. *Born* Clapton, 12 March, 1978
S.Middleweight. Former British Masters S.Middleweight Champion. *Ht* 5'11"
Manager D. Ingle

28.03.01 Danny Smith L PTS 6 Piccadilly
18.08.01 Rob Stevenson W PTS 6 Dewsbury
24.09.01 Colin McCash L PTS 6 Cleethorpes
01.11.01 Rob Stevenson L PTS 6 Hull
16.11.01 Jon O'Brien L PTS 6 Dublin
24.11.01 Darren Rhodes L RSC 5 Wakefield
31.01.02 Shpetim Hoti W PTS 6 Piccadilly
13.04.02 Earl Ling L CO 4 Norwich
13.05.02 Roddy Doran DREW 8 Birmingham
02.06.02 Gary Dixon W PTS 6 Shaw
03.08.02 Mike Duffield W RSC 2 Derby
14.09.02 Ivan Botton L PTS 6 Newark
05.12.02 Mark Brookes L RSC 3 Sheffield
15.02.03 Peter Jackson W RSC 2 Wolverhampton
23.02.03 Roddy Doran L PTS 10 Shrewsbury
  (Vacant British Masters S.Middleweight Title)
22.03.03 Barry Connell L PTS 4 Renfrew
12.04.03 Danny Smith L CO 5 Norwich
08.06.03 Ivan Botton W PTS 6 Nottingham
25.07.03 Steven Spartacus L CO 3 Norwich
  (Vacant British Masters L.Heavyweight Title)
06.10.03 Hamed Jamali L PTS 6 Birmingham
17.10.03 Barry Connell L PTS 6 Glasgow
14.11.03 Terry Morrill W PTS 6 Hull

01.12.03 Clint Johnson L PTS 6 Leeds
15.12.03 Lee Nicholson W RSC 4 Cleethorpes
06.02.04 Mark Brookes L RSC 4 Sheffield
12.03.04 Hastings Rasani L CO 6 Irvine
07.05.04 Dean Cockburn L PTS 6 Doncaster
15.05.04 Gary Thompson W PTS 6 Aberdeen
04.06.04 Danny Norton L RSC 3 Dudley
10.09.04 Matthew Barney L PTS 4 Wembley
05.10.04 Andrew Flute W PTS 4 Dudley
04.11.04 Gary Thompson W PTS 6 Piccadilly
13.12.04 Hamed Jamali W PTS 10 Birmingham
(Vacant British Masters S.Middleweight Title)
21.01.05 Jamie Hearn L PTS 4 Brentford
23.03.05 Jamie Hearn W CO 7 Leicester Square
(Vacant British Masters S.Middleweight Title)
30.04.05 Lee Blundell L PTS 10 Wigan
(Vacant British Masters Middleweight Title)
14.05.05 Danny Thornton DREW 6 Aberdeen
03.06.05 Paul Smith L PTS 6 Manchester
20.06.05 Ryan Walls L RSC 8 Longford
16.09.05 Dean Cockburn W PTS 10 Doncaster
(British Masters S.Middleweight Title Defence)
25.09.05 Danny Thornton L PTS 6 Leeds
03.11.05 Ryan Kerr L PTS 10 Sunderland
(English S.Middleweight Title Challenge)
02.02.06 Jimi Hendricks W PTS 4 Holborn
26.02.06 JJ Ojuederie L PTS 4 Dagenham
30.03.06 Joey Vegas L PTS 10 Piccadilly
(British Masters S.Middleweight Title Defence)
01.06.06 Tony Quigley L PTS 4 Barnsley
16.06.06 Steve McGuire L PTS 6 Liverpool
12.07.06 Joey Vegas L PTS 4 Bethnal Green
15.09.06 Kreshnik Qato L PTS 6 Muswell Hill
06.10.06 Michael Monaghan W PTS 6 Mansfield
28.10.06 Tony Oakey L PTS 6 Bethnal Green
08.12.06 Kreshnik Qato L PTS 10 Dagenham
(Vacant Southern Area S.Middleweight Title)
28.09.07 Neil Tidman L RSC 2 Coventry
09.11.07 Tyrone Wright L PTS 4 Nottingham
02.12.07 Darren Stubbs L PTS 6 Oldham

15.12.07 Kenny Anderson L CO 6 Edinburgh
20.04.08 Darren Stubbs L RTD 7 Shaw
(Vacant British Masters L.Heavyweight Title)
21.06.08 Jon Ibbotson L PTS 6 Sheffield
Career: 58 contests, won 16, drew 2, lost 40.

Andy Cox

Cleethorpes. *Born* Grimsby, 22 February, 1986
L.Welterweight. *Ht* 5'11"
Manager D. Coldwell

14.05.07 Amir Nadi W PTS 6 Cleethorpes
25.09.07 Leonard Lothian L PTS 6 Hull
Career: 2 contests, won 1, lost 1.

Jamie Cox

Swindon. *Born* Swindon, 24 August, 1986
Welterweight. *Ht* 5'11"
Manager F. Warren

14.07.07 Johnny Greaves W PTS 4 Greenwich
13.10.07 Duncan Cottier W PTS 4 Bethnal Green
03.11.07 David Kirk W PTS 4 Cardiff
08.12.07 Surinder Sekhon W RSC 3 Bolton
22.03.08 David Kehoe W RSC 1 Cardiff
21.06.08 Billy Smith W PTS 6 Birmingham
Career: 6 contests, won 6.

Danny Coyle

Atherstone. *Born* Nuneaton, 1 December, 1982
Welterweight. *Ht* 5'9¼"
Manager P. Carpenter

01.03.08 Steve Cooper W PTS 6 Coventry
13.04.08 Craig Tomes W PTS 6 Edgbaston
Career: 2 contests, won 2.

Jamie Coyle

Bannockburn. *Born* Stirling, 24 August, 1976
L. Middleweight. *Ht* 6'0"
Manager T. Gilmour

Jamie Cox

Philip Sharkey

02.06.03 Richard Inquieti W RSC 2 Glasgow
20.10.03 Jed Tytler W RSC 2 Glasgow
04.12.03 George Robshaw DREW 6 Huddersfield
28.02.04 Geraint Harvey W PTS 4 Bridgend
22.04.04 Peter Dunn W PTS 6 Glasgow
15.10.04 Terry Adams W RSC 3 Glasgow
17.12.04 Arv Mittoo W RSC 5 Huddersfield
25.04.05 Tony Montana W RSC 3 Glasgow
16.06.05 Michael Lomax L PTS 6 Dagenham
30.09.05 Arek Malek W PTS 6 Kirkcaldy
04.11.05 Arek Malek W PTS 6 Glasgow
17.03.06 Karl David L RSC 1 Kirkcaldy
23.06.06 Ben Hudson W PTS 6 Blackpool
10.11.06 Franny Jones L RSC 2 Hartlepool
23.04.07 Rocky Muscas W PTS 8 Glasgow
08.06.07 Graham Delehedy W RSC 4 Motherwell
24.11.07 Ernie Smith W PTS 6 Clydebank
29.02.08 Tye Williams W RSC 2 Glasgow
28.04.08 Tony Randell W PTS 8 Glasgow
06.06.08 Andrew Butlin W RTD 3 Glasgow
Career: 20 contests, won 16, drew 1, lost 3.

Lloyd Creighton

Darlington. *Born* Darlington, 11 May, 1977
Middleweight. *Ht* 5' 9¼"
Manager M. Marsden

26.04.08 Ricky Strike W PTS 6 Darlington
Career: 1 contest, won 1.

Anthony Crolla

Manchester. *Born* Manchester, 16 November, 1986
Lightweight. *Ht* 5'8¾"
Manager T. Jones/F. Warren

14.10.06 Abdul Rashid W PTS 4 Manchester
09.12.06 Arial Krasnopolski W RSC 3 Canning Town
10.03.07 Rom Krauklis W PTS 4 Liverpool
31.05.07 Neal McQuade W RSC 1 Manchester
06.10.07 Johnny Greaves W RSC 3 Nottingham
08.12.07 Daniel Thorpe W RTD 2 Bolton
19.01.08 Tomasz Kwiecien W CO 5 Dusseldorf, Germany
14.03.08 Steve Gethin W PTS 6 Manchester
05.04.08 Youssef Al Hamidi L PTS 8 Bolton
Career: 9 contests, won 8, lost 1.

Michael Crossan

Glasgow. *Born* Glasgow, 21 June, 1975
Featherweight. *Ht* 5'5¼"
Manager Self

17.10.03 Hussain Nasser W PTS 6 Glasgow
07.12.03 Rocky Dean W PTS 6 Glasgow
23.04.04 Dean Ward W PTS 6 Glasgow
19.06.04 Colin Moffett DREW 4 Renfrew
01.04.05 John Bothwell W PTS 6 Glasgow
17.11.07 Jason Hastie L PTS 4 Glasgow
09.12.07 James Ancliff L RSC 1 Glasgow
Career: 7 contests, won 4, drew 1, lost 2.

Duane Cumberbatch

Manchester. *Born* Manchester, 27 June, 1987
S.Featherweight. *Ht* 5'10¼"
Manager G. Hunter

01.03.08 Paul Economides L PTS 6 Stoke
20.03.08 Billy Bell L PTS 6 South Shields
Career: 2 contests, lost 2.

D

Howard Daley

Preston. *Born* Preston, 4 July, 1976
Heavyweight. *Ht* 6'1¼"
Manager A. Penarski

28.09.07	David Ingleby W PTS 6 Preston
12.10.07	David Dolan L RSC 2 Peterlee
02.12.07	Billy Bessey L PTS 6 Oldham
29.02.08	Ben Harding DREW 4 Plymouth
14.03.08	Tony Booth W RTD 2 Manchester
12.04.08	Mike Perez L RSC 1 Castlebar
13.06.08	Dave Ferguson L PTS 4 Sunderland
21.06.08	Dean O'Loughlin L PTS 6 Hull

Career: 8 contests, won 2, drew 1, lost 5.

Paul David   Les Clark

Paul David

Sheffield. *Born* Northampton, 2 September, 1984
Midlands Area S.Middleweight Champion. *Ht* 6'0½"
Manager J. Ingle

27.02.06	Peter McCormack W RTD 2 Birmingham
17.03.06	Steve McGuire L PTS 6 Kirkcaldy
25.03.06	Duane Reid W RSC 3 Burton
12.05.06	Daniel Cadman W RSC 6 Bethnal Green
23.06.06	Richard Turba W PTS 6 Blackpool
21.10.06	Gary Thompson W PTS 6 Glasgow
03.11.06	Brian Magee L PTS 6 Barnsley
26.01.07	Tony Salam L PTS 4 Dagenham
18.05.07	Peter Haymer W PTS 8 Canning Town
05.10.07	Andrew Lowe W PTS 8 Bethnal Green
09.11.07	Michael Monaghan W PTS 10 Nottingham
	(Vacant Midlands Area S.Middleweight Title)
29.03.08	Ayitey Powers W PTS 6 Aberdeen
10.05.08	Tyrone Wright L PTS 10 Nottingham
	(Midlands Area L.Heavyweight Title Challenge)

Career: 13 contests, won 9, lost 4.

Dai Davies   Les Clark

Dai Davies

Merthyr Tydfil. *Born* Merthyr Tydfil, 20 April, 1983
Welsh S.Featherweight Champion. *Ht* 5'6"
Manager Self

08.07.04	Neil Marston W PTS 6 Birmingham
01.10.04	Riaz Durgahed W PTS 4 Bristol
02.12.04	Martin Lindsay L RSC 1 Crystal Palace
25.02.05	Matthew Marsh L PTS 4 Wembley
16.07.05	Derry Matthews L RSC 2 Bolton
12.12.05	Riaz Durgahed L PTS 6 Peterborough
13.04.06	Gary Sykes L CO 3 Leeds
09.06.06	Jamie McDonnell DREW 4 Doncaster
29.06.06	Jed Syger W PTS 6 Bethnal Green
08.10.06	Henry Jones W PTS 10 Swansea
	(Vacant Welsh Area S.Featherweight Title)
16.02.07	Riaz Durgahed W PTS 8 Merthyr Tydfil
27.04.07	Akaash Bhatia L PTS 4 Wembley
13.07.07	Rendall Munroe L RSC 5 Barnsley
30.03.08	Ricky Owen L CO 5 Port Talbot
13.06.08	Jason Booth L PTS 6 Portsmouth

Career: 15 contests, won 5, drew 1, lost 9.

Sara Davies

Nottingham. *Born* Stockton, 24 August, 1971
L.Middleweight. *Ht* 5'8"
Manager C. Mitchell

31.03.07	Borislava Goranova W PTS 4 Derby
03.11.07	Angel McKenzie W PTS 4 Derby

Career: 2 contests, won 2.

Shon Davies

Llanelli. *Born* Carmarthen, 6 September, 1986
Welsh Area L.Heavyweight Champion. *Ht* 5'1½"
Manager D. Davies

23.07.06	Richard Horton W RSC 1 Dagenham
08.10.06	Mark Phillips W PTS 4 Swansea
26.10.06	Nicki Taylor W RSC 1 Wolverhampton
16.02.07	Jamie Ambler W PTS 6 Merthyr Tydfil
03.03.07	Tyrone Wright L PTS 6 Alfreton
21.10.07	Leon Owen W PTS 6 Swansea
17.11.07	Kenny Anderson L RSC 3 Glasgow

30.03.08	Wayne Brooks W RSC 7 Port Talbot
	(Vacant Welsh Area L.Heavyweight Title)

Career: 8 contests, won 6, lost 2.

Tristan Davies

Telford. *Born* Shrewsbury, 13 October, 1978
Welterweight. Former Undefeated Midlands Area Lightweight Champion. *Ht* 5'10"
Manager E. Johnson

04.06.04	Pete Buckley W PTS 6 Dudley
05.10.04	Gavin Tait W PTS 6 Dudley
17.02.05	Stuart Phillips W PTS 6 Dudley
16.09.05	Karl Taylor W PTS 4 Telford
04.12.05	Jonathan Whiteman W PTS 4 Telford
14.04.06	Kristian Laight W PTS 6 Telford
01.06.06	Carl Allen W PTS 6 Birmingham
09.10.06	Peter Dunn W PTS 6 Birmingham
10.11.06	Carl Allen W PTS 10 Telford
	(Vacant Midlands Area Lightweight Title)
01.04.07	Peter Dunn W PTS 6 Shrewsbury
25.10.07	Billy Smith W PTS 4 Wolverhampton
01.12.07	Graeme Higginson L RSC 5 Telford
	(Vacant British Masters L.Welterweight Title)

Career: 12 contests, won 11, lost 1.

Tristan Davies   Les Clark

Andy Davis

Abercynon. *Born* Aberdare, 28 December, 1985
Featherweight. *Ht* 5'7"
Manager B. Coleman

10.03.06	Shaun Walton W PTS 6 Walsall
28.04.06	Paul Appleby L RSC 1 Hartlepool
15.09.06	Sergei Rozhakmens W RSC 4 Newport
02.12.07	Kallum De'Ath L PTS 4 Oldham

Career: 4 contests, won 2, lost 2.

Gary Davis (Harding)

St Helens. *Born* Liverpool, 17 October, 1982
British Masters S.Bantamweight Champion. Former Undefeated Central Area S.Bantamweight Champion. *Ht* 5'6"
Manager Self

01.06.02	Steve Gethin L RSC 2 Manchester

05.10.02	Jason Thomas W RSC 5 Liverpool
29.11.02	Simon Chambers W RSC 2 Liverpool
15.11.04	Furhan Rafiq W PTS 6 Glasgow
18.09.05	Rocky Dean L RSC 4 Bethnal Green
24.02.06	Chris Hooper W RSC 1 Scarborough

(Vacant Central Area S.Bantamweight Title. Vacant British Masters S.Bantamweight Title)

30.09.06	Barrington Brown DREW 6 Stoke
24.02.07	Abdul Mougharbel W PTS 6 Stoke
15.06.08	Sumaila Badu W RSC 2 St Helens

Career: 9 contests, won 6, drew 1, lost 2.

Paul Davis

Lowestoft. *Born* Dublin, 10 August, 1979
L.Heavyweight. *Ht* 6'1"
Manager G. Everett

15.10.06	Phillip Callaghan W RSC 4 Norwich
16.03.07	Omid Bourzo W RSC 4 Norwich
21.06.08	Billy Boyle L CO 5 Sheffield

Career: 3 contests, won 2, lost 1.

Mark Dawes

Sedgefield. *Born* Stockton, 9 April, 1981
L.Welterweight. *Ht* 5'9"
Manager Self

06.05.07	Peter Dunn W PTS 6 Darlington
09.06.07	Karl Taylor W PTS 6 Middlesbrough
15.07.07	Carl Allen W PTS 6 Hartlepool
23.09.07	Sergei Rozhakmens W PTS 6 Hartlepool

Career: 4 contests, won 4.

Lenny Daws Philip Sharkey

Lenny Daws

Morden. *Born* Carshalton, 29 December, 1978
L.Welterweight. Former British L.Welterweight Champion. Former Undefeated Southern Area L.Welterweight Champion. *Ht* 5'10½"
Manager Self

16.04.03	Danny Gwilym W RSC 2 Nottingham
27.05.03	Ben Hudson W RSC 2 Dagenham
25.07.03	Karl Taylor W RTD 2 Norwich
04.10.03	Ernie Smith W PTS 4 Muswell Hill
28.11.03	Tony Montana W PTS 6 Derby
11.12.03	Keith Jones W PTS 6 Bethnal Green

30.01.04	Denis Alekseev W CO 3 Dagenham
24.09.04	Ernie Smith W PTS 6 Nottingham
12.11.04	Keith Jones W PTS 8 Wembley
10.04.05	Silence Saheed W PTS 6 Brentwood
09.07.05	Ivor Bonavic W PTS 6 Nottingham
28.10.05	Oscar Hall W RTD 7 Hartlepool

(Elim. English L.Welterweight Title)

20.01.06	Colin Lynes W RTD 9 Bethnal Green

(Elim. British L.Welterweight Title. Vacant Southern Area L.Welterweight Title)

12.05.06	Nigel Wright W PTS 12 Bethnal Green

(Vacant British L.Welterweight Title)

20.01.07	Barry Morrison L PTS 12 Muswell Hill

(British L.Welterweight Title Defence)

18.05.07	Billy Smith W PTS 6 Canning Town
14.11.07	Nigel Wright DREW 10 Bethnal Green

(English L.Welterweight Title Challenge)

27.06.08	Mihaita Mutu W PTS 10 Bethnal Green

Career: 18 contests, won 16, drew 1, lost 1.

Gavin Deacon

Northampton. *Born* Northampton, 5 June, 1982
Welterweight. *Ht* 5'9¼"
Manager G. Earl

12.11.05	Colin Bain L PTS 6 Glasgow
12.02.06	Danny Harding L PTS 6 Manchester
20.02.06	Ryan Brawley L PTS 4 Glasgow
03.03.06	Wez Miller L PTS 4 Doncaster
17.03.06	David Appleby L PTS 4 Kirkcaldy
15.10.06	Neal McQuade W PTS 6 Norwich
07.12.06	Tony McQuade DREW 6 Peterborough
14.12.06	Daniel Thorpe L PTS 6 Leicester
23.02.07	Waz Hussain W PTS 4 Birmingham
03.03.07	Deniss Sirjatovs W PTS 4 Alfreton
30.03.07	Neal McQuade W PTS 6 Peterborough
13.04.07	Rendall Munroe L PTS 6 Altrincham
11.05.07	George Watson L PTS 6 Sunderland
08.06.07	Charles Paul King L PTS 4 Motherwell
13.10.07	Andrew Ward W PTS 6 Barnsley
25.11.07	Tom Glover L PTS 6 Colchester
10.12.07	Craig Johnson L PTS 6 Cleethorpes

Career: 17 contests, won 5, drew 1, lost 11.

Robin Deakin Les Clark

Robin Deakin

Crawley. *Born* Crawley, 19 April, 1986
Lightweight. *Ht* 5'8½"
Manager F. Warren

28.10.06	Shaun Walton W PTS 4 Bethnal Green
17.02.07	Rom Krauklis L PTS 4 Wembley
13.10.07	Eddie Hyland L PTS 4 Belfast
02.11.07	Ricky Owen L RSC 2 Irvine
12.01.08	Vinny Mitchell L PTS 4 Bethnal Green
23.02.08	Steve Gethin L PTS 4 Crawley
08.03.08	Ryan Walsh L PTS 4 Greenwich
16.03.08	Josh Wale L PTS 6 Sheffield
29.03.08	Jason Hastie L PTS 4 Glasgow
26.04.08	Jon Kays L PTS 4 Wigan
31.05.08	Patrick Hyland L RSC 5 Belfast

Career: 11 contests, won 1, lost 10.

Rocky Dean Philip Sharkey

Rocky Dean

Thetford. *Born* Bury St Edmonds, 17 June, 1978
Featherweight. Former Southern Area Featherweight Champion. *Ht* 5'5"
Manager Self

14.10.99	Lennie Hodgkins W PTS 6 Bloomsbury
30.10.99	Lennie Hodgkins W PTS 6 Southwark
18.05.00	Danny Lawson W RSC 1 Bethnal Green
29.09.00	Anthony Hanna W PTS 4 Bethnal Green
10.11.00	Chris Jickells L RSC 1 Mayfair
19.04.02	Peter Svendsen W PTS 6 Aarhus, Denmark
19.10.02	Sean Grant W RSC 3 Norwich
21.12.02	Darren Cleary W PTS 4 Millwall
08.02.03	Steve Gethin DREW 4 Norwich
11.07.03	Isaac Ward DREW 4 Darlington
26.07.03	Michael Hunter L RSC 1 Plymouth
10.10.03	Isaac Ward L PTS 6 Darlington
06.11.03	Martin Power L PTS 6 Dagenham
07.12.03	Michael Crossan L PTS 6 Glasgow
24.09.04	Simon Wilson W PTS 4 Millwall
19.12.04	Jim Betts W PTS 8 Bethnal Green
05.03.05	Mickey Coveney W PTS 10 Dagenham

(Vacant Southern Area Featherweight Title)

20.05.05	Andy Morris L PTS 10 Southwark

(Vacant English Featherweight Title)

18.09.05 Gary Davis W RSC 4 Bethnal Green
21.10.05 Andrey Isaev L RSC 12 Kharkov,
Ukraine
*(Vacant WBF Inter-Continental
Featherweight Title)*
26.02.06 Vinesh Rungea W PTS 6 Dagenham
09.12.06 Matthew Marsh L PTS 10 Canning
Town
*(Southern Area Featherweight Title
Defence)*
14.07.07 Matthew Marsh L PTS 10 Greenwich
*(Vacant Southern Area S.Bantamweight
Title)*
01.12.07 Steve Gethin W RSC 5 Bethnal Green
Career: 24 contests, won 13, drew 2, lost 9.

Kallum De'Ath

Manchester. *Born* Manchester, 29 May,
1989
S.Bantamweight. *Ht* 5'9¼"
Manager T. Jones

02.12.07 Andy Davis W PTS 4 Oldham
14.03.08 Delroy Spencer W PTS 6 Manchester
Career: 2 contests, won 2.

Graham Delehedy

Liverpool. *Born* Liverpool, 7 October, 1978
L.Middleweight. *Ht* 5'8"
Manager T. Gilmour

17.05.03 Joel Ani W RSC 4 Liverpool
27.10.03 Rocky Muscus W RSC 2 Glasgow
01.12.03 Gary Cummings W RSC 1 Bradford
27.05.04 Ernie Smith W RSC 3 Huddersfield
08.10.04 David Kehoe W RSC 2 Brentwood
26.11.04 Tony Montana W PTS 6 Altrincham
30.04.05 Cafu Santos W RSC 1 Wigan
23.09.05 Arek Malek W PTS 6 Manchester
28.04.06 Taz Jones L CO 6 Hartlepool
30.03.07 Martin Marshall W CO 2 Crawley
08.06.07 Jamie Coyle L RSC 4 Motherwell
11.08.07 Lee Murtagh L PTS 6 Liverpool
08.10.07 Tony Randell L PTS 10 Glasgow
*(Vacant International Masters
Middleweight Title)*
09.06.08 James Tucker DREW 6 Glasgow
Career: 14 contests, won 9, drew 1, lost 4.

Graham Delehedy Les Clark

(Dennis) Buster Dennis (Mwanze)

Canning Town. *Born* Mawokota, Uganda,
31 December, 1981
Featherweight. *Ht* 5'0"
Manager Self

28.03.03 Vitali Makarov W RSC 2 Millwall
03.04.03 Chris Hooper L RSC 1 Hull
15.05.03 Mark Alexander L PTS 4 Mayfair
24.05.03 Haider Ali L PTS 4 Bethnal Green
21.11.03 Anthony Hanna W PTS 6 Millwall
30.11.03 Daleboy Rees W PTS 6 Swansea
20.02.04 Chris Hooper W RSC 2 Bethnal Green
01.04.04 Kevin O'Hara L PTS 4 Bethnal Green
19.06.04 Riaz Durgahed L PTS 4 Muswell Hill
03.09.04 Jamie Arthur L PTS 6 Newport
10.09.04 Derry Matthews L PTS 6 Liverpool
26.11.04 Eddie Hyland L PTS 4 Altrincham
13.12.04 Matt Teague W PTS 6 Cleethorpes
11.02.05 Andy Morris L PTS 6 Manchester
08.04.05 Ricky Burns L PTS 6 Edinburgh
20.05.05 John Bothwell W RTD 4 Glasgow
03.06.05 Steve Bell DREW 6 Manchester
18.06.05 Musa Njue W RSC 7 Kampala, Uganda
18.09.05 Paul Griffin W PTS 4 Bethnal Green
04.11.05 Lee Cook DREW 4 Bethnal Green
10.12.05 Steve Foster DREW 6 Canning Town
24.03.06 Jadgar Abdulla DREW 4 Bethnal Green
18.10.06 Harry Ramogoadi L RSC 9 Bayswater
*(Vacant British Masters Featherweight
Title)*
16.02.07 Paul Appleby L PTS 8 Kirkcaldy
30.03.07 Martin Lindsay L PTS 6 Crawley
14.03.08 James Ancliff W RSC 3 Glasgow
Career: 26 contests, won 9, drew 4, lost 13.

Craig Denton

Hartlepool. *Born* Hartlepool, 7 April, 1981
Middleweight. *Ht* 6'1"
Manager Self

13.04.07 Jeff Hamilton W PTS 6 Houghton le
Spring
06.05.07 Jon Foster W PTS 6 Darlington
15.07.07 Matt Scriven W PTS 6 Hartlepool
23.09.07 Ernie Smith W PTS 8 Hartlepool
18.11.07 Eder Kurti W PTS 4 Tooting
09.05.08 Ernie Smith W RSC 2 Middlesbrough
25.05.08 Robert Burton W RSC 3 Hartlepool
Career: 7 contests, won 7.

Mark Denton

Hartlepool. *Born* Hartlepool, 5 October, 1982
L.Heavyweight. *Ht* 6'1¼"
Manager D. Garside

25.05.08 Pawel Trebinski W RSC 3 Hartlepool
Career: 1 contest, won 1.

Senol Dervis

Salford. *Born* Hammersmith, 1 February,
1969
L.Welterweight. *Ht* 5'6¼"
Manager O. Harrison

23.11.07 Chris Kitson L PTS 6 Sheffield
16.02.08 Rick Godding L PTS 6 Blackpool
28.02.08 Rob Hunt L PTS 4 Wolverhampton
26.04.08 Tamao Dwyer L RTD 2 Wigan
31.05.08 Eddie O'Rourke L PTS 6 Newark
15.06.08 Stuart McFadyen L PTS 6 St Helens
Career: 6 contests, lost 6.

Senol Dervis Philip Sharkey

Craig Dickson

Glasgow. *Born* Glasgow, 6 March, 1979
L.Middleweight. *Ht* 5'11"
Manager T. Gilmour

21.10.02 Paul Rushton W RSC 2 Glasgow
18.11.02 Ernie Smith W PTS 6 Glasgow
17.02.03 Jon Hilton W RSC 2 Glasgow
14.04.03 Richard Inquieti W PTS 4 Glasgow
20.10.03 Danny Moir W RSC 3 Glasgow
19.01.04 Dean Nicholas W RSC 5 Glasgow
19.04.04 Ernie Smith W PTS 6 Glasgow
30.09.04 Taz Jones DREW 6 Glasgow
15.11.04 Tony Montana W PTS 8 Glasgow
21.03.05 David Keir W RTD 3 Glasgow
30.09.05 Vadzim Astapuk W RSC 4 Kirkcaldy
21.11.05 David Kehoe W PTS 8 Glasgow
20.02.06 Arek Malek W RSC 5 Glasgow
17.03.06 Kevin Anderson L RSC 7 Kirkcaldy
*(Commonwealth Welterweight Title
Challenge)*
01.06.06 Darren Gethin L PTS 6 Birmingham
23.10.06 Martin Marshall W RTD 4 Glasgow
02.12.06 Franny Jones L RSC 6 Clydebank
10.09.07 Darren Gethin W PTS 6 Glasgow
24.11.07 Billy Smith W PTS 6 Clydebank
25.01.08 Michael Lomax L PTS 6 Dagenham
Career: 20 contests, won 15, drew 1, lost 4.

Craig Dickson Philip Sharkey

Carl Dilks

Liverpool. *Born* Liverpool, 29 September, 1983
L.Heavyweight. *Ht* 5'11"
Manager S. Wood

06.05.07	Carl Wild W PTS 6 Altrincham
16.06.07	Carl Wild W PTS 6 Bolton
28.09.07	Michael Banbula W PTS 6 Preston
26.10.07	Lee Nicholson W RSC 4 Wigan
01.12.07	Brian Wood W RSC 1 Liverpool
16.03.08	Dean Walker W PTS 6 Liverpool
15.06.08	Adam Wilcox W RSC 3 St Helens

Career: 7 contests, won 7.

Craig Docherty

Glasgow. *Born* Glasgow, 27 September, 1979
Lightweight. Former Commonwealth S.Featherweight Champion. *Ht* 5'7"
Manager A. Morrison

16.11.98	Kevin Gerowski W PTS 6 Glasgow
22.02.99	Des Gargano W PTS 6 Glasgow
19.04.99	Paul Quarmby W RSC 4 Glasgow
07.06.99	Simon Chambers W PTS 6 Glasgow
20.09.99	John Barnes W PTS 6 Glasgow
15.11.99	Peter Allen W RSC 1 Glasgow
24.01.00	Lee Williamson W PTS 6 Glasgow
19.02.00	Steve Hanley W PTS 6 Prestwick
05.06.00	Sebastian Hart W RSC 1 Glasgow
23.10.00	Lee Armstrong DREW 8 Glasgow
22.01.01	Nigel Senior W RSC 4 Glasgow
20.03.01	Jamie McKeever W RSC 3 Glasgow
11.06.01	Rakhim Mingaleev W PTS 8 Nottingham
27.10.01	Michael Gomez L RSC 2 Manchester *(British S.Featherweight Title Challenge)*
18.03.02	Joel Viney W CO 1 Glasgow
13.07.02	Dariusz Snarski W PTS 6 Coventry
25.01.03	Nikolai Eremeev W PTS 6 Bridgend
12.04.03	Dean Pithie W CO 8 Bethnal Green *(Commonwealth S. Featherweight Title Challenge)*
01.11.03	Abdul Malik Jabir W PTS 12 Glasgow *(Commonwealth S.Featherweight Title Defence)*
22.04.04	Kpakpo Allotey W RSC 6 Glasgow *(Commonwealth S.Featherweight Title Defence)*
15.10.04	Boris Sinitsin L PTS 12 Glasgow *(European S.Featherweight Title Challenge)*
08.04.05	Alex Arthur L CO 9 Edinburgh *(Vacant British S.Featherweight Title. Commonwealth S.Featherweight Title Defence)*
30.09.05	John Mackay W RSC 7 Kirkcaldy
25.05.07	Billy Smith W PTS 6 Glasgow
06.10.07	Lee McAllister L RSC 9 Aberdeen *(Vacant WBU Lightweight Title)*
09.12.07	Silence Saheed W PTS 6 Glasgow
14.03.08	Jay Morris W PTS 6 Glasgow

Career: 27 contests, won 22, drew 1, lost 4.

Tony Dodson

Liverpool. *Born* Liverpool, 2 July, 1980
Former Undefeated British & English S.Middleweight Champion. Former Undefeated Central Area S.Middleweight Champion. Former WBF Inter-Continental S.Middleweight Champion. *Ht* 6'0½"
Manager Self

31.07.99	Michael McDermott W RTD 1 Carlisle
02.10.99	Sean Pritchard W RSC 3 Cardiff
22.01.00	Mark Dawson W PTS 4 Birmingham
11.03.00	Paul Bonson W PTS 4 Kensington
19.08.00	Jimmy Steel W RSC 3 Brentwood
09.09.00	Danny Southam W RSC 2 Manchester
09.10.00	Elvis Michailenko DREW 6 Liverpool
03.02.01	Paul Bonson W PTS 4 Manchester
25.09.01	Paul Wesley W PTS 6 Liverpool
13.10.01	Roman Divisek W CO 1 Budapest, Hungary
10.11.01	Valery Odin W RSC 4 Wembley
10.12.01	Jon Penn W RSC 2 Liverpool *(Vacant Central Area S.Middleweight Title)*
23.02.02	Jason Hart W RSC 2 Nottingham
09.03.02	Varuzhan Davtyan L PTS 6 Manchester
13.04.02	Brian Barbosa W PTS 8 Liverpool
07.09.02	Mike Algoet W PTS 10 Liverpool *(Vacant WBF Inter-Continental S.Middleweight Title)*
26.10.02	Albert Rybacki L RSC 9 Maesteg *(WBF Inter-Continental S.Middleweight Title Defence)*
19.04.03	Pierre Moreno L RSC 9 Liverpool *(Vacant WBF Inter-Continental S.Middleweight Title)*
26.07.03	Varuzhan Davtyan W RTD 3 Plymouth
22.11.03	Allan Foster W RSC 11 Belfast *(Vacant British S.Middleweight Title)*
23.09.05	Varuzhan Davtyan W PTS 4 Manchester
25.11.05	Szabolcs Rimovszky W RSC 3 Liverpool
03.03.06	Dmitry Adamovich W PTS 4 Hartlepool
16.06.06	Jamie Hearn W RSC 4 Liverpool *(Vacant English S.Middleweight Title)*
24.11.06	Carl Froch L CO 3 Nottingham *(British & Commonwealth S.Middleweight Title Challenges)*
06.07.07	Nick Okoth W PTS 4 Wigan
29.09.07	Yuri Tsarenko W PTS 6 Sheffield

Career: 27 contests, won 22, drew 1, lost 4.

Jimmy Doherty

Stoke. *Born* Stafford, 15 August, 1985
L.Middleweight. *Ht* 5'11"
Manager M. Carney

12.11.05	Surinder Sekhon W PTS 6 Stoke
18.02.06	Pete Buckley W PTS 6 Stoke
06.05.06	Jason Nesbitt W PTS 6 Stoke
30.09.06	Aldon Stewart W PTS 6 Stoke
24.02.07	Chris Brophy W PTS 6 Stoke
12.05.07	Steve Cooper W PTS 6 Stoke
17.11.07	Matt Seawright W PTS 4 Stoke
17.05.08	Dale Miles L PTS 6 Stoke

Career: 8 contests, won 7, lost 1.

Shaun Doherty

Bradford. *Born* Bradford, 15 November, 1982
S.Bantamweight. *Ht* 5'7"
Manager C. Aston

23.11.05	Eylon Kedem DREW 6 Mayfair
24.02.06	Neil Marston L PTS 6 Birmingham
27.10.06	Stephen Russell L PTS 6 Glasgow
07.12.06	Anthony Hanna W PTS 6 Bradford

12.05.07	Imran Khan W PTS 6 Stoke
19.10.07	Ross Burkinshaw DREW 6 Doncaster

Career: 6 contests, won 2, drew 2, lost 2.

Tony Doherty   Les Clark

Tony Doherty

Pontypool. *Born* London, 8 April, 1983
Welsh Area Welterweight Champion. Former Celtic Welterweight Champion. *Ht* 5'8"
Manager F. Warren/Brian Hughes

08.05.03	Karl Taylor W PTS 4 Widnes
28.06.03	Paul McIlwaine W RSC 1 Cardiff
13.09.03	Darren Covill W PTS 4 Newport
06.12.03	James Paisley W RSC 3 Cardiff
21.02.04	Chris Brophy W RSC 2 Cardiff
24.04.04	Keith Jones W PTS 6 Reading
22.05.04	Karl Taylor W RTD 2 Widnes
03.07.04	David Kirk W PTS 4 Newport
30.07.04	Ernie Smith W PTS 6 Bethnal Green
03.09.04	Keith Jones W PTS 6 Newport
10.09.04	Peter Dunn W RSC 2 Bethnal Green
19.11.04	Karl Taylor W RSC 2 Bethnal Green
21.01.05	Emmanuel Fleury W RSC 3 Bridgend
22.04.05	Belaid Yahiaoui W PTS 8 Barnsley
16.07.05	Ernie Smith NC 2 Bolton
10.09.05	Taz Jones W PTS 10 Cardiff *(Vacant Celtic Welterweight Title)*
28.01.06	Ernie Smith W PTS 6 Nottingham
13.05.06	Andrzej Butowicz W PTS 6 Bethnal Green
08.07.06	Ihar Filonau W CO 1 Cardiff
18.11.06	Gary O'Connor W PTS 6 Newport
07.04.07	Taz Jones W RSC 7 Cardiff *(Celtic Welterweight Title Defence)*
21.07.07	Kevin McIntyre L PTS 10 Cardiff *(Celtic Welterweight Title Defence)*
22.03.08	Barrie Jones W PTS 10 Cardiff *(Vacant Welsh Area Welterweight Title)*

Career: 23 contests, won 21, lost 1, no contest 1.

David Dolan   Philip Sharkey

David Dolan

Sunderland. *Born* Sunderland, 7 October, 1979
Heavyweight. *Ht* 6'2"
Manager Self

13.05.06	Nabil Haciani W PTS 4 Sheffield
03.11.06	Paul King W PTS 4 Barnsley
13.04.07	Paul King W PTS 4 Houghton le Spring
27.07.07	Luke Simpkin W RSC 6 Houghton le Spring
12.10.07	Howard Daley W RSC 2 Peterlee
23.11.07	Tony Booth W RSC 3 Houghton le Spring
08.02.08	Lee Swaby W PTS 6 Peterlee
11.04.08	Darren Morgan W PTS 3 Bethnal Green
11.04.08	Paul Butlin W PTS 3 Bethnal Green
11.04.08	Martin Rogan L PTS 3 Bethnal Green

Career: 10 contests, won 9, lost 1.

James Dolan

Sunderland. *Born* Sunderland, 14 August, 1977
Heavyweight. *Ht* 6'2½"
Manager D. Hobson

27.07.07	David Ingleby W PTS 4 Houghton le Spring

Career: 1 contest, won 1.

John Donnelly

Croxteth. *Born* Liverpool, 15 July, 1984
Featherweight. *Ht* 5'4½"
Manager T. Gilmour

05.06.07	Shaun Walton W PTS 6 Glasgow
14.09.07	Sergei Rozhakmens W PTS 4 Kirkcaldy

05.11.07	Delroy Spencer W PTS 6 Glasgow
01.12.07	David Keogan W RSC 1 Liverpool
23.02.08	Gheorghe Ghiompirica W PTS 6 Liverpool
14.03.08	Tony McQuade W PTS 6 Manchester
09.05.08	Gavin Reid L CO 4 Middlesbrough
07.06.08	Gheorghe Ghiompirica W PTS 6 Wigan

Career: 8 contests, won 7, lost 1.

Mark Douglas

Wokingham. *Born* Reading, 28 December, 1984
Welterweight. *Ht* 5'9¼"
Manager J. Evans

15.06.08	Nathan Weise W PTS 4 Bethnal Green

Career: 1 contest, won 1.

Wayne Downing

West Bromwich. *Born* Sandwell, 30 December, 1979
L.Middleweight. *Ht* 5'9"
Manager Self

16.02.06	Peter Dunn L PTS 4 Dudley
18.05.06	Malik Khan L RSC 3 Walsall
18.09.06	Tye Williams L RSC 2 Glasgow
17.11.06	Peter Dunn W PTS 6 Brierley Hill
06.12.06	Martin Gordon W PTS 6 Stoke
03.03.07	Pete Buckley W PTS 4 Burton
19.05.07	Dennis Corpe L PTS 4 Nottingham
20.07.07	Dennis Corpe L RSC 3 Wolverhampton
28.11.07	Martin Gordon W PTS 4 Walsall
21.06.08	Curtis Woodhouse L CO 1 Birmingham

Career: 10 contests, won 4, lost 6.

Wayne Downing   Les Clark

Carl Drake

Plymouth. *Born* Plymouth, 22 February, 1975
Western Area L.Middleweight Champion.
Ht 5'8"
Manager J. Evans

02.06.07	Tommy Marshall W RSC 4 Bristol
15.09.07	Danny Butler L PTS 6 Bristol
06.10.07	Simon Fleck DREW 8 Leicester
01.12.07	Ryan Mahoney W PTS 4 Chigwell
29.02.08	Jon Harrison W RSC 7 Plymouth
	(Vacant Western Area L.Middleweight Title)
20.06.08	Taz Jones L RSC 1 Plymouth
	(Vacant International Masters L.Middleweight Title)

Career: 6 contests, won 3, drew 1, lost 2.

Ciaran Duffy

Glasgow. *Born* Donegal, 11 September, 1980
L. Middleweight. *Ht* 5'11"
Manager Self

03.11.01	Wayne Shepherd W PTS 6 Glasgow
03.12.01	Pedro Thompson W PTS 6 Leeds
22.04.02	Richard Inquieti W PTS 6 Glasgow
20.11.02	Gavin Pearson DREW 6 Leeds
17.03.03	Danny Moir W PTS 6 Glasgow
10.12.06	Paddy Pollock L PTS 6 Glasgow
10.02.07	Rocky Muscas W PTS 4 Letterkenny
26.10.07	Martin Sweeney L RSC 4 Glasgow

Career: 8 contests, won 5, drew 1, lost 2

Lee Duncan

Sheffield. *Born* Barnsley, 14 November, 1988
Middleweight. *Ht* 6'1¼"
Manager J. Ingle

10.05.08	Keiron Gray L RSC 3 Nottingham

Career: 1 contest, lost 1.

Peter Dunn

Pontefract. *Born* Doncaster, 15 February, 1975
Middleweight. *Ht* 5'8"
Manager Self

08.12.97	Leigh Daniels W PTS 6 Bradford
15.05.98	Peter Lennon W PTS 6 Nottingham
18.09.98	Jan Cree L RSC 5 Belfast
23.10.98	Bobby Lyndon W PTS 6 Wakefield
03.12.98	Craig Smith L RSC 3 Sunderland
17.03.99	Des Sowden W PTS 6 Kensington
15.05.99	Ray Wood DREW 4 Blackpool
29.05.99	Dean Nicholas L PTS 6 South Shields
01.10.99	Jon Honney L PTS 4 Bethnal Green
18.10.99	Jan Cree W PTS 6 Glasgow
26.11.99	Gavin Pearson DREW 6 Wakefield
18.02.00	John T. Kelly L PTS 6 Pentre Halkyn
11.03.00	Iain Eldridge L RSC 2 Kensington
18.09.00	Joe Miller L PTS 6 Glasgow
26.10.00	Ram Singh W PTS 6 Stoke
27.11.00	Young Muttley L RSC 3 Birmingham
22.02.01	Darren Spencer W PTS 6 Sunderland
03.03.01	Glenn McClarnon L PTS 4 Wembley
20.03.01	Robert Burton L PTS 6 Leeds
08.04.01	Martyn Bailey L PTS 6 Wrexham
17.05.01	Gavin Pearson L PTS 6 Leeds
25.09.01	Darren Spencer L PTS 4 Liverpool
06.10.01	Lee Byrne L RSC 4 Manchester
13.11.01	Richard Inquieti DREW 6 Leeds

24.11.01 Robert Burton W PTS 6 Wakefield
28.01.02 Robert Burton L RSC 8 Barnsley
(Vacant Central Area Welterweight Title)
23.03.02 Colin Lynes L PTS 4 Southwark
19.04.02 Oscar Hall L PTS 6 Darlington
28.05.02 Matt Scriven L PTS 8 Leeds
29.06.02 Darren Bruce L PTS 6 Brentwood
28.09.02 Surinder Sekhon L PTS 6 Wakefield
13.09.03 Wayne Shepherd W PTS 6 Wakefield
20.09.03 Michael Lomax L PTS 6 Nottingham
04.10.03 Andy Gibson L PTS 6 Belfast
25.10.03 Gary Young L PTS 6 Edinburgh
13.12.03 Michael Jennings L PTS 6 Manchester
19.02.04 Young Muttley L PTS 4 Dudley
26.02.04 Matthew Hatton L PTS 6 Widnes
06.03.04 Jason Rushton L PTS 6 Renfrew
10.04.04 Ali Nuumembe L PTS 6 Manchester
22.04.04 Jamie Coyle L PTS 6 Glasgow
06.05.04 Jason Rushton L PTS 4 Barnsley
19.06.04 Chris Saunders L PTS 4 Muswell Hill
03.07.04 Oscar Hall L PTS 6 Blackpool
10.09.04 Tony Doherty L RSC 2 Bethnal Green
09.10.04 Steve Russell W PTS 6 Norwich
23.10.04 Geraint Harvey L PTS 6 Wakefield
11.12.04 Gary Woolcombe L PTS 4 Canning Town
19.12.04 Freddie Luke L PTS 4 Bethnal Green
25.02.05 Chas Symonds L PTS 4 Wembley
07.04.05 Jonjo Finnegan L PTS 6 Birmingham
26.04.05 Tyrone McInerney L RSC 6 Leeds
03.06.05 Oscar Hall L PTS 6 Hull
19.06.05 Gary Woolcombe L RSC 6 Bethnal Green
21.09.05 Danny Moir L PTS 6 Bradford
30.09.05 Paul McInnes L PTS 6 Burton
10.10.05 Joe Mitchell L PTS 6 Birmingham
13.11.05 Khurram Hussain L PTS 4 Leeds
21.11.05 Muhsen Nasser L RSC 4 Glasgow
16.02.06 Wayne Downing W PTS 4 Dudley
23.02.06 Darren Rhodes L PTS 6 Leeds
05.03.06 Muhsen Nasser L PTS 6 Sheffield
30.03.06 Oscar Milkitas L PTS 6 Bloomsbury
14.04.06 Gary Round L PTS 4 Telford
21.04.06 Jason Rushton L PTS 6 Doncaster
29.04.06 Lee McAllister L PTS 6 Edinburgh
09.05.06 Ryan Ashworth L PTS 6 Leeds
18.05.06 Stuart Elwell L PTS 6 Walsall
29.06.06 Marcus Portman L PTS 6 Dudley
18.09.06 Marcus Portman L PTS 6 Glasgow
29.09.06 Paul Burns L PTS 6 Motherwell
09.10.06 Tristan Davies L PTS 6 Birmingham
27.10.06 Lee Noble L PTS 6 Glasgow
04.11.06 Matt Scriven L PTS 6 Mansfield
17.11.06 Wayne Downing L PTS 6 Brierley Hill
24.11.06 Tyan Booth L PTS 4 Nottingham
05.12.06 Rob Kenney DREW 4 Wolverhampton
14.12.06 Simon Fleck L PTS 6 Leicester
22.12.06 Abul Taher L PTS 6 Coventry
01.02.07 Wayne Alwan Arab L PTS 6 Piccadilly
15.02.07 Rob Kenney L PTS 6 Dudley
23.02.07 Max Maxwell L PTS 6 Birmingham
02.03.07 Mark Hastie L PTS 6 Irvine
17.03.07 James McKinley L PTS 6 Birmingham
24.03.07 Sean McKervey L PTS 6 Coventry
01.04.07 Tristan Davies L PTS 6 Shrewsbury
14.04.07 Rob Kenney L PTS 4 Wakefield
06.05.07 Mark Dawes L PTS 6 Darlington
19.05.07 Karl Chiverton L PTS 6 Nottingham
27.05.07 Khurram Hussain L PTS 4 Bradford
03.06.07 Curtis Woodhouse L PTS 4 Barnsley
21.06.07 Clint Smith L PTS 6 Peterborough
30.06.07 Lee Murtagh L PTS 6 Belfast
27.07.07 Muhsen Nasser L PTS 6 Houghton le Spring
08.09.07 Ollie Newham L PTS 6 Sutton in

Ashfield
21.09.07 Duane Parker L PTS 6 Burton
04.10.07 Wayne Alwan Arab L PTS 6 Piccadilly
13.10.07 Willie Thompson L PTS 6 Belfast
26.10.07 Karl Chiverton L PTS 6 Birmingham
03.11.07 Jack Perry L PTS 6 Derby
18.11.07 Dee Mitchell L PTS 6 Birmingham
25.11.07 Chris Johnson L PTS 6 Colne
08.12.07 Damian Taggart L PTS 4 Belfast
26.01.08 Gary O'Sullivan L RSC 6 Cork
02.03.08 Paul Dyer L PTS 6 Portsmouth
17.03.08 Charles Paul King L PTS 6 Glasgow
30.03.08 Paul Royston W PTS 4 Colne
10.04.08 Jimmy Beech L PTS 6 Piccadilly
20.04.08 Dave Murray L PTS 6 Shaw
30.04.08 Russ Colley L PTS 4 Wolverhampton
16.05.08 Duane Parker L PTS 6 Burton
13.06.08 Stuart Kennedy L PTS 6 Sunderland
28.06.08 Joe Hockenhull L PTS 6 Leicester
Career: 113 contests, won 12, drew 4, lost 97.

Peter Dunn   Philip Sharkey

Riaz Durgahed

Bristol. *Born* Mauritius, 4 May, 1977
S.Featherweight. *Ht* 5'6"
Manager Self

29.02.04 Jason Thomas W RSC 1 Bristol
19.06.04 Buster Dennis W PTS 4 Muswell Hill
01.10.04 Dai Davies L PTS 4 Bristol
02.12.04 Lloyd Otte L PTS 6 Crystal Palace
08.04.05 Scott Flynn L PTS 4 Edinburgh
02.06.05 Jason Nesbitt W PTS 6 Peterborough
02.09.05 Rendall Munroe L PTS 6 Derby
16.10.05 Dave Hinds W PTS 6 Peterborough
18.11.05 Lloyd Otte DREW 4 Dagenham
12.12.05 Dai Davies W PTS 6 Peterborough
03.03.06 Jamie McKeever L PTS 6 Hartlepool
15.09.06 Billy Corcoran L CO 3 Muswell Hill
10.11.06 Sean Hughes W PTS 6 Hartlepool
03.12.06 Ryan Barrett L PTS 6 Bethnal Green
16.02.07 Dai Davies L PTS 8 Merthyr Tydfil

20.04.07 Paul Truscott L PTS 4 Dudley
12.10.07 Paul Appleby L RSC 3 Peterlee
30.11.07 Akaash Bhatia L PTS 6 Newham
02.02.08 Ryan Walsh L CO 1 Canning Town
24.05.08 Rob Turley W PTS 6 Cardiff
Career: 20 contests, won 7, drew 1, lost 12.

Tamao Dwyer

Manchester. *Born* Blackburn, 19 September, 1983
Lightweight. *Ht* 5'8¼"
Manager S. Wood

26.04.08 Senol Dervis W RTD 2 Wigan
Career: 1 contest, won 1.

Craig Dyer

Swansea. *Born* Swansea, 23 August, 1986
L.Welterweight. *Ht* 5'7¼"
Manager N. Hodges

21.09.07 Jamie Spence L PTS 6 Peterborough
10.11.07 Darryl Still L PTS 6 Portsmouth
25.01.08 Lee Purdy L RSC 1 Dagenham
30.03.08 Danny Stewart L PTS 4 Port Talbot
Career: 4 contests, lost 4.

Paul Dyer

Portsmouth. *Born* Portsmouth, 11 July, 1970
L.Middleweight. Former Southern Area Welterweight Champion. *Ht* 5'11¼"
Manager J. Bishop

24.09.91 Mike Reed W PTS 6 Basildon
19.11.91 Dave Andrews W PTS 6 Norwich
23.02.93 Kevin Mabbutt L PTS 6 Kettering
17.06.94 Dewi Roberts W PTS 6 Plymouth
27.10.94 George Wilson W PTS 4 Bayswater
25.01.95 John Janes W PTS 6 Cardiff
08.03.95 Anthony Huw Williams W PTS 6 Cardiff
06.05.95 Wahid Fats W PTS 4 Shepton Mallet
15.09.95 Mark Ramsey W PTS 6 Mansfield
16.12.95 Dennis Gardner W RSC 1 Cardiff
26.01.96 Danny Quacoe W PTS 6 Brighton
30.11.96 Mark Winters L PTS 6 Tylorstown
09.12.96 Paul Miles W PTS 6 Bristol
08.02.97 Michael Carruth L PTS 4 Millwall
14.03.97 Harry Dhami L PTS 10 Reading
(Southern Area Welterweight Title Challenge)
24.03.99 Steve Brumant W PTS 4 Bayswater
16.10.99 Neil Sinclair L RSC 8 Belfast
16.05.00 Neil Sinclair L RSC 6 Warrington
01.12.00 Paul Denton W PTS 4 Peterborough
02.02.01 David Baptiste W PTS 10 Portsmouth
(Vacant Southern Area Welterweight Title)
16.03.01 Peter Nightingale W PTS 6 Portsmouth
01.12.01 Paul Knights L PTS 10 Bethnal Green
(Southern Area Welterweight Title Defence)
16.03.02 David Walker L RSC 6 Bethnal Green
(Vacant Southern Area Welterweight Title)
16.09.07 Kenroy Lambert W PTS 6 Southampton
10.11.07 Duncan Cottier W PTS 6 Portsmouth
02.03.08 Peter Dunn W PTS 6 Portsmouth
13.06.08 Sam Webb L PTS 6 Portsmouth
Career: 27 contests, won 18, lost 9.

Graham Earl

Luton. *Born* Luton, 26 August, 1978
Lightweight. Former Undefeated WBU,
British & Commonwealth Lightweight
Champion. Former Undefeated Southern
Area Lightweight Champion. *Ht* 5'5¾"
Manager F. Warren

02.09.97	Mark O'Callaghan W RSC 2 Southwark
06.12.97	Mark McGowan W PTS 4 Wembley
11.04.98	Danny Lutaaya W RSC 2 Southwark
23.05.98	David Kirk W PTS 4 Bethnal Green
12.09.98	Brian Coleman W PTS 4 Bethnal Green
10.12.98	Marc Smith W RSC 1 Barking
16.01.99	Lee Williamson W RSC 4 Bethnal Green
08.05.99	Benny Jones W PTS 6 Bethnal Green
15.07.99	Simon Chambers W CO 6 Peterborough
04.03.00	Ivo Golakov W RSC 1 Peterborough
29.04.00	Marco Fattore W PTS 6 Wembley
21.10.00	Lee Williamson W RSC 3 Wembley
10.03.01	Brian Gentry W RSC 8 Bethnal Green *(Vacant Southern Area Lightweight Title)*
22.09.01	Liam Maltby W CO 1 Bethnal Green *(Southern Area Lightweight Title Defence)*
15.12.01	Mark Winters W PTS 10 Wembley *(Elim. British Lightweight Title)*
12.10.02	Chill John W PTS 10 Bethnal Green *(Southern Area Lightweight Title Defence)*
15.02.03	Steve Murray W RSC 2 Wembley *(Southern Area Lightweight Title Defence. Final Elim. British Lightweight Title)*
24.05.03	Nikolai Eremeev W PTS 8 Bethnal Green
17.07.03	Bobby Vanzie W PTS 12 Dagenham *(British Lightweight Title Challenge)*
11.10.03	Jon Honney W PTS 8 Portsmouth
05.06.04	Bobby Vanzie W PTS 12 Bethnal Green *(Vacant British Lightweight Title)*
30.07.04	Steve Murray W RSC 6 Bethnal Green *(British Lightweight Title Defence)*
25.02.05	Ricky Burns L PTS 8 Wembley
19.06.05	Kevin Bennett W RSC 9 Bethnal Green *(Commonwealth Lightweight Title Challenge. British Lightweight Title Defence)*
27.01.06	Yuri Romanov W PTS 12 Dagenham
28.10.06	Angel Hugo Ramirez W PTS 12 Bethnal Green *(Vacant WBU Lightweight Title)*
17.02.07	Michael Katsidis L RTD 5 Wembley *(Vacant Interim WBO Lightweight Title)*
08.12.07	Amir Khan L RSC 1 Bolton *(Commonwealth Lightweight Title Challenge)*

Career: 28 contests, won 25, lost 3.

Gilbert Eastman

Balham. *Born* Guyana, 16 November, 1972
L.Middleweight. Former Southern Area
L.Middleweight Champion. *Ht* 5'10¼"
Manager Self

22.04.96	Wayne Shepherd W PTS 4 Crystal Palace
09.07.96	Costas Katsantonis W RSC 1 Bethnal Green
11.01.97	Mike Watson W RSC 1 Bethnal Green
25.03.97	Danny Quacoe W RSC 3 Lewisham
30.08.97	Karl Taylor W PTS 4 Cheshunt
08.11.97	Ray Newby W PTS 6 Southwark
14.02.98	Cam Raeside W RSC 5 Southwark
21.04.98	Dennis Berry W RSC 6 Edmonton
23.05.98	Shaun O'Neill W RSC 1 Bethnal Green
12.09.98	Everald Williams W RTD 5 Bethnal Green
21.11.98	Lindon Scarlett W RTD 3 Southwark
06.03.99	Kofi Jantuah L RSC 11 Southwark *(Commonwealth Welterweight Title Challenge)*
25.10.02	Ojay Abrahams W PTS 4 Bethnal Green
21.12.02	Pedro Thompson W RSC 2 Dagenham
05.03.03	Howard Clarke W PTS 6 Bethnal Green
16.04.03	Andrew Facey L RSC 3 Nottingham
25.07.03	Jason Collins W RSC 1 Norwich
04.10.03	Spencer Fearon W RSC 4 Muswell Hill *(Vacant Southern Area L.Middleweight Title)*
28.11.03	Eugenio Monteiro L PTS 8 Derby
30.01.04	Craig Lynch W PTS 6 Dagenham
16.04.04	Delroy Mellis W RSC 5 Bradford *(Southern Area L.Middleweight Title Defence)*
24.09.04	Clive Johnson W PTS 6 Nottingham
19.12.05	Duncan Cottier W RTD 3 Longford
11.03.06	Gary Lockett L RSC 1 Newport *(Vacant WBU Middleweight Title)*
26.05.06	Gary Woolcombe L RSC 7 Bethnal Green *(Southern Area L.Middleweight Title Defence)*
23.02.08	George Katsimpas L PTS 6 Crawley

Career: 26 contests, won 20, lost 6.

Howard Eastman

Battersea. *Born* New Amsterdam, Guyana,
8 December, 1970
Former Undefeated Commonwealth
Middleweight Champion. Former British
Middleweight Champion. Former
Undefeated European, IBO Inter-
Continental, WBA Inter-Continental &
Southern Area Middleweight Champion.
Ht 5'11"
Manager Self

06.03.94	John Rice W RSC 1 Southwark
14.03.94	Andy Peach W PTS 6 Mayfair
22.03.94	Steve Phillips W RSC 5 Bethnal Green
17.10.94	Barry Thorogood W RSC 6 Mayfair
06.03.95	Marty Duke W RSC 1 Mayfair
20.04.95	Stuart Dunn W RSC 2 Mayfair
23.06.95	Peter Vosper W RSC 1 Bethnal Green
16.10.95	Carlo Colarusso W RSC 1 Mayfair
29.11.95	Brendan Ryan W RSC 2 Bethnal Green
31.01.96	Paul Wesley W RSC 1 Birmingham
13.03.96	Steve Goodwin W RSC 5 Wembley
29.04.96	John Duckworth W RSC 5 Mayfair
11.12.96	Sven Hamer W RSC 10 Southwark *(Vacant Southern Area Middleweight Title)*
18.02.97	John Duckworth W CO 7 Cheshunt
25.03.97	Rachid Serdjane W RSC 7 Lewisham
14.02.98	Vitali Kopitko W PTS 8 Southwark
28.03.98	Terry Morrill W RTD 4 Hull
23.05.98	Darren Ashton W RSC 4 Bethnal Green
30.11.98	Steve Foster W RSC 7 Manchester *(Vacant British Middleweight Title)*
04.02.99	Jason Barker W RSC 6 Lewisham
06.03.99	Jon Penn W RSC 3 Southwark *(Vacant IBO Inter-Continental S. Middleweight Title)*
22.05.99	Roman Babaev W RSC 6 Belfast *(WBA Inter-Continental Middleweight Title Challenge)*
10.07.99	Teimouraz Kikelidze W RSC 6 Southwark *(WBA Inter-Continental Middleweight Title Defence)*
13.09.99	Derek Wormald W RSC 3 Bethnal Green *(British Middleweight Title Defence)*
13.11.99	Mike Algoet W RSC 8 Hull *(WBA Inter-Continental Middleweight Title Defence)*
18.01.00	Ojay Abrahams W RSC 2 Mansfield
04.03.00	Viktor Fesetchko W RTD 4 Peterborough
29.04.00	Anthony Ivory W RTD 6 Wembley
25.07.00	Ahmet Dottouev W RTD 5 Southwark *(WBA Inter-Continental Middleweight Title Defence)*
16.09.00	Sam Soliman W PTS 12 Bethnal Green *(Commonwealth Middleweight Title Challenge)*
05.02.01	Mark Baker W RTD 5 Hull
10.04.01	Robert McCracken W RSC 10 Wembley *(British & Commonwealth Middleweight Title Defences. Vacant European Middleweight Title)*
17.11.01	William Joppy L PTS 12 Las Vegas, Nevada, USA *(Vacant WBA Interim Middleweight Title)*
25.10.02	Chardan Ansoula W RSC 1 Bethnal Green
21.12.02	Hussain Osman W RTD 4 Dagenham
28.01.03	Christophe Tendil W RTD 4 Nottingham *(Vacant European Middleweight Title)*
05.03.03	Gary Beardsley W RSC 2 Bethnal Green
16.04.03	Scott Dann W RSC 3 Nottingham *(British, Commonwealth & European Middleweight Title Defences)*
25.07.03	Hacine Cherifi W RTD 8 Norwich *(European Middleweight Title Defence)*
30.01.04	Sergei Tatevosyan W PTS 12 Dagenham *(European Middleweight Title Defence)*
24.09.04	Jerry Elliott W PTS 10 Nottingham
19.02.05	Bernard Hopkins L PTS 12 Los Angeles, California, USA *(WBC, WBA, IBF & WBO Middleweight Title Challenges)*
16.07.05	Arthur Abraham L PTS 12 Nuremburg, Germany *(WBA Inter-Continental Middleweight Title Challenge)*
24.03.06	Edison Miranda L RSC 7 Hollywood, Florida, USA

(Final Elim. IBF Middleweight Title)

15.12.06   Richard Williams W CO 12 Bethnal Green
(Vacant British Middleweight Title)
20.04.07   Evans Ashira W PTS 12 Dudley
(Vacant Commonwealth Middleweight Title)
28.09.07   Wayne Elcock L PTS 12 Coventry
(British Middleweight Title Defence)
08.12.07   John Duddy L PTS 10 Belfast
Career: 48 contests, won 42, lost 6.

Paul Economides

Connah's Quay. *Born* Chester, 19 November, 1986
S.Bantamweight. *Ht* 5'5¼"
Manager S. Goodwin

01.03.08   Duane Cumberbatch W PTS 6 Stoke
17.05.08   Delroy Spencer W PTS 6 Stoke
Career: 2 contests, won 2.

Steve Ede   Les Clark

Steve Ede

Gosport. *Born* Southampton, 22 June,1976
Middleweight. Former Undefeated British Masters Middleweight Champion. *Ht* 5'10"
Manager J. Bishop

06.02.05   Jed Tytler W RSC 4 Southampton
26.06.05   Mark Wall W PTS 6 Southampton
25.09.05   Rocky Muscus W PTS 6 Southampton
16.12.05   Lee Hodgson W PTS 4 Bracknell
05.03.06   Anthony Young W RSC 3 Southampton
26.05.06   Jake Guntert W RSC 2 Bethnal Green
24.09.06   Lee Hodgson W RSC 3 Southampton
25.02.07   Conroy McIntosh W PTS 10 Southampton
(Vacant British Masters Middleweight Title)
16.09.07   Cello Renda L RSC 2 Southampton
(Vacant British Masters Middleweight Title)
02.03.08   Sherman Alleyne W PTS 6 Portsmouth
Career: 10 contests, won 9, lost 1.

Matthew Edmonds

Newport. *Born* Newport, 12 February, 1984
International Masters Bantamweight Champion. *Ht* 5'6"
Manager C. Sanigar

15.09.06   Delroy Spencer W PTS 4 Newport
07.10.06   Colin Moffett W PTS 4 Belfast
10.11.06   Mo Khaled W PTS 6 Newport
03.03.07   Sumaila Badu W PTS 6 Newport
16.06.07   Jamil Hussain W RTD 3 Newport
(Vacant International Masters Bantamweight Title)
05.10.07   Kris Hughes L PTS 6 Newport
08.12.07   Jason Booth L RSC 9 Wigan
(Vacant Commonwealth Bantamweight Title)
05.04.08   Sumaila Badu W PTS 10 Newport
(International Masters Bantamweight Title Defence)
24.05.08   Herbert Quartey W RSC 6 Cardiff
Career: 9 contests, won 7, lost 2.

Chris Edwards

Stoke. *Born* Stoke, 6 May, 1976
Former British S.Flyweight Champion. Former Undefeated English Flyweight Champion. Former Undefeated British Masters S.Bantamweight Champion. *Ht* 5'3"
Manager M. Carney

03.04.98   Chris Thomas W RSC 2 Ebbw Vale
21.09.98   Russell Laing L PTS 6 Glasgow
26.02.99   Delroy Spencer L PTS 6 West Bromwich
17.04.99   Stevie Quinn L RSC 4 Dublin
19.10.99   Lee Georgiou L RSC 2 Bethnal Green
03.12.99   Daniel Ring L PTS 4 Peterborough
15.05.00   Paddy Folan L PTS 6 Bradford
07.10.00   Andy Roberts W PTS 4 Doncaster
27.11.00   Levi Pattison W PTS 4 Birmingham
16.03.01   Jamie Evans L PTS 6 Portsmouth
03.06.01   Darren Taylor DREW 6 Hanley
08.10.01   Levi Pattison L PTS 4 Barnsley
06.12.01   Neil Read W PTS 8 Stoke
10.10.02   Neil Read W PTS 6 Stoke
13.06.03   Lee Haskins L PTS 6 Bristol
23.04.04   Delroy Spencer DREW 6 Leicester
26.09.04   Neil Read W RSC 2 Stoke
(Vacant British Masters S.Bantamweight Title)
28.10.04   Colin Moffett L PTS 4 Belfast
12.11.05   Delroy Spencer W PTS 4 Stoke
18.02.06   Gary Ford L PTS 6 Stoke
10.03.06   Andrea Sarritzu L CO 4 Bergamo, Italy
06.05.06   Gary Sheil W PTS 6 Stoke
30.09.06   Usman Ahmed W PTS 6 Stoke
24.11.06   Dale Robinson W RSC 8 Stoke
(Vacant English Flyweight Title)
13.04.07   Dale Robinson DREW 12 Altrincham
(Vacant British & Commonwealth Flyweight Titles)
08.12.07   Jamie McDonnell W PTS 12 Wigan
(Vacant British S.Flyweight Title)
28.03.08   Andy Bell L PTS 12 Barnsley
(British S.Flyweight Title Defence)
Career: 27 contests, won 11, drew 3, lost 13.

Lee Edwards

Sheffield. *Born* Huntingdon, 25 May, 1984
Middleweight. *Ht* 5'11"
Manager Self

08.05.05   Sergey Haritonov W PTS 6 Sheffield
24.07.05   Lee Williamson W PTS 6 Sheffield
30.10.05   Joe Mitchell L RSC 2 Sheffield
17.02.06   Malik Khan W RSC 6 Sheffield
20.04.07   Howard Clarke W PTS 6 Sheffield
16.09.07   Jon Musgrave W PTS 6 Sheffield
23.11.07   Paul Royston W PTS 6 Sheffield
15.02.08   Matt Scriven W PTS 6 Sheffield
Career: 8 contests, won 7, lost 1.

Franklin Egobi

Tooting. *Born* Lagos, Nigeria, 14 July, 1976
Heavyweight. Former Undefeated IBF Inter-Continental Heavyweight Champion. *Ht* 6'2¾"
Manager F. Maloney/B. Baker

22.02.00   Donovan Luff W PTS 4 Cape Town, South Africa
02.07.00   Goodman Kwinana W RSC 5 Cape Town, South Africa
08.07.00   Egan Norman W RSC 2 George, South Africa
23.07.00   Brian Butler W RSC 1 Cape Town, South Africa
13.08.00   Rocky Floris W CO 1 Cape Town, South Africa
27.02.01   Sibusiso Mhlophe W RSC 1 Cape Town, South Africa
13.05.01   Lance O'Connor W CO 1 Khayelitsha, South Africa
08.06.01   Petrus Kapp W CO 1 Cape Town, South Africa
25.09.01   Isaac Mahlangu W RSC 6 Cape Town, South Africa
(Vacant IBF Inter-Continental Heavyweight Title)
29.10.02   Said Diab W CO 1 Cape Town, South Africa
10.12.02   Aleh Dubiaha W PTS 6 Constanta, Romania
04.03.03   JC Hilliard W RSC 1 Iasi, Romania
24.06.03   Petr Sedlak L PTS 6 Ploiesti, Romania
09.09.03   Marcel Beresoaie W PTS 8 Varna, Bulgaria
21.05.04   Zoran Manojlovic W PTS 6 Iasi, Romania
18.11.07   Chris Burton L PTS 6 Tooting
Career: 16 contests, won 14, lost 2.

Wayne Elcock   Philip Sharkey

Wayne Elcock

Birmingham. *Born* Birmingham, 12 February, 1974
British Middleweight Champion. Former Undefeated English Middleweight Champion. Former WBU Middleweight Champion. *Ht* 5'9½"
Manager Self

02.12.99	William Webster W PTS 6 Peterborough
04.03.00	Sonny Pollard W RSC 3 Peterborough
07.07.01	Darren Rhodes W PTS 4 Manchester
09.10.01	Valery Odin W PTS 4 Cardiff
02.03.02	Charles Shodiya W RSC 1 Bethnal Green
20.04.02	Howard Clarke W PTS 4 Cardiff
01.06.02	Jason Collins W RSC 2 Manchester
17.08.02	Ojay Abrahams W PTS 4 Cardiff
23.11.02	Jason Collins W RSC 1 Derby
15.02.03	Yuri Tsarenko W PTS 10 Wembley
05.04.03	Anthony Farnell W PTS 12 Manchester *(WBU Middleweight Title Challenge)*
29.11.03	Lawrence Murphy L CO 1 Renfrew *(WBU Middleweight Title Defence)*
07.02.04	Farai Musiiwa W PTS 6 Bethnal Green
05.06.04	Michael Monaghan W PTS 4 Bethnal Green
07.04.05	Darren Rhodes W CO 1 Birmingham
16.09.05	Scott Dann L PTS 12 Plymouth *(British Middleweight Title Challenge)*
06.05.06	Lawrence Murphy W RSC 5 Birmingham *(Elim. British Middleweight Title)*
08.09.06	Vince Baldassara W CO 6 Birmingham *(Vacant WBF Inter-Continental Middleweight Title)*
01.12.06	Steven Bendall W RSC 8 Birmingham *(English Middleweight Title Challenge)*
28.09.07	Howard Eastman W PTS 12 Coventry *(British Middleweight Title Challenge)*
08.12.07	Arthur Abraham L RSC 5 Basle, Switzerland *(IBF Middleweight Title Challenge)*
20.06.08	Darren McDermott W RSC 2 Wolverhampton *(British Middleweight Title Defence)*

Career: 22 contests, won 19, lost 3.

Joe Elfidh
Doncaster. *Born* Doncaster, 5 April, 1980
L.Welterweight. *Ht* 5'7¼"
Manager D. Hobson

23.11.07	Darren Askew W PTS 6 Rotherham
22.03.08	Karl Taylor W PTS 6 Sheffield
21.06.08	Abdul Rashid W PTS 6 Sheffield

Career: 3 contests, won 3.

Matthew Ellis
Blackpool. *Born* Oldham, 12 April, 1974
Heavyweight. *Ht* 5'11¾"
Manager Self

03.02.96	Laurent Rouze W CO 1 Liverpool
01.04.96	Ladislav Husarik W RTD 4 Den Bosch, Holland
06.09.96	Darren Fearn W RSC 6 Liverpool
26.10.96	Daniel Beun W RSC 1 Liverpool
01.03.97	Yuri Yelistratov L RSC 5 Liverpool
20.07.97	Ricardo Phillips W PTS 4 Indio, California, USA
26.09.97	Albert Call DREW 6 Liverpool
12.03.98	Yuri Yelistratov W RSC 1 Liverpool
21.07.98	Chris Woollas W RSC 5 Widnes
24.10.98	Peter Hrivnak W RSC 1 Liverpool
12.12.98	Harry Senior W PTS 8 Southwark
27.02.99	Michael Murray W PTS 8 Bethnal Green
15.05.99	Biko Botowamungu W PTS 8 Blackpool
27.05.00	Alex Vasiliev W CO 4 Southwark
16.09.00	Dimitri Bakhtov W PTS 4 Bethnal Green
18.11.00	Chris Woollas W PTS 4 Dagenham
17.02.01	Alexei Osokin W PTS 8 Bethnal Green
12.07.01	Ronnie Smith W PTS 6 Houston, Texas, USA
22.09.01	Colin Abelson W CO 1 Bethnal Green
02.03.02	Dennis Bakhtov L RSC 5 Bethnal Green *(WBC International Heavyweight Title Challenge)*
29.03.03	Derek McCafferty W PTS 4 Wembley
31.05.03	Audley Harrison L RSC 2 Bethnal Green
27.10.03	Tony Moran L RSC 4 Glasgow
26.10.06	Chris Woollas W PTS 4 Dudley
08.02.08	Chris Burton L RTD 2 Peterlee

Career: 25 contests, won 19, drew 1, lost 5.

Yassine El Maachi
Balham. *Born* Morocco, 19 September, 1979
L.Middleweight. *Ht* 5'7¼"
Manager W. Fuller

02.09.01	Rudolf Murko W PTS 4 Den Haag, Netherlands
20.12.01	Anthony Armstead W PTS 6 Rotterdam, Netherlands
20.05.02	Jackson Osei Bonsu L CO 3 Roeselare, Belgium
21.06.03	Alex Solcsanyi W RSC 3 Den Haag, Netherlands
06.07.07	Brett Flournoy L RSC 4 Wigan
21.09.07	Scott Woolford W PTS 4 Bethnal Green
08.12.07	Denton Vassell L PTS 4 Bolton
30.03.08	Thomas McDonagh L PTS 6 Colne

Career: 8 contests, won 4, lost 4.

Yassine El Maachi　　　　Les Clark

Stuart Elwell
Darlaston. *Born* Walsall, 14 December, 1977
L.Middleweight. Former Undefeated Midlands Area Welterweight Champion. *Ht* 5'9"
Manager E. Johnson

06.11.00	Ernie Smith W PTS 6 Wolverhampton
28.01.01	Arv Mittoo W PTS 6 Wolverhampton
01.04.01	Richard Inquieti W PTS 6 Wolverhampton
06.10.05	Ernie Smith W PTS 6 Dudley
25.11.05	Ben Hudson W PTS 4 Walsall
10.03.06	David Kirk W PTS 10 Walsall *(Vacant Midlands Area Welterweight Title)*
18.05.06	Peter Dunn W PTS 6 Walsall
23.06.06	Franny Jones W RSC 1 Blackpool
10.11.06	Ben Hudson W PTS 4 Telford
23.03.07	John O'Donnell L PTS 10 Nottingham *(Vacant English Welterweight Title)*
20.07.07	Alexander Matviechuk W PTS 6 Wolverhampton
18.02.08	Chris Brophy W PTS 6 Glasgow
25.03.08	Vyacheslav Senchenko L RSC 2 Donetsk, Ukraine *(WBA Inter-Continental Welterweight Title Challenge)*

Career: 13 contests, won 11, lost 2.

Johnny Enigma (Nelson)
Bolton. *Born* Farnworth, 12 July, 1973
Middleweight. *Ht* 5'11"
Manager S. Wood/A. Penarski

06.05.07	Paul Royston W PTS 6 Altrincham
24.06.07	Tony Randell L RSC 5 Wigan
25.01.08	Max Maxwell L RSC 2 Birmingham

Career: 3 contests, won 1, lost 2.

James Evans
Cardiff, *Born* Cardiff, 3 May, 1989
Middleweight. *Ht* 5'9¼"
Manager C. Sanigar

05.04.08	Gavin Brook DREW 6 Newport

Career: 1 contest, drew 1.

Scott Evans
Stourbridge. *Born* Wordsley, 1 March, 1988
L.Welterweight. *Ht* 5'8¾"
Manager P. Rowson

25.10.07	Amir Nadi W PTS 4 Wolverhampton
28.11.07	Karl Taylor W RSC 3 Walsall
28.02.08	Kristian Laight W PTS 6 Wolverhampton
30.04.08	Amir Nadi W RSC 3 Wolverhampton

Career: 4 contests, won 4.

Scott Evans　　　　Philip Sharkey

Andrew Facey

Sheffield. *Born* Wolverhampton, 20 May, 1972
English L.Middleweight Champion. Former Undefeated Central Area Middleweight Champion. *Ht* 6'0"
Manager D. Ingle

06.12.99	Peter McCormack W CO 2 Birmingham
09.06.00	Matthew Pepper W RSC 1 Hull
04.11.00	Earl Ling W PTS 6 Derby
11.12.00	Gary Jones W PTS 6 Cleethorpes
10.02.01	Louis Swales W RSC 3 Widnes
17.03.01	Darren Rhodes L PTS 4 Manchester
24.03.01	Matthew Tait W PTS 4 Chigwell
16.06.01	Earl Ling DREW 6 Derby
09.12.01	Michael Pinnock W PTS 6 Shaw
02.03.02	Darren Rhodes W RSC 6 Wakefield *(Vacant Central Area Middleweight Title)*
20.04.02	Darren Ashton W PTS 6 Derby
13.04.02	Leigh Wicks W PTS 6 Norwich
03.08.02	Damon Hague L CO 5 Derby *(Final Elim. WBF Middleweight Title)*
25.10.02	William Webster W PTS 4 Cotgrave
16.04.03	Gilbert Eastman W RSC 3 Nottingham
06.11.03	Matthew Macklin W PTS 10 Dagenham *(Vacant English L.Middleweight Title)*
22.11.03	Jamie Moore L RSC 7 Belfast *(British & Commonwealth L.Middleweight Title Challenges)*
04.06.04	Howard Clarke W PTS 6 Hull
17.09.04	Jason Collins W PTS 4 Sheffield
03.09.05	Jason Collins W PTS 4 Norwich
29.10.05	Howard Clarke W PTS 6 Aberdeen
27.05.06	Ojay Abrahams W PTS 6 Aberdeen
18.11.06	Bradley Pryce L PTS 12 Newport *(Commonwealth L.Middleweight Title Challenge)*
26.01.07	Gary Woolcombe W RSC 5 Dagenham *(English L.Middleweight Title Defence)*
26.10.07	Jamie Moore L RSC 11 Wigan *(British L.Middleweight Title Challenge)*
24.05.08	Thomas McDonagh DREW 10 Manchester *(English L.Middleweight Title Defence)*

Career: 26 contests, won 19, drew 2, lost 5.

Shaun Farmer

Hartlepool. *Born* Hull, 7 March, 1977
L.Middleweight. *Ht* 6'0"
Manager T. Conroy

05.10.06	Lee Noble W PTS 6 Sunderland
17.12.06	Craig Bunn L PTS 6 Bolton
25.02.07	Alex Matvienko L PTS 6 Manchester
11.05.07	Matt Scriven W PTS 6 Sunderland
25.05.07	Paddy Pollock L PTS 6 Glasgow
24.06.07	Jon Foster W PTS 6 Sunderland
11.08.07	Paddy Pollock W PTS 6 Liverpool
19.10.07	Chris Black L CO 1 Motherwell
08.12.07	Brian Rose L RSC 3 Wigan
23.02.08	Paul Royston W PTS 6 Liverpool
20.03.08	Jon Musgrave W PTS 6 South Shields

15.05.08	Jon Musgrave L PTS 6 Sunderland
13.06.08	Ryan Ashworth L CO 3 Sunderland

Career: 13 contests, won 6, lost 7.

Graham Fearn

York. *Born* York, 1 December, 1974
L.Welterweight. *Ht* 5'7¼"
Manager M. Marsden

10.12.07	Kristian Laight W PTS 6 Leicester
18.02.08	Brian Murphy W RSC 6 Glasgow
24.04.08	Bheki Moyo W PTS 6 Piccadilly
05.06.08	Karl Taylor W PTS 6 Leeds

Career: 4 contests, won 4.

Graham Fearn   Philip Sharkey

Femi Fehintola

Bradford. *Born* Bradford, 1 July, 1982
English Featherweight Champion. *Ht* 5'7"
Manager D. Hobson

26.09.03	John-Paul Ryan W PTS 6 Reading
07.11.03	Pete Buckley W PTS 6 Sheffield
10.12.03	Jason Nesbitt W PTS 6 Sheffield
06.02.04	Jason Nesbitt W PTS 6 Sheffield
20.04.04	Kristian Laight W PTS 6 Sheffield
17.06.04	Anthony Hanna W PTS 6 Sheffield
24.10.04	John-Paul Ryan W PTS 6 Sheffield
10.12.04	Philippe Meheust W PTS 6 Sheffield
04.03.05	Daniel Thorpe W PTS 6 Rotherham
24.07.05	Jason Nesbitt W PTS 6 Sheffield
14.10.05	Rakhim Mingaleev W PTS 8 Huddersfield
16.12.05	Frederic Gosset W PTS 8 Bracknell
18.03.06	Ivo Golakov W RSC 2 Monte Carlo, Monaco
13.05.06	Nikita Lukin W PTS 8 Sheffield
03.11.06	Carl Johanneson L RSC 6 Barnsley *(British S.Featherweight Title Challenge)*
27.05.07	Carl Allen W PTS 6 Bradford
23.06.07	Barbaro Zepeda W PTS 4 Las Vegas, Nevada, USA
07.09.07	Karl Taylor W PTS 4 Doncaster
06.10.07	Steve Bell W PTS 10 Nottingham *(Vacant English S.Featherweight Title)*
22.03.08	John Baguley W PTS 6 Sheffield

Career: 20 contests, won 19, lost 1.

Femi Fehintola   Philip Sharkey

Dave Ferguson

Wallsend. *Born* North Shields, 28 February, 1976
Heavyweight. *Ht* 6'4"
Manager T. Conroy

16.02.07	David Ingleby W PTS 4 Sunderland
24.06.07	David Ingleby W PTS 4 Sunderland
23.09.07	Paul Malcolm W RTD 3 Hartlepool
06.12.07	Lee Mountford W PTS 6 Sunderland
20.03.08	Mark Walker W RSC 1 South Shields
11.04.08	Billy Bessey W PTS 3 Bethnal Green
11.04.08	Martin Rogan L PTS 3 Bethnal Green
13.06.08	Howard Daley W PTS 4 Sunderland

Career: 8 contests, won 7, lost 1.

Dave Ferguson   Philip Sharkey

Andrew Ferrans

New Cumnock. *Born* Irvine, 4 February, 1981
Welterweight. Former Undefeated British Masters S.Featherweight Champion.
Ht 5'9"
Manager T. Gilmour

19.02.00	Chris Lyons W PTS 6 Prestwick	
03.03.00	Gary Groves W RSC 1 Irvine	
20.03.00	John Barnes DREW 6 Glasgow	
06.06.00	Duncan Armstrong W PTS 6 Motherwell	
18.09.00	Steve Brook W PTS 6 Glasgow	
20.11.00	Duncan Armstrong W PTS 6 Glasgow	
23.02.01	Dave Cotterill L RSC 2 Irvine	
30.04.01	Dave Cotterill W RSC 1 Glasgow	
04.06.01	Jason Nesbitt W RSC 2 Glasgow	
17.09.01	Gary Flear W PTS 8 Glasgow	
10.12.01	Jamie McKeever L PTS 6 Liverpool	
21.01.02	Joel Viney W PTS 8 Glasgow	
01.03.02	Peter Allen W PTS 8 Irvine	
13.04.02	Tony Mulholland L PTS 4 Liverpool	
11.05.02	Marc Callaghan L PTS 6 Dagenham	
23.09.02	Greg Edwards W RTD 4 Glasgow	
08.10.02	Peter Allen W PTS 8 Glasgow	
18.11.02	Joel Viney W PTS 6 Glasgow	
30.11.02	Colin Toohey L PTS 6 Liverpool	
28.02.03	Simon Chambers W RSC 7 Irvine	
28.04.03	Craig Spacie L PTS 6 Nottingham	
26.07.03	Baz Carey DREW 4 Plymouth	
01.11.03	Anthony Hanna W PTS 4 Glasgow	
19.01.04	Dariusz Snarski W PTS 6 Glasgow	
15.03.04	Baz Carey W PTS 10 Glasgow	
	(Vacant British Masters S.Featherweight Title)	
08.05.04	Carl Johanneson L RSC 6 Bristol	
	(WBF S.Featherweight Title Challenge)	
26.02.05	Stephen Chinnock W RTD 5 Burton	
24.10.05	Kristian Laight W PTS 8 Glasgow	
23.02.06	Carl Johanneson L RSC 2 Leeds	
	(Final Elim. British S.Featherweight Title)	
06.05.06	Sergii Tertii W PTS 6 Irvine	
13.10.06	Frederic Gosset W PTS 6 Irvine	
19.02.07	Billy Smith W PTS 6 Glasgow	
05.06.07	Jay Morris W RSC 3 Glasgow	
06.06.08	Simon Fleck W RSC 2 Glasgow	

Career: 34 contests, won 24, drew 2, lost 8.

John Fewkes

Sheffield. *Born* Sheffield, 16 July, 1985
Central Area L.Welterweight Champion.
Ht 5'8"
Manager G. Rhodes

17.09.04	Mark Dane W RSC 2 Sheffield	
24.10.04	Lea Handley W PTS 6 Sheffield	
10.12.04	Jason Nesbitt W PTS 6 Sheffield	
04.03.05	Jason Nesbitt W PTS 6 Rotherham	
08.05.05	Chris Long W PTS 8 Sheffield	
25.06.05	Billy Smith W PTS 6 Wakefield	
24.07.05	Karl Taylor W PTS 6 Sheffield	
09.09.05	Rakhim Mingaleev W PTS 4 Sheffield	
30.10.05	Tony Montana W PTS 6 Sheffield	
17.02.06	Tony Montana W PTS 10 Sheffield	
	(Central Area L.Welterweight Title Challenge)	
21.07.06	Kristian Laight W RSC 5 Altrincham	
29.09.06	Thomas Mazurkiewicz W PTS 4 Manchester	
03.11.06	Scott Haywood W PTS 8 Barnsley	
09.02.07	Craig Watson W PTS 8 Leeds	
13.07.07	Tontcho Tontchev W PTS 8 Barnsley	
19.10.07	Gary Reid W PTS 8 Doncaster	
28.03.08	Frederic Gosset W PTS 4 Barnsley	

Career: 17 contests, won 17.

(John Joseph) Jonjo Finnegan

Burton on Trent. *Born* Burton on Trent, 25 April, 1980
S.Middleweight. *Ht* 6'1"
Manager E. Johnson

08.07.04	Paul Billington W PTS 6 Birmingham	
25.11.04	Nick Okoth DREW 6 Birmingham	
26.02.05	Arv Mittoo W PTS 4 Burton	
07.04.05	Peter Dunn W PTS 6 Birmingham	
24.04.05	Omid Bourzo L PTS 6 Derby	
30.09.05	Robert Burton DREW 4 Burton	
25.11.05	Paul Billington W PTS 6 Walsall	
28.01.06	Dave Pearson W PTS 4 Nottingham	
25.03.06	Dave Pearson W PTS 8 Burton	
13.05.06	Ernie Smith W PTS 6 Sutton in Ashfield	
01.06.06	Mark Phillips W PTS 4 Birmingham	
16.09.06	Jamie Ambler W PTS 6 Burton	
30.09.06	Dave Pearson W PTS 6 Middlesbrough	
24.11.06	Dean Walker DREW 4 Nottingham	
03.03.07	Neil Tidman L PTS 10 Burton	
	(Vacant Midlands Area S.Middleweight Title)	
21.09.07	Mark Phillips L PTS 10 Burton	
	(Vacant British Masters L.Heavyweight Title)	
16.05.08	Dave Pearson W PTS 4 Burton	

Career: 17 contests, won 11, drew 3, lost 3.

Simon Fleck

Leicester. *Born* Leicester, 26 March, 1979
Middleweight. *Ht* 6'0"
Manager M. Shinfield

22.10.05	Simone Lucas W RSC 5 Mansfield	
08.12.05	Tommy Jones W PTS 6 Derby	
02.03.06	Mark Thompson L CO 3 Blackpool	
24.04.06	Karl Taylor W PTS 6 Cleethorpes	
14.12.06	Peter Dunn W PTS 6 Leicester	
14.05.07	Rocky Muscas W PTS 6 Cleethorpes	
06.10.07	Carl Drake DREW 8 Leicester	
06.06.08	Andrew Ferrans L RSC 2 Glasgow	

Career: 8 contests, won 5, drew 1, lost 2.

James Flinn

Coventry. *Born* Coventry, 28 February, 1982
Welterweight. *Ht* 5'10¼"
Manager E. Johnson

16.05.08	Lance Verallo W RSC 3 Burton	
20.06.08	Paddy Pollock W PTS 4 Wolverhampton	

Career: 2 contests, won 2.

James Flinn   Philip Sharkey

Brett Flournoy

Bromborough. *Born* Birkenhead, 7 August, 1979
L.Middleweight. *Ht* 5'10"
Manager D. Waul/F. Maloney

21.07.06	Tommy Jones W RSC 1 Altrincham	
29.09.06	Gatis Skuja W PTS 4 Manchester	
09.02.07	Ernie Smith W PTS 4 Leeds	
13.04.07	Alexander Spitjo W PTS 4 Altrincham	
06.07.07	Yassine El Maachi W RSC 4 Wigan	
26.10.07	Ryan Ashworth W PTS 6 Wigan	
01.12.07	Lewis Byrne W RSC 2 Liverpool	
16.03.08	Alan Sebire W CO 3 Liverpool	
23.05.08	Vladimir Borovski W PTS 6 Wigan	

Career: 9 contests, won 9.

Jon Foster

Oldham. *Born* Nottingham, 18 October, 1979
Middleweight. *Ht* 6'1"
Manager M. Scriven

31.10.97	David Thompson W RSC 4 Ilkeston	
26.11.97	Billy McDougall W RSC 2 Stoke	
20.03.98	Phil Molyneux W PTS 6 Ilkeston	
03.04.98	Harry Butler W PTS 6 Ebbw Vale	
23.04.98	Hughie Davey L PTS 8 Newcastle	
11.09.98	Brian Dunn W RTD 3 Cleethorpes	
07.12.98	Darren Christie W RSC 6 Cleethorpes	
06.06.99	Jason Collins DREW 6 Nottingham	
20.09.99	Joe Townsley L PTS 6 Glasgow	
11.12.99	Jacek Bielski L PTS 6 Merthyr	
12.02.00	Zoltan Sarossy L RSC 1 Sheffield	
06.06.00	James Docherty L PTS 6 Motherwell	
24.09.00	Lee Murtagh L PTS 6 Shaw	
25.04.05	Jed Tytler L RSC 2 Cleethorpes	
28.01.06	Matthew Hall L RSC 3 Nottingham	
04.03.06	Nathan Cleverly L PTS 4 Manchester	
13.04.06	Brendan Halford L PTS 6 Leeds	
14.05.06	Adie Whitmore L RSC 6 Derby	
08.09.06	Leigh Hallet L PTS 6 Birmingham	
29.09.06	Alex Matvienko L RTD 3 Manchester	
04.11.06	Davey Jones W DIS 6 Mansfield	
17.11.06	Sam Horton L PTS 6 Brierley Hill	
22.02.07	Franny Jones L CO 3 Leeds	
23.03.07	Adie Whitmore L RTD 4 Nottingham	
29.04.07	James McKinley L PTS 6 Birmingham	
06.05.07	Craig Denton L PTS 6 Darlington	
24.06.07	Shaun Farmer L PTS 6 Sunderland	
16.09.07	Jezz Wilson L RSC 1 Sheffield	
01.12.07	Ollie Newham L RSC 2 Nottingham	

Career: 29 contests, won 7, drew 1, lost 21.

Steve Foster

Salford. *Born* Salford, 16 September, 1980
Featherweight. Former WBU Featherweight Champion. Former Undefeated English Featherweight Champion. *Ht* 5'6"
Manager F. Warren

15.09.01	Andy Greenaway W PTS 4 Manchester	
27.10.01	Gareth Wiltshaw W PTS 4 Manchester	
02.03.02	Andy Greenaway W RSC 1 Bethnal Green	
04.05.02	Gareth Wiltshaw W PTS 4 Bethnal Green	
08.07.02	Ian Turner W RSC 1 Mayfair	
20.07.02	Paddy Folan W CO 1 Bethnal Green	
28.09.02	Jason White W RSC 3 Manchester	
14.12.02	Sean Green W RSC 3 Newcastle	
22.03.03	David McIntyre W PTS 4 Renfrew	
24.05.03	Henry Janes W PTS 6 Bethnal Green	
12.07.03	David McIntyre W RTD 3 Renfrew	

18.09.03 Alexander Abramenko W RTD 4
Dagenham
06.11.03 Vladimir Borov W RSC 8 Dagenham
13.12.03 Steve Gethin W RTD 3 Manchester
26.02.04 Sean Hughes W RSC 6 Widnes
(Vacant English Featherweight Title)
30.07.04 Jean-Marie Codet W PTS 8 Bethnal
Green
01.10.04 Gary Thornhill W RSC 9 Manchester
(English Featherweight Title Defence)
11.02.05 Livinson Ruiz W CO 10 Manchester
(Vacant WBU Featherweight Title)
16.07.05 Jim Betts W RTD 5 Bolton

10.12.05 Buster Dennis DREW 8 Canning Town
01.04.06 John Simpson W PTS 12 Bethnal
Green
(WBU Featherweight Title Defence)
08.07.06 Frederic Bonifai W RSC 2 Cardiff
14.10.06 Derry Matthews L PTS 12 Manchester
(WBU Featherweight Title Defence)
14.07.07 Wladimir Borov W RSC 3 Greenwich
13.10.07 Jean-Marie Codet W CO 1 Bethnal
Green
15.12.07 Alex Arthur L PTS 12 Edinburgh
*(WBO Interim S.Featherweight Title
Challenge)*

Career: 26 contests, won 23, drew 1, lost 2.

Dean Francis

Basingstoke. *Born* Basingstoke, 23 January,
1974
British, Commonwealth & IBO Inter-
Continental L.Heavyweight Champion.
Former Undefeated English Cruiserweight
Champion. Former Undefeated British,
European & WBO Inter-Continental
S.Middleweight Champion. *Ht* 5'10½"
Manager Self

Carl Froch

Les Clark

28.05.94	Darren Littlewood W PTS 4 Queensway
17.06.94	Martin Jolley W PTS 6 Plymouth
21.07.94	Horace Fleary W RSC 4 Tooting
02.09.94	Steve Osborne W RTD 4 Spitalfields
27.10.94	Tony Booth W CO 1 Bayswater
22.11.94	Darron Griffiths W RTD 1 Bristol
30.03.95	Paul Murray W RSC 2 Bethnal Green
25.05.95	Hunter Clay W RSC 8 Reading
16.06.95	Paul Murray W RTD 3 Southwark
20.10.95	Zafarou Ballogou L RSC 10 Ipswich *(WBC International S. Middleweight Title Challenge)*
16.12.95	Kid Milo W RSC 3 Cardiff
13.02.96	Mike Bonislawski W RSC 2 Bethnal Green
26.04.96	Neil Simpson W RSC 3 Cardiff
08.06.96	John Marceta W RSC 8 Newcastle
14.09.96	Larry Kenny W RSC 2 Sheffield
19.10.96	Rolando Torres W RSC 4 Bristol *(Vacant WBO Inter-Continental S. Middleweight Title)*
14.03.97	Cornelius Carr W RSC 7 Reading *(WBO Inter-Continental S. Middleweight Title Defence)*
15.05.97	Kit Munro W RSC 2 Reading *(WBO Inter-Continental S. Middleweight Title Defence)*
19.07.97	David Starie W RSC 6 Wembley *(British S. Middleweight Title Challenge)*
19.12.97	Frederic Seillier W RSC 9 Millwall *(Vacant European S. Middleweight Title)*
07.03.98	Mark Baker W RSC 12 Reading *(British & WBO Inter-Continental S. Middleweight Title Defences)*
22.08.98	Xolani Ngemntu W CO 2 Hammanskraal, South Africa *(WBO Inter-Continental S. Middleweight Title Defence)*
31.10.98	Undra White L RTD 4 Basingstoke *(Vacant IBO Inter-Continental S. Middleweight Title)*
20.04.02	Mondili Mbonambi W PTS 8 Wembley
29.03.03	Matthew Barney L PTS 12 Wembley *(Vacant British S.Middleweight Title)*
09.07.05	Paul Bonson W PTS 6 Bristol
12.11.05	Hastings Rasani W RSC 6 Bristol
25.02.06	Tommy Eastwood W PTS 10 Bristol *(Vacant English Cruiserweight Title)*
07.10.06	Hastings Rasani W CO 2 Weston super Mare
09.02.07	Ovill McKenzie W RSC 1 Bristol *(Commonwealth L.Heavyweight Title Challenge)*
02.06.07	Ayitey Powers W CO 9 Bristol *(Vacant IBO Inter-Continental L.Heavyweight Title)*
08.12.07	Michael Gbenga W PTS 12 Bolton *(Commonwealth L.Heavyweight Title Defence)*
13.06.08	Tony Oakey W RSC 9 Portsmouth *(British L.Heavyweight Title Challenge. Commonwealth L.Heavyweight Title Defence)*

Career: 33 contests, won 30, lost 3.

Carl Froch

Nottingham. *Born* Nottingham, 2 July, 1977
British S.Middleweight Champion. Former
Undefeated Commonwealth & English
S.Middleweight Champion. *Ht* 6'4"
Manager Self

16.03.02	Michael Pinnock W RSC 4 Bethnal Green
10.05.02	Ojay Abrahams W RSC 1 Bethnal Green
23.08.02	Darren Covill W RSC 1 Bethnal Green
25.10.02	Paul Bonson W PTS 6 Bethnal Green
21.12.02	Mike Duffield W RSC 1 Dagenham
28.01.03	Valery Odin W RSC 6 Nottingham
05.03.03	Varuzhan Davtyan W RSC 5 Bethnal Green
16.04.03	Michael Monaghan W RSC 3 Nottingham
04.10.03	Vage Kocharyan W PTS 8 Muswell Hill
28.11.03	Alan Page W RSC 7 Derby *(Vacant English S.Middleweight Title. Elim. British S.Middleweight Title)*
30.01.04	Dmitri Adamovich W RSC 2 Dagenham
12.03.04	Charles Adamu W PTS 12 Nottingham *(Commonwealth S.Middleweight Title Challenge)*
02.06.04	Mark Woolnough W RSC 11 Nottingham *(Commonwealth S.Middleweight Title Defence)*
24.09.04	Damon Hague W RSC 1 Nottingham *(Vacant British S.Middleweight Title. Commonwealth S.Middleweight Title Defence)*
21.04.05	Henry Porras W RSC 8 Hollywood, California, USA
09.07.05	Matthew Barney W PTS 12 Nottingham *(British & Commonwealth S.Middleweight Title Defences)*
02.12.05	Ruben Groenewald W RSC 5 Nottingham *(Commonwealth S.Middleweight Title Defence)*
17.02.06	Dale Westerman W RSC 9 Bethnal Green *(Commonwealth S.Middleweight Title Defence)*
26.05.06	Brian Magee W RSC 11 Bethnal Green *(British & Commonwealth S.Middleweight Title Defences)*
24.11.06	Tony Dodson W CO 3 Nottingham *(British & Commonwealth S.Middleweight Title Defences)*
23.03.07	Sergei Tatevosyan W RSC 2 Nottingham
09.11.07	Robin Reid W RTD 5 Nottingham *(British S.Middleweight Title Defence)*
10.05.08	Albert Rybacki W RSC 4 Nottingham

Career: 23 contests, won 23.

Michael Frontin

Edmonton. *Born* Mauritius, 25 November, 1977
L.Welterweight. *Ht* 5'6¼"
Manager C. Sanigar

01.12.07	Ben Murphy W PTS 4 Bethnal Green
10.12.07	Alexander Spitjo L PTS 6 Birmingham
01.03.08	Scott Lawton L PTS 6 Stoke
22.03.08	Nicki Smedley L PTS 6 Sheffield

Career: 4 contests, won 1, lost 3.

Michael Frontin   Philip Sharkey

Courtney Fry

Wood Green. *Born* Enfield, 19 May, 1975
L.Heavyweight. *Ht* 6'1¼"
Manager C. Sanigar

29.03.03	Harry Butler W RSC 3 Wembley
31.05.03	Darren Ashton W PTS 4 Bethnal Green
24.10.03	Ovill McKenzie W PTS 4 Bethnal Green
20.03.04	Clint Johnson W RSC 2 Wembley
02.04.04	Paulie Silva W PTS 4 Plymouth
08.05.04	Radcliffe Green W PTS 6 Bristol
19.06.04	Valery Odin W PTS 8 Muswell Hill
17.12.04	Varuzhan Davtyan W RTD 2 Liverpool
13.05.05	Ovill McKenzie L PTS 4 Liverpool
07.04.06	Vasyl Kondor W PTS 6 Bristol
21.09.07	Nick Okoth W RSC 1 Bethnal Green
01.02.08	Tony Salam W CO 6 Bethnal Green

Career: 12 contests, won 11, lost 1.

Courtney Fry   Les Clark

113

Luke Gallear

Derby. *Born* Derby, 20 December, 1984
L.Middleweight. *Ht* 5'9"
Manager C. Mitchell

31.03.07   Surinder Sekhon L PTS 6 Derby
10.12.07   John Wainwright L RSC 3 Cleethorpes
16.05.08   Kevin McCauley W PTS 6 Burton
Career: 3 contests, won 1, lost 2.

Scott Gammer

Pembroke Dock. *Born* Pembroke Dock, 24 October, 1976
Heavyweight. Former British Heavyweight Champion. *Ht* 6'2"
Manager P. Boyce

15.09.02   Leighton Morgan W RSC 1 Swansea
26.10.02   James Gilbert W RSC 1 Maesteg
08.01.03   Dave Clarke W PTS 4 Aberdare
25.01.03   Ahmad Cheleh W CO 1 Bridgend
28.06.03   Dave Clarke W RSC 1 Cardiff
13.09.03   Derek McCafferty W PTS 6 Newport
08.11.03   Mendauga Kulikauskas DREW 6 Bridgend
28.02.04   James Zikic W PTS 6 Bridgend
01.05.04   Paul Buttery W CO 1 Bridgend
02.06.04   Paul King W RSC 3 Hereford
17.09.04   Carl Baker W PTS 4 Plymouth
05.11.04   Roman Bugaj W RSC 2 Hereford
18.02.05   Micky Steeds W PTS 6 Brighton
15.05.05   Mark Krence W RSC 8 Sheffield
            (Elim. British Heavyweight Title)
30.09.05   Julius Francis W PTS 8 Carmarthen
10.12.05   Suren Kalachyan W PTS 6 Canning Town
16.06.06   Mark Krence W RSC 9 Carmarthen
            (Vacant British Heavyweight Title)
13.10.06   Micky Steeds W PTS 12 Aberavon
            (British Heavyweight Title Defence)
02.03.07   Danny Williams L CO 9 Neath
            (British Heavyweight Title Defence)
10.06.07   Paul King W PTS 6 Neath
29.09.07   John McDermott L PTS 10 Sheffield
            (Elim. British Heavyweight Title)
Career: 21 contests, won 18, drew 1, lost 2.

David Gentles   Philip Sharkey

David Gentles

Cardiff. *Born* Cardiff, 28 June, 1975
S.Middleweight. *Ht* 6'0"
Manager B. Coleman

05.10.07   Rasham Sohi L PTS 6 Newport
10.11.07   Danny Tombs L PTS 4 Stalybridge
10.12.07   John Ruddock W PTS 6 Birmingham
31.01.08   Leon Senior W PTS 6 Piccadilly
25.02.08   John Ruddock W RSC 2 Birmingham
30.03.08   Jamie Ambler W PTS 6 Port Talbot
Career: 6 contests, won 4, lost 2.

Darren Gethin

Walsall. *Born* Walsall, 19 August, 1976
Former Midlands Area Welterweight Champion. Former Undefeated British Masters L.Middleweight Champion. *Ht* 5'8"
Manager E. Johnson

08.07.04   Joe Mitchell DREW 6 Birmingham
12.09.04   Joe Mitchell W PTS 6 Shrewsbury
12.11.04   Tyrone McInerney L PTS 4 Halifax
26.02.05   Tye Williams DREW 4 Burton
18.04.05   Joe Mitchell W PTS 6 Bradford
25.04.05   Terry Carruthers L RSC 3 Cleethorpes
02.06.05   Franny Jones L PTS 8 Yarm
02.09.05   Scott Conway W RSC 1 Derby
10.09.05   Nathan Cleverly L PTS 4 Cardiff
01.10.05   Jonathan Hussey L PTS 6 Wigan
22.10.05   Joe McCluskey DREW 6 Coventry
12.02.06   Mark Thompson L PTS 4 Manchester
23.02.06   Khurram Hussain DREW 4 Leeds
03.03.06   Jason Rushton W PTS 6 Doncaster
24.04.06   Gary McArthur L PTS 6 Glasgow
09.05.06   Danny Reynolds DREW 4 Leeds
18.05.06   Lance Hall W PTS 6 Walsall
01.06.06   Craig Dickson W PTS 6 Birmingham
12.07.06   John O'Donnell L PTS 8 Bethnal Green
11.12.06   Simon Sherrington W PTS 10 Birmingham
            (Vacant British Masters L.Middleweight Title)
19.02.07   Lee Noble L PTS 6 Glasgow
23.03.07   Tyan Booth W RSC 10 Nottingham
            (Vacant Midlands Area Welterweight Title)
10.09.07   Craig Dickson L PTS 6 Glasgow
09.11.07   Adnan Amar L RSC 10 Nottingham
            (Midlands Area Welterweight Title Defence)
01.02.08   Mark Thompson L RTD 2 Bethnal Green
22.03.08   Kell Brook L RTD 3 Cardiff
16.05.08   Chris Black L PTS 6 Motherwell
23.05.08   Chris Johnson L RSC 5 Wigan
Career: 28 contests, won 8, drew 5, lost 15.

Martin Gethin

Walsall. *Born* Walsall, 16 November, 1983
Midlands Area Lightweight Champion. Former Undefeated British Masters L.Welterweight Champion. *Ht* 5'6"
Manager Self

18.11.04   Kristian Laight W RSC 4 Shrewsbury
15.04.05   Jason Nesbitt W PTS 6 Shrewsbury
06.10.05   John-Paul Ryan W RSC 2 Dudley
25.11.05   Michael Medor W PTS 4 Walsall
10.03.06   Carl Allen W PTS 4 Walsall
01.06.06   Baz Carey W PTS 4 Birmingham
07.11.06   Kristian Laight W PTS 6 Leeds
05.12.06   Judex Meemea W RSC 3 Wolverhampton
            (Vacant British Masters L.Welterweight Title)
20.04.07   Carl Allen DREW 6 Dudley
15.09.07   Craig Johnson W PTS 10 Birmingham
            (Vacant Midlands Area Lightweight Title)
08.10.07   Darren Broomhall W RSC 3 Birmingham
07.12.07   Fabian Luque W RSC 4 Las Vegas, Nevada, USA
25.01.08   Carl Allen W PTS 6 Dagenham
25.02.08   Ali Wyatt W PTS 8 Birmingham
Career: 14 contests, won 13, drew 1.

Steve Gethin   Philip Sharkey

Steve Gethin

Walsall. *Born* Walsall, 30 July, 1978
Lightweight. *Ht* 5'9"
Manager Self

03.09.99   Ike Halls W RSC 3 West Bromwich
24.10.99   Ricky Bishop W RSC 4 Wolverhampton
22.01.00   Sebastian Hart L PTS 4 Birmingham
10.09.00   Nigel Senior DREW 6 Walsall
03.06.01   Richmond Asante L PTS 4 Southwark
28.11.01   Mickey Coveney L PTS 4 Bethnal Green
09.12.01   Gary Groves W PTS 6 Shaw
17.02.02   Gary Groves W PTS 6 Wolverhampton
01.06.02   Gary Davis W RSC 2 Manchester
21.09.02   Marc Callaghan L PTS 6 Brentwood
02.12.02   Neil Read W RTD 3 Leicester
14.12.02   Isaac Ward L PTS 4 Newcastle
08.02.03   Rocky Dean DREW 4 Norwich
15.02.03   Anthony Hanna W PTS 6 Wolverhampton
08.05.03   Derry Matthews L RSC 3 Widnes
07.09.03   Henry Janes L PTS 4 Shrewsbury
02.10.03   Mark Moran L PTS 4 Liverpool
20.10.03   John Simpson L PTS 8 Glasgow
30.10.03   Gareth Payne W PTS 6 Dudley
13.12.03   Steve Foster L RTD 3 Manchester
05.03.04   Isaac Ward L PTS 6 Darlington
27.05.04   Marc Callaghan L PTS 6 Huddersfield
30.07.04   Chris Hooper L PTS 4 Bethnal Green
08.10.04   Ian Napa L PTS 6 Brentwood
22.10.04   Andy Bell L RSC 5 Mansfield

17.12.04 Mark Moran L PTS 4 Liverpool
13.02.05 Patrick Hyland L PTS 4 Brentwood
24.04.05 Darren Broomhall W CO 5 Derby
09.07.05 Billy Corcoran L PTS 6 Nottingham
05.11.05 Amir Khan L RSC 3 Renfrew
24.03.06 Ian Wilson L PTS 4 Bethnal Green
06.05.06 Paul Newby L PTS 4 Birmingham
13.05.06 Andy Bell W RSC 2 Sutton in Ashfield
21.05.06 Mark Alexander L PTS 4 Bethnal Green
30.09.06 Paul Truscott L PTS 4 Middlesbrough
13.10.06 Gary McArthur L PTS 6 Irvine
21.10.06 Ryan Barrett L PTS 6 Southwark
28.10.06 Steve Bell L RTD 5 Bethnal Green
02.12.06 Mitch Prince L PTS 6 Clydebank
15.12.06 Ben Jones L PTS 4 Bethnal Green
22.01.07 Darren Johnstone L PTS 10 Glasgow
(British Masters S.Featherweight Title Challenge)
30.03.07 David Mulholland L PTS 4 Crawley
20.04.07 Billy Corcoran L PTS 8 Dudley
13.07.07 Akaash Bhatia L RSC 5 Barnsley
13.10.07 Esham Pickering L RTD 3 Newark
01.12.07 Rocky Dean L RSC 5 Bethnal Green
25.01.08 Ben Jones L PTS 4 Dagenham
16.02.08 Jon Kays L PTS 6 Blackpool
23.02.08 Robin Deakin W PTS 4 Crawley
14.03.08 Anthony Crolla L PTS 6 Manchester
Career: 50 contests, won 11, drew 2, lost 37.

Ruben Giles
Virginia Water. *Born* Woking, 1 April, 1987
L.Middleweight. *Ht* 5'7½"
Manager Self

28.05.06 Barry Downes W PTS 4 Longford
17.11.06 Bheki Moyo W RSC 4 Bethnal Green
24.02.07 Mahamadou Traore W RSC 3 Bracknell
27.04.07 Kristian Laight W PTS 4 Wembley
23.09.07 Karl Taylor W PTS 6 Heathrow
Career: 5 contests, won 5.

Tom Glover
Maldon, Essex. *Born* Maldon, 21 June, 1981
L. Welterweight. Former Undefeated British Masters Lightweight Champion. *Ht* 5'6½"
Manager A. Sims

11.02.06 Billy Smith W PTS 4 Bethnal Green
24.03.06 Gavin Tait L PTS 4 Bethnal Green
03.06.06 Ben Hudson W PTS 4 Chigwell
26.10.06 James Gorman DREW 6 Belfast
09.12.06 Rocky Muscas W PTS 4 Chigwell
26.01.07 Nathan Weise DREW 4 Dagenham
01.07.07 John Baguley W PTS 10 Colchester
(Vacant British Masters Lightweight Title)
07.09.07 Nadeem Siddique L PTS 6 Doncaster
05.10.07 Leonard Lothian L PTS 4 Bethnal Green
25.11.07 Gavin Deacon W PTS 6 Colchester
04.04.08 Gareth Couch L PTS 6 Bethnal Green
10.05.08 Jack Perry DREW 4 Nottingham
Career: 12 contests, won 5, drew 3, lost 4.

Rick Godding
Bolton. *Born* Bolton, 18 February, 1985
L.Welterweight. *Ht* 5'10¼"
Manager S. Wood

23.12.07 Kristian Laight W PTS 6 Bolton

16.02.08 Senol Dervis W PTS 6 Blackpool
15.06.08 Carl Allen W PTS 6 St Helens
Career: 3 contests, won 3.

Michael Gomez (Armstrong)
Manchester. *Born* Dublin, 21 June, 1977
Lightweight. Former WBU S.Featherweight Champion. Former Undefeated WBO Inter-Continental & British S.Featherweight Champion. Former WBO Inter-Continental S.Featherweight Champion. Former Undefeated Central Area & IBF Inter-Continental Featherweight Champion. *Ht* 5'5"
Manager Self

10.06.95 Danny Ruegg W PTS 6 Manchester
15.09.95 Greg Upton L PTS 4 Mansfield
24.11.95 Danny Ruegg L PTS 4 Manchester
19.09.96 Martin Evans W RSC 1 Manchester
09.11.96 David Morris W PTS 4 Manchester
22.03.97 John Farrell W RSC 2 Wythenshawe
03.05.97 Chris Williams L PTS 4 Manchester
11.09.97 Wayne Jones W RSC 2 Widnes
18.04.98 Benny Jones W PTS 4 Manchester
16.05.98 Craig Spacie W RSC 3 Bethnal Green
05.09.98 Pete Buckley W PTS 6 Telford
14.11.98 David Jeffrey W RSC 1 Cheshunt
19.12.98 Kevin Sheil W RSC 4 Liverpool
13.02.99 Dave Hinds W PTS 6 Newcastle
27.02.99 Chris Jickells W RSC 5 Oldham
(Vacant Central Area Featherweight Title)
29.05.99 Nigel Leake W RSC 2 Halifax
(Vacant IBF Inter-Continental Featherweight Title)
07.08.99 William Alverzo W PTS 6 Atlantic City, New Jersey, USA
04.09.99 Gary Thornhill W RSC 2 Bethnal Green
(Vacant British S. Featherweight Title)
06.11.99 Jose Juan Manjarrez W PTS 12 Widnes
(WBO Inter-Continental S. Featherweight Title Defence)
11.12.99 Oscar Galindo W RSC 11 Liverpool
(WBO Inter-Continental S. Featherweight Title Defence)
29.01.00 Chris Jickells W RSC 4 Manchester
29.02.00 Dean Pithie W PTS 12 Widnes
(British S. Featherweight Title Defence)
24.06.00 Carl Allen W CO 2 Glasgow
08.07.00 Carl Greaves W CO 2 Widnes
(British S. Featherweight Title Defence)
19.10.00 Awel Abdulai W PTS 8 Harrisburg, USA
11.12.00 Ian McLeod W PTS 12 Widnes
(British S.Featherweight Title Defence)
10.02.01 Laszlo Bognar L RSC 9 Widnes
(WBO Inter-Continental S. Featherweight Title Defence)
07.07.01 Laszlo Bognar W RSC 3 Manchester
(WBO Inter-Continental S. Featherweight Title Challenge)
27.10.01 Craig Docherty W RSC 2 Manchester
(British S.Featherweight Title Defence)
01.06.02 Kevin Lear L RTD 8 Manchester
(Vacant WBU S. Featherweight Title)
28.09.02 Jimmy Beech W RSC 4 Manchester
18.01.03 Rakhim Mingaleev W RTD 4 Preston
05.04.03 Vladimir Borov W RSC 3 Manchester
25.10.03 Alex Arthur W RSC 5 Edinburgh
(British S.Featherweight Title Challenge)

03.04.04 Ben Odamattey W RSC 3 Manchester
(Vacant WBU S.Featherweight Title)
22.05.04 Justin Juuko W RSC 2 Widnes
(WBU S.Featherweight Title Defence)
01.10.04 Leva Kirakosyan W RTD 6 Manchester
(WBU S.Featherweight Title Defence)
11.02.05 Javier Osvaldo Alvarez L RSC 6 Manchester
(WBU S.Featherweight Title Defence)
28.01.06 Peter McDonagh L RSC 5 Dublin
(Vacant All-Ireland Lightweight Title)
06.05.07 Daniel Thorpe W RSC 3 Altrincham
24.06.07 Youssef Al Hamidi W RTD 3 Wigan
19.10.07 Carl Johanneson L RSC 6 Doncaster
(British S.Featherweight Title Challenge)
29.03.08 Baz Carey W PTS 6 Glasgow
21.06.08 Amir Khan L RSC 5 Birmingham
(Commonwealth Lightweight Title Challenge)
Career: 44 contests, won 35, lost 9.

Danny Goode   Philip Sharkey

Danny Goode
New Milton. *Born* Wimbledon, 15 January, 1980
Middleweight. *Ht* 5'8"
Manager Self

16.10.04 Geraint Harvey W PTS 4 Dagenham
06.02.05 Neil Jarmolinski W PTS 4 Southampton
23.03.05 Tony Randell W PTS 6 Leicester Square
30.04.05 John-Paul Temple W PTS 4 Dagenham
26.06.05 John-Paul Temple W PTS 4 Southampton
18.09.05 Rocky Muscus W PTS 4 Bethnal Green
05.03.06 Terry Adams W PTS 8 Southampton
07.04.06 Jamie Ambler W PTS 4 Longford
23.07.06 Ben Hudson W PTS 4 Dagenham
24.09.06 Mark Franks W RSC 3 Southampton
25.02.07 Duncan Cottier W PTS 6 Southampton
19.10.07 Sherman Alleyne W PTS 4 Mayfair
01.12.07 Jay Morris L PTS 4 Bethnal Green
17.05.08 Gary McMillan L PTS 6 Glasgow
27.06.08 George Hillyard L RSC 2 Bethnal Green
Career: 15 contests, won 12, lost 3.

Chris Goodwin

Chester. *Born* Chester, 31 October, 1988
Welterweight. *Ht* 5'7½"
Manager S. Goodwin

07.12.06 Chris Mullen L PTS 6 Sunderland
24.02.07 Kristian Laight W PTS 6 Stoke
12.05.07 James Lilley W PTS 4 Stoke
17.11.07 Pete Buckley W PTS 4 Stoke
01.03.08 Johnny Greaves W PTS 6 Stoke
17.05.08 Baz Carey W PTS 4 Stoke
06.06.08 Carl Allen W PTS 4 Stoke
Career: 7 contests, won 6, lost 1.

Phil Goodwin

Hull. *Born* Hull, 2 May, 1980
L.Heavyweight. *Ht* 5'10"
Manager C. Greaves

25.09.07 Phillip Callaghan W PTS 6 Hull
30.11.07 James Tucker W PTS 6 Hull
07.03.08 Rasham Sohi L RSC 3 Nottingham
21.06.08 Dave Pearson W RSC 2 Hull
Career: 4 contests, won 3, lost 1.

Martin Gordon

Brierley Hill. *Born* Wordsley, 23 July, 1982
Welterweight. *Ht* 5'9"
Manager E. Johnson

26.10.06 Bheki Moyo DREW 6 Dudley
17.11.06 Billy Smith L PTS 6 Brierley Hill
06.12.06 Wayne Downing L PTS 6 Stoke
20.04.07 Kristian Laight L PTS 4 Dudley
28.11.07 Wayne Downing L PTS 4 Walsall
28.02.08 Matt Seawright L PTS 4 Wolverhampton
Career: 6 contests, drew 1, lost 5.

James Gorman   Les Clark

James Gorman

Belfast. *Born* Belfast, 1 August, 1979
Northern Ireland Area L.Welterweight
Champion.. *Ht* 5'8"
Manager Self

28.06.03 Jamie Arthur L PTS 4 Cardiff
11.10.03 Lee Beavis L PTS 4 Portsmouth
25.10.03 George Telfer L PTS 4 Edinburgh
22.11.03 Peter McDonagh W PTS 4 Belfast

28.02.04 Ceri Hall L PTS 6 Bridgend
01.04.04 Lee Beavis L RTD 2 Bethnal Green
24.09.04 Silence Saheed L PTS 6 Millwall
12.11.04 Jas Malik W RTD 2 Belfast
18.03.05 Stephen Haughian L PTS 4 Belfast
14.05.05 Pete Buckley W PTS 6 Dublin
24.06.05 Daniel Thorpe W PTS 6 Belfast
30.09.05 George Hillyard L RSC 1 Kirkcaldy
24.11.05 Stephen Haughian L PTS 6 Lurgan
27.01.06 Wayne Goddard L PTS 4 Dagenham
07.10.06 Steve Anning W PTS 6 Belfast
26.10.06 Tom Glover DREW 6 Belfast
25.11.06 Jonathan Whiteman W RSC 2 Belfast
17.02.07 Chris Long W RSC 3 Cork
13.10.07 Gary Hamilton W PTS 10 Belfast
(Vacant Northern Ireland Area L.Welterweight Title)
08.12.07 Andrew Murray L TD 4 Belfast
(Vacant All-Ireland L.Welterweight Title)
26.01.08 Billy Walsh L PTS 10 Cork
(Vacant All-Ireland Welterweight Title)
Career: 21 contests, won 8, drew 1, lost 12.

Danny Grainger

Chesterfield. *Born* Chesterfield, 1
September, 1979
Cruiserweight. *Ht* 5'11¼"
Manager Self

05.10.02 Jamie Wilson W PTS 6 Chesterfield
21.10.02 Jamie Wilson W PTS 6 Cleethorpes
29.11.02 Gary Jones W PTS 6 Hull
08.06.03 Darren Stubbs W RSC 2 Shaw
12.10.03 Paul Billington W PTS 6 Sheffield
03.04.04 Terry Morrill W RSC 5 Sheffield
04.06.04 Patrick Cito W PTS 6 Hull
15.05.05 Hastings Rasani L RSC 5 Sheffield
05.03.06 Jimi Hendrix W PTS 6 Sheffield
07.09.07 Danny Thornton L PTS 4 Doncaster
Career: 10 contests, won 8, lost 2.

Keiron Gray   Philip Sharkey

Keiron Gray

Telford. *Born* West Bromwich, 8 January,
1978
Middleweight. *Ht* 5'10¼"
Manager E. Johnson

10.05.08 Lee Duncan W RSC 3 Nottingham
20.06.08 Tony Stones W PTS 4 Wolverhampton
Career: 2 contests, won 2.

Johnny Greaves

East Ham. *Born* Forest Gate, 4 March, 1979
L.Welterweight. *Ht* 5'9"
Manager C. Greaves

09.06.07 Rob Hunt L PTS 6 Middlesbrough
28.06.07 Dean Harrison L PTS 6 Dudley
14.07.07 Jamie Cox L PTS 4 Greenwich
11.08.07 John Watson L PTS 4 Liverpool
16.09.07 Dwayne Hill L PTS 6 Sheffield
06.10.07 Anthony Crolla L RSC 3 Nottingham
25.11.07 Lee Purdy L PTS 6 Colchester
10.12.07 Darren Hamilton L RSC 3 Peterborough
01.02.08 Jamie Radford L PTS 4 Bethnal Green
15.02.08 Paul Holborn L PTS 6 Sunderland
23.02.08 Sergei Rozhakmens W RSC 1 Newark
01.03.08 Chris Goodwin L PTS 6 Stoke
08.03.08 Eddie Corcoran L PTS 4 Greenwich
17.03.08 Stuart Green L PTS 8 Glasgow
18.04.08 Scott Woolford L RSC 3 Bethnal Green
14.06.08 Liam Walsh L CO 4 Bethnal Green
Career: 16 contests, won 1, lost 15.

Johnny Greaves   Philip Sharkey

Radcliffe Green   Philip Sharkey

Radcliffe Green

Balham. *Born* Jamaica, 24 November, 1973
Cruiserweight. *Ht* 5'9¼"
Manager W. Fuller

26.03.01	Peter Haymer L PTS 4 Wembley
22.04.01	Adam Cale W CO 5 Streatham
03.06.01	Rob Hayes-Scott W RSC 4 Southwark
21.07.01	John Keeton L PTS 4 Sheffield
28.10.01	Michael Pinnock W PTS 4 Southwark
16.11.01	Darren Corbett L PTS 8 Dublin
10.02.02	Valery Odin L PTS 6 Southwark
20.04.02	Nathan King L PTS 6 Cardiff
04.05.02	Andrew Lowe L PTS 4 Bethnal Green
22.09.02	Mark Baker L PTS 6 Southwark
27.10.02	Neil Linford DREW 10 Southwark
	(Vacant British Masters L.Heavyweight Title)
08.02.03	Eric Teymour L RTD 1 Norwich
29.03.03	Andrew Lowe L PTS 10 Wembley
	(Vacant Southern Area L.Heavyweight Title)
26.09.03	Tony Booth L PTS 6 Millwall
07.11.03	Andrew Lowe L PTS 6 Sheffield
07.02.04	Bruce Scott L PTS 6 Bethnal Green
08.05.04	Courtney Fry L PTS 6 Bristol
15.12.04	Simon Francis L PTS 6 Sheffield
04.02.05	Gareth Hogg L PTS 4 Plymouth
20.02.05	Henry Smith L PTS 6 Bristol
08.04.05	Neil Hosking W RSC 2 Bristol
19.06.05	Junior MacDonald L RTD 1 Bethnal Green
25.11.05	Gyorgy Hidvegi L RTD 2 Liverpool
25.02.06	Darren Morgan L RSC 3 Canning Town
13.10.07	Martin Rogan L RSC 2 Belfast
01.12.07	Ali Adams W CO 4 Bethnal Green
13.06.08	Micky Steeds L RTD 4 Portsmouth

Career: 27 contests, won 5, drew 1, lost 21.

Stuart Green

Glenrothes. *Born* Kirkcaldy, 13 December, 1984
L.Welterweight. *Ht* 5'6"
Manager T. Gilmour

17.11.03	Chris Long W PTS 6 Glasgow
12.03.04	Jason Nesbitt W PTS 8 Irvine
07.06.04	Gavin Tait W PTS 6 Glasgow
11.10.04	Paul Holborn L PTS 6 Glasgow
21.02.05	Pete Buckley W PTS 6 Glasgow
11.06.05	Dave Hinds W PTS 6 Kirkcaldy
30.09.05	Fred Janes W PTS 4 Kirkcaldy
17.03.06	Adam Kelly W PTS 4 Kirkcaldy
21.04.06	Michael Kelly L PTS 4 Belfast
27.05.06	Lee McAllister L RSC 8 Aberdeen
	(Vacant Scottish Area Lightweight Title)
09.09.06	Pete Buckley W PTS 8 Inverurie

Roman Greenberg

Philip Sharkey

18.09.06	Pete Buckley W PTS 6 Glasgow
06.10.06	Dean Hickman L PTS 6 Wolverhampton
03.11.06	Martin Kristjansen L PTS 6 Skive, Denmark
13.12.06	Chris Long W PTS 6 Strand
01.02.07	Sam Rukundo L PTS 6 Piccadilly
02.03.07	Ceri Hall L RSC 9 Neath *(Vacant Celtic L.Welterweight Title)*
17.03.08	Johnny Greaves W PTS 8 Glasgow

Career: 18 contests, won 11, lost 7.

Roman Greenberg

Finchley. *Born* Russia, 18 May, 1982
IBO Inter-Continental Heavyweight
Champion. *Ht* 6'2½"
Manager J. Evans

22.11.01	Dave Clarke W RSC 5 Paddington
25.02.02	Paul Bonson W PTS 6 Slough
25.04.02	Jakarta Nakyru W RSC 4 Las Vegas, Nevada, USA
28.11.02	Tony Booth W PTS 4 Finchley
05.12.02	Dave Clarke W RSC 1 Sheffield
20.12.02	Derek McCafferty W PTS 4 Bracknell
24.01.03	Piotr Jurczk W CO 1 Sheffield
04.03.03	Calvin Miller W RSC 2 Miami, Florida, USA
18.03.03	Gary Williams W RSC 1 Reading
15.05.03	Tracy Williams W RTD 2 Miami, Florida, USA
29.05.03	Troy Beets W RSC 3 Miami, Florida, USA
05.09.03	Luke Simpkin W RTD 4 Sheffield
18.09.03	Konstantin Prizyuk W RSC 1 Mayfair
26.11.03	Mendauga Kulikauskas W RSC 5 Mayfair
15.04.04	Jason Gethers W RSC 6 NYC, New York, USA
10.09.04	Vitaly Shkraba W PTS 6 Wembley
10.12.04	Julius Francis W PTS 10 Sheffield
28.01.05	Marcus McGee W RSC 4 NYC, New York, USA
11.06.05	Josh Gutcher W RSC 4 Las Vegas, Nevada, USA
20.07.05	Mamadou Sacko W PTS 8 Monte Carlo, Monaco
16.12.05	Kendrick Releford W PTS 10 Bracknell
18.03.06	Alex Vassilev W RSC 6 Monte Carlo, Monaco *(Vacant IBO Inter-Continental Heavyweight Title)*
04.11.06	Alexei Varakin W CO 6 Monte Carlo, Monaco *(IBO Inter-Continental Heavyweight Title Defence)*
09.12.06	Steve Pannell W RSC 3 Hollywood, Florida, USA
10.03.07	Michael Simms W PTS 10 NYC, New York, USA
18.08.07	Damon Reed W RSC 9 Salt Lake City, Utah, USA
31.10.07	Colin Kenna W PTS 8 Bayswater

Career: 27 contests, won 27.

Carl Griffiths

Oakham. *Born* Leicester, 4 July, 1984
Lightweight. *Ht* 5'5¾"
Manager D. Cowland

30.03.07	Tony McQuade L PTS 6 Peterborough
21.06.07	Sergei Rozhakmens W PTS 6 Peterborough
21.09.07	Sebastian Hart L CO 2 Peterborough
10.12.07	Leroy Smedley W RSC 2 Leicester
16.02.08	Dean Mills L RSC 6 Leicester
20.06.08	Dezzie O'Connor L PTS 6 Plymouth

Career: 6 contests, won 2, lost 4.

Ruben Groenewald

London. *Born* Brakpan South Africa, 13
October, 1977
S.Middleweight. Former Undefeated
WBF Inter-Continental S.Middleweight
Champion. Former Undefeated WBU
Middleweight Champion. Former
Undefeated British Masters S.Middleweight
Champion. Former Undefeated All-African
Middleweight Champion. *Ht* 5'10¼"
Manager M. Helliet

27.03.96	Andries Gogome DREW 4 Johannesburg, South Africa
21.04.96	Clifford Smith W PTS 4 Thabong, South Africa
03.07.96	Michael Ramabele W PTS 4 Johannesburg, South Africa
11.08.96	Alpheus Phungula W PTS 4 Durban, South Africa
01.09.96	Andries Gogome L PTS 4 Johannesburg, South Africa
22.06.97	Edward Ramathape W RSC 2 Johannesburg, South Africa
25.11.97	David Ramantsi W RSC 1 Temba, South Africa
31.05.98	Roland Francis DREW 6 Durban, South Africa
24.06.98	Sipho Ndele W RSC 4 Johannesburg, South Africa
26.08.98	Boyisela Mashalele W PTS 6 Johannesburg, South Africa
14.10.98	Mondli Mbonambi W PTS 8 Secunda, South Africa
03.08.99	Sipho Sibeko DREW 6 Temba, South Africa
23.11.99	John Tshabalala W PTS 6 Temba, South Africa
10.03.00	Delroy Leslie L PTS 12 Bethnal Green *(Vacant Interim WBF Middleweight Title)*
20.09.00	Elvis Adonisi W CO 10 Brakpan, South Africa
24.10.00	Cyprian Emeti W RSC 11 Brakpan, South Africa *(Vacant All-African L.Middleweight Title)*
24.02.01	Ojay Abrahams W PTS 6 Bethnal Green
03.04.01	Paul Bowen W PTS 6 Bethnal Green
21.07.01	Terry Morrill W RSC 4 Sheffield
20.09.01	Harry Butler W PTS 4 Blackfriars
09.10.01	Leigh Wicks W PTS 6 Cardiff
10.02.02	Wayne Asker W PTS 10 Southwark *(Vacant British Masters S.Middleweight Title)*
01.06.02	Anthony Farnell W PTS 12 Manchester *(Vacant WBU Middleweight Title)*
28.09.02	Anthony Farnell L PTS 12 Manchester *(WBU Middleweight Title Defence)*
23.10.04	Danilo Haussler L PTS 8 Berlin, Germany
24.04.05	Alan Gilbert W RSC 10 Leicester Square *(Vacant WBF Inter-Continental S.Middleweight Title)*

02.12.05	Carl Froch L RSC 5 Nottingham *(Commonwealth S.Middleweight Title Challenge)*
28.11.07	Mark Nilsen W PTS 6 Piccadilly
04.04.08	Richard Horton L PTS 6 Bethnal Green

Career: 29 contests, won 20, drew 3, lost 6.

Ruben Groenewald   Philip Sharkey

Omar Gumati

Chester. *Born* Chester, 18 May, 1984
Middleweight. *Ht* 5'9¼"
Manager S. Goodwin

07.05.03	Craig Goodman W PTS 6 Ellesmere Port
02.10.03	Danny Moir L PTS 6 Sunderland
01.12.03	Ojay Abrahams W PTS 6 Leeds
05.12.05	Ryan Ashworth L PTS 6 Leeds
15.12.05	Davey Jones L PTS 6 Cleethorpes
11.02.06	Paul Porter W RSC 3 Bethnal Green
09.03.06	Martin Marshall DREW 6 Sunderland
20.03.06	Mark Franks W RTD 4 Leeds
23.04.06	Joe Mitchell W PTS 4 Chester
26.05.06	Wayne Goddard L PTS 4 Bethnal Green
17.05.08	Davey Jones W PTS 6 Stoke

Career: 11 contests, won 6, drew 1, lost 4.

Danny Gwilym

Bristol. *Born* Bristol, 15 January, 1975
L.Middleweight. *Ht* 5'7"
Manager Self

16.12.01	Wayne Wheeler L RSC 2 Bristol
11.02.02	James Lee L PTS 6 Southampton
12.07.02	Mo W PTS 6 Southampton
26.02.03	Wasim Hussain W PTS 6 Bristol
17.03.03	Danny Cooper L PTS 6 Southampton
16.04.03	Lenny Daws L RSC 2 Nottingham
26.09.03	Darren Covill W PTS 6 Millwall
12.10.03	Mo L PTS 6 Sheffield
06.12.03	Martin Concepcion L RSC 2 Cardiff
09.07.05	Arv Mittoo W RSC 4 Bristol
24.07.05	Garry Buckland L RSC 2 Leicester Square
12.11.05	Kristian Laight W PTS 6 Bristol
28.04.07	Paul Burns L PTS 6 Clydebank
06.05.07	Chris Johnson L RSC 4 Altrincham
21.10.07	Adam Wilcox W PTS 6 Swansea

Career: 15 contests, won 6, lost 9.

H

Saud Hafiz
Watford. *Born* Watford, 20 August, 1979
S.Featherweight. *Ht* 5'7¼"
Manager M. Helliet
31.01.08 Shaun Walton W PTS 4 Piccadilly
10.04.08 Shaun Walton W RSC 3 Piccadilly
Career: 2 contests, won 2.

Saud Hafiz   Philip Sharkey

Matthew Hainy
Derby. *Born* Dewsbury, 29 September, 1981
S.Middleweight. *Ht* 5'11¼"
Manager C. Mitchell
18.01.08 James Tucker W PTS 4 Burton
16.02.08 Ricky Strike W PTS 4 Leicester
22.06.08 Manoocha Salari W PTS 6 Derby
Career: 3 contests, won 3.

Matthew Hall
Manchester. *Born* Manchester, 5 July, 1984
Middleweight. *Ht* 5'7¾"
Manager F. Warren/Brian Hughes
28.09.02 Pedro Thompson W RSC 1 Manchester
14.12.02 Pedro Thompson W PTS 4 Newcastle
18.01.03 Clive Johnson W PTS 4 Preston
05.04.03 Brian Coleman W RSC 1 Manchester
08.05.03 Patrick Cito W PTS 4 Widnes
06.05.04 Craig Lynch W PTS 6 Barnsley
12.06.04 Isidro Gonzalez W RSC 3 Manchester
01.10.04 Howard Clarke W RSC 5 Manchester
12.11.04 Ojay Abrahams W RSC 1 Halifax
03.12.04 Jason Collins W PTS 6 Edinburgh
21.01.05 Leigh Wicks W PTS 4 Bridgend
11.02.05 Sylvestre Marianini W CO 1 Manchester
04.06.05 Matt Scriven W RSC 2 Manchester
28.01.06 Jon Foster W RSC 3 Nottingham
11.03.06 Robert Burton W CO 1 Newport
08.07.06 Kevin Phelan W RSC 1 Cardiff
14.07.07 Martin Concepcion L RSC 1 Greenwich
03.12.07 Tyan Booth W PTS 8 Manchester
22.03.08 Kerry Hope W RSC 8 Cardiff
Career: 19 contests, won 18, lost 1.

Richard Hall
Ripley. *Born* Belper, 17 July, 1982
L.Welterweight. *Ht* 5'9¼"
Manager M. Shinfield
10.12.07 Byron Vince W PTS 6 Cleethorpes
Career: 1 contest, won 1.

Stuart Hall
Darlington. *Born* Darlington, 24 February, 1980
S.Bantamweight. *Ht* 5'8¼"
Manager M. Marsden
26.04.08 Abdul Mougharbel W PTS 6 Darlington
Career: 1 contest, won 1.

Leigh Hallet
Walsall. *Born* Sutton Coldfield, 29 July, 1980
Middleweight. *Ht* 5'10"
Manager R. Woodhall
08.09.06 Jon Foster W PTS 6 Birmingham
28.09.07 Paul Royston L RSC 3 Birmingham
Career: 2 contests, won 1, lost 1.

Darren Hamilton
Bristol. *Born* Bristol, 6 September, 1978
L.Welterweight. *Ht* 5'9"
Manager C. Sanigar
03.11.06 Neal McQuade W PTS 6 Bristol
07.12.06 Jaz Virdee W PTS 6 Peterborough
24.02.07 James Lilley W PTS 6 Bristol
28.11.07 Byron Vince W PTS 6 Piccadilly
10.12.07 Johnny Greaves W RSC 3 Peterborough
Career: 5 contests, won 5.

Darren Hamilton   Philip Sharkey

Gary Hamilton
Belfast. *Born* Belfast, 27 May, 1980
Lightweight. *Ht* 5'8¼"
Manager P. McCausland
20.10.00 Gyula Zabo W PTS 4 Belfast
10.12.00 Patrick Dominguez L RSC 3 Elgin, Illinois, USA
21.01.02 John Marshall L PTS 4 Glasgow
18.02.02 Tony McPake L PTS 4 Glasgow
24.04.02 Robert Murray L PTS 6 Dublin
05.04.03 Dafydd Carlin L PTS 10 Belfast
(*Vacant Northern Ireland Area Lightweight Title*)
13.10.07 James Gorman L PTS 10 Belfast
(*Vacant Northern Ireland Area L.Welterweight Title*)
31.05.08 Andrew Ward W CO 1 Belfast
Career: 8 contests, won 2, lost 6.

Kevin Hammond
Lincoln. *Born* Lincoln, 8 November, 1980
Middleweight. *Ht* 5'9¼"
Manager M. Shinfield
01.12.07 David Kirk W PTS 4 Nottingham
02.05.08 Gavin Brook W RTD 1 Nottingham
31.05.08 Lester Walsh DREW 4 Newark
Career: 3 contests, won 2, drew 1.

Anthony Hanna
Birmingham. *Born* Birmingham, 22 September, 1974
British Masters Featherweight Champion.
Former Undefeated Midlands Area Flyweight Champion. *Ht* 5'6"
Manager Self
19.11.92 Nick Tooley L PTS 6 Evesham
10.12.92 Daren Fifield L RSC 6 Bethnal Green
11.05.93 Tiger Singh W PTS 6 Norwich
24.05.93 Lyndon Kershaw L PTS 6 Bradford
16.09.93 Chris Lyons W PTS 6 Southwark
06.10.93 Tiger Singh W PTS 6 Solihull
03.11.93 Mickey Cantwell L PTS 8 Bristol
25.01.94 Marty Chestnut W PTS 4 Piccadilly
10.02.94 Allan Mooney W RTD 1 Glasgow
13.04.94 Allan Mooney L PTS 6 Glasgow
22.04.94 Jesper Jensen L PTS 6 Aalborg, Denmark
03.08.94 Paul Ingle L PTS 6 Bristol
01.10.94 Mark Hughes L PTS 4 Cardiff
30.11.94 Shaun Norman W PTS 10 Solihull
(*Vacant Midlands Area Flyweight Title*)
24.02.95 Darren Greaves W RSC 5 Weston super Mare
06.03.95 Mark Hughes L PTS 6 Mayfair
27.04.95 Mickey Cantwell L PTS 6 Bethnal Green
05.05.95 Mark Cokely W RSC 4 Swansea
04.06.95 Mark Reynolds L PTS 10 Bethnal Green
(*Elim. British Flyweight Title*)
02.07.95 Mickey Cantwell L PTS 6 Dublin
02.11.95 Shaun Norman DREW 10 Mayfair
(*Midlands Area Flyweight Title Defence*)
31.01.96 Marty Chestnut DREW 6 Stoke
20.03.96 Harry Woods L PTS 6 Cardiff
22.04.96 Neil Parry W PTS 6 Manchester
14.05.96 Dharmendra Singh Yadav L PTS 4 Dagenham
08.10.96 Marty Chestnut W PTS 6 Battersea
11.12.96 Mark Reynolds DREW 8 Southwark
28.01.97 Colin Moffett L PTS 4 Belfast
28.02.97 Paul Weir L PTS 8 Kilmarnock
14.03.97 Jesper Jensen L PTS 6 Odense, Denmark
30.04.97 Clinton Beeby DREW 6 Acton

119

10.05.97   Jason Booth L PTS 6 Nottingham
02.06.97   Keith Knox L PTS 6 Glasgow
14.10.97   Louis Veitch L PTS 6 Kilmarnock
27.10.97   Russell Laing W PTS 4 Musselburgh
13.11.97   Noel Wilders L PTS 6 Bradford
24.11.97   Shaun Anderson L PTS 8 Glasgow
20.12.97   Damaen Kelly L PTS 4 Belfast
31.01.98   Jason Booth L PTS 6 Edmonton
23.02.98   David Coldwell W PTS 6 Salford
19.03.98   Andy Roberts L PTS 6 Doncaster
18.05.98   Chris Emanuele W RSC 3 Cleethorpes
11.09.98   Nicky Booth DREW 6 Cleethorpes
18.09.98   Colin Moffett DREW 4 Belfast
29.10.98   Nick Tooley W RTD 6 Bayswater
25.11.98   Nicky Booth W PTS 6 Clydach
21.01.99   Ola Dali W PTS 6 Piccadilly
13.03.99   Damaen Kelly L PTS 12 Manchester
           (Vacant British Flyweight Title.
           Commonwealth Flyweight Title
           Challenge)
24.04.99   Noel Wilders L PTS 6 Peterborough
07.06.99   Alston Buchanan W RSC 3 Glasgow
29.06.99   Tommy Waite L PTS 4 Bethnal Green
16.10.99   Stevie Quinn W PTS 4 Belfast
22.11.99   Frankie DeMilo L PTS 6 Piccadilly
04.12.99   Ady Lewis L PTS 6 Manchester
19.02.00   Ian Napa L PTS 6 Dagenham
13.03.00   Mzukisi Sikali L PTS 6 Bethnal Green
27.05.00   Nicky Cook L PTS 6 Mayfair
25.07.00   David Lowry L PTS 4 Southwark
19.08.00   Marc Callaghan L PTS 4 Brentwood
29.09.00   Rocky Dean L PTS 4 Bethnal Green
07.10.00   Oleg Kiryukhin L PTS 6 Doncaster
14.10.00   Danny Costello DREW 4 Wembley
31.10.00   Dmitri Kirilov L PTS 6 Hammersmith
10.02.01   Tony Mulholland L PTS 4 Widnes
19.02.01   Alex Moon L PTS 6 Glasgow
03.03.01   Marc Callaghan L PTS 6 Wembley
24.04.01   Silence Mabuza L PTS 6 Liverpool
06.05.01   Michael Hunter L PTS 4 Hartlepool
26.05.01   Mickey Bowden L PTS 4 Bethnal
           Green
04.06.01   Michael Hunter L PTS 4 Hartlepool
01.11.01   Nigel Senior L PTS 6 Hull
24.11.01   Martin Power L PTS 4 Bethnal Green
08.12.01   Faprakob Rakkiatgym L PTS 8
           Dagenham
24.03.02   Mickey Coveney L PTS 4 Streatham
23.06.02   Johannes Maisa L PTS 4 Southwark
30.10.02   Mickey Bowden L PTS 4 Leicester
           Square
08.11.02   Sean Green L PTS 6 Doncaster
17.11.02   Shinny Bayaar L PTS 6 Shaw
14.12.02   Michael Hunter L PTS 6 Newcastle
15.02.03   Steve Gethin L PTS 6 Wolverhampton
24.02.03   Jackson Williams W PTS 6
           Birmingham
08.06.03   Darryn Walton L PTS 6 Shaw
25.09.03   Rob Jeffries L PTS 6 Bethnal Green
01.11.03   Andrew Ferrans L PTS 4 Glasgow
14.11.03   Mickey Bowden L PTS 4 Bethnal Green
21.11.03   Buster Dennis L PTS 6 Millwall
29.11.03   Willie Limond L PTS 4 Renfrew
09.04.04   Rendall Munroe L PTS 6 Rugby
16.04.04   Billy Corcoran L PTS 4 Bradford
24.04.04   Lee Beavis L PTS 4 Reading
12.05.04   Chris McDonagh L PTS 4 Reading
02.06.04   John Murray L PTS 4 Nottingham
17.06.04   Femi Fehintola L PTS 6 Sheffield
03.07.04   Jeff Thomas L PTS 6 Blackpool
12.11.06   Stuart McFadyen L PTS 6 Manchester
07.12.06   Shaun Doherty L PTS 6 Bradford
15.04.07   Josh Wale L PTS 6 Barnsley
02.06.07   Darryl Mitchell W RTD 5 Bristol

20.07.07   Ricky Owen L RSC 5 Wolverhampton
09.06.08   Furhan Rafiq W RSC 10 Glasgow
           (Vacant British Masters Featherweight
           Title)
Career: 100 contests, won 21, drew 7, lost 72.

Ben Harding

Fowey. *Born* Amersham, 28 September,
1971
Heavyweight. *Ht* 6'3¼"
Manager N. Christian

09.11.07   Tony Booth W PTS 4 Plymouth
29.02.08   Howard Daley DREW 4 Plymouth
Career: 2 contests, won 1, drew 1.

Audley Harrison

Wembley. *Born* Park Royal, 26 October,
1971
Heavyweight. Former Undefeated WBF
Heavyweight Champion. *Ht* 6'4¾"
Manager Self

19.05.01   Michael Middleton W RSC 1 Wembley
22.09.01   Derek McCafferty W PTS 6 Newcastle
20.10.01   Piotr Jurczyk W RSC 2 Glasgow
20.04.02   Julius Long W CO 2 Wembley
21.05.02   Mark Krence W PTS 6 Custom House
10.07.02   Dominic Negus W PTS 6 Wembley
05.10.02   Wade Lewis W RSC 2 Liverpool
23.11.02   Shawn Robinson W RSC 1 Atlantic
           City, New Jersey, USA
08.02.03   Rob Calloway W RSC 5 Brentford
29.03.03   Ratko Draskovic W PTS 8 Wembley
31.05.03   Matthew Ellis W RSC 2 Bethnal Green
09.09.03   Quinn Navarre W RSC 3 Miami,
           Florida, USA
03.10.03   Lisandro Diaz W RSC 4 Las Vegas,
           Nevada, USA
12.12.03   Brian Nix W RSC 3 Laughlin, Nevada,
           USA
20.03.04   Richel Hersisia W CO 4 Wembley
           (WBF Heavyweight Title Challenge)
08.05.04   Julius Francis W PTS 12 Bristol
           (WBF Heavyweight Title Defence)
19.06.04   Tomasz Bonin W RSC 9 Muswell Hill
           (WBF Heavyweight Title Defence)
09.06.05   Robert Davis W RSC 7 Temecula,
           California, USA
18.08.05   Robert Wiggins W RTD 4 San Jose,
           California, USA
10.12.05   Danny Williams L PTS 12 Canning
           Town
           (Vacant Commonwealth Heavyweight
           Title)
14.04.06   Dominick Guinn L PTS 10 Rancho
           Mirage, California, USA
09.06.06   Andrew Greeley W CO 3 Atlantic City,
           New Jersey, USA
09.12.06   Danny Williams W RSC 3 Canning
           Town
17.02.07   Michael Sprott L RSC 3 Wembley
           (European Union Heavyweight Title
           Challenge.Vacant English Heavyweight
           Title)
19.04.08   Jason Barnett W RSC 5 Las Vegas,
           Nevada, USA
Career: 25 contests, won 22, lost 3.

Dean Harrison

Wolverhampton. *Born* Wolverhampton, 9
August, 1983
Welterweight. *Ht* 5'8"
Manager Self

06.10.06   Joe Mitchell W PTS 4 Wolverhampton
26.10.06   Kristian Laight W PTS 4 Dudley
05.12.06   Baz Carey W PTS 4 Wolverhampton
15.02.07   Daniel Thorpe W PTS 4 Dudley
23.03.07   Kristian Laight W PTS 4 Nottingham
20.04.07   Judex Meemea W RSC 6 Dudley
28.06.07   Johnny Greaves W PTS 6 Dudley
21.09.07   Jason Nesbitt W PTS 6 Burton
25.10.07   Rakhim Mingaleev W PTS 6
           Wolverhampton
07.12.07   Ramon Guevara W RSC 5 Las Vegas,
           Nevada, USA
28.02.08   Alex Brew W RSC 7 Wolverhampton
30.04.08   Gary Reid W PTS 8 Wolverhampton
Career: 12 contests, won 12.

Dean Harrison   Les Clark

Jon Harrison

Plymouth. *Born* Scunthorpe, 18 March,
1977
Former Undefeated International Masters L.
Middleweight Champion. *Ht* 5'11½"
Manager Self

13.01.96   Mark Haslam L PTS 6 Manchester
13.02.96   Paul Samuels L CO 1 Cardiff
16.05.96   Dave Fallon W RSC 4 Dunstable
03.07.96   Allan Gray L PTS 6 Wembley
01.10.96   Cam Raeside L PTS 6 Birmingham
07.11.96   Nicky Bardle L PTS 6 Battersea
14.12.96   James Hare L PTS 4 Sheffield
19.04.97   Jason Williams W PTS 6 Plymouth
11.07.97   Pat Larner L PTS 6 Brighton
07.10.97   Paul Salmon L PTS 6 Plymouth
23.02.98   Alan Gilbert L PTS 6 Windsor
24.03.98   Brian Coleman DREW 6
           Wolverhampton
14.07.98   Jason Williams L RTD 2 Reading
12.05.01   Ernie Smith W PTS 4 Plymouth
15.09.01   Darren Williams L PTS 6 Swansea
02.04.04   Nathan Wyatt W PTS 6 Plymouth
27.05.04   Ady Clegg W PTS 4 Huddersfield
17.09.04   Geraint Harvey W PTS 6 Plymouth
13.12.04   Simon Sherrington L RSC 5
           Birmingham
04.02.05   Joe Mitchell W PTS 6 Plymouth
29.04.05   Neil Jarmolinski W PTS 6 Plymouth
10.02.06   Jamie Ambler W PTS 4 Plymouth
15.09.06   Taz Jones L PTS 6 Newport

09.11.07 Gatis Skuja W PTS 10 Plymouth
(Vacant International Masters L.Middleweight Title)
29.02.08 Carl Drake L RSC 7 Plymouth
(Vacant Western Area L.Middleweight Title)
Career: 25 contests, won 10, drew 1, lost 14.

Sebastian Hart
Wisbech. *Born* Burnley, 10 May, 1980
L.Welterweight. *Ht* 5'4¼"
Manager Self

26.11.99 Gary Wilson W PTS 6 Wakefield
08.12.99 Phil Lashley W RSC 3 Stoke
22.01.00 Steve Gethin W PTS 4 Birmingham
24.02.00 John Barnes W PTS 6 Sunderland
05.03.00 Chris Lyons W PTS 6 Peterborough
27.03.00 Lee Armstrong W CO 5 Barnsley
13.05.00 James Rooney L PTS 6 Barnsley
05.06.00 Craig Docherty L RSC 1 Glasgow
04.11.00 Gavin Down L RSC 4 Derby
25.09.01 Jamie McKeever L PTS 4 Liverpool
21.09.07 Carl Griffiths W CO 2 Peterborough
Career: 11 contests, won 7, lost 4.

Lee Haskins   Philip Sharkey

Lee Haskins
Bristol. *Born* Bristol, 29 November, 1983
Bantamweight. Former Undefeated
Commonwealth & English Flyweight
Champion. *Ht* 5'5"
Manager C. Sanigar

06.03.03 Ankar Miah W RSC 1 Bristol
13.06.03 Chris Edwards W PTS 6 Bristol
09.10.03 Neil Read W PTS 4 Bristol
05.12.03 Jason Thomas W PTS 6 Bristol
13.02.04 Marty Kayes W PTS 6 Bristol
08.05.04 Colin Moffett W RSC 2 Bristol
03.07.04 Sergei Tasimov W RSC 5 Bristol
01.10.04 Junior Anderson W CO 3 Bristol
03.12.04 Delroy Spencer W RTD 3 Bristol
(Vacant English Flyweight Title)
18.02.05 Hugo Cardinale W CO 1 Torrevieja, Spain
08.04.05 Moses Kinyua W PTS 10 Bristol
29.04.05 Andrzej Ziora W RSC 1 Bristol
16.09.05 Delroy Spencer W RTD 2 Plymouth
10.02.06 Anthony Mathias W RSC 2 Plymouth
(Vacant Commonwealth Flyweight Title)

07.04.06 Zolile Mbityi W PTS 12 Bristol
(Commonwealth Flyweight Title Defence)
06.10.06 Tshifhiwa Munyai L RSC 6 Bethnal Green
(Commonwealth Bantamweight Title Challenge)
24.02.07 Sumaila Badu W PTS 6 Bristol
21.09.07 Ian Napa L RTD 7 Bethnal Green
(British Bantamweight Title Challenge)
28.03.08 Jamie McDonnell W PTS 8 Barnsley
Career: 19 contests, won 17, lost 2.

Jason Hastie
Edinburgh. *Born* Edinburgh, 24 October, 1986
Featherweight. *Ht* 5'8¼"
Manager Barry Hughes

17.11.07 Michael Crossan W PTS 4 Glasgow
15.12.07 Shaun Walton W PTS 4 Edinburgh
29.03.08 Robin Deakin W PTS 4 Glasgow
Career: 3 contests, won 3.

Mark Hastie
Motherwell. *Born* Bellshill, 28 July, 1981
Welterweight. *Ht* 5'10¾"
Manager T. Gilmour

29.09.06 Steve Cooper W PTS 6 Motherwell
03.11.06 Surinder Sekhon W RSC 1 Glasgow
02.12.06 Geraint Harvey W PTS 6 Clydebank
19.02.07 Pete Buckley W PTS 6 Glasgow
02.03.07 Peter Dunn W PTS 6 Irvine
08.06.07 Alex Stoda W PTS 4 Motherwell
19.10.07 Karl Taylor W PTS 6 Motherwell
Career: 7 contests, won 7.

Matthew Hatton
Manchester. *Born* Stockport, 15 May, 1981
Former Undefeated IBF Inter-Continental
Welterweight Champion. Former
Undefeated Central Area Welterweight
Champion. Former Undefeated Central
Area L.Middleweight Champion. *Ht* 5'8½"
Manager R. Hatton

23.09.00 David White W PTS 4 Bethnal Green
25.11.00 David White W PTS 4 Manchester
11.12.00 Danny Connelly W PTS 4 Widnes
15.01.01 Keith Jones W PTS 4 Manchester
10.02.01 Karl Taylor W PTS 4 Widnes
17.03.01 Assen Vassilev W RSC 5 Manchester
09.06.01 Brian Coleman W RTD 2 Bethnal Green
21.07.01 Ram Singh W RSC 2 Sheffield
15.09.01 Marcus Portman W RSC 3 Manchester
15.12.01 Dafydd Carlin W PTS 6 Wembley
09.02.02 Paul Denton W PTS 6 Manchester
04.05.02 Karl Taylor W RSC 3 Bethnal Green
20.07.02 Karl Taylor W RTD 2 Bethnal Green
28.09.02 David Kirk L PTS 6 Manchester
14.12.02 Paul Denton W PTS 6 Newcastle
15.02.03 David Keir L RSC 4 Wembley
08.05.03 Jay Mahoney W PTS 6 Widnes
17.07.03 Jay Mahoney W RSC 1 Dagenham
27.09.03 Taz Jones W PTS 6 Manchester
13.12.03 Franny Jones DREW 6 Manchester
26.02.04 Peter Dunn W PTS 6 Widnes
06.05.04 Robert Burton W PTS 10 Barnsley
(Central Area Welterweight Title Challenge)
12.06.04 Matt Scriven W RSC 4 Manchester
01.10.04 Lee Armstrong W PTS 8 Manchester

12.11.04 Robert Burton W PTS 10 Halifax
(Central Area L.Middleweight Title Challenge)
11.03.05 Franny Jones W RTD 6 Doncaster
03.06.05 Adnan Hadoui W PTS 8 Manchester
09.09.05 Dmitry Yanushevich W RSC 4 Sheffield
26.11.05 Sergey Starkov W PTS 10 Sheffield
18.03.06 Alexander Abramenko W RTD 6 Monte Carlo, Monaco
13.05.06 Jose Medina W PTS 8 Boston, Massachusetts, USA
20.10.06 Alan Bosworth L DIS 10 Sheffield
(Elim. British Welterweight Title)
10.12.06 Vladimir Borovski W PTS 6 Sheffield
20.01.07 Frank Houghtaling W RTD 7 Las Vegas, Nevada, USA
(Vacant IBF Inter-Continental Welterweight Title)
23.06.07 Edwin Vazquez W PTS 12 Las Vegas, Nevada, USA
(IBF Inter-Continental Welterweight Title Defence)
20.10.07 Samuli Leppiaho W RSC 6 Dublin
08.12.07 Frankie Santos W PTS 8 Las Vegas, Nevada, USA
24.05.08 Craig Watson L PTS 12 Manchester
(Commonwealth Welterweight Title Challenge)
Career: 38 contests, won 33, drew 1, lost 4.

Ricky Hatton   Philip Sharkey

Ricky Hatton
Manchester. *Born* Stockport, 6 October, 1978
IBO L.Welterweight Champion.
Former Undefeated WBC International
L.Welterweight Champion. Former
Undefeated WBA Welterweight Champion.
Former Undefeated WBA, IBF & WBU
L.Welterweight Champion. Former
Undefeated British, WBO Inter-Continental
& Central Area L.Welterweight Champion.
Ht 5'7½"
Manager Self

11.09.97 Kid McAuley W RTD 1 Widnes
19.12.97 Robert Alvarez W PTS 4 NYC, New York, USA
17.01.98 David Thompson W RSC 1 Bristol

27.03.98	Paul Salmon W RSC 1 Telford
18.04.98	Karl Taylor W RSC 1 Manchester
30.05.98	Mark Ramsey W PTS 6 Bristol
18.07.98	Anthony Campbell W PTS 6 Sheffield
19.09.98	Pascal Montulet W CO 2 Oberhausen, Germany
31.10.98	Kevin Carter W RSC 1 Atlantic City, New Jersey, USA
19.12.98	Paul Denton W RSC 6 Liverpool
27.02.99	Tommy Peacock W RSC 2 Oldham *(Vacant Central Area L.Welterweight Title)*
03.04.99	Brian Coleman W CO 2 Kensington
29.05.99	Dillon Carew W RSC 5 Halifax *(Vacant WBO Inter-Continental L. Welterweight Title)*
17.07.99	Mark Ramsey W PTS 6 Doncaster
09.10.99	Bernard Paul W RTD 4 Manchester *(WBO Inter-Continental L.Welterweight Title Defence)*
11.12.99	Mark Winters W RSC 4 Liverpool *(WBO Inter-Continental L. Welterweight Title Defence)*
29.01.00	Leoncio Garces W RSC 3 Manchester
25.03.00	Pedro Teran W RSC 4 Liverpool *(WBO Inter-Continental L. Welterweight Title Defence)*
16.05.00	Ambioris Figuero W RSC 4 Warrington *(WBO Inter-Continental L. Welterweight Title Defence)*
10.06.00	Gilbert Quiros W CO 2 Detroit, Michigan, USA *(WBO Inter-Continental L. Welterweight Title Defence)*
23.09.00	Giuseppe Lauri W RSC 5 Bethnal Green *(WBO Inter-Continental L.Welterweight Title Defence. WBA Inter-Continental L.Welterweight Title Challenge)*
21.10.00	Jonathan Thaxton W PTS 12 Wembley *(Vacant British L.Welterweight Title)*
26.03.01	Tony Pep W CO 4 Wembley *(Vacant WBU L. Welterweight Title)*
07.07.01	Jason Rowland W CO 4 Manchester *(WBU L.Welterweight Title Defence)*
15.09.01	John Bailey W RSC 5 Manchester *(WBU L.Welterweight Title Defence)*
27.10.01	Fred Pendleton W CO 2 Manchester *(WBU L.Welterweight Title Defence)*
15.12.01	Justin Rowsell W RSC 2 Wembley *(WBU L.Welterweight Title Defence)*
09.02.02	Mikhail Krivolapov W RSC 9 Manchester *(WBU L. Welterweight Title Defence)*
01.06.02	Eamonn Magee W PTS 12 Manchester *(WBU L. Welterweight Title Defence)*
28.09.02	Stephen Smith W DIS 2 Manchester *(WBU L.Welterweight Title Defence)*
14.12.02	Joe Hutchinson W CO 4 Newcastle *(WBU L.Welterweight Title Defence)*
05.04.03	Vince Phillips W PTS 12 Manchester *(WBU L.Welterweight Title Defence)*
27.09.03	Aldi Rios W RTD 9 Manchester *(WBU L.Welterweight Title Defence)*
13.12.03	Ben Tackie W PTS 12 Manchester *(WBU L.Welterweight Title Defence)*
03.04.04	Dennis Holbaek Pedersen W RSC 6 Manchester *(WBU L.Welterweight Title Defence)*
12.06.04	Wilfredo Carlos Vilches W PTS 12 Manchester *(WBU L.Welterweight Title Defence)*
01.10.04	Michael Stewart W RSC 5 Manchester *(WBU L.Welterweight Title Defence. Final Elim. IBF L.Welterweight Title)*

11.12.04	Ray Oliveira W CO 10 Canning Town *(WBU L.Welterweight Title Defence)*
04.06.05	Kostya Tszyu W RSC 11 Manchester *(IBF L.Welterweight Title Challenge)*
26.11.05	Carlos Maussa W CO 9 Sheffield *(IBF L.Welterweight Title Challenge. WBA L.Welterweight Title Defence)*
13.05.06	Luis Collazo W PTS 12 Boston, Massachusetts, USA *(WBA Welterweight Title Challenge)*
20.01.07	Juan Urango W PTS 12 Las Vegas, Nevada, USA *(IBF L.Welterweight Title Challenge. Vacant IBO L.Welterweight Title)*
23.06.07	Jose Luis Castillo W CO 4 Las Vegas, Nevada, USA *(IBO L.Welterweight Title Defence. Vacant WBC International L.Welterweight Title)*
08.12.07	Floyd Mayweather L RSC 10 Las Vegas, Nevada, USA *(WBC Welterweight Title Challenge)*
24.05.08	Juan Lazcano W PTS 12 Manchester *(IBO L.Welterweight Title Defence)*

Career: 45 contests, won 44, lost 1.

Stephen Haughian　　　　Philip Sharkey

Stephen Haughian

Lurgan Co. Armagh. *Born* Craigavon, 20 November, 1984
L.Welterweight. *Ht* 5'10½"
Manager J. Breen

18.03.05	James Gorman W PTS 4 Belfast
14.10.05	Imad Khamis W RSC 4 Dublin
24.11.05	James Gorman W PTS 6 Lurgan
28.01.06	Duncan Cottier W PTS 4 Dublin
20.05.06	Pete Buckley W PTS 4 Belfast
26.10.06	Denis Alekseevs W RSC 1 Belfast
11.11.06	Silence Saheed W PTS 6 Dublin
17.02.07	Dwayne Hill W RSC 2 Cork
25.03.07	Chill John W PTS 6 Dublin
14.07.07	Gary O'Connor W RSC 6 Dublin
20.10.07	Thomas Hengstberger W RSC 1 Dublin
11.11.07	Tye Williams W PTS 8 Dunshaughlin
08.12.07	Giammario Grassellini L PTS 12 Belfast *(IBF Inter-Continental Welterweight Title Challenge)*
15.12.07	Artur Jashkul W PTS 6 Dublin
20.06.08	Raul Saiz W RSC 2 Wolverhampton

Career: 15 contests, won 14, lost 1.

David Haye

Bermondsey. *Born* London, 13 October, 1980
WBO Cruiserweight Champion. Former Undefeated WBC, WBA, European & English Cruiserweight Champion. *Ht* 6'3"
Manager Self

08.12.02	Tony Booth W RTD 2 Bethnal Green
24.01.03	Saber Zairi W RSC 4 Sheffield
04.03.03	Roger Bowden W RSC 2 Miami, Florida, USA
18.03.03	Phill Day W RSC 2 Reading
15.07.03	Vance Wynn W RSC 1 Los Angeles, California, USA
01.08.03	Greg Scott-Briggs W CO 1 Bethnal Green
26.09.03	Lolenga Mock W RSC 4 Reading
14.11.03	Tony Dowling W RSC 1 Bethnal Green *(Vacant English Cruiserweight Title)*
20.03.04	Hastings Rasani W RSC 1 Wembley
12.05.04	Arthur Williams W RSC 3 Reading
10.09.04	Carl Thompson L RSC 5 Wembley *(IBO Cruiserweight Title Challenge)*
10.12.04	Valery Semishkur W RSC 1 Sheffield
21.01.05	Garry Delaney W RTD 3 Brentford
04.03.05	Glen Kelly W CO 2 Rotherham
14.10.05	Vincenzo Rossitto W RSC 2 Huddersfield
16.12.05	Alexander Gurov W CO 1 Bracknell *(European Cruiserweight Title Challenge)*
24.03.06	Lasse Johansen W RSC 8 Bethnal Green *(European Cruiserweight Title Defence)*
21.07.06	Ismail Abdoul W PTS 12 Altrincham *(European Cruiserweight Title Defence)*
17.11.06	Giacobbe Fragomeni W RSC 9 Bethnal Green *(European Cruiserweight Title Defence)*
27.04.07	Tomasz Bonin W RSC 1 Wembley
10.11.07	Jean Marc Mormeck W RSC 7 Paris, France *(WBC & WBA Cruiserweight Title Challenges)*
08.03.08	Enzo Maccarinelli W RSC 2 Greenwich *(WBC & WBA Cruiserweight Title Defences. WBO Cruiserweight Title Challenge)*

Career: 22 contests, won 21, lost 1.

Peter Haymer

Enfield. *Born* London, 10 July, 1978
Former Undefeated English L.Heavyweight Champion.
Ht 6'1¼"
Manager Self

25.11.00	Adam Cale W RSC 1 Manchester
27.01.01	Darren Ashton W PTS 4 Bethnal Green
10.03.01	Daniel Ivanov W CO 2 Bethnal Green
26.03.01	Radcliffe Green W PTS 4 Wembley
05.05.01	Terry Morrill W PTS 4 Edmonton
22.09.01	Tony Booth W PTS 4 Bethnal Green
24.11.01	Nathan King L PTS 4 Bethnal Green
12.02.02	Nathan King L PTS 4 Bethnal Green
09.05.02	Mark Snipe W PTS 4 Leicester Square
15.06.02	Paul Bonson W PTS 4 Tottenham
30.10.02	Jimmy Steel W PTS 4 Leicester Square
18.03.03	Mark Brookes W PTS 6 Reading

18.09.03	Ovill McKenzie W PTS 4 Mayfair
10.12.03	Mark Brookes DREW 6 Sheffield
12.11.04	Steven Spartacus W PTS 10 Wembley
	(English L.Heavyweight Title Challenge)
10.12.04	Mark Brookes W RSC 10 Sheffield
	(English L.Heavyweight Title Defence)
24.04.05	Ryan Walls W PTS 6 Leicester Square
19.06.05	Tony Oakey W PTS 10 Bethnal Green
	(English L.Heavyweight Title Defence)
07.04.06	Leigh Alliss W RSC 9 Bristol
	(English L.Heavyweight Title Defence)
21.05.06	Varuzhan Davtyan W RSC 4 Bethnal Green
24.09.06	Ovill McKenzie L RSC 2 Bethnal Green
	(Vacant Commonwealth L.Heavyweight Title)
18.05.07	Paul David L PTS 8 Canning Town
01.02.08	Tony Oakey L CO 9 Bethnal Green
	(British L.Heavyweight Title Challenge)

Career: 23 contests, won 17, drew 1, lost 5.

Peter Haymer   Philip Sharkey

Scott Haywood

Derby. *Born* Derby, 5 June, 1981
L.Welterweight. *Ht* 6'0"
Manager Self

06.10.03	Pete Buckley W PTS 6 Barnsley
23.11.03	Arv Mittoo W PTS 6 Rotherham
16.02.04	Pete Buckley W PTS 6 Scunthorpe
26.04.04	Chris Brophy W RSC 5 Cleethorpes
27.09.04	Judex Meemea W PTS 6 Cleethorpes
16.12.04	Tony Montana L PTS 6 Cleethorpes
26.02.05	Jimmy Beech W PTS 6 Burton
24.04.05	Chris Long W PTS 6 Derby
02.09.05	Kristian Laight W PTS 6 Derby
08.12.05	Dave Hinds W RTD 3 Derby
28.01.06	Jus Wallie W PTS 4 Nottingham
25.03.06	Billy Smith W PTS 6 Burton
14.05.06	Surinder Sekhon W RSC 1 Derby
03.11.06	John Fewkes L PTS 8 Barnsley
09.02.07	Billy Smith W PTS 4 Leeds
13.04.07	Gary O'Connor W PTS 6 Altrincham
11.05.07	Billy Smith W PTS 4 Motherwell
08.12.07	Gavin Tait W PTS 6 Wigan
07.03.08	Gary Reid W PTS 6 Nottingham
02.05.08	Frederic Gosset W RSC 2 Nottingham

Career: 20 contests, won 18, lost 2.

Eugene Heagney

Huddersfield. *Born* Dublin, 4 April, 1983
Featherweight. *Ht* 5'8"
Manager M. Marsden

29.06.06	Neil Marston W PTS 6 Dudley
11.11.06	Delroy Spencer W PTS 4 Dublin
03.12.06	Neil Read W PTS 6 Wakefield
14.04.07	Delroy Spencer W PTS 6 Wakefield
14.06.07	Shaun Walton W PTS 6 Leeds
14.07.07	Colin Moffett W PTS 8 Dublin
15.12.07	Colin Moffett L RSC 8 Dublin
	(Vacant All-Ireland Bantamweight Title)

Career: 7 contests, won 6, lost 1.

Ciaran Healy

Belfast. *Born* Belfast, 25 December, 1974
All-Ireland L.Middleweight Champion.
Ht 5'11"
Manager Self

05.04.03	Tomas da Silva W PTS 4 Belfast
18.09.03	Patrick Cito W PTS 4 Mayfair
04.10.03	Joel Ani W PTS 4 Belfast
22.11.03	Neil Addis W RSC 1 Belfast
26.06.04	Jason McKay L PTS 6 Belfast
25.04.05	Vince Baldassara L RSC 4 Glasgow
17.06.05	Chris Black DREW 4 Glasgow
18.02.06	Karoly Domokos W PTS 4 Dublin
21.04.06	George Hillyard L CO 6 Belfast
18.11.06	Anthony Small L RSC 3 Newport
23.06.07	Lukasz Wawrzyczek L PTS 8 Dublin
18.08.07	Martins Kukuls W PTS 6 Cork
25.08.07	Andy Lee L RTD 4 Dublin
08.12.07	Lee Murtagh W CO 5 Belfast
	(Vacant All-Ireland L.Middleweight Title)
02.02.08	Pavel Lotah L PTS 6 Limerick
29.03.08	Pavel Lotah W PTS 8 Letterkenny

Career: 16 contests, won 8, drew 1, lost 7.

Gareth Hearns

Sidcup. *Born* Dublin, 26 October, 1980
Heavyweight. *Ht* 6'2¼"
Manager A. Forbes

16.05.08	Ali Adams W PTS 4 Holborn

Career: 1 contest, won 1.

Tommy Heffron

Oldham. *Born* Oldham, 23 July, 1982
Middleweight. *Ht* 5'9"
Manager J. Pennington

07.10.07	Kenroy Lambert W RSC 3 Shaw
10.11.07	Paul Royston W PTS 6 Stalybridge
02.12.07	JJ Bird DREW 6 Oldham

Career: 3 contests, won 2, drew 1.

Daniel Herdman

Stevenage. *Born* Stevenage, 15 September, 1984
Middleweight. *Ht* 6'0¼"
Manager T. Sims

05.10.07	Gatis Skuja L PTS 4 Bethnal Green
22.02.08	Ben Hudson W PTS 4 Bethnal Green
04.04.08	Duncan Cottier W PTS 4 Bethnal Green
27.06.08	Russell Pearce W RTD 2 Bethnal Green

Career: 4 contests, won 3, lost 1.

Daniel Herdman   Philip Sharkey

Ross Hewitt

Romford. *Born* Romford, 24 June, 1982
L.Welterweight. *Ht* 5'7¼"
Manager F. Maloney

30.11.07	Kristian Laight W PTS 4 Newham

Career: 1 contest, won 1.

Dean Hickman

West Bromwich. *Born* West Bromwich, 24 November, 1979
L.Welterweight. Former Undefeated Midlands Area L.Welterweight Champion.
Ht 5'7"
Manager E. Johnson

17.02.02	Wayne Wheeler DREW 6 Wolverhampton
13.04.02	Wayne Wheeler W PTS 6 Wolverhampton
13.07.02	Dai Bando W RSC 1 Wolverhampton
02.11.02	Darren Goode W RSC 2 Wolverhampton
15.02.03	Gareth Wiltshaw W PTS 6 Wolverhampton
21.03.03	David Vaughan W PTS 6 West Bromwich
30.06.03	Dave Hinds W RSC 4 Shrewsbury
17.07.03	Lee McAllister W PTS 6 Walsall
30.10.03	John-Paul Ryan W PTS 6 Dudley
15.04.04	Tony Montana W PTS 6 Dudley
04.06.04	Adnan Amar W RSC 8 Dudley
	(Vacant Midlands Area L.Welterweight Title)
25.11.04	Ceri Hall W PTS 4 Birmingham
17.02.05	Gary Reid W PTS 10 Dudley
	(Midlands Area L.Welterweight Title Defence)
11.03.05	Nigel Wright L CO 7 Doncaster
	(Vacant English L.Welterweight Title)
16.02.06	Ernie Smith W PTS 4 Dudley
17.03.06	Barry Morrison L RSC 1 Kirkcaldy
	(Elim. British L.Welterweight Title)
29.06.06	Tom Hogan W RSC 2 Dudley
06.10.06	Stuart Green W PTS 6 Wolverhampton
20.04.07	Gary Reid L RSC 5 Dudley
	(Vacant Midlands Area L.Welterweight Title)
09.11.07	John Murray L RSC 4 Nottingham
	(Vacant English Lightweight Title)

Career: 20 contests, won 15, drew 1, lost 4.

Dean Hickman   Les Clark

Herbie Hide

Norwich. *Born* Nigeria, 27 August, 1971
WBC International Cruiserweight
Champion. Former WBO Heavyweight
Champion. Former Undefeated British,
WBC International & Penta-Continental
Heavyweight Champion. *Ht* 6'1½"
Manager Self

24.10.89	L. A. Williams W CO 2 Bethnal Green
05.11.89	Gary McCrory W RTD 1 Kensington
19.12.89	Steve Osborne W RSC 6 Bethnal Green
27.06.90	Alek Penarski W RSC 3 Kensington
05.09.90	Steve Lewsam W RSC 4 Brighton
26.09.90	Jonjo Greene W RSC 1 Manchester
17.10.90	Gus Mendes W RSC 2 Bethnal Green
18.11.90	Steve Lewsam W RSC 1 Birmingham
29.01.91	Lennie Howard W RSC 1 Wisbech
09.04.91	David Jules W RSC 1 Mayfair
14.05.91	John Westgarth W RTD 4 Dudley
03.07.91	Tucker Richards W RSC 3 Brentwood
15.10.91	Eddie Gonzalez W CO 2 Hamburg, Germany
29.10.91	Chris Jacobs W RSC 1 Cardiff
21.01.92	Conroy Nelson W RSC 2 Norwich *(Vacant WBC International Heavyweight Title)*
03.03.92	Percell Davis W CO 1 Amsterdam, Holland
08.09.92	Jean Chanet W RSC 7 Norwich
06.10.92	Craig Peterson W RSC 7 Antwerp, Belgium *(WBC International Heavyweight Title Defence)*
12.12.92	James Pritchard W RSC 2 Muswell Hill
30.01.93	Juan Antonio Diaz W RSC 3 Brentwood *(Vacant Penta-Continental Heavyweight Title)*
27.02.93	Michael Murray W RSC 5 Dagenham *(Vacant British Heavyweight Title)*
11.05.93	Jerry Halstead W RSC 4 Norwich *(Penta-Continental Heavyweight Title Defence)*
18.09.93	Everett Martin W PTS 10 Leicester
06.11.93	Mike Dixon W RSC 9 Bethnal Green *(Penta-Continental Heavyweight Title Defence)*

04.12.93	Jeff Lampkin W RSC 2 Sun City, South Africa *(WBC International Heavyweight Title Defence)*
19.03.94	Michael Bentt W CO 7 Millwall *(WBO Heavyweight Title Challenge)*
11.03.95	Riddick Bowe L CO 6 Las Vegas, Nevada, USA *(WBO Heavyweight Title Defence)*
06.07.96	Michael Murray W RSC 6 Manchester
09.11.96	Frankie Swindell W CO 1 Manchester
28.06.97	Tony Tucker W RSC 2 Norwich *(Vacant WBO Heavyweight Title)*
18.04.98	Damon Reed W RSC 1 Manchester *(WBO Heavyweight Title Defence)*
26.09.98	Willi Fischer W RSC 2 Norwich *(WBO Heavyweight Title Defence)*
26.06.99	Vitali Klitschko L CO 2 Millwall *(WBO Heavyweight Title Defence)*
14.07.01	Alexei Osokin W RSC 3 Liverpool
22.09.01	Joseph Chingangu L RSC 2 Newcastle
16.04.03	Derek McCafferty W RSC 7 Nottingham
27.05.03	Joseph Chingangu W CO 1 Dagenham
04.10.03	Alex Vasiliev W RSC 5 Muswell Hill
12.03.04	Mendauga Kulikauskas L RSC 4 Nottingham
23.09.06	Mitch Hicks W RSC 1 Fort Smith, Arkansas, USA
24.03.07	Valery Semishkur W CO 1 Hamburg, Germany
27.04.07	Pavol Polakovic W CO 6 Hamburg, Germany
16.06.07	Aleh Dubiaha W CO 1 Ankara, Turkey
21.09.07	Mircea Telecan W RSC 1 Luebeck, Germany
23.12.07	Mikhail Nasyrov W RSC 6 Halle, Germany *(Vacant WBC International Cruiserweight Title)*
11.03.08	Ruediger May W RSC 2 Halle, Germany *(WBC International Cruiserweight Title Defence)*
30.05.08	Ehinomen Ehikhamenor W PTS 12 Baracaldo, Spain *(WBC International Cruiserweight Title Defence)*

Career: 47 contests, won 43, lost 4.

Graeme Higginson

Blackburn. *Born* Blackburn, 31 July, 1982
British Masters L.Welterweight Champion.
Ht 5'8¼"
Manager Self

14.10.05	Darren Johnstone L PTS 6 Motherwell
03.11.05	Tom Hogan L PTS 6 Sunderland
19.11.05	Mark Alexander L PTS 4 Southwark
23.01.06	Paul Appleby L RTD 3 Glasgow
04.03.06	Dougie Walton DREW 6 Coventry
27.05.06	Omar Akram W RSC 2 Glasgow
01.06.06	Paul Appleby L RSC 2 Birmingham
21.07.06	James Brown W PTS 4 Altrincham
06.12.06	Andrew Ward W PTS 6 Rotherham
28.01.07	Paul Truscott L PTS 4 Yarm
15.11.07	Adil Anwar W PTS 6 Leeds
01.12.07	Tristan Davies W RSC 5 Telford *(Vacant British Masters L.Welterweight Title)*
06.06.08	Gary Reid W RSC 10 Stoke *(British Masters L.Welterweight Title Defence)*

Career: 13 contests, won 6, drew 1, lost 6.

Graeme Higginson   Les Clark

Dwayne Hill

Sheffield. *Born* Sheffield, 31 January, 1986
Lightweight. *Ht* 5'8"
Manager Self

08.05.05	Anthony Christopher W PTS 6 Sheffield
24.07.05	Gary Coombes W RSC 3 Sheffield
30.10.05	Gavin Tait W PTS 6 Sheffield
12.11.05	Lance Verallo W PTS 6 Sheffield
17.02.06	Carl Allen W PTS 6 Sheffield
16.06.06	Daniel Thorpe W PTS 4 Liverpool
28.10.06	Youssef Al Hamidi L RSC 3 Sheffield
17.02.07	Stephen Haughian L RSC 2 Cork
13.07.07	Danny Wallace L RTD 3 Barnsley
16.09.07	Johnny Greaves W PTS 6 Sheffield
29.09.07	Vadzim Astapuk W PTS 4 Sheffield
19.10.07	Gary Sykes L RSC 4 Doncaster
06.12.07	George Watson L PTS 6 Sunderland
15.02.08	Carl Allen W PTS 6 Sheffield
01.03.08	Kevin Buckley L PTS 6 Stoke
20.03.08	Paul Holborn L PTS 6 South Shields
13.06.08	Paul Holborn L PTS 10 Sunderland *(Vacant International Masters L.Welterweight Title)*

Career: 17 contests, won 9, lost 8.

George Hillyard

Canning Town. *Born* Forest Gate, 19
November, 1984
Former Undefeated British Masters
L.Middleweight Champion. *Ht* 5'9¼"
Manager A. Sims

16.06.05	Geraint Harvey W RSC 1 Dagenham
30.09.05	James Gorman W RSC 1 Kirkcaldy
21.10.05	Ernie Smith L PTS 4 Bethnal Green
18.11.05	Richard Mazurek W PTS 6 Dagenham
24.02.06	Gary Harrison W RTD 4 Dagenham
21.04.06	Ciaran Healy W CO 6 Belfast
22.09.06	Tyan Booth L PTS 6 Bethnal Green
15.12.06	Marcus Portman L PTS 8 Bethnal Green
20.01.07	Tony Randell DREW 4 Muswell Hill
18.05.07	Matt Scriven W PTS 4 Canning Town
16.06.07	Dave Wakefield W PTS 10 Chigwell *(Vacant British Masters L.Middleweight Title)*
05.10.07	Lee Noble W PTS 6 Bethnal Green
27.06.08	Danny Goode W RSC 2 Bethnal Green

Career: 13 contests, won 9, drew 1, lost 3.

George Hillyard   Philip Sharkey

Mark Hobson

Huddersfield. *Born* Workington, 7 May, 1976
Former Undefeated WBU, British & Commonwealth Cruiserweight Champion.
Ht 6'5"
Manager C. Aston

09.06.97	Michael Pinnock W PTS 6 Bradford
06.10.97	P. R. Mason W PTS 6 Bradford
13.11.97	P. R. Mason W PTS 6 Bradford
27.02.98	Colin Brown DREW 6 Irvine
21.05.98	Paul Bonson W PTS 6 Bradford
15.06.98	Martin Jolley W RSC 3 Bradford
25.10.98	Mark Snipe W RSC 3 Shaw
26.11.98	Danny Southam W RSC 5 Bradford
19.04.99	Mark Levy L PTS 8 Bradford
11.09.99	Paul Bonson W PTS 4 Sheffield
06.12.99	Brian Gascoigne W RSC 3 Bradford
11.03.00	Nikolai Ermenkov W RSC 3 Kensington
27.03.00	Luke Simpkin W PTS 4 Barnsley
13.05.00	Paul Bonson W PTS 4 Barnsley
25.09.00	Mark Dawson W CO 1 Barnsley
26.02.01	Billy Bessey W PTS 4 Nottingham
24.04.01	Sebastiaan Rothmann L RTD 9 Liverpool *(WBU Cruiserweight Title Challenge)*
08.10.01	Firat Arslan L RSC 7 Barnsley
10.12.01	Luke Simpkin W RTD 3 Liverpool
23.02.02	Valery Semishkur W PTS 6 Nottingham
27.04.02	Lee Swaby W PTS 10 Huddersfield *(Final Elim. British Cruiserweight Title)*
05.10.02	Varuzhan Davtyan W RSC 3 Huddersfield
25.01.03	Abdul Kaddu W RSC 4 Bridgend *(Vacant Commonwealth Cruiserweight Title)*
10.05.03	Muslim Biarslanov W RSC 2 Huddersfield
05.09.03	Robert Norton W PTS 12 Sheffield *(Commonwealth Cruiserweight Title Defence. Vacant British Cruiserweight Title)*
13.03.04	Tony Moran W RSC 3 Huddersfield *(British & Commonwealth Cruiserweight Title Defences)*
27.05.04	Lee Swaby W RSC 6 Huddersfield *(British & Commonwealth Cruiserweight Title Defences)*
17.12.04	Bruce Scott W PTS 12 Huddersfield *(British & Commonwealth Cruiserweight Title Defences)*
04.03.06	Enzo Maccarinelli L PTS 12 Manchester *(WBU Cruiserweight Title Challenge)*
01.06.06	John Keeton W RSC 4 Barnsley *(British & Commonwealth Cruiserweight Title Defences)*
08.09.06	Pavol Polakovic W PTS 12 Mayfair *(Vacant WBU Cruiserweight Title)*
14.10.06	Enzo Maccarinelli L RSC 1 Manchester *(WBO Cruiserweight Title Challenge)*
29.09.07	John Keeton W RSC 4 Sheffield *(British Cruiserweight Title Challenge)*

Career: 33 contests, won 27, drew 1, lost 5.

Joe Hockenhull

Leicester. *Born* Leicester, 15 March, 1984
L.Middleweight. *Ht* 5'11¼"
Manager P. Carpenter

28.06.08	Peter Dunn W PTS 6 Leicester

Career: 1 contest, won 1.

Paul Holborn

Sunderland. *Born* Sunderland, 1 March, 1984
International Masters L.Welterweight Champion.
Ht 5'8½"
Manager Self

11.10.04	Stuart Green W PTS 6 Glasgow
15.12.04	Amir Ali L PTS 6 Sheffield
06.10.05	Daniel Thorpe W PTS 6 Sunderland
03.11.05	Haroon Din DREW 6 Sunderland
28.04.06	Billy Smith W PTS 4 Hartlepool
11.05.06	Kristian Laight W PTS 6 Sunderland
05.10.06	Youssef Al Hamidi W PTS 6 Sunderland
15.02.08	Johnny Greaves W PTS 6 Sunderland
20.03.08	Dwayne Hill W PTS 6 South Shields
13.06.08	Dwayne Hill W PTS 10 Sunderland *(Vacant International Masters L.Welterweight Title)*

Career: 10 contests, won 8, drew 1, lost 1.

Mike Holloway

Leeds. *Born* Leeds, 22 December, 1982
S.Bantamweight. *Ht* 5'7¼"
Manager T. O'Neill

28.03.08	Delroy Spencer W PTS 4 Barnsley
23.05.08	Mike Robinson L PTS 4 Wigan
06.06.08	Davey Savage L RSC 4 Glasgow

Career: 3 contests, won 1, lost 2.

Kerry Hope

Merthyr Tydfil. *Born* Merthyr Tydfil, 21 October, 1981
Middleweight. *Ht* 5'10"
Manager Self

21.01.05	Brian Coleman W PTS 4 Bridgend
08.04.05	Ernie Smith W PTS 4 Edinburgh
27.05.05	Lee Williamson W PTS 4 Spennymoor
10.09.05	John-Paul Temple W PTS 4 Cardiff
04.03.06	Matt Scriven W PTS 4 Manchester
01.06.06	Joe Mitchell W PTS 4 Barnsley
08.07.06	Ryan Rowlinson W PTS 4 Cardiff
18.11.06	Manoocha Salari W RSC 2 Newport
07.04.07	Jamie Ambler W PTS 6 Cardiff
21.07.07	Sherman Alleyne W PTS 6 Cardiff
03.11.07	Ernie Smith W PTS 4 Cardiff
22.03.08	Matthew Hall L RSC 8 Cardiff

Career: 12 contests, won 11, lost 1.

Shaun Horsfall

Colne. *Born* Burnley, 15 November, 1975
L.Middleweight. *Ht* 5'7¼"
Manager S. Wood

19.09.99	Danny Bance W PTS 6 Shaw
28.10.99	Lee Molyneux W PTS 6 Burnley
05.03.00	Dave Gibson W PTS 6 Shaw
21.05.00	Tony Smith W RSC 4 Shaw
24.09.00	Ernie Smith W PTS 6 Shaw
03.12.00	Ernie Smith W PTS 6 Shaw
03.03.02	Dean Walker L PTS 6 Shaw
30.03.08	Jimmy Beech W PTS 6 Colne

Career: 8 contests, won 7, lost 1.

Richard Horton

Romford. *Born* Romford, 12 November, 1981
S.Middleweight. *Ht* 6'0¾"
Manager D. Powell

25.02.06	Nick Okoth W CO 3 Canning Town
01.04.06	Ojay Abrahams W PTS 4 Bethnal Green
13.05.06	Mark Phillips W PTS 4 Bethnal Green
23.07.06	Shon Davies L RSC 1 Dagenham
24.09.06	Mark Phillips W PTS 4 Bethnal Green
01.12.07	Michael Banbula W PTS 4 Bethnal Green
04.04.08	Ruben Groenewald W PTS 6 Bethnal Green

Career: 7 contests, won 6, lost 1.

Richard Horton   Philip Sharkey

Sam Horton

Stourbridge. *Born* Wordsley, 20 August, 1985
S.Middleweight. *Ht* 5'11"
Manager E. Johnson

07.10.06	Tony Randell W PTS 6 Walsall
17.11.06	Jon Foster W PTS 6 Brierley Hill
15.02.07	Dave Pearson W RSC 4 Dudley
20.04.07	Tony Stones W PTS 4 Dudley
28.06.07	Ernie Smith W PTS 4 Dudley
26.10.07	Davey Jones W PTS 6 Birmingham
18.01.08	Lee Noble W PTS 4 Burton

10.04.08   Tony Stones W PTS 6 Piccadilly
12.05.08   Lee Noble W PTS 8 Birmingham
Career: 9 contests, won 9.

Shpetim Hoti

New Cross. *Born* Montenegro, 29
November, 1974
L.Heavyweight. *Ht* 5'11¼"
Manager D. Cowland

21.09.00   Elvis Michailenko L PTS 4
            Bloomsbury
30.11.00   Harry Butler L PTS 4 Bloomsbury
21.06.01   Harry Butler L PTS 4 Earls Court
31.01.02   Simeon Cover L PTS 6 Piccadilly
26.09.02   Mark Ellwood L PTS 6 Hull
17.11.02   Darren Stubbs L RSC 2 Shaw
20.06.03   David Louzan W RSC 5 Gatwick
05.09.03   Amer Khan L RTD 4 Sheffield
19.02.04   Danny Norton L PTS 4 Dudley
01.05.04   Scott Baker W PTS 4 Gravesend
11.02.05   Tony Quigley L CO 1 Manchester
10.11.07   Danny Couzens L PTS 6 Portsmouth
01.12.07   Victor Smith L PTS 4 Chigwell
Career: 13 contests, won 2, lost 11.

Matthew Hough

Walsall. *Born* Walsall, 5 January, 1977
L.Heavyweight. *Ht* 6'2"
Manager E. Johnson

17.02.05   Paddy Ryan W PTS 6 Dudley
21.04.05   Mark Phillips W PTS 4 Dudley
25.11.05   Robert Burton W PTS 4 Walsall
10.03.06   John Ruddock W PTS 6 Walsall
18.05.06   Dean Walker W PTS 4 Walsall
07.10.06   Danny McIntosh L RSC 6 Walsall
15.02.07   Nicki Taylor L RSC 2 Dudley
28.09.07   John Ruddock W RSC 3 Coventry
08.10.07   Mark Phillips W PTS 6 Birmingham
28.11.07   Jamie Ambler DREW 4 Walsall
28.02.08   Max Maxwell L RSC 3 Wolverhampton
            *(Vacant Midlands Area Middleweight
            Title)*
Career: 11 contests, won 7, drew 1, lost 3.

Ben Hudson

Cambridge. *Born* Cambridge, 29 March,
1973
L.Middleweight. *Ht* 5'6"
Manager Self

23.08.02   Pete Buckley DREW 4 Bethnal Green
06.09.02   Scott Lawton L PTS 4 Bethnal Green
26.09.02   Jas Malik W CO 3 Fulham
27.10.02   Peter McDonagh W PTS 6 Southwark
08.12.02   Daffyd Carlin W PTS 6 Bethnal Green
18.02.03   Brian Coleman W PTS 6 Bethnal Green
08.04.03   Peter McDonagh L PTS 4 Bethnal
            Green
26.04.03   Robert Lloyd-Taylor W PTS 4
            Brentford
27.05.03   Lenny Daws L RSC 2 Dagenham
25.09.03   Chas Symonds L PTS 6 Bethnal Green
09.07.05   John O'Donnell L RTD 3 Nottingham
30.09.05   Mike Reid L PTS 4 Kirkcaldy
07.10.05   Craig Watson L PTS 4 Bethnal Green
21.10.05   John O'Donnell L PTS 4 Bethnal Green
30.10.05   Wayne Goddard L PTS 4 Bethnal
            Green
12.11.05   Scott Lawton L PTS 6 Stoke
25.11.05   Stuart Elwell L PTS 4 Walsall
11.12.05   Surinder Sekhon W PTS 6 Chigwell
28.01.06   Adnan Amar L PTS 4 Nottingham

17.02.06   Lee Meager L PTS 4 Bethnal Green
03.03.06   Franny Jones L PTS 6 Hartlepool
24.03.06   Robert Lloyd-Taylor L PTS 6 Bethnal
            Green
06.04.06   Duncan Cottier L PTS 4 Piccadilly
14.04.06   Mark Lloyd L PTS 4 Telford
12.05.06   Allan Gray W PTS 4 Bethnal Green
03.06.06   Tom Glover L PTS 4 Chigwell
23.06.06   Jamie Coyle L PTS 6 Blackpool
23.07.06   Danny Goode L PTS 4 Dagenham
15.09.06   Grzegorz Proksa L PTS 4 Muswell Hill
23.09.06   Kevin Concepcion L PTS 6 Coventry
30.09.06   Franny Jones L PTS 6 Middlesbrough
07.10.06   Marcus Portman L PTS 6 Walsall
28.10.06   Lee McAllister L PTS 8 Aberdeen
10.11.06   Stuart Elwell L PTS 4 Telford
24.11.06   Aaron Thomas L PTS 6 Stoke
02.12.06   Nathan Ward L PTS 6 Longford
23.03.07   Adnan Amar L PTS 4 Nottingham
27.04.07   Glen Matsell L PTS 6 Hull
06.05.07   Danny Reynolds L PTS 8 Leeds
18.05.07   David Walker L PTS 6 Canning Town
15.06.07   Sam Webb L PTS 4 Crystal Palace
01.07.07   Lee Purdy L PTS 6 Colchester
01.12.07   Dave Stewart L PTS 6 Chigwell
08.12.07   Jack Arnfield L PTS 4 Wigan
12.01.08   Grant Skehill L PTS 4 Bethnal Green
22.02.08   Daniel Herdman L PTS 4 Bethnal
            Green
16.03.08   Andrew Butlin L PTS 6 Sheffield
04.04.08   Steve O'Meara L PTS 4 Bethnal Green
13.04.08   Alex Strutt L PTS 4 Edgbaston
Career: 49 contests, won 7, drew 1, lost 41.

Ben Hudson   Philip Sharkey

Barry Hughes

Glasgow. *Born* Glasgow, 18 November,
1978
L.Welterweight. *Ht* 5'8"
Manager Self

07.12.98   Woody Greenaway L PTS 6 Acton
18.02.99   Leon Dobbs W RSC 1 Glasgow
09.04.99   Gareth Dooley W PTS 6 Glasgow
26.06.99   Des Sowden W CO 1 Glasgow
04.10.99   Tony Smith W RSC 5 Glasgow
12.11.99   Brendan Ahearne W RSC 5 Glasgow
13.12.99   Jason Vlasman W RSC 2 Glasgow
24.02.00   No No Junior W RSC 1 Glasgow
18.03.00   Gary Flear W RSC 4 Glasgow
07.04.00   Billy Smith W PTS 6 Glasgow

12.08.00   Dave Travers W PTS 4 Wembley
15.03.02   Woody Greenaway W PTS 8 Glasgow
19.10.02   Arsen Vassilev W CO 3 Renfrew
08.12.02   Paul McIlwaine W RSC 2 Glasgow
16.05.03   Martin Watson L RTD 8 Glasgow
            (Vacant Scottish Lightweight Title)
06.03.04   Peter McDonagh W PTS 6 Renfrew
23.04.04   Brian Coleman W PTS 8 Glasgow
28.05.04   Charles Shepherd DREW 12 Glasgow
            *(Vacant WBU Inter-Continental
            Lightweight Title)*
19.06.04   Nigel Senior W RSC 3 Renfrew
04.11.06   Baz Carey W PTS 4 Glasgow
17.11.07   Nugzar Margvelashvili L RSC 4
            Glasgow
            *(Vacant WBU Inter-Continental
            Lightweight Title)*
Career: 21 contests, won 17, drew 1, lost 3.

Danny Hughes

Sunderland. *Born* Sunderland, 3 March,
1986
Heavyweight. *Ht* 6'5¼"
Manager T. Conroy

24.06.07   Lee Webb W RSC 4 Sunderland
05.10.07   David Ingleby DREW 6 Sunderland
15.02.08   Lee Mountford W PTS 6 Sunderland
15.05.08   Steve Bodger W PTS 6 Sunderland
13.06.08   David Ingleby W PTS 4 Sunderland
Career: 5 contests, won 4, drew 1.

Kris Hughes

Bellshill. *Born* Bellshill, 23 November,
1987
Bantamweight. *Ht* 5'11¼"
Manager Barry Hughes/F. O'Connor

27.10.06   Delroy Spencer W PTS 6 Glasgow
26.01.07   Robert Bunford W PTS 6 Glasgow
05.10.07   Matthew Edmonds W PTS 6 Newport
Career: 3 contests, won 3.

Sean Hughes

Pontefract. *Born* Pontefract, 5 June, 1982
S.Featherweight. Former Undefeated
Central Area S.Bantamweight Champion.
Ht 5'9"
Manager Self

02.03.02   Paddy Folan W PTS 6 Wakefield
25.06.02   John Paul Ryan W PTS 6 Rugby
05.10.02   Paddy Folan W PTS 4 Huddersfield
10.02.03   Neil Read W PTS 6 Sheffield
24.05.03   John-Paul Ryan W PTS 6 Sheffield
13.09.03   Daniel Thorpe W PTS 6 Wakefield
05.10.03   Paddy Folan W RSC 4 Bradford
            *(Vacant Central Area S.Bantamweight
            Title)*
07.12.03   Marty Kayes W PTS 6 Bradford
26.02.04   Steve Foster L RSC 6 Widnes
            (Vacant English Featherweight Title)
23.10.04   Kristian Laight W PTS 6 Wakefield
04.03.05   Michael Hunter L RSC 6 Hartlepool
            *(British S.Bantamweight Title
            Challenge)*
08.05.05   Billy Smith W PTS 6 Bradford
25.06.05   Pete Buckley DREW 6 Wakefield
14.10.05   Bernard Dunne L RSC 2 Dublin
            (Vacant IBC S.Bantamweight Title)
03.03.06   Marc Callaghan L PTS 10 Hartlepool
            (Vacant English S.Bantamweight Title)
28.05.06   Shaun Walton W PTS 6 Wakefield

10.11.06	Riaz Durgahed L PTS 6 Hartlepool	
24.11.06	Billy Corcoran L RSC 8 Nottingham	
14.04.07	Sergei Rozhakmens W PTS 6 Wakefield	
05.10.07	Sergei Rozhakmens W PTS 6 Sunderland	
09.11.07	Esham Pickering W PTS 8 Nottingham	
18.01.08	Esham Pickering L RSC 9 Burton *(British S.Bantamweight Title Challenge)*	

Career: 22 contests, won 14, drew 1, lost 7.

Albi Hunt

Ealing. *Born* Hammersmith, 20 April, 1974
L.Welterweight. *Ht* 5'9"
Manager Self

28.04.02	Jason Gonzales W PTS 6 Southwark	
22.09.02	Daniel Thorpe W PTS 6 Southwark	
18.02.07	Pawel Jas W PTS 4 Bethnal Green	
08.06.07	Daniel Thorpe W PTS 4 Mayfair	
16.09.07	Dave Ryan L RSC 2 Derby	

Career: 5 contests, won 4, lost 1.

Albi Hunt   Les Clark

Rob Hunt

Stafford. *Born* Stafford, 9 November, 1985
Welterweight. *Ht* 6'0"
Manager P. Dykes

18.05.06	Ian Clyde W RSC 1 Walsall	
29.06.06	Pete Buckley W PTS 6 Dudley	
07.10.06	Karl Taylor W PTS 6 Walsall	
15.02.07	Kristian Laight W PTS 6 Dudley	
09.06.07	Johnny Greaves W PTS 6 Middlesbrough	
20.07.07	Karl Taylor W PTS 4 Wolverhampton	
25.10.07	Leonard Lothian W PTS 4 Wolverhampton	
28.02.08	Senol Dervis W PTS 4 Wolverhampton	
30.04.08	Baz Carey W PTS 6 Wolverhampton	
20.06.08	Alex Brew W PTS 6 Wolverhampton	

Career: 10 contests, won 10.

Michael Hunter

Hartlepool. *Born* Hartlepool, 5 May, 1978
Featherweight. Former Undefeated British,
European, Commonwealth, WBF &
Northern Area S.Bantamweight Champion.
Ht 5'7½"
Manager Self

23.07.00	Sean Grant W PTS 6 Hartlepool	
01.10.00	Chris Emanuele W PTS 6 Hartlepool	
24.11.00	Gary Groves W RSC 2 Darlington	
09.12.00	Chris Jickells W PTS 4 Southwark	
11.02.01	Paddy Folan W RSC 6 Hartlepool	
06.05.01	Anthony Hanna W PTS 4 Hartlepool	
04.06.01	Anthony Hanna W PTS 4 Hartlepool	
09.09.01	John Barnes W RSC 8 Hartlepool *(Vacant Northern Area S.Bantamweight Title)*	
29.11.01	Joel Viney W PTS 6 Hartlepool	
26.01.02	Stevie Quinn W CO 2 Dagenham	
18.03.02	Marc Callaghan DREW 6 Crawley	
18.05.02	Mark Payne W PTS 8 Millwall	
18.10.02	Frankie DeMilo W PTS 12 Hartlepool *(Vacant WBF S. Bantamweight Title)*	
14.12.02	Anthony Hanna W PTS 8 Newcastle	
07.06.03	Afrim Mustafa W RSC 5 Trieste, Italy	
26.07.03	Rocky Dean W RSC 1 Plymouth	
04.10.03	Nikolai Eremeev W PTS 6 Belfast	
08.11.03	Gennadiy Delisandru W PTS 6 Bridgend	
16.04.04	Mark Payne W RSC 7 Hartlepool *(Vacant British S.Bantamweight Title)*	
02.06.04	Vladimir Borov W PTS 6 Hereford	
19.11.04	Marc Callaghan W RSC 10 Hartlepool *(British S.Bantamweight Title Defence)*	
04.03.05	Sean Hughes W RSC 6 Hartlepool *(British S.Bantamweight Title Defence)*	
27.05.05	Kamel Guerfi W RSC 6 Spennymoor	
28.10.05	Esham Pickering W PTS 12 Hartlepool *(European & Commonwealth S.Bantamweight Title Challenges. British S.Bantamweight Title Defence)*	
03.03.06	Yersin Jailauov W RSC 2 Hartlepool *(European S.Bantamweight Title Defence)*	
28.04.06	German Guartos W RTD 3 Hartlepool *(European S.Bantamweight Title Defence)*	
23.06.06	Tuncay Kaya W CO 9 Blackpool *(European S.Bantamweight Title Defence)*	
10.11.06	Steve Molitor L CO 5 Hartlepool *(Vacant IBF S.Bantamweight Title)*	
30.03.07	Ben Odamattey W PTS 8 Crawley	
08.02.08	Youssef Al Hamidi W PTS 6 Peterlee	

Career: 30 contests, won 28, drew 1, lost 1.

Jonathan Hussey

Manchester. *Born* Manchester, 18 August,
1982
Welterweight. *Ht* 6'0"
Manager Self

08.07.05	Joe Mitchell W PTS 4 Altrincham	
01.10.05	Darren Gethin W PTS 6 Wigan	
18.12.05	Karl Taylor W PTS 6 Bolton	
12.02.06	Tye Williams W PTS 6 Manchester	
06.05.06	Geraint Harvey W PTS 6 Blackpool	
18.06.06	Barry Downes W PTS 6 Manchester	
10.07.06	Imad Khamis W PTS 6 Manchester	
26.10.06	Billy Smith L PTS 6 Dudley	
24.02.07	Khurram Hussain W PTS 6 Manchester	
28.09.07	Jason Nesbitt W PTS 6 Preston	
14.03.08	Chris Brophy W RSC 6 Manchester	
07.06.08	Russell Pearce W PTS 4 Wigan	

Career: 12 contests, won 11, lost 1.

Eddie Hyland

Wellingborough. *Born* Dublin, 24 April,
1981
All-Ireland S.Featherweight Champion.
Ht 5'6½"
Manager J. Harding

26.11.04	Buster Dennis W PTS 4 Altrincham	
04.06.05	Stefan Berza W RSC 1 Dublin	
17.09.05	Peter Batora W RSC 1 Dublin	
11.03.06	Tibor Rafael W RSC 2 Dublin	
16.06.06	Steve Mullin L RTD 4 Liverpool	
10.02.07	Gheorghe Ghiompirica W PTS 4 Letterkenny	
30.06.07	Daniel Thorpe W PTS 4 Belfast	
13.10.07	Robin Deakin W PTS 4 Belfast	
15.12.07	Wladimir Borov W PTS 8 Dublin	
19.04.08	Kevin O'Hara W PTS 10 Dublin *(Vacant All-Ireland S.Featherweight Title)*	

Career: 10 contests, won 9, lost 1.

Eddie Hyland   Les Clark

Patrick Hyland

Wellingborough. *Born* Dublin, 16
September, 1983
All-Ireland Featherweight Champion.
Ht 5'7¼"
Manager J. Harding

24.09.04	Dean Ward W PTS 4 Dublin	
13.02.05	Steve Gethin W PTS 4 Brentwood	
04.06.05	Pete Buckley W PTS 4 Dublin	
17.09.05	Imrich Parlagi W PTS 4 Dublin	
18.11.05	Craig Morgan W PTS 4 Dagenham	
11.03.06	Tibor Besze W CO 1 Dublin	
23.06.07	Lajos Beller W RSC 1 Dublin	
14.07.07	Roman Rafael W RSC 1 Dublin	
26.01.08	Gheorghe Ghiompirica W PTS 8 Cork	
15.03.08	Mike Dobbs W RSC 1 Boston, Mass, USA	
19.04.08	Paul Griffin W RSC 3 Dublin *(Vacant All-Ireland Featherweight Title)*	
31.05.08	Robin Deakin W RSC 5 Belfast	

Career: 12 contests, won 12.

Jon Ibbotson

Sheffield. *Born* Sheffield, 2 September, 1982
L.Heavyweight. *Ht* 6'3½"
Manager D. Hobson

15.12.04 Paul Billington W PTS 4 Sheffield
20.02.05 Nick Okoth W PTS 6 Sheffield
22.04.05 Daniel Teasdale W RSC 1 Barnsley
18.06.05 Ojay Abrahams W PTS 4 Barnsley
05.03.06 Tony Booth W PTS 4 Sheffield
13.05.06 Magid Ben Driss W RSC 2 Sheffield
22.06.06 Robert Burton DREW 6 Sheffield
20.10.06 Robert Burton W CO 2 Sheffield
20.01.07 Shannon Anderson W RSC 1 Las Vegas, Nevada, USA
03.05.07 Darren Stubbs L RSC 4 Sheffield
22.03.08 Ayitey Powers W PTS 6 Sheffield
21.06.08 Simeon Cover W PTS 6 Sheffield
Career: 12 contests, won 10, drew 1, lost 1.

Alex Ibbs   Philip Sharkey

Alex Ibbs

Stoke. *Born* Stoke, 17 August, 1985
Heavyweight. *Ht* 6'4"
Manager Self

01.12.06 Istvan Kecskes W PTS 4 Birmingham
12.05.07 David Ingleby W PTS 6 Stoke
17.11.07 Lee Mountford W PTS 6 Stoke
01.03.08 David Ingleby L RSC 4 Stoke
11.04.08 Martin Rogan L RSC 2 Bethnal Green
Career: 5 contests, won 3, lost 2.

Egbui Ikeagwu

Luton. *Born* Ibadan Nigeria, 14 October, 1975
L.Heavyweight. *Ht* 6'0¼"
Manager C. Sanigar

12.05.03 Michael Matthewsian W PTS 6 Southampton
13.06.03 Leigh Alliss L PTS 6 Bristol
06.02.04 Paul Owen W PTS 4 Sheffield
27.01.05 Joey Vegas L PTS 4 Piccadilly

04.02.05 Dan Guthrie DREW 4 Plymouth
26.03.05 Joey Vegas L PTS 4 Hackney
24.04.08 Hastings Rasani DREW 4 Piccadilly
Career: 7 contests, won 2, drew 2, lost 3.

Egbui Ikeagwu   Philip Sharkey

David Ingleby

Lancaster. *Born* Lancaster, 14 June, 1980
Heavyweight. *Ht* 6'3"
Manager Self

09.06.03 Costi Marin L RSC 1 Bradford
01.12.03 Paul Bonson L PTS 6 Leeds
28.02.04 Paul King L RSC 3 Manchester
01.05.04 Jason Callum L PTS 6 Coventry
10.07.04 Scott Lansdowne L RSC 4 Coventry
20.09.04 Dave Clarke W RTD 5 Glasgow
06.12.04 Paul Butlin L CO 5 Leicester
30.04.05 Paul Butlin W PTS 6 Coventry
02.06.05 Chris Burton L RSC 3 Yarm
12.12.05 Scott Lansdowne L RSC 1 Leicester
18.03.06 Paul Butlin L PTS 6 Coventry
06.04.06 Matt Paice L PTS 4 Piccadilly
13.05.06 Carl Baker L RSC 4 Sheffield
07.10.06 Henry Smith W PTS 6 Weston super Mare
16.02.07 Dave Ferguson L PTS 4 Sunderland
20.04.07 Billy Boyle L PTS 4 Sheffield
03.05.07 Scott Brookes L PTS 6 Sheffield
12.05.07 Alex Ibbs L PTS 6 Stoke
24.06.07 Dave Ferguson L PTS 4 Sunderland
06.07.07 Scott Mitchell L PTS 4 Wigan
15.07.07 Paul Malcolm L PTS 6 Hartlepool
27.07.07 James Dolan L PTS 4 Houghton le Spring
28.09.07 Howard Daley L PTS 6 Preston
05.10.07 Danny Hughes DREW 6 Sunderland
19.10.07 Dean O'Loughlin W RSC 5 Doncaster
01.03.08 Alex Ibbs W RSC 4 Stoke
13.06.08 Danny Hughes L PTS 4 Sunderland
Career: 27 contests, won 5, drew 1, lost 21.

Simon Ivekich

Nottingham. *Born* Derby, 21 February, 1983
Welterweight. *Ht* 5'8¼"
Manager M. Shinfield

16.05.08 Steve Cooper DREW 6 Burton
Career: 1 contest, drew 1.

Hamed Jamali

Birmingham. *Born* Iran, 23 November, 1973
S.Middleweight. *Ht* 5'9"
Manager Self

09.12.02 Dale Nixon W CO 1 Birmingham
24.02.03 Harry Butler W PTS 6 Birmingham
06.10.03 Simeon Cover W PTS 6 Birmingham
08.12.03 JJ Ojuederie W PTS 6 Birmingham
08.03.04 Ojay Abrahams W PTS 8 Birmingham
10.05.04 Jason Collins W PTS 8 Birmingham
11.10.04 Hastings Rasani W PTS 8 Birmingham
13.12.04 Simeon Cover L PTS 10 Birmingham
(*Vacant British Masters S.Middleweight Title*)
21.02.05 Michael Pinnock W PTS 8 Birmingham
02.03.06 Lee Blundell L PTS 6 Blackpool
07.04.06 Dan Guthrie L RSC 3 Bristol
08.09.06 Cello Renda L RSC 1 Birmingham
25.01.08 Mark Nilsen W PTS 4 Birmingham
07.03.08 Adie Whitmore L PTS 4 Nottingham
16.05.08 Rod Anderton L PTS 10 Burton
(*Vacant International Masters L.Heavyweight Title*)
Career: 15 contests, won 9, lost 6.

Robbie James

Rhymney. *Born* Merthyr, 23 August, 1984
L.Middleweight. *Ht* 5'11"
Manager C. Sanigar

15.09.06 Jav Jerome W PTS 4 Newport
03.03.07 Gatis Skuja W PTS 6 Newport
16.06.07 Lewis Byrne W PTS 4 Newport
05.10.07 Steve Cooper W PTS 6 Newport
Career: 4 contests, won 4.

Lee Jennings

Liverpool. *Born* Liverpool, 14 July, 1981
Lightweight. *Ht* 5'2¼"
Manager S. Wood

15.06.08 Kristian Laight W PTS 6 St Helens
Career: 1 contest, won 1.

Michael Jennings

Chorley. *Born* Preston, 9 September, 1977
WBU Welterweight Champion. Former British Welterweight Champion. Former Undefeated English Welterweight Champion. Former Undefeated WBU Inter-Continental Welterweight Champion.
Ht 5'9¼"
Manager F. Warren/BrianHughes

15.05.99 Tony Smith W RSC 1 Blackpool
11.12.99 Lee Molyneux W PTS 4 Liverpool
29.02.00 Lee Molyneux W PTS 6 Widnes
25.03.00 Brian Coleman W PTS 6 Liverpool
16.05.00 Brian Coleman W PTS 6 Warrington
29.05.00 William Webster W PTS 6 Manchester
08.07.00 Paul Denton W PTS 6 Widnes
04.09.00 Mark Ramsey W PTS 6 Manchester
25.11.00 Ernie Smith W PTS 4 Manchester
11.12.00 Paul Denton W PTS 6 Widnes
10.02.01 Mark Haslam W RSC 2 Widnes
07.07.01 David Kirk W PTS 6 Manchester
15.09.01 Gary Harrison W PTS 6 Manchester
09.02.02 James Paisley W RSC 3 Manchester
01.06.02 Lee Williamson W PTS 6 Manchester
28.09.02 Karl Taylor W RSC 4 Manchester
01.11.02 Richard Inquieti W RSC 2 Preston
18.01.03 Lee Williamson W RTD 4 Preston

08.05.03	Jimmy Gould W RTD 6 Widnes *(Vacant WBU Inter-Continental Welterweight Title)*
27.09.03	Sammy Smith W RTD 4 Manchester *(WBU Inter-Continental Welterweight Title Defence)*
13.12.03	Peter Dunn W PTS 6 Manchester
01.04.04	Brett James W RTD 5 Bethnal Green *(WBU Inter-Continental Welterweight Title Defence)*
22.05.04	Rafal Jackiewicz W PTS 8 Widnes
01.10.04	Chris Saunders W RTD 5 Manchester *(English Welterweight Title Challenge)*
11.02.05	Vasile Dragomir W CO 3 Manchester
03.06.05	Gavin Down W RSC 9 Manchester *(English Welterweight Title Defence)*
16.07.05	Jimmy Vincent W CO 1 Bolton *(Vacant British Welterweight Title)*
25.10.05	Bradley Pryce W PTS 12 Preston *(British Welterweight Title Defence)*
28.01.06	Young Muttley L PTS 12 Nottingham *(British Welterweight Title Defence)*
02.09.06	Rastislav Kovac W CO 3 Bolton
07.04.07	Takaloo W PTS 12 Cardiff

	(WBU Welterweight Title Challenge)
28.09.07	Vladimir Khodokovski W PTS 8 Preston
02.02.08	Ross Minter W RSC 9 Canning Town *(WBU Welterweight Title Defence)*
05.04.08	George Ungiadze W RSC 7 Bolton

Career: 34 contests, won 33, lost 1.

Mick Jenno

Liverpool. *Born* Liverpool, 16 July, 1977
S.Middleweight. *Ht* 5'11"
Manager W. Dixon

30.06.07	Martin Gillick W RSC 1 Manchester
01.12.07	Gary Cooper W PTS 4 Liverpool

Career: 2 contests, won 2.

Steve Jevons

Swanwick. *Born* Mansfield, 8 June, 1988
Welterweight. *Ht* 6'0¼"
Manager M. Shinfield

02.05.08	Bheki Moyo W PTS 4 Nottingham

Career: 1 contest, won 1.

Carl Johanneson

Leeds. *Born* Leeds, 1 August, 1978
Former British S.Featherweight
Champion. Former Undefeated Central
Area S.Featherweight Champion. Former
Undefeated WBF S.Featherweight
Champion. *Ht* 5'5"
Manager F. Maloney

08.07.00	Calvin Sheppard W PTS 3 North Carolina, USA
15.09.00	Sean Thomassen W RSC 1 Paterson, New Jersey, USA
14.10.00	Hiep Bui W RSC 1 Scranton, Pennsylvania, USA
08.12.00	Walusimbi Kizito W PTS 4 Atlantic City, New Jersey, USA
12.04.01	Efrain Guzman W PTS 4 Melville, New York, USA
04.05.01	Calvin Sheppard W RSC 4 Atlantic City, New Jersey, USA
26.06.01	Joey Figueroa W PTS 6 NYC, New York, USA
26.10.01	Jose Ramon Disla W RSC 5 Atlantic

Michael Jennings

Philip Sharkey

City, New Jersey, USA
14.12.01	Angel Rios W PTS 6 Uncasville, Connecticut, USA
03.03.02	Kema Muse W PTS 6 Scranton, Pennsylvania, USA
02.07.02	James Baker W RSC 4 Washington DC, USA
16.01.03	Juan R. Llopis W RSC 5 Philadelphia, Pennsylvania, USA
05.06.03	Koba Gogoladze L PTS 8 Detroit, Michigan, USA
18.07.03	Reggie Sanders W PTS 6 Dover, Delaware, USA
21.08.03	Steve Trumble W RSC 2 Philadelphia, Pennsylvania, USA
30.01.04	Harold Grey W RSC 5 Philadelphia, Pennsylvania, USA
20.03.04	Carl Greaves W RTD 3 Wembley *(WBF S.Featherweight Title Challenge)*
08.05.04	Andrew Ferrans W RSC 6 Bristol *(WBF S.Featherweight Title Defence)*
19.06.04	Alexander Abramenko W RSC 5 Muswell Hill *(WBF S.Featherweight Title Defence)*
02.12.04	Leva Kirakosyan L RSC 1 Crystal Palace
08.05.05	Jimmy Beech W CO 2 Bradford
09.07.05	Daniel Thorpe W RSC 3 Bristol
25.09.05	Peter Allen W RTD 9 Leeds *(Vacant Central Area S.Featherweight Title)*
13.11.05	Carl Allen W RTD 2 Leeds
23.02.06	Andrew Ferrans W RSC 2 Leeds *(Final Elim. British S.Featherweight Title)*
12.07.06	Billy Corcoran W RSC 4 Bethnal Green *(Vacant British S.Featherweight Title)*
03.11.06	Femi Fehintola W RSC 6 Barnsley *(British S.Featherweight Title Defence)*
09.02.07	Ricky Burns W PTS 12 Leeds *(British S.Featherweight Title Defence)*
13.07.07	Leva Kirakosyan L CO 4 Barnsley *(European S.Featherweight Title Challenge)*
19.10.07	Michael Gomez W RSC 6 Doncaster *(British S.Featherweight Title Defence)*
08.03.08	Kevin Mitchell L RSC 9 Greenwich *(British S.Featherweight Title Defence. Commonwealth S.Featherweight Title Challenge)*

Career: 31 contests, won 27, lost 4.

Carl Johanneson   Les Clark

Chris Johnson

Manchester. *Born* Chorley, 8 March, 1981
L.Middleweight. *Ht* 5'10"
Manager S. Wood

29.09.06	Paul Porter L RSC 2 Manchester
17.12.06	Geraint Harvey W PTS 6 Bolton
11.03.07	Karl Taylor W RTD 3 Shaw
06.05.07	Danny Gwilym W RSC 4 Altrincham
24.06.07	David Kirk W PTS 4 Wigan
25.11.07	Peter Dunn W PTS 6 Colne
23.12.07	Steve Cooper W RSC 4 Bolton
16.02.08	Dave Murray W RSC 4 Blackpool
23.05.08	Darren Gethin W RSC 5 Wigan

Career: 9 contests, won 8, lost 1.

Clint Johnson

Leeds. *Born* Leeds, 13 April, 1974
Cruiserweight. *Ht* 6'2"
Manager M. Bateson

11.11.97	Jon Penn W RSC 2 Leeds
04.12.97	John O'Byrne L PTS 6 Sunderland
17.02.98	Rob Galloway W PTS 6 Leeds
20.09.98	Rob Galloway W PTS 6 Sheffield
29.10.98	Mike White L PTS 6 Newcastle
06.11.98	Gerard Zdiarski W PTS 4 Mayfair
07.12.98	Carl Nicholson W PTS 6 Bradford
16.02.99	Danny Southam L RSC 5 Leeds
15.09.99	Steve Loftus W PTS 6 Harrogate
28.03.00	Martin Jolley W PTS 6 Hartlepool
17.04.00	Alex Mason L PTS 6 Birmingham
20.05.00	Jason Barker L RSC 1 Rotherham
23.10.00	Joe Gillon L CO 4 Glasgow
17.05.01	Paul Bonson L PTS 6 Leeds
18.06.01	Mark Brookes L PTS 6 Bradford
13.09.01	Darren Littlewood W PTS 6 Sheffield
03.11.01	Joe Gillon W CO 3 Glasgow
03.12.01	Jimmy Steel DREW 6 Leeds
15.12.01	Mark Brookes L PTS 4 Sheffield
18.02.02	Billy McClung L PTS 6 Glasgow
01.03.02	Billy McClung L PTS 6 Irvine
16.03.02	Clinton Woods L RSC 3 Bethnal Green
08.10.02	Allan Foster L PTS 6 Glasgow
02.12.02	Greg Scott-Briggs W PTS 6 Leeds
08.02.03	Andrew Lowe L PTS 6 Brentford
05.04.03	Darren Corbett L RSC 4 Belfast
12.10.03	Scott Lansdowne L PTS 4 Sheffield
01.12.03	Simeon Cover W PTS 6 Leeds
20.03.04	Courtney Fry L RSC 2 Wembley
28.02.06	Keiran O'Donnell L RSC 1 Leeds
21.04.06	Stewart Mitchell L PTS 4 Doncaster
01.10.06	John Anthony L PTS 6 Rotherham
15.11.07	Carl Wild L PTS 6 Leeds
23.11.07	Billy Boyle L RSC 2 Sheffield

Career: 34 contests, won 11, drew 1, lost 22.

Craig Johnson

Clay Cross. *Born* Chesterfield, 10 November, 1980
Lightweight. *Ht* 5'7"
Manager M. Shinfield

25.04.04	Peter Allen W PTS 6 Nottingham
18.09.04	David Bailey L PTS 6 Newark
22.10.04	Carl Allen W PTS 6 Mansfield
10.12.04	Pete Buckley W PTS 6 Mansfield
06.03.05	Ian Reid W PTS 6 Mansfield
11.09.05	Billy Smith W PTS 4 Kirkby in Ashfield
12.11.05	Jason Nesbitt W PTS 6 Sheffield
29.04.07	Sergei Rozhakmens W PTS 6 Birmingham
15.09.07	Martin Gethin L PTS 10 Birmingham

(Vacant Midlands Area Lightweight Title)
10.12.07	Gavin Deacon W PTS 6 Cleethorpes

Career: 10 contests, won 8, lost 2.

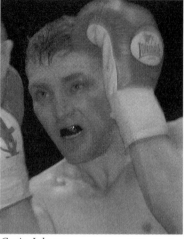

Craig Johnson   Philip Sharkey

Barrie Jones

Rhondda. *Born* Tylorstown, South Wales, 1 March, 1985
Welterweight. *Ht* 5'11¼"
Manager D. Powell/F. Warren

03.07.04	Pete Buckley W PTS 4 Newport
03.09.04	Dave Hinds W PTS 4 Newport
21.01.05	Lea Handley W PTS 4 Bridgend
17.06.05	Marco Cittadini W RSC 2 Glasgow
10.09.05	Jas Malik W RSC 1 Cardiff
11.03.06	Terry Carruthers W RSC 1 Newport
29.04.06	David Kehoe W RTD 2 Edinburgh
08.07.06	James Paisley W RSC 2 Cardiff
18.11.06	Ernie Smith W PTS 4 Newport
16.02.07	Chris Brophy W PTS 4 Merthyr Tydfil
07.04.07	Daniel Thorpe W RSC 2 Cardiff
05.05.07	Rocky Muscas W PTS 6 Glasgow
21.07.07	Billy Smith W PTS 4 Cardiff
07.09.07	Jay Morris W RTD 4 Mayfair
03.11.07	Silence Saheed W PTS 4 Cardiff
22.03.08	Tony Doherty L PTS 10 Cardiff *(Vacant Welsh Area Welterweight Title)*
14.06.08	Kell Brook L RSC 7 Bethnal Green *(Vacant British Welterweight Title)*

Career: 17 contests, won 15, lost 2.

Barrie Jones   Philip Sharkey

Ben Jones

Crawley. *Born*: Crawley, 12 June, 1982
Lightweight. *Ht* 5'8"
Manager M. Alldis

22.09.06 Carl Allen W PTS 4 Bethnal Green
15.12.06 Steve Gethin W PTS 4 Bethnal Green
30.03.07 Rom Krauklis L RSC 1 Crawley
25.01.08 Steve Gethin W PTS 4 Dagenham
23.02.08 Shaun Walton W RSC 4 Crawley
Career: 5 contests, won 4, lost 1.

Ben Jones   Philip Sharkey

Davey Jones

Epworth. *Born* Grimsby, 30 May, 1977
S.Middleweight. *Ht* 5'11"
Manager M. Shinfield

23.09.02 William Webster W PTS 6 Cleethorpes
08.11.02 William Webster W PTS 6 Doncaster
30.11.02 Matt Scriven W PTS 6 Newark
16.12.02 Gary Jones W PTS 6 Cleethorpes
21.02.03 Jimi Hendricks W PTS 6 Doncaster
09.05.03 Wayne Shepherd W PTS 6 Doncaster
22.09.03 Steve Brumant L PTS 6 Cleethorpes
26.02.04 Paul Smith L PTS 4 Widnes
06.03.04 Paul Buchanan L PTS 4 Renfrew
23.05.05 Ernie Smith DREW 6 Cleethorpes
15.12.05 Omar Gumati W PTS 6 Cleethorpes
16.02.06 Mark Lloyd L PTS 6 Dudley
04.11.06 Jon Foster L DIS 6 Mansfield
11.12.06 Terry Adams W PTS 6 Cleethorpes
23.02.07 Jason Rushton L CO 7 Doncaster
*(Vacant Central Area L.Middleweight
Title)*
24.03.07 Kevin Concepcion L RSC 1 Coventry
28.06.07 Rob Kenney L PTS 4 Dudley
20.07.07 Steven Bendall L RTD 2
Wolverhampton
13.10.07 Charlie Chiverton L PTS 4 Newark
26.10.07 Sam Horton L PTS 6 Birmingham
16.02.08 Alex Matvienko L RSC 2 Blackpool
17.05.08 Omar Gumati L PTS 6 Stoke
Career: 22 contests, won 8, drew 1, lost 13.

Franny Jones

Darlington. *Born* Burnley, 7 February, 1981
L.Middleweight. *Ht* 5'9¼"
Manager M. Marsden

05.05.02 Surinder Sekhon W PTS 6 Hartlepool
28.09.02 Martin Scotland W PTS 6 Wakefield
18.10.02 Richard Inquieti W PTS 6 Hartlepool
27.02.03 Danny Moir DREW 6 Sunderland
17.03.03 Gary Porter W PTS 6 Glasgow
11.07.03 Gary Cummings W RSC 2 Darlington
10.10.03 Pedro Thompson W PTS 6 Darlington
13.12.03 Matthew Hatton DREW 6 Manchester
05.03.04 Danny Moir NC 3 Darlington
*(Vacant Northern Area L.Middleweight
Title)*
16.04.04 Brian Coleman W PTS 6 Hartlepool
19.11.04 Paul Lomax W RSC 2 Hartlepool
04.03.05 Ali Nuumbembe L PTS 6 Hartlepool
11.03.05 Matthew Hatton L RTD 6 Doncaster
02.06.05 Darren Gethin W PTS 8 Yarm
28.10.05 Ernie Smith W PTS 4 Hartlepool
03.03.06 Ben Hudson W PTS 6 Hartlepool
28.04.06 Richard Mazurek W PTS 6 Hartlepool
23.06.06 Stuart Elwell L RSC 1 Blackpool
30.09.06 Ben Hudson W PTS 6 Middlesbrough
10.11.06 Jamie Coyle W RSC 2 Hartlepool
02.12.06 Craig Dickson W RSC 4 Clydebank
22.02.07 Jon Foster W CO 3 Leeds
23.06.07 Neil Sinclair W CO 5 Dublin
14.09.07 Kevin Anderson L RSC 12 Kirkcaldy
(British Welterweight Title Challenge)
Career: 24 contests, won 17, drew 2, lost 4, no
contest 1.

Henry Jones

Pembroke. *Born* Haverfordwest, 23
December, 1975
Lightweight. *Ht* 5'0¼"
Manager Self

17.06.95 Abdul Mannon W PTS 6 Cardiff
07.07.95 Harry Woods L PTS 4 Cardiff
07.10.95 Frankie Slane L PTS 4 Belfast
28.11.95 Jason Thomas L PTS 4 Cardiff
20.12.95 Brendan Bryce W PTS 6 Usk
20.03.96 Danny Lawson W CO 1 Cardiff
29.05.96 Ian Turner L PTS 6 Ebbw Vale
02.10.96 Jason Thomas W PTS 4 Cardiff
26.10.96 Danny Costello L RSC 3 Liverpool
29.04.97 Tommy Waite L PTS 4 Belfast
19.05.97 Francky Leroy L RSC 1 Coudekerque,
France
02.12.97 Ian Turner L RSC 8 Swansea
*(Vacant Welsh Area Bantamweight
Title)*
30.10.98 Tiger Singh W CO 4 Peterborough
05.05.00 Jason Edwards L PTS 6 Pentre Halkyn
28.11.02 Jon Honney L PTS 4 Finchley
23.02.03 David Vaughan L PTS 6 Aberystwyth
10.04.03 Daleboy Rees L PTS 4 Clydach
07.05.03 Jason Nesbitt W PTS 6 Ellesmere Port
15.06.03 Dean Lambert L RSC 4 Bradford
20.04.04 Scott Lawton L PTS 6 Sheffield
19.06.04 Colin Bain L PTS 4 Renfrew
03.07.04 Michael Graydon DREW 6 Bristol
30.09.05 Jason Nesbitt W PTS 6 Carmarthen
24.04.06 Darren Johnstone L CO 4 Glasgow
*(Vacant British Masters
S.Featherweight Title)*
16.06.06 Furhan Rafiq W PTS 6 Carmarthen
08.10.06 Dai Davies L PTS 10 Swansea
*(Vacant Welsh Area S.Featherweight
Title)*
10.06.07 John Baguley L RSC 4 Neath

24.11.07 Gary McArthur L RSC 7 Clydebank
*(British Masters Lightweight
Title Challenge)*
Career: 28 contests, won 8, drew 1, lost 19.

Justin Jones

Burslem. *Born* Burslem, 5 April, 1982
L.Heavyweight. *Ht* 6'3"
Manager P. Boyce

24.02.07 Richard Collins DREW 6 Stoke
14.03.08 Tony Stones W PTS 4 Manchester
Career: 2 contests, won 1, drew 1..

(Lee) Taz Jones

Abercynon. *Born* Aberdare, 24 August,
1982
International Masters L.Middleweight
Champion. Former Undefeated British
Masters L.Middleweight Champion.
Ht 5'11"
Manager B. Coleman

15.09.02 David White DREW 4 Swansea
02.11.02 Gerard McAuley DREW 4 Belfast
21.12.02 Luke Rudd W RTD 1 Millwall
08.01.03 Elroy Edwards W PTS 6 Aberdare
27.09.03 Matthew Hatton L PTS 6 Manchester
06.12.03 Ernie Smith W PTS 4 Cardiff
21.02.04 Craig Lynch W PTS 4 Cardiff
17.04.04 Andy Gibson W PTS 6 Belfast
03.09.04 Karl Taylor W PTS 4 Newport
30.09.04 Craig Dickson DREW 6 Glasgow
08.12.04 Kevin Phelan W PTS 10 Longford
*(British Masters L.Middleweight Title
Challenge)*
18.03.05 Neil Sinclair W RSC 1 Belfast
23.07.05 Colin McNeil L PTS 10 Edinburgh
(Vacant Celtic L.Middleweight Title)
10.09.05 Tony Doherty L PTS 10 Cardiff
(Vacant Celtic Welterweight Title)
28.04.06 Graham Delehedy W CO 6 Hartlepool
15.09.06 Jon Harrison W PTS 6 Newport
07.04.07 Tony Doherty L RSC 7 Cardiff
(Celtic Welterweight Title Challenge)
20.06.08 Carl Drake W RSC 1 Plymouth
*(Vacant International Masters
L.Middleweight Title)*
Career: 18 contests, won 11, drew 3, lost 4.

Scott Jordan

Belfast. *Born* Dundonald, 22 April, 1984
L.Middleweight. *Ht* 5'9¼"
Manager Self

21.04.06 Jamie Ambler W PTS 4 Belfast
25.11.06 Geraint Harvey W PTS 4 Belfast
15.12.06 Greg Barton W PTS 4 Bethnal Green
25.03.07 Duncan Cottier W PTS 6 Dublin
30.06.07 Alexander Spitjo L RSC 5 Belfast
13.10.07 Denis Alekseevs W RSC 1 Belfast
Career: 6 contests, won 5, lost 1.

Shane Junior (Walford)

Coventry. *Born* Coventry, 14 July, 1976
Welterweight. *Ht* 5'10"
Manager P. Carpenter

25.03.99 Richard Inquieti W CO 2 Edgbaston
22.04.99 Lee Bird L RSC 2 Dudley
27.06.99 Matt Scriven W RSC 2 Alfreton
21.09.07 Tony Stones W RSC 2 Burton
Career: 4 contests, won 3, lost 1.

Zahir Kahut

Batley. *Born* Pakistan, 25 September, 1973
Heavyweight. *Ht* 6'6"
Manager Self

16.06.07	Scott Mitchell W PTS 6 Bolton
29.11.07	Lee Mountford W PTS 6 Bradford

Career: 2 contests, won 2.

George Katsimpas

Cheddar. *Born* Bristol, 8 June, 1980
Middleweight. *Ht* 5'7¾"
Manager J. Evans

05.03.06	Leon Owen W RSC 2 Southampton
20.05.06	Tony Randell W RSC 1 Bristol
11.09.06	Geraint Harvey W RSC 2 Manchester
26.10.06	Cello Renda W RSC 2 Wolverhampton
18.02.07	Prince Arron L PTS 8 Bethnal Green
15.12.07	Lukasz Wawrzyczek W RSC 9 Dublin
23.02.08	Gilbert Eastman W PTS 6 Crawley
14.06.08	Anthony Small L RSC 8 Bethnal Green
	(*Southern Area L.Middleweight Title Challenge*)

Career: 8 contests, won 6, lost 2.

Jon Kays

Ashton-under-Lyne. *Born* Tameside, 24 May, 1983
Welterweight. *Ht* 5'8½"
Manager Self

24.06.07	Pete Buckley W PTS 6 Wigan
12.10.07	Sergei Rozhakmens W RSC 4 Leeds
23.12.07	Craig O'Neile W RSC 2 Bolton
16.02.08	Steve Gethin W PTS 6 Blackpool
26.04.08	Robin Deakin W PTS 4 Wigan

Career: 5 contests, won 5.

Gokhan Kazaz   Philip Sharkey

Gokhan Kazaz

Walthamstow. *Born* Turkey, 21 November, 1977
Middleweight. *Ht* 5'8¼"
Manager J. Eames

17.07.03	Joel Ani W PTS 4 Dagenham
18.09.03	Jimi Hendrix W PTS 4 Dagenham
06.11.03	Tomas da Silva W PTS 4 Dagenham
07.02.04	Patrick Cito W PTS 4 Bethnal Green
13.05.04	Alan Gilbert W PTS 4 Bethnal Green
30.07.04	Dean Powell W RSC 2 Bethnal Green
10.09.04	Dimitry Donetskiy W RSC 4 Bethnal Green
11.12.04	Darren McDermott DREW 4 Canning Town
19.06.05	Alan Gilbert W PTS 6 Bethnal Green
30.10.05	John Humphrey L PTS 10 Bethnal Green
	(*Vacant British Masters Middleweight Title*)
26.02.06	Manoocha Salari DREW 4 Dagenham
16.05.08	Sherman Alleyne W PTS 4 Holborn
15.06.08	Anthony Young W PTS 6 Bethnal Green

Career: 13 contests, won 10, drew 2, lost 1.

John Keeton

Sheffield. *Born* Sheffield, 19 May, 1972
Former British Cruiserweight Champion.
Former Undefeated WBF & WBO Inter-Continental Cruiserweight Champion.
Ht 6'0"
Manager Self

11.08.93	Tony Colclough W RSC 1 Mansfield
15.09.93	Val Golding L PTS 6 Ashford
27.10.93	Darren McKenna W RSC 3 Stoke
01.12.93	Julius Francis L PTS 4 Bethnal Green
19.01.94	Dennis Bailey W RTD 2 Stoke
17.02.94	Dermot Gascoyne L RSC 1 Dagenham
09.04.94	Eddie Knight W RTD 5 Mansfield
11.05.94	John Rice W RSC 5 Sheffield
02.06.94	Devon Rhooms W RSC 2 Tooting
06.09.94	Mark Walker W RSC 5 Stoke
24.09.94	Dirk Wallyn L CO 3 Middlekerke, Belgium
26.10.94	Lee Archer W PTS 6 Stoke
09.12.94	Bruce Scott L CO 2 Bethnal Green
11.02.95	Rudiger May L PTS 6 Frankfurt, Germany
06.03.95	Simon McDougall W RSC 5 Mayfair
07.07.95	Nicky Piper L RTD 2 Cardiff
15.09.95	Steve Osborne W RSC 4 Mansfield
27.10.95	Nicky Wadman W RSC 1 Brighton
03.11.95	Monty Wright W RSC 4 Dudley
11.11.95	Denzil Browne W RSC 4 Halifax
30.01.96	Cesar Kazadi W RSC 3 Lille, France
11.05.96	Terry Dunstan L RSC 1 Bethnal Green
	(*British Cruiserweight Title Challenge*)
14.09.96	John Pierre W PTS 4 Sheffield
14.12.96	Nigel Rafferty W RTD 3 Sheffield
12.04.97	Nigel Rafferty W RSC 6 Sheffield
11.10.97	Kelly Oliver L RSC 8 Sheffield
	(*Vacant WBO Inter-Continental Cruiserweight Title*)
16.05.98	Jacob Mofokeng L RTD 4 Hammanskraal, South Africa
18.07.98	Kelly Oliver W RSC 2 Sheffield
23.01.99	Garry Delaney W PTS 12 Cheshunt
	(*Vacant WBO Inter-Continental Cruiserweight Title*)
15.05.99	William Barima W RTD 3 Sheffield
29.02.00	Tony Booth W RSC 2 Widnes

16.12.00	Bruce Scott L CO 6 Sheffield
	(*Vacant British Cruiserweight Title*)
21.07.01	Radcliffe Green W PTS 4 Sheffield
19.03.02	Butch Lesley W PTS 12 Slough
	(*Vacant WBF Cruiserweight Title*)
16.04.04	Paul Bonson W PTS 4 Bradford
14.05.05	Paul Bonson W PTS 4 Aberdeen
11.06.05	Krzysztof Wlodarczyk L RTD 3 Gorzow Wielkopolski, Poland
	(*WBC Youth Cruiserweight Title Challenge*)
10.09.05	Don Diego Poeder L CO 1 Rotterdam, Netherlands
01.06.06	Mark Hobson L RSC 4 Barnsley
	(*British & Commonwealth Cruiserweight Title Challenges*)
20.10.06	Lee Swaby W RSC 7 Sheffield
	(*Vacant British Cruiserweight Title*)
19.03.07	Troy Ross L CO 2 Montreal, Canada
	(*Vacant Commonwealth Cruiserweight Title*)
29.09.07	Mark Hobson L RSC 4 Sheffield
	(*British Cruiserweight Title Defence*)

Career: 42 contests, won 26, lost 16.

David Kehoe   Philip Sharkey

David Kehoe

Northampton. *Born* Northampton, 24 December, 1972
Welterweight. *Ht* 5'10½"
Manager J. Gill

06.02.96	Simon Frailing W CO 1 Basildon
20.04.96	Paul Salmon W PTS 6 Brentwood
12.11.96	Peter Nightingale L PTS 6 Dudley
28.04.97	Craig Kelley L DIS 3 Enfield
18.11.97	Peter Nightingale DREW 4 Mansfield
27.01.98	Paul Miles L PTS 4 Bethnal Green
11.03.98	Trevor Tacy W RTD 1 Bethnal Green

28.03.98	David Thompson W PTS 6 Crystal Palace
26.05.98	Dave Hinds W RSC 5 Mayfair
08.09.98	Marc Smith W PTS 6 Bethnal Green
12.01.99	Gary Flear L PTS 4 Bethnal Green
25.01.99	Roger Sampson L PTS 4 Glasgow
12.03.99	Jamie McKeever L RSC 2 Bethnal Green
02.07.99	Mark McGowan L RSC 3 Bristol *(Vacant British Masters Lightweight Title)*
13.09.99	Stephen Smith L DIS 2 Bethnal Green
05.10.99	John Humphrey L PTS 4 Bloomsbury
24.10.99	Young Muttley L RTD 1 Wolverhampton
02.12.99	Liam Maltby L PTS 4 Peterborough
19.02.00	Dariusz Snarski DREW 6 Prestwick
10.03.00	Ted Bami L PTS 4 Bethnal Green
17.04.00	Mark Hawthorne L PTS 4 Birmingham
25.07.00	P.J.Gallagher L PTS 6 Southwark
08.09.00	Dariusz Snarski W PTS 4 Hammersmith
27.11.00	Anthony Maynard L RSC 5 Birmingham
16.03.02	Wayne Wheeler DREW 6 Northampton
28.05.02	Ricky Eccleston L RSC 4 Liverpool
14.09.02	Danny Hunt L RSC 3 Bethnal Green
16.11.02	Gwyn Wale L PTS 4 Nottingham
01.02.03	Mark Winters L RSC 2 Belfast
29.10.03	Pete Buckley W PTS 6 Leicester Square
08.07.04	Rocky Muscus W PTS 6 The Strand
08.10.04	Graham Delehedy L RSC 2 Brentwood
18.03.05	Paul McCloskey L RSC 3 Belfast
24.04.05	Ashley Theophane L PTS 4 Leicester Square
26.06.05	Jay Morris L PTS 4 Southampton
24.07.05	Michael Grant L PTS 4 Leicester Square
30.09.05	Ceri Hall L PTS 6 Carmarthen
09.10.05	Ashley Theophane L PTS 4 Hammersmith
12.11.05	George Telfer L PTS 6 Glasgow
21.11.05	Craig Dickson L PTS 8 Glasgow
02.12.05	Stefy Bull L PTS 6 Doncaster
09.12.05	Grzegorz Proksa L RSC 3 Iver Heath
11.02.06	Lee Cook L RTD 2 Bethnal Green
13.03.06	Paul Burns L PTS 6 Glasgow
01.04.06	Dean Smith L PTS 4 Bethnal Green
13.04.06	Nadeem Siddique L PTS 6 Leeds
29.04.06	Barrie Jones L RTD 2 Edinburgh
30.05.06	Scott Woolford L PTS 4 Bethnal Green
16.06.06	Karl David L RSC 1 Carmarthen
09.12.06	Eddie Corcoran L RSC 3 Canning Town
16.02.07	Willie Bilan L RSC 1 Kirkcaldy
03.05.07	Nicki Smedley L RSC 4 Sheffield
07.10.07	Dave Murray L PTS 6 Shaw
17.11.07	Kris Carslaw L PTS 4 Glasgow
02.02.08	Thomas Costello L RSC 2 Canning Town
02.03.08	Darryl Still L PTS 4 Portsmouth
14.03.08	Mark Bett L PTS 6 Glasgow
22.03.08	Jamie Cox L RSC 1 Cardiff
07.06.08	Steve Williams L RSC 1 Wigan

Career: 59 contests, won 9, drew 3, lost 47.

Paul Keir
Wirral. *Born* Liverpool, 26 November, 1980
Cruiserweight. *Ht* 6'2¼"
Manager S. Wood

16.03.08	Paul Bonson W PTS 4 Liverpool
15.06.08	Hastings Rasani W PTS 4 St Helens

Career: 2 contests, won 2.

Lee Kellett   Les Clark

Lee Kellett
Barrow. *Born* Barrow, 28 September, 1978
Cruiserweight. *Ht* 6'2"
Manager M. Helliet

12.02.06	John Anthony L RSC 1 Manchester
23.06.06	Gary Thompson L PTS 4 Blackpool
13.10.06	Gary Neville W RSC 1 Irvine
25.02.07	Mervyn Langdale W RSC 1 Southampton
05.10.07	Victor Smith W PTS 4 Bethnal Green

Career: 5 contests, won 3, lost 2.

Adam Kelly
Sheffield. *Born* Sheffield, 8 August, 1987
L.Welterweight. *Ht* 5'8"
Manager J. Ingle

08.12.05	Tom Hogan L PTS 6 Sunderland
05.03.06	Tye Williams W PTS 4 Sheffield
17.03.06	Stuart Green L PTS 4 Kirkcaldy
27.05.06	Mike Reid DREW 6 Aberdeen
20.10.06	Tye Williams W PTS 4 Sheffield
24.11.06	Pete Buckley W PTS 6 Hull
06.12.06	Rom Krauklis W PTS 6 Stoke
03.05.07	Matt Seawright W PTS 4 Sheffield
07.09.07	Matthew Martin Lewis W PTS 4 Doncaster
29.09.07	Matt Seawright W PTS 4 Sheffield
06.10.07	Mark Bett L RTD 3 Aberdeen
29.03.08	Mark Bett W PTS 6 Aberdeen
21.06.08	Amir Nadi W PTS 6 Sheffield

Career: 13 contests, won 9, drew 1, lost 3.

Colin Kenna
Southampton. *Born* Dublin, 28 July, 1976
Heavyweight. Former Southern Area
Heavyweight Champion. *Ht* 6'1"
Manager J. Bishop

25.02.01	Slick Miller W RSC 3 Streatham
22.04.01	Eamonn Glennon W PTS 4 Streatham
15.10.01	Tony Booth W PTS 6 Southampton
11.02.02	Dave Clarke W RSC 4 Southampton
08.04.02	James Gilbert W RSC 1 Southampton
12.07.02	Gary Williams W RSC 3 Southampton
01.11.02	Paul Buttery DREW 6 Preston
17.03.03	Derek McCafferty W PTS 6 Southampton
12.05.03	Paul Bonson W PTS 6 Southampton

01.08.03	Michael Sprott L RSC 1 Bethnal Green *(Southern Area Heavyweight Title Challenge)*
26.10.03	Darren Ashton W CO 1 Longford
20.02.04	Paul Bonson W PTS 6 Southampton
30.03.04	Chris Woollas W PTS 6 Southampton
12.05.04	Mark Krence L RTD 3 Reading
06.02.05	Oneal Murray W RTD 3 Southampton
19.02.05	Paul King DREW 6 Dublin
26.06.05	Julius Francis W PTS 4 Southampton
04.12.05	Wayne Llewelyn W CO 2 Portsmouth *(Vacant Southern Area Heavyweight Title)*
28.01.06	Luke Simpkin W PTS 8 Dublin
05.03.06	Micky Steeds L PTS 10 Southampton *(Southern Area Heavyweight Title Defence)*
22.04.06	Oleg Platov L RSC 5 Mannheim, Germany
25.02.07	Keith Long W PTS 8 Southampton
31.10.07	Roman Greenberg L PTS 8 Bayswater
25.01.08	Albert Sosnowski L PTS 10 Dagenham
11.04.08	Paul Butlin L RSC 2 Bethnal Green

Career: 25 contests, won 16, drew 2, lost 7.

Colin Kenna   Philip Sharkey

Stuart Kennedy
Sunderland. *Born* Sunderland, 15 May, 1985
L.Welterweight. *Ht* 5'7¼"
Manager D. Garside

23.11.07	Kristian Laight W PTS 6 Houghton le Spring
18.04.08	Billy Smith W PTS 6 Houghton le Spring
13.06.08	Peter Dunn W PTS 6 Sunderland

Career: 3 contests, won 3.

Rob Kenney
Wolverhampton. *Born* Wolverhampton, 1 August, 1977
Middleweight. *Ht* 5'9"
Manager E. Johnson

05.12.06	Peter Dunn DREW 4 Wolverhampton
15.02.07	Peter Dunn W PTS 4 Dudley

14.04.07 Peter Dunn W PTS 4 Wakefield
28.06.07 Davey Jones W PTS 4 Dudley
25.10.07 Paul Royston W PTS 6 Wolverhampton
28.02.08 Lance Verallo W PTS 4
          Wolverhampton
30.04.08 Paul Royston W PTS 6 Wolverhampton
20.06.08 Drew Campbell W PTS 4
          Wolverhampton
Career: 8 contests, won 7, drew 1.

Rob Kenney   Les Clark

David Keogan

Liverpool. *Born* Liverpool, 1 May, 1987
Flyweight. *Ht* 5'5¼"
Manager S. Goodwin

01.12.07 John Donnelly L RSC 1 Liverpool
15.06.08 Najah Ali L RSC 1 Bethnal Green
Career: 2 contests, lost 2.

Mo Khaled (Al Saroodi)

Sheffield. *Born* Doha, Qatar, 19 January,
1988
S.Bantamweight. *Ht* 5'4"
Manager J. Ingle

26.05.06 Neil Marston L DIS 5 Hull
12.07.06 Neil Marston W PTS 4 Bethnal Green
29.09.06 Danny Wallace L RSC 1 Manchester
10.11.06 Matthew Edmonds L PTS 6 Newport
11.03.07 Stuart McFadyen L PTS 6 Shaw
27.05.07 Robert Nelson DREW 6 Bradford
17.06.07 Andy Bell L PTS 10 Mansfield
          (Vacant British Masters Bantamweight
          Title)
05.12.07 Josh Wale L RSC 4 Sheffield
          (Vacant Central Area S.Bantamweight
          Title)
Career: 8 contests, won 1, drew 1, lost 6.

Amir Khan

Bolton. *Born* Bolton, 8 December, 1986
Commonwealth & WBO Inter-Continental
Lightweight Champion. *Ht* 5'10"
Manager Self

16.07.05 David Bailey W RSC 1 Bolton
10.09.05 Baz Carey W PTS 4 Cardiff
05.11.05 Steve Gethin W RSC 3 Renfrew
10.12.05 Daniel Thorpe W RSC 2 Canning Town
28.01.06 Vitali Martynov W RSC 1 Nottingham
25.02.06 Jackson Williams W RSC 3 Canning
          Town
20.05.06 Laszlo Komjathi W PTS 6 Belfast
08.07.06 Colin Bain W RSC 2 Cardiff
02.09.06 Ryan Barrett W RSC 1 Bolton
09.12.06 Rachid Drilzane W PTS 10 Canning
          Town
          Vacant IBF Inter-Continental
          L.Welterweight Title)
17.02.07 Mohammed Medjadji W RSC 1
          Wembley
07.04.07 Stefy Bull W RSC 3 Cardiff
14.07.07 Willie Limond W RTD 8 Greenwich
          (Commonwealth Lightweight Title
          Challenge)
06.10.07 Scott Lawton W RSC 4 Nottingham
          (Commonwealth Lightweight Title
          Defence)
08.12.07 Graham Earl W RSC 1 Bolton
          (Commonwealth Lightweight Title
          Defence)
02.02.08 Gairy St Clair W PTS 12 Canning
          Town
          (Commonwealth Lightweight Title
          Defence)
05.04.08 Martin Kristjansen W RSC 7 Bolton
          (Vacant WBO Inter-Continental
          Lightweight Title)
21.06.08 Michael Gomez W RSC 5 Birmingham
          (Commonwealth Lightweight Title
          Defence)
Career: 18 contests, won 18.

Tasif Khan   Les Clark

Tasif Khan

Bradford. *Born* Bradford, 29 December,
1982
S.Bantamweight. *Ht* 5'7"
Manager Self

20.11.05 Gary Ford DREW 6 Shaw
23.02.06 Neil Read W RSC 6 Leeds
28.05.06 Delroy Spencer W PTS 6 Wakefield
06.07.07 Stuart McFadyen L PTS 4 Wigan
Career: 4 contests, won 2, drew 1, lost 1.

(Maciej) Magic Kidem (Brzostek)

Birmingham. *Born* Poland,18 June, 1981
S.Middleweight. *Ht* 5'10½"
Manager Self

25.02.06 Danny Butler L PTS 6 Bristol
05.03.06 Stuart Brookes L RSC 1 Sheffield
24.04.06 Dave Pearson L PTS 6 Cleethorpes
23.09.06 Sam Gorman W PTS 6 Coventry
11.03.07 Lee Noble L PTS 4 Shaw
13.10.07 Jamie Norkett L CO 3 Newark
Career: 6 contests, won 1, lost 5.

Charles Paul King

Motherwell. *Born* Bellshill, 26 October,
1982
L.Welterweight. Ht. 5'10"
Manager T. Gilmour

22.01.07 Rom Krauklis W PTS 6 Glasgow
26.03.07 Pete Buckley W PTS 6 Glasgow
28.04.07 Amir Nadi W PTS 6 Clydebank
08.06.07 Gavin Deacon W PTS 4 Motherwell
08.10.07 Karl Taylor W PTS 6 Glasgow
19.10.07 Matt Seawright W PTS 6 Motherwell
29.02.08 Abdul Rashid W PTS 4 Glasgow
17.03.08 Peter Dunn W PTS 6 Glasgow
28.04.08 Karl Taylor W PTS 6 Glasgow
16.05.08 Mark Bett W PTS 6 Motherwell
Career: 10 contests, won 10.

Nathan King

Mountain Ash. *Born* Aberdare, 19 March,
1981
L.Heavyweight. *Ht* 6'3"
Manager Self

27.01.01 Tony Oakey L PTS 6 Bethnal Green
28.04.01 Pinky Burton W PTS 4 Cardiff
09.06.01 Michael Pinnock W PTS 4 Bethnal Green
09.10.01 Darren Ashton W PTS 6 Cardiff
24.11.01 Peter Haymer W PTS 4 Bethnal Green
12.02.02 Peter Haymer W PTS 4 Bethnal Green
20.04.02 Radcliffe Green W PTS 6 Cardiff
17.08.02 Valery Odin L PTS 6 Cardiff
14.12.02 Paul Bonson L PTS 4 Newcastle
10.04.03 Ovill McKenzie L PTS 4 Clydach
28.06.03 Varuzhan Davtyan W PTS 4 Cardiff
21.02.04 Daniel Sackey L PTS 4 Cardiff
12.03.04 Elvis Michailenko L PTS 6 Millwall
03.07.04 Nick Okoth W PTS 4 Newport
22.10.04 Hastings Rasani W PTS 6 Edinburgh
24.11.04 Eric Teymour L PTS 12 Mayfair
          (Vacant WBU S.Middleweight Title)
13.02.05 Malik Dziarra W PTS 6 Brentwood
28.06.05 Malik Dziarra L PTS 8 Cuaxhaven,
          Germany
13.05.06 Tony Oakey L PTS 6 Bethnal Green
15.09.06 Tyrone Wright W RTD 3 Newport
10.11.06 Neil Tidman W PTS 6 Newport
14.09.07 Steve McGuire L PTS 10 Kirkcaldy
          (Vacant Celtic S.Middleweight Title)
Career: 22 contests, won 12, lost 10.

David Kirk

Sutton in Ashfield. *Born* Mansfield, 5 October, 1974
Middleweight. Former Undefeated WBF European Welterweight Champion. *Ht* 5'8"
Manager Self

01.11.96	Arv Mittoo W PTS 6 Mansfield
04.12.96	Stuart Rimmer W PTS 6 Stoke
20.02.97	Chris Price W PTS 6 Mansfield
16.03.97	Gary Hibbert L PTS 6 Shaw
25.03.97	Miguel Matthews W PTS 6 Wolverhampton
28.04.97	Mark Breslin L PTS 8 Glasgow
06.10.97	Christian Brady L PTS 6 Birmingham
30.10.97	Trevor Tacy L PTS 6 Newark
08.12.97	Nick Hall L PTS 6 Nottingham
12.01.98	Juha Temonen DREW 6 Helsinki, Finland
24.01.98	Jason Cook L RSC 3 Cardiff
24.02.98	Roy Rutherford L PTS 6 Edgbaston
11.03.98	Patrick Gallagher L PTS 6 Bethnal Green
27.04.98	Tommy Peacock L PTS 6 Manchester
08.05.98	Chris Barnett L PTS 6 Manchester
23.05.98	Graham Earl L PTS 4 Bethnal Green
04.06.98	Mark Richards L PTS 6 Dudley
21.09.98	Steve McLevy L PTS 8 Glasgow
12.10.98	Malcolm Melvin L PTS 10 Birmingham
	(Midlands Area L. Welterweight Title Challenge)
31.10.98	Bernard Paul L PTS 6 Southend
28.11.98	Glenn McClarnon L PTS 4 Belfast
11.12.98	Charlie Kane L PTS 8 Prestwick
20.02.99	Dennis Berry L PTS 10 Thornaby
	(Vacant Continental European Welterweight Title)
09.05.99	Sammy Smith L PTS 6 Bracknell
20.05.99	Steve Brumant W PTS 4 Kensington
05.06.99	Neil Sinclair L PTS 8 Cardiff
11.09.99	Glenn McClarnon L PTS 6 Sheffield
20.10.99	Dave Gibson W PTS 6 Stoke
18.11.99	Adrian Chase W PTS 10 Mayfair
	(Vacant WBF European Welterweight Title)
26.11.99	Gerard Murphy L RTD 3 Hull
25.03.00	Jacek Bielski L PTS 6 Liverpool
29.04.00	Eamonn Magee L RSC 8 Wembley
13.08.00	Ram Singh W PTS 6 Nottingham
09.09.00	Mally McIver L PTS 6 Newark
23.09.00	Steve Murray L PTS 4 Bethnal Green
09.10.00	Steve Saville W PTS 8 Birmingham
19.11.00	Gavin Down L PTS 10 Chesterfield
	(Vacant British Masters L.Welterweight Title)
01.12.00	Alan Bosworth DREW 8 Peterborough
04.02.01	Mark Winters L PTS 6 Queensferry
28.02.01	Ossie Duran L PTS 8 Kensington
	(Vacant WBF European Welterweight Title)
10.03.01	Junior Witter L RSC 2 Bethnal Green
10.04.01	Colin Lynes L PTS 6 Wembley
20.04.01	Mark Winters L PTS 6 Dublin
16.06.01	Oscar Hall L PTS 6 Derby
07.07.01	Michael Jennings L PTS 6 Manchester
28.07.01	Jonathan Thaxton L PTS 4 Wembley
13.09.01	David Walker DREW 8 Sheffield
17.11.01	Kevin McIntyre L PTS 4 Glasgow
24.11.01	Ivan Kirpa L PTS 4 Bethnal Green
08.12.01	Chris Saunders L CO 2 Chesterfield
26.01.02	Colin Lynes L PTS 6 Dagenham
09.02.02	David Barnes L RTD 1 Manchester
11.03.02	Matthew Macklin L PTS 4 Glasgow
25.05.02	Francis Barrett L PTS 6 Portsmouth
08.06.02	Kevin McIntyre L RTD 4 Renfrew
28.09.02	Matthew Hatton W PTS 6 Manchester
22.03.03	Kevin McIntyre L RSC 1 Renfrew
24.05.03	Nigel Wright L PTS 4 Bethnal Green
31.05.03	Sammy Smith L PTS 4 Bethnal Green
08.06.03	Adnan Amar L PTS 6 Nottingham
04.10.03	Francis Barrett L PTS 6 Muswell Hill
10.04.04	Albert Sosnowski L PTS 4 Manchester
07.05.04	Gary Woolcombe L PTS 4 Bethnal Green
19.06.04	Gary Young L PTS 4 Renfrew
03.07.04	Tony Doherty L PTS 4 Newport
19.11.04	Ross Minter L PTS 6 Bethnal Green
03.12.04	Martin Concepcion L PTS 4 Edinburgh
11.09.05	Gatis Skuja L PTS 6 Kirkby in Ashfield
12.11.05	Joe Mitchell W PTS 6 Sheffield
10.03.06	Stuart Elwell L PTS 10 Walsall
	(Vacant Midlands Area Welterweight Title)
04.11.06	Colin McNeil L PTS 6 Glasgow
17.11.06	Sam Webb L PTS 4 Bethnal Green
09.12.06	Kell Brook L RSC 1 Canning Town
06.05.07	Brian Rose L PTS 6 Altrincham
18.05.07	Matthew Thirlwall L PTS 4 Canning Town
24.06.07	Chris Johnson L PTS 4 Wigan
15.09.07	Gary Young L PTS 6 Paisley
06.10.07	Kevin Concepcion L PTS 6 Leicester
13.10.07	Billy Saunders L PTS 4 Bethnal Green
03.11.07	Jamie Cox L PTS 4 Cardiff
01.12.07	Kevin Hammond L PTS 4 Nottingham
16.02.08	Jack Arnfield L PTS 6 Blackpool
01.03.08	Joe McCluskey L RSC 3 Coventry
05.04.08	Thomas Costello L PTS 4 Bolton
02.05.08	Sam Webb L PTS 6 Nottingham

Career: 85 contests, won 11, drew 3, lost 71.

David Kirk   Philip Sharkey

Chris Kitson

Kettering. *Born* Shefield, 5 June, 1988
Lightweight. *Ht* 5'6¼"
Manager G. Rhodes

23.11.07	Senol Dervis W PTS 6 Sheffield

Career: 1 contest, won 1.

Giovanni Kopogo

London. *Born* Libourne, France, 15 March, 1984
L.Welterweight. *Ht* 5'7"
Manager S. Fearon

09.10.07	Daniel Thorpe L RSC 2 Tower Hamlets

Career: 1 contest, lost 1.

Mark Krence

Chesterfield. *Born* Chesterfield, 24 August, 1976
Cruiserweight. Former Undefeated English & Midlands Area Heavyweight Champion. *Ht* 6'5¼"
Manager Self

09.04.00	Slick Miller W PTS 6 Alfreton
21.10.00	Neil Kirkwood W PTS 6 Sheffield
11.12.00	Tony Booth W PTS 6 Sheffield
20.01.01	Nigel Rafferty W PTS 4 Bethnal Green
24.03.01	Mark Williams W PTS 4 Sheffield
27.07.01	Shane Woollas W PTS 4 Sheffield
13.09.01	Luke Simpkin W PTS 4 Sheffield
25.09.01	Darren Chubbs W PTS 4 Liverpool
15.12.01	Eamonn Glennon W RSC 2 Sheffield
16.03.02	Neil Kirkwood W RSC 4 Bethnal Green
11.05.02	Gary Williams W PTS 6 Chesterfield
21.05.02	Audley Harrison L PTS 6 Custom House
03.08.02	Tony Booth W PTS 4 Derby
05.10.02	Gary Williams W RSC 4 Chesterfield
24.01.03	Petr Horacek W RSC 4 Sheffield
18.03.03	Paul Bonson W PTS 6 Reading
10.06.03	Luke Simpkin W RTD 8 Sheffield
	(Vacant Midlands Area Heavyweight Title)
01.08.03	Derek McCafferty W PTS 4 Bethnal Green
05.09.03	Collice Mutizwa W CO 2 Sheffield
06.02.04	Mindaugas Kulikauskas W PTS 8 Sheffield
12.05.04	Colin Kenna W RTD 3 Reading
10.09.04	Konstantin Prizyuk L RSC 6 Wembley
11.12.04	John McDermott W PTS 10 Canning Town
	(Vacant English Heavyweight Title)
15.05.05	Scott Gammer L RSC 8 Sheffield
	(Elim. British Heavyweight Title)
16.07.05	Matt Skelton L RTD 7 Bolton
	(British Heavyweight Title Challenge)
22.10.05	Ruslan Chagaev L CO 5 Halle, Germany
16.06.06	Scott Gammer L RSC 9 Carmarthen
	(Vacant British Heavyweight Title)
22.03.08	Hastings Rasani W PTS 4 Sheffield
21.06.08	Paul Bonson W PTS 4 Sheffield

Career: 29 contests, won 23, lost 6.

Eder Kurti

Kennington. *Born* Albania, 29 August, 1984
S.Middleweight. *Ht* 5'10¾"
Manager Self

04.11.04	Cafu Santos W RSC 1 Piccadilly
02.12.04	Craig Lynch W DIS 4 Crystal Palace
27.01.05	Ojay Abrahams W PTS 6 Piccadilly
19.11.05	JJ Ojuederie L RSC 4 Southwark
06.10.06	Stuart Brookes L PTS 6 Mexborough
02.12.06	Dave Pearson W PTS 6 Southwark
18.02.07	Greg Barton L PTS 4 Bethnal Green
18.11.07	Craig Denton L PTS 4 Tooting

Career: 8 contests, won 4, lost 4.

Kristian Laight

Nuneaton. *Born* Nuneaton, 15 June, 1980
Welterweight. *Ht* 5'10"
Manager J. Gill

26.09.03	James Paisley L PTS 6 Millwall
14.11.03	Matt Teague L PTS 6 Hull
05.12.03	Justin Hicks L PTS 6 Bristol
07.02.04	Kevin Mitchell L PTS 4 Bethnal Green
30.03.04	Chris McDonagh L PTS 6 Southampton
08.04.04	Jaz Virdee W PTS 6 Peterborough
20.04.04	Femi Fehintola L PTS 6 Sheffield
04.06.04	Gary Coombes DREW 6 Dudley
19.06.04	Ryan Barrett L PTS 4 Muswell Hill
23.10.04	Sean Hughes L PTS 6 Wakefield
18.11.04	Martin Gethin L RSC 4 Shrewsbury
17.12.04	Baz Carey L PTS 6 Coventry
08.05.05	Nadeem Siddique L RSC 7 Bradford
25.06.05	John-Paul Ryan DREW 6 Melton Mowbray
09.07.05	Chris Long L PTS 6 Bristol
02.09.05	Scott Haywood L PTS 6 Derby
06.10.05	Tom Hogan L PTS 6 Sunderland
24.10.05	Andrew Ferrans L PTS 8 Glasgow
12.11.05	Danny Gwilym L PTS 6 Bristol
20.11.05	Barry Downes DREW 6 Shaw
02.12.05	Charlie Thompson DREW 6 Doncaster
18.12.05	Gary O'Connor L PTS 6 Bolton
16.02.06	Haider Ali L PTS 4 Dudley
02.03.06	Jeff Thomas L PTS 6 Blackpool
30.03.06	Jaz Virdee L PTS 6 Peterborough
14.04.06	Tristan Davies L PTS 6 Telford
21.04.06	Wez Miller W PTS 6 Doncaster
11.05.06	Paul Holborn L PTS 6 Sunderland
21.05.06	Chris Long L PTS 6 Bristol
30.05.06	Akaash Bhatia L PTS 4 Bethnal Green
15.06.06	Neal McQuade W PTS 6 Peterborough
21.07.06	John Fewkes L RSC 5 Altrincham
09.10.06	Baz Carey DREW 6 Bedworth
26.10.06	Dean Harrison L PTS 4 Dudley
07.11.06	Martin Gethin L PTS 6 Leeds
24.11.06	Jack Perry L PTS 4 Nottingham
07.12.06	Ali Hussain W PTS 6 Bradford
15.02.07	Rob Hunt L PTS 6 Dudley
24.02.07	Chris Goodwin L PTS 6 Stoke
16.03.07	Lee Purdy L PTS 4 Norwich
23.03.07	Dean Harrison L PTS 4 Nottingham
13.04.07	Gary Sykes L PTS 4 Altrincham
20.04.07	Martin Gordon W PTS 4 Dudley
27.04.07	Ruben Giles L PTS 4 Wembley
05.10.07	George Watson L PTS 6 Sunderland
19.10.07	Stefy Bull L PTS 4 Doncaster
23.11.07	Stuart Kennedy L PTS 6 Houghton le Spring
30.11.07	Ross Hewitt L PTS 4 Newham
10.12.07	Graham Fearn L PTS 6 Leicester
23.12.07	Rick Godding L PTS 6 Bolton
18.01.08	Jack Perry L PTS 4 Burton
15.02.08	John Wainwright L PTS 6 Sheffield
28.02.08	Scott Evans L PTS 6 Wolverhampton
28.03.08	Tyrone Nurse L PTS 4 Barnsley
20.04.08	Darren Askew L PTS 6 Shaw
02.05.08	Chris Long L PTS 4 Bristol
12.05.08	Dean Arnold L PTS 6 Birmingham
23.05.08	Chris O'Brian L PTS 6 Wigan
15.06.08	Lee Jennings L PTS 6 St Helens
22.06.08	Jack Perry L PTS 6 Derby

Career: 60 contests, won 5, drew 5, lost 50.

Kristian Laight Philip Sharkey

Kenroy Lambert

Luton. *Born* Grenada, WI, 14 March, 1972
Middleweight. *Ht* 5'9¼"
Manager Self

17.02.02	Mark Nilsen L PTS 6 Salford
27.03.02	Freddie Yemofio W PTS 6 Mayfair
17.09.02	Leigh Wicks W PTS 6 Bethnal Green
10.10.02	William Webster L PTS 6 Piccadilly
16.09.07	Paul Dyer L PTS 6 Southampton
07.10.07	Tommy Heffron L RSC 3 Shaw
29.02.08	Paul Brown L RSC 6 Plymouth

Career: 7 contests, won 2, lost 5.

Ben Lawler

Skegness. *Born* Boston, 24 November, 1984
L.Welterweight. *Ht* 5'10¼"
Manager C. Greaves

31.05.08	Sid Razak W PTS 6 Newark

Career: 1 contest, won 1

Scott Lawton

Stoke. *Born* Stoke, 23 September, 1976
Former Undefeated English & Midlands
Area Lightweight Champion. *Ht* 5'10"
Manager M. Carney

29.09.01	Dave Hinds W RSC 2 Southwark
08.12.01	Ilias Miah W PTS 4 Dagenham
26.01.02	Pete Buckley W PTS 4 Bethnal Green
26.04.02	Pete Buckley W PTS 4 Coventry
06.09.02	Ben Hudson W PTS 4 Bethnal Green
30.01.03	Dave Stewart L PTS 6 Piccadilly
26.04.03	Chris McDonagh W RSC 2 Brentford
13.06.03	Jason Nesbitt W PTS 6 Queensway
14.11.03	Jimmy Beech W RSC 5 Bethnal Green
20.04.04	Henry Jones W PTS 6 Sheffield
17.06.04	Carl Allen W PTS 10 Sheffield *(Vacant Midlands Area Lightweight Title)*
17.09.04	Silence Saheed W PTS 6 Sheffield
10.12.04	Roger Sampson W PTS 6 Sheffield
04.03.05	Peter McDonagh W PTS 6 Rotherham
15.05.05	Carl Allen W PTS 6 Sheffield
24.07.05	Pete Buckley W PTS 6 Sheffield
09.09.05	Alan Temple L PTS 6 Sheffield
12.11.05	Ben Hudson W PTS 6 Stoke
18.02.06	Surinder Sekhon DREW 8 Stoke
06.05.06	Baz Carey W PTS 10 Stoke *(Midlands Area Lightweight Title*

Defence)

09.06.06	Stefy Bull W RSC 8 Doncaster *(Vacant English Lightweight Title)*
30.09.06	Judex Meemea W DIS 7 Stoke
24.11.06	Karl Taylor W PTS 4 Stoke
16.03.07	Jonathan Thaxton L RSC 7 Norwich *(British Lightweight Title Challenge)*
06.10.07	Amir Khan L RSC 4 Nottingham *(Commonwealth Lightweight Title Challenge)*
17.11.07	Carl Allen W PTS 6 Stoke
01.03.08	Michael Frontin W PTS 6 Stoke
17.05.08	Youssef Al Hamidi W PTS 6 Stoke

Career: 28 contests, won 23, drew 1, lost 4.

Dwayne Lewis

Canning Town. *Born* London, 12 June, 1979
S.Middleweight. *Ht.* 5'11¼"
Manager Self

18.02.07	Nick Okoth DREW 4 Bethnal Green
21.09.07	Michael Banbula W PTS 4 Bethnal Green
30.11.07	Lee Nicholson W RTD 2 Newham
27.06.08	Jamie Ambler W RSC 2 Bethnal Green

Career: 4 contests, won 3, drew 1.

Matthew Martin Lewis

Colchester. *Born* Colchester, 13 October, 1974
Lightweight. *Ht* 5'7½"
Manager A. Sims

07.11.06	John Baguley W PTS 6 Leeds
17.11.06	Ian Wilson L PTS 4 Bethnal Green
16.03.07	Leonard Lothian DREW 4 Norwich
01.07.07	Leonard Lothian L PTS 4 Colchester
07.09.07	Adam Kelly L PTS 4 Doncaster
28.09.07	Erick Roth L PTS 4 Stockholm, Sweden

Career: 6 contests, won 1, drew 1, lost 4.

James Lilley

Swansea. *Born* Swansea, 14 November, 1986
L.Welterweight. *Ht* 5'10"
Manager N. Hodges

08.10.06	Anthony Christopher W RSC 1 Swansea
24.02.07	Darren Hamilton L PTS 6 Bristol
12.05.07	Chris Goodwin L PTS 4 Stoke
21.10.07	Chris Brophy W PTS 4 Swansea
29.02.08	Ben Wakeham L PTS 6 Plymouth
30.03.08	Russell Pearce W PTS 6 Port Talbot

Career: 6 contests, won 3, lost 3.

Willie Limond

Glasgow. *Born* Glasgow, 2 February, 1979
IBO Inter-Continental Lightweight
Champion. Former Commonwealth
Lightweight Champion. Former Undefeated
Celtic & European Union S.Featherweight
Champion. *Ht* 5'7"
Manager Barry Hughes

12.11.99	Lennie Hodgkins W RTD 1 Glasgow
13.12.99	Steve Hanley W PTS 6 Glasgow
24.02.00	Nigel Senior W RSC 6 Glasgow
18.03.00	Phil Lashley W RSC 1 Glasgow
07.04.00	Jimmy Beech W RSC 2 Glasgow
26.05.00	Billy Smith W PTS 4 Glasgow

24.06.00	Haroon Din W PTS 4 Glasgow
10.11.00	Danny Connelly W PTS 6 Glasgow
17.12.00	Billy Smith W PTS 6 Glasgow
15.02.01	Marcus Portman W PTS 6 Glasgow
03.04.01	Trevor Smith W PTS 4 Bethnal Green
27.04.01	Choi Tseveenpurev W PTS 6 Glasgow
07.09.01	Gary Reid W PTS 8 Glasgow
03.11.01	Rakhim Mingaleev W PTS 6 Glasgow
17.11.01	Keith Jones W PTS 4 Glasgow
11.03.02	Dave Hinds W PTS 6 Glasgow
06.09.02	Assen Vassilev W RSC 3 Glasgow
22.03.03	Jimmy Beech W CO 4 Renfrew
12.07.03	Alex Arthur L RSC 8 Renfrew
	(British S.Featherweight Title Challenge)
01.11.03	Dariusz Snarski W RSC 1 Glasgow
29.11.03	Anthony Hanna W PTS 4 Renfrew
06.03.04	Dafydd Carlin W RSC 1 Renfrew
19.06.04	Youssouf Djibaba W PTS 10 Renfrew
	(Vacant European Union S.Featherweight Title)
29.10.04	Frederic Bonifai W PTS 8 Glasgow
03.12.04	Alberto Lopez W PTS 10 Edinburgh
	(European Union S.Featherweight Title Defence)
20.05.05	John Mackay W RSC 5 Glasgow
17.06.05	Kevin O'Hara W PTS 10 Glasgow
	(Vacant Celtic S.Featherweight Title)
05.11.05	Jus Wallie W PTS 6 Renfrew
04.11.06	Kpakpo Allotey W PTS 12 Glasgow
	(Vacant Commonwealth Lightweight Title)
14.07.07	Amir Khan L RTD 8 Greenwich
	(Commonwealth Lightweight Title Defence)
29.03.08	Martin Watson W PTS 12 Glasgow
	(Vacant IBO Inter-Continental Lightweight Title)

Career: 31 contests, won 29, lost 2.

Martin Lindsay

Belfast. *Born* Belfast, 10 May, 1982
IBF Youth Featherweight Champion.
Ht 5'7"
Manager J. Rooney

02.12.04	Dai Davies W RSC 1 Crystal Palace
24.04.05	Rakhim Mingaleev W PTS 4 Leicester Square
02.07.05	Henry Janes W RSC 2 Dundalk
17.09.05	Peter Feher W PTS 4 Dublin
21.04.06	Chris Hooper W RSC 1 Belfast
13.10.06	Nikita Lukin W PTS 6 Aberavon
30.03.07	Buster Dennis W PTS 6 Crawley
14.07.07	Jose Silveira W PTS 6 Rama, Canada
27.10.07	Uriel Barrera W PTS 4 Rama, Canada
	(Vacant IBF Youth Featherweight Title)
08.12.07	Edison Torres W PTS 8 Belfast
19.01.08	Jason Hayward W CO 1 Rama, Canada
16.05.08	Marc Callaghan W PTS 8 Turin, Italy

Career: 12 contests, won 12.

Mark Lloyd

Telford. *Born* Walsall, 21 October, 1975
Midlands Area Welterweight Champion.
Former Undefeated International & British
Masters L.Middleweight Champion.
Ht 5'10"
Manager Self

16.09.05	Dennis Corpe W PTS 6 Telford
04.12.05	Gatis Skuja W PTS 4 Telford
16.02.06	Davey Jones W PTS 6 Dudley
14.04.06	Ben Hudson W PTS 4 Telford

13.05.06	Tommy Jones W PTS 6 Sutton in Ashfield
29.06.06	Tommy Jones W PTS 6 Dudley
06.10.06	Terry Adams W RSC 7 Wolverhampton
	(Vacant British Masters L.Middleweight Title)
28.06.07	Neil Bonner W PTS 4 Dudley
15.09.07	Vladimir Borovski W PTS 10 Birmingham
	(Vacant International Masters L.Middleweight Title)
01.12.07	Martin Marshall W RTD 8 Telford
	(International Masters L.Middleweight Title Defence)
10.05.08	Adnan Amar L PTS 10 Nottingham
	(Vacant English Welterweight Title)
20.06.08	Andrew Alan Lowe W RSC 8 Wolverhampton
	(Vacant Midlands Area Welterweight Title)

Career: 12 contests, won 11, lost 1.

Mark Lloyd   Les Clark

Matthew Lloyd

Llanelli. *Born* Morriston, 24 May, 1977
L.Heavyweight. *Ht* 5'11"
Manager D.H. Davies

21.07.07	Harry Miles L CO 4 Cardiff

Career: 1 contest, lost 1.

Robert Lloyd-Taylor (Lloyd)

Northolt. *Born* Perivale, 1 September, 1980
Welterweight. *Ht* 5'11¼"
Manager Self

27.09.02	Wayne Wheeler W PTS 6 Bracknell
25.10.02	Nicky Leech L PTS 6 Cotgrave
20.12.02	Dean Larter W PTS 4 Bracknell
26.04.03	Ben Hudson L PTS 4 Brentford
31.05.03	Aidan Mooney W PTS 4 Bethnal Green
26.10.03	Arv Mittoo W PTS 6 Longford
14.11.03	Michael Lomax L PTS 6 Bethnal Green
07.04.04	Joe Mitchell W RSC 5 Leicester Square
07.05.04	Chas Symonds L RTD 5 Bethnal Green
08.07.04	Ivor Bonavic W PTS 4 The Strand
18.09.04	Matt Scriven W RTD 4 Newark
21.11.04	Geraint Harvey W PTS 4 Bracknell
21.01.05	Ivor Bonavic W CO 2 Brentford
16.06.05	Duncan Cottier W RSC 1 Mayfair
16.12.05	Karl David W PTS 4 Bracknell
24.03.06	Ben Hudson W PTS 6 Bethnal Green

17.11.06	James Hare W PTS 6 Bethnal Green
27.04.07	Craig Watson L PTS 8 Wembley
21.09.07	Craig Watson L RSC 1 Bethnal Green
30.11.07	Christopher Sebire L PTS 6 Newham

Career: 20 contests, won 13, lost 7.

Robert Lloyd-Taylor   Philip Sharkey

Gary Lockett

Cwmbran. *Born* Pontypool, 25 November, 1976
WBU Middleweight Champion. Former
WBO Inter-Continental L.Middleweight
Champion. *Ht* 5'10"
Manager Self

06.09.96	Ernie Loveridge W PTS 4 Liverpool
26.10.96	Charlie Paine W RSC 4 Liverpool
24.10.98	Lee Bird W RSC 2 Liverpool
27.02.99	Carl Smith W RSC 2 Bethnal Green
15.05.99	Mike Whittaker W RSC 2 Blackpool
19.06.99	Kid Halls W CO 1 Dublin
09.03.00	Kevin Thompson W CO 2 Liverpool
04.11.00	David Baptiste W PTS 4 Bethnal Green
23.01.01	Abdul Mehdi W RSC 2 Crawley
03.03.01	Hussain Osman W CO 2 Wembley
07.04.01	Howard Clarke W RSC 2 Wembley
08.05.01	Mike Algoet W PTS 6 Barnsley
14.07.01	Howard Clarke W CO 1 Wembley
25.09.01	Denny Dalton W RSC 1 Liverpool
24.11.01	Chris Nembhard W RSC 2 Bethnal Green
09.02.02	Kevin Kelly W CO 4 Manchester
	(Vacant WBO Inter-Continental L.Middleweight Title)
20.04.02	Youri Tsarenko L PTS 12 Cardiff
	(WBO Inter-Continental L.Middleweight Title Defence)
23.11.02	Viktor Fesetchko W PTS 8 Derby
29.03.03	Jason Collins W CO 1 Portsmouth
08.05.03	Yuri Tsarenko W PTS 10 Widnes
28.06.03	Michael Monaghan W PTS 10 Cardiff
21.02.04	Kreshnik Qato W RSC 2 Cardiff
12.06.04	Matt Galer W RSC 4 Manchester
03.09.04	Michael Monaghan W RSC 3 Newport
10.09.05	Allan Gray W CO 2 Cardiff
26.11.05	Victor Kpadenue W PTS 8 Rome, Italy
11.03.06	Gilbert Eastman W RSC 1 Newport
	(Vacant WBU Middleweight Title)
08.07.06	Ryan Rhodes W PTS 12 Cardiff
	(WBU Middleweight Title Defence)
18.11.06	Ayitey Powers W PTS 10 Newport

07.04.07 Lee Blundell W RSC 3 Cardiff
(*WBU Middleweight Title Defence*)
15.12.07 Kai Kauramaki W RSC 2 Edinburgh
07.06.08 Kelly Pavlik L RSC 3 Atlantic City,
New Jersey, USA
(*WBC & WBO Middleweight Title Challenges*)
Career: 32 contests, won 30, lost 2.

Michael Lomax

Chingford. *Born* London, 25 September, 1978
Welterweight. *Ht* 6'0"
Manager Self

05.07.03 Ernie Smith W PTS 4 Brentwood
20.09.03 Peter Dunn W PTS 4 Nottingham
14.11.03 Robert Lloyd-Taylor W PTS 6 Bethnal Green
16.01.04 Craig Lynch W PTS 6 Bradford
31.01.04 Steve Brumant W PTS 6 Bethnal Green
08.05.04 David Keir W RTD 4 Dagenham
13.02.05 Terry Adams W RSC 1 Brentwood
16.06.05 Jamie Coyle W PTS 6 Dagenham
18.11.05 Kevin Phelan W PTS 8 Dagenham
15.12.06 Billy Smith W PTS 6 Bethnal Green
30.03.07 Silence Saheed DREW 6 Crawley
06.07.07 Craig Watson L PTS 8 Wigan
25.01.08 Craig Dickson W PTS 6 Dagenham
Career: 13 contests, won 11, drew 1, lost 1.

Michael Lomax   Philip Sharkey

Chris Long

Calne. *Born* Gloucester, 5 March, 1980
L.Welterweight. *Ht* 5'9"
Manager Self

15.05.03 Darren Goode W RSC 1 Clevedon
21.09.03 Daniel Thorpe L PTS 6 Bristol
17.11.03 Stuart Green L PTS 6 Glasgow
13.02.04 Justin Hicks W RSC 4 Bristol
29.02.04 Gareth Perkins L PTS 6 Bristol
12.03.04 Ivor Bonavic W PTS 6 Millwall
01.05.04 Stuart Phillips W RSC 1 Bridgend
19.06.04 Ceri Hall L PTS 4 Muswell Hill
12.09.04 Ernie Smith DREW 6 Shrewsbury
24.09.04 John O'Donnell L RSC 4 Nottingham
02.12.04 Gavin Tait W PTS 6 Bristol
27.01.05 Sam Rukundo L PTS 4 Piccadilly
24.04.05 Scott Haywood L PTS 6 Derby
08.05.05 John Fewkes L PTS 8 Sheffield

09.07.05 Kristian Laight W PTS 6 Bristol
25.02.06 Muhsen Nasser L PTS 4 Bristol
05.03.06 Shane Watson L PTS 4 Southampton
25.03.06 Ryan Brawley L PTS 8 Irvine
21.05.06 Kristian Laight W PTS 6 Bristol
08.10.06 Stuart Phillips L PTS 4 Swansea
03.12.06 Rocky Chakir W PTS 6 Bristol
13.12.06 Stuart Green L PTS 6 Strand
17.02.07 James Gorman L RSC 3 Cork
18.03.07 Chris Brophy DREW 6 Bristol
30.03.07 Tibor Dudas L PTS 4 Crawley
28.04.07 Gary McArthur L PTS 10 Clydebank
(*Vacant British Masters Lightweight Title*)
21.10.07 Damian Owen L PTS 4 Swansea
02.12.07 Russell Pearce DREW 6 Bristol
03.02.08 Billy Smith L PTS 6 Bristol
02.05.08 Kristian Laight W PTS 4 Bristol
16.05.08 Martin Watson L PTS 10 Motherwell
(*International Masters Lightweight Title Defence*)
Career: 31 contests, won 9, drew 3, lost 19.

Leonard Lothian

Sheffield. *Born* Northampton, 11 February, 1988
Welterweight. *Ht* 5'6"
Manager J. Ingle

16.03.07 Matthew Martin Lewis DREW 4 Norwich
19.05.07 Dave Ryan L PTS 6 Nottingham
26.05.07 Mike Reid W PTS 6 Aberdeen
01.07.07 Matthew Martin Lewis W PTS 4 Colchester
15.09.07 Marco Cittadini DREW 6 Paisley
25.09.07 Andy Cox W PTS 6 Hull
05.10.07 Tom Glover W PTS 4 Bethnal Green
12.10.07 Scott Sandmann L PTS 4 Peterlee
25.10.07 Rob Hunt L PTS 4 Wolverhampton
09.11.07 Amir Unsworth L PTS 4 Nottingham
30.11.07 Daniel Thorpe W PTS 6 Hull
10.12.07 Pete Buckley W PTS 6 Leicester
15.02.08 George Watson L PTS 6 Sunderland
14.03.08 Nathan Brough L PTS 6 Manchester
22.03.08 Andrew Murray L RSC 3 Dublin
Career: 15 contests, won 6, drew 2, lost 7.

Andrew Lowe

Hackney. *Born* Hackney, 23 June, 1974
Former Southern Area L.Heavyweight Champion. *Ht* 5'10"
Manager Self

19.05.01 Rob Stevenson W PTS 4 Wembley
16.06.01 William Webster W RSC 2 Dagenham
20.10.01 Tom Cannon W PTS 4 Glasgow
24.11.01 Paul Wesley W PTS 4 Bethnal Green
15.12.01 Mark Snipe W PTS 4 Chigwell
12.02.02 Ali Forbes W PTS 4 Bethnal Green
04.05.02 Radcliffe Green W PTS 4 Bethnal Green
12.10.02 Paul Bonson W PTS 4 Bethnal Green
08.02.03 Clint Johnson W PTS 6 Brentford
29.03.03 Radcliffe Green W PTS 10 Wembley
(*Vacant Southern Area L.Heavyweight Title*)
31.05.03 Neil Linford W PTS 10 Bethnal Green
(*Elim. British L. Heavyweight Title*)
07.11.03 Radcliffe Green W PTS 6 Sheffield
20.03.04 Varuzhan Davtyan W PTS 6 Wembley
12.05.04 Peter Oboh L RTD 10 Reading
(*British & Commonwealth

L.Heavyweight Title Challenges)
10.04.05 Varuzhan Davtyan W PTS 6 Brentwood
03.06.06 John Anthony W PTS 6 Chigwell
09.12.06 Neil Tidman W PTS 6 Chigwell
26.01.07 Brian Magee L PTS 10 Dagenham
(*Final Elim.British L.Heavyweight Title*)
05.10.07 Paul David L PTS 8 Bethnal Green
16.05.08 JJ Ojuederie L PTS 10 Holborn
(*Southern Area L.Heavyweight Title Defence*)
Career: 20 contests, won 16, lost 4.

Andrew Alan Lowe

Newark Born Newark, 28 February, 1980
L.Middleweight. *Ht* 5'11¾"
Manager C. Greaves

30.09.06 Jon Musgrave L PTS 6 Stoke
24.11.06 Pawel Jas W PTS 6 Stoke
24.02.07 Barry Downes W PTS 6 Stoke
28.04.07 Steve Cooper W PTS 6 Newark
08.09.07 Lance Verallo W PTS 6 Sutton in Ashfield
13.10.07 Ernie Smith W PTS 6 Newark
23.02.08 Jon Musgrave W PTS 6 Newark
31.05.08 Chris Brophy W RSC 4 Newark
20.06.08 Mark Lloyd L RSC 8 Wolverhampton
(*Vacant Midlands Area Welterweight Title*)
Career: 9 contests, won 7, lost 2.

Colin Lynes

Hornchurch. *Born* Whitechapel, 26 November, 1977
Former European L.Welterweight Champion. Former Undefeated IBO & British L.Welterweight Champion. Former IBO Inter-Continental L.Welterweight Champion. *Ht* 5'7½"
Manager Self

04.06.98 Les Frost W CO 1 Barking
23.07.98 Ram Singh W CO 1 Barking
22.10.98 Brian Coleman W RSC 2 Barking
31.10.98 Marc Smith W PTS 4 Basingstoke
10.12.98 Trevor Smith W RSC 1 Barking
25.02.99 Dennis Griffin W PTS 6 Kentish Town
20.05.99 Mark Haslam W PTS 4 Barking
18.05.00 Jason Vlasman W RSC 2 Bethnal Green
16.09.00 Karl Taylor W PTS 6 Bethnal Green
14.10.00 Brian Coleman W PTS 6 Wembley
09.12.00 Jimmy Phelan W PTS 6 Southwark
17.02.01 Mark Ramsey W PTS 6 Bethnal Green
10.04.01 David Kirk W PTS 6 Wembley
10.11.01 Keith Jones W PTS 6 Wembley
01.12.01 Leonti Voronchuk W PTS 6 Bethnal Green
26.01.02 David Kirk W PTS 6 Dagenham
23.03.02 Peter Dunn W PTS 4 Southwark
18.05.02 Kevin Bennett W RSC 4 Millwall
29.06.02 Ian Smith W RSC 7 Brentwood
21.09.02 Abdelilah Touil W CO 7 Brentwood
07.12.02 Richard Kiley W RSC 9 Brentwood
(*Vacant IBO Inter-Continental L.Welterweight Title*)
08.03.03 Samuel Malinga L RTD 8 Bethnal Green
(*IBO Inter-Continental L.Welterweight Title Defence*)
18.10.03 Brian Coleman W PTS 4 Manchester
22.11.03 Fabrice Colombel W PTS 6 Belfast

31.01.04 Cesar Levia W PTS 8 Bethnal Green
08.05.04 Pablo Sarmiento W PTS 12 Dagenham
(IBO L.Welterweight Title Challenge)
13.02.05 Juaquin Gallardo W PTS 12 Brentwood
(IBO L.Welterweight Title Defence)
21.10.05 Junior Witter L PTS 12 Bethnal Green
*(British, Commonwealth & European
L.Welterweight Title Challenges)*
20.01.06 Lenny Daws L RTD 9 Bethnal Green
*(Elim. British L.Welterweight Title.
Vacant Southern Area L.Welterweight
Title)*
15.12.06 Janos Petrovics W RSC 6 Bethnal

Green
30.03.07 Arek Malek W RTD 2 Crawley
08.06.07 Barry Morrison W PTS 12 Motherwell
*(British L.Welterweight Title
Challenge)*
20.07.07 Young Muttley W RSC 8
Wolverhampton
*(Vacant European L.Welterweight
Title. British L.Welterweight Title
Defence)*
25.01.08 Juho Tolppola W PTS 12 Dagenham
*(European L.Welterweight Title
Defence)*

16.05.08 Gianluca Branco L PTS 12 Turin, Italy
*(European L.Welterweight Title
Defence)*
Career: 35 contests, won 31, lost 4.

Craig Lyon

St Helens. *Born* Whiston, 3 February, 1982
Bantamweight. *Ht* 5'3¼"
Manager O. Harrison
07.06.08 Delroy Spencer W PTS 6 Wigan
Career: 1 contest, won 1.

Colin Lynes

Philip Sharkey

Pat McAleese

Newmarket. *Born* Newmarket, 27 June, 1986
L.Middleweight. *Ht* 5'10¼"
Manager J. Eames
15.06.08 Steve Cooper W RSC 4 Bethnal Green
Career: 1 contest, won 1.

Pat McAleese   Philip Sharkey

Lee McAllister

Aberdeen. *Born* Aberdeen, 5 October, 1982
WBU L.Welterweight Champion. Former
Undefeated Scottish Area & WBF Inter-
Continental Lightweight Champion. Former
Undefeated British Masters L.Welterweight
Champion. *Ht* 5'9"
Manager Self
19.10.02 Baz Carey W PTS 4 Renfrew
17.11.02 Arv Mittoo W PTS 6 Bradford
23.02.03 Lee Williamson W PTS 6 Shrewsbury
13.04.03 Ernie Smith W PTS 4 Bradford
12.05.03 Ernie Smith W PTS 6 Birmingham
15.06.03 Brian Coleman W PTS 6 Bradford
11.07.03 John-Paul Ryan W RTD 2 Darlington
17.07.03 Dean Hickman L PTS 6 Walsall
03.08.03 Brian Coleman W PTS 4 Stalybridge
06.09.03 Jeff Thomas W PTS 10 Aberdeen
            (Vacant British Masters L.Welterweight Title)
28.11.03 Ernie Smith W PTS 6 Hull
30.01.04 Karl Taylor W PTS 4 Dagenham
08.03.04 Lee Williamson W PTS 6 Birmingham
15.05.04 Martin Hardcastle W PTS 8 Aberdeen
13.02.05 Daniel Thorpe W PTS 4 Bradford
26.04.05 Mark Wall W PTS 6 Leeds
14.05.05 Karl Taylor W RTD 3 Aberdeen
23.07.05 Billy Smith W PTS 4 Edinburgh
29.10.05 Jackson Williams W RSC 5 Aberdeen
18.02.06 Silence Saheed W PTS 4 Edinburgh
29.04.06 Peter Dunn W PTS 6 Edinburgh
12.05.06 Billy Smith W PTS 4 Bethnal Green
27.05.06 Stuart Green W RSC 8 Aberdeen

(Vacant Scottish Area Lightweight Title)
28.10.06 Ben Hudson W PTS 8 Aberdeen
26.05.07 Ben Odamattey W PTS 10 Aberdeen
            (Vacant WBF Inter-Continental Lightweight Title)
06.10.07 Craig Docherty W RSC 9 Aberdeen
            (Vacant WBU Lightweight Title)
29.03.08 Mihaita Mutu W PTS 12 Aberdeen
            (Vacant WBU L.Welterweight Title)
Career: 27 contests, won 26, lost 1.

Gary McArthur

Clydebank. *Born* Glasgow, 27 July, 1982
British Masters Lightweight Champion.
Ht 5'9"
Manager T. Gilmour
23.01.06 Lance Verallo W PTS 6 Glasgow
13.03.06 Pete Buckley W PTS 6 Glasgow
24.04.06 Darren Gethin W PTS 6 Glasgow
18.09.06 Billy Smith W PTS 8 Glasgow
13.10.06 Steve Gethin W PTS 6 Irvine
02.12.06 Frederic Gosset W PTS 6 Clydebank
28.04.07 Chris Long W PTS 10 Clydebank
            (Vacant British Masters Lightweight Title)
08.06.07 Egon Szabo W PTS 6 Motherwell
14.09.07 Dariusz Snarski W PTS 6 Kirkcaldy
24.11.07 Henry Jones W RSC 7 Clydebank
            (British Masters Lightweight Title Defence)
21.01.08 Billy Smith W PTS 8 Glasgow
Career: 11 contests, won 11.

Enzo Maccarinelli

Swansea. *Born* Swansea, 20 August, 1980
Former WBO Cruiserweight Champion.
Former Undefeated WBU Cruiserweight
Champion. *Ht* 6'4"
Manager F. Warren
02.10.99 Paul Bonson W PTS 4 Cardiff
11.12.99 Mark Williams W RSC 1 Merthyr
26.02.00 Nigel Rafferty W RSC 3 Swansea
12.05.00 Lee Swaby L CO 3 Swansea
11.12.00 Chris Woollas W PTS 4 Widnes
28.04.01 Darren Ashton W CO 1 Cardiff
09.10.01 Eamonn Glennon W RSC 2 Cardiff
15.12.01 Kevin Barrett W RSC 2 Wembley
12.02.02 James Gilbert W RSC 2 Bethnal Green
20.04.02 Tony Booth W PTS 4 Cardiff
17.08.02 Tony Booth W RTD 2 Cardiff
12.10.02 Dave Clarke W RSC 2 Bethnal Green
18.01.03 Paul Bonson W PTS 4 Preston
29.03.03 Valery Shemishkur W RSC 1 Portsmouth
28.06.03 Bruce Scott W RSC 4 Cardiff
            (Vacant WBU Cruiserweight Title)
13.09.03 Andrei Kiarsten W CO 1 Newport
            (WBU Cruiserweight Title Defence)
06.12.03 Earl Morais W RSC 1 Cardiff
            (WBU Cruiserweight Title Defence)
21.02.04 Garry Delaney W RSC 8 Cardiff
            (WBU Cruiserweight Title Defence)
03.07.04 Ismail Abdoul W PTS 12 Newport
            (WBU Cruiserweight Title Defence)
03.09.04 Jesper Kristiansen W CO 3 Newport
            (WBU Cruiserweight Title Defence)
21.01.05 Rich LaMontagne W RSC 4 Bridgend
            (WBU Cruiserweight Title Defence)
04.06.05 Roman Bugaj W RSC 1 Manchester
26.11.05 Marco Heinichen W RSC 1 Rome, Italy
04.03.06 Mark Hobson W PTS 12 Manchester
            (WBU Cruiserweight Title Defence)

08.07.06 Marcelo Dominguez W RSC 9 Cardiff
            (Vacant WBO Interim Cruiserweight Title)
14.10.06 Mark Hobson W RSC 1 Manchester
            (WBO Cruiserweight Title Defence)
07.04.07 Bobby Gunn W RSC 1 Cardiff
            (WBO Cruiserweight Title Defence)
21.07.07 Wayne Braithwaite W PTS 12 Cardiff
            (WBO Cruiserweight Title Defence)
03.11.07 Mohamed Azzaoui W RSC 4 Cardiff
            (WBO Cruiserweight Title Defence)
08.03.08 David Haye L RSC 2 Greenwich
            (WBA & WBC Cruiserweight Title Challenges.WBO Cruiserweight Title Defence)
Career: 30 contests, won 28, lost 2.

Kevin McCauley

Stourbridge. *Born* Stourbridge, 21
September, 1979
L.Welterweight. *Ht* 5'9¼"
Manager P. Rowson
16.05.08 Luke Gallear L PTS 6 Burton
Career: 1 contest, lost 1.

Paul McCloskey

Dungiven. *Born* Londonderry, 3 August, 1979
IBF International L.Welterweight
Champion. *Ht* 5'8½"
Manager J. Breen
18.03.05 David Kehoe W RSC 3 Belfast
17.06.05 Oscar Milkitas W PTS 4 Glasgow
05.11.05 Billy Smith W PTS 4 Renfrew
24.11.05 Henry Janes W RSC 3 Lurgan
18.02.06 Duncan Cottier W PTS 6 Edinburgh
11.03.06 Surinder Sekhon W RSC 1 Newport
04.11.06 Daniel Thorpe W RTD 3 Glasgow
09.12.06 Silence Saheed W PTS 4 Canning Town
10.02.07 Eugen Stan W PTS 6 Letterkenny
17.02.07 Chill John W PTS 6 Cork
14.07.07 Ivan Orlando Bustos W CO 4 Dublin
25.08.07 Alfredo Di Feto W PTS 8 Dublin
20.10.07 Dariusz Snarski W RTD 6 Dublin
08.12.07 Tontcho Tontchev W RSC 4 Belfast
            (Vacant IBF International L.Welterweight Title)
02.02.08 Manuel Garnica W PTS 10 Limerick
29.03.08 Cesar Bazan W PTS 10 Letterkenny
Career: 16 contests, won 16.

Joe McCluskey

Coventry. *Born* Coventry, 26 November, 1977
Welterweight. *Ht* 5'9"
Manager Self
01.05.04 John-Paul Ryan W RTD 2 Coventry
10.07.04 Declan English W RSC 4 Coventry
20.11.04 Judex Meemea DREW 6 Coventry
18.06.05 Carl Allen W PTS 6 Coventry
22.10.05 Darren Gethin DREW 6 Coventry
04.03.06 Khurram Hussain L PTS 6 Coventry
23.09.06 Thomas Mazurkiewicz L RSC 2 Coventry
02.12.06 Duncan Cottier W PTS 6 Coventry
26.02.07 Ali Wyatt L RSC 5 Birmingham
13.05.07 Ali Wyatt DREW 8 Birmingham
01.03.08 David Kirk W RSC 3 Coventry
Career: 11 contests, won 5, drew 3, lost 3.

Mark McCullough   Philip Sharkey

Mark McCullough

High Wycombe. *Born* High Wycombe, 10 February, 1983
L.Welterweight. *Ht* 5'8¼"
Manager J. Evans

16.09.07	Darryl Still L PTS 4 Southampton	
31.10.07	Daniel Thorpe W PTS 6 Bayswater	
28.03.08	Lloyd Smith W RSC 3 Piccadilly	
01.05.08	Dezzie O'Connor W CO 1 Piccadilly	
15.06.08	Silence Saheed L PTS 4 Bethnal Green	

Career: 5 contests, won 3, lost 2.

Darren McDermott

Dudley. *Born* Dudley, 17 July, 1978
Former Undefeated Midlands Area & British Masters Middleweight Champion. *Ht* 6'1"
Manager D. Powell

26.04.03	Leigh Wicks W PTS 4 Brentford
13.06.03	Gary Jones W RSC 1 Queensway
30.10.03	Harry Butler W PTS 4 Dudley
21.02.04	Freddie Yemofio W RSC 3 Cardiff
15.04.04	Mark Phillips W PTS 4 Dudley
03.07.04	Neil Addis W PTS 4 Newport
11.12.04	Gokhan Kazaz DREW 4 Canning Town
21.04.05	Howard Clarke W RTD 1 Dudley
06.10.05	Andy Halder W RTD 5 Dudley
	(Midlands Area Middleweight Title Challenge)
16.02.06	Michael Monaghan W RTD 9 Dudley
	(Midlands Area Middleweight Title Defence)
29.06.06	Andrzej Butowicz W RSC 3 Dudley
26.10.06	Hussain Osman W PTS 10 Dudley
	(Vacant British Masters Middleweight Title)
15.02.07	Darren Rhodes W RSC 5 Dudley
	(Elim.British Middleweight Title)
28.06.07	Conroy McIntosh W RSC 2 Dudley
	(Midlands Area Middleweight Title Defence)
25.10.07	Kai Kauramaki W RSC 4 Wolverhampton
20.06.08	Wayne Elcock L RSC 2 Wolverhampton
	(British Middleweight Title Challenge)

Career: 16 contests, won 14, drew 1, lost 1.

John McDermott

Horndon. *Born* Basildon, 26 February, 1980
English Heavyweight Champion. *Ht* 6'3"
Manager J. Branch

23.09.00	Slick Miller W RSC 1 Bethnal Green
21.10.00	Gary Williams W PTS 4 Wembley
13.11.00	Geoff Hunter W RSC 1 Bethnal Green
27.01.01	Eamonn Glennon W RSC 1 Bethnal Green
24.02.01	Alexei Osokin W PTS 4 Bethnal Green
26.03.01	Mal Rice W RSC 2 Wembley
09.06.01	Luke Simpkin W PTS 6 Bethnal Green
22.09.01	Gary Williams W RSC 4 Bethnal Green
24.11.01	Gordon Minors W RSC 3 Bethnal Green
19.01.02	Tony Booth W RSC 1 Bethnal Green
04.05.02	Martin Roothman W RSC 1 Bethnal Green
14.09.02	Alexander Mileiko W RSC 2 Bethnal Green
12.10.02	Mendauga Kulikauskas W PTS 6 Bethnal Green
14.12.02	Jason Brewster W RSC 1 Newcastle
15.02.03	Derek McCafferty W PTS 4 Wembley
08.05.03	Konstantin Prizyuk W PTS 8 Widnes
18.09.03	Nicolai Popov L RSC 2 Dagenham
13.05.04	James Zikic W RSC 4 Bethnal Green
30.07.04	Suren Kalachyan W CO 7 Bethnal Green
11.12.04	Mark Krence L PTS 10 Canning Town
	(Vacant English Heavyweight Title)
08.04.05	Slick Miller W RSC 1 Edinburgh
10.12.05	Matt Skelton L RSC 1 Canning Town
	(British Heavyweight Title Challenge)
26.01.07	Vitaly Shkraba W RSC 1 Dagenham
02.03.07	Paul King W PTS 6 Neath
15.06.07	Luke Simpkin W RSC 2 Crystal Palace
29.09.07	Scott Gammer W PTS 10 Sheffield
	(Elim. British Heavyweight Title)
01.02.08	Daniel Peret W PTS 6 Bethnal Green
18.04.08	Pele Reid W RSC 2 Bethnal Green
	(Vacant English Heavyweight Title)

Career: 28 contests, won 25, lost 3.

John McDermott   Philip Sharkey

Peter McDonagh

Bermondsey. *Born* Galway, 21 December, 1977
L.Welterweight. All-Ireland Lightweight Champion. Former Southern Area

Lightweight Champion. *Ht* 5'9"
Manager M. Roe

28.04.02	Arv Mittoo W PTS 6 Southwark
23.06.02	Dave Hinds W PTS 6 Southwark
14.09.02	Pete Buckley W PTS 4 Bethnal Green
27.10.02	Ben Hudson L PTS 6 Southwark
18.02.03	Daffyd Carlin L PTS 4 Bethnal Green
08.04.03	Ben Hudson W PTS 4 Bethnal Green
08.11.03	Ceri Hall L PTS 4 Bridgend
22.11.03	James Gorman L PTS 4 Belfast
21.02.04	Chill John W RTD 2 Brighton
06.03.04	Barry Hughes L PTS 6 Renfrew
07.04.04	Jon Honney W PTS 10 Leicester Square
	(Vacant Southern Area Lightweight Title)
19.11.04	David Burke L PTS 8 Bethnal Green
21.01.05	Ryan Barrett L PTS 8 Brentford
04.03.05	Scott Lawton L PTS 6 Rotherham
30.04.05	Rob Jeffries L PTS 10 Dagenham
	(Southern Area Lightweight Title Defence)
14.05.05	Robbie Murray L PTS 10 Dublin
	(Vacant All-Ireland L.Welterweight Title)
07.08.05	Brunet Zamora L PTS 6 Rimini, Italy
04.11.05	Anthony Christopher W PTS 4 Bethnal Green
28.01.06	Michael Gomez W RSC 5 Dublin
	(Vacant All-Ireland Lightweight Title)
24.09.06	Jason Nesbitt W PTS 4 Bethnal Green
01.12.06	Karl Taylor W PTS 4 Tower Hill
05.10.07	Duncan Cottier W PTS 4 Bethnal Green
29.02.08	Giuseppe Lauri L RSC 6 Milan, Italy
	(European Union L.Welterweight Title Challenge)

Career: 23 contests, won 11, lost 12.

Thomas McDonagh

Manchester. *Born* Manchester, 8 December, 1980
Middleweight. Former Undefeated WBU Inter-Continental L.Middleweight Champion. *Ht* 6'0"
Manager Brian Hughes

09.10.99	Lee Molyneux W PTS 4 Manchester
06.11.99	Lee Molyneux W PTS 4 Widnes
11.12.99	Arv Mittoo W RSC 2 Liverpool
29.01.00	Emmanuel Marcos W PTS 4 Manchester
29.02.00	William Webster W RTD 2 Widnes
25.03.00	Lee Molyneux W PTS 6 Liverpool
16.05.00	Richie Murray W PTS 4 Warrington
29.05.00	David Baptiste W PTS 6 Manchester
04.09.00	Colin Vidler W PTS 6 Manchester
11.12.00	Richie Murray W PTS 6 Widnes
15.01.01	Kid Halls W RSC 4 Manchester
10.02.01	Harry Butler W PTS 6 Widnes
17.03.01	David Baptiste W PTS 4 Manchester
07.07.01	Paul Denton W PTS 6 Manchester
15.09.01	Howard Clarke W PTS 6 Manchester
27.10.01	Mark Richards DREW 4 Manchester
09.02.02	Tomas da Silva DREW 4 Manchester
01.06.02	Delroy Mellis W PTS 4 Manchester
28.09.02	Brian Coleman W RSC 1 Manchester
18.01.03	Tomas da Silva W PTS 4 Preston
05.04.03	Paul Wesley W PTS 6 Manchester
08.05.03	Marcus Portman W PTS 6 Widnes
27.09.03	Eugenio Monteiro W PTS 12 Manchester
	(Vacant WBU Inter-Continental

L.Middleweight Title)
26.02.04 Bobby Banghar W CO 2 Widnes
*(WBU Inter-Continental
L.Middleweight Title Defence)*
03.04.04 Craig Lynch W PTS 6 Manchester
06.05.04 Bradley Pryce W PTS 12 Barnsley
*(WBU Inter-Continental
L.Middleweight Title Defence)*
12.11.04 Darren Rhodes W PTS 10 Halifax
(Elim. British L.Middleweight Title)
03.06.05 Barrie Lee W RSC 7 Manchester
*(WBU Inter-Continental
L.Middleweight Title Defence)*
25.10.05 Dean Walker W PTS 6 Preston
04.03.06 Wayne Alexander L PTS 12
Manchester
(WBU L.Middleweight Title Challenge)
14.10.06 Martin Concepcion W PTS 6
Manchester
21.04.07 Vladimir Borovski W PTS 6
Manchester
30.06.07 Alexander Matviechuk W PTS 6
Manchester
30.03.08 Yassine El Maachi W PTS 6 Colne
24.05.08 Andrew Facey DREW 10 Manchester
*(English L.Middleweight Title
Challenge)*
Career: 35 contests, won 31, drew 3, lost 1.

Jamie McDonnell
Doncaster. *Born* Doncaster, 3 March, 1986
English Bantamweight Champion. *Ht* 5'8"
Manager D. Hobson

16.09.05 Neil Read W PTS 6 Doncaster
02.12.05 Delroy Spencer W PTS 6 Doncaster
03.03.06 Gary Sheil W PTS 6 Doncaster
21.04.06 Neil Marston W PTS 4 Doncaster
09.06.06 Dai Davies DREW 4 Doncaster
13.10.06 Wayne Bloy W PTS 4 Doncaster
01.12.06 Andy Bell W RSC 3 Doncaster
23.02.07 Wayne Bloy W RSC 3 Doncaster
(Vacant English Bantamweight Title)
21.09.07 Nikita Lukin W PTS 8 Bethnal Green
08.12.07 Chris Edwards L PTS 12 Wigan
(Vacant British S.Flyweight Title)
28.03.08 Lee Haskins L PTS 8 Barnsley
Career: 11 contests, won 8, drew 1, lost 2.

Jamie McDonnell   Les Clark

James McElvaney
Middlesbrough. *Born* Middlesbrough, 30
December, 1986
Lightweight. *Ht* 5'8"
Manager Self

06.05.07 Shaun Walton W PTS 6 Darlington
09.06.07 Sergei Rozhakmens W PTS 6
Middlesbrough
15.07.07 John Baguley W PTS 6 Hartlepool
12.10.07 Mariusz Bak W PTS 4 Peterlee
Career: 4 contests, won 4.

Stuart McFadyen   Les Clark

Stuart McFadyen
Colne. *Born* Burnley, 27 January, 1982
S.Bantamweight. *Ht* 5'4"
Manager S. Wood

21.07.06 Neil Read W RSC 1 Altrincham
29.09.06 Abdul Mougharbel W PTS 4
Manchester
12.11.06 Anthony Hanna W PTS 6 Manchester
09.02.07 John Baguley W PTS 4 Leeds
11.03.07 Mo Khaled W PTS 6 Shaw
06.07.07 Tasif Khan W PTS 4 Wigan
22.09.07 Delroy Spencer W PTS 6 Wigan
25.11.07 Gavin Reid L RSC 5 Colne
30.03.08 Abdul Mougharbel W PTS 6 Colne
15.06.08 Senol Dervis W PTS 6 St Helens
Career: 10 contests, won 9, lost 1.

Steve McGuire
Glenrothes. *Born* Kirkcaldy, 1 June, 1981
Celtic S.Middleweight Champion. *Ht* 6'2¼"
Manager T. Gilmour

17.11.03 Shane White W CO 2 Glasgow
22.04.04 Paul Billington W RTD 3 Glasgow
15.10.04 Karl Wheeler W PTS 4 Glasgow
11.06.05 Varuzhan Davtyan W PTS 6 Kirkcaldy
30.09.05 Marcin Radola W RSC 1 Kirkcaldy
17.03.06 Paul David W PTS 6 Kirkcaldy
28.04.06 Valery Odin W PTS 6 Hartlepool
16.06.06 Simeon Cover W PTS 6 Liverpool
10.11.06 Richard Turba DREW 6 Hartlepool
16.02.07 Roman Vanicky W RSC 1 Kirkcaldy
11.05.07 Neil Tidman W PTS 8 Motherwell
14.09.07 Nathan King W PTS 10 Kirkcaldy
(Vacant Celtic S.Middleweight Title)
29.02.08 Jamie Ambler W PTS 6 Glasgow
06.06.08 Anthony Young W PTS 6 Glasgow
Career: 14 contests, won 13, drew 1.

George McIlroy
Stevenston. *Born* Irvine, 12 March, 1984
L.Middleweight. *Ht* 5'10¼"
Manager Self

28.02.03 Paul McIlwaine W PTS 6 Irvine
14.04.03 Paul Rushton W RSC 1 Glasgow
20.10.03 Norman Dhalie W PTS 6 Glasgow
15.10.04 Ivor Bonavic DREW 4 Glasgow
31.01.05 Chris Brophy W RSC 6 Glasgow
06.05.06 Deniss Sirjatovs W RSC 2 Irvine
02.11.07 Billy Smith L PTS 6 Irvine
Career: 7 contests, won 5, drew 1, lost 1.

Danny McIntosh
Norwich. *Born* Norwich, 1 March, 1980
L. Heavyweight. *Ht* 6'2"
Manager Self

09.04.05 Omid Bourzo W PTS 6 Norwich
03.09.05 Howard Clarke W PTS 4 Norwich
06.10.05 Michael Banbula W PTS 6 Longford
07.10.06 Matthew Hough W RSC 6 Walsall
16.03.07 Robert Burton W PTS 4 Norwich
04.10.07 Joey Vegas W PTS 6 Piccadilly
22.02.08 Nick Okoth W RSC 3 Bethnal Green
Career: 7 contests, won 7.

Eddie McIntosh
Birmingham. *Born* Birmingham, 21
September, 1982
S.Middleweight. *Ht* 6'0¼"
Manager R. Woodhall

28.09.07 Nicki Taylor W CO 2 Birmingham
18.11.07 Mark Phillips W PTS 4 Birmingham
25.01.08 Phillip Callaghan W PTS 4
Birmingham
13.04.08 Dave Pearson W PTS 4 Edgbaston
30.05.08 James Tucker W PTS 4 Birmingham
Career: 5 contests, won 5.

Nathan McIntosh
Nottingham. *Born* Nottingham, 2 February,
1988
L.Welterweight. *Ht* 5'8¼"
Manager J. Ingle

10.05.08 Danny Stewart W PTS 4 Nottingham
Career: 1 contest, won 1.

Kevin McIntyre
Paisley. *Born* Paisley, 5 May, 1978
Former Undefeated British, Celtic &
Scottish Area Welterweight Champion.
Ht 5'10½"
Manager Barry Hughes

13.11.98 Ray Wood W RSC 4 Glasgow
18.02.99 Gareth Dooley W RSC 3 Glasgow
21.05.99 Mohamed Helel W PTS 6 Glasgow
26.06.99 Karim Bouali L RTD 1 Glasgow
18.03.00 Chris Hall W RSC 3 Glasgow
07.04.00 Dave Travers W RSC 4 Glasgow
26.05.00 Tommy Peacock W RSC 5 Glasgow
24.06.00 Lee Williamson W PTS 4 Glasgow
02.10.00 Paul Denton W PTS 6 Glasgow
10.11.00 Mark Ramsey W PTS 4 Glasgow
17.12.00 Ernie Smith W PTS 6 Glasgow
15.02.01 John Humphrey L RSC 4 Glasgow
27.04.01 Michael Smyth W PTS 6 Glasgow
17.11.01 David Kirk W PTS 4 Glasgow
16.12.01 Manzo Smith W PTS 6 Glasgow
11.03.02 Karl Taylor W PTS 4 Glasgow

26.04.02	Craig Lynch W PTS 10 Glasgow
	(Vacant Scottish Area Welterweight Title)
08.06.02	David Kirk W RTD 5 Renfrew
19.10.02	Nigel Wright W PTS 6 Renfrew
22.03.03	David Kirk W RSC 1 Renfrew
12.07.03	Paul Denton W PTS 4 Renfrew
25.10.03	Karim Hussine W PTS 6 Edinburgh
13.12.03	David Barnes L RTD 8 Manchester
	(British Welterweight Title Challenge)
02.06.04	Keith Jones W PTS 6 Hereford
17.12.04	Sergey Starkov W PTS 6 Huddersfield
05.11.05	Nigel Wright L RSC 1 Renfrew
	(Final Elim. British L.Welterweight Title)
06.05.06	Gary Reid L RSC 6 Stoke
	(Vacant British Masters L.Welterweight Title)
05.05.07	Dave Wakefield W PTS 6 Glasgow
21.07.07	Tony Doherty W PTS 10 Cardiff
	(Celtic Welterweight Title Challenge)
02.11.07	Kevin Anderson W PTS 12 Irvine
	(British Welterweight Title Challenge)
29.02.08	Kevin Anderson W PTS 12 Glasgow
	(British Welterweight Title Defence)

Career: 31 contests, won 26, lost 5.

Jason McKay

Banbridge. *Born* Craigavon, NI, 11 October, 1977
S.Middleweight. Former Undefeated All-Ireland L.Heavyweight Champion. *Ht* 6'1"
Manager F. Warren/J. Breen

18.02.02	Jimmy Steel W PTS 4 Glasgow
11.05.02	Harry Butler W PTS 4 Dagenham
27.07.02	Simon Andrews W RSC 3 Nottingham
08.10.02	Dean Cockburn W PTS 4 Glasgow
08.02.03	William Webster W RSC 1 Liverpool
12.04.03	Marcin Radola W RSC 1 Bethnal Green
17.05.03	Varuzhan Davtyan W PTS 6 Liverpool
04.10.03	Jamie Hearn W PTS 8 Belfast
22.11.03	Ojay Abrahams W PTS 4 Belfast
17.04.04	Alan Gilbert W PTS 4 Belfast
26.06.04	Ciaran Healy W PTS 6 Belfast
05.11.04	Paul Buchanan L PTS 6 Hereford
24.11.05	Ojay Abrahams W PTS 4 Lurgan
18.02.06	Dean Walker W RTD 1 Belfast
20.05.06	Conroy McIntosh W PTS 6 Belfast
26.10.06	Sandris Tomson W RSC 6 Belfast
11.11.06	Michael Monaghan W PTS 10 Dublin
	(Vacant All-Ireland L.Heavyweight Title)
25.03.07	Darren Rhodes W PTS 6 Dublin
18.08.07	Mugurel Sebe W PTS 8 Cork
15.12.07	Andy Lee L RTD 6 Dublin
	(Vacant All-Ireland S.Middleweight Title)
02.02.08	Martins Kukuls W PTS 6 Limerick

Career: 21 contests, won 19, lost 2.

Jamie McKeever

Birkenhead. *Born* Birkenhead, 7 July, 1979
S.Featherweight. Former British Featherweight Champion. Former Undefeated Central Area Featherweight Champion. *Ht* 5'6½"
Manager Self

12.03.98	Dave Hinds W PTS 4 Liverpool
08.04.98	Kid McAuley W RTD 1 Liverpool
06.06.98	Brian Coleman W PTS 4 Liverpool
21.07.98	Stuart Rimmer W PTS 4 Widnes
31.10.98	John T. Kelly L PTS 6 Southend

22.01.99	Garry Burrell W RSC 2 Carlisle
12.03.99	David Kehoe W RSC 2 Bethnal Green
28.05.99	Arv Mittoo W PTS 6 Liverpool
02.10.99	Lee Armstrong DREW 6 Cardiff
27.11.99	Nigel Leake W RSC 2 Liverpool
01.07.00	Gary Flear L PTS 4 Manchester
09.10.00	Marc Callaghan W PTS 6 Liverpool
20.03.01	Craig Docherty L RSC 3 Glasgow
25.09.01	Sebastian Hart W PTS 4 Liverpool
10.12.01	Andrew Ferrans W PTS 6 Liverpool
09.03.02	James Rooney W PTS 6 Manchester
13.04.02	Barry Hawthorne W PTS 6 Liverpool
07.09.02	Tony Mulholland W PTS 10 Liverpool
	(Vacant Central Area Featherweight Title)
08.02.03	Tony Mulholland W RSC 6 Liverpool
	(Vacant British Featherweight Title)
17.05.03	Roy Rutherford L PTS 12 Liverpool
	(British Featherweight Title Defence)
28.02.04	Dazzo Williams L PTS 12 Bridgend
	(British Featherweight Title Challenge)
23.09.05	Jim Betts W RSC 4 Manchester
25.11.05	Dariusz Snarski W PTS 6 Liverpool
03.03.06	Riaz Durgahed W PTS 6 Hartlepool
16.06.06	Jackson Asiku L RSC 1 Liverpool
	(Commonwealth Featherweight Title Challenge)
18.02.07	Ryan Barrett L PTS 10 Bethnal Green
	(Vacant British Masters Featherweight Title)
10.03.07	Steve Bell L RSC 7 Liverpool
	(Vacant Central Area S.Featherweight Title)
06.06.08	Ryan Brawley L RSC 7 Glasgow

Career: 28 contests, won 18, drew 1, lost 9.

Dave McKenna

Port Glasgow. *Born* Greenock, 8 January, 1975
Heavyweight. *Ht* 6'3"
Manager Self

18.03.02	Leighton Morgan L DIS 3 Glasgow
14.04.03	Costi Marin L DIS 5 Glasgow
07.06.04	Dave Clarke W PTS 6 Glasgow
29.03.08	Lee Mountford W PTS 6 Glasgow

Career: 4 contests, won 2, lost 2.

(Helen) Angel McKenzie (Hobbs)

Thornton Heath. *Born* Russia, 10 June, 1973
L.Welterweight. *Ht* 5'7"
Manager Self

26.02.06	Alena Kokavcova W PTS 4 Dagenham
01.10.06	Elena Schmitt W PTS 4 Bruchsal, Germany
11.11.06	Galina Gumliiska L PTS 4 Rheinstetten, Germany
31.03.07	Ramona Kuehne L PTS 6 Berlin, Germany
23.06.07	Jill Emery L PTS 8 Dublin
14.09.07	Vinni Skovgaard L PTS 6 Horsens, Denmark
03.11.07	Sara Davies L PTS 4 Derby
01.12.07	Anna Ingman L PTS 4 Tidaholm, Sweden
22.12.07	Nathalie Toro L PTS 6 Beyne, Belgium
03.05.08	Myriam Lamare L RSC 6 Marseille, France
27.06.08	Myriam Lamare L RTD 3 Toulon, France

Career: 11 contests, won 2, lost 9.

Ovill McKenzie

Canning Town. *Born* Jamaica, 26 November, 1979
L.Heavyweight. Former Commonwealth L.Heavyweight Champion. *Ht* 5'9"
Manager C. Mitchell

06.03.03	Leigh Alliss W PTS 4 Bristol
10.04.03	Nathan King W PTS 4 Clydach
02.06.03	Pinky Burton L PTS 8 Glasgow
18.09.03	Peter Haymer L PTS 4 Mayfair
24.10.03	Courtney Fry L PTS 4 Bethnal Green
15.11.03	Edwin Cleary W PTS 4 Coventry
30.01.04	Steven Spartacus W PTS 6 Dagenham
12.03.04	Harry Butler W RSC 2 Millwall
03.04.04	Denis Inkin L PTS 8 Manchester
10.09.04	Tommy Eastwood L PTS 8 Wembley
04.12.04	Stipe Drews L PTS 8 Berlin, Germany
06.02.05	Paul Bonson W PTS 4 Southampton
13.02.05	Gyorgy Hidvegi W RSC 3 Brentwood
13.05.05	Courtney Fry W PTS 4 Liverpool
01.07.05	Hastings Rasani W PTS 6 Fulham
26.02.06	Tony Booth W PTS 4 Dagenham
23.03.06	Paul Bonson W PTS 6 The Strand
30.03.06	Paul Bonson W RSC 3 Bloomsbury
24.09.06	Peter Haymer W RSC 2 Bethnal Green
	(Vacant Commonwealth L.Heavyweight Title)
09.02.07	Dean Francis L RSC 1 Bristol
	(Commonwealth L.Heavyweight Title Defence)
16.09.07	Mark Nilsen W RSC 1 Derby
19.10.07	Tony Salam L PTS 6 Doncaster

Career: 22 contests, won 14, lost 8.

Sean McKervey

Coventry. *Born* Coventry, 17 July, 1983
L.Middleweight. *Ht* 5'8½"
Manager O. Delargy

04.03.06	Ernie Smith W PTS 6 Coventry
09.10.06	Steve Cooper DREW 6 Birmingham
11.12.06	Steve Cooper W PTS 6 Birmingham
26.02.07	Terry Carruthers L PTS 6 Birmingham
24.03.07	Peter Dunn W PTS 6 Coventry
22.09.07	Steve Cooper W PTS 6 Coventry
10.12.07	Karl Chiverton L PTS 6 Birmingham

Career: 7 contests, won 4, drew 1, lost 2.

James McKinley

Birmingham. *Born* Birmingham, 21 August, 1981
Middleweight. *Ht* 6'0"
Manager R. Woodhall

08.09.06	Mark Phillips W PTS 4 Birmingham
26.10.06	Thomas Flynn W PTS 4 Wolverhampton
01.12.06	Jon Musgrave W PTS 4 Birmingham
23.02.07	Matt Scriven W PTS 6 Birmingham
17.03.07	Peter Dunn W PTS 6 Birmingham
29.04.07	Jon Foster W PTS 6 Birmingham
13.07.07	Ernie Smith W PTS 6 Birmingham

Career: 7 contests, won 7.

Matthew Macklin

Birmingham. *Born* Birmingham, 14 May, 1982
L.Middleweight. Former Undefeated All-Ireland Middleweight Champion. *Ht* 5'10"
Manager Self

17.11.01	Ram Singh W RSC 1 Glasgow
15.12.01	Christian Hodorogea W CO 1 Wembley

09.02.02 Dimitri Protkunas W RTD 3 Manchester
11.03.02 David Kirk W PTS 4 Glasgow
20.04.02 Illia Spassov W CO 3 Cardiff
01.06.02 Guy Alton W RSC 3 Manchester
28.09.02 Leonti Voronchuk W RSC 5 Manchester
15.02.03 Ruslan Yakupov W PTS 6 Wembley
24.05.03 Paul Denton W PTS 6 Bethnal Green
06.11.03 Andrew Facey L PTS 10 Dagenham
 (Vacant English L.Middleweight Title)
21.02.04 Dean Walker W CO 1 Cardiff
24.04.04 Scott Dixon W RTD 5 Reading
12.06.04 Ojay Abrahams W PTS 4 Manchester
14.05.05 Michael Monaghan W CO 5 Dublin
 (Vacant All-Ireland Middleweight Title)
04.08.05 Leo Laudat W RSC 3 Atlantic City, New Jersey, USA
28.10.05 Anthony Little W RSC 2 Philadelphia, Pennsylvania, USA
26.11.05 Alexey Chirkov W CO 1 Sheffield
01.06.06 Marcin Piatkowski W RSC 4 Birmingham
29.09.06 Jamie Moore L RSC 10 Manchester
 (British L.Middleweight Title Challenge)
20.07.07 Anatoliy Udalov W CO 1 Wolverhampton
25.08.07 Darren Rhodes W CO 4 Dublin
20.10.07 Alessio Furlan W RSC 8 Dublin
22.03.08 Luis Ramon Campas W PTS 10 Dublin
Career: 23 contests, won 21, lost 2.

Gary McMillan

Edinburgh. *Born* Edinburgh, 12 January, 1987
Welterweight. *Ht* 5'10"
Manager A. Morrison

17.11.06 Scott Woolford L PTS 4 Bethnal Green
16.02.07 Thomas Mazurkiewicz DREW 4 Kirkcaldy
26.10.07 Craig Tomes W PTS 6 Glasgow
09.12.07 Mark Bett W RSC 1 Glasgow
14.03.08 Duncan Cottier W PTS 6 Glasgow
17.05.08 Danny Goode W PTS 6 Glasgow
Career: 6 contests, won 4, drew 1, lost 1.

Joe McNally

Liverpool. *Born* Liverpool, 30 October, 1984
Middleweight. *Ht* 5'9¾"
Manager Self

10.03.07 Rocky Muscas W PTS 4 Liverpool
23.02.08 Drew Campbell W PTS 4 Liverpool
16.03.08 Mark Phillips W RTD 2 Liverpool
07.06.08 Paul Royston W PTS 4 Wigan
Career: 4 contests, won 4.

Colin McNeil

Fauldhouse. *Born* Lanark, 21 December, 1972
Scottish Area L.Middleweight Champion. Former Undefeated Celtic L.Middleweight Champion. *Ht* 5'8"
Manager A. Morrison/F. Warren

06.03.04 Arv Mittoo W PTS 4 Renfrew
27.03.04 Lee Williamson W PTS 4 Edinburgh
19.06.04 Andrei Ivanov W RSC 2 Renfrew
22.10.04 Ivor Bonavic W PTS 4 Edinburgh
03.12.04 Geraint Harvey W PTS 6 Edinburgh
28.01.05 Matt Scriven W PTS 4 Renfrew
20.05.05 Duncan Cottier W PTS 6 Glasgow

23.07.05 Taz Jones W PTS 10 Edinburgh
 (Vacant Celtic L.Middleweight Title)
23.09.05 Ossie Duran L PTS 12 Mayfair
 (Commonwealth L.Middleweight Title Challenge)
29.04.06 Gary Young W CO 1 Edinburgh
 (Elim.British Welterweight Title)
04.11.06 David Kirk W PTS 6 Glasgow
10.12.06 Barrie Lee W RSC 4 Glasgow
 (Scottish Area L.Middleweight Title Challenge)
30.03.07 Cornelius Bundrage L RSC 7 Newcastle
29.03.08 Tyan Booth L CO 1 Aberdeen
Career: 14 contests, won 11, lost 3.

Neal McQuade

Peterborough. *Born* London, 17 November, 1977
L.Welterweight. *Ht* 5'4½"
Manager I. Pauly

15.06.06 Kristian Laight L PTS 6 Peterborough
21.07.06 Danny Harding L PTS 4 Altrincham
15.10.06 Gavin Deacon L PTS 6 Norwich
03.11.06 Darren Hamilton L PTS 6 Bristol
01.12.06 Waz Hussain DREW 4 Birmingham
24.02.07 Abdul Rashid W PTS 6 Manchester
30.03.07 Gavin Deacon L PTS 6 Peterborough
31.05.07 Anthony Crolla L RSC 1 Manchester
29.06.07 Lewis Smith L PTS 6 Manchester
13.07.07 Ben Murphy L RSC 2 Birmingham
Career: 10 contests, won 1, drew 1, lost 8.

Tony McQuade   Philip Sharkey

Tony McQuade

Peterborough. *Born* Peterborough, 2 June, 1988
S.Featherweight. *Ht* 5'5½"
Manager I. Pauly

07.12.06 Gavin Deacon DREW 6 Peterborough
30.03.07 Carl Griffiths W PTS 6 Peterborough
18.04.07 Leroy Smedley L PTS 6 Strand
21.06.07 Shaun Walton W PTS 6 Peterborough
20.07.07 Kevin Buckley L PTS 4 Wolverhampton
10.12.07 John Vanemmenis DREW 6 Peterborough
08.02.08 Gavin Reid L PTS 4 Peterlee
29.02.08 Davey Savage L PTS 4 Glasgow
14.03.08 John Donnelly L PTS 6 Manchester

05.04.08 Rob Turley L PTS 6 Newport
13.06.08 Billy Bell L PTS 6 Sunderland
Career: 11 contests, won 2, drew 2, lost 7.

Brian Magee

Belfast. *Born* Lisburn, 9 June, 1975
L.Heavyweight. Former IBO S.Middleweight Champion. Former Undefeated IBO Inter-Continental S.Middleweight Champion. *Ht* 6'0"
Manager Self

13.03.99 Dean Ashton W RSC 2 Manchester
22.05.99 Richard Glaysher W RSC 1 Belfast
22.06.99 Chris Howarth W RSC 1 Ipswich
13.09.99 Dennis Doyley W RSC 3 Bethnal Green
16.10.99 Michael Pinnock W RSC 3 Belfast
12.02.00 Terry Morrill W RTD 4 Sheffield
21.02.00 Rob Stevenson W RSC 5 Southwark
20.03.00 Darren Ashton W RTD 5 Mansfield
15.04.00 Pedro Carragher W CO 2 Bethnal Green
12.06.00 Jason Barker W PTS 8 Belfast
11.11.00 Teimouraz Kikelidze W RSC 4 Belfast
29.01.01 Neil Linford W PTS 12 Peterborough
 (Vacant IBO Inter-Continental S. Middleweight Title)
31.07.01 Chris Nembhard W RSC 6 Bethnal Green
10.12.01 Ramon Britez W CO 1 Liverpool
 (IBO S.Middleweight Title Challenge)
18.03.02 Vage Kocharyan W PTS 8 Crawley
15.06.02 Mpush Makambi W RSC 7 Leeds
 (IBO S. Middleweight Title Defence)
09.11.02 Jose Spearman W PTS 12 Altrincham
 (IBO S. Middleweight Title Defence)
22.02.03 Miguel Jimenez W PTS 12 Huddersfield
 (IBO S. Middleweight Title Defence)
21.06.03 Andre Thysse W RSC 10 Manchester
 (IBO S.Middleweight Title Defence)
04.10.03 Omar Eduardo Gonzalez W RSC 1 Belfast
 (IBO S.Middleweight Title Defence)
22.11.03 Hacine Cherifi W RTD 8 Belfast
 (IBO S.Middleweight Title Defence)
17.04.04 Jerry Elliott W PTS 12 Belfast
 (IBO S.Middleweight Title Defence)
26.06.04 Robin Reid L PTS 12 Belfast
 (IBO S.Middleweight Title Defence)
26.11.04 Neil Linford W RSC 7 Altrincham
16.07.05 Vitali Tsypko L PTS 12 Nurnberg, Germany
 (Vacant European S.Middleweight Title)
14.10.05 Varuzhan Davtyan W RSC 2 Dublin
28.01.06 Daniil Prakapsou W RSC 2 Dublin
26.05.06 Carl Froch L RSC 11 Bethnal Green
 (British & Commonwealth S.Middleweight Title Challenges)
03.11.06 Paul David W PTS 6 Barnsley
26.01.07 Andrew Lowe W PTS 10 Dagenham
 (Final Elim.British L.Heavyweight Title)
08.06.07 Danny Thornton W RTD 2 Motherwell
25.08.07 Tony Oakey DREW 12 Dublin
 (British L.Heavyweight Title Challenge)
08.02.08 Mark Nilsen W PTS 4 Peterlee
07.03.08 Tyrone Wright W PTS 6 Nottingham
Career: 34 contests, won 30, drew 1, lost 3.

Ryan Mahoney

Canvey Island. *Born* Lambeth, 3 February, 1985
Middleweight. *Ht* 5'11½"
Manager J. Eames

01.12.07 Carl Drake L PTS 4 Chigwell
Career: 1 contest, lost 1.

Paul Malcolm

Hartlepool. *Born* Hartlepool, 22 June, 1970
Heavyweight. *Ht* 6'2"
Manager D. Garside

15.07.07 David Ingleby W PTS 6 Hartlepool
23.09.07 Dave Ferguson L RTD 3 Hartlepool
Career: 2 contests, won 1, lost 1.

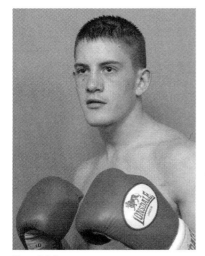

Rory Malone   Philip Sharkey

Rory Malone

Peterborough. *Born* Peterborough, 12 September, 1989
L.Welterweight. *Ht* 5'8½"
Manager G. De'Roux/D. Powell

10.11.07 Lloyd Smith W PTS 6 Portsmouth
Career: 1 contest, won 1.

Matthew Marsh

West Ham. *Born* Sidcup, 1 August, 1982
British S.Bantamweight Champion. Former Undefeated Southern Area Featherweight & S.Bantamweight Champion. *Ht* 5'5¾"
Manager F. Warren/J. Eames

10.09.04 Fred Janes W PTS 4 Bethnal Green
19.11.04 Dean Ward W PTS 4 Bethnal Green
11.12.04 Abdul Mougharbel W PTS 4 Canning Town
25.02.05 Dai Davies W PTS 4 Wembley
10.12.05 Darren Cleary W PTS 4 Canning Town
29.06.06 Frederic Gosset W PTS 6 Bethnal Green
09.12.06 Rocky Dean W PTS 10 Canning Town
           (Southern Area Featherweight Title Challenge)
14.07.07 Rocky Dean W PTS 10 Greenwich
           (Vacant Southern Area S.Bantamweight Title)
13.10.07 Derry Matthews L RSC 11 Bethnal

Green
           (WBU Featherweight Title Challenge)
02.02.08 Ajibu Salum W CO 1 Canning Town
27.06.08 Esham Pickering W PTS 12 Bethnal Green
           (British S.Bantamweight Title Challenge)
Career: 11 contests, won 10, lost 1.

Martin Marshall

Sunderland. *Born* Sunderland, 28 January, 1983
Middleweight. *Ht* 6'1"
Manager T. Conroy

14.05.04 Richard Mazurek DREW 6 Sunderland
23.09.04 Richard Inquieti W PTS 6 Gateshead
28.10.04 Richard Inquieti W PTS 6 Sunderland
09.12.04 Gary Porter L PTS 6 Sunderland
19.12.04 John Marshall L CO 5 Bolton
12.05.05 Muhsen Nasser L PTS 6 Sunderland
27.05.05 Gary Porter L PTS 6 Motherwell
11.06.05 Keith Ellwood W PTS 6 Kirkcaldy
06.10.05 Alex Stoda W PTS 6 Sunderland
03.11.05 Malik Khan W PTS 6 Sunderland
08.12.05 Brendan Halford L RSC 5 Sunderland
09.03.06 Omar Gumati DREW 6 Sunderland
11.09.06 Prince Arron L PTS 6 Manchester
23.10.06 Craig Dickson L RTD 4 Glasgow
24.11.06 Danny Johnston L PTS 6 Stoke
07.12.06 Thomas Mazurkiewicz W PTS 6 Sunderland
16.02.07 Paddy Pollock W PTS 4 Sunderland
30.03.07 Graham Delehedy L CO 2 Crawley
24.06.07 Matt Scriven W PTS 6 Sunderland
06.07.07 Alex Matvienko DREW 4 Wigan
22.09.07 Alex Matvienko L PTS 6 Wigan
12.10.07 Prince Arron L PTS 4 Peterlee
01.12.07 Mark Lloyd L RTD 8 Telford
           (International Masters L.Middleweight Title Challenge)
08.02.08 Danny Thornton L PTS 4 Peterlee
15.05.08 James Tucker W PTS 6 Sunderland
Career: 25 contests, won 9, drew 3, lost 13.

Shanee Martin   Philip Sharkey

Shanee Martin

Colchester. *Born* Dagenham, 31 January, 1982
Bantamweight. *Ht* 5'2"
Manager Self

16.10.04 Iliana Boneva W RSC 4 Dagenham
05.03.05 Svetla Taskova W PTS 6 Dagenham
18.09.05 Albena Atseva W RSC 3 Bethnal Green
19.11.05 Valerie Rangeard W PTS 6 Southwark
26.02.06 Maya Frenzel W RSC 5 Dagenham
23.07.06 Juliette Winter L PTS 8 Dagenham
21.10.06 Tatiana Puchkova W RSC 2 Southwark
03.12.06 Rebekka Herrmann W PTS 8 Bethnal Green
18.02.07 Oksana Romanova L RSC 7 Bethnal Green
04.05.07 Viktoria Milo L PTS 10 Szombathely, Hungary
           (Womens IBF-GBU Flyweight Title Challenge)
29.06.07 Svetla Taskova W PTS 6 Manchester
07.09.07 Susi Kentikian L RSC 3 Dusseldorf, Germany
           (Womens WBA Flyweight Title Challenge)
01.12.07 Juliette Winter DREW 6 Bethnal Green
Career: 13 contests, won 8, drew 1, lost 4.

Glen Matsell

Hull. *Born* Hull, 24 March, 1975
L.Middleweight. *Ht* 5'9"
Manager Self

26.11.04 Ali Mateen W RTD 3 Hull
27.04.07 Ben Hudson W PTS 6 Hull
25.09.07 Alex Stoda W PTS 6 Hull
Career: 3 contests, won 3.

Derry Matthews

Liverpool. *Born* Liverpool, 23 September, 1983
Former WBU Featherweight Champion. Former Undefeated English Featherweight Champion. *Ht* 5'8½"
Manager Self

18.01.03 Sergei Tasimov W CO 1 Preston
05.04.03 Jus Wallie W PTS 4 Manchester
08.05.03 Steve Gethin W RSC 3 Widnes
20.06.03 Henry Janes W RSC 1 Liverpool
29.08.03 Marty Kayes W RTD 2 Liverpool
02.10.03 Alexei Volchan W RSC 2 Liverpool
13.12.03 Pete Buckley W PTS 4 Manchester
26.02.04 Gareth Payne W RSC 4 Widnes
03.04.04 Henry Janes W PTS 4 Manchester
10.09.04 Buster Dennis W PTS 6 Liverpool
17.12.04 Dean Ward W RSC 1 Liverpool
13.05.05 John Mackay W PTS 6 Liverpool
16.07.05 Dai Davies W RSC 2 Bolton
25.10.05 Frederic Bonifai W PTS 6 Preston
28.01.06 Stephen Chinnock W RTD 6 Nottingham
           (Vacant English Featherweight Title)
01.06.06 Mickey Coveney W PTS 8 Barnsley
14.10.06 Steve Foster W PTS 12 Manchester
           (WBU Featherweight Title Challenge)
10.03.07 John Simpson W PTS 12 Liverpool
           (WBU Featherweight Title Defence)
13.10.07 Matthew Marsh W RSC 11 Bethnal Green
           (WBU Featherweight Title Defence)
02.02.08 Nikoloz Berkatsashvili W CO 1 Canning Town

05.04.08 Choi Tseveenpurev L CO 5 Bolton
(WBU Featherweight Title Defence)
Career: 21 contests, won 20, lost 1.

Derry Matthews   Philip Sharkey

Harry Matthews

York. *Born* Beverley, 21 February, 1988
Middleweight. *Ht* 5'9¼"
Manager C. Greaves

21.06.08 Jason Smith W PTS 6 Hull
Career: 1 contest, won 1.

Alex Matvienko   Les Clark

Alex Matvienko

Bolton. *Born* Bolton, 9 May, 1978
Middleweight. *Ht* 5'11"
Manager Self

18.12.05	Tommy Jones W PTS 6 Bolton
02.04.06	Tony Randell W PTS 6 Shaw
21.07.06	Simone Lucas W PTS 4 Altrincham
29.09.06	Jon Foster W RTD 3 Manchester
12.11.06	Thomas Flynn W RSC 5 Manchester
25.02.07	Shaun Farmer W PTS 6 Manchester
13.04.07	Ryan Ashworth DREW 4 Altrincham
24.06.07	Ronnie Daniels W PTS 6 Wigan
06.07.07	Martin Marshall DREW 4 Wigan
22.09.07	Martin Marshall W PTS 6 Wigan
08.12.07	Jamie Ambler W PTS 4 Wigan

16.02.08 Davey Jones W RSC 2 Blackpool
26.04.08 Drew Campbell W RSC 4 Wigan
Career: 13 contests, won 11, drew 2.

Max Maxwell

Birmingham. *Born* Jamaica, 26 July, 1979
Midlands Area Middleweight Champion.
Ht 5'10"
Manager R. Woodhall

26.10.06	Anthony Young L PTS 4 Wolverhampton
01.12.06	Ernie Smith W PTS 6 Birmingham
23.02.07	Peter Dunn W PTS 6 Birmingham
17.03.07	Sherman Alleyne W PTS 6 Birmingham
29.04.07	Matt Scriven W PTS 4 Birmingham
28.09.07	Duncan Cottier W PTS 6 Birmingham
25.01.08	Johnny Enigma W RSC 2 Birmingham
28.02.08	Matthew Hough W RSC 3 Wolverhampton
	(Vacant Midlands Area Middleweight Title)

Career: 8 contests, won 7, lost 1.

Max Maxwell   Philip Sharkey

Patrick J. Maxwell

Sheffield. *Born* USA, 20 March, 1979
S.Middleweight. *Ht* 5'8¼"
Manager Self

17.03.98	Danny Thornton W PTS 6 Sheffield
12.08.00	Matthew Ashmole W RSC 3 Wembley
26.03.01	Jason Collins L PTS 4 Wembley
27.10.01	Prince Kasi Kaihau W CO 4 Manchester
09.02.02	Leigh Wicks W PTS 4 Manchester
09.03.03	Surinder Sekhon W RSC 1 Shaw
10.06.03	Andy Halder W RSC 1 Sheffield
05.09.03	Isidro Gonzalez W RSC 6 Sheffield
07.11.03	Conroy McIntosh W RSC 4 Sheffield
17.06.04	Howard Clarke W RSC 1 Sheffield
21.09.05	Conroy McIntosh W RSC 2 Bradford
14.10.06	Anthony Little W RSC 3 Philadelphia, Pennsylvania, USA
17.11.06	Charden Ansoula W PTS 6 Cabazon, California, USA
09.03.07	Kevin Phelan W RSC 2 Dagenham
27.04.07	Geard Ajetovic DREW 6 Wembley
13.07.07	Geard Ajetovic L RSC 3 Barnsley
08.03.08	Anthony Young W RTD 4 Greenwich

Career: 17 contests, won 14, drew 1, lost 2.

Richard Mazurek

Leamington. *Born* Leamington, 20 January, 1977
L.Middleweight. *Ht* 5'10"
Manager Self

15.11.03	Neil Addis W PTS 6 Coventry
21.02.04	Simon Hopkins W RSC 3 Brighton
01.05.04	Brian Coleman W PTS 6 Coventry
14.05.04	Martin Marshall DREW 6 Sunderland
10.07.04	Richard Inquieti W RSC 1 Coventry
20.11.04	David Payne W PTS 6 Coventry
18.06.05	Ernie Smith L PTS 6 Coventry
09.09.05	Jozsef Matolcsi L PTS 6 Sheffield
22.10.05	Rob Burton L PTS 6 Coventry
18.11.05	George Hillyard L PTS 6 Dagenham
15.12.05	Ali Mateen L PTS 6 Coventry
20.01.06	Darren Barker L PTS 8 Bethnal Green
04.03.06	Tommy Jones W PTS 6 Coventry
28.04.06	Franny Jones L PTS 6 Hartlepool
25.02.08	Rocky Chakir L RSC 2 Birmingham

Career: 15 contests, won 7, drew 1, lost 7.

Lee Meager   Philip Sharkey

Lee Meager

Salford. *Born* Salford, 18 January, 1978
Lightweight. Former British Lightweight
Champion. *Ht* 5'8"
Manager Self

16.09.00	Pete Buckley W PTS 4 Bethnal Green
14.10.00	Chris Jickells W PTS 4 Wembley
18.11.00	Billy Smith W RSC 1 Dagenham
09.12.00	Jason Nesbitt W RSC 2 Southwark
05.02.01	Carl Allen DREW 6 Hull
13.03.01	Lennie Hodgkins W RSC 3 Plymouth
12.05.01	Jason White W PTS 4 Plymouth
31.07.01	Steve Hanley W PTS 6 Bethnal Green
13.09.01	Arv Mittoo W PTS 6 Sheffield
16.03.02	Jason Nesbitt W PTS 6 Bethnal Green
10.05.02	Pete Buckley W PTS 6 Bethnal Green
25.10.02	Iain Eldridge W RSC 5 Bethnal Green
21.12.02	Chill John W RSC 5 Dagenham
28.01.03	Carl Allen W PTS 8 Nottingham
28.11.03	Pete Buckley W PTS 4 Derby
11.12.03	Charles Shepherd W RTD 7 Bethnal Green
02.06.04	Michael Muya W PTS 8 Nottingham
19.11.04	Danny Hunt L PTS 10 Bethnal Green
	(English Lightweight Title Challenge)
09.07.05	Martin Watson W PTS 10 Nottingham

02.12.05	Tony Montana W PTS 8 Nottingham
17.02.06	Ben Hudson W PTS 4 Bethnal Green
12.05.06	Dave Stewart W RSC 6 Bethnal Green
	(Vacant British Lightweight Title)
08.12.06	Jonathan Thaxton L PTS 12 Dagenham
	(British Lightweight Title Defence)
07.09.07	Laszlo Komjathi W RTD 4 Doncaster
07.12.07	Jose Alberto Gonzalez DREW 8 Las Vegas, Nevada, USA

Career: 25 contests, won 21, drew 2, lost 2.

Dale Miles   Les Clark

Dale Miles

Alfreton. *Born* Mansfield, 19 November, 1984
L.Middleweight. *Ht* 5'11"
Manager M. Shinfield

13.05.06	Karl Taylor W RSC 3 Sutton in Ashfield
16.09.06	Steve Cooper W PTS 6 Burton
11.11.06	Jimmy Maile W RSC 5 Sutton in Ashfield
17.05.08	Jimmy Doherty W PTS 6 Stoke

Career: 4 contests, won 4.

Harry Miles

Blackwood. *Born* Hereford, 18 November, 1985
L.Heavyweight. *Ht* 6'4¼"
Manager E. Calzaghe/F. Warren

21.07.07	Matthew Lloyd W CO 4 Cardiff
03.11.07	Mark Phillips W PTS 4 Cardiff
22.03.08	Jamie Norkett W PTS 4 Cardiff

Career: 3 contests, won 3.

Ian Millarvie

Hamilton. *Born* Bellshill, 7 April, 1980
Heavyweight. *Ht* 6'5¾"
Manager T. Gilmour

31.01.05	Mal Rice W RTD 3 Glasgow
21.02.05	Luke Simpkin W PTS 6 Glasgow

27.05.05	Sergey Voron W RSC 1 Motherwell
17.03.06	Jason Callum W CO 3 Kirkcaldy
11.04.07	Sean McClain W PTS 4 NYC, New York, USA
14.09.07	Chris Woollas W RSC 2 Kirkcaldy
05.11.07	Jevgenijs Stamburskis W RSC 2 Glasgow

Career: 7 contests, won 7.

Scott Miller

Stoke. *Born* Stoke, 7 July, 1982
Welterweight. *Ht* 5'11¼"
Manager Self

17.11.07	Karl Taylor W PTS 6 Stoke
01.03.08	Craig Tomes W RSC 6 Stoke
20.03.08	Chris Mullen W PTS 6 South Shields
17.05.08	Jimmy Beech W RTD 2 Stoke
06.06.08	Ade Adebolu W RSC 2 Stoke

Career: 5 contests, won 5.

Dean Mills

Bridgewater. *Born* Bridgewater, 13 October, 1987
S.Featherweight. *Ht* 5'5¾"
Manager N. Christian

09.11.07	Dezzie O'Connor L PTS 6 Plymouth
16.02.08	Carl Griffiths W RSC 6 Leicester
18.04.08	Billy Bell W PTS 6 Houghton le Spring
02.05.08	Barrington Brown DREW 4 Nottingham

Career: 4 contests, won 2, drew 1, lost 1.

Ross Minter

Crawley. *Born* Crawley, 10 November, 1978
Welterweight. Former Undefeated Southern Area & English Welterweight Champion. *Ht* 5'7¾"
Manager F. Warren

26.03.01	Brian Coleman W PTS 4 Wembley
05.05.01	Trevor Smith W RTD 3 Edmonton
28.07.01	Lee Williamson W PTS 4 Wembley
24.11.01	Karl Taylor W PTS 4 Bethnal Green
15.12.01	Ernie Smith W RSC 2 Wembley
02.03.02	Paul Denton W PTS 6 Bethnal Green
25.05.02	Howard Clarke L RSC 2 Portsmouth
12.10.02	Dafydd Carlin W RSC 1 Bethnal Green
15.02.03	Karl Taylor W PTS 6 Wembley
29.03.03	Jay Mahoney W RSC 2 Portsmouth
24.05.03	Jay Mahoney W RSC 6 Bethnal Green
18.09.03	John Marshall DREW 6 Dagenham
19.11.04	David Kirk W PTS 6 Bethnal Green
25.02.05	Ernie Smith W PTS 4 Wembley
29.04.05	Chas Symonds W RSC 3 Southwark
	(Southern Area Welterweight Title Challenge)
23.09.05	Sammy Smith W RSC 3 Mayfair
	(Southern Area Welterweight Title Defence)
10.12.05	Brett James W RSC 4 Canning Town
	(Vacant English Welterweight Title. Southern Area Welterweight Title Defence)
08.07.06	Duncan Cottier W PTS 6 Cardiff
17.02.07	Sasha Shnip W RSC 2 Wembley
30.03.07	Freddy Curiel L RSC 8 Newcastle
02.02.08	Michael Jennings L RSC 9 Canning Town
	(WBU Welterweight Title Challenge)

Career: 21 contests, won 17, drew 1, lost 3.

(Delroy) Dee Mitchell

Birmingham. *Born* Birmingham, 16 November, 1976
L.Middleweight. *Ht* 5'9"
Manager R. Woodhall

08.09.06	Chris Brophy W RSC 2 Birmingham
26.10.06	Tony Randell W PTS 4 Wolverhampton
01.12.06	Billy Smith W PTS 4 Birmingham
23.02.07	Geraint Harvey W PTS 4 Birmingham
17.03.07	Matt Scriven W RSC 2 Birmingham
29.04.07	Tye Williams W PTS 8 Birmingham
13.07.07	Gatis Skuja L RSC 5 Birmingham
18.11.07	Peter Dunn W PTS 6 Birmingham
21.06.08	Martin Concepcion L PTS 4 Birmingham

Career: 9 contests, won 7, lost 2.

Kevin Mitchell   Les Clark

Kevin Mitchell

Dagenham. *Born* Dagenham, 29 October, 1984
British, Commonwealth, IBF & WBO Inter-Continental S.Featherweight Champion. *Ht* 5'8"
Manager F. Warren

17.07.03	Stevie Quinn W CO 1 Dagenham
18.09.03	Csabi Ladanyi W RSC 1 Dagenham
06.11.03	Vlado Varhegyi W RSC 3 Dagenham
24.01.04	Jaz Virdee W RSC 1 Wembley
07.02.04	Kristian Laight W PTS 4 Bethnal Green
24.04.04	Eric Patrac W RSC 1 Reading
13.05.04	Slimane Kebaili W RSC 1 Bethnal Green
05.06.04	Jason Nesbitt W RSC 3 Bethnal Green
10.09.04	Arpad Toth W RSC 3 Bethnal Green
22.10.04	Mounir Guebbas W PTS 6 Edinburgh
19.11.04	Alain Rakow W CO 1 Bethnal Green
11.12.04	Henry Janes W PTS 4 Canning Town
08.04.05	Frederic Bonifai W PTS 6 Edinburgh
29.04.05	Karim Chakim W PTS 8 Southwark
23.09.05	Wladimir Borov W RSC 2 Mayfair
25.10.05	Daniel Thorpe W RSC 4 Preston
10.12.05	Mohammed Medjadji W RSC 6 Canning Town
	(Vacant IBF Inter-Continental S.Featherweight Title)
25.02.06	Youssef Djibaba W PTS 12 Canning Town
	(IBF Inter-Continental S.Featherweight

Title Defence)

13.05.06 Kirkor Kirkorov W RTD 2 Bethnal
Green
*(IBF Inter-Continental S.Featherweight
Title Defence)*
08.07.06 Imad Ben Khalifa W RSC 2 Cardiff
08.09.06 Andrey Isaev W RSC 11 Mayfair
*(IBF Inter-Continental S.Featherweight
Title Defence)*
28.10.06 George Ashie W PTS 12 Bethnal Green
*(Vacant Commonwealth
S.Featherweight Title)*
10.03.07 Harry Ramogoadi W RSC 6 Liverpool
*(Commonwealth S.Featherweight Title
Defence)*
14.07.07 Alexander Hrulev W CO 2 Greenwich
*(Vacant WBO Inter-Continental
S.Featherweight Title. IBF Inter-
Continental S.Featherweight Title
Defence)*
12.01.08 Edison Torres W RSC 3 Bethnal Green
08.03.08 Carl Johanneson W RSC 9 Greenwich
*(British S.Featherweight Title
Challenge. Commonwealth
S.Featherweight Title Defence)*
07.06.08 Walter Estrada W RSC 5 Atlantic City,
New Jersey, USA
*(Vacant WBO Inter-Continental
S.Featherweight Title)*
Career: 27 contests, won 27.

Scott Mitchell

Bolton. *Born* Bolton, 3 February, 1979
Heavyweight. *Ht.* 6'3"
Manager Self
16.06.07 Zahir Kahut L PTS 6 Bolton
06.07.07 David Ingleby W PTS 4 Wigan
23.05.08 Paul Bonson W PTS 6 Wigan
Career: 3 contests, won 2, lost 1.

Vinny Mitchell   Les Clark

Vinny Mitchell

Dagenham. *Born* Dagenham, 1 May, 1987
Lightweight. Ht. 5'7¼"
Manager F. Warren
17.02.07 Shaun Walton W PTS 4 Wembley
14.07.07 Sergei Rozhakmens W RSC 3
Greenwich
12.01.08 Robin Deakin W PTS 4 Bethnal Green
08.03.08 John Baguley W PTS 4 Greenwich
14.06.08 Wladimir Borov W PTS 4 Bethnal
Green
Career: 5 contests, won 5.

Colin Moffett

Belfast. *Born* Belfast, 15 April, 1975
All-Ireland Bantamweight Champion.
Ht 5'6"
Manager O. McMahon
05.11.96 Shane Mallon W RSC 2 Belfast
28.01.97 Anthony Hanna W PTS 4 Belfast
29.04.97 Gary Hickman W PTS 4 Belfast
02.06.97 Jason Thomas L RSC 3 Belfast
20.12.97 Graham McGrath DREW 4 Belfast
18.09.98 Anthony Hanna DREW 4 Belfast
28.11.98 Shaun Norman W PTS 4 Belfast
31.07.99 Waj Khan W CO 1 Carlisle
16.10.99 Delroy Spencer L PTS 4 Bethnal Green
31.03.00 Steffen Norskov L PTS 4 Esbjerg,
Denmark
05.06.00 Keith Knox L RSC 3 Glasgow
02.12.00 Dale Robinson L PTS 4 Bethnal Green
15.09.01 Chris Emanuele L RSC 4 Nottingham
27.04.02 Levi Pattison L RSC 2 Huddersfield
27.07.02 Jim Betts L RSC 3 Nottingham
30.10.03 John Bothwell DREW 4 Belfast
08.05.04 Lee Haskins L RSC 2 Bristol
19.06.04 Michael Crossan DREW 4 Renfrew
28.10.04 Chris Edwards W PTS 4 Belfast
20.05.06 Delroy Spencer W PTS 4 Belfast
07.10.06 Matthew Edmonds L PTS 4 Belfast
14.07.07 Eugene Heagney L PTS 8 Ireland
15.12.07 Eugene Heagney W RSC 8 Dublin
*(Vacant All-Ireland Bantamweight
Title)*
02.05.08 Ian Napa L PTS 12 Nottingham
(British Bantamweight Title Challenge)
Career: 24 contests, won 8, drew 4, lost 12.

Michael Monaghan

Lincoln. *Born* Nottingham, 31 May, 1976
L.Heavyweight. Former Midlands Area
L.Heavyweight Champion. *Ht* 5'10¾"
Manager M. Scriven
23.09.96 Lee Simpkin W PTS 6 Cleethorpes
24.10.96 Lee Bird W RSC 6 Lincoln
09.12.96 Lee Simpkin W PTS 6 Chesterfield
16.12.96 Carlton Williams W PTS 6 Cleethorpes
20.03.97 Paul Miles W PTS 6 Newark
26.04.97 Paul Ryan L RSC 2 Swadlincote
05.07.97 Ali Khattab W PTS 4 Glasgow
18.08.97 Trevor Meikle W PTS 6 Nottingham
12.09.97 Willie Quinn L PTS 6 Glasgow
19.09.97 Roy Chipperfield W PTS 6 Salford
30.09.97 George Richards L PTS 6 Edgbaston
10.03.98 Anthony van Niekirk L RTD 6
Hammanskraal, South Africa
23.04.98 Darren Sweeney L PTS 10 Edgbaston
*(Midlands Area Middleweight Title
Challenge)*
19.09.98 Jim Rock L PTS 12 Dublin

*(Vacant WAA Inter-Continental
S. Middleweight Title)*
27.11.98 Mark Dawson W PTS 6 Nottingham
07.12.98 Mike Whittaker L PTS 6 Manchester
14.09.02 Paul Billington W RSC 4 Newark
30.11.02 Gary Beardsley W PTS 6 Newark
24.02.03 Jason Collins W PTS 8 Birmingham
16.04.03 Carl Froch L RSC 3 Nottingham
28.06.03 Gary Lockett L PTS 10 Cardiff
13.09.03 Tomas da Silva W PTS 6 Newport
25.04.04 Jason Collins W PTS 6 Nottingham
05.06.04 Wayne Elcock L PTS 4 Bethnal Green
03.09.04 Gary Lockett L RSC 3 Newport
29.10.04 Lawrence Murphy L PTS 6 Renfrew
20.02.05 Howard Clarke W PTS 6 Sheffield
18.03.05 Jim Rock L PTS 8 Belfast
27.03.05 Michal Bilak W PTS 6 Prague, Czech
Republic
30.04.05 John Humphrey L PTS 6 Dagenham
14.05.05 Matthew Macklin L CO 5 Dublin
(Vacant All-Ireland Middleweight Title)
16.02.06 Darren McDermott W RTD 9 Dudley
*(Midlands Area Middleweight Title
Challenge)*
06.10.06 Simeon Cover L PTS 6 Mansfield
11.11.06 Jason McKay L PTS 10 Dublin
*(Vacant All-Ireland L.Heavyweight
Title)*
30.11.06 Joey Vegas L PTS 10 Piccadilly
*(British Masters S.Middleweight Title
Challenge)*
03.03.07 Rod Anderton W PTS 10 Alfreton
*(Vacant Midlands Area L.Heavyweight
Title)*
19.05.07 Tyrone Wright L RSC 10 Nottingham
*(Midlands Area L.Heavyweight
Defence. Vacant British Masters
L.Heavyweight Title)*
06.10.07 Neil Tidman L PTS 6 Leicester
09.11.07 Paul David L PTS 10 Nottingham
*(Vacant Midlands Area S.Middleweight
Title)*
Career: 39 contests, won 17, lost 22.

Michael Monaghan   Les Clark

Jamie Moore

Salford. *Born* Salford, 4 November, 1978
Former Undefeated British L.Middleweight
Champion. Former Commonwealth
L.Middleweight Champion. *Ht* 5'8"
Manager Self

09.10.99	Clive Johnson W RSC 3 Manchester
13.11.99	Peter Nightingale W PTS 4 Hull
19.12.99	Paul King W PTS 6 Salford
29.02.00	David Baptiste W RSC 3 Manchester
20.03.00	Harry Butler W RSC 2 Mansfield
14.04.00	Jimmy Steel W PTS 6 Manchester
27.05.00	Koba Kulu W RTD 3 Southwark
07.10.00	Leigh Wicks W PTS 4 Doncaster
12.11.00	Prince Kasi Kaihau W RSC 2 Manchester
25.11.00	Wayne Shepherd W RSC 3 Manchester
17.03.01	Richie Murray W RSC 1 Manchester
27.05.01	Paul Denton W RSC 3 Manchester
07.07.01	Scott Dixon L CO 5 Manchester
	(Vacant WBO Inter-Continental L.Middleweight Title)
26.01.02	Harry Butler W RSC 3 Dagenham
09.03.02	Andrzej Butowicz W RSC 5 Manchester
07.09.02	Delroy Mellis W CO 6 Liverpool
08.02.03	Akhmed Oligov W PTS 6 Liverpool
19.04.03	Michael Jones W PTS 12 Liverpool
	(Vacant British L. Middleweight Title. Commonwealth L. Middleweight Title Challenge)
18.10.03	Gary Logan W CO 5 Manchester
	(British & Commonwealth L.Middleweight Title Defences)
22.11.03	Andrew Facey W RSC 7 Belfast
	(British & Commonwealth L.Middleweight Title Defences)
10.04.04	Adam Katumwa W RSC 5 Manchester
	(Vacant Commonwealth L.Middleweight Title)
26.06.04	Ossie Duran L RSC 3 Belfast
	(Commonwealth L.Middleweight Title Defence)
26.11.04	Michael Jones L DIS 3 Altrincham
	(British L.Middleweight Title Defence)
08.07.05	Michael Jones W RSC 6 Altrincham
	(British L.Middleweight Title Challenge)
23.09.05	David Walker W RSC 4 Manchester
	(British L.Middleweight Title Defence)
27.01.06	Vladimir Borovski W RSC 3 Dagenham
21.07.06	Mike Algoet W RSC 5 Altrincham
29.09.06	Matthew Macklin W RSC 10 Manchester
	(British L.Middleweight Title Defence)
09.03.07	Mugurel Sebe W PTS 8 Dagenham
13.04.07	Sebastian Andres Lujan W PTS 12 Altrincham
26.10.07	Andrew Facey W RSC 11 Wigan
	(British L.Middleweight Title Defence)
24.05.08	Esau Herrera W RSC 5 Manchester

Career: 32 contests, won 29, lost 3.

Mark Moran

Liverpool. *Born* Liverpool, 16 February,
1982 English S.Bantamweight Champion.
Ht 5'5"
Manager S. Wood

02.10.03	Steve Gethin W PTS 4 Liverpool
13.12.03	Delroy Spencer W PTS 4 Manchester
26.02.04	Darren Cleary W PTS 4 Widnes
03.04.04	Neil Read W RSC 2 Manchester
22.05.04	Darren Cleary DREW 4 Widnes
17.12.04	Steve Gethin W PTS 4 Liverpool
22.09.07	John Baguley W PTS 4 Wigan
26.10.07	Gavin Reid W PTS 4 Wigan
08.12.07	Iordan Vasilev W CO 3 Wigan
16.03.08	Abdul Mougharbel W PTS 4 Liverpool
24.05.08	Danny Wallace W RSC 9 Manchester
	(Vacant English S.Bantamweight Title)

Career: 11 contests, won 10, drew 1.

Paul Morby

Portsmouth. Born Portsmouth, 15 October,
1979
Middleweight. *Ht* 5'11"
Manager J. Bishop

24.09.06	Jamie Ambler W PTS 4 Southampton
25.02.07	Dave Wakefield W PTS 6 Southampton
10.06.07	Philip Dowse L RSC 4 Neath
16.09.07	John-Paul Temple W PTS 4 Southampton
10.11.07	JJ Bird W PTS 6 Portsmouth
02.03.08	John-Paul Temple W PTS 4 Portsmouth
13.06.08	Chas Symonds L PTS 6 Portsmouth

Career: 7 contests, won 5, lost 2.

Darren Morgan   Philip Sharkey

Darren Morgan

Swansea. *Born* Swansea, 26 October, 1976
Heavyweight. *Ht* 6'1¼"
Manager Self

21.01.05	Ebrima Secka W RSC 1 Bridgend
04.06.05	Dave Clarke W RSC 1 Manchester
10.09.05	Tony Booth W PTS 4 Cardiff
25.02.06	Radcliffe Green W RSC 3 Canning Town
11.03.06	Istvan Kecskes W PTS 4 Newport
20.05.06	Martin Rogan L PTS 4 Belfast
13.10.07	Derek Chisora L PTS 4 Bethnal Green
12.01.08	Sam Sexton L PTS 6 Bethnal Green
11.04.08	David Dolan L PTS 3 Bethnal Green

Career: 9 contests, won 5, lost 4.

Andy Morris

Wythenshawe. *Born* Manchester, 10 March,
1983
Featherweight. Former British
Featherweight Champion. Former
Undefeated English Featherweight
Champion. *Ht* 5'6½"
Manager F. Warren

18.01.03	Jason Nesbitt W PTS 4 Preston
05.04.03	Haroon Din W RSC 1 Manchester
08.05.03	Daniel Thorpe W PTS 4 Widnes
06.11.03	Dave Hinds W PTS 4 Dagenham
13.12.03	Henry Janes W PTS 4 Manchester
26.02.04	Daniel Thorpe W RSC 3 Widnes
03.04.04	Carl Allen W PTS 4 Manchester
12.06.04	Jus Wallie W PTS 6 Manchester
01.10.04	Chris Hooper W RSC 3 Manchester
11.02.05	Buster Dennis W PTS 6 Manchester
20.05.05	Rocky Dean W PTS 10 Southwark
	(Vacant English Featherweight Title)
23.09.05	Mickey Coveney W RSC 4 Mayfair
05.11.05	John Simpson W PTS 12 Renfrew
	(Vacant British Featherweight Title)
29.04.06	Rendall Munroe W PTS 12 Edinburgh
	(British Featherweight Title Defence)
09.12.06	John Simpson L RSC 5 Canning Town
	(British Featherweight Title Defence)
21.07.07	Daniel Thorpe W RSC 2 Cardiff
07.09.07	John Simpson L RSC 7 Mayfair
	(British Featherweight Title Challenge)

Career: 17 contests, won 15, lost 2.

Jack Morris

Margate. *Born* Greenwich, 15 August, 1982
L.Heavyweight. *Ht* 5'11½"
Manager S. Fearon

09.10.07	Michael Banbula L PTS 6 Tower Hamlets
28.03.08	Ricky Strike W PTS 4 Piccadilly

Career: 2 contests, won 1, lost 1.

Jay Morris   Philip Sharkey

Jay Morris

Newport, IoW. *Born* Newport, IoW, 8 May,
1978
Welterweight. *Ht* 5'7"
Manager J. Feld

21.02.04	Judex Meemea DREW 4 Brighton
30.03.04	Casey Brooke W RSC 1 Southampton
21.11.04	Chris Brophy W RSC 1 Bracknell
12.02.05	Pete Buckley W PTS 6 Portsmouth
26.06.05	David Kehoe W RSC 1 Southampton
25.09.05	Ivor Bonavic L PTS 6 Southampton
04.12.05	Ivor Bonavic W PTS 6 Portsmouth
05.03.06	Duncan Cottier L RSC 2 Southampton
24.09.06	Duncan Cottier W PTS 4 Southampton
02.12.06	Alex Stoda L RSC 4 Southwark

03.05.07	David Barnes L RSC 1 Sheffield
05.06.07	Andrew Ferrans L RSC 3 Glasgow
07.09.07	Barrie Jones L RTD 4 Mayfair
01.12.07	Danny Goode W PTS 4 Bethnal Green
09.12.07	Paddy Pollock W PTS 6 Glasgow
23.02.08	Terry Adams W RSC 2 Crawley
14.03.08	Craig Docherty L PTS 6 Glasgow
13.06.08	Jason Rushton L PTS 6 Portsmouth
27.06.08	John O'Donnell L RSC 6 Bethnal Green

Career: 19 contests, won 9, drew 1, lost 9.

Ally Morrison

Penrith. *Born* Penrith, 26 October, 1977
S.Middleweight. *Ht* 5' 11¼"
Manager S. Wood

26.04.08	Dave Pearson W PTS 6 Wigan

Career: 1 contest, won 1.

Barry Morrison

Motherwell. *Born* Bellshill, 8 May, 1980
L.Welterweight. Former British
L.Welterweight Champion. Former
Undefeated British Masters L.Welterweight
Champion. *Ht* 5'7"
Manager T. Gilmour

12.04.03	Keith Jones W PTS 4 Bethnal Green
28.04.03	Arv Mittoo W RSC 3 Nottingham
05.07.03	Cristian Hodorogea W RSC 3 Brentwood
06.09.03	Jay Mahoney W RSC 2 Huddersfield
04.10.03	Sergei Starkov W PTS 6 Belfast
01.11.03	Tarik Amrous W PTS 8 Glasgow
28.02.04	Zoltan Surman W RSC 3 Bridgend
22.04.04	Andrei Devyataykin W PTS 8 Glasgow
15.10.04	Adam Zadworny W RSC 2 Glasgow
27.05.05	Gary Reid W RTD 8 Motherwell *(British Masters L.Welterweight Title Challenge)*
14.10.05	Tony Montana W PTS 10 Motherwell *(British Masters L.Welterweight Title Defence)*
17.03.06	Dean Hickman W RSC 1 Kirkcaldy *(Elim. British L.Welterweight Title)*
21.04.06	Mihaita Mutu L PTS 8 Belfast
22.09.06	Mounir Guebbas W PTS 6 Bethnal Green
20.01.07	Lenny Daws W PTS 12 Muswell Hill *(British L.Welterweight Title Challenge)*
08.06.07	Colin Lynes L PTS 12 Motherwell *(British L.Welterweight Title Defence)*
19.10.07	Arek Malek W PTS 6 Motherwell
29.02.08	Billy Smith W PTS 6 Glasgow

Career: 18 contests, won 16, lost 2.

(Moses) Olufemi Moses (Ajayi)

Droylsden. *Born* Nigeria, 28 May, 1985
Welterweight. *Ht* 5'10"
Manager W. Barker

23.02.07	Silence Saheed W PTS 4 Manchester
02.03.07	Ysopov Karium W PTS 4 Coventry
26.04.07	Duncan Cottier W PTS 4 Manchester
22.09.07	Prince Arron L PTS 6 Coventry
13.10.07	Ryan Rhodes L RSC 2 Barnsley

Career: 5 contests, won 3, lost 2.

Abdul Mougharbel (Almgharbel)

Dewsbury. *Born* Syria, 10 November, 1975
S.Bantamweight. *Ht* 5'4"
Manager Self

15.03.04	Hussain Nasser W RTD 3 Bradford
19.04.04	Sandy Bartlett W PTS 6 Glasgow
11.10.04	Sandy Bartlett L PTS 6 Glasgow
22.10.04	Scott Flynn L PTS 4 Edinburgh
19.11.04	Isaac Ward L PTS 4 Hartlepool
11.12.04	Matthew Marsh L PTS 4 Canning Town
06.03.05	Andy Bell L PTS 4 Mansfield
18.04.05	Neil Read W PTS 6 Bradford
27.05.05	Kevin Townsley L PTS 6 Motherwell
06.06.05	Gary Ford W PTS 6 Glasgow
16.09.05	Shaun Walton DREW 6 Telford
28.10.05	Isaac Ward L PTS 6 Hartlepool
20.11.05	Shinny Bayaar L PTS 4 Shaw
04.12.05	Shaun Walton DREW 6 Telford
24.02.06	Wayne Bloy L PTS 6 Scarborough
29.09.06	Stuart McFadyen L PTS 4 Manchester
03.11.06	Jason Booth L PTS 6 Barnsley
26.01.07	Stephen Russell L PTS 6 Glasgow
24.02.07	Gary Davis L PTS 6 Stoke
15.02.08	Ross Burkinshaw W RSC 2 Sheffield
16.03.08	Mark Moran L PTS 4 Liverpool
30.03.08	Stuart McFadyen L PTS 6 Colne
26.04.08	Stuart Hall L PTS 6 Darlington

Career: 23 contests, won 5, drew 2, lost 16.

Lee Mountford   Philip Sharkey

Lee Mountford

Pudsey. *Born* Leeds, 1 September, 1972
Heavyweight. *Ht* 6'2"
Manager Self

19.04.02	Gary Thompson DREW 4 Darlington
24.06.02	Eamonn Glennon L PTS 6 Bradford
20.11.02	Nate Joseph W PTS 6 Leeds
03.02.03	Eamonn Glennon DREW 6 Bradford
28.02.03	Gary Thompson W PTS 6 Irvine
13.05.03	Nate Joseph L PTS 6 Leeds
01.12.03	Dave Clarke W PTS 6 Bradford
15.03.04	Greg Scott-Briggs DREW 6 Bradford
09.04.04	Carl Wright L PTS 4 Rugby
20.04.04	Lee Swaby L RSC 1 Sheffield
26.09.04	Paul Butlin L PTS 6 Stoke
28.10.04	Martin Rogan L RSC 1 Belfast
13.02.05	Nate Joseph L PTS 6 Bradford
13.05.05	Tony Moran L RSC 1 Liverpool
18.06.05	John Anthony L RSC 5 Barnsley
25.09.05	Dave Clarke W PTS 4 Leeds
22.10.05	Tyrone Wright L CO 3 Mansfield
03.03.06	Stewart Mitchell L PTS 4 Doncaster

26.05.06	Tony Booth L PTS 6 Hull
15.10.06	Sam Sexton L RSC 2 Norwich
25.09.07	Dean O'Loughlin L PTS 6 Hull
19.10.07	Billy Boyle L PTS 6 Doncaster
17.11.07	Alex Ibbs L PTS 6 Stoke
29.11.07	Zahir Kahut L PTS 6 Bradford
06.12.07	Dave Ferguson L PTS 6 Sunderland
25.01.08	Tom Owens L PTS 6 Birmingham
15.02.08	Danny Hughes L PTS 6 Sunderland
28.02.08	Neil Perkins L PTS 4 Wolverhampton
29.03.08	Dave McKenna L PTS 6 Glasgow

Career: 29 contests, won 4, drew 3, lost 22.

Bheki Moyo   Les Clark

Bheki Moyo

Earls Court. *Born* Pretoria, South Africa, 6
October, 1974
L.Welterweight. *Ht* 5'7"
Manager J. Gill

24.07.05	Judex Meemea L PTS 4 Leicester Square
28.10.05	Damian Owen L PTS 6 Hartlepool
17.11.05	Garry Buckland L RSC 3 Bristol
21.05.06	Ali Wyatt L RSC 3 Bristol
29.06.06	Nathan Weise L PTS 4 Bethnal Green
26.10.06	Martin Gordon DREW 6 Dudley
17.11.06	Ruben Giles L RSC 4 Bethnal Green
24.04.08	Graham Fearn L PTS 6 Piccadilly
02.05.08	Steve Jevons L PTS 4 Nottingham
20.06.08	Jimmy Briggs L PTS 6 Plymouth

Career: 10 contests, drew 1, lost 9.

Chris Mullen

South Shields. *Born* South Shields, 24 May,
1986
Welterweight. *Ht* 5'9"
Manager M. Gates

07.12.06	Chris Goodwin W PTS 6 Sunderland
13.04.07	Martin Sweeney W RSC 6 Houghton le Spring
23.11.07	Scott Sandmann W PTS 6 Houghton le Spring
20.03.08	Scott Miller L PTS 6 South Shields

Career: 4 contests, won 3, lost 1.

Rendall Munroe

Leicester. *Born* Leicester, 1 June, 1980
European S.Bantamweight Champion.
Former Undefeated English
S.Bantamweight Champion. *Ht* 5'7"
Manager M. Shinfield

20.09.03	Joel Viney W RTD 3 Nottingham
23.11.03	John-Paul Ryan W PTS 6 Rotherham
14.02.04	Neil Read W RSC 1 Nottingham
09.04.04	Anthony Hanna W PTS 6 Rugby
26.04.04	Baz Carey W PTS 6 Cleethorpes
27.09.04	David Bailey W PTS 6 Cleethorpes
08.10.04	David Killu W PTS 6 Brentwood
18.06.05	Darren Broomhall W RSC 3 Barnsley
02.09.05	Riaz Durgahed W PTS 6 Derby
28.01.06	Jonathan Whiteman W RSC 2 Nottingham
29.04.06	Andy Morris L PTS 12 Edinburgh *(British Featherweight Title Challenge)*
13.04.07	Gavin Deacon W PTS 6 Altrincham
13.07.07	Dai Davies W RSC 5 Barnsley
12.10.07	Marc Callaghan W RTD 6 Peterlee *(English S.Bantamweight Title Challenge)*
07.03.08	Kiko Martinez W PTS 12 Nottingham *(European S.Bantamweight Title Challenge)*
02.05.08	Salem Bouaita W RTD 7 Nottingham *(European S.Bantamweight Title Defence)*

Career: 16 contests, won 15, lost 1.

Ben Murphy   Philip Sharkey

Ben Murphy

Hove. *Born* Hove, 11 March, 1980
L.Welterweight. *Ht* 5'3¾"
Manager B. Lawrence

17.03.07	Deniss Sirjatovs W PTS 4 Birmingham
29.04.07	Barry Downes W RSC 1 Birmingham
13.07.07	Neal McQuade W RSC 2 Birmingham
21.09.07	Lewis Smith W RSC 4 Peterborough
01.12.07	Michael Frontin L PTS 4 Bethnal Green
13.06.08	Garry Buckland W PTS 6 Portsmouth

Career: 6 contests, won 5, lost 1.

Brian Murphy

Cambuslang. *Born* Rutherglen, 16 August, 1987
Lightweight. *Ht* 5'8½"
Manager T. Gilmour

25.03.06	Pete Buckley W PTS 6 Irvine
29.06.06	Ian Wilson L RTD 1 Bethnal Green
29.09.06	Jimmy Gilhaney L RSC 1 Motherwell
20.11.06	Sergei Rozhakmens W PTS 6 Glasgow
02.12.06	Sandy Bartlett L RSC 5 Clydebank
23.04.07	Shaun Walton L RSC 5 Glasgow
18.02.08	Graham Fearn L RSC 6 Glasgow

Career: 7 contests, won 2, lost 5.

Andrew Murray   Les Clark

Andrew Murray

St Albans. *Born* Cavan, 10 September, 1982
All-Ireland L.Welterweight Champion.
Ht 5'10¼"
Manager Self

18.03.05	Jonathan Jones W RSC 4 Belfast
09.10.05	Billy Smith W PTS 4 Hammersmith
17.11.05	Silence Saheed W PTS 4 Piccadilly
02.02.06	Ian Reid W RSC 4 Holborn
30.03.06	Frederic Gosset W PTS 6 Piccadilly
21.05.06	Carl Allen W PTS 4 Bethnal Green
03.06.06	Tony Jourda W RSC 3 Dublin
04.10.07	Billy Smith W PTS 8 Piccadilly
08.12.07	James Gorman W TD 4 Belfast *(Vacant All-Ireland L.Welterweight Title)*
22.03.08	Leonard Lothian W RSC 3 Dublin
29.03.08	Juris Ivanovs W RSC 3 Letterkenny
12.04.08	Wellington De Jesus W CO 1 Castlebar

Career: 12 contests, won 12.

Dave Murray

Manchester. *Born* Manchester, 19 January, 1974
L.Middleweight. *Ht* 5'10¼"
Manager J. Pennington

07.10.07	David Kehoe W PTS 6 Shaw
10.11.07	Lance Verallo W PTS 6 Stalybridge
30.11.07	Jamie Radford L RSC 1 Newham
16.02.08	Chris Johnson L RSC 4 Blackpool
20.04.08	Peter Dunn W PTS 6 Shaw
17.05.08	Curtis Woodhouse L RSC 2 Sheffield

Career: 6 contests, won 3, lost 3.

John Murray

Manchester. *Born* Manchester, 20 December, 1984
Former Undefeated English & WBC Youth
Lightweight Champion. *Ht* 5'8"
Manager Self

06.09.03	Pete Buckley W PTS 4 Huddersfield
18.10.03	Matthew Burke W RSC 1 Manchester
21.12.03	Jason Nesbitt W PTS 6 Bolton
30.01.04	Norman Dhalie W CO 2 Dagenham
12.03.04	John-Paul Ryan W RSC 1 Nottingham
02.06.04	Anthony Hanna W PTS 4 Nottingham
24.09.04	Dariusz Snarski W RSC 2 Nottingham
31.10.04	Ernie Smith W PTS 4 Shaw
26.11.04	Daniel Thorpe W RSC 2 Altrincham
09.12.04	Harry Ramogoadi W RSC 4 Stockport
06.03.05	Karl Taylor W PTS 6 Shaw
08.07.05	Mounir Guebbas W PTS 8 Altrincham
06.08.05	Johnny Walker W PTS 6 Tampa, Florida, USA
23.09.05	Azad Azizov W RSC 3 Manchester
29.10.05	Tyrone Wiggins W RSC 4 Gatineau, Canada
02.12.05	Nacho Mendoza W TD 8 Nottingham *(Vacant WBC Youth Lightweight Title)*
12.07.06	Billy Smith W RSC 6 Bethnal Green
15.09.06	Moebi Sarouna W PTS 10 Muswell Hill *(WBC Youth Lightweight Title Defence)*
08.12.06	Billy Smith W PTS 6 Dagenham
20.01.07	Ben Odamattey W RSC 5 Muswell Hill
05.05.07	Lorenzo Bethea W RSC 7 Las Vegas, Nevada, USA
09.11.07	Dean Hickman W RSC 4 Nottingham *(Vacant English Lightweight Title)*
07.12.07	Miguel Angel Munguia W PTS 10 Las Vegas, Nevada, USA
10.05.08	Youssef Al Hamidi W PTS 8 Nottingham

Career: 24 contests, won 24.

Martin Murray   Philip Sharkey

Martin Murray

Manchester. *Born* Knowsley, 27 September, 1982
S.Middleweight. *Ht* 6'0¼"
Manager S. Wood

22.09.07	Jamie Ambler W PTS 6 Wigan
26.10.07	Phillip Callaghan W RSC 1 Wigan
16.02.08	Dean Walker W PTS 6 Blackpool
16.03.08	Michael Banbula W PTS 6 Liverpool

18.04.08 James Tucker W PTS 4 Bethnal Green
23.05.08 Dean Walker W PTS 6 Wigan
15.06.08 Michael Recloux W PTS 6 St Helens
Career: 7 contests, won 7.

Lee Murtagh

Leeds. *Born* Leeds, 30 September, 1973
Middleweight. Former Undefeated Central
Area L.Middleweight Champion. Former
Undefeated Central Area Middleweight
Champion. Former British Masters
Middleweight Champion. Former British
Masters L.Middleweight Champion.
Ht 5'9¼"
Manager Self

12.06.95 Dave Curtis W PTS 6 Bradford
25.09.95 Roy Gbasai W PTS 6 Bradford
30.10.95 Cam Raeside L PTS 6 Bradford
11.12.95 Donovan Davey W PTS 6 Bradford
13.01.96 Peter Varnavas W PTS 6 Halifax
05.02.96 Shamus Casey W PTS 6 Bradford
20.05.96 Shaun O'Neill W PTS 6 Bradford
24.06.96 Michael Alexander W PTS 6 Bradford
28.10.96 Jimmy Vincent L RSC 2 Bradford
14.04.97 Lee Simpkin W PTS 6 Bradford
09.10.97 Brian Dunn W PTS 6 Leeds
05.03.98 Wayne Shepherd W PTS 6 Leeds
08.08.98 Alan Gilbert W PTS 4 Scarborough
13.03.99 Keith Palmer DREW 6 Manchester
27.09.99 Jawaid Khaliq L RSC 5 Leeds
　　　*(Vacant WBF European
　　　L. Middleweight Title)*
27.02.00 Gareth Lovell W PTS 6 Leeds
24.09.00 Jon Foster W PTS 6 Shaw
03.12.00 Michael Alexander W PTS 6 Shaw
17.05.01 Ojay Abrahams L RSC 2 Leeds
　　　*(Vacant British Masters
　　　L. Middleweight Title)*
03.03.02 Howard Clarke NC 2 Shaw
19.04.02 Neil Bonner W PTS 6 Darlington
21.06.02 Wayne Shepherd W PTS 10 Leeds
　　　*(Vacant British Masters Middleweight
　　　Title)*
02.12.02 Martyn Bailey L RSC 6 Leeds
　　　*(British Masters Middleweight Title
　　　Defence)*
10.05.03 Darren Rhodes L PTS 6 Huddersfield
15.09.03 Matt Scriven W DIS 9 Leeds
　　　*(British Masters L.Middleweight Title
　　　Challenge)*
01.12.03 Gary Beardsley L RSC 6 Leeds
　　　*(British Masters L.Middleweight Title
　　　Defence)*
08.06.04 Robert Burton L CO 3 Sheffield
　　　*(Vacant Central Area L.Middleweight
　　　Title)*
15.12.04 Dean Walker W PTS 10 Sheffield
　　　*(Vacant Central Area Middleweight
　　　Title)*
20.05.05 Jason Rushton W PTS 10 Doncaster
　　　*(Central Area L.Middleweight Title
　　　Challenge)*
27.01.06 Gary Woolcombe L RSC 4 Dagenham
03.06.07 John Musgrave W PTS 6 Barnsley
30.06.07 Peter Dunn W PTS 6 Belfast
11.08.07 Graham Delehedy W PTS 6 Liverpool
13.10.07 Tye Williams W PTS 6 Belfast
08.12.07 Ciaran Healy L CO 5 Belfast
　　　*(Vacant All-Ireland L.Middleweight
　　　Title)*
Career: 35 contests, won 23, drew 1, lost 10, no
　　　contest 1.

(Nikos) Rocky Muscus (Agrapidis Israel)

Chertsey. *Born* Athens, Greece, 5 August,
1983
S.Middleweight. *Ht* 5'6½"
Manager Self

12.05.03 Danny Cooper L PTS 6 Southampton
18.09.03 Wayne Wheeler L PTS 6 Mayfair
27.10.03 Graham Delehedy L RSC 2 Glasgow
08.07.04 David Kehoe L PTS 6 The Strand
30.09.04 Richard Inquieti W PTS 4 Glasgow
23.10.04 Tye Williams L PTS 6 Wakefield
24.11.04 Ivor Bonavic L PTS 4 Mayfair
18.09.05 Danny Goode L PTS 4 Bethnal Green
25.09.05 Steve Ede L PTS 6 Southampton
23.07.06 Dean Marcantonio L PTS 4 Dagenham
09.10.06 Jay Allen L PTS 6 Bedworth
18.10.06 Anthony Young L PTS 4 Bayswater
11.11.06 Billy Walsh L PTS 4 Dublin
23.11.06 Prince Arron L PTS 6 Manchester
02.12.06 Kevin Concepcion L PTS 6 Coventry
09.12.06 Tom Glover L PTS 4 Chigwell
26.01.07 Eamonn Goodbrand L PTS 6 Glasgow
10.02.07 Ciaran Duffy L PTS 4 Letterkenny
24.02.07 Nobby Cain L PTS 4 Bracknell
10.03.07 Joe McNally L PTS 4 Liverpool
14.04.07 Andrew Butlin L PTS 6 Wakefield
23.04.07 Jamie Coyle L PTS 8 Glasgow
05.05.07 Barrie Jones L PTS 6 Glasgow
14.05.07 Simon Fleck L PTS 6 Cleethorpes
25.05.07 Colin Baxter L PTS 6 Glasgow
01.06.07 Sherman Alleyne L PTS 6
　　　Peterborough
13.10.07 Grant Skehill L PTS 4 Bethnal Green
15.11.07 Danny Reynolds L PTS 6 Leeds
25.11.07 Drew Campbell L PTS 6 Colchester
01.12.07 Ashley Theophane L RSC 1 Bethnal
　　　Green
21.02.08 Danny Reynolds L RSC 2 Leeds
Career: 31 contests, won 1, lost 30.

Rocky Muscus 　　　　　Philip Sharkey

Jon Musgrave

Barnsley. *Born* Barnsley, 26 July, 1982
L.Middleweight. *Ht* 5'11"
Manager Self

30.09.06 Andrew Alan Lowe W PTS 6 Stoke
01.12.06 James McKinley L PTS 4 Birmingham
26.03.07 Paul Royston W PTS 6 Glasgow
15.04.07 Sherman Alleyne W PTS 6 Barnsley
03.06.07 Lee Murtagh L PTS 6 Barnsley
16.09.07 Lee Edwards L PTS 6 Sheffield
13.10.07 Steve Cooper W PTS 6 Barnsley
23.02.08 Andrew Alan Lowe L PTS 6 Newark
20.03.08 Shaun Farmer L PTS 6 South Shields
15.05.08 Shaun Farmer W PTS 5 Sunderland
Career: 10 contests, won 5, lost 5.

(Lee) Young Muttley (Woodley)

West Bromwich. *Born* West Bromwich, 17
May, 1976
L.Welterweight. Former British
Welterweight Champion. Former
Undefeated WBF Inter-Continental,
English & Midlands Area L.Welterweight
Champion. *Ht* 5'8½"
Manager Self

03.09.99 Dave Hinds W RSC 4 West Bromwich
24.10.99 David Kehoe W RTD 1 Wolverhampton
22.01.00 Wahid Fats L PTS 4 Birmingham
18.02.00 Stuart Rimmer W RSC 1 West
　　　Bromwich
27.11.00 Peter Dunn W RSC 3 Birmingham
07.09.01 Jon Honney W RSC 1 West Bromwich
16.11.01 Tony Montana W PTS 6 West
　　　Bromwich
26.11.01 Lee Byrne W RSC 1 Manchester
23.02.02 Brian Coleman W PTS 4 Nottingham
23.03.02 Adam Zadworny W RSC 3 Southwark
02.11.02 Tony Montana W PTS 4
　　　Wolverhampton
21.03.03 Gary Reid W RSC 7 West Bromwich
　　　*(Vacant Midlands Area L.Welterweight
　　　Title)*
28.04.03 John Marshall W RSC 5 Nottingham
17.07.03 Tony Montana W PTS 4 Walsall
19.02.04 Peter Dunn W PTS 4 Dudley
08.05.04 Sammy Smith W RSC 1 Bristol
　　　(Vacant English L.Welterweight Title)
05.10.04 Gavin Down W RSC 6 Dudley
　　　*(English L.Welterweight Title Defence.
　　　Vacant WBF Inter-Continental
　　　L.Welterweight Title)*
17.02.05 Geraint Harvey W PTS 6 Dudley
21.04.05 Oscar Hall W PTS 10 Dudley
　　　*(WBF Inter-Continental L.Welterweight
　　　Title Defence)*
30.09.05 Surinder Sekhon W PTS 4 Burton
28.01.06 Michael Jennings W PTS 12 Nottingham
　　　(British Welterweight Title Challenge)
01.06.06 Kevin Anderson L RSC 10 Birmingham
　　　*(British Welterweight Title Defence.
　　　Commonwealth Welterweight Title
　　　Challenge)*
22.09.06 Alexander Abramenko W CO 1 Bethnal
　　　Green
25.01.07 Arek Malek W PTS 6 Milan, Italy
20.07.07 Colin Lynes L RSC 8 Wolverhampton
　　　*(Vacant European L.Welterweight
　　　Title. British L.Welterweight Title
　　　Challenge)*
28.11.07 Vladimir Borovski W PTS 6 Walsall
14.03.08 Kevin Placide W RSC 4 Manchester
Career: 27 contests, won 24, lost 3.

Amir Nadi

Birmingham. *Born* Iraq, 21 November, 1981
L.Welterweight. *Ht* 5'10"
Manager M. Helliet

16.02.07	Steve Anning L PTS 4 Merthyr Tydfil	
02.03.07	Abul Taher L PTS 6 Coventry	
28.04.07	Charles Paul King L PTS 6 Clydebank	
14.05.07	Andy Cox L PTS 6 Cleethorpes	
16.09.07	Jack Perry L PTS 4 Derby	
25.10.07	Scott Evans L PTS 4 Wolverhampton	
10.11.07	Darren Askew L PTS 6 Stalybridge	
20.04.08	Ali Shah L PTS 4 Shaw	
30.04.08	Scott Evans L RSC 3 Wolverhampton	
21.06.08	Adam Kelly L PTS 6 Sheffield	

Career: 10 contests, lost 10.

Ian Napa

Hackney. *Born* Zimbabwe, 14 March, 1978
British Bantamweight Champion. Former
Undefeated Southern Area Flyweight
Champion. *Ht* 5'1"
Manager B. Lawrence

06.06.98	Nick Tooley W PTS 6 Liverpool
14.07.98	Nicky Booth W PTS 6 Reading
10.10.98	Sean Green W PTS 6 Bethnal Green
30.01.99	Delroy Spencer W PTS 6 Bethnal Green
15.11.99	Mark Reynolds W PTS 10 Bethnal Green *(Southern Area Flyweight Title Challenge)*
19.02.00	Anthony Hanna W PTS 6 Dagenham
08.04.00	Delroy Spencer W PTS 8 Bethnal Green
15.07.00	Jamie Evans W PTS 4 Millwall
13.11.00	Jason Booth L PTS 12 Bethnal Green *(British & Commonwealth Flyweight Title Challenges)*
24.02.01	Oleg Kiryukhin W PTS 6 Bethnal Green
09.06.01	Peter Culshaw L RSC 8 Bethnal Green *(WBU Flyweight Title Challenge)*
08.05.04	Danny Costello W PTS 4 Dagenham
08.10.04	Steve Gethin W PTS 6 Brentwood
13.02.05	Alexey Volchan W PTS 4 Brentwood
16.06.05	Marc Callaghan W PTS 10 Dagenham *(Vacant Southern Area S.Bantamweight Title)*
04.11.05	Martin Power L PTS 12 Bethnal Green *(British Bantamweight Title Challenge)*
25.11.05	Damaen Kelly L PTS 10 Liverpool
06.10.06	Delroy Spencer W PTS 6 Bethnal Green
09.03.07	Simone Maludrottu L PTS 12 Dagenham *(European Bantamweight Title Challenge)*
06.07.07	Jason Booth W PTS 12 Wigan *(Vacant British Bantamweight Title)*
21.09.07	Lee Haskins W RTD 7 Bethnal Green *(British Bantamweight Title Defence)*

Ian Napa

Les Clark

30.11.07 Martin Power W PTS 12 Newham
        (*British Bantamweight Title Defence*)
02.05.08 Colin Moffett W PTS 12 Nottingham
        (*British Bantamweight Title Defence*)
Career: 23 contests, won 17, lost 6.

Muhsen Nasser   Les Clark

Muhsen Nasser

Sheffield. *Born* Yemen, 10 April, 1986
L.Middleweight. *Ht* 5'11"
Manager J. Ingle

11.10.04 Andy Cosnett W PTS 6 Birmingham
26.11.04 Rocky Flanagan W PTS 6 Hull
27.01.05 Ernie Smith W PTS 6 Piccadilly
12.05.05 Martin Marshall W PTS 6 Sunderland
30.10.05 Lance Verallo W PTS 6 Sheffield
12.11.05 Dave Hinds W PTS 6 Sheffield
21.11.05 Peter Dunn W RSC 4 Glasgow
25.02.06 Chris Long W PTS 4 Bristol
05.03.06 Peter Dunn W PTS 4 Sheffield
06.10.06 Thomas Flynn W PTS 4 Mexborough
10.12.06 Karl Taylor W PTS 6 Sheffield
27.07.07 Peter Dunn W PTS 6 Houghton le
        Spring
06.10.07 James Barker W RSC 1 Aberdeen
14.11.07 Billy Smith DREW 4 Bethnal Green
29.11.07 Ryan Ashworth W PTS 4 Bradford
18.01.08 Tye Williams W PTS 4 Burton
20.04.08 Jimmy Beech W PTS 6 Shaw
17.05.08 Paul Royston W PTS 4 Sheffield
Career: 18 contests, won 17, drew 1.

Robert Nelson

Bradford. *Born* Bradford, 15 January, 1980
S.Bantamweight. *Ht* 5'5"
Manager Self

27.05.05 Delroy Spencer W PTS 4 Spennymoor
25.06.05 Delroy Spencer W PTS 6 Wakefield
13.11.05 Neil Marston W PTS 6 Leeds
09.05.06 Delroy Spencer DREW 6 Leeds
28.05.06 Neil Read W PTS 6 Wakefield
03.12.06 Robert Bunford W PTS 4 Wakefield
14.04.07 Shaun Walton W PTS 8 Wakefield
27.05.07 Mo Khaled DREW 6 Bradford
07.09.07 Andy Bell L RSC 7 Doncaster
        (*Vacant English S.Flyweight Title*)
Career: 9 contests, won 6, drew 2, lost 1.

Jason Nesbitt

Nuneaton. *Born* Birmingham, 15
December, 1973
Welterweight. *Ht* 5'9"
Manager Self

06.11.00 Stephen Chinnock L PTS 6
        Wolverhampton
09.12.00 Lee Meager L RSC 2 Southwark
29.01.01 Henry Castle L CO 6 Peterborough
27.03.01 Billy Smith W PTS 6 Brierley Hill
21.05.01 Sid Razak L PTS 6 Birmingham
04.06.01 Andrew Ferrans L RSC 2 Glasgow
07.07.01 Colin Toohey L PTS 4 Manchester
15.09.01 Colin Toohey L PTS 4 Manchester
22.09.01 John Mackay L PTS 4 Canning Town
01.11.01 Chris Hooper L RSC 6 Hull
16.03.02 Lee Meager L PTS 6 Bethnal Green
27.03.02 Greg Edwards W RSC 5 Mayfair
20.04.02 Henry Castle L PTS 4 Cardiff
04.05.02 Danny Hunt L PTS 4 Bethnal Green
15.06.02 Jesse James Daniel L PTS 4 Leeds
27.07.02 Craig Spacie L PTS 4 Nottingham
23.08.02 Billy Corcoran L PTS 4 Bethnal Green
25.10.02 Billy Corcoran L RSC 2 Bethnal Green
03.12.02 Mark Bowen L PTS 6 Shrewsbury
11.12.02 Matt Teague L PTS 6 Hull
20.12.02 Chris McDonagh L PTS 6 Bracknell
18.01.03 Andy Morris L PTS 4 Preston
09.02.03 Mally McIver L PTS 6 Bradford
09.03.03 Choi Tseveenpurev L PTS 8 Shaw
29.03.03 Kevin O'Hara L RSC 3 Portsmouth
07.05.03 Henry Jones L PTS 6 Ellesmere Port
02.06.03 Stefy Bull L PTS 6 Cleethorpes
13.06.03 Scott Lawton L PTS 6 Queensway
17.07.03 Haider Ali L PTS 4 Dagenham
29.08.03 Gary Thornhill L CO 1 Liverpool
05.10.03 Nadeem Siddique L PTS 6 Bradford
08.11.03 Harry Ramogoadi L PTS 6 Coventry
23.11.03 Amir Ali L PTS 6 Rotherham
10.12.03 Femi Fehintola L PTS 6 Sheffield
21.12.03 John Murray L PTS 6 Bolton
06.02.04 Femi Fehintola L PTS 6 Sheffield
23.02.04 Carl Greaves L PTS 6 Nottingham
05.03.04 Haroon Din L PTS 6 Darlington
12.03.04 Stuart Green L PTS 8 Irvine
03.04.04 Daniel Thorpe L PTS 6 Sheffield
16.04.04 John O'Donnell L PTS 4 Bradford
27.04.04 Jim Betts L PTS 6 Leeds
07.05.04 Jus Wallie L PTS 6 Bethnal Green
28.05.04 John Bothwell W RSC 3 Glasgow
05.06.04 Kevin Mitchell L RSC 3 Bethnal Green
30.07.04 Lee Beavis L PTS 4 Bethnal Green
20.09.04 Matt Teague L PTS 6 Cleethorpes
30.09.04 Eddie Nevins L PTS 6 Hull
18.11.04 Joel Viney W PTS 6 Blackpool
26.11.04 John Davidson W RSC 1 Altrincham
10.12.04 John Fewkes L PTS 6 Sheffield
17.12.04 Gwyn Wale L PTS 4 Huddersfield
13.02.05 Nadeem Siddique L PTS 6 Bradford
04.03.05 John Fewkes L PTS 6 Rotherham
01.04.05 Martin McDonagh L PTS 6 Glasgow
15.04.05 Martin Gethin L PTS 6 Shrewsbury
28.04.05 Ceri Hall L RTD 2 Clydach
02.06.05 Riaz Durgahed L PTS 6 Peterborough
24.07.05 Femi Fehintola L PTS 6 Sheffield
09.09.05 Nicki Smedley L PTS 4 Sheffield
30.09.05 Henry Jones L PTS 6 Carmarthen
16.10.05 Michael Medor L PTS 6 Peterborough
12.11.05 Craig Johnson L PTS 6 Sheffield
25.11.05 Nadeem Siddique L RSC 6 Hull
17.02.06 Dave Stewart L PTS 4 Bethnal Green
04.03.06 Tony Delaney L PTS 4 Manchester
01.04.06 Steve Bell L PTS 6 Bethnal Green
28.04.06 Davis Kamara L PTS 6 Manchester

06.05.06 Jimmy Doherty L PTS 6 Stoke
20.05.06 Anthony Christopher W RSC 4 Bristol
05.06.06 Mitch Prince L PTS 6 Glasgow
24.09.06 Peter McDonagh L PTS 4 Bethnal
        Green
01.10.06 Andrew Ward DREW 6 Rotherham
24.11.06 Chris Hooper DREW 6 Hull
02.12.06 Shane Watson L PTS 6 Longford
25.02.07 Danny Harding L PTS 6 Manchester
10.03.07 John Watson L PTS 4 Liverpool
28.04.07 Jonathan Whiteman W RTD 5 Newark
18.05.07 Dave Stewart L PTS 4 Canning Town
09.06.07 Davey Watson L PTS 6 Middlesbrough
13.07.07 Thomas Costello L PTS 4 Birmingham
21.09.07 Dean Harrison L PTS 6 Burton
28.09.07 Jonathan Hussey L PTS 6 Preston
Career: 83 contests, won 7, drew 2, lost 74.

Paul Newby

Keighley. *Born* Eastburn, 13 September,
1977
L.Welterweight. *Ht* 5'6½"
Manager D. Coldwell

13.11.05 Ian Reid W PTS 6 Leeds
13.04.06 Pete Buckley W PTS 4 Leeds
06.05.06 Steve Gethin W PTS 4 Birmingham
13.10.07 Baz Carey W PTS 6 Barnsley
Career: 4 contests, won 4.

Ollie Newham

Nottingham. *Born* Nottingham, 8 October,
1986
Middleweight. *Ht* 6'2¼"
Manager M. Shinfield

08.09.07 Peter Dunn W PTS 6 Sutton in Ashfield
01.12.07 Jon Foster W RSC 2 Nottingham
02.05.08 Paul Brown W RSC 4 Nottingham
Career: 3 contests, won 3.

Lee Nicholson   Philip Sharkey

Lee Nicholson

Doncaster. *Born* Mexborough, 10
November, 1976
Cruiserweight. *Ht* 5'11"
Manager Self

24.09.01 Jason Brewster L PTS 6 Cleethorpes
17.02.02 Jason Brewster L PTS 6
        Wolverhampton

11.05.02	Fola Okesola L RSC 1 Dagenham
07.09.03	Stewart West L RSC 2 Shrewsbury
01.12.03	Mike Duffield W PTS 6 Barnsley
15.12.03	Simeon Cover L RSC 4 Cleethorpes
29.10.04	Dean Cockburn L RSC 2 Doncaster
13.12.04	Dean Cockburn L RSC 3 Cleethorpes
23.05.05	Slick Miller W PTS 6 Cleethorpes
03.03.06	Jimmy Harrington DREW 4 Doncaster
21.04.06	Jimmy Harrington L RTD 3 Doncaster
13.10.06	Billy Wilson L RSC 5 Doncaster
19.10.07	Ryan Rowlinson W PTS 4 Doncaster
26.10.07	Carl Dilks L RSC 4 Wigan
30.11.07	Dwayne Lewis L RTD 2 Newham

Career: 15 contests, won 3, drew 1, lost 11.

Mark Nilsen   Philip Sharkey

Mark Nilsen

Sale. *Born* Manchester, 26 July, 1978
L.Heavyweight. *Ht* 6'0"
Manager W. Dixon

17.02.02	Kenroy Lambert W PTS 6 Salford
26.10.06	Chris Harman W PTS 6 Dudley
06.12.06	Simon Wood W PTS 4 Stoke
24.02.07	Carl Wild W PTS 6 Manchester
21.04.07	Tomas Da Silva W RSC 5 Manchester
30.06.07	Nicki Taylor W CO 4 Manchester
16.09.07	Ovill McKenzie L RSC 1 Derby
28.11.07	Ruben Groenewald L PTS 6 Piccadilly
25.01.08	Hamed Jamali L PTS 4 Birmingham
08.02.08	Brian Magee L PTS 4 Peterlee
23.02.08	Joey Ainscough L PTS 4 Liverpool
07.03.08	Rod Anderton L PTS 4 Nottingham
28.03.08	Billy Boyle L RTD 1 Barnsley
31.05.08	Jamie Norkett L PTS 4 Newark

Career: 14 contests, won 6, lost 8.

Lee Noble

Sheffield. *Born* Barnsley, 23 April, 1987
Middleweight. Former Undefeated British
Masters Middleweight Champion. *Ht* 6'0"
Manager J. Ingle

05.10.06	Shaun Farmer L PTS 6 Sunderland
13.10.06	Jason Rushton W PTS 6 Doncaster
20.10.06	Jak Hibbert W RSC 6 Sheffield
27.10.06	Peter Dunn W PTS 6 Glasgow
10.12.06	Jak Hibbert W PTS 6 Sheffield
09.02.07	Mark Thompson L PTS 6 Leeds
19.02.07	Darren Gethin W PTS 6 Glasgow

11.03.07	Magic Kidem W PTS 4 Shaw
03.05.07	Stuart Brookes L PTS 10 Sheffield
	(Vacant British Masters L.Heavyweight Title)
17.06.07	Alexander Spitjo W PTS 4 Mansfield
22.09.07	Brian Rose L PTS 4 Wigan
05.10.07	George Hillyard L PTS 6 Bethnal Green
03.11.07	Thomas Povlsen L PTS 6 Cardiff
20.11.07	William Ruiz W RSC 4 Vilamoura, Portugal
02.12.07	Drew Campbell W PTS 6 Oldham
18.01.08	Sam Horton L PTS 4 Burton
23.02.08	Anthony Young W PTS 10 Crawley
	(Vacant British Masters Middleweight Title)
12.05.08	Sam Horton L PTS 8 Birmingham

Career: 18 contests, won 10, lost 8.

Jamie Norkett

Newark. *Born* Harpenden, 15 February,
1977
L.Heavyweight. *Ht* 6'3¼"
Manager C. Greaves

08.09.07	Carl Wild L PTS 4 Sutton in Ashfield
13.10.07	Magic Kidem W CO 3 Newark
14.11.07	Victor Smith L PTS 4 Bethnal Green
23.02.08	Dave Pearson W PTS 6 Newark
22.03.08	Harry Miles L PTS 4 Cardiff
26.04.08	Bob Ajisafe L PTS 4 Darlington
31.05.08	Mark Nilsen W PTS 4 Newark

Career: 7 contests, won 3, lost 4.

Robert Norton

Stourbridge. *Born* Dudley, 20 January, 1972
English Cruiserweight Champion. Former
Undefeated British Masters Cruiserweight
Champion. Former WBU Cruiserweight
Champion. *Ht* 6'2"
Manager Self

30.09.93	Stuart Fleet W CO 2 Walsall
27.10.93	Kent Davis W PTS 6 West Bromwich
02.12.93	Eddie Pyatt W RSC 2 Walsall
26.01.94	Lennie Howard W PTS 6 Birmingham
17.05.94	Steve Osborne W PTS 6 Kettering
05.10.94	Chris Woollas DREW 6 Wolverhampton
30.11.94	L. A. Williams W RSC 2 Wolverhampton
10.02.95	Newby Stevens W RSC 3 Birmingham
22.02.95	Steve Osborne W PTS 6 Telford
21.04.95	Cordwell Hylton W PTS 6 Dudley
25.10.95	Nigel Rafferty W RSC 6 Telford
31.01.96	Gary Williams W RSC 2 Birmingham
25.04.96	Steve Osborne W RSC 5 Mayfair
01.10.96	Andrew Benson W RSC 6 Birmingham
12.11.96	Nigel Rafferty W PTS 8 Dudley
11.02.97	Touami Benhamed W RSC 5 Bethnal Green
16.04.97	Tony Booth W RSC 4 Bethnal Green
20.12.97	Darren Corbett L PTS 12 Belfast
	(Commonwealth Cruiserweight Title Challenge)
03.04.98	Adrian Nicolai W RSC 2 West Bromwich
03.10.98	Tim Brown W CO 3 West Bromwich
01.04.99	Jacob Mofokeng W PTS 12 Birmingham
	(WBU Cruiserweight Title Challenge)
24.09.99	Sebastiaan Rothmann L RSC 8 Merthyr
	(WBU Cruiserweight Title Defence)
30.09.00	Tony Booth W RSC 3 Peterborough
18.11.00	Darron Griffiths W PTS 10 Dagenham

	(Elim. British Cruiserweight Title)
05.02.01	Lee Swaby W PTS 8 Hull
30.11.02	Paul Bonson W PTS 6 Coventry
05.09.03	Mark Hobson L PTS 12 Sheffield
	(Commonwealth Cruiserweight Title Challenge. Vacant British Cruiserweight Title)
09.04.04	Greg Scott-Briggs W CO 1 Rugby
10.07.04	Chris Woollas W RSC 4 Coventry
06.12.04	Paul Bonson W CO 6 Leicester
	(Vacant British Masters Cruiserweight Title)
22.10.05	Dmitry Adamovich W CO 2 Coventry
09.10.06	Roland Horvath W RSC 3 Bedworth
02.03.07	Tommy Eastwood W RSC 8 Coventry
	(Vacant English Cruiserweight Title)
08.12.07	Enad Licina L PTS 8 Basle, Switzerland

Career: 34 contests, won 29, drew 1, lost 4.

Tyrone Nurse

Huddersfield. *Born* Huddersfield, 4 January,
1990
L.Welterweight. *Ht* 5'11¼"
Manager S. Wood/C. Aston

28.03.08	Kristian Laight W PTS 4 Barnsley

Career: 1 contest, won 1.

(Paulus) Ali Nuumbembe

Glossop. *Born* Oshakati, Namibia, 24 June,
1978
WBA Pan-African Welterweight Champion.
Former Commonwealth Welterweight
Champion. *Ht* 5'8½"
Manager S. Wood

16.04.03	Dai Bando W PTS 4 Nottingham
15.06.03	Ernie Smith W PTS 4 Bradford
03.08.03	Lee Williamson W PTS 6 Stalybridge
29.08.03	Ernie Smith W PTS 6 Liverpool
05.10.03	Keith Jones W PTS 6 Bradford
07.12.03	Brian Coleman W RTD 2 Bradford
16.01.04	Wayne Wheeler W RSC 1 Bradford
29.02.04	William Webster W RSC 3 Shaw
10.04.04	Peter Dunn W PTS 6 Manchester
09.10.04	Bethuel Ushona L PTS 10 Windhoek, Namibia
	(Vacant Namibian Welterweight Title)
09.12.04	Lee Armstrong W PTS 6 Stockport
04.03.05	Franny Jones W PTS 6 Hartlepool
22.04.05	David Barnes DREW 12 Barnsley
	(Vacant WBO Inter-Continental Welterweight Title)
08.07.05	Dmitry Yanushevich W RSC 2 Altrincham
23.09.05	Gavin Down W RSC 3 Manchester
18.12.05	Ernie Smith W CO 4 Bolton
12.02.06	Sergey Starkov W PTS 8 Manchester
29.06.06	Ajose Olusegun L CO 6 Bethnal Green
29.09.06	Vladimir Borovski W PTS 6 Manchester
16.02.07	Kevin Anderson W PTS 12 Kirkcaldy
	(Commonwealth Welterweight Title Challenge)
06.07.07	Vladimir Borovski W PTS 6 Wigan
08.12.07	Craig Watson L RSC 8 Wigan
	(Commonwealth Welterweight Title Defence)
20.06.08	Welcome Ntshingila W PTS 12 Windhoek, Namibia
	(Vacant WBA Pan-African Welterweight Title)

Career: 23 contests, won 19, drew 1, lost 3.

Tony Oakey   Les Clark

Tony Oakey

Havant. *Born* Portsmouth, 2 January, 1976
Former British & WBU L.Heavyweight
Champion. Former Undefeated
Commonwealth & Southern Area
L.Heavyweight Champion. *Ht* 5'8"
Manager Self

12.09.98	Smokey Enison W RSC 2 Bethnal Green
21.11.98	Zak Chelli W RSC 1 Southwark
16.01.99	Jimmy Steel W PTS 4 Bethnal Green
06.03.99	Mark Dawson W PTS 4 Southwark
10.07.99	Jimmy Steel W PTS 4 Southwark
01.10.99	Michael Pinnock W PTS 4 Bethnal Green
21.02.00	Darren Ashton W PTS 4 Southwark
13.03.00	Martin Jolley W PTS 6 Bethnal Green
21.10.00	Darren Ashton W PTS 4 Wembley
27.01.01	Nathan King W PTS 6 Bethnal Green
26.03.01	Butch Lesley W PTS 10 Wembley *(Southern Area L. Heavyweight Title Challenge)*
08.05.01	Hastings Rasani W RSC 10 Barnsley *(Vacant Commonwealth L. Heavyweight Title)*
09.09.01	Konstantin Ochrej W RSC 4 Southwark
20.10.01	Chris Davies W PTS 12 Portsmouth *(Commonwealth L.Heavyweight Title Defence)*
02.03.02	Konstantin Shvets W PTS 12 Bethnal Green *(Vacant WBU L. Heavyweight Title)*
25.05.02	Neil Simpson W PTS 12 Portsmouth *(WBU L. Heavyweight Title Defence)*
12.10.02	Andrei Kaersten W PTS 12 Bethnal Green *(WBU L. Heavyweight Title Defence)*
29.03.03	Neil Linford W PTS 12 Portsmouth *(WBU L. Heavyweight Title Defence)*
11.10.03	Matthew Barney L PTS 12 Portsmouth *(WBU L.Heavyweight Title Defence)*
12.02.05	Varuzhan Davtyan W RTD 5 Portsmouth
19.06.05	Peter Haymer L PTS 10 Bethnal Green *(English L.Heavyweight Title Challenge)*
01.04.06	Radek Seman W PTS 8 Bethnal Green
13.05.06	Nathan King W PTS 6 Bethnal Green
28.10.06	Simeon Cover W PTS 6 Bethnal Green
09.03.07	Josip Jalusic W PTS 6 Dagenham
18.05.07	Steven Spartacus W RSC 12 Canning Town *(Vacant British L.Heavyweight Title)*
25.08.07	Brian Magee DREW 12 Dublin *(British L.Heavyweight Title Defence)*
01.02.08	Peter Haymer W CO 9 Bethnal Green *(British L.Heavyweight Title Defence)*
13.06.08	Dean Francis L RSC 9 Portsmouth *(British L.Heavyweight Title Defence. Commonwealth L.Heavyweight Title Challenge)*

Career: 29 contests, won 25, drew 1, lost 3.

Chris O'Brian

Nelson. *Born* Burnley, 24 September, 1981
Welterweight. *Ht* 6'0¼"
Manager S. Wood

26.04.08	Russell Pearce W PTS 6 Wigan
23.05.08	Kristian Laight W PTS 6 Wigan

Career: 2 contests, won 2.

(David) Dezzie O'Connor

Plymouth. *Born* Plymouth, 26 September, 1984
L.Welterweight. *Ht* 5'6"
Manager C. Sanigar

23.02.07	Jamie Spence L RSC 3 Peterborough
09.11.07	Dean Mills W PTS 6 Plymouth
29.02.08	John Vanemmenis W RSC 5 Plymouth
01.05.08	Mark McCullough L CO 1 Piccadilly
20.06.08	Carl Griffiths W PTS 6 Plymouth

Career: 5 contests, won 3, lost 2.

John O'Donnell

Shepherds Bush. *Born* Croydon, 13 November, 1985
Former Undefeated English Welterweight Champion. *Ht* 5'11"
Manager Self

16.04.04	Jason Nesbitt W PTS 4 Bradford
02.06.04	Dave Hinds W PTS 4 Nottingham
24.09.04	Chris Long W RSC 4 Nottingham
12.11.04	Ernie Smith W PTS 6 Wembley
10.04.05	Duncan Cottier W PTS 4 Brentwood
09.07.05	Ben Hudson W RTD 3 Nottingham
21.10.05	Ben Hudson W PTS 4 Bethnal Green
20.01.06	Matt Scriven W RSC 4 Bethnal Green
28.01.06	Zaid Bediouri W PTS 6 Dublin
17.02.06	Karl Taylor W PTS 4 Bethnal Green
12.05.06	Duncan Cottier W RTD 3 Bethnal Green
12.07.06	Darren Gethin W PTS 8 Bethnal Green
15.09.06	Silence Saheed W PTS 6 Muswell Hill
08.12.06	Ernie Smith W CO 2 Dagenham
23.03.07	Stuart Elwell W PTS 10 Nottingham *(Vacant English Welterweight Title)*
05.05.07	Christian Solano L RSC 2 Las Vegas, Nevada, USA
10.05.08	Billy Smith W PTS 4 Nottingham
27.06.08	Jay Morris W RSC 6 Bethnal Green

Career: 18 contests, won 17, lost 1.

Kevin O'Hara

Belfast. *Born* Belfast, 21 September, 1981
Welterweight. *Ht* 5'6"
Manager Self

02.11.02	Mike Harrington W RSC 1 Belfast
01.02.03	Jus Wallie W RSC 2 Belfast
29.03.03	Jason Nesbitt W RSC 3 Portsmouth
14.06.03	Piotr Niesporek W PTS 4 Magdeburg, Germany
02.10.03	Vladimir Borov W PTS 6 Liverpool
30.10.03	Henry Janes W PTS 6 Belfast
29.11.03	Gareth Payne W PTS 4 Renfrew
06.03.04	Henry Janes W PTS 6 Renfrew
01.04.04	Buster Dennis W PTS 4 Bethnal Green
06.05.04	Choi Tsveenpurev L PTS 8 Barnsley
28.10.04	Jean-Marie Codet W PTS 8 Belfast
17.06.05	Willie Limond L PTS 10 Glasgow *(Vacant Celtic S.Featherweight Title)*
24.11.05	Damian Owen W PTS 6 Lurgan
20.05.06	Daniel Thorpe W PTS 6 Belfast
26.10.06	Eric Patrac W PTS 6 Belfast
30.11.07	Henry Castle L PTS 8 Newham
19.04.08	Eddie Hyland L PTS 10 Dublin *(Vacant All-Ireland S.Featherweight Title)*

Career: 17 contests, won 13, lost 4.

(Gary) JJ Ojuederie

Watford. *Born* Watford, 13 September, 1979
Southern Area L.Heavyweight Champion.
International Masters Cruiserweight
Champion.. *Ht* 6'0"
Manager J. Feld

29.09.00	Chris Nembhard L RSC 1 Bethnal Green
08.12.03	Hamid Jamali L PTS 6 Birmingham
13.02.04	Jason Samuels L DIS 3 Bristol
28.02.04	Mike Allen W RSC 1 Bridgend
16.10.05	Karl Wheeler DREW 4 Peterborough
19.11.05	Eder Kurti W RSC 4 Southwark
16.12.05	Sam Price W PTS 6 Bracknell
26.02.06	Simeon Cover W PTS 4 Dagenham
23.07.06	Carl Wright W PTS 4 Dagenham
03.12.06	Tony Booth W PTS 4 Bethnal Green
15.04.07	John Anthony W PTS 6 Barnsley
19.10.07	Ayitey Powers W PTS 10 Mayfair *(Vacant International Masters Cruiserweight Title)*
01.12.07	Hastings Rasani W PTS 6 Bethnal Green
16.05.08	Andrew Lowe W PTS 10 Holborn *(Southern Area L.Heavyweight Title Challenge)*

Career: 14 contests, won 10, drew 1, lost 3.

Nick Okoth

Battersea. *Born* Camden Town, 19 July, 1973
L. Heavyweight. *Ht* 5'11"
Manager Self

18.09.03	Mark Phillips W PTS 4 Mayfair
28.02.04	Paulie Silva L PTS 6 Manchester
08.04.04	Karl Wheeler L PTS 6 Peterborough
24.04.04	Daniel Sackey L RSC 2 Reading
03.07.04	Nathan King L PTS 4 Newport
31.10.04	Darren Stubbs L PTS 6 Shaw
25.11.04	Jonjo Finnegan DREW 6 Birmingham
03.12.04	Paul Henry W RSC 5 Bristol
21.01.05	Sam Price L PTS 6 Brentford
06.02.05	Mervyn Langdale DREW 6 Southampton
20.02.05	Jon Ibbotson L PTS 6 Sheffield
08.04.05	Dan Guthrie L RSC 2 Bristol
09.09.05	Steven Birch W PTS 4 Sheffield
28.01.06	Rod Anderton L PTS 6 Nottingham
25.02.06	Richard Horton L CO 3 Canning Town
29.09.06	Chris Harman W PTS 4 Cardiff
14.10.06	Kenny Anderson L RSC 4 Manchester

18.02.07	Dwayne Lewis DREW 4 Bethnal Green
02.03.07	Wayne Brooks DREW 4 Neath
07.04.07	Nathan Cleverly L PTS 8 Cardiff
15.06.07	Tony Salam L PTS 4 Crystal Palace
06.07.07	Tony Dodson L PTS 4 Wigan
14.09.07	Gordon Brennan W PTS 4 Kirkcaldy
21.09.07	Courtney Fry L RSC 1 Bethnal Green
27.10.07	Ladislav Kutil W RSC 4 Prague, Czech Republic
21.12.07	Roman Kracik L PTS 6 Brno, Czech Republic
15.02.08	Billy Boyle L PTS 4 Sheffield
22.02.08	Danny McIntosh L RSC 3 Bethnal Green
01.05.08	Neil Simpson L RSC 10 Piccadilly *(British Masters Cruiserweight Title Challenge)*

Career: 29 contests, won 6, drew 4, lost 19.

Kelly Oliver

Lincoln. *Born* Lincoln, 11 November, 1973
Cruiserweight. Former Undefeated WBO Inter-Continental & British Masters Cruiserweight Champion. *Ht* 6'3¼"
Manager C. Sanigar

20.01.96	Steve Osborne W RSC 4 Mansfield
16.03.96	Marvin O'Brien W RSC 2 Glasgow
13.04.96	Andrew Benson W PTS 4 Wythenshawe
06.07.96	John Pierre W PTS 4 Manchester
14.09.96	Tony Booth W RSC 2 Sheffield
30.11.96	Nigel Rafferty W PTS 6 Tylorstown
18.01.97	Tony Booth W RSC 4 Swadlincote
14.03.97	Chris Woollas W PTS 4 Reading
05.06.97	Darren Westover W RTD 1 Bristol
02.08.97	Chris Woollas W RSC 3 Barnsley
11.10.97	John Keeton W RSC 8 Sheffield *(Vacant WBO Inter-Continental Cruiserweight Title)*
15.11.97	Sergei Korolev W PTS 12 Bristol *(WBO Inter-Continental Cruiserweight Title Defence)*
21.03.98	Brian la Spada W RSC 6 Bethnal Green *(WBO Inter-Continental Cruiserweight Title Defence)*
18.04.98	Nigel Rafferty W RSC 4 Manchester
18.07.98	John Keeton L RSC 2 Sheffield
19.06.99	Chris P. Bacon W PTS 8 Dublin
03.12.99	John Wyborn W RSC 2 Peterborough
05.03.00	Lee Swaby W PTS 8 Peterborough *(Vacant British Masters Cruiserweight Title)*
17.05.00	John Kiser W PTS 10 NYC, New York, USA
01.09.00	Sebastiaan Rothmann L RSC 10 Brakpan, South Africa *(WBU Cruiserweight Title Challenge)*
26.07.03	Tony Booth W PTS 4 Plymouth
09.11.07	John Anthony L RSC 5 Nottingham
23.02.08	Hastings Rasani W PTS 4 Newark

Career: 23 contests, won 20, lost 3.

Dean O'Loughlin

Hull. *Born* Beverley, 25 September, 1982
Heavyweight. *Ht* 6'5"
Manager J. Rushton

01.12.06	Lee Webb W RSC 3 Doncaster
23.02.07	Lee Webb W RSC 2 Doncaster
25.09.07	Lee Mountford W PTS 6 Hull
19.10.07	David Ingleby L RSC 5 Doncaster
21.06.08	Howard Daley W PTS 6 Hull

Career: 5 contests, won 4, lost 1.

Ajose Olusegun

Kentish Town. *Born* Nigeria, 6 December, 1979
Commonwealth L.Welterweight Champion. Former Undefeated ABU L.Welterweight Champion. *Ht* 5'9"
Manager Self

24.05.01	Tony Montana W RSC 1 Kensington
21.06.01	Woody Greenaway W RSC 1 Earls Court
09.09.01	Sunni Ajayi W PTS 6 Lagos, Nigeria
04.10.01	Stuart Rimmer W RTD 2 Finsbury
13.03.02	Gary Flear W PTS 4 Mayfair
13.06.02	Keith Jones W PTS 6 Leicester Square
30.10.02	Martin Holgate W RSC 7 Leicester Square
27.11.02	Vladimir Kortovski W RSC 1 Tel Aviv, Israel
15.12.02	Adewale Adegbusi W RSC 6 Lagos, Nigeria
20.03.03	Cristian Hodorogea W PTS 4 Queensway
26.04.03	Keith Jones W PTS 6 Brentford
29.10.03	Karl Taylor W PTS 6 Leicester Square
10.04.04	Victor Kpadenue W PTS 12 Carabas, Nigeria *(ABU L.Welterweight Title Challenge)*
03.09.04	Bradley Pryce W RSC 4 Newport
26.03.05	Vasile Dragomir W PTS 8 Hackney
26.05.06	Alexander Abramenko W RSC 2 Bethnal Green
29.06.06	Ali Nuumbembe W CO 6 Bethnal Green
17.11.06	Franck Aiello W RSC 2 Bethnal Green
09.03.07	Vladimir Khodokovski W PTS 6 Dagenham
15.06.07	Gary Reid W PTS 12 Crystal Palace *(Vacant Commonwealth L.Welterweight Title)*
26.10.07	Armando Candel W RSC 3 Wigan
08.02.08	Nigel Wright W PTS 12 Peterlee *(Commonwealth L.Welterweight Title Defence)*
18.04.08	Alexander Spitjo W RSC 3 Bethnal Green

Career: 23 contests, won 23.

Steve O'Meara

West Drayton. *Born* West Drayton, 31 December, 1983
L.Middleweight. *Ht* 5'11¼"
Manager J. McDonnell

04.04.08	Ben Hudson W PTS 4 Bethnal Green
06.06.08	Dontre King W RSC 2 Philadelphia, Pennsylvania, USA

Career: 2 contests, won 2.

Craig O'Neile

Leeds. *Born* Leeds, 7 March, 1979
Featherweight. *Ht* 5'2"
Manager M. Bateson

15.11.07	Sergei Rozhakmens W RSC 2 Leeds
23.12.07	Jon Kays L RSC 2 Bolton

Career: 2 contests, won 1, lost 1.

Eddie O'Rourke

Newark. *Born* Nottingham, 20 October, 1989
Lightweight. *Ht* 5'8¼"
Manager C. Greaves

31.05.08	Senol Dervis W PTS 6 Newark

Career: 1 contest, won 1.

Luke Osman

Merthyr. *Born* Merthyr, 10 March, 1986
Middleweight. *Ht* 6'1"
Manager D. Gardiner

28.06.08	Lester Walsh L PTS 6 Leicester

Career: 1 contest, lost 1.

Damian Owen

Swansea. *Born* Swansea, 7 May, 1985
Welsh Area Lightweight Champion. *Ht* 5'7"
Manager T. Gilmour

01.10.04	Darren Payne W RSC 4 Bristol
05.11.04	Peter Allen W RSC 1 Hereford
08.04.05	Jus Wallie W PTS 4 Bristol
28.10.05	Bheki Moyo W PTS 6 Hartlepool
24.11.05	Kevin O'Hara L PTS 6 Lurgan
25.02.06	Carl Allen W PTS 6 Bristol
21.04.06	Steve Mullin W RSC 6 Belfast
13.10.06	Yauhen Kruhlik W PTS 6 Aberavon
02.03.07	Dean Phillips W CO 4 Neath *(Vacant Welsh Area Lightweight Title)*
08.06.07	Pedro Verdu L RSC 3 Motherwell
21.10.07	Chris Long W PTS 4 Swansea

Career: 11 contests, won 9, lost 2.

Leon Owen

Swansea. *Born* Mountain Ash, 7 October, 1983
S.Middleweight. *Ht* 6'1"
Manager N. Hodges

26.02.06	Greg Barton W RSC 1 Dagenham
05.03.06	George Katsimpas L RSC 2 Southampton
20.05.06	Jav Jerome W PTS 6 Bristol
08.10.06	Dave Pearson W PTS 4 Swansea
11.05.07	Gordon Brennan L PTS 4 Motherwell
21.10.07	Shon Davies L PTS 6 Swansea

Career: 6 contests, won 3, lost 3.

Ricky Owen

Swansea. *Born* Swansea, 10 May, 1985
Featherweight. *Ht* 5'6"
Manager Self

05.11.04	Sandy Bartlett W RSC 2 Hereford
16.06.05	Billy Smith W PTS 4 Dagenham
30.09.05	Rakhim Mingaleev W PTS 4 Carmarthen
03.03.06	Alexander Vladimirov W PTS 6 Hartlepool
02.03.07	Egon Szabo W PTS 6 Neath
20.07.07	Anthony Hanna W RSC 5 Wolverhampton
02.11.07	Robin Deakin W RSC 2 Irvine
25.01.08	Frederic Gosset W PTS 6 Dagenham
30.03.08	Dai Davies W CO 5 Port Talbot
06.06.08	Sumaila Badu W PTS 6 Glasgow

Career: 10 contests, won 10.

Tom Owens

Birmingham. *Born* Birmingham, 1 May, 1983
Cruiserweight. *Ht* 6'4"
Manager R. Woodhall

01.06.07	Gary Thompson L RTD 1 Birmingham
13.07.07	Tony Booth W PTS 4 Birmingham
18.11.07	Bob Ajisafe L RSC 2 Birmingham
25.01.08	Lee Mountford W PTS 6 Birmingham

Career: 4 contests, won 2, lost 2.

Duane Parker

Swadlincote. *Born* Burton, 14 September, 1987
L.Middleweight. *Ht* 5'11¼"
M*anager* E. Johnson

21.09.07	Peter Dunn W PTS 6 Burton
18.01.08	Lance Verallo W PTS 4 Burton
16.05.08	Peter Dunn W PTS 6 Burton
22.06.08	Chris Thompson W PTS 4 Derby

Career: 4 contests, won 4.

Yanko Pavlov

Fife. *Born* Bulgaria, 27 July, 1982
Cruiserweight. *Ht* 6'0¼"
Manager T. Gilmour

09.05.08	Bob Ajisafe L PTS 4 Middlesbrough

Career: 1 contest, lost 1.

Russell Pearce   Philip Sharkey

Russell Pearce

Welshpool. *Born* Shrewsbury, 28 October, 1986
Welterweight. *Ht* 5'10¼"
Manager N. Hodges

21.10.07	Steve Cooper W PTS 4 Swansea
02.12.07	Chris Long DREW 6 Bristol
30.03.08	James Lilley L PTS 6 Port Talbot
26.04.08	Chris O'Brian L PTS 6 Wigan
12.05.08	Callum Archer DREW 6 Birmingham
07.06.08	Jonathan Hussey L PTS 4 Wigan
27.06.08	Daniel Herdman L RTD 2 Bethnal Green

Career: 7 contests, won 1, drew 2, lost 4.

Dave Pearson

Middlesbrough. *Born* Middlesbrough, 1 April, 1974
L.Heavyweight. *Ht* 6'2¾"
Manager Self

15.04.02	Ian Thomas L CO 3 Shrewsbury

03.10.02	Gary Firby W CO 3 Sunderland
21.10.02	Gary Jones L RSC 3 Cleethorpes
05.12.02	Chris Steele W PTS 6 Sunderland
24.03.03	Reagan Denton L PTS 6 Barnsley
31.05.03	Gary Jones L RSC 2 Barnsley
11.07.03	Ben Coward L PTS 6 Darlington
16.02.04	Brian Coleman L PTS 6 Scunthorpe
26.02.04	Tony Quigley L RSC 1 Widnes
26.04.04	Mark Phillips L RSC 6 Cleethorpes
25.06.04	Gerard London L PTS 4 Bethnal Green
06.11.04	Brian Coleman W PTS 6 Coventry
16.12.04	Peter McCormack W PTS 6 Cleethorpes
25.04.05	Peter McCormack W PTS 6 Cleethorpes
02.09.05	Mark Phillips L PTS 6 Derby
15.12.05	Ryan Rowlinson L PTS 6 Cleethorpes
28.01.06	Jonjo Finnegan L PTS 4 Nottingham
25.03.06	Jonjo Finnegan L PTS 8 Burton
24.04.06	Magic Kidem W PTS 6 Cleethorpes
30.09.06	Jonjo Finnegan L PTS 6 Middlesbrough
08.10.06	Leon Owen L PTS 4 Swansea
02.12.06	Eder Kurti L PTS 6 Southwark
15.02.07	Sam Horton L RSC 4 Dudley
14.05.07	Tony Stones DREW 6 Cleethorpes
25.10.07	Richard Collins L RSC 3 Wolverhampton
23.02.08	Jamie Norkett L PTS 6 Newark
13.04.08	Eddie McIntosh L PTS 4 Edgbaston
26.04.08	Ally Morrison L PTS 6 Wigan
16.05.08	Jonjo Finnegan L PTS 4 Burton
21.06.08	Phil Goodwin L RSC 2 Hull

Career: 30 contests, won 6, drew 1, lost 23.

Dave Pearson   Les Clark

Neil Perkins

Birmingham. *Born* Shrewsbury, 2 October, 1981
Heavyweight. *Ht* 6'5¼"
Manager P. Rowson

28.02.08	Lee Mountford W PTS 4 Wolverhampton
30.04.08	Paul Bonson W PTS 6 Wolverhampton

Career: 2 contests, won 2.

Neil Perkins   Philip Sharkey

Jack Perry

Derby. *Born* Derby, 20 June, 1987
L.Welterweight. *Ht* 6'1"
Manager J. Ingle

16.09.06	Deniss Sirjatovs W PTS 6 Burton
24.11.06	Kristian Laight W PTS 4 Nottingham
03.03.07	Matt Seawright W RSC 2 Burton
16.09.07	Amir Nadi W PTS 4 Derby
03.11.07	Peter Dunn W PTS 6 Derby
18.01.08	Kristian Laight W PTS 4 Burton
10.05.08	Tom Glover DREW 4 Nottingham
22.06.08	Kristian Laight W PTS 6 Derby

Career: 8 contests, won 7, drew 1.

Mark Phillips

St Clare's. *Born* Carmarthen, 28 April, 1975
L.Heavyweight. Former Undefeated British Masters L.Heavyweight Champion. *Ht* 6'0"
Manager Self

26.10.00	Shayne Webb W PTS 6 Clydach
12.12.00	Tommy Matthews W PTS 6 Clydach
13.03.01	William Webster W RTD 1 Plymouth
07.10.01	Danny Norton L PTS 6 Wolverhampton
12.12.01	Simon Andrews W PTS 6 Clydach
25.04.02	Mark Ellwood L PTS 6 Hull
10.05.02	Scott Dann L PTS 6 Bethnal Green
23.06.02	Gareth Hogg L PTS 4 Southwark
10.07.02	Scott Dann L PTS 4 Wembley
03.12.02	Jamie Hearn L PTS 4 Bethnal Green
20.12.02	Ryan Walls L PTS 4 Bracknell
06.03.03	Darren Dorrington L PTS 8 Bristol
21.03.03	Steve Timms L PTS 6 West Bromwich
05.04.03	Dale Nixon L PTS 6 Coventry
13.04.03	Donovan Smillie L PTS 6 Bradford
12.05.03	Leigh Alliss L PTS 6 Southampton
27.05.03	Steven Spartacus L RSC 2 Dagenham
30.06.03	Roddy Doran L PTS 6 Shrewsbury
06.09.03	Alan Page L PTS 6 Huddersfield
18.09.03	Nick Okoth L PTS 4 Mayfair
09.10.03	Leigh Alliss L PTS 4 Bristol
30.11.03	Jimi Hendricks W PTS 6 Swansea
16.01.04	Donovan Smillie L PTS 4 Bradford
07.04.04	Christian Imaga L PTS 6 Leicester Square
15.04.04	Darren McDermott L PTS 4 Dudley
26.04.04	Dave Pearson W RSC 6 Cleethorpes
04.06.04	Steve Timms L PTS 6 Dudley
03.12.04	Dan Guthrie L RSC 1 Bristol

26.02.05	Matt Galer L PTS 6 Burton
21.04.05	Matthew Hough L PTS 4 Dudley
09.07.05	Liam Stinchcombe L PTS 4 Bristol
02.09.05	Dave Pearson W PTS 6 Derby
25.09.05	Lee Hodgson L PTS 6 Southampton
10.10.05	Peter McCormack W PTS 6 Birmingham
04.11.05	Gary Woolcombe L PTS 4 Bethnal Green
24.11.05	Glenn McClarnon L PTS 4 Lurgan
04.03.06	James Davenport L PTS 4 Manchester
30.03.06	Danny Tombs L PTS 4 Bloomsbury
13.05.06	Richard Horton L PTS 4 Bethnal Green
01.06.06	Jonjo Finnegan L PTS 4 Birmingham
09.06.06	Jason Rushton L PTS 6 Doncaster
08.07.06	Nathan Cleverly L PTS 4 Cardiff
08.09.06	James McKinley L PTS 4 Birmingham
24.09.06	Richard Horton L PTS 4 Bethnal Green
08.10.06	Shon Davies L PTS 4 Swansea
28.10.06	Carl Wild L PTS 6 Sheffield
02.12.06	Neil Tidman L PTS 6 Coventry
17.12.06	Robin White L PTS 4 Bolton
23.04.07	Kenny Davidson L PTS 6 Glasgow
06.05.07	Joey Ainscough L PTS 6 Altrincham
13.05.07	Kevin Concepcion L PTS 6 Birmingham
02.06.07	Robert Boardman L PTS 6 Bristol
28.06.07	Richard Collins L PTS 4 Dudley
21.09.07	Jonjo Finnegan W PTS 10 Burton
	(Vacant British Masters L.Heavyweight Title)
08.10.07	Matthew Hough L PTS 6 Birmingham
03.11.07	Harry Miles L PTS 4 Cardiff
18.11.07	Eddie McIntosh L PTS 4 Birmingham
28.11.07	Wayne Alwan Arab L PTS 4 Piccadilly
16.02.08	Rasham Sohi L PTS 6 Leicester
16.03.08	Joe McNally L RTD 2 Liverpool

Career: 60 contests, won 9, lost 51.

Mark Phillips   Philip Sharkey

Esham Pickering
Newark. *Born* Newark, 7 August, 1976
Former British, European &
Commonwealth S.Bantamweight
Champion. Former Undefeated British
Masters Bantamweight Champion. *Ht* 5'5"

Manager C. Greaves

23.09.96	Brendan Bryce W RSC 5 Cleethorpes
24.10.96	Kevin Sheil W PTS 6 Lincoln
22.11.96	Amjid Mahmood W RSC 2 Hull
09.12.96	Des Gargano W RTD 2 Chesterfield
16.12.96	Graham McGrath W PTS 6 Cleethorpes
20.03.97	Robert Braddock W RSC 6 Newark
12.04.97	Graham McGrath W PTS 4 Sheffield
26.04.97	Mike Deveney W PTS 4 Swadlincote
16.05.97	Chris Price W PTS 6 Hull
26.06.97	Graham McGrath W PTS 6 Salford
01.11.97	Mike Deveney W RSC 8 Glasgow
	(Elim. British Featherweight Title)
09.05.98	Jonjo Irwin L PTS 12 Sheffield
	(Vacant British Featherweight Title)
11.09.98	Louis Veitch W PTS 6 Newark
15.08.99	Chris Lyons W RSC 2 Derby
23.10.99	Ian Turner W PTS 6 Telford
20.11.99	Marc Smith W PTS 6 Grantham
19.02.00	Kevin Gerowski W PTS 10 Newark
	(Vacant British Masters Bantamweight Title. Elim. British Bantamweight Title)
13.08.00	Lee Williamson W PTS 6 Nottingham
16.12.00	Mauricio Martinez L RSC 1 Sheffield
	(WBO Bantamweight Title Challenge)
15.09.01	Carl Allen W PTS 6 Derby
08.12.01	Carl Allen W PTS 8 Chesterfield
20.04.02	Carl Allen W PTS 6 Derby
24.09.02	Alejandro Monzon L PTS 12 Gran Canaria, Spain
	(Vacant WBA Inter-Continental S.Featherweight Title)
02.12.02	Carl Allen W PTS 6 Leicester
08.02.03	Duncan Karanja W CO 5 Brentford
	(Vacant Commonwealth S.Bantamweight Title)
12.07.03	Brian Carr W RSC 4 Renfrew
	(Vacant British S.Bantamweight Title. Commonwealth S.Bantamweight Title Defence)
24.10.03	Alfred Tetteh W RSC 7 Bethnal Green
	(Commonwealth S.Bantamweight Title Defence)
16.01.04	Vincenzo Gigliotti W CO 10 Bradford
	(Vacant European S.Bantamweight Title)
12.05.04	Juan Garcia Martin W RSC 8 Reading
	(European S.Bantamweight Title Defence)
08.05.05	Noel Wilders W PTS 8 Bradford
09.06.05	Miguel Mallon W RSC 10 Alcobendas, Madrid, Spain
	(European S.Bantamweight Title Defence)
28.10.05	Michael Hunter L PTS 12 Hartlepool
	(European & Commonwealth S.Bantamweight Title Defences. British S.Bantamweight Title Challenge)
02.12.05	Frederic Bonifai W PTS 6 Nottingham
11.11.06	Bernard Dunne L PTS 12 Dublin
	(Vacant European S.Bantamweight Title)
20.01.07	Frederic Gosset W PTS 6 Muswell Hill
16.03.07	Marc Callaghan W PTS 12 Norwich
	(Vacant British S.Bantamweight Title)
13.10.07	Steve Gethin W RTD 3 Newark
09.11.07	Sean Hughes L PTS 8 Nottingham
18.01.08	Sean Hughes W RSC 9 Burton
	(British S.Bantamweight Title Defence)
27.06.08	Matthew Marsh L PTS 12 Bethnal Green
	(British S.Bantamweight Title Defence)

Career: 40 contests, won 33, lost 7.

Esham Pickering   Philip Sharkey

(Patrick) Paddy Pollock
Wishaw. *Born* Bellshill, 10 October, 1985
L.Middleweight. *Ht* 5'10½"
Manager A. Morrison

22.04.06	Duncan Cottier W PTS 6 Glasgow
21.10.06	Tyrone McInerney DREW 6 Glasgow
10.12.06	Ciaran Duffy W PTS 6 Glasgow
26.01.07	Dave Wakefield L PTS 6 Glasgow
16.02.07	Martin Marshall L PTS 4 Sunderland
16.03.07	Tom Hogan W RSC 3 Glasgow
25.05.07	Shaun Farmer W PTS 6 Glasgow
11.08.07	Shaun Farmer L PTS 6 Liverpool
26.10.07	Mark Bett DREW 6 Glasgow
09.12.07	Jay Morris L PTS 6 Glasgow
17.05.08	Duncan Cottier W PTS 6 Glasgow
20.06.08	James Flinn L PTS 4 Wolverhampton

Career: 12 contests, won 5, drew 2, lost 5.

Paddy Pollock   Philip Sharkey

Paul Porter

Luton. *Born* Luton, 4 October, 1978
L.Middleweight. *Ht* 5'9¼"
Manager Self

11.02.06	Omar Gumati L RSC 3 Bethnal Green	
02.04.06	Steve Anning DREW 4 Bethnal Green	
29.09.06	Chris Johnson W RSC 2 Manchester	
17.11.06	Gareth Perkins DREW 4 Bethnal Green	
09.03.07	Thomas Mazurkiewicz L PTS 4 Dagenham	
23.09.07	Rocky Chakir L RSC 1 Longford	
28.03.08	Duncan Cottier DREW 6 Piccadilly	

Career: 7 contests, won 1, drew 3, lost 3.

Paul Porter   Les Clark

Marcus Portman

West Bromwich. *Born* West Bromwich, 26
September, 1980
L.Middleweight. Former Undefeated
WBF L.Middleweight Champion. Former
Undefeated British Masters Welterweight
Champion. *Ht* 6'0"
Manager E. Johnson

18.02.00	Ray Wood W PTS 6 West Bromwich	
28.03.00	Billy Smith W PTS 6 Wolverhampton	
10.09.00	Alan Kershaw W RSC 2 Walsall	
15.02.01	Willie Limond L PTS 6 Glasgow	
01.04.01	Tony Smith W PTS 6 Wolverhampton	
20.04.01	Darren Melville L RSC 3 Millwall	
07.09.01	Tony Smith W PTS 6 West Bromwich	
15.09.01	Matthew Hatton L RSC 3 Manchester	
12.12.01	Ross McCord DREW 4 Clydach	
18.01.02	Andy Egan W PTS 4 Coventry	
25.02.02	Sammy Smith W PTS 6 Slough	
27.04.02	Gavin Wake W PTS 4 Huddersfield	
08.05.03	Thomas McDonagh L PTS 6 Widnes	
17.05.03	Scott Dixon W PTS 6 Liverpool	
30.06.03	Wayne Wheeler W RSC 3 Shrewsbury	
07.09.03	Jason Williams L PTS 6 Shrewsbury	
19.02.04	Richard Swallow W PTS 10 Dudley	
	(British Masters Welterweight Title Challenge)	

03.04.04	Chris Saunders L RSC 1 Sheffield	
	(Vacant English Welterweight Title)	
29.06.06	Peter Dunn W PTS 6 Dudley	
18.09.06	Peter Dunn W PTS 6 Glasgow	
07.10.06	Ben Hudson W PTS 6 Walsall	
15.12.06	George Hillyard W PTS 8 Bethnal Green	
20.07.07	Jozsef Matolcsi W RSC 6 Wolverhampton	
	(WBF L.Middleweight Title Challenge)	
12.10.07	Jozsef Matolcsi W PTS 12 Peterlee	
	(WBF L.Middleweight Title Defence)	
08.12.07	Gary Woolcombe L RTD 8 Wigan	
	(Vacant British L.Middleweight Title)	
28.04.08	Dean Walker W PTS 6 Glasgow	
21.06.08	Bradley Pryce L RSC 6 Birmingham	
	(Commonwealth L.Middleweight Title Challenge)	

Career: 27 contests, won 19, drew 1, lost 7.

Martin Power   Philip Sharkey

Martin Power

St Pancras. *Born* London, 14 February,
1980
Bantamweight. Former Undefeated British
Bantamweight Champion. *Ht* 5'6"
Manager Self

09.06.01	Sean Grant W PTS 4 Bethnal Green	
28.07.01	Andrew Greenaway W RSC 3 Wembley	
22.09.01	Stevie Quinn W RSC 2 Bethnal Green	
24.11.01	Anthony Hanna W PTS 4 Bethnal Green	
19.01.02	Gareth Wiltshaw W PTS 4 Bethnal Green	
08.07.02	Darren Cleary W PTS 4 Mayfair	
12.10.02	Stevie Quinn W RSC 4 Bethnal Green	
15.02.03	Stevie Quinn W RTD 1 Wembley	
29.03.03	Dave Hinds W PTS 4 Portsmouth	
17.07.03	Darren Cleary W PTS 6 Dagenham	
06.11.03	Rocky Dean W PTS 6 Dagenham	
24.01.04	Delroy Spencer W RTD 1 Wembley	
01.04.04	Fred Janes W RSC 2 Bethnal Green	
13.05.04	Jean-Marie Codet W PTS 8 Bethnal Green	
30.07.04	Delroy Spencer W CO 2 Bethnal Green	
11.12.04	Shinny Bayaar W PTS 10 Canning	

	Town	
20.05.05	Dale Robinson W PTS 12 Southwark	
	(Vacant British Bantamweight Title)	
04.11.05	Ian Napa W PTS 12 Bethnal Green	
	(British Bantamweight Title Defence)	
30.05.06	Isaac Ward W RSC 8 Bethnal Green	
	(British Bantamweight Title Defence)	
29.06.06	Tshifhiwa Munyai L RSC 9 Bethnal Green	
	(Vacant Commonwealth Bantamweight Title)	
26.01.07	Tshifhiwa Munyai L RTD 5 Dagenham	
	(Commonwealth Bantamweight Title Challenge)	
30.11.07	Ian Napa L PTS 12 Newham	
	(British Bantamweight Title Challenge)	

Career: 22 contests, won 19, lost 3.

Ayitey Powers

Edmonton. *Born* Mamprobi, Ghana, 3 July,
1980
L.Heavyweight. Former Undefeated
Ghanaian & West AFrican Middleweight &
S.Middleweight Champion. *Ht* 5'10¼"
Manager J. Feld

30.09.00	Joshua Okine W RSC 4 Kaneshie, Ghana	
26.01.01	Ashiaquaye Aryee DREW 8 Kaneshie, Ghana	
12.10.01	George Amuzu W PTS 6 Kaneshie, Ghana	
03.05.02	Akeem Alarape W RSC 8 Accra, Ghana	
02.06.02	Marciano Commey W RSC 6 Kaneshie, Ghana	
	(Vacant Ghanaian & West African Middleweight Titles)	
02.11.02	Victor Kpadenue W PTS 8 Accra, Ghana	
	(Ghanaian & West African Middleweight Title Defences)	
06.12.02	Joshua Clottey L PTS 10 Accra, Ghana	
27.12.02	Kojo Adaho W RSC 6 Cotonou, Benin	
	(Ghanaian & West African Middleweight Title Defences)	
20.01.03	Dornu Kwame W RSC 4 Lome, Togo	
	(Ghanaian & West African Middleweight Title Defences)	
06.03.03	Samuel Shegu W PTS 10 Accra, Ghana	
	(Ghanaian & West African Middleweight Title Defences)	
28.06.03	Madaga Solomon W CO 1 Accra, Ghana	
15.08.03	Osumanu Adama L PTS 12 Kaneshie, Ghana	
	(Ghanaian & West African L.Middleweight Title Challenges)	
31.01.04	Richard Williams L RSC 7 Bethnal Green	
	(Vacant Commonwealth L.Middleweight Title)	
03.07.04	James Obede Toney L PTS 12 Accra, Ghana	
	(Vacant WBC International & Commonwealth Middleweight Titles)	
18.12.04	Mohammed Konde W CO 12 Accra, Ghana	
	(Vacant Ghanaian West African S.Middleweight Titles)	
26.08.05	Flash Issaka W RSC 4 Kaneshie, Ghana	
	(Vacant Ghanaian S.Middleweight Title)	
18.11.06	Gary Lockett L PTS 10 Newport	
08.12.06	Steven Spartacus W PTS 6 Dagenham	

23.02.07 Matthew Barney L PTS 6 Peterborough
23.03.07 Amer Khan L PTS 6 Nottingham
30.03.07 Cello Renda W RSC 2 Peterborough
02.06.07 Dean Francis L CO 9 Bristol
 *(Vacant IBO Inter-Continental
 L.Heavyweight Title)*
21.07.07 Nathan Cleverly L CO 6 Cardiff
19.10.07 JJ Ojuederie L PTS 10 Mayfair
 *(Vacant International Masters
 Cruiserweight Title)*
22.03.08 Jon Ibbotson L PTS 6 Sheffield
29.03.08 Paul David L PTS 6 Aberdeen
16.05.08 Matthew Barney L PTS 6 Holborn
15.06.08 Tony Quigley L PTS 6 St Helens
Career: 28 contests, won 13, drew 1, lost 14.

Bradley Pryce (Price)

Newbridge. *Born* Newport, 15 March, 1981
Commonwealth L.Middleweight Champion.
Former Undefeated Welsh Welterweight
Champion. Former Undefeated IBF Inter-
Continental L.Welterweight Champion.
Former Undefeated WBO Inter-Continental
Lightweight Champion. *Ht* 5'11"
Manager F. Warren/E. Calzaghe

17.07.99 Dave Hinds W PTS 4 Doncaster
23.10.99 David Jeffrey W RSC 3 Telford
06.11.99 Eddie Nevins W RSC 2 Widnes
29.01.00 Pete Buckley W PTS 4 Manchester
29.02.00 Carl Allen W PTS 4 Widnes
16.05.00 Carl Allen W RSC 3 Warrington
15.07.00 Gary Flear W RSC 1 Millwall
07.10.00 Gary Reid W RSC 5 Doncaster
27.01.01 Joel Viney W RSC 3 Bethnal Green
17.03.01 Brian Coleman W PTS 4 Manchester
28.04.01 Jason Hall W PTS 12 Cardiff
 *(Vacant WBO Inter-Continental
 Lightweight Title)*
21.07.01 Stuart Patterson W RSC 5 Sheffield
09.10.01 Lucky Sambo W PTS 12 Cardiff
 *(WBO Inter-Continental Lightweight
 Title Defence)*
12.02.02 Gavin Down W RSC 9 Bethnal Green
 *(Vacant IBF Inter-Continental
 L.Welterweight Title)*
20.04.02 Dafydd Carlin W RSC 8 Cardiff
08.06.02 Pete Buckley W RSC 1 Renfrew
17.08.02 Ted Bami L RSC 6 Cardiff
23.11.02 Craig Lynch W CO 4 Derby
01.02.03 Neil Sinclair L RSC 8 Belfast
 (British Welterweight Title Challenge)
08.05.03 Ivan Kirpa W PTS 10 Widnes
21.02.04 Farai Musiiwa L PTS 6 Cardiff
06.05.04 Thomas McDonagh L PTS 12 Barnsley
 *(WBU International L.Middleweight
 Title Challenge)*
03.07.04 Keith Jones W RSC 8 Newport
 (Vacant Welsh Area Welterweight Title)
03.09.04 Ajose Olusegun L RSC 4 Newport
11.12.04 Sergey Styopkin W RSC 10 Canning
 Town
25.10.05 Michael Jennings L PTS 12 Preston
 (British Welterweight Title Challenge)
11.03.06 Ossie Duran W PTS 12 Newport
 *(Commonwealth L.Middleweight Title
 Challenge)*
08.07.06 Hassan Matumla W RSC 4 Cardiff
 *(Commonwealth L.Middleweight Title
 Defence)*
18.11.06 Andrew Facey W PTS 12 Newport
 *(Commonwealth L.Middleweight Title
 Defence)*
07.04.07 Thomas Awinbono W PTS 12 Cardiff

 *(Commonwealth L.Middleweight Title
 Defence)*
14.07.07 Anthony Small W RSC 7 Greenwich
 *(Commonwealth L.Middleweight Title
 Defence)*
06.10.07 Martin Concepcion W RSC 3
 Nottingham
 *(Commonwealth L.Middleweight Title
 Defence)*
21.06.08 Marcus Portman W RSC 6 Birmingham
 *(Commonwealth L.Middleweight Title
 Defence)*
Career: 33 contests, won 27, lost 6.

Lee Purdy

Colchester. *Born* Colchester, 29 May, 1987
Welterweight. *Ht* 5'7"
Manager A. Sims

08.12.06 Deniss Sirjatovs W RSC 3 Dagenham
16.03.07 Kristian Laight W PTS 4 Norwich
16.06.07 Duncan Cottier W PTS 4 Chigwell
01.07.07 Ben Hudson W PTS 6 Colchester
25.11.07 Johnny Greaves W PTS 6 Colchester
25.01.08 Craig Dyer W RSC 1 Dagenham
04.04.08 Jamie Spence W RSC 1 Bethnal Green
27.06.08 Geoffrey Munika DREW 6 Bethnal
 Green
Career: 8 contests, won 7, drew 1.

Lee Purdy   Les Clark

Kreshnik Qato

Wembley. *Born* Albania, 13 August, 1978
WBF Middleweight Champion. Former
Undefeated European Union EE &
Southern Area S.Middleweight Champion.
Former Undefeated Eastern European
Boxing Association S.Middleweight
Champion. *Ht* 5'9½"
Manager P. Fondu

28.09.01 Erik Teymour L PTS 6 Millwall
16.12.01 Lawrence Murphy L PTS 6 Glasgow
08.04.02 Ty Browne W PTS 4 Southampton
10.05.02 Paul Jones L PTS 6 Millwall
20.03.03 Jason Collins W PTS 4 Queensway
13.04.03 Mark Thornton W RSC 3 Streatham
13.05.03 Danny Thornton W PTS 6 Leeds
26.07.03 Scott Dann L RSC 2 Plymouth
26.09.03 Joel Ani W PTS 6 Millwall
14.11.03 Steven Bendall L PTS 8 Bethnal Green
21.02.04 Gary Lockett L RSC 2 Cardiff
16.10.04 Vladimir Zavgorodniy W PTS 10 Yalta,
 Ukraine
 *(Vacant Eastern European Boxing
 Association S.Middleweight Title)*
05.03.05 Rizvan Magomedov W PTS 12 Durres,
 Albania
 *(Eastern European Boxing Association
 S.Middleweight Title Defence)*
12.06.05 Dmitry Donetskiy W RSC 6 Leicester
 Square
09.10.05 Daniil Prakapsou W PTS 8
 Hammersmith
02.04.06 Laurent Goury W PTS 6 Bethnal Green
26.05.06 Simone Lucas W PTS 4 Bethnal Green
15.07.06 Sylvain Touzet W PTS 6 Tirana,
 Albania
15.09.06 Simeon Cover W PTS 6 Muswell Hill
08.12.06 Simeon Cover W PTS 10 Dagenham
 *(Vacant Southern Area S.Middleweight
 Title)*
03.03.07 Alexander Zaitsev W PTS 12 Tirana,
 Albania
 *(Vacant European Union-EE
 S.Middleweight Title)*
14.11.07 Ernie Smith W PTS 6 Bethnal Green
04.04.08 Vitor Sa W PTS 12 Tirana, Albania
 (Vacant WBF Middleweight Title)
Career: 23 contests, won 17, lost 6.

Scott Quigg

Bury. *Born* Bury, 9 October, 1988
S.Bantamweight. *Ht* 5'8"
Manager Brian Hughes/W. Dixon

21.04.07 Gary Sheil W PTS 6 Manchester
30.06.07 Shaun Walton W RSC 1 Manchester
11.08.07 Shaun Walton W PTS 6 Liverpool
28.09.07 Sandy Bartlett W RSC 3 Preston
03.12.07 Delroy Spencer W PTS 6 Manchester
14.03.08 Gheorghe Ghiompirica W PTS 4
 Manchester
07.06.08 Sid Razak W RSC 2 Wigan
Career: 7 contests, won 7.

Tony Quigley

Liverpool. *Born* Liverpool, 1 October, 1984
L.Heavyweight. *Ht* 5'10"
Manager S. Wood

26.02.04 Dave Pearson W RSC 1 Widnes
22.05.04 Patrick Cito W PTS 4 Widnes
01.10.04 Leigh Wicks W PTS 4 Manchester
11.02.05 Shpetim Hoti W CO 1 Manchester
03.06.05 Varuzhan Davtyan W PTS 4
 Manchester
04.03.06 Ojay Abrahams W PTS 4 Manchester
01.06.06 Simeon Cover W PTS 4 Barnsley
14.10.06 Nathan Cleverly L RSC 5 Manchester
10.03.07 Dean Walker W RSC 2 Liverpool
26.04.07 Ricky Strike W RSC 3 Manchester
11.08.07 Jevgenijs Andrejevs W PTS 4
 Liverpool
15.06.08 Ayitey Powers W PTS 6 St Helens
Career: 12 contests, won 11, lost 1.

Jamie Radford

Woolwich. *Born* Newham, 2 August, 1987
Welterweight. *Ht* 5'7¾"
Manager J. Eames

09.03.07	Barry Downes W PTS 4 Dagenham
30.11.07	Dave Murray W RSC 1 Newham
01.02.08	Johnny Greaves W PTS 4 Bethnal Green

Career: 3 contests, won 3.

Furhan Rafiq

Glasgow. *Born* Glasgow, 16 December, 1977
Scottish Area Featherweight Champion.
Ht 5'8"
Manager T. Gilmour

19.04.04	Paddy Folan W PTS 6 Glasgow
15.11.04	Gary Davis L PTS 6 Glasgow
05.06.06	Shaun Walton W PTS 6 Glasgow
16.06.06	Henry Jones L PTS 6 Carmarthen
09.09.06	Shaun Walton W PTS 6 Inverurie
10.11.06	Neil Marston L PTS 6 Telford
22.01.07	Shaun Walton W PTS 6 Glasgow
02.03.07	Sandy Bartlett W PTS 6 Irvine
28.04.07	Pete Buckley W PTS 6 Clydebank
05.11.07	John Baguley L PTS 6 Glasgow
18.02.08	Sandy Bartlett W RSC 10 Glasgow (*Vacant Scottish Area Featherweight Title*)
09.06.08	Anthony Hanna L RSC 10 Glasgow (*Vacant British Masters Featherweight Title*)

Career: 12 contests, won 7, lost 5

Tony Randell (Webster)

Birmingham. *Born* Peterborough, 11 April, 1982
Middleweight. *Ht* 5'11½"
Manager Self

16.12.04	Scott Conway W PTS 6 Cleethorpes
13.02.05	Gavin Smith L PTS 6 Bradford
23.03.05	Danny Goode L PTS 6 Leicester Square
01.04.05	Chris Black L PTS 6 Glasgow
16.05.05	Sergey Haritonov W RSC 4 Birmingham
24.07.05	Stuart Brookes L PTS 6 Sheffield
09.09.05	Stuart Brookes L RSC 3 Sheffield
10.10.05	Simon Sherrington L PTS 6 Birmingham
30.10.05	Jake Guntert L PTS 4 Bethnal Green
18.12.05	Mark Thompson L RSC 2 Bolton
17.02.06	Reagan Denton L PTS 6 Sheffield
18.03.06	Sam Gorman W PTS 6 Coventry
02.04.06	Alex Matvienko L PTS 6 Shaw
13.04.06	Danny Wright L PTS 6 Leeds
20.05.06	George Katsimpas L RSC 1 Bristol
16.09.06	Karl Chiverton L PTS 6 Burton
07.10.06	Sam Horton L PTS 6 Walsall
26.10.06	Dee Mitchell L PTS 4 Wolverhampton
06.12.06	Ryan Rowlinson DREW 6 Rotherham
20.01.07	George Hillyard DREW 4 Muswell Hill
31.05.07	Brian Rose L PTS 6 Manchester

24.06.07	Johnny Enigma W RSC 5 Wigan
08.10.07	Graham Delehedy W PTS 10 Glasgow (*Vacant International Masters Middleweight Title*)
22.02.08	Chris Black L PTS 6 Motherwell
28.04.08	Jamie Coyle L PTS 8 Glasgow

Career: 25 contests, won 5, drew 2, lost 18.

Hastings Rasani   Philip Sharkey

Hastings Rasani

Birmingham. *Born* Zimbabwe, 16 April, 1974
Cruiserweight. *Ht* 6'2"
Manager Self

21.12.97	Elias Chikwanda W RSC 4 Harare, Zimbabwe
28.02.98	Victor Ndebele W CO 1 Harare, Zimbabwe
04.04.98	William Mpoku W PTS 8 Harare, Zimbabwe
03.05.98	Nightshow Mafukidze W CO 3 Harare, Zimbabwe
30.05.98	Frank Mutiyaya W RSC 4 Harare, Zimbabwe
24.07.98	Ambrose Mlilo L RSC 9 Harare, Zimbabwe
13.01.99	Tobia Wede W RSC 4 Harare, Zimbabwe
27.02.99	Ambrose Mlilo L CO 9 Harare, Zimbabwe
27.03.99	Gibson Mapfumo W CO 1 Harare, Zimbabwe
17.04.99	Eric Sauti W RSC 2 Harare, Zimbabwe
05.06.99	Gibson Mapfumo W RSC 2 Harare, Zimbabwe
18.12.99	Gibson Mapfumo W RSC 3 Harare, Zimbabwe
02.01.01	Neil Simpson L CO 4 Coventry (*Vacant Commonwealth L.Heavyweight Title*)
24.03.01	Gibson Mapfumo W CO 3 Harare, Zimbabwe
28.04.01	Arigoma Chiponda W DIS Harare, Zimbabwe
08.05.01	Tony Oakey L RSC 10 Barnsley (*Vacant Commonwealth L.Heavyweight Title*)
06.10.01	Sipho Moyo L CO 9 Harare, Zimbabwe
15.03.02	Elvis Michailenko L RSC 5 Millwall
24.05.03	Elvis Michailenko L RSC 4 Bethnal Green

31.07.03	Mark Brookes L PTS 6 Sheffield
05.09.03	Carl Thompson L RSC 1 Sheffield
04.10.03	Steven Spartacus L RSC 1 Muswell Hill
11.11.03	Denzil Browne L PTS 6 Leeds
13.02.04	Leigh Alliss L PTS 6 Bristol
21.02.04	Earl Ling DREW 6 Norwich
12.03.04	Simeon Cover W CO 6 Irvine
20.03.04	David Haye L RSC 1 Wembley
12.05.04	Jamie Hearn L RSC 4 Reading
17.06.04	Amer Khan L PTS 6 Sheffield
17.09.04	Mark Brookes L PTS 6 Sheffield
11.10.04	Hamed Jamali L PTS 8 Birmingham
22.10.04	Nathan King L PTS 6 Edinburgh
08.12.04	Sam Price L PTS 6 Longford
17.12.04	Neil Simpson L PTS 6 Coventry
21.02.05	Karl Wheeler L PTS 6 Peterborough
24.04.05	Nicki Taylor W RTD 4 Askern
08.05.05	Nate Joseph W RSC 4 Bradford
15.05.05	Danny Grainger W RSC 5 Sheffield
02.06.05	Karl Wheeler W RSC 5 Peterborough
01.07.05	Ovill McKenzie L PTS 6 Fulham
09.09.05	Lee Swaby L PTS 4 Sheffield
24.09.05	Neil Linford W RSC 5 Coventry
12.11.05	Dean Francis L RSC 6 Bristol
19.12.05	Valery Odin W PTS 4 Longford
11.03.06	Bruce Scott W PTS 8 Newport
07.10.06	Dean Francis L CO 2 Weston super Mare
02.12.06	Tommy Eastwood L PTS 6 Longford
20.01.07	Troy Ross L CO 3 Muswell Hill
11.03.07	Darren Stubbs L RSC 5 Shaw
29.09.07	Scott Brookes L PTS 4 Sheffield
07.10.07	Darren Stubbs L PTS 6 Shaw
03.11.07	Anders Hugger L PTS 6 Cardiff
01.12.07	JJ Ojuederie L PTS 6 Bethnal Green
23.02.08	Kelly Oliver L PTS 4 Newark
22.03.08	Mark Krence L PTS 4 Sheffield
24.04.08	Egbui Ikeagwu DREW 4 Piccadilly
15.06.08	Paul Keir L PTS 4 St Helens

Career: 57 contests, won 20, drew 2, lost 35.

Abdul Rashid

Manchester. *Born* Manchester, 17 February, 1975
Lightweight. *Ht* 5'7"
Manager Self

18.06.06	Sergei Rozhakmens W PTS 6 Manchester
14.10.06	Anthony Crolla L PTS 4 Manchester
24.02.07	Neal McQuade L PTS 6 Manchester
29.02.08	Charles Paul King L PTS 4 Glasgow
21.06.08	Joe Elfidh L PTS 6 Sheffield

Career: 5 contests, won 1, lost 4.

(Shahid) Sid Razak

Birmingham. *Born* Birmingham, 9 March, 1973
Lightweight. *Ht* 5'7"
Manager R. Woodhall

13.02.01	Neil Read W PTS 6 Brierley Hill
27.03.01	Tommy Thomas W RSC 2 Brierley Hill
21.05.01	Jason Nesbitt W PTS 6 Birmingham
08.10.01	Gareth Wiltshaw L PTS 6 Birmingham
14.09.02	J.J.Moore L PTS 6 Newark
26.09.02	Chris Hooper L PTS 6 Hull
08.12.03	Steve Mullin L PTS 6 Birmingham
08.03.04	Steve Mullin L PTS 6 Birmingham
01.06.07	Sergei Rozhakmens L PTS 6 Birmingham
31.05.08	Ben Lawler L PTS 6 Newark
07.06.08	Scott Quigg L RSC 2 Wigan

Career: 11 contests, won 3, lost 8.

Joe Rea
Birmingham. *Born* Ballymena, 24 July, 1983
S.Middleweight. *Ht* 6'0¼"
Manager R. Woodhall

11.06.04	Devin Womack W RSC 1 Plymouth, Mass, USA	
10.08.04	Henry Dukes NC 2 Hyannis, Mass, USA	
01.10.04	Robert Muhammad W PTS 4 Boston, Mass, USA	
25.03.05	Jerald Lowe W RSC 3 Dorchester, Mass, USA	
01.04.05	Cory Phelps W RSC 2 New Haven, Connecticut, USA	
19.11.05	Michael Rayner W RSC 1 Dorchester, USA	
07.07.06	Valentino Jalomo DREW 4 Hyannis, Mass, USA	
13.04.08	Jamie Ambler W PTS 4 Edgbaston	

Career: 8 contests, won 6, drew 1, no contest 1.

Gavin Rees   Philip Sharkey

Gavin Rees
Newbridge. *Born* Newport, 10 May, 1980
L.Welterweight. Former WBA L.Welterweight Champion. Former Undefeated WBO Inter-Continental Featherweight Champion. *Ht* 5'7"
Manager F. Warren/E. Calzaghe

05.09.98	John Farrell W PTS 4 Telford	
05.12.98	Ernie Smith W PTS 4 Bristol	
27.03.99	Graham McGrath W RSC 2 Derby	
05.06.99	Wayne Jones W RSC 2 Cardiff	
11.12.99	Dave Hinds W RSC 2 Liverpool	
19.02.00	Pete Buckley W PTS 4 Dagenham	
29.05.00	Willie Valentine W RSC 3 Manchester	
23.09.00	Pete Buckley W PTS 4 Bethnal Green	
13.11.00	Steve Hanley W RSC 1 Bethnal Green	
15.01.01	Chris Jickells W RSC 2 Manchester	
28.04.01	Vladimir Borov W RSC 4 Cardiff	
	(Vacant WBO Inter-Continental Featherweight Title)	
21.07.01	Nigel Senior W RSC 2 Sheffield	
09.10.01	Nikolai Eremeev W PTS 12 Cardiff	
	(WBO Inter-Continental Featherweight Title Defence)	
12.02.02	Rakhim Mingaleev W PTS 6 Bethnal Green	

20.04.02	Gary Flear W RTD 4 Cardiff	
08.07.02	Ernie Smith W RSC 5 Mayfair	
17.08.02	Sergei Andreychikov W RTD 1 Cardiff	
14.12.02	Jimmy Beech W PTS 4 Newcastle	
15.02.03	Andrei Devyataykin W PTS 6 Wembley	
28.06.03	Daniel Thorpe W RSC 1 Cardiff	
03.07.04	Michael Muya W RSC 2 Newport	
03.09.04	Carl Allen W PTS 6 Newport	
11.03.06	Daniel Thorpe W RSC 5 Newport	
08.07.06	Martin Watson W PTS 6 Cardiff	
18.11.06	Chill John W PTS 8 Newport	
07.04.07	Billy Smith W PTS 6 Cardiff	
21.07.07	Souleymane M'Baye W PTS 12 Cardiff	
	(WBA L.Welterweight Title Challenge)	
22.03.08	Andreas Kotelnik L RSC 12 Cardiff	
	(WBA L.Welterweight Title Defence)	

Career: 28 contests, won 27, lost 1.

Gary Reid
Stoke. *Born* Jamaica, 20 November, 1972
L.Welterweight. Former Undefeated Midlands Area & British Masters L.Welterweight Champion. *Ht* 5'5½"
Manager M. Carney

09.12.98	Carl Tilley W CO 1 Stoke	
11.02.99	Ted Bami L RSC 2 Dudley	
23.03.99	Lee Williamson W PTS 6 Wolverhampton	
07.10.99	Stuart Rimmer W RSC 2 Mere	
19.12.99	No No Junior L PTS 6 Salford	
14.04.00	Lee Molyneux W PTS 6 Manchester	
18.05.00	Sammy Smith W RSC 1 Bethnal Green	
23.07.00	Kevin Bennett L RSC 4 Hartlepool	
21.09.00	Karim Bouali L PTS 4 Bloomsbury	
07.10.00	Bradley Pryce L RSC 5 Doncaster	
07.09.01	Willie Limond L PTS 8 Glasgow	
22.09.01	Francis Barrett L PTS 4 Bethnal Green	
17.02.02	Richie Caparelli W PTS 6 Salford	
02.03.02	Paul Halpin L RSC 3 Bethnal Green	
26.04.02	Martin Watson L PTS 6 Glasgow	
28.05.02	Gareth Jordan DREW 6 Liverpool	
13.07.02	Gary Greenwood L RSC 5 Coventry	
05.10.02	Joel Viney W CO 2 Coventry	
18.11.02	Martin Watson L RSC 4 Glasgow	
21.03.03	Young Muttley L RSC 7 West Bromwich	
	(Vacant Midlands Area L.Welterweight Title)	
10.10.03	Oscar Hall W RSC 2 Darlington	
26.09.04	Tony Montana W PTS 10 Stoke	
	(Vacant British Masters L.Welterweight Title)	
17.02.05	Dean Hickman L PTS 10 Dudley	
	(Midlands Area L.Welterweight Title Challenge)	
27.05.05	Barry Morrison L RTD 8 Motherwell	
	(British Masters L.Welterweight Title Defence)	
25.11.05	Jason Cook L DIS 2 Liverpool	
18.02.06	Davis Kamara W PTS 6 Stoke	
06.05.06	Kevin McIntyre W RSC 6 Stoke	
	(Vacant British Masters L.Welterweight Title)	
26.05.06	Leo O'Reilly W RSC 2 Bethnal Green	
04.11.06	Nigel Wright L PTS 10 Glasgow	
	(English L.Welterweight Title Challenge)	
20.04.07	Dean Hickman W RSC 5 Dudley	
	(Vacant Midlands Area L.Welterweight Title)	
15.06.07	Ajose Olusegun L PTS 12 Crystal Palace	

	(Vacant Commonwealth L.Welterweight Title)	
19.10.07	John Fewkes L PTS 8 Doncaster	
07.03.08	Scott Haywood L PTS 6 Nottingham	
30.04.08	Dean Harrison L PTS 8 Wolverhampton	
06.06.08	Graeme Higginson L RSC 10 Stoke	
	(British Masters L.Welterweight Title Challenge)	

Career: 35 contests, won 13, drew 1, lost 21.

Gavin Reid   Philip Sharkey

Gavin Reid
Redcar. *Born* Aberdeen, 17 November, 1978
S.Bantamweight. *Ht* 5'8½"
Manager M. Marsden

09.06.07	Neil Marston W CO 2 Middlesbrough	
15.07.07	Delroy Spencer W PTS 6 Hartlepool	
26.10.07	Mark Moran L PTS 4 Wigan	
25.11.07	Stuart McFadyen W RSC 5 Colne	
08.02.08	Tony McQuade W PTS 4 Peterlee	
22.02.08	Andrew Kooner L RSC 8 Bethnal Green	
09.05.08	John Donnelly W CO 4 Middlesbrough	

Career: 7 contests, won 5, lost 2.

Pele Reid   Philip Sharkey

Pele Reid

Birmingham. *Born* Birmingham, 11 January, 1973
Heavyweight. Former Undefeated WBO Inter-Continental Heavyweight Champion. *Ht* 6'3"
Manager R. Woodhall

24.11.95	Gary Williams W RSC 1 Manchester
20.01.96	Joey Paladino W RSC 1 Mansfield
26.01.96	Vance Idiens W RSC 1 Brighton
11.05.96	Keith Fletcher W CO 1 Bethnal Green
25.06.96	Andy Lambert W CO 1 Mansfield
12.10.96	Eduardo Carranza W CO 2 Milan, Italy
02.11.96	Ricky Sullivan W RSC 2 Garmisch, Germany
25.02.97	Michael Murray W RSC 1 Sheffield
28.06.97	Ricardo Kennedy W RSC 1 Norwich *(Vacant WBO Inter-Continental Heavyweight Title)*
11.10.97	Eli Dixon W CO 9 Sheffield *(WBO Inter-Continental Heavyweight Title Defence)*
15.11.97	Albert Call W RSC 2 Bristol
06.06.98	Wayne Llewelyn W CO 1 Liverpool *(Elim. British Heavyweight Title)*
19.09.98	Biko Botowamungo W RTD 3 Oberhausen, Germany
30.01.99	Julius Francis L RSC 3 Bethnal Green *(British & Commonwealth Heavyweight Title Challenges)*
26.06.99	Orlin Norris L RSC 1 Millwall
22.01.00	Jacklord Jacobs L RSC 2 Birmingham
04.10.01	Mal Rice W PTS 4 Finsbury
13.12.01	Derek McCafferty W RSC 3 Leicester Square
27.01.02	Luke Simpkin DREW 4 Streatham
09.05.02	Michael Sprott L RSC 7 Leicester Square *(Vacant WBF European Heavyweight Title)*
06.09.02	Derek McCafferty DREW 4 Bethnal Green
15.10.02	Joseph Chingangu W RSC 3 Bethnal Green
01.12.06	Paul King W RSC 6 Birmingham
17.03.07	Roman Suchoterin W PTS 6 Birmingham
01.06.07	Chris Woollas W CO 1 Birmingham
18.04.08	John McDermott L RSC 2 Bethnal Green *(Vacant English Heavyweight Title)*

Career: 26 contests, won 19, drew 2, lost 5.

Robin Reid

Runcorn. Liverpool, 19 February, 1971
S.Middleweight. Former IBO S.Middleweight Champion. Former Undefeated WBF S.Middleweight Champion. Former WBC S.Middleweight Champion. *Ht* 5'9"
Manager Self

27.02.93	Mark Dawson W RSC 1 Dagenham
06.03.93	Julian Eavis W RSC 2 Glasgow
10.04.93	Andrew Furlong W PTS 6 Swansea
10.09.93	Juan Garcia W PTS 6 San Antonio, Texas, USA
09.10.93	Ernie Loveridge W PTS 4 Manchester
18.12.93	Danny Juma DREW 6 Manchester
09.04.94	Kesem Clayton W RSC 1 Mansfield
04.06.94	Andrew Furlong W RSC 2 Cardiff
17.08.94	Andrew Jervis W RSC 1 Sheffield
19.11.94	Chris Richards W RSC 3 Cardiff
04.02.95	Bruno Westenberghs W RSC 1 Cardiff
04.03.95	Marvin O'Brien W RSC 6 Livingston
06.05.95	Steve Goodwin W CO 1 Shepton Mallet
10.06.95	Martin Jolley W CO 1 Manchester
22.07.95	John Duckworth W PTS 8 Millwall
15.09.95	Trevor Ambrose W CO 5 Mansfield
10.11.95	Danny Juma W PTS 8 Derby
26.01.96	Stinger Mason W RSC 2 Brighton
16.03.96	Andrew Flute W RSC 7 Glasgow
26.04.96	Hunter Clay W RSC 1 Cardiff
08.06.96	Mark Dawson W RSC 5 Newcastle
31.08.96	Don Pendleton W RTD 4 Dublin
12.10.96	Vincenzo Nardiello W CO 7 Milan, Italy *(WBC S. Middleweight Title Challenge)*
08.02.97	Giovanni Pretorius W RSC 7 Millwall *(WBC S. Middleweight Title Defence)*
03.05.97	Henry Wharton W PTS 12 Manchester *(WBC S. Middleweight Title Defence)*
11.09.97	Hassine Cherifi W PTS 12 Widnes *(WBC S. Middleweight Title Defence)*
19.12.97	Thulani Malinga L PTS 12 Millwall *(WBC S. Middleweight Title Defence)*
18.04.98	Graham Townsend W RSC 6 Manchester
13.02.99	Joe Calzaghe L PTS 12 Newcastle *(WBO S. Middleweight Title Challenge)*
24.06.00	Silvio Branco L PTS 12 Glasgow *(WBU S. Middleweight Title Challenge)*
08.12.00	Mike Gormley W RSC 1 Crystal Palace *(Vacant WBF S. Middleweight Title)*
19.05.01	Roman Babaev W RSC 3 Wembley *(WBF S. Middleweight Title Defence)*
14.07.01	Soon Botes W RSC 4 Liverpool *(WBF S.Middleweight Title Defence)*
20.10.01	Jorge Sclarandi W CO 3 Glasgow *(WBF S. Middleweight Title Defence)*
19.12.01	Julio Cesar Vasquez W PTS 12 Coventry *(WBF S. Middleweight Title Defence)*
10.07.02	Francisco Mora W PTS 12 Wembley *(WBF S. Middleweight Title Defence)*
29.11.02	Mondili Mbonambi W RSC 2 Liverpool
05.04.03	Enrique Carlos Campos W RSC 8 Leipzig, Germany
04.10.03	Willard Lewis W RSC 6 Zwickau, Germany
24.10.03	Dmitri Adamovich W CO 4 Bethnal Green
13.12.03	Sven Ottke L PTS 12 Nuremberg, Germany *(WBA & IBF S.Middleweight Title Challenges)*
26.06.04	Brian Magee W PTS 12 Belfast *(IBO S.Middleweight Title Challenge)*
13.02.05	Ramdane Serdjane W PTS 6 Brentwood
06.08.05	Jeff Lacy L RTD 8 Tampa, Florida, USA *(IBF S.Middleweight Title Challenge. IBO S.Middleweight Title Defence)*
30.03.07	Jesse Brinkley W PTS 8 Newcastle
09.11.07	Carl Froch L RTD 5 Nottingham *(British S.Middleweight Title Challenge)*

Career: 46 contests, won 39, drew 1, lost 6.

(Marcello) Cello Renda

Peterborough. *Born* Peterborough, 4 June, 1985
Middleweight. Former Undefeated British Masters Middleweight Champion. *Ht* 5'11"
Manager I. Pauly

30.09.04	Mark Ellwood W RSC 2 Hull
04.11.04	Joey Vegas L RSC 3 Piccadilly
12.12.04	Scott Forsyth W RSC 1 Glasgow
21.02.05	Tom Cannon W PTS 6 Peterborough
11.03.05	Ricardo Samms L PTS 4 Doncaster
02.06.05	Michael Banbula DREW 6 Peterborough
16.10.05	Howard Clarke W PTS 4 Peterborough
12.12.05	Robert Burton W CO 1 Peterborough
10.02.06	Conroy McIntosh W RSC 1 Plymouth
30.03.06	Terry Adams W PTS 4 Peterborough
15.06.06	Gatis Skuja W PTS 4 Peterborough
23.06.06	Howard Clarke W PTS 8 Birmingham
08.09.06	Hamed Jamali W RSC 1 Birmingham
26.10.06	George Katsimpas L RSC 2 Wolverhampton
07.12.06	Hussain Osman W RSC 4 Peterborough
23.02.07	Vince Baldassara W CO 3 Birmingham
30.03.07	Ayitey Powers L RSC 2 Peterborough
29.06.07	Prince Arron L PTS 10 Manchester *(Vacant British Masters Middleweight Title)*
16.09.07	Steve Ede W RSC 2 Southampton *(Vacant British Masters Middleweight Title)*
10.12.07	Ryan Rowlinson W RTD 4 Peterborough *(British Masters Middleweight Title Defence)*
08.03.08	Paul Smith L RSC 6 Greenwich *(Vacant English Middleweight Title)*

Career: 21 contests, won 14, drew 1, lost 6.

Danny Reynolds

Leeds. *Born* Leeds, 12 May, 1978
Central Area L.Middleweight Champion. *Ht* 5'8"
Manager M. Bateson

08.11.05	Karl Taylor W RSC 4 Leeds
28.02.06	Gary Coombes W CO 1 Leeds
20.03.06	Geraint Harvey W RTD 2 Leeds
09.05.06	Darren Gethin DREW 4 Leeds
28.05.06	Terry Adams W RSC 1 Wakefield
03.12.06	Prince Arron W PTS 6 Wakefield
22.02.07	Anthony Young W RSC 4 Leeds
06.05.07	Ben Hudson W PTS 8 Leeds
14.06.07	Surinder Sekhon W PTS 6 Leeds
19.10.07	Gatis Skuja W PTS 6 Doncaster
15.11.07	Rocky Muscus W PTS 6 Leeds
21.02.08	Rocky Muscus W RSC 2 Leeds
28.03.08	Jason Rushton W RSC 1 Barnsley *(Central Area L.Middleweight Title Challenge)*

Career: 13 contests, won 12, drew 1.

Darren Rhodes

Leeds. *Born* Leeds, 16 September, 1975
S.Middleweight. *Ht* 5'11"
Manager Self

18.07.98	Andy Kemp W RSC 1 Sheffield
10.10.98	Perry Ayres W CO 2 Bethnal Green
27.02.99	Gareth Lovell W PTS 4 Oldham
01.05.99	Carlton Williams W RSC 4 Crystal Palace
29.05.99	Sean Pritchard DREW 4 Halifax
09.10.99	Leigh Wicks W PTS 4 Manchester
11.12.99	Leigh Wicks W PTS 4 Liverpool
25.03.00	Leigh Wicks W PTS 4 Liverpool
29.05.00	Dean Ashton W RSC 3 Manchester
08.07.00	Jason Collins DREW 4 Widnes

04.09.00	Jason Collins L PTS 4 Manchester
11.12.00	Paul Wesley W PTS 4 Widnes
17.03.01	Andrew Facey W PTS 4 Manchester
07.07.01	Wayne Elcock L PTS 4 Manchester
24.11.01	Simeon Cover W RSC 5 Wakefield
02.03.02	Andrew Facey L RSC 6 Wakefield
	(Vacant Central Area Middleweight Title)
21.05.02	Hussain Osman L PTS 10 Custom House
15.06.02	Harry Butler W PTS 4 Leeds
28.09.02	Martin Thompson W PTS 8 Wakefield
09.11.02	Wayne Pinder L RSC 4 Altrincham
12.04.03	Mihaly Kotai L PTS 10 Bethnal Green
10.05.03	Lee Murtagh W PTS 6 Huddersfield
05.07.03	Darren Bruce W RSC 3 Brentwood
06.09.03	Scott Dixon DREW 6 Huddersfield
04.12.03	Steve Roberts W CO 6 Huddersfield
10.04.04	Michael Jones L RSC 3 Manchester
	(Final Elim. British L.Middleweight Title)
12.11.04	Thomas McDonagh L PTS 10 Halifax
	(Elim. British L.Middleweight Title)
07.04.05	Wayne Elcock L CO 1 Birmingham
25.09.05	Howard Clarke W PTS 6 Leeds
13.11.05	Ernie Smith W PTS 6 Leeds
23.02.06	Peter Dunn W PTS 6 Leeds
09.09.06	Jozsef Nagy L PTS 12 Szentes, Hungary
	(Vacant IBF Inter-Continental S.Middleweight Title)
03.12.06	Robert Burton W PTS 6 Wakefield
15.02.07	Darren McDermott L RSC 5 Dudley
	(Elim.British Middleweight Title)
25.03.07	Jason McKay L PTS 6 Dublin
06.05.07	Dean Walker W PTS 4 Leeds
25.08.07	Matthew Macklin L CO 4 Dublin
01.12.07	Kevin Concepcion L RSC 5 Coventry
28.03.08	Kevin Concepcion L CO 4 Barnsley
Career: 39 contests, won 21, drew 3, lost 15.	

Ryan Rhodes   Philip Sharkey

Ryan Rhodes

Sheffield. *Born* Sheffield, 20 November, 1976
British L.Middleweight Champion.
Former Undefeated WBO Inter-Continental Middleweight Champion.
Former Undefeated IBF Inter-Continental L.Middleweight Champion. *Ht* 5'8½"
Manager F. Warren/D. Coldwell

04.02.95	Lee Crocker W RSC 2 Cardiff
04.03.95	Shamus Casey W CO 1 Livingston
06.05.95	Chris Richards W PTS 6 Shepton Mallet
15.09.95	John Rice W RSC 2 Mansfield
10.11.95	Mark Dawson W PTS 6 Derby
20.01.96	John Duckworth W RSC 2 Mansfield
26.01.96	Martin Jolley W CO 3 Brighton
11.05.96	Martin Jolley W RSC 2 Bethnal Green
25.06.96	Roy Chipperfield W RSC 1 Mansfield
14.09.96	Del Bryan W PTS 6 Sheffield
14.12.96	Paul Jones W RSC 8 Sheffield
	(Vacant British L. Middleweight Title)
25.02.97	Peter Waudby W CO 1 Sheffield
	(British L. Middleweight Title Defence)
14.03.97	Del Bryan W RSC 7 Reading
	(British L. Middleweight Title Defence)
12.04.97	Lindon Scarlett W RSC 1 Sheffield
	(Vacant IBF Inter-Continental L. Middleweight Title)
02.08.97	Ed Griffin W RSC 2 Barnsley
	(IBF Inter-Continental L. Middleweight Title Defence. Vacant WBO L. Middleweight Title)
11.10.97	Yuri Epifantsev W RSC 2 Sheffield
	(Final Elim. WBO Middleweight Title)
13.12.97	Otis Grant L PTS 12 Sheffield
	(Vacant WBO Middleweight Title)
18.07.98	Lorant Szabo W RSC 8 Sheffield
	(WBO Inter-Continental Middleweight Title Challenge)
28.11.98	Fidel Avendano W RSC 1 Sheffield
	(WBO Inter-Continental Middleweight Title Defence)
27.03.99	Peter Mason W RSC 1 Derby
17.07.99	Jason Matthews L CO 2 Doncaster
	(Vacant WBO Middleweight Title)
15.01.00	Eddie Haley W RSC 5 Doncaster
16.05.00	Ojay Abrahams W PTS 6 Warrington
21.10.00	Michael Alexander W PTS 6 Wembley
16.12.00	Howard Clarke W PTS 6 Sheffield
21.07.01	Youri Tsarenko W PTS 6 Sheffield
27.10.01	Jason Collins W PTS 4 Manchester
16.03.02	Lee Blundell L RSC 3 Bethnal Green
	(Vacant WBF Inter-Continental Middleweight Title)
16.04.03	Paul Wesley W CO 3 Nottingham
25.07.03	Alan Gilbert W RSC 5 Norwich
11.12.03	Peter Jackson W PTS 6 Bethnal Green
12.03.04	Scott Dixon W PTS 8 Nottingham
16.04.04	Tomas da Silva W RSC 4 Bradford
22.04.05	Peter Jackson W PTS 6 Barnsley
03.06.05	Craig Lynch W RSC 3 Manchester
16.07.05	Alan Gilbert W RSC 2 Bolton
25.10.05	Hussain Osman W RTD 4 Preston
01.06.06	Jevgenijs Andrejevs W PTS 8 Barnsley
08.07.06	Gary Lockett L PTS 12 Cardiff
	(WBU Middleweight Title Challenge)
03.06.07	Paul Buchanan W RSC 1 Barnsley
13.10.07	Olufemi Moses W RSC 2 Barnsley
05.12.07	Manoocha Salari W RSC 4 Sheffield
18.04.08	Gary Woolcombe W CO 9 Bethnal Green
	(British L.Middleweight Title Challenge)
Career: 43 contests, won 39, lost 4.	

Rhys Roberts

Manchester. *Born* Manchester, 3 June, 1989
S.Bantamweight. *Ht* 5'6"
Manager Brian Hughes/W. Dixon

30.06.07	Delroy Spencer W PTS 6 Manchester
11.08.07	Delroy Spencer W PTS 6 Liverpool
07.06.08	Shaun Walton W PTS 4 Wigan
Career: 3 contests, won 3.	

Mike Robinson

Liverpool. *Born* Liverpool, 30 April, 1985
S.Bantamweight. *Ht* 5'5¼"
Manager S. Wood

26.04.08	Delroy Spencer W PTS 6 Wigan
23.05.08	Mike Holloway W PTS 4 Wigan
Career: 2 contests, won 2.	

Martin Rogan   Philip Sharkey

Martin Rogan

Belfast. *Born* Belfast, 1 May, 1971
Heavyweight. *Ht* 6'3"
Manager Self

28.10.04	Lee Mountford W RSC 1 Belfast
18.03.05	Billy Bessey W PTS 4 Belfast
04.06.05	Tony Booth W RSC 2 Manchester
20.05.06	Darren Morgan W PTS 4 Belfast
07.10.06	Paul King W PTS 6 Belfast
26.10.06	Jevgenijs Stamburskis W RSC 3 Belfast
13.10.07	Radcliffe Green W RSC 2 Belfast
11.04.08	Alex Ibbs W RSC 2 Bethnal Green
11.04.08	Dave Ferguson W PTS 3 Bethnal Green
11.04.08	David Dolan W PTS 3 Bethnal Green
Career: 10 contests, won 10.	

Brian Rose

Blackpool. *Born* Birmingham, 2 February, 1985
Middleweight. *Ht* 6'0"
Manager S. Wood

14.12.05	Geraint Harvey W PTS 6 Blackpool
25.02.07	Ernie Smith W PTS 6 Manchester
06.05.07	David Kirk W PTS 6 Altrincham
31.05.07	Tony Randell W PTS 6 Manchester
24.06.07	Justin Barnes W RSC 2 Wigan
22.09.07	Lee Noble W PTS 4 Wigan
08.12.07	Shaun Farmer W RSC 3 Wigan
16.02.08	Manoocha Salari DREW 6 Blackpool
26.04.08	Ernie Smith W PTS 4 Wigan
15.06.08	Kobe Vandekerkhove W PTS 6 St Helens
Career: 10 contests, won 9, drew 1.	

165

Ryan Rowlinson

Rotherham. *Born* Mexborough, 4 June, 1979
S.Middleweight. *Ht* 6'0"
Manager Self

15.12.05	Dave Pearson W PTS 6 Cleethorpes
18.02.06	Craig Lynch DREW 4 Edinburgh
01.06.06	Robert Burton LPTS 4 Barnsley
18.06.06	Craig Bunn L PTS 6 Manchester
08.07.06	Kerry Hope L PTS 4 Cardiff
01.10.06	Ernie Smith W PTS 6 Rotherham
09.10.06	Kevin Concepcion L PTS 6 Bedworth
06.12.06	Tony Randell DREW 6 Rotherham
16.06.07	Nigel Travis L PTS 6 Bolton
19.10.07	Lee Nicholson L PTS 4 Doncaster
10.12.07	Cello Renda L RTD 4 Peterborough
	(British Masters Middleweight Title Challenge)

Career: 11 contests, won 2, drew 2, lost 7.

Paul Royston   Philip Sharkey

Paul Royston

Sheffield. *Born* Rotherham, 16 January, 1985
L.Middleweight. *Ht* 5'10"
Manager D. Coldwell

24.02.07	Stuart Jeffrey L PTS 6 Manchester
26.03.07	Jon Musgrave L PTS 6 Glasgow
15.04.07	Thomas Flynn W RSC 3 Barnsley
06.05.07	Johnny Enigma L PTS 6 Altrincham
03.06.07	Steve Cooper L PTS 6 Barnsley
30.06.07	Willie Thompson L PTS 4 Belfast
08.09.07	Danny Connors L PTS 4 Sutton in Ashfield
15.09.07	Stevie Weir L PTS 6 Paisley
28.09.07	Leigh Hallet W RSC 3 Birmingham
13.10.07	Craig Tomes L PTS 6 Barnsley
25.10.07	Rob Kenney L PTS 6 Wolverhampton
10.11.07	Tommy Heffron L PTS 6 Stalybridge
23.11.07	Lee Edwards L PTS 6 Sheffield
15.12.07	Kris Carslaw L PTS 4 Edinburgh
02.02.08	Sam Webb L PTS 6 Canning Town
16.02.08	Lester Walsh L PTS 6 Leicester
23.02.08	Shaun Farmer L PTS 6 Liverpool
16.03.08	Chris Thompson W PTS 6 Sheffield
30.03.08	Peter Dunn L PTS 4 Colne
18.04.08	Ryan Ashworth L PTS 6 Houghton le Spring
30.04.08	Rob Kenney L PTS 6 Wolverhampton

17.05.08	Muhsen Nasser L PTS 4 Sheffield
30.05.08	Nasser Al Harbi L PTS 6 Birmingham
07.06.08	Joe McNally L PTS 4 Wigan
20.06.08	Jamie Ball L PTS 4 Wolverhampton

Career: 25 contests, won 3, lost 22.

Sergei Rozhakmens

Sutton in Ashfield. *Born* Riga, Latvia, 6 May, 1979
Lightweight. *Ht* 5'7"
Manager M. Scriven

13.11.02	Sergei Lazarenko W RSC 1 Tallin, Estonia
22.02.03	Leonti Voronchuk L RSC 3 Narva, Estonia
20.02.06	Jimmy Gilhaney L PTS 6 Glasgow
06.05.06	Jamie McIlroy L PTS 6 Irvine
18.06.06	Abdul Rashid L PTS 6 Manchester
15.09.06	Andy Davis L RSC 4 Newport
10.11.06	Shaun Walton L PTS 6 Telford
20.11.06	Brian Murphy L PTS 6 Glasgow
30.11.06	Neil Marston L PTS 6 Piccadilly
01.02.07	Kim Poulsen L RSC 5 Piccadilly
01.04.07	Shaun Walton DREW 6 Shrewsbury
14.04.07	Sean Hughes L PTS 6 Wakefield
29.04.07	Craig Johnson L PTS 6 Birmingham
06.05.07	Davey Watson L PTS 6 Darlington
01.06.07	Sid Razak W PTS 6 Birmingham
09.06.07	James McElvaney L PTS 6 Middlesbrough
21.06.07	Carl Griffiths L PTS 6 Peterborough
30.06.07	Amir Unsworth L PTS 6 Manchester
14.07.07	Vinny Mitchell L RSC 3 Greenwich
14.09.07	John Donnelly L PTS 4 Kirkcaldy
23.09.07	Mark Dawes L PTS 6 Hartlepool
05.10.07	Sean Hughes L PTS 6 Sunderland
12.10.07	Jon Kays L RSC 4 Leeds
15.11.07	Craig O'Neile L RSC 2 Leeds
23.02.08	Johnny Greaves L RSC 1 Newark

Career: 25 contests, won 2, drew 1, lost 22.

Sergei Rozhakmens   Philip Sharkey

John Ruddock

Stoke. *Born* Coventry, 28 October, 1973
S.Middleweight. *Ht* 5'9¼"
Manager Self

10.03.06	Matthew Hough L PTS 6 Walsall
28.09.07	Matthew Hough L RSC 3 Coventry
10.12.07	David Gentles L PTS 6 Birmingham
25.02.08	David Gentles L RSC 2 Birmingham

Career: 4 contests, lost 4.

Jason Rushton

Doncaster. *Born* Doncaster, 15 February, 1983
Former Central Area L.Middleweight Champion. *Ht* 5'10"
Manager Self

27.10.01	Ram Singh W PTS 6 Manchester
09.02.02	Brian Gifford W RSC 1 Manchester
01.06.02	Tony Smith W PTS 4 Manchester
08.11.02	Gary Hadwin W CO 4 Doncaster
21.02.03	Wayne Shepherd W PTS 6 Doncaster
05.09.03	Harry Butler W PTS 4 Doncaster
27.09.03	Jimi Hendricks W PTS 4 Manchester
06.03.04	Peter Dunn W PTS 6 Renfrew
06.05.04	Peter Dunn W PTS 4 Barnsley
03.09.04	Ernie Smith W PTS 4 Doncaster
29.10.04	Brian Coleman W PTS 6 Doncaster
04.02.05	Howard Clarke W PTS 4 Doncaster
11.03.05	Lee Armstrong W PTS 10 Doncaster
	(Vacant Central Area L.Middleweight Title)
20.05.05	Lee Murtagh L PTS 10 Doncaster
	(Central Area L.Middleweight Title Defence)
02.12.05	Joe Mitchell W PTS 6 Doncaster
03.03.06	Darren Gethin L PTS 6 Doncaster
21.04.06	Peter Dunn W PTS 6 Doncaster
09.06.06	Mark Phillips W PTS 6 Doncaster
13.10.06	Lee Noble L PTS 6 Doncaster
23.02.07	Davey Jones W CO 7 Doncaster
	(Vacant Central Area L.Middleweight Title)
21.09.07	Gary Woolcombe L RSC 7 Bethnal Green
28.03.08	Danny Reynolds L RSC 1 Barnsley
	(Central Area L.Middleweight Title Defence)
13.06.08	Jay Morris W PTS 6 Portsmouth

Career: 23 contests, won 18, lost 5.

Stephen Russell

Paisley. *Born* Paisley, 29 December, 1987
Featherweight. *Ht* 5'6"
Manager Barry Hughes

27.10.06	Shaun Doherty W PTS 6 Glasgow
26.01.07	Abdul Mougharbel W PTS 6 Glasgow
05.05.07	Delroy Spencer W PTS 4 Glasgow
15.09.07	Robert Bunford W PTS 6 Paisley
29.03.08	Shaun Walton W PTS 4 Glasgow

Career: 5 contests, won 5.

Dave Ryan

Derby. *Born* Derby, 6 May, 1988
Welterweight. *Ht* 5'10"
Manager C. Mitchell

31.03.07	Deniss Sirjatovs W PTS 6 Derby
19.05.07	Leonard Lothian W PTS 6 Nottingham
16.09.07	Albi Hunt W RSC 2 Derby
03.11.07	Baz Carey W PTS 6 Derby
30.11.07	Scott Woolford L PTS 4 Newham
10.05.08	Carl Allen W PTS 4 Nottingham
22.06.08	Carl Allen W PTS 8 Derby

Career: 7 contests, won 6, lost 1.

Silence Saheed   Philip Sharkey

(Saheed) Silence Saheed (Salawu)

Canning Town. *Born* Ibadan, Nigeria, 1
January, 1978
L.Welterweight. *Ht* 5'6"
Manager D. Lutaaya

28.03.03	Martin Hardcastle W PTS 4 Millwall
10.04.03	Ceri Hall DREW 4 Clydach
27.05.03	Francis Barrett W RSC 1 Dagenham
11.10.03	Wayne Wheeler W RSC 1 Portsmouth
15.11.03	Gary Greenwood W RTD 1 Coventry
21.11.03	Jaz Virdee W RSC 2 Millwall
01.05.04	Alan Temple L DIS 8 Gravesend
	(Vacant British Masters Lightweight Title)
17.09.04	Scott Lawton L PTS 6 Sheffield
24.09.04	James Gorman W PTS 6 Millwall
09.10.04	Jonathan Thaxton L PTS 6 Norwich
22.10.04	Nigel Wright L PTS 8 Edinburgh
10.04.05	Lenny Daws L PTS 6 Brentwood
01.07.05	Gareth Couch L PTS 4 Fulham
30.09.05	Karl David W PTS 6 Carmarthen
21.10.05	Ted Bami L PTS 6 Bethnal Green
17.11.05	Andrew Murray L PTS 4 Piccadilly
24.11.05	Ceri Hall L PTS 6 Clydach
02.02.06	Sam Rukundo L PTS 10 Holborn
	(Vacant British Masters Lightweight Title)
18.02.06	Lee McAllister L PTS 4 Edinburgh
04.03.06	David Barnes L PTS 4 Manchester
23.03.06	Imad Khamis W RSC 5 The Strand
02.04.06	Leo O'Reilly DREW 6 Bethnal Green
10.07.06	Gary O'Connor L PTS 6 Manchester
15.09.06	John O'Donnell L PTS 6 Muswell Hill
11.06.06	Stephen Haughian L PTS 6 Dublin
01.12.06	Anthony Maynard L PTS 6 Birmingham
09.12.06	Paul McCloskey L PTS 4 Canning Town
23.02.07	Olufemi Moses L PTS 4 Manchester
30.03.07	Michael Lomax DREW 6 Crawley
03.11.07	Barrie Jones L PTS 4 Cardiff
09.12.07	Craig Docherty L PTS 6 Glasgow
22.02.08	Ricky Burns L RSC 3 Motherwell
15.06.08	Mark McCullough W PTS 4 Bethnal Green

Career: 33 contests, won 9, drew 3, lost 21.

Tony Salam

Romford. *Born* Nigeria, 24 September,
1983
L.Heavyweight. *Ht* 6'0"
Manager Self

03.11.06	Csaba Andras W RSC 2 Barnsley
26.01.07	Paul David W PTS 4 Dagenham
09.03.07	Nicki Taylor W RSC 1 Dagenham
27.04.07	John Anthony W PTS 4 Wembley
15.06.07	Nick Okoth W PTS 4 Crystal Palace
19.10.07	Ovill McKenzie W PTS 6 Doncaster
30.11.07	Carl Wild W RTD 4 Newham
01.02.08	Courtney Fry L CO 6 Bethnal Green

Career: 8 contests, won 7, lost 1.

Manoocha Salari   Les Clark

Manoocha Salari

Worksop. *Born* Iran, 25 May, 1974
Midlands Area L.Middleweight Champion.
Ht 5'9½"
Manager J. Ingle

12.11.05	Danny Johnston W RSC 5 Stoke
25.11.05	Paul McInnes W PTS 6 Walsall
12.12.05	Simon Sherrington DREW 6 Birmingham
28.01.06	Martin Concepcion W RSC 2 Nottingham
26.02.06	Gokhan Kazaz DREW 4 Dagenham
13.05.06	Geard Ajetovic L RSC 4 Sheffield
18.11.06	Kerry Hope L RSC 2 Newport
03.03.07	Matt Galer W RSC 8 Burton
	(Midlands Area L.Middleweight Title Challenge)
13.04.07	Mark Thompson L RSC 1 Altrincham
23.11.07	Stuart Brookes L PTS 6 Rotherham
05.12.07	Ryan Rhodes L RSC 4 Sheffield
16.02.08	Brian Rose DREW 6 Blackpool
05.04.08	Denton Vassell L PTS 4 Bolton
22.06.08	Matthew Hainy L PTS 6 Derby

Career: 14 contests, won 4, drew 3, lost 7

Scott Sandmann

Manchester. *Born* London, 4 October, 1981
L.Welterweight. *Ht* 5'10¼"
Manager J. Gallagher

28.09.07	Craig Tomes W PTS 6 Preston
12.10.07	Leonard Lothian W PTS 4 Peterlee
23.11.07	Chris Mullen L PTS 6 Houghton le Spring
05.06.08	Adil Anwar L RSC 1 Leeds

Career: 4 contests, won 2, lost 2.

Laura Saperstein   Philip Sharkey

Laura Saperstein

Tottenham. *Born* Australia, 29 August, 1971
Lightweight. *Ht* 5'6¼"
Manager C. Hall

18.11.07	Borislava Goranova W PTS 4 Tooting
01.02.08	Olga Varchenko W PTS 4 Bethnal Green
18.04.08	Kristine Shergold W PTS 4 Bethnal Green

Career: 3 contests, won 3.

Billy Saunders

Sidcup. *Born* Harold Wood, 25 December, 1987
L.Middleweight. *Ht* 5'9¼"
Manager F. Warren

13.10.07	David Kirk W PTS 4 Bethnal Green

Career: 1 contest, won 1.

Chris Saunders

Barnsley. *Born* Barnsley, 15 August, 1969
Welterweight. Former British & English
Welterweight Champion. *Ht* 5'8"
Manager Self

22.02.90	Malcolm Melvin W PTS 4 Hull
10.04.90	Mike Morrison W PTS 6 Doncaster
20.05.90	Justin Graham W RSC 3 Sheffield
29.11.90	Ross Hale L PTS 6 Bayswater
05.03.91	Rocky Ferrari L PTS 4 Glasgow
19.03.91	Richard Woolgar W RSC 3 Leicester
26.03.91	Felix Kelly L PTS 6 Bethnal Green
17.04.91	Billy Schwer L RSC 1 Kensington
16.05.91	Richard Burton L PTS 6 Liverpool
06.06.91	Mark Tibbs W RSC 6 Barking
30.06.91	Billy Schwer L RSC 3 Southwark
01.08.91	James Jiora W PTS 6 Dewsbury

167

03.10.91 Gary Flear L PTS 6 Burton
24.10.91 Ron Shinkwin W PTS 6 Dunstable
21.11.91 J. P. Matthews L RSC 4 Burton
30.01.92 John O. Johnson L PTS 6 Southampton
11.02.92 Eddie King W RSC 4 Wolverhampton
27.02.92 Richard Burton L PTS 10 Liverpool
(*Vacant Central Area L. Welterweight Title*)
09.09.92 John O. Johnson DREW 6 Stoke
01.10.92 Mark McCreath L RSC 4 Telford
01.12.92 Shea Neary L PTS 6 Liverpool
22.02.93 Cham Joof L PTS 4 Eltham
16.03.93 Mark Elliot L PTS 6 Wolverhampton
26.04.93 Dean Hollington W RSC 5 Lewisham
23.10.93 Michael Smyth L PTS 6 Cardiff
02.12.93 Rob Stewart L PTS 4 Sheffield
03.03.94 Kevin Lueshing W RSC 4 Ebbw Vale
04.06.94 Jose Varela W CO 2 Dortmund, Germany
26.08.94 Julian Eavis W PTS 6 Barnsley
26.09.94 Julian Eavis W PTS 6 Cleethorpes
26.10.94 Lindon Scarlett W PTS 8 Leeds
17.12.94 Roberto Welin W RSC 7 Cagliari, Italy
15.09.95 Del Bryan W PTS 12 Mansfield
(*British Welterweight Title Challenge*)
13.02.96 Kevin Lueshing L RSC 3 Bethnal Green
(*British Welterweight Title Defence*)
25.06.96 Michael Carruth L RSC 10 Mansfield
09.06.97 Derek Roche L RSC 4 Bradford
(*Central Area Welterweight Title Challenge. Elim. British Welterweight Title*)
27.02.98 Scott Dixon L PTS 10 Glasgow
(*Elim. British Welterweight Title*)
17.04.99 Michael Carruth L RSC 5 Dublin
08.12.01 David Kirk W CO 2 Chesterfield
15.06.02 Arv Mittoo W PTS 6 Norwich
24.09.02 Robert Pacuraru W RTD 4 Gran Canaria, Spain
09.02.03 Richard Swallow W PTS 4 Bradford
03.04.04 Marcus Portman W RSC 1 Sheffield
(*Vacant English Welterweight Title*)
19.06.04 Peter Dunn W PTS 4 Muswell Hill
01.10.04 Michael Jennings L RTD 5 Manchester
(*English Welterweight Title Defence*)
15.04.07 Tye Williams W PTS 6 Barnsley
20.11.07 Frank Shabani L RTD 4 Vilamoura, Portugal
Career: 47 contests, won 23, drew 1, lost 23.

Tommy Saunders

Hatfield. *Born* Hatfield, 17 February, 1987
Cruiserweight. *Ht* 5'11¼"
Manager F. Warren

28.10.06 Varuzhan Davtyan W PTS 4 Bethnal Green
17.02.07 Gary Thompson W PTS 4 Wembley
02.02.08 James Tucker W PTS 4 Canning Town
14.06.08 Michael Banbula W RSC 1 Bethnal Green
Career: 4 contests, won 4.

Davey Savage

Glasgow. *Born* Glasgow, 2 July, 1986
S.Bantamweight. *Ht* 5'9¼"
Manager T. Gilmour

08.10.07 Delroy Spencer W PTS 6 Glasgow
24.11.07 Shaun Walton W PTS 6 Clydebank
21.01.08 Shaun Walton W PTS 6 Glasgow
29.02.08 Tony McQuade W PTS 4 Glasgow
06.06.08 Mike Holloway W RSC 4 Glasgow
Career: 5 contests, won 5.

Steve Saville   Philip Sharkey

Steve Saville

Wolverhampton. *Born* Wolverhampton, 29 September, 1976
L.Welterweight. *Ht* 5'4¼"
Manager E. Johnson

08.06.98 Simon Chambers W RSC 2 Birmingham
07.10.98 Dave Hinds W PTS 6 Stoke
26.11.98 Dave Hinds W PTS 6 Edgbaston
14.12.98 Woody Greenaway L PTS 6 Birmingham
27.01.99 Darren Woodley W PTS 6 Stoke
23.03.99 Benny Jones W PTS 6 Wolverhampton
14.06.99 Trevor Tacy L PTS 8 Birmingham
12.10.99 Gary Flear W PTS 6 Wolverhampton
20.10.99 Arv Mittoo W PTS 8 Stoke
08.02.00 Marc Smith W PTS 6 Wolverhampton
13.03.00 Dave Gibson W RSC 6 Birmingham
09.10.00 David Kirk L PTS 8 Birmingham
06.11.00 Woody Greenaway W CO 5 Wolverhampton
28.11.00 Danny Connelly W PTS 8 Brierley Hill
11.12.00 Keith Jones W PTS 8 Birmingham
01.04.01 Gavin Down L RSC 3 Alfreton
(*Vacant Midlands Area L.Welterweight Title*)
13.07.02 Wayne Wheeler W CO 2 Wolverhampton
07.10.02 Gareth Wiltshaw W RSC 3 Birmingham
09.12.02 Keith Jones W PTS 8 Birmingham
20.06.08 Baz Carey W PTS 4 Wolverhampton
11.07.08 Mark Bett W RSC 4 Wigan
Career: 21 contests, won 17, lost 4.

Lindsay Scragg

Wolverhampton. *Born* Wolverhampton, 19 April, 1979
S.Featherweight. *Ht* 5'3¼"
Manager E. Johnson

15.02.07 Valerie Rangeard W RSC 2 Dudley
28.06.07 Yarkor Chavez Annan W PTS 4 Dudley
25.10.07 Olga Michenko W RSC 2 Wolverhampton
28.02.08 Yarkor Chavez Annan W RSC 6 Wolverhampton

30.04.08 Viktoria Oleynik W PTS 6 Wolverhampton
20.06.08 Galina Gumliiska W PTS 4 Wolverhampton
Career: 6 contests, won 6.

Lindsay Scragg   Les Clark

Matt Scriven

Nottingham. *Born* Nottingham, 1 September, 1973
Middleweight. Former Undefeated Midlands Area L.Middleweight Champion. Former British Masters L.Middleweight Champion. *Ht* 5'10"
Manager Self

26.11.97 Shamus Casey W PTS 6 Stoke
08.12.97 Shane Thomas W PTS 6 Bradford
20.03.98 C. J. Jackson L PTS 6 Ilkeston
15.05.98 Lee Bird W RSC 5 Nottingham
08.10.98 Stevie McCready L RTD 3 Sunderland
01.04.99 Adrian Houldey W PTS 6 Birmingham
25.04.99 Danny Thornton L RSC 4 Leeds
27.06.99 Shane Junior L RSC 2 Alfreton
11.09.99 David Arundel L RTD 1 Sheffield
20.03.00 James Docherty L PTS 8 Glasgow
27.03.00 Matt Mowatt L PTS 4 Barnsley
09.04.00 David Matthews W PTS 6 Alfreton
06.06.00 Jackie Townsley L RSC 3 Motherwell
04.11.00 Brett James L RTD 1 Bethnal Green
04.02.01 Mark Paxford L PTS 6 Queensferry
26.02.01 Pedro Thompson W RTD 1 Nottingham
12.03.01 Ernie Smith W PTS 6 Birmingham
20.03.01 James Docherty L RSC 1 Glasgow
21.05.01 Christian Brady L RSC 5 Birmingham
(*Vacant Midlands Area Welterweight Title*)
21.10.01 Neil Bonner NC 1 Glasgow
04.03.02 Danny Parkinson L PTS 6 Bradford
22.04.02 Gary Porter L PTS 6 Glasgow
28.05.02 Peter Dunn W PTS 8 Leeds
14.09.02 Ernie Smith W PTS 6 Newark
29.09.02 James Lee L RTD 4 Shrewsbury
30.11.02 Davey Jones L PTS 6 Newark
16.03.03 Lee Williamson W PTS 10 Nottingham
(*Vacant Midlands Area & British Masters L. Middleweight Titles*)
08.06.03 Wayne Shepherd W PTS 10 Nottingham
(*British Masters L.Middleweight Title Defence*)

15.09.03 Lee Murtagh L DIS 9 Leeds
(British Masters L.Middleweight Title Defence)
12.03.04 David Walker L RSC 3 Nottingham
12.06.04 Matthew Hatton L RSC 4 Manchester
18.09.04 Robert Lloyd-Taylor L RTD 4 Newark
28.01.05 Colin McNeil L PTS 4 Renfrew
06.03.05 Mark Wall W PTS 4 Mansfield
29.04.05 Gary Woolcombe L RSC 4 Southwark
04.06.05 Matthew Hall L RSC 2 Manchester
20.01.06 John O'Donnell L RSC 4 Bethnal Green
04.03.06 Kerry Hope L PTS 4 Manchester
04.11.06 Peter Dunn W PTS 6 Mansfield
23.02.07 James McKinley L PTS 6 Birmingham
17.03.07 Dee Mitchell L RSC 2 Birmingham
29.04.07 Max Maxwell L PTS 4 Birmingham
11.05.07 Shaun Farmer L PTS 6 Sunderland
18.05.07 George Hillyard L PTS 4 Canning Town
31.05.07 Dave Wakefield L PTS 6 Manchester
24.06.07 Martin Marshall L PTS 6 Sunderland
15.07.07 Craig Denton L PTS 6 Hartlepool
15.02.08 Lee Edwards L PTS 6 Sheffield
22.02.08 Paul Burns L PTS 6 Motherwell
21.06.08 Joe Selkirk L PTS 4 Birmingham
Career: 50 contests, won 13, lost 36, no contest 1.

Matt Seawright — Philip Sharkey

Matt Seawright
Tamworth. *Born* Bathgate, 8 February, 1978
Welterweight. *Ht* 5'7"
Manager Self
03.03.07 Jack Perry L RSC 2 Burton
03.05.07 Adam Kelly L PTS 4 Sheffield
29.09.07 Adam Kelly L PTS 4 Sheffield
19.10.07 Charles Paul King L PTS 6 Motherwell
17.11.07 Jimmy Doherty L PTS 4 Stoke
28.02.08 Martin Gordon W PTS 4 Wolverhampton
16.03.08 Curtis Woodhouse L RTD 3 Sheffield
09.06.08 Mark Bett L RSC 5 Glasgow
Career: 8 contests, won 1, lost 7.

Surinder Sekhon
Barnsley. *Born* Birmingham, 4 October, 1979
L.Middleweight. *Ht* 5'9"
Manager T. Schofield/D. Coldwell
05.05.02 Franny Jones L PTS 6 Hartlepool
28.09.02 Peter Dunn W PTS 6 Wakefield
27.02.03 Ryan Kerr L PTS 6 Sunderland
09.03.03 P.J.Maxwell L RSC 1 Shaw
09.09.05 Grzegorz Proksa L PTS 4 Sheffield
30.09.05 Young Muttley L PTS 4 Burton
14.10.05 Paul Burns L PTS 6 Motherwell
12.11.05 Jimmy Doherty L PTS 6 Stoke
11.12.05 Ben Hudson L PTS 6 Chigwell
18.02.06 Scott Lawton DREW 8 Stoke
11.03.06 Paul McCloskey L RSC 1 Newport
14.05.06 Scott Haywood L RSC 1 Derby
03.11.06 Mark Hastie L RSC 1 Glasgow
31.03.07 Luke Gallear W PTS 6 Derby
12.05.07 Aaron Thomas L PTS 4 Stoke
01.06.07 Danny Butler L PTS 6 Birmingham
14.06.07 Danny Reynolds L PTS 6 Leeds
25.08.07 Nicki Smedley L PTS 4 Dublin
15.09.07 Kris Carslaw L PTS 4 Paisley
08.12.07 Jamie Cox L RSC 3 Bolton
Career: 20 contests, won 2, drew 1, lost 17.

Joe Selkirk
Liverpool. *Born* Liverpool, 2 August, 1985
Middleweight. *Ht* 6'0¾"
Manager F. Warren
21.06.08 Matt Scriven W PTS 4 Birmingham
Career: 1 contest, won 1.

Leon Senior
Sydenham. *Born* London, 20 November, 1980
L.Heavyweight. *Ht* 5'11¼"
Manager A. Forbes
18.11.07 Michael Banbula W PTS 4 Tooting
31.01.08 David Gentles L PTS 6 Piccadilly
22.03.08 Sandris Tomson W PTS 4 Dublin
16.05.08 Ricky Strike W PTS 4 Holborn
Career: 4 contests, won 3, lost 1.

Leon Senior — Philip Sharkey

Sam Sexton — Les Clark

Sam Sexton
Norwich. *Born* Norwich, 18 July, 1984
Heavyweight. *Ht* 6'2"
Manager G. Everett
03.09.05 Paul Bonson W PTS 6 Norwich
11.12.05 Jason Callum W PTS 6 Norwich
12.05.06 Istvan Kecskes W PTS 4 Bethnal Green
15.10.06 Lee Mountford W RSC 2 Norwich
16.03.07 Paul King W PTS 6 Norwich
13.10.07 Luke Simpkin W RSC 5 Bethnal Green
12.01.08 Darren Morgan W PTS 6 Bethnal Green
14.06.08 Derek Chisora L RSC 6 Bethnal Green
Career: 8 contests, won 7, lost 1.

Ali Shah
Sheffield. *Born* Blackburn, 16 October, 1986
Welterweight. *Ht* 6'2¼"
Manager J. Ingle
20.04.08 Amir Nadi W PTS 4 Shaw
Career: 1 contest, won 1.

Gary Sheil
Chester. *Born* Chester, 29 June, 1983
Bantamweight. *Ht* 5'2¾"
Manager Self
03.03.06 Jamie McDonnell L PTS 6 Doncaster
23.04.06 Delroy Spencer L PTS 6 Chester
06.05.06 Chris Edwards L PTS 6 Stoke
03.03.07 Usman Ahmed L PTS 6 Alfreton
21.04.07 Scott Quigg L PTS 6 Manchester
16.09.07 Usman Ahmed L PTS 6 Derby
06.10.07 Don Broadhurst L PTS 6 Nottingham
Career: 7 contests, lost 7.

Kristine Shergold
Paignton. *Born* Torquay, 2 March, 1981
S.Featherweight. *Ht* 5'1¼"
Manager J. Feld
18.04.08 Laura Saperstein L PTS 4 Bethnal Green
Career: 1 contest, lost 1.

169

Nadeem Siddique   Philip Sharkey

Nadeem Siddique

Bradford. *Born* Bradford, 28 October, 1977
Central Area Welterweight Champion.
Former Undefeated British Masters
Welterweight Champion. *Ht* 5'8"
Manager J. Ingle

17.11.02	Daniel Thorpe W PTS 4 Bradford
09.02.03	Norman Dhalie W PTS 4 Bradford
13.04.03	Dave Hinds W PTS 4 Bradford
15.06.03	Nigel Senior W PTS 6 Bradford
05.10.03	Jason Nesbitt W PTS 6 Bradford
27.10.03	Daniel Thorpe W PTS 6 Glasgow
07.12.03	Chris Duggan W RSC 2 Bradford
16.01.04	Pete Buckley W PTS 4 Bradford
16.04.04	Arv Mittoo W PTS 6 Bradford
15.05.04	Joel Viney W PTS 6 Aberdeen
24.09.04	Dave Hinds W PTS 4 Nottingham
13.02.05	Jason Nesbitt W PTS 6 Bradford
09.04.05	Pete Buckley W PTS 6 Norwich
08.05.05	Kristian Laight W RSC 7 Bradford
03.06.05	Daniel Thorpe W PTS 6 Hull
13.11.05	Billy Smith W PTS 6 Leeds
25.11.05	Jason Nesbitt W RSC 6 Hull
13.04.06	David Kehoe W PTS 6 Leeds
27.05.07	Tye Williams W RSC 4 Bradford
	(Vacant Central Area & British Masters Welterweight Titles)
07.09.07	Tom Glover W PTS 6 Doncaster
29.03.08	Salaheddine Sarhani W RSC 4 Aberdeen
10.05.08	Alex Brew W CO 2 Nottingham

Career: 22 contests, won 22.

(Paulino) Paulie Silva

Droylsden. *Born* Almada, Portugal, 29 April, 1978
Central Area S.Middleweight Champion. *Ht* 5'10"
Manager Self

28.02.04	Nick Okoth W PTS 6 Manchester
02.04.04	Courtney Fry L PTS 4 Plymouth
24.10.04	Amer Khan L PTS 6 Sheffield
16.09.05	Dan Guthrie W RSC 2 Plymouth
21.04.07	Tony Booth W PTS 6 Manchester
30.06.07	Lee Jones W PTS 6 Manchester
03.12.07	Joey Ainscough W PTS 10 Manchester
	(Vacant Central Area S.Middleweight Title)

Career: 7 contests, won 5, lost 2.

Luke Simpkin

Swadlincote. *Born* Derby, 5 May, 1979
Heavyweight. *Ht* 6'2"
Manager Self

24.09.98	Simon Taylor W CO 3 Edgbaston
16.10.98	Chris P. Bacon L PTS 6 Salford
10.12.98	Jason Flisher W RSC 5 Barking
04.02.99	Danny Watts L CO 3 Lewisham
28.05.99	Tommy Bannister W RSC 4 Liverpool
07.08.99	Owen Beck L PTS 4 Dagenham
11.09.99	Scott Lansdowne L PTS 4 Sheffield
11.03.00	Albert Sosnowski L PTS 4 Kensington
27.03.00	Mark Hobson L PTS 4 Barnsley
29.04.00	Johan Thorbjoernsson L PTS 4 Wembley
23.09.00	Mark Potter L PTS 6 Bethnal Green
30.09.00	Gordon Minors DREW 4 Peterborough
18.11.00	Keith Long L RSC 3 Dagenham
03.02.01	Paul Buttery W RSC 1 Manchester
01.04.01	Wayne Llewelyn L PTS 6 Southwark
24.04.01	Darren Chubbs L PTS 4 Liverpool
06.05.01	Billy Bessey L PTS 6 Hartlepool
09.06.01	John McDermott L PTS 6 Bethnal Green
13.09.01	Mark Krence L PTS 4 Sheffield
10.12.01	Mark Hobson L RTD 3 Liverpool
27.01.02	Pele Reid DREW 4 Streatham
15.03.02	Mike Holden L PTS 6 Millwall
13.04.02	Fola Okesola W PTS 4 Liverpool
10.05.02	Julius Francis DREW 6 Millwall
23.08.02	Mark Potter L PTS 6 Bethnal Green
10.06.03	Mark Krence L RTD 8 Sheffield
	(Vacant Midlands Area Heavyweight Title)
05.09.03	Roman Greenberg L RTD 4 Sheffield
25.04.04	Dave Clarke W RSC 2 Nottingham
18.09.04	Paul King L PTS 6 Newark
02.12.04	Micky Steeds L RSC 3 Crystal Palace
21.02.05	Ian Millarvie L PTS 6 Glasgow
26.04.05	Carl Baker W RSC 4 Leeds
09.07.05	Henry Smith W RSC 3 Bristol
11.09.05	Carl Baker L PTS 10 Kirkby in Ashfield
	(British Masters Heavyweight Title Challenge)
28.01.06	Colin Kenna L PTS 8 Dublin
25.03.06	Istvan Kecskes W PTS 4 Burton
02.12.06	Micky Steeds L PTS 6 Southwark
03.03.07	Paul Butlin L PTS 4 Burton
15.06.07	John McDermott L RSC 2 Crystal Palace
27.07.07	David Dolan L RSC 6 Houghton le Spring
16.09.07	Billy Bessey W CO 6 Southampton
13.10.07	Sam Sexton L RSC 5 Bethnal Green

Career: 42 contests, won 10, drew 3, lost 29.

John Simpson

Greenock. *Born* Greenock, 26 July, 1983
Former British Featherweight Champion. *Ht* 5'7"
Manager F. Warren/A. Morrison

23.09.02	Simon Chambers W RSC 1 Glasgow
06.10.02	Lee Holmes L PTS 6 Rhyl
07.12.02	Matthew Burke W PTS 4 Brentwood
20.01.03	John-Paul Ryan W PTS 6 Glasgow
17.02.03	Joel Viney W RTD 1 Glasgow
14.04.03	Simon Chambers W PTS 6 Glasgow
20.10.03	Steve Gethin W PTS 8 Glasgow
01.11.03	Mark Alexander W PTS 4 Glasgow
19.01.04	Henry Janes W PTS 8 Glasgow
31.01.04	Gennadiy Delisandru W PTS 4 Bethnal Green

22.04.04	Jus Wallie W PTS 6 Glasgow
02.06.04	Fred Janes W PTS 6 Hereford
20.09.04	Marc Callaghan W PTS 8 Glasgow
05.11.04	Dazzo Williams L PTS 12 Hereford
	(British Featherweight Title Challenge)
06.06.05	Dariusz Snarski W RSC 3 Glasgow
05.11.05	Andy Morris L PTS 12 Renfrew
	(Vacant British Featherweight Title)
01.04.06	Steve Foster L PTS 12 Bethnal Green
	(WBU Featherweight Title Challenge)
09.12.06	Andy Morris W RSC 5 Canning Town
	(British Featherweight Title Challenge)
10.03.07	Derry Matthews L PTS 12 Liverpool
	(WBU Featherweight Title Challenge)
08.06.07	Ryan Barrett W CO 5 Mayfair
	(British Featherweight Title Defence)
07.09.07	Andy Morris W RSC 7 Mayfair
	(British Featherweight Title Defence)
15.12.07	Youssef Al Hamidi W PTS 8 Edinburgh
06.06.08	Paul Appleby L PTS 12 Glasgow
	(British Featherweight Title Defence)

Career: 23 contests, won 17, lost 6.

John Simpson   Philip Sharkey

Neil Simpson

Coventry. *Born* London, 5 July, 1970
British Masters Cruiserweight
Champion. Former Undefeated British &
Commonwealth L.Heavyweight Champion.
Former Midlands Area L.Heavyweight
Champion. *Ht* 6'2¼"
Manager Self

04.10.94	Kenny Nevers W PTS 4 Mayfair
20.10.94	Johnny Hooks W RSC 2 Walsall
05.12.94	Chris Woollas L PTS 6 Cleethorpes
15.12.94	Paul Murray W PTS 6 Walsall
06.03.95	Greg Scott-Briggs W RTD 5 Leicester
17.03.95	Thomas Hansvoll L PTS 4 Copenhagen, Denmark
26.04.95	Craig Joseph L PTS 6 Solihull
11.05.95	Andy McVeigh L CO 2 Dudley
24.06.95	Dave Owens W RSC 1 Cleethorpes
25.09.95	Tony Booth L PTS 8 Cleethorpes
11.10.95	Darren Ashton W RSC 3 Solihull
29.11.95	Greg Scott-Briggs W DIS 7 Solihull
	(Vacant Midlands Area L.Heavyweight Title)
19.02.96	Stephen Wilson L PTS 6 Glasgow
27.03.96	Tony Booth W PTS 6 Whitwick
26.04.96	Dean Francis L RSC 3 Cardiff

02.10.96 Chris Davies W PTS 4 Cardiff
28.10.96 Nigel Rafferty W PTS 8 Leicester
03.12.96 Danny Peters L PTS 6 Liverpool
03.02.97 Michael Pinnock W PTS 6 Leicester
25.04.97 Stuart Fleet L PTS 10 Cleethorpes
(Midlands Area L.Heavyweight Title Defence)
20.10.97 Slick Miller W RTD 1 Leicester
15.12.97 Chris Woollas L PTS 6 Cleethorpes
11.05.98 Greg Scott-Briggs W PTS 6 Leicester
30.11.98 Slick Miller W CO 3 Leicester
26.02.99 Adam Cale W RSC 3 Coventry
12.07.99 Tony Booth W PTS 10 Coventry
(Elim. British L.Heavyweight Title)
14.12.99 Darren Corbett L PTS 12 Coventry
(Vacant IBO Inter-Continental L.Heavyweight Title)
22.05.00 Mark Baker W PTS 12 Coventry
(Vacant British L.Heavyweight Title)
18.11.00 Mark Delaney W RSC 1 Dagenham
(British L.Heavyweight Title Defence)
02.01.01 Hastings Rasani W RSC 4 Coventry
(Vacant Commonwealth L.Heavyweight Title)
06.04.01 Yawe Davis L RSC 3 Grosseto, Italy
(Vacant European L.Heavyweight Title)
25.05.02 Tony Oakey L PTS 12 Portsmouth
(WBU L.Heavyweight Title Challenge)
08.03.03 Peter Oboh L RSC 11 Coventry
(Vacant British L.Heavyweight Title. Commonwealth L.Heavyweight Title Challenge)
20.04.04 Mark Brookes L PTS 10 Sheffield
(Elim. British L.Heavyweight Title)
17.12.04 Hastings Rasani W PTS 6 Coventry
18.06.05 Paul Bonson W PTS 6 Coventry
16.09.05 Leigh Alliss L RSC 3 Plymouth
10.02.06 Gareth Hogg L PTS 6 Plymouth
18.03.06 Varuzhan Davtyan W RSC 1 Coventry
25.09.07 Tony Booth W PTS 10 Hull
(Vacant British Masters Cruiserweight Title)
01.12.07 John Anthony W PTS 4 Coventry
01.03.08 Tony Booth W PTS 4 Coventry
01.05.08 Nick Okoth W RSC 10 Piccadilly
(British Masters Cruiserweight Title Defence)
Career: 43 contests, won 26, lost 17.

Neil Simpson   Philip Sharkey

Neil Sinclair
Belfast. *Born* Belfast, 23 February, 1974
L.Middleweight. Former Undefeated British
Welterweight Champion. *Ht* 5'10½"
Manager Self

14.04.95 Marty Duke W RSC 2 Belfast
27.05.95 Andrew Jervis L RSC 3 Belfast
17.07.95 Andy Peach W RSC 1 Mayfair
26.08.95 George Wilson W PTS 4 Belfast
07.10.95 Wayne Shepherd W PTS 6 Belfast
02.12.95 Brian Coleman W RTD 1 Belfast
13.04.96 Hughie Davey W PTS 6 Liverpool
28.05.96 Prince Kasi Kaihau W RSC 2 Belfast
03.09.96 Dennis Berry L PTS 6 Belfast
27.09.97 Trevor Meikle W RSC 5 Belfast
20.12.97 Chris Pollock W RTD 3 Belfast
21.02.98 Leigh Wicks W RSC 1 Belfast
19.09.98 Paul Denton W RSC 1 Dublin
07.12.98 Michael Smyth W CO 1 Acton
22.01.99 Mark Ramsey W CO 3 Dublin
05.06.99 David Kirk W PTS 8 Cardiff
16.10.99 Paul Dyer W RSC 8 Belfast
18.03.00 Dennis Berry W RSC 2 Glasgow
16.05.00 Paul Dyer W RSC 6 Warrington
24.06.00 Chris Henry W RSC 1 Glasgow
12.08.00 Adrian Chase W RSC 2 Wembley
16.12.00 Daniel Santos L CO 2 Sheffield
(WBO Welterweight Title Challenge)
28.04.01 Zoltan Szilii W CO 2 Cardiff
22.09.01 Viktor Fesetchko W PTS 6 Bethnal Green
19.11.01 Harry Dhami W RSC 5 Glasgow
(British Welterweight Title Challenge)
20.04.02 Leonti Voronchuk W RSC 4 Cardiff
15.06.02 Derek Roche W CO 1 Leeds
(British Welterweight Title Defence)
17.08.02 Dmitri Kashkan W RSC 4 Cardiff
02.11.02 Paul Knights W RSC 2 Belfast
(British Welterweight Title Defence)
01.02.03 Bradley Pryce W RSC 8 Belfast
(British Welterweight Title Defence)
30.07.04 Craig Lynch W PTS 6 Bethnal Green
18.03.05 Taz Jones L RSC 1 Belfast
05.07.06 Jerome Ellis L CO 6 Colorado Springs, Colorado, USA
17.02.07 Arek Malek W RSC 4 Cork
23.06.07 Franny Jones L CO 5 Dublin
18.08.07 Sergejs Savrinovics W PTS 6 Cork
29.03.08 Juan Martinez Bas W PTS 8 Letterkenny
07.06.08 Daniele Petrucci L PTS 12 Rome, Italy
(European Union Welterweight Title Challenge)
Career: 38 contests, won 31, lost 7.

Deniss Sirjatovs
Sutton in Ashfield. *Born* Riga, Latvia, 14
November, 1984
L.Welterweight. *Ht* 5'10¾"
Manager M. Scriven

06.05.06 George McIlroy L RSC 2 Irvine
16.09.06 Jack Perry L PTS 6 Burton
01.12.06 John Baguley L PTS 4 Doncaster
08.12.06 Lee Purdy L RSC 3 Dagenham
03.03.07 Gavin Deacon L PTS 4 Alfreton
17.03.07 Ben Murphy L PTS 4 Birmingham
31.03.07 Dave Ryan L PTS 6 Derby
15.04.07 Andrew Ward L PTS 6 Barnsley
29.04.07 Thomas Costello L RSC 1 Birmingham
01.06.07 Jamie Spence L RSC 3 Peterborough
30.06.07 Kevin Maxwell L PTS 4 Belfast
13.07.07 Gary Sykes L RSC 2 Barnsley
Career: 12 contests, lost 12.

Deniss Sirjatovs   Les Clark

Grant Skehill
Wanstead. *Born* London, 1 October, 1985
L.Middleweight. *Ht* 5'11¼"
Manager F. Warren

13.05.06 Geraint Harvey W PTS 4 Bethnal Green
28.10.06 Ernie Smith W PTS 4 Bethnal Green
17.02.07 Duncan Cottier W PTS 4 Wembley
13.10.07 Rocky Muscus W PTS 4 Bethnal Green
12.01.08 Ben Hudson W PTS 4 Bethnal Green
14.06.08 Duncan Cottier W PTS 4 Bethnal Green
Career: 6 contests, won 6.

Grant Skehill   Les Clark

Matt Skelton
Bedford. *Born* Bedford, 23 January, 1968
Commonwealth Heavyweight Champion.
Former Undefeated British, WBU &
English Heavyweight Champion. *Ht* 6'3"
Manager Self

22.09.02 Gifford Shillingford W RSC 2 Southwark

171

27.10.02	Slick Miller W CO 1 Southwark
08.12.02	Neil Kirkwood W RSC 1 Bethnal Green
18.02.03	Jacklord Jacobs W RSC 4 Bethnal Green
08.04.03	Alexei Varakin W CO 2 Bethnal Green
15.05.03	Dave Clarke W RSC 1 Mayfair
17.07.03	Antoine Palatis W RSC 4 Dagenham
18.09.03	Mike Holden W RSC 6 Dagenham *(Vacant English Heavyweight Title)*
11.10.03	Costi Marin W RSC 1 Portsmouth
25.10.03	Ratko Draskovic W RSC 3 Edinburgh
15.11.03	Patriche Costel W CO 1 Bayreuth, Germany
07.02.04	Julius Francis W PTS 10 Bethnal Green *(English Heavyweight Title Defence)*
24.04.04	Michael Sprott W CO 12 Reading *(British & Commonwealth Heavyweight Title Challenges)*
05.06.04	Bob Mirovic W RTD 4 Bethnal Green *(Commonwealth Heavyweight Title Defence)*
19.11.04	Keith Long W RSC 11 Bethnal Green *(British & Commonwealth Heavyweight Title Defences)*
25.02.05	Fabio Eduardo Moli W RSC 6 Wembley *(Vacant WBU Heavyweight Title)*
16.07.05	Mark Krence W RTD 7 Bolton *(British Heavyweight Title Defence)*
10.12.05	John McDermott W RSC 1 Canning Town *(British Heavyweight Title Defence)*
25.02.06	Danny Williams L PTS 12 Canning Town *(Commonwealth Heavyweight Title Challenge)*
01.04.06	Suren Kalachyan W CO 4 Bethnal Green
08.07.06	Danny Williams W PTS 12 Cardiff *(Commonwealth Heavyweight Title Challenge)*
14.07.07	Michael Sprott W PTS 12 Greenwich *(Commonwealth Heavyweight Title Defence)*
19.01.08	Ruslan Chagaev L PTS 12 Dusseldorf, Germany *(WBA Heavyweight Title Challenge)*

Career: 23 contests, won 21, lost 2.

Gatis Skuja

Bethnal Green. *Born* Latvia, 23 June, 1982
L.Middleweight. *Ht* 5'9"
Manager C. Sanigar

26.03.05	Nathan Graham L RSC 1 Hackney
11.09.05	David Kirk W PTS 6 Kirkby in Ashfield
04.12.05	Mark Lloyd L PTS 4 Telford
24.02.06	Terry Adams DREW 4 Birmingham
24.03.06	Sam Webb L PTS 4 Bethnal Green
22.05.06	Simon Sherrington DREW 8 Birmingham
15.06.06	Cello Renda L PTS 4 Peterborough
14.07.06	Laurent Gomis L RSC 2 Alicante, Spain
29.09.06	Brett Flournoy L PTS 4 Manchester
03.11.06	Gavin Smith DREW 6 Barnsley
03.12.06	Daley Oujederie DREW 4 Bethnal Green
03.03.07	Robbie James L PTS 6 Newport
13.07.07	Dee Mitchell W RSC 5 Birmingham
11.08.07	Denton Vassell L PTS 4 Liverpool
23.09.07	Fred Smith W RSC 1 Heathrow

05.10.07	Daniel Herdman W PTS 4 Bethnal Green
19.10.07	Danny Reynolds L PTS 6 Doncaster
09.11.07	Jon Harrison L PTS 10 Plymouth *(Vacant International Masters L.Middleweight Title)*

Career: 18 contests, won 4, drew 4, lost 10.

Anthony Small Philip Sharkey

Anthony Small

Deptford. *Born* London, 28 June, 1981
Southern Area L.Middleweight Champion.
Ht 5'9"
Manager Self

12.05.04	Lance Hall W RSC 1 Reading
10.09.04	Emmanuel Marcos W RSC 1 Wembley
10.12.04	Howard Clarke W PTS 4 Sheffield
21.01.05	Andrei Sherel W RSC 3 Brentford
24.04.05	Dmitry Donetskiy W PTS 4 Leicester Square
16.06.05	Howard Clarke W PTS 6 Mayfair
20.07.05	David le Franc W RSC 1 Monte Carlo, Monaco
14.10.05	Ismael Kerzazi W RSC 1 Huddersfield
23.11.05	Ernie Smith W PTS 6 Mayfair
24.03.06	Kai Kauramaki W CO 3 Bethnal Green
30.05.06	Alexander Matviechuk W RSC 6 Bethnal Green
21.07.06	Vladimir Borovski W PTS 6 Altrincham
21.10.06	Prince Arron W RSC 2 Southwark
18.11.06	Ciaran Healy W RSC 3 Newport
09.12.06	Kevin Phelan W RSC 1 Canning Town
17.02.07	Sergey Starkov W RSC 2 Wembley
30.03.07	Walter Wright W PTS 8 Newcastle
14.07.07	Bradley Pryce L RSC 7 Greenwich *(Commonwealth L.Middleweight Title Challenge)*
12.01.08	Takaloo W RSC 7 Bethnal Green *(Vacant Southern Area L.Middleweight Title)*
14.06.08	George Katsimpas W RSC 8 Bethnal Green *(Southern Area L.Middleweight Title Defence)*

Career: 20 contests, won 19, lost 1.

Leroy Smedley

Leeds. *Born* Scarborough, 14 January, 1982
Lightweight. Ht. 5'9"
Manager M. Marsden

18.04.07	Tony McQuade W PTS 6 Strand
10.12.07	Carl Griffiths L RSC 2 Leicester

Career: 2 contests, won 1, lost 1.

Leroy Smedley Philip Sharkey

Nicki Smedley

Sheffield. *Born* Sheffield, 3 February, 1986
Welterweight. *Ht* 5'10"
Manager Self

24.07.05	Lance Verallo W PTS 6 Sheffield
09.09.05	Jason Nesbitt W PTS 4 Sheffield
26.11.05	Rakhim Mingaleev W PTS 4 Sheffield
05.03.06	Davis Kamara W PTS 6 Sheffield
13.05.06	Artak Tsironyan W PTS 4 Sheffield
22.06.06	Martin Sweeney W RSC 3 Sheffield
20.10.06	Jon Honney W PTS 6 Sheffield
10.12.06	Imad Khamis W RSC 4 Sheffield
03.05.07	David Kehoe W RSC 4 Sheffield
25.08.07	Surinder Sekhon W PTS 4 Dublin
22.03.08	Michael Frontin W PTS 6 Sheffield

Career: 11 contests, won 11.

Billy Smith

Stourport. *Born* Kidderminster, 10 June, 1978
Welterweight. Former Undefeated Midlands Area L.Welterweight Champion. *Ht* 5'7"
Manager Self

28.03.00	Marcus Portman L PTS 6 Wolverhampton
07.04.00	Barry Hughes L PTS 6 Glasgow
18.05.00	Manzo Smith L PTS 4 Bethnal Green
26.05.00	Willie Limond W PTS 4 Glasgow
07.07.00	Gareth Jordan L PTS 6 Chigwell
15.07.00	David Walker L RTD 2 Millwall
09.09.00	Ricky Eccleston L PTS 4 Manchester
24.09.00	Choi Tsveenpurev L RTD 2 Shaw
18.11.00	Lee Meager L RSC 1 Dagenham
17.12.00	Willie Limond L PTS 6 Glasgow
03.02.01	Scott Spencer L PTS 6 Brighton
09.03.01	Darren Melville L PTS 4 Millwall
27.03.01	Jason Nesbitt L PTS 6 Brierley Hill
05.03.05	Lee Cook L PTS 4 Southwark
23.03.05	Sam Rukundo L RSC 3 Leicester Square

30.04.05 Baz Carey L PTS 6 Coventry
08.05.05 Sean Hughes L PTS 6 Bradford
20.05.05 Stefy Bull L PTS 6 Doncaster
02.06.05 Isaac Ward L PTS 8 Yarm
16.06.05 Ricky Owen L PTS 4 Dagenham
25.06.05 John Fewkes L PTS 6 Wakefield
16.07.05 Craig Watson L PTS 4 Bolton
23.07.05 Lee McAllister L PTS 4 Edinburgh
11.09.05 Craig Johnson L PTS 4 Kirkby in Ashfield
24.09.05 Baz Carey NC 5 Coventry
01.10.05 John Davidson W PTS 6 Wigan
09.10.05 Andrew Murray L PTS 4 Hammersmith
22.10.05 Jonathan Whiteman L PTS 6 Mansfield
05.11.05 Paul McCloskey L PTS 4 Renfrew
13.11.05 Nadeem Siddique L PTS 6 Leeds
25.11.05 Steve Mullin L PTS 4 Liverpool
03.12.05 Baz Carey L PTS 6 Coventry
12.12.05 Judex Meemea L PTS 6 Peterborough
11.02.06 Tom Glover L PTS 4 Bethnal Green
24.02.06 Lance Hall W PTS 4 Birmingham
25.03.06 Scott Haywood L PTS 6 Burton
07.04.06 Michael Graydon W PTS 4 Bristol
28.04.06 Paul Holborn L PTS 4 Hartlepool
12.05.06 Lee McAllister L PTS 4 Bethnal Green
21.05.06 Ashley Theophane L PTS 4 Bethnal Green
30.05.06 Chris Pacy L PTS 4 Bethnal Green
16.06.06 Ceri Hall L PTS 6 Carmarthen
23.06.06 Paul Truscott L PTS 4 Blackpool
12.07.06 John Murray L RSC 6 Bethnal Green
02.09.06 Stephen Burke L PTS 4 Bolton
09.09.06 Mike Reid W PTS 8 Inverurie
18.09.06 Gary McArthur L PTS 8 Glasgow
29.09.06 Gwyn Wale W PTS 6 Motherwell
26.10.06 Jonathan Hussey W PTS 6 Dudley
04.11.06 Jonathan Whiteman W PTS 6 Mansfield
17.11.06 Martin Gordon W PTS 6 Brierley Hill
01.12.06 Dee Mitchell L PTS 4 Birmingham
08.12.06 John Murray L PTS 6 Dagenham
15.12.06 Michael Lomax L PTS 4 Bethnal Green
09.02.07 Scott Haywood L PTS 4 Leeds
19.02.07 Andrew Ferrans L PTS 6 Glasgow
24.03.07 Baz Carey W PTS 10 Coventry
(Vacant Midlands Area L.Welterweight Title)
07.04.07 Gavin Rees L PTS 6 Cardiff
11.05.07 Scott Haywood L PTS 4 Motherwell
18.05.07 Lenny Daws L PTS 6 Canning Town
25.05.07 Craig Docherty L PTS 4 Motherwell
08.06.07 Nathan Brough L PTS 4 Motherwell
21.07.07 Barrie Jones L PTS 4 Cardiff
15.09.07 Carl Allen W PTS 10 Birmingham
(Vacant Midlands Area L.Welterweight Title)
04.10.07 Andrew Murray L PTS 8 Piccadilly
13.10.07 Eddie Corcoran L PTS 4 Bethnal Green
25.10.07 Tristan Davies L PTS 4 Wolverhampton
02.11.07 George McIlroy W PTS 6 Irvine
14.11.07 Muhsen Nasser DREW 4 Bethnal Green
24.11.07 Craig Dickson L PTS 6 Clydebank
01.12.07 Stephen Burke L PTS 6 Liverpool
15.12.07 Ricky Burns L PTS 6 Edinburgh
21.01.08 Gary McArthur L PTS 8 Glasgow
03.02.08 Chris Long L PTS 6 Bristol
22.02.08 Dave Stewart L PTS 6 Bethnal Green
29.02.08 Barry Morrison L PTS 6 Glasgow
08.03.08 Christopher Sebire L PTS 4 Greenwich
22.03.08 Ricky Burns L PTS 4 Cardiff
30.03.08 Jack Arnfield L PTS 6 Colne
18.04.08 Stuart Kennedy L PTS 6 Houghton le Spring

02.05.08 Kevin Concepcion L PTS 6 Nottingham
10.05.08 John O'Donnell L PTS 4 Nottingham
21.06.08 Jamie Cox L PTS 6 Birmingham
28.06.08 Liam Anthony L PTS 6 Leicester
Career: 84 contests, won 12, drew 1, lost 70, no contest 1.

Billy Smith   Les Clark

Ernie Smith
Stourport. *Born* Kidderminster, 10 June, 1978
S.Middleweight. *Ht* 5'8"
Manager Self

24.11.98 Woody Greenaway L PTS 6 Wolverhampton
05.12.98 Gavin Rees L PTS 4 Bristol
27.01.99 Arv Mittoo DREW 6 Stoke
11.02.99 Tony Smith W PTS 6 Dudley
22.02.99 Liam Maltby W PTS 4 Peterborough
08.03.99 Wayne Jones W PTS 6 Birmingham
18.03.99 Carl Greaves L PTS 6 Doncaster
25.03.99 Brian Coleman L PTS 6 Edgbaston
27.05.99 Brian Coleman W PTS 6 Edgbaston
14.06.99 Dave Gibson W PTS 6 Birmingham
22.06.99 Koba Gogoladze L RSC 1 Ipswich
03.10.99 Gavin Down L RSC 1 Chesterfield
30.11.99 Brian Coleman L PTS 8 Wolverhampton
13.12.99 Richie Murray L RSC 5 Cleethorpes
24.02.00 Brian Coleman L PTS 6 Edgbaston
02.03.00 Oscar Hall L PTS 6 Birkenhead
10.03.00 John Tiftik L PTS 4 Chigwell
18.03.00 Biagio Falcone L PTS 4 Glasgow
07.04.00 Barry Connell L PTS 6 Glasgow
14.04.00 Jose Luis Castro L PTS 6 Madrid, Spain
06.05.00 Matthew Barr L PTS 4 Southwark
15.05.00 Harry Butler L PTS 6 Birmingham
26.05.00 Biagio Falcone L PTS 4 Glasgow
06.06.00 Chris Henry L PTS 8 Brierley Hill
08.07.00 Takaloo L RSC 4 Widnes
13.08.00 Jawaid Khaliq L RSC 4 Nottingham
(Vacant Midlands Area Welterweight Title)
24.09.00 Shaun Horsfall L PTS 6 Shaw
09.10.00 Dave Gibson W PTS 6 Birmingham
22.10.00 Matthew Barr L PTS 4 Streatham
06.11.00 Stuart Elwell L PTS 6 Wolverhampton
25.11.00 Michael Jennings L PTS 4 Manchester
03.12.00 Shaun Horsfall L PTS 6 Shaw
17.12.00 Kevin McIntyre L PTS 6 Glasgow
20.01.01 David Walker L RTD 1 Bethnal Green

12.03.01 Matt Scriven L PTS 6 Birmingham
24.03.01 Bobby Banghar L PTS 4 Chigwell
12.05.01 Jon Harrison L PTS 4 Plymouth
21.05.01 Brian Coleman W PTS 6 Birmingham
03.06.01 Babatunde Ajayi L PTS 4 Southwark
16.06.01 Bobby Banghar L PTS 4 Dagenham
26.07.01 Andy Abrol L PTS 6 Blackpool
13.09.01 Leo O'Reilly L PTS 6 Sheffield
29.09.01 Brett James L PTS 6 Southwark
01.11.01 Lance Crosby L PTS 6 Hull
17.11.01 Nigel Wright L PTS 4 Glasgow
15.12.01 Ross Minter L RSC 2 Wembley
11.02.02 Tony Montana L PTS 6 Shrewsbury
13.05.02 Martin Scotland W RTD 2 Birmingham
15.06.02 Gavin Wake L PTS 4 Leeds
08.07.02 Gavin Rees L RSC 5 Mayfair
06.09.02 Ricky Burns L PTS 6 Glasgow
14.09.02 Matt Scriven L PTS 6 Newark
29.09.02 Anthony Christopher L PTS 6 Shrewsbury
18.11.02 Craig Dickson L PTS 6 Glasgow
03.12.02 Anthony Christopher W PTS 6 Shrewsbury
23.02.03 Gary Greenwood L PTS 4 Shrewsbury
24.03.03 Darrell Grafton L PTS 6 Barnsley
13.04.03 Lee McAllister L PTS 4 Bradford
28.04.03 Adnan Amar L PTS 6 Cleethorpes
12.05.03 Lee McAllister L PTS 6 Birmingham
31.05.03 Robbie Sivyer L PTS 6 Barnsley
08.06.03 Jonathan Woollins W PTS 4 Nottingham
15.06.03 Ali Nuumembe L PTS 4 Bradford
05.07.03 Michael Lomax L PTS 4 Brentwood
29.08.03 Ali Nuumembe L PTS 6 Liverpool
04.10.03 Lenny Daws L PTS 4 Muswell Hill
18.11.03 Chas Symonds L PTS 6 Bethnal Green
28.11.03 Lee McAllister L PTS 6 Hull
06.12.03 Taz Jones L PTS 4 Cardiff
07.02.04 Gary Woolcombe L PTS 4 Bethnal Green
09.04.04 Richard Swallow L PTS 4 Rugby
19.04.04 Craig Dickson L PTS 6 Glasgow
10.05.04 Adnan Amar L PTS 6 Birmingham
27.05.04 Graham Delehedy L RSC 3 Huddersfield
08.07.04 Steve Brumant L PTS 8 Birmingham
30.07.04 Tony Doherty L PTS 6 Bethnal Green
03.09.04 Jason Rushton L PTS 4 Doncaster
12.09.04 Chris Long DREW 6 Shrewsbury
24.09.04 Lenny Daws L PTS 6 Nottingham
23.10.04 Steve Conway L PTS 6 Wakefield
31.10.04 John Murray L PTS 4 Shaw
12.11.04 John O'Donnell L PTS 6 Wembley
25.11.04 Joe Mitchell W PTS 4 Birmingham
03.12.04 George Telfer L PTS 4 Edinburgh
13.12.04 Luke Teague L PTS 6 Cleethorpes
27.01.05 Muhsen Nasser L PTS 6 Piccadilly
12.02.05 Nathan Ward L PTS 4 Portsmouth
25.02.05 Ross Minter L PTS 4 Wembley
05.03.05 Gary Woolcombe L PTS 6 Southwark
23.03.05 Delroy Mellis L PTS 6 Leicester Square
08.04.05 Kerry Hope L PTS 4 Edinburgh
21.04.05 Jimmy Gould L PTS 4 Dudley
30.04.05 Andy Egan DREW 6 Coventry
08.05.05 Danny Parkinson L PTS 6 Bradford
15.05.05 Kell Brook L PTS 6 Sheffield
23.05.05 Davey Jones DREW 6 Cleethorpes
03.06.05 Martin Concepcion L PTS 4 Manchester
18.06.05 Richard Mazurek W PTS 6 Coventry
25.06.05 Adnan Amar L PTS 6 Melton Mowbray
09.07.05 Darren Barker L PTS 6 Nottingham
16.07.05 Tony Doherty NC 2 Bolton

23.07.05 Nathan Cleverly L PTS 4 Edinburgh
10.09.05 Kell Brook L PTS 4 Cardiff
25.09.05 Gavin Smith DREW 6 Leeds
06.10.05 Stuart Elwell L PTS 4 Dudley
21.10.05 George Hillyard W PTS 4 Bethnal Green
28.10.05 Franny Jones L PTS 4 Hartlepool
13.11.05 Darren Rhodes L PTS 6 Leeds
23.11.05 Anthony Small L PTS 6 Mayfair
02.12.05 Matthew Thirlwall L PTS 4 Nottingham
18.12.05 Ali Nuumbembe L CO 4 Bolton
28.01.06 Tony Doherty L PTS 6 Nottingham
16.02.06 Dean Hickman L PTS 4 Dudley
24.02.06 Joe Mitchell L PTS 6 Birmingham
04.03.06 Sean McKervey L PTS 6 Coventry
02.04.06 Mark Thompson L PTS 6 Shaw
29.04.06 Kell Brook L PTS 6 Edinburgh
06.05.06 Terry Adams L PTS 6 Birmingham
13.05.06 Jonjo Finnegan L PTS 6 Sutton in Ashfield
01.06.06 James Hare L CO 5 Barnsley
21.07.06 Mark Thompson L RSC 3 Altrincham
02.09.06 Denton Vassell L RSC 3 Bolton
01.10.06 Ryan Rowlinson L PTS 6 Rotherham
28.10.06 Grant Skehill L PTS 4 Bethnal Green
04.11.06 Gary Young L PTS 6 Glasgow
11.11.06 Karl Chiverton L PTS 6 Sutton in Ashfield
18.11.06 Barrie Jones L PTS 4 Newport
01.12.06 Max Maxwell L PTS 6 Birmingham
08.12.06 John O'Donnell L CO 2 Dagenham
09.02.07 Brett Flournoy L PTS 4 Leeds
16.02.07 Philip Dowse L PTS 6 Merthyr Tydfil
25.02.07 Brian Rose L PTS 6 Manchester
16.06.07 Sean Crompton L PTS 6 Bolton
28.06.07 Sam Horton L PTS 4 Dudley
13.07.07 James McKinley L PTS 6 Birmingham
11.08.07 Joey Ainscough L PTS 6 Liverpool
15.09.07 Ricky Burns L PTS 6 Paisley
23.09.07 Craig Denton L PTS 8 Hartlepool
06.10.07 Adnan Amar L PTS 4 Nottingham
13.10.07 Andrew Alan Lowe L PTS 6 Newark
03.11.07 Kerry Hope L PTS 4 Cardiff
14.11.07 Kreshnik Qato L PTS 6 Bethnal Green
24.11.07 Jamie Coyle L PTS 6 Clydebank
01.12.07 Greg Barton L PTS 4 Bethnal Green
29.03.08 Stevie Weir L PTS 4 Glasgow
13.04.08 Nasser Al Harbi L PTS 4 Edgbaston
26.04.08 Brian Rose L PTS 4 Wigan
09.05.08 Craig Denton L RSC 2 Middlesbrough
Career: 148 contests, won 13, drew 5, lost 129, no contest 1.

Ernie Smith   Philip Sharkey

Fred Smith
Wormley. *Born* Lambeth, 11 January, 1978
L.Middleweight. *Ht* 5'9¾"
Manager G. Carman
23.09.07 Gatis Skuja L RSC 1 Longford
Career: 1 contest, lost 1.

Gavin Smith
Bradford. *Born* Bradford, 16 December, 1981
L.Middleweight. *Ht* 5'7¾"
Manager D. Hobson
23.10.04 Mark Wall W PTS 6 Wakefield
10.12.04 Mark Wall W PTS 4 Sheffield
13.02.05 Tony Randell W PTS 6 Bradford
24.07.05 Terry Adams L PTS 6 Sheffield
25.09.05 Ernie Smith DREW 6 Leeds
23.02.06 Jav Jerome W RSC 5 Leeds
13.05.06 Aleksandr Zhuk W RSC 3 Sheffield
03.11.06 Gatis Skuja DREW 6 Barnsley
22.03.08 Drew Campbell W PTS 6 Sheffield
Career: 9 contests, won 6, drew 2, lost 1.

Jason Smith
Barnsley. *Born* Sheffield, 9 January, 1979
S.Middleweight. *Ht* 5'11¼"
Manager T. Schofield
09.11.07 Paul Brown L PTS 6 Plymouth
21.02.08 Kurt Bromberg L PTS 6 Leeds
21.06.08 Harry Matthews L PTS 6 Hull
Career: 3 contests, lost 3.

Lewis Smith
Accrington. *Born* Blackburn, 25 November, 1987
Welterweight. *Ht* 5'8"
Manager W. Barker
23.11.06 Duncan Cottier W PTS 6 Manchester
23.02.07 Baz Carey W PTS 6 Manchester
29.06.07 Neal McQuade W PTS 6 Manchester
21.09.07 Ben Murphy L RSC 4 Peterborough
Career: 4 contests, won 3, lost 1.

Lloyd Smith
Portsmouth. *Born* Portsmouth, 18 November, 1988
Welterweight. *Ht* 5'9¼"
Manager J. Bishop
10.11.07 Rory Malone L PTS 6 Portsmouth
02.03.08 Jimmy Briggs L PTS 6 Portsmouth
28.03.08 Mark McCullough L RSC 3 Piccadilly
Career: 3 contests, lost 3.

Paul Smith
Liverpool. *Born* Liverpool, 6 October, 1982
Central Area Middleweight Champion.
Former English Middleweight Champion.
Ht 5'11"
Manager F. Warren
05.04.03 Howard Clarke W PTS 4 Manchester
08.05.03 Andrei Ivanov W RSC 2 Widnes
20.06.03 Elroy Edwards W RSC 2 Liverpool
29.08.03 Patrick Cito W PTS 4 Liverpool
02.10.03 Mike Duffield W RSC 1 Liverpool
13.12.03 Joel Ani W PTS 4 Manchester
26.02.04 Davey Jones W PTS 4 Widnes
03.04.04 Howard Clarke W PTS 4 Manchester
12.06.04 Steve Timms W RSC 1 Manchester
10.09.04 Ojay Abrahams W PTS 4 Liverpool

01.10.04 Jason Collins W RSC 1 Manchester
17.12.04 Howard Clarke W CO 1 Liverpool
11.02.05 Robert Burton W CO 1 Manchester
03.06.05 Simeon Cover W PTS 6 Manchester
11.03.06 Hussain Osman W RSC 4 Newport
01.06.06 Conroy McIntosh W PTS 8 Barnsley
14.10.06 Dean Walker W RSC 3 Manchester
(Vacant Central Area Middleweight Title)
18.11.06 Ryan Walls W RSC 4 Newport
10.03.07 Alexander Polizzi W RSC 8 Liverpool
30.03.07 Jonathan Reid W RSC 7 Newcastle
09.10.07 David Banks W PTS 5 Los Angeles, Calforina, USA
08.12.07 Francis Cheka W PTS 8 Bolton
08.03.08 Cello Renda W RSC 6 Greenwich
(Vacant English Middleweight Title)
21.06.08 Steven Bendall L PTS 10 Birmingham
(English Middleweight Title Defence)
Career: 24 contests, won 23, lost 1.

Stephen Smith
Liverpool. *Born* Liverpool, 22 July, 1985
Featherweight. *Ht* 5'6½"
Manager F. Warren
21.06.08 Shaun Walton W CO 3 Birmingham
Career: 1 contest, won 1.

Victor Smith   Philip Sharkey

Victor Smith
Edmonton. *Born* Edmonton, 3 October, 1978
L.Heavyweight. *Ht* 5'9"
Manager T. Sims
05.10.07 Lee Kellett L PTS 4 Bethnal Green
14.11.07 Jamie Norkett W PTS 4 Bethnal Green
01.12.07 Shpetim Hoti W PTS 4 Chigwell
22.02.08 Bob Ajisafe L PTS 4 Bethnal Green
04.04.08 Michael Banbula L PTS 4 Bethnal Green
Career: 5 contests, won 2, lost 3.

Rasham Sohi
Leicester. *Born* Leicester, 7 April, 1981
L.Heavyweight. *Ht* 6'2¼"
Manager J. Gill/T. Harris
05.10.07 David Gentles W PTS 6 Newport
16.02.08 Mark Phillips W PTS 6 Leicester
07.03.08 Phil Goodwin W RSC 3 Nottingham
Career: 3 contests, won 3.

Albert Sosnowski   Philip Sharkey

Albert Sosnowski

Brentwood. *Born* Warsaw, Poland, 7 March, 1979
WBF Heavyweight Champion. *Ht* 6'3½"
Manager B. Hearn

22.07.98	Jan Drobena W RSC 1 Outrup, Denmark
25.09.98	Andrzej Dziewulski W RSC 4 Poznan, Poland
02.10.98	Rene Hanl W PTS 4 Wroclaw, Poland
13.02.99	Viktor Juhasz W RSC 1 Jastrzebie Zdroj, Poland
12.03.99	Chris Woollas W PTS 4 Bethnal Green
17.04.99	Stipe Balic W PTS 4 Warsaw, Poland
28.05.99	Gary Williams W RSC 4 Liverpool
26.06.99	Biko Botowamungu W PTS 4 Wroclaw, Poland
17.07.99	Bruno Foster W RSC 6 Gdansk, Poland
18.09.99	Ignacio Orsola W CO 1 Gdansk, Poland
22.10.99	Jeff Lally W RSC 3 Detroit, Michigan, USA
20.11.99	Henry Kolle Njume W PTS 6 Gliwice, Poland
11.03.00	Luke Simpkin W PTS 4 Kensington
08.04.00	Slobodan Popovic W CO 1 Gdansk, Poland
27.05.00	Neil Kirkwood W RSC 1 Mayfair
24.06.00	Clarence Goins W RSC 2 Torun, Poland
19.08.00	Dan Conway W PTS 4 Mashantucket, Connecticut, USA
30.09.00	Everett Martin W RSC 7 Rotterdam, Holland
27.11.00	Michael Murray W RSC 5 Birmingham
17.03.01	Arthur Cook L CO 9 Budapest, Hungary
	(Vacant WBC World Youth Heavyweight Title)
07.07.01	Dirk Wallyn W PTS 6 Amsterdam, Holland
13.10.01	Stanislav Tomkatchov W RSC 3 Budapest, Hungary
27.10.01	Robert Magureanu W RSC 4 Kolobrzeg, Poland
22.01.02	Catalin Zmarandescu W CO 1 Gdynia, Poland
09.03.02	Jacob Odhiambo W CO 1 Budapest, Hungary
27.07.02	Paul Bonson W PTS 4 Nottingham
07.12.02	Jacklord Jacobs W PTS 6 Brentwood
08.03.03	Mindaugas Kulikauskas W RSC 2 Bethnal Green
12.04.03	Mike Holden W PTS 6 Bethnal Green
05.07.03	Jason Brewster W RSC 2 Brentwood
22.11.03	Chris Woollas W RSC 1 Belfast
31.01.04	Greg Scott-Briggs W CO 2 Bethnal Green
10.04.04	Paul King W PTS 4 Manchester
26.06.04	Wojciech Bartnik W PTS 6 Belfast
11.09.04	Kenny Craven W CO 2 Budapest, Hungary
22.01.05	Tommy Connelly W RSC 2 Miami, Florida, USA
19.03.05	Travis Fulton W RSC 2 Las Vegas, Nevada, USA
28.05.05	Orlin Norris W PTS 6 Los Angeles, California, USA
25.06.05	Osborne Machimana W PTS 10 Brakpan, South Africa
04.11.06	Lawrence Tauasa W PTS 12 Kempton Park, South Africa
	(Vacant WBF Heavyweight Title)
08.06.07	Steve Herelius W RSC 9 Motherwell
14.09.07	Manuel Alberto Pucheta W CO 2 Kirkcaldy
	(WBF Heavyweight Title Defence)
25.01.08	Colin Kenna W PTS 10 Dagenham
25.04.08	Terrell Nelson W RSC 5 NYC, New York, USA

Career: 44 contests, won 43, lost 1.

Jamie Spence

Northampton. *Born* Northampton, 9 June, 1984
L.Welterweight. *Ht* 5'7¼"
Manager Self

03.12.06	Gavin Tait L RSC 4 Bethnal Green
23.02.07	Dezzie O'Connor W RSC 3 Peterborough
01.06.07	Deniss Sirjatovs W RSC 3 Peterborough
21.09.07	Craig Dyer W PTS 6 Peterborough
22.02.08	Baz Carey W PTS 4 Bethnal Green
04.04.08	Lee Purdy L RSC 1 Bethnal Green

Career: 6 contests, won 4, lost 2.

Jamie Spence   Les Clark

Delroy Spencer

Walsall. *Born* Walsall, 25 July, 1968
Bantamweight. British Masters Flyweight Champion. *Ht* 5'4"
Manager Self

30.10.98	Gwyn Evans L PTS 4 Peterborough
21.11.98	Jamie Evans W PTS 4 Southwark
30.01.99	Ian Napa L PTS 6 Bethnal Green
26.02.99	Chris Edwards W PTS 6 West Bromwich
30.04.99	Nicky Booth L PTS 6 Scunthorpe
06.06.99	Nicky Booth L PTS 4 Nottingham
19.06.99	Willie Valentine L PTS 4 Dublin
16.10.99	Colin Moffett W PTS 4 Bethnal Green
31.10.99	Shane Mallon W PTS 6 Raynes Park
29.11.99	Lee Georgiou L PTS 4 Wembley
19.02.00	Steffen Norskov L PTS 4 Aalborg, Denmark
08.04.00	Ian Napa L PTS 8 Bethnal Green
15.04.00	Lee Georgiou L PTS 4 Bethnal Green
04.07.00	Ankar Miah W RSC 3 Tooting
13.07.00	Darren Hayde W PTS 4 Bethnal Green
30.09.00	Paul Weir L PTS 8 Chigwell
28.10.00	Dale Robinson L PTS 4 Coventry
02.12.00	Keith Knox W PTS 6 Bethnal Green
08.05.01	Levi Pattison L PTS 4 Barnsley
22.05.01	Mimoun Chent L DIS 5 Telde, Gran Canaria
16.06.01	Sunkanmi Ogunbiyi L PTS 4 Wembley
22.11.01	Darren Taylor W PTS 8 Paddington
	(Vacant British Masters Flyweight Title)
09.12.01	Shinny Bayaar L PTS 4 Shaw
19.12.01	Gareth Payne L PTS 4 Coventry
18.01.02	Gareth Payne W PTS 4 Coventry
28.01.02	Levi Pattison L RSC 2 Barnsley
19.10.03	Shinny Bayaar L PTS 6 Shaw
13.12.03	Mark Moran L PTS 4 Manchester
24.01.04	Martin Power L RTD 1 Wembley
23.04.04	Chris Edwards DREW 6 Leicester
26.06.04	Damaen Kelly L RSC 4 Belfast
30.07.04	Martin Power L CO 2 Bethnal Green
31.10.04	Shinny Bayaar L PTS 6 Shaw
12.11.04	Stevie Quinn L PTS 6 Belfast
03.12.04	Lee Haskins L RTD 3 Bristol
	(Vacant English Flyweight Title)
27.05.05	Robert Nelson L PTS 4 Spennymoor
25.06.05	Robert Nelson L PTS 6 Wakefield
16.09.05	Lee Haskins L RTD 2 Plymouth
16.10.05	Moses Kinyua L PTS 6 Peterborough
30.10.05	Lee Fortt L PTS 4 Bethnal Green
12.11.05	Chris Edwards L PTS 4 Stoke
02.12.05	Jamie McDonnell L PTS 6 Doncaster
11.02.06	John Armour L PTS 6 Bethnal Green
04.03.06	Dale Robinson L RSC 3 Manchester
02.04.06	Shinny Bayaar L PTS 6 Shaw
23.04.06	Gary Sheil W PTS 6 Chester
09.05.06	Robert Nelson DREW 6 Leeds
20.05.06	Colin Moffett L PTS 4 Belfast
28.05.06	Tasif Khan L PTS 6 Wakefield
02.09.06	Don Broadhurst L PTS 4 Bolton
15.09.06	Matthew Edmonds L PTS 4 Newport
06.10.06	Ian Napa L PTS 6 Bethnal Green
27.10.06	Kris Hughes L PTS 6 Glasgow
11.11.06	Eugene Heagney L PTS 4 Dublin
11.12.06	Usman Ahmed DREW 6 Cleethorpes
09.02.07	Ross Burkinshaw L PTS 4 Leeds
26.02.07	Dougie Walton L PTS 6 Birmingham
07.04.07	Don Broadhurst L PTS 4 Cardiff
14.04.07	Eugene Heagney L PTS 6 Wakefield
05.05.07	Stephen Russell L PTS 4 Glasgow
19.05.07	Andy Bell L PTS 4 Nottingham
03.06.07	Josh Wale L PTS 6 Barnsley

16.06.07	Rob Turley L PTS 6 Newport	
30.06.07	Rhys Roberts L PTS 6 Manchester	
15.07.07	Gavin Reid L PTS 6 Hartlepool	
22.07.07	Andy Bell L PTS 6 Mansfield	
11.08.07	Rhys Roberts L PTS 6 Liverpool	
08.09.07	Wayne Bloy L PTS 4 Sutton in Ashfield	
22.09.07	Stuart McFadyen L PTS 6 Wigan	
08.10.07	Davey Savage L PTS 6 Glasgow	
26.10.07	Dougie Walton L PTS 6 Birmingham	
05.11.07	John Donnelly L PTS 6 Glasgow	
03.12.07	Scott Quigg L PTS 6 Manchester	
02.02.08	Michael Walsh L RSC 3 Canning Town	
14.03.08	Kallum De'Ath L PTS 6 Manchester	
28.03.08	Mike Holloway L PTS 4 Barnsley	
19.04.08	Luke Wilton L PTS 4 Dublin	
26.04.08	Mike Robinson L PTS 6 Wigan	
17.05.08	Paul Economides L PTS 6 Stoke	
07.06.08	Craig Lyon L PTS 6 Wigan	
15.06.08	Ian Bailey L PTS 6 Bethnal Green	

Career: 81 contests, won 10, drew 3, lost 68.

Delroy Spencer   Philip Sharkey

Alexander Spitjo   Philip Sharkey

Alexander Spitjo

Mansfield. *Born* Riga, Latvia, 21 February, 1986
L.Middleweight. *Ht* 5'10½"
Manager M. Scriven/J. Gill

13.04.07	Brett Flournoy L PTS 4 Altrincham
27.04.07	Sam Webb L RSC 1 Wembley
17.06.07	Lee Noble L PTS 4 Mansfield
30.06.07	Scott Jordan W RSC 5 Belfast
14.09.07	Willie Bilan W CO 1 Kirkcaldy
08.10.07	Ali Wyatt W RTD 5 Birmingham
10.12.07	Michael Frontin W PTS 6 Birmingham
07.03.08	Garry Buckland L RSC 3 Nottingham
18.04.08	Ajose Olusegun L RSC 3 Bethnal Green

Career: 9 contests, won 4, lost 5.

Michael Sprott   Les Clark

Michael Sprott

Reading. *Born* Reading, 16 January, 1975
Former Undefeated English & European Union Heavyweight Champion. Former British & Commonwealth Heavyweight Champion. Former Undefeated Southern Area & WBF European Heavyweight Champion.
Ht 6'0¾"
Manager Self

20.11.96	Geoff Hunter W RSC 1 Wembley
19.02.97	Johnny Davison W CO 2 Acton
17.03.97	Slick Miller W CO 1 Mayfair
16.04.97	Tim Redman W CO 2 Bethnal Green
20.05.97	Waldeck Fransas W PTS 6 Edmonton
02.09.97	Gary Williams W PTS 6 Southwark
08.11.97	Darren Fearn W PTS 6 Southwark
06.12.97	Nick Howard W RSC 1 Wembley
10.01.98	Johnny Davison W RSC 2 Bethnal Green
14.02.98	Ray Kane W RTD 1 Southwark
14.03.98	Michael Murray W PTS 6 Bethnal Green
12.09.98	Harry Senior L RSC 6 Bethnal Green *(Vacant Southern Area Heavyweight Title)*
16.01.99	Gary Williams W PTS 6 Bethnal Green
10.07.99	Chris Woollas W RTD 4 Southwark

18.01.00	Tony Booth W PTS 6 Mansfield
14.10.00	Wayne Llewelyn L RSC 3 Wembley
17.02.01	Timo Hoffmann W PTS 8 Bethnal Green
24.03.01	Timo Hoffmann L PTS 8 Magdeburg, Germany
03.11.01	Corrie Sanders L RSC 1 Brakpan, South Africa
20.12.01	Jermell Lamar Barnes W PTS 8 Rotterdam, Holland
12.02.02	Danny Williams L RTD 8 Bethnal Green *(British & Commonwealth Heavyweight Title Challenges)*
09.05.02	Pele Reid W RSC 7 Leicester Square *(Vacant WBF European Heavyweight Title)*
10.07.02	Garing Lane W PTS 6 Wembley
17.09.02	Derek McCafferty W PTS 8 Bethnal Green
12.12.02	Tamas Feheri W RSC 2 Leicester Square
24.01.03	Mike Holden W RSC 4 Sheffield
18.03.03	Mark Potter W RSC 3 Reading *(Southern Area Heavyweight Title Challenge. Elim. British Heavyweight Title)*
10.06.03	Petr Horacek W CO 1 Sheffield
01.08.03	Colin Kenna W RSC 1 Bethnal Green *(Southern Area Heavyweight Title Defence)*
26.09.03	Danny Williams L RSC 5 Reading *(British & Commonwealth Heavyweight Title Challenges)*
24.01.04	Danny Williams W PTS 12 Wembley *(British & Commonwealth Heavyweight Title Challenges)*
24.04.04	Matt Skelton L CO 12 Reading *(British & Commonwealth Heavyweight Title Defences)*
10.09.04	Robert Sulgan W RSC 1 Bethnal Green
23.04.05	Cengiz Koc W PTS 10 Dortmund, Germany *(Vacant European Union Heavyweight Title)*
01.10.05	Paolo Vidoz L PTS 12 Oldenburg, Germany *(European Heavyweight Title Challenge)*
13.12.05	Vladimir Virchis L PTS 12 Solden, Austria *(WBO Inter-Continental Heavyweight Title Challenge)*
18.02.06	Antoine Palatis W PTS 10 Edinburgh *(Vacant European Union Heavyweight Title)*
15.07.06	Ruslan Chagaev L RSC 8 Hamburg, Germany *(Vacant WBO Asia-Pacific Heavyweight Title)*
04.11.06	Rene Dettweiler W PTS 12 Mülheim an der Ruhr, Germany *(European Union Heavyweight Title Defence)*
17.02.07	Audley Harrison W RSC 3 Wembley *(European Union Heavyweight Title Defence. Vacant English Heavyweight Title)*
14.07.07	Matt Skelton L PTS 12 Greenwich *(Commonwealth Heavyweight Title Challenge)*
31.05.08	Taras Bidenko L PTS 10 Dusseldorf, Germany

Career: 42 contests, won 30, lost 12.

Micky Steeds

Isle of Dogs. *Born* London, 14 September, 1983
Cruiserweight. Former Undefeated Southern Area Heavyweight Champion. *Ht* 6'0"
Manager Self

18.09.03 Slick Miller W PTS 4 Mayfair
21.02.04 Brodie Pearmaine W RSC 1 Brighton
12.03.04 Paul King W PTS 6 Millwall
02.12.04 Luke Simpkin W RSC 3 Crystal Palace
18.02.05 Scott Gammer L PTS 6 Brighton
24.04.05 Julius Francis W PTS 8 Leicester Square
12.06.05 Mal Rice W PTS 6 Leicester Square
24.07.05 Garry Delaney W PTS 6 Leicester Square
05.03.06 Colin Kenna W PTS 10 Southampton
(Southern Area Heavyweight Title Challenge)
13.10.06 Scott Gammer L PTS 12 Aberavon
(British Heavyweight Title Challenge)
02.12.06 Luke Simpkin W PTS 6 Southwark
18.05.07 John Anthony W PTS 6 Canning Town
18.04.08 Paul Bonson W PTS 8 Bethnal Green
13.06.08 Radcliffe Green W RTD 4 Portsmouth
Career: 14 contests, won 12, lost 2.

Micky Steeds   Philip Sharkey

Danny Stewart

Bristol. *Born* Bristol, 3 January, 1986
L.Welterweight. *Ht* 5'11¼"
Manager J. Feld

23.02.08 John Baguley L RSC 2 Crawley
30.03.08 Craig Dyer W PTS 4 Port Talbot
10.05.08 Nathan McIntosh L PTS 4 Nottingham
Career: 3 contests, won 1, lost 2.

Dave Stewart

Ayr. *Born* Irvine, 5 September, 1975
Welterweight. Former Undefeated British Masters Lightweight Champion. *Ht* 6'0¼"
Manager Self

15.02.01 Danny Connelly W PTS 6 Glasgow

27.04.01 Woody Greenaway W PTS 6 Glasgow
07.09.01 John Marshall W PTS 6 Glasgow
15.06.02 Dave Hinds W PTS 6 Tottenham
06.09.02 Pete Buckley W PTS 6 Bethnal Green
17.09.02 James Paisley W RSC 5 Bethnal Green
30.01.03 Scott Lawton W PTS 6 Piccadilly
26.04.03 Nigel Senior W RSC 2 Brentford
(British Masters Lightweight Title Challenge)
27.05.03 Pete Buckley W PTS 4 Dagenham
01.08.03 Norman Dhalie W RTD 2 Bethnal Green
26.09.03 Jimmy Beech W RTD 2 Reading
14.11.03 Pete Buckley W PTS 4 Bethnal Green
16.04.04 Carl Allen W PTS 6 Bradford
10.09.04 Bobby Vanzie W PTS 6 Wembley
10.04.05 Daniel Thorpe W RSC 3 Brentwood
16.07.05 Anthony Mezaache W PTS 8 Chigwell
21.10.05 Judex Meemea W PTS 6 Bethnal Green
17.02.06 Jason Nesbitt W PTS 4 Bethnal Green
12.05.06 Lee Meager L RSC 6 Bethnal Green
(Vacant British Lightweight Title)
24.11.06 Kpakpo Allotey W PTS 10 Nottingham
(Elim. Commonwealth Lightweight Title)
18.05.07 Jason Nesbitt W PTS 4 Canning Town
05.10.07 Jonathan Thaxton L RSC 12 Bethnal Green
(British Lightweight Title Challenge)
01.12.07 Ben Hudson W PTS 6 Chigwell
22.02.08 Billy Smith W PTS 6 Bethnal Green
Career: 24 contests, won 22, lost 2.

Darryl Still

Basingstoke. *Born* Basingstoke, 26 November, 1980
Welterweight. *Ht* 5'8¼"
Manager J. Bishop

16.09.07 Mark McCullough W PTS 4 Southampton
10.11.07 Craig Dyer W PTS 6 Portsmouth
02.03.08 David Kehoe W PTS 4 Portsmouth
Career: 3 contests, won 3.

(Alexei) Alex Stoda

Wisbech. *Born* Venemaa, Estonia, 21 February, 1978
L.Middleweight. *Ht* 5'10"
Manager Self

22.12.99 Ivan Dragov L PTS 4 Tallin, Estonia
06.10.05 Martin Marshall L PTS 6 Sunderland
30.10.05 Anthony Young L PTS 6 Bethnal Green
30.05.06 Sam Webb W RSC 3 Bethnal Green
18.06.06 Mark Thompson L RSC 1 Manchester
03.11.06 Gary Woolcombe L DIS 4 Barnsley
02.12.06 Jay Morris W RSC 4 Southwark
02.03.07 Karl David L PTS 6 Neath
08.06.07 Mark Hastie L PTS 4 Motherwell
14.09.07 Nathan Brough L DIS 2 Kirkcaldy
25.09.07 Glen Matsell L PTS 6 Hull
06.10.07 Kell Brook L PTS 6 Nottingham
Career: 12 contests, won 2, lost 10.

Tony Stones

Bradford. *Born* Manchester, 18 February, 1978
S.Middleweight. *Ht* 5'10"
Manager M. Marsden

16.03.07 Colin Baxter L PTS 6 Glasgow
20.04.07 Sam Horton L PTS 4 Dudley
14.05.07 Dave Pearson DREW 6 Cleethorpes

21.09.07 Shane Junior L RSC 2 Burton
29.11.07 Peter Cannon DREW 6 Bradford
14.03.08 Justin Jones L PTS 4 Manchester
10.04.08 Sam Horton L PTS 6 Piccadilly
20.06.08 Keiron Gray L PTS 4 Wolverhampton
Career: 8 contests, drew 2, lost 6.

Tony Stones   Philip Sharkey

Ricky Strike

Sheffield. *Born* Rotherham, 28 November, 1978
L.Heavyweight. *Ht* 5'9"
Manager D. Coldwell

23.02.07 Jorge Gomez L PTS 4 Peterborough
26.03.07 Jamie Ambler L CO 6 Glasgow
26.04.07 Tony Quigley L RSC 3 Manchester
22.07.07 Charlie Chiverton L RSC 1 Mansfield
16.02.08 Matthew Hainy L PTS 4 Leicester
28.03.08 Jack Morris L PTS 4 Piccadilly
26.04.08 Lloyd Creighton L PTS 6 Darlington
16.05.08 Leon Senior L PTS 4 Holborn
20.06.08 Russ Colley L PTS 4 Wolverhampton
Career: 9 contests, lost 9.

Ricky Strike   Philip Sharkey

Alex Strutt

Ombersley. *Born* Banbury, 9 April, 1982
Middleweight. *Ht* 5'11¼"
Manager R. Woodhall

28.09.07 Lance Verallo W RSC 2 Birmingham
13.04.08 Ben Hudson W PTS 4 Edgbaston
Career: 2 contests, won 2.

Darren Stubbs

Oldham. *Born* Manchester, 16 October, 1971
British Masters L.Heavyweight Champion.
Ht 5'10"
Manager J. Doughty

02.06.02 Adam Cale W RSC 6 Shaw
21.06.02 Dean Cockburn L RSC 1 Leeds
17.11.02 Shpetim Hoti W RTD 2 Shaw
29.11.02 Jamie Wilson W PTS 6 Hull
09.03.03 Martin Thompson W RSC 3 Shaw
18.03.03 Jamie Hearn W RSC 3 Reading
08.06.03 Danny Grainger L RSC 2 Shaw
19.10.03 Paul Wesley W PTS 6 Shaw
29.02.04 Patrick Cito W PTS 6 Shaw
10.04.04 Alan Page L PTS 4 Manchester
20.04.04 Paul Owen W PTS 6 Sheffield
31.10.04 Nick Okoth W PTS 6 Shaw
20.11.05 Paul Bonson W PTS 6 Shaw
02.04.06 Howard Clarke W PTS 6 Shaw
18.06.06 Amer Khan L PTS 10 Manchester
         (Vacant Central Area L.Heavyweight Title)
11.03.07 Hastings Rasani W RSC 5 Shaw
03.05.07 Jon Ibbotson W RSC 4 Sheffield
07.10.07 Hastings Rasani W PTS 6 Shaw
02.12.07 Simeon Cover W PTS 6 Oldham
20.04.08 Simeon Cover W RTD 7 Shaw
         (Vacant British Masters L.Heavyweight Title)
Career: 20 contests, won 16, lost 4.

Lee Swaby

Lincoln. *Born* Lincoln, 14 May, 1976
Cruiserweight. Former Undefeated British
Masters Cruiserweight Champion. *Ht* 6'2"
Manager Self

29.04.97 Naveed Anwar W PTS 6 Manchester
19.06.97 Liam Richardson W RSC 4 Scunthorpe
30.10.97 Phil Ball W RSC 3 Newark
17.11.97 L. A. Williams W PTS 6 Manchester
02.02.98 Tim Redman L PTS 6 Manchester
27.02.98 John Wilson W CO 3 Glasgow
07.03.98 Phill Day L PTS 4 Reading
08.05.98 Chris P. Bacon L RSC 3 Manchester
17.07.98 Chris P. Bacon L PTS 6 Mere
19.09.98 Cathal O'Grady L RSC 1 Dublin
20.12.98 Mark Levy L RTD 5 Salford
23.06.99 Lee Archer W PTS 6 West Bromwich
04.09.99 Garry Delaney L PTS 8 Bethnal Green
03.10.99 Brian Gascoigne DREW 6 Chesterfield
11.12.99 Owen Beck L PTS 4 Liverpool
05.03.00 Kelly Oliver L PTS 10 Peterborough
         (Vacant British Masters Cruiserweight Title)
15.04.00 Mark Levy W PTS 4 Bethnal Green
12.05.00 Enzo Maccarinelli W CO 3 Swansea
26.05.00 Steffen Nielsen L PTS 4 Holbaek, Denmark
09.09.00 Tony Dowling W RSC 9 Newark
         (Vacant British Masters Cruiserweight Title)

05.02.01 Robert Norton L PTS 8 Hull
24.03.01 Crawford Ashley L PTS 8 Sheffield
30.04.01 Eamonn Glennon W PTS 6 Glasgow
02.06.01 Denzil Browne DREW 8 Wakefield
31.07.01 Stephane Allouane W PTS 4 Bethnal Green
13.09.01 Kevin Barrett W PTS 4 Sheffield
15.12.01 Chris Woollas W RSC 4 Sheffield
27.04.02 Mark Hobson L PTS 10 Huddersfield
         (Final Elim. British Cruiserweight Title)
03.08.02 Greg Scott-Briggs W RSC 4 Derby
05.12.02 Eamonn Glennon W PTS 4 Sheffield
24.01.03 Tommy Eastwood W PTS 6 Sheffield
10.06.03 Paul Bonson W PTS 4 Sheffield
05.09.03 Brodie Pearmaine W RTD 4 Sheffield
20.04.04 Lee Mountford W RSC 1 Sheffield
27.05.04 Mark Hobson L RSC 6 Huddersfield
         (British & Commonwealth Cruiserweight Title Challenges)
24.10.04 Denzil Browne W RSC 7 Sheffield
         (Elim. British Cruiserweight Title)
09.09.05 Hastings Rasani W PTS 4 Sheffield
26.11.05 Vitaly Shkraba W RSC 3 Sheffield
04.03.06 Marco Huck L RTD 6 Oldenburg, Germany
20.10.06 John Keeton L RSC 7 Sheffield
         (Vacant British Cruiserweight Title)
02.12.06 Alexander Alexeev L RSC 5 Berlin, Germany
07.12.07 Sebastian Koeber L PTS 6 Alsterdorf, Germany
08.02.08 David Dolan L PTS 6 Peterlee
09.05.08 Chris Burton L PTS 8 Middlesbrough
Career: 44 contests, won 22, drew 2, lost 20.

Lee Swaby   Philip Sharkey

Martin Sweeney

Darwen. *Born* Rochdale, 19 August, 1981
L.Middleweight. *Ht* 5'7¾"
Manager Self

11.05.06 Zahoor Hussain L PTS 6 Sunderland
21.05.06 Danny Butler L PTS 6 Bristol
22.06.06 Nicki Smedley L RSC 3 Sheffield
30.09.06 Aaron Thomas L CO 2 Stoke
13.04.07 Chris Mullen L RSC 6 Houghton le Spring
26.10.07 Ciaran Duffy W RSC 4 Glasgow
05.12.07 Faizal Zahid L RSC 5 Sheffield
23.02.08 Steve Williams L PTS 6 Liverpool
28.03.08 Karl Chiverton L PTS 4 Barnsley
Career: 9 contests, won 2, lost 7.

James Swindells

Aldershot. *Born* Aylesbury, 24 July, 1975
Cruiserweight. *Ht* 5'10½"
Manager J. Evans

05.06.07 Andrew Young L RSC 2 Glasgow
16.09.07 Billy Boyle L RSC 4 Sheffield
Career: 2 contests, lost 2.

Gary Sykes

Dewsbury. *Born* Dewsbury, 13 February, 1984
Lightweight. *Ht* 5'8"
Manager C. Aston/S. Wood

23.02.06 Dave Hinds W PTS 6 Leeds
13.04.06 Dai Davies W CO 3 Leeds
13.04.07 Kristian Laight W PTS 4 Altrincham
24.06.07 Rom Krauklis W PTS 4 Wigan
13.07.07 Deniss Sirjatovs W RSC 2 Barnsley
19.10.07 Dwayne Hill W RSC 4 Doncaster
08.12.07 Carl Allen W PTS 6 Wigan
28.03.08 Peter Allen W PTS 6 Barnsley
Career: 8 contests, won 8.

Chas Symonds

Croydon. *Born* Croydon, 8 July, 1982
Welterweight. Former Undefeated British
Masters Welterweight Champion. Former
Southern Area Welterweight Champion.
Ht 5'6¼"
Manager S. Barrett

18.02.03 Darren Goode W RSC 2 Bethnal Green
08.04.03 Lee Bedell W PTS 4 Bethnal Green
03.06.03 Arv Mittoo W PTS 6 Bethnal Green
22.07.03 Pete Buckley W PTS 6 Bethnal Green
25.09.03 Ben Hudson W PTS 6 Bethnal Green
18.11.03 Ernie Smith W PTS 6 Bethnal Green
20.02.04 Dave Wakefield W RSC 5 Bethnal Green
24.04.04 Geraint Harvey W PTS 4 Reading
07.05.04 Robert Lloyd-Taylor W RTD 5 Bethnal Green
25.06.04 Brett James W RSC 4 Bethnal Green
         (Southern Area Welterweight Title Challenge)
24.09.04 Keith Jones W PTS 10 Bethnal Green
         (Vacant British Masters Welterweight Title)
25.02.05 Peter Dunn W PTS 4 Wembley
29.04.05 Ross Minter L RSC 3 Southwark
         (Southern Area Welterweight Title Defence)
13.06.08 Paul Morby W PTS 6 Portsmouth
Career: 14 contests, won 13, lost 1.

Gavin Tait

Carmarthen. *Born* Carmarthen, 2 March, 1976
Welterweight. *Ht* 5'7"
Manager Self

07.06.04	Stuart Green L PTS 6 Glasgow	
03.07.04	Justin Hicks W RSC 5 Bristol	
05.10.04	Tristan Davies L PTS 6 Dudley	
24.11.04	David Pereira L PTS 6 Mayfair	
02.12.04	Chris Long L PTS 6 Bristol	
07.04.05	Gary Coombes W RSC 3 Birmingham	
27.05.05	Darren Johnstone L PTS 6 Motherwell	
30.10.05	Dwayne Hill L PTS 6 Sheffield	
24.03.06	Tom Glover W PTS 4 Bethnal Green	
21.10.06	Calvin White W PTS 4 Southwark	
03.12.06	Jamie Spence W RSC 4 Bethnal Green	
08.12.07	Scott Haywood L PTS 6 Wigan	
16.05.08	Paul Burns L PTS 10 Motherwell	

(Vacant International Masters Welterweight Title)
Career: 13 contests, won 5, lost 8.

(Mehrdud) Takaloo (Takalobigashi)

Margate. *Born* Iran, 23 September, 1975
Welterweight. Former WBU Welterweight Champion. Former Undefeated WBU L.Middleweight Champion. Former Undefeated IBF Inter-Continental L.Middleweight Champion. *Ht* 5'9"
Manager F. Warren

19.07.97 Harry Butler W RSC 1 Wembley
13.09.97 Michael Alexander W PTS 4 Millwall
15.11.97 Koba Kulu W RSC 3 Bristol
19.12.97 Mark Sawyers W PTS 4 Millwall
07.02.98 Jawaid Khaliq L RSC 4 Cheshunt
16.05.98 Anas Oweida W RSC 1 Bethnal Green
10.10.98 Michael Jones L PTS 6 Bethnal Green
30.01.99 Darren McInulty W RSC 5 Bethnal Green
03.04.99 Gareth Lovell W RSC 6 Kensington
26.06.99 Leigh Wicks W CO 3 Millwall
04.09.99 Carlton Williams W RSC 4 Bethnal Green
23.10.99 Prince Kasi Kaihau W RSC 3 Telford
29.01.00 Paul King W RSC 2 Manchester
08.04.00 Biagio Falcone W RTD 4 Bethnal Green
08.07.00 Ernie Smith W RSC 4 Widnes
12.08.00 Howard Clarke W PTS 12 Wembley
(Vacant IBF Inter-Continental L.Middleweight Title)
13.11.00 Jason Collins W RSC 2 Bethnal Green
24.02.01 James Lowther W PTS 12 Bethnal Green
(IBF Inter-Continental L.Middleweight Title Defence)
07.07.01 Anthony Farnell W RSC 1 Manchester
(Vacant WBU L.Middleweight Title)
22.09.01 Scott Dixon W CO 1 Bethnal Green
(WBU L. Middleweight Title Defence)
04.05.02 Gary Logan W RSC 10 Bethnal Green
(WBU L.Middleweight Title Defence)
17.08.02 Daniel Santos L PTS 12 Cardiff
(WBO L.Middleweight Title Challenge.

WBU L.Middleweight Title Defence)
01.02.03 Jim Rock W RSC 9 Belfast
(Vacant WBU L. Middleweight Title)
24.05.03 Jose Rosa W PTS 12 Bethnal Green
(WBU L.Middleweight Title Defence)
13.09.03 Vladimir Borovski W CO 3 Newport
24.01.04 Eugenio Monteiro L PTS 8 Wembley
10.09.04 Wayne Alexander L RSC 2 Bethnal Green
(Vacant WBU L.Middleweight Title)
23.07.05 Delroy Mellis W PTS 8 Edinburgh
25.02.06 Turgay Uzun W PTS 10 Canning Town
20.05.06 Eamonn Magee W PTS 12 Belfast
(WBU Welterweight Title Challenge)
07.04.07 Michael Jennings L PTS 12 Cardiff
(WBU Welterweight Title Defence)
12.01.08 Anthony Small L RSC 7 Bethnal Green
(Vacant Southern Area L.Middleweight Title)
Career: 32 contests, won 25, lost 7.

Takaloo   Philip Sharkey

Karl Taylor

Birmingham. *Born* Birmingham, 5 January, 1966
Welterweight. Former Undefeated Midlands Area Lightweight Champion. *Ht* 5'5"
Manager Self

18.03.87 Steve Brown W PTS 6 Stoke
06.04.87 Paul Taylor L PTS 6 Southampton
12.06.87 Mark Begley W RSC 1 Leamington
18.11.87 Colin Lynch W RSC 4 Solihull
29.02.88 Peter Bradley L PTS 8 Birmingham
04.10.89 Mark Antony W CO 2 Stafford
30.10.89 Tony Feliciello L PTS 8 Birmingham
06.12.89 John Davison L PTS 8 Leicester
23.12.89 Regilio Tuur L RTD 1 Hoogvliet, Holland
22.02.90 Mark Ramsey L RSC 4 Hull
29.10.90 Steve Walker DREW 6 Birmingham
10.12.90 Elvis Parsley L PTS 6 Birmingham
16.01.91 Wayne Windle W PTS 8 Stoke
02.05.91 Billy Schwer L PTS 6 Northampton
25.07.91 Peter Till L RSC 4 Dudley
(Midlands Area Lightweight Title Challenge)
24.02.92 Charlie Kane L PTS 8 Glasgow
28.04.92 Richard Woolgar W PTS 6 Wolverhampton
29.05.92 Alan McDowall L PTS 6 Glasgow
25.07.92 Michael Armstrong L RSC 3

Manchester
02.11.92 Hugh Forde L PTS 6 Wolverhampton
23.11.92 Dave McHale L PTS 8 Glasgow
22.12.92 Patrick Gallagher L RSC 3 Mayfair
13.02.93 Craig Dermody L RSC 5 Manchester
31.03.93 Craig Dermody W PTS 6 Barking
07.06.93 Mark Geraghty W PTS 8 Glasgow
13.08.93 Giorgio Campanella L CO 6 Arezzo, Italy
05.10.93 Paul Harvey W PTS 6 Mayfair
21.10.93 Charles Shepherd L RTD 5 Bayswater
21.12.93 Patrick Gallagher L PTS 6 Mayfair
09.02.94 Alan Levene W RSC 2 Brentwood
01.03.94 Shaun Cogan L PTS 6 Dudley
15.03.94 Patrick Gallagher L PTS 6 Mayfair
18.04.94 Peter Till W PTS 10 Walsall
(Midlands Area Lightweight Title Challenge)
24.05.94 Michael Ayers DREW 8 Sunderland
12.11.94 P. J. Gallagher L PTS 6 Dublin
29.11.94 Dingaan Thobela W PTS 8 Cannock
31.03.95 Michael Ayers L RSC 8 Crystal Palace
(British Lightweight Title Challenge)
06.05.95 Cham Joof W PTS 8 Shepton Mallet
23.06.95 Poli Diaz L PTS 8 Madrid, Spain
02.09.95 Paul Ryan L RSC 3 Wembley
04.11.95 Carl Wright L PTS 6 Liverpool
15.12.95 Peter Richardson L PTS 8 Bethnal Green
23.01.96 Paul Knights DREW 6 Bethnal Green
05.03.96 Andy Holligan L PTS 6 Barrow
20.03.96 Mervyn Bennett W PTS 8 Cardiff
21.05.96 Malcolm Melvin L PTS 10 Edgbaston
(Midlands Area L. Welterweight Title Challenge)
07.10.96 Joshua Clottey L RSC 2 Lewisham
20.12.96 Anatoly Alexandrov L RSC 7 Bilbao, Spain
28.01.97 Eamonn Magee L PTS 6 Belfast
28.02.97 Mark Breslin L RSC 6 Kilmarnock
30.08.97 Gilbert Eastman L PTS 4 Cheshunt
25.10.97 Tontcho Tontchev L PTS 4 Queensferry
22.11.97 Bobby Vanzie L PTS 6 Manchester
18.04.98 Ricky Hatton L RSC 1 Manchester
18.07.98 James Hare L PTS 4 Sheffield
26.09.98 Oktay Urkal L PTS 8 Norwich
28.11.98 Junior Witter L PTS 4 Sheffield
06.03.99 George Scott L RSC 4 Southwark
15.05.99 Jon Thaxton L PTS 6 Sheffield
10.07.99 Eamonn Magee L RTD 3 Southwark
06.11.99 Alan Sebire W PTS 6 Widnes
15.11.99 Steve Murray L RSC 1 Bethnal Green
19.08.00 Iain Eldridge L PTS 4 Brentwood
04.09.00 Tomas Jansson L PTS 6 Manchester
16.09.00 Colin Lynes L PTS 6 Bethnal Green
09.12.00 David Walker L PTS 6 Southwark
10.02.01 Matthew Hatton L PTS 4 Widnes
10.03.01 Francis Barrett L RSC 3 Bethnal Green
10.04.01 Costas Katsantonis L PTS 4 Wembley
16.06.01 Brett James DREW 4 Wembley
15.09.01 David Barnes L PTS 4 Manchester
28.10.01 Babatunde Ajayi L PTS 4 Southwark
24.11.01 Ross Minter L PTS 4 Bethnal Green
15.12.01 Alexandra Vetoux L PTS 4 Wembley
12.02.02 Brett James DREW 4 Bethnal Green
11.03.02 Kevin McIntyre L PTS 4 Glasgow
04.05.02 Matthew Hatton L RSC 3 Bethnal Green
25.06.02 Rimell Taylor DREW 6 Rugby
20.07.02 Matthew Hatton L RTD 2 Bethnal Green
28.09.02 Michael Jennings L RSC 4 Manchester
16.11.02 Gavin Wake L PTS 4 Nottingham

179

30.11.02	Tony Conroy L PTS 4 Coventry
14.12.02	Alexander Vetoux L RTD 3 Newcastle
15.02.03	Ross Minter L PTS 6 Wembley
29.03.03	Alexander Vetoux L RSC 1 Portsmouth
08.05.03	Tony Doherty L PTS 4 Widnes
25.07.03	Lenny Daws L RTD 2 Norwich
06.10.03	Jonathan Woollins W PTS 6 Birmingham
29.10.03	Ajose Olusegun L PTS 6 Leicester Square
29.11.03	Gary Young L RSC 3 Renfrew
30.01.04	Lee McAllister L PTS 4 Dagenham
05.03.04	Oscar Hall L PTS 6 Darlington
27.03.04	Jamie Arthur L PTS 6 Edinburgh
06.05.04	Ashley Theophane L PTS 4 Barnsley
22.05.04	Tony Doherty L RTD 2 Widnes
03.09.04	Taz Jones L PTS 4 Newport
18.09.04	Karl Chiverton L PTS 6 Newark
26.09.04	Danny Johnston L PTS 6 Stoke
19.11.04	Tony Doherty L RSC 2 Bethnal Green
19.12.04	Kell Brook L PTS 6 Bolton
06.03.05	John Murray L PTS 6 Shaw
14.05.05	Lee McAllister L RTD 3 Aberdeen
26.06.05	Henry Castle L PTS 6 Southampton
24.07.05	John Fewkes L PTS 6 Sheffield
16.09.05	Tristan Davies L PTS 4 Telford
08.11.05	Danny Reynolds L RSC 4 Leeds
11.12.05	Paul Halpin L PTS 4 Chigwell
18.12.05	Jonathan Hussey L PTS 6 Bolton
17.02.06	John O'Donnell L PTS 4 Bethnal Green
01.04.06	Ashley Theophane L PTS 4 Bethnal Green
24.04.06	Simon Fleck L PTS 6 Cleethorpes
13.05.06	Dale Miles L RSC 3 Sutton in Ashfield
18.06.06	Prince Arron L PTS 6 Manchester
15.09.06	Garry Buckland L PTS 6 Newport
07.10.06	Rob Hunt L PTS 6 Walsall
24.11.06	Scott Lawton L PTS 4 Stoke
01.12.06	Peter McDonagh L PTS 4 Tower Hill
10.12.06	Muhsen Nasser L PTS 6 Sheffield
17.02.07	Eddie Corcoran L PTS 4 Wembley
11.03.07	Chris Johnson L RTD 3 Shaw
06.05.07	Khurram Hussain L PTS 4 Leeds
09.06.07	Mark Dawes L PTS 6 Middlesbrough
20.07.07	Rob Hunt L PTS 4 Wolverhampton
07.09.07	Femi Fehintola L PTS 4 Doncaster
23.09.07	Ruben Giles L PTS 6 Longford
08.10.07	Charles Paul King L PTS 6 Glasgow
19.10.07	Mark Hastie L PTS 6 Motherwell
17.11.07	Scott Miller L PTS 6 Stoke
28.11.07	Scott Evans L RSC 3 Walsall
22.03.08	Joe Elfidh L PTS 6 Sheffield
28.04.08	Charles Paul King L PTS 6 Glasgow
05.06.08	Graham Fearn L PTS 6 Leeds
15.06.08	Danny Chamberlain L PTS 6 Bethnal Green

Career: 133 contests, won 16, drew 6, lost 111.

Nicki Taylor

Askern. *Born* Doncaster, 6 July, 1979
L.Heavyweight. *Ht* 5'11"
Manager Self

20.09.04	Sandy Robb L RSC 5 Glasgow
24.04.05	Hastings Rasani L RTD 4 Askern
18.06.05	Rod Anderton L RSC 4 Barnsley
22.10.05	Michael Pinnock W PTS 6 Mansfield
12.11.05	Danny Tombs DREW 4 Sheffield
12.12.05	Karl Wheeler L PTS 4 Peterborough
14.05.06	Duane Reid L RSC 2 Derby
06.10.06	Scott Brookes L PTS 6 Mexborough
26.10.06	Shon Davies L RSC 1 Wolverhampton
01.12.06	Lee Jones L PTS 4 Birmingham

15.02.07	Matthew Hough W RSC 2 Dudley
25.02.07	Robin White L PTS 4 Manchester
09.03.07	Tony Salam L RSC 1 Dagenham
30.06.07	Mark Nilsen L CO 4 Manchester
16.09.07	Carl Wild L PTS 6 Sheffield
28.09.07	Eddie McIntosh L CO 2 Birmingham
01.12.07	Adie Whitmore L CO 1 Nottingham

Career: 17 contests, won 2, drew 1, lost 14.

John-Paul Temple

Brighton. *Born* London, 30 May, 1973
L.Middleweight. *Ht* 5'11"
Manager R. Davies

11.02.97	Mark O'Callaghan W PTS 6 Bethnal Green
17.03.97	Les Frost W CO 4 Mayfair
24.04.97	Chris Lyons W PTS 6 Mayfair
23.10.97	Chris Lyons W PTS 8 Mayfair
26.03.98	Trevor Smith L RSC 5 Piccadilly
28.04.98	Chris Price L PTS 6 Brentford
05.10.99	Jason Hall L PTS 6 Bloomsbury
25.02.00	Daniel James L PTS 10 Newmarket *(Vacant Southern Area L.Welterweight Title)*
21.11.04	Neil Jarmolinski DREW 4 Bracknell
03.12.04	Barrie Lee L PTS 4 Edinburgh
30.04.05	Danny Goode L PTS 4 Dagenham
26.06.05	Danny Goode L PTS 4 Southampton
10.09.05	Kerry Hope L PTS 4 Cardiff
06.10.05	Kevin Phelan L PTS 6 Longford
02.12.05	Darren Barker L RSC 6 Nottingham
29.09.06	Karl David L PTS 6 Cardiff
16.09.07	Paul Morby L PTS 4 Southampton
02.03.08	Paul Morby L PTS 4 Portsmouth

Career: 18 contests, won 4, drew 1, lost 13.

Jonathan Thaxton

Norwich. *Born* Norwich, 10 September, 1974
Former Undefeated British & WBF Lightweight Champion. Former Southern Area, IBF & WBO Inter-Continental L.Welterweight Champion. *Ht* 5'6"
Manager J. Ingle

09.12.92	Scott Smith W PTS 6 Stoke
03.03.93	Dean Hiscox W PTS 6 Solihull
17.03.93	John O. Johnson W PTS 6 Stoke
23.06.93	Brian Coleman W PTS 8 Gorleston
22.09.93	John Smith W PTS 6 Wembley
07.12.93	Dean Hollington W RSC 3 Bethnal Green
10.03.94	B. F. Williams W RSC 4 Watford *(Vacant Southern Area L.Welterweight Title)*
18.11.94	Keith Marner L PTS 10 Bracknell *(Southern Area L.Welterweight Title Defence)*
26.05.95	David Thompson W RSC 6 Norwich
23.06.95	Delroy Leslie W PTS 6 Bethnal Green
12.08.95	Rene Prins L PTS 8 Zaandam, Holland
08.12.95	Colin Dunne L RSC 5 Bethnal Green *(Vacant Southern Area Lightweight Title)*
20.01.96	John O. Johnson W RSC 4 Mansfield
13.02.96	Paul Ryan W RSC 1 Bethnal Green
25.06.96	Mark Elliot W CO 5 Mansfield *(Vacant IBF Inter-Continental L.Welterweight Title)*
14.09.96	Bernard Paul W PTS 12 Sheffield *(Vacant WBO Inter-Continental L.Welterweight Title)*

Jonathan Thaxton   Philip Sharkey

27.03.97 Paul Burke W RSC 9 Norwich
(IBF & WBO Inter-Continental
L.Welterweight Title Defences)
28.06.97 Gagik Chachatrian W RSC 2 Norwich
(IBF & WBO Inter-Continental
L.Welterweight Title Defences)
29.11.97 Rimvidas Billius W PTS 12 Norwich
(IBF & WBO Inter-Continental
L.Welterweight Title Defences)
26.09.98 Emanuel Burton L RSC 7 Norwich
(IBF & WBO Inter-Continental
L.Welterweight Title Defences)
15.05.99 Karl Taylor W PTS 6 Sheffield
07.08.99 Brian Coleman W PTS 6 Dagenham
15.11.99 Jason Rowland L RSC 5 Bethnal Green
(British L.Welterweight Title
Challenge)
15.07.00 Kimoun Kouassi W RSC 3 Norwich
21.10.00 Ricky Hatton L PTS 12 Wembley
(Vacant British L.Welterweight Title)
26.03.01 Alan Temple W PTS 4 Wembley
28.07.01 David Kirk W PTS 4 Wembley
09.02.02 Eamonn Magee L RSC 6 Manchester
(Commonwealth L.Welterweight Title
Challenge)
13.04.02 Chill John W RSC 2 Norwich
15.06.02 Marc Waelkens W RSC 7 Norwich
21.09.02 Viktor Baranov W RSC 1 Norwich
09.10.04 Silence Saheed W PTS 6 Norwich
13.12.04 Carl Allen W RSC 1 Birmingham
09.04.05 Christophe de Busillet W CO 4
Norwich
(Vacant WBF Lightweight Title)
03.09.05 Vasile Dragomir W CO 4 Norwich
(WBF Lightweight Title Defence)
17.02.06 Alan Temple W RSC 5 Bethnal Green
13.05.06 Jorge Daniel Miranda W PTS 10
Sheffield
08.12.06 Lee Meager W PTS 12 Dagenham
(British Lightweight Title Challenge)
16.03.07 Scott Lawton W RSC 7 Norwich
(British Lightweight Title Defence)
05.10.07 Dave Stewart W RSC 12 Bethnal
Green
(British Lightweight Title Defence)
04.04.08 Yuri Romanov L RSC 6 Bethnal Green
(European Lightweight Title
Challenge)
Career: 41 contests, won 33, lost 8.

Ashley Theophane

Kilburn. *Born* London, 20 August, 1980
L.Welterweight. Former Undefeated Global
Boxing Council Welterweight Champion.
Ht 5'7"
Manager Self

03.06.03 Lee Bedell W RSC 4 Bethnal Green
22.07.03 Brian Coleman W PTS 6 Bethnal Green
25.04.04 David Kirk W PTS 6 Nottingham
06.05.04 Karl Taylor W PTS 4 Barnsley
05.06.04 Chris Brophy W RSC 3 Bethnal Green
19.06.04 Arv Mittoo W PTS 4 Muswell Hill
02.12.04 Keith Jones W PTS 6 Crystal Palace
26.03.05 Judex Meemea L PTS 6 Hackney
24.04.05 David Kehoe W PTS 4 Leicester Square
12.06.05 Jus Wallie W PTS 4 Leicester Square
18.09.05 Oscar Milkitas L PTS 4 Bethnal Green
09.10.05 David Kehoe W PTS 4 Hammersmith
19.11.05 Duncan Cottier W PTS 6 Southwark
25.02.06 Daniel Thorpe DREW 4 Canning Town
17.03.06 Josef Holub W CO 3 Horka, Germany
01.04.06 Karl Taylor W PTS 4 Bethnal Green

21.05.06 Billy Smith W PTS 4 Bethnal Green
24.09.06 Jon Honney W PTS 6 Bethnal Green
07.10.06 Ibrahim Barakat W PTS 6 Horka,
Germany
02.12.06 Omar Siala W RSC 11 Berlin, Germany
(Vacant GBC Welterweight Title)
20.01.07 Alan Bosworth W RSC 7 Muswell Hill
(Elim. British Welterweight Title)
16.11.07 Marcos Hernandez W RSC 3 Gros
Islet, Saint Lucia
01.12.07 Rocky Muscus W RSC 1 Bethnal
Green
15.02.08 Ali Oubaali L PTS 10 Uncasville,
Connecticut, USA
15.06.08 Geoffrey Munika W PTS 6 Bethnal
Green
Career: 25 contests, won 21, drew 1, lost 3.

Matthew Thirlwall

Bermondsey. *Born* Middlesbrough, 28
November, 1980
S.Middleweight. *Ht* 5'9½"
Manager Self

16.03.02 William Webster W RSC 1 Bethnal
Green
10.05.02 Leigh Wicks W PTS 4 Bethnal Green
23.08.02 Harry Butler W RSC 3 Bethnal Green
25.10.02 Jason Collins W RSC 5 Bethnal Green
21.12.02 Howard Clarke W PTS 6 Dagenham
28.01.03 Gary Beardsley L PTS 6 Nottingham
16.04.03 Gary Beardsley W PTS 6 Nottingham
27.05.03 Leigh Wicks W PTS 6 Dagenham
04.10.03 Dean Powell W RSC 2 Muswell Hill
11.12.03 Harry Butler W PTS 6 Bethnal Green
12.03.04 Patrick Cito W RSC 3 Nottingham
24.09.04 Jason Collins L PTS 6 Nottingham
02.12.04 Ernie Smith W PTS 4 Nottingham
20.01.06 Donovan Smillie W CO 9 Bethnal
Green
(Final Elim. English S.Middleweight
Title)
24.03.06 Moises Martinez W RSC 6 Hollywood,
Florida, USA
08.12.06 Howard Clarke W PTS 4 Dagenham
20.01.07 Hussain Osman W RSC 5 Muswell Hill
18.05.07 David Kirk W PTS 4 Canning Town
14.11.07 Danny Thornton L RSC 3 Bethnal
Green
Career: 19 contests, won 16, lost 3.

Chris Thompson   Philip Sharkey

Chris Thompson

Leeds. *Born* Leeds, 5 April, 1984
L.Middleweight. *Ht* 5'11¼"
Manager M. Marsden

31.01.08 Steve Cooper L RSC 2 Piccadilly
16.03.08 Paul Royston L PTS 6 Sheffield
22.06.08 Duane Parker L PTS 4 Derby
Career: 3 contests, lost 3.

Mark Thompson   Philip Sharkey

Mark Thompson

Heywood. *Born* Rochdale, 28 May, 1981
L.Middleweight. Former Undefeated
International Masters Welterweight
Champion. *Ht* 5'11"
Manager S. Wood

23.09.05 Geraint Harvey W PTS 4 Manchester
20.11.05 Danny Moir W RSC 2 Shaw
18.12.05 Tony Randell W RSC 2 Bolton
12.02.06 Darren Gethin W PTS 4 Manchester
02.03.06 Simon Fleck W CO 3 Blackpool
02.04.06 Ernie Smith W PTS 6 Shaw
18.06.06 Alex Stoda W RSC 1 Manchester
21.07.06 Ernie Smith W RSC 3 Altrincham
29.09.06 Alexander Matviechuk W PTS 8
Manchester
09.02.07 Lee Noble W PTS 6 Leeds
13.04.07 Manoocha Salari W RSC 1 Altrincham
06.07.07 Vincent Vuma L RSC 8 Wigan
(Vacant WBC International
L.Middleweight Title)
22.09.07 Ronny Daniels W RSC 1 Wigan
26.10.07 Frank Harroche Horta W PTS 8 Wigan
01.02.08 Darren Gethin W RTD 2 Bethnal Green
26.04.08 Maurycy Gojko W RSC 1 Wigan
(Vacant International Masters
Welterweight Title)
13.06.08 Artur Jashkul W CO 1 Portsmouth
Career: 17 contests, won 16, lost 1.

Willie Thompson

Ballyclare. *Born* Larne, 2 January, 1980
L.Middleweight. *Ht* 6'0"
Manager A. Wilton

30.06.07 Paul Royston W PTS 4 Belfast
25.08.07 Artur Jashkul W PTS 4 Dublin
13.10.07 Peter Dunn W PTS 6 Belfast
08.12.07 Duncan Cottier W PTS 4 Belfast
22.03.08 Semens Moroshek W PTS 4 Dublin
31.05.08 Janis Chernouskis W PTS 6 Belfast
Career: 6 contests, won 6.

Danny Thornton

Leeds. *Born* Leeds, 20 July, 1978
Cruiserweight. Former Undefeated Central
Area Middleweight Champion. *Ht* 5'10"
Manager Self

06.10.97	Pedro Carragher L PTS 6 Bradford
13.11.97	Shaun O'Neill DREW 6 Bradford
08.12.97	Shaun O'Neill DREW 6 Bradford
09.02.98	Roy Chipperfield W RSC 4 Bradford
17.03.98	Patrick J. Maxwell L PTS 6 Sheffield
30.03.98	Mark Owens W PTS 6 Bradford
15.05.98	Danny Bell W PTS 6 Nottingham
15.06.98	Jimmy Hawk W PTS 6 Bradford
12.10.98	Wayne Shepherd W PTS 6 Bradford
21.02.99	Shaun O'Neill W RSC 5 Bradford
25.04.99	Matt Scriven W RSC 4 Leeds
14.06.99	Martin Thompson W PTS 6 Bradford
18.10.99	Paul Henry W PTS 4 Bradford
14.11.99	Dean Ashton W PTS 4 Bradford
06.12.99	Lee Blundell L PTS 6 Bradford
05.02.00	Steve Roberts L PTS 6 Bethnal Green
25.03.00	Lee Molloy W RSC 2 Liverpool
06.06.00	Joe Townsley L RSC 7 Motherwell
	(IBO Inter-Continental
	L. Middleweight Title Challenge)
30.11.00	Lee Blundell L RSC 8 Blackpool
	(Vacant Central Area L. Middleweight
	Title)
20.03.01	Ian Toby W PTS 8 Leeds
13.11.01	Matt Galer L RSC 4 Leeds
02.12.02	Gary Thompson W PTS 6 Leeds
13.05.03	Kreshnik Qato L PTS 6 Leeds
06.06.03	Jason Collins W PTS 10 Hull
	(Vacant Central Area Middleweight
	Title)
28.11.03	Jason Collins W PTS 10 Hull
	(Central Area Middleweight Title
	Defence)
10.02.04	Mo W PTS 6 Barnsley
08.05.04	Scott Dann L RSC 3 Bristol
	(Vacant English Middleweight Title)
14.05.05	Simeon Cover DREW 6 Aberdeen
01.06.05	Gary Thompson W PTS 4 Leeds
25.09.05	Simeon Cover W PTS 6 Leeds
29.10.05	Jozsef Nagy L PTS 12 Szentes, Hungary
	(Vacant EBA S.Middleweight Title)
23.02.06	Howard Clarke W PTS 6 Leeds
20.03.06	Ojay Abrahams W PTS 6 Leeds
12.05.06	Darren Barker L RSC 6 Bethnal Green
01.06.07	Jorge Gomez W PTS 4 Peterborough
08.06.07	Brian Magee L RTD 2 Motherwell
07.09.07	Danny Grainger W PTS 4 Doncaster
12.10.07	Carl Wild W PTS 6 Leeds
14.11.07	Matthew Thirlwall W RSC 3 Bethnal Green
08.02.08	Martin Marshall W PTS 4 Peterlee

Career: 40 contests, won 25, drew 3, lost 12.

Daniel Thorpe

Sheffield. *Born* Sheffield, 24 September, 1977
Lightweight. Former Central Area
Lightweight Champion. *Ht* 5'7½"
Manager D. Coldwell

07.09.01	Brian Gifford DREW 4 Bethnal Green
24.09.01	Ram Singh W RSC 4 Cleethorpes
17.11.01	Mally McIver L PTS 6 Dewsbury
10.12.01	Jason Gonzales W RSC 2 Birmingham
17.12.01	Joel Viney L RSC 2 Cleethorpes
11.02.02	Gareth Wiltshaw L PTS 6 Shrewsbury
04.03.02	Dave Travers W PTS 6 Birmingham
13.04.02	Jackson Williams L PTS 6 Norwich
11.05.02	Dean Scott W RSC 1 Chesterfield
21.05.02	Chris McDonagh L PTS 6 Custom House
08.06.02	Gary Young L RSC 1 Renfrew
12.07.02	Chill John L PTS 4 Southampton
21.07.02	John Marshall L RSC 1 Salford
22.09.02	Albi Hunt L PTS 6 Southwark
05.10.02	Gavin Down L RSC 2 Chesterfield
17.11.02	Nadeem Siddique L PTS 4 Bradford
29.11.02	Pete Buckley W PTS 6 Hull
21.12.02	Billy Corcoran L CO 2 Dagenham
16.02.03	Eddie Nevins L RSC 8 Salford
	(Vacant Central Area S.Featherweight
	Title)
22.03.03	Jamie Arthur L PTS 4 Renfrew
29.03.03	Danny Hunt L PTS 6 Portsmouth
12.04.03	Jackson Williams L PTS 6 Norwich
19.04.03	Steve Mullin W RSC 1 Liverpool
28.04.03	Jeff Thomas L PTS 6 Cleethorpes
08.05.03	Andy Morris L PTS 4 Widnes
08.06.03	Choi Tsveenpurev L PTS 8 Shaw
20.06.03	Colin Toohey L PTS 6 Liverpool
28.06.03	Gavin Rees L RSC 1 Cardiff
03.08.03	Joel Viney L PTS 6 Stalybridge
06.09.03	Joel Viney W PTS 6 Aberdeen
13.09.03	Sean Hughes L PTS 6 Wakefield
21.09.03	Chris Long W PTS 6 Bristol
12.10.03	Baz Carey DREW 6 Sheffield
19.10.03	Charles Shepherd L PTS 6 Shaw
27.10.03	Nadeem Siddique L PTS 6 Glasgow
06.11.03	Lee Beavis L PTS 4 Dagenham
07.12.03	Mally McIver W PTS 10 Bradford
	(Vacant Central Area Lightweight Title)
21.12.03	Pete Buckley W PTS 6 Bolton
26.02.04	Andy Morris L RSC 3 Widnes
03.04.04	Jason Nesbitt W PTS 6 Sheffield
23.04.04	Dave Hinds W PTS 6 Leicester
07.05.04	Stefy Bull L PTS 10 Doncaster
	(Central Area Lightweight Title
	Defence)
22.05.04	Gary Thornhill L RSC 4 Manchester
03.07.04	Joel Viney W RSC 1 Blackpool
10.09.04	Mickey Bowden W PTS 6 Wembley
18.09.04	Carl Greaves L PTS 6 Newark
01.10.04	Steve Bell L PTS 6 Manchester
08.10.04	Ricky Burns L PTS 6 Glasgow
16.10.04	Ryan Barrett L PTS 4 Dagenham
29.10.04	Adnan Amar L PTS 4 Worksop
06.11.04	Baz Carey W PTS 6 Coventry
26.11.04	John Murray L RSC 2 Altrincham
13.02.05	Lee McAllister L PTS 4 Bradford
04.03.05	Femi Fehintola L PTS 6 Rotherham
10.04.05	Dave Stewart L RSC 3 Brentwood
14.05.05	Tye Williams W RSC 3 Aberdeen
26.05.05	Baz Carey W PTS 6 Mayfair
03.06.05	Nadeem Siddique L PTS 6 Hull
24.06.05	James Gorman L PTS 6 Belfast
02.07.05	Michael Kelly L PTS 4 Dundalk
09.07.05	Carl Johanneson L RSC 3 Bristol
25.09.05	Jon Honney W PTS 4 Southampton
06.10.05	Paul Holborn L PTS 6 Sunderland
25.10.05	Kevin Mitchell L RSC 4 Preston
25.11.05	Haider Ali W RTD 4 Walsall
10.12.05	Amir Khan L RSC 2 Canning Town
27.01.06	Ian Wilson L PTS 4 Dagenham
25.02.06	Ashley Theophane DREW 4 Canning Town
11.03.06	Gavin Rees L RSC 5 Newport
13.05.06	Dean Smith L PTS 4 Bethnal Green
20.05.06	Kevin O'Hara L PTS 6 Belfast
28.05.06	Shane Watson L PTS 6 Longford
16.06.06	Dwayne Hill L PTS 4 Liverpool
23.06.06	Anthony Maynard L PTS 4 Birmingham
02.09.06	Steve Bell L RTD 4 Bolton
06.10.06	Jonathan Whiteman L PTS 6 Mansfield
18.10.06	Gareth Couch L PTS 4 Bayswater
04.11.06	Paul McCloskey L RTD 3 Glasgow
06.12.06	Pete Buckley W PTS 6 Rotherham
14.12.06	Gavin Deacon W PTS 6 Leicester
22.12.06	Harry Ramogoadi L PTS 6 Coventry
15.02.07	Dean Harrison L PTS 4 Dudley
10.03.07	Stephen Burke L PTS 4 Liverpool
07.04.07	Barrie Jones L RSC 2 Cardiff
06.05.07	Michael Gomez L RSC 3 Altrincham
08.06.07	Albi Hunt L PTS 4 Mayfair
30.06.07	Eddie Hyland L PTS 4 Belfast
21.07.07	Andy Morris L RSC 2 Cardiff
09.10.07	Giovanni Kopogo W RSC 2 Tower Hamlets
12.10.07	Paul Truscott L PTS 4 Peterlee
31.10.07	Mark McCullough L PTS 6 Bayswater
17.11.07	Marco Cittadini L PTS 4 Glasgow
30.11.07	Leonard Lothian L PTS 6 Hull
08.12.07	Anthony Crolla L RTD 2 Bolton
02.02.08	Liam Walsh L CO 1 Canning Town

Career: 95 contests, won 22, drew 3, lost 70.

Daniel Thorpe   Philip Sharkey

Neil Tidman   Philip Sharkey

Neil Tidman

Bedworth. *Born* Nuneaton, 16 April, 1978
Midlands Area S.Middleweight Champion.
Ht 5'10"
Manager P. Carpenter

18.06.05	Lee Williamson W PTS 6 Coventry
22.10.05	Michael Banbula W PTS 6 Coventry
15.12.05	Omid Bourzo W RSC 3 Coventry
09.10.06	Ojay Abrahams W PTS 4 Bedworth
10.11.06	Nathan King L PTS 6 Newport
02.12.06	Mark Phillips W PTS 6 Coventry
09.12.06	Andrew Lowe L PTS 6 Chigwell
03.03.07	Jonjo Finnegan W PTS 10 Burton
	(Vacant Midlands Area S.Middleweight Title)
18.04.07	Joey Vegas L PTS 4 Strand
11.05.07	Steve McGuire L PTS 8 Motherwell
28.09.07	Simeon Cover W RSC 2 Coventry
06.10.07	Michael Monaghan W PTS 6 Leicester

Career: 12 contests, won 8, lost 4.

Danny Tombs

Sheffield. *Born* London, 26 May, 1986
L.Heavyweight. *Ht* 5'10½"
Manager D. Hobson (senior)

12.11.05	Nicki Taylor DREW 4 Sheffield
19.11.05	Michael Banbula W RSC 2 Southwark
30.03.06	Mark Phillips W PTS 4 Bloomsbury
21.10.06	Tony Booth L PTS 4 Southwark
10.11.07	David Gentles W PTS 4 Stalybridge

Career: 5 contests, won 3, drew 1, lost 1.

Craig Tomes

Barnsley. *Born* Barnsley, 22 November, 1980
Welterweight. *Ht* 5'7"
Manager Self

14.06.07	Adil Anwar L PTS 6 Leeds
11.08.07	Stephen Burke L RSC 1 Liverpool
28.09.07	Scott Sandmann L PTS 6 Preston
13.10.07	Paul Royston W PTS 6 Barnsley
26.10.07	Gary McMillan L PTS 6 Glasgow
05.12.07	Curtis Woodhouse L RSC 1 Sheffield
01.03.08	Scott Miller L RSC 6 Stoke
13.04.08	Danny Coyle L PTS 6 Edgbaston

Career: 8 contests, won 1, lost 7.

Nigel Travis

Manchester. *Born* Oldham, 5 July, 1972
S.Middleweight. *Ht* 6'0"
Manager S. Wood

16.06.07	Ryan Rowlinson W PTS 6 Bolton
23.11.07	Jezz Wilson L RSC 4 Sheffield
23.12.07	Jamie Ambler L PTS 6 Bolton

Career: 3 contests, won 1, lost 2.

Pawel Trebinski　　　　Philip Sharkey

Pawel Trebinski

Tooting. *Born* Poland, 21 October, 1983
L.Heavyweight. *Ht* 5'10¼"
Manager D. Cowland

01.05.08	Michael Banbula W PTS 6 Piccadilly
25.05.08	Mark Denton L RSC 3 Hartlepool

Career: 2 contests, won 1, lost 1.

Paul Truscott

Middlesbrough. *Born* Middlesbrough, 1 May, 1986
Commonwealth Featherweight Champion.
Ht 5'9"
Manager M. Marsden

23.06.06	Billy Smith W PTS 4 Blackpool
30.09.06	Steve Gethin W PTS 4 Middlesbrough
10.11.06	Rakhim Mingaleev W PTS 4 Hartlepool
28.01.07	Graeme Higginson W PTS 4 Yarm
25.03.07	Peter Feher W RSC 1 Dublin
20.04.07	Riaz Durgahed W PTS 4 Dudley
09.06.07	Ben Odamattey W PTS 6 Middlesbrough
12.10.07	Daniel Thorpe W PTS 4 Peterlee
15.12.07	Nikita Lukin W PTS 6 Dublin
08.02.08	Samir Kasmi W PTS 8 Peterlee
09.05.08	Osumanu Akaba W PTS 12 Middlesbrough
	(Vacant Commonwealth Featherweight Title)

Career: 11 contests, won 11.

Choi Tseveenpurev

Oldham. *Born* Mongolia, 6 October, 1971
WBU Featherweight Champion. Former
Undefeated WBF Featherweight Champion.
Former Undefeated British Masters
Featherweight Champion. *Ht* 5'5¾"
Manager J. Doughty

22.11.96	Jeun-Tae Kim W CO 8 Seoul, South Korea
28.06.97	Hee-Youn Kwon W CO 9 Busan, South Korea
19.08.98	Veeraphol Sahaprom L PTS 10 Bangkok, Thailand
02.10.98	Surapol Sithnaruepol W CO 1 Bangkok, Thailand
07.01.99	Ekarat 13Reintower W CO 2 Krabi, Thailand
01.05.99	Bulan Bugiarso L PTS 12 Kalimanton, Indonesia
12.08.99	Jiao Hasabayar W RSC 4 Ulan-Bator, Mongolia
22.08.99	Con Roksa W CO 3 Seinyeng, China
22.08.99	Thongdang Sorvoraphin W CO 4 Seinyeng, China
21.05.00	David Jeffrey W RSC 2 Shaw
24.09.00	Billy Smith W RTD 2 Shaw
03.12.00	Chris Williams W PTS 4 Shaw
27.04.01	Willie Limond L PTS 6 Glasgow
23.09.01	Steve Hanley W PTS 6 Shaw
06.10.01	Livinson Ruiz W PTS 4 Manchester
09.12.01	Kevin Gerowski W RSC 5 Shaw
	(Vacant British Masters Featherweight Title)
22.03.02	Chris Emanuele W PTS 4 Coventry
02.06.02	John Mackay W RSC 5 Shaw
17.11.02	Peter Allen W RSC 4 Shaw
09.03.03	Jason Nesbitt W PTS 8 Shaw
08.06.03	Daniel Thorpe W PTS 8 Shaw
29.02.04	John Mackay W RSC 3 Shaw
13.03.04	Lehlohonolo Ledwaba L PTS 8 Copenhagen, Denmark
06.05.04	Kevin O'Hara W PTS 8 Barnsley
10.07.04	Harry Ramogoadi W RTD 6 Coventry
	(British Masters Featherweight Title Defence)
06.03.05	Harry Ramogoadi W RSC 5 Shaw
	(British Masters Featherweight Title Defence)
20.11.05	Alexey Volchan W RSC 10 Shaw
02.04.06	David Kiilu W RSC 3 Shaw
	(Vacant WBF Featherweight Title)
11.03.07	Nikoloz Berkatsashvili W RSC 4 Shaw
	(WBF Featherweight Title Defence)
07.10.07	Abdu Tebazalwa W PTS 12 Shaw
	(WBF Featherweight Title Defence)
02.12.07	Ajibu Salum W CO 2 Oldham
05.04.08	Derry Matthews W CO 5 Bolton
	(WBU Featherweight Title Challenge)

Career: 32 contests, won 28, lost 4.

James Tucker　　　　Philip Sharkey

James Tucker

Doncaster. *Born* Doncaster, 8 February, 1985
S.Middleweight. *Ht* 5'10¼"
Manager D. Coldwell

30.11.07	Phil Goodwin L PTS 6 Hull
18.01.08	Matthew Hainy L PTS 4 Burton
02.02.08	Tommy Saunders L PTS 4 Canning Town
16.03.08	Carl Wild L PTS 6 Sheffield
28.03.08	Michael Banbula L PTS 4 Piccadilly
18.04.08	Martin Murray L PTS 4 Bethnal Green
15.05.08	Martin Marshall L PTS 6 Sunderland
30.05.08	Eddie McIntosh L PTS 4 Birmingham
09.06.08	Graham Delehedy DREW 6 Glasgow
21.06.08	Richard Collins L PTS 4 Birmingham

Career: 10 contests, drew 1, lost 9.

Rob Turley

Cefn Fforest. *Born* Newport, 24 November, 1986
S.Featherweight. *Ht* 5'7"
Manager C. Sanigar

16.06.07 Delroy Spencer W PTS 6 Newport
05.10.07 John Vanemmenis W RSC 3 Newport
05.04.08 Tony McQuade W PTS 6 Newport
24.05.08 Riaz Durgahed L PTS 6 Cardiff
Career: 4 contests, won 3, lost 1.

Amir Unsworth (Morshedi)

Sleaford. *Born* Warrington, 12 January, 1981
L.Welterweight. *Ht* 5'7"
Manager C. Greaves

30.06.07 Sergei Rozhakmens W PTS 6 Manchester
11.08.07 Mark Bett W RSC 4 Liverpool
09.11.07 Leonard Lothian W PTS 4 Nottingham
23.02.08 Carl Allen W PTS 4 Newark
31.05.08 Baz Carey W PTS 4 Newark
Career: 5 contests, won 5.

Vadim Usenko

Enfield. *Born* Ukraine, 18 August 1986
Cruiserweight. *Ht* 6'5½"
Manager P. Fondu

16.12.05 Csaba Andras W RSC 1 Bracknell
18.03.06 Nabil Haciani L RSC 6 Monte Carlo, Monaco
19.05.06 Olivier Bonvin W RSC 1 Grenoble, France
29.06.06 Tomas Mrazek W PTS 6 Carouge, Switzerland
09.03.07 Vyacheslav Sherbakov W CO 2 Donetsk, Ukraine
16.10.07 Anatoliy Kusenko W CO 1 Minsk, Belarus
31.10.07 John Anthony W PTS 6 Bayswater
Career: 7 contests, won 6, lost 1.

John Vanemmenis   Philip Sharkey

John Vanemmenis

Bideford. *Born* Barnstaple, 17 September, 1981
Lightweight. *Ht* 5'6¼"
Manager N. Christian

05.10.07 Rob Turley L RSC 3 Newport
01.12.07 Shaun Walton W PTS 6 Telford
10.12.07 Tony McQuade DREW 6 Peterborough
29.02.08 Dezzie O'Connor L RSC 5 Plymouth
20.06.08 Ali Wyatt L PTS 4 Plymouth
Career: 5 contests, won 1, drew 1, lost 3.

Denton Vassell

Manchester. *Born* Manchester, 13 September, 1984
L.Middleweight. *Ht* 5'9¾"
Manager F. Warren

02.09.06 Ernie Smith W RSC 3 Bolton
09.12.06 Duncan Cottier W PTS 4 Canning Town
10.03.07 Steve Cooper W RSC 2 Liverpool
11.08.07 Gatis Skuja W PTS 4 Liverpool
07.09.07 Sherman Alleyne W RSC 1 Mayfair
08.12.07 Yassine El Maachi W PTS 4 Bolton
05.04.08 Manoocha Salari W PTS 4 Bolton
Career: 7 contests, won 7.

Joey Vegas (Lubega)

Tottenham. *Born* Namirembe Uganda, 1 January, 1982
Cruiserweight. Former Undefeated British Masters S.Middleweight Champion.
Ht 5'8½"
Manager M. Helliet

04.11.04 Cello Renda W RSC 3 Piccadilly
27.01.05 Egbui Ikeagwo W PTS 4 Piccadilly
26.03.05 Egbui Ikeagwo W PTS 4 Hackney
26.05.05 Gareth Lawrence W PTS 4 Mayfair
17.11.05 Conroy McIntosh W RSC 3 Piccadilly
30.03.06 Simeon Cover W PTS 10 Piccadilly
          (British Masters S.Middleweight Title Challenge)
12.07.06 Simeon Cover W PTS 4 Bethnal Green
30.11.06 Michael Monaghan W PTS 10 Piccadilly
          (British Masters S.Middleweight Title Defence)
13.12.06 Varuzhan Davtyan W RSC 1 Strand
18.04.07 Neil Tidman W PTS 4 Strand
04.10.07 Danny McIntosh L PTS 6 Piccadilly
03.11.07 Nathan Cleverly L PTS 8 Cardiff
14.11.07 Geard Ajetovic L RSC 4 Bethnal Green
Career: 13 contests, won 10, lost 3.

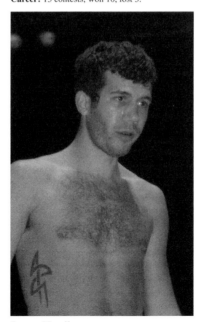

Lance Verallo   Philip Sharkey

Lance Verallo

Birmingham. *Born* Cardiff, 25 July, 1984
Welterweight. *Ht* 5'11"
Manager Self

08.05.05 Sujad Elahi L PTS 6 Sheffield
11.06.05 Mike Reid L PTS 6 Kirkcaldy
19.06.05 Ian Wilson L PTS 4 Bethnal Green
24.07.05 Nicki Smedley L PTS 6 Sheffield
19.09.05 Kyle Taylor L PTS 6 Glasgow
30.09.05 Stephen Chinnock L PTS 4 Burton
14.10.05 Ryan Brawley L PTS 6 Motherwell
30.10.05 Muhsen Nasser L PTS 6 Sheffield
12.11.05 Dwayne Hill L PTS 6 Sheffield
21.11.05 Darren Johnstone L PTS 6 Glasgow
08.12.05 Scott Conway L PTS 6 Derby
23.01.06 Gary McArthur L PTS 6 Glasgow
12.02.06 Gary O'Connor L RSC 4 Manchester
31.03.06 Thomas Moran L PTS 6 Inverurie
22.07.07 Karl Chiverton L PTS 6 Mansfield
08.09.07 Andrew Alan Lowe L PTS 6 Sutton in Ashfield
21.09.07 JJ Bird L PTS 6 Peterborough
28.09.07 Alex Strutt L RSC 2 Birmingham
10.11.07 Dave Murray L PTS 6 Stalybridge
25.11.07 Jack Arnfield L RSC 4 Colne
18.01.08 Duane Parker L PTS 4 Burton
28.02.08 Rob Kenney L PTS 4 Wolverhampton
16.03.08 Faizal Zahid L PTS 6 Sheffield
02.05.08 Brock Cato L PTS 6 Bristol
16.05.08 James Flinn L RSC 3 Burton
Career: 25 contests, lost 25.

Byron Vince

Northampton. *Born* Bury St Edmunds, 3 March, 1984
Welterweight. *Ht* 5'10¼"
Manager J. Cox

18.11.07 Charlie Collins W RSC 3 Tooting
28.11.07 Darren Hamilton L PTS 6 Piccadilly
10.12.07 Richard Hall L PTS 6 Cleethorpes
Career: 3 contests, won 1, lost 2.

Byron Vince   Philip Sharkey

WXYZ

John Wainwright
Sheffield. *Born* Sheffield, 18 August, 1987
Welterweight. *Ht* 5'10¼"
Manager G. Rhodes

10.12.07 Luke Gallear W RSC 3 Cleethorpes
15.02.08 Kristian Laight W PTS 6 Sheffield
Career: 2 contests, won 2.

Dave Wakefield
Tooting. *Born* London, 8 January, 1979
L.Middleweight. *Ht* 5'11"
Manager D. Powell

12.12.02 Mark Thornton L PTS 4 Leicester
 Square
13.04.03 Jon Hilton W PTS 4 Streatham
26.04.03 Kevin Phelan L PTS 4 Brentford
03.06.03 Justin Hudson L PTS 4 Bethnal Green
13.06.03 William Webster DREW 6 Queensway
25.10.03 Barrie Lee L PTS 4 Edinburgh
27.11.03 Kevin Phelan L PTS 6 Longford
20.02.04 Chas Symonds L RSC 5 Bethnal Green
15.05.04 Alan Campbell DREW 6 Aberdeen
26.02.06 Dean Marcantonio W RSC 3
 Dagenham
06.05.06 Lance Hall W PTS 6 Birmingham
23.06.06 Joe Mitchell W PTS 6 Birmingham
26.01.07 Paddy Pollock W PTS 6 Glasgow
25.02.07 Paul Morby L PTS 6 Southampton
05.05.07 Kevin McIntyre L PTS 6 Glasgow
31.05.07 Matt Scriven W PTS 6 Manchester
16.06.07 George Hillyard L PTS 10 Chigwell
 *(Vacant British Masters L.Middleweight
 Title)*
03.02.08 Danny Butler L RTD 7 Bristol
 *(British Masters L.Middleweight Title
 Challenge)*
29.03.08 Kris Carslaw L PTS 4 Glasgow
14.06.08 Eddie Corcoran L PTS 6 Bethnal Green
Career: 20 contests, won 6, drew 2, lost 12.

Ben Wakeham
Torquay. *Born* Torquay, 3 December, 1988
Welterweight. *Ht* 5'10¼"
Manager C. Sanigar

09.11.07 Jimmy Briggs W PTS 6 Plymouth
29.02.08 James Lilley W PTS 6 Plymouth
Career: 2 contests, won 2.

Josh Wale
Brampton. *Born* Barnsley, 8 April, 1988
Central Area S.Bantamweight Champion
Ht 5'7"
Manager D. Coldwell

13.10.06 Neil Read W RSC 1 Doncaster
15.04.07 Anthony Hanna W PTS 6 Barnsley
03.06.07 Delroy Spencer W PTS 6 Barnsley
13.10.07 Shaun Walton W PTS 4 Barnsley
05.12.07 Mo Khaled W RSC 4 Sheffield
 *(Vacant Central Area S.Bantamweight
 Title)*
16.03.08 Robin Deakin W PTS 6 Sheffield
17.05.08 Ayittey Mettle W RSC 1 Sheffield
Career: 7 contests, won 7.

David Walker   Philip Sharkey

David Walker
Bermondsey. *Born* Bromley, 17 June, 1976
L.Middleweight. Former Undefeated
Southern Area L.Middleweight Champion.
Former Undefeated Southern Area
Welterweight Champion. *Ht* 5'10"
Manager Self

29.04.00 Dave Fallon W RSC 1 Wembley
27.05.00 Stuart Rimmer W RSC 2 Southwark
15.07.00 Billy Smith W RTD 2 Millwall
16.09.00 Keith Jones W PTS 6 Bethnal Green
14.10.00 Jason Vlasman W RSC 1 Wembley
18.11.00 Gary Flear W PTS 4 Dagenham
09.12.00 Karl Taylor W PTS 6 Southwark
20.01.01 Ernie Smith W RTD 1 Bethnal Green
17.02.01 Paul Denton W PTS 4 Bethnal Green
19.05.01 Mark Ramsey W PTS 4 Wembley
14.07.01 David White W PTS 4 Liverpool
13.09.01 David Kirk DREW 8 Sheffield
16.03.02 Paul Dyer W RSC 6 Bethnal Green
 *(Vacant Southern Area Welterweight
 Title)*
10.05.02 Pedro Thompson W RSC 3 Bethnal
 Green
23.08.02 Robert Burton W RSC 2 Bethnal Green
25.10.02 Brett James W RSC 4 Bethnal Green
 *(Southern Area Welterweight Title
 Defence)*
21.12.02 Jimmy Vincent L RSC 8 Dagenham
 (Final Elim. British Welterweight Title)
05.03.03 Ojay Abrahams W PTS 6 Bethnal
 Green
16.04.03 Leigh Wicks W PTS 6 Nottingham
27.05.03 John Humphrey W CO 2 Dagenham
 *(Southern Area L.Middleweight
 Title Challenge. Elim. British
 L.Middleweight Title)*
25.07.03 Spencer Fearon W RSC 4 Norwich
 *(Southern Area L.Middleweight Title
 Defence)*
04.10.03 Roman Karmazin L RTD 3 Muswell
 Hill
 *(European L.Middleweight Title
 Challenge)*

12.03.04 Matt Scriven W RSC 3 Nottingham
02.06.04 Kevin Phelan W PTS 6 Nottingham
12.11.04 Danny Moir W RSC 5 Wembley
09.07.05 Howard Clarke W PTS 4 Nottingham
23.09.05 Jamie Moore L RSC 4 Manchester
 *(British L.Middleweight Title
 Challenge)*
18.05.07 Ben Hudson W PTS 6 Canning Town
22.02.08 Andrew Butlin W PTS 6 Bethnal Green
27.06.08 JJ Bird L PTS 4 Bethnal Green
Career: 30 contests, won 25, drew 1, lost 4.

Dean Walker
Sheffield. *Born* Sheffield, 25 April, 1979
L.Heavyweight. *Ht* 5'11"
Manager D. Coldwell

21.10.00 Colin McCash DREW 6 Sheffield
11.12.00 James Lee L PTS 6 Sheffield
27.07.01 Chris Duggan W RSC 4 Sheffield
15.12.01 William Webster W PTS 6 Sheffield
03.03.02 Shaun Horsfall W PTS 6 Shaw
02.06.02 Wayne Shepherd W PTS 6 Shaw
03.08.02 Richard Inquieti W PTS 6 Derby
05.10.02 Martin Scotland W PTS 6 Chesterfield
24.05.03 Neil Bonner W PTS 6 Sheffield
12.10.03 Paul Lomax W PTS 6 Sheffield
10.02.04 Neil Addis W PTS 6 Sheffield
21.02.04 Matthew Macklin L CO 1 Cardiff
08.06.04 Andrei Ivanov W PTS 6 Sheffield
03.09.04 Dean Cockburn L PTS 10 Doncaster
 *(Vacant Central Area S.Middleweight
 Title)*
15.12.04 Lee Murtagh L PTS 10 Sheffield
 *(Vacant Central Central Area
 Middleweight Title)*
20.02.05 Mo W PTS 6 Sheffield
19.03.05 Jozsef Nagy L RTD 8 Tapolca,
 Hungary
 *(IBF Inter-Continental Middleweight
 Title Challenge)*
16.07.05 Darren Barker L PTS 6 Chigwell
25.10.05 Thomas McDonagh L PTS 6 Preston
18.02.06 Jason McKay L RTD 1 Edinburgh
18.05.06 Matthew Hough L PTS 6 Walsall
14.10.06 Paul Smith L RSC 3 Manchester
 *(Vacant Central Area Middleweight
 Title)*
12.11.06 Craig Bunn DREW 6 Manchester
24.11.06 Jonjo Finnegan DREW 4 Nottingham
11.12.06 Tyrone Wright L PTS 6 Cleethorpes
10.03.07 Tony Quigley L RSC 2 Liverpool
15.04.07 Robert Burton L PTS 6 Barnsley
06.05.07 Darren Rhodes L PTS 4 Leeds
21.07.07 Kenny Anderson L RSC 2 Cardiff
08.09.07 Brian Wood W PTS 6 Sutton in
 Ashfield
21.09.07 Rod Anderton L PTS 6 Burton
16.02.08 Martin Murray L PTS 6 Blackpool
16.03.08 Carl Dilks L PTS 6 Liverpool
29.03.08 Kenny Anderson L RTD 4 Glasgow
28.04.08 Marcus Portman L PTS 6 Glasgow
23.05.08 Martin Murray L PTS 6 Wigan
Career: 36 contests, won 12, drew 3, lost 21.

Mark Walker
Boldon Colliery. *Born* South Shields, 14
December, 1973
Heavyweight. *Ht* 6'2"
Manager M. Gates

04.11.06 Chris Woollas DREW 4 Glasgow
20.03.08 Dave Ferguson L RSC 1 South Shields
Career: 2 contests, drew 1, lost 1.

Danny Wallace

Leeds. *Born* Leeds, 12 July, 1980
S.Featherweight. *Ht* 5'7"
Manager Self

24.08.01	Roger Glover W PTS 4 Atlantic City, USA	
12.04.02	Michael Weaver DREW 4 Philadelphia, USA	
22.02.03	Jamil Hussain W RSC 1 Huddersfield	
12.04.03	Ian Turner W RSC 4 Bethnal Green	
10.05.03	Marcel Kasimov L RSC 3 Huddersfield	
06.09.03	Alexei Volchan W PTS 4 Huddersfield	
31.01.04	Jamie Yelland W PTS 6 Bethnal Green	
13.03.04	Henry Janes L PTS 4 Huddersfield	
11.09.04	Joseph Barela W RSC 2 Philadelphia, Pennsylvania, USA	
06.12.04	Fred Janes W RSC 2 Leeds	
01.06.05	Harry Ramogoadi L PTS 6 Leeds	
05.12.05	Matt Teague L PTS 10 Leeds	

(Vacant British Masters & Central Area Featherweight Titles)

29.09.06	Mo Khaled W RSC 1 Manchester	
03.11.06	Barrington Brown W PTS 4 Barnsley	
09.02.07	Chris Hooper W PTS 4 Leeds	
13.07.07	Dwayne Hill W RTD 3 Barnsley	
28.03.08	Rakhim Mingaleev W PTS 6 Barnsley	
24.05.08	Mark Moran L RSC 9 Manchester	

(Vacant English S.Bantamweight Title)

Career: 18 contests, won 12, drew 1, lost 5.

Lester Walsh

Leicester. *Born* Greenock, 26 January, 1976
Middleweight. *Ht* 5'8"
Manager P. Carpenter

01.12.07	Rocky Chakir L PTS 6 Coventry
16.02.08	Paul Royston W PTS 6 Leicester
31.05.08	Kevin Hammond DREW 4 Newark
28.06.08	Luke Osman W PTS 6 Leicester

Career: 4 contests, won 2, drew 1, lost 1.

Liam Walsh

Cromer. *Born* Rochdale, 18 May, 1986
Lightweight. *Ht* 5'7¼"
Manager G. Everett

02.02.08	Daniel Thorpe W CO 1 Canning Town
14.06.08	Johnny Greaves W CO 4 Bethnal Green

Career: 2 contests, won 2.

Liam Walsh   Philip Sharkey

Michael Walsh   Philip Sharkey

Michael Walsh

Cromer. *Born* Rochdale, 4 August, 1984
S.Bantamweight. *Ht* 5'5¼"
Manager G. Everett

02.02.08	Delroy Spencer W RSC 3 Canning Town	
08.03.08	Khvicha Papiashvili W RSC 4 Greenwich	
14.06.08	Fouad El Bahji W RSC 3 Bethnal Green	

Career: 3 contests, won 3.

Ryan Walsh

Cromer. *Born* Rochdale, 18 May, 1986
Featherweight. *Ht* 5'4¼"
Manager G. Everett

02.02.08	Riaz Durgahed W CO 1 Canning Town
08.03.08	Robin Deakin W PTS 4 Greenwich
14.06.08	Gheorghe Ghiompirica W PTS 4 Bethnal Green

Career: 3 contests, won 3.

Ryan Walsh   Philip Sharkey

Dougie Walton

Coventry. *Born* Coventry, 9 August, 1981
Featherweight. *Ht* 5'4"
Manager Self

04.03.06	Graeme Higginson DREW 6 Coventry
09.10.06	Neil Marston W PTS 6 Birmingham
11.12.06	Neil Read W RSC 5 Birmingham
26.02.07	Delroy Spencer W PTS 6 Birmingham
13.05.07	Shaun Walton W PTS 4 Birmingham
28.09.07	Shaun Walton W PTS 6 Coventry
26.10.07	Delroy Spencer W PTS 6 Birmingham

Career: 7 contests, won 6, drew 1.

Shaun Walton   Les Clark

Shaun Walton

Telford. *Born* West Bromwich, 2 January, 1975
Lightweight. *Ht* 5'10"
Manager E. Johnson

15.04.05	Dave Hinds W PTS 6 Shrewsbury
16.09.05	Abdul Mougharbel DREW 6 Telford
14.10.05	Craig Bromley L PTS 4 Huddersfield
04.12.05	Abdul Mougharbel DREW 6 Telford
10.03.06	Andy Davis L PTS 6 Walsall
28.05.06	Sean Hughes L PTS 6 Wakefield
05.06.06	Furhan Rafiq L PTS 6 Glasgow
09.09.06	Furhan Rafiq L PTS 6 Inverurie
06.10.06	Andy Bell L PTS 6 Mansfield
13.10.06	Jamie McIlroy L PTS 6 Irvine
21.10.06	Mark Alexander L PTS 6 Southwark
28.10.06	Robin Deakin L PTS 4 Bethnal Green
10.11.06	Sergei Rozhakmens W PTS 6 Telford
30.11.06	Kim Poulsen L PTS 6 Piccadilly
13.12.06	Darryl Mitchell L PTS 4 Strand
22.01.07	Furhan Rafiq L PTS 6 Glasgow
17.02.07	Vinny Mitchell L PTS 4 Wembley
03.03.07	Kevin Buckley L PTS 6 Burton
01.04.07	Sergei Rozhakmens DREW 6 Shrewsbury
14.04.07	Robert Nelson L PTS 8 Wakefield
23.04.07	Brian Murphy W RSC 5 Glasgow
06.05.07	James McElvaney L PTS 6 Darlington
13.05.07	Dougie Walton L PTS 4 Birmingham
05.06.07	John Donnelly L PTS 6 Glasgow
14.06.07	Eugene Heagney L PTS 6 Leeds
21.06.07	Tony McQuade L PTS 6 Peterborough
30.06.07	Scott Quigg L RSC 1 Manchester
11.08.07	Scott Quigg L PTS 6 Liverpool
10.09.07	John Bothwell W PTS 6 Glasgow
28.09.07	Dougie Walton L PTS 6 Coventry

13.10.07	Josh Wale L PTS 4 Barnsley	
24.11.07	Davey Savage L PTS 6 Clydebank	
01.12.07	John Vanemmenis L PTS 6 Telford	
15.12.07	Jason Hastie L PTS 4 Edinburgh	
21.01.08	Davey Savage L PTS 6 Glasgow	
31.01.08	Saud Hafiz L PTS 4 Piccadilly	
23.02.08	Ben Jones L RSC 4 Crawley	
29.03.08	Stephen Russell L PTS 4 Glasgow	
10.04.08	Saud Hafiz L RSC 3 Piccadilly	
07.06.08	Rhys Roberts L PTS 4 Wigan	
21.06.08	Stephen Smith L CO 3 Birmingham	

Career: 41 contests, won 4, drew 3, lost 34.

Andrew Ward

Maltby. *Born* Rotherham, 19 September, 1982 L.Welterweight. *Ht* 5'7"
Manager D. Coldwell

01.10.06	Jason Nesbitt DREW 6 Rotherham
06.12.06	Graeme Higginson L PTS 6 Rotherham
15.04.07	Deniss Sirjatovs W PTS 6 Barnsley
03.06.07	Pete Buckley W PTS 4 Barnsley
13.10.07	Gavin Deacon L PTS 6 Barnsley
31.05.08	Gary Hamilton L CO 1 Belfast

Career: 6 contests, won 2, drew 1, lost 3.

Isaac Ward

Darlington. *Born* Darlington, 7 April, 1977
Former Commonwealth S.Bantamweight
Champion. *Ht* 5'5"
Manager M. Marsden

03.08.02	Neil Read W RSC 1 Blackpool
18.10.02	John-Paul Ryan W PTS 6 Hartlepool
14.12.02	Steve Gethin W PTS 4 Newcastle
11.07.03	Rocky Dean DREW 4 Darlington
13.09.03	Pete Buckley W PTS 6 Wakefield
10.10.03	Rocky Dean W PTS 6 Darlington
04.12.03	Jamie Yelland W PTS 6 Huddersfield
05.03.04	Steve Gethin W PTS 6 Darlington
16.04.04	Pete Buckley W PTS 6 Hartlepool
03.07.04	Dave Hinds W PTS 6 Blackpool
19.11.04	Abdul Mougharbel W PTS 4 Hartlepool
04.03.05	Peter Allen DREW 6 Hartlepool
02.06.05	Billy Smith W PTS 8 Yarm
28.10.05	Abdul Mougharbel W PTS 6 Hartlepool
28.04.06	Rakhim Mingaleev W PTS 4 Hartlepool
30.05.06	Martin Power L RSC 8 Bethnal Green *(British Bantamweight Title Challenge)*
30.09.06	Neil Marston W PTS 6 Middlesbrough
28.01.07	Francis Miyeyusho W CO 2 Yarm *(Vacant Commonwealth S.Bantamweight Title)*
12.10.07	Anyetei Laryea L RTD 4 Peterlee *(Commonwealth S.Bantamweight Title Defence)*

Career: 19 contests, won 15, drew 2, lost 2.

Craig Watson

Manchester. *Born* Oldham, 7 February, 1983
Commonwealth Welterweight Champion.
Ht 5'10"
Manager F. Maloney

20.05.05	Willie Valentine W RTD 2 Southwark
19.06.05	Jus Wallie W PTS 4 Bethnal Green
16.07.05	Billy Smith W PTS 4 Bolton
07.10.05	Ben Hudson W PTS 4 Bethnal Green
04.11.05	Sergii Tertii W PTS 6 Bethnal Green
29.09.06	Michael Medor W RSC 1 Manchester
25.11.06	Rakhim Mingaleev W PTS 6 Belfast
09.02.07	John Fewkes L PTS 8 Leeds
27.04.07	Robert Lloyd-Taylor W PTS 8 Wembley
06.07.07	Michael Lomax W PTS 8 Wigan
21.09.07	Robert Lloyd-Taylor W RSC 1 Bethnal Green
26.10.07	Frederic Gosset W PTS 6 Wigan
08.12.07	Ali Nuumbembe W RSC 8 Wigan *(Commonwealth Welterweight Title Challenge)*
08.03.08	Daniele Petrucci L RSC 3 Rome, Italy *(Vacant European Union Welterweight Title)*
24.05.08	Matthew Hatton W PTS 12 Manchester *(Commonwealth Welterweight Title Defence)*

Career: 15 contests, won 13, lost 2.

Craig Watson   Philip Sharkey

George Watson

Newcastle. *Born* Newcastle, 13 December, 1983
Lightweight. *Ht* 6'0"
Manager T. Conroy

11.05.07	Gavin Deacon W PTS 6 Sunderland
05.10.07	Kristian Laight W PTS 6 Sunderland
02.11.07	Ryan Brawley L PTS 6 Irvine
06.12.07	Dwayne Hill W PTS 6 Sunderland
15.02.08	Leonard Lothian W PTS 6 Sunderland
20.03.08	Youssef Al Hamidi W PTS 6 South Shields

Career: 6 contests, won 5, lost 1.

John Watson

Liverpool. *Born* Whiston, 9 June, 1983
L.Welterweight. *Ht* 5'9¾"
Manager Self

10.03.07	Jason Nesbitt W PTS 4 Liverpool
11.08.07	Johnny Greaves W PTS 4 Liverpool
01.12.07	Ade Adebolu W RSC 4 Liverpool
23.02.08	Darren Broomhall W CO 1 Liverpool
16.03.08	Baz Carey W PTS 4 Liverpool
07.06.08	John Baguley W PTS 4 Wigan

Career: 6 contests, won 6.

Martin Watson

Coatbridge. *Born* Bellshill, 12 May, 1981
International Masters Lightweight
Champion. Former Celtic Lightweight
Champion. Former Undefeated Scottish
Lightweight Champion. *Ht* 5'8"
Manager R. Bannon

24.05.01	Shaune Danskin W RSC 3 Glasgow
20.10.01	Jon Honney W RSC 3 Glasgow
16.12.01	Richie Caparelli W PTS 6 Glasgow
11.03.02	Pete Buckley W PTS 4 Glasgow
26.04.02	Gary Reid W PTS 6 Glasgow
08.06.02	Scott Miller W RSC 2 Renfrew
18.11.02	Gary Reid W RSC 4 Renfrew
22.03.03	Joel Viney W RSC 2 Renfrew
16.05.03	Barry Hughes W RTD 8 Glasgow *(Vacant Scottish Lightweight Title)*
30.10.03	Mark Winters DREW 8 Belfast
01.04.04	Steve Murray L PTS 10 Bethnal Green
19.06.04	Jus Wallie W PTS 6 Renfrew
29.10.04	Mark Winters W PTS 10 Renfrew *(Vacant Celtic Lightweight Title)*
28.01.05	Jimmy Beech W PTS 4 Renfrew
09.07.05	Lee Meager L PTS 10 Nottingham
01.04.06	Ryan Barrett W PTS 10 Bethnal Green *(Elim. British Lightweight Title)*
29.04.06	George Ashie W PTS 10 Edinburgh
08.07.06	Gavin Rees L PTS 6 Cardiff
05.10.07	Garry Buckland L PTS 10 Newport *(Celtic Lightweight Title Defence)*
29.03.08	Willie Limond L PTS 12 Glasgow *(Vacant IBO Inter-Continental Lightweight Title)*
16.05.08	Chris Long W PTS 10 Motherwell *(Vacant International Masters Lightweight Title)*

Career: 21 contests, won 15, drew 1, lost 5.

Shane Watson

Ruislip. *Born* Hillingdon, 12 August, 1984
L.Welterweight. *Ht* 5'9½"
Manager Self

23.11.05	Pete Buckley W PTS 6 Mayfair
04.12.05	Duncan Cottier W PTS 4 Portsmouth
05.03.06	Chris Long W PTS 4 Southampton
07.04.06	Anthony Christopher W RSC 1 Longford
28.05.06	Daniel Thorpe W PTS 6 Longford
02.12.06	Jason Nesbitt W PTS 6 Longford
23.09.07	Pete Buckley W PTS 6 Longford

Career: 7 contests, won 7.

Jamie Way

Abercarn. *Born* Newport, 11 December, 1981 Welterweight. *Ht* 5'7"
Manager B. Powell

15.09.06	Jimmy Maile W RSC 4 Newport
10.11.06	Pawel Jas W PTS 6 Newport
03.03.07	Geraint Harvey W PTS 6 Newport
16.06.07	Steve Cooper W PTS 6 Newport
05.10.07	Lewis Byrne W PTS 4 Newport
05.04.08	Jimmy Briggs W PTS 6 Newport
24.05.08	Rocky Chakir W PTS 6 Cardiff

Career: 7 contests, won 7.

Sam Webb

Chislehurst. *Born* Sidcup, 11 April, 1981
Middleweight. *Ht* 5'8¾"
Manager F. Maloney

07.10.05	Geraint Harvey W CO 1 Bethnal Green
04.11.05	Vadzim Astapuk W RSC 2 Bethnal Green
27.01.06	Aleksandr Zhuk W PTS 4 Dagenham
24.03.06	Gatis Skuja W PTS 4 Bethnal Green
30.05.06	Alex Stoda L RSC 3 Bethnal Green
17.11.06	David Kirk W PTS 4 Bethnal Green
27.04.07	Alexander Spitjo W RSC 1 Wembley
15.06.07	Ben Hudson W PTS 4 Crystal Palace

12.01.08 Duncan Cottier W PTS 4 Bethnal Green
02.02.08 Paul Royston W PTS 6 Canning Town
02.05.08 David Kirk W PTS 6 Nottingham
13.06.08 Paul Dyer W PTS 6 Portsmouth
Career: 12 contests, won 11, lost 1.

Stevie Weir
Paisley. *Born* Paisley, 7 July, 1982
L.Middleweight. *Ht* 5'10¼"
Manager J. McIntyre

15.09.07 Paul Royston W PTS 6 Paisley
29.03.08 Ernie Smith W PTS 4 Glasgow
Career: 2 contests, won 2.

Nathan Weise   Les Clark

Nathan Weise
Thameside. *Born* Bath, 7 July, 1984
Welterweight. *Ht* 5'11½"
Manager F. Maloney

29.06.06 Bheki Moyo W PTS 4 Bethnal Green
26.01.07 Tom Glover DREW 4 Dagenham
15.06.08 Mark Douglas L PTS 4 Bethnal Green
Career: 3 contests, won 1, drew 1, lost 1.

Jonathan Whiteman
Mansfield. *Born* Sutton in Ashfield, 1 May, 1984 Welterweight. *Ht* 5'11"
Manager C. Greaves

22.10.04 Pete Buckley W PTS 6 Mansfield
10.12.04 Joel Viney W RSC 4 Mansfield
06.03.05 Terry Carruthers DREW 6 Mansfield
24.04.05 Dave Curran L DIS 2 Askern
09.07.05 Kell Brook L RSC 2 Nottingham
11.09.05 Ian Reid W PTS 4 Kirkby in Ashfield
22.10.05 Billy Smith W PTS 6 Mansfield
04.11.05 Darren Johnstone L RSC 3 Glasgow
04.12.05 Tristan Davies L PTS 4 Telford
28.01.06 Rendall Munroe L RSC 2 Nottingham
06.10.06 Daniel Thorpe W PTS 6 Mansfield
04.11.06 Billy Smith L PTS 6 Mansfield
25.11.06 James Gorman L RSC 2 Belfast
28.04.07 Jason Nesbitt L RTD 5 Newark
22.07.07 Darren Broomhall L PTS 6 Mansfield
Career: 15 contests, won 5, drew 1, lost 9.

Adie Whitmore
Derby. *Born* Alfreton, 28 July, 1987
S.Middleweight. *Ht* 6'2"
Manager M. Shinfield

08.12.05 Jimi Hendricks W RSC 1 Derby
14.05.06 Jon Foster W RSC 6 Derby
11.11.06 Ojay Abrahams W PTS 6 Sutton in Ashfield
23.03.07 Jon Foster W RTD 4 Nottingham
21.09.07 Robert Burton W PTS 6 Burton
01.12.07 Nicki Taylor W CO 1 Nottingham
07.03.08 Hamed Jamali W PTS 4 Nottingham
02.05.08 Carl Wild W CO 1 Nottingham
Career: 8 contests, won 8.

Adam Wilcox
Cross Hands. *Born* Blacktown, Australia, 1 June, 1979 L.Heavyweight. *Ht* 5'8¼"
Manager N. Hodges

21.10.07 Danny Gwilym L PTS 6 Swansea
03.11.07 Tony Bellew L RSC 3 Cardiff
02.12.07 Robert Boardman L PTS 4 Bristol
15.06.08 Carl Dilks L RSC 3 St Helens
Career: 4 contests, lost 4.

Carl Wild
Sheffield. *Born* Sheffield, 3 April, 1986
L.Heavyweight. *Ht* 6'2"
Manager Self

28.10.06 Mark Phillips W PTS 6 Sheffield
24.02.07 Mark Nilsen L PTS 6 Manchester
20.04.07 Phillip Callaghan W RSC 1 Sheffield
06.05.07 Carl Dilks L PTS 6 Altrincham
16.06.07 Carl Dilks L PTS 6 Bolton
13.07.07 Rod Anderton L PTS 4 Barnsley
08.09.07 Jamie Norkett W PTS 4 Sutton in Ashfield
16.09.07 Nicki Taylor W PTS 6 Sheffield
12.10.07 Danny Thornton L PTS 6 Leeds
15.11.07 Clint Johnson W PTS 6 Leeds
23.11.07 Scott Brookes L PTS 4 Rotherham
30.11.07 Tony Salam L RTD 4 Newham
16.03.08 James Tucker W PTS 6 Sheffield
02.05.08 Adie Whitmore L CO 1 Nottingham
Career: 14 contests, won 6, lost 8.

Danny Williams
Brixton. *Born* London, 13 July, 1973
British Heavyweight Champion. Former Commonwealth Heavyweight Champion. Former Undefeated WBO & WBU Inter-Continental Heavyweight Champion.
Ht 6'3"
Manager Self

21.10.95 Vance Idiens W CO 2 Bethnal Green
09.12.95 Joey Paladino W RSC 1 Bethnal Green
13.02.96 Slick Miller W RSC 1 Bethnal Green
09.03.96 James Wilder W PTS 4 Millstreet
13.07.96 John Pierre W PTS 4 Bethnal Green
31.08.96 Andy Lambert W RSC 2 Dublin
09.11.96 Michael Murray W CO 1 Manchester
08.02.97 Shane Woollas W RSC 2 Millwall
03.05.97 Albert Call W RSC 4 Manchester
19.07.97 R. F. McKenzie W RSC 2 Wembley
15.11.97 Bruce Douglas W RSC 2 Bristol
19.12.97 Derek Amos W RSC 4 NYC, New York, USA
21.02.98 Shane Woollas W RSC 2 Belfast
16.05.98 Antonio Diaz W CO 3 Bethnal Green
10.10.98 Antoine Palatis W PTS 12 Bethnal Green
(Vacant WBO Inter-Continental Heavyweight Title)
03.04.99 Julius Francis L PTS 12 Kensington
(British & Commonwealth Heavyweight Title Challenges)
02.10.99 Ferenc Deak W RTD 1 Namur, Belgium
18.12.99 Harry Senior W PTS 12 Southwark
(Vacant Commonwealth Heavyweight Title)
19.02.00 Anton Nel W CO 5 Dagenham
06.05.00 Michael Murray W RSC 6 Frankfurt, Germany
24.06.00 Craig Bowen-Price W CO 1 Glasgow
23.09.00 Quinn Navarre W RSC 6 Bethnal Green
21.10.00 Mark Potter W RSC 6 Wembley
(Commonwealth & WBO Inter-Continental Heavyweight Title Defences. Vacant British Heavyweight Title)
09.06.01 Kali Meehan W RSC 1 Bethnal Green

Danny Williams   Philip Sharkey

(Commonwealth Heavyweight Title Defence)

28.07.01 Julius Francis W CO 4 Wembley
(British & Commonwealth Heavyweight Title Defences)

15.12.01 Shawn Robinson W RSC 2 Mashantucket Connecticut, USA

12.02.02 Michael Sprott W RTD 7 Bethnal Green
(British & Commonwealth Heavyweight Title Defences)

17.09.02 Keith Long W PTS 12 Bethnal Green
(British & Commonwealth Heavyweight Title Defences)

08.02.03 Sinan Samil Sam L RSC 6 Berlin, Germany
(European Heavyweight Title Challenge)

26.04.03 Bob Mirovic W RSC 4 Brentford
(Commonwealth Heavyweight Title Defence)

26.09.03 Michael Sprott W RSC 5 Reading
(British & Commonwealth Heavyweight Title Defences)

24.01.04 Michael Sprott L PTS 12 Wembley
(British & Commonwealth Heavyweight Title Defences)

01.04.04 Ratko Draskovic W RSC 1 Bethnal Green

13.05.04 Augustin N'Gou W RTD 3 Bethnal Green
(Vacant WBU Inter-Continental Heavyweight Title)

30.07.04 Mike Tyson W CO 4 Louisville, Kentucky, USA

11.12.04 Vitali Klitschko L RSC 8 Las Vegas, USA
(WBC Heavyweight Title Challenge)

04.06.05 Zoltan Petranyi W RSC 3 Manchester

10.12.05 Audley Harrison W PTS 12 Canning Town
(Vacant Commonwealth Heavyweight Title)

25.02.06 Matt Skelton W PTS 12 Canning Town
(Commonwealth Heavyweight Title Defence)

20.05.06 Adnan Serin W RTD 3 Belfast

08.07.06 Matt Skelton L PTS 12 Cardiff
(Commonwealth Heavyweight Title Defence)

09.12.06 Audley Harrison L RSC 3 Canning Town

02.03.07 Scott Gammer W CO 9 Neath
(British Heavyweight Title Challenge)

08.12.07 Oleg Platov NC 4 Basle, Switzerland
(IBF Inter-Continental Heavyweight Title Challenge)

12.04.08 Marcus McGee W PTS 6 Tampa, Florida, USA

30.05.08 Konstantin Airich W RSC 7 Baracaldo, Spain

Career: 46 contests, won 39, lost 6, no contest 1.

Steve Williams

Wallasey. *Born* Wallasey, 29 February, 1984
Welterweight. *Ht* 5'8¼"
Manager T. Gilmour

23.02.08 Martin Sweeney W PTS 6 Liverpool
17.03.08 Steve Cooper W PTS 6 Glasgow
07.06.08 David Kehoe W RSC 1 Wigan
Career: 3 contests, won 3.

Tye Williams

Dewsbury. *Born* London, 9 June, 1976
Welterweight. *Ht* 5'9"
Manager Self

23.10.04 Rocky Muscus W PTS 6 Wakefield
09.11.04 Lea Handley L RSC 1 Leeds
26.02.05 Darren Gethin DREW 4 Burton
14.05.05 Daniel Thorpe L RSC 3 Aberdeen
25.06.05 Gary Connolly W CO 4 Wakefield
11.12.05 Jackson Williams L PTS 6 Norwich
12.02.06 Jonathan Hussey L PTS 6 Manchester
05.03.06 Adam Kelly L PTS 4 Sheffield
25.03.06 Scott Conway DREW 4 Burton
14.05.06 Scott Conway W RSC 5 Derby
28.05.06 Khurram Hussain L PTS 6 Wakefield
18.09.06 Wayne Downing W RSC 2 Glasgow
20.10.06 Adam Kelly L PTS 4 Sheffield
03.11.06 Mike Reid W RSC 6 Glasgow
15.04.07 Chris Saunders L PTS 6 Barnsley
29.04.07 Dee Mitchell L PTS 8 Birmingham
27.05.07 Nadeem Siddique L RSC 4 Bradford
(Vacant Central Area & British Masters Welterweight Titles)
13.10.07 Lee Murtagh L PTS 6 Belfast
11.11.07 Stephen Haughian L PTS 8 Dunshaughlin
18.01.08 Muhsen Nasser L PTS 4 Burton
29.02.08 Jamie Coyle L RSC 2 Glasgow
19.04.08 Gary O'Sullivan L RSC 1 Dublin
Career: 22 contests, won 5, drew 2, lost 15.

(Jeremy) Jezz Wilson

Sheffield. *Born* Wolverhampton, 22 June, 1979
S.Middleweight. *Ht* 5'9"
Manager G. Rhodes

20.04.07 Peter Cannon W RSC 5 Sheffield
16.09.07 Jon Foster W RSC 1 Sheffield
23.11.07 Nigel Travis W RSC 4 Sheffield
15.02.08 Jamie Ambler W PTS 6 Sheffield
Career: 4 contests, won 4.

Luke Wilton

Crossgar. *Born* Barking, 12 May, 1988
Bantamweight. *Ht* 5'5¼"
Manager A. Wilton

29.03.08 Istvan Ajtai W RSC 1 Letterkenny
19.04.08 Delroy Spencer W PTS 4 Dublin
31.05.08 Kemal Plavci W PTS 4 Belfast
Career: 3 contests, won 3.

Juliette Winter   Philip Sharkey

Juliette Winter

Derby. *Born* Whitehaven, 21 February, 1973 Bantamweight. *Ht* 5'6"
Manager C. Mitchell

16.06.01 Sara Hall L RTD 4 Derby
20.09.01 Claire Cooper L RSC 4 Blackfriars
20.03.03 Cathy Brown W PTS 4 Queensway
24.01.04 Esther Schouten L RTD 3 Amsterdam, Holland
23.07.06 Shanee Martin W PTS 8 Dagenham
24.09.06 Cathy Brown L PTS 10 Bethnal Green
(Vacant Womens English Bantamweight Title)
12.05.07 Yarkor Chavez Annan W PTS 4 Stoke
17.11.07 Nadia Raoui L PTS 10 Schwedt, Germany
(Vacant Womens IBF Inter-Continental Flyweight Title)
01.12.07 Shanee Martin DREW 6 Bethnal Green
19.04.08 Magdalena Dahlen L PTS 6 Magdeburg, Germany
Career: 10 contests, won 3, drew 1, lost 6.

Junior Witter

Bradford. *Born* Bradford, 10 March, 1974
Former WBC L.Welterweight Champion. Former Undefeated British, Commonwealth, European, European Union, WBU Inter-Continental & WBF L.Welterweight Champion. *Ht* 5'7"
Manager D. Ingle

18.01.97 Cam Raeside DREW 6 Swadlincote
04.03.97 John Green W PTS 6 Yarm
20.03.97 Lee Molyneux W RSC 6 Salford
25.04.97 Trevor Meikle W PTS 6 Mere
15.05.97 Andreas Panayi W RSC 5 Reading
02.08.97 Brian Coleman W PTS 4 Barnsley
04.10.97 Michael Alexander W PTS 4 Hannover, Germany
07.02.98 Mark Ramsey DREW 6 Cheshunt
05.03.98 Brian Coleman W PTS 6 Leeds
18.04.98 Jan Bergman W PTS 6 Manchester
05.09.98 Mark Winters W PTS 8 Telford
28.11.98 Karl Taylor W PTS 4 Sheffield
13.02.99 Malcolm Melvin W RSC 2 Newcastle
(Vacant WBF L. Welterweight Title)
17.07.99 Isaac Cruz W PTS 8 Doncaster
06.11.99 Harry Butler W PTS 6 Widnes
21.03.00 Mrhai Iourgh W RSC 1 Telde, Gran Canaria
08.04.00 Arv Mittoo W PTS 4 Bethnal Green
24.06.00 Zab Judah L PTS 12 Glasgow
(IBF L. Welterweight Title Challenge)
20.10.00 Steve Conway W RTD 4 Belfast
25.11.00 Chris Henry W RSC 3 Manchester
10.03.01 David Kirk W RSC 2 Bethnal Green
22.05.01 Fabrice Faradji W RSC 1 Telde, Gran Canaria
21.07.01 Alan Temple W CO 5 Sheffield
27.10.01 Colin Mayisela W RSC 2 Manchester
(Vacant WBU Inter-Continental L.Welterweight Title)
16.03.02 Alan Bosworth W RSC 3 Northampton
(Vacant British L.Welterweight Title)
08.07.02 Laatekwi Hammond W RSC 2 Mayfair
(Vacant Commonwealth L.Welterweight Title)
19.10.02 Lucky Samba W RSC 2 Renfrew
23.11.02 Giuseppe Lauri W RSC 2 Derby
(Final Elim. WBO L. Welterweight Title)

05.04.03 Jurgen Haeck W RTD 4 Manchester
(Vacant European Union L.Welterweight Title)
27.09.03 Fred Kinuthia W RSC 2 Manchester
(Commonwealth L.Welterweight Title Defence)
16.04.04 Oscar Hall W RSC 3 Bradford
02.06.04 Salvatore Battaglia W RSC 2 Nottingham
(Vacant European L.Welterweight Title)
12.11.04 Krzysztof Bienias W RSC 2 Wembley
(European L.Welterweight Title Defence)
19.02.05 Lovemore Ndou W PTS 12 Los Angeles, California, USA
(Commonwealth L.Welterweight Title Defence)
09.07.05 Andreas Kotelnik W PTS 12 Nottingham
(European L.Welterweight Title Defence)
21.10.05 Colin Lynes W PTS 12 Bethnal Green
(British, Commonwealth & European L.Welterweight Title Defences)
15.09.06 DeMarcus Corley W PTS 12 Muswell Hill
(Vacant WBC L.Welterweight Title)
20.01.07 Arturo Morua W RSC 9 Muswell Hill
(WBC L.Welterweight Title Defence)

07.09.07 Vivian Harris W CO 7 Doncaster
(WBC L.Welterweight Title Defence)
10.05.08 Tim Bradley L PTS 12 Nottingham
(WBC L.Welterweight Title Defence)
Career: 40 contests, won 36, drew 2, lost 2.

Brian Wood

South Normanton. *Born* Sutton in Ashfield, 5 September, 1981
S.Middleweight. *Ht* 5'10"
Manager S. Calow

28.04.07 Howard Clarke W PTS 6 Newark
08.09.07 Dean Walker L PTS 6 Sutton in Ashfield
01.12.07 Carl Dilks L RSC 1 Liverpool
Career: 3 contests, won 1, lost 2.

Curtis Woodhouse

Hull. *Born* Beverley, 17 April, 1980
L.Middleweight. *Ht* 5'8¼"
Manager D. Powell

08.09.06 Dean Marcantonio W PTS 4 Mayfair
15.04.07 Duncan Cottier W PTS 4 Barnsley
03.06.07 Peter Dunn W PTS 4 Barnsley
05.12.07 Craig Tomes W RSC 1 Sheffield
16.03.08 Matt Seawright W RTD 3 Sheffield
17.05.08 Dave Murray W RSC 2 Sheffield

21.06.08 Wayne Downing W CO 1 Birmingham
Career: 7 contests, won 7.

Clinton Woods

Sheffield. *Born* Sheffield, 1 May, 1972
Former IBF L.Heavyweight Champion. Former Undefeated British, European, WBC International & Commonwealth L.Heavyweight Champion. Former Commonwealth S.Middleweight Champion. Former Undefeated Central Area S.Middleweight Champion. *Ht* 6'2"
Manager Self

17.11.94 Dave Proctor W PTS 6 Sheffield
12.12.94 Earl Ling W RSC 5 Cleethorpes
23.02.95 Paul Clarkson W RSC 1 Hull
06.04.95 Japhet Hans W RSC 3 Sheffield
16.05.95 Kevin Burton W PTS 6 Cleethorpes
14.06.95 Kevin Burton W RSC 6 Batley
21.09.95 Paul Murray W PTS 6 Sheffield
20.10.95 Phil Ball W RSC 4 Mansfield
22.11.95 Andy Ewen W RSC 3 Sheffield
05.02.96 Chris Walker W RSC 6 Bradford
16.03.96 John Duckworth W PTS 8 Sheffield
13.06.96 Ernie Loveridge W PTS 6 Sheffield
14.11.96 Craig Joseph W PTS 10 Sheffield
(Vacant Central Area S. Middleweight Title)
20.02.97 Rocky Shelly W RSC 2 Mansfield

Clinton Woods   Philip Sharkey

10.04.97	Darren Littlewood W RSC 6 Sheffield
	(Central Area S. Middleweight Title Defence)
26.06.97	Darren Ashton W PTS 6 Sheffield
25.10.97	Danny Juma W PTS 8 Queensferry
26.11.97	Jeff Finlayson W PTS 8 Sheffield
06.12.97	Mark Baker W PTS 12 Wembley
	(Vacant Commonwealth S.Middleweight Title)
28.03.98	David Starie L PTS 12 Hull
	(Commonwealth S. Middleweight Title Defence)
18.06.98	Peter Mason W RTD 4 Sheffield
30.11.98	Mark Smallwood W RSC 7 Manchester
13.03.99	Crawford Ashley W RSC 8 Manchester
	(British, Commonwealth & European L. Heavyweight Title Challenges)
10.07.99	Sam Leuii W RSC 6 Southwark
	(Commonwealth L. Heavyweight Title Defence)
11.09.99	Lenox Lewis W RSC 10 Sheffield
	(Commonwealth L. Heavyweight Title Defence)
10.12.99	Terry Ford W RTD 4 Warsaw, Poland
12.02.00	Juan Perez Nelongo W PTS 12 Sheffield
	(European L. Heavyweight Title Defence)
29.04.00	Ole Klemetsen W RSC 9 Wembley
	(European L. Heavyweight Title Defence)
15.07.00	Greg Scott-Briggs W RSC 3 Millwall
24.03.01	Ali Forbes W RTD 10 Sheffield
	(Vacant WBC International L. Heavyweight Title)
27.07.01	Paul Bonson W PTS 6 Sheffield
13.09.01	Yawe Davis W PTS 12 Sheffield
	(Final Elim.WBC L.Heavyweight Title)
16.03.02	Clint Johnson W RSC 3 Bethnal Green
07.09.02	Roy Jones L RSC 6 Portland, Oregon, USA
	(WBC, WBA & IBF L.Heavyweight Title Challenges)
24.01.03	Sergio Martin Beaz W RSC 3 Sheffield
18.03.03	Arturo Rivera W RSC 2 Reading
10.06.03	Demetrius Jenkins W RSC 7 Sheffield
07.11.03	Glengoffe Johnson DREW 12 Sheffield
	(Vacant IBF L.Heavyweight Title)
06.02.04	Glengoffe Johnson L PTS 12 Sheffield
	(Vacant IBF L.Heavyweight Title)
24.10.04	Jason DeLisle W RSC 12 Sheffield
	(Elim. IBF L.Heavyweight Title)
04.03.05	Rico Hoye W RSC 5 Rotherham
	(Vacant IBF L.Heavyweight Title)
09.09.05	Julio Gonzalez W PTS 12 Sheffield
	(IBF L.Heavyweight Title Defence)
13.05.06	Jason DeLisle W RSC 6 Sheffield
	(IBF L.Heavyweight Title Defence)
02.09.06	Glengoffe Johnson W PTS 12 Bolton
	(IBF L.Heavyweight Title Defence)
29.09.07	Julio Cesar Gonzalez W PTS 12 Sheffield
	(IBF L.Heavyweight Title Defence)
12.04.08	Antonio Tarver L PTS 12 Tampa, Florida, USA
	(IBF L.Heavyweight Title Defence. IBO L.Heavyweight Title Challenge)

Career: 46 contests, won 41, drew 1, lost 4.

Gary Woolcombe

Welling. *Born* London, 4 August, 1982
Former British L.Middleweight Champion.
Former Undefeated Southern Area &

British Masters L.Middleweight Champion.
Ht 5'10¾"
Manager F. Maloney

15.05.03	Paul McIlwaine W RSC 2 Mayfair
22.07.03	Arv Mittoo W PTS 6 Bethnal Green
25.09.03	Pete Buckley W PTS 6 Bethnal Green
18.11.03	John Butler W PTS 4 Bethnal Green
07.02.04	Ernie Smith W PTS 4 Bethnal Green
14.02.04	Lee Williamson W PTS 6 Hol*Born*
07.05.04	David Kirk W PTS 4 Bethnal Green
05.06.04	Ivor Bonavic W PTS 4 Bethnal Green
24.09.04	Geraint Harvey W PTS 4 Bethnal Green
19.11.04	Keith Jones W PTS 4 Bethnal Green
11.12.04	Peter Dunn W PTS 4 Canning Town
12.02.05	Howard Clarke W PTS 6 Portsmouth
05.03.05	Ernie Smith W PTS 6 Southwark
29.04.05	Matt Scriven W RSC 4 Southwark
20.05.05	Danny Parkinson W RSC 3 Southwark
19.06.05	Peter Dunn W RSC 6 Bethnal Green
07.10.05	Delroy Mellis W RTD 8 Bethnal Green
	(Vacant British Masters L.Middleweight Title)
04.11.05	Mark Phillips W PTS 4 Bethnal Green
27.01.06	Lee Murtagh W RSC 4 Dagenham
24.03.06	Eugenio Monteiro W PTS 8 Bethnal Green
26.05.06	Gilbert Eastman W RSC 7 Bethnal Green
	(Southern Area L.Middleweight Title Challenge)
03.11.06	Alex Stoda W DIS 4 Barnsley
26.01.07	Andrew Facey L RSC 5 Dagenham
	(English L.Middleweight Title Challenge)
15.06.07	Anthony Young W RSC 4 Crystal Palace
21.09.07	Jason Rushton W RSC 7 Bethnal Green
08.12.07	Marcus Portman W RTD 8 Wigan
	(Vacant British L.Middleweight Title)
18.04.08	Ryan Rhodes L CO 9 Bethnal Green
	(British L.Middleweight Title Defence)

Career: 27 contests, won 25, lost 2.

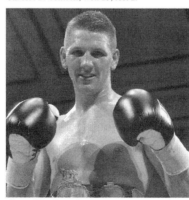

Gary Woolcombe   Les Clark

Scott Woolford

Ramsgate. *Born* Rush Green, 6 September, 1983
L.Middleweight. *Ht* 5'7"
Manager F. Maloney

30.05.06	David Kehoe W PTS 4 Bethnal Green
06.10.06	Tommy Jones W PTS 4 Bethnal Green
17.11.06	Gary McMillan W PTS 4 Bethnal Green

15.06.07	Tyrone McInerney W PTS 4 Crystal Palace
21.09.07	Yassine El Maachi L PTS 4 Bethnal Green
30.11.07	Dave Ryan W PTS 4 Newham
01.02.08	Terry Adams W PTS 4 Bethnal Green
18.04.08	Johnny Greaves W RSC 3 Bethnal Green

Career: 8 contests, won 7, lost 1.

Scott Woolford   Les Clark

Chris Woollas

Epworth. *Born* Scunthorpe, 22 November, 1973
Heavyweight. Former Undefeated Midlands Area Cruiserweight Champion. *Ht* 5'11"
Manager M. Shinfield

17.08.94	Darren Littlewood W RSC 4 Sheffield
05.10.94	Robert Norton DREW 6 Wolverhampton
05.12.94	Neil Simpson W PTS 6 Cleethorpes
10.02.95	Monty Wright L RSC 4 Birmingham
30.06.95	Kenny Nevers L RSC 2 Doncaster
25.09.95	Cliff Elden DREW 6 Cleethorpes
08.11.95	Stevie Pettit W PTS 6 Walsall
17.11.95	Markku Salminen L PTS 6 Helsinki, Finland
11.12.95	Cliff Elden DREW 6 Cleethorpes
15.02.96	Pele Lawrence W RSC 6 Sheffield
29.02.96	John Pierre DREW 6 Scunthorpe
16.03.96	David Jules W PTS 6 Sheffield
22.04.96	Jacklord Jacobs DREW 4 Crystal Palace
30.05.96	Martin Langtry L RSC 6 Lincoln
	(Midlands Area Cruiserweight Title Challenge)
03.09.96	Darren Corbett L RSC 7 Belfast
02.10.96	Rocky Shelly W RSC 6 Stoke
09.10.96	Nigel Rafferty W PTS 6 Stoke
28.10.96	Colin Brown L PTS 8 Glasgow
10.11.96	Michael Gale DREW 6 Glasgow
25.11.96	Albert Call L PTS 6 Cleethorpes
17.12.96	Darren Corbett L RSC 1 Doncaster
16.01.97	Mark Smallwood L PTS 8 Solihull
31.01.97	Tim Redman L PTS 6 Pentre Halkyn
14.03.97	Kelly Oliver L PTS 6 Reading
24.03.97	Mikael Lindblad L RSC 7 Helsinki, Finland
19.06.97	Ian Henry W PTS 6 Scunthorpe
02.08.97	Kelly Oliver L RSC 3 Barnsley
15.12.97	Neil Simpson W PTS 6 Cleethorpes

26.01.98 Colin Brown W PTS 6 Glasgow
26.03.98 Cliff Elden L PTS 4 Scunthorpe
06.05.98 Simon McDougall W PTS 6 Blackpool
21.07.98 Matthew Ellis L RSC 5 Widnes
11.09.98 Lennox Williams W PTS 6 Cleethorpes
12.03.99 Albert Sosnowski L PTS 4 Bethnal
Green
27.05.99 Nigel Rafferty W PTS 10 Edgbaston
(*Midlands Area Cruiserweight Title*
Challenge)
10.07.99 Michael Sprott L RTD 4 Southwark
13.09.99 Dominic Negus L PTS 10 Bethnal
Green
(*Elim. British Cruiserweight Title*)
09.10.99 Chris P. Bacon L PTS 4 Manchester
30.10.99 Terry Dunstan L RSC 1 Southwark
08.04.00 Bruce Scott L RSC 2 Bethnal Green
13.07.00 Firat Aslan L RSC 2 Bethnal Green
08.09.00 Petr Horacek L PTS 4 Hammersmith
21.10.00 Danny Percival L PTS 4 Wembley
18.11.00 Matthew Ellis L PTS 4 Dagenham
11.12.00 Enzo Maccarinelli L PTS 4 Widnes
15.12.01 Lee Swaby L RSC 4 Sheffield
21.10.02 Greg Scott-Briggs W PTS 6
Cleethorpes
01.11.02 Spencer Wilding DREW 6 Preston
28.04.03 Eamonn Glennon W PTS 6 Cleethorpes
22.11.03 Albert Sosnowski L RSC 1 Belfast
16.02.04 Dave Clarke W PTS 6 Scunthorpe
30.03.04 Colin Kenna L PTS 6 Southampton
10.07.04 Robert Norton L RSC 4 Coventry
30.09.04 Paul King L PTS 4 Glasgow
06.11.04 Carl Wright L RSC 1 Coventry
16.12.04 Billy Wilson W PTS 6 Cleethorpes
26.10.06 Mathew Ellis L PTS 4 Dudley
04.11.06 Mark Walker DREW 4 Glasgow
11.12.06 Istvan Kecskes W PTS 6 Cleethorpes
28.01.07 Chris Burton L RSC 3 Yarm
01.06.07 Pele Reid L CO 1 Birmingham
30.06.07 Scott Belshaw L CO 1 Belfast
14.09.07 Ian Millarvie L RSC 2 Kirkcaldy
Career: 63 contests, won 18, drew 8, lost 37.

Nigel Wright
Crook. *Born* Bishop Auckland, 22 June,
1979
English L.Welterweight Champion. *Ht* 5'9"
Manager G. Robinson

10.02.01 Keith Jones W PTS 4 Widnes
15.09.01 Tommy Peacock W RSC 1 Manchester
17.11.01 Ernie Smith W PTS 4 Glasgow
19.01.02 Woody Greenaway W CO 2 Bethnal
Green
11.03.02 James Paisley W PTS 4 Glasgow
19.10.02 Kevin McIntyre L PTS 6 Renfrew
29.03.03 Darren Melville W PTS 6 Portsmouth
24.05.03 David Kirk W PTS 4 Bethnal Green
02.10.03 Nigel Senior W RSC 5 Liverpool
29.11.03 Jason Hall W PTS 6 Renfrew
06.03.04 George Telfer W RSC 3 Renfrew
22.05.04 Jon Honney W RSC 2 Widnes
22.10.04 Silence Saheed W PTS 8 Edinburgh
11.03.05 Dean Hickman W CO 7 Doncaster
(*Vacant English L.Welterweight Title*)
27.05.05 Alan Bosworth W PTS 10 Spennymoor
(*English L.Welterweight Title Defence*)
05.11.05 Kevin McIntyre W RSC 1 Renfrew
(*Final Elim. British L.Welterweight*
Title)
18.02.06 Valery Kharyanov W CO 4 Edinburgh
12.05.06 Lenny Daws L PTS 12 Bethnal Green
(*Vacant British L.Welterweight Title*)

04.11.06 Gary Reid W PTS 10 Glasgow
(*English L.Welterweight Title Defence*)
30.03.07 Jonathan Nelson W RTD 2 Newcastle
14.11.07 Lenny Daws DREW 10 Bethnal Green
(*English L.Welterweight Title Defence*)
08.02.08 Ajose Olusegun L PTS 12 Peterlee
(*Commonwealth L.Welterweight Title*
Challenge)
Career: 22 contests, won 18, drew 1, lost 3.

Tyrone Wright
Nottingham. *Born* Nottingham, 7
September, 1978
Midlands Area L.Heavyweight Champion.
Former Undefeated British Masters
L.Heavyweight Champion. *Ht* 6'2"
Manager M. Scriven

22.10.05 Lee Mountford W CO 3 Mansfield
15.12.05 Gary Thompson DREW 6 Cleethorpes
24.04.06 Csaba Andras W CO 2 Cleethorpes
15.09.06 Nathan King L RTD 3 Newport
11.11.06 Gordon Brennan W PTS 6 Sutton in
Ashfield
11.12.06 Dean Walker W PTS 6 Cleethorpes
03.03.07 Shon Davies W PTS 6 Alfreton
19.05.07 Michael Monaghan W RSC 10
Nottingham
(*Midlands Area L.Heavyweight Title*
Challenge. Vacant British Masters
L.Heavyweight Title)
09.11.07 Simeon Cover W PTS 4 Nottingham
07.03.08 Brian Magee L PTS 6 Nottingham
10.05.08 Paul David W PTS 10 Nottingham
(*Midlands Area L.Heavyweight Title*
Defence)
Career: 11 contests, won 8, drew 1, lost 2.

Ali Wyatt   Philip Sharkey

Ali Wyatt
Torquay. *Born* Iran, 15 May, 1977
Welterweight. *Ht* 5'5¾"
Manager C. Sanigar

09.10.05 Michael Grant DREW 4 Hammersmith
17.11.05 Stuart Phillips L PTS 4 Bristol
21.05.06 Bheki Moyo W RSC 3 Bristol

03.06.06 Michael Grant L PTS 4 Chigwell
23.06.06 Lance Hall W RSC 5 Birmingham
26.02.07 Joe McCluskey W RSC 5 Birmingham
13.05.07 Joe McCluskey DREW 8 Birmingham
08.10.07 Alexander Spitjo L RTD 5 Birmingham
25.02.08 Martin Gethin L PTS 8 Birmingham
05.04.08 Garry Buckland L PTS 6 Newport
20.06.08 John Vanemmenis W PTS 4 Plymouth
Career: 11 contests, won 4, drew 2, lost 5.

Anthony Young
Crawley. *Born* Crawley, 10 April, 1984
S.Middleweight. *Ht* 5'11¼"
Manager J. Evans

30.10.05 Alex Stoda W PTS 6 Bethnal Green
05.03.06 Steve Ede L RSC 3 Southampton
18.10.06 Rocky Muscas W PTS 4 Bayswater
26.10.06 Max Maxwell W PTS 4
Wolverhampton
22.02.07 Danny Reynolds L RSC 4 Leeds
08.06.07 Greg Barton W PTS 4 Mayfair
15.06.07 Gary Woolcombe L RSC 4 Crystal
Palace
23.09.07 Simon O'Donnell L PTS 6 Longford
27.10.07 Pavel Dostal L PTS 6 Prague, Czech
Republic
21.12.07 Tomas Kugler L PTS 6 Brno, Czech
Republic
23.02.08 Lee Noble L PTS 10 Crawley
(*Vacant British Masters Middleweight*
Title)
08.03.08 Patrick J. Maxwell L RTD 2 Greenwich
06.06.08 Steve McGuire L PTS 6 Glasgow
15.06.08 Gokhan Kazaz L PTS 6 Bethnal Green
Career: 14 contests, won 4, lost 10.

Gary Young
Edinburgh. *Born* Edinburgh, 23 May, 1983
Welterweight. *Ht* 5'7"
Manager Self

11.03.02 Paul McIlwaine W CO 2 Glasgow
08.06.02 Daniel Thorpe W RSC 1 Renfrew
02.11.02 Keith Jones W PTS 4 Belfast
22.03.03 Dean Larter W RSC 2 Renfrew
12.07.03 Lee Williamson W PTS 4 Renfrew
25.10.03 Peter Dunn W PTS 6 Edinburgh
29.11.03 Karl Taylor W RSC 3 Renfrew
06.03.04 Anthony Christopher W CO 1 Renfrew
27.03.04 Keith Jones W PTS 6 Edinburgh
19.06.04 David Kirk W PTS 4 Renfrew
22.10.04 Lionel Saraille W RSC 3 Edinburgh
28.01.05 Thomas Hengstberger W RSC 3
Renfrew
08.04.05 Viktor Baranov W PTS 8 Edinburgh
05.11.05 Ivor Bonavic W RSC 8 Renfrew
18.02.06 Oscar Milkitas W PTS 8 Edinburgh
29.04.06 Colin McNeil L CO 1 Edinburgh
(*Elim. British Welterweight Title*)
04.11.06 Ernie Smith W PTS 6 Glasgow
15.09.07 David Kirk W PTS 6 Paisley
Career: 18 contests, won 17, lost 1.

Faizal Zahid
Sheffield. *Born* Sangot, Pakistan, 8
November, 1989
Welterweight. *Ht* 6'1¼"
Manager D. Coldwell

05.12.07 Martin Sweeney L RSC 5 Sheffield
16.03.08 Lance Verallo W PTS 6 Sheffield
Career: 2 contests, won 1, lost 1.

British Area Title Bouts, 2007-2008

Please note that BBBoC Regulations state that any Area champion who wins English, Celtic, British, Commonwealth, European and world championships have to automatically relinquish their titles.

Central Area

Titleholders at 30 June 2008

Fly: *vacant*. **S.Fly:** *vacant*. **Bantam:** *vacant*. **S.Bantam:** Josh Wale. **Feather:** *vacant*. **S.Feather:** Steve Bell. **Light:** Stefy Bull. **L.Welter:** John Fewkes. **Welter:** Nadeem Siddique. **L.Middle:** Danny Reynolds. **Middle:** Paul Smith. **S.Middle:** Paulie Silva. **L.Heavy:** Amer Khan. **Cruiser:** *vacant*. **Heavy:** *vacant*.

Title Bouts Held Between 1 July 2007 and 30 June 2008

3 December   Paulie Silva W PTS 10 Joey Ainscough, Manchester (Vacant S.Middleweight Title)

5 December   Josh Wale W RSC 4 Mo Khaled, Sheffield (Vacant S.Bantamweight Title)

28 March   Jason Rushton L RSC 1 Danny Reynolds, Barnsley (L.Middleweight Title Defence)

Between 1 July 2007 and 30 June 2008, Gary Davis (S.Bantam) relinquished his title and Matt Teague (Feather) retired.

Midlands Area

Titleholders at 30 June 2008

Fly: *vacant*. **S.Fly:** *vacant*. **Bantam:** *vacant*. **S.Bantam:** *vacant*. **Feather:** *vacant*. **S.Feather:** *vacant*. **Light:** Martin Gethin. **L.Welter:** *vacant*. **Welter:** Mark Lloyd. **L.Middle:** Manoocha Salari. **Middle:** Max Maxwell. **S.Middle:** Paul David. **L.Heavy:**

Following the abdication of Adnan Amar, the vacant Midlands Area welterweight title was won by Mark Lloyd (right), who stopped Andrew Alan Lowe inside eight rounds at Wolverhampton last June   Philip Sharkey

Tyrone Wright. **Cruiser:** Carl Wright. **Heavy:** *vacant.*

Title Bouts Held Between 1 July 2007 and 30 June 2008

15 September	Martin Gethin W PTS 10 Craig Johnson, Birmingham (Vacant Lightweight Title)
15 September	Billy Smith W PTS 10 Carl Allen, Birmingham (Vacant L.Welterweight Title)
7 November	Darren Gethin L RSC 10 Adnan Amar, Nottingham (Welterweight Title Defence)
9 November	Paul David W PTS 10 Michael Monaghan, Nottingham (Vacant S.Middleweight Title)
28 February	Max Maxwell W RSC 3 Matthew Hough, Wolverhampton (Vacant Middleweight Title)
10 May	Tyrone Wright W PTS 10 Paul David, Nottingham (L.Heavyweight Title Defence)
20 June	Mark Lloyd W RSC 8 Andrew Alan Lowe, Wolverhampton (Vacant Welterweight Title)

Between 1 July 2007 and 30 June 2008, Andy Bell (Bantam), Billy Smith (L.Welter), Adnan Amar (Welter), Darren McDermott (Middle) and Neil Tidman (S.Middle) all relinquished their titles.

Northern Area

Titleholders at 30 June 2008

Fly: *vacant.* **S.Fly:** *vacant.* **Bantam:** *vacant.* **S.Bantam:** *vacant.* **Feather:** *vacant.* **S.Feather:** *vacant.* **Light:** *vacant.* **L.Welter:** *vacant.* **Welter:** *vacant.* **L.Middle:** *vacant.* **Middle:** *vacant.* **S.Middle:** *vacant.* **L.Heavy:** *vacant.* **Cruiser:** *vacant.* **Heavy:** *vacant.*

Title Bouts Held Between 1 July 2007 and 30 June 2008

None

Northern Ireland Area

Titleholders at 30 June 2008

Fly: *vacant.* **S.Fly:** *vacant.* **Bantam:** *vacant.* **S.Bantam:** *vacant.* **Feather:** *vacant.* **S.Feather:** *vacant.* **Light:** *vacant.* **L.Welter:** James Gorman. **Welter:** *vacant.* **L.Middle:** *vacant.* **Middle:** *vacant.* **S.Middle:** *vacant.* **L.Heavy:** *vacant.* **Cruiser:** *vacant.* **Heavy:** *vacant.*

Title Bouts Held Between 1 July 2007 and 30 June 2008

13 October	James Gorman W PTS 10 Gary Hamilton, Belfast (Vacant L.Welterweight Title)

Scottish Area

Titleholders at 30 June 2008

Fly: *vacant.* **S.Fly:** *vacant.* **Bantam:** *vacant.* **S.Bantam:** *vacant.* **Feather:** Furham Rafiq. **S.Feather:** *vacant.* **Light:** *vacant.* **L.Welter:** *vacant.* **Welter:** *vacant.* **L.Middle:** Colin McNeil. **Middle:** Vince Baldassara. **S.Middle:** Tom Cannon. **L.Heavy:** *vacant.* **Cruiser:** *vacant.* **Heavy:** *vacant.*

Title Bouts Held Between 1 July 2007 and 30 June 2008

18 February	Furhan Rafiq W RSC 10 Sandy Bartlett, Glasgow (Vacant Featherweight Title)

Between 1 July 2007 and 30 June 2008, Jimmy Gilhaney (Feather), Lee McAllister (Light) and Kevin McIntyre (Welter) relinquished their titles.

Southern Area

Titleholders at 30 June 2008

Fly: *vacant.* **S.Fly:** *vacant.* **Bantam:** *vacant.* **S.Bantam:** *vacant.* **Feather:** *vacant.* **S.Feather:** *vacant.* **Light:** *vacant..* **L.Welter:** Jon Honney. **Welter:** *vacant.* **L.Middle:** Anthony Small. **Middle:** *vacant.* **S.Middle:** *vacant..* **L.Heavy:** JJ Ojuederie. **Cruiser:** Tommy Eastwood. **Heavy:** *vacant.*

Title Bouts Held Between 1 July 2006 and 30 June 2007

14 July	Matthew Marsh W PTS 10 Rocky Dean, Greenwich (Vacant S.Bantamweight Title)
12 January	Anthony Small W RSC 7 Takaloo, Bethnal Green (Vacant L.Middleweight Title)
16 May	Andrew Lowe L PTS 10 JJ Ojuederie, Holborn (L.Heavyweight Title Defence)
14 June	Anthony Small W RSC 8 George Katsimpas, Bethnal Green (L.Middleweight Title Defence)

Between 1 July 2007 and 30 June 2008, Matthew Marsh (S.Bantam/Feather), Gary Woolcombe (L.Middle), Darren Barker (Middle) and Kreshnik Qato (S.Middle) all relinquished their titles, while Rob Jeffries (Light) forfeited his belt.

Welsh Area

Titleholders at 30 June 2008

Fly: *vacant.* **S.Fly:** *vacant.* **Bantam:** *vacant.* **S.Bantam:** *vacant.* **Feather:** *vacant.* **S.Feather:** Dai Davies. **Light:** Damian Owen. **L.Welter:** *vacant.* **Welter:** Tony Doherty. **L.Middle:** *vacant.* **Middle:** *vacant.* **S.Middle:** *vacant.* **L.Heavy:** Shon Davies **Cruiser:** *vacant.* **Heavy:** *vacant.*

Title Bouts Held Between 1 July 2007 and 30 June 2008

22 March	Tony Doherty W PTS 10 Barrie Jones, Cardiff (Vacant Welterweight Title)
30 March	Shon Davies W RSC 7 Wayne Brooks, Port Talbot (Vacant L.Heavyweight Title)

Between 1 July 2007 and 30 June 2008, Garry Buckland (L.Welter) relinquished his title.

Western Area

Titleholders at 30 June 2008

Fly: *vacant.* **S.Fly:** *vacant.* **Bantam:** *vacant.* **S.Bantam:** *vacant.* **Feather:** *vacant.* **S.Feather:** *vacant.* **Light:** *vacant.* **L.Welter:** *vacant.* **Welter:** *vacant.* **L.Middle:** Carl Drake. **Middle:** *vacant.* **S.Middle:** *vacant.* **L.Heavy:** *vacant.* **Cruiser:** *vacant.* **Heavy:** *vacant.*

Title Bouts Held Between 1 July 2006 and 30 June 2007

29 February	Carl Drake W RSC 7 Jon Harrison, Plymouth (Vacant L.Middleweight Title)

Between 1 July 2007 and 30 June 2008, Leigh Alliss (L.Heavy) retired.

English and Celtic Title Bouts, 2007-2008

English Championships

Titleholders at 30 June 2008

Fly: *vacant.* **S.Fly:** *vacant.* **Bantam:** Jamie McDonnell. **S.Bantam:** Mark Moran. **Feather:** *vacant.* **S.Feather:** Femi Fehintola. **Light:** *vacant.* **L.Welter:** Nigel Wright. **Welter:** Adnan Amar. **L.Middle:** Andrew Facey. **Middle:** Steven Bendall. **S.Middle:** *vacant.* **L.Heavy:** *vacant.* **Cruiser:** Robert Norton. **Heavy:** John McDermott.

Title bouts held between 1 July 2007 and 30 June 2008

7 September	Andy Bell W RSC 7 Robert Nelson, Doncaster (Vacant S.Flyweight Title)
6 October	Femi Fehintola W PTS 10 Steve Bell, Nottingham (Vacant S.Featherweight Title)
12 October	Marc Callaghan L RTD 6, Rendall Munroe, Peterlee (S.Bantamweight Title Challenge)
9 November	John Murray W RSC 4 Dean Hickman, Nottingham (Vacant Lightweight Title)
14 November	Nigel Wright DREW 10 Lenny Daws, Bethnal Green (L.Welterweight Title Defence)
1 December	Andy Bell W PTS 10 Wayne Bloy, Nottingham (S.Flyweight Title Defence)
8 March	Paul Smith W RSC 6 Cello Renda, Greenwich (Vacant Middleweight Title)
18 April	John McDermott W RSC 2 Pele Reid, Bethnal Green (Vacant Heavyweight Title)
10 May	Adnan Amar W PTS 10 Mark Lloyd, Nottingham (Vacant Welterweight Title)
24 May	Mark Moran W RSC 9 Danny Wallace, Manchester (Vacant S.Bantamweight Title)
24 May	Andrew Facey DREW 10 Thomas McDonagh, Manchester (L.Middleweight Title Defence)
21 June	Paul Smith L PTS 10 Steven Bendall, Birmingham (Middleweight Title Defence)

Between 1 July 2007 and 30 June 2008, Chris Edwards (Fly), Andy Bell (S.Fly), Rendall Munroe (S.Bantam), Scott Lawton and John Murray (Light), John O'Donnell (Welter), Wayne Elcock (Middle), Tony Dodson (S.Middle), Peter Haymer (L. Heavy) and Michael Sprott (Heavy), all relinquished their titles.

Celtic Championships

Titleholders at 30 June 2008

Fly: *vacant.* **S.Fly:** *vacant.* **Bantam:** *vacant.* **S.Bantam:** *vacant.* **Feather:** *vacant.* **S.Feather:** *vacant.* **Light:** Garry Buckland. **L.Welter:** Stuart Phillips. **Welter:** *vacant.* **L.Middle:** *vacant.* **Middle:** *vacant.* **S.Middle:** Steve McGuire. **L.Heavy:** *vacant.* **Cruiser:** *vacant.* **Heavy:** *vacant.*

Title bouts held between 1 July 2006 and 30 June 2007

21 July	Tony Doherty L PTS 10 Kevin McIntyre, Cardiff (Welterweight Title Defence)
14 September	Steve McGuire W PTS 10 Nathan King, Kirkcaldy (Vacant S.Middleweight Title)
5 October	Martin Watson L PTS 10 Garry Buckland, Newport (Lightweight Title Defence)

Between 1 July 2007 and 30 June 2008, Kevin McIntyre (Welter) relinquished his title.

John McDermott (right) won the vacant English heavyweight title when stopping the dangerous Pele Reid inside two rounds last April

Philip Sharkey

PROFESSIONAL BOXING PROMOTERS' ASSOCIATION

PRESENTS

THE BRITISH & INTERNATIONAL MASTERS CHAMPIONS

UNDER BBB OF C RULES

	BRITISH	INTERNATIONAL
HEAVY:	VACANT	VACANT
CRUISER	NEIL SIMPSON	JJ OJUEDERIE
LIGHT-HEAVY	DARREN STUBBS	ROD ANDERTON
SUPER-MIDDLE	VACANT	VACANT
MIDDLE	KEVIN CONCEPCION	VACANT
LIGHT-MIDDLE	DANNY BUTLER	TAZ JONES
WELTER	VACANT	PAUL BURNS
LIGHT-WELTER	GRAEME HIGGINSON	PAUL HOLBORN
LIGHT	GARY McARTHUR	MARTIN WATSON
SUPER-FEATHER	DARREN JOHNSTONE	RICKY BURNS
FEATHER	ANTHONY HANNA	VACANT
SUPER-BANTAM	GARY DAVIS	VACANT
BANTAM	VACANT	MATTHEW EDMONDS
SUPER-FLY	VACANT	VACANT
FLY	DELROY SPENCER	VACANT

THE ONLY ALL-COMERS TITLE OPERATING IN BRITISH BOXING. OUR CHAMPIONS HAVE TO DEFEND WHEN A VALID CHALLENGE IS MADE WITH MORE THAN 30 DAYS NOTICE. TO CHALLENGE FOR OUR TITLE, PROMOTERS SHOULD APPLY TO:

THE PBPA
UNIT 2
SIX ACRES
STODDARDS LANE
BECKLEY
EAST SUSSEX TN31 6UG

TEL: 01797 260616
FAX: 01797 260642
EMAIL: info@pbpauk.com

PRESIDENT: Keith Walker
CHAIRMAN: Bruce Baker
GENERAL SECRETARY: Greg Steene
DIRECTORS: B. Baker, G. Steene, J. Gill, J. Evans, T. Brogan

MEMBERSHIP IS OPEN TO PROMOTERS AND MANAGERS. THOSE INTERESTED PLEASE APPLY

British Title Bouts, 2007-2008

All of last season's title bouts are shown in date order within their weight divisions and give the boxers' respective weights, the names of the referees and judges involved, and the scorecard if going to a decision. Foreign-born boxers who contest a British title, having been qualified by being British citizens for more than five years, are shown by domicile/country of birth. To benefit men whose natural fighting weight is around 115lbs the super-flyweight division was introduced during this period

Flyweight

There were no championship fights during the period, the last one being held on 13 April 2006 when Dale Robinson and Chris Edwards drew in a contest for the vacant title. The title remains vacant.

S. Flyweight

8 December   Chris Edwards 114 (England) W PTS 12 Jamie McDonnell 114 (England), Robin Park Centre, Wigan. Referee: Victor Loughlin. Scorecards: Dave Parris 115-114, Phil Edwards 116-113, Marcus McDonnell 113-116. This was the inaugural title contest at the weight.

28 March   Chris Edwards 114½ (England) L PTS 12 Andy Bell 115 (England), The Metrodome, Barnsley. Referee: Victor Loughlin. Scorecards: Phil Edwards 111-117, Terry O'Connor 111-117, John Keane 113-115.

Bantamweight

6 July   Ian Napa 118 (England/Zimbabwe) W PTS 12 Jason Booth 116 (England), Robin Park Centre, Wigan. Referee: John Keane. Scorecards: Howard Foster 115-113, Dave Parris 116-113, Phil Edwards 117-113. Contested for the vacant title after Martin Power, due to make a defence against Jason Booth before suffering an injured shoulder, handed back his belt on 26 June. Nappa stepped in to meet Booth at short notice

21 September   Ian Napa 117½ (England/Zimbabwe) W RTD 7 Lee Haskins 117¼ (England), York Hall, Bethnal Green, London. Referee: Mark Green. Judges: Richie Davies, Ian John-Lewis, Marcus McDonnell.

30 November   Ian Napa 117¼ (England/Zimbabwe) W PTS 12 Martin Power 117¼ (England), Leisure Centre, Newham, London. Referee: John Keane. Scorecards: Richie Davies 117-111, Mark Green 117-110, Marcus McDonnell 117-112.

2 May   Ian Napa 117½ (England/Zimbabwe) W PTS 12 Colin Moffett 117¾ (Northern Ireland), Harvey Hadden Leisure Centre, Nottingham. Referee: Mickey Vann. Scorecards: John Keane 119-108, Richie Davies 119-109, Howard Foster 117-111. On making his third successful defence, Napa won the Lonsdale Belt outright.

S.Bantamweight

18 January   Esham Pickering 121¾ (England) W RSC 9 Sean Hughes 122 (England), Meadowside Leisure Centre, Burton. Referee: Howard Foster. Judges: Phil Edwards, Victor Loughlin, Terry O'Connor.

27 June   Esham Pickering 121¼ (England) L PTS 12 Matthew Marsh 121 (England), York Hall, Bethnal Green, London. Referee: Mickey Vann. Scorecards: John Keane 113-116, Dave Parris 113-115, Ian John-Lewis 111-117.

Featherweight

7 September   John Simpson 125¾ (Scotland) W RSC 7 Andy Morris 125½ (England), Grosvenor House, Mayfair, London. Referee: Marcus McDonnell. Judges: Richie Davies, Mark Green, Terry O'Connor.

6 June   John Simpson 125¾ (Scotland) L PTS 12 Paul Appleby 125¾ (England), Kelvin Hall, Glasgow. Referee: Victor Loughlin. Scorecards: Terry O'Connor 113-115, Phil Edwards 114-115, Marcus McDonnell 114-115.

S.Featherweight

19 October   Carl Johanneson 129½ (England) W RSC 6 Michael Gomez 129½ (England), The Dome, Doncaster. Referee: Mickey Vann. Judges: Phil Edwards, Dave Parris, Howard Foster. Johanneson won the Lonsdale Belt outright following his win over Gomez.

8 March   Carl Johanneson 129¼ (England) L RSC 9 Kevin Mitchell 129½ (England), O2 Arena, Greenwich, London. Referee: Ian John-Lewis. Judges: Richie Davies, John Keane, Marcus McDonnell. Mitchell's Commonwealth title was also at stake.

Lightweight

5 October   Jonathan Thaxton 134 (England) W RSC 12 Dave Stewart 134 (Scotland), York Hall, Bethnal Green, London. Referee: Dave Parris. Judges: Marcus McDonnell, Mark Green, Ian John-Lewis. Thaxton handed back his belt on 17 June, needing more time to allow an eye wound to heal before making a defence against Lee Meager. Also taken into consideration was a forthcoming European title challenge.

L.Welterweight

20 July   Colin Lynes 139½ (England) W RSC 8 Young Muttley 139 (England), Civic Hall, Wolverhampton. Referee: Richie Davies. Judges: Terry O'Connor, Marcus McDonnell, Ian John-Lewis. Also at stake was the vacant European title. Lynes relinquished the title on 12 March in order to prepare for a defence of his European crown.

14 March   David Barnes 139¼ (England) W PTS 12 Ted Bami 138 (England/Zaire), George Carnall Leisure Centre, Manchester. Referee: Howard Foster. Scorecards: Dave Parris 117-111, Mickey Vann 117-111, Phil Edwards 119-110.

Welterweight

14 September Kevin Anderson 146¾ (Scotland) W RSC 12 Franny Jones 146 (England), Ice Rink, Kirkcaldy. Referee: Victor Loughlin. Judges: Howard Foster, Terry O'Connor, John Keane.

2 November Kevin Anderson 146¾ (Scotland) L PTS 12 Kevin McIntyre 147 (Scotland), Magnum Centre, Irvine. Referee: Mickey Vann. Scorecards: John Keane 110-118, Victor Loughlin 110-118, Richie Davies 107-120.

29 February Kevin McIntyre 146¾ (Scotland) W PTS 12 Kevin Anderson 146¾ (Scotland), Kelvin Hall, Glasgow. Referee: Dave Parris. Scorecards: Mark Green 117-112, Victor Loughlin 117-112, John Keane 114-115. Matched to make a defence against Kell Brook, McIntyre forfeited his title on 4 June after twice pulling out with an injured back, and Barrie Jones substituted in what became a battle for the vacant crown.

14 June Kell Brook 147 (England) W RSC 7 Barrie Jones 146 (Wales), York Hall, Bethnal Green, London. Referee: Mickey Vann. Judges: Dave Parris, Mark Green, Richie Davies.

L.Middleweight

26 October Jamie Moore 153 (England) W RSC 11 Andrew Facey 153¼ (England), Robin Park Centre, Wigan. Referee: Howard Foster. Judges: Richie Davies, Phil Edwards, Mickey Vann. Moore relinquished the title on 30 November to have a minor operation and allow Gary Woolcombe and Marcus Portman to contest the vacant title.

8 December Gary Woolcombe 153¼ (England) W RTD 8 Marcus Portman 152¼ (England), Robin Park Centre, Wigan. Referee: Phil Edwards. Judges: Victor Loughlin, Dave Parris, Marcus McDonnell.

18 April Gary Woolcombe 153¼ (England) L CO 9 Ryan Rhodes 152¼ (England), Robin Park Centre, Wigan. Referee: Phil Edwards. Judges: Victor Loughlin, Dave Parris, Marcus McDonnell. Rhodes re-won the same title that he had relinquished back in 1997.

Middleweight

28 September Howard Eastman 160 (England/Guyana) L PTS 12 Wayne Elcock 159 (England), The Skydrome, Coventry. Referee: Phil Edwards. Scorecards: Terry O'Connor 113-115, Mark Green 113-116, Howard Foster 114-115. Although this contest did not involve Eastman's Commonwealth title, he forfeited any further right to it on the result.

20 June Wayne Elcock 158³/₄ (England) W RSC 2 Darren McDermott 159 (England), Civic Hall, Wolverhampton. Referee: Howard Foster. Judges: Mark Green, John Keane, Terry O'Connor.

S.Middleweight

9 November Carl Froch 167½ (England) W RTD 5 Robin Reid 167¼ (England), The Arena, Nottingham. Referee:

Tony Oakey (right) storms into Peter Haymer prior to scoring a ninth-round count-out victory in defence of his British light-heavyweight title last February Philip Sharkey

Dave Parris. Judges: Howard Foster, Ian John-Lewis, Terry O'Connor.

L.Heavyweight

25 August Tony Oakey 173 (England) DREW 12 Brian Magee 175 (Northern Ireland), The Point, Dublin. Referee: John Keane. Scorecards: Mickey Vann 113-116, Ian John-Lewis 114-114, Terry O'Connor 114-114.

1 February Tony Oakey 173½ (England) W CO 9 Peter Haymer 174¼ (England), York Hall, Bethnal Green, London. Referee: Mickey Vann. Judges: Dave Parris, Marcus McDonnell, Howard Foster.

13 June Tony Oakey 173 (England) L RSC 9 Dean Francis 174½ (England), Mountbatten Centre, Portsmouth. Referee: Richie Davies. Judges: Mark Green, Ian John-Lewis, Marcus McDonnell. While Oakey failed to win a Lonsdale Belt outright, also at stake was Francis' Commonwealth title

Cruiserweight

29 September John Keeton 199 (England) L RSC 4 Mark Hobson 199½ (England), Hallam FM Arena, Sheffield. Referee: Phil Edwards. Judges: Howard Foster, Dave Parris, Victor Loughlin. The title became vacant after Hobson retired on 25 April.

Heavyweight

There were no championship defences made by Danny Williams (England) during the period.

Lord Lonsdale Challenge Belts: Outright Winners

Outright Winners of the National Sporting Club's Challenge Belt, 1909-1935 (21)

Under pressure from other promoters with bigger venues, and in an effort to sustain their monopoly – having controlled championship fights in Britain up until that point in time – the National Sporting Club launched the belt in 1909. They did so on the proviso that there should be eight weight divisions – fly, bantam, feather, light, welter, middle, light-heavy, and heavy – and that to win a belt outright a champion must score three title-match victories at the same weight, but not necessarily consecutively. Worth a substantial amount of money, and carrying a £1 a week pension from the age of 50, the President of the NSC, Lord Lonsdale, donated the first of 22 belts struck. Known as the Lonsdale Belt, despite the inscription reading: 'The National Sporting Club's Challenge Belt', the first man to put a notch on a belt was Freddie Welsh, who outpointed Johnny Summers for the lightweight title on 8 November 1909, while Jim Driscoll became the first man to win one outright. The record time for winning the belt is held by Jim Higgins (279 days).

FLYWEIGHT	Jimmy Wilde; Jackie Brown
BANTAMWEIGHT	Digger Stanley; Joe Fox; Jim Higgins; Johnny Brown; Dick Corbett; Johnny King
FEATHERWEIGHT	Jim Driscoll; Tancy Lee; Johnny Cuthbert; Nel Tarleton
LIGHTWEIGHT	Freddie Welsh
WELTERWEIGHT	Johnny Basham; Jack Hood
MIDDLEWEIGHT	Pat O'Keefe; Len Harvey; Jock McAvoy
L. HEAVYWEIGHT	Dick Smith
HEAVYWEIGHT	Bombardier Billy Wells; Jack Petersen

Note: Both Dick Corbett and Johnny King – with one notch apiece on the 'special' British Empire Lonsdale Belt that was struck in 1933 and later presented to the winner of the Tommy Farr v Joe Louis fight – were allowed to keep their Lonsdale Belts with just two notches secured; Freddie Welsh, also with two notches, was awarded a belt due to his inability to defend because of the First World War; the first bantam belt came back into circulation and was awarded to Johnny Brown; Al Foreman, with just one notch on the second lightweight belt, took it back to Canada with him without the consent of the BBBoC; while the second light-heavy belt was awarded to Jack Smith of Worcester for winning a novices heavyweight competition. Having emigrated to New Zealand, Smith later presented the visiting Her Majesty The Queen with the belt and it now hangs in the BBBoC's offices.

Outright Winners of the BBBoC Lord Lonsdale Challenge Belt, 1936-2008 (123)

Re-introduced by the British Boxing Board of Control as the Lord Lonsdale Challenge Belt, but of less intrinsic value, Benny Lynch's eight-round win over Pat Palmer (16 September 1936 at Shawfield Park, Glasgow) got the new version underway, while Eric Boon became the first man to win one outright, in 1939, following victories over Dave Crowley (2) and Arthur Danahar. Since those early days, six further weight divisions have been added and, following on from Henry Cooper's feat of winning three Lonsdale Belts outright, on 10 June 1981 the BBBoC's rules and regulations were amended to read that no boxer shall receive more than one belt as his own property, in any one weight division. A later amendment stated that from 1 September 1999, any boxer putting a notch on a Lonsdale Belt for the first time would require three more notches at the same weight before he could call the belt his own. However, men who already had a notch on the Lonsdale Belt prior to 1 September 1999 could contest it under the former ruling of three winning championship contests at the same weight. Incidentally, the fastest of the modern belt winners is Ryan Rhodes (90 days), while Chris and Kevin Finnegan are the only brothers to have each won a belt outright.

FLYWEIGHT	Jackie Paterson; Terry Allen; Walter McGowan; John McCluskey; Hugh Russell; Charlie Magri; Pat Clinton; Robbie Regan; Francis Ampofo; Ady Lewis
BANTAMWEIGHT	Johnny King; Peter Keenan (2); Freddie Gilroy; Alan Rudkin; Johnny Owen; Billy Hardy; Drew Docherty; Nicky Booth; Ian Napa
S. BANTAMWEIGHT	Richie Wenton; Michael Brodie; Michael Alldis; Michael Hunter
FEATHERWEIGHT	Nel Tarleton; Ronnie Clayton (2); Charlie Hill; Howard Winstone (2); Evan Armstrong; Pat Cowdell; Robert Dickie; Paul Hodkinson; Colin McMillan; Sean Murphy; Jonjo Irwin; Dazzo Williams
S. FEATHERWEIGHT	Jimmy Anderson; John Doherty; Floyd Havard; Charles Shepherd; Michael Gomez; Alex Arthur;

	Carl Johanneson
LIGHTWEIGHT	Eric Boon; Billy Thompson; Joe Lucy; Dave Charnley; Maurice Cullen; Ken Buchanan; Jim Watt; George Feeney; Tony Willis; Carl Crook; Billy Schwer; Michael Ayers; Bobby Vanzie; Graham Earl
L. WELTERWEIGHT	Joey Singleton; Colin Power; Clinton McKenzie; Lloyd Christie; Andy Holligan; Ross Hale; Junior Witter
WELTERWEIGHT	Ernie Roderick; Wally Thom; Brian Curvis (2); Ralph Charles; Colin Jones; Lloyd Honeyghan; Kirkland Laing; Del Bryan; Geoff McCreesh; Derek Roche; Neil Sinclair; David Barnes
L. MIDDLEWEIGHT	Maurice Hope; Jimmy Batten; Pat Thomas; Prince Rodney; Andy Till; Robert McCracken; Ryan Rhodes; Ensley Bingham; Jamie Moore
MIDDLEWEIGHT	Pat McAteer; Terry Downes; Johnny Pritchett; Bunny Sterling; Alan Minter; Kevin Finnegan; Roy Gumbs; Tony Sibson; Herol Graham; Neville Brown; Howard Eastman; Scott Dann
S. MIDDLEWEIGHT	Sammy Storey; David Starie; Carl Froch
L. HEAVYWEIGHT	Randy Turpin; Chic Calderwood; Chris Finnegan; Bunny Johnson; Tom Collins; Dennis Andries; Tony Wilson; Crawford Ashley
CRUISERWEIGHT	Johnny Nelson; Terry Dunstan; Bruce Scott; Mark Hobson
HEAVYWEIGHT	Henry Cooper (3); Horace Notice; Lennox Lewis; Julius Francis; Danny Williams; Matt Skelton

Note: Walter McGowan, Charlie Magri and Junior Witter, with one notch apiece, kept their belts under the three years/no available challengers' ruling, while Johnny King, with two notches, was awarded the belt on the grounds that the Second World War stopped him from making further defences. Incidentally, King and Nel Tarleton are the only men to have won both the NSC and BBBoC belts outright.

Ian Napa, the British bantamweight champion, won a Lonsdale Belt outright following four straight title wins at the weight during the season

Les Clark

British Champions Since Gloves, 1878-2008

The listings below show the tenure of all British champions at each weight since gloves (two ounces or more) were introduced to British rings under Queensberry Rules. Although Charley Davis (147 lbs) had beaten Ted Napper (140 lbs) with gloves in 1873, we start with Denny Harrington, who defeated George Rooke for both the English and world middleweight titles in London on 12 March 1878. We also make a point of ignoring competition winners, apart from Anthony Diamond who beat Dido Plumb for the middles title over 12 rounds, basically because full championship conditions or finish fights of three-minute rounds were not applied. Another point worth bearing in mind, is that prior to the 1880s there were only five weights – heavy, middle, light, feather and bantam. Anything above 154 lbs, the middleweight limit, was classified a heavyweight contest, whereas lightweight, feather and bantamweight poundages were much looser. Therefore, to put things into current perspective, in many cases we have had to ascertain the actual poundage of fighters concerned and relate them to the modern weight classes. Another point worth remembering is that men born outside Britain who won international titles in this country, are not recorded for fear of added confusion and, although many of the champions or claimants listed before 1909 were no more than English titleholders, having fought for the 'championship of England', for our purposes they carry the 'British' label.

Prior to 1909, the year that the Lord Lonsdale Challenge Belt was introduced and weight classes subsequently standardised, poundages within divisions could vary quite substantially, thus enabling men fighting at different weights to claim the same 'title' at the same time. A brief history of the weight fluctuations between 1891 and 1909, shows:

Bantamweight   With the coming of gloves, the division did not really take off until Nunc Wallace established himself at 112 lbs on beating (small) Bill Goode after nine rounds in London on 12 March 1889. Later, with Wallace fighting above the weight, Billy Plimmer was generally recognised as the country's leading eight stoner, following victories over Charles Mansford and Jem Stevens, and became accepted as world champion when George Dixon, the number one in America's eyes, gradually increased his weight. In 1895, Pedlar Palmer took the British title at 112 lbs, but by 1900 he had developed into a 114 pounder. Between 1902 and 1904, Joe Bowker defended regularly at 116 lbs and in 1909 the NSC standardised the weight at 118 lbs, even though the USA continued for a short while to accept only 116 lbs.

Featherweight   Between 1886 and 1895, one of the most prestigious championship belts in this country was fought for at 126 lbs and, although George Dixon was recognised in the USA as world featherweight champion – gradually moving from 114 to 122 lbs – no major international contests took place in Britain during the above period at his weight. It was only in 1895, when Fred Johnson took the British title at 120 lbs, losing it to Ben Jordan two years later, that we came into line with the USA. Ben Jordan became an outstanding champion who, between 1898 and 1899, was seen by the NSC as world champion at 120 lbs. However, first Harry Greenfield, then Jabez White and Will Curley, continued to claim the 126 lbs version of the British title and it was only in 1900, when Jack Roberts beat Curley, that the weight limit was finally standardised at nine stone.

Lightweight   Outstanding champions often carried their weights as they grew in size. A perfect example of this was Dick Burge, the British lightweight champion from 1891-1901, who gradually increased from 134 to 144 lbs, while still maintaining his right to the title. It was not until 1902 that Jabez White brought the division into line with the USA. Later, both White, and then Goldswain, carried their weight up to 140 lbs and it was left to Johnny Summers to set the current limit of 135 lbs.

Welterweight   The presence of Dick Burge fighting from 134 to 144 lbs plus up until 1900, explains quite adequately why the welterweight division, although very popular in the USA, did not take off in this country until 1902. The championship was contested between 142 and 146 lbs in those days and was not really supported by the NSC, but by 1909 with their backing it finally became established at 147 lbs.

On 8 September 1970, Bunny Sterling became the first immigrant to win a British title under the ten-year residential ruling, while earlier, on 28 June 1948, Dick Turpin won the British middleweight title and, in doing so, became the first coloured fighter to win the title, thus breaking down the so-called 'colour bar'. On 20 May 1998, the BBBoC passed a ruling allowing fighters from abroad, who take out British citizenship, the opportunity to fight for the British title after five years residency instead of ten.

Note that the Lonsdale Belt notches (title bout wins) relate to NSC, 1909-1935, and BBBoC, 1936-2008.

Title Holder	Lonsdale Belt Notches	Tenure	Title Holder	Lonsdale Belt Notches	Tenure	Title Holder	Lonsdale Belt Notches	Tenure
Flyweight (112 lbs)			Joe Symonds		1914	Elky Clark*	2	1924-1927
Sid Smith		1911	**Tancy Lee**	1	1914-1915	Johnny Hill*	1	1927-1929
Sid Smith	1	1911-1913	Jimmy Wilde		1914-1915	Jackie Brown		1929-1930
Bill Ladbury		1913-1914	**Joe Symonds**	1	1915-1916	**Bert Kirby**	1	1930-1931
Percy Jones	1	1914	**Jimmy Wilde***	3	1916-1923	**Jackie Brown**	3	1931-1935

Title Holder	Lonsdale Belt Notches	Tenure
Benny Lynch*	2	1935-1938
Jackie Paterson	4	1939-1948
Rinty Monaghan*	1	1948-1950
Terry Allen	1	1951-1952
Teddy Gardner*	1	1952
Terry Allen*	2	1952-1954
Dai Dower*	1	1955-1957
Frankie Jones	2	1957-1960
Johnny Caldwell*	1	1960-1961
Jackie Brown	1	1962-1963
Walter McGowan*	1	1963-1966
John McCluskey*	3	1967-1977
Charlie Magri*	1	1977-1981
Kelvin Smart	1	1982-1984
Hugh Russell	3	1984-1985
Duke McKenzie*	2	1985-1986
Dave Boy McAuley*	1	1986-1988
Pat Clinton*	3	1988-1991
Robbie Regan	1	1991
Francis Ampofo	1	1991
Robbie Regan*	2	1991-1992
Francis Ampofo	3	1992-1996
Mickey Cantwell*	1	1996-1997
Ady Lewis*	3	1997-1998
Damaen Kelly	1	1999
Keith Knox	1	1999
Jason Booth*	2	1999-2003

S. Flyweight (115 lbs)

Title Holder	Lonsdale Belt Notches	Tenure
Chris Edwards	1	2007-2008
Andy Bell	1	2008-

Bantamweight (118 lbs)

Title Holder	Lonsdale Belt Notches	Tenure
Nunc Wallace*		1889-1891
Billy Plimmer		1891-1895
Tom Gardner		1892
Willie Smith		1892-1896
Nunc Wallace		1893-1895
George Corfield		1893-1896
Pedlar Palmer		1895-1900
Billy Plimmer		1896-1898
Harry Ware		1899-1900
Harry Ware		1900-1902
Andrew Tokell		1901-1902
Jim Williams		1902
Andrew Tokell		1902
Harry Ware		1902
Joe Bowker		1902-1910
Owen Moran		1905-1907
Digger Stanley		1906-1910
Digger Stanley	2	1910-1913
Bill Beynon	1	1913
Digger Stanley	1	1913-1914
Curley Walker*	1	1914-1915
Joe Fox*	3	1915-1917
Tommy Noble	1	1918-1919
Walter Ross*	1	1919-1920
Jim Higgins	3	1920-1922
Tommy Harrison		1922-1923
Bugler Harry Lake	1	1923
Johnny Brown	3	1923-1928
Alf Pattenden	2	1928-1929
Johnny Brown		1928
Teddy Baldock		1928-1929
Teddy Baldock*	1	1929-1931
Dick Corbett	1	1931-1932
Johnny King	1	1932-1934
Dick Corbett*	1	1934

Title Holder	Lonsdale Belt Notches	Tenure
Johnny King	1+2	1935-1947
Jackie Paterson	2	1947-1949
Stan Rowan*	1	1949
Danny O'Sullivan	1	1949-1951
Peter Keenan	3	1951-1953
John Kelly	1	1953-1954
Peter Keenan	3	1954-1959
Freddie Gilroy*	4	1959-1963
Johnny Caldwell	1	1964-1965
Alan Rudkin	1	1965-1966
Walter McGowan	1	1966-1968
Alan Rudkin*	4	1968-1972
Johnny Clark*	1	1973-1974
Dave Needham	1	1974-1975
Paddy Maguire	1	1975-1977
Johnny Owen*	4	1977-1980
John Feeney	1	1981-1983
Hugh Russell	1	1983
Davy Larmour	1	1983
John Feeney	1	1983-1985
Ray Gilbody	2	1985-1987
Billy Hardy*	5	1987-1991
Joe Kelly	1	1992
Drew Docherty	4	1992-1997
Paul Lloyd	2	1997-1999
Noel Wilders*	2	1999-2000
Ady Lewis	1	2000
Tommy Waite	1	2000
Nicky Booth	5	2000-2004
Martin Power*	3	2005-2007
Ian Napa	4	2007-

S. Bantamweight (122 lbs)

Title Holder	Lonsdale Belt Notches	Tenure
Richie Wenton*	3	1994-1996
Michael Brodie*	3	1997-1999
Patrick Mullings	1	1999
Drew Docherty*	1	1999
Michael Alldis	3	1999-2001
Patrick Mullings	1	2001
Michael Alldis*	1	2002
Esham Pickering*	1	2003-2004
Michael Hunter*	4	2004-2006
Esham Pickering	2	2006-2008
Matthew Marsh	1	2008-

Featherweight (126 lbs)

Title Holder	Lonsdale Belt Notches	Tenure
Bill Baxter		1884-1891
Harry Overton		1890-1891
Billy Reader		1891-1892
Fred Johnson		1891-1895
Harry Spurden		1892-1895
Jack Fitzpatrick		1895-1897
Fred Johnson		1895-1897
Harry Greenfield		1896-1899
Ben Jordan*		1897-1900
Jabez White		1899-1900
Will Curley		1900-1901
Jack Roberts		1901-1902
Will Curley		1902-1903
Ben Jordan*		1902-1905
Joe Bowker		1905
Johnny Summers		1906
Joe Bowker		1905-1906
Jim Driscoll		1906-1907
Spike Robson		1906-1907
Jim Driscoll*	3	1907-1913
Spike Robson		1907-1910
Ted Kid Lewis*	1	1913-1914

Title Holder	Lonsdale Belt Notches	Tenure
Llew Edwards*	1	1915-1917
Charlie Hardcastle	1	1917
Tancy Lee*	3	1917-1919
Mike Honeyman	2	1920-1921
Joe Fox*	1	1921-1922
George McKenzie	2	1924-1925
Johnny Curley	2	1925-1927
Johnny Cuthbert	1	1927-1928
Harry Corbett	1	1928-1929
Johnny Cuthbert	2	1929-1931
Nel Tarleton	1	1931-1932
Seaman Tommy Watson	2	1932-1934
Nel Tarleton	2	1934-1936
Johnny McGrory	1	1936-1938
Jim Spider Kelly	1	1938-1939
Johnny Cusick	1	1939-1940
Nel Tarleton*	3	1940-1947
Ronnie Clayton	6	1947-1954
Sammy McCarthy	1	1954-1955
Billy Spider Kelly	1	1955-1956
Charlie Hill	3	1956-1959
Bobby Neill	1	1959-1960
Terry Spinks	2	1960-1961
Howard Winstone*	7	1961-1969
Jimmy Revie	2	1969-1971
Evan Armstrong	2	1971-1972
Tommy Glencross	1	1972-1973
Evan Armstrong*	2	1973-1975
Vernon Sollas	1	1975-1977
Alan Richardson	2	1977-1978
Dave Needham	2	1978-1979
Pat Cowdell*	3	1979-1982
Steve Sims*	1	1982-1983
Barry McGuigan*	2	1983-1986
Robert Dickie	3	1986-1988
Peter Harris	1	1988
Paul Hodkinson*	3	1988-1990
Sean Murphy	2	1990-1991
Gary de Roux	1	1991
Colin McMillan*	3	1991-1992
John Davison*	1	1992-1993
Sean Murphy	1	1993
Duke McKenzie*	1	1993-1994
Billy Hardy*	1	1994
Michael Deveney	1	1995
Jonjo Irwin	2	1995-1996
Colin McMillan	1	1996-1997
Paul Ingle*	3	1997-1998
Jonjo Irwin*	2	1998-1999
Gary Thornhill	1	2000
Scott Harrison*	3	2001-2002
Jamie McKeever	1	2003
Roy Rutherford	1	2003
Dazzo Williams	4	2003-2005
Nicky Cook*	1	2005
Andy Morris	2	2005-2006
John Simpson	3	2006-2008
Paul Appleby	1	2008-

S. Featherweight (130 lbs)

Title Holder	Lonsdale Belt Notches	Tenure
Jimmy Anderson*	3	1968-1970
John Doherty	1	1986
Pat Cowdell	1	1986
Najib Daho	1	1986-1987
Pat Cowdell	1	1987-1988
Floyd Havard	1	1988-1989
John Doherty	1	1989-1990
Joey Jacobs	1	1990

Title Holder	Lonsdale Belt Notches	Tenure
Hugh Forde	1	1990
Kevin Pritchard	1	1990-1991
Robert Dickie	1	1991
Sugar Gibiliru	1	1991
John Doherty	1	1991-1992
Michael Armstrong	1	1992
Neil Haddock	2	1992-1994
Floyd Havard*	3	1994-1995
P. J. Gallagher	2	1996-1997
Charles Shepherd	3	1997-1999
Michael Gomez*	5	1999-2002
Alex Arthur	3	2002-2003
Michael Gomez	1	2003-2004
Alex Arthur*	2	2005-2006
Carl Johanneson	4	2006-2008
Kevin Mitchell	1	2008-

Lightweight (135 lbs)

Title Holder	Lonsdale Belt Notches	Tenure
Dick Burge		1891-1897
Harry Nickless		1891-1894
Tom Causer		1894-1897
Tom Causer		1897
Dick Burge*		1897-1901
Jabez White		1902-1906
Jack Goldswain		1906-1908
Johnny Summers		1908-1909
Freddie Welsh	1	1909-1911
Matt Wells	1	1911-1912
Freddie Welsh*	1	1912-1919
Bob Marriott*	1	1919-1920
Ernie Rice	1	1921-1922
Seaman Nobby Hall		1922-1923
Harry Mason		1923-1924
Ernie Izzard	2	1924-1925
Harry Mason		1924-1925
Harry Mason*	1	1925-1928
Sam Steward		1928-1929
Fred Webster		1929-1930
Al Foreman*	1	1930-1932
Johnny Cuthbert		1932-1934
Harry Mizler		1934
Jackie Kid Berg		1934-1936
Jimmy Walsh	1	1936-1938
Dave Crowley	1	1938
Eric Boon	3	1938-1944
Ronnie James*	1	1944-1947
Billy Thompson	3	1947-1951
Tommy McGovern	1	1951-1952
Frank Johnson	1	1952-1953
Joe Lucy	1	1953-1955
Frank Johnson	1	1955-1956
Joe Lucy	2	1956-1957
Dave Charnley*	3	1957-1965
Maurice Cullen	4	1965-1968
Ken Buchanan*	2	1968-1971
Willie Reilly*	1	1972
Jim Watt	1	1972-1973
Ken Buchanan*	1	1973-1974
Jim Watt*	2	1975-1977
Charlie Nash*	1	1978-1979
Ray Cattouse	2	1980-1982
George Feeney*	3	1982-1985
Tony Willis	3	1985-1987
Alex Dickson	1	1987-1988
Steve Boyle	2	1988-1990
Carl Crook	5	1990-1992
Billy Schwer	1	1992-1993
Paul Burke	1	1993
Billy Schwer*	2	1993-1995
Michael Ayers*	5	1995-1997
Wayne Rigby	2	1998
Bobby Vanzie	5	1998-2003
Graham Earl	1	2003-2004
Graham Earl*	3	2004-2006
Lee Meager	1	2006
Jonathan Thaxton*	3	2006-2008

L. Welterweight (140 lbs)

Title Holder	Lonsdale Belt Notches	Tenure
Des Rea	1	1968-1969
Vic Andreetti*	2	1969-1970
Des Morrison	1	1973-1974
Pat McCormack	1	1974
Joey Singleton	3	1974-1976
Dave Boy Green*	1	1976-1977
Colin Power*	2	1977-1978
Clinton McKenzie	1	1978-1979
Colin Power	1	1979
Clinton McKenzie	5	1979-1984
Terry Marsh*	1	1984-1986
Tony Laing*	1	1986
Tony McKenzie	2	1986-1987
Lloyd Christie	3	1987-1989
Clinton McKenzie*	1	1989
Pat Barrett*	2	1989-1990
Tony Ekubia	1	1990-1991
Andy Holligan	3	1991-1994
Ross Hale	4	1994-1995
Paul Ryan	1	1995-1996
Andy Holligan*	1	1996-1997
Mark Winters	2	1997-1998
Jason Rowland*	2	1998-2000
Ricky Hatton*	1	2000-2001
Junior Witter*	2	2002-2006
Lenny Daws	1	2006-2007
Barry Morrison	1	2007
Colin Lynes*	2	2007-2008
David Barnes	1	2008-

Welterweight (147 lbs)

Title Holder	Lonsdale Belt Notches	Tenure
Charlie Allum		1903-1904
Charlie Knock		1904-1906
Curly Watson		1906-1910
Young Joseph		1908-1910
Young Joseph	1	1910-1911
Arthur Evernden		1911-1912
Johnny Summers		1912
Johnny Summers	2	1912-1914
Tom McCormick		1914
Matt Wells		1914
Johnny Basham	3	1914-1920
Matt Wells		1914-1919
Ted Kid Lewis		1920-1924
Tommy Milligan*		1924-1925
Hamilton Johnny Brown		1925
Harry Mason		1925-1926
Jack Hood*	3	1926-1934
Harry Mason		1934
Pat Butler*		1934-1936
Dave McCleave		1936
Jake Kilrain	1	1936-1939
Ernie Roderick	5	1939-1948
Henry Hall	1	1948-1949
Eddie Thomas	2	1949-1951
Wally Thom	1	1951-1952
Cliff Curvis*	1	1952-1953
Wally Thom	2	1953-1956
Peter Waterman*	2	1956-1958
Tommy Molloy	2	1958-1960
Wally Swift	1	1960
Brian Curvis*	7	1960-1966
Johnny Cooke	2	1967-1968
Ralph Charles*	3	1968-1972
Bobby Arthur	1	1972-1973
John H. Stracey*	1	1973-1975
Pat Thomas	2	1975-1976
Henry Rhiney	2	1976-1979
Kirkland Laing	1	1979-1980
Colin Jones*	3	1980-1982
Lloyd Honeyghan*	2	1983-1985
Kostas Petrou	1	1985
Sylvester Mittee	1	1985
Lloyd Honeyghan*	1	1985-1986
Kirkland Laing	4	1987-1991
Del Bryan	2	1991-1992
Gary Jacobs*	2	1992-1993
Del Bryan	4	1993-1995
Chris Saunders	1	1995-1996
Kevin Lueshing	1	1996-1997
Geoff McCreesh*	4	1997-1999
Derek Roche	3	1999-2000
Harry Dhami	3	2000-2001
Neil Sinclair*	4	2001-2003
David Barnes	4	2003-2005
Michael Jennings	2	2005-2006
Young Muttley	1	2006
Kevin Anderson	3	2006-2007
Kevin McIntyre	1	2008
Kell Brook	1	2008-

L. Middleweight (154 lbs)

Title Holder	Lonsdale Belt Notches	Tenure
Larry Paul	2	1973-1974
Maurice Hope*	3	1974-1977
Jimmy Batten	3	1977-1979
Pat Thomas	3	1979-1981
Herol Graham*	2	1981-1983
Prince Rodney*	1	1983-1984
Jimmy Cable	2	1984-1985
Prince Rodney	2	1985-1986
Chris Pyatt*	1	1986
Lloyd Hibbert*	1	1987
Gary Cooper	1	1988
Gary Stretch	2	1988-1990
Wally Swift Jnr	2	1991-1992
Andy Till	3	1992-1994
Robert McCracken*	3	1994-1995
Ensley Bingham*	2	1996
Ryan Rhodes*	3	1996-1997
Ensley Bingham	3	1997-1999
Wayne Alexander*	2	2000-2003
Jamie Moore	3	2003-2004
Michael Jones	1	2004-2005
Jamie Moore	4	2005-2007
Gary Woolcombe	1	2007-2008
Ryan Rhodes	1	2008-

Middleweight (160 lbs)

Title Holder	Lonsdale Belt Notches	Tenure
Denny Harrington		1878-1880
William Sheriff*		1880-1883
Bill Goode		1887-1890
Toff Wall*		1890
Ted Pritchard		1890-1895
Ted White		1893-1895
Ted White*		1895-1896
Anthony Diamond*		1898

Title Holder	Lonsdale Belt Notches	Tenure
Dick Burge*		1898-1900
Jack Palmer		1902-1903
Charlie Allum		1905-1906
Pat O'Keefe		1906
Tom Thomas	1	1906-1910
Jim Sullivan*	1	1910-1912
Jack Harrison*	1	1912-1913
Pat O'Keefe	2	1914-1916
Bandsman Jack Blake	1	1916-1918
Pat O'Keefe*	1	1918-1919
Ted Kid Lewis		1920-1921
Tom Gummer	1	1920-1921
Gus Platts		1921
Johnny Basham		1921
Ted Kid Lewis	2	1921-1923
Johnny Basham		1921
Roland Todd		1923-1925
Roland Todd		1925-1927
Tommy Milligan	1	1926-1928
Frank Moody		1927-1928
Alex Ireland		1928-1929
Len Harvey	5	1929-1933
Jock McAvoy	3+2	1933-1944
Ernie Roderick	1	1945-1946
Vince Hawkins	1	1946-1948
Dick Turpin	2	1948-1950
Albert Finch	1	1950
Randy Turpin*	1	1950-1954
Johnny Sullivan	1	1954-1955
Pat McAteer*	3	1955-1958
Terry Downes	1	1958-1959
John Cowboy McCormack	1	1959
Terry Downes	2	1959-1962
George Aldridge	1	1962-1963
Mick Leahy	1	1963-1964
Wally Swift	1	1964-1965
Johnny Pritchett*	4	1965-1969
Les McAteer	1	1969-1970
Mark Rowe	1	1970
Bunny Sterling	4	1970-1974
Kevin Finnegan*	1	1974
Bunny Sterling*	1	1975
Alan Minter	3	1975-1977
Kevin Finnegan	1	1977
Alan Minter*	1	1977-1978
Tony Sibson	1	1979
Kevin Finnegan*	1	1979-1980
Roy Gumbs	3	1981-1983
Mark Kaylor	1	1983-1984
Tony Sibson*	1	1984
Herol Graham*	1	1985-1986
Brian Anderson	1	1986-1987
Tony Sibson*	1	1987-1988
Herol Graham	4	1988-1992
Frank Grant	2	1992-1993
Neville Brown	6	1993-1998
Glenn Catley*	1	1998
Howard Eastman*	4	1998-2004
Scott Dann*	4	2004-2006
Howard Eastman	1	2006-2007
Wayne Elcock	2	2007-

S. Middleweight (168 lbs)

Title Holder	Lonsdale Belt Notches	Tenure
Sammy Storey	2	1989-1990
James Cook*	1	1990-1991
Fidel Castro	2	1991-1992
Henry Wharton*	1	1992-1993
James Cook	1	1993-1994
Cornelius Carr*	1	1994
Ali Forbes	1	1995
Sammy Storey*	1	1995
Joe Calzaghe*	2	1995-1997
David Starie	1	1997
Dean Francis*	2	1997-1998
David Starie*	5	1998-2003
Matthew Barney*	1	2003
Tony Dodson*	1	2003-2004
Carl Froch	5	2004-

L. Heavyweight (175lbs)

Title Holder	Lonsdale Belt Notches	Tenure
Dennis Haugh		1913-1914
Dick Smith	2	1914-1916
Harry Reeve*	1	1916-1917
Dick Smith*	1	1918-1919
Boy McCormick*	1	1919-1921
Jack Bloomfield*	1	1922-1924
Tom Berry	1	1925-1927
Gipsy Daniels*	1	1927
Frank Moody	1	1927-1929
Harry Crossley	1	1929-1932
Jack Petersen*	1	1932
Len Harvey*	1	1933-1934
Eddie Phillips		1935-1937
Jock McAvoy	1	1937-1938
Len Harvey	2	1938-1942
Freddie Mills*	1	1942-1950
Don Cockell	2	1950-1952
Randy Turpin*	1	1952
Dennis Powell	1	1953
Alex Buxton	2	1953-1955
Randy Turpin*	1	1955
Ron Barton*	1	1956
Randy Turpin*	2	1956-1958
Chic Calderwood	3	1960-1963
Chic Calderwood*	1	1964-1966
Young John McCormack	2	1967-1969
Eddie Avoth	2	1969-1971
Chris Finnegan	2	1971-1973
John Conteh*	2	1973-1974
Johnny Frankham	1	1975
Chris Finnegan	1	1975-1976
Tim Wood	1	1976-1977
Bunny Johnson*	3	1977-1981
Tom Collins	3	1982-1984
Dennis Andries*	5	1984-1986
Tom Collins*	1	1987
Tony Wilson	3	1987-1989
Tom Collins*	1	1989-1990
Steve McCarthy	1	1990-1991
Crawford Ashley*	3	1991-1992
Maurice Core*	2	1992-1994
Crawford Ashley	3	1994-1999
Clinton Woods*	1	1999-2000
Neil Simpson*	2	2000-2002
Peter Oboh	2	2003-2007
Tony Oakey	3	2007-2008
Dean Francis	1	2008-

Cruiserweight (200 lbs)

Title Holder	Lonsdale Belt Notches	Tenure
Sam Reeson*	1	1985-1986
Andy Straughn	1	1986-1987
Roy Smith	1	1987
Tee Jay	1	1987-1988
Glenn McCrory*	2	1988
Andy Straughn	1	1988-1989
Johnny Nelson*	3	1989-1991
Derek Angol*	2	1991-1992
Carl Thompson*	1	1992-1994
Dennis Andries	1	1995
Terry Dunstan*	3	1995-1996
Johnny Nelson*	1	1996-1998
Bruce Scott	1	1998-1999
Carl Thompson*	1	1999-2000
Bruce Scott	2	2000-2003
Mark Hobson*	5	2003-2006
John Keeton	1	2006-2007
Mark Hobson*	1	2008

Heavyweight (200 lbs +)

Title Holder	Lonsdale Belt Notches	Tenure
Tom Allen*		1878-1882
Charlie Mitchell*		1882-1894
Jem Smith		1889-1891
Ted Pritchard		1891-1895
Jem Smith*		1895-1896
George Chrisp		1901
Jack Scales		1901-1902
Jack Palmer		1903-1906
Gunner Moir		1906-1909
Iron Hague		1909-1910
P.O. Curran		1910-1911
Iron Hague		1910-1911
Bombardier Billy Wells	3	1911-1919
Joe Beckett		1919
Frank Goddard	1	1919
Joe Beckett*	1	1919-1923
Frank Goddard		1923-1926
Phil Scott*		1926-1931
Reggie Meen		1931-1932
Jack Petersen	3	1932-1933
Len Harvey		1933-1934
Jack Petersen		1934-1936
Ben Foord		1936-1937
Tommy Farr*	1	1937-1938
Len Harvey*	1	1938-1942
Jack London	1	1944-1945
Bruce Woodcock	2	1945-1950
Jack Gardner	1	1950-1952
Johnny Williams	1	1952-1953
Don Cockell*	1	1953-1956
Joe Erskine	2	1956-1958
Brian London	1	1958-1959
Henry Cooper*	9	1959-1969
Jack Bodell	1	1969-1970
Henry Cooper	1	1970-1971
Joe Bugner	1	1971
Jack Bodell	1	1971-1972
Danny McAlinden	1	1972-1975
Bunny Johnson	1	1975
Richard Dunn	2	1975-1976
Joe Bugner*	1	1976-1977
John L. Gardner*	2	1978-1980
Gordon Ferris	1	1981
Neville Meade	1	1981-1983
David Pearce*	1	1983-1985
Hughroy Currie	1	1985-1986
Horace Notice*	4	1986-1988
Gary Mason	2	1989-1991
Lennox Lewis*	3	1991-1993
Herbie Hide*	1	1993-1994
James Oyebola	1	1994-1995
Scott Welch*	1	1995-1996
Julius Francis	4	1997-2000
Mike Holden*	1	2000
Danny Williams	5	2000-2004
Michael Sprott	1	2004
Matt Skelton	4	2004-2006
Scott Gammer	2	2006-2007
Danny Williams	1	2007-

Commonwealth Title Bouts, 2007-2008

All of last season's title bouts are shown in date order within their weight divisions and give the boxers' respective weights, the names of all referees and British judges where applicable, along with the scorecard if going to a decision. Boxers are denoted by their country of citizenship/birthplace.

Flyweight
No title fights took place during the period in question, the last champion being Lee Haskins who handed his belt in on 28 March 2007.

S. Flyweight
The inaugural championship bout is expected to take place in the early part of 2008-2009.

Bantamweight
8 December Jason Booth 117 (England) W RSC 9 Matthew Edmonds 117½ (Wales), Robin Park Centre, Wigan. Referee: Marcus McDonnell. Judges: Dave Parris, Victor Loughlin, Phil Edwards. Contested for the vacant title after Tshifhiwa Munyai (South Africa) returned the belt on 4 December to chase a world title shot.

7 March Jason Booth 115¾ (England) W PTS 12 Lante Addy 116½ (Ghana), Harvey Hadden Leisure Centre, Nottingham. Referee: Phil Edwards. Scorecards: Terry O'Connor 118-110, Dave Parris 117-111, Mickey Vann 118-111.

S.Bantamweight
12 October Isaac Ward 120¼ (England) L RTD 4 Anyetei Laryea 121¾ (Ghana), Leisure Centre, Peterlee. Referee: Phil Edwards. Judges: Howard Foster, John Keane, Victor Loughlin.

Featherweight
16 December Jackson Asiku 125½ (Australia/Uganda) W RSC 4 Matt Powell 125¾ (Australia), Challenge Stadium, Perth, Australia. Referee: Gary Ingraham. This contest also involved the Australian title at the weight. After Asiku turned in his belt on 24 April to concentrate on getting a crack at the WBA champion, Chris John, England's Paul Truscott was matched against Osumana Akaba (Ghana) to decide the vacant title.

9 May Paul Truscott 125 (England) W PTS 12 Osumana Akaba 125¾ (Ghana), Eston Sports Academy, Middlesbrough. Referee: Ian John-Lewis. Scorecards: Richie Davies 116-112, Howard Foster 115-113, Mickey Vann 116-112.

S.Featherweight
8 March Kevin Mitchell 129½ (England) W RSC 9 Carl Johanneson 129¼ (England), O2 Arena, Greenwich, London. Referee: Ian John-Lewis. Judges: Richie Davies, John Keane, Marcus McDonnell. Johanneson's British title

was also at stake in this one.

Lightweight
14 July Willie Limond 134¾ (Scotland) L RTD 8 Amir Khan 134¾ (England), O2 Arena, Greenwich, London. Referee: Marcus McDonnell. Judges: Howard Foster, Ian John-Lewis, Mickey Vann.

6 October Amir Khan 134½ (England) W RSC 4 Scott Lawton 134½ (England), The Arena, Nottingham. Referee: Victor Loughlin. Judges: John Keane, Richie Davies, Terry O'Connor.

8 December Amir Khan 134½ (England) W RSC 1 Graham Earl 134¼ (England), The Arena, Bolton. Referee: Howard Foster. Judges: Mickey Vann, John Keane, Richie Davies.

2 February Amir Khan 134½ (England) W PTS 12 Gairy St Clair 135 (Australia/Ghana), ExCel Arena, Canning Town, London. Referee: Ian John-Lewis. Scorecards: Mark Green 120-108, Dave Parris 120-108, Mickey Vann 120-108.

21 June Amir Khan 134½ (England) W RSC 5 Michael Gomez 134¾ (England), National Indoor Arena, Birmingham. Referee: John Keane. Judges: Marcus McDonnell, Mark Green, Terry O'Connor.

L.Welterweight
8 February Ajose Olusegun 139¼ (Nigeria) W PTS 12 Nigel Wright 140 (England), Leisure Centre, Peterlee. Referee: Victor Loughlin. Scorecards: Howard Foster 116-113, John Keane 116-113, Phil Edwards 116-113.

Welterweight
8 December Ali Nuumbembe 146¼ (Namibia) L RSC 8 Craig Watson 146¼ (England), Robin Park Centre, Wigan. Referee: Dave Parris. Judges: Phil Edwards, Marcus McDonnell, Victor Loughlin.

24 May Craig Watson 146¼ (England) W PTS 12 Matthew Hatton 146½ (England), City of Manchester Stadium, Manchester. Referee: Dave Parris. Scorecards: Mickey Vann 116-112, Howard Foster 117-112, Victor Loughlin 118-111.

L.Middleweight
14 July Bradley Pryce 153 (Wales) W RSC 7 Anthony Small 153 (England), O2 Arena, Greenwich, London. Referee: Howard Foster. Judges: Ian John-Lewis, Marcus McDonnell, Mickey Vann.

6 October Bradley Pryce 153½ (Wales) W RSC 3 Martin Concepcion 153½ (England), The Arena, Nottingham.

Darren Barker (right) retained his Commonwealth middleweight title with a seventh-round stoppage over Steven Bendall

Philip Sharkey

Referee: Howard Foster. Judges: John Keane, Victor Loughlin, Terry O'Connor.

21 June Bradley Pryce 153¼ (Wales) W RSC 6 Marcus Portman 153½ (England), National Indoor Arena, Birmingham. Referee: Marcus McDonnell. Judges: Terry O'Connor, Mark Green, John Keane.

Middleweight

14 November Darren Barker 158½ (England) W PTS 12 Ben Crampton 158½ (Australia), York Hall, Bethnal Green, London. Referee: Ian John-Lewis. Scorecards: Richie Davies 120-108, Phil Edwards 120-108, Dave Parris 119-110. Contested for the vacant title after Howard Eastman (England/Guyana) had forfeited his championship belt when losing his British crown to Wayne Elcock on 28 September.

22 February Darren Barker 158½ (England) W RSC 7 Steven Bendall 159¾ (England), York Hall, Bethnal Green, London. Referee: Richie Davies. Judges: Ian John-Lewis, Terry O'Connor, Dave Parris.

S.Middleweight

There were no title bouts held during the period and the championship remains vacant after England's Carl Froch handed back his belt on 12 June 2007. Following postponement and the withdrawal of Charles Adamu (Ghana) through injury, Jermain Mackey (Bahamas) will face either Michael Gbenga (Nigeria) or fellow Bahamian, Elkenu Saunders, to decide the title.

L.Heavyweight

8 December Dean Francis 173½ (England) W PTS 12 Michael Gbenga 173½ (Nigeria), The Arena, Bolton. Referee: John Keane. Scorecards: Howard Foster 117-112, Richie Davies 117-112, Mickey Vann 118-110.

13 June Dean Francis 175 (England) W RSC 9 Tony Oakey 173 (England), Mountbatten Centre, Portsmouth. Referee: Richie Davies. Judges: Mark Green, Marcus McDonnell, Ian John-Lewis. Francis also picked up Oakey's British title on the result.

Cruiserweight

There were no title bouts held during the period in question and the champion, Troy Ross (Canada), has been given until 31 October to make a defence or risk being stripped of the title.

Heavyweight

14 July Matt Skelton 248¾ (England) W PTS 12 Michael Sprott 243¾ (England), O2 Arena, Greenwich, London. Referee: Mickey Vann. Scorecards: Howard Foster 115-114, Marcus McDonnell 117-113, Ian John-Lewis 114-114.

Commonwealth Champions, 1887-2008

Since the 1997 edition, Harold Alderman's magnificent research into Imperial British Empire title fights has introduced many more claimants/champions than were shown previously. Prior to 12 October 1954, the date that the British Commonwealth and Empire Boxing Championships Committee was formed, there was no official body as such and the Australian and British promoters virtually ran the show, with other members of the British Empire mainly out in the cold. We have also listed Canadian representatives, despite championship boxing in that country being contested over ten or 12 rounds at most, but they are not accorded the same kind of recognition that their British and Australian counterparts are. Boxers who became Commonwealth champions while being licensed and qualified to contest national titles outside of their country of birth are recorded by domicile/birthplace. Reconstituted as the British Commonwealth Boxing Championships Committee on 22 November 1972, and with a current membership that includes Australia, Bahamas, Barbados, Canada, Ghana, Guyana, Jamaica, Kenya, Namibia, New Zealand, Nigeria, South Africa, Tanzania, Trinidad &Tobago, Uganda and Zambia, in 1989 the 'British' tag was dropped.

COMMONWEALTH COUNTRY CODE
A = Australia; ANT = Antigua; BAH = Bahamas; BAR = Barbados; BER = Bermuda; C = Canada; E = England; F = Fiji; GH = Ghana; GU = Guyana; I = Ireland; J = Jamaica; K = Kenya; MAU = Mauritius; N = Nigeria; NAM = Namibia; NZ = New Zealand; NI = Northern Ireland; PNG = Papua New Guinea; SA = South Africa; SAM = Samoa; S = Scotland; SK = St Kitts; SL = St Lucia; T = Tonga; TR = Trinidad; U = Uganda; W = Wales; ZA = Zambia; ZI = Zimbabwe.

Champions in **bold** denote those recognised by the British Commonwealth and Empire Boxing Championships Committee (1954 to date) and, prior to that, those with the best claims

*Undefeated champions (Does not include men who forfeited titles)

Flyweight (112 lbs)

Name	Country	Years
Elky Clark*	S	1924-1927
Harry Hill	E	1929
Frenchy Belanger	C	1929
Vic White	A	1929-1930
Teddy Green	A	1930-1931
Jackie Paterson	S	1940-1948
Rinty Monaghan*	NI	1948-1950
Teddy Gardner	E	1952
Jake Tuli	SA	1952-1954
Dai Dower*	W	1954-1957
Frankie Jones	S	1957
Dennis Adams*	SA	1957-1962
Jackie Brown	S	1962-1963
Walter McGowan*	S	1963-1969
John McCluskey	S	1970-1971
Henry Nissen	A	1971-1974
Big Jim West*	A	1974-1975
Patrick Mambwe	ZA	1976-1979
Ray Amoo	N	1980
Steve Muchoki	K	1980-1983
Keith Wallace*	E	1983-1984
Richard Clarke	J	1986-1987
Nana Yaw Konadu*	GH	1987-1989
Alfred Kotey*	GH	1989-1993
Francis Ampofo*	E/GH	1993
Daren Fifield	E	1993-1994
Francis Ampofo	E/GH	1994-1995
Danny Ward	SA	1995-1996
Peter Culshaw	E	1996-1997
Ady Lewis*	E	1997-1998
Alfonso Zvenyika	ZI	1998
Damaen Kelly	NI	1998-1999
Keith Knox	S	1999
Jason Booth*	E	1999-2003
Dale Robinson	E	2003-2004
Lee Haskins*	E	2006-2007

Bantamweight (118 lbs)

Name	Country	Years
Digger Stanley	E	1904-1905
Owen Moran	E	1905
Ted Green	A	1905-1911
Charlie Simpson*	A	1911-1912
Jim Higgins	S	1920-1922
Tommy Harrison	E	1922-1923
Bugler Harry Lake	E	1923
Johnny Brown	E	1923-1928
Billy McAllister	A	1928-1930
Teddy Baldock*	E	1928-1930
Johnny Peters	E	1930
Dick Corbett	E	1930-1932
Johnny King	E	1932-1934
Dick Corbett	E	1934
Frankie Martin	C	1935-1937
Baby Yack	C	1937
Johnny Gaudes	C	1937-1939
Lefty Gwynn	C	1939
Baby Yack	C	1939-1940
Jim Brady	S	1941-1945
Jackie Paterson	S	1945-1949
Stan Rowan	E	1949
Vic Toweel	SA	1949-1952
Jimmy Carruthers*	A	1952-1954
Peter Keenan	S	1955-1959
Freddie Gilroy*	NI	1959-1963
Johnny Caldwell	NI	1964-1965
Alan Rudkin	E	1965-1966
Walter McGowan	S	1966-1968
Alan Rudkin	E	1968-1969
Lionel Rose*	A	1969
Alan Rudkin*	E	1970-1972
Paul Ferreri	A	1972-1977
Sulley Shittu	GH	1977-1978
Johnny Owen*	W	1978-1980
Paul Ferreri	A	1981-1986
Ray Minus*	BAH	1986-1991
John Armour*	E	1992-1996
Paul Lloyd*	E	1996-2000
Ady Lewis	E	2000
Tommy Waite	NI	2000
Nicky Booth	E	2000-2002
Steve Molitor	C	2002-2004
Joseph Agbeko	GH	2004-2006
Tshifhiwa Munyai*	SA	2006-2007
Jason Booth	E	2007-

S. Bantamweight (122 lbs)

Name	Country	Years
Neil Swain	W	1995
Neil Swain	W	1996-1997
Michael Brodie	E	1997-1999
Nedal Hussein*	A	2000-2001
Brian Carr	S	2001-2002
Michael Alldis	E	2002
Esham Pickering	E	2003-2005
Michael Hunter*	E	2005-2006
Isaac Ward	E	2007
Anyeti Laryea	GH	2007-

Featherweight (126 lbs)

Name	Country	Years
Jim Driscoll*	W	1908-1913
Llew Edwards	W	1915-1916
Charlie Simpson*	A	1916
Tommy Noble	E	1919-1921
Bert Spargo	A	1921-1922
Bert McCarthy	A	1922
Bert Spargo	A	1922-1923
Billy Grime	A	1923
Ernie Baxter	A	1923
Leo Kid Roy	C	1923
Bert Ristuccia	A	1923-1924
Barney Wilshur	C	1923

Title Holder	Domicile/ Birthplace	Tenure
Benny Gould	C	1923-1924
Billy Grime	A	1924
Leo Kid Roy	C	1924-1932
Johnny McGrory	S	1936-1938
Jim Spider Kelly	NI	1938-1939
Johnny Cusick	E	1939-1940
Nel Tarleton	E	1940-1947
Tiger Al Phillips	E	1947
Ronnie Clayton	E	1947-1951
Roy Ankrah	GH	1951-1954
Billy Spider Kelly	NI	1954-1955
Hogan Kid Bassey*	N	1955-1957
Percy Lewis	TR	1957-1960
Floyd Robertson	GH	1960-1967
John O'Brien	S	1967
Johnny Famechon*	A	1967-1969
Toro George	NZ	1970-1972
Bobby Dunne	A	1972-1974
Evan Armstrong	S	1974
David Kotey*	GH	1974-1975
Eddie Ndukwu	N	1977-1980
Pat Ford*	GU	1980-1981
Azumah Nelson*	GH	1981-1985
Tyrone Downes	BAR	1986-1988
Thunder Aryeh	GH	1988-1989
Oblitey Commey	GH	1989-1990
Modest Napunyi	K	1990-1991
Barrington Francis*	C	1991
Colin McMillan*	E	1992
Billy Hardy*	E	1992-1996
Jonjo Irwin	E	1996-1997
Paul Ingle*	E	1997-1999
Patrick Mullings	E	1999-2000
Scott Harrison*	S	2000-2002
Nicky Cook*	E	2003-2005
Jackson Asiku*	A/U	2005-2008
Paul Truscott	E	2008-

S. Featherweight (130 lbs)

Title Holder	Domicile/ Birthplace	Tenure
Billy Moeller	A	1975-1977
Johnny Aba*	PNG	1977-1982
Langton Tinago	ZI	1983-1984
John Sichula	ZA	1984
Lester Ellis*	A/E	1984-1985
John Sichula	ZA	1985-1986
Sam Akromah	GH	1986-1987
John Sichula	ZA	1987-1989
Mark Reefer*	E	1989-1990
Thunder Aryeh	GH	1990-1991
Hugh Forde	E	1991
Paul Harvey	E	1991-1992
Tony Pep	C	1992-1995
Justin Juuko*	U	1995-1998
Charles Shepherd*	E	1999
Mick O'Malley	A	1999-2000
Ian McLeod*	S	2000
James Armah*	GH	2000-2001
Alex Moon	E	2001-2002
Dean Pithie	E	2002-2003

Title Holder	Domicile/ Birthplace	Tenure
Craig Docherty	S	2003-2004
Alex Arthur*	S	2004-2006
Kevin Mitchell	E	2006-

Lightweight (135 lbs)

Title Holder	Domicile/ Birthplace	Tenure
Jim Burge	A	1890
George Dawson*	A	1890
Harry Nickless	E	1892-1894
Arthur Valentine	E	1894-1895
Dick Burge*	E	1894-1895
Jim Murphy*	NZ	1894-1897
Eddie Connolly*	C	1896-1897
Jack Goldswain	E	1906-1908
Jack McGowan	A	1909
Hughie Mehegan	A	1909-1910
Johnny Summers*	E	1910
Hughie Mehegan	A	1911
Freddie Welsh*	W	1912-1914
Ernie Izzard	E	1928
Tommy Fairhall	A	1928-1930
Al Foreman	E	1930-1933
Jimmy Kelso	A	1933
Al Foreman*	E	1933-1934
Laurie Stevens*	SA	1936-1937
Dave Crowley	E	1938
Eric Boon	E	1938-1944
Ronnie James*	W	1944-1947
Arthur King	C	1948-1951
Frank Johnson	E	1953
Pat Ford	A	1953-1954
Ivor Germain	BAR	1954
Pat Ford	A	1954-1955
Johnny van Rensburg	SA	1955-1956
Willie Toweel	SA	1956-1959
Dave Charnley	E	1959-1962
Bunny Grant	J	1962-1967
Manny Santos*	NZ	1967
Love Allotey	GH	1967-1968
Percy Hayles	J	1968-1975
Jonathan Dele	N	1975-1977
Lennox Blackmore	GU	1977-1978
Hogan Jimoh	N	1978-1980
Langton Tinago	ZI	1980-1981
Barry Michael	A/E	1981-1982
Claude Noel	T	1982-1984
Graeme Brooke	A	1984-1985
Barry Michael*	A/E	1985-1986
Langton Tinago	ZI	1986-1987
Mo Hussein	E	1987-1989
Pat Doherty	E	1989
Najib Daho	E	1989-1990
Carl Crook	E	1990-1992
Billy Schwer	E	1992-1993
Paul Burke	E	1993
Billy Schwer	E	1993-1995
David Tetteh	GH	1995-1997
Billy Irwin	C	1997
David Tetteh	GH	1997-1999
Bobby Vanzie	E	1999-2001

Title Holder	Domicile/ Birthplace	Tenure
James Armah*	GH	2001-2002
David Burke*	E	2002
Michael Muya	K	2003
Kevin Bennett	E	2003-2005
Graham Earl*	E	2005-2006
Willie Limond	S	2006-2007
Amir Khan	E	2007-

L. Welterweight (140 lbs)

Title Holder	Domicile/ Birthplace	Tenure
Joe Tetteh	GH	1972-1973
Hector Thompson	A	1973-1977
Baby Cassius Austin	A	1977-1978
Jeff Malcolm	A	1978-1979
Obisia Nwankpa	N	1979-1983
Billy Famous	N	1983-1986
Tony Laing	E	1987-1988
Lester Ellis	A/E	1988-1989
Steve Larrimore	BAH	1989
Tony Ekubia	E/N	1989-1991
Andy Holligan	E	1991-1994
Ross Hale	E	1994-1995
Paul Ryan	E	1995-1996
Andy Holligan	E	1996-1997
Bernard Paul	E/MAU	1997-1999
Eamonn Magee	NI	1999-
Paul Burke	E	1997
Felix Bwalya*	ZA	1997
Paul Burke	E	1998-1999
Eamonn Magee*	NI	1999-2002
Junior Witter*	E	2002-2006
Ajose Olusegun	N	2007-

Welterweight (147 lbs)

Title Holder	Domicile/ Birthplace	Tenure
Tom Williams	A	1892-1895
Dick Burge	E	1895-1897
Eddie Connolly*	C	1903-1905
Joe White*	C	1907-1909
Johnny Summers	E	1912-1914
Tom McCormick	I	1914
Matt Wells	E	1914-1919
Fred Kay	A	1915
Tommy Uren	A	1915-1916
Fritz Holland	A	1916
Tommy Uren	A	1916-1919
Fred Kay	A	1919-1920
Johnny Basham	W	1919-1920
Bermondsey Billy Wells	E	1922
Ted Kid Lewis	E	1920-1924
Tommy Milligan*	S	1924-1925
Jack Carroll	A	1928
Charlie Purdie	A	1928-1929
Wally Hancock	A	1929-1930
Tommy Fairhall*	A	1930
Jack Carroll	A	1934-1938
Eddie Thomas	W	1951
Wally Thom	E	1951-1952
Cliff Curvis	W	1952
Gerald Dreyer	SA	1952-1954

Title Holder	Domicile/Birthplace	Tenure
Barry Brown	NZ	1954
George Barnes	A	1954-1956
Darby Brown	A	1956
George Barnes	A	1956-1958
Johnny van Rensburg	SA	1958
George Barnes	A	1958-1960
Brian Curvis*	W	1960-1966
Johnny Cooke	E	1967-1968
Ralph Charles*	E	1968-1972
Clyde Gray	C	1973-1979
Chris Clarke	C	1979
Clyde Gray*	C	1979-1980
Colin Jones*	W	1981-1984
Sylvester Mittee	E/SL	1984-1985
Lloyd Honeyghan*	E/J	1985-1986
Brian Janssen	A	1987
Wilf Gentzen	A	1987-1988
Gary Jacobs	S	1988-1989
Donovan Boucher	C	1989-1992
Eamonn Loughran*	NI	1992-1993
Andrew Murray*	GU	1993-1997
Kofi Jantuah*	GH	1997-2000
Scott Dixon*	S	2000

Title Holder	Domicile/Birthplace	Tenure
Jawaid Khaliq*	E	2000-2001
Julian Holland	A	2001-2002
James Hare*	E	2002-2003
Ossie Duran*	GH	2003-2004
Fatai Onikeke	NI	2004-2005
Joshua Okine	GH	2005
Kevin Anderson	S	2005-2007
Ali Nuumbembe	NAM	2007-2007
Craig Watson	E	2007-

L. Middleweight (154 lbs)

Title Holder	Domicile/Birthplace	Tenure
Charkey Ramon*	A	1972-1975
Maurice Hope*	E/ANT	1976-1979
Kenny Bristol	GU	1979-1981
Herol Graham*	E	1981-1984
Ken Salisbury	A/E	1984-1985
Nick Wilshire	E	1985-1987
Lloyd Hibbert	E	1987
Troy Waters*	A/E	1987-1991
Chris Pyatt*	E	1991-1992
Mickey Hughes	E	1992-1993
Lloyd Honeyghan	E/J	1993-1994
Leo Young	A	1994-1995

Title Holder	Domicile/Birthplace	Tenure
Kevin Kelly	A	1995
Chris Pyatt	E	1995-1996
Steve Foster	E	1996-1997
Kevin Kelly	A	1997-1999
Tony Badea	C	1999-2001
Richard Williams*	E	2001
Joshua Onyango	K	2002
Michael Jones	E	2002-2003
Jamie Moore*	E	2003-2004
Richard Williams*	E	2004
Jamie Moore	E	2004
Ossie Duran	GH	2004-2006
Bradley Pryce	W	2006-

Middleweight (160 lbs)

Title Holder	Domicile/Birthplace	Tenure
Chesterfield Goode	E	1887-1890
Toff Wall	E	1890-1891
Jim Hall	A	1892-1893
Bill Heffernan	NZ	1894-1896
Bill Doherty	A	1896-1897
Billy Edwards	A	1897-1898
Dido Plumb*	E	1898-1901
Tom Duggan	A	1901-1903

Bradley Price (right) retained his Commonwealth light-welter title when he stopped the brash Anthony Small inside seven rounds in July 2007

Les Clark

Title Holder	Domicile/ Birthplace	Tenure
Jack Palmer*	E	1902-1904
Jewey Cooke	E	1903-1904
Tom Dingey	C	1904-1905
Jack Lalor	SA	1905
Ted Nelson	A	1905
Tom Dingey	C	1905
Sam Langford*	C	1907-1911
Ed Williams	A	1908-1910
Arthur Cripps	A	1910
Dave Smith	A	1910-1911
Jerry Jerome	A	1913
Arthur Evernden	E	1913-1914
Mick King	A	1914-1915
Les Darcy*	A	1915-1917
Ted Kid Lewis	E	1922-1923
Roland Todd	E	1923-1926
Len Johnson	E	1926-1928
Tommy Milligan	S	1926-1928
Alex Ireland	S	1928-1929
Len Harvey	E	1929-1933
Del Fontaine	C	1931
Ted Moore	E	1931
Jock McAvoy	E	1933-1939
Ron Richards*	A	1940
Ron Richards*	A	1941-1942
Bos Murphy	NZ	1948
Dick Turpin	E	1948-1949
Dave Sands*	A	1949-1952
Randy Turpin	E	1952-1954
Al Bourke	A	1952-1954
Johnny Sullivan	E	1954-1955
Pat McAteer	E	1955-1958
Dick Tiger	N	1958-1960
Wilf Greaves	C	1960
Dick Tiger*	N	1960-1962
Gomeo Brennan	BAH	1963-1964
Tuna Scanlon*	NZ	1964
Gomeo Brennan	BAH	1964-1966
Blair Richardson*	C	1966-1967
Milo Calhoun	J	1967
Johnny Pritchett*	E	1967-1969
Les McAteer	E	1969-1970
Mark Rowe	E	1970
Bunny Sterling	E/J	1970-1972
Tony Mundine*	A	1972-1975
Monty Betham	NZ	1975-1978
Al Korovou	A	1978
Ayub Kalule	U	1978-1980
Tony Sibson*	E	1980-1983
Roy Gumbs	E/SK	1983
Mark Kaylor	E	1983-1984
Tony Sibson*	E	1984-1988
Nigel Benn	E	1988-1989
Michael Watson*	E	1989-1991
Richie Woodhall	E	1992-1995
Robert McCracken	E	1995-1997
Johnson Tshuma	SA	1997-1998
Paul Jones	E	1998-1999
Jason Matthews*	E	1999
Alain Bonnamie*	C	1999-2000
Sam Soliman	A	2000
Howard Eastman*	E/GU	2000-2004
James Obede Toney	GH	2004-2006
Scott Dann*	E	2006-2007
Howard Eastman*	E/GU	2007
Darren Barker	E	2007-

S. Middleweight (168 lbs)

Title Holder	Domicile/ Birthplace	Tenure
Rod Carr	A	1989-1990
Lou Cafaro	A	1990-1991
Henry Wharton*	E	1991-1997
Clinton Woods	E	1997-1998
David Starie	E	1998-2003
Andre Thysse	SA	2003
Charles Adamu	GH	2003-2004
Carl Froch*	E	2004-2007

L. Heavyweight (175 lbs)

Title Holder	Domicile/ Birthplace	Tenure
Dave Smith*	A	1911-1915
Jack Bloomfield*	E	1923-1924
Tom Berry	E	1927
Gipsy Daniels*	W	1927
Len Harvey	E	1939-1942
Freddie Mills*	E	1942-1950
Randy Turpin*	E	1952-1955
Gordon Wallace	C	1956-1957
Yvon Durelle*	C	1957-1959
Chic Calderwood	S	1960-1963
Bob Dunlop*	A	1968-1970
Eddie Avoth	W	1970-1971
Chris Finnegan	E	1971-1973
John Conteh*	E	1973-1974
Steve Aczel	A	1975
Tony Mundine	A	1975-1978
Gary Summerhays	C	1978-1979
Lottie Mwale	ZA	1979-1985
Leslie Stewart*	TR	1985-1987
Willie Featherstone	C	1987-1989
Guy Waters*	A/E	1989-1993
Brent Kosolofski	C	1993-1994
Garry Delaney	E	1994-1995
Noel Magee	I	1995
Nicky Piper*	W	1995-1997
Crawford Ashley	E	1998-1999
Clinton Woods*	E	1999-2000
Neil Simpson	E	2001
Tony Oakey*	E	2001-2002
Peter Oboh*	E/N	2002-2006
Ovill McKenzie	J	2006-2007
Dean Francis	E	2007-

Cruiserweight (200 lbs)

Title Holder	Domicile/ Birthplace	Tenure
Stewart Lithgo	E	1984
Chisanda Mutti	ZA	1984-1987
Glenn McCrory*	E	1987-1989
Apollo Sweet	A	1989
Derek Angol*	E	1989-1993
Francis Wanyama	U	1994-1995
Chris Okoh	E	1995-1997
Darren Corbett	NI	1997-1998
Bruce Scott	E/J	1998-1999
Adam Watt*	A	2000-2001
Bruce Scott*	E/J	2001-2003
Mark Hobson*	E	2003-2006
Troy Ross	C	2007-

Heavyweight (200 lbs +)

Title Holder	Domicile/ Birthplace	Tenure
Peter Jackson*	A	1889-1901
Dan Creedon	NZ	1896-1903
Billy McColl	A	1902-1905
Tim Murphy	A	1905-1906
Bill Squires	A	1906-1909
Bill Lang	A	1909-1910
Tommy Burns*	C	1910-1911
P.O. Curran	I	1911
Dan Flynn	I	1911
Bombardier Billy Wells	E	1911-1919
Bill Lang	A	1911-1913
Dave Smith	A	1913-1917
Joe Beckett*	E	1919-1923
Phil Scott	E	1926-1931
Larry Gains	C	1931-1934
Len Harvey	E	1934
Jack Petersen	W	1934-1936
Ben Foord	SA	1936-1937
Tommy Farr	W	1937
Len Harvey*	E	1939-1942
Jack London	E	1944-1945
Bruce Woodcock	E	1945-1950
Jack Gardner	E	1950-1952
Johnny Williams	W	1952-1953
Don Cockell	E	1953-1956
Joe Bygraves	J	1956-1957
Joe Erskine	W	1957-1958
Brian London	E	1958-1959
Henry Cooper	E	1959-1971
Joe Bugner	E	1971
Jack Bodell	E	1971-1972
Danny McAlinden	NI	1972-1975
Bunny Johnson	E/J	1975
Richard Dunn	E	1975-1976
Joe Bugner*	E	1976-1977
John L. Gardner*	E	1978-1981
Trevor Berbick	C/J	1981-1986
Horace Notice*	E	1986-1988
Derek Williams	E	1988-1992
Lennox Lewis*	E	1992-1993
Henry Akinwande	E	1993-1995
Scott Welch	E	1995-1997
Julius Francis*	E	1997-1999
Danny Williams	E	1999-2004
Michael Sprott	E	2004
Matt Skelton*	E	2004-2005
Danny Williams	E	2005-2006
Matt Skelton	E	2006-

European Title Bouts, 2007-2008

All of last season's title bouts are shown in date order within their weight divisions and give the boxers' respective weights, along with the scorecard if going to a decision. Referees are names, as are British judges where applicable.

Flyweight
22 December   Andrea Sarritzu (Italy) 111 (Italy) W RSC 7 Lahcene Zemmouri 112 (France, born Algeria), Datch Forum, Milan, Italy. Referee: Robin Dolpierre. Judge: Dave Parris.
3 May   Andrea Sarritzu 110¾ (Italy) L RSC 8 Bernard Inom 110¼ (France, born Reunion), Santoru Sports Palace, Sassari, Sardinia, Italy. Referee: Richie Davies. Judge: John Keane.

Bantamweight
3 August   Simone Maludrottu 117¾ (Italy) W PTS 12 Mohamed Bouleghcha 116 (France), Piccola Marina Open-Air Arena, Cagliari, Sardinia, Italy. Referee: Francisco Vazquez. Scorecards: 115-113, 115-114, 115-113. Maudrottu handed in his belt on 28 September to prepare for a WBC title challenge against Hozumi Hasegawa.
21 December   Carmelo Ballone 117¼ (Belgium) W RSC 8 Eugen Sorin Tanasi 116½ (Romania), Bouvy Omnisports Hall, La Louviere, Hainaut, Belgium. Referee: Luigi Muratore.
23 May Carmelo Ballone 115½ (Belgium) W RSC 10 Valery Yanchy 118 (Belarus), Bouvy Omnisports Hall, La Louviere, Hainautm Belgium. Referee: Guido Cavalleri.

S.Bantamweight
25 August   Bernard Dunne 121 (Republic of Ireland) L RSC 1 Kiko Martinez 121 (Spain), The Point, Dublin, Ireland. Referee: Terry O'Connor. Judges: John Keane, Mickey Vann, Ian John-Lewis.
7 March   Kiko Martinez 120½ (Spain) L PTS 12 Rendall Munroe 120¾ (England), Harvey Hadden Leisure Centre, Nottingham, England. Referee: Adrio Zannoni. Scorecards: 113-115, 113-115, 114-114.
2 May   Rendall Munroe 121¼ (England) W RTD 7 Salem Bouaita 120¾ (France), Harvey Hadden Leisure Centre, Nottingham, England. Referee: Jesus Morata Garcia.

Featherweight
31 October   Alberto Servidei 126 (Italy) TECH DRAW 8 Sergio Blanco 126 (Spain), Mauro de Andre Sports Palace, Ravenna, Italy. Referee: Mickey Vann. Scorecards: 77-76, 76-78, 76-76. Servidei forfeited his title on 4 April after pulling out of a defence against Blanco for personal reasons.

Colin Lynes (right) made the first defence of his European light-welterweight title a successful one when outscoring Finland's Juho Tolppola at the Goresbrook Leisure Centre last January

Philip Sharkey

It was decided that Blanco would meet Oleg Yefimovich (Ukraine) for the vacant title in July.

S.Featherweight

13 July   Leva Kirakosyan 129¾ (Armenia) W CO 4 Carl Johanneson 130 (England), The Metrodome, Barnsley, England. Referee: Robin Dolpierre.

22 December   Leva Kirakosyan 129 (Armenia) L PTS 12 Sergei Gulyakevich 128½ (Belarus), Datch Forum, Milan, Italy. Referee: Erkki Meronen. Judge: Terry O'Connor. Scorecards: 113-115, 108-120, 110-118.

Lightweight

16 October   Yuri Romanov 134½ (Belarus) W PTS 12 Steffano Zoff 133½ (Italy), Sports Palace, Minsk, Belarus. Referee: Terry O'Connor. Scorecards: 116-113, 115-113, 119-112.

4 April   Yuri Romanov 134½ (Belarus) W RSC 6 Jonathan Thaxton 134¼ (England), York Hall, Bethnal Green, London, England. Referee: Massimo Barrovecchio. Romanov relinquished the title on 23 April 2008 for reasons unknown.

L.Welterweight

20 July   Colin Lynes 139½ (England) W RSC 8 Young Muttley 139 (England), Civic Hall, Wolverhampton, England. Referee: Richie Davies. Judges: Terry O'Connor, Ian John-Lewis, Marcus McDonnell. Contested for the vacant title after Ted Bami (England) handed in his belt on 12 July, having pulled out of his defence against Muttley, citing an injured hand. Lynes stepped in at short notice, putting his British title on the line.

25 January   Colin Lynes 139¾ (England) W PTS 12 Juho Tolppola 139¾ (Finland), Goresbrook Leisure Centre, Dagenham, England. Referee: Jesus Morata Garcia. Scorecards: 120-108, 120-108, 119-109.

16 May   Colin Lynes 137½ (England) L PTS 12 Gianluca Branco 139 (Italy), Ruffini Park Sports Palace, Turin, Italy. Referee: Manuel Oliver Palomo. Scorecards: 115-113, 113-114, 113-114.

Welterweight

27 October   Jackson Osei Bonsu 146¼ (Belgium, born Ghana) W CO 3 Nordine Mouchi 145½ (France), Vieilles Forges Conference Centre, Ardennes, France. Referee: Franco Ciminale.

12 January   Jackson Osei Bonsu 146¼ (Belgium, born Ghana) W PTS 12 Brice Feradji 146 (France, born Algeria), Lotto Arena, Antwerp, Belgium. Referee: Terry O'Connor. Scorecards: 116-111, 115-113, 118-109.

3 May   Jackson Osei Bonsu 146¼ (Belgium, born Ghana) W PTS 12 Viktor Plotnikov 147 (Ukraine), Lotto Arena, Antwerp, Belgium. Referee: Terry O'Connor. Scorecards: 116-112, 116-113, 116-112.

L.Middleweight

7 July   Zaurbek Baysangurov 152½ (Russia) W PTS 12 Hussein Bayram 151½ (France), The Arena, Cologne, Germany. Referee: Massimo Barrovecchio. Scorecards: 114-113, 114-113, Mickey Vann 115-113. Contested for the vacant title after Michele Piccirillo (Italy) handed in his belt on 19 April.

23 March   Zaurbek Baysangurov 151 (Russia) W RSC 8 Roman Dzuman 151½ (Ukraine), Meteor Sports Palace, Dnipropetrovsk, Ukraine. Referee: Erkki Meronen.

Middleweight

27 October   Sebastian Sylvester 159½ (Germany) W PTS 12 Simone Rotala 158½ (Italy), Exhibition Hall, Erfurt, Germany. Referee: Jesus Morata Garcia. Judge: John Keane. Scorecards: 115-114, 115-114, 112-116.

26 January   Sebastian Sylvester 159¾ (Germany) W PTS 12 Francois Bastient 159½ (France), Kreuzberg Tempodrome, Berlin, Germany. Referee: Guido Cavaleri. Scorecards: 118-109, 120-108, 119-108.

12 April   Sebastian Sylvester 159½ (Germany) W CO 12 Javier Castillejo 159 (Spain), Sports Forum, Neubrandenberg, Germany. Referee: Erkki Meronen.

S.Middleweight

8 December   Cristian Sanavia 165 (Italy) DREW 12 Danilio Haussler 167¼ (Germany), St Jakob Hall, Basle, Switzerland. Referee: Erkki Meronen. Scorecards: 114-112, 112-114, 113-113.

12 April   Cristian Sanavia 167¼ (Italy) L PTS 12 Karo Murat 166¾ (Germany), Sports Forum, Neubrandenberg, Germany. Referee: Dave Parris. Scorecards: 112-115, 113-114, 111-116.

L.Heavyweight

23 February   Thomas Ulrich 174¾ (Germany) L CO 8 Yuri Barashian 174¾ (Ukraine), Brandberge Arena, Halle, Germany. Referee: Massimo Barrovecchio.

Cruiserweight

14 December   Vincenzo Cantatore 198¾ (Italy) L CO 2 Johny Jensen 197¼ (Denmark), Sports Palace, Rome, Italy. Referee: Ian John-Lewis. Judge: Mark Green.

3 May   Johny Jensen 197¼ (Denmark) L RSC 1 Jean-Marc Monrose 195½ (France), Sports Palace, Marseille, France. Referee: Dave Parris. Judge: Mickey Vann.

Heavyweight

There were co contests during the period. Vladimir Virchis (Ukraine) relinquished his title on 8 October to concentrate on getting a WBC world title shot. Eventually Turkey's Sinan Samil Sam and Paolo Vidoz (Italy) were selected to contest the vacancy in July 2008.

European Champions, 1909-2008

Prior to 1946, the championship was contested under the auspices of the International Boxing Union, re-named that year as the European Boxing Union (EBU). The IBU had come into being when Victor Breyer, a Paris-based journalist and boxing referee who later edited the Annuaire du Ring (first edition in 1910), warmed to the idea of an organisation that controlled boxing right across Europe, regarding rules and championship fights between the champions of the respective countries. He first came to London at the end of 1909 to discuss the subject with the NSC, but went away disappointed. However, at a meeting between officials from Switzerland and France in March 1912, the IBU was initially formed and, by June of that year, had published their first ratings. By April 1914, Belgium had also joined the organisation, although it would not be until the war was over that the IBU really took off. Many of the early champions shown on the listings were the result of promoters, especially the NSC, billing their own championship fights. Although the (French dominated) IBU recognised certain champions, prior to being re-formed in May 1920, they did not find their administrative 'feet' fully until other countries such as Italy (1922), Holland (1923), and Spain (1924), produced challengers for titles. Later in the 1920s, Germany (1926), Denmark (1928), Portugal (1929) and Romania (1929) also joined the fold. Unfortunately, for Britain, its representatives (Although the BBBoC, as we know it today, was formed in 1929, an earlier attempt to form a Board of Control had been initiated in April 1918 by the NSC and it was that body who were involved here) failed to reach agreement on the three judges' ruling, following several meetings with the IBU early in 1920 and, apart from Elky Clark (fly), Ernie Rice and Alf Howard (light), and Jack Hood (welter), who conformed to that stipulation, fighters from these shores would not be officially recognised as champions until the EBU was formed in 1946. This led to British fighters claiming the title after beating IBU titleholders, or their successors, under championship conditions in this country. The only men who did not come into this category were Kid Nicholson (bantam), and Ted Kid Lewis and Tommy Milligan (welter), who defeated men not recognised by the IBU. For the record, the first men recognised and authorised, respectively, as being champions of their weight classes by the IBU were: Sid Smith and Michel Montreuil (fly), Charles Ledoux (bantam), Jim Driscoll and Louis de Ponthieu (feather), Freddie Welsh and Georges Papin (light), Georges Carpentier and Albert Badoud (welter), Georges Carpentier and Ercole Balzac (middle), Georges Carpentier and Battling Siki (light-heavy and heavy).

EUROPEAN COUNTRY CODE
ARM = Armenia; AU = Austria; BE = Belarus; BEL = Belgium; BUL = Bulgaria; CRO = Croatia; CZ = Czechoslovakia; DEN = Denmark; E = England; FIN = Finland; FR = France; GEO = Georgia; GER = Germany; GRE = Greece; HOL = Holland; HUN = Hungary; ITA = Italy; KAZ = Kazakhstan; LUX = Luxembourg; NI= Northern Ireland; NOR = Norway; POL = Poland; POR = Portugal; RoI = Republic of Ireland; ROM = Romania; RUS = Russia; S = Scotland; SP = Spain; SWE = Sweden; SWI = Switzerland; TU = Turkey; UK = Ukraine; W= Wales; YUG = Yugoslavia.

Champions in **bold** denote those recognised by the IBU/EBU

*Undefeated champions (Does not include men who may have forfeited titles)

Title Holder	Birthplace/ Domicile	Tenure	Title Holder	Birthplace/ Domicile	Tenure	Title Holder	Birthplace/ Domicile	Tenure
Flyweight (112 lbs)			**Dai Dower**	W	1955	**Andrea Sarritzu**	ITA	2006-
Sid Smith	E	1913	**Young Martin**	SP	1955-1959			
Bill Ladbury	E	1913-1914	**Risto Luukkonen**	FIN	1959-1961	**Bantamweight (118 lbs)**		
Percy Jones	W	1914	**Salvatore Burruni***	ITA	1961-1965	Joe Bowker	E	1910
Joe Symonds	E	1914	**Rene Libeer**	FR	1965-1966	Digger Stanley	E	1910-1912
Tancy Lee	S	1914-1916	**Fernando Atzori**	ITA	1967-1972	**Charles Ledoux**	FR	1912-1921
Jimmy Wilde	W	1914-1915	**Fritz Chervet**	SWI	1972-1973	Bill Beynon	W	1913
Jimmy Wilde*	W	1916-1923	**Fernando Atzori**	ITA	1973	Tommy Harrison	E	1921-1922
Michel Montreuil	BEL	1923-1925	**Fritz Chervet***	SWI	1973-1974	**Charles Ledoux**	FR	1922-1923
Elky Clark*	S	1925-1927	**Franco Udella**	ITA	1974-1979	Bugler Harry Lake	E	1923
Victor Ferrand	SP	1927	**Charlie Magri***	E	1979-1983	Johnny Brown	E	1923-1928
Emile Pladner	FR	1928-1929	**Antoine Montero**	FR	1983-1984	**Henry Scillie***	BEL	1925-1928
Johnny Hill	S	1928-1929	**Charlie Magri***	E	1984-1985	Kid Nicholson	E	1928
Eugene Huat	FR	1929	**Franco Cherchi**	ITA	1985	Teddy Baldock	E	1928-1931
Emile Degand	BEL	1929-1930	**Charlie Magri**	E	1985-1986	**Domenico Bernasconi**	ITA	1929
Kid Oliva	FR	1930	**Duke McKenzie***	E	1986-1988	**Carlos Flix**	SP	1929-1931
Lucien Popescu	ROM	1930-1931	**Eyup Can***	TU	1989-1990	**Lucien Popescu**	ROM	1931-1932
Jackie Brown	E	1931-1935	**Pat Clinton***	S	1990-1991	**Domenico Bernasconi**	ITA	1932
Praxile Gyde	FR	1932-1935	**Salvatore Fanni**	ITA	1991-1992	**Nicholas Biquet**	BEL	1932-1935
Benny Lynch	S	1935-1938	**Robbie Regan***	W	1992-1993	**Maurice Dubois**	SWI	1935-1936
Kid David*	BEL	1935-1936	**Luigi Camputaro**	ITA	1993-1994	**Joseph Decico**	FR	1936
Ernst Weiss	AU	1936	**Robbie Regan***	W	1994-1995	**Aurel Toma**	ROM	1936-1937
Valentin Angelmann*	FR	1936-1938	**Luigi Camputaro***	ITA	1995-1996	**Nicholas Biquet**	BEL	1937-1938
Enrico Urbinati*	ITA	1938-1943	**Jesper Jensen**	DEN	1996-1997	**Aurel Toma**	ROM	1938-1939
Raoul Degryse	BEL	1946-1947	**David Guerault***	FR	1997-1999	**Ernst Weiss**	AU	1939
Maurice Sandeyron	FR	1947-1949	**Alexander Mahmutov**	RUS	1999-2000	**Gino Cattaneo**	ITA	1939-1941
Rinty Monaghan*	NI	1949-1950	**Damaen Kelly***	NI	2000	**Gino Bondavilli***	ITA	1941-1943
Terry Allen	E	1950	**Alexander Mahmutov**	RUS	2000-2002	**Jackie Paterson**	S	1946
Jean Sneyers*	BEL	1950-1951	**Mimoun Chent**	FR	2002-2003	**Theo Medina**	FR	1946-1947
Teddy Gardner*	E	1952	**Alexander Mahmutov***	RUS	2003	**Peter Kane**	E	1947-1948
Louis Skena*	FR	1953-1954	**Brahim Asloum***	FR	2003-2005	**Guido Ferracin**	ITA	1948-1949
Nazzareno Giannelli	ITA	1954-1955	**Ivan Pozo**	SP	2005-2006	**Luis Romero**	SP	1949-1951

Title Holder	Birthplace/ Domicile	Tenure
Peter Keenan	S	1951-1952
Jean Sneyers*	BEL	1952-1953
Peter Keenan	S	1953
John Kelly	NI	1953-1954
Robert Cohen*	FR	1954-1955
Mario D'Agata	ITA	1955-1958
Piero Rollo	ITA	1958-1959
Freddie Gilroy	NI	1959-1960
Pierre Cossemyns	BEL	1961-1962
Piero Rollo	ITA	1962
Alphonse Halimi	FR	1962
Piero Rollo	ITA	1962-1963
Mimoun Ben Ali	SP	1963
Risto Luukkonen	FIN	1963-1964
Mimoun Ben Ali	SP	1965
Tommaso Galli	ITA	1965-1966
Mimoun Ben Ali	SP	1966-1968
Salvatore Burruni*	ITA	1968-1969
Franco Zurlo	ITA	1969-1971
Alan Rudkin	E	1971
Agustin Senin*	SP	1971-1973
Johnny Clark*	E	1973-1974
Bob Allotey	SP	1974-1975
Daniel Trioulaire	FR	1975-1976
Salvatore Fabrizio	ITA	1976-1977
Franco Zurlo	ITA	1977-1978
Juan Francisco Rodriguez	SP	1978-1980
Johnny Owen*	W	1980
Valerio Nati	ITA	1980-1982
Giuseppe Fossati	ITA	1982-1983
Walter Giorgetti	ITA	1983-1984
Ciro de Leva*	ITA	1984-1986
Antoine Montero	FR	1986-1987
Louis Gomis*	FR	1987-1988
Fabrice Benichou	FR	1988
Vincenzo Belcastro*	ITA	1988-1990
Thierry Jacob*	FR	1990-1992
Johnny Bredahl*	DEN	1992
Vincenzo Belcastro	ITA	1993-1994
Prince Naseem Hamed*	E	1994-1995
John Armour*	E	1995-1996
Johnny Bredahl	DEN	1996-1998
Paul Lloyd*	E	1998-1999
Johnny Bredahl*	DEN	1999-2000
Luigi Castiglione	ITA	2000-2001
Fabien Guillerme	FR	2001
Alex Yagupov	RUS	2001
Spend Abazi	SWE	2001-2002
Noel Wilders	E	2003
David Guerault	FR	2003-2004
Frederic Patrac	FR	2004
Simone Maludrottu	ITA	2004-

S. Bantamweight (122 lbs)

Title Holder	Birthplace/ Domicile	Tenure
Vincenzo Belcastro	ITA	1995-1996
Salim Medjkoune	FR	1996
Martin Krastev	BUL	1996-1997
Spencer Oliver	E	1997-1998
Sergei Devakov	UK	1998-1999
Michael Brodie*	E	1999-2000
Vladislav Antonov	RUS	2000-2001
Salim Medjkoune*	FR	2001-2002
Mahyar Monshipour*	FR	2002-2003
Esham Pickering	E	2003-2005
Michael Hunter*	E	2005-2006
Bernard Dunne	RoI	2006-

Featherweight (126 lbs)

Title Holder	Birthplace/ Domicile	Tenure
Young Joey Smith	E	1911
Jean Poesy	FR	1911-1912
Jim Driscoll*	W	1912-1913
Ted Kid Lewis*	E	1913-1914
Louis de Ponthieu*	FR	1919-1920
Arthur Wyns	BEL	1920-1922
Billy Matthews	E	1922
Eugene Criqui*	FR	1922-1923
Edouard Mascart	FR	1923-1924
Charles Ledoux	FR	1924
Henri Hebrans	BEL	1924-1925
Antonio Ruiz	SP	1925-1928
Luigi Quadrini	ITA	1928-1929
Knud Larsen	DEN	1929
Jose Girones	SP	1929-1934
Maurice Holtzer*	FR	1935-1938
Phil Dolhem	BEL	1938-1939
Lucien Popescu	ROM	1939-1941
Ernst Weiss	AU	1941
Gino Bondavilli	ITA	1941-1945
Ermanno Bonetti*	ITA	1945-1946
Tiger Al Phillips	E	1947
Ronnie Clayton	E	1947-1948
Ray Famechon	FR	1948-1953
Jean Sneyers	BEL	1953-1954
Ray Famechon	FR	1954-1955
Fred Galiana*	SP	1955-1956
Cherif Hamia	FR	1957-1958
Sergio Caprari	ITA	1958-1959
Gracieux Lamperti	FR	1959-1962
Alberto Serti	ITA	1962-1963
Howard Winstone	W	1963-1967
Jose Legra*	SP	1967-1968
Manuel Calvo	SP	1968-1969
Tommaso Galli	ITA	1969-1970
Jose Legra*	SP	1970-1972
Gitano Jiminez	SP	1973-1975
Elio Cotena	ITA	1975-1976
Nino Jimenez	SP	1976-1977
Manuel Masso	SP	1977
Roberto Castanon*	SP	1977-1981
Salvatore Melluzzo	ITA	1981-1982
Pat Cowdell*	E	1982-1983
Loris Stecca*	ITA	1983
Barry McGuigan*	NI	1983-1985
Jim McDonnell*	E	1985-1987
Valerio Nati*	ITA	1987
Jean-Marc Renard*	BEL	1988-1989
Paul Hodkinson*	E	1989-1991
Fabrice Benichou	FR	1991-1992
Maurizio Stecca	ITA	1992-1993
Herve Jacob	FR	1993
Maurizio Stecca	ITA	1993
Stephane Haccoun	FR	1993-1994
Stefano Zoff	ITA	1994
Medhi Labdouni	FR	1994-1995
Billy Hardy	E	1995-1998
Paul Ingle*	E	1998-1999
Steve Robinson	W	1999-2000
Istvan Kovacs*	HUN	2000-2001
Manuel Calvo*	SP	2001-2002
Cyril Thomas	FR	2002-2004
Nicky Cook*	E	2004-2006
Cyril Thomas*	FR	2006-2007
Alberto Servidei	ITA	2007-

S. Featherweight (130 lbs)

Title Holder	Birthplace/ Domicile	Tenure
Tommaso Galli	ITA	1971-1972
Domenico Chiloiro	ITA	1972
Lothar Abend	GER	1972-1974
Sven-Erik Paulsen*	NOR	1974-1976
Roland Cazeaux	FR	1976
Natale Vezzoli	ITA	1976-1979
Carlos Hernandez	SP	1979
Rodolfo Sanchez	SP	1979
Carlos Hernandez	SP	1979-1982
Cornelius Boza-Edwards*	E	1982
Roberto Castanon	SP	1982-1983
Alfredo Raininger	ITA	1983-1984
Jean-Marc Renard	BEL	1984
Pat Cowdell	E	1984-1985
Jean-Marc Renard*	BEL	1986-1987
Salvatore Curcetti	ITA	1987-1988
Piero Morello	ITA	1988
Lars Lund Jensen	DEN	1988
Racheed Lawal	DEN	1988-1989
Daniel Londas*	FR	1989-1991
Jimmy Bredahl*	DEN	1992
Regilio Tuur	HOL	1992-1993
Jacobin Yoma	FR	1993-1995
Anatoly Alexandrov*	KAZ	1995-1996
Julian Lorcy*	FR	1996
Djamel Lifa	FR	1997-1998
Anatoly Alexandrov*	RUS	1998
Dennis Holbaek Pedersen	DEN	1999-2000
Boris Sinitsin	RUS	2000
Dennis Holbaek Pedersen*	DEN	2000
Tontcho Tontchev*	BUL	2001
Boris Sinitsin	RUS	2001-2002
Pedro Oscar Miranda	SP	2002
Affif Djelti	FR	2002-2003
Boris Sinitsin	RUS	2003-2005
Alex Arthur*	S	2005-2006
Leva Kirakosyan	ARM	2007-

Lightweight (135 lbs)

Title Holder	Birthplace/ Domicile	Tenure
Freddie Welsh	W	1909-1911
Matt Wells	E	1911-1912
Freddie Welsh*	W	1912-1914
Georges Papin	FR	1920-1921
Ernie Rice	E	1921-1922
Seaman Nobby Hall	E	1922-1923
Harry Mason	E	1923-1926
Fred Bretonnel	FR	1924
Lucien Vinez	FR	1924-1927
Luis Rayo*	SP	1927-1928
Aime Raphael	FR	1928-1929
Francois Sybille	BEL	1929-1930
Alf Howard	E	1930
Harry Corbett	E	1930-1931
Francois Sybille	BEL	1930-1931
Bep van Klaveren	HOL	1931-1932
Cleto Locatelli	ITA	1932
Francois Sybille	BEL	1932-1933
Cleto Locatelli*	ITA	1933
Francois Sybille	BEL	1934
Carlo Orlandi*	ITA	1934-1935
Enrico Venturi*	ITA	1935-1936
Vittorio Tamagnini	ITA	1936-1937
Maurice Arnault	FR	1937
Gustave Humery	FR	1937-1938
Aldo Spoldi*	ITA	1938-1939
Karl Blaho	AU	1940-1941
Bruno Bisterzo	ITA	1941
Ascenzo Botta	ITA	1941
Bruno Bisterzo	ITA	1941-1942
Ascenzo Botta	ITA	1942
Roberto Proietti	ITA	1942-1943
Bruno Bisterzo	ITA	1943-1946
Roberto Proietti*	ITA	1946
Emile Dicristo	FR	1946-1947
Kid Dussart	BEL	1947
Roberto Proietti	ITA	1947-1948
Billy Thompson	E	1948-1949
Kid Dussart	BEL	1949
Roberto Proietti*	ITA	1949-1950
Pierre Montane	FR	1951
Elis Ask	FIN	1951-1952
Jorgen Johansen	DEN	1952-1954
Duilio Loi*	ITA	1954-1959
Mario Vecchiatto	ITA	1959-1960
Dave Charnley	E	1960-1963
Conny Rudhof*	GER	1963-1964
Willi Quatuor*	GER	1964-1965
Franco Brondi	ITA	1965
Maurice Tavant	FR	1965-1966
Borge Krogh	DEN	1966-1967
Pedro Carrasco*	SP	1967-1969
Miguel Velazquez	SP	1970-1971
Antonio Puddu	ITA	1971-1974
Ken Buchanan*	S	1974-1975
Fernand Roelandts	BEL	1976
Perico Fernandez*	SP	1976-1977
Jim Watt*	S	1977-1979

Title Holder	Birthplace/ Domicile	Tenure	Title Holder	Birthplace/ Domicile	Tenure	Title Holder	Birthplace/ Domicile	Tenure
Charlie Nash*	NI	1979-1980	Leo Darton	BEL	1928	Remo Golfarini	ITA	1968-1969
Francisco Leon	SP	1980	Alf Genon	BEL	1928-1929	Gerhard Piaskowy	GER	1969-1970
Charlie Nash	NI	1980-1981	Gustave Roth	BEL	1929-1932	Jose Hernandez	SP	1970-1972
Joey Gibilisco	ITA	1981-1983	Adrien Aneet	BEL	1932-1933	Juan Carlos Duran	ITA	1972-1973
Lucio Cusma	ITA	1983-1984	Jack Hood*	E	1933	Jacques Kechichian	FR	1973-1974
Rene Weller	GER	1984-1986	Gustav Eder	GER	1934-1936	Jose Duran	SP	1974-1975
Gert Bo Jacobsen	DEN	1986-1988	Felix Wouters	BEL	1936-1938	Eckhard Dagge	GER	1975-1976
Rene Weller*	GER	1988	Saverio Turiello	ITA	1938-1939	Vito Antuofermo	ITA	1976
Policarpo Diaz*	SP	1988-1990	Marcel Cerdan*	FR	1939-1942	Maurice Hope*	E	1976-1978
Antonio Renzo	ITA	1991-1992	Ernie Roderick	E	1946-1947	Gilbert Cohen	FR	1978-1979
Jean-Baptiste Mendy*	FR	1992-1994	Robert Villemain*	FR	1947-1948	Marijan Benes	YUG	1979-1981
Racheed Lawal	DEN	1994	Livio Minelli	ITA	1949-1950	Louis Acaries	FR	1981
Jean-Baptiste Mendy*	FR	1994-1995	Michele Palermo	ITA	1950-1951	Luigi Minchillo*	ITA	1981-1983
Angel Mona	FR	1995-1997	Eddie Thomas	W	1951	Herol Graham*	E	1983-1984
Manuel Carlos Fernandes	FR	1997	Charles Humez*	FR	1951-1952	Jimmy Cable	E	1984
Oscar Garcia Cano	SP	1997	Gilbert Lavoine	FR	1953-1954	Georg Steinherr	GER	1984-1985
Billy Schwer*	E	1997-1999	Wally Thom	E	1954-1955	Said Skouma*	FR	1985-1986
Oscar Garcia Cano	SP	1999-2000	Idrissa Dione	FR	1955-1956	Chris Pyatt	E	1986-1987
Lucien Lorcy*	FR	2000-2001	Emilio Marconi	ITA	1956-1958	Gianfranco Rosi*	ITA	1987
Stefano Zoff*	ITA	2001-2002	Peter Waterman*	E	1958	Rene Jacquot*	FR	1988-1989
Jason Cook	W	2002-2003	Emilio Marconi	ITA	1958-1959	Edip Secovic	AU	1989
Stefano Zoff*	ITA	2003-2005	Duilio Loi*	ITA	1959-1963	Giuseppe Leto	ITA	1989
Juan Carlos Diaz Melero	SP	2005-2006	Fortunato Manca*	ITA	1964-1965	Gilbert Dele*	FR	1989-1990
Yuri Romanov	BE	2006-	Jean Josselin	FR	1966-1967	Said Skouma	FR	1991
			Carmelo Bossi	ITA	1967-1968	Mourad Louati	HOL	1991
L. Welterweight (140 lbs)			Fighting Mack	HOL	1968-1969	Jean-Claude Fontana	FR	1991-1992
Olli Maki	FIN	1964-1965	Silvano Bertini	ITA	1969	Laurent Boudouani	FR	1992-1993
Juan Sombrita-Albornoz	SP	1965	Jean Josselin	FR	1969	Bernard Razzano	FR	1993-1994
Willi Quatuor*	GER	1965-1966	Johann Orsolics	AU	1969-1970	Javier Castillejos	SP	1994-1995
Conny Rudhof	GER	1967	Ralph Charles	E	1970-1971	Laurent Boudouani*	FR	1995-1996
Johann Orsolics	AU	1967-1968	Roger Menetrey	FR	1971-1974	Faouzi Hattab	FR	1996
Bruno Arcari*	ITA	1968-1970	John H. Stracey*	E	1974-1975	Davide Ciarlante*	ITA	1996-1997
Rene Roque	FR	1970-1971	Marco Scano	ITA	1976-1977	Javier Castillejo*	SP	1998
Pedro Carrasco*	SP	1971-1972	Jorgen Hansen	DEN	1977	Mamadou Thiam*	FR	1998-2000
Roger Zami	FR	1972	Jorg Eipel	GER	1977	Roman Karmazin*	RUS	2000
Cemal Kamaci	TU	1972-1973	Alain Marion	FR	1977-1978	Mamadou Thiam*	FR	2001
Toni Ortiz	SP	1973-1974	Jorgen Hansen	DEN	1978	Wayne Alexander*	E	2002
Perico Fernandez*	SP	1974	Josef Pachler	AU	1978	Roman Karmazin*	RUS	2003-2004
Jose Ramon Gomez-Fouz	SP	1975	Henry Rhiney	E	1978-1979	Sergei Dzindziruk*	UK	2004-2005
Cemal Kamaci*	TU	1975-1976	Dave Boy Green	E	1979	Michele Piccirillo*	ITA	2006-2007
Dave Boy Green*	E	1976-1977	Jorgen Hansen*	DEN	1979-1981			
Primo Bandini	ITA	1977	Hans-Henrik Palm	DEN	1982	**Middleweight (160 lbs)**		
Jean-Baptiste Piedvache	FR	1977-1978	Colin Jones*	W	1982-1983	Georges Carpentier*	FR	1912-1918
Colin Power	E	1978	Gilles Elbilia	FR	1983-1984	Ercole Balzac	FR	1920-1921
Fernando Sanchez	SP	1978-1979	Gianfranco Rosi	ITA	1984-1985	Gus Platts	E	1921
Jose Luis Heredia	SP	1979	Lloyd Honeyghan*	E	1985-1986	Willem Westbroek	HOL	1921
Jo Kimpuani	FR	1979-1980	Jose Varela	GER	1986-1987	Johnny Basham	W	1921
Giuseppe Martinese	ITA	1980	Alfonso Redondo	SP	1987	Ted Kid Lewis	E	1921-1923
Antonio Guinaldo	SP	1980-1981	Mauro Martelli*	SWI	1987-1988	Roland Todd	E	1923-1924
Clinton McKenzie	E	1981-1982	Nino la Rocca	ITA	1989	Ted Kid Lewis	E	1924-1925
Robert Gambini	FR	1982-1983	Antoine Fernandez	FR	1989-1990	Bruno Frattini	ITA	1924-1925
Patrizio Oliva*	ITA	1983-1985	Kirkland Laing	E	1990	Tommy Milligan	S	1925-1928
Terry Marsh	E	1985-1986	Patrizio Oliva*	ITA	1990-1992	Rene Devos	BEL	1926-1927
Tusikoleta Nkalankete	FR	1987-1989	Ludovic Proto	FR	1992-1993	Barthelemy Molina	FR	1928
Efren Calamati	ITA	1989-1990	Gary Jacobs*	S	1993-1994	Alex Ireland	S	1928-1929
Pat Barrett	E	1990-1992	Jose Luis Navarro	SP	1994-1995	Mario Bosisio	ITA	1928
Valery Kayumba	ITA	1992-1993	Valery Kayumba	FR	1995	Leone Jacovacci	ITA	1928-1929
Christian Merle	FR	1993-1994	Patrick Charpentier*	FR	1995-1996	Len Johnson	E	1928-1929
Valery Kayumba	FR	1994	Andrei Pestriaev*	RUS	1997	Marcel Thil	FR	1929-1930
Khalid Rahilou*	FR	1994-1996	Michele Piccirillo*	ITA	1997-1998	Mario Bosisio	ITA	1930-1931
Soren Sondergaard*	DEN	1996-1998	Maxim Nesterenko	RUS	1998-1999	Poldi Steinbach	AU	1931
Thomas Damgaard*	DEN	1998-2000	Alessandro Duran	ITA	1999	Hein Domgoergen	GER	1931-1932
Oktay Urkal*	GER	2000-2001	Andrei Pestriaev	RUS	1999-2000	Ignacio Ara	SP	1932-1933
Gianluca Branco*	ITA	2001-2002	Alessandro Duran	ITA	2000	Gustave Roth*	BEL	1933-1934
Oktay Urkal*	GER	2002-2003	Thomas Damgaard	DEN	2000-2001	Marcel Thil*	FR	1934-1938
Junior Witter*	E	2004-2006	Alessandro Duran	ITA	2001-2002	Edouard Tenet	FR	1938
Ted Bami	E	2006-	Christian Bladt*	DEN	2002	Bep van Klaveren	HOL	1938
			Michel Trabant*	GER	2002-2003	Anton Christoforidis	GRE	1938-1939
Welterweight (147 lbs)			Frederic Klose*	FR	2003-2005	Edouard Tenet	FR	1939
Young Joseph	E	1910-1911	Oktay Urkal*	GER	2005	Josef Besselmann*	GER	1942-1943
Georges Carpentier*	FR	1911-1912	Frederic Klose*	FR	2006	Marcel Cerdan	FR	1947-1948
Albert Badoud*	SWI	1915-1921	Jackson Osei Bonsu	BEL	2007-	Cyrille Delannoit	BEL	1948
Johnny Basham	W	1919-1920				Marcel Cerdan*	FR	1948
Ted Kid Lewis	E	1920-1924	**L. Middleweight (154 lbs)**			Cyrille Delannoit	BEL	1948-1949
Piet Hobin	BEL	1921-1925	Bruno Visintin	ITA	1964-1966	Tiberio Mitri*	ITA	1949-1950
Billy Mack	E	1923	Bo Hogberg	SWE	1966	Randy Turpin	E	1951-1954
Tommy Milligan	S	1924-1925	Yolande Leveque	FR	1966	Tiberio Mitri	ITA	1954
Mario Bosisio*	ITA	1925-1928	Sandro Mazzinghi*	ITA	1966-1968	Charles Humez	FR	1954-1958

Title Holder	Birthplace/Domicile	Tenure
Gustav Scholz*	GER	1958-1961
John Cowboy McCormack	S	1961-1962
Chris Christensen	DEN	1962
Laszlo Papp*	HUN	1962-1965
Nino Benvenuti*	ITA	1965-1967
Juan Carlos Duran	ITA	1967-1969
Tom Bogs	DEN	1969-1970
Juan Carlos Duran	ITA	1970-1971
Jean-Claude Bouttier	FR	1971-1972
Tom Bogs*	DEN	1973
Elio Calcabrini	ITA	1973-1974
Jean-Claude Bouttier	FR	1974
Kevin Finnegan	E	1974-1975
Gratien Tonna*	FR	1975
Bunny Sterling	E	1976
Angelo Jacopucci	ITA	1976
Germano Valsecchi	ITA	1976-1977
Alan Minter	E	1977
Gratien Tonna	FR	1977-1978
Alan Minter*	E	1978-1979
Kevin Finnegan	E	1980
Matteo Salvemini	ITA	1980
Tony Sibson*	E	1980-1982
Louis Acaries	FR	1982-1984
Tony Sibson	E	1984-1985
Ayub Kalule	DEN	1985-1986
Herol Graham	E	1986-1987
Sumbu Kalambay*	ITA	1987
Pierre Joly	FR	1987-1988
Christophe Tiozzo*	FR	1988-1989
Francesco dell' Aquila	ITA	1989-1990
Sumbu Kalambay*	ITA	1990-1993
Agostino Cardamone*	ITA	1993-1994
Richie Woodhall*	E	1995-1996
Alexandre Zaitsev	RUS	1996
Hassine Cherifi*	FR	1996-1998
Agostino Cardamone*	ITA	1998
Erland Betare*	FR	1999-2000
Howard Eastman*	E	2001
Cristian Sanavia	ITA	2001-2002
Morrade Hakkar*	FR	2002
Howard Eastman*	E	2003-2004
Morrade Hakkar	FR	2005
Sebastian Sylvester	GER	2005-2006
Amin Asikainen	FIN	2006-2007
Sebastian Sylvester	GER	2007-

S. Middleweight (168 lbs)

Title Holder	Birthplace/Domicile	Tenure
Mauro Galvano*	ITA	1990-1991
James Cook	E	1991-1992
Franck Nicotra*	FR	1992
Vincenzo Nardiello	ITA	1992-1993
Ray Close*	NI	1993
Vinzenzo Nardiello	ITA	1993-1994
Frederic Seillier*	FR	1994-1995
Henry Wharton*	E	1995-1996
Frederic Seillier*	FR	1996
Andrei Shkalikov*	RUS	1997
Dean Francis*	E	1997-1998
Bruno Girard*	FR	1999
Andrei Shkalikov	RUS	2000-2001
Danilo Haeussler	GER	2001-2003
Mads Larsen*	DEN	2003-2004
Rudy Markussen*	DEN	2004-2005
Vitali Tsypko	UK	2005
Jackson Chanet	FR	2005-2006
Mger Mkrtchian	ARM	2006
David Gogoya	GEO	2006-2007
Cristian Sanavia	ITA	2007-

L. Heavyweight (175 lbs)

Title Holder	Birthplace/Domicile	Tenure
Georges Carpentier	FR	1913-1922
Battling Siki	FR	1922-1923
Emile Morelle	FR	1923
Raymond Bonnel	FR	1923-1924
Louis Clement	SWI	1924-1926
Herman van T'Hof	HOL	1926
Fernand Delarge	BEL	1926-1927
Max Schmeling*	GER	1927-1928
Michele Bonaglia*	ITA	1929-1930
Ernst Pistulla*	GER	1931-1932
Adolf Heuser	GER	1932
John Andersson	SWE	1933
Martinez de Alfara	SP	1934
Marcel Thil	FR	1934-1935
Merlo Preciso	ITA	1935
Hein Lazek	AU	1935-1936
Gustave Roth	BEL	1936-1938
Adolf Heuser*	GER	1938-1939
Luigi Musina*	ITA	1942-1943
Freddie Mills*	E	1947-1950
Albert Yvel	FR	1950-1951
Don Cockell*	E	1951-1952
Conny Rux*	GER	1952
Jacques Hairabedian	FR	1953-1954
Gerhard Hecht	GER	1954-1955
Willi Hoepner	GER	1955
Gerhard Hecht	GER	1955-1957
Artemio Calzavara	ITA	1957-1958
Willi Hoepner	GER	1958
Erich Schoeppner	GER	1958-1962
Giulio Rinaldi	ITA	1962-1964
Gustav Scholz*	GER	1964-1965
Giulio Rinaldi	ITA	1965-1966
Piero del Papa	ITA	1966-1967
Lothar Stengel	GER	1967-1968
Tom Bogs*	DEN	1968-1969
Yvan Prebeg	YUG	1969-1970
Piero del Papa	ITA	1970-1971
Conny Velensek	GER	1971-1972
Chris Finnegan	E	1972
Rudiger Schmidtke	GER	1972-1973
John Conteh*	E	1973-1974
Domenico Adinolfi	ITA	1974-1976
Mate Parlov*	YUG	1976-1977
Aldo Traversaro	ITA	1977-1979
Rudi Koopmans	HOL	1979-1984
Richard Caramonolis	FR	1984
Alex Blanchard	HOL	1984-1987
Tom Collins	E	1987-1988
Pedro van Raamsdonk	HOL	1988
Jan Lefeber	HOL	1988-1989
Eric Nicoletta	FR	1989-1990
Tom Collins	E	1990-1991
Graciano Rocchigiani*	GER	1991-1992
Eddie Smulders	HOL	1993-1994
Fabrice Tiozzo*	FR	1994-1995
Eddy Smulders	HOL	1995-1996
Crawford Ashley	E	1997
Ole Klemetsen*	NOR	1997-1998
Crawford Ashley	E	1998-1999
Clinton Woods*	E	1999-2000
Yawe Davis	ITA	2001-2002
Thomas Ulrich*	GER	2002-2003
Stipe Drews*	CRO	2003-2004
Thomas Ulrich*	GER	2004-2005
Stipe Drews*	CRO	2006
Thomas Ulrich	GER	2007-

Cruiserweight (200 lbs)

Title Holder	Birthplace/Domicile	Tenure
Sam Reeson*	E	1987-1988
Angelo Rottoli	ITA	1989
Anaclet Wamba*	FR	1989-1990
Johnny Nelson*	E	1990-1992
Akim Tafer*	FR	1992-1993
Massimiliano Duran	ITA	1993-1994
Carl Thompson	E	1994
Alexander Gurov	UK	1995
Patrice Aouissi	FR	1995
Alexander Gurov*	UK	1995-1996
Akim Tafer*	FR	1996-1997
Johnny Nelson	E	1997-1998
Terry Dunstan*	E	1998
Alexei Iliin	RUS	1999
Torsten May*	GER	1999-2000
Carl Thompson*	E	2000-2001
Alexander Gurov*	UK	2001-2002
Pietro Aurino*	ITA	2002-2003
Vincenzo Cantatore	ITA	2004
Alexander Gurov	UK	2004-2005
David Haye*	E	2005-2007
Vincenzo Cantatore	ITA	2007-

Heavyweight (200 lbs +)

Title Holder	Birthplace/Domicile	Tenure
Georges Carpentier	FR	1913-1922
Battling Siki	FR	1922-1923
Erminio Spalla	ITA	1923-1926
Paolino Uzcudun	SP	1926-1928
Harry Persson	SWE	1926
Phil Scott	E	1927
Pierre Charles	BEL	1929-1931
Hein Muller	GER	1931-1932
Pierre Charles	BEL	1932-1933
Paolino Uzcudun	SP	1933
Primo Carnera	ITA	1933-1935
Pierre Charles	BEL	1935-1937
Arno Kolblin	GER	1937-1938
Hein Lazek	AU	1938-1939
Adolf Heuser	GER	1939
Max Schmeling*	GER	1939-1941
Olle Tandberg	SWE	1943
Karel Sys*	BEL	1943-1946
Bruce Woodcock	E	1946-1949
Joe Weidin	AU	1950-1951
Jack Gardner	E	1951
Hein Ten Hoff	GER	1951-1952
Karel Sys	BEL	1952
Heinz Neuhaus	GER	1952-1955
Franco Cavicchi	ITA	1955-1956
Ingemar Johansson*	SWE	1956-1959
Dick Richardson	W	1960-1962
Ingemar Johansson*	SWE	1962-1963
Henry Cooper*	E	1964
Karl Mildenberger	GER	1964-1968
Henry Cooper*	E	1968-1969
Peter Weiland	GER	1969-1970
Jose Urtain	SP	1970
Henry Cooper	E	1970-1971
Joe Bugner	E	1971
Jack Bodell	E	1971
Jose Urtain	SP	1971-1972
Jurgen Blin	GER	1972
Joe Bugner*	E	1972-1975
Richard Dunn	E	1976
Joe Bugner	E	1976-1977
Jean-Pierre Coopman	BEL	1977
Lucien Rodriguez	FR	1977
Alfredo Evangelista	SP	1977-1979
Lorenzo Zanon*	SP	1979-1980
John L. Gardner*	E	1980-1981
Lucien Rodriguez	FR	1981-1984
Steffen Tangstad	NOR	1984-1985
Anders Eklund	SWE	1985
Frank Bruno*	E	1985-1986
Steffen Tangstad	NOR	1986
Alfredo Evangelista	SP	1987
Anders Eklund	SWE	1987
Francesco Damiani*	ITA	1987-1989
Derek Williams	E	1989-1990
Jean Chanet	FR	1990
Lennox Lewis*	E	1990-1992
Henry Akinwande*	E	1993-1995
Zeljko Mavrovic*	CRO	1995-1998
Vitali Klitschko*	UK	1998-1999
Vladimir Klitschko*	UK	1999-2000
Vitali Klitschko*	UK	2000-2001
Luan Krasniqi	GER	2002
Przemyslaw Saleta	POL	2002
Sinan Samil Sam	TU	2002-2004
Luan Krasniqi	GER	2004-2005
Paolo Vidoz	ITA	2005-2006
Vladimir Virchis	UK	2006-

A-Z of Current World Champions

by Eric Armit

Shows the record since 1 July 2007, plus career summary and pen portrait, of all men holding IBF, WBA, WBC and WBO titles as at 30 June 2008. The author has also produced the same data for those who first won titles during that period but were no longer champions on 30 June 2008. World champions belonging to other bodies are shown if they are considered to be the best man at the weight. Incidentally, the place name given is the respective boxer's domicile and may not necessarily be his birthplace, while all nicknames are shown where applicable in brackets. Not included are British fighters, Alex Arthur (WBO super-featherweight), Joe Calzaghe (WBO/WBA super-middleweight champion), Ricky Hatton (IBO light-welterweight champion) and David Haye (WBO cruiserweight champion). Their full records can be found among the Active British-Based Boxers: Career Records section.

Arthur (King Arthur) Abraham

Berlin, Germany. *Born* Yerevan, Armenia, 20 February, 1980
IBF Middleweight Champion
Major Amateur Honours: Competed in the 200 European Olympic qualifiers
Turned Pro: August 2003
Significant Results: Cristian Zanabria W CO 5, Nader Hamdan W RSC 12, Ian Gardner W PTS 12, Hector Velazco W CO 5, Howard Eastman W PTS 12, Kingsley Ikeke W CO 5, Shannon Taylor W PTS 12, Kofi Jantuah W PTS 12, Edison Miranda W PTS 12, Sebastien Demers W CO 3
Type/Style: Recognised as a tough, strong and aggressive fighter
Points of Interest: 5'10 " tall. Arthur's real name is Avetik Abrahamyan and although *Born* in Armenia he received German citizenship in 2006 and is with the Sauerland Group, as is his brother Alex who boxes as a pro at light-middleweight. Has 20 wins by stoppage or kayo after winning his first 14 bouts inside the distance. Won the vacant IBF title by beating Kingsley Ikeke in December 2005 and has made seven defences. He is played into the ring by the Smurf Song from the TV programme which featured a Father Abraham. Having had to survive a fractured draw when beating Edison Miranda in 2006, their return fight was a catchweight contest so the IBF title was not on the line.

18.08.07	Khoren Gevar W CO 11 Berlin *(IBF Middleweight Title Defence)*
08.12.07	Wayne Elcock W RSC 5 Basle *(IBF Middleweight Title Defenc*
29.03.08	Elvin Ayala W CO 12 Kiel *(IBF Middleweight Title Defence)*
21.06.08	Edison Miranda W RSC 4 Hollywood

Career: 27 contests, won 27.

Joseph (King Kong) Agbeko

Accra, Ghana. *Born* 22 March, 1980
IBF Bantamweight Champion,
Former Undefeated Commonwealth & African Boxing Union Bantamweight Champion
Major Amateur Honours: Champion of Ghana in 1998 and competed in the Commonwealth Games the same year
Turned Pro: December 1988
Significant Results: Johannes Maisa W PTS 12, Michael Kizza W RSC 2, Wladimir Sidorenko L PTS 12, Sumaila Badu W PTS 12
Type/Style: Is an upright orthodox fighter with a strong jab and a hard punch
Points of Interest: 5'6" tall. Was inactive from October 2004, when he won the vacant Commonwealth bantamweight title, until March 2007 due to contractual problems, something that has marked his career. Showed his potential in taking Wladimir Sidorenko to a majority verdict when losing to the future WBA super-bantamweight champion in Germany in 2004. Is now based in New York and has 22 wins inside the distance

09.08.07	Fidencio Reyes W RSC 4 Las Vegas
29.09.07	Luis Perez W RSC Sacramento *(IBF Bantamweight Title Challenge)*

Career: 26 contests, won 25, lost 1.

Joachim (Ti-Joa) Alcine

Gonaive, Haiti. *Born* 26 March, 1976
WBA L.Middleweight Champion.
Major Amateur Honours: Competed in the 1997 Francophile Games for Canada and claims 40 wins in 46 fights.
Turned Pro: May 1999
Significant Results: Marcos Primera W PTS 12, Stephane Ouellet W CO 1, Carlos Bojorquez W RSC 7, Carl Daniels W RTD 5, Elio Ortiz W CO 10, Anderson Clayton W PTS 12, Javier Mamani W PTS 12
Type/Style: An aggressive, two-fisted fighter, he is a good body puncher with an effective jab
Points of Interest: 5'11" tall. Having moved to Quebec with his parents when just a child, he is trained by the former Commonwealth lightweight title challenger, Howard Grant. Has 19 wins inside the distance

07.07.07	Travis Simms W PTS 12 Bridgeport *(WBA 'Interim' L.Heavyweight Title)*
28.04.07	Stipe Drews L PTS 12 Oberhausen *(WBA L.Heavyweight Title Defence)*

Career: 66 contests, won 55, drew 2, lost 9.

Firat (The Lion) Arslan

Friedburg, Germany. *Born* 28 September, 1970
WBA Cruiserweight Champion

Major Amateur Honours: No major honours, but fought with considerable success in the German League
Turned Pro: January 1997
Significant Results: Chris Woolas W RSC 2, Tony Booth W RSC 2, Collice Mutizawa L PTS 6, Rudiger May L PTS 10, Mark Hobson W RSC 7, Vadim Tokarev DREW 12, Lubos Suda L PTS 12, Lee Manuel Osie W PTS 10, Alex Petkovic W RSC 7, Carlos Cruzat W PTS 12, Grigory Drozd W RSC 5, Valery Brudov W PTS 12
Type/Style: Firat is a tough, strong and aggressive southpaw with a solid left-hand punch
Points of Interest: 5'11½" tall. He is of Turkish descent and his elder brother boxed as an amateur. Firat, who is fluent in four languages, served an apprenticeship as a mechanic before taking up boxing full time. In his early days he was signed with Panix Promotions and was a stable mate to Lennox Lewis. He won the WBA 'interim' title by beating Valery Brudov in June 2007, retaining it when beating Virgil Hill, before finally gaining

sole recognition when David Haye relinquished the 'super champion' title. Is unbeaten since 2003 and has 18 wins by stoppage or kayo.

24.11.07 Virgil Hill W PTS 12 Dresden
(WBA 'Interim' Cruiserweight Title Defence)
03.05.08 Darnell Wilson W PTS 12 Stuttgart
(WBA 'Interim' Cruiserweight Title Defence)

Career: 33 contests, won 29, drew 1, lost 3.

Brahim Asloum

Bourgoin Jallieu, France *Born* 31 January, 1979
WBA L.Flyweight Champion. Former Undefeated European & French Flyweight Champion
Major Amateur Honours: Competed in the 1997 European Junior Championships in Birmingham and reached the quarter-finals of the 1999 World Championships, losing to Brian Viloria. Won a silver medal in the 1999 French Championships and a gold medal in the French Championships and Acropolis Cup in 2000. Won the gold medal in the 2000 Olympics at 106lbs
Turned Pro: January 2001
Significant Results: Zolile Mbityi W PTS 8, Jose Lopez Bueno W PTS 12 (twice), Ivan Pozo W PTS 12, Alex Mahmutov W PTS 12, Nohel Arambulet W PTS 12, Edgar Velasquez W TD 8, Lorenzo Parra L PTS 12, Jose Jimenez W PTS 12, Omar Narvaez L PTS 12
Type/Style: Is a hard-working, switch-hitting combination puncher
Points of Interest: 5'5" tall. His Olympic gold was the first won by a Frenchman since 1936. Lost to Lorenzo Parra in a challenge for the WBA flyweight title in December 2005 and to Omar Narvaez for the WBO flyweight crown in March 2007 before moving down to light-flyweight. His brother Redouane competed in the 2004 Olympics. He has nine wins by stoppage or kayo

15.09.07 Wellington Vicente W CO 9 Rostock
08.12.07 Juan Carlos Reveco W CO 9 Rostock
(WBA Sl. Flyweight Title Challenge)

Career: 25 contests, won 23, lost 2.

Cassius (Mr Shy Guy) Baloyi

Giyana, South Africa. *Born* 5 November, 1974
IBF S.Featherweight Champion
Major Amateur Honours: Was the South African national champion in 1993 and competed in the World Championships during the same year
Turned Pro: January 1994
Significant Results: Frank Toledo W PTS 12, Anton Gilmore W PTS 12, Sergio Liendo W PTS 12, Brian Carr W RSC 10, Hector Lizarraga W CO 1, Steve Robinson W PTS 12, Phillip Ndou L PTS 12, Tiger Ari W RSC 6, Mbulelo Botile W RSC 11, Lehlohonolo Ledwaba W PTS 12 (twice), Isaac Hlatshwayo L PTS 12, Manuel Medina W RSC 11 & T DRAW 4, Gairy St Clair L PTS 12
Type/ Style: Is a tall stylish fighter
Points of Interest: 5'10" tall with a 75" reach. He was actually christened Cassuis by mistake as his father intended to name him Cassius after Cassius Clay but he uses the right spelling. Managed by the former WBA champion Brian Mitchell, he won the IBF title in May 2006 when halting Manuel Medina, but lost it in his first defence in July 2006 to Gairy St Clair. Has 18 wins inside the distance

12.11.07 Gairy St Clair W PTS 12 Gauten
28.04.07 Mzonke Fana W PTS 12 Mafikeng
(IBF S.Featherweight Title Challenge)

Career: 39 contests won 35, drew 1, lost 3.

Andre Berto

Miami, USA. *Born* 7 September, 1983
WBC Welterweight Champion
Major Amateur Honours: In 2000 he won a gold medal in the PAL and a silver medal in the US Junior National Championships; in 2001 he won a gold medal in the National Golden Gloves, a gold medal in the PAL Championships; in 2002 he won a silver medal in the US Championships, a bronze medal in the US under-19 Championships and represented the USA in the World Cup. Won a gold medal in the 2003 National Golden Gloves, a silver medal in the US Championships and a bronze medal in the World Championships, where he beat Darren Barker. Was disqualified in the 2004 US Olympic trials, but as he had dual US and Haitian citizenship he re-entered the Olympic qualifiers representing Haiti, winning a berth for Athens by finishing as runner-up in the Americas qualifiers in Tijuana. In the Games he was eliminated by France's Xavier Noel

Turned Pro: December 2004
Significant Results: Sam Sparkman W RSC 2, James Crayton W CO 5, Miguel Figueroa W RSC 6, Norberto Bravo W RSC 1
Type/Style: Has an excellent jab and is a strong body puncher with fast hands
Points of Interest: 5'9" tall. Although Andre was born in Miami, his parents were both from Haiti. His father fought in Ultimate Fighting contests, a brother is a State champion wrestler and one of his sisters also boxes. His loss in the Olympic trials was a disqualification for wrestling his opponent to the canvas. This decision was overturned by a committee, but re-instated by another committee. Although he represented Haiti in the Olympics, he had never set foot in the country before then. Has 19 wins by stoppage or kayo

27.07.07 Cosme Rivera W PTS 10 Saratoga Springs
29.09.07 David Estrada W RSC 11 Atlantic City
12.05.07 Michael Trabant W RTD 6 Temecula
21.06.08 Miguel Angel Rodriguez W RSC 7 Memphis
(Vacant WBC Welterweight Title)

Career: 22 contests, won 22.

Tim (Desert Storm) Bradley

Palm Springs, USA. *Born* 29 August, 1983
WBC Welterweight Champion
Major Amateur Honours: In 2000 he won a silver medal in the PAL Championships; in 2001 he took gold in the PAL Championships and was the US under-19 champion; in 2002 he took bronze in the PAL Championships and a silver medal in the National Golden Gloves
Turned Pro: August 2004
Significant Results: Francisco Rincon W PTS 10, Rafael Ortiz W RTD 2, Arturo Urena W RSC 3, Alfonso Sanchez W CO 1, Manuel Garnica W PTS 8, Donald Camarena W PTS 10
Type/Style: A compact fighter with a busy, aggressive style and a good right-hand punch
Points of Interest: The 'Desert Storm' nickname relates to his Palm Springs residency and not the military campaign of that name. He is jointly trained by his father, Tim Senior, and Joel Diaz, a former IBF lightweight title challenger. The Junior Witter fight was his first fight outside California. Has 11 wins by

stoppage or kayo

27.07.07 Miguel Vazquez W PTS 10 Corona
10.05.08 Junior Witter W PTS 12 Nottingham
(*WBC L.Weltrweight Title Challenge)*)
Career: 22 contests, won 22.

Lucien (Le Tombeur) Bute

Galati, Romania *Born* 28 February, 1980
IBF S.Middleweight Champion.

Major Amateur Honours: Took a silver medal in the first European Cadets Championships in 1996; won bronze medals at both the 1998 World Junior and 1999 World Senior Championships; won gold medals in the 2001 Francophone Games and the Ahmet Comert tournament, but was eliminated in the quarter-finals of the 2002 European Championships by Karoly Balzsay. Also competed in the 2003 World Championships
Turned Pro: November 2003
Significant Results: Dingaan Thobela W RSC 4, Jose Spearman W CO 8, Kabary Salem W RSC 8, Andre Thysse W PTS 12, Lolenga Mock W PTS 12, James Obede Toney W RSC 8, Sergey Tatesvoyan W PTS 12, Sakio Bika W PTS 12
Type/Style: Is a stylish southpaw and a sound technician with good hand and foot speed. Also has plenty of stamina
Points of Interest: 6'2" tall, he is based in Montreal and has only fought back home in Romania once. Has also campaigned as a light-heavyweight, but has no problems with the super-middleweight limit. Has won 18 bouts by stoppage or kayo

19.10.07 Alejandro Berrio W RSC 11 Montreal
(*IBF S.Middleweight Title Challenge*)
02.12.06 William Joppy W RSC 10 Montreal
(*IBF S.Middleweight Title Defence*)
Career: 22 contests, won 22.

Celestino (Pelenchin) Caballero

Colon, Panama *Born* 21 June, 1976
WBA S.Bantamweight Champion
Major Amateur Honours: None known
Turned Pro: November 1988
Significant Results: Jose Rojas L CO 3, Giovanni Andrade W DIS 10, Ricardo Cordoba L PTS 12, Daniel Ponce de Leon W PTS 12, Yober Ortega W PTS 12, Roberto Bonilla W RSC 7, Somsak Sithchatchawal W RSC 3, Ricardo Castillo W DIS 9
Type/Style: Is a tall, rangy southpaw

Points of Interest: 5'11" tall. Also known as 'The Towering Inferno, Celestino wanted to be a footballer but took up boxing instead for financial reasons and started boxing at the age of 14. First won the 'interim' WBA title by beating Yober Ortega in October 2005 and became full champion with his crushing victory over Somsak Sithchatchawal in Thailand in October 2006. Promoted by Sycuan Ringside promotions, who are a native American promotions group, he has 20 wins by stoppage or kayo. His title winning fight with Sithchatchawal was staged at an ancient Temple and he has since defended his title four times. He is trained by Francisco Arroyo who had fights in England in 1988, 1990 and 1991

04.08.07 Jorge Lacierva W PTS 12 Hidalgo
(*WBA S.Bantamweight Title Defence*)
01.12.07 Mauricio Pastrana W RSC 8 Panama City
(*WBA S.Bantamweight Title Defence*)
07.06.08 Lorenzo Parra W RTD 12 San Juan de los Morros
(*WBA S.Bantamweight Title Defence*)
Career:31 contests, won 29, lost 2.

Ivan (Iron Boy) Calderon

Guaynabo, Puerto Rico. *Born* 7 January, 1975
WBO L.Flyweight Champion. Former Undefeated WBO M.Flyweight Champion
Major Amateur Honours: A bronze medallist in the 1999 Pan-American Games and the winner of a silver medal in the Central American Games that year, he also competed in the 1999 World Championships and the 2000 Olympic Games. Claims 110 wins in 130 bouts
Turned Pro: February 2001
Significant Results: Jorge Romero W RTD 4, Alejandro Moreno W PTS 10, Eduardo Marquez W TD 9, Lorenzo Trejo W PTS 12, Alex Sanchez W PTS 12, Edgar Cardenas W CO 11, Roberto Leyva W PTS 12, Carlos Fajardo W PTS 12, Noel Tunacao W RSC 8, Gerard Verde W PTS 12, Daniel Reyes W PTS 12, Isaac Bustos W PTS 12, Miguel Tellez W RSC 9, Jose Luis Valera W PTS 12, Ronald Barrera W PTS 12
Type/Style: Southpaw. Although an excellent boxer, technically sound, and good counter-puncher, he lacks power
Points of Interest: 5'0" tall. Won

the WBO mini-flyweight title with a technical verdict over Eduardo Marquez in May 2003 and made 11 defences before moving up to win the light-flyweight title. An extrovert who is tremendously popular in Puerto Rico, being voted 'Boxer of the Year' there in 2002, he has only six wins by stoppage or kayo. Revenged an amateur defeat when beating Jose Luis Varela

25.08.07 Hugo Cazares W PTS 12 Bayamon
(*WBO L. Flyweight Title Challenge*)
18.11.06 Juan Esquer W PTS 12 Albuquerque
(*WBO L. Flyweight Title Challenge*)
14.04.07 Nelson Dieppa W PTS 12 San Juan
(*WBO L. Flyweight Title Challenge*)
Career: 31 contests, won 31.

Nate (The Galaxxy Warrior) Campbell

Jacksonvile, Florida. *Born* 7 March, 1972
IBF, WBC & WBO Lightweight Champion
Major Amateur Honours: Competed in the 1998 and 1999 US Championships and the 1998 PAL Championships. Claims 30 wins in 36 amateur fights
Turned Pro: February 2000
Significant Results: Carlos Navarro W CO 5, Danny Alicea W CO 3, Joel Casamayor L PTS 10, Daniel Attah W PTS 12, Robbie Peden L RSC 5 & L RSC 8, Francisco Lorenzo L PTS 10, Almazbek Raiymulkov W RSC 10, Isaac Hlatshwayo L PTS 12, Matt Zegan W PTS 12, Ricky Quiles W PTS 12,
Type/Style: Although a fast, sharp, crafty veteran and a hard-hitting box-puncher he can also be an inconsistent performer
Points of Interest: 5'7" tall. Had a terrible start in life, his father dying when Nate was ten-years-old, at a time when his mother was in jail. This resulted in him spending much of his early life in foster homes. He now has three teenage daughters of his own. Nate began boxing at the age of five but did not turn pro until he was 27, starting out as a lightweight before moving down to super-featherweight. After winning his first 23 contests, he was kayoed by Robbie Peden in February 2005 for the vacant IBF super-featherweight title before moving back up to lightweight. Now trained by Buddy McGirt, he has 25 wins by stoppage or kayo

06.07.07 Wilson Alcorro W RSC 6 Tampa

17.12.06 Juan Diaz W PTS 12 Cancun
(IBF, WBA & WBO Lightweight Title Challenges)
Career: 38 contests, won 32, drew 1, lost 5.

Ruslan Chagaev   Les Clark

Ruslan (White Tyson) Chagaev
Andizhan, Uzbekistan. *Born* 19 October, 1978
WBA Heavyweight Champion
Major Amateur Honours:: Won gold medals in the 1995 and 1999 Asian Championships and 1998 Asian Games. Competed in the 1996 and 2000 Olympic Games and won a bronze medal in the 1997 World Junior Championships. Also won gold medals in both the 1997 and 2001 World Championships, having competed unsuccessfully in the 1999 Championships. Claims 82 wins in 86 amateur fights
Turned Pro: October 1997
Significant Results: Rob Calloway T DRAW 3 & W CO 2, Sherman Williams W PTS 8, Marc Krenec W CO 5, Vladimir Virchis W PTS 12
Type/Style: Ruslan is a stocky, strong southpaw counter puncher with fast hands and a good chin
Points of Interest: 6'1" tall. Having started boxing at 13, he was stripped of his first World Amateur title in 1997 when it was discovered that he had taken part in two fights as a professional in the United States. These were later changed to exhibition bouts so that he could continue as an amateur, but they were genuine paid bouts so are included on his record. Although possessing a

74" reach, he gave away 11" in height and 90lbs in weight to Nikolay Valuev when winning the WBA title in April 2007. Has 17 wins by stoppage or kayo but is injury prone

19.01.08 Matt Skelton W PTS 12 Dusseldorf
(WBA Heavyweight Title Defence)
Career: 25 contests, won 24, drew 1.

Florante (Little Pacquiao) Condes
Sampaguita, Philippines. *Born* 20 May, 1980
Former IBF M.Flyweight Champion. Former Undefeated Philippines M.Flyweight Champion
Major Amateur Honours: None known
Turned Pro: June 2002
Significant Results: Philip Parcon W CO 6, Elmer Gejon W CO 5, Arman de la Cruz W RSC 5, Fabio Marfa W RSC 6
Type/Style: An aggressive, hard-punching southpaw
Points of Interest: 5'2" tall. Contract disputes kept him out of the ring after his title win over Muhammad Rachman until his split decision loss to Raul Garcia. Reputedly received only $3,000 for beating Rachman. Has 20 wins by stoppage or kayo

07.07.07 Muhammed Rachman W PTS 12 Jakarta
(IBF M.Flyweight Title Challenge)
03.03.07 Raul Garca L PTS 12 La Paz
(IBF M.Flyweight Title Defence)
Career: 27 contests, won 22, drew 1, lost 4.

Migeul Cotto
Caguas, Puerto Rico. *Born* 29 October, 1980
WBA Welterweight Champion. Former Undefeated WBO L.Welterweight Champion
Major Amateur Honours: He won a gold medal in the 1997 Pan-American Championships, a bronze medal in the 1997 Central American Games and silver medals in the 1997 and 1998 World Junior Championships. He collected silver medals from the Pan-American Cadet Championships and the Central American Games in 1998. Competed without success, in both the World Championships and the Pan-American Games in 1999. Won a gold medal in the 2000 Central American Games, having earlier competed in the 2000 Olympics where he lost to Mohamad Abdulaev
Turned Pro: February 2001

Significant Results: Justin Juuko W RSC 5, John Brown W PTS 10, Cesar Bazan W RSC 11, Joel Perez W CO 4, Demetrio Ceballos W RSC 7, Charles Maussa W RSC 8, Victoriano Sosa W RSC 4, Lovemore Ndou W PTS 12, Kelson Pinto W RSC 6, Randall Bailey W RSC 6, DeMarcus Corley W RSC 5, Mohamad Abdullaev W RSC 9, Ricardo Torres W CO 7, Gianluca Branco W RSC 8, Paulie Malignaggi W PTS 12, Carlos Quintana W RTD 5, Oktay Urkal W RSC 11, Zab Judah W RSC 11
Type/Style: Miguel is a classy, hard-hitting box puncher with an exciting style but has been rocked a few times
Points of Interest: 5'8" tall with a 67" reach. His father, uncle and cousin all boxed and his brother Jose Miguel Cotto lost to Juan Diaz in a fight for the IBF lightweight title in April 2006. Is trained by his uncle Evangelista and has 26 wins inside the distance. Won the WBO light-welterweight title in September 2004 by beating Kelson Pinto, making six title defences before moving up to win the WBA welterweight title. Has now made four defences of that title.

10.11.07 Shane Mosley W PTS 12 New York City
(WBA Welterweight Title Defence)
12.04.08 Alfonso Gomez W RTD 5 Atlantic City
(WBA Welterweight Title Defence)
Career: 27 contests, won 22, drew 1, lost 4.

Steve (USS) Cunningham
Philadelphia, USA. *Born* 15 July, 1976
IBF Cruiserweight Champion
Major Amateur Honours: National Golden Gloves champion in 1998 and also competed in the 2000 US Championships, losing a box-off for third place
Turned Pro: October 2000
Significant Results: Terry McGroom W PTS 8, Sebastiaan Rothmann W PTS 10, Guillermo Jones W PTS 10, Kelvin Davis W PTS 12, Krzysztof Wlodarczyk L PTS 12 & W PTS 12
Type/Style: A classy, slick boxer but not a big puncher
Points of Interest: 6'3" tall with an 82" reach, Steve is trained by Richie Giachetti who also trained Larry Holmes. Steve is a reformed street fighter and former sailor who worked as an aircraft refueller and started his boxing in the Navy in 1996. The loss

to Krzysztof Wlodarczyk in November 2006 for the vacant IBF title was by a split decision, with the American judge having Steve nine points in front. However, he beat Wlodarczyk clearly in the return in May 2007 to win the title. Has 11 wins inside the distance

29.12.07 Marco Huck W RSC 12 Bielefeld
(IBF Cruiserweight Title Defence)
Career: 21 contests, won 20, lost 1.

Chad (Bad) Dawson
Hartsville, USA. *Born* 13 July,1983
WBC L.Heavyweight Champion
Major Amateur Honours: Finished as runner up in the 1998 US Junior Championships and won a bronze medal in the 2000 World Junior Championships before taking the gold medal in the US under-19 Championships. Claims a 67-13 amateur record
Turned Pro: August 2001
Significant Results: Brett Lally W RSC 4, Darnell Wilson W PTS 10, Carl Daniels W RTD 7, Ian Gardner W RSC 11, Eric Harding W PTS 12, Tomasz Adamek W PTS 12, Jesus Ruiz W RSC 6
Type/Style: Tall southpaw who has a fast, hard jab and a big right cross
Points of Interest: 6'3" tall. Chad's father was a pro boxer back in the 1980s, winning only one of his six bouts, and Chad, who has four brothers and two sisters, started boxing at the age of 11. His dad works as a volunteer at the local YMCA and brings his son into the ring before each fight. Although a big puncher with 17 wins by stoppage or kayo, he had to climb off the floor to beat Tomasz Adamek for the WBC title in February 2007. Has made three title defences

29.09.07 Epifanio Mendoza W RSC 4 Sacramento
(WBC L.Heavyweight Title Defence)
09.06.07 Glengoffe Johnson W PTS 12 Tampa
(WBC L.Heavyweight Title Defence)
Career: 26 contests, won 26.

Juan (Baby Bull) Diaz
Houston, USA. *Born* 17 September, 1983
Former IBF, WBA & WBO Lightweight Champion
Major Amateur Honours: The Mexican Junior and Senior champion in 1999, he claims 105 wins in 110 fights, but was too young for the Sydney Olympics
Turned Pro: June 2002

Significant Results: John Bailey W RSC 7, Eleazar Contreras W PTS 10, Joel Perez W RSC 6, Martin O'Malley W CO 2, Lakva Sim W PTS 12, Julien Lorcy W PTS 12, Billy Irwin W RSC 9, Jose Miguel Cotto W PTS 12, Randy Suico W RSC 9, Fernando Angulo W PTS 12, Acelino Freitas W RTD 8
Type/Style: Juan is a solid, busy fighter with great hand speed and is developing as a puncher.
Points of Interest: 5'6" tall. Started boxing when he was eight years old, becoming the fourth youngest fighter to win a version of the lightweight title and was still a high school student at the time he beat Lakva Sim in July 2004. Now at College taking Government studies, he is trained by ex-pro Ronnie Shields and has 17 wins by stoppage or kayo. Had made four defences of his WBA title before beating Acelino Freitas in April 2007 to unify the WBA and WBO titles. He then stopped Julio Diaz to add the IBF title to his collection

13.10.07 Julio Diaz W RSC 9 Chicago
(WBA & WBO Lightweight Title Defence)
08.03.08 Nate Campbell L PTS 12 Cancun
(IBF, WBA & WBO Lightweight Title Defence)
Career: 34 contests, won 33, lost 1.

Nonito (The Filipino Flash) Donaire
Talibon, Philippines. *Born* 16 November, 1982
IBF Flyweight Champion
Major Amateur Honours: Won a gold medal in the US National Silver Gloves in 1998 and gold medals in both the 1999 and 2000 US Junior Olympics at 106lbs. He also competed in the 1999 National Golden Gloves. In 2000 he won the gold medal in the US Championships, but lost to Brian Viloria, as did his brother Glenn, and to Karoz Norman in the Olympic trials. He claims a 68-8 amateur record
Turned Pro: February 2001
Significant Results: JRosendo Sanchez L PTS 5, Kaichon Sorvoraphin W CO 2, Paulino Villalobos W RSC 6, Ildo Julio W PTS 8, Oscar Andrade W PTS 12
Type/Style: Is a sharp, fast boxer who has a dangerous left hook and hits hard with both hands
Points of Interest: 5'7" tall. Trained by his father, his elder brother Glenn

was also a successful amateur and is himself a world-rated flyweight. In addition, two of Nonito's cousins work his corner and his girlfriend is a martial arts expert. Brother Glenn lost on a technical decision to Vic Darchinyan for the IBF flyweight title in October 2006 before Nonito took the title from Darchinyan in what was a massive upset. Has 12 wins inside the distance

07.07.07 Vic Darchinyan W RSC 5 Bridgeport
(IBF Flyweight Title Challenge)
01.12.07 Luis Maldonado W RSC 8 Mashantucket
(IBF Flyweight Title Defence)
Career:20 contests, won 19, lost 1.

Sergei (Razor) Dzindziruk
Nozewska, Ukraine. *Born* 1 March, 1976
WBO L.Middleweight Champion. Former Undefeated European L.Middleweight Champion
Major Amateur Honours: Competed in both the 1993 European and 1994 World Junior Championships. Despite failing at the 1996 Olympics, he went on to win a bronze medal in the 1996 European Championships and a silver medal in the 1997 World Championships. He also won a silver in the 1998 European Championships and competed in the 1998 Goodwill Games. Claims 195 wins in 220 fights
Turned Pro: February 1999
Significant Results: Ariel Chavez W RSC 7, Andrei Pestriaev W RSC 5, Mamadou Thiam W RTD 3, Hussein Bayram W CO 11, Jimmy Colas W PTS 12, Daniel Santos W PTS 12, Sebastian Lujan W PTS 12, Alisultan Nadirbegov W PTS 12, Carlos Nascimento W RSC 11
Type/Style: A tall, lean southpaw, who is a good boxer with a hard right hook
Points of Interest: 6'0" tall. He started boxing in 1985 and is based in Germany but three of his first four pro fights were in Britain. However, his first fight in Poland was not sanctioned by the Polish federation and so is not included on the record given below. He won the European title by beating Mamadou Thiam in July 2004 and made two defences before winning the WBO title in December 2005 when beating Daniel Santos. Has 22 wins inside the distance and has made just four defences in 30 months

26.04.08 Lukas Konecny W PTS 12 Dresden
    (WBO L.Middleweight Title Defence)
Career: 34 contests, won 34.

Zsolt (Firebird) Erdei

Budapest, Hungary. *Born* 31 May, 1974
WBO L.Heavyweight Champion
Major Amateur Honours: The European Junior champion in 1992, he competed in the 1995 World Championships and 1996 Olympics and won a silver medal in the 1996 European Championships. He went on to win gold medals in the 1997 World Championship, the 1998 and 2000 European Championships, and a bronze medal in the 2000 Olympics.
Turned Pro: December 2000
Significant Results: Jim Murray W CO 5, Juan Carlos Gimenez W RSC 8, Massimiliano Saiani W RSC 7, Julio Gonzalez W PTS 12, Hugo Garay W PTS 12 twice, Alejandro Lakatus W PTS 12, Mehdi Sahnoune W RSC 12, Paul Murdoch W RSC 10, Thomas Ulrich W PTS 12, Danny Santiago W RSC 8
Type/Style: He is an excellent, clever technical craftsman with a strong, accurate jab, but despite having a good inside the distance record he is not a puncher
Points of Interest: 5' 10" tall with a 72" reach. Floored twice in early fights, he is based in Germany. When beating Julio Gonzalez in January 2004 he brought the WBO title back to his stable after fellow Universum fighter, Dariusz Michalczewski, had lost it to the same fighter. Has 17 wins inside the distance and has made ten defences, although the opposition has generally been mediocre
24.11.07 Tito Mendoza W PTS 12 Dresden
    (WBO L.Heavyweight Title Defence)
27.01.07 DeAudrey Abron W PTS 12
    (WBO L.Heavyweight Title Defence)
Career: 29 contests, won 29.

Vernon (The Viper) Forrest

Augusta, USA. *Born* 21 February, 1971
Former WBC L.Middleweight Champion. Former WBC & IBF Welterweight Champion
Major Amateur Honours: Having been runner-up to Kostya Tszyu in the 1991 World Championships, he competed in the 1992 Olympics before taking a gold medal in the 1992 World Championships.
Turned Pro: November 1992
Significant Results: Adrian Stone W RSC 11, Steve Martinez W RSC 1, Santiago Samaniego W CO 7, Vince Phillips W PTS 12, Raul Frank NC 3 & W PTS 12, Shane Mosley W PTS 12, Ricardo Mayorga L RSC 3 & L PTS 12, Ike Quartey W PTS 10
Type/Style: Is a tall, quick boxer with a long reach and a strong jab
Points of Interest: 6'0" tall. Lost to Kostya Tszyu in the 1991 World Championships, but beat Shane Mosley and Stevie Johnston in the Olympic Trials. Attended College under a boxing scholarship. 6'0" tall. His first fight with Raul Frank in May 2001 for the vacant IBF title was declared a no contest when Frank was cut. Won the vacant IBF title by outpointing Frank in return in May 2001 but relinquished the title to challenge Shane Mosley for the WBC title in July 2002. Lost the WBC title in a unification bout against the WBA champion Ricardo Mayorga in January 2003 and failed in a challenge for the same titles against Mayorga in July 2003. Has 29 wins by stoppage or knockout
28.07.07 Carlos Baldomir W PTS 12 Tacoma
    (Vacant WBC L.Middleweight Title)
20.04.07 Michele Piccirillo W RSC 11 Mashantucket
    (WBC L.Middleweight Title Defence)
20.04.07 Sergio Mora L PTS 12 Uncasville
    (WBC L.Middleweight Title Defence)
Career: 44 contests, won 40, lost 3, no contest 1.

Raul (Rayito) Garcia

La Paz, Mexico.
WBO Bantamweight Champion IBF M.Flyweight Champion. Former Undefeated Mexican M.Flyweight Champion
Major Amateur Honours: None known
Turned Pro: July 2004
Significant Results: Jesus Iribe W RSC 8, Sammy Gutierrez DREW 12 & W PTS 12
Type/Style: Southpaw. Is a good, stylish boxer
Points of Interest: Is the first boxer from Baja California to win a world title and has never boxed outside of Baja California. Won the Mexican title in June 2007 by beating Sammy Gutierrez but made only one defence. Has 15 wins by stoppage or kayo but had to climb off the floor to beat

Florante Condes

31.08.07 Noe Floes W CO 1 La Paz
19.10.07 Oscar Satumino W PTS 12 La Paz
    (Mexican M.Flyweight Title Defence)
29.02.08 Ronald Barrera W PTS 12 La Paz
14.06.08 Florante Condes W PTS 12 La Paz
    (IBF M.Flyweight Title Challenge)
 Career: 24 contests, won 23, lost 1.

Danny (Green Machine) Green

Perth, Australia. *Born* 9 March, 1973
WBA L.Heavyweight Champion
Major Amateur Honours: : Surprisingly eliminated in the quarter-finals of the 1998 Commonwealth Games, he won a gold medal in the 2000 Oceania Games and competed in the 2000 Olympics
Turned Pro: June 2001
Significant Results: Heath Stenton W RSC 2, Paul Smallman W CO 8, Jason DeLisle W CO 5 & W CO 9, Markus Beyer L DIS 5 & L PTS 12, Eric Lucas W RSC 6, Kirino Garcia W PTS 10, Anthony Mundine L PTS 12, Paul Murdoch W RSC 2
Type/Style: A tall, angular and tough fighter with a hard punch and a good chin
Points of Interest: 6'1" tall. At one time trained by Jeff Fenech, Danny suffered so badly from heat stroke in beating Sean Sullivan in 2004 that he almost died after the bout. Received an award for bravery for rescuing a man from the sea in 2006. The losses to Markus Beyer and Anthony Mundine were in challenges for versions of the WBC and WBA super-middleweight titles, respectively. Announced his retirement in March with 22 wins by stoppage or kayo on his record
18.07.07 Otis Griffin W CO 3 Perth
16.12.07 Stipe Drews W PTS 12 Perth
    (WBA L.Heavyweight Title Challenge)
Career: 28 contests, won 25, lost 3.

Hozumi Hasegawa

Nishiwaki City. Japan. *Born* 16 December, 1980
WBC Bantamweight Champion
Major Amateur Honours: None known
Turned Pro: November 1999
Significant Results: Jess Maca W PTS 12, Gunao Uno W PTS 12, Alvin Felisilda W CO 10, Jun Toriumi W PTS 10, Veerapol Sahaprom W PTS 12 (twice), Gerard Martinez W RSC 7, Genaro Garcia W PTS 12, Simpiwe Vetyeka W PTS 12
Type/ Style: He is a tall, fast and stylish

southpaw who utilises a counter-punching style

Points of Interest: 5'5" tall. With only seven wins inside the distance, he was once known as the 'Japanese Pernell Whittaker' due to his boxing skills. Lost two of his first five fights but is now unbeaten in 21 bouts and Veerapol Sahaprom had not tasted defeat in his last 45 fights before Hozumi beat him for the WBC title in April 2005. He has since made six defences and has eight wins inside the distance

10.01.08 Simone Maludrottu W PTS 12 Osaka
(WBC Bantamweight Title Defence)
12.06.08 Cristian Faccio W RSC 2 Tokyo
(WBC Bantamweight Title Defence)

Career: 26 contests, won 24, lost 2.

Chris (The Smiling Dragon) John
Semarang, Indonesia. *Born* September 4, 1981
WBA Featherweight Champion.
Former Undefeated Indonesian Featherweight Champion
Major Amateur Honours: None known
Turned Pro: June 1998
Significant Results: Ratanchai Sorvoraphin W PTS 10, Oscar Leon W PTS 10, Osamu Sato W PTS 12, Jose Rojas T DRAW 4 & W PTS 12, Derrick Gainer W PTS 12, Tommy Browne W RTD 9, Juan Manuel Marquez W PTS 12, Renan Acosta W PTS 12
Type/Style: He is a tall, switch-hitting, counter-puncher with good footwork
Points of Interest: 5' 7½" tall with a 65" reach. Christened Johannes Christian John, his original nickname was 'Thin Man', which he took as a tribute to Alexis Arguello, before eventually deciding that it was no longer suitable for his improved muscular build. His father was a former amateur boxer and Chris has been boxing since he was six, originally training in a garage before being based in a gym in Australia. He is also an international standard competitor at martial arts, winning a gold medal in the South East Asia Games in 1997. He won the vacant 'interim' WBA title in September 2003 by beating Oscar Leon and made three defences until he was recognised as full champion when Juan Manuel Marquez was stripped of the title in 2005. Has made five defences of the full title and has 22 wins inside the distance.

19.08.07 Zaiki Takemoto W RTD 9 Kobe
(WBA Featherweight Title Defence)

26.01.08 Roinet Caballero W RTD 7 Jakarta
(WBA Featherweight Title Defence)

Career: 42 contests, won 41, drew 1.

Dimitri (The Baby) Kirilov
St Petersburg, Russia. *Born* 24 November, 1978
IBF S.Flyweight Champion. Former Undefeated Russian Bantamweight Champion
Major Amateur Honours: No major titles but represented Russia in international matches
Turned Pro: May 1998
Significant Results: Daniel Ward W PTS 8, Junver Halog W PTS 10, Nat Sting W PTS 6, Spend Abazi L PTS 12, Masamori Tokuyama L PTS 12, Reynaldo Lopez W PTS 12, Luis Perez L PTS 12
Type/Style: Busy little fighter with an excellent defence and a heavy hitter with his hooks
Points of Interest: 5'4" tall. IBF title winning effort was his third try, having lost to Masamori Tokuyama for the WBC title in 2004 and to Luis Perez on a disputed split decision for the IBF title in 2006. Also lost to Spend Abazi for the European bantamweight title in 2002. Trained by Freddie Roach, he has just nine wins inside the distance

13.10.07 Jose Navarro W PTS 12 Moscow
(Vacant IBF S.Flyweight Title)
28.02.08 Cecilio Santos DREW 12 New York City
(IBF S.Flyweight Title Defence)

Career: 33 contests, won 29, drew 1, lost 3.

Vladimir Klitschko
Kiev, Ukraine. *Born* 25 March, 1976
IBF & WBC Heavyweight Champion. Former WBO Heavyweight Champion. Former Undefeated European Heavyweight Champion
Major Amateur Honours: Having won a gold medal in the 1993 European Junior Championships, a year later he took silver medals in the 1994 World Junior Championships and World Military Championships. He then went one better in the 1995 World Military Championship, winning the gold medal. In 1996 he won a silver medal in the European Championships prior to picking up a gold medal in the Olympics
Turned Pro: November 1996
Significant Results: Ross Puritty L RSC 11, Axel Schulz W RSC 8, Chris Byrd

W PTS 12 & W RSC 7, Frans Botha W RSC 8, Ray Mercer W RSC 6, Jameel McCline W RSC 10, Corrie Sanders L RSC 2, Lamon Brewster L RSC 5 , DaVarryl Williamson W TD 5, Eliseo Castillo W RSC 4, Samuel Peter W PTS 12, Calvin Brock W RSC 7, Ray Austin W RSC 2,
Type/Style: Although he relies on a mechanical jab and cross approach, his reach and punching power makes him dangerous, if unpredictable. Despite being a double champion there are still some questions over his stamina and chin
Points of Interest: 6' 6" tall. Despite losing his first amateur fight he was not deterred and has 44 wins inside the distance as a pro. After winning the European title by beating Axel Schulz in September 1999 he made only one defence before relinquishing it and going on to win the WBO title when outpointing Chris Byrd in October 2000. He made five defences before dropping the title in a shock stoppage loss to Corrie Sanders in March 2003. The younger brother of the former WBO and WBC champion, Vitali, he was then stopped by Lamon Brewster in a fight for the vacant WBO title in April 2004. Now self managed, he won the IBF title by beating Chris Byrd in April 2006 and the WBC title by outpointing Sultan Ibragimov in February 2008

07.07.07 Lamon Brewster W RTD 6 Cologne
(IBF Heavyweight Title Defence)
23.02.08 Sultan Ibragimov W PTS 12 New York City
(IBF Heavyweight Title Defence. WBC Heavyweight Title Challenge)

Career: 53 contests, won 50, lost 3.

Andreas Kotelnik
Lvov, Ukraine. *Born* 29 December,1977
WBA L.Welterweight Champion
Major Amateur Honours: Won gold medals in the 1995 European Junior and the 1999 European Senior Championships. Having competed without winning a medal in the 1997 World Championships, he won a silver in the 2000 Olympics and claims 135 wins in 150 amateur bouts
Turned Pro: December 2000
Significant Results: Fabrice Colombel W PTS 12, Arturo Urena W RSC 10, Sayan Sanchat W PTS 8, Gabriel Mapouka W PTS 12, Souleymane

M'Baye L PTS 12 & DREW 12, Junior Witter L PTS 12, Mohamad Abdulla W PTS 12, William Gonzalez W RSC 8

Type/Style: An upright stylish boxer with a good defence, who can be one-paced

Points of Interest: 5'7½" tall, he is trained by the former European amateur champion Michael Trimm. Was unsuccessful in his first challenge for the WBA title when he was held to a draw by Souleymane M'Baye in March 2007. Has 13 wins inside the distance

16.06.07 Laszlo Komjathi W PTS 8 Budapest
22.03.08 Gavin Rees W RSC 12 Cardiff
(WBA L.Welterweight Title Challenge)

Career: 32 contests, won 29, drew 1, lost 2.

Jorge (Golden Boy) Linares

Barinitas, Venezuela. *Born* 22 August, 1985

WBC Featherweight Champion

Major Amateur Honours: Won the Venezuelan Junior Championship four times and picked up a silver medal from the 2001 Venezuelan Senior Championships

Turned Pro: December 2002

Significant Results: Pedrito Laurente W PTS 10, Hugo Soto W PTS 10, Mike Domingo W PTS 10, Renan Acosta W PTS 10, Saohin Condo W PTS 10, Pedro Navarrete W PTS 10

Type/Style: A combination puncher, who is fast with real power in both hands

Points of Interest: 5'2" tall. Turned pro as a super-bantamweight at the age of 17 under the Akihiko Honda banner in Japan and is still based there. His brother Nelson Linares is also unbeaten as a pro. Has 16 wins by stoppage or kayo

21.07.07 Oscar Larios W RSC 10 Las Vegas
(Vacant WBC 'Interim' Featherweight Title)
15.12.07 Gamaliel Diaz W CO 8 Cancun
(WBC Featherweight Title Defence)

Career: 25 contests, won 25.

Juan Manuel (Juanma) López

Rio Piedras, Puerto Rico. *Born* 30 June, 1983

WBO S.Bantamweight Champion

Major Amateur Honours: Was five-time Puerto Rico national champion. Won gold medals in the 2001 and 2004 Jose Che Aponte Tournament. He also won a silver medal in the 2001

Pan-American Championships and a bronze medal in the 2002 Central American Games. Lost to Abner Mares in the quarter-finals of the 2003 Pan-American Games, but won a place at the 2004 Olympics by finishing runner-up in the Tijuana qualifier. Lost in the first series in Athens.

Turned Pro: January 2005

Significant Results: Luis Bolano W RTD 2, Edel Ruiz W RTD 6, Jose Alonso W RSC 3, Cuauhtemoc Vargas W RTD 6, Giovanni Andrade W RSC 1

Type/Style: Is a strong, hard-punching southpaw who can box or brawl and has real kayo power in both hands

Points of Interest: 5'7" tall. His father was tired of Juan Manuel fighting in the street so took him to the gym when he was just ten years old. It was no surprise that he took to boxing with one of his brothers fighting as an amateur. He is a stablemate of Miguel Cotto and always has his partner Barbara de Jesus as part of his corner team when he fights. Has won 20 of his 22 fights by stoppage or kayo

04.08.07 Hugo Dianzo W RSC 10 Rosemont
31.10.07 Omar Adorno W RSC 2 San Juan
23.02.08 Jonathan Oquendo W RSC 3 Caguas
07.06.08 Daniel Ponce de Leon W RSC 1 Atlantic City
(WBO S.Bantamweight Title Challenge)

Career: 22 contests, won 22.

Steve Luevano   Les Clark

Steve Luevano
Los Angeles, USA. *Born* 3 March, 1981
WBO Featherweight Champion
Major Amateur Honours: Won the Californian Junior Silver Gloves in 1996; was US Junior Olympics champion in 1997; won a gold medal in the 1998 US under-19 Championships; competed in the 1998 under-19 World Championships and won a silver medal in both the 1999 US Senior Championships and the National Golden Gloves but lost to Rocky Juarez in the Olympic trials. Claims 187 wins in 205 amateur and junior contests
Turned Pro: June 2000
Significant Results: Freddie Neal W RTD 9, Aldo Valtierra W PTS 10, Genaro Trazancos W RSC 5, Ruben Estanislao W PTS 12, Jorge Martinez W PTS 10, Martin Honorio L PTS 10, Cristobal Cruz W PTS 12
Type/Style: A Southpaw, he is a good technical fighter with an excellent jab and solid defence
Points of Interest: 5'7" tall. Started boxing in 1998 and is trained by the former IBF super-featherweight champion Roberto Garcia. He is married with two children and has plans to join the police force when he retires. Has 15 wins by stoppage or kayo

14.07.07	Nicky Cook W RSC 11 Greenwich *(Vacant WBO Featherweight Title)*
06.10.07	Antonio Davis W PTS 12 Las Vegas *(WBO Featherweight Title Defence)*
15.03.08	Terdsak Jandaeng W PTS 12 Las Vegas *(WBO Featherweight Title Defence)*
28.06.08	Mario Santiago DREW 12 Las Vegas *(WBO Featherweight Title Defence)*

Career: 37 contests, won 35, drew 1, lost 1.

Paul (Magic Man) Malignaggi
Brooklyn, USA. *Born* 23 November, 1980
IBF L.Welterweight Champion
Major Amateur Achievements: Won a gold medal in the 1998 New York Golden Gloves novice category and a silver medal in the 2000 New York Golden Gloves senior division, before taking a bronze medal in the 2000 PAL Championships. Although he failed to win a medal in the 2000 National Golden Gloves, he put this right in 2001 when he won the gold medal at the US Championships
Turned Pro: July 2001
Significant Results: Ray Martinez W PTS 10, Sandro Casamonica W TD 7, Jeremy Yelton W PTS 8, Donald Camarena W PTS 10, Miguel Cotto L PTS 12
Type/Style: Is a speedy, skilful boxer with a great jab but no real punching power
Points of Interest: 5'8½" tall, he is managed by Lou DiBella and trained by Buddy McGirt who once held the same IBF title. His parents were Sicilian immigrants but his father abandoned the family when Paul was six. Plagued by injuries to his right hand, which he has fractured four times, Paul climbed off the floor and overcame a fractured orbital eye socket to last the distance in a challenge to Miguel Cotto for the WBO light-welterweight title in June 2006. He then won the IBF title by beating Lovemore Ndou in June 2007. Still working as a Telemarketer, he has only five wins by stoppage or kayo

05.01.08	Herman Ngoudjo W PTS 12 Atlantic City *(IBF L.Welterweight Title Defence)*
24.05.08	Lovemore Ndou W PTS 12 Manchester *(IBF L.Welterweight Title Defence)*

Career: 26 contests, won 25, lost 1.

Antonio Margarito
Tijuana, Mexico. *Born* 18 March, 1978
Former Undefeated IBF Welterweight Champion. Former WBO Welterweight Champion
Major Amateur Honours: None known, but he claims 18 wins in 23 contests
Turned Pro: January 1994
Significant Results: Larry Dixon L PTS 10, Rodney Jones L PTS 10, Alfred Ankamah W CO 4, Danny Perez W PTS 8 & W PTS 12, David Kamau W CO 2, Frankie Randall W RSC 4, Daniel Santos NC 1 & L TD 9, Antonio Diaz W RSC 10, Andrew Lewis W RSC 2, Hercules Kyvelos W RSC 2, Sebastien Lujan W RSC 10, Kermit Cintron W RSC 5
Type/Style: Is a tall, strong, aggressive banger. Although a bit one-paced, he has a good jab and a strong chin
Points of Interest: 6'0" tall. Turned pro at the age of 15 and suffered three early defeats. His first fight with Daniel Santos for the WBO welterweight title in July 2001 was stopped and declared a no contest due to Antonio suffering a bad cut, and when Santos handed in the belt Antonio won the vacant title by beating Antonio Diaz in March 2002. His challenge against Santos for the WBO light-middleweight title in September 2004 title also went to a technical decision due to a cut. Relinquished the IBF title in May 2008 in order to take on Miguel Cotto for the latter's WBA crown. Has 26 wins inside the distance

14.07.07	Paul Williams L PTS 12 Carson *(WBO Welterweight Title Defence)*
10.11.07	Golden Johnson W RSC 1 New York City
12.04.08	Kermit Cintron W CO 6 Atlantic City *(IBF Welterweight Title Challenge)*

Career: 42 contests, won 36, lost 5, no contest 1.

Cristian Mijares
Gomez Palacio, Mexico. *Born* 2 October, 1981
WBC & WBA S.Flyweight Champion. Former Undefeated Mexican S.Flyweight Champion.
Major Amateur Honours: None known
Turned Pro: August 1997
Significant Results: Tomas Rojas W PTS 12, Gerson Guerrero W RSC 8, Alimi Goitia W RSC 3, Luis Maldonado DREW 12, Katsushige Kawashima W PTS 12 & W RSC 10, Reynaldo Lopez W PTS 12, Jorge Arce W PTS 12
Type/Style: Lanky, fast and accurate, this busy southpaw is also an excellent tactical boxer
Points of Interest: 5'6" tall. His trainer is his uncle Vicente Saldivar Mijares, who lost to Esteban DeJesus in challenge for the WBC lightweight title in 1977. Has two brothers who are also pros. Cristian had never fought outside Mexico until he climbed off the floor to beat Katsushige Kawashima for the vacant WBC 'interim' title in September 2006. The fight with Reynaldo Lopez in 2006 was a defence of the 'interim' title and he was recognised as full champion when reigning champion Masamori Tokuyama retired at the end of 2006. He is 5'6" tall, and has 14 wins inside the distance being unbeaten since July 2002

13.07.07	Teppei Kikui W RSC 10 Durango *(WBC S.Flyweight Title Defence)*
20.10.07	Franck Gorjux W RSC 1 Cancun *(WBC S.Flyweight Title Defence)*
16.02.08	Jose Navarro W PTS 12 Las Vegas *(WBC S.Flyweight Title Defence)*
17.05.08	Alexander Munoz W PTS 12 Durango *(WBC S.Flyweight Title Defence. WBA S.Flyweight Title Challenge)*

Career: 40 contests, won 35, drew 2, lost 3.

225

Steve (The Canadian Kid) Molitor
Sarnia, Canada. *Born* 4 April, 1980
IBF S.Bantamweight Champion.
Former Undefeated Commonwealth
Bantamweight Champion
Major Amateur Honours: The Canadian
national champion at flyweight in
1999, Steve competed in the 1998
Americas Championships, the 1999
Pan-American Games and 1999 World
Championships, where he lost to the
current WBO flyweight champion
Omar Narvaez
Turned Pro: May 2000
Significant Results: Scotty Olson W
RSC 5, Nicky Booth W PTS 12, Julio
Coronel W PTS 10, John MacKay W
PTS 8, Hugo Dianzo W PTS 12, Debind
Thapa W RSC 8, Michael Hunter W
CO 5
Type/Style: Tall, skinny southpaw who
is a cool, slick and clever boxer
Points of Interest: 5'7" tall. Steve was
inactive for over a year before beating
Michael Hunter for the vacant IBF title
in November 2006. This was partially
due to Gabula Vabaza failing a medical
when he and Steve were scheduled to
fight for the vacant title in South Africa.
Steve's brother Johnny was also an
outstanding boxer but has finished up in
jail. Trained by ex-pro Chris Johnson,
who won a bronze medal in the 1992
Olympics, he has defended his title
four times and has ten wins inside the
distance

14.07.07	Takalani Ndlovu W RSC 9 Orillia	
	(IBF S.Bantamweight Title Defence)	
27.10.07	Fahsan 3-K Battery W PTS 12 Orillia	
	(IBF S.Bantamweight Title Defence)	
19.01.08	Ricardo Castillo W PTS 12 Orillia	
	(IBF S.Bantamweight Title Defence)	
05.04.08	Fernando Beltran W PTS 12 Orillia	
	(IBF S.Bantamweight Title Defence)	

Career: 27 contests, won 27.

Fernando (Cochulito) Montiel
Los Mochis, Mexico. *Born* 1 March,
1979
WBO S.Flyweight Champion.
Former Undefeated WBO Flyweight
Champion
Major Amateur Honours: Claiming 33
wins in 36 fights, he was a local Golden
Gloves champion.
Turned Pro: December 1996
Significant Results: Paulino Villalobos
DREW 10 & W PTS 10, Sergio Millan
W PTS 10, Cruz Carbajal W RSC 4,
Isidro Garcia W RSC 7, Zoltan Lunka
W RSC 7, Juan Domingo Cordoba W

Steve Molitor   Philip Sharkey

CO 1, Jose Lopez W PTS 12, Pedro
Alcazar W RSC 6, Roy Doliguez
W RSC 3, Mark Johnson L PTS 12,
Reynaldo Hurtado W CO 7, Ivan
Hernandez W RSC 7, Evert Briceno
W PTS 12, Pramuansak Posuwan W
PTS 12, Jhonny Gonzalez L PTS 12, Z
Gorres W PTS 12
Type/ Style: Clever and stylish, he has a
good uppercut
Points of Interest: 5'4" tall. The
youngest of a fighting family, his father
and four brothers all being boxers, he
won his first 11 bouts inside the distance.
Jointly trained by his father Manuel
and a Japanese trainer based in Mexico,
Fernando has 28 wins by knockout
or stoppage. He won the WBO title,

stopping Isidro Garcia in December
2000, and made three defences before
moving up to win the super-flyweight
title by beating Pedro Alcazar in June
2002. Sadly, Alcazar collapsed and died
after the fight. Having lost the title in
his second defence to Mark Johnson in
August 2003, Fernando came back to
regain it when stopping Ivan Hernandez
in April 2005. He made an unsuccessful
challenge to Jhonny Gonzales for the
WBO bantamweight title in May 2006,
but has since made five more defences
of his super-flyweight title

14.07.07	Cecilio Santos W RSC 10 Ciudad	
	Obregon	
	(WBO S.Flyweight Title Defence)	
04.10.07	Luis Melendez W RSC 12 Las Vegas	

(WBO S.Flyweight Title Defence)
16.02.08 Martin Castillo W CO 4 Las Vegas
(WBO S.Flyweight Title Defence)
31.05.08 Luis Maldonado W RSC 3 San Luis
Potosi
(WBO S.Flyweight Title Defence)
Career: 40 contests, won 37, drew 1, lost 2.

Sergio (The Latin Snake) Mora
East Los Angeles, California, USA.
Born 4 December, 1980
WBC L.Middleweight Champion
Major Amateur Honours: A Californian
Golden Gloves champion, he beat Peter
Manfredo in the 1998 National Golden
Gloves but was eliminated in the
quarter-finals. Won a bronze medal in
the 1999 US Championships, losing to
Anthony Hanshaw. Went on to win the
Western Olympic trials in 2000, before
losing to Jermain Taylor in the final
Olympic trials
Turned Pro: August 2000
Significant Results: Les Ralston W
PTS 8, Jesse Brinkley W PTS 7, Peter
Manfredo W PTS 7 & W PTS 8, Archak
TerMeliksetian W RSC 7, Elvin Ayala
DREW 10, Eric Regan W PTS 10, Rito
Ruvalcaba W RSC 6
Type/Style: Is a quick, awkward fighter
with an elusive style but has good
stamina and a sound chin
Points of Interest: 6'0" tall with a 73"
reach. He and his three brothers were
brought up by their mother after their
father left home when Sergio was very
young. A street fighter who entered the
amateurs at the age of 15, he came to
prominence when he won the initial
series of the reality television show
The Contenders. He won $1,000,000
when his highest purse previous to this
had been just $7,000. A High School
graduate he studied law enforcement
and is also an accomplished artist. Has
only five wins inside the distance
16.10.07 Elvin Ayala DREW 10 Carson
11.01.08 Rito Ruvalcaba W RSC 6 Cabazon
07.06.08 Vernon Forrest W PTS 12 Uncasville
*(WBC L.Middleweight Title
Challenge)*
Career: 22 contests, won 21, drew 1.

Anselmo (Chemito) Moreno
San Miguel, Panama. *Born* 28 June,
1985
WBA Bantamweight Champion
Major Amateur Honours: Was mini-
flyweight champion of Panama in 2001
Turned Pro: March 2002
Significant Results: David Arosemena

W PTS 6, Felix Machado W PTS 10,
Jose de Jesus Lopez W RSC 5, Nestor
Paniagua W PTS 10, Luis Benavidez W
CO 2, Tomas Rojas W PTS 10
Type/Style: Fast, lanky, and a slick
counter-punching southpaw
Points of Interest: Turned pro as a
flyweight and even fought at light-
flyweight, but made so little money
early in his career that he took a job
as a house painter. Things looked up
after his 2006 win over former super-
flyweight champion Felix Machado. He
is Panama's 25th world champion. Has
eight wins inside the distance
16.08.07 Ricardo Vargas W RSC 1 Panama City
31.05.08 Wladimir Sidorenko W PTS 12
Dusseldorf
(WBA Bantamweight Title Challenge)
Career: 24 contests, won 22, drew 1, lost 1.

Daisuke Naito
Hokkaido, Japan. *Born* 30 August,
1974
WBC Flyweight Champion. Former
Undefeated Japanese Flyweight
Champion
Major Amateur Honours: None known
Turned Pro: October 1996
Significant Results: Takefumi Sakata
DREW 10, Pongsaklek Wonjongkam
L CO 1 & L TD 7, Teppei Kikui W
PTS 10, Hiroshi Nakano W TD 6,
Daigo Nakahiro W PTS 10, Noriyuki
Komatsu W RSC 6,
Type/Style: An unorthodox, aggressive
swinger
Points of Interest: 5'4" tall. His
first round kayo loss to Pongsaklek
Wonjongkam in a challenge for the
WBC title in April 2002 took just 34
seconds, making it the fastest finish in
a flyweight title fight bout. Daisuke had
been unbeaten in 21 bouts up to that
time. Their second fight went to the
cards after Naito was badly cut. Has 20
wins inside the distance
18.07.07 Pongsaklek Wonjongkam W PTS 12
Tokyo
(WBC Flyweight Title Challenge)
11.10.07 Daiki Kameda W PTS 12 Tokyo
(WBC Flyweight Title Defence)
08.03.08 Pongsaklek Wonjongkam DREW 12
Tokyo
(WBC Flyweight Title Defence)
Career: 37 contests, won 32, drew 3, lost 2.

Omar (Huracan) Narvaez
Trelew, Argentina. *Born* 7 October,
1975
WBO Flyweight Champion

Major Amateur Honours: Won
a bronze medal in 1997 World
Championships; a silver in the 1999
Championships, and gold medals in the
1999 Pan-American Games and South
American Championships. Earlier he
had competed in the 1996 Olympics,
where he beat the future double WBO
champion Joan Guzman. He also
competed in the 2000 Olympics
Turned Pro: December 2000
Significant Results: Carlos Montiveros
DREW 4, Wellington Vicente W
PTS 10, Marcos Obregon W PTS 10,
Adonis Rivas W PTS 12, Luis Lazarate
W DIS 10, Andrea Sarritzu W PTS 12
& DREW 12, Everardo Morales W
RSC 5, Alexander Mahmutov W RSC
10, Bernard Inom W RSC 11, Dario
Azuaga W RSC 6, Rexon Flores W
PTS 12, Walberto Ramos W PTS 12,
Brahim Asloum W PTS 12
Type/Style: Is a stocky, tough and
aggressive southpaw with fast hands
Points of Interest: 5'3" tall. Became
the first of the 2000 Olympians to win
a version of a world title when he beat
Adolfo Rivas in only his 12th paid fight
in July 2002. Was originally trained by
Cuban Sarbelio Fuentes but now has a
local trainer and has made 13 defences.
Has 17 wins by stoppage or kayo
14.09.07 Marlon Marquez W RSC 4 Trelew
(WBO Flyweight Title Defence)
25.01.08 Carlos Tamara W PTS 12 Puerto
Madryn
(WBO Flyweight Title Defence)
09.05.08 Ivan Pozo W RTD 7 Vigo
(WBO Flyweight Title Defence)
Career: 29 contests, won 27, drew 2.

Donnie (Ahas) Nietes
Bacolod City, Philippines. *Born* 13
May, 1982
WBO M.Flyweight Champion
Major Amateur Honours: None known
Turned Pro: April 2003
Significant Results: Abrin Matta W
RSC 5, Angky Angkota L PTS 10,
Ricardo Albia w RSC 7, Henri Amol
W CO 2
Type/Style: Skilful boxer who can also
punch a bit
Points of Interest: 5'3" tall. Donnie
was the first world champion for the
Antonio Aldeguer stable after they had
lost in three attempts in the previous
12 months. Has 13 wins inside the
distance
07.07.07 Saengpetch Sor Sakulphan W CO 7
Cebu City

30.09.07 Pornsawan Kratingdaenggym W
PTS 12 Cebu City
(Vacant WBO M.Flyweight Title)
Career: 26 contests, won 22, drew 3, lost 1.

Yutaka Niida

Kanagawa, Japan. *Born* 2 October, 1978
WBA M.Flyweight Champion. Former Undefeated Japanese M.Flyweight Champion
Major Amateur Honours: None known
Turned Pro: November 1996
Significant Results: Makoto Suzuki W RSC 9, Daisuke Iida DREW 10, Chana Porpaoin W PTS 12, Nohel Arambulet L PTS 12 & W PTS 12, Juan Landaeta W PTS 12, Jaewon Kim W PTS 12, Eriberto Gejon W TD 10, Ronald Barrera W PTS 12, Katsunari Takayama W PTS 12
Type/Style: Aggressive, with good speed and a big right hand punch, he has, however, a suspect chin
Points of Interest: 5'2" tall. Managed by the late Mitsunori Seki, who failed in five attempts to win versions of the world featherweight title. Yutaka climbed off the floor twice in the first round for his draw with Daisuke Iida. Although surprisingly retiring immediately after winning the WBA title when beating Chana Porpaoin in August 2001, he returned to action in July 2003 and lost to Nohel Arambulet for the WBA title. In a return in July 2004, Arambulet failed to make the weight and Yutaka won the vacant title after outpointing the Venezuelan. He has made seven defences

01.09.07 Eriberto Gejon W PTS 12 Tokyo
(WBA M.Flyweight Title Defence)
01.03.08 Jose Luis Varela W CO 6 Tokyo
(WBA M.Flyweight Title Defence)
Career: 27 contests, won 23, drew 3, lost 1.

Manny Pacquiao

Bukidnon, Philippines. *Born* 17 December, 1976
WBC Lightweight Champion. Former Undefeated WBC S.Featherweight Champion. Former Undefeated IBF S. Bantamweight Champion. Former WBC Flyweight Champion
Major Amateur Honours: None known, but started at 13 and won 60 of 64 fights
Turned Pro: January 1995
Significant Results: Rostico Torrecampo L CO 3, Chockchai Chokwiwat W CO

5, Chatchai Sasakul W CO 8, Medgoen Singsurat L CO 3, Nedal Hussein W RSC 10, Lehlohonolo Ledwaba W RSC 6, Agapito Sanchez T DRAW 6, Jorge Julio W RSC 2, Emmanuel Lucero W RSC 3, Marco Antonio Barrera W RSC 11, Juan Manuel Marquez DREW 12, Oscar Larios W PTS 12, Erik Morales L PTS 10, W RSC 10 & W CO 3, Jorge Solis W CO 8
Type/Style: Stocky and aggressive, he is an exciting and hard-punching southpaw
Points of Interest: Turning pro at the age of 18 as a mini-flyweight, he won the WBC flyweight title by knocking out Chatchai Sasakul in December 1998. Made one defence and then, when struggling to make the weight, lost the title on a kayo to Medgoen Singsurat in September 1999. Promptly moved straight up to super-bantamweight and won the IBF title in June 2001 with an upset stoppage victory over Lehlohonolo Ledwaba, when coming in as a substitute at two weeks notice. Made six defences and then drew in a dramatic battle with Juan Manuel Marquez in a challenge for the IBF and WBA featherweight titles. Moved up again to super-featherweight to add the WBC title and win two out of three dramatic battles against Erik Morales. Added a fourth division title by beating David Diaz and is the only fighter to have spanned from flyweight to lightweight in winning world titles. Trained by Freddie Roach, he has 36 wins by stoppage or kayo. His brother Bobby is also a pro

06.10.07 Marco Antonio Barrera W PTS 12 Las Vegas
15.03.08 Juan Manuel Marquez W PTS 12 Las Vegas
(WBC S.Featherweight Title Challenge)
28.06.08 David Diaz W RSC 9 Las Vegas
(WBC Lightweight Title Challenge)
Career: 52 contests, won 47, drew 2, lost 3.

Kelly (Ghost) Pavlik

Youngstown, USA. *Born* 4 April, 1982
WBC & WBO Middleweight Champion
Major Amateur Honours: 1998 National Police Athletic League Junior champion and National Golden Gloves Junior champion; 1999 US under-19 champion and bronze medallist in the 2000 US Championships. Claims 89 wins in 98 contests

Turned Pro: June 2000
Significant Results: Ross Thompson W PTS 8, Fulgencio Zuniga W RTD 9, Bronco McKart W RSC 6, Lenord Pierre W RSC 4, Jose Luis Zertuche W CO 8, Edison Miranda W RSC 7
Type/Style: Skilled and polished, he is a pressure fighter with a hard jab, a big right-hand punch and a strong chin
Points of Interest: 6'2 ½" tall with a 75" reach. His father Michael is his joint manager and trainer and he had two brothers who boxed as amateurs. After flirting with martial arts he was inspired to take up boxing by former IBF lightweight champion Harry Arroyo, who also hails from Youngstown. He lost to Jermain Taylor in the 2000 Olympic trials. A college student, who graduated in computer graphics, he has stopped or kayoed 30 opponents

29.09.07 Jermain Taylor W RSC 7 Atlantic City
(WBC & WBO Middleweight Title Challenges)
16.02.08 Jermain Taylor W PTS 12 Las Vegas
07.06.08 Gary Lockett W RSC 3 Atlantic City
(WBC & WBO Middleweight Title Defences)
Career: 34 contests, won 34.

Gerry (Fearless) Penalosa

San Carlos City, Philippines. *Born* 7 August, 1972
WBO Bantamweight Champion. Former WBC S.Flyweight Champion
Major Amateur Honours: None known
Turned Pro: May 1989
Significant Results: Sammy Duran L PTS 12, Rolando Bohol W PTS 10, Rolando Pascua W CO 8, Hiroshi Kawashima W PTS 12, Seung-Koo Lee W CO 9, Joel Luna Zarate T DRAW 2, In-Joo Cho L PTS 12 (twice), Ramon Hurtado W CO 2, Masamori Tokuyama L PTS 12, Tomas Rojas W PTS 10, Mauricio Martinez W RSC 9, Daniel Ponce de Leon L PTS 12
Type/Style: This experienced southpaw is a good craftsman with a sound defence a great chin and a hard punch
Points of Interest: 5'4" tall. From a fighting family, his father Carl was the Philippines' light-welterweight champion and elder brother Dodi was IBF light-flyweight and flyweight champion. Dodi lost in a challenge for the IBF flyweight title to Dave McAuley in 1989. A third brother, Jonathan, was also a pro. Turning pro at the age of 16,

Gerry, real name Geronimo, won the WBC super-flyweight title by beating Hiroshi Kawashima in 1997 and made five defences before losing the title to In-Joo Cho in 1998. Unsuccessful in three subsequent challenges for the title, he did not fight in 2003 and returned in 2004 as a bantamweight. Lost to Daniel Ponce de Leon on a hotly disputed verdict in a challenge for the WBO super-bantamweight title in March 2007. Is trained by Freddie Roach and has 36 wins inside the distance

11.08.07 Jhonny Gonzalez W CO 7
Sacramento
(WBO Bantamweight Title Challenge)
06.04.08 Ratanchai Sorvoraphin W RSC 8
Quezon City
(WBO Bantamweight Title Defence)
Career: 61 contests, won 53, drew 2, lost 6.

Luis (The Demolisher) Perez

Managua, Nicaragua. *Born* 6 April, 1978
Former IBF Bantamweight Champion. Former undefeated IBF S.Flyweight Champion
Major Amateur Honours: None known
Turned Pro: November 1996
Significant Results: Leon Salazar W RSC 4, Justo Zuniga W CO 1, Vernie Torres L PTS 12, Moises Castro W PTS 10, Edicson Torres W PTS 12 (twice), Felix Machado W PTS 12 (twice), Luis Bolano W RSC 6, Dimitri Kirilov W PTS 12
Type/Style: He is a very skilful southpaw with a strong jab, but not a big puncher
Points of Interest: 5'5" tall with a 67" reach. Had only five days notice of the first fight with Felix Machado in January 2003 when he won the IBF super-flyweight title, but showed it was no fluke in the rematch. At one time he was managed by Anna Alvarez, the wife of the former WBA light-flyweight champion Rosendo Alvarez. Luis failed to make the weight for his May 2006 defence against Dimitri Kirilov and was stripped of the title. After 13 months of inactivity he moved up to bantamweight and won the vacant IBF title

07.07.07 Genaro Garcia W RSC 7 Bridgeport
(Vacant IBF Bantamweight Title)
29.09.07 Joseph Agbeko L RSC 7 Sacramento
(IBF Bantamweight Title Defence)
Career: 27 contests, won 25, lost 2.

Samuel (The Nigerian Nightmare) Peter

Akwaibon, Nigeria. *Born* 6 September, 1980
WBC Heavyweight Champion
Major Amateur Honours: Nigerian and All-Africa heavyweight champion in 2000, he lost to Paolo Vidoz in the quarter-finals of the Olympics that year
Turned Pro: February 2001
Significant Results: Charles Shufford W PTS 10, Jovo Pudar W PTS 10, Jeremy Williams W CO 2, Yanqui Diaz W RSC 5, Taurus Sykes W CO 2, Vladimir Klitschko L PTS 12, James Toney W PTS 12 (twice)
Type/Style: Not big by today's standards at 6'2", Samuel is a strong and powerful fighter with a good jab and heavy overhand right punch.
Points of Interest: Was adopted as a youngster by the Nigerian police force and is still a member of the force. As an amateur he lost to Audley Harrison in 2000. Although he had Vladimir Klitschko on the floor three times in their September 2005 fight, he lost the decision. Was floored three times by Jameel McCline, but claimed that this, the first time he had been floored as a professional, was due to a perforated ear drum. Samuel was recognised as WBC 'interim' champion when Oleg Maskaev withdrew with an injury from their proposed fight in October 2007 and then won the full title when beating Maskaev in March this year. Has 23 wins by knockout or stoppage

06.10.07 Jameel McCline W PTS 12 New York City
08.03.08 Oleg Maskaev W RSC 6 Cancun
(WBC Heavyweight Title Challenge)
Career: 31 contests, won 30, lost 1.

Verno Phillips

Troy, USA. *Born* Belize, 29 November, 1969
IBF L.Middleweight Champion. Former WBO L.Middleweight Champion
Major Amateur Honours: None known
Turned Pro: January 1988
Significant Results: Larry Barnes L PTS 10, Hector Vilte W RSC 4, Lupe Aquino W RSC 7, Santos Cardona W PTS 12 (twice), Gianfranco Rosi L PTS 12 and W PTS 12, Paul Jones L PTS 12, Godfrey Nyakana W CO 11, Julian Jackson W CO 9, Kassim Ouma L PTS 10 & L PTS 12, Bronco McKart W PTS 10, Carlos Bojorquez W RSC 6, Ike Quarry L PTS 10
Type/Style: A slick, experienced boxer with a real kayo punch
Points of Interest: 5'8" tall. Was an ordinary club fighter in New York State with a 10-4 record before moving his base to Argentina where he established a winning run that took him to a victory over Lupe Aquino in 1993 for the WBO title. Having lost to Gianfranco Rosi in 1995 in his fourth defence, he looked jaded in losing to Paul Jones in a challenge for the WBO title in November 1995. Was an in-and-out performer until beating Bronco McKart in April 2003 and went on to win the vacant IBF title by halting Carlos Bojorquez in June 2004. After losing the title in his first defence to Kassim Ouma in October 2004, Verno had been inactive for 13 months before beating Cory Spinks in a big upset. Has 21 wins by stoppage or kayo

27.03.08 Cory Spinks W PTS 12 St Louis
(IBF L.Middleweight Title Challenge)
Career: 54 contests, won 42, drew 1, lost 10, no contest 1.

Carlos (Indio) Quintana

Moca, Puerto Rico. *Born* 6 November, 1976
Former WBO Welterweight Champion
Major Amateur Honours: Was the Puerto Rican amateur champion and claims 62 wins in 70 contests, with 48 victories inside the distance
Turned Pro: June 1997
Significant Results: Edwin Cassiani W CO 3, Nurhan Suleymanoglu W RSC 4, Raul Bejerano W RSC 10, Joel Julio W PTS 12, Miguel Cotta L RTD 5
Type/Style: Clever, capable southpaw
Points of Interest: 5'9½" tall. He started boxing at the age of 19 and his brother Jose is also a pro. Married with three children, Carlos' fifth-round loss to Miguel Cotto in December 2006 was for the vacant WBA welterweight title. Trained by Felix Trinidad senior, he has 19 wins inside the distance

29.09.07 Chris Henry W RSC 4 Atlantic City
09.02.08 Paul Williams W PTS 12 Temecula
(WBO Welterweight Title Challenge)
07.06.08 Paul Williams L RSC 1 Uncasville
(WBO Welterweight Title Defence)
Career: 27 contests, won 25, lost 2.

229

Takefumi Sakata

Hiroshima, Japan. *Born* 29 January, 1980
WBA Flyweight Champion. Former Undefeated Japanese Flyweight Champion
Major Amateur Honours: None known
Turned Pro: December 1998
Significant Results: Masaki Kawabata W PTS 10, Daisuke Naito DREW 10, Shiro Yahiro W RSC 9, Trash Nakamura L PTS 10 & W PTS 10, Robert Vasquez L PTS 12, Lorenzo Parra L PTS 12 (twice) & W RSC 3
Type/Style: A slow starter out of his peek-a-boo style but strong and durable with great stamina, he is a good body puncher
Points of Interest: 5'4" tall. Had two spells as Japanese champion, taking part in eight title fights. Lost twice on majority decisions to Lorenzo Parra in title challenges, suffering a broken jaw but going the distance in their first bout in 2004. In their third bout Parra failed to make the weight but the fight went ahead and Sakata won the vacant title when the Venezuelan retired at the end of the second round. Takefumi, who dedicated his win to the late founder of his gym Masaki Kanehira, has 15 wins by stoppage or kayo

01.07.07	Roberto Vasquez W PTS 12 Tokyo	
	(WBA Flyweight Title Defence)	
04.11.07	Denkaosaen Kaovichit DREW 12 Saitama	
	(WBA Flyweight Title Defence)	
29.03.08	Shingo Yamaguchi W PTS 12 Chiba City	
	(WBA Flyweight Title Defence)	

Career: 35 contests, won 30, drew 1, lost 4.

Olyedong Sithsamerchai

Bangkok, Thailand. *Born* 17 July, 1985
WBC M.Flyweight Champion
Major Amateur Honours: None, but was a star in Muay Thai contests
Turned Pro: September 2002
Significant Results: Arman del a Cruz W PTS 10, Alex Aroy W PTS 10, Rollen del Castillo W PTS 10, Omar Soto W PTS 12
Type/Style: Is a fast moving, counter-punching southpaw with good stamina
Points of Interest: 5'2" tall. His real name is Kittipong Jaikajang and he was fighting ten-round bouts after only three contests. Has 11 wins inside the distance

18.07.07	Sawangchai Sithchalermchai W RSC 9 Bangkok

29.11.07	Eagle Kyowa W PTS 12 Bangkok	
	(WBC M.Flyweight Title Challenge)	
28.03.08	John Cut Siregar W RSC 4 Bangkok	
18.06.08	Junichi Ebisuoka W RSC 9 Phuket	
	(WBC M.Flyweight Title Defence)	

Career: 27 contests, won 27.

Ulises (Archie) Solis

Guadalajara, Mexico. *Born* 28 August, 1981
IBF L.Flyweight Champion. Former Undefeated Mexican L.Flyweight Champion
Major Amateur Honours: None known, but he claims only two losses in 38 fights
Turned Pro: April 2000
Significant Results: Omar Soto W PTS 10, Juan Keb Baas W RSC 9, Edgar Sosa W PTS 12, Lee Sandoval W RTD 8, Gabriel Munoz W CO 3, Nelson Dieppa L PTS 12, Carlos Fajardo W RSC 8, Will Grigsby W PTS 12 & W RTD 8, Erik Ortiz W RSC 9, Omar Salado DREW 12, Jose Antonio Aguirre W RSC 9
Type/Style: Although not a big puncher he is an accomplished stand-up boxer with an excellent jab
Points of Interest: 5'3" tall. Ulises is a member of a fighting family and his elder brother Jorge has lost only once in 38 fights, and that was to Manny Pacquiao. Has 20 wins inside the distance with his only defeat coming when he lost a majority verdict to Nelson Dieppa in a challenge for the WBO title in July 2004. He then went on to win the IBF title with a win over Will Grigsby in January 2006 and has made six defences

04.08.07	Rodel Mayol W RSC 8 Rosemont	
	(IBF L.Flyweight Title Defence)	
15.12.07	Bert Batawang W RSC 9 Guadalajara	
	(IBF L.Flyweight Title Defence)	

Career: 29 contests, won 26, drew 2, lost 1.

Edgar Sosa

Mexico City, Mexico. *Born* 23 August, 1979
WBC L.Flyweight Champion
Major Amateur Honours: None known
Turned Pro: April 2002
Significant Results: Ulises Solis L PTS 6 & L PTS 12, Manuel Vargas L RSC 8, Omar Nino Romero L PTS 10, Isaac Bustos L PTS 12, Domingo Guillen W RSC 6, Francisco Rosas W PTS 12, Gilberto Keb Baas W PTS 12, Nohel Aramabulet W TD 10, Brian Viloria

W PTS 12
Type/Style: A good tactical boxer with a strong jab and plenty of movement, he has a tough chin to go with his punching power
Points of Interest: A couple of his uncles were fighters and he started boxing at the age of ten. Trained by Miguel 'Raton' Gonzalez, who is the father of the former WBO bantamweight titleholder Jhonny Gonzalez, and managed by Haitian businessman Jacques Deschamps, in late 2003 his record was a mediocre 12-5. However, four of those losses were close decisions to fighters who went on to win versions of world titles and Edgar is now unbeaten in his last 20 contests, winning the vacant IBF title with a victory over Brian Viloria in April 2007. He has made five defences of his title and has 16 wins by stoppage or kayo

28.07.07	Luis Alberto Lazarte W DIS 10 Cancun	
	(WBC L.Flyweight Title Defence)	
16.09.07	Lorenzo Trejo W RSC 9 Las Vegas	
	(WBC L.Flyweight Title Defence)	
24.11.07	Roberto Leyva W RSC 4 Veracruz	
	(WBC L.Flyweight Title Defence)	
09.02.08	Jesus Iribe W PTS 12 Leon	
	(WBC L.Flyweight Title Defence)	
14.06.08	Takashi Kunishige W RSC 8 Mexico City	
	(WBC L.Flyweight Title Defence)	

Career: 37 contests, won 32, lost 5.

Felix (Storm) Sturm

Leverkusen, Germany. *Born* 31 January, 1979
WBA Middleweight Champion. Former WBO Middleweight Champion
Major Amateur Honours: Won a gold medal in the 1997 European Junior Championships and was German champion in 1995, 1998 and 1999. He was a quarter-finalist in both the 1999 World Championships and 2000 Olympics and won a gold medal in the European Championships in 2000. Claims 113 wins in 122 fights
Turned Pro: January 2001
Significant Results: Hector Velazco W PTS 12, Ruben Varon W PTS 12, Oscar de la Hoya L PTS 12, Robert Frazier W PTS 10, Hacine Cherifi W CO 3, Bert Schenk W CO 2, Jorge Sendra W PTS 12, Maselino Maseo W PTS 12, Javier Castillejo L RSC 10 & W PTS 12, Noe Gonzalez W PTS 12
Type/Style: Is a tall, strong, technically sound, box-puncher with a solid jab

Points of Interest: 5'11" tall. Fought in the amateurs under his real name Adnan Catic but took the name Sturm, which means storm in German, as a pro. Won the WBO middleweight title by beating Hector Velazco in September 2003 and made one defence before losing the title on a close decision to Oscar de la Hoya in June 2004. Won the WBA 'secondary' title when beating Maselino Maseo in March 2006 and was recognised as full WBA champion when Jermain Taylor was stripped of the 'super' title in 2006. Lost the title to Javier Castillejo in July 2006 but regained it when beating Castillejo in April 2007 and has made three defences since then. Surprisingly, has only 13 wins inside the distance

20.10.07 Randy Griffin DREW 12 Halle
(WBA Middleweight Title Defence)
05.04.08 Jamie Pittman W RSC 7 Dusseldorf

(WBA Middleweight Title Defence)
Career: 32 contests, won 29, drew 1, lost 2.

Antonio (The Magic Man) Tarver
Orlando, USA. *Born* 21 November, 1968
IBF & IBO L.Heavyweight Champion. Former Undefeated IBF, WBA & WBC L.Heavyweight Champion
Major Amateur Honours: US champion 1993; National Golden Gloves champion 1994 and 1995; US champion in 1995; gold medallist in both the 1995 Pan-American Games and the 1995 World Championships; bronze medallist in the 1996 Olympic Games
Turned Pro: February 1997
Significant Results: Mohamed Ben Guesima W RSC 9, Ernest Mateen W RSC 1, Eric Harding L PTS 12, Chris Johnson W RSC 10, Reggie Johnson

W PTS 12, Eric Harding W RSC 5, Montell Griffin W PTS 12, Roy Jones L PTS 12, W CO 2 & W PTS 12, Glengoffe Johnson L PTS 12 & W PTS 12, Bernard Hopkins L PTS 12, Elvir Muriqi W PTS 12
Type/Style: Tall, skinny southpaw with a good jab and a fair puncher
Points of Interest: 6'2" tall. Trained by Buddy McGirt, he has been known to wear a top hat and cape into the ring. Was awarded the keys to the City of Orlando for his exploits as an amateur. Won the vacant IBF and WBC titles by beating Montell Griffin in April 2003 but was stripped of the IBF title in the same year. Lost the WBC title to Roy Jones in November 2003, but regained the WBC title and won the WBA crown by kayoing Jones in May 2004,

Antonio Tarver

Les Clark

only to subsequently be stripped of both titles for failing to defend them. Declared himself bankrupt just before the second fight with Jones. Became involved in film work, seeming to be out of the picture after losing to Bernard Hopkins in June 2006, and did not fight for another year before coming back to beat Elvir Murqi, Danny Santiago and then Clinton Woods for the IBF title. Has 19 wins inside the distance

01.12.07 Danny Santiago W RSC 4 Mashantucket
(IBO Middleweight Title Defence)
12.04.08 Clinton Woods W PTS 12 Tampa
(IBF L.Heavyweight Title Challenge. IBO L.Heavyweight Title Defence)
Career: 31 contests, won 27, lost 4.

Ricardo (Mochuelo)Torres

Magangue, Colombia. *Born* 16 February, 1980
WBO L.Welterweight Champion
Major Amateur Honours: Won a gold medal in the 1998 Pan-American Junior Championships and in the same year competed in the World Junior Championships. Lost to Miguel Cotto in the Americas qualifiers for the 2000 Olympics
Turned Pro: March 2001
Significant Results: Emilio Julio W RSC 3, Ignacio Solar W CO 5, Edwin Vazquez W RSC 3, Miguel Cotto L CO 7, Carlos Donquiz W CO 2, Mike Arnaoutis W PTS 12, Arturo Morua W PTS 12
Type/Style: Aggressive come-forward banger who can adapt
Points of Interest: 5'8" tall. Ricardo won 26 of his first 28 fights by stoppage or kayo, 11 of them in the first round. Had Miguel Cotto on the floor in his challenge for the WBO title in 2005, but was floored four times himself. Won the vacant WBO title by beating Mike Arnaoutis in November 2006 and has made two defences. His brother Jose Miguel Torres is a successful pro at light-middleweight

01.09.08 Kendall Holt W RSC 11 Barranquilla
(WBO L.Welterweight Title Defence)
Career: 33 contests, won 32, lost 1.

Edwin (Dinamita) Valero

Merida, Venezuela. *Born* 3 December, 1981
WBA S.Featherweight Champion
Major Amateur Honours: Three times Venezuelan amateur champion, he won a gold medal in the 2000 Central American Games and competed in the 2000 Olympics qualifiers. Claims only six losses in 92 fights
Turned Pro: July 2002
Significant Results: Roque Cassiani W CO 1, Esteban Morales W CO 1, Aram Ramazyan W CO 1, Whyber Garcia W CO 1, Genaro Trazancos W RSC 2, Vicente Mosquera W RSC 10, Miguel Lozada W RSC 1, Nobuhito Honmo W RSC 8
Type/Style: Loose-limbed, wide open, aggressive southpaw banger with a devastating punch in both hands
Points of Interest: 5'7" tall. Having started boxing as an amateur at the age of 12, he set a record by winning all of his first 18 pro bouts inside the first round. Based in Japan, he was banned from fighting in the United States after failing an MRI in New York in 2004, due to an injury suffered in a motor cycle accident in Venezuela, but has since fought in Argentina, Panama, Venezuela, Japan, France and Mexico and is now licensed in Texas. Won the WBA title by halting Vicente Mosquera in August 2006 and has made four defences. All of his fights have ended inside the distance and only five have lasted more than one round

15.12.07 Zaid Zavaleta W RSC 3 Cancun
(WBA S.Featherweight Title Defence)
12.06.08 Takehiro Shimada W RSC 7 Tokyo
(WBA S.Featherweight Title Defence)
Career: 24 contests, won 24.

Israel (Magnifico) Vazquez

Mexico City, Mexico. *Born* 25 December, 1977
WBC S.Bantamweight Champion. Former Undefeated IBF S.Bantamweight Champion
Major Amateur Honours: None known, although he claims 58 wins
Turner Pro: March 1995
Significant Results: Marcos Licona L PTS 12, Eddy Saenz W CO 3, Ever Beleno W CO 2, Osvaldo Guerrero W PTS 10, Oscar Larios L CO 12 & W RSC 3, Jorge Julio W RSC 10, Trinidad Mendoza W CO 7, Jose Luis Valbuena W RSC 12, Art Simonyan W RSC 5, Armando Guerrero W PTS 12, Ivan Hernandez W RTD 4 Atlantic City, Jhonny Gonzalez W RSC 10, Rafael Marquez L RTD 7
Type/Style: Quick, upright boxer with a high, tight guard and a hard puncher
Points of Interest: 5'6" tall with a 66" reach. He idolised Ruben Olivares, which inspired him to give up karate to concentrate on boxing. Israel lost to Oscar Larios for the vacant WBC 'interim' super-bantamweight title in May 2002 and then won the vacant IBF title in March 2004 by beating Jose Luis Valbuena. He made two defences before winning the WBC title when halting Larios in a return in December 2005, but was stripped of the IBF title for failing to make a mandatory defence. Lost the WBC title to Rafael Marquez in March 2007 in the first of a three bout series that is sure to go down in boxing history as one of the great rivalries. Has 31 wins inside the distance

04.08.07 Rafael Marquez W RSC 6 Hidalgo
(WBC S.Bantamweight Title Challenge)
01.03.08 Rafael Marquez W PTS 12 Carson
(WBC S.Bantamweight Title Defence)
Career: 47 contests, won 43, lost 4.

Paul (The Punisher) Williams

Aiken, Georgia. *Born* 27 July, 1981
WBO Welterweight Champion
Major Amateur Honours: No major titles and lost to James Webb in the 1999 Police Athletic League championships
Turned Pro: July 2000
Significant Results: Rodolfo Gomez W RSC 4, Luis Hernandez W PTS 10, Terrance Cauthen W PTS 10, Alfonso Sanchez W CO 5, Sergio Rios W CO 2, Walter Matthysse W RSC 10, Sharmba Mitchell W CO 4, Santos Pakau W RSC 6
Type/Style: is an all-action, aggressive southpaw
Points of Interest: 6'1" tall. Started in boxing when his mother took him to the gymnasium on the recommendation of a school bus driver who was tired of Paul making trouble. Did not really take his amateur time that seriously which is why he never won a major title. Has 25 wins by kayo or stoppage

14.07.07 Antonio Margarito W PTS 12 Carson
(WBO Welterweight Title Challenge)
09.02.08 Carlos Quintana L PTS 12 Temecula
(WBO Welterweight Title Defence)
07.06.08 Carlos Quintana W RSC 1 Uncasville
(WBO Welterweight Title Challenge)
Career: 35 contests, won 34, lost 1.

World Title Bouts, 2007-2008

by Bob Yalen

All of last season's title bouts for the IBF, WBA, WBC and WBO are shown in date order within their weight division and give the boxers' respective weights as well as the scorecard if going to a decision. British officials, where applicable, are also listed. Yet again there were no WORLD TITLE FIGHTS as such, just a proliferation of champions recognised by the above four commissions and spread over 17 weight divisions. Below the premier league, come other commissions such as the WBU, IBO, IBC and WBF, etc, etc, which would devalue the world championships even further if one recognised their champions as being the best in the world. Despite that, we have shown IBO title defences attributed to Ricky Hatton (IBO light-welterweight champion) and Antonio Tarver (IBO light-heavyweight champion), as they are arguably the top men in their respective divisions. Right now, the WBA have decided to continue recognising their champions who move on to claim other commissions' titles as super champions – despite vacating the title and creating a new champion, who, for our purposes, is classified as a 'secondary' champion – which if taken up in general could eventually lead to the best man at his weight being recognised universally as a world champion if the fights can be made.

M.Flyweight

7 July Muhammad Rachman 104½ (Indonesia) L PTS 12 Florante Condes 104 (Philippines), RCTI TV Studio, Jakarta, Indonesia - IBF. Referee: Wayne Hedgepeth. Scorecards: 111-115, 112-114, 114-112.

1 September Yutaka Niida 104¾ (Japan) W PTS 12 Eriberto Gejon 105 (Philippines), Korakuen Hall, Tokyo, Japan - WBA. Referee: Derek Milham. Scorecards: 117-111, 117-112, 117-112.

30 September Donnie Nietes 105 (Philippines) W PTS 12 Pornsawan Kratingdaenggym 105 (Thailand), Waterfront Hotel, Cebu City, Philippines - WBO. Referee: Raul Caiz (junior). Scorecards: 114-113, 116-110, 115-111. Contested for the vacant title after Ivan Calderon (Puerto Rico) handed in his belt on beating Hugo Cazares for the WBO junior flyweight title on 25 August.

29 November Eagle Kyowa 104¾ (Thailand) L PTS 12 Oleydong Sithsamerchai 105 (Thailand), 11th Infantry Arena, Bangkok, Thailand - WBC. Referee: Laurentino Ramirez. Scorecards: 112-115, 114-115, 112-117.

1 March Yutaka Niida 105 (Japan) W CO 6 Jose Luis Varela 104¾ (Venezuela), Korakuen Hall, Tokyo, Japan - WBA. Referee: Raul Caiz.

14 June Florante Condes 103½ (Philippines) L PTS 12 Raul Garcia 103½ (Mexico), Arturo C. Nahl Stadium, La Paz, Baja California, Mexico - IBF. Referee: Wayne Hedgepeth. Scorecards: 110-118, 112-115, 115-112.

18 June Oleydong Sithsamerchai 105 (Thailand) W RSC 9 Junichi Ebisuoka 105 (Japan), Saphanhin Boxing Arena, Phuket, Thailand - WBC. Referee: Malcolm Bulner.

L.Flyweight

28 July Edgar Sosa 107 (Mexico) W DISQ 10 Luis Alberto Lazarte 105 (Argentina), Union of Taxi Drivers Arena, Cancun, Mexico - WBC. Referee: Hector Afu.

4 August Ulises Solis 108 (Mexico) W RSC 8 Rodel Mayor 108 (Philippines), Allstate Arena, Rosemont, Illinois, USA - IBF. Referee: John O'Brien.

25 August Hugo Cazares 107¾ (Mexico) L PTS 12 Ivan Calderon 107 (Puerto Rico), Ruben Rodriguez Coliseum, Bayamon, Puerto Rico - WBO. Referee: Jose Rivera. Scorecards: 112-115, 112-115, 116-111.

16 September Edgar Sosa 107 (Mexico) W RSC 9 Lorenzo Trejo 108 (Mexico), Hard Rock Hotel & Casino, Las Vegas, Nevada, USA - WBC. Referee: Tony Weeks.

13 October Juan Carlos Reveco 107¾ (Argentina) W CO 5 Humberto Pool 107½ (Mexico), Luna Park Stadium, Buenos Aires, Argentina - WBA. Referee: Hector Afu.

24 November Edgar Sosa 108 (Mexico) W RSC 4 Roberto Leyva 108 (Mexico), Beto Avila Baseball Stadium, Veracruz, Mexico - WBC. Referee: Toby Gibson.

1 December Ivan Calderon 107 (Puerto Rico) W PTS 12 Juan Esquer 108 (Mexico), Tingley Coliseum, Albuquerque, New Mexico, USA - WBO. Referee: Russell Mora. Scorecards: 115-113, 116-112, 118-110.

8 December Juan Carlos Reveco 107½ (Argentina) L PTS 12 Brahim Asloum 107½ (France), Ice Palace, Le Cannet, France - WBA. Referee: Russell Mora. Scorecards: 113-115, 113-116, 112-116.

15 December Ulises Solis 107½ (Mexico) W RSC 9 Bert Batawang 106½ (Philippines), Benito Juarez Auditorium, Guadalajara, Mexico - IBF. Referee: Pat Russell.

9 February Edgar Sosa 107 (Mexico) W PTS 12 Jesus Iribe 106¾ (Mexico), Fair Dome Arena, Leon, Guadalajara, Mexico - WBC. Referee: Laurentino Ramirez. Scorecards: 120-108, 119-109, 120-108.

5 April Ivan Calderon 107¾ (Puerto Rico) W PTS 12 Nelson Dieppa 108 (Puerto Rico), Roberto Clemente Coliseum, San Juan, Puerto Rico - WBO. Referee: Jose Rivera. Scorecards: 120-108, 120-108, 120-108.

14 June Edgar Sosa 108 (Mexico) W RSC 8 Takashi Kunishige 107¼ (Japan), Sports Palace, Mexico City, Mexico - WBC. Referee: Hector Afu.

Flyweight

1 July Takefumi Sakata 111¾ (Japan) W PTS 12 Roberto Vasquez 112 (Panama), Ariake Coliseum, Tokyo, Japan - WBA. Referee: Stan Christodoulou. Scorecards: 116-113, 116-112, 115-113.

7 July Vic Darchinyan 112 (Armenia) L RSC 5 Nonito Donaire 112 (Philippines), Harbor Yard Arena, Bridgeport, Connecticut, USA - IBF. Referee: Eddie Claudio.

18 July Pongsaklek Wonjongkam 112 (Thailand) L PTS 12 Daisuke Naito 112 (Japan), Korakuen Hall, Tokyo, Japan - WBC. Referee: Toby Gibson. Scorecards: 113-115, 113-116, 113-116.

14 September Omar Narvaez 112 (Argentina) W RSC 4 Marlon Marquez 112 (Nicaragua), Number 1 Municipal

Gymnasium, Trelew, Chubut, Argentina - WBO. Referee: Roberto Ramirez.

11 October Daisuke Naito 112 (Japan) W PTS 12 Daiki Kameda 112 (Japan), Ariake Colisium, Tokyo, Japan - WBC. Referee: Vic Drakulich. Scorecards: 117-107, 117-107, 116-108.

4 November Takefumi Sakata 112 (Japan) DREW 12 Denkaosaen Kaovichit 111½ (Thailand), Super Arena, Saitama, Japan - WBA. Referee: Mark Nelson. Scorecards: 113-113, 114-112, 112-115.

1 December Nonito Donaire 111 (Philippines) W RSC 8 Luis Maldonado 111 (Mexico), Foxwoods Casino, Mashantucket, Connecticut, USA - IBF. Referee: Charles Dwyer.

25 January Omar Narvaez 111½ (Argentina) W PTS 12 Carlos Tamara 112 (Colombia), Aurinegro New Palace Arena, Puerto Madryn, Chubut, Argentina - WBO. Referee: Joe Cortez. Scorecards: 119-109, 119-109, 120-108.

8 March Daisuke Naito 112 (Japan) DREW 12 Pongsaklek Wonjongkam 112 (Thailand), Ryogoku Sumo Arena, Tokyo, Japan - WBC. Referee: Hector Afu. Scorecards: 115-113, 114-115, 114-114.

29 March Takefumi Sakata 112 (Japan) W PTS 12 Shingo Yamaguchi 111¾ (Japan), Makuhari-Messe Exhibition Centre, Chiba City, Japan - WBA. Referee: Takeshi Shimakawa. Scorecards: 116-112, 116-112, 115-113.

9 May Omar Narvaez 111½ (Argentina) W RTD 7 Ivan Pozo 111½ (Spain), Central Pavilion, Vigo, Spain - WBO. Referee: Samuel Viruet.

S.Flyweight

13 July Cristian Mijares 115 (Mexico) W RSC 10 Teppei Kikui 115 (Japan), Gomez Palace, Durango, Mexico - WBC. Referee: Frank Garza.

14 July Fernando Montiel 115 (Mexico) W RSC 10 Cecilio Santos 112¾ (Mexico), Tecate Esplanade, Ciudad Obregon, Sonora, Mexico - WBO. Referee: Alejandro Garcia.

24 September Alexander Munoz 115 (Venezuela) W PTS 12 Kuniyuki Aizawa 114¾ (Japan), Korakuen Hall, Tokyo, Japan - WBA. Referee: Luis Pabon. Scorecards: 120-106, 120-107, 118-109.

4 October Fernando Montiel 115 (Mexico) W RSC 12 Luis Melendez 114½ (Colombia), Hard Rock Hotel & Casino, Las Vegas, Nevada, USA - WBO. Referee: Kenny Bayless.

13 October Dimitri Kirilov 114¾ (Russia) W PTS 12 Jose Navarro 114 (USA), Khodynka Ice Palace, Moscow, Russia - IBF. Referee: Samuel Viruet. Scorecards: 116-112, 114-113, 114-113. Contested for the vacant title after Luis Perez (Nicaragua) had been stripped in November 2006.

20 October Cristian Mijares 115 (Mexico) W RSC 1 Franck Gorjux 113¼ (France), Go-Kart Auditorium, Cancun, Mexico - WBC. Referee: Gelasio Perez.

14 January Alexander Munoz 115 (Venezuela) W PTS 12 Katsushige Kawashima 115 (Japan), Cultural Gymnasium, Yokohama, Japan - WBA. Referee: Steve Smoger. Scorecards: 115-113, 117-111, 115-114.

16 February Cristian Mijares 115 (Mexico) W PTS 12 Jose Navarro 115 (USA), MGM Grand, Las Vegas, Nevada, USA - WBC. Referee: Russell Mora. Scorecards: 117-111, 115-113, 108-120.

16 February Fernando Montiel 115 (Mexico) W CO 4 Martin Castillo 115 (Mexico), MGM Grand, Las Vegas, Nevada, USA - WBO. Referee: Joe Cortez.

28 February Dimitri Kirilov 113½ (Russia) DREW 12 Cecilio Santos 115 (Mexico), Roseland Ballroom, NYC, New York - IBF. Referee: Steve Willis. Scorecards: 116-112, 114-114, 114-114.

17 May Cristian Mijares 114¾ (Mexico) W PTS 12 Alexander Munoz 114¾ (Mexico), Centenary Auditorium, Gomez Palacio, Durango, Mexico - WBC/WBA. Referee: Jon Schorle. Scorecards: 115-112, 116-111, 113-115. Following his victory, Mijares was promoted to 'super' champion status by the WBA, thus allowing Rafael Concepcion and AJ Banal to contest the 'secondary' championship.

31 May Fernando Montiel 115 (Mexico) W RSC 3 Luis Maldonado 115 (Mexico), The Bullring, San Luis Potosi, Mexico - WBO. Referee: Raul Caiz (junior).

Bantamweight

7 July Luis Perez 118 (Nicaragua) W RSC 7 Genaro Garcia 118 (Mexico), Harbor Yard Arena, Bridgeport, Connecticut - IBF. Referee: Charles Dyer. Contested for the vacant title after Rafael Marquez (Mexico) handed in his belt just days after winning the WBC super-bantamweight title on 3 March 2007.

11 August Jhonny Gonzalez 117 (Mexico) L CO 7 Gerry Penalosa 118 (Philippines), ARCO Arena, Sacramento, California, USA - WBO. Referee: Pat Russell.

29 September Luis Perez 118 (Nicaragua) L RSC 7 Joseph Agbeko 116¾ (Ghana), Arco Arena, Sacramento, California, USA - IBF. Referee: Dan Stell.

10 January Wladimir Sidorenko 117¾ (Ukraine) W PTS 12 Nobuto Ikehara 118 (Japan), Prefectural Gymnasium, Osaka, Japan - WBA. Referee: Rafael Ramos. Scorecards: 118-110, 116-112, 119-110.

10 January Hozumi Hasegawa 117¾ (Japan) W PTS 12 Simone Maludrottu 117½ (Italy), Prefectural Gymnasium, Osaka, Japan - WBC. Referee: Kenny Bayless. Scorecards: 117-111, 116-112, 118-110.

6 April Gerry Penalosa 118 (Philippines) W RSC 8 Ratanchai Sorvoraphin 118 (Thailand), Araneta Coliseum, Quezon City, Philippines - WBO. Referee: Genaro Rodriguez.

31 May Wladimir Sidorenko 118 (Ukraine) L PTS 12 Anselmo Moreno 117¾ (Panama), Castello Castle-Keeper Arena, Dusseldorf, Germany - WBA. Referee: Luis Pabon. Scorecards: 113-116, 112-116, 112-116.

12 June Hozumi Hasegawa 117½ (Japan) W RSC 2 Cristian Faccio 117¾ (Uruguay), Nihon Budokan Arena, Tokyo, Japan - WBC. Referee: Toby Gibson.

S.Bantamweight

14 July Steve Molitor 120¾ (Canada) W RSC 9 Takalani Ndlovu 121 (South Africa), Rama Casino, Orillia, Ontario, Canada - IBF. Referee: Hubert Earle.

4 August Rafael Marquez 121 (Mexico) L RSC 6 Israel Vazquez 121 (Mexico), Dodge Arena, Hidalgo, Texas, USA - WBC. Referee: Guadalupe Garcia.

4 August Celestino Caballero 121 (Panama) W PTS 12 Jorge Lacierva 121½ (Mexico), Dodge Arena, Hidalgo,

Texas, USA - WBA. Referee: Laurence Cole. Scorecards: 116-110, 115-112, 116-111.

11 August Daniel Ponce de Leon 121¾ (Mexico) W RSC 1 Rey Bautista 121½ (Philippines), ARCO Arena, Sacramento, California, USA - WBO. Referee: Jon Schorle.

27 October Steve Molitor 122 (Canada) W PTS 12 Fahsan 3-K Battery 121½ (Thailand), Rama Casino, Orillia, Ontario, Canada - IBF. Referee: Rocky Zolnierczyk. Scorecards: 119-109, 119-109, 120-108.

1 December Celestino Caballero 122 (Panama) W RSC 8 Mauricio Pastrana 121 (Colombia), Roberto Duran Gymnasium, Panama City, Panama - WBA. Referee: Roberto Ramirez.

8 December Daniel Ponce de Leon 121 (Mexico) W PTS 12 Eduardo Escobedo 122 (Mexico), MGM Grand Garden Arena, Las Vegas, Nevada, USA - WBO. Referee: Kenny Bayless. Scorecards: 115-113, 117-111, 118-110.

19 January Steve Molitor 121½ (Canada) W PTS 12 Ricardo Castillo 122 (Mexico), Rama Casino, Orillia, Ontario, Canada - IBF. Referee: Sam Williams. Scorecards: 118-109, 118-109, 118-109.

1 March Israel Vazquez 122 (Mexico) W PTS 12 Rafael Marquez 121½ (Mexico), Home Depot Centre, Carson, California - WBC. Referee: Pat Russell. Scorecards: 114-111, 113-112, 111-114.

5 April Steve Molitor 121¾ (Canada) W PTS 12 Fernando Beltran 121¼ (Mexico), Rama Casino, Orillia, Ontario, Canada - IBF. Referee: Mark Nelson. Scorecards: 120-107, 120-107, 119-108.

7 June Daniel Ponce de Leon 121 (Mexico) L RSC 1 Juan Manuel Lopez 121 (Puerto Rico), Boardwalk Hall, Atlantic City, New Jersey, USA - WBO. Referee: Michael Ortega.

7 June Celestino Caballero 121 (Panama) W RTD 12 Lorenzo Parra 121 (Venezuela), National Olympic Centre, San Juan de los Morros, Venezuela - WBA. Referee: Luis Pabon.

Featherweight

14 July Steve Luevano 125¾ (USA) W RSC 11 Nicky Cook 125¾ (England), 02 Arena, Greenwich, London, England - WBO. Referee: Dave Parris. Contested for the vacant title after Juan Manuel Marquez (Mexico) had handed back the belt when winning the WBC super-featherweight title on 17 March 2007.

19 August Chris John 125¾ (Indonesia) W RTD 9 Zaiki Takemoto 126 (Japan), Fashion Mart Arena, Kobe, Japan - WBA. Referee: Steve Smoger.

6 October Steve Luevano 126 (USA) W PTS 12 Antonio Davis 126 (USA), Mandalay Bay Events Centre, Las Vegas, Nevada, USA - WBO. Referee: Toby Gibson. Scorecards: 118-109, 119-108, 119-108.

3 November Robert Guerrero 126 (USA) W RSC 1 Martin Honorio 126 (Mexico), Desert Diamond Casino, Tucson, Arizona, USA - IBF. Referee: Tony Weeks.

15 December Jorge Linares 126 (Venezuela) W CO 8 Gamaliel Diaz 126 (Mexico), The Bullring, Cancun, Mexico - WBC. Referee: Laurence Cole. Earlier, on 21 July 2007, in Las Vegas, Nevada, USA, Linares had stopped Oscar Larios (Mexico) in the tenth round of a contest to decide the vacant WBC 'interim' title. Ten days later, on 31 July, South

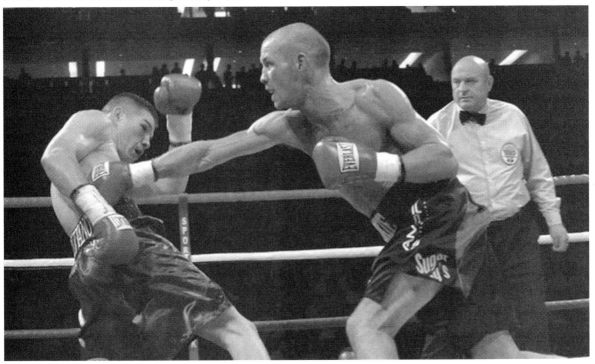

Despite going well at times, England's Nicky Cook (right) was well beaten by Steve Luevano in their contest for the vacant WBO featherweight title last year

Les Clark

Korea's In-Jin Chi announced that he was relinquishing the main title and following that Linares was proclaimed the new champion. On 31 May 2008, Oscar Larios (Mexico) stopped Feider Viloria (Colombia) in the fifth round at Chetumal, Quintana Roo, Mexico to win the vacant WBC 'interim' title.

26 January Chris John 126 (Indonesia) W RTD 7 Roinet Caballero 125½ (Panama), Gelora Bung Karno Stadium, Jakarta, Indonesia - WBA. Referee: Raul Caiz (junior). Judge: Paul Thomas.

29 February Robert Guerrero 126 (USA) W CO 8 Jason Litzau 125 (USA), Tachi Palace Hotel & Casino, Lemoore, California, USA - IBF. Referee: David Mendoza. Guerrero relinquished the IBF title in June to move up a weight division.

15 March Steve Luevano 126 (USA) W PTS 12 Terdsak Jandaeng 126 (Thailand), Mandalay Bay Events Centre, Las Vegas, Nevada, USA - WBO. Referee: Robert Byrd. Scorecards: 118-109, 119-109, 119-109.

28 June Steve Luevano 126 (USA) DREW 12 Mario Santiago 125 (Puerto Rico), Mandalay Bay Resort & Casino, Las Vegas, Nevada, USA - WBO. Referee: Tony Weeks. Scorecards: 117-111, 113-115, 114-114.

S.Featherweight

31 August Mzonke Fana 128¼ (South Africa) W CO 9 Javier Alvarez 129 (Argentina), Civic Centre, Klerksdorp, South Africa - IBF. Referee: Deon Dwarte.

3 November Juan Manuel Marquez 128 (Mexico) W PTS 12 Rocky Juarez 129 (USA), Desert Diamond Casino, Tucson, Arizona, USA - WBC. Referee: Bobby Ferrara. Scorecards: 117-111, 118-110, 120-108.

17 November Joan Guzman 129¾ (Dominican Republic) W PTS 12 Humberto Sosa 130 (Mexico), Borgata Hotel Casino, Atlantic City, New Jersey, USA - WBO. Referee: Harvey Dock. Scorecards: 117-111, 117-111, 118-110. On 15 December, Alex Arthur (Scotland) successfully defended the WBO 'interim' title when outpointing Steve Foster (England) over 12 rounds in Edinburgh, Scotland and with Guzman being forced to move up in weight the Scot was confirmed as being the WBO champion in May 2008.

15 December Edwin Valero 130 (Venezuela) W RSC 3 Zaid Zavaleta 130 (Mexico), The Bullring, Cancun, Mexico - WBA. Referee: Luis Pabon.

15 March Juan Manuel Marquez 130 (Mexico) L PTS 12 Manny Pacquiao 129 (Philippines), (Mexico), Mandalay Bay Events Centre, Las Vegas, Nevada, USA - WBC. Referee: Kenny Bayless. Scorecards: 112-115, 113-114, 115-112. Pacquiao relinquished the title in June in order to challenge David Diaz for the WBC lightweight crown in Las Vegas on 28 June. On that same bill, Francisco Lorenzo (Dominican Republic) beat Mexico's Humberto Soto by a fourth-round disqualification to win the vacant WBC 'interim' title.

12 April Mzonke Fana 128¾ (South Africa) L PTS 12 Cassius Baloyi 129 (South Africa), University Sports Complex, Mafikeng, South Africa - IBF. Referee: Luis Pabon. Scorecards: 111-117, Mickey Vann 112-116, 114-114.

12 June Edwin Valero 129¾ (Venezuela) W RSC 7 Takehiro

Shimada 129¾ (Japan), Nihon Budokan Arena, Tokyo, Japan - WBA. Referee: Guillermo Perez Pineda.

Lightweight

4 August David Diaz 133¾ (USA) W PTS 12 Erik Morales 135 (Mexico), Allstate Arena, Rosemont, Illinois, USA - WBC. Referee: Benji Estevez. Scorecards: 114-113, 115-113, 115-112. On 10 November, Joel Casamayor (Cuba) retained the WBC 'interim' title when outpointing Jose Armando Santa Cruz (Mexico) in NYC, New York.

13 October Juan Diaz 135 (USA) W RSC 9 Julio Diaz 135 (USA), Sears Centre, Hoffman Estates, Illinois, USA - WBA/IBF/WBO. Referee: Genaro Rodriguez. In a battle of namesakes, Juan Diaz captured Julio Diaz's IBF title following his victory. With Diaz being proclaimed the WBA 'super' champion, Jose Alfaro (Nicaragua) outpointed Prawet Singwancha (Thailand) over 12 rounds in Bielefeld, Germany on 29 December to win the WBA 'secondary' title.

8 March Juan Diaz 134 (USA) L PTS 12 Nate Campbell 134½ (USA, The Bullring, Cancun, Mexico - WBA/WBO/IBF. Referee: Jesus Salcedo. Scorecards: 111-116, 112-15, 114-113. On 22 March at the Morongo Casino Resort, Cabazon, California, USA, Joel Casamayor (Cuba) won the WBO 'interim' title when beating Australia's Michael Katsidis (w rsc 10). Casemayor already held the WBC version. The WBA 'secondary' title changed hands when Yusuke Kobori (Japan) stopped Jose Alfaro (Nicaragua) in Tokyo, Japan on 19 May.

28 June David Diaz 135 (USA) L RSC 9 Manny Pacquiao 134½ (Philippines), Mandalay Bay Resort & Casino, Las Vegas, Nevada, USA - WBC. Referee: Vic Drakulich.

L.Welterweight

21 July Souleymane M'Baye 139½ (France) L PTS 12 Gavin Rees 139½ (Wales), International Arena, Cardiff, Wales - WBA. Referee: Stan Christodoulou. Scorecards: Paul Thomas 112-117, John Coyle 113-117, 110-118.

1 September Ricardo Torres 140 (Colombia) W RSC 11 Kendall Holt 139¾ (USA), Jumbo Saloon Country Club, Barranquilla, Colombia - WBO. Referee: Genaro Rodriguez.

7 September Junior Witter 139½ (England) W CO 7 Vivian Harris 139½ (Guyana), Dome Leisure Centre, Doncaster, England - WBC. Referee: Daniel van der Wiele.

5 January Paul Malignaggi 139 (USA) W PTS 12 Herman Ngoudjo 140 (Cameroon), Bally's Hotel & Casino, Atlantic City, New Jersey, USA - IBF. Referee: Allan Huggins. Scorecards: 117-111, 115-113, 116-113.

22 March Gavin Rees 140 (Wales) L RSC 12 Andreas Kotelnik 140 (Ukraine), International Arena, Cardiff, Wales - WBA. Referee: Luis Pabon.

10 May Junior Witter 139¾ (England) L PTS 12 Tim Bradley 139½ (USA), Trent FM Arena, Nottingham, England - WBC. Referee: Massimo Barrovecchio. Scorecards: 113-115, 113-114, 115-112.

24 May Paul Malignaggi 139¾ (USA) W PTS 12 Lovemore Ndou 139 (South Africa), City of Manchester Stadium, Manchester, England - IBF. Referee: Mickey Vann. Scorecards: Dave Parris 116-112, Victor Loughlin 116-113,

Phil Edwards 114-115.

24 May Ricky Hatton 140 (England) W PTS 12 Juan Lazcano 139¾ (Mexico), City of Manchester Stadium, Manchester, England - IBO. Referee: Howard Foster. Scorecards: Marcus McDonnell 120-110, 118-110, 120-108.

Welterweight

14 July Kermit Cintron 146 (Puerto Rico) W CO 2 Walter Matthysse 147 (Argentina), Boardwalk Hall, Atlantic City, New Jersey, USA - IBF. Referee: Earl Morton.

14 July Antonio Margarito 145¾ (Mexico) L PTS 12 Paul Williams 145½ (USA), Home Depot Centre, Carson, California, USA - WBO. Referee: Lou Moret. Scorecards: 113-115, 113-115, 112-116.

10 November Miguel Cotto 146¼ (Puerto Rico) W PTS 12 Shane Mosley 146¼ (USA), Madison Square Garden, NYC, New York, USA - WBA. Referee: Benji Estevez (junior). Scorecards: 115-113, 116-113, 115-113. On 8 December, in Le Cannet, France, Yuri Nuzhnenko (Ukraine) outpointed Frederic Klose (France) over 12 rounds to win the WBA 'interim' title.

23 November Kermit Cintron 146¾ (Puerto Rico) W RSC 10 Jesse Feliciano 147 (USA), Staples Centre, Los Angeles, California, USA - IBF. Referee: Jon Schorle.

8 December Floyd Mayweather 147 (USA) W RSC 10 Ricky Hatton 145 (England), MGM Grand Garden Arena, Las Vegas, Nevada, USA - WBC. Referee: Joe Cortez. Following Mayweather's announcement on 6 June 2008 that he was retiring, a forthcoming match between Andre Berto (USA) and Miguel Angel Rodriguez (Mexico) was recognised by the WBC as being for the vacant title.

9 February Paul Williams 146¾ (USA) L PTS 12 Carlos Quintana 146¾ (Puerto Rico), Pechanga Resort & Casino, Temecula, California, USA - WBO. Referee: Jack Reese. Scorecards: 113-115, 112-116, 112-116.

12 April Miguel Cotto 146½ (Puerto Rico) W RTD 5 Alfonso Gomez 147 (USA), Boardwalk Hall, Atlantic City, New Jersey, USA - WBA. Referee: Randy Neumann. Defending the WBA 'interim' title, Yuri Nuzhnenko (Ukraine) retained his title following a ten-round technical draw against Irving Garcia (Puerto Rico) on 19 April in Kiev, Ukraine.

12 April Kermit Cintron 146½ (Puerto Rico) L CO 6 Antonio Margarito 146½ (Mexico), Boardwalk Hall, Atlantic City, New Jerset, USA - IBF. Referee: Earl Brown. Margarito relinquished the IBF title in May in order to take on Miguel Cotto for the latter's WBA crown.

7 June Carlos Quintana 146 (Puerto Rico) L RSC 1 Paul Williams 145¾ (USA), Mohegan Sun Casino, Uncasville, Connecticut, USA - WBO. Referee: Eddie Claudio.

21 June Andre Berto 146 (USA) W RSC 7 Miguel Angel Rodriguez 145 (Mexico), FedEx Forum, Memphis, Tennessee, USA - WBC. Referee: Laurence Cole.

L.Middleweight

7 July Travis Simms 152½ (USA) L PTS 12 Joachim Alcine 152¼ (Haiti), Harbour Yard Arena, Bridgeport, Connecticut, USA - WBA. Referee: Michael Ortega. Scorecards: 110-115, 109-116, 111-114.

28 July Vernon Forrest 154 (USA) W PTS 12 Carlos

Baldomir 154 (Argentina), Emerald Queen Casino, Tacoma, Washington - WBC. Referee: Michael Ortega. Referee: Jose Rivera. Scorecards: 118-109, 116-111, 118-109. Contested for the vacant title after Floyd Mayweather (USA) handed back his belt in June, preferring to hold on to the WBC welterweight crown.

1 December Vernon Forrest 153 (USA) W RSC 11 Michele Piccirillo 152 (Italy), Foxwoods Casino, Mashantucket, Connecticut, USA - WBC. Referee: Arthur Mercante (junior).

7 December Joachim Alcine 152¼ (Haiti) W RSC 12 Alfonso Mosquera 153 (Panama), Bell Centre, Montreal, Quebec, Canada - WBA. Referee: Michael Griffin.

27 March Cory Spinks 153 (USA) L PTS 12 Verno Phillips 153 (Belize), Scot Trade Centre, St Louis, Missouri, USA - IBF. Referee: Gerald Scott. Scorecards: 113-115, 112-116, 115-113.

26 April Sergei Dzindziruk 153 (Ukraine) W PTS 12 Lukas Konecny 153 (Czech Republic), Freiberger Arena, Dresden, Germany - WBO. Referee: Samuel Viruet. Scorecards: 118-110, 115-113, 114-114.

7 June Vernon Forrest 153¾ (USA) L PTS 12 Sergio Mora 154 (Mexico), Mohegan Sun Casino, Uncasville, Connecticut, USA - WBC. Referee: Dick Flaherty. Scorecards: 112-116, 113-115, 114-114.

Middleweight

18 August Arthur Abraham 160 (Armenia) W CO 11 Khoren Gevor 160 (Armenia), Max Schmeling Hall, Berlin, Germany - IBF. Referee: Pete Podgorski. Judges: Mickey Vann, Dave Parris.

29 September Jermain Taylor 159 (USA) L RSC 7 Kelly Pavlik 159½ (USA), Boardwalk Hall, Atlantic City, New Jersey, USA - WBC/WBO. Referee: Steve Smoger. A return match made six pounds above the middleweight limit saw Pavlik outpoint Taylor over 12 rounds at the MGM Grand, Nevada on 16 February 2008.

20 October Felix Sturm 159¾ (Germany) DREW 12 Randy Griffin 159½ (USA), Gerry Weber Stadium, Halle, Germany - WBA. Referee: Guillermo Perez Pineda. Scorecards: 115-114, 114-117, 114-114.

8 December Arthur Abraham 160 (Armenia) W RSC 5 Wayne Elcock 159 (England), St Jakob Hall, Basle, Switzerland - IBF. Referee: Wayne Kelly.

29 March Arthur Abraham 159¾ (Armenia) W CO 12 Elvin Ayala 159¾ (USA), Sparkassen Arena, Kiel, Germany - IBF. Referee: Roberto Ramirez.

5 April Felix Sturm 158¾ (Germany) W RSC 7 Jamie Pittman 160 (Australia), Castello Castle-Keeper Arena, Dusseldorf, Germany - WBA. Referee: Russell Mora.

7 June Kelly Pavlik 159 (USA) W RSC 3 Gary Lockett 159½ (Wales), Boardwalk Hall, Atlantic City, New Jersey, USA - WBO/WBC. Referee: Eddie Cotton.

S.Middleweight

19 October Alejandro Berrio 167 (Colombia) L RSC 11 Lucian Bute 167¾ (Romania), Bell Centre, Montreal, Canada - IBF. Referee: Marlon Wright.

3 November Joe Calzaghe 167½ (Wales) W PTS 12 Mikkel

Kessler 168 (Denmark), Millenium Stadium, Cardiff, Wales - WBA/WBC/WBO. Referee: Michael Ortega. Scorecards: 117-111, 116-112, 116-112. Following his victory, Calzaghe took over Kessler's WBC/WBA titles. On 10 December, in Sydney, Australia, Anthony Mundine (Australia) knocked out Jose Alberto Clavero (Argentina) inside four rounds to retain the WBA 'secondary' title prior to outpointing Nader Hamdan (Australia) over 12 rounds on 27 February 2008 at the Entertainment Centre, Sydney, Australia in another defence. The day after Mundine made another successful defence when outpointing fellow-Australian Sam Soliman over 12 rounds in Melbourne, Australia on 28 May 2008 he relinquished the title in order to drop down a weight division. Following that, Kessler knocked out Kazakhstan's Dimitri Sartison inside 12 rounds in Copenhagen, Denmark on 21 June 2008 to regain his old title, bearing in mind that Calzaghe continued to be recognised as the 'super' champion. At the end of June, Calzaghe relinquished the WBC title to pursue a fight at the light-heavyweight limit against Roy Jones and England's Carl Froch was selected to meet Jermain Taylor (USA) to decide the vacant crown.

29 February Lucian Bute 167½ (Romania) W RSC 10 William Joppy 167¾ (USA), Bell Centre, Montreal, Canada - IBF. Referee: Marlon Wright.

L.Heavyweight

29 September Chad Dawson 172¾ (USA) W RSC 4 Epifanio Mendoza 175 (Colombia), Arco Arena, Sacramento, California, USA - WBC. Referee: Jon Schorle. Judge: John Keane.

29 September Clinton Woods 174½ (England) W PTS 12 Julio Gonzalez 173½ (Mexico), Hallam FM Arena, Sheffield, England - IBF. Referee: Dave Parris. Scorecards: 115-113, 117-111, 116-112.

24 November Zsolt Erdei 173½ (Hungary) W PTS 12 Tito Mendoza 174 (Panama), Freiberger Arena, Dresden, Germany - WBO. Referee: Samuel Viruet. Scorecards: 116-112, 117-111, 111-117.

1 December Antonio Tarver 175 (USA) W RSC 4 Danny Santiago 174 (USA), Foxwoods Casino, Mashantucket, Connecticut, USA - IBO. Referee: Steve Smoger.

16 December Stipe Drews 174½ (Croatia) L PTS 12 Danny Green 174½ (Australia), Challenge Stadium, Mount Claremont, Perth, Australia - WBA. Referee: Takeshi Shimakawa. Scorecards: 111-118, 110-118, 108-120. Having fulfilled his lifetime ambition of winning a title, Green announced at the end of March 2008 that he was hanging up his gloves with immediate effect to concentrate on his family and to preserve his health.

12 April Clinton Woods 175 (England) L PTS 12 Antonio Tarver 173¾ (USA), St Petersburg Times Forum, Tampa, Florida, USA - IBF/IBO. Referee: Frank Santore junior. Scorecards: Howard Foster 109-119, 111-117, 112-116.

12 April Chad Dawson 173¾ (USA) W PTS 12 Glengoffe Johnson 172½ (Jamaica), St Petersburg Times Forum, Tampa, Florida, USA - WBC. Referee: Tommy Kimmons. Scorecards: 116-112, 116-112, 116-112. On 19 April in Bucharest, Romania, Adrian Diaconu (Romania) outpointed Chris Henry (USA) over 12 rounds to win the vacant WBC

'interim' title.

26 April Zsolt Erdei 173¼ (Hungary) W PTS 12 DeAndrey Abron 173 (USA), Freiberger Arena, Dresden, Germany - WBO. Referee: Roberto Ramirez. Scorecards: 119-109, 119-109, 119-109.

Cruiserweight

21 July Enzo Maccarinelli 194 (Wales) W PTS 12 Wayne Braithwaite 195¼ (Guyana), International Arena, Cardiff, Wales - WBO. Referee: Mickey Vann. Scorecards: 118-109, 120-107, 119-108.

3 November Enzo Maccarinelli 197¾ (Wales) W RSC 4 Mohamed Azzaoui 197¾ (Algeria), Millennium Stadium, Cardiff, Wales - WBO. Referee: Dave Parris. Judge: Roy Francis.

10 November Jean-Marc Mormeck 199 (Guadeloupe) L RSC 7 David Haye 199½ (England), Marcel Cerdan Sports Palace, Paris, France - WBC/WBA. Referee: Franco Ciminale. On 24 November, at the Freiberger Arena, Dresden, Germany, Firat Arslan (Germany) retained his WBA 'interim' title when outpointing Virgil Hill (USA) over 12 rounds.

29 December Steve Cunningham 192¾ (USA) W RSC 12 Marco Huck 198½ (Germany), Seidensticker Hall, Bielefeld, Germany - IBF. Referee: Marlon Wright.

8 March David Haye 198 (England) W RSC 2 Enzo Maccarinelli 197 (Wales), O2 Arena, Greenwich, London, England - WBA/WBC/WBO. Referee: John Keane. Judges: John Coyle, Paul Thomas, Larry O'Connell. By his victory, Haye took over Maccarinelli's WBO title. On 3 May Firat Arslan outpointed Darnell Wilson (USA) over 12 rounds in Stuttgart, Germany to retain the WBA 'interim' title. Having decided to move up to the heavyweight division, Haye relinquished the WBC title on 12 May and a short while later notified the WBA that he would be sending back his belt. Following that Arslan was handed full title honours on 16 June.

Heavyweight

7 July Vladimir Klitschko 243½ (Kazakhstan) W RTD 6 Lamon Brewster 228¼ (USA), The Arena, Cologne, Germany - IBF. Referee: Sam Williams.

13 October Sultan Ibragimov 219 (Russia) W PTS 12 Evander Holyfield 211½ (USA), Khodynka Ice Palace, Moscow, Russia - WBO. Referee: Raul Caiz. Scorecards: 117-111, 117-111, 118-110.

19 January Ruslan Chagaev 229¼ (Uzbekistan) W PTS 12 Matt Skelton 254¾ (England), Castello Castle-Keeper Arena, Dusseldorf, Germany - WBA. Referee: Guillermo Pineda Perez. Scorecards: 117-110, 117-112, 117-111.

23 February Vladimir Klitschko 238 (Kazakhstan) W PTS 12 Sultan Ibragimov 219 (Russia), Madison Square Garden, NYC, New York, USA - IBF/WBO. Referee: Wayne Kelly. Scorecards: 119-110, 117-111, 118-110. By his victory, Klitschko picked up Ibragimov's WBO title belt as well as making a successful defence of the IBF championship.

8 March Oleg Maskaev 243 (Kazakhstan) L RSC 6 Samuel Peter 250 (Nigeria), The Bullring, Cancun, Mexico - WBC. Referee: Lupe Garcia.

World Champions Since Gloves, 1889-2008

Since I began to carry out extensive research into world championship boxing from the very beginnings of gloved action, I discovered much that needed to be amended regarding the historical listings as we know them, especially prior to the 1920s. Although yet to finalise my researches, despite making considerable changes, the listings are the most comprehensive ever published. Bearing all that in mind, and using a wide range of American newspapers, the aim has been to discover just who had claims, valid or otherwise. Studying the records of all the recognised champions, supplied by Professor Luckett Davis and his team, fights against all opposition have been analysed to produce the ultimate data. Because there were no boxing commissions as such in America prior to the 1920s, the yardstick used to determine valid claims were victories over the leading fighters of the day and recognition given within the newspapers. Only where that criteria has been met have I adjusted previous information. Please note that weight limits for the bantam (1919), feather (1921), light (1913), welter (1921) and middleweight (1921) divisions were only universally recognised in the years stated in brackets. Prior to that the champions shown would have won title claims at varying weights, which were massaged in later years to fit the modern weight classes.

Championship Status Code:

AU = Austria; AUST = Australia; CALIF = California; CAN = Canada; CLE = Cleveland Boxing Commission; EBU = European Boxing Union; FL = Florida; FR = France; GB = Great Britain; GEO = Georgia; H = Hawaii; IBF = International Boxing Federation; IBU = International Boxing Union; ILL = Illinois; LOUIS = Louisiana; MARY = Maryland; MASS = Massachusetts; MICH = Michigan; NBA = National Boxing Association; NC = North Carolina; NY = New York; PEN = Pennsylvania; SA = South Africa; TBC = Territorial Boxing Commission; USA = United States; WBA = World Boxing Association; WBC = World Boxing Council; WBO = World Boxing Organisation.

Champions in **bold** are accorded universal recognition.

*Undefeated champions (Only relates to universally recognised champions prior to 1962 and thereafter WBA/WBC/IBF/ WBO champions, apart from the odd occasion. Does not include men who forfeited titles).

Title Holder	Birthplace	Tenure	Status
M. Flyweight (105 lbs)			
Kyung-Yung Lee*	S Korea	1987	IBF
Hiroki Ioka	Japan	1987-1988	WBC
Silvio Gamez*	Venezuela	1988-1989	WBA
Samuth Sithnaruepol	Thailand	1988-1989	IBF
Napa Kiatwanchai	Thailand	1988-1989	WBC
Bong-Jun Kim	S Korea	1989-1991	WBA
Nico Thomas	Indonesia	1989	IBF
Rafael Torres	Dom Republic	1989-1992	WBO
Eric Chavez	Philippines	1989-1990	IBF
Jum-Hwan Choi	S Korea	1989-1990	WBC
Hideyuki Ohashi	Japan	1990	WBC
Fahlan Lukmingkwan	Thailand	1990-1992	IBF
Ricardo Lopez*	Mexico	1990-1997	WBC
Hi-Yon Choi	S Korea	1991-1992	WBA
Manny Melchor	Philippines	1992	IBF
Hideyuki Ohashi	Japan	1992-1993	WBA
Ratanapol Sowvoraphin	Thailand	1992-1996	IBF
Chana Porpaoin	Thailand	1993-1995	WBA
Paul Weir*	Scotland	1993-1994	WBO
Alex Sanchez	Puerto Rico	1993-1997	WBO
Rosendo Alvarez	Nicaragua	1995-1998	WBA
Ratanapol Sowvoraphin	Thailand	1996-1997	IBF
Ricardo Lopez*	Mexico	1997-1998	WBC/WBO
Zolani Petelo*	S Africa	1997-2000	IBF
Ricardo Lopez*	Mexico	1998	WBC
Eric Jamili	Philippines	1998	WBO
Kermin Guardia*	Colombia	1998-2002	WBO
Ricardo Lopez*	Mexico	1998-1999	WBA/WBC
Wandee Chor Chareon	Thailand	1999-2000	WBC
Nohel Arambulet	Venezuela	1999-2000	WBA
Jose Antonio Aguirre	Mexico	2000-2004	WBC
Jomo Gamboa	Philippines	2000	WBA
Keitaro Hoshino	Japan	2000-2001	WBA
Chana Porpaoin	Thailand	2001	WBA
Roberto Levya	Mexico	2001-2003	IBF
Yutaka Niida*	Japan	2001	WBA
Keitaro Hoshino	Japan	2002	WBA
Jorge Mata	Spain	2002-2003	WBO
Nohel Arambulet	Venezuela	2002-2004	WBA
Miguel Barrera	Colombia	2002-2003	IBF
Eduardo Marquez	Nicaragua	2003	WBO
Ivan Calderon*	Puerto Rico	2003-2007	WBO
Edgar Cardenas	Mexico	2003	IBF
Daniel Reyes	Colombia	2003-2004	IBF
Eagle Kyowa	Thailand	2004	WBC
Muhammad Rachman	Indonesia	2004-2007	IBF
Yutaka Niida	Japan	2004-	WBA
Isaac Bustos	Mexico	2004-2005	WBC
Katsunari Takayama	Japan	2005	WBC
Eagle Kyowa	Thailand	2005-2007	WBC
Florante Condes	Philippines	2007-2008	IBF
Donnie Nietes	Philippines	2007-	WBO
Oleydong Sithsamerchai	Thailand	2007-	WBC
Raul Garcia	Mexico	2008-	IBF
L. Flyweight (108 lbs)			
Franco Udella	Italy	1975	WBC
Jaime Rios	Panama	1975-1976	WBA
Luis Estaba	Venezuela	1975-1978	WBC
Juan Guzman	Dom Republic	1976	WBA
Yoko Gushiken	Japan	1976-1981	WBA
Freddie Castillo	Mexico	1978	WBC
Sor Vorasingh	Thailand	1978	WBC
Sun-Jun Kim	S Korea	1978-1980	WBC
Shigeo Nakajima	Japan	1980	WBC
Hilario Zapata	Panama	1980-1982	WBC
Pedro Flores	Mexico	1981	WBA
Hwan-Jin Kim	S Korea	1981	WBA
Katsuo Tokashiki	Japan	1981-1983	WBA
Amado Ursua	Mexico	1982	WBC
Tadashi Tomori	Japan	1982	WBC
Hilario Zapata	Panama	1982-1983	WBC
Jung-Koo Chang*	S Korea	1983-1988	WBC
Lupe Madera	Mexico	1983-1984	WBA
Dodie Penalosa	Philippines	1983-1986	IBF
Francisco Quiroz	Dom Republic	1984-1985	WBA
Joey Olivo	USA	1985	WBA

Title Holder	Birthplace	Tenure	Status
Myung-Woo Yuh	S Korea	1985-1991	WBA
Jum-Hwan Choi	S Korea	1986-1988	IBF
Tacy Macalos	Philippines	1988-1989	IBF
German Torres	Mexico	1988-1989	WBC
Yul-Woo Lee	S Korea	1989	WBC
Muangchai Kitikasem	Thailand	1989-1990	IBF
Jose de Jesus	Puerto Rico	1989-1992	WBO
Humberto Gonzalez	Mexico	1989-1990	WBC
Michael Carbajal*	USA	1990-1993	IBF
Rolando Pascua	Philippines	1990-1991	WBC
Melchor Cob Castro	Mexico	1991	WBC
Humberto Gonzalez	Mexico	1991-1993	WBC
Hiroki Ioka	Japan	1991-1992	WBA
Josue Camacho	Puerto Rico	1992-1994	WBO
Myung-Woo Yuh*	S Korea	1992-1993	WBA
Michael Carbajal	USA	1993-1994	IBF/WBC
Silvio Gamez	Venezuela	1993-1995	WBA
Humberto Gonzalez	Mexico	1994-1995	WBC/IBF
Michael Carbajal*	USA	1994	WBO
Paul Weir	Scotland	1994-1995	WBO
Hi-Yong Choi	S Korea	1995-1996	WBA
Saman Sorjaturong*	Thailand	1995	WBC/IBF
Jacob Matlala*	South Africa	1995-1997	WBO
Saman Sorjaturong	Thailand	1995-1999	WBC
Carlos Murillo	Panama	1996	WBA
Michael Carbajal	USA	1996-1997	IBF
Keiji Yamaguchi	Japan	1996	WBA
Pichitnoi Chor Siriwat	Thailand	1996-2000	WBA
Mauricio Pastrana	Colombia	1997-1998	IBF
Jesus Chong	Mexico	1997	WBO
Melchor Cob Castro	Mexico	1997-1998	WBO
Mauricio Pastrana	Colombia	1997-1998	IBF
Juan Domingo Cordoba	Argentina	1998	WBO
Jorge Arce	Mexico	1998-1999	WBO
Will Grigsby	USA	1998-1999	IBF
Michael Carbajal*	USA	1999-2000	WBO
Ricardo Lopez*	Mexico	1999-2002	IBF
Yo-Sam Choi	S Korea	1999-2002	WBC
Masibuleke Makepula*	S Africa	2000	WBO
Will Grigsby	USA	2000	WBO
Beibis Mendoza	Colombia	2000-2001	WBA
Rosendo Alvarez	Nicaragua	2001-2004	WBA
Nelson Dieppa	Puerto Rico	2001-2005	WBO
Jorge Arce*	Mexico	2002-2005	WBC
Jose Victor Burgos	Mexico	2003-2004	IBF
Erick Ortiz	Mexico	2005	WBC
Roberto Vasquez*	Panama	2005-2006	WBA
Hugo Cazares	Mexico	2005-2007	WBO
Will Grigsby	USA	2005-2006	IBF
Brian Viloria	USA	2005-2006	WBC
Ulises Solis	Mexico	2006-	IBF
Koki Kameda*	Japan	2006-2007	WBA
Omar Nino	Mexico	2006-2007	WBC
Edgar Sosa	Mexico	2007-	WBC
Juan Carlos Reveco	Argentina	2007	WBA
Ivan Calderon	Puerto Rico	2007-	WBO
Brahim Asloum	France	2007-	WBA

Flyweight (112 lbs)

Title Holder	Birthplace	Tenure	Status
Johnny Coulon	Canada	1910	USA
Sid Smith	England	1911-1913	GB
Sid Smith	England	1913	GB/IBU
Bill Ladbury	England	1913-1914	GB/IBU
Percy Jones	Wales	1914	GB/IBU
Tancy Lee	Scotland	1915	GB/IBU
Joe Symonds	England	1915-1916	GB/IBU
Jimmy Wilde	Wales	1916	GB/IBU
Jimmy Wilde	Wales	1916-1923	
Pancho Villa*	Philippines	1923-1925	
Fidel la Barba	USA	1925-1927	NBA/CALIF
Fidel la Barba*	USA	1927	
Pinky Silverberg	USA	1927	NBA

Title Holder	Birthplace	Tenure	Status
Johnny McCoy	USA	1927-1928	CALIF
Izzy Schwartz	USA	1927-1929	NY
Frenchy Belanger	Canada	1927-1928	NBA
Newsboy Brown	Russia	1928	CALIF
Johnny Hill	Scotland	1928-1929	GB
Frankie Genaro	USA	1928-1929	NBA
Emile Pladner	France	1929	NBA/IBU
Frankie Genaro	USA	1929-1931	NBA/IBU
Midget Wolgast	USA	1930-1935	NY
Young Perez	Tunisia	1931-1932	NBA/IBU
Jackie Brown	England	1932-1935	NBA/IBU
Jackie Brown	England	1935	GB/NBA
Benny Lynch	Scotland	1935-1937	GB/NBA
Small Montana	Philippines	1935-1937	NY/CALIF
Valentin Angelmann	France	1936-1938	IBU
Peter Kane*	England	1938-1939	NBA/NY/GB/IBU
Little Dado	Philippines	1938-1939	CALIF
Little Dado	Philippines	1939-1943	NBA/CALIF
Jackie Paterson	Scotland	1943-1947	
Jackie Paterson	Scotland	1947-1948	GB/NY
Rinty Monaghan	Ireland	1947-1948	NBA
Rinty Monaghan*	Ireland	1948-1950	
Terry Allen	England	1950	
Dado Marino	Hawaii	1950-1952	
Yoshio Shirai	Japan	1952-1954	
Pascual Perez	Argentina	1954-1960	
Pone Kingpetch	Thailand	1960-1962	

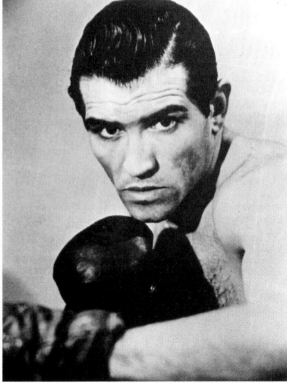

Pascual Perez

Title Holder	Birthplace	Tenure	Status
Fighting Harada	Japan	1962-1963	
Pone Kingpetch	Thailand	1963	
Hiroyuki Ebihara	Japan	1963-1964	
Pone Kingpetch	Thailand	1964-1965	
Salvatore Burruni	Italy	1965	
Salvatore Burruni	Italy	1965-1966	WBC

Terry Allen

Title Holder	Birthplace	Tenure	Status
Horacio Accavallo*	Argentina	1966-1968	WBA
Walter McGowan	Scotland	1966	WBC
Chartchai Chionoi	Thailand	1966-1969	WBC
Efren Torres	Mexico	1969-1970	WBC
Hiroyuki Ebihara	Japan	1969	WBA
Bernabe Villacampo	Philippines	1969-1970	WBA
Chartchai Chionoi	Thailand	1970	WBC
Berkrerk Chartvanchai	Thailand	1970	WBA
Masao Ohba*	Japan	1970-1973	WBA
Erbito Salavarria	Philippines	1970-1971	WBC
Betulio Gonzalez	Venezuela	1971-1972	WBC
Venice Borkorsor*	Thailand	1972-1973	WBC
Chartchai Chionoi	Thailand	1973-1974	WBA
Betulio Gonzalez	Venezuela	1973-1974	WBC
Shoji Oguma	Japan	1974-1975	WBC
Susumu Hanagata	Japan	1974-1975	WBA
Miguel Canto	Mexico	1975-1979	WBC
Erbito Salavarria	Philippines	1975-1976	WBA
Alfonso Lopez	Panama	1976	WBA
Guty Espadas	Mexico	1976-1978	WBA
Betulio Gonzalez	Venezuela	1978-1979	WBA
Chan-Hee Park	S Korea	1979-1980	WBC
Luis Ibarra	Panama	1979-1980	WBA
Tae-Shik Kim	S Korea	1980	WBA
Shoji Oguma	Japan	1980-1981	WBC
Peter Mathebula	S Africa	1980-1981	WBA
Santos Laciar	Argentina	1981	WBA
Antonio Avelar	Mexico	1981-1982	WBC
Luis Ibarra	Panama	1981	WBA
Juan Herrera	Mexico	1981-1982	WBA
Prudencio Cardona	Colombia	1982	WBC
Santos Laciar*	Argentina	1982-1985	WBA
Freddie Castillo	Mexico	1982	WBC
Eleonicio Mercedes	Dom Republic	1982-1983	WBC
Charlie Magri	Tunisia	1983	WBC
Frank Cedeno	Philippines	1983-1984	WBC
Soon-Chun Kwon	S Korea	1983-1985	IBF
Koji Kobayashi	Japan	1984	WBC
Gabriel Bernal	Mexico	1984	WBC
Sot Chitalada	Thailand	1984-1988	WBC
Hilario Zapata	Panama	1985-1987	WBA
Chong-Kwan Chung	S Korea	1985-1986	IBF
Bi-Won Chung	S Korea	1986	IBF
Hi-Sup Shin	S Korea	1986-1987	IBF
Fidel Bassa	Colombia	1987-1989	WBA
Dodie Penalosa	Philippines	1987	IBF
Chang-Ho Choi	S Korea	1987-1988	IBF
Rolando Bohol	Philippines	1988	IBF
Yong-Kang Kim	S Korea	1988-1989	WBC
Duke McKenzie	England	1988-1989	IBF
Elvis Alvarez*	Colombia	1989	WBO
Sot Chitalada	Thailand	1989-1991	WBC
Dave McAuley	Ireland	1989-1992	IBF
Jesus Rojas	Venezuela	1989-1900	WBA
Yukihito Tamakuma	Japan	1990-1991	WBA
Isidro Perez	Mexico	1990-1992	WBO
Yul-Woo Lee	S Korea	1990	WBA
Muangchai Kitikasem	Thailand	1991-1992	WBC
Elvis Alvarez	Colombia	1991	WBA
Yong-Kang Kim	S Korea	1991-1992	WBA
Pat Clinton	Scotland	1992-1993	WBO
Rodolfo Blanco	Colombia	1992	IBF
Yuri Arbachakov	Russia	1992-1997	WBC
Aquiles Guzman	Venezuela	1992	WBA
Pichit Sitbangprachan*	Thailand	1992-1994	IBF
David Griman	Venezuela	1992-1994	WBA
Jacob Matlala	S Africa	1993-1995	WBO
Saen Sorploenchit	Thailand	1994-1996	WBA
Alberto Jimenez	Mexico	1995-1996	WBO
Francisco Tejedor	Colombia	1995	IBF
Danny Romero*	USA	1995-1996	IBF
Mark Johnson*	USA	1996-1998	IBF

Title Holder	Birthplace	Tenure	Status
Jose Bonilla	Venezuela	1996-1998	WBA
Carlos Salazar	Argentina	1996-1998	WBO
Chatchai Sasakul	Thailand	1997-1998	WBC
Hugo Soto	Argentina	1998-1999	WBA
Ruben Sanchez	Mexico	1998-1999	WBO
Manny Pacquiao	Philippines	1998-1999	WBC
Silvio Gamez	Venezuela	1999	WBA
Irene Pacheco	Colombia	1999-2004	IBF
Jose Antonio Lopez	Spain	1999	WBO
Sornpichai Pisanurachan	Thailand	1999-2000	WBA
Medgoen Singsurat	Thailand	1999-2000	WBC
Isidro Garcia	Mexico	1999-2000	WBO
Malcolm Tunacao	Philippines	2000-2001	WBC
Eric Morel	USA	2000-2003	WBA
Fernando Montiel*	Mexico	2000-2002	WBO
Pongsaklek Wonjongkam	Thailand	2001-2007	WBC
Adonis Rivas	Nicaragua	2002	WBO
Omar Narvaez	Argentina	2002-	WBO
Lorenzo Parra	Venezuela	2003-2007	WBA
Vic Darchinyan	Armenia	2004-2007	IBF
Takefumi Sakata	Japan	2007-	WBA
Nonito Donaire	Philippines	2007-	IBF
Daisuke Naito	Japan	2007-	WBC

S. Flyweight (115 lbs)

Title Holder	Birthplace	Tenure	Status
Rafael Orono	Venezuela	1980-1981	WBC
Chul-Ho Kim	S Korea	1981-1982	WBC
Gustavo Ballas	Argentina	1981	WBA
Rafael Pedroza	Panama	1981-1982	WBA
Jiro Watanabe	Japan	1982-1984	WBA
Rafael Orono	Venezuela	1982-1983	WBC
Payao Poontarat	Thailand	1983-1984	WBC
Joo-Do Chun	S Korea	1983-1985	IBF
Jiro Watanabe	Japan	1984-1986	WBC
Kaosai Galaxy*	Thailand	1984-1992	WBA
Elly Pical	Indonesia	1985-1986	IBF
Cesar Polanco	Dom Republic	1986	IBF
Gilberto Roman	Mexico	1986-1987	WBC
Elly Pical	Indonesia	1986-1987	IBF
Santos Laciar	Argentina	1987	WBC
Tae-Il Chang	S Korea	1987	IBF
Jesus Rojas	Colombia	1987-1988	WBC
Elly Pical	Indonesia	1987-1989	IBF
Gilberto Roman	Mexico	1988-1989	WBC
Jose Ruiz	Puerto Rico	1989-1992	WBO
Juan Polo Perez	Colombia	1989-1990	IBF
Nana Yaw Konadu	Ghana	1989-1990	WBC
Sung-Il Moon	S Korea	1990-1993	WBC
Robert Quiroga	USA	1990-1993	IBF
Jose Quirino	Mexico	1992	WBO
Katsuya Onizuka	Japan	1992-1994	WBA
Johnny Bredahl	Denmark	1992-1994	WBO
Julio Cesar Borboa	Mexico	1993-1994	IBF
Jose Luis Bueno	Mexico	1993-1994	WBC
Hiroshi Kawashima	Japan	1994-1997	WBC
Harold Grey	Colombia	1994-1995	IBF
Hyung-Chul Lee	S Korea	1994-1995	WBA
Johnny Tapia*	USA	1994-1997	WBO
Alimi Goitia	Venezuela	1995-1996	WBA
Carlos Salazar	Argentina	1995-1996	IBF
Harold Grey	Colombia	1996	IBF
Yokthai Sith-Oar	Thailand	1996-1997	WBA
Danny Romero	USA	1996-1997	IBF
Gerry Penalosa	Philippines	1997-1998	WBC
Johnny Tapia*	USA	1997-1998	IBF/WBO
Satoshi Iida	Japan	1997-1998	WBA
In-Joo Cho	S Korea	1998-2000	WBC
Victor Godoi	Argentina	1998-1999	WBO
Jesus Rojas	Venezuela	1998-1999	WBA
Mark Johnson	USA	1999-2000	IBF
Diego Morales	Mexico	1999	WBO
Hideki Todaka	Japan	1999-2000	WBA

Title Holder	Birthplace	Tenure	Status
Adonis Rivas	Nicaragua	1999-2001	WBO
Felix Machado	Venezuela	2000-2003	IBF
Masamori Tokuyama	Japan	2000-2004	WBC
Silvio Gamez	Venezuela	2000-2001	WBA
Celes Kobayashi	Japan	2001-2002	WBA
Pedro Alcazar	Panama	2001-2002	WBO
Alexander Munoz	Venezuela	2002-2004	WBA
Fernando Montiel	Mexico	2002-2003	WBO
Luis Perez	Nicaragua	2003-2006	IBF
Mark Johnson	USA	2003-2004	WBO
Katsushige Kawashima	Japan	2004-2005	WBC
Ivan Hernandez	Mexico	2004-2005	WBO
Martin Castillo	Mexico	2004-2006	WBA
Fernando Montiel	Mexico	2005-	WBO
Masamori Tokuyama*	Japan	2005-2006	WBC
Nobuo Nashiro	Japan	2006-2007	WBA
Cristian Mijares	Mexico	2007-	WBC
Alexander Munoz	Venezuela	2007-	WBA
Dimitri Kirilov	Russia	2007-	IBF

Bantamweight (118 lbs)

Title Holder	Birthplace	Tenure	Status
Tommy Kelly	USA	1889	
George Dixon	Canada	1889-1890	
Chappie Moran	England	1889-1890	
Tommy Kelly	USA	1890-1892	
Billy Plimmer	England	1892-1895	
Pedlar Palmer	England	1895-1899	
Terry McGovern	USA	1899	USA
Pedlar Palmer	England	1899-1900	GB
Terry McGovern*	USA	1899-1900	
Clarence Forbes	USA	1900	
Johnny Reagan	USA	1900-1902	
Harry Ware	England	1900-1902	GB
Harry Harris	USA	1901	
Harry Forbes	USA	1901-1902	
Kid McFadden	USA	1901	
Dan Dougherty	USA	1901	
Andrew Tokell	England	1902	GB
Harry Ware	England	1902	GB
Harry Forbes	USA	1902-1903	USA
Joe Bowker	England	1902-1904	GB
Frankie Neil	USA	1903-1904	USA
Joe Bowker*	England	1904-1905	
Frankie Neil	USA	1905	USA
Digger Stanley	England	1905-1907	
Owen Moran	England	1905-1907	
Jimmy Walsh	USA	1905-1908	USA
Owen Moran	England	1907	GB
Monte Attell	USA	1908-1910	
Jimmy Walsh	USA	1908-1911	
Digger Stanley	England	1909-1912	GB
Frankie Conley	Italy	1910-1911	
Johnny Coulon	Canada	1910-1911	
Monte Attell	USA	1910-1911	
Johnny Coulon	Canada	1911-1913	USA
Charles Ledoux	France	1912-1913	GB/IBU
Eddie Campi	USA	1913-1914	
Johnny Coulon	Canada	1913-1914	
Kid Williams	Denmark	1913-1914	
Kid Williams	Denmark	1914-1915	
Kid Williams	Denmark	1915-1917	
Johnny Ertle	USA	1915-1918	
Pete Herman	USA	1917-1919	
Pal Moore	USA	1918-1919	
Pete Herman	USA	1919-1920	
Joe Lynch	USA	1920-1921	
Pete Herman	USA	1921	
Johnny Buff	USA	1921-1922	
Joe Lynch	USA	1922-1923	
Joe Lynch	USA	1923-1924	NBA
Joe Burman	England	1923	NY
Abe Goldstein	USA	1923-1924	NY

Title Holder	Birthplace	Tenure	Status
Joe Lynch	USA	1924	
Abe Goldstein	USA	1924	
Eddie Martin	USA	1924-1925	
Charley Rosenberg	USA	1925-1926	
Charley Rosenberg	USA	1926-1927	NY
Bud Taylor*	USA	1926-1928	NBA
Bushy Graham*	Italy	1928-1929	NY
Al Brown	Panama	1929-1931	
Al Brown	Panama	1931	NY/IBU
Pete Sanstol	Norway	1931	CAN
Al Brown	Panama	1931-1933	
Al Brown	Panama	1933-1934	NY/NBA/IBU
Speedy Dado	Philippines	1933	CALIF
Baby Casanova	Mexico	1933-1934	CALIF
Sixto Escobar	Puerto Rico	1934	CAN
Sixto Escobar	Puerto Rico	1934-1935	NBA
Al Brown	Panama	1934-1935	NY/IBU
Lou Salica	USA	1935	CALIF
Baltazar Sangchilli	Spain	1935-1938	IBU
Lou Salica	USA	1935	NBA/NY
Sixto Escobar	Puerto Rico	1935-1937	NBA/NY
Harry Jeffra	USA	1937-1938	NY/NBA
Sixto Escobar	Puerto Rico	1938-1939	NY/NBA
Al Brown	Panama	1938	IBU
Sixto Escobar	Puerto Rico	1939	
George Pace	USA	1939-1940	NBA
Lou Salica	USA	1939	CALIF
Tony Olivera	USA	1939-1940	CALIF
Little Dado	Philippines	1940	CALIF
Lou Salica	USA	1940-1941	
Kenny Lindsay	Canada	1941	CAN
Lou Salica	USA	1942	NY
David Kui Kong Young	Hawaii	1941-1943	TBC
Lou Salica	USA	1941-1942	NY/NBA
Manuel Ortiz	USA	1942-1943	NBA
Manuel Ortiz	USA	1943-1945	NY/NBA
David Kui Kong Young	Hawaii	1943	TBC
Rush Dalma	Philippines	1943-1945	TBC
Manuel Ortiz	USA	1945-1947	
Harold Dade	USA	1947	
Manuel Ortiz	USA	1947-1950	
Vic Toweel	S Africa	1950-1952	
Jimmy Carruthers*	Australia	1952-1954	
Robert Cohen	Algeria	1954	
Robert Cohen	Algeria	1954-1956	NY/EBU
Raton Macias	Mexico	1955-1957	NBA
Mario D'Agata	Italy	1956-1957	NY/EBU
Alphonse Halimi	Algeria	1957	NY/EBU
Alphonse Halimi	Algeria	1957-1959	
Joe Becerra*	Mexico	1959-1960	
Alphonse Halimi	Algeria	1960-1961	EBU
Eder Jofre	Brazil	1960-1962	NBA
Johnny Caldwell	Ireland	1961-1962	EBU
Eder Jofre	Brazil	1962-1965	
Fighting Harada	Japan	1965-1968	
Lionel Rose	Australia	1968-1969	
Ruben Olivares	Mexico	1969-1970	
Chuchu Castillo	Mexico	1970-1971	
Ruben Olivares	Mexico	1971-1972	
Rafael Herrera	Mexico	1972	
Enrique Pinder	Panama	1972	
Enrique Pinder	Panama	1972-1973	WBC
Romeo Anaya	Mexico	1973	WBA
Rafael Herrera	Mexico	1973-1974	WBC
Arnold Taylor	S Africa	1973-1974	WBA
Soo-Hwan Hong	S Korea	1974-1975	WBA
Rodolfo Martinez	Mexico	1974-1976	WBC
Alfonso Zamora	Mexico	1975-1977	WBA
Carlos Zarate	Mexico	1976-1979	WBC
Jorge Lujan	Panama	1977-1980	WBA
Lupe Pintor*	Mexico	1979-1983	WBC
Julian Solis	Puerto Rico	1980	WBA

Title Holder	Birthplace	Tenure	Status
Jeff Chandler	USA	1980-1984	WBA
Albert Davila	USA	1983-1985	WBC
Richard Sandoval	USA	1984-1986	WBA
Satoshi Shingaki	Japan	1984-1985	IBF
Jeff Fenech*	Australia	1985-1987	IBF
Daniel Zaragoza	Mexico	1985	WBC
Miguel Lora	Colombia	1985-1988	WBC
Gaby Canizales	USA	1986	WBA
Bernardo Pinango*	Venezuela	1986-1987	WBA
Takuya Muguruma	Japan	1987	WBA
Kelvin Seabrooks	USA	1987-1988	IBF
Chang-Yung Park	S Korea	1987	WBA
Wilfredo Vasquez	Puerto Rico	1987-1988	WBA
Kaokor Galaxy	Thailand	1988	WBA
Orlando Canizales*	USA	1988-1994	IBF
Sung-Il Moon	S Korea	1988-1989	WBA
Raul Perez	Mexico	1988-1991	WBC
Israel Contrerras*	Venezuela	1989-1991	WBO
Kaokor Galaxy	Thailand	1989	WBA
Luisito Espinosa	Philippines	1989-1991	WBA
Greg Richardson	USA	1991	WBC
Gaby Canizales	USA	1991	WBO
Duke McKenzie	England	1991-1992	WBO
Joichiro Tatsuyushi*	Japan	1991-1992	WBC
Israel Contrerras	Venezuela	1991-1992	WBA
Eddie Cook	USA	1992	WBA
Victor Rabanales	Mexico	1992-1993	WBC
Rafael del Valle	Puerto Rico	1992-1994	WBO
Jorge Elicier Julio	Colombia	1992-1993	WBA
Il-Jung Byun	S Korea	1993	WBC
Junior Jones	USA	1993-1994	WBA
Yasuei Yakushiji	Japan	1993-1995	WBC
John Michael Johnson	USA	1994	WBA
Daorung Chuwatana	Thailand	1994-1995	WBA
Alfred Kotey	Ghana	1994-1995	WBO
Harold Mestre	Colombia	1995	IBF
Mbulelo Botile	S Africa	1995-1997	IBF
Wayne McCullough	Ireland	1995-1997	WBC
Veeraphol Sahaprom	Thailand	1995-1996	WBA
Daniel Jimenez	Puerto Rico	1995-1996	WBO
Nana Yaw Konadu	Ghana	1996	WBA
Robbie Regan*	Wales	1996-1998	WBO
Daorung Chuwatana	Thailand	1996-1997	WBA
Sirimongkol Singmanassak	Thailand	1997	WBC
Nana Yaw Konadu	Ghana	1997-1998	WBA
Tim Austin	USA	1997-2003	IBF
Joichiro Tatsuyoshi	Japan	1997-1998	WBC
Jorge Elicier Julio	Colombia	1998-2000	WBO
Johnny Tapia	USA	1998-1999	WBA
Veeraphol Sahaprom	Thailand	1998-2005	WBC
Paulie Ayala	USA	1999-2001	WBA
Johnny Tapia*	USA	2000	WBO
Mauricio Martinez	Panama	2000-2002	WBO
Eidy Moya	Venezuela	2001-2002	WBA
Cruz Carbajal	Mexico	2002-2004	WBO
Johnny Bredahl*	Denmark	2002-2004	WBA
Rafael Marquez*	Mexico	2003-2007	IBF
Ratanchai Sowvoraphin	Thailand	2004-2005	WBO
Julio Zarate	Mexico	2004-2005	WBA
Wladimir Sidorenko	Ukraine	2005-2008	WBA
Hozumi Hasegawa	Japan	2005-	WBC
Jhonny Gonzalez	Mexico	2005-2007	WBO
Luis Perez	Nicaragua	2007	IBF
Gerry Penalosa	Philippines	2007-	WBO
Joseph Agbeko	Ghana	2007-	IBF
Anselmo Moreno	Panama	2008-	WBA

S. Bantamweight (122 lbs)

Title Holder	Birthplace	Tenure	Status
Rigoberto Riasco	Panama	1976	WBC
Royal Kobayashi	Japan	1976	WBC
Dong-Kyun Yum	S Korea	1976-1977	WBC
Wilfredo Gomez*	Puerto Rico	1977-1983	WBC

Title Holder	Birthplace	Tenure	Status
Soo-Hwan Hong	S Korea	1977-1978	WBA
Ricardo Cardona	Colombia	1978-1980	WBA
Leo Randolph	USA	1980	WBA
Sergio Palma	Argentina	1980-1982	WBA
Leonardo Cruz	Dom Republic	1982-1984	WBA
Jaime Garza	USA	1983-1984	WBC
Bobby Berna	Philippines	1983-1984	IBF
Loris Stecca	Italy	1984	WBA
Seung-In Suh	S Korea	1984-1985	IBF
Victor Callejas	Puerto Rico	1984-1986	WBA
Juan Meza	Mexico	1984-1985	WBC
Ji-Won Kim*	S Korea	1985-1986	IBF
Lupe Pintor	Mexico	1985-1986	WBC
Samart Payakarun	Thailand	1986-1987	WBC
Louie Espinosa	USA	1987	WBA
Seung-Hoon Lee*	S Korea	1987-1988	IBF
Jeff Fenech*	Australia	1987-1988	WBC
Julio Gervacio	Dom Republic	1987-1988	WBA
Bernardo Pinango	Venezuela	1988	WBA
Daniel Zaragoza	Mexico	1988-1990	WBC
Jose Sanabria	Venezuela	1988-1989	IBF
Juan J. Estrada	Mexico	1988-1989	WBA
Fabrice Benichou	Spain	1989-1990	IBF
Kenny Mitchell	USA	1989	WBO
Valerio Nati	Italy	1989-1990	WBO
Jesus Salud	USA	1989-1990	WBA
Welcome Ncita	S Africa	1990-1992	IBF
Paul Banke	USA	1990	WBC
Orlando Fernandez	Puerto Rico	1990-1991	WBO
Luis Mendoza	Colombia	1990-1991	WBA
Pedro Decima	Argentina	1990-1991	WBC
Kiyoshi Hatanaka	Japan	1991	WBC
Jesse Benavides	USA	1991-1992	WBO
Daniel Zaragoza	Mexico	1991-1992	WBC
Raul Perez	Mexico	1991-1992	WBA
Thierry Jacob	France	1992	WBC
Wilfredo Vasquez	Puerto Rico	1992-1995	WBA
Tracy Harris Patterson	USA	1992-1994	WBC
Duke McKenzie	England	1992-1993	WBO
Kennedy McKinney	USA	1992-1994	IBF
Daniel Jimenez	Puerto Rico	1993-1995	WBO
Vuyani Bungu *	S Africa	1994-1999	IBF
Hector Acero-Sanchez	Dom Republic	1994-1995	WBC
Marco Antonio Barrera	Mexico	1995-1996	WBO
Antonio Cermeno *	Venezuela	1995-1997	WBA
Daniel Zaragoza	Mexico	1995-1997	WBC
Junior Jones	USA	1996-1997	WBO
Erik Morales*	Mexico	1997-2000	WBC
Kennedy McKinney*	USA	1997-1998	WBO
Enrique Sanchez	Mexico	1998	WBA
Marco Antonio Barrera	Mexico	1998-2000	WBO
Nestor Garza	Mexico	1998-2000	WBA
Lehlohonolo Ledwaba	S Africa	1999-2001	IBF
Erik Morales	Mexico	2000	WBC/WBO
Erik Morales*	Mexico	2000	WBC
Marco Antonio Barrera*	Mexico	2000-2001	WBO
Clarence Adams	USA	2000-2001	WBA
Willie Jorrin	USA	2000-2002	WBC
Manny Pacquiao*	Philippines	2001-2003	IBF
Agapito Sanchez*	Dom Republic	2001-2002	WBO
Yober Ortega	Venezuela	2001-2002	WBA
Yoddamrong Sithyodthong	Thailand	2002	WBA
Osamu Sato	Japan	2002	WBA
Joan Guzman*	Dom Republic	2002-2005	WBO
Salim Medjkoune	France	2002-2003	WBA
Oscar Larios	Mexico	2002-2005	WBC
Mahyar Monshipour	Iran	2003-2006	WBA
Israel Vazquez*	Mexico	2004-2005	IBF
Daniel Ponce de Leon	Mexico	2005-2008	WBO
Israel Vazquez	Mexico	2005-2006	IBF/WBC
Somsak Sithchatchawal	Thailand	2006	WBA
Israel Vazquez	Mexico	2006-2007	WBC

WORLD CHAMPIONS SINCE GLOVES, 1889-2008

Title Holder	Birthplace	Tenure	Status	Title Holder	Birthplace	Tenure	Status
Celestino Caballero	Panama	2006-	WBA	Chalky Wright	Mexico	1941-1942	NY/MARY
Steve Molitor	Canada	2006-	IBF	Jackie Wilson	USA	1941-1943	NBA
Rafael Marquez	Mexico	2007	WBC	Willie Pep	USA	1942-1946	NY
Israel Vazquez	Mexico	2007-	WBC	Jackie Callura	Canada	1943	NBA
Juan Manuel Lopez	Puerto Rico	2008-	WBO	Phil Terranova	USA	1943-1944	NBA
				Sal Bartolo	USA	1944-1946	NBA

Featherweight (126 lbs)

Title Holder	Birthplace	Tenure	Status	Title Holder	Birthplace	Tenure	Status
Ike Weir	Ireland	1889-1890		**Willie Pep**	USA	1946-1948	
Billy Murphy	New Zealand	1890-1893		**Sandy Saddler**	USA	1948-1949	
George Dixon	Canada	1890-1893		**Willie Pep**	USA	1949-1950	
Young Griffo	Australia	1890-1893		**Sandy Saddler***	USA	1950-1957	
Johnny Griffin	USA	1891-1893		**Hogan Kid Bassey**	Nigeria	1957-1959	
Solly Smith	USA	1893		**Davey Moore**	USA	1959-1963	
George Dixon	Canada	1893-1896		**Sugar Ramos**	Cuba	1963-1964	
Solly Smith	USA	1896-1898		**Vicente Saldivar***	Mexico	1964-1967	
Frank Erne	USA	1896-1897		Raul Rojas	USA	1967	CALIF
George Dixon	Canada	1896-1900		Howard Winstone	Wales	1968	WBC
Harry Greenfield	England	1897-1899		Raul Rojas	USA	1968	WBA
Ben Jordan	England	1897-1899		Johnny Famechon	France	1968-1969	AUST
Will Curley	England	1897-1899		Jose Legra	Cuba	1968-1969	WBC
Dave Sullivan	Ireland	1898		Shozo Saijyo	Japan	1968-1971	WBA
Ben Jordan	England	1899-1905	GB	Johnny Famechon	France	1969-1970	WBC
Eddie Santry	USA	1899-1900		Vicente Saldivar	Mexico	1970	WBC
Terry McGovern	USA	1900		Kuniaki Shibata	Japan	1970-1972	WBC
Terry McGovern	USA	1900-1901	USA	Antonio Gomez	Venezuela	1971-1972	WBA
Young Corbett II	USA	1901-1903	USA	Clemente Sanchez	Mexico	1972	WBC
Eddie Hanlon	USA	1903		Ernesto Marcel*	Panama	1972-1974	WBA
Young Corbett II	USA	1903-1904		Jose Legra	Cuba	1972-1973	WBC
Abe Attell	USA	1903-1904		Eder Jofre	Brazil	1973-1974	WBC
Abe Attell	USA	1904-1911	USA	Ruben Olivares	Mexico	1974	WBA
Joe Bowker	England	1905-1907	GB	Bobby Chacon	USA	1974-1975	WBC
Jim Driscoll	Wales	1907-1912	GB	Alexis Arguello*	Nicaragua	1974-1977	WBA
Abe Attell	USA	1911-1912		Ruben Olivares	Mexico	1975	WBC
Joe Coster	USA	1911		David Kotey	Ghana	1975-1976	WBC
Joe Rivers	Mexico	1911		Danny Lopez	USA	1976-1980	WBC
Johnny Kilbane	USA	1911-1912		Rafael Ortega	Panama	1977	WBA
Jim Driscoll*	Wales	1912-1913	GB/IBU	Cecilio Lastra	Spain	1977-1978	WBA
Johnny Kilbane	USA	1912-1922	USA	Eusebio Pedroza	Panama	1978-1985	WBA
Johnny Kilbane	USA	1922-1923	NBA	Salvador Sanchez*	Mexico	1980-1982	WBC
Johnny Dundee	Italy	1922-1923	NY	Juan Laporte	Puerto Rico	1982-1984	WBC
Eugene Criqui	France	1923		Min-Keun Oh	S Korea	1984-1985	IBF
Johnny Dundee*	Italy	1923-1924		Wilfredo Gomez	Puerto Rico	1984	WBC
Kid Kaplan	Russia	1925	NY	Azumah Nelson*	Ghana	1984-1988	WBC
Kid Kaplan*	Russia	1925-1926		Barry McGuigan	Ireland	1985-1986	WBA
Honeyboy Finnegan	USA	1926-1927	MASS	Ki-Yung Chung	S Korea	1985-1986	IBF
Benny Bass	Russia	1927-1928	NBA	Steve Cruz	USA	1986-1987	WBA
Tony Canzoneri	USA	1928		Antonio Rivera	Puerto Rico	1986-1988	IBF
Andre Routis	France	1928-1929		Antonio Esparragoza	Venezuela	1987-1991	WBA
Bat Battalino	USA	1929-1932		Calvin Grove	USA	1988	IBF
Bat Battalino	USA	1932	NBA	Jeff Fenech*	Australia	1988-1989	WBC
Tommy Paul	USA	1932-1933	NBA	Jorge Paez*	Mexico	1988-1990	IBF
Kid Chocolate*	Cuba	1932-1934	NY	Maurizio Stecca	Italy	1989	WBO
Baby Arizmendi	Mexico	1932-1933	CALIF	Louie Espinosa	USA	1989-1990	WBO
Freddie Miller	USA	1933-1936	NBA	Jorge Paez*	Mexico	1990-1991	IBF/WBO
Baby Arizmendi	Mexico	1934-1935	NY	Marcos Villasana	Mexico	1990-1991	WBC
Baby Arizmendi	Mexico	1935-1936	NY/MEX	Kyun-Yung Park	S Korea	1991-1993	WBA
Baby Arizmendi	Mexico	1936	MEX	Troy Dorsey	USA	1991	IBF
Petey Sarron	USA	1936-1937	NBA	Maurizio Stecca	Italy	1991-1992	WBO
Henry Armstrong	USA	1936-1937	CALIF/MEX	Manuel Medina	Mexico	1991-1993	IBF
Mike Belloise	USA	1936	NY	Paul Hodkinson	England	1991-1993	WBC
Maurice Holtzer	France	1937-1938	IBU	Colin McMillan	England	1992	WBO
Henry Armstrong*	USA	1937-1938	NBA/NY	Ruben Palacio	Colombia	1992-1993	WBO
Leo Rodak	USA	1938	MARY	Tom Johnson	USA	1993-1997	IBF
Joey Archibald	USA	1938-1939	NY	Steve Robinson	Wales	1993-1995	WBO
Leo Rodak	USA	1938-1939	NBA	Gregorio Vargas	Mexico	1993	WBC
Joey Archibald	USA	1939-1940		Kevin Kelley	USA	1993-1995	WBC
Joey Archibald	USA	1940	NY	Eloy Rojas	Venezuela	1993-1996	WBA
Petey Scalzo	USA	1940-1941	NBA	Alejandro Gonzalez	Mexico	1995	WBC
Jimmy Perrin	USA	1940	LOUIS	Manuel Medina	Mexico	1995	WBC
Harry Jeffra	USA	1940-1941	NY/MARY	Prince Naseem Hamed*	England	1995-1997	WBO
Joey Archibald	USA	1941	NY/MARY	Luisito Espinosa	Philippines	1995-1999	WBC
Richie Lemos	USA	1941	NBA	Wilfredo Vasquez	Puerto Rico	1996-1998	WBA
				Prince Naseem Hamed *	England	1997	WBO/IBF

Title Holder	Birthplace	Tenure	Status
Prince Naseem Hamed*	England	1997-1999	WBO
Hector Lizarraga	Mexico	1997-1998	IBF
Freddie Norwood	USA	1998	WBA
Manuel Medina	Mexico	1998-1999	IBF
Antonio Cermeno	Venezuela	1998-1999	WBA
Cesar Soto	Mexico	1999	WBC
Freddie Norwood	USA	1999-2000	WBA
Prince Naseem Hamed	England	1999-2000	WBC/WBO
Paul Ingle	England	1999-2000	IBF
Prince Naseem Hamed*	England	2000	WBO
Gustavo Espadas	Mexico	2000-2001	WBC
Derrick Gainer	USA	2000-2003	WBA
Mbulelo Botile	S Africa	2000-2001	IBF
Istvan Kovacs	Hungary	2001	WBO
Erik Morales	Mexico	2001-2002	WBC
Frankie Toledo	USA	2001	IBF
Julio Pablo Chacon	Argentina	2001-2002	WBO
Manuel Medina	Mexico	2001-2002	IBF
Johnny Tapia	USA	2002	IBF
Marco Antonio Barrera*	Mexico	2002	WBC
Scott Harrison	Scotland	2002-2003	WBO
Erik Morales*	Mexico	2002-2003	WBC
Juan Manuel Marquez*	Mexico	2003	IBF
Manuel Medina	Mexico	2003	WBO
Juan Manuel Marquez	Mexico	2003-2005	IBF/WBA
Scott Harrison	Scotland	2003-2006	WBO
In-Jin Chi	S Korea	2004-2006	WBC
Juan Manuel Marquez	Mexico	2005-2006	WBA
Valdemir Pereira	Brazil	2005-2006	IBF
Takashi Koshimoto	Japan	2006	WBC
Chris John	Indonesia	2006-	WBA
Eric Aiken	USA	2006	IBF
Rodolfo Lopez	Mexico	2006	WBC
Robert Guerrero	USA	2006	IBF
Orlando Salido	Mexico	2006	IBF
Juan Manuel Marquez*	Mexico	2006-2007	WBO
In-Jin Chi*	S Korea	2006-2007	WBC
Robert Guerrero*	USA	2007-2008	IBF
Steve Luevano	USA	2007-	WBO
Jorge Linares	Venezuela	2007-	WBC

S. Featherweight (130 lbs)

Title Holder	Birthplace	Tenure	Status
Johnny Dundee	Italy	1921-1923	NY
Jack Bernstein	USA	1923	NY
Jack Bernstein	USA	1923	NBA/NY
Johnny Dundee	Italy	1923-1924	NBA/NY
Kid Sullivan	USA	1924-1925	NBA/NY
Mike Ballerino	USA	1925	NBA/NY
Tod Morgan	USA	1925-1929	NBA/NY
Benny Bass	Russia	1929-1930	NBA/NY
Benny Bass	Russia	1930-1931	NBA
Kid Chocolate	Cuba	1931-1933	NBA
Frankie Klick	USA	1933-1934	NBA
Sandy Saddler	USA	1949-1950	NBA
Sandy Saddler	USA	1950-1951	CLE
Harold Gomes	USA	1959-1960	NBA
Flash Elorde	Philippines	1960-1962	NBA
Flash Elorde	Philippines	1962-1967	WBA
Raul Rojas	USA	1967	CALIF
Yoshiaki Numata	Japan	1967	WBA
Hiroshi Kobayashi	Japan	1967-1971	WBA
Rene Barrientos	Philippines	1969-1970	WBC
Yoshiaki Numata	Japan	1970-1971	WBC
Alfredo Marcano	Venezuela	1971-1972	WBA
Ricardo Arredondo	Mexico	1971-1974	WBC
Ben Villaflor	Philippines	1972-1973	WBA
Kuniaki Shibata	Japan	1973	WBA
Ben Villaflor	Philippines	1973-1976	WBA
Kuniaki Shibata	Japan	1974-1975	WBC
Alfredo Escalera	Puerto Rico	1975-1978	WBC
Sam Serrano	Puerto Rico	1976-1980	WBA
Alexis Arguello*	Nicaragua	1978-1980	WBC

Title Holder	Birthplace	Tenure	Status
Yasutsune Uehara	Japan	1980-1981	WBA
Rafael Limon	Mexico	1980-1981	WBC
Cornelius Boza-Edwards	Uganda	1981	WBC
Sam Serrano	Puerto Rico	1981-1983	WBA
Rolando Navarrete	Philippines	1981-1982	WBC
Rafael Limon	Mexico	1982	WBC
Bobby Chacon	USA	1982-1983	WBC
Roger Mayweather	USA	1983-1984	WBA
Hector Camacho*	Puerto Rico	1983-1984	WBC
Rocky Lockridge	USA	1984-1985	WBA
Hwan-Kil Yuh	S Korea	1984-1985	IBF
Julio Cesar Chavez*	Mexico	1984-1987	WBC
Lester Ellis	England	1985	IBF
Wilfredo Gomez	Puerto Rico	1985-1986	WBA
Barry Michael	England	1985-1987	IBF
Alfredo Layne	Panama	1986	WBA
Brian Mitchell*	S Africa	1986-1991	WBA
Rocky Lockridge	USA	1987-1988	IBF
Azumah Nelson	Ghana	1988-1994	WBC
Tony Lopez	USA	1988-1989	IBF
Juan Molina*	Puerto Rico	1989	WBO
Juan Molina	Puerto Rico	1989-1990	IBF
Kamel Bou Ali	Tunisia	1989-1992	WBO
Tony Lopez	USA	1990-1991	IBF
Joey Gamache*	USA	1991	WBA
Brian Mitchell*	S Africa	1991-1992	IBF
Genaro Hernandez	USA	1991-1995	WBA
Juan Molina*	Puerto Rico	1992-1995	IBF
Daniel Londas	France	1992	WBO
Jimmy Bredahl	Denmark	1992-1994	WBO
Oscar de la Hoya*	USA	1994	WBO
James Leija	USA	1994	WBC
Gabriel Ruelas	USA	1994-1995	WBC
Regilio Tuur*	Surinam	1994-1997	WBO
Eddie Hopson	USA	1995	IBF
Tracy Harris Patterson	USA	1995	IBF
Yong-Soo Choi	S Korea	1995-1998	WBA
Arturo Gatti*	Canada	1995-1997	IBF
Azumah Nelson	Ghana	1996-1997	WBC
Genaro Hernandez	USA	1997-1998	WBC
Barry Jones*	Wales	1997-1998	WBO
Roberto Garcia	USA	1998-1999	IBF
Anatoly Alexandrov	Kazakhstan	1998-1999	WBO
Takenori Hatakeyama	Japan	1998-1999	WBA
Floyd Mayweather*	USA	1998-2002	WBC
Lakva Sim	Mongolia	1999	WBA
Acelino Freitas*	Brazil	1999-2002	WBO
Diego Corrales*	USA	1999-2000	IBF
Jong-Kwon Baek	S Korea	1999-2000	WBA
Joel Casamayor	Cuba	2000-2002	WBA
Steve Forbes	USA	2000-2002	IBF
Acelino Freitas*	Brazil	2002-2004	WBO/WBA
Sirimongkol Singmanassak	Thailand	2002-2003	WBC
Carlos Hernandez	El Salvador	2003-2004	IBF
Jesus Chavez	Mexico	2003-2004	WBC
Yodesnan Sornontachai	Thailand	2004-2005	WBA
Erik Morales	Mexico	2004	WBC
Diego Corrales*	USA	2004	WBO
Erik Morales	Mexico	2004	IBF
Mike Anchondo	USA	2004-2005	WBO
Marco Antonio Barrera*	Mexico	2004-2005	WBC
Robbie Peden	Australia	2005	IBF
Jorge Barrios	Argentina	2005-2006	WBO
Vincente Mosquera	Panama	2005-2006	WBA
Marco Antonio Barrera*	Mexico	2005-2006	WBC/IBF
Marco Antonio Barrera	Mexico	2006-2007	WBC
Cassius Baloyi	South Africa	2006	IBF
Gairy St Clair	Guyana	2006	IBF
Edwin Valero	Venezuela	2006-	WBA
Malcolm Klassen	S Africa	2006-2007	IBF
Joan Guzman*	Dom Republic	2006-2008	WBO
Juan Manuel Marquez	Mexico	2007-2008	WBC

245

Title Holder	Birthplace	Tenure	Status
Mzonke Fana	S Africa	2007-2008	IBF
Manny Pacquiao*	Philippines	2008	WBC
Cassius Baloyi	South Africa	2008-	IBF
Alex Arthur	Scotland	2008-	WBO

Lightweight (135 lbs)

Title Holder	Birthplace	Tenure	Status
Jack McAuliffe	Ireland	1889-1894	USA
Jem Carney	England	1889-1891	
Jimmy Carroll	England	1889-1891	
Dick Burge	England	1891-1896	GB
George Lavigne	USA	1894-1896	USA
George Lavigne	USA	1896	
George Lavigne	USA	1896-1897	
Eddie Connolly	Canada	1896-1897	
George Lavigne	USA	1897-1899	
Frank Erne	Switzerland	1899-1902	
Joe Gans	USA	1902	
Joe Gans	USA	1902-1906	
Jabez White	England	1902-1905	GB
Jimmy Britt	USA	1902-1905	
Battling Nelson	Denmark	1905-1907	
Joe Gans	USA	1906-1908	
Battling Nelson	Denmark	1908-1910	
Ad Wolgast	USA	1910-1912	
Willie Ritchie	USA	1912	
Freddie Welsh	Wales	1912-1914	GB
Willie Ritchie	USA	1912-1914	USA
Freddie Welsh	Wales	1914-1917	
Benny Leonard*	USA	1917-1925	
Jimmy Goodrich	USA	1925	NY
Rocky Kansas	USA	1925-1926	
Sammy Mandell	USA	1926-1930	
Al Singer	USA	1930	
Tony Canzoneri	USA	1930-1933	
Barney Ross*	USA	1933-1935	
Tony Canzoneri	USA	1935-1936	
Lou Ambers	USA	1936-1938	
Henry Armstrong	USA	1938-1939	
Lou Ambers	USA	1939-1940	
Sammy Angott	USA	1940-1941	NBA
Lew Jenkins	USA	1940-1941	NY
Sammy Angott*	USA	1941-1942	
Beau Jack	USA	1942-1943	NY
Slugger White	USA	1943	MARY
Bob Montgomery	USA	1943	NY
Sammy Angott	USA	1943-1944	NBA
Beau Jack	USA	1943-1944	NY
Bob Montgomery	USA	1944-1947	NY
Juan Zurita	Mexico	1944-1945	NBA
Ike Williams	USA	1945-1947	NBA
Ike Williams	USA	1947-1951	
Jimmy Carter	USA	1951-1952	
Lauro Salas	Mexico	1952	
Jimmy Carter	USA	1952-1954	
Paddy de Marco	USA	1954	
Jimmy Carter	USA	1954-1955	
Wallace Bud Smith	USA	1955-1956	
Joe Brown	USA	1956-1962	
Carlos Ortiz	Puerto Rico	1962-1963	
Carlos Ortiz*	Puerto Rico	1963-1964	WBA/WBC
Kenny Lane	USA	1963-1964	MICH
Carlos Ortiz	Puerto Rico	1964-1965	
Ismael Laguna	Panama	1965	
Carlos Ortiz	Puerto Rico	1965-1966	
Carlos Ortiz*	Puerto Rico	1966-1967	WBA
Carlos Ortiz	Puerto Rico	1967-1968	
Carlos Teo Cruz	Dom Republic	1968-1969	
Mando Ramos	USA	1969-1970	
Ismael Laguna	Panama	1970	
Ismael Laguna	Panama	1970	WBA
Ken Buchanan*	Scotland	1970-1971	WBA
Ken Buchanan	Scotland	1971	
Ken Buchanan	Scotland	1971-1972	WBA
Pedro Carrasco	Spain	1971-1972	WBC
Mando Ramos	USA	1972	WBC
Roberto Duran*	Panama	1972-1978	WBA
Chango Carmona	Mexico	1972	WBC
Rodolfo Gonzalez	Mexico	1972-1974	WBC
Guts Ishimatsu	Japan	1974-1976	WBC
Esteban de Jesus	Puerto Rico	1976-1978	WBC
Roberto Duran*	Panama	1978-1979	
Jim Watt	Scotland	1979-1981	WBC
Ernesto Espana	Venezuela	1979-1980	WBA
Hilmer Kenty	USA	1980-1981	WBA
Sean O'Grady	USA	1981	WBA
Alexis Arguello*	Nicaragua	1981-1983	WBC
Claude Noel	Trinidad	1981	WBA
Arturo Frias	USA	1981-1982	WBA
Ray Mancini	USA	1982-1984	WBA
Edwin Rosario	Puerto Rico	1983-1984	WBC
Charlie Choo Choo Brown	USA	1984	IBF
Harry Arroyo	USA	1984-1985	IBF
Livingstone Bramble	USA	1984-1986	WBA
Jose Luis Ramirez	Mexico	1984-1985	WBC
Jimmy Paul	USA	1985-1986	IBF
Hector Camacho*	Puerto Rico	1985-1987	WBC
Edwin Rosario	Puerto Rico	1986-1987	WBA
Greg Haugen	USA	1986-1987	IBF
Vinny Pazienza	USA	1987-1988	IBF
Jose Luis Ramirez	Mexico	1987-1988	WBC
Julio Cesar Chavez*	Mexico	1987-1988	WBA
Greg Haugen	USA	1988-1989	IBF
Julio Cesar Chavez*	Mexico	1988-1989	WBA/WBC
Mauricio Aceves	Mexico	1989-1990	WBO
Pernell Whitaker*	USA	1989	IBF
Edwin Rosario	Puerto Rico	1989-1990	WBA
Pernell Whitaker*	USA	1989-1990	IBF/WBC
Juan Nazario	Puerto Rico	1990	WBA
Pernell Whitaker*	USA	1990-1992	IBF/WBC/WBA
Dingaan Thobela*	S Africa	1990-1992	WBO
Joey Gamache	USA	1992	WBA
Miguel Gonzalez*	Mexico	1992-1996	WBC
Giovanni Parisi*	Italy	1992-1994	WBO
Tony Lopez	USA	1992-1993	WBA

Ken Buchanan

Title Holder	Birthplace	Tenure	Status		Title Holder	Birthplace	Tenure	Status
Fred Pendleton	USA	1993-1994	IBF		Bruno Arcari*	Italy	1970-1974	WBC
Dingaan Thobela	S Africa	1993	WBA		Alfonso Frazer	Panama	1972	WBA
Orzubek Nazarov	Kyrghyzstan	1993-1998	WBA		Antonio Cervantes	Colombia	1972-1976	WBA
Rafael Ruelas	USA	1994-1995	IBF		Perico Fernandez	Spain	1974-1975	WBC
Oscar de la Hoya*	USA	1994-1995	WBO		Saensak Muangsurin	Thailand	1975-1976	WBC
Oscar de la Hoya*	USA	1995	WBO/IBF		Wilfred Benitez	USA	1976	WBA
Oscar de la Hoya*	USA	1995-1996	WBO		Miguel Velasquez	Spain	1976	WBC
Phillip Holiday	S Africa	1995-1997	IBF		Saensak Muangsurin	Thailand	1976-1978	WBC
Jean-Baptiste Mendy	France	1996-1997	WBC		Antonio Cervantes	Colombia	1977-1980	WBA
Artur Grigorian	Uzbekistan	1996-2004	WBO		Wilfred Benitez*	USA	1977-1978	NY
Steve Johnston	USA	1997-1998	WBC		Sang-Hyun Kim	S Korea	1978-1980	WBC
Shane Mosley*	USA	1997-1999	IBF		Saoul Mamby	USA	1980-1982	WBC
Jean-Baptiste Mendy	France	1998-1999	WBA		Aaron Pryor*	USA	1980-1984	WBA
Cesar Bazan	Mexico	1998-1999	WBC		Leroy Haley	USA	1982-1983	WBC
Steve Johnston	USA	1999-2000	WBC		Bruce Curry	USA	1983-1984	WBC
Julien Lorcy	France	1999	WBA		Johnny Bumphus	USA	1984	WBA
Stefano Zoff	Italy	1999	WBA		Bill Costello	USA	1984-1985	WBC
Paul Spadafora*	USA	1999-2003	IBF		Gene Hatcher	USA	1984-1985	WBA
Gilberto Serrano	Venezuela	1999-2000	WBA		Aaron Pryor	USA	1984-1985	IBF
Takanori Hatakeyama	Japan	2000-2001	WBA		Ubaldo Sacco	Argentina	1985-1986	WBA
Jose Luis Castillo	Mexico	2000-2002	WBC		Lonnie Smith	USA	1985-1986	WBC
Julien Lorcy	France	2001	WBA		Patrizio Oliva	Italy	1986-1987	WBA
Raul Balbi	Argentina	2001-2002	WBA		Gary Hinton	USA	1986	IBF
Leonardo Dorin	Romania	2002-2003	WBA		Rene Arredondo	Mexico	1986	WBC
Floyd Mayweather*	USA	2002-2004	WBC		Tsuyoshi Hamada	Japan	1986-1987	WBC
Javier Jauregui	Mexico	2003-2004	IBF		Joe Manley	USA	1986-1987	IBF
Acelino Freitas	Brazil	2004	WBO		Terry Marsh*	England	1987	IBF
Lakva Sim	Mongolia	2004	WBA		Juan M. Coggi	Argentina	1987-1990	WBA
Julio Diaz*	Mexico	2004-2005	IBF		Rene Arredondo	Mexico	1987	WBC
Jose Luis Castillo	Mexico	2004-2005	WBC		Roger Mayweather	USA	1987-1989	WBC
Juan Diaz*	USA	2004-2007	WBA		James McGirt	USA	1988	IBF
Diego Corrales*	USA	2004-2005	WBO		Meldrick Taylor	USA	1988-1990	IBF
Diego Corrales	USA	2005-2006	WBC/WBO		Hector Camacho	Puerto Rico	1989-1991	WBO
Leavander Johnson	USA	2005	IBF					
Jesus Chavez	Mexico	2005-2007	IBF					
Diego Corrales	USA	2006	WBC					
Acelino Freitas	Brazil	2006-2007	WBO					
Joel Casamayor	Cuba	2006-2007	WBC					
Julio Diaz	USA	2007	IBF					
David Diaz	USA	2007-2008	WBC					
Juan Diaz*	USA	2007	WBA/WBO					
Juan Diaz	USA	2007-2008	WBA/WBO/IBF					
Nate Campbell	USA	2008-	WBA/WBO/IBF					
Manny Pacquiao	Philippines	2008-	WBC					

L. Welterweight (140 lbs)

Title Holder	Birthplace	Tenure	Status
Pinkey Mitchell	USA	1922-1926	NBA
Mushy Callahan	USA	1926-1927	NBA
Mushy Callahan	USA	1927-1930	NBA/NY
Mushy Callahan	USA	1930	NBA
Jackie Kid Berg	England	1930-1931	NBA
Tony Canzoneri	USA	1931-1932	NBA
Johnny Jadick	USA	1932	NBA
Johnny Jadick	USA	1932-1933	PEN
Battling Shaw	Mexico	1933	LOUIS
Tony Canzoneri	USA	1933	LOUIS
Barney Ross*	USA	1933-1935	ILL
Maxie Berger	Canada	1939	CAN
Harry Weekly	USA	1941-1942	LOUIS
Tippy Larkin	USA	1946-1947	NY/NBA
Carlos Ortiz	Puerto Rico	1959-1960	NBA
Duilio Loi	Italy	1960-1962	NBA
Duilio Loi	Italy	1962	WBA
Eddie Perkins	USA	1962	WBA
Duilio Loi*	Italy	1962-1963	WBA
Roberto Cruz	Philippines	1963	WBA
Eddie Perkins	USA	1963-1965	WBA
Carlos Hernandez	Venezuela	1965-1966	WBA
Sandro Lopopolo	Italy	1966-1967	WBA
Paul Fujii	Hawaii	1967-1968	WBA
Nicolino Loche	Argentina	1968-1972	WBA
Pedro Adigue	Philippines	1968-1970	WBC

Mushy Callahan

Title Holder	Birthplace	Tenure	Status	Title Holder	Birthplace	Tenure	Status
Julio Cesar Chavez*	Mexico	1989-1990	WBC	Rube Ferns	USA	1900	
Julio Cesar Chavez*	Mexico	1990-1991	IBF/WBC	Matty Matthews	USA	1900	
Loreto Garza	USA	1990-1991	WBA	Eddie Connolly	Canada	1900	
Greg Haugen	USA	1991	WBO	Matty Matthews	USA	1900-1901	
Hector Camacho	Puerto Rico	1991-1992	WBO	Rube Ferns	USA	1901	
Edwin Rosario	Puerto Rico	1991-1992	WBA	Joe Walcott	Barbados	1901-1906	
Julio Cesar Chavez	Mexico	1991-1994	WBC	Eddie Connolly	Canada	1902-1903	GB
Rafael Pineda	Colombia	1991-1992	IBF	Matty Matthews	USA	1902-1903	
Akinobu Hiranaka	Japan	1992	WBA	Rube Ferns	USA	1903	
Carlos Gonzalez	Mexico	1992-1993	WBO	Martin Duffy	USA	1903-1904	
Pernell Whitaker*	USA	1992-1993	IBF	Honey Mellody	USA	1904	
Morris East	Philippines	1992-1993	WBA	Jack Clancy	USA	1904-1905	GB
Juan M. Coggi	Argentina	1993-1994	WBA	Dixie Kid	USA	1904-1905	
Charles Murray	USA	1993-1994	IBF	Buddy Ryan	USA	1904-1905	
Zack Padilla*	USA	1993-1994	WBO	Sam Langford	Canada	1904-1905	
Frankie Randall	USA	1994	WBC	George Petersen	USA	1905	
Jake Rodriguez	USA	1994-1995	IBF	Jimmy Gardner	USA	1905	
Julio Cesar Chavez	Mexico	1994-1996	WBC	Mike Twin Sullivan	USA	1905-1906	
Frankie Randall	USA	1994-1996	WBA	Joe Gans	USA	1906	
Konstantin Tszyu	Russia	1995-1997	IBF	Joe Walcott	Barbados	1906	USA
Sammy Fuentes	Puerto Rico	1995-1996	WBO	Honey Mellody	USA	1906	USA
Juan M. Coggi	Argentina	1996	WBA	Honey Mellody	USA	1906-1907	
Giovanni Parisi	Italy	1996-1998	WBO	Joe Thomas	USA	1906-1907	
Oscar de la Hoya*	USA	1996-1997	WBC	Mike Twin Sullivan	USA	1907-1911	
Frankie Randall	USA	1996-1997	WBA	Jimmy Gardner	USA	1907-1908	
Khalid Rahilou	France	1997-1998	WBA	Frank Mantell	USA	1907-1908	
Vince Phillips	USA	1997-1999	IBF	Harry Lewis	USA	1908-1910	
Carlos Gonzalez	Mexico	1998-1999	WBO	Jack Blackburn	USA	1908	
Sharmba Mitchell	USA	1998-2001	WBA	Jimmy Gardner	USA	1908-1909	
Terron Millett	USA	1999	IBF	Willie Lewis	USA	1909-1910	
Randall Bailey	USA	1999-2000	WBO	Harry Lewis	USA	1910-1911	GB/FR
Kostya Tszyu*	Russia	1999-2001	WBC	Jimmy Clabby	USA	1910-1911	
Zab Judah	USA	2000-2001	IBF	Dixie Kid	USA	1911-1912	GB/FR
Ener Julio	Colombia	2000-2001	WBO	Ray Bronson	USA	1911-1914	
Kostya Tszyu*	Russia	2001	WBA/WBC	Marcel Thomas	France	1912-1913	FR
DeMarcus Corley	USA	2001-2003	WBO	Wildcat Ferns	USA	1912-1913	
Kostya Tszyu*	Russia	2001-2004	WBA/WBC/IBF	Spike Kelly	USA	1913-1914	
Zab Judah*	USA	2003-2004	WBO	Mike Glover	USA	1913-1915	
Kostya Tszyu	Russia	2004-2005	IBF	Mike Gibbons	USA	1913-1914	
Arturo Gatti	Canada	2004-2005	WBC	Waldemar Holberg	Denmark	1914	
Vivien Harris	Guyana	2004-2005	WBA	Tom McCormick	Ireland	1914	
Miguel Cotto*	Puerto Rico	2004-2006	WBO	Matt Wells	England	1914-1915	AUSTR
Ricky Hatton*	England	2005	IBF	Kid Graves	USA	1914-1917	
Carlos Maussa	Colombia	2005	WBA	Jack Britton	USA	1915	
Floyd Mayweather*	USA	2005-2006	WBC	Ted Kid Lewis	England	1915-1916	
Ricky Hatton*	England	2005-2006	IBF/WBA	Jack Britton	USA	1916-1917	
Juan Urango	Colombia	2006-2007	IBF	Ted Kid Lewis	England	1917	
Souleymane M'Baye	France	2006-2007	WBA	**Ted Kid Lewis**	England	1917-1919	
Junior Witter	England	2006-2008	WBC	**Jack Britton**	USA	1919-1922	
Ricardo Torres	Colombia	2006-	WBO	**Mickey Walker**	USA	1922-1923	
Ricky Hatton	England	2007	IBF	Mickey Walker	USA	1923-1924	NBA
Lovemore Ndou	S Africa	2007	IBF	Dave Shade	USA	1923	NY
Paul Malignaggi	USA	2007-	IBF	Jimmy Jones	USA	1923	NY/MASS
Ricky Hatton	England	2007-	IBO	**Mickey Walker**	USA	1924-1926	
Gavin Rees	Wales	2007-2008	WBA	**Pete Latzo**	USA	1926-1927	
Andreas Kotelnik	Ukraine	2008-	WBA	**Joe Dundee**	Italy	1927-1928	
Tim Bradley	USA	2008-	WBC	Joe Dundee	Italy	1928-1929	NY
				Jackie Fields	USA	1929	NBA
Welterweight (147 lbs)				**Jackie Fields**	USA	1929-1930	
Paddy Duffy	USA	1889-1890		**Young Jack Thompson**	USA	1930	
Tommy Ryan	USA	1891-1894		**Tommy Freeman**	USA	1930-1931	
Mysterious Billy Smith	USA	1892-1894		**Young Jack Thompson**	USA	1930	
Tommy Ryan	USA	1894-1897	USA	**Lou Brouillard**	Canada	1931-1932	
Tommy Ryan	USA	1897-1899		**Jackie Fields**	USA	1932-1933	
Dick Burge	GB	1897		**Young Corbett III**	Italy	1933	
George Green	USA	1897		**Jimmy McLarnin**	Ireland	1933-1934	
Tom Causer	GB	1897		**Barney Ross**	USA	1934	
Joe Walcott	Barbados	1897		**Jimmy McLarnin**	Ireland	1934-1935	
George Lavigne	USA	1897-1899		**Barney Ross**	USA	1935-1938	
Dick Burge	GB	1897-1898		Barney Ross	USA	1938	NY/NBA
Mysterious Billy Smith	USA	1898-1900		Felix Wouters	Belgium	1938	IBU
Bobby Dobbs	USA	1898-1902		**Henry Armstrong**	USA	1938-1940	

Title Holder	Birthplace	Tenure	Status
Fritzie Zivic	USA	1940	
Fritzie Zivic	USA	1940-1941	NY/NBA
Izzy Jannazzo	USA	1940-1942	MARY
Red Cochrane	USA	1941-1942	NY/NBA
Red Cochrane	USA	1942-1946	
Marty Servo	USA	1946	
Sugar Ray Robinson*	USA	1946-1951	
Johnny Bratton	USA	1951	NBA
Kid Gavilan	Cuba	1951-1952	NBA/NY
Kid Gavilan	Cuba	1952-1954	
Johnny Saxton	USA	1954-1955	
Tony de Marco	USA	1955	
Carmen Basilio	USA	1955-1956	
Johnny Saxton	USA	1956	
Carmen Basilio*	USA	1956-1957	
Virgil Akins	USA	1957-1958	MASS
Virgil Akins	USA	1958	
Don Jordan	Dom Republic	1958-1960	
Benny Kid Paret	Cuba	1960-1961	
Emile Griffith	Virgin Islands	1961	
Benny Kid Paret	Cuba	1961-1962	
Emile Griffith	Virgin Islands	1962-1963	
Luis Rodriguez	Cuba	1963	
Emile Griffith*	Virgin Islands	1963-1966	
Willie Ludick	S Africa	1966-1968	SA
Curtis Cokes*	USA	1966	WBA
Curtis Cokes*	USA	1966-1967	WBA/WBC
Charley Shipes	USA	1966-1967	CALIF
Curtis Cokes	USA	1968-1969	
Jose Napoles	Cuba	1969-1970	
Billy Backus	USA	1970-1971	
Jose Napoles	Cuba	1971-1972	
Jose Napoles*	Cuba	1972-1974	WBA/WBC
Hedgemon Lewis	USA	1972-1974	NY
Jose Napoles	Cuba	1974-1975	
Jose Napoles	Cuba	1975	WBC
Angel Espada	Puerto Rico	1975-1976	WBA
John H. Stracey	England	1975-1976	WBC
Carlos Palomino	Mexico	1976-1979	WBC
Pipino Cuevas	Mexico	1976-1980	WBA
Wilfred Benitez	USA	1979	WBC
Sugar Ray Leonard	USA	1979-1980	WBC
Roberto Duran	Panama	1980	WBC
Thomas Hearns	USA	1980-1981	WBA
Sugar Ray Leonard	USA	1980-1981	WBC
Sugar Ray Leonard*	USA	1981-1982	
Don Curry*	USA	1983-1984	WBA
Milton McCrory	USA	1983-1985	WBC
Don Curry*	USA	1984-1985	WBA/IBF
Don Curry	USA	1985-1986	
Lloyd Honeyghan	Jamaica	1986	
Lloyd Honeyghan	Jamaica	1986-1987	WBC/IBF
Mark Breland	USA	1987	WBA
Marlon Starling	USA	1987-1988	WBA
Jorge Vaca	Mexico	1987-1988	WBC
Lloyd Honeyghan	Jamaica	1988-1989	WBC
Simon Brown*	Jamaica	1988-1991	IBF
Tomas Molinares	Colombia	1988-1989	WBA
Mark Breland	USA	1989-1990	WBA
Marlon Starling	USA	1989-1990	WBC
Genaro Leon*	Mexico	1989	WBO
Manning Galloway	USA	1989-1993	WBO
Aaron Davis	USA	1990-1991	WBA
Maurice Blocker	USA	1990-1991	WBC
Meldrick Taylor	USA	1991-1992	WBA
Simon Brown*	Jamaica	1991	WBC/IBF
Simon Brown	Jamaica	1991	WBC
Maurice Blocker	USA	1991-1993	IBF
James McGirt	USA	1991-1993	WBC
Crisanto Espana	Venezuela	1992-1994	WBA
Gert Bo Jacobsen*	Denmark	1993	WBO
Pernell Whitaker	USA	1993-1997	WBC

Title Holder	Birthplace	Tenure	Status
Felix Trinidad*	Puerto Rico	1993-2000	IBF
Eamonn Loughran	Ireland	1993-1996	WBO
Ike Quartey	Ghana	1994-1998	WBA
Jose Luis Lopez	Mexico	1996-1997	WBO
Michael Loewe*	Romania	1997-1998	WBO
Oscar de la Hoya	USA	1997-1999	WBC
Ahmed Kotiev	Russia	1998-2000	WBO
James Page	USA	1998-2000	WBA
Oscar de la Hoya	USA	2000	WBC
Daniel Santos*	Puerto Rico	2000-2002	WBO
Shane Mosley	USA	2000-2002	WBC
Andrew Lewis	Guyana	2001-2002	WBA
Vernon Forrest	USA	2001	IBF
Vernon Forrest	USA	2002-2003	WBC
Antonio Margarito	Mexico	2002-2007	WBO
Ricardo Mayorga*	Nicaragua	2002-2003	WBA
Michele Piccirillo	Italy	2002-2003	IBF
Ricardo Mayorga	Nicaragua	2003	WBA/WBC
Cory Spinks*	USA	2003	IBF
Cory Spinks	USA	2003-2005	IBF/WBA/WBC
Zab Judah	USA	2005-2006	IBF/WBA/WBC
Carlos Baldomir	Argentina	2006	WBC
Zab Judah	USA	2006	IBF
Luis Collazo	USA	2006	WBA
Floyd Mayweather*	USA	2006	IBF
Ricky Hatton*	England	2006	WBA
Kermin Cintron	Puerto Rico	2006-2008	IBF
Floyd Mayweather*	USA	2006-2008	WBC
Miguel Cotto	Puerto Rico	2006-	WBA
Paul WIlliams	USA	2007-2008	WBO
Carlos Quintana	Puerto Rico	2008	WBO
Antonio Margarito*	Mexico	2008	IBF
Paul Williams	USA	2008-	WBO
Andre Berto	USA	2008-	WBC

Sugar Ray Leonard

Title Holder	Birthplace	Tenure	Status	Title Holder	Birthplace	Tenure	Status
L. Middleweight (154 lbs)				Harry Simon*	Namibia	1998-2001	WBO
Emile Griffith*	USA	1962-1963	AU	Fernando Vargas	USA	1998-2000	IBF
Denny Moyer	USA	1962-1963	WBA	Javier Castillejo	Spain	1999-2001	WBC
Ralph Dupas	USA	1963	WBA	David Reid	USA	1999-2000	WBA
Sandro Mazzinghi	Italy	1963-1965	WBA	Felix Trinidad*	Puerto Rico	2000	WBA
Nino Benvenuti	Italy	1965-1966	WBA	Felix Trinidad*	Puerto Rico	2000-2001	IBF/WBA
Ki-Soo Kim	S Korea	1966-1968	WBA	Oscar de la Hoya*	USA	2001-2002	WBC
Sandro Mazzinghi	Italy	1968-1969	WBA	Fernando Vargas	USA	2001-2002	WBA
Freddie Little	USA	1969-1970	WBA	Ronald Wright*	USA	2001-2004	IBF
Carmelo Bossi	Italy	1970-1971	WBA	Daniel Santos	Puerto Rico	2002-2005	WBO
Koichi Wajima	Japan	1971-1974	WBA	Oscar de la Hoya	USA	2002-2003	WBA/WBC
Oscar Albarado	USA	1974-1975	WBA	Shane Mosley	USA	2003-2004	WBA/WBC
Koichi Wajima	Japan	1975	WBA	Ronald Wright	USA	2004	IBF/WBA/WBC
Miguel de Oliveira	Brazil	1975	WBC	Ronald Wright	USA	2004-2005	WBA/WBC
Jae-Do Yuh	S Korea	1975-1976	WBA	Verno Phillips	USA	2004	IBF
Elisha Obed	Bahamas	1975-1976	WBC	Kassim Ouma	Uganda	2004-2005	IBF
Koichi Wajima	Japan	1976	WBA	Ronald Wright*	USA	2005	WBC
Jose Duran	Spain	1976	WBA	Travis Simms	USA	2005	WBA
Eckhard Dagge	Germany	1976-1977	WBC	Javier Castillejo	Spain	2005	WBC
Miguel Castellini	Argentina	1976-1977	WBA	Alejandro Garcia	Mexico	2005-2006	WBA
Eddie Gazo	Nicaragua	1977-1978	WBA	Roman Karmazin	Russia	2005-2006	IBF
Rocky Mattioli	Italy	1977-1979	WBC	Ricardo Mayorga	Nicaragua	2005-2006	WBC
Masashi Kudo	Japan	1978-1979	WBA	Sergei Dzindziruk	Ukraine	2005-	WBO
Maurice Hope	Antigua	1979-1981	WBC	Jose Antonio Rivera	USA	2006-2007	WBA
Ayub Kalule	Uganda	1979-1981	WBA	Oscar de la Hoya	USA	2006-2007	WBC
Wilfred Benitez	USA	1981-1982	WBC	Cory Spinks	USA	2006-2008	IBF
Sugar Ray Leonard*	USA	1981	WBA	Travis Simms	USA	2007	WBA
Tadashi Mihara	Japan	1981-1982	WBA	Floyd Mayweather*	USA	2007	WBC
Davey Moore	USA	1982-1983	WBA	Joachim Alcine	Haiti	2007-	WBA
Thomas Hearns*	USA	1982-1986	WBC	Vernon Forrest	USA	2007-2008	WBC
Roberto Duran*	Panama	1983-1984	WBA	Verno Phillips	Belize	2008-	IBF
Mark Medal	USA	1984	IBF	Sergio Mora	Mexico	2008-	WBC
Mike McCallum*	Jamaica	1984-1987	WBA				
Carlos Santos	Puerto Rico	1984-1986	IBF	**Middleweight (160 lbs)**			
Buster Drayton	USA	1986-1987	IBF	Nonpareil Jack Dempsey	Ireland	1889-1891	USA
Duane Thomas	USA	1986-1987	WBC	Bob Fitzsimmons	England	1891-1893	USA
Matthew Hilton	Canada	1987-1988	IBF	Jim Hall	Australia	1892-1893	GB
Lupe Aquino	Mexico	1987	WBC	**Bob Fitzsimmons**	England	1893-1894	
Gianfranco Rosi	Italy	1987-1988	WBC	Bob Fitzsimmons	England	1894-1899	
Julian Jackson*	Virgin Islands	1987-1990	WBA	Frank Craig	USA	1894-1895	GB
Don Curry	USA	1988-1989	WBC	Dan Creedon	New Zealand	1895-1897	GB
Robert Hines	USA	1988-1989	IBF	Tommy Ryan	USA	1895-1896	
John David Jackson*	USA	1988-1993	WBO	Kid McCoy	USA	1896-1898	
Darrin van Horn	USA	1989	IBF	Tommy Ryan	USA	1898-1905	
Rene Jacqot	France	1989	WBC	Charley McKeever	USA	1900-1902	
John Mugabi	Uganda	1989-1990	WBC	George Gardner	USA	1901-1902	
Gianfranco Rosi	Italy	1989-1994	IBF	Jack O'Brien	USA	1901-1905	
Terry Norris	USA	1990-1993	WBC	George Green	USA	1901-1902	
Gilbert Dele	France	1991	WBA	Jack Palmer	England	1902-1903	GB
Vinny Pazienza*	USA	1991-1992	WBA	Hugo Kelly	USA	1905-1908	
Julio Cesar Vasquez	Argentina	1992-1995	WBA	Jack Twin Sullivan	USA	1905-1908	
Verno Phillips	USA	1993-1995	WBO	Sam Langford	Canada	1907-1911	
Simon Brown	USA	1993-1994	WBC	Billy Papke	USA	1908	
Terry Norris	USA	1994	WBC	Stanley Ketchel	USA	1908	
Vince Pettway	USA	1994-1995	IBF	Billy Papke	USA	1908	
Luis Santana	Dom Republic	1994-1995	WBC	Stanley Ketchel	USA	1908-1910	
Pernell Whitaker*	USA	1995	WBA	Billy Papke	USA	1910-1913	
Gianfranco Rosi	Italy	1995	WBO	Stanley Ketchel*	USA	1910	
Carl Daniels	USA	1995	WBA	Hugo Kelly	USA	1910-1912	
Verno Phillips	USA	1995	WBO	Cyclone Johnny Thompson	USA	1911-1912	
Paul Vaden	USA	1995	IBF	Harry Lewis	USA	1911	
Terry Norris*	USA	1995	WBC	Leo Houck	USA	1911-1912	
Paul Jones	England	1995-1996	WBO	Georges Carpentier	France	1911-1912	
Terry Norris	USA	1995-1997	IBF/WBC	Jack Dillon	USA	1912	
Julio Cesar Vasquez	Argentina	1995-1996	WBA	Frank Mantell	USA	1912-1913	
Bronco McKart	USA	1996	WBO	Frank Klaus	USA	1912-1913	
Ronald Wright	USA	1996-1998	WBO	Georges Carpentier	France	1912	IBU
Laurent Boudouani	France	1996-1999	WBA	Jack Dillon	USA	1912-1915	
Terry Norris	USA	1997	WBC	Eddie McGoorty	USA	1912-1913	
Raul Marquez	USA	1997	IBF	Frank Klaus	USA	1913	IBU
Luis Campas	Mexico	1997-1998	IBF	Jimmy Clabby	USA	1913-1914	
Keith Mullings	USA	1997-1999	WBC	George Chip	USA	1913-1914	

Title Holder	Birthplace	Tenure	Status
Joe Borrell	USA	1913-1914	
Jeff Smith	USA	1913-1914	
Eddie McGoorty	USA	1914	AUSTR
Jeff Smith	USA	1914	AUSTR
Al McCoy	USA	1914-1917	
Jimmy Clabby	USA	1914-1915	
Mick King	Australia	1914	AUSTR
Jeff Smith	USA	1914-1915	AUSTR
Young Ahearn	England	1915-1916	
Les Darcy*	Australia	1915-1917	AUSTR
Mike Gibbons	USA	1916-1917	
Mike O'Dowd	USA	1917-1920	
Johnny Wilson	USA	1920-1921	
Johnny Wilson	USA	1921-1922	NBA/NY
Bryan Downey	USA	1921-1922	OHIO
Johnny Wilson	USA	1922-1923	NBA
Dave Rosenberg	USA	1922	NY
Jock Malone	USA	1922-1923	OHIO
Mike O'Dowd	USA	1922-1923	NY
Johnny Wilson	USA	1923	
Harry Greb	USA	1923-1926	
Tiger Flowers	USA	1926	
Mickey Walker	USA	1926-1931	
Gorilla Jones	USA	1932	NBA
Marcel Thil	France	1932-1933	NBA/IBU
Marcel Thil	France	1933-1937	IBU
Ben Jeby	USA	1933	NY
Lou Brouillard	Canada	1933	NY
Lou Brouillard	Canada	1933	NY/NBA
Vearl Whitehead	USA	1933	CALIF
Teddy Yarosz	USA	1933-1934	PEN
Vince Dundee	USA	1933-1934	NY/NBA
Teddy Yarosz	USA	1934-1935	NY/NBA
Babe Risko	USA	1935-1936	NY/NBA
Freddie Steele	USA	1936-1938	NY/NBA
Fred Apostoli	USA	1937-1938	IBU
Edouard Tenet	France	1938	IBU
Young Corbett III	Italy	1938	CALIF
Freddie Steele	USA	1938	NBA
Al Hostak	USA	1938	NBA
Solly Krieger	USA	1938-1939	NBA
Fred Apostoli	USA	1938-1939	NY
Al Hostak	USA	1939-1940	NBA
Ceferino Garcia	Philippines	1939-1940	NY
Ken Overlin	USA	1940-1941	NY
Tony Zale	USA	1940-1941	NBA
Billy Soose	USA	1941	NY
Tony Zale	USA	1941-1947	
Rocky Graziano	USA	1947-1948	
Tony Zale	USA	1948	
Marcel Cerdan	Algeria	1948-1949	
Jake la Motta	USA	1949-1950	
Jake la Motta	USA	1950-1951	NY/NBA
Sugar Ray Robinson	USA	1950-1951	PEN
Sugar Ray Robinson	USA	1951	
Randy Turpin	England	1951	
Sugar Ray Robinson*	USA	1951-1952	
Randy Turpin	England	1953	GB/EBU
Carl Bobo Olson	Hawaii	1953-1955	
Sugar Ray Robinson	USA	1955-1957	
Gene Fullmer	USA	1957	
Sugar Ray Robinson	USA	1957	
Carmen Basilio	USA	1957-1958	
Sugar Ray Robinson	USA	1958-1959	
Sugar Ray Robinson	USA	1959-1960	NY/EBU
Gene Fullmer	USA	1959-1962	NBA
Paul Pender	USA	1960-1961	NY/EBU
Terry Downes	England	1961-1962	NY/EBU
Paul Pender	USA	1962	NY/EBU
Dick Tiger	Nigeria	1962-1963	NBA
Dick Tiger	Nigeria	1963	
Joey Giardello	USA	1963-1965	

Title Holder	Birthplace	Tenure	Status
Dick Tiger	Nigeria	1965-1966	
Emile Griffith	Virgin Islands	1966-1967	
Nino Benvenuti	Italy	1967	
Emile Griffith	Virgin Islands	1967-1968	
Nino Benvenuti	Italy	1968-1970	
Carlos Monzon	Argentina	1970-1974	
Carlos Monzon*	Argentina	1974-1976	WBA
Rodrigo Valdez	Colombia	1974-1976	WBC
Carlos Monzon*	Argentina	1976-1977	
Rodrigo Valdez	Colombia	1977-1978	
Hugo Corro	Argentina	1978-1979	

Nino Benvenuti

Title Holder	Birthplace	Tenure	Status
Vito Antuofermo	Italy	1979-1980	
Alan Minter	England	1980	
Marvin Hagler	USA	1980-1987	
Marvin Hagler	USA	1987	WBC/IBF
Sugar Ray Leonard	USA	1987	WBC
Frank Tate	USA	1987-1988	IBF
Sumbu Kalambay	Zaire	1987-1989	WBA
Thomas Hearns	USA	1987-1988	WBC
Iran Barkley	USA	1988-1989	WBC
Michael Nunn	USA	1988-1991	IBF
Roberto Duran	Panama	1989-1990	WBC
Doug de Witt	USA	1989-1990	WBO
Mike McCallum	Jamaica	1989-1991	WBA
Nigel Benn	England	1990	WBO
Chris Eubank*	England	1990-1991	WBO
Julian Jackson	Virgin Islands	1990-1993	WBC
James Toney*	USA	1991-1993	IBF
Gerald McClellan*	USA	1991-1993	WBO
Reggie Johnson	USA	1992-1993	WBA
Gerald McClellan*	USA	1993-1995	WBC
Chris Pyatt	England	1993-1994	WBO

251

Title Holder	Birthplace	Tenure	Status
Roy Jones*	USA	1993-1994	IBF
John David Jackson	USA	1993-1994	WBA
Steve Collins*	Ireland	1994-1995	WBO
Jorge Castro	Argentina	1994	WBA
Julian Jackson	Virgin Islands	1995	WBC
Bernard Hopkins*	USA	1995-2001	IBF
Lonnie Bradley*	USA	1995-1998	WBO
Quincy Taylor	USA	1995-1996	WBC
Shinji Takehara	Japan	1995-1996	WBA
Keith Holmes	USA	1996-1998	WBC
William Joppy	USA	1996-1997	WBA
Julio Cesar Green	Dom Republic	1997-1998	WBA
William Joppy	USA	1998-2001	WBA
Hassine Cherifi	France	1998-1999	WBC
Otis Grant*	Canada	1998	WBO
Bert Schenk	Germany	1999	WBO
Keith Holmes	USA	1999-2001	WBC
Jason Matthews	England	1999	WBO
Armand Krajnc	Slovenia	1999-2002	WBO
Bernard Hopkins*	USA	2001	WBC/IBF
Felix Trinidad	Puerto Rico	2001	WBA
Bernard Hopkins*	USA	2001-2004	WBC/WBA/IBF
Harry Simon	Namibia	2002-2003	WBO
Hector Javier Velazco	Argentina	2003	WBO
Felix Sturm	Germany	2003-2004	WBO
Oscar de la Hoya	USA	2004	WBO
Bernard Hopkins	USA	2004-2005	IBF/WBA/WBC/WBO
Jermain Taylor*	USA	2005	IBF/WBA/WBC/WBO
Jermain Taylor*	USA	2005	WBA/WBC/WBO
Arthur Abraham	Armenia	2005-	IBF
Jermain Taylor	USA	2006-2007	WBC/WBO
Javier Castillejo	Spain	2006	WBA
Mariano Carrera	Argentina	2006-2007	WBA
Javier Castillejo	Spain	2007	WBA
Felix Sturm	Germany	2007-	WBA
Kelly Pavlik	USA	2007-	WBC/WBO

S. Middleweight (168 lbs)

Title Holder	Birthplace	Tenure	Status
Murray Sutherland	Scotland	1984	IBF
Chong-Pal Park*	S Korea	1984-1987	IBF
Chong-Pal Park	S Korea	1987-1988	WBA
Graciano Rocchigiani*	Germany	1988-1989	IBF
Fully Obelmejias	Venezuela	1988-1989	WBA
Sugar Ray Leonard*	USA	1988-1990	WBC
Thomas Hearns*	USA	1988-1991	WBO
In-Chul Baek	S Korea	1989-1990	WBA
Lindell Holmes	USA	1990-1991	IBF
Christophe Tiozzo	France	1990-1991	WBA
Mauro Galvano	Italy	1990-1992	WBC
Victor Cordoba	Panama	1991-1992	WBA
Darrin van Horn	USA	1991-1992	IBF
Chris Eubank	England	1991-1995	WBO
Iran Barkley	USA	1992-1993	IBF
Michael Nunn	USA	1992-1994	WBA
Nigel Benn	England	1992-1996	WBC
James Toney	USA	1993-1994	IBF
Steve Little	USA	1994	WBA
Frank Liles	USA	1994-1999	WBA
Roy Jones*	USA	1994-1997	IBF
Steve Collins*	Ireland	1995-1997	WBO
Thulani Malinga	S Africa	1996	WBC
Vincenzo Nardiello	Italy	1996	WBC
Robin Reid	England	1996-1997	WBC
Charles Brewer	USA	1997-1998	IBF
Joe Calzaghe*	Wales	1997-2006	WBO
Thulani Malinga	S Africa	1997-1998	WBC
Richie Woodhall	England	1998-1999	WBC
Sven Ottke*	Germany	1998-2003	IBF
Byron Mitchell	USA	1999-2000	WBA
Markus Beyer	Germany	1999-2000	WBC

Title Holder	Birthplace	Tenure	Status
Bruno Girard	France	2000-2001	WBA
Glenn Catley	England	2000	WBC
Dingaan Thobela	S Africa	2000	WBC
Dave Hilton	Canada	2000-2001	WBC
Byron Mitchell	USA	2001-2003	WBA
Eric Lucas	Canada	2001-2003	WBC
Sven Ottke*	Germany	2003-2004	IBF/WBA
Markus Beyer	Germany	2003-2004	WBC
Anthony Mundine	Australia	2004	WBA
Manny Sica	Puerto Rico	2004	WBA
Cristian Sanavia	Italy	2004	WBC
Jeff Lacy	USA	2004-2006	IBF
Markus Beyer	Germany	2004-2006	WBC
Mikkel Kessler*	Denmark	2004-2006	WBA
Joe Calzaghe*	Wales	2006	WBO/IBF
Mikkel Kessler	Denmark	2006-2007	WBC/WBA
Joe Calzaghe*	Wales	2006-2007	WBO
Alejandro Berrio	Colombia	2007	IBF
Lucien Bute	Romania	2007-	IBF
Joe Calzaghe*	Wales	2007-2008	WBA/WBC/WBO
Joe Calzaghe	Wales	2008-	WBA/WBO

L. Heavyweight (175 lbs)

Title Holder	Birthplace	Tenure	Status
Jack Root	Austria	1903	
George Gardner	Ireland	1903	
George Gardner	Ireland	1903	USA
Bob Fitzsimmons	England	1903-1905	USA
Jack O'Brien	USA	1905-1911	
Sam Langford	Canada	1911-1913	
Georges Carpentier	France	1913-1920	IBU
Jack Dillon	USA	1914-1916	USA
Battling Levinsky	USA	1916-1920	USA
Georges Carpentier	France	1920-1922	
Battling Siki	Senegal	1922-1923	
Mike McTigue	Ireland	1923-1925	
Paul Berlenbach	USA	1925-1926	
Jack Delaney*	Canada	1926-1927	
Jimmy Slattery	USA	1927	NBA
Tommy Loughran	USA	1927	NY
Tommy Loughran*	USA	1927-1929	
Jimmy Slattery	USA	1930	NY
Maxie Rosenbloom	USA	1930-1931	
Maxie Rosenbloom	USA	1931-1933	NY
George Nichols	USA	1932	NBA
Bob Godwin	USA	1933	NBA
Maxie Rosenbloom	USA	1933-1934	
Maxie Rosenbloom	USA	1934	NY
Joe Knight	USA	1934-1935	FL/NC/GEO
Bob Olin	USA	1934-1935	NY
Al McCoy	Canada	1935	CAN
Bob Olin	USA	1935	NY/NBA
John Henry Lewis	USA	1935-1938	NY/NBA
Gustav Roth	Belgium	1936-1938	IBU
Ad Heuser	Germany	1938	IBU
John Henry Lewis	USA	1938	
John Henry Lewis	USA	1938-1939	NBA
Melio Bettina	USA	1939	NY
Len Harvey	England	1939-1942	GB
Billy Conn	USA	1939-1940	NY/NBA
Anton Christoforidis	Greece	1941	NBA
Gus Lesnevich	USA	1941	NBA
Gus Lesnevich	USA	1941-1946	NY/NBA
Freddie Mills	England	1942-1946	GB
Gus Lesnevich	USA	1946-1948	
Freddie Mills	England	1948-1950	
Joey Maxim	USA	1950-1952	
Archie Moore	USA	1952-1960	
Archie Moore	USA	1960-1962	NY/EBU
Harold Johnson	USA	1961-1962	NBA
Harold Johnson	USA	1962-1963	
Willie Pastrano	USA	1963	
Willie Pastrano*	USA	1963-1964	WBA/WBC

Title Holder	Birthplace	Tenure	Status
Eddie Cotton	USA	1963-1964	MICH
Willie Pastrano	USA	1964-1965	
Jose Torres	Puerto Rico	1965-1966	
Dick Tiger	Nigeria	1966-1968	
Bob Foster	USA	1968-1970	
Bob Foster*	USA	1970-1972	WBC
Vicente Rondon	Venezuela	1971-1972	WBA
Bob Foster*	USA	1972-1974	
John Conteh	England	1974-1977	WBC
Victor Galindez	Argentina	1974-1978	WBA
Miguel Cuello	Argentina	1977-1978	WBC
Mate Parlov	Yugoslavia	1978	WBC
Mike Rossman	USA	1978-1979	WBA
Marvin Johnson	USA	1978-1979	WBC
Victor Galindez	Argentina	1979	WBA
Matt Saad Muhammad	USA	1979-1981	WBC
Marvin Johnson	USA	1979-1980	WBA
Mustafa Muhammad	USA	1980-1981	WBA
Michael Spinks*	USA	1981-1983	WBA
Dwight Muhammad Qawi	USA	1981-1983	WBC
Michael Spinks*	USA	1983-1985	
J. B. Williamson	USA	1985-1986	WBC
Slobodan Kacar	Yugoslavia	1985-1986	IBF
Marvin Johnson	USA	1986-1987	WBA
Dennis Andries	Guyana	1986-1987	WBC
Bobby Czyz	USA	1986-1987	IBF
Thomas Hearns*	USA	1987	WBC
Leslie Stewart	Trinidad	1987	WBA
Virgil Hill	USA	1987-1991	WBA
Charles Williams	USA	1987-1993	IBF
Don Lalonde	Canada	1987-1988	WBC
Sugar Ray Leonard*	USA	1988	WBC
Michael Moorer*	USA	1988-1991	WBO
Dennis Andries	Guyana	1989	WBC
Jeff Harding	Australia	1989-1990	WBC
Dennis Andries	Guyana	1990-1991	WBC
Leonzer Barber	USA	1991-1994	WBO
Thomas Hearns	USA	1991-1992	WBA
Jeff Harding	Australia	1991-1994	WBC
Iran Barkley*	USA	1992	WBA
Virgil Hill*	USA	1992-1996	WBA
Henry Maske	Germany	1993-1996	IBF
Mike McCallum	Jamaica	1994-1995	WBC
Dariusz Michalczewski*	Poland	1994-1997	WBO
Fabrice Tiozzo	France	1995-1997	WBC
Virgil Hill	USA	1996-1997	IBF/WBA
Roy Jones	USA	1997	WBC
Montell Griffin	USA	1997	WBC
Dariusz Michalczewski*	Poland	1997	WBO/IBF/WBA
Dariusz Michalczewski	Poland	1997-2003	WBO
William Guthrie	USA	1997-1998	IBF
Roy Jones*	USA	1997-1998	WBC
Lou del Valle	USA	1997-1998	WBA
Reggie Johnson	USA	1998-1999	IBF
Roy Jones*	USA	1998-1999	WBC/WBA
Roy Jones*	USA	1999-2002	WBC/WBA/IBF
Roy Jones*	USA	2002-2003	WBA/WBC
Mehdi Sahnoune	France	2003	WBA
Antonio Tarver*	USA	2003	IBF/WBC
Silvio Branco	Italy	2003-2004	WBA
Julio Gonzalez	Mexico	2003-2004	WBO
Antonio Tarver*	USA	2003-2004	WBC
Zsolt Erdei	Hungary	2004-	WBO
Glengoffe Johnson*	Jamaica	2004	IBF
Antoine Tarver	USA	2004-2006	IBO
Fabrice Tiozzo*	France	2004-2006	WBA
Clinton Woods	England	2005-2008	IBF
Tomasz Adamek	Poland	2005-2007	WBC
Bernard Hopkins*	USA	2006	IBO
Silvio Branco	Italy	2006-2007	WBA
Chad Dawson	USA	2006-	WBC
Stipe Drews	Croatia	2007	WBA

Title Holder	Birthplace	Tenure	Status
Antonio Tarver*	USA	2007-2008	IBO
Danny Green*	Australia	2007-2008	WBA
Antonio Tarver	USA	2008-	IBO/IBF

Cruiserweight (200 lbs)

Title Holder	Birthplace	Tenure	Status
Marvin Camel	USA	1979-1980	WBC
Carlos de Leon	Puerto Rico	1980-1982	WBC
Ossie Ocasio	Puerto Rico	1982-1984	WBA
S. T. Gordon	USA	1982-1983	WBC
Marvin Camel	USA	1983-1984	IBF
Carlos de Leon	Puerto Rico	1983-1985	WBC
Lee Roy Murphy	USA	1984-1986	IBF
Piet Crous	S Africa	1984-1985	WBA
Alfonso Ratliff	USA	1985	WBC
Dwight Muhammad Qawi	USA	1985-1986	WBA
Bernard Benton	USA	1985-1986	WBC
Carlos de Leon	Puerto Rico	1986-1988	WBC
Evander Holyfield*	USA	1986-1987	WBA
Rickey Parkey	USA	1986-1987	IBF
Evander Holyfield*	USA	1987-1988	WBA/IBF
Evander Holyfield*	USA	1988	
Taoufik Belbouli*	France	1989	WBA
Carlos de Leon	Puerto Rico	1989-1990	WBC
Glenn McCrory	England	1989-1990	IBF
Robert Daniels	USA	1989-1991	WBA
Boone Pultz	USA	1989-1990	WBO
Jeff Lampkin*	USA	1990-1991	IBF
Magne Havnaa*	Norway	1990-1992	WBO
Masimilliano Duran	Italy	1990-1991	WBC
Bobby Czyz	USA	1991-1993	WBA
Anaclet Wamba	Congo	1991-1995	WBC
James Warring	USA	1991-1992	IBF
Tyrone Booze	USA	1992-1993	WBO
Al Cole*	USA	1992-1996	IBF
Marcus Bott	Germany	1993	WBO
Nestor Giovannini	Argentina	1993-1994	WBO
Orlin Norris	USA	1993-1995	WBA
Dariusz Michalczewski*	Poland	1994-1995	WBO
Ralf Rocchigiani	Germany	1995-1997	WBO
Nate Miller	USA	1995-1997	WBA
Marcelo Dominguez	Argentina	1995-1998	WBC
Adolpho Washington	USA	1996-1997	IBF
Uriah Grant	USA	1997	IBF
Carl Thompson	England	1997-1999	WBO
Imamu Mayfield	USA	1997-1998	IBF
Fabrice Tiozzo	France	1997-2000	WBA
Juan Carlos Gomez*	Cuba	1998-2002	WBC
Arthur Williams	USA	1998-1999	IBF
Johnny Nelson*	England	1999-2006	WBO
Vassily Jirov	Kazakhstan	1999-2003	IBF
Virgil Hill	USA	2000-2002	WBA
Jean-Marc Mormeck*	Guadeloupe	2002-2005	WBA
Wayne Braithwaite	Guyana	2002-2005	WBC
James Toney*	USA	2003-2004	IBF
Kelvin Davis	USA	2004-2005	IBF
Jean-Marc Mormeck	Guadaloupe	2005-2006	WBA/WBC
O'Neil Bell*	USA	2005-2006	IBF
O'Neil Bell	USA	2006	IBF/WBA/WBC
O'Neil Bell	USA	2006-2007	WBA/WBC
Enzo Maccarinelli	Wales	2006-2008	WBO
Krzysztof Wlodarczyk	Poland	2006-2007	IBF
Jean-Marc Mormeck	Guadaloupe	2007	WBA/WBC
Steve Cunningham	USA	2007-	IBF
David Haye*	England	2007-2008	WBC/WBA
David Haye*	England	2008	WBC/WBA/WBO
Firat Arslan	Germany	2008-	WBA
David Haye	England	2008-	WBO

Heavyweight (200 lbs+)

Title Holder	Birthplace	Tenure	Status
John L. Sullivan	USA	1889-1892	USA
Peter Jackson	Australia	1889-1892	
Frank Slavin	Australia	1890-1892	GB/AUST

WORLD CHAMPIONS SINCE GLOVES, 1889-2008

Title Holder	Birthplace	Tenure	Status
Peter Jackson	Australia	1892-1893	GB/AUST
James J. Corbett	USA	1892-1894	USA
James J. Corbett	USA	1894-1895	
James J. Corbett	USA	1895-1897	
Peter Maher	Ireland	1895-1896	
Bob Fitzsimmons	England	1896-1897	
Bob Fitzsimmons	England	1897-1899	
James J. Jeffries	USA	1899-1902	
James J. Jeffries	USA	1902-1903	
Denver Ed Martin	USA	1902-1903	
Jack Johnson	USA	1902-1908	
Bob Fitzsimmons	England	1905	
Marvin Hart	USA	1905-1906	
Jack O'Brien	USA	1905-1906	
Tommy Burns	Canada	1906-1908	
Jack Johnson	USA	1908-1909	
Jack Johnson	USA	1909-1915	
Sam Langford	USA	1909-1911	
Sam McVey	USA	1911-1912	
Sam Langford	USA	1912-1914	
Luther McCarty	USA	1913	
Arthur Pelkey	Canada	1913-1914	
Gunboat Smith	USA	1914	
Harry Wills	USA	1914	
Georges Carpentier	France	1914	
Sam Langford	USA	1914-1915	
Jess Willard	USA	1915-1919	
Joe Jeannette	USA	1915	
Sam McVey	USA	1915	
Harry Wills	USA	1915-1916	
Sam Langford	USA	1916-1917	
Bill Tate	USA	1917	
Sam Langford	USA	1917-1918	
Harry Wills	USA	1918-1926	
Jack Dempsey	USA	1919-1926	
Gene Tunney*	USA	1926-1928	
Max Schmeling	Germany	1930-1932	
Jack Sharkey	USA	1932-1933	
Primo Carnera	Italy	1933-1934	
Max Baer	USA	1934-1935	
James J. Braddock	USA	1935	
James J. Braddock	USA	1935-1936	NY/NBA
George Godfrey	USA	1935-1936	IBU
James J. Braddock	USA	1936-1937	
Joe Louis*	USA	1937-1949	
Ezzard Charles	USA	1949-1950	NBA
Lee Savold	USA	1950-1951	GB/EBU
Ezzard Charles	USA	1950-1951	NY/NBA
Joe Louis	USA	1951	GB/EBU
Jersey Joe Walcott	USA	1951	NY/NBA
Jersey Joe Walcott	USA	1951-1952	
Rocky Marciano*	USA	1952-1956	
Floyd Patterson	USA	1956-1959	
Ingemar Johansson	Sweden	1959-1960	
Floyd Patterson	USA	1960-1962	
Sonny Liston	USA	1962-1964	
Muhammad Ali	USA	1964	
Muhammad Ali*	USA	1964-1967	WBC
Ernie Terrell	USA	1965-1967	WBA
Muhammad Ali	USA	1967	
Muhammad Ali	USA	1967-1968	WBC
Joe Frazier*	USA	1968-1970	NY/MASS
Jimmy Ellis	USA	1968-1970	WBA
Joe Frazier	USA	1970-1973	
George Foreman	USA	1973-1974	
Muhammad Ali	USA	1974-1978	
Leon Spinks	USA	1978	
Leon Spinks	USA	1978	WBA
Ken Norton	USA	1978	WBC
Larry Holmes*	USA	1978-1983	WBC
Muhammad Ali*	USA	1978-1979	WBA
John Tate	USA	1979-1980	WBA
Mike Weaver	USA	1980-1982	WBA
Michael Dokes	USA	1982-1983	WBA
Gerrie Coetzee	S Africa	1983-1984	WBA
Larry Holmes	USA	1983-1985	IBF
Tim Witherspoon	USA	1984	WBC
Pinklon Thomas	USA	1984-1986	WBC
Greg Page	USA	1984-1985	WBA
Tony Tubbs	USA	1985-1986	WBA
Michael Spinks	USA	1985-1987	IBF
Tim Witherspoon	USA	1986	WBA
Trevor Berbick	Jamaica	1986	WBC
Mike Tyson*	USA	1986-1987	WBC
James Smith	USA	1986-1987	WBA
Mike Tyson*	USA	1987	WBA/WBC
Tony Tucker	USA	1987	IBF
Mike Tyson	USA	1987-1989	
Mike Tyson	USA	1989-1990	IBF/WBA/WBC
Francesco Damiani	Italy	1989-1991	WBO
James Douglas	USA	1990	IBF/WBA/WBC
Evander Holyfield	USA	1990-1992	IBF/WBA/WBC
Ray Mercer	USA	1991-1992	WBO
Michael Moorer*	USA	1992-1993	WBO
Riddick Bowe	USA	1992	IBF/WBA/WBC
Riddick Bowe	USA	1992-1993	IBF/WBA
Lennox Lewis	England	1992-1994	WBC
Tommy Morrison	USA	1993	WBO
Michael Bentt	England	1993-1994	WBO
Evander Holyfield	USA	1993-1994	WBA/IBF
Herbie Hide	England	1994-1995	WBO
Michael Moorer	USA	1994	WBA/IBF
Oliver McCall	USA	1994-1995	WBC
George Foreman	USA	1994-1995	WBA/IBF
Riddick Bowe*	USA	1995-1996	WBO
George Foreman*	USA	1995	IBF
Bruce Seldon	USA	1995-1996	WBA
Frank Bruno	England	1995-1996	WBC
Frans Botha	S Africa	1995-1996	IBF
Mike Tyson	USA	1996	WBC
Michael Moorer	USA	1996-1997	IBF
Henry Akinwande*	England	1996-1997	WBO
Mike Tyson	USA	1996	WBA
Evander Holyfield*	USA	1996-1997	WBA
Lennox Lewis*	England	1997-1999	WBC
Herbie Hide	England	1997-1999	WBO
Evander Holyfield	USA	1997-1999	IBF/WBA
Vitali Klitschko	Ukraine	1999-2000	WBO
Lennox Lewis*	England	1999-2000	IBF/WBA/WBC
Chris Byrd	USA	2000	WBO
Lennox Lewis	England	2000-2001	IBF/WBC
Evander Holyfield	USA	2000-2001	WBA
Vladimir Klitschko	Ukraine	2000-2003	WBO
John Ruiz	USA	2001-2003	WBA
Hasim Rahman	USA	2001	WBC/IBF
Lennox Lewis*	England	2001-2002	WBC/IBF
Lennox Lewis*	England	2002-2004	WBC
Chris Byrd	USA	2002-2006	IBF
Roy Jones*	USA	2003	WBA
Corrie Sanders*	S Africa	2003	WBO
Lamon Brewster	USA	2004-2006	WBO
John Ruiz	Puerto Rico	2004-2005	WBA
Vitali Klitschko*	Ukraine	2004-2005	WBC
James Toney	USA	2005	WBA
John Ruiz	Puerto Rico	2005	WBA
Nikolai Valuev	Russia	2005-2007	WBA
Hasim Rahman	USA	2005-2006	WBC
Sergei Lyakhovich	Belarus	2006	WBO
Vladimir Klitschko	Ukraine	2006-	IBF
Oleg Maskaev	Kazakhstan	2006-2008	WBC
Shannon Briggs	USA	2006-2007	WBO
Ruslan Chagaev	Uzbekistan	2007-	WBA
Sultan Ibragimov	Russia	2007-	WBO
Samuel Peter	Nigeria	2008-	WBC

ABA National Championships, 2007-2008

Note: Only men who fought at some stage of the competition are included.

Combined Services v Southern Counties

Combined Services

Maida Gymnasium, Aldershot – 27 March

L.Fly: *final:* K. Subhan (Army) wo. **Fly:** *final:* A. Whitfield (Army) wo. **Bantam:** *final:* G. Smith (RN) w co 3 S. Southey (Army). **Feather:** *final:* J. Allen (Army) wo. **L.Welter:** *final:* S. Turner (Army) w pts P. Ferguson (RN). **Welter:** *final:* M. Flowers (RN) w rsc 4 G. McGhee (Army). **Middle:** *final:* N. Gittus (Army) w pts A. Neylon (RN).**L.Heavy:** *final:* T. Richardson (Army) w rsc 3 N. McGarry (RN). **Cruiser:** *final:* P. Ormston (RN) w pts G. Jones (Army). **Heavy:** *final:* J. Harvey (RN) w rsc 1 A. MacDonald (Army). **S.Heavy:** *final:* M. O'Connell (RN) w rsc 3 L. John (Army).

Southern Counties

Prince of Wales Gymnasium, Canterbury – 29 March & Town Hall, Dover – 4 April

L.Fly: no entries. **Fly:** no entries. **Bantam:** no entries. **Feather:** *final:* J. Fernandez (Golden Ring) wo. **Light:** *semi-finals:* S. Attrell (Hastings West Hill) wo, N. Yahyaoui (Tunbridge Wells) w pts M. Page (Golden Ring); *final:* N. Yahyaoui w pts S. Attrell. **L.Welter:** *quarter-finals:* A. Battle (Woking) wo, S. Ellis (Foley) wo, R. Goodfellow (Whitstable SoB), L. Ellett (Hove) w rsc 3 D. Debruin (Eastern); *semi-finals:* A. Battle w pts S. Ellis, L. Ellett w pts R. Goodfellow; *final:* A. Battle w pts L. Ellett. **Welter:** *semi-finals:* B. Buchanan (Hastings West Hill) w pts V. Woolford (The Grange), A. Neunie (Crawley) w rsc 3 S. Ayers (Guildford City); *final:* B. Buchanan w pts A. Neunie. **Middle:** *semi-finals:* T. Hill (Golden Ring) w pts S. James (Ramsgate); T. Pluckrose (Shepway) w pts P. Lawther (Woking); *final:* T. Hill w pts T. Pluckrose. **L.Heavy:** *quarter-finals:* K. Baker (Shepway) wo, A. Haniver (Hastings West Hill) wo, R. Moore (Waterlooville) w pts M. Atkins (Golden Ring), S. Couzens (Gosport) w pts J. Lawrence (Sandwich); *semi-finals:* R. Moore w rsc 1 K. Baker, S. Couzens w rsc 4 A. Haniver; *final:* R. Moore w pts S. Couzens. **Cruiser:** *final:* M. Matthewsian (Golden Ring) w pts D. Woodgate (The Grange). **Heavy:** No entries. **S.Heavy:** *final:* T. Dallas (St Mary's) wo.

Combined Services v Southern Counties

Maida Gymnasium, Aldershot – 19 April

L.Fly: K. Subhan (Army) wo. **Fly:** A. Whitfield (Army) wo. **Bantam:** G. Smith (RN) wo. **Feather:** J. Allen (Army) w rsc 3 J. Fernandez (Golden Ring). **Light:** M. Stead (Army) w co 1 N. Yahyaoui (Tunbridge Wells). **L.Welter:** S. Turner (Army) w pts A. Battle (Woking). **Welter:** B. Buchanan (Hastings West Hill) w pts M. Flowers (RN). **Middle:** N. Gittus (Army) w pts T. Hill (Golden Ring). **L.Heavy:** T. Richardson (Army) w pts R. Moore (Waterlooville). **Cruiser:** P. Ormston (RN) w pts M. Matthewsian (Golden Ring). **Heavy:** J. Harvey (RN) wo. **S.Heavy:** M. O'Connell (RN) w disq 2 T. Dallas (St Mary's).

Eastern Counties v Home Counties

Eastern Counties   Eastgate ABC, Bury St Edmunds – 28 March & Kingfisher ABC, Great Yarmouth – 5 April
L.Fly: no entries. **Fly:** no entries. **Bantam:** no entries. **Feather:** *semi-finals:* J. Taylor (Brentwood Youth) wo, M. Romani (St Ives) w pts D. Naylor (Ferry Street); *final:* J. Taylor w pts M. Romani. **Light:** no entries. **L.Welter:** *semi-finals:* J. Payne (Chatteris) wo, J. Homer (Rayleigh Mill) w pts K. Allen (Eastgate); *final:* J. Payne w pts J. Homer. **Welter:** *final:* A. Ogogo (Triple A) wo. **Middle:** *semi-finals:* J. Burnett (Triple A) wo, P. Smith (New Astley) w pts K. Wootton (Harlow); *final:* J. Burnett w pts P. Smith. **L.Heavy:** *semi-finals:* C. Brown (Chatteris) w pts R. Beck (Kingfisher), H. Bacon (Triple A) w pts F. Douglas (Chadwell & Corringham); *final:* C. Brown wo H. Bacon. **Cruiser:** *final:* H. Javed (Iceni) wo. **Heavy:** no entries. **S.Heavy:** no entries.

Home Counties   Auction Rooms, Luton – 5 & 11 April
L.Fly: *final:* B. Fowl (Hoddesdon BA) wo. **Fly:** *final:* D. Culling (Stevenage) wo. **Bantam:** no entries. **Feather:** *final:* B. Evans (Stevenage) w pts L. Lewis (Oxford BA). **Light:** *final:* R. O'Brian (Reading) wo. **L.Welter:** *semi-finals:* B. Crotty (Stevenage) w pts D. Phillips (Luton Shamrock), A. Lever (Bedford) w pts M. Randell (Berinsfield); *final:* A. Lever w pts B. Crotty. **Welter:** *final:* P. Gill (Cheshunt) w pts P. Samuels (Welwyn Garden City). **Middle:** *final:* C. Wood (Oxford BA) w pts T. Skipper (Cheshunt). **L.Heavy:** *semi-finals:* M. Churcher (Thames Valley) wo, A. Dennis (Welwyn Garden City) w pts M. Stephenson (Luton Shamrock); *final:* A. Dennis w pts M. Churcher. **Cruiser:** *final:* S. Jury (Thames Valley) w pts S. Richardson (Slough). **Heavy:** no entries. **S.Heavy:** no entries.

Eastern Counties v Home Counties   Great Parndon Recreation Centre, Harlow – 19 April
L.Fly: B. Fowl (Hoddesdon BA) wo. **Fly:** D. Culling (Stevenage) wo. **Bantam:** no entries. **Feather:** B. Evans (Stevenage) w pts J. Taylor (Brentwood Youth). **Light:** R. O'Brian (Reading) wo. **L.Welter:** J. Payne (Chatteris) w rsc 2 A. Lever (Bedford). **Welter:** A. Ogogo (Triple A) w pts P. Gill (Cheshunt). **Middle:** J. Burnett (Kingfisher) w pts C. Wood (Oxford BA). **L.Heavy:** A. Dennis (Welwyn Garden City) w pts C. Brown (Chatteris). **Cruiser:** H. Javed (Iceni) w pts S. Jury (Thames Valley). **Heavy:** no entries. **S.Heavy:** no entries.

London

North-East Division   Leisure Centre, Newham – 28 March
L.Fly: no entries. **Fly:** no entries. **Bantam:** *final:* D. Burrell (Peacock) wo. **Feather:** *final:* L. Ballard (Repton) w pts S. Burrell (Peacock). **Light:** *semi-finals:* S. Marson (Barking) wo, D. Clark (Repton) w pts P. Akubuko (West Ham); *final:* D. Clarke w pts S. Marson. **L.Welter:** *final:* I. Sheikh (Repton) wo. **Welter:** *final:* L. Newman (Repton) w pts D. Miller (Peacock). **Middle:** *final:* J. Gosling (Barking) w pts G. Thomas (Peacock). **L.Heavy:** no entries. **Cruiser:** *final:* R. Newland (Peacock) w pts T. Conquest (Dagenham). **Heavy:** *final:* W. Camacho (Peacock) w rtd 1 O. Ossai (Repton). **S.Heavy:** *final:* D. Campbell (Repton) wo.

North-West Division   **Town Hall, Wembley – 27 March & Dacorium Banqueting Suite, Wood Green – 4 April**
L.Fly: no entries. **Fly:** *final:* A. Sexton (Haringey Police) wo. **Bantam:** no entries. **Feather:** *final:* D. Rowe (Ruslip & District) wo. **Light:** *final:* M. Mellish (Times) wo. **L.Welter:** *quarter-finals:* C. Webb (Haringey Police) wo, B. Zakarani (Haringey Police) wo, R. Taylor (Haringey Police) w rtd 3 E. Ajayi (All Stars), T. Tear (Dale Youth) w pts M. McKray (Haringey Police); *semi-finals:* C. Webb w pts B. Zakarani, R. Taylor w pts T. Tear; *final:* R. Taylor w pts C. Webb. **Welter:** *final:* E. Ochieng (Haringey Police) w pts O. Ekundayo (Haringey Police). **Middle:** *semi-finals:* G. Groves (Dale Youth) wo, J. Ryder (Angel) w pts L. Reid (Dale Youth); *final:* G. Groves w pts J. Ryder. **L.Heavy:** *final:* I. Szucs (All Stars) wo. **Cruiser:** *final:* J. McDermott (Dale Youth) wo. **Heavy:** *final:* D. Reed (Dale Youth) w co 2 M. Onda (Finchley). **S.Heavy:** no entries.

South-East Division   **Fairfield Halls, Croydon – 30 March**
L.Fly: no entries. **Fly:** no entries. **Bantam:** *semi-finals:* M. Casey (Fisher) wo, D. Pettitt (Nemesis) w pts T. Ajagbe (Fitzroy Lodge); *final:* M. Casey w pts D. Pettitt. **Feather:** *final:* J. Saeed (Eltham & District) wo. **Light:** *final:* L. Gibb (Nemesis) w rsc 2 D. Davies (Fitzroy Lodge). **L.Welter:** *final:* A. Ideh (Lynn) w pts M. White-Dowe (Marvels Lane). **Welter:** *semi-finals:* M. Welsh (Fitzroy Lodge) wo, A. Patterson (Fitzroy Lodge) w pts L. Calvert (Fisher); *final:* M. Welsh w pts A. Patterson. **Middle:** *semi-finals:* F. Makenda (Hollington) wo, D. Burton (Honour Oak) w pts T. Ladeh (Lynn); *final:* F. Makenda w pts D. Burton. **L.Heavy:** *final:* O. Mbwakongo (Lynn) wo. **Cruiser:** *final:* L. Williams (Fitzroy Lodge) wo. **Heavy:** *final:* M.O. McDonagh (Hollington) w pts W. Byrne (Fitzroy Lodge). **S.Heavy:** *final:* J. Kaczorowski (Lynn) wo.

South-West Division   **Fairfield Halls, Croydon – 30 March**
L.Fly: no entries. **Fly:** no entries. **Bantam:** no entries. **Feather:** no entries. **Light:** no entries. **L.Welter:** *final:* B. Skeete (Earlsfield) wo. **Welter:** *final:* R. Garvey (Earlsfield) wo. **Middle:** *final:* G. Boulden (Kingston) wo. **L.Heavy:** no entries. **Cruiser:** no entries. **Heavy:** no entries. **S.Heavy:** *final:* F. Nortey (Kingston University) wo.

London Semi-Finals & Finals   **York Hall, Bethnal Green – 12 April**
L.Fly: no entries. **Fly:** *final:* A. Sexton (Haringey Police) wo. **Bantam:** *final:* D. Burrell (Peacock) w pts M. Casey (Fisher). **Feather:** *semi-finals:* D. Rowe (Ruislip & District) wo, J. Saeed (Eltham & District) w pts L. Ballard (Repton), *final:* J. Saeed w pts D. Rowe. **Light:** *semi-finals:* M. Mellish (Times) wo, L. Gibb (Nemesis) w pts D. Clark (Repton), *final:* L. Gibb w pts D. Clark. **L. Welter:** *semi-finals:* B. Skeete (Earlsfield) wo, R. Taylor (Haringey Police) w pts A. Ideh (Lynn), *final:* B. Skeete w pts R. Taylor. **Welter:** *semi-finals:* M. Welsh (Fitzroy Lodge) wo, E. Ochieng (Haringey Police), L. Newman (Repton) w pts R. Garvey (Earlsfield); *final:* M. Welsh w pts L. Newman. **Middle:** *semi-finals:* G. Groves (Dale Youth) w rtd 1 F. Makenda (Hollington), J. Gosling (Barking) w pts G. Boulden (Kingston); *final:* G. Groves w pts J. Gosling. **L.Heavy:** *final:* I. Szucs (All Stars) w pts O. Mbwakongo (Lynn). **Cruiser:** *semi-finals:* R. Newland (Peacock) wo, L. Williams (Fitzroy Lodge) w co 1 J. McDermott (Dale Youth); *final:* R. Newland w pts L. Williams. **Heavy:** *semi-finals:* M.O. McDonagh (Hollington) wo, D. Reed (Dale Youth) w pts W. Camacho (Peacock); *final:* M.O. McDonagh w pts D. Reed. **S.Heavy:** *semi-finals:* J. Kaczorowski (Lynn) wo, D. Campbell (Repton) w pts F. Nortey (Kingston University); *final:* D. Campbell w pts J. Kaczorowski.

Midland Counties

Standard Triumph Club, Coventry – 16, 30 March & 13 April ☐
L.Fly: no entries. **Fly:** *final:* W. Hussain (Aston Police) w pts U. Malik (Merlin). **Bantam:** *semi-finals:* Y. Naseer (Donnington) wo, M. Maguire (Kettering SoB) w pts l. Wood; *final:* M. Maguire w pts Y. Naseer. **Feather:** *semi-finals:* D. Rogers (Kettering SoB) wo, L. Glover (William Perry) w pts T. James (Capitol); *final:* L. Glover w pts D. Rogers. **Light:** *semi-finals:* J. Mason (Heart of England) w pts N. Rafiq (Queensberry Police), R. Bennett (Kettering SoB) w pts N. Heaney (Hulton Abbey); *final:* R. Bennett w pts J. Mason. **L.Welter:** *semi-finals:* I. Kiyemba (Belgrave) wo, S. Morrison (Birmingham City Police) w pts C. Speed (Standard Triumph); *final:* S. Morrison w pts I. Kiyemba. **Welter:** *quarter-finals:* C. Lewis (Graisley) w rtd 3 D. Woolery (Pleck), N. Hill (Trinity) w pts M. Lerwill (Donington), J. McGough (Standard Triumph) w pts N. Khan (Small Heath), K. Hooper (Grimsby) w pts A. Hardy (St George's); *semi-finals:* J. McGough w pts N. Hill, K. Hooper w pts C. Lewis; *final:* J. McGough w pts K. Hooper. **Middle:** *quarter-finals:* L. Morris (Benny's) wo, T. Staples (Grimsby) wo, A. Johnson (St Georges) w pts Q. Hillocks (Lions), J. Turner (Kettering SoB) w pts G. Cunningham (Warley); *semi-finals:* L. Morris w pts T. Staples, A. Johnson w pts J. Turner; *final:* L. Morris w pts A. Johnson. **L.Heavy:** *quarter-finals:* J. Ingram (Aston Police) wo, M. Till (Tom Lowe) wo, J. McCann (Kettering SoB) wo, M. Smith (Heartlands) w pts E. Dube (Merlin); *semi-finals:* J. McCann w rsc 3 M. Smith, J.Ingram w rsc M. Till; *final:* J. Ingram w pts J. McCann. **Cruiser:** *semi-finals:* V. Petkovic (One Nation) w disq 4 C. Owen (Bilborough Community), L. Robinson (Trinity) w pts D. Denvey (Droitwich); *final:* L. Robinson w v Petkovic. **Heavy:** *final:* R. Stepien (Birmingham City Police) wo. **S.Heavy:** *semi-finals:* T. Cope (Tamworth) wo, S. McPhilbin (Bilborough Community) w pts C. Kean (Pleck); *final:* S. McPhilbin w pts T. Cope.

North-West Counties

East Lancs & Cheshire Division   **The Forum, Wythenshawe – 30 March & 6 April**
L.Fly: *final:* T. Stubbs (Northside) wo. **Fly:** no entries. **Bantam:** *final:* T. Flanagan (Northside) w pts R. Todd (Hamer). **Feather:** *final:* L. Gillespie (Bridgewater Salford) w pts B. Younis (Northside). **Light:** *final:* K. Place (Northside) w pts J. Cosgrove (Barton). **L.Welter:** *semi-finals:* J. Bailey (Whitehaven) wo, A. Delaney (Northside) w pts S. Rice (Dynamics); *final:* A. Delaney w pts J. Bailey. **Welter:** *final:* W. Warburton (Pool of Life) w rsc 2 S. Cardle (Kirkham). **Middle:** *final:* K. Kirkham (Northside) w pts L. Brewster (Ashton Albion). **L.Heavy:** *semi-finals:* K. Borucki (Manx) wo, L. Holland (Egan's Academy) w pts C. Healey (Bredbury Stockport); *final:* K. Borucki w pts L. Holland. **Cruiser:** *final:* M. Askin (Pool of Life) wo. **Heavy:** no entries. **S.Heavy:** *final:* T. Fury (Egan's Academy) w rsc 2 D. Hodgson (Kirkham).

West Lancs & Cheshire Division   **Our Lady Queen of Peace Social Club, Sefton – 31 March, Rotunda ABC, Liverpool – 1 April & Austin Rawlingson Sports Centre, Speke – 4 April**
L.Fly: *final:* P. Butler (Vauxhall Motors) wo. **Fly:** *final:* A. Smith (Stockbridge) w pts I. Halsall (Lowe House). **Bantam:** *semi-finals:* J. Gilbertson (St Aloysius) wo, P. Edwards (Salisbury) w pts K. Satchell (Everton Red Triangle); *final:* P. Edwards w pts J. Gilbertson. **Feather:** *final:* G. Greenwood (Kirkdale) wo. **Light:** *final:* S. Jennings (Tower Hill) w pts C. Greenwood (Kirkdale). **L.Welter:** *quarter-finals:* S. Sweeney (Salisbury) wo, P. Jones (Stockbridge) wo, L .Smith (Rotunda) w pts C. Court (Transport), C. Callaghan (Sefton) w rtd 3 C. Kelly (Kirkdale); *semi-finals:* S.

Sweeney w pts C. Callaghan, L. Smith w pts P. Jones; *final:* L. Smith w pts S. Sweeney. **Welter:** *semi-finals:* A. Ismail (Salisbury) wo, G. Ormerod (Lowe House) w pts J. Spencer (Rotunda); *final:* A. Ismail w pts G. Ormrod. **Middle:** *final:* J. Seddon (Transport) w pts M. Phillips (Vauxhall Motors). **L.Heavy:** *final:* M. Fielding (Rotunda) wo. **Cruiser:** no entries. **Heavy:** *final:* W. Adeniyi (Mersey) wo. **S.Heavy:** no entries.

North-West Counties Finals   The Forum, Wythenshawe – 11 April

L.Fly: T. Stubbs (Northside) w pts P. Butler (Vauxhall Motors). **Fly:** A. Smith (Stockbridge) wo. **Bantam:** P. Edwards (Salisbury) w pts T. Flanagan (Northside). **Feather:** L. Gillespie (Bridgewater Salford) w pts G. Greenwood (Kirkdale). **Light:** K. Place (Northside) w pts S. Jennings (Tower Hill). **L.Welter:** L. Smith (Rotunda) w pts A. Delaney (Northside). **Welter:** A. Ismail (Salisbury) w pts W. Warburton (Pool of Life). **Middle:** K. Kirkham (Northside) w rsc 2 J. Seddon (Transport). **L.Heavy:** M. Fielding (Rotunda) w pts K. Borucki (Manx). **Cruiser:** M. Askin (Pool of Life) wo. **Heavy:** W. Adeniyi (Mersey) wo. **S.Heavy:** T. Fury (Egan's Academy) wo.

Tyne, Tees & Wear

Lancastrian Suite, Dunston – 4 & 10 April

L.Fly: *final:* A. Dillon (North Benwell) wo. **Fly:** *final:* D. Candlish (Empire SoB) wo. **Bantam:** no entries. **Feather:** *semi-finals:* M. Hadfield (Headland) wo, M. Ward (Birtley) w rsc 3 M. Ogara (Brambles Farm); *final:* M. Ward w pts M. Hadfield. **Light:** *final:* G. Reay (East Durham College) w rsc 3 D. Curran (Grainger Park). **L.Welter:** *quarter-finals:* D. Ferguson (Newcastle East End) wo, D. Oldham (North Benwell) w rsc 3 P. Boyle (Brambles Farm), M. Robinson (Sunderland) w pts P. Robinson (Hartlepool Catholic), C. Dixon (Birley) w pts S. Moore (Bilton Hall); *semi-finals:* D. Oldham w pts D. Ferguson, C. Dixon w pts M. Robinson; *final:* C. Dixon w rsc 3 D. Oldham. **Welter:** *semi-finals:* B. Falaja (Phil Thomas SoB) wo, G. Foot (Sunderland) w pts S. Buckley (Hartlepool Catholic); *final:* G. Foot w rsc 4 B. Falaja. **Middle:** *final:* I. Turnbull (Hylton Castle) w pts T. Crewe (Plains Farm). **L.Heavy:** *final:* S. McCrone (Spennymoor BA) w pts G. Barr (Birtley). **Cruiser:** *final:* D. Cullerton (Sunderland) wo. **Heavy:** *final:* W. Baister (Sunderland) wo. **S.Heavy:** *final:* M. Smith (Hartlepool Catholic) wo.

Western Counties

Northern Division   Town Hall, Lydney – 29 March

L.Fly: no entries. **Fly:** *final:* M. Hussain (Walcot Boys) wo. **Bantam:** no entries. **Feather:** *semi-finals:* W. Lilly (Sydenham) w pts J. Jameson (Yeovil), D. Webb (Empire) w pts S. Hussain (Walcot Boys); *final:* D. Webb w pts W. Lilly. **Light:** *final:* C. Higgs (Lydney) w pts D. Bharj (Walcot Boys). **L.Welter:** *final:* L. Horgan (Broad Plain) w pts J. Hicks (Yeovil). **Welter:** *semi-finals:* R. Gammon (Gloucester) wo, A. Grigg (Salisbury City) w pts S. Wilcox (Lydney); *final:* A. Grigg w co 1 R. Gammon. **Middle:** *final:* M. Reid (Walcot Boys) wo. **L.Heavy:** no entries. **Cruiser:** no entries. **Heavy:** no entries. **S.Heavy:** no entries.

Southern Division   Bideford ABC – 29 March

L.Fly: no entries. **Fly:** no entries. **Bantam:** *final:* L. Browning (Exeter) wo. **Feather:** *final:* P. Barney (Bournemouth) wo. **Light:** *final:* J. Speight (Apollo) w pts B. Zacharkiw (Pilgrims). **L.Welter:** *final:* T. Watson (Bournemouth) w pts J. Eddy (Devonport). **Welter:** *final:* F. Khan (Kingsteignton). **Middle:** *final:* L. Whane (Apollo) w pts A. Coles (Camborne & Redruth). **L.Heavy:** no

entries. **Cruiser:** *final:* M. Jennings (Amalgamated) wo. **Heavy:** no entries. **S.Heavy:** no entries.

Western Counties Finals   Oaklands, Cinderford – 12 April

L.Fly: no entries. **Fly:** M. Hussain (Walcot Boys) wo. **Bantam:** L. Browning (Exeter) wo. **Feather:** D. Webb (Empire) w pts P. Barney (Bournemouth). **Light:** C. Higgs (Lydney) w pts J. Speight (Apollo). **L.Welter:** T. Watson (Bournemouth) w pts L. Horgan (Broad Plain). **Welter:** A. Grigg (Salisbury City) w pts F. Khan (Kingsteignton). **Middle:** L. Whane (Apollo) w pts M. Reid (Walcot Boys). **L.Heavy:** no entries. **Cruiser:** M. Jennings (Amalgamated) wo. **Heavy:** no entries. **S.Heavy:** no entries.

Yorkshire

Light Waves Leisure Centre, Wakefield – 3 & 17 April

L.Fly: *final:* R. Downie (Scarborough) wo. **Fly:** no entries. **Bantam:** *final:* L. Campbell (St Paul's) w pts J. Cunningham (Doncaster Plant). **Feather:** *final:* S. Fadye (Rawthorpe) wo. **Light:** *semi-finals:* R. Urry (Fish Trades) wo, A. Townend (Hard & Fast) w rsc 4 T. Coyle (St Paul's); *final:* A. Townend w co 4 R. Urry. **L.Welter:** *final:* S. Newlove (St Paul's) wo. **Welter:** *final:* L. Robinson (White Rose) wo. **Middle:** *final:* L. Allon (St Paul's) wo. **L.Heavy:** *final:* A. Warren (Huddersfield University) wo. **Cruiser:** no entries. **Heavy:** no entries. **S.Heavy:** no entries.

English ABA Quarter-Finals, Semi-Finals & Finals

English Institute of Sport's Badminton Hall, Sheffield – 25 & 26 April & York Hall, Bethnal Green – 16 May

L.Fly: quarter- *finals:* K. Subhan (Army) wo, B. Fowl (Hoddesdon BA) wo, R. Downie (Scarborough) wo, T. Stubbs (Northside) w pts A. Dillon (North Benwell), *semi-finals:* T. Stubbs w pts R. Downie, B. Fowl w pts K. Subhan; *final:* T. Stubbs w pts B. Fowl. **Fly:** *quarter-finals:* W. Hussain (Aston Police) wo, A. Smith (Stockbridge) w pts D. Candish (Empire SoB), A. Sexton (Haringey Police) w pts M. Hussain (Walcot Boys), A. Whitfield (Army) w pts D. Culling (Stevenage); *semi-finals:* A. Smith w pts W. Hussain, A. Whitfield w pts A. Sexton; *final:* A. Whitfield w pts A. Smith. **Bantam:** *quarter-finals:* G. Smith (Army) wo, P. Edwards (Salisbury) wo, L. Browning (Exeter) w pts D. Burrell (Peacock), L. Campbell (St Paul's) w pts M. Maguire (Kettering SoB); *semi-finals:* L. Campbell w pts P. Edwards, G. Smith w pts L. Browning; *final:* L. Campbell w pts G. Smith. **Feather:** *quarter-finals:* L. Glover (William Perry) w pts S. Fadye (Rawthorpe), L. Gillespie (Bridgewater Salford) w pts M. Ward (Birtley), J. Saeed (Eltham & District) w pts D. Webb (Empire), B. Evans (Stevenage) w pts J. Allen (Army); *semi-finals:* L. Gillespie w pts L. Glover, B. Evans w pts J. Saeed; *final:* B. Evans w pts L. Gillespie. **Light:** *quarter-finals:* A. Townend (Hard & Fast) w co 1 R. Bennett (Kettering SoB), G. Reay (East Durham College) w pts K. Place (Northside), C. Higgs (Lydney) w pts L. Gibb (Nemesis), M. Stead (Army) w pts R. O'Brian (Reading); *semi-finals:* G. Reay w pts A. Townend, M. Stead w pts C. Higgs; *final:* M. Stead w pts G. Reay. **L.Welter:** *quarter-finals:* S. Morrison (Birmingham City Police) w pts S. Newlove (St Paul's), L. Smith (Rotunda) w rsc 1 C. Dixon (Birtley), B. Skeete (Earlsfield) w pts T. Watson (Bournemouth), S. Turner (Army) w rsc 2 J. Payne (Chatteris); *semi-finals:* L. Smith wo S. Morrison, S. Turner w pts B. Skeete; *final:* L. Smith w pts S. Turner. **Welter:** *quarter-finals:* L. Robinson (White Rose) w rsc 4 J. McGough (Standard Triumph), G. Foot (Sunderland) w pts A. Ismael (Salisbury), A. Grigg (Salisbury City) w pts M. Welsh

257

(Fitzroy Lodge), A. Ogogo (Triple A) w pts B. Buchanan (Hastings West Hill); *semi-finals:* L. Robinson w pts G. Foot, A. Ogogo w pts A. Grigg; *final:* A. Ogogo w pts L. Robinson. **Middle:** *quarter-finals:* L. Allon (St Paul's) w pts L. Morris (Benny's), K. Kirkham (Northside) w pts I. Turnbull (Hylton Castle), G. Groves (Dale Youth) w rsc 2 L. Whane (Apollo), N. Gittus (Army) w rsc 2 J. Burnett (Kingfisher); *semi-finals:* K. Kirkham w pts L. Allon, G.Groves w rsc 2 N. Gittus; *final:* G. Groves w pts K. Kirkham. **L.Heavy:** *quarter-finals:* I. Szucs (All Stars) wo, J. Ingram (Aston Police) w pts A. Warren (Huddersfield University), M. Fielding (Rotunda) w pts S. McCrone (Spennymoor BA), T. Richardson (Army) w pts A. Dennis (Welwyn Garden City); *semi-finals:* M. Fielding w pts J. Ingram, I. Szucs w pts T. Richardson; *final:* I. Szucs w pts M. Fielding. **Cruiser:** *quarter-finals:* L. Robinson

(Trinity) wo, D. Cullerton (Sunderland) w pts M. Askin (Pool of Life), R. Newland (Peacock) w rsc 2 M. Jennings (Amalgamated), P. Ormston (RN) w rsc 4 H. Javed (Iceni); *semi-finals:* M. Askin w rsc 3 L. Robinson (Trinity), R. Newland w rsc 3 P. Ormston; *final:* M. Askin w pts R. Newland. **Heavy:** *quarter-finals:* B. Atkin (Unity) wo, P. Stepien (Birmingham City Police) wo, M.O. McDonagh (Hollington) wo, J. Harvey (RN) wo, W. Baister (Sunderland) w pts W. Adeniyi (Mersey); *semi-finals:* W. Baister w rsc 3 P. Stepien, J. Harvey w pts M.O. McDonagh; *final:* W. Baister w pts J. Harvey. **S.Heavy:** *quarter-finals:* M. O'Connell (RN) – ruled out due to 28 day suspension, S. McPhilbin (Bilborough) wo, D. Campbell (Repton) wo, T. Fury (Egan's Academy) w rtd 1 M. Smith (Hartlepool Catholic); *semi-finals:* D. Campbell wo, T. Fury w rsc 4 S. McPhilbin; *final:* T. Fury w pts D. Campbell.

St Paul's Luke Campbell (right) on his way to a points win over the Royal Navy's Garath Smith in the ABA bantamweight final   Philip Sharkey

ABA Champions, 1881-2008

L. Flyweight
1971 M. Abrams
1972 M. Abrams
1973 M. Abrams
1974 C. Magri
1975 M. Lawless
1976 P. Fletcher
1977 P. Fletcher
1978 J. Dawson
1979 J. Dawson
1980 T. Barker
1981 J. Lyon
1982 J. Lyon
1983 J. Lyon
1984 J. Lyon
1985 M. Epton
1986 M. Epton
1987 M. Epton
1988 M. Cantwell
1989 M. Cantwell
1990 N. Tooley
1991 P. Culshaw
1992 D. Fifield
1993 M. Hughes
1994 G. Jones
1995 D. Fox
1996 R. Mercer
1997 I. Napa
1998 J. Evans
1999 G. Jones
2000 J. Mulherne
2001 C. Lyon
2002 D. Langley
2003 C. Lyon
2004 S. McDonald
2005 D. Langley
2006 J. Fowl
2007 K. Saeed
2008 T. Stubbs

Flyweight
1920 H. Groves
1921 W. Cuthbertson
1922 E. Warwick
1923 L. Tarrant
1924 E. Warwick
1925 E. Warwick
1926 J. Hill
1927 J. Roland
1928 C. Taylor
1929 T. Pardoe
1930 T. Pardoe
1931 T. Pardoe
1932 T. Pardoe
1933 T. Pardoe
1934 P. Palmer
1935 G. Fayaud
1936 G. Fayaud
1937 P. O'Donaghue
1938 A. Russell
1939 D. McKay
1944 J. Clinton
1945 J. Bryce
1946 R. Gallacher
1947 J. Clinton
1948 H. Carpenter
1949 H. Riley
1950 A. Jones
1951 G. John
1952 D. Dower
1953 R. Currie
1954 R. Currie
1955 D. Lloyd
1956 T. Spinks
1957 R. Davies
1958 J. Brown
1959 M. Gushlow
1960 D. Lee
1961 W. McGowan
1962 M. Pye
1963 M. Laud
1964 J. McCluskey
1965 J. McCluskey
1966 P. Maguire
1967 S. Curtis
1968 J. McGonigle
1969 D. Needham
1970 D. Needham
1971 P. Wakefield
1972 M. O'Sullivan
1973 R. Hilton
1974 M. O'Sullivan
1975 C. Magri
1976 C. Magri
1977 C. Magri
1978 G. Nickels
1979 R. Gilbody
1980 K. Wallace
1981 K. Wallace
1982 J. Kelly
1983 S. Nolan
1984 P. Clinton
1985 P. Clinton
1986 J. Lyon
1987 J. Lyon
1988 J. Lyon
1989 J. Lyon
1990 J. Armour
1991 P. Ingle
1992 K. Knox
1993 P. Ingle
1994 D. Costello
1995 D. Costello
1996 D. Costello
1997 M. Hunter
1998 J. Hegney
1999 D. Robinson
2000 D. Robinson
2001 M. Marsh
2002 D. Barriball
2003 D. Broadhurst
2004 S. Langley
2005 S. Langley
2006 P. Edwards
2007 M. Walsh
2008 A. Whitfield

Bantamweight
1884 A. Woodward
1885 A. Woodward
1886 T. Isley
1887 T. Isley
1888 H. Oakman
1889 H. Brown
1890 J. Rowe
1891 E. Moore
1892 F. Godbold
1893 E. Watson
1894 P. Jones
1895 P. Jones
1896 P. Jones
1897 C. Lamb
1898 F. Herring
1899 A. Avent
1900 J. Freeman
1901 W. Morgan
1902 A. Miner
1903 H. Perry
1904 H. Perry
1905 W. Webb
1906 T. Ringer
1907 E. Adams
1908 H. Thomas
1909 J. Condon
1910 W. Webb
1911 W. Allen
1912 W. Allen
1913 A. Wye
1914 W. Allen
1919 W. Allen
1920 G. McKenzie
1921 L. Tarrant
1922 W. Boulding
1923 A. Smith
1924 L. Tarrant
1925 A. Goom
1926 F. Webster
1927 E. Warwick
1928 J. Garland
1929 F. Bennett
1930 H. Mizler
1931 F. Bennett
1932 J. Treadaway
1933 G. Johnston
1934 A. Barnes
1935 L. Case
1936 A. Barnes
1937 A. Barnes
1938 J. Pottinger
1939 R. Watson
1944 R. Bissell
1945 P. Brander
1946 C. Squire
1947 D. O'Sullivan
1948 T. Profitt
1949 T. Miller
1950 K. Lawrence
1951 T. Nicholls
1952 T. Nicholls
1953 J. Smillie
1954 J. Smillie
1955 G. Dormer
1956 O. Reilly
1957 J. Morrissey
1958 H. Winstone
1959 D. Weller
1960 F. Taylor
1961 P. Benneyworth
1962 P. Benneyworth
1963 B. Packer
1964 B. Packer
1965 R. Mallon
1966 J. Clark
1967 M. Carter
1968 M. Carter
1969 M. Piner
1970 A. Oxley
1971 G. Turpin
1972 G. Turpin
1973 P. Cowdell
1974 S. Ogilvie
1975 S. Ogilvie
1976 J. Bambrick
1977 J. Turner
1978 J. Turner
1979 R. Ashton
1980 R. Gilbody
1981 P. Jones
1982 R. Gilbody
1983 J. Hyland
1984 J. Hyland
1985 S. Murphy
1986 S. Murphy
1987 J. Sillitoe
1988 K. Howlett
1989 K. Howlett
1990 P. Lloyd
1991 D. Hardie
1992 P. Mullings
1993 R. Evatt
1994 S. Oliver
1995 N. Wilders
1996 L. Eedle
1997 S. Oates
1998 L. Pattison
1999 M. Hunter
2000 S. Foster
2001 S. Foster
2002 D. Matthews
2003 N. McDonald
2004 M. Marsh
2005 N. McDonald
2006 N. McDonald
2007 L. Campbell
2008 L. Campbell

Featherweight
1881 T. Hill
1882 T. Hill
1883 T. Hill
1884 E. Hutchings
1885 J. Pennell
1886 T. McNeil
1887 J. Pennell
1888 J. Taylor
1889 G. Belsey
1890 G. Belsey
1891 F. Curtis
1892 F. Curtis
1893 T. Davidson
1894 R. Gunn
1895 R. Gunn
1896 R. Gunn
1897 N. Smith
1898 P. Lunn
1899 J. Scholes
1900 R. Lee
1901 C. Clarke
1902 C. Clarke
1903 J. Godfrey
1904 C. Morris
1905 H. Holmes
1906 A. Miner
1907 C. Morris
1908 T. Ringer
1909 A. Lambert
1910 C. Houghton
1911 H. Bowers
1912 G. Baker
1913 G. Baker
1914 G. Baker
1919 G. Baker
1920 J. Fleming
1921 G. Baker
1922 E. Swash
1923 E. Swash
1924 A. Beavis
1925 A. Beavis
1926 R. Minshull
1927 F. Webster
1928 F. Meachem
1929 F. Meachem
1930 J. Duffield
1931 B. Caplan
1932 H. Mizler
1933 J. Walters
1934 J. Treadaway
1935 E. Ryan
1936 J. Treadaway
1937 A. Harper
1938 C. Gallie
1939 C. Gallie
1944 D. Sullivan
1945 J. Carter
1946 P. Brander
1947 S. Evans
1948 P. Brander
1949 H. Gilliland
1950 P. Brander
1951 J. Travers
1952 P. Lewis
1953 P. Lewis
1954 D. Charnley
1955 T. Nicholls
1956 T. Nicholls
1957 M. Collins
1958 M. Collins
1959 G. Judge
1960 P. Lundgren
1961 P. Cheevers
1962 B. Wilson
1963 A. Riley
1964 R. Smith
1965 K. Buchanan
1966 H. Baxter
1967 K. Cooper
1968 J. Cheshire
1969 A. Richardson
1970 D. Polak
1971 T. Wright
1972 K. Laing
1973 J. Lynch
1974 G. Gilbody
1975 R. Beaumont
1976 P. Cowdell
1977 P. Cowdell
1978 M. O'Brien
1979 P. Hanlon
1980 M. Hanif
1981 P. Hanlon
1982 H. Henry
1983 P. Bradley
1984 K. Taylor
1985 F. Havard
1986 P. Hodkinson

1987 P. English
1988 D. Anderson
1989 P. Richardson
1990 B. Carr
1991 J. Irwin
1992 A. Temple
1993 J. Cook
1994 D. Pithie
1995 D. Burrows
1996 T. Mulholland
1997 S. Bell
1998 D. Williams
1999 S. Miller
2000 H. Castle
2001 S. Bell
2002 D. Mulholland
2003 K. Mitchell
2004 D. Mulholland
2005 G. Sykes
2006 S. Smith
2007 S. Smith
2008 B. Evans

Lightweight
1881 F. Hobday
1882 A. Bettinson
1883 A. Diamond
1884 A. Diamond
1885 A. Diamond
1886 G. Roberts
1887 J. Hair
1888 A. Newton
1889 W. Neale
1890 A. Newton
1891 E. Dettmer
1892 E. Dettmer
1893 W. Campbell
1894 W. Campbell
1895 A. Randall
1896 A. Vanderhout
1897 A. Vanderhout
1898 H. Marks
1899 H. Brewer
1900 G. Humphries
1901 A. Warner
1902 A. Warner
1903 H. Fergus
1904 M. Wells
1905 M. Wells
1906 M. Wells
1907 M. Wells
1908 H. Holmes
1909 F. Grace
1910 T. Tees
1911 A. Spenceley
1912 R. Marriott
1913 R. Grace
1914 R. Marriott
1919 F. Grace
1920 F. Grace
1921 G. Shorter
1922 G. Renouf
1923 G. Shorter
1924 W. White
1925 E. Viney
1926 T. Slater
1927 W. Hunt
1928 F. Webster
1929 W. Hunt
1930 J. Waples
1931 D. McCleave

1932 F. Meachem
1933 H. Mizler
1934 J. Rolland
1935 F. Frost
1936 F. Simpson
1937 A. Danahar
1938 T. McGrath
1939 H. Groves
1944 W. Thompson
1945 J. Williamson
1946 E. Thomas
1947 C. Morrissey
1948 R. Cooper
1949 A. Smith
1950 R. Latham
1951 R. Hinson
1952 F. Reardon
1953 D. Hinson
1954 G. Whelan
1955 S. Coffey
1956 R. McTaggart
1957 J. Kidd
1958 R. McTaggart
1959 P. Warwick
1960 R. McTaggart
1961 P. Warwick
1962 B. Whelan
1963 B. O'Sullivan
1964 J. Dunne
1965 A. White
1966 J. Head
1967 T. Waller
1968 J. Watt
1969 H. Hayes
1970 N. Cole
1971 J. Singleton
1972 N. Cole
1973 T. Dunn
1974 J. Lynch
1975 P. Cowdell
1976 S. Mittee
1977 G. Gilbody
1978 T. Marsh
1979 G. Gilbody
1980 G. Gilbody
1981 G. Gilbody
1982 J. McDonnell
1983 K. Willis
1984 A. Dickson
1985 E. McAuley
1986 J. Jacobs
1987 M. Ayers
1988 C. Kane
1989 M. Ramsey
1990 P. Gallagher
1991 P. Ramsey
1992 D. Amory
1993 B. Welsh
1994 A. Green
1995 R. Rutherford
1996 K. Wing
1997 M. Hawthorne
1998 A. McLean
1999 S. Burke
2000 A. McLean
2001 S. Burke
2002 A. Morris
2003 S. Burke
2004 C. Pacy
2005 F. Gavin
2006 A. Crolla

2007 F. Gavin
2008 M. Stead

L. Welterweight
1951 W. Connor
1952 P. Waterman
1953 D. Hughes
1954 G. Martin
1955 F. McQuillan
1956 D. Stone
1957 D. Stone
1958 R. Kane
1959 R. Kane
1960 R. Day
1961 B. Brazier
1962 B. Brazier
1963 R. McTaggart
1964 R. Taylor
1965 R. McTaggart
1966 W. Hiatt
1967 B. Hudspeth
1968 E. Cole
1969 J. Stracey
1970 D. Davies
1971 M. Kingwell
1972 T. Waller
1973 N. Cole
1974 P. Kelly
1975 J. Zeraschi
1976 C. McKenzie
1977 J. Douglas
1978 D. Williams
1979 E. Copeland
1980 A. Willis
1981 A. Willis
1982 A. Adams
1983 D. Dent
1984 D. Griffiths
1985 I. Mustafa
1986 J. Alsop
1987 A. Holligan
1988 A. Hall
1989 A. Hall
1990 J. Pender
1991 J. Matthews
1992 D. McCarrick
1993 P. Richardson
1994 A. Temple
1995 A. Vaughan
1996 C. Wall
1997 R. Hatton
1998 N. Wright
1999 D. Happe
2000 N. Wright
2001 G. Smith
2002 L. Daws
2003 L. Beavis
2004 J. Watson
2005 M. Grant
2006 J. Cox
2007 B. Saunders
2008 L. Smith

Welterweight
1920 F. Whitbread
1921 A. Ireland
1922 E. White
1923 P. Green
1924 P. O'Hanrahan
1925 P. O'Hanrahan
1926 B. Marshall

1927 H. Dunn
1928 H. Bone
1929 T. Wigmore
1930 F. Brooman
1931 J. Barry
1932 D. McCleave
1933 P. Peters
1934 D. McCleave
1935 D. Lynch
1936 W. Pack
1937 D. Lynch
1938 C. Webster
1939 R. Thomas
1944 H. Hall
1945 R. Turpin
1946 J. Ryan
1947 J. Ryan
1948 M. Shacklady
1949 A. Buxton
1950 T. Ratcliffe
1951 J. Maloney
1952 J. Maloney
1953 L. Morgan
1954 N. Gargano
1955 N. Gargano
1956 N. Gargano
1957 R. Warnes
1958 B. Nancurvis
1959 J. McGrail
1960 C. Humphries
1961 A. Lewis
1962 J. Pritchett
1963 J. Pritchett
1964 M. Varley
1965 P. Henderson
1966 P. Cragg
1967 D. Cranswick
1968 A. Tottoh
1969 T. Henderson
1970 T. Waller
1971 D. Davies
1972 T. Francis
1973 T. Waller
1974 T. Waller
1975 W. Bennett
1976 C. Jones
1977 C. Jones
1978 E. Byrne
1979 J. Frost
1980 T. Marsh
1981 T. Marsh
1982 C. Pyatt
1983 R. McKenley
1984 M. Hughes
1985 E. McDonald
1986 D. Dyer
1987 M. Elliot
1988 M. McCreath
1989 M. Elliot
1990 A. Carew
1991 J. Calzaghe
1992 M. Santini
1993 C. Bessey
1994 K. Short
1995 M. Hall
1996 J. Khaliq
1997 F. Barrett
1998 D. Walker
1999 A. Cesay
2000 F. Doherty
2001 M. Macklin

2002 M. Lomax
2003 D. Happe
2004 M. Murray
2005 B. Flournoy
2006 D. Vassell
2007 J. Selkirk
2008 A. Ogogo

L. Middleweight
1951 A. Lay
1952 B. Foster
1953 B. Wells
1954 B. Wells
1955 B. Foster
1956 J. McCormack
1957 J. Cunningham
1958 S. Pearson
1959 S. Pearson
1960 W. Fisher
1961 J. Gamble
1962 J. Lloyd
1963 A. Wyper
1964 W. Robinson
1965 P. Dwyer
1966 T. Imrie
1967 A. Edwards
1968 E. Blake
1969 T. Imrie
1970 D. Simmonds
1971 A. Edwards
1972 L. Paul
1973 R. Maxwell
1974 R. Maxwell
1975 A. Harrison
1976 W. Lauder
1977 C. Malarkey
1978 E. Henderson
1979 D. Brewster
1980 J. Price
1981 E. Christie
1982 D. Milligan
1983 R. Douglas
1984 R. Douglas
1985 R. Douglas
1986 T. Velinor
1987 N. Brown
1988 W. Ellis
1989 N. Brown
1990 T. Taylor
1991 T. Taylor
1992 J. Calzaghe
1993 D. Starie
1994 W. Alexander
1995 C. Bessey
1996 S. Dann
1997 C. Bessey
1998 C. Bessey
1999 C. Bessey
2000 C. Bessey
2001 M. Thirwall
2002 P. Smith

Middleweight
1881 T. Bellhouse
1882 A. H. Curnick
1883 A. J. Curnick
1884 W. Brown
1885 M. Salmon
1886 W. King
1887 R. Hair
1888 R. Hair

1889 G. Sykes	1969 D. Wallington	1954 A. Madigan	1886 A. Diamond	1966 A. Brogan

1889 G. Sykes
1890 J. Hoare
1891 J. Steers
1892 J. Steers
1893 J. Steers
1894 W. Sykes
1895 G. Townsend
1896 W. Ross
1897 W. Dees
1898 G. Townsend
1899 R. Warnes
1900 E. Mann
1901 R. Warnes
1902 E. Mann
1903 R. Warnes
1904 E. Mann
1905 J. Douglas
1906 A. Murdock
1907 R. Warnes
1908 W. Child
1909 W. Child
1910 R. Warnes
1911 W. Child
1912 E. Chandler
1913 W. Bradley
1914 H. Brown
1919 H. Mallin
1920 H. Mallin
1921 H. Mallin
1922 H. Mallin
1923 H. Mallin
1924 J. Elliot
1925 J. Elliot
1926 F. P. Crawley
1927 F. P. Crawley
1928 F. Mallin
1929 F. Mallin
1930 F. Mallin
1931 F. Mallin
1932 F. Mallin
1933 A. Shawyer
1934 J. Magill
1935 J. Magill
1936 A. Harrington
1937 M. Dennis
1938 H. Tiller
1939 H. Davies
1944 J. Hockley
1945 R. Parker
1946 R. Turpin
1947 R. Agland
1948 J. Wright
1949 S. Lewis
1950 P. Longo
1951 E. Ludlam
1952 T. Gooding
1953 R. Barton
1954 K. Phillips
1955 F. Hope
1956 R. Redrup
1957 P. Burke
1958 P. Hill
1959 F. Elderfield
1960 R. Addison
1961 J. Caiger
1962 A. Matthews
1963 A. Matthews
1964 W. Stack
1965 W. Robinson
1966 C. Finnegan
1967 A. Ball
1968 P. McCann

1969 D. Wallington
1970 J. Conteh
1971 A. Minter
1972 F. Lucas
1973 F. Lucas
1974 D. Odwell
1975 D. Odwell
1976 E. Burke
1977 R. Davies
1978 H. Graham
1979 N. Wilshire
1980 M. Kaylor
1981 B. Schumacher
1982 J. Price
1983 T. Forbes
1984 B. Schumacher
1985 D. Cronin
1986 N. Benn
1987 R. Douglas
1988 M. Edwards
1989 S. Johnson
1990 S. Wilson
1991 M. Edwards
1992 L. Woolcock
1993 J. Calzaghe
1994 D. Starie
1995 J. Matthews
1996 J. Pearce
1997 I. Cooper
1998 J. Pearce
1999 C. Froch
2000 S. Swales
2001 C. Froch
2002 N. Perkins
2003 N. Perkins
2004 D. Guthrie
2005 J. Degale
2006 J. Degale
2007 G. Groves
2008 G. Groves

L. Heavyweight
1920 H. Franks
1921 L. Collett
1922 H. Mitchell
1923 H. Mitchell
1924 H. Mitchell
1925 H. Mitchell
1926 D. McCorkindale
1927 A. Jackson
1928 A. Jackson
1929 J. Goyder
1930 J. Murphy
1931 J. Petersen
1932 J. Goyder
1933 G. Brennan
1934 G. Brennan
1935 R. Hearns
1936 J. Magill
1937 J. Wilby
1938 A. S. Brown
1939 B. Woodcock
1944 E. Shackleton
1945 A. Watson
1946 J. Taylor
1947 A. Watson
1948 D. Scott
1949 *Declared no contest*
1950 P. Messervy
1951 G. Walker
1952 H. Cooper
1953 H. Cooper

1954 A. Madigan
1955 D. Rent
1956 D. Mooney
1957 T. Green
1958 J. Leeming
1959 J. Ould
1960 J. Ould
1961 J. Bodell
1962 J. Hendrickson
1963 P. Murphy
1964 J. Fisher
1965 E. Whistler
1966 R. Tighe
1967 M. Smith
1968 R. Brittle
1969 J. Frankham
1970 J. Rafferty
1971 J. Conteh
1972 W. Knight
1973 W. Knight
1974 W. Knight
1975 M. Heath
1976 G. Evans
1977 C. Lawson
1978 V. Smith
1979 A. Straughn
1980 A. Straughn
1981 A. Straughn
1982 G. Crawford
1983 A. Wilson
1984 A. Wilson
1985 J. Beckles
1986 J. Moran
1987 J. Beckles
1988 N. Lawson
1989 N. Piper
1990 J. McCluskey
1991 A. Todd
1992 K. Oliver
1993 K. Oliver
1994 K. Oliver
1995 K. Oliver
1996 C. Fry
1997 P. Rogers
1998 C. Fry
1999 J. Ainscough
2000 P. Haymer
2001 C. Fry
2002 T. Marsden
2003 J. Boyd
2004 M. Abdusalem
2005 D. Pendleton
2006 T. Jeffries
2007 O. Mbwakongo
2008 I. Szucs

Cruiserweight
1998 T. Oakey
1999 M. Krence
2000 J. Dolan
2001 J. Dolan
2002 J. Dolan
2007 J-L Dickinson
2008 M. Askin

Heavyweight
1881 R. Frost-Smith
1882 H. Dearsley
1883 H. Dearsley
1884 H. Dearsley
1885 W. West

1886 A. Diamond
1887 E. White
1888 W. King
1889 A. Bowman
1890 J. Steers
1891 V. Barker
1892 J. Steers
1893 J. Steers
1894 H. King
1895 W. E. Johnstone
1896 W. E. Johnstone
1897 G. Townsend
1898 G. Townsend
1899 F. Parks
1900 W. Dees
1901 F. Parks
1902 F. Parks
1903 F. Dickson
1904 A. Horner
1905 F. Parks
1906 F. Parks
1907 H. Brewer
1908 S. Evans
1909 C. Brown
1910 F. Storbeck
1911 W. Hazell
1912 R. Smith
1913 R. Smith
1914 E. Chandler
1919 H. Brown
1920 R. Rawson
1921 R. Rawson
1922 T. Evans
1923 E. Eagan
1924 A. Clifton
1925 D. Lister
1926 T. Petersen
1927 C. Capper
1928 J. L. Driscoll
1929 P. Floyd
1930 V. Stuart
1931 M. Flanagan
1932 V. Stuart
1933 C. O'Grady
1934 P. Floyd
1935 P. Floyd
1936 V. Stuart
1937 V. Stuart
1938 G. Preston
1939 A. Porter
1944 M. Hart
1945 D. Scott
1946 P. Floyd
1947 G. Scriven
1948 J. Gardner
1949 A. Worrall
1950 P. Toch
1951 A. Halsey
1952 E. Hearn
1953 J. Erskine
1954 B. Harper
1955 D. Rowe
1956 D. Rent
1957 D. Thomas
1958 D. Thomas
1959 D. Thomas
1960 L. Hobbs
1961 W. Walker
1962 R. Dryden
1963 R. Sanders
1964 C. Woodhouse
1965 W. Wells

1966 A. Brogan
1967 P. Boddington
1968 W. Wells
1969 A. Burton
1970 J. Gilmour
1971 L. Stevens
1972 T. Wood
1973 G. McEwan
1974 N. Meade
1975 G. McEwan
1976 J. Rafferty
1977 G. Adair
1978 J. Awome
1979 A. Palmer
1980 F. Bruno
1981 A. Elliott
1982 H. Hylton
1983 H. Notice
1984 D. Young
1985 H. Hylton
1986 E. Cardouza
1987 J. Moran
1988 H. Akinwande
1989 H. Akinwande
1990 K. Inglis
1991 P. Lawson
1992 S. Welch
1993 P. Lawson
1994 S. Burford
1995 M. Ellis
1996 T. Oakey
1997 B. Stevens
1998 N. Hosking
1999 S. St John
2000 D. Dolan
2001 D. Dolan
2002 D. Dolan
2003 M. O'Connell
2004 T. Bellew
2005 T. Bellew
2006 T. Bellew
2007 Daniel Price
2008 W. Baister

S. Heavyweight
1982 A. Elliott
1983 K. Ferdinand
1984 R. Wells
1985 G. Williamson
1986 J. Oyebola
1987 J. Oyebola
1988 K. McCormack
1989 P. Passley
1990 M. McCormack
1991 K. McCormack
1992 M. Hopper
1993 M. McKenzie
1994 D. Watts
1995 R. Allen
1996 D. Watts
1997 A. Harrison
1998 A. Harrison
1999 W. Bessey
2000 J. McDermott
2001 M. Grainger
2002 M. Grainger
2003 David Price
2004 J. Young
2005 David Price
2006 D. Chisora
2007 David Price
2008 T. Fury

Irish Championships, 2007-2008

Senior Tournament

The National Stadium, Dublin – 8 to 11 January
L.Fly: *final*: P. Barnes (Holy Family, Belfast) w rtd 4 J. Moore (St Francis, Limerick). **Fly**: *semi-finals*: R. Dalton (St John's, Antrim) wo, S. Cox (Gorey) w pts J. Conlon (St John Bosco, Belfast); *final*: S. Cox w pts R. Dalton. **Bantam**: *quarter-finals*: R. Lindberg (Immaculata, Belfast) wo, T.J. Doherty (Portlaoise, Laois) wo, J.J. Nevin (Cavan) w pts D. Coughlin (St Anne's, Westport), D. Thorpe (St Aiden's, Wexford) w pts F. Campbell (Edenderry, Ofally); *semi-finals*: T.J. Doherty w pts D. Thorpe, J.J. Nevin w pts R. Lindberg; *final*: J.J. Nevin w pts T.J. Doherty. **Feather**: *quarter-finals*: C. Frampton (Midland White City, Belfast), D.O. Joyce (St Michael's, Athy) wo, E. Touhy (Moate, Westmeath) w pts W. Casey (Our Lady of Lourdes, Limerick), K. Fennessy (Clonmel, Tipperary) w pts S. Kilroy (Holy Family, Drogheda); *semi-finals*: D.O. Joyce w pts E. Touhy, K. Fennessy w pts C. Frampton; *final*: D.O. Joyce w pts K. Fennessy. **Light**: *quarter-finals*: E. Donovan (St Michael's, Athy) wo, S. Ormond (St Matthew's, Dublin) wo, R. Hickey (Grangecon, Kildare) w pts C. Bates (St Mary's, Dublin), A. Cacace (Holy Trinity, Belfast) w pts D. McCombe (Holy Trinity, Belfast); *semi-finals*: R. Hickey w pts E. Donovan, A. Cacace w pts S. Ormond; *final*: R. Hickey w pts A. Cacace. **L. Welter**: *quarter-finals*: J.J. Joyce (St Michael's, Athy) w rsc 3 D. Barrett (Rylane, Cork), P. Sutcliffe (Crumlin, Dublin) w rsc 4 J. Dowling (Paulstown, Kilkenny), J. Kavanagh (Crumlin, Dublin) w rsc 3 M. Wickham (St Anthony's/St Patrick's, Wexford), J. Murray (Crumlin, Dublin) w pts T. Dwyer (St Aiden's, Wexford); *semi-finals*: J.J. Joyce w rsc 3 P. Sutcliffe, J. Kavanagh w pts J. Murray; *final*: J.J. Joyce w rsc 3 J. Kavanagh. **Welter**: *quarter-finals*: R. Sheahan (St Michael's, Athy) wo, W. McLoughlin (Illies Golden Gloves, Donegal) w pts T. O'Neill (St Saviour's, Dublin), R. Brennan (Dealgan, Louth) w disq 4 Z. Bujuskus (Arklow, Wicklow), J.J. McDonagh (Brosna, Offaly) w pts F. Redmond (Arklow, Wicklow); *semi-finals*: R. Sheahan w rsc 3 W. McLoughlin, J.J. McDonagh w rsc 4 R. Brennan; *final*: R. Sheahan w pts J.J. McDonagh. **Middle**: *quarter-finals*: D. Sutherland (St Saviour's, Dublin) wo, S. Shevlin (Dealgan, Louth) wo, D. O'Neill (Paulstown, Kilkenny) wo, E. Healy (Portlaoise, Laois) w pts E. O'Kane (Immaculata, Belfast); *semi-finals*: D. Sutherland w rsc 2 S. Shevlin, D. O'Neill w pts E. Healy; *final*: D. Sutherland w pts D. O'Neill. **L.Heavy**: *semi-finals*: K. Egan (Neilstown, Dublin) wo, C. Curtis (Dealgan, Louth) w pts M. Mullaney (Claremorris, Mayo); *final*: K. Egan w pts C. Curtis. **Heavy**: *prelims*: John Sweeney (Dungloe, Donegal) wo, W. Byrne (Knocknagoshel, Kerry) wo, P. Kearns (Golden Cobra, Dublin) wo, C. Sheehan (Clonmel, Tipperary) w pts P. Phelan (St Michael's, Athy), T. Sheehan (St Michael's, Athy) w pts Jim Sweeney (Drimnagh, Dublin), N. Kennedy (Gorey) w pts M. Donovan (Our Lady of Lourdes, Limerick), P. Corcoran (Galway) w pts J. Power (St Francis, Limerick), G. Riggs (St Saviour's, Dublin) w pts M. Oshun (Arklow, Wicklow); *quarter-finals*: W. Byrne w pts P. Kearns, C. Sheehan w pts John Sweeney, T. Sheehan w pts N. Kennedy, P. Corcoran w pts G. Riggs; *semi-finals*: C. Sheehan w pts W. Byrne, T. Sheehan w pts P. Corcoran; *final*: C. Sheehan w pts T. Sheehan. **S.Heavy**: *final*: C. McMonagle (Holy Trinity, Belfast) wo.

Intermediate finals

The National Stadium, Dublin – 7 December
L.Fly: P. Brady (Holy Trinity, Belfast) wo D. Geraghty (Docklands, Dublin). **Fly**: T. McCullough (Illies Golden Gloves, Donegal) w rsc 3 C. Rice (Immaculata, Belfast). **Bantam**: D. Coughlin (St Anne's, Westport) w pts G. Murray (St Saviour's, Dublin). **Feather**: Gavin Keating (St Saviour's, Dublin) w pts Graham Keating (St Saviour's, Dublin). **Light**: J. Murray (Gorey) w pts G. Casey (Our Lady of Lourdes, Limerick). **L.Welter**: J. Kavanagh (Crumlin, Dublin) w pts N. McGinley (Bishop Kelly, Omagh). **Welter**: M. McNamara (St Francis, Limerick) w pts S. McKeown (Sacred Heart, Belfast). **L.Middle**: M. Collins (Darndale, Dublin) w pts M. Carlyle (Crumlin, Dublin). **Middle**: B. Brosnan (Olympic, Galway) w pts S. O'Reilly (Twintowns, Donegal). **L.Heavy**: B. Barrett (Olympic, Galway) w rtd 4 D. Tourish (Twintowns, Donegal) **Cruiser**: M. Collins (Darndale, Dublin) w pts P. Halligan (Midfield, Mayo). **Heavy**: W. Byrne (Knocknagoshel, Kerry) w pts J. Connors (Darndale, Dublin). **S.Heavy**: D. Joyce (Moate, Westmeath) w co 1 E. Higgins (UCC, Cork).

Under-21 finals

National Stadium, Dublin – 19 October
L.Fly: D. Geraghty (Docklands, Dublin). wo. **Fly**: G. McDonagh (Kilcullen, Kildare) w rsc 3 S. Donnellan (Monivea, Galway). **Bantam**: M. McCullagh (Cairn Lodge, Belfast) w pts R. Dalton (St John's, Antrim). **Feather**: Gavin Keating (St Saviour's, Dublin) w pts J. Upton (Westside, Dublin). **Light**: J. Murray (Gorey) w pts S. Donnelly (Saints, Belfast). **L.Welter**: J. Kavanagh (Crumlin, Dublin) w pts A. Nolan (The Ballagh, Wicklow). **Welter**: C. Boyle (Dunfanaghy, Donegal) w pts P. Upton (Westside, Dublin). **L.Middle**: S. O'Reilly (Twintowns, Donegal) w pts M. Collins (Darndale, Dublin). **Middle**: B. Brosnan (Olympic, Galway) w pts M. Lynch (Illies Golden Gloves, Donegal). **L.Heavy**: M. Ward (Galway) w pts C. McAuley (Holy Family, Belfast). **Cruiser**: P. Corcoran (Galway) w pts J. Stokes (Loughglynn, Roscommon). **Heavy**: C. Sheehan (Clonmel, Tipperary) w pts L. Cadden (Cavan). **S.Heavy**: D. Joyce (Moate, Westmeath) w pts M. Stokes (Crumlin, Dublin).

Under-19 finals

National Stadium, Dublin – 6 June
L.Fly: D. Geraghty (Docklands, Dublin) w pts G. Molloy (Moate, Westmeath). **Fly**: R. Dalton (St John's Antrim) w pts M. Stevens (Crumlin, Dublin). **Bantam**: T. McCullagh (Illies Golden Gloves, Donegal) w pts B. McDonagh (St Paul's, Waterford). **Feather**: T. McKenna (Oliver Plunkett, Belfast) w rsc 2 C. Haggerty (Golden Cobra, Dublin). **Light**: R. Moylett (St Anne's, Mayo) w pts M. McDonagh (St Anne's, Mayo). **L.Welter**: J. Kavanagh (Crumlin, Dublin) w pts P. Ward (Olympic, Galway). **Welter**: D.J. Joyce (St Michael's, Athy) w pts C. Boyle (Dunfanaghy, Donegal). **Middle**: D. Barrett (Geesala, Mayo) w pts M. O'Sullivan (Frenchpark, Roscommon). **L.Heavy**: T. McCarthy (Oliver Plunkett, Belfast) w rsc 1 S. Ward (Monkstown, Antrim). **Heavy**: R. Lacey (St Nicholas, Tipperary) w pts L. Cadden (Cavan). **S.Heavy**: D. Cruise (Annagh/Ballhaunis, Mayo) w pts J. Stokes (Loughglynn, Roscommon).

Scottish and Welsh Senior Championships, 2007-2008

Scotland ABA

High School Gymnasium, Lasswade – 1 & 28 March, Hilton Hotel & Aberdeen – 7 March, Miners' Club, Dalkeith

L.Fly: no entries. **Fly**: no entries. **Bantam**: *semi-finals*: B. Parker (Linwood) wo, J. Thomson (Dennistoun) w pts G. Stemp (Sparta); *final*: J. Thomson w pts B. Parker. **Feather**: *quarter-finals*: M. Roberts (Forgewood) wo, D. McNally Doon Valley) wo, S. Cunningham (Lochee) wo, L. Moles (Denny) w pts D. Cowan (Sparta); *semi-finals*: M. Roberts w pts D. McNally, L. Moles w pts S. Cunningham; *final*: M. Roberts w pts L. Moles. **Light**: *quarter-finals*: J. Kelso (Blantyre) w rsc 1 C. Duffy (Barn), S. Dick (Paisley) w rsc 2 K. Whyte (Alloa), T. Graham (Auchengeich) w pts A. McKelvie (St Francis), S. Sharoudi (Forgewood) w pts S. Carroll (Granite City); *semi-finals*: J. Kelso w pts S. Dick, S. Sharoudi w pts T. Graham; *final*: S. Sharoudi w pts J. Kelso. **L.Welter**: *prelims*: D. Foster (Arbroath) wo, M. Kelly (Forgewood) wo, E. Doyle (Glenboig) wo, E. Finney (Kingdom) wo, D. Love (Holyrood) wo, J. Thain (Gilmerton) wo, R. McMurdie (Newarthill) wo, D. Brown (Port Glasgow) w pts D. McCulloch (Lochside); *quarter-finals*: D. Foster w pts M. Kelly, E. Doyle w rsc 1 E. Finney, D. Brown w pts D. Love, J. Thain w pts R. McMurdie; *semi-finals*: E. Doyle w pts D. Foster, J. Thain w pts D. Brown; *final*: J. Thain w pts E. Doyle. **Welter**: *prelims*: A. Gonsalves (Kinross) wo, G. Thomson (Stirling) wo, M. McAllister (Granite City) wo, M. Jammeh (Leith Victoria) wo, S. Banks (Jerviston) w pts A. Hardie (Leith Victoria), P. Allison (Millennium) w rsc 3 A. Chisholm (Inverness), K. Guthrie (Kingdom) w pts D. Armstrong (Cleland), S. Ross (Inverness) w pts R. Singh (Bellahouston); *quarter-finals*: S. Banks w pts M. Jammeh, M. McAllister w pts P. Allison, G. Thomson w rsc 4 A. Gonsalves, S. Ross w pts K. Guthrie; *semi-finals*: S. Banks w pts G. Thomson, M. McAllister w pts S. Ross; *final*: M. McAllister w pts S. Banks. **Middle**: *quarter-finals*: D. Drummond (Lochee) wo, A. Montgomery (Jerviston) w pts J. Cunningham (Dennistoun), F. Mhura (Leith Victoria) w co 3 A. McKelvie (St Francis), K. Finn (Lochend) w pts D. Campbell (Denbeath); *semi-finals*: D. Drummond wo F. Mhura, A. Montgomery w pts K. Finn; *final*: A. Montgomery w pts D. Drummond. **L.Heavy**: *quarter-finals*: T. Carter (Glenrothes) wo, C. Johnson (Newarthill) wo, K. McCallum (Dunfermline) wo, M. Davidson (Lochside) w pts J. Thomson (Springhill); *semi-finals*: T. Carter w rtd 4 K. McCallum, C. Johnson wo M. Davidson; *final*: T. Carter w pts M. Davidson – replaced C. Johnson. **Heavy**: *semi-finals*: Y. Pavlov (Glenrothes) wo, M. Warner (Springhill) w pts M. McDonagh (Port Glasgow Victoria); *final*: M. Warner w pts Y. Pavlov. **S.Heavy**: *quarter-finals*: F. Thirde (Arbroath) wo, R. Henderson (Springhill) w co 1 C. McFadden (Alloa), R. Parnez (Dennistoun) w pts S. Palmer (Inverness), J. McAvoy (Stirling) w pts J. McKechnie (Wellmeadow); *semi-finals*: F. Thirde w pts R. Henderson, J. McAvoy w pts R. Parnez; *final*: F. Thirde w pts J. McAvoy.

Wales ABA

Welsh Institute of Sport, Cardiff – 16 February, The Leisure Centre, Cowbridge – 24 February & Afan Lido, Port Talbot – 7 March

L.Fly: *final*: A. Perry (Colcot) wo. **Fly**: *final*: J.Beasley (Aberystwyth) wo. **Bantam**: *semi-finals*: A. Selby (Splott Adventure) wo, J. Gage (Cwmavon Hornets) w pts C.Jenkins (Cwmgors); *final*: A.Selby w pts J. Gage. **Feather**: *quarter-finals*: S. Kilroy (St Joseph's, Cardiff) wo, L. Earls (Ferndale) wo, L. Davies (Cwmgors) w pts S. Davies (Carmarthen), R. Evans (Church Place) w rsc 1 K. Hardcastle (Cwmavon Hornets); *semi-finals*: S. Kilroy w rsc 3 L. Earls, R. Evans w rsc 1 L. Davies; *final*: S.Kilroy w pts R. Evans. **Light**: *quarter-finals*: K. Wisniewski (Army) wo, P. Harris (Bonymaen) wo, L. Selby (Splott Adventure) wo, R. Griffiths (Merthyr Ex-Servicemen) w pts D. Harty (Heads of the Valley); *semi-finals*: K. Wisniewski w pts P. Harris, L. Selby w pts R. Griffiths; *final*: L. Selby w pts K. Wisniewski. **L.Welter**: *quarter-finals*: L. Rees (Rhondda) wo, J. Flinn (Standard Triumph, Coventry) wo, C. Nagel (Stable) w pts C. D. Lynch (Swansea), S. Jamma (Cardiff YMCA); *semi-finals*: L. Rees w pts J. Flinn, C. Nagel w co 4 S. Jamma; *final*: L. Rees w pts C. Nagel. **Welter**: *prelims*: M. Innes (Cwmbran) wo, P. Hayhurst (Carmarthen) wo, L. Trott (Towy) wo, J. Weetch (Cwmcarn) wo, D. Hazeldene (Maesgwl) wo, J. Moss (Cwmbran) w pts N. Davies (Dowlais), J. Todd (Bonymaen) w pts D. Jones (Fleur-de-Lys), R. Evans (Dowlais) w pts Z. Ummar (St Joseph's, Newport); *quarter-finals*: M. Innes w rsc 2 P. Hayhurst, L. Trott w pts J. Weetch, J. Moss w pts D. Hazeldene, R. Evans w pts J. Todd; *semi-finals*: M. Innes w pts L. Trott, R. Evans w pts J. Moss; *final*: M. Innes w pts R. Evans. **Middle**: *quarter-finals*: G. Straddon (Trostre) wo, M. Saint (Glyncorrwg) wo, D. Smith (Pontypool & Panteg) w pts S. Scourfield (Clwyd), L. Bunce (Merthyr Ex-Servicemen) w rsc 2 S. Weaver (Carmarthen); *semi-finals*: G. Straddon w rsc 3 M. Saint, D. Smith w pts L. Bunce; *final*: D. Smith w pts G. Straddon. **L.Heavy**: *quarter-finals*: T. Webb (Bonymaen) w pts J. Hughes (St Joseph's, Newport), J. Evans (Pontypool & Panteg) w pts J. Morris (Fleur-de-Lys), G. Jones (Army) w pts G. Millington (Shotton), R. Davies (Standard Triumph, Coventry) w pts J. Asare (Mertyr Ex-Servicemen); *semi-finals*: R Davies wo T. Webb, G. Jones w pts J. Evans; *final*: R. Davies w pts G. Jones. **Heavy**: *quarter-finals*: S. Frith (Maesteg) wo, L. Milsjen (Rhoose) wo, J. Bunce (Merthyr Ex-Servicemen) wo, J. Phillips (Gwent) w pts J. O'Kelly (Barry Eastend); *semi-finals*: S. Frith w pts L. Milsjen, J. Phillips w pts J. Bunce. *final*: J.Phillips w rsc 3 S. Frith. **S.Heavy**: *quarter-finals*: A. W. Jones (Shotton) wo, F. Williams (All Saints) wo, S. Brown (Gwent) wo, D. Cronin (All Saints) w pts J. Higgins (All Saints); *semi-finals*: A. W. Jones w pts F. Williams, S. Brown w pts D. Cronin; *final*: A. W. Jones w pts S. Brown.

British Junior Championship Finals, 2007-2008

National Association of Clubs for Young People (NACYP)

The Festival Hall, Kirkby in Ashfield – 3 March

Class A: 46kg: M. Smith (Bushey) w ptd G. Venness (Newham). 48kg: D. Harker (Darlington) w pts Z. Davies (Chelmsley Wood). 50kg: R. Cawley (Chelmsley Wood) w pts L. Coppin (Newham). 52kg: B. Beadon (Repton) w pts B. Dolan (Birtley). 54kg: T. Simpson (Stockbridge) w pts M. Hedges (Repton). 57kg: S. Asif (South Bank) w pts L. Adolphe (Earlsfield). 60kg: J. Evans (St Joseph's East) w pts S. Lewis (Long Lane). 63kg: J. Ward (Repton) w pts J. Kelly (Egan's Academy). 66kg: T. Ghent (Priory Park) w rsc 1 P. Fannerman (Dale Youth). 70kg: L. Richards (Repton) w pts J. Allan (Phil Thomas SoB). 75kg: H. Amjad (Bury) w pts N. Nichols (Cwmcarn). 80kg: J. Millen (Hailsham) wo. 85kg: S. Delaney (Hornchurch & Elm Park) w pts W. Cassap (Lambton Street).

Ponds Forge Leisure Centre, Sheffield – 6 March

Class B: 48kg: M. Ward (Repton) w pts B. Joyce (Kingsthorpe). 50kg: J. Dickens (Golden Gloves) w pts J. Bloor (Queensberry Police). 52kg: G. Yafai (Birmingham City Police) w pts J. Brain (Premier). 54kg: M. Morrison (Pembroke) w pts M. Mongon (Bridgewater Salford). 57kg: S. Jenkins (St Michael's) w pts J. Kennedy (Shepway). 60kg: F. Evans (St Joseph's East) w pts S. Barnes (Manor). 63kg: J. Kerr (West Ham) w pts N. Dale (Kingfisher). 66kg: C. Gaynor (Millennium) w pts D. Innes (Cwmbran). 70kg: R. Aston (Priory Park) w pts L. Thomas (Gwynfi). 75kg: L. Camp-Hayward (Chadwell & Corringham) w pts A. Rees (St Joseph's East). 80kg: D. Price (Skelmersdale) w pts C. Burgess (Lawrence). 85kg: N. Smith (Pinewood Starr) w pts D. Hodge (Bridgefoot). 91kg: K. Tierney (North Mersey) w pts O. Siuabdellah (Benny's).

Chelsea Football Club, London – 7 March

Class C: 48kg: T. Stubbs (Northside) w pts J. Harries (Premier). 51kg: W. Hussain (Aston Police) w pts D. Chapman (Gwynfi). 54kg: D. Walton (Hall Green) w pts J. Otwell (Oxford BA). 57kg: L. Cooksey (Prince of Wales) w pts K. Goodings (Sunderland). 60kg: J. Rogers (Parsons Cross) w pts L. McGoldrick (St Joseph's East). 64kg: J. Hughes (Malmesbury) w pts T. Langford (Hall Green). 69kg: S. Henty (Eltham) w pts C. Burton (Egan's Academy). 75kg: F. Buglioni (Repton) w rsc 2 J. Scotter (Scarborough). 81kg: L. Holland (Egan's Academy) w pts W. Evans (Splott Adventure). 86kg: K. Pitman (Earl Shilton) wo. 91kg: S. Robbins (Chelmsley Wood) w pts J. Creek (Barnstaple). 91+kg: J. Radford (Hard & Fast) w pts S. Gunther (Stable).

Golden Gloves (Schools)

The Leisure Centre, Knottingley – 8 March

Class 1: 34kg: A. Lee (Eltham & District) w pts D. Manning (Northside). 32kg: D. Chalk (Guildford City) w pts R. Burrows (Pleck). 34kg: A. Sharp (Eltham & District) w pts C. O'Regan (Cleckheaton). 36kg: A. Middleton (Nemesis) w pts C. Farley (Salisbury). 38kg: D. Arnold (Repton) w pts T. Aitchinson (Skelmersdale). 40kg: C. Stevens (March) w rsc 2 J. Wood (Wednesbury). 42kg: J. James (Northside) w pts S. McDonagh (Stowe). 44kg: J. Weedon (Five Star) w pts L. Parrock (Priory Park). 46kg: J. King (Repton) w pts K. Ward (Darnhill & Heywood). 48kg: J. McDonagh (Walcot Boys) w pts R. Bolton (Broad Plain). 50kg: J. Bradley (Benny's) w pts S. Baker (Repton). 52kg: M. Dumphey (Guildford City) w pts I. Shah (Audley Police). 54kg: H. Fury (Skerton) w pts L. Joseph (Marlow). 57kg: B. Ako (Salisbury) w pts A. Little (Brompton). 60kg: N. Halton (Apollo) w pts R. Bithell (Queensberry Police).

Class 2: 34kg: J. Bateson (Burmantofts) w pts J. Budge (St Mary's). 36kg: M. Leach (Bridgewater Salford) w pts P. Lovejoy (Repton). 38kg: I. Greenwell (Sunderland) w pts J. Smith (Bushey). 40kg: T. Beaney (West Ham) w pts T. Ward (Birtley). 42kg: A. Price (West Ham) w pts Z. Parker (Bunton). 44kg: T. McDonagh (Dale Youth) w pts R. Fillingham (Bracebridge).

46kg: R. Wallace (Repton) w pts J. Maphosa (Middlesbrough). 48kg: J. Collins (Priory Park) w pts L. Keller (Repton). 50kg: F. Smith (Hailsham) w rsc 2 L. Hatfield (Brambles Farm). 52kg: M. Joynson (Kirkby) w pts J. Gill (Chatteris). 54kg: G. Grotty (Stevenage) w pts C. Sugden (Newark). 57kg: M. Baker (Repton) w pts R. Morgan (Middlesbrough). 60kg: P. Miller (Skerton) w pts R. Martin (Walcot Boys). 63kg: S. O'Driscoll (West Ham) w rsc 2 M. Hussain (Northside). 66kg: N. Pemberton (Darnhill & Heywood) w pts G. Jones (Bedworth Ex-Servicemen).

Class 3: 38kg: C. Driscoll (West Ham) w pts J. Dring (Gemini). 40kg: C. Edwards (Newham) w pts C. Gibbs (Chelmsley Wood). 42kg: L. Patel (Dale Youth) w disq 3 C. Nixon (Wombwell & Dearne). 44kg: M. Cousins (West Ham) w pts J. Crossley (Vauxhall Motors). 46kg: J. Costello (Chelmsley Wood) w pts C. Smith (Newham). 48kg: J. Cooke (Rayleigh Mill) w pts L. Garrett (Shildon). 50kg: H. Thomas (Darlington) w pts R. Jackson (Fisher). 52kg: J. McDonagh (Stowe) w pts D. Craven (Bridgefoot). 54kg: M. Lee (Guildford City) w pts M. McDonnell (Northside). 57kg: J. Reay (Lancaster) w pts A. Doe (Bushey). 60kg: J. Coyle (Newham) w pts D. Jones (Bateson's). 63kg: W. Ingram (Gloucester) w pts T. Aitchinson (Salisbury). 66kg: E. Matthews (Guildford City) w pts J. Newell (Ancoats). 70kg: L. Coneley (Sporting Ring) w pts E. Wharton (Phoenix). 75kg: S. Smith (Pinewood Starr) w pts J. Rough (Lambton Street).

ABA Youth

Everton Park Sports Centre, Liverpool – 31 May

Class 4: 46kg: G. Venness (Newham) w pts R. Hamza (Aston Police). 48kg: C. Johnson (Tower Hill) w pts J. Dennard (Nemesis). 50kg: J. Beer (Newham) w pts J. Glover (Kirkby). 52kg: C. Pearson (Barrow) w pts D. Fernandez (Woking). 54kg: B. Beadon (Repton) w disq 3 B. Dolan (Birtley). 57kg: S. Asif (South Bank) w pts L. Adolphe (Earlsfield). 60kg: C. Winston (Hartlepool Catholic) w pts S. McNess (Repton). 63kg: J. Kelly (Egan's Academy) w pts M. Cash (St Albans). 66kg: D. Saunders (St Mary's) w pts J. Turner (Wigan). 70kg: L. Richards (Repton) w pts J. Steffe (Roche). 75kg: E. Duraku (Reading) w pts M. Davies (Salisbury). 80kg: M. Watson (Northumbria SoB) w pts K. Thompson (Portsmouth). 85kg: W. Cassap (Lambton Street) w pts S. Delaney (Hornchurch & Elm Park).

Class 5: 48kg: M. Ward (Repton) w pts C. Blinkhorn (Withern School). 50kg: J. Dickens (Golden Gloves) w rsc 2 J. Pomphrey (Gloucester). 52kg: P. O'Sullivan (Rotunda) w rsc 3 M. Shannon (Marvels Lane). 54kg: S. Brar (Kingsthorpe Boys) w pts D. Benham (Blandford). 57kg: J. Saunders (South Durham) w pts J. Kennedy (Shepway). 60kg: A. Counihan (Chelmsley Wood) w pts J. Winson (Finchley). 63kg: J. Kerr (West Ham) w pts A. Keates (Tamworth). 66kg: A. Fowler (Golden Gloves) w pts T. Horgan (Marvels Lane). 70kg: T. Goodjohn (Haddenham) w pts K. Haywood (Earl Shilton). 75kg: J. Cetaj (Walcot Boys) w pts R. Aston (Priory Park). 80kg: D. Fusco (East Durham Colliery) w pts M. Neilson (Tom Hill). 85kg: M. Jorat (Haringey Police) w pts K. Skill (Woodseats). 91kg: D. Benson (Tameside Elite) w pts M. Raza (Repton).

Class 6: 50kg: K. Farrell (Boarshaw) w rsc 2 A. Seldon (Exeter). 52kg: L. Goodings (Lambton Street) w rsc 4 R. Murray (Golden Ring). 54kg: J. Quigley (Tower Hill) w pts L. Pettitt (Nemesis). 57kg: I. Weaver (Golden Ring) w pts J. McLaren (Queensberry Police). 60kg: S. McBride (Redcar) w pts G. Evans (Golden Ring). 63kg: R. Heffron (Boarshaw) w pts J. Hughes (Malmesbury). 66kg: C. Smith (Rotunda) w pts D. Docherty (Bushey). 70kg: C. Gould (Gloucester) w pts K. Hardman (Handsworth). 75kg: K. Garvey (Earlsfield) w pts M. Laws (Plains Farm). 80kg: C. Delve (Droitwich) w rsc 2 D. Pagan (Berry Boys). 85kg: L. Rennie (King's) w rsc 4 C. Grout (Perth Green). 91kg: S. Robbins (Chelmsley Wood) w pts L. Ford (Ramsgate). 91+kg: M. Wilson (Kettering SoB) w pts S. Virgo (Forest Oaks).

International Amateur Champions, 1904-2008

Shows all Olympic, World, European & Commonwealth champions since 1904. British silver and bronze medal winners are shown throughout, where applicable.

Country Code

ALG = Algeria; ARG = Argentina; ARM = Armenia; AUS = Australia; AUT = Austria; AZE = Azerbaijan; BE = Belarus; BEL = Belgium; BUL = Bulgaria; CAN = Canada; CEY = Ceylon (now Sri Lanka); CI = Channel Islands; CHI = China; CUB = Cuba; DEN = Denmark; DOM = Dominican Republic; ENG = England; ESP = Spain; EST = Estonia; FIJ = Fiji Islands; FIN = Finland; FRA = France; GBR = United Kingdom; GDR = German Democratic Republic; GEO = Georgia; GER = Germany (but West Germany only from 1968-1990); GHA = Ghana; GUY = Guyana; HOL = Netherlands; HUN = Hungary; IND = India; IRL = Ireland; ITA = Italy; JAM = Jamaica; JPN = Japan; KAZ = Kazakhstan; KEN = Kenya; LIT= Lithuania; MAS = Malaysia; MEX = Mexico; MON=Mongolia; MOR = Morocco; MRI = Mauritius; NAM = Nambia; NKO = North Korea; NIG = Nigeria; NIR = Northern Ireland; NOR = Norway; NZL = New Zealand; PAK = Pakistan; POL = Poland; PUR = Puerto Rico; ROM = Romania; RUS = Russia; SAF = South Africa; SCO = Scotland; SER = Serbia; SKO = South Korea; SR = Southern Rhodesia; STV = St Vincent; SWE = Sweden; TCH = Czechoslovakia; THA = Thailand; TUR = Turkey; UGA = Uganda; UKR = Ukraine; URS = USSR; USA = United States of America; UZB = Uzbekistan; VEN = Venezuela; WAL = Wales; YUG = Yugoslavia; ZAM = Zambia.

Olympic Champions, 1904-2008

St Louis, USA - 1904
Fly: G. Finnegan (USA). **Bantam:** O. Kirk (USA). **Feather:** O. Kirk (USA). **Light:** H. Spangler (USA). **Welter:** A. Young (USA). **Middle:** C. May (USA). **Heavy:** S. Berger (USA).

London, England - 1908
Bantam: H. Thomas (GBR). **Feather:** R. Gunn (GBR). **Light:** F. Grace (GBR). **Middle:** J.W.H.T. Douglas (GBR). **Heavy:** A. Oldman (GBR).
Silver medals: J. Condon (GBR), C. Morris (GBR), F. Spiller (GBR), S. Evans (GBR).
Bronze medals: W. Webb (GBR), H. Rodding (GBR), T. Ringer (GBR), H. Johnson (GBR), R. Warnes (GBR), W. Philo (GBR), F. Parks (GBR).

Antwerp, Belgium - 1920
Fly: F. Genaro (USA). **Bantam:** C. Walker (SAF). **Feather:** R. Fritsch (FRA). **Light:** S. Mossberg (USA). **Welter:** T. Schneider (CAN). **Middle:** H. Mallin (GBR). **L. Heavy:** E. Eagan (USA). **Heavy:** R. Rawson (GBR).
Silver medal: A. Ireland (GBR).
Bronze medals: W. Cuthbertson (GBR), G. McKenzie (GBR), H. Franks (GBR).

Paris, France - 1924
Fly: F. la Barba (USA). **Bantam:** W. Smith (SAF). **Feather:** J. Fields (USA). **Light:** H. Nielson (DEN). **Welter:** J. Delarge (BEL). **Middle:** H. Mallin (GBR). **L. Heavy:** H. Mitchell (GBR). **Heavy:** O. von Porat (NOR).
Silver medals: J. McKenzie (GBR), J. Elliot (GBR).

Amsterdam, Holland - 1928
Fly: A. Kocsis (HUN). **Bantam:** V. Tamagnini (ITA). **Feather:** B. van Klaveren (HOL). **Light:** C. Orlando (ITA). **Welter:** E. Morgan (NZL). **Middle:** P. Toscani (ITA). **L. Heavy:** V. Avendano (ARG). **Heavy:** A. Rodriguez Jurado (ARG).

Los Angeles, USA - 1932
Fly: I. Enekes (HUN). **Bantam:** H. Gwynne (CAN). **Feather:** C. Robledo (ARG). **Light:** L. Stevens (SAF). **Welter:** E. Flynn (USA). **Middle:** C. Barth (USA). **L. Heavy:** D. Carstens (SAF). **Heavy:** A. Lovell (ARG).

Berlin, West Germany - 1936
Fly: W. Kaiser (GER). **Bantam:** U. Sergo (ITA). **Feather:** O. Casanova (ARG). **Light:** I. Harangi (HUN). **Welter:** S. Suvio (FIN). **Middle:** J. Despeaux (FRA). **L. Heavy:** R. Michelot (FRA). **Heavy:** H. Runge (GER).

London, England - 1948
Fly: P. Perez (ARG). **Bantam:** T. Csik (HUN). **Feather:** E. Formenti (ITA). **Light:** G. Dreyer (SAF). **Welter:** J. Torma (TCH). **Middle:** L. Papp (HUN). **L. Heavy:** G. Hunter (SAF). **Heavy:** R. Iglesas (ARG).
Silver medals: J. Wright (GBR), D. Scott (GBR).

Helsinki, Finland - 1952
Fly: N. Brooks (USA). **Bantam:** P. Hamalainen (FIN). **Feather:** J. Zachara (TCH). **Light:** A. Bolognesi (ITA). **L. Welter:** C. Adkins (USA). **Welter:** Z. Chychla (POL). **L. Middle:** L. Papp (HUN). **Middle:** F. Patterson (USA). **L. Heavy:** N. Lee (USA). **Heavy:** E. Sanders (USA).
Silver medal: J. McNally (IRL).

Melbourne, Australia - 1956
Fly: T. Spinks (GBR). **Bantam:** W. Behrendt (GER). **Feather:** V. Safronov (URS). **Light:** R. McTaggart (GBR). **L. Welter:** V. Jengibarian (URS). **Welter:** N. Linca (ROM). **L. Middle:** L. Papp (HUN). **Middle:** G. Schatkov (URS). **L. Heavy:** J. Boyd (USA). **Heavy:** P. Rademacher (USA).

Silver medals: T. Nicholls (GBR), F. Tiedt (IRL).
Bronze medals: J. Caldwell (IRL), F. Gilroy (IRL), A. Bryne (IRL), N. Gargano (GBR), J. McCormack (GBR).

Rome, Italy - 1960
Fly: G. Torok (HUN). **Bantam:** O. Grigoryev (URS). **Feather:** F. Musso (ITA). **Light:** K. Pazdzior (POL). **L. Welter:** B. Nemecek (TCH). **Welter:** N. Benvenuti (ITA). **L. Middle:** W. McClure (USA). **Middle:** E. Crook (USA). **L. Heavy:** C. Clay (USA). **Heavy:** F. de Piccoli (ITA).
Bronze medals: R. McTaggart (GBR), J. Lloyd (GBR), W. Fisher (GBR).

Tokyo, Japan - 1964
Fly: F. Atzori (ITA). **Bantam:** T. Sakurai (JPN). **Feather:** S. Stepashkin (URS). **Light:** J. Grudzien (POL). **L. Welter:** J. Kulej (POL). **Welter:** M. Kasprzyk (POL). **L. Middle:** B. Lagutin (URS). **Middle:** V. Popenchenko (URS). **L. Heavy:** C. Pinto (ITA). **Heavy:** J. Frazier (USA).
Bronze medal: J. McCourt (IRL).

Mexico City, Mexico - 1968
L. Fly: F. Rodriguez (VEN). **Fly:** R. Delgado (MEX). **Bantam:** V. Sokolov (URS). **Feather:** A. Roldan (MEX). **Light:** R. Harris (USA). **L. Welter:** J. Kulej (POL). **Welter:** M. Wolke (GDR). **L. Middle:** B. Lagutin (URS). **Middle:** C. Finnegan (GBR). **L. Heavy:** D. Poznyak (URS). **Heavy:** G. Foreman (USA).

Munich, West Germany - 1972
L. Fly: G. Gedo (HUN). **Fly:** G. Kostadinov (BUL). **Bantam:** O. Martinez (CUB). **Feather:** B. Kusnetsov (URS). **Light:** J. Szczepanski (POL). **L. Welter:** R. Seales (USA). **Welter:** E. Correa (CUB). **L. Middle:** D. Kottysch (GER). **Middle:** V. Lemeschev (URS). **L. Heavy:** M. Parlov (YUG). **Heavy:** T. Stevenson (CUB).
Bronze medals: R. Evans (GBR), G. Turpin (GBR), A. Minter (GBR).

Montreal, Canada - 1976
L. Fly: J. Hernandez (CUB). **Fly:** L. Randolph (USA). **Bantam:** Y-J. Gu (NKO). **Feather:** A. Herrera (CUB). **Light:** H. Davis (USA). **L. Welter:** R. Leonard (USA). **Welter:** J. Bachfield (GDR). **L. Middle:** J. Rybicki (POL). **Middle:** M. Spinks (USA). **L. Heavy:** L. Spinks (USA). **Heavy:** T. Stevenson (CUB).
Bronze medal: P. Cowdell (GBR).

Moscow, USSR - 1980
L. Fly: S. Sabirov (URS). **Fly:** P. Lessov (BUL). **Bantam:** J. Hernandez (CUB). **Feather:** R. Fink (GDR). **Light:** A. Herrera (CUB). **L. Welter:** P. Oliva (ITA). **Welter:** A. Aldama (CUB). **L. Middle:** A. Martinez (CUB). **Middle:** J. Gomez (CUB). **L. Heavy:** S. Kacar (YUG). **Heavy:** T. Stevenson (CUB).
Bronze medals: H. Russell (IRL), A. Willis (GBR).

Los Angeles, USA - 1984
L. Fly: P. Gonzalez (USA). **Fly:** S. McCrory (USA). **Bantam:** M. Stecca (ITA). **Feather:** M. Taylor (USA). **Light:** P. Whitaker (USA). **L. Welter:** J. Page (USA). **Welter:** M. Breland (USA). **L. Middle:** F. Tate (USA). **Middle:** J-S. Shin (SKO). **L. Heavy:** A. Josipovic (YUG). **Heavy:** H. Tillman (USA). **S. Heavy:** T. Biggs (USA).
Bronze medal: B. Wells (GBR).

Seoul, South Korea - 1988
L. Fly: I. Mustafov (BUL). **Fly:** H-S. Kim (SKO). **Bantam:** K. McKinney (USA). **Feather:** G. Parisi (ITA). **Light:** A. Zuelow (GDR). **L. Welter:** V. Yanovsky (URS). **Welter:** R. Wangila (KEN). **L. Middle:** S-H. Park (SKO). **Middle:** H. Maske (GDR). **L. Heavy:** A. Maynard (USA). **Heavy:** R. Mercer (USA). **S. Heavy:** L. Lewis (CAN).
Bronze medal: R. Woodhall (GBR).

Barcelona, Spain - 1992
L. Fly: R. Marcelo (CUB). **Fly:** C-C. Su (NKO). **Bantam:** J. Casamayor (CUB).

265

Feather: A. Tews (GER). **Light:** O. de la Hoya (USA). **L. Welter:** H. Vinent (CUB). **Welter:** M. Carruth (IRL). **L. Middle:** J. Lemus (CUB). **Middle:** A. Hernandez (CUB). **L. Heavy:** T. May (GER). **Heavy:** F. Savon (CUB). **S. Heavy:** R. Balado (CUB).
Silver medal: W. McCullough (IRL).
Bronze medal: R. Reid (GBR).

Atlanta, USA - 1996
L. Fly: D. Petrov (BUL). **Fly:** M. Romero (CUB). **Bantam:** I. Kovacs (HUN). **Feather:** S. Kamsing (THA). **Light:** H. Soltani (ALG). **L. Welter:** H. Vinent (CUB). **Welter:** O. Saitov (RUS). **L. Middle:** D. Reid (USA). **Middle:** A. Hernandez (CUB). **L. Heavy:** V. Jirov (KAZ). **Heavy:** F. Savon (CUB). **S. Heavy:** Vladimir Klitschko (UKR).

Sydney, Australia - 2000
L. Fly: B. Aslom (FRA). **Fly:** W. Ponlid (THA). **Bantam:** G. Rigondeaux (CUB). **Feather:** B. Sattarkhanov (KAZ). **Light:** M. Kindelan (CUB). **L. Welter:** M. Abdullaev (UZB). **Welter:** O. Saitov (RUS). **L. Middle:** Y. Ibraimov (KAZ). **Middle:** J. Gutierrez Espinosa (CUB). **L. Heavy:** A. Lebziak (RUS). **Heavy:** F. Savon (CUB). **S. Heavy:** A. Harrison (ENG).

Athens, Greece - 2004
L. Fly: Y. Bartelemi (CUB). **Fly:** Y. Gamboa (CUB). **Bantam:** G. Rigondeaux (CUB). **Feather:** A. Tischenko (RUS). **Light:** M. Kindelan (CUB). **L. Welter:** M. Boonjumnong (THA). **Welter:** B. Artayev (KAZ). **Middle:** G. Gaiderbekov (RUS). **L. Heavy:** A. Ward (USA). **Heavy:** O. Solis (CUB). **S. Heavy:** A. Povetkin (RUS).
Silver medal: A. Khan (ENG).

Beijing, China - 2008
L. Fly: Zou Shiming (CHI). **Fly:** S. Jongjohor (THA). **Bantam:** B-U Enkhbat (MON). **Fly:** V.Lomachenko (UKR). **Light:** A.Tishchenko (RUS). **L. Welter:** F. Diaz (DOM). **Welter:** B. Sarsekbayev (KAZ). **Middle:** J. Degale (ENG). **L. Heavy:** Xiaoping Zhang (CHI). **Heavy:** R. Chakhiev (RUS). **S. Heavy:** R.Cammarelle (ITA).
Silver medal: K.Egan (IRL).
Bronze medals: P. Barnes (IRL), D. Sutherland (IRL), T. Jeffries (ENG), D. Price (ENG)

World Champions, 1974-2007

Havana, Cuba - 1974
L. Fly: J. Hernandez (CUB). **Fly:** D. Rodriguez (CUB). **Bantam:** W. Gomez (PUR). **Feather:** H. Davis (USA). **Light:** V. Solomin (URS). **L. Welter:** A. Kalule (UGA). **Welter:** E. Correa (CUB). **L. Middle:** R. Garbey (CUB). **Middle:** R. Riskiev (URS). **L. Heavy:** M. Parlov (YUG). **Heavy:** T. Stevenson (CUB).

Belgrade, Yugoslavia - 1978
L. Fly: S. Muchoki (KEN). **Fly:** H. Strednicki (POL). **Bantam:** A. Horta (CUB). **Feather:** A. Herrera (CUB). **Light:** D. Andeh (NIG). **L. Welter:** V. Lvov (URS). **Welter:** V. Rachkov (URS). **L. Middle:** V. Savchenko (URS). **Middle:** J. Gomez (CUB). **L. Heavy:** S. Soria (CUB). **Heavy:** T. Stevenson (CUB).

Munich, West Germany - 1982
L. Fly: I. Mustafov (BUL). **Fly:** Y. Alexandrov (URS). **Bantam:** F. Favors (USA). **Feather:** A. Horta (CUB). **Light:** A. Herrera (CUB). **L. Welter:** C. Garcia (CUB). **Welter:** M. Breland (USA). **L. Middle:** A. Koshkin (URS). **Middle:** B. Comas (CUB). **L. Heavy:** P. Romero (CUB). **Heavy:** A. Jagubkin (URS). **S. Heavy:** T. Biggs (USA).
Bronze medal: T. Corr (IRL).

Reno, USA - 1986
L. Fly: J. Odelin (CUB). **Fly:** P. Reyes (CUB). **Bantam:** S-I. Moon (SKO). **Feather:** K. Banks (USA). **Light:** A. Horta (CUB). **L. Welter:** V. Shishov (URS). **Welter:** K. Gould (USA). **L. Middle:** A. Espinosa (CUB). **Middle:** D. Allen (USA). **L. Heavy:** P. Romero (CUB). **Heavy:** F. Savon (CUB). **S. Heavy:** T. Stevenson (CUB).

Moscow, USSR - 1989
L. Fly: E. Griffin (USA). **Fly:** Y. Arbachakov (URS). **Bantam:** E. Carrion (CUB). **Feather:** A. Khamatov (URS). **Light:** J. Gonzalez (CUB). **L. Welter:** I. Ruzinkov (URS). **Welter:** F. Vastag (Rom). **L. Middle:** I. Akopokhian (URS). **Middle:** A. Kurniavka (URS). **L. Heavy:** H. Maske (GDR). **Heavy:** F. Savon (CUB). **S. Heavy:** R. Balado (CUB).
Bronze medal: M. Carruth (IRL).

Sydney, Australia - 1991
L. Fly: E. Griffin (USA). **Fly:** I. Kovacs (HUN). **Bantam:** S. Todorov (BUL). **Feather:** K. Kirkorov (BUL). **Light:** M. Rudolph (GER). **L. Welter:** K. Tszyu (URS). **Welter:** J. Hernandez (CUB). **L. Middle:** J. Lemus (CUB). **Middle:** T. Russo (ITA). **L. Heavy:** T. May (GER). **Heavy:** F. Savon (CUB). **S. Heavy:** R. Balado (CUB).

Tampere, Finland - 1993
L. Fly: N. Munchian (ARM). **Fly:** W. Font (CUB). **Bantam:** A. Christov (BUL). **Feather:** S. Todorov (BUL). **Light:** D. Austin (CUB). **L. Welter:** H. Vinent (CUB). **Welter:** J. Hernandez (CUB). **L. Middle:** F. Vastag (ROM). **Middle:** A. Hernandez (CUB). **L. Heavy:** R. Garbey (CUB). **Heavy:** F. Savon (CUB). **S. Heavy:** R. Balado (CUB).
Bronze medal: D. Kelly (IRL).

Berlin, Germany - 1995
L. Fly: D. Petrov (BUL). **Fly:** Z. Lunka (GER). **Bantam:** R. Malachbekov (RUS). **Feather:** S. Todorov (BUL). **Light:** L. Doroftei (ROM). **L. Welter:** H. Vinent (CUB). **Welter:** J. Hernandez (CUB). **L. Middle:** F. Vastag (ROM). **Middle:** A. Hernandez (CUB). **L. Heavy:** A. Tarver (USA). **Heavy:** F. Savon (CUB). **S. Heavy:** A. Lezin (RUS).

Budapest, Hungary - 1997
L. Fly: M. Romero (CUB). **Fly:** M. Mantilla (CUB). **Bantam:** R Malakhbekov (RUS). **Feather:** I. Kovacs (HUN). **Light:** A. Maletin (RUS). **L. Welter:** D. Simion (ROM). **Welter:** O. Saitov (RUS). **L. Middle:** A. Duvergel (CUB). **Middle:** Z. Erdei (HUN). **L. Heavy:** A. Lebsiak (RUS). **Heavy:** F. Savon (CUB). **S. Heavy:** G. Kandelaki (GEO).
Bronze medal: S. Kirk (IRL).

Houston, USA - 1999
L. Fly: B. Viloria (USA). **Fly:** B. Jumadilov (KAZ). **Bantam:** R. Crinu (ROM). **Feather:** R. Juarez (USA). **Light:** M. Kindelan (CUB). **L. Welter:** M. Abdullaev (UZB). **Welter:** J. Hernandez (CUB). **L. Middle:** M. Simion (ROM). **Middle:** U. Haydarov (UZB). **L. Heavy:** M. Simms (USA). **Heavy:** M. Bennett (USA). **S. Heavy:** S. Samilsan (TUR).
Bronze medal: K. Evans (WAL).

Belfast, Northern Ireland - 2001
L. Fly: Y. Bartelemi (CUB). **Fly:** J. Thomas (FRA). **Bantam:** G. Rigondeaux (CUB). **Feather:** R. Palyani (TUR). **Light:** M. Kindelan (CUB). **L. Welter:** D. Luna Martinez (CUB). **Welter:** L. Aragon (CUB). **L. Middle:** D. Austin (CUB). **Middle:** A. Gogolev (RUS). **L. Heavy:** Y. Makarenko (RUS). **Heavy:** O. Solis (CUB). **S. Heavy:** R. Chagaev (UZB).
Silver medal: D. Haye (ENG).
Bronze medals: J. Moore (IRL), C. Froch (ENG).

Bangkok, Thailand - 2003
L. Fly: S. Karazov (RUS). **Fly:** S. Jongjohor (THA). **Bantam:** A. Mamedov (AZE). **Feather:** G. Jafarov (KAZ). **Light:** M. Kindelan (CUB). **L. Welter:** W. Blain (FRA). **Welter:** L. Aragon (CUB). **Middle:** G. Golovkin (KAZ). **L. Heavy:** Y. Makarenko (RUS). **Heavy:** O. Solis (CUB). **S. Heavy:** A. Povetkin (RUS).

Mianyang City, China - 2005
L. Fly: Zou Shiming (CHI). **Fly:** O-S Lee (SKO). **Bantam:** G. Rigondeaux (CUB). **Feather:** A. Tischenko (RUS). **Light:** Y. Ugas (CUB). **L. Welter:** S. Sapiyev (KAZ). **Welter:** E. Lara (CUB). **Middle:** M. Korobev (RUS). **L. Heavy:** Y. Dzhanabergenov (KAZ). **Heavy:** A. Alexeev (RUS). **S. Heavy:** O. Solis (CUB). **Bronze medal:** N. Perkins (ENG).

Chicago, USA - 2007
L. Fly: Zou Shiming (CHI). **Fly:** R. Warren (USA). **Bantam:** S.Vodopyanov (RUS). **Feather:** A. Selimov (RUS). **Light:** F. Gavin (ENG). **L. Welter:** S. Sapiyev (KAZ). **Welter:** D. Andrade (USA). **Middle:** M. Korobov (RUS). **L. Heavy:** A. Atoev (UZB). **Heavy:** C. Russo (ITA). **S. Heavy:** R. Cammarelle (ITA).

World Junior Champions, 1979-2006

Yokohama, Japan - 1979
L. Fly: R. Shannon (USA). **Fly:** P. Lessov (BUL). **Bantam:** P-K Choi (SKO). **Feather:** Y. Gladychev (URS). **Light:** R. Blake (USA). **L. Welter:** I. Akopokhian (URS). **Welter:** M. McCrory (USA). **L. Middle:** A. Mayes (USA). **Middle:** A. Milov (URS). **L. Heavy:** A. Lebedev (URS). **Heavy:** M. Frazier (USA).
Silver medals: N. Wilshire (ENG), D. Cross (ENG).
Bronze medal: I. Scott (SCO).

Santo Domingo, Dominican Republic - 1983
L. Fly: M. Herrera (DOM). **Fly:** J. Gonzalez (CUB). **Bantam:** J. Molina (PUR). **Feather:** A. Miesses (DOM). **Light:** A. Beltre (DOM). **L. Welter:** A. Espinoza (CUB). **Welter:** M. Watkins (USA). **L. Middle:** U. Castillo (CUB). **Middle:** R. Batista (CUB). **L. Heavy:** O. Pought (USA). **Heavy:** A. Williams (USA). **S. Heavy:** L. Lewis (CAN).

Bucharest, Romania - 1985
L. Fly: R-S. Hwang (SKO). **Fly:** T. Marcelica (ROM). **Bantam:** R. Diaz (CUB). **Feather:** D. Maeran (ROM). **Light:** J. Teiche (GDR). **L. Welter:** W. Saeger (GDR). **Welter:** A. Stoianov (BUL). **L. Middle:** M. Franek (TCH). **Middle:** O. Zahalotskih (URS). **L. Heavy:** B. Riddick (USA). **Heavy:** F. Savon (CUB). **S. Heavy:** A. Prianichnikov (URS).

Havana, Cuba - 1987
L. Fly: E. Paisan (CUB). **Fly:** C. Daniels (USA). **Bantam:** A. Moya (CUB). **Feather:** G. Iliyasov (URS). **Light:** J. Hernandez (CUB). **L. Welter:** L. Mihai (ROM). **Welter:** F. Vastag (ROM). **L. Middle:** A. Lobsyak (URS). **Middle:** W. Martinez (CUB). **L. Heavy:** D. Yeliseyev (URS). **Heavy:** R. Balado (CUB). **S. Heavy:** L. Martinez (CUB).
Silver medal: E. Loughran (IRL).
Bronze medal: D. Galvin (IRL).

266

San Juan, Puerto Rico - 1989

L. Fly: D. Petrov (BUL). **Fly:** N. Monchai (FRA). **Bantam:** J. Casamayor (CUB). **Feather:** C. Febres (PUR). **Light:** A. Acevedo (PUR). **L. Welter:** E. Berger (GDR). **Welter:** A. Hernandez (CUB). **L. Middle:** L. Bedey (CUB). **Middle:** R. Garbey (CUB). **L. Heavy:** R. Alvarez (CUB). **Heavy:** K. Johnson (CAN). **S. Heavy:** A. Burdiantz (URS).
Silver medals: E. Magee (IRL), R. Reid (ENG), S. Wilson (SCO).

Lima, Peru - 1990

L. Fly: D. Alicea (PUR). **Fly:** K. Pielert (GDR). **Bantam:** K. Baravi (URS). **Feather:** A. Vaughan (ENG). **Light:** J. Mendez (CUB). **L. Welter:** H. Vinent (CUB). **Welter:** A. Hernandez (CUB). **L. Middle:** A. Kakauridze (URS). **Middle:** J. Gomez (CUB). **L. Heavy:** B. Torsten (GDR). **Heavy:** I. Andreev (URS). **S. Heavy:** J. Quesada (CUB).
Bronze medal: P. Ingle (ENG).

Montreal, Canada - 1992

L. Fly: W. Font (CUB). **Fly:** J. Oragon (CUB). **Bantam:** N. Machado (CUB). **Feather:** M. Stewart (CAN). **Light:** D. Austin (CUB). **L. Welter:** O. Saitov (RUS). **Welter:** L. Brors (GER). **L. Middle:** J. Acosta (CUB). **Middle:** I. Arsangaliev (RUS). **L. Heavy:** S. Samilsan (TUR). **Heavy:** G. Kandeliaki (GEO). **S. Heavy:** M. Porchnev (RUS).
Bronze medal: N. Sinclair (IRL).

Istanbul, Turkey - 1994

L. Fly: J. Turunen (FIN). **Fly:** A. Jimenez (CUB). **Bantam:** J. Despaigne (CUB). **Feather:** D. Simion (ROM). **Light:** L. Diogenes (CUB). **L. Welter:** V. Romero (CUB). **Welter:** E. Aslan (TUR). **L. Middle:** G. Ledsvanys (CUB). **Middle:** M. Genc (TUR). **L. Heavy:** P. Aurino (ITA). **Heavy:** M. Lopez (CUB). **S. Heavy:** P. Carrion (CUB).

Havana, Cuba - 1996

L. Fly: L. Hernandez (CUB). **Fly:** L. Cabrera (CUB). **Bantam:** P. Miradal (CUB). **Feather:** E. Rodriguez (CUB). **Light:** R. Vaillan (CUB). **L. Welter:** T. Mergadze (RUS). **Welter:** J. Brahmer (GER). **L. Middle:** L. Mezquia (CUB). **Middle:** V. Pletniov (RUS). **L. Heavy:** O. Simon (CUB). **Heavy:** A. Yatsenko (UKR). **S. Heavy:** S. Fabre (CUB).
Bronze medal: R. Hatton (ENG).

Buenos Aires, Argentina - 1998

L. Fly: S. Tanasie (ROM). **Fly:** S. Yeledov (KAZ). **Bantam:** S. Suleymanov (UKR). **Feather:** I. Perez (ARG). **Light:** A. Solopov (RUS). **L. Welter:** Y. Tomashov (UKR). **Welter:** K. Oustarkhanov (RUS). **L. Middle:** S. Kostenko (UKR). **Middle:** M. Kempe (GER). **L. Heavy:** H. Yohanson Martinez (CUB). **Heavy:** O. Solis Fonte (CUB). **S. Heavy:** B. Ohanyan (ARM).
Silver medal: H. Cunningham (IRL).
Bronze medal: D. Campbell (IRL).

Budapest, Hungary - 2000

L. Fly: Y. Leon Alarcon (CUB). **Fly:** O. Franco Vaszquez (CUB). **Bantam:** V. Tajbert (GER). **Feather:** G. Kate (HUN). **Light:** F. Adzsanalov (AZE). **L. Welter:** G. Galovkin (KAZ). **Welter:** S. Ustunel (TUR). **L. Middle:** D. Chernysh (RUS). **Middle:** F. Sullivan Barrera (CUB). **L. Heavy:** A. Shekmourov (RUS). **Heavy:** D. Medzhydov (UKR). **S. Heavy:** A. Dmitrienko (RUS).
Bronze medal: C. Barrett (IRL).

Santiago, Cuba - 2002

L. Fly: D. Acripitian (RUS). **Fly:** Y. Fabregas (CUB). **Bantam:** S. Bahodirijan (UZB). **Feather:** A. Tichtchenko (RUS). **Light:** S. Mendez (CUB). **L. Welter:** K. Iliyasov (KAZ). **Welter:** J. McPherson (USA). **L. Middle:** V. Diaz (CUB). **Middle:** A. Duarte (CUB). **L. Heavy:** R. Zavalnyuyk (UKR). **Heavy:** Y. P. Hernandez (CUB). **S. Heavy:** P. Portal (CUB).
Silver medal: A. Lee (IRL).
Bronze medal: N. Brough (ENG).

Jeju Island, South Korea - 2004

L. Fly: P. Bedak (Hun). **Fly:** I. Rahimov (UZB). **Bantam:** A. Abdimomunov (KAZ). **Feather:** E. Ambartsumyan (RUS). **Light:** A. Khan (ENG). **L. Welter:** C. Banteur (CUB). **Welter:** E. Rasulov (UZB). **Middle:** D. Tchudinov (RUS). **L. Heavy:** I. Perez (CUB). **Heavy:** E. Romanov (RUS). **S.Heavy:** D. Boytsov (RUS).
Bronze medal: D. Price (ENG).

Agadir, Morocco - 2006

L.Fly: A.Collado Acosta (CUB). **Fly:** V.Lomachenko (UKR). **Bantam:** M.Ouatine (MOR). **Feather:** Y.Frometa (CUB). **Light:** R.Iglesias (CUB). **L.Welter:** B.Bacskai (HUN). **Welter:** J.Iglesias (CUB). **Middle:** L.Garcia (CUB). **L.Heavy:** I.Yandiev (RUS). **Heavy:** S.Kalchugin (RUS). **S.Heavy:** C.Ciocan (ROM).
Bronze medals: O.Mbwakongo (ENG), T.Fury (ENG).

European Champions, 1924-2006

Paris, France - 1924

Fly: J. McKenzie (GBR). **Bantam:** J. Ces (FRA). **Feather:** R. de Vergnie (BEL). **Light:** N. Nielsen (DEN). **Welter:** J. Delarge (BEL). **Middle:** H. Mallin (GBR). **L.**

Heavy: H. Mitchell (GBR). **Heavy:** O. von Porat (NOR).

Stockholm, Sweden - 1925

Fly: E. Pladner (FRA). **Bantam:** A. Rule (GBR). **Feather:** P. Andren (SWE). **Light:** S. Johanssen (SWE). **Welter:** H. Nielsen (DEN). **Middle:** F. Crawley (GBR). **L. Heavy:** T. Petersen (DEN). **Heavy:** B. Persson (SWE).
Silver medals: J. James (GBR), E. Viney (GBR), D. Lister (GBR).

Berlin, Germany - 1927

Fly: L. Boman (SWE). **Bantam:** K. Dalchow (GER). **Feather:** F. Dubbers (GER). **Light:** H. Domgoergen (GER). **Welter:** R. Caneva (ITA). **Middle:** J. Christensen (NOR). **L. Heavy:** H. Muller (GER). **Heavy:** N. Ramm (SWE).

Amsterdam, Holland - 1928

Fly: A. Kocsis (HUN). **Bantam:** V. Tamagnini (ITA). **Feather:** B. van Klaveren (HOL). **Light:** C. Orlandi (ITA). **Welter:** R. Galataud (FRA). **Middle:** P. Toscani (ITA). **L. Heavy:** E. Pistulla (GER). **Heavy:** N. Ramm (SWE).

Budapest, Hungary - 1930

Fly: I. Enekes (HUN). **Bantam:** J. Szeles (HUN). **Feather:** G. Szabo (HUN). **Light:** M. Bianchini (ITA). **Welter:** J. Besselmann (GER). **Middle:** C. Meroni (ITA). **L. Heavy:** T. Petersen (DEN). **Heavy:** J. Michaelson (DEN).

Los Angeles, USA - 1932

Fly: I. Enekes (HUN). **Bantam:** H. Ziglarski (GER). **Feather:** J. Schleinkofer (GER). **Light:** T. Ahlqvist (SWE). **Welter:** E. Campe (GER). **Middle:** R. Michelot (FRA). **L. Heavy:** G. Rossi (ITA). **Heavy:** L. Rovati (ITA).

Budapest, Hungary - 1934

Fly: P. Palmer (GBR). **Bantam:** I. Enekes (HUN). **Feather:** O. Kaestner GER). **Light:** E. Facchini (ITA). **Welter:** D. McCleave (GBR). **Middle:** S. Szigetti (HUN). **L. Heavy:** P. Zehetmayer (AUT). **Heavy:** G. Baerlund (FIN).
Bronze medal: P. Floyd (GBR).

Milan, Italy - 1937

Fly: I. Enekes (HUN). **Bantam:** U. Sergo (ITA). **Feather:** A. Polus (POL). **Light:** H. Nuremberg (GER). **Welter:** M. Murach (GER). **Middle:**H. Chmielewski (POL). **L. Heavy:** S. Szigetti (HUN). **Heavy:** O. Tandberg (SWE).

Dublin, Eire - 1939

Fly: J. Ingle (IRL). **Bantam:** U. Sergo (ITA). **Feather:** P. Dowdall (IRL). **Light:** H. Nuremberg (GER). **Welter:** A. Kolczyski (POL). **Middle:** A. Raadik (EST). **L. Heavy:** L. Musina (ITA). **Heavy:** O. Tandberg (SWE).
Bronze medal: C. Evenden (IRL).

Dublin, Eire - 1947

Fly: L. Martinez (ESP). **Bantam:** L. Bogacs (HUN). **Feather:** K. Kreuger (SWE). **Light:** J. Vissers (BEL). **Welter:** J. Ryan (ENG). **Middle:** A. Escudie (FRA). **L. Heavy:** H. Quentemeyer (HOL). **Heavy:** G. O'Colmain (IRL).
Silver medals: J. Clinton (SCO), P. Maguire (IRL), W. Thom (ENG), G. Scriven (ENG).
Bronze medals: J. Dwyer (SCO), A. Sanderson (ENG), W. Frith (SCO), E. Cantwell (IRL), K. Wyatt (ENG).

Oslo, Norway - 1949

Fly: J. Kasperczak (POL). **Bantam:** G. Zuddas (ITA). **Feather:** J. Bataille (FRA). **Light:** M. McCullagh (IRL). **Welter:** J. Torma (TCH). **Middle:** L. Papp (HUN). **L. Heavy:** G. di Segni (ITA). **Heavy:** L. Bene (HUN).
Bronze medal: D. Connell (IRL).

Milan, Italy - 1951

Fly: A. Pozzali (ITA). **Bantam:** V. Dall'Osso (ITA). **Feather:** J. Ventaja (FRA). **Light:** B. Visintin (ITA). **L. Welter:** H. Schelling (GER). **Welter:** Z. Chychla (POL). **L. Middle:** L. Papp (HUN). **Middle:** S. Sjolin (SWE). **L. Heavy:** M. Limage (BEL). **Heavy:** G. di Segni (ITA).
Silver medal: J. Kelly (IRL).
Bronze medals: D. Connell (IRL), T. Milligan (IRL), A. Lay (ENG).

Warsaw, Poland - 1953

Fly: H. Kukier (POL). **Bantam:** Z. Stefaniuk (POL). **Feather:** J. Kruza (POL). **Light:** V. Jengibarian (URS). **L. Welter:** L. Drogosz (POL). **Welter:** Z. Chychla (POL). **L. Middle:** B. Wells (ENG). **Middle:** D. Wemhoner (GER). **L. Heavy:** U. Nietchke (GER). **Heavy:** A. Schotzikas (URS).
Silver medal: T. Milligan (IRL).
Bronze medals: J. McNally (IRL), R. Barton (ENG).

Berlin, West Germany - 1955

Fly: E. Basel (GER). **Bantam:** Z. Stefaniuk (POL). **Feather:** T. Nicholls (ENG). **Light:** H. Kurschat (GER). **L. Welter:** L. Drogosz (POL). **Welter:** N. Gargano (ENG). **L. Middle:** Z. Pietrzykowski (POL). **Middle:** G. Schatkov (URS). **L. Heavy:** E. Schoeppner (GER). **Heavy:** A. Schotzikas (URS).

Prague, Czechoslovakia - 1957

Fly: M. Homberg (GER). **Bantam:** O. Grigoryev (URS). **Feather:** D. Venilov (BUL). **Light:** K. Pazdzior (POL). **L. Welter:** V. Jengibarian (URS). **Welter:** M. Graus (GER). **L. Middle:** N. Benvenuti (ITA). **Middle:** Z. Pietrzykowski (POL). **L. Heavy:** G. Negrea (ROM). **Heavy:** A. Abramov (URS).

Bronze medals: R. Davies (WAL), J. Morrissey (SCO), J. Kidd (SCO), F. Teidt (IRL).

Lucerne, Switzerland - 1959
Fly: M. Homberg (GER). **Bantam:** H. Rascher (GER). **Feather:** J. Adamski (POL). **Light:** O. Maki (FIN). **L. Welter:** V. Jengibarian (URS). **Welter:** L. Drogosz (POL). **L. Middle:** N. Benvenuti (ITA). **Middle:** G. Schatkov (URS). **L. Heavy:** Z. Pietrzykowski (POL). **Heavy:** A. Abramov (URS).
Silver medal: D. Thomas (ENG).
Bronze medals: A. McClean (IRL), H. Perry (IRL), C. McCoy (IRL), H. Scott (ENG).

Belgrade, Yugoslavia - 1961
Fly: P. Vacca (ITA). **Bantam:** S. Sivko (URS). **Feather:** F. Taylor (ENG). **Light:** R. McTaggart (SCO). **L. Welter:** A. Tamulis (URS). **Welter:** R. Tamulis (URS). **L. Middle:** B. Lagutin (URS). **Middle:** T. Walasek (POL). **L. Heavy:** G. Saraudi (ITA). **Heavy:** A. Abramov (URS).
Bronze medals: P. Warwick (ENG), I. McKenzie (SCO), J. Bodell (ENG).

Moscow, USSR - 1963
Fly: V. Bystrov (URS). **Bantam:** O. Grigoryev (URS). **Feather:** S. Stepashkin (URS). **Light:** J. Kajdi (HUN). **L. Welter:** J. Kulej (POL). **Welter:** R. Tamulis (URS). **L. Middle:** B. Lagutin (URS). **Middle:** V. Popenchenko (URS). **L. Heavy:** Z. Pietrzykowski (POL). **Heavy:** J. Nemec (TCH).
Silver medal: A. Wyper (SCO).

Berlin, East Germany - 1965
Fly: H. Freisdadt (GER). **Bantam:** O. Grigoryev (URS). **Feather:** S. Stepashkin (URS). **Light:** V. Barranikov (URS). **L. Welter:** J. Kulej (POL). **Welter:** R. Tamulis (URS). **L. Middle:** V. Ageyev (URS). **Middle:** V. Popenchenko (URS). **L. Heavy:** D. Poznyak (URS). **Heavy:** A. Isosimov (URS).
Silver medal: B. Robinson (ENG).
Bronze medals: J. McCluskey (SCO), K. Buchanan (SCO), J. McCourt (IRL).

Rome, Italy - 1967
Fly: H. Skrzyczak (POL). **Bantam:** N. Giju (ROM). **Feather:** R. Petek (POL). **Light:** J. Grudzien (POL). **L. Welter:** V. Frolov (URS). **Welter:** B. Nemecek (TCH). **L. Middle:** V. Ageyev (URS). **Middle:** M. Casati (ITA). **L. Heavy:** D. Poznyak (URS). **Heavy:** M. Baruzzi (ITA).
Silver medal: P. Boddington (ENG).

Bucharest, Romania - 1969
L. Fly: G. Gedo (HUN). **Fly:** C. Ciuca (ROM). **Bantam:** A. Dumitrescu (ROM). **Feather:** L. Orban (HUN). **Light:** S. Cutov (ROM). **L. Welter:** V. Frolov (URS). **Welter:** G. Meier (GER). **L. Middle:** V. Tregubov (URS). **Middle:** V. Tarasenkov (URS). **L. Heavy:** D. Poznyak (URS). **Heavy:** I. Alexe (ROM).
Bronze medals: M. Dowling (IRL), M. Piner (ENG), A. Richardson (ENG), T. Imrie (SCO).

Madrid, Spain - 1971
L. Fly: G. Gedo (HUN). **Fly:** J. Rodriguez (ESP). **Bantam:** T. Badar (HUN). **Feather:** R. Tomczyk (POL). **Light:** J. Szczepanski (POL). **L. Welter:** U. Beyer (GDR). **Welter:** J. Kajdi (HUN). **L. Middle:** V. Tregubov (URS). **Middle:** J. Juotsiavitchus (URS). **L. Heavy:** M. Parlov (YUG). **Heavy:** V. Tchernishev (URS).
Bronze medals: N. McLaughlin (IRL), M. Dowling (IRL), B. McCarthy (IRL), M. Kingwell (ENG), L. Stevens (ENG).

Belgrade, Yugoslavia - 1973
L. Fly: V. Zasypko (URS). **Fly:** C. Gruescu (ROM). **Bantam:** A. Cosentino (FRA). **Feather:** S. Forster (GDR). **Light:** S. Cutov (ROM). **L. Welter:** M. Benes (YUG). **Welter:** S. Csjef (HUN). **L. Middle:** A. Klimanov (URS). **Middle:** V. Lemechev (URS). **L. Heavy:** M. Parlov (YUG). **Heavy:** V. Ulyanich (URS).
Bronze medal: J. Bambrick (SCO).

Katowice, Poland - 1975
L. Fly: A. Tkachenko (URS). **Fly:** V. Zasypko (URS). **Bantam:** V. Rybakov (URS). **Feather:** T. Badari (HUN). **Light:** S. Cutov (ROM). **L. Welter:** V. Limasov (URS). **Welter:** K. Marjaama (FIN). **L. Middle:** W. Rudnowski (POL). **Middle:** V. Lemechev (URS). **L. Heavy:** A. Klimanov (URS). **Heavy:** A. Biegalski (POL).
Bronze medals: C. Magri (ENG), P. Cowdell (ENG), G. McEwan (ENG).

Halle, East Germany - 1977
L. Fly: H. Srednicki (POL). **Fly:** L. Blazynski (POL). **Bantam:** S. Forster (GDR). **Feather:** R. Nowakowski (GDR). **Light:** A. Rusevski (YUG). **L. Welter:** B. Gajda (POL). **Welter:** V. Limasov (URS). **L. Middle:** V. Saychenko (URS). **Middle:** I. Shaposhnikov (URS). **L. Heavy:** D. Kvachadze (URS). **Heavy:** E. Gorstkov (URS).
Bronze medal: P. Sutcliffe (IRL).

Cologne, West Germany - 1979
L. Fly: S. Sabirov (URS). **Fly:** H. Strednicki (POL). **Bantam:** N. Khrapzov (URS). **Feather:** V. Rybakov(URS). **Light.:** V. Demianenko (URS). **L. Welter:** S. Konakbaev (URS). **Welter:** E. Muller (GER). **L. Middle:** M. Perunovic (YUG). **Middle:** T. Uusiverta (FIN). **L. Heavy:** A. Nikolyan (URS). **Heavy:** E. Gorstkov (URS). **S. Heavy:** P. Hussing (GER).
Bronze medal: P. Sutcliffe (IRL).

Tampere, Finland - 1981
L. Fly: I. Mustafov (BUL). **Fly:** P. Lessov (BUL). **Bantam:** V. Miroschnichenko (URS). **Feather:** R. Nowakowski (GDR). **Light:** V. Rybakov (URS). **L. Welter:** V. Shisov (URS). **Welter:** S. Konakvbaev (URS). **L. Middle:** A. Koshkin (URS). **Middle:** J. Torbek (URS). **L. Heavy:** A Krupin (URS). **Heavy:** A. Jagupkin (URS). **S. Heavy:** F. Damiani (ITA).
Bronze medal: G. Hawkins (IRL).

Varna, Bulgaria - 1983
L. Fly: I. Mustafov (BUL). **Fly:** P. Lessov (BUL). **Bantam:** Y. Alexandrov (URS). **Feather:** S. Nurkazov (URS). **Light:** E. Chuprenski (BUL). **L. Welter:** V. Shishov (URS). **Welter:** P. Galkin (URS). **L. Middle:** V. Laptev (URS). **Middle:** V. Melnik (URS). **L. Heavy:** V. Kokhanovski (URS). **Heavy:** A. Jagubkin (URS). **S. Heavy:** F. Damiani (ITA).
Bronze medal: K. Joyce (IRL).

Budapest, Hungary - 1985
L. Fly: R. Breitbarth (GDR). **Fly:** D. Berg (GDR). **Bantam:** L. Simic (YUG). **Feather:** S. Khachatrian (URS). **Light:** E. Chuprenski (BUL) **L. Welter:** S. Mehnert (GDR). **Welter:** I. Akopokhian (URS). **L. Middle:** M. Timm (GDR). **Middle:** H. Maske (GDR). **L. Heavy:** N. Shanavasov (URS). **Heavy:** A. Jagubkin (URS). **S. Heavy:** F. Somodi (HUN).
Bronze medals: S. Casey(IRL), J. Beckles (ENG).

Turin, Italy - 1987
L. Fly: N. Munchyan (URS). **Fly:** A. Tews (GDR). **Bantam:** A. Hristov (BUL). **Feather:** M. Kazaryan (URS). **Light:** O. Nazarov (URS). **L. Welter:** B. Abadjier (BUL). **Welter:** V. Shishov (URS). **L. Middle:** E. Richter (GDR). **Middle:** H. Maske (GDR). **L. Heavy:** Y. Vaulin (URS). **Heavy:** A. Vanderlijde (HOL). **S. Heavy:** U. Kaden (GDR).
Bronze medal: N. Brown (ENG).

Athens, Greece - 1989
L. Fly: I.Mustafov (BUL). **Fly:** Y. Arbachakov (URS). **Bantam:** S. Todorov (BUL). **Feather:** K. Kirkorov (BUL). **Light:** M. Tsziu (URS). **L. Welter:** I. Ruznikov (URS). **Welter:** S. Mehnert (GDR). **L. Middle:** I. Akopokhian (URS). **Middle:** H. Maske (GDR). **L. Heavy:** S. Lange (GDR). **Heavy:** A. Vanderlijde (HOL). **S. Heavy:** U. Kaden (GDR).
Bronze Medal: D. Anderson (SCO).

Gothenburg, Sweden - 1991
L. Fly: I. Marinov (BUL). **Fly:** I. Kovacs (HUN). **Bantam:** S. Todorov (BUL). **Feather:** P. Griffin (IRL). **Light:** V. Nistor (ROM). **L. Welter:** K. Tsziu (URS). **Welter:** R. Welin (SWE). **L. Middle:** I. Akopokhian (URS). **Middle:** S. Otke (GER). **L. Heavy:** D. Michalczewski (GER). **Heavy:** A. Vanderlijde (HOL). **S. Heavy:** E. Beloussov (URS).
Bronze medals: P. Weir (SCO), A. Vaughan (ENG).

Bursa, Turkey - 1993
L. Fly: D. Petrov (BUL). **Fly:** R. Husseinov (AZE). **Bantam:** R. Malakhbetov (RUS). **Feather:** S. Todorov (BUL). **Light:** J. Bielski (POL). **L. Welter:** N. Suleymanogiu (TUR). **Welter:** V. Karpaclauskas (LIT). **L. Middle:** F. Vastag (ROM). **Middle:** D. Eigenbrodt (GER). **L. Heavy:** I. Kshinin (RUS). **Heavy:** G. Kandelaki (GEO). **S. Heavy:** S. Rusinov (BUL).
Bronze medals: P. Griffin (IRL), D. Williams (ENG), K. McCormack (WAL).

Vejle, Denmark - 1996
L. Fly: D. Petrov (BUL). **Fly:** A. Pakeev (RUS). **Bantam:** I. Kovacs (HUN). **Feather:** R. Paliani (RUS). **Light:** L. Doroftei (ROM). **L. Welter:** O. Urkal (GER). **Welter:** H. Al (DEN). **L. Middle:** F. Vastag (ROM). **Middle:** S. Ottke (GER). **L. Heavy:** P. Aurino (ITA). **Heavy:** L. Krasniqi (GER). **S. Heavy:** A. Lezin (RUS).
Bronze medals: S. Harrison (SCO), D. Burke (ENG), D. Kelly (IRL).

Minsk, Belarus - 1998
L. Fly: S. Kazakov (RUS). **Fly:** V. Sidorenko (UKR). **Bantam:** S. Danilchenko (UKR). **Feather:** R. Paliani (TUR). **Light:** K. Huste (GER). **L. Welter:** D. Simion (ROM). **Welter:** O. Saitov (RUS). **L. Middle:** F. Esther (FRA). **Middle:** Z. Erdei (HUN). **L. Heavy:** A. Lebsiak (RUS). **Heavy:** G. Fragomeni (ITA). **S. Heavy:** A. Lezin (RUS).
Silver Medals: B. Magee (IRL), C. Fry (ENG).
Bronze medal: C. Bessey (ENG).

Tampere, Finland - 2000
L. Fly: Valeri Sidorenko (UKR). **Fly:** Vladimir Sidorenko (UKR). **Bantam:** A. Agagueloglu (TUR). **Feather:** R. Paliani (TUR). **Light:** A. Maletin (RUS). **L. Welter:** A. Leonev (RUS). **Welter:** B. Ueluesoy (TUR). **L. Middle:** A. Catic (GER). **Middle:** Z. Erdei (HUN). **L. Heavy:** A. Lebsiak (RUS). **Heavy:** J. Chanet (FRA). **S. Heavy:** A. Lezin (RUS).

Perm, Russia - 2002
L. Fly: S. Kazakov (RUS). **Fly:** G. Balakshin (RUS). **Bantam:** K. Khatsygov (BE). **Feather:** R. Malakhbekov (RUS). **Light:** A. Maletin (RUS). **L. Welter:** D. Panayotov (BUL). **Welter:** T. Gaidalov (RUS). **L. Middle:** A. Mishin (RUS). **Middle:** O. Mashkin (UKR). **L. Heavy:** M. Gala (RUS). **Heavy:** E. Makarenko (RUS). **S. Heavy:** A. Povetkin (RUS).

Pula, Croatia - 2004
L. Fly: S. Kazakov (RUS). **Fly:** G. Balakchine (RUS). **Bantam:** G. Kovalev (RUS).

Feather: V. Tajbert (GER). **Light:** D. Stilianov (BUL). **L. Welter:** A. Maletin (RUS). **Welter:** O. Saitov (RUS). **Middle:** G. Gaiderbekov (RUS). **L. Heavy:** E. Makarenko (RUS). **Heavy:** A. Alekseev (RUS). **S. Heavy:** A. Povetkin (RUS).
Bronze medal: A. Lee (IRL).

Plovdiv, Bulgaria - 2006
L. Fly: D. Ayrapetyan (RUS). **Fly:** G. Balakshin (RUS). **Bantam:** A. Aliev (RUS). **Feather:** A. Selimov (RUS). **Light:** A. Tishchenko (RUS). **L. Welter:** B. Georgiev (BUL). **Welter:** A. Balanov (RUS). **Middle:** M. Korobov (RUS). **L. Heavy:** A. Beterbiev (RUS). **Heavy:** D. Poyatsika (UKR). **S. Heavy:** I. Timurziev (RUS).
Bronze medals: S. Smith (ENG), F. Mhura (SCO), K. Egan (IRL).

Note: Gold medals were awarded to the Europeans who went the furthest in the Olympic Games of 1924, 1928 & 1932.

European Junior (Youth) Champions, 1970-2007

Miskolc, Hungary - 1970
L. Fly: Gluck (HUN). **Fly:** Z. Kismeneth (HUN). **Bantam:** A. Levitschev (URS). **Feather:** Andrianov (URS). **Light:** L. Juhasz (HUN). **L. Welter:** K. Nemec (HUN). **Welter:** Davidov (URS). **L. Middle:** A. Lemeschev (URS). **Middle:** N. Anfimov (URS). **L. Heavy:** O. Sasche (GDR). **Heavy:** J. Reder (HUN).
Bronze medals: D. Needham (ENG), R. Barlow (ENG), L. Stevens (ENG).

Bucharest, Romania - 1972
L. Fly: A. Turei (ROM). **Fly:** Condurat (ROM). **Bantam:** V. Solomin (URS). **Feather:** V. Lvov (URS). **Light:** S. Cutov (ROM). **L. Welter:** K. Pierwieniecki (POL). **Welter:** Zorov (URS). **L. Middle:** Babescu (ROM). **Middle:** V. Lemeschev (URS). **L. Heavy:** Mirounik (URS). **Heavy:** Subutin (URS).
Bronze medals: J. Gale (ENG), R. Maxwell (ENG), D. Odwell (ENG).

Kiev, Russia - 1974
L. Fly: A. Tkachenko (URS). **Fly:** V. Rybakov (URS). **Bantam:** C. Andreikovski (BUL). **Feather:** V. Sorokin (URS). **Light:** V. Limasov (URS). **L. Welter:** N. Sigov (URS). **Welter:** M. Bychkov (URS). **L. Middle:** V. Danshin (URS). **Middle:** D. Jende (GDR). **L. Heavy:** K. Dafinoiu (ROM). **Heavy:** K. Mashev (BUL).
Silver medal: C. Magri (ENG).
Bronze medals: G. Gilbody (ENG), K. Laing (ENG).

Izmir, Turkey - 1976
L. Fly: C. Seican (ROM). **Fly:** G. Khratsov (URS). **Bantam:** M. Navros (URS). **Feather:** V. Demoianeko (URS). **Light:** M. Puzovic (YUG). **L. Welter:** V. Zverev (URS). **Welter:** K. Ozoglouz (TUR). **L. Middle:** W. Lauder (SCO). **Middle:** H. Lenhart (GER). **L. Heavy:** I. Yantchauskas (URS). **Heavy:** B. Enjenyan (URS).
Silver medal: J. Decker (ENG).
Bronze medals: I. McLeod (SCO), N. Croombes (ENG).

Dublin, Ireland - 1978
L. Fly: R. Marx (GDR). **Fly:** D. Radu (ROM). **Bantam:** S. Khatchatrian (URS). **Feather:** H. Loukmanov (URS). **Light:** P. Oliva (ITA). **L. Welter:** V. Laptiev (URS). **Welter:** R. Filimanov (URS). **L. Middle:** A. Beliave (URS). **Middle:** G. Zinkovitch (URS). **L. Heavy:** I. Jolta (ROM). **Heavy:** P. Stoimenov (BUL).
Silver medals: M. Holmes (IRL), P. Hanlon (ENG), M. Courtney (ENG).
Bronze medals: T. Thompson (IRL), J. Turner (ENG), M. Bennett (WAL), J. McAllister (SCO), C. Devine (ENG).

Rimini, Italy - 1980
L. Fly: A. Mikoulin (URS). **Fly:** J. Varadi (HUN). **Bantam:** F. Rauschning (GDR). **Feather:** J. Gladychev (URS). **Light:** V. Shishov (URS). **L. Welter:** R. Lomski (BUL). **Welter:** T. Holonics (GDR). **L. Middle:** N. Wilshire (ENG). **Middle:** S. Laptiev (URS). **L. Heavy:** V. Dolgoun (URS). **Heavy:** V. Tioumentsev (URS). **S. Heavy:** S. Kormihtsine (URS).
Bronze medals: N. Potter (ENG), B. McGuigan (IRL), M. Brereton (IRL), D. Cross (ENG).

Schwerin, East Germany - 1982
L. Fly: R. Kabirov (URS). **Fly:** I. Filchev (BUL). **Bantam:** M. Stecca (ITA). **Feather:** B. Blagoev (BUL). **Light:** E. Chakimov (URS). **L. Welter:** S. Mehnert (GDR). **Welter:** T. Schmitz (GDR). **L. Middle:** B. Shararov (URS). **Middle:** E. Christie (ENG). **L. Heavy:** Y. Waulin (URS). **Heavy:** A. Popov (URS). **S. Heavy:** V. Aldoshin (URS).
Silver medal: D. Kenny (ENG).
Bronze medal: O. Jones (ENG).

Tampere, Finland - 1984
L. Fly: R. Breitbart (GDR). **Fly:** D. Berg (GDR). **Bantam:** K. Khdrian (URS). **Feather:** O. Nazarov (URS). **Light:** C. Furnikov (BUL). **L. Welter:** W. Schmidt (GDR). **Welter:** K. Doinov (BUL). **L. Middle:** O. Volkov (URS). **Middle:** R. Ryll (GDR). **L. Heavy:** G. Peskov (URS). **Heavy:** R. Draskovic (YUG). **S. Heavy:** L. Kamenov (BUL).
Bronze medals: J. Lowey (IRL), F. Harding (ENG), N. Moore (ENG).

Copenhagen, Denmark - 1986
L. Fly: S. Todorov (BUL). **Fly:** S. Galotian (URS). **Bantam:** D. Drumm (GDR). **Feather:** K. Tsziu (URS). **Light:** G. Akopkhian (URS). **L. Welter:** F. Vastag (ROM). **Welter:** S. Karavayev (URS). **L. Middle:** E. Elibaev (URS). **Middle:** A. Kurnabka

(URS). **L. Heavy:** A. Schultz (GDR). **Heavy:** A. Golota (POL). **S. Heavy:** A. Prianichnikov (URS).

Gdansk, Poland - 1988
L. Fly: I. Kovacs (HUN). **Fly:** M. Beyer (GDR). **Bantam:** M. Aitzanov (URS). **Feather:** M. Rudolph (GDR). **Light:** M. Shaburov (URS). **L. Welter:** G. Campanella (ITA). **Welter:** D. Konsun (URS). **L. Middle:** K. Kiselev (URS). **Middle:** A. Rudenko (URS). **L. Heavy:** O. Velikanov (URS). **Heavy:** A. Ter-Okopian (URS). **S. Heavy:** E. Belusov (URS).
Bronze medals: P. Ramsey (ENG), M. Smyth (WAL).

Usti Nad Labem, Czechoslovakia - 1990
L. Fly: Z. Paliani (URS). **Fly:** K. Pielert (GDR). **Bantam:** K. Baravi (URS). **Feather:** P. Gvasalia (URS). **Light:** J. Hildenbrandt (GDR). **L. Welter:** N. Smanov (URS). **Welter:** A. Preda (ROM). **L. Middle:** A. Kakauridze (URS). **Middle:** J. Schwank (GDR). **L. Heavy:** Iljin (URS). **Heavy:** I. Andrejev (URS). **S. Heavy:** W. Fischer (GDR).
Silver medal: A. Todd (ENG).
Bronze medal: P. Craig (ENG).

Edinburgh, Scotland - 1992
L. Fly: M. Ismailov (URS). **Fly:** F. Brennfuhrer (GER). **Bantam:** S. Kuchler (GER). **Feather:** M. Silantiev (URS). **Light:** S. Shcherbakov (URS). **L. Welter:** O. Saitov (URS). **Welter:** H. Kurlumaz (TUR). **L. Middle:** Z. Erdie (HUN). **Middle:** V. Zhirov (URS). **L. Heavy:** D. Gorbachev (URS). **Heavy:** L. Achkasov (URS). **S. Heavy:** A. Mamedov (URS).
Silver medals: M. Hall (ENG), B. Jones (WAL).
Bronze medals: F. Slane (IRL), G. Stephens (IRL), C. Davies (WAL).

Salonika, Greece - 1993
L. Fly: O. Kiroukhine (UKR). **Fly:** R. Husseinov (AZE). **Bantam:** M. Kulbe (GER). **Feather:** E. Zakharov (RUS). **Light:** O. Sergeev (RUS). **L. Welter:** A. Selihanov (RUS). **Welter:** O. Kudinov (UKR). **L. Middle:** E. Makarenko (RUS). **Middle:** D. Droukovski (RUS). **L. Heavy:** A. Voida (RUS). **Heavy:** Vladimir Klitschko (UKR). **S. Heavy:** A. Moiseev (RUS).
Bronze medal: D. Costello (ENG).

Sifok, Hungary - 1995
L. Fly: D. Gaissine (RUS). **Fly:** A. Kotelnik (UKR). **Bantam:** A. Loutsenko (UKR). **Feather:** S. Harrison (SCO). **Light:** D. Simon (ROM). **L. Welter:** B. Ulusoy (TUR). **Welter:** O. Bouts (UKR). **L. Middle:** O. Bukalo (UKR). **Middle:** V. Plettnev (RUS). **L. Heavy:** A. Derevtsov (RUS). **Heavy:** C. O'Grady (IRL). **S. Heavy:** D. Savvine (RUS).
Silver medal: G. Murphy (SCO).
Bronze medal: N. Linford (ENG).

Birmingham, England - 1997
L. Fly: G. Balakshine (RUS). **Fly:** K. Dzhamoloudinov (RUS). **Bantam:** A. Shaiduline (RUS). **Feather:** D. Marciukaitis (LIT). **Light:** D. Baranov (RUS). **L. Welter:** A. Mishine (RUS). **Welter:** D. Yuldashev (UKR). **L. Middle:** A. Catic (GER). **Middle:** D. Lebedev (RUS). **L. Heavy:** V. Uzelkov (UKR). **Heavy:** S. Koeber (GER). **S. Heavy:** D. Pirozhenko (RUS).
Silver medal: S. Miller (ENG).
Bronze medals: S. Burke (ENG), M. Dean (ENG), P. Pierson (ENG), M. Lee (IRE).

Rijeka, Croatia - 1999
L. Fly: K. Kibalyuk (UKR). **Fly:** A. Bakhtin (RUS). **Bantam:** V. Simion (ROM). **Feather:** Kiutkhukow (BUL). **Light:** Pontilov (RUS). **L. Welter:** G. Ajetovic (YUG). **Welter:** S. Nouaouria (FRA). **L. Middle:** S. Kazantsev (RUS). **Middle:** D. Tsariouk (RUS). **L. Heavy:** Alexeev (RUS). **Heavy:** Alborov (RUS). **S. Heavy:** Soukhoverkov (RUS).
Bronze medal: S. Birch (ENG).

Sarajevo, Croatia - 2001
L. Fly: A. Taratokin (RUS). **Fly:** E. Abzalimov (RUS). **Bantam:** G. Kovaljov (RUS). **Feather:** M. Hratchev (RUS). **Light:** S. Aydin (TUR). **L. Welter:** D. Mikulin (RUS). **Welter:** O. Bokalo (UKR). **L. Middle:** M. Korobov (RUS). **Middle:** I. Bogdanov (UKR). **L. Heavy:** R. Kahkijev (RUS). **Heavy:** V. Zuyev (BE). **S. Heavy:** I. Timurziejev (RUS).
Bronze medal: K. Anderson (SCO).

Warsaw, Poland - 2003
L. Fly: P. Bedak (HUN). **Fly:** A. Ganev (RUS). **Bantam:** M. Tretiak (UKR). **Feather:** A. Alexandru (ROM). **Light:** A. Aleksiev (RUS). **L. Welter:** T. Tabotadze (UKR). **Welter:** Z. Baisangurov (RUS). **Middle:** J. Machoncev (RUS). **L. Heavy:** I. Michalkin (RUS). **Heavy:** Y. Romanov (RUS). **S. Heavy:** D. Arshba (RUS).
Bronze medal: S. Smith (ENG), F. Gavin (ENG), J. O'Donnell (ENG), T. Jeffries (ENG).

Tallinn, Estonia - 2005
L. Fly: S. Vodopyanov (RUS). **Fly:** S. Mamodov (AZE). **Bantam:** A. Akhba (RUS). **Feather:** M. Ignatev (RUS). **Light:** I. Iksanov (RUS). **L. Welter:** A.Zamkovoy (RUS). **Welter:** M. Koptyakov (RUS). **Middle:** S. Skiarov (RUS). **L.Heavy:** D. Chudinov (RUS). **Heavy:** S. Kalchugin (RUS). **S. Heavy:** A.Volkov (RUS).
Bronze Medal: J. Joyce (IRL).

Sombor, Serbia - 2007

L.Fly: M.Dvinskiy (RUS). **Fly:** M.Aloyan (RUS). **Bantam:** M.Maguire (ENG). **Feather:** B.Shelestyuk (UKR). **Light:** V.Shipunov (RUS). **L.Welter:** D.Lazarev (UKR). **Welter:** Y.Khytrov (UKR). **Middle:** N.Jovanovic (SER). **L.Heavy:** E.Yakushev (RUS). **Heavy:** V.Kudukhov (RUS). **S.Heavy:** M.Babanin (RUS). **Silver medals:** K.Saeed (ENG), T.Fury (ENG).

Note: The age limit for the championships were reduced from 21 to 19 in 1976.

Commonwealth Champions, 1930-2006

Hamilton, Canada - 1930
Fly: W. Smith (SAF). **Bantam:** H. Mizler (ENG). **Feather:** F. Meacham (ENG). **Light:** J. Rolland (SCO). **Welter:** L. Hall (SAF). **Middle:** F. Mallin (ENG). **L. Heavy:** J. Goyder (ENG). **Heavy:** V. Stuart (ENG).
Silver medals: T. Pardoe (ENG), T. Holt (SCO).
Bronze medals: A. Lyons (SCO), A. Love (ENG), F. Breeman (ENG).

Wembley, England - 1934
Fly: P. Palmer (ENG). **Bantam:** F. Ryan (ENG). **Feather:** C. Cattarall (SAF). **Light:** L. Cook (AUS). **Welter:** D. McCleave (ENG). **Middle:** A. Shawyer (ENG). **L. Heavy:** G. Brennan (ENG). **Heavy:** P. Floyd (ENG).
Silver medals: A. Barnes (WAL), J. Jones (WAL), F. Taylor (WAL), J. Holton (SCO).
Bronze medals: J. Pottinger (WAL), T. Wells (SCO), H. Moy (ENG), W. Duncan (NIR), J. Magill (NIR), Lord D. Douglas-Hamilton (SCO).

Melbourne, Australia - 1938
Fly: J. Joubert (SAF). **Bantam:** W. Butler (ENG). **Feather:** A. Henricus (CEY). **Light:** H. Groves (ENG). **Welter:** W. Smith (AUS). **Middle:** D. Reardon (WAL). **L. Heavy:** N. Wolmarans (SAF). **Heavy:** T. Osborne (CAN).
Silver medals: J. Watson (SCO), M. Dennis (ENG).
Bronze medals: H. Cameron (SCO), J. Wilby (ENG).

Auckland, New Zealand - 1950
Fly: H. Riley (SCO). **Bantam:** J. van Rensburg (SAF). **Feather:** H. Gilliland (SCO). **Light:** R. Latham (ENG). **Welter:** T. Ratcliffe (ENG). **Middle:** T. van Schalkwyk (SAF). **L. Heavy:** D. Scott (ENG). **Heavy:** F. Creagh (NZL).
Bronze medal: P. Brander (ENG).

Vancouver, Canada - 1954
Fly: R. Currie (SCO). **Bantam:** J. Smillie (SCO). **Feather:** L. Leisching (SAF). **Light:** P. van Staden (SR). **L. Welter:** M. Bergin (CAN). **Welter:** N. Gargano (ENG). **L. Middle:** W. Greaves (CAN). **Middle:** J. van de Kolff (SAF). **L. Heavy:** P. van Vuuren (SAF). **Heavy:** B. Harper (ENG).
Silver medals: M. Collins (WAL), F. McQuillan (SCO).
Bronze medals: D. Charnley (ENG), B. Wells (ENG).

Cardiff, Wales - 1958
Fly: J. Brown (SCO). **Bantam:** H. Winstone (WAL). **Feather:** W. Taylor (AUS). **Light:** R. McTaggart (SCO). **L. Welter:** H. Loubscher (SAF). **Welter:** J. Greyling (SAF). **L. Middle:** G. Webster (SAF). **Middle:** T. Milligan (NIR). **L. Heavy:** A. Madigan (AUS). **Heavy:** D. Bekker (SAF).
Silver medals: T. Bache (ENG), M. Collins (WAL), J. Jordan (NIR), R. Kane (SCO), S. Pearson (ENG), A. Higgins (WAL), D. Thomas (ENG).
Bronze medals: P. Lavery (NIR), D. Braithwaite (WAL), R. Hanna (NIR), A. Owen (SCO), J. McClory (NIR), J. Cooke (ENG), J. Jacobs (ENG), B. Nancurvis (ENG), R. Scott (SCO), W. Brown (WAL), J. Caiger (ENG), W. Bannon (SCO), R. Pleace (WAL).

Perth, Australia - 1962
Fly: R. Mallon (SCO). **Bantam:** J. Dynevor (AUS). **Feather:** J. McDermott (SCO). **Light:** E. Blay (GHA). **L. Welter:** C. Quartey (GHA). **Welter:** W. Coe (NZL). **L. Middle:** H. Mann (CAN). **Middle:** M. Calhoun (JAM). **L. Heavy:** A. Madigan (AUS). **Heavy:** G. Oywello (UGA).
Silver medals: R. McTaggart (SCO), J. Pritchett (ENG).
Bronze medals: M. Pye (ENG), P. Benneyworth (ENG), B. Whelan (ENG), B. Brazier (ENG), C. Rice (NIR), T. Menzies (SCO), H. Christie (NIR), A. Turmel (CI).

Kingston, Jamaica - 1966
Fly: S. Shittu (GHA). **Bantam:** E. Ndukwu (NIG). **Feather:** P. Waruinge (KEN). **Light:** A. Andeh (NIG). **L. Welter:** J. McCourt (NIR). **Welter:** E. Blay (GHA). **L. Middle:** M. Rowe (ENG). **Middle:** J. Darkey (GHA). **L. Heavy:** R. Tighe (ENG). **Heavy:** W. Kini (NZL).
Silver medals: P. Maguire (NIR), R. Thurston (ENG), R. Arthur (ENG), T. Imrie (SCO).
Bronze medals: S. Lockhart (NIR), A. Peace (SCO), F. Young (NIR), J. Turpin (ENG), D. McAlinden (NIR).

Edinburgh, Scotland - 1970
L. Fly: J. Odwori (UGA). **Fly:** D. Needham (ENG). **Bantam:** S. Shittu (GHA). **Feather:** P. Waruinge (KEN). **Light:** A. Adeyemi (NIG). **L. Welter:** M. Muruli (UGA). **Welter:** E. Ankudey (GHA). **L. Middle:** T. Imrie (SCO). **Middle:** J. Conteh (ENG). **L. Heavy:** F. Ayinla (NIG). **Heavy:** B. Masanda (UGA).
Silver medals: T. Davies (WAL), J. Gillan (SCO), D. Davies (WAL), J. McKinty (NIR).

Bronze medals: M. Abrams (ENG), A. McHugh (SCO), D. Larmour (NIR), S. Oglivie (SCO), A. Richardson (ENG), T. Joyce (SCO), P. Doherty (NIR), J. Rafferty (SCO), L. Stevens (ENG).

Christchurch, New Zealand - 1974
L. Fly: S. Muchoki (KEN). **Fly:** D. Larmour (NIR). **Bantam:** P. Cowdell (ENG). **Feather:** E. Ndukwu (NIG). **Light:** A. Kalule (UGA). **L. Welter:** O. Nwankpa (NIG). **Welter:** M. Muruli (UGA). **L. Middle:** L. Mwale (ZAM). **Middle:** F. Lucas (STV). **L. Heavy:** W. Knight (ENG). **Heavy:** N. Meade (ENG).
Silver medals: E. McKenzie (WAL), A. Harrison (SCO).
Bronze medals: J. Bambrick (SCO), J. Douglas (SCO), J. Rodgers (NIR), S. Cooney (SCO), R. Davies (ENG), C. Speare (ENG), G. Ferris (NIR).

Edmonton, Canada - 1978
L. Fly: S. Muchoki (KEN). **Fly:** M. Irungu (KEN). **Bantam:** B. McGuigan (NIR). **Feather:** A. Nelson (GHA). **Light:** G. Hamill (NIR). **L. Welter:** W. Braithwaite (GUY). **Welter:** M. McCallum (JAM). **L. Middle:** K. Perlette (ENG). **Middle:** P. McElwaine (AUS). **L. Heavy:** R. Fortin (CAN). **Heavy:** J. Awome (ENG).
Silver medals: J. Douglas (SCO), K. Beattie (NIR), D. Parkes (ENG), V. Smith (ENG).
Bronze medals: H. Russell (NIR), M. O'Brien (ENG), J. McAllister (SCO), T. Feal (WAL).

Brisbane, Australia - 1982
L. Fly: A. Wachire (KEN). **Fly:** M. Mutua (KEN). **Bantam:** J. Orewa (NIG). **Feather:** P. Konyegwachie (NIG). **Light:** H. Khalili (KEN). **L. Welter:** C. Ossai (NIG). **Welter:** C. Pyatt (ENG). **L. Middle:** S. O'Sullivan (CAN). **Middle:** J. Price (ENG). **L. Heavy:** F. Sani (FIJ). **Heavy:** W. de Wit (CAN).
Silver medals: J. Lyon (ENG), J. Kelly (SCO), R. Webb (NIR), P. Hanlon (ENG), J. McDonnell (ENG), N. Croombes (ENG), H. Hylton (ENG).
Bronze medals: R. Gilbody (ENG), C. McIntosh (ENG), R. Corr (NIR).

Edinburgh, Scotland - 1986
L. Fly: S. Olson (CAN). **Fly:** J. Lyon (ENG). **Bantam:** S. Murphy (ENG). **Feather:** B. Downey (CAN). **Light:** A. Dar (CAN). **L. Welter:** H. Grant (CAN). **Welter:** D. Dyer (ENG). **L. Middle:** D. Sherry (CAN). **Middle:** R. Douglas (ENG). **L. Heavy:** J. Moran (ENG). **Heavy:** J. Peau (NZL). **S. Heavy:** L. Lewis (CAN).
Silver medals: M. Epton (ENG), R. Nash (NIR), P. English (ENG), N. Haddock (WAL), J. McAlister (SCO), H. Lawson (SCO), D. Young (SCO), A. Evans (WAL).
Bronze medals: W. Docherty (SCO), J. Todd (NIR), K. Webber (WAL), G. Brooks (SCO), J. Wallace (SCO), C. Carleton (NIR), J. Jacobs (ENG), B. Lowe (NIR), D. Denny (NIR), G. Thomas (WAL), A. Mullen (SCO), G. Ferrie (SCO), P. Tinney (NIR), B. Pullen (WAL), E. Cardouza (ENG), J. Oyebola (ENG), J. Sillitoe (CI).

Auckland, New Zealand - 1990
L. Fly: J. Juuko (UGA). **Fly:** W. McCullough (NIR). **Bantam:** S. Mohammed (NIG). **Feather:** J. Irwin (ENG). **Light:** G. Nyakana (UGA). **L. Welter:** C. Kane (SCO). **Welter:** D. Defiagbon (NIG). **L. Middle:** R. Woodhall (ENG). **Middle:** C. Johnson (CAN). **L. Heavy:** J. Akhasamba (KEN). **Heavy:** G. Onyango (KEN). **S. Heavy:** M. Kenny (NZL).
Bronze medals: D. Anderson (SCO), M. Edwards (ENG), P. Douglas (NIR).

Victoria, Canada - 1994
L. Fly: H. Ramadhani (KEN). **Fly:** P. Shepherd (SCO). **Bantam:** R. Peden (AUS). **Feather:** C. Patton (CAN). **Light:** M. Strange (CAN). **L. Welter:** P. Richardson (ENG). **Welter:** N. Sinclair (NIR). **L. Middle:** J. Webb (ENG). **Middle:** R. Donaldson (CAN). **L. Heavy:** D. Brown (CAN). **Heavy:** O. Ahmed (KEN). **S. Heavy:** D. Dokiwari (NIG).
Silver medals: S. Oliver (ENG), J. Cook (WAL), M. Renaghan (NIR), M. Winters (NIR), J. Wilson (SCO).
Bronze medals: D. Costello (ENG), J. Townsley (SCO), D. Williams (ENG).

Kuala Lumpar, Malaysia - 1998
L. Fly: S. Biki (MAS). **Fly:** R. Sunee (MRI). **Bantam:** M. Yomba (TAN). **Feather:** A. Arthur (SCO). **Light:** R. Narh (GHA). **L. Welter:** M. Strange (CAN). **Welter:** J. Molitor (CAN). **L. Middle:** C. Bessey (ENG). **Middle:** J. Pearce (ENG). **L. Heavy:** C. Fry (ENG). **Heavy:** M. Simmons (CAN). **S. Heavy:** A. Harrison (ENG).
Silver medal: L. Cunningham (NIR).
Bronze medals: G. Jones (ENG), A. McLean (ENG), C. McNeil (SCO), J. Townsley (SCO), B. Magee (NIR), K. Evans (WAL).

Manchester, England - 2002
L. Fly: M. Ali Qamar (IND). **Fly:** K. Kanyanta (ZAM). **Bantam:** J. Kane (AUS). **Feather:** H. Ali (PAK). **Light:** J. Arthur (WAL). **L. Welter:** D. Barker (ENG). **Welter:** D. Geale (AUS). **L. Middle:** J. Pascal (CAN). **Middle:** P. Miller (AUS). **L. Heavy:** J. Albert (NIG). **Heavy:** J. Douglas (CAN). **S. Heavy:** D. Dolan (ENG).
Silver medals: D. Langley (ENG), P. Smith (ENG), S. Birch (ENG).
Bronze medals: M. Moran (ENG), A. Morris (ENG), C. McEwan (SCO), A. Young (SCO), K. Evans (WAL).

Melbourne, Australia - 2006
L. Fly: J. Utoni (NAM). **Fly:** D. Broadhurst (ENG). **Bantam:** G. Kumar (FIJ). **Feather:** S. Smith (ENG). **Light:** F. Gavin (ENG). **L. Welter:** J. Cox (ENG). **Welter:** B. Mwelase (SA). **Middle:** J. Fletcher (AUS). **L. Heavy:** K. Anderson (SCO). **Heavy:** B. Pitt (AUS). **S. Heavy:** D. Price (ENG).
Silver medals: D. Langley (ENG), K. Evans (WAL).
Bronze medals: M. Nasir (WAL), D. Edwards (WAL), J. Crees (WAL), N. Perkins (ENG), J. Degale (ENG).

The Triple Hitters' Boxing Quiz: Part 13

Compiled by Ralph Oates

QUESTIONS

1. In which weight division was Solly Kreiger an NBA world champion?
   A. Welterweight.   B. Middleweight.
   C. Light-Heavyweight.

2. On 22 March 1948, Ronnie Clayton lost his European featherweight title when Ray Famechon outpointed him over 15 rounds. Where did this contest take place?
   A. Liverpool.   B. Manchester.
   C. Nottingham.

3. Giuseppe Antonio Berardinelli was the real name of which former world light-heavyweight champion?
   A. Joey Maxim.   B. Billy Conn.   C. Melio Bettina.

4. On 30 September 1949, Rinty Monaghan defended his British, British Empire, European and world flyweight titles against Terry Allen. What was the result?
   A. 15-round points win for Allen.   B. A draw.
   C. 15-round points win for Monaghan.

5. During his career how many professional bouts did former world middleweight champion Jake LaMotta have?
   A. 105.   B. 106.   C. 107.

6. Jack Gardner lost his European heavyweight title to Germany's Hein Ten Hoff when outpointed over 15 rounds on 23 September 1951. In which country did this contest take place?
   A. England.   B. Austria.   C. West Germany.

7. During his career, which boxer did the former British, European and British Empire lightweight champion Dave Charnley not meet in the professional ranks?
   A. Carlos Ortiz.   B. Emile Griffith.
   C. Ismael Laguna.

8. Who was the first boxer to defeat the future British and British Empire featherweight champion Evan Armstrong in the professional ranks on 3 September 1964, by way of a stoppage in round six?
   A. Bobby Fisher.   B. Tony Riley.
   C. Brian Cartwright.

9. Nino Benventui won the world middleweight title on 17 April 1967 when he outpointed the defending champion Emile Griffith over 15 rounds in New York. Who was the referee for this contest?
   A. Tommy Walsh.   B. Mark Conn.
   C. Arthur Mercante.

10. During his professional career, heavyweight Billy Walker boxed abroad on just one occasion. Name the country?
    A. France.   B. Spain.   C. Italy.

11. In a non-title bout that took place on 9 April 1968, the reigning WBC featherweight champion Howard Winstone outpointed the British super-featherweight king Jimmy Anderson over ten rounds. Up to that time Anderson was on a winning streak of how many contests?
    A. Two.   B. Three.   C. Four.

12. How many European lightweight title bouts did Ken Buchanan participate in during the course of his professional career?
    A. Three.   B. Four.   C. Five.

13. On 22 March 1971, Bunny Sterling retained his Commonwealth middleweight title by outpointing Johann Louw over 15 rounds. In which country did this contest take place?
    A. Australia.   B. Canada.   C. Jamaica.

14. On how many occasions did former WBC world lightweight champion Jim Watt box in Glasgow during his professional career?
    A. Eight.   B. Nine.   C. Ten.

15. Dave Boy Green lost in his bid for the WBC world welterweight title when he was knocked out in round 11 by defending champion Carlos Palomino on 14 June 1977. Prior to this setback, Green had been undefeated in how many bouts?
    A. 24.   B. 25.   C. 26.

16. On 20 June 1978, future three times WBC world light-heavyweight champion Dennis Andries met Bonny McKenzie in a contest scheduled for eight rounds. What was the result?
    A. Points win for McKenzie.   B. A draw.
    C. Points win for Andries.

17. During his professional career, which British title did Hugh Russell not hold?
    A. Flyweight.   B. Bantamweight.
    C. Featherweight.

18. In defence of his WBA lightweight title on 2 August 1980, Hilmer Kenty stopped Yong-Ho Oh. Name the round that the stoppage occured?
    A. Eight.   B. Nine.   C. Ten.

19. What was the nationality of former world WBO featherweight champion Maurizio Stecca?
    A. Italian.   B. French.   C. Spanish.

20. In which weight division was Andy Till a British champion?
    A. Welterweight.
    B. Light-Middleweight.
    C. Middleweight.

21. In which year was former world light-heavyweight champion Jose Torres born?
    A. 1936.   B. 1937.   C. 1938.

22. In which round did Gary De'Roux stop Alan McKay on 14 December 1990 to win the vacant Southern Area featherweight title?
    A. Three.   B. Four.   C. Five.

23. Robbie Regan won the vacant British flyweight title on 28 May 1991 when he outpointed Joe Kelly over 12 rounds. Where did this contest take place?
    A. Glasgow.   B. Cardiff.   C. Belfast.

24. On 10 February 1993, John Armour retained his Commonwealth bantamweight title against Morgan Mpande when winning on points over 12 rounds. At that stage of his career, Armour was undefeated in how many professional contests?
    A. 11.   B. 12.   C. 13.

25. Over how many rounds did former WBO world, British and Commonwealth featherweight champion Colin McMillan outpoint opponent Harry Escott on 4 February 1995?
    A. Six.   B. Eight.   C. Ten.

26. Charles Brewer won the vacant IBF world super-middleweight title on 21 June 1997 when he stopped Gary Ballard. In which round did the fight end?
    A. Five.   B. Six.   C. Seven.

27. Wayne Alexander won the vacant British light-middleweight title on 19 February 2000 when he stopped Paul Samuels in the third round. Who held the crown prior to Alexander?
    A. Ryan Rhodes.
    B. Robert McCracken.
    C. Ensley Bingham.

28. On 19 August 2000, Jane Couch lost a six-round points decision to Liz Mueller. In which country did this contest take place?
    A. America.   B. Canada.   C. England.

29. Tony Booth lost a four-round points decision to Tommy Eastwood on 9 September 2001. At this stage of his career, Booth had taken part in how many professional bouts?
    A. 103.   B. 104.   C. 105.

30. In defence of his WBU cruiserweight title, Enzo Maccarinelli stopped Earl Morais in the first round on 6 December 2003. At this stage in his career how many times had Maccarinelli achieved victory in the opening round?
    A. Three.   B. Four.   C. Five.

31. On 3 December 2004, Alex Arthur retained his IBF Inter-Continental super-featherweight title when he defeated Narazeno Ruiz. Name the means of victory?
    A. Four-round count out.
    B. Eight-round stoppage.
    C. 12-round points decision.

32. Carl Baker won the vacant British Masters heavyweight title on 26 June 2005 when he stopped Scott Lansdowne in round eight. How many professional bouts had Baker participated in at that stage of his career?
    A. Eight.   B. Nine.   C. Ten.

33. Miguel Cotto retained his WBO world light-welterweight title on 24 September 2005 when he knocked out Ricardo Torres in round seven. In which part of America did this contest take place?
    A. Las Vegas.   B. Atlantic City.   C. New York.

34. In his professional debut on 16 December 2005, heavyweight Matt Paice outpointed Simon Goodwin over four rounds. Who was Paice's manager?
    A. Tania Follett.   B. Bruce Baker.   C. Frank Maloney.

35. Young Muttley won the British welterweight title on 28 January 2006 when he outpointed defending champion Michael Jennings over 12 rounds. Who was the referee for this contest?
    A. Terry O'Connor.   B. Mark Green.   C. John Keane.

36. Nicky Cook retained his European featherweight title on 24 February 2006 when he outpointed Yuri Voronin over 12 rounds. At this stage of his career, Cook was undefeated in how many professional contests?
A. 24.   B. 25.   C. 26.

37. In defence of his European cruiserweight title, on 24 March 2006 David Haye retained his crown when he stopped Lasse Johansen. In which round did the stoppage occur?
A. Six.   B. Seven.   C. Eight.

38. Which one of the following was born in the year of 1972?
A. Joe Calzaghe. B. Ricky Hatton.   C. Scott Gammer.

39. In which weight division did former WBC world super-middleweight champion Richie Woodhall win a European title during his professional career?
A. Middleweight.   B. Super-Middleweight.
C. Light-Heavyweight.

40. Kevin Mitchell retained his IBF Inter-Continental super-featherweight title on 13 May 2006 when Kirkor Kirkorov retired in the second round. At this stage in his career Mitchell was undefeated in 19 contests. How many had he won inside the distance?
A. 11.   B. 12.   C. 13.

41. How tall is the former British and Commonwealth heavyweight champion Julius Francis?
A. 6'1".   B. 6'2".   C. 6'3".

42. Ricky Hatton won the WBA world welterweight title in Boston on 13 May 2006 when he defeated the holder Luis Collazo. By which method was victory secured?
A. Five-round knockout.
B. Eight-round stoppage.
C. 12-round points decision.

43. On 20 May 2006, Amir Khan outpointed Laszlo Komjathi over six rounds. Where did this contest take place?
A. Cardiff.   B. Glasgow.   C. Belfast.

44. Carl Froch retained his British and Commonwealth super-middleweight titles on 26 May 2006 when he stopped Brian Magee in round 11. Who was the referee for this contest?
A. Richie Davis.   B. Paul Thomas.
C. Mickey Vann.

45. Which of the following former British holders of a world title did not box in America during their professional career?
A. Alan Minter. B. John Conteh.   C. Charlie Magri.

46. Clinton Woods retained his IBF light-heavyweight world crown on 2 September 2006 when he outpointed the former champion Glengoffe Johnson over 12 rounds. Where did this contest take place?
A. Bolton.   B. Nottingham.   C. Liverpool.

47. Junior Witter won the vacant WBC world light-welterweight title on 15 September 2006 when he outpointed DeMarcus Corley over 12 rounds. As a former world champion, which version of the title did Corley once hold?
A. IBF.   B. WBO.   C. WBA.

48. On 24 September 2006, Cathy Brown won the inaugural English bantamweight title for women when she defeated Juliette Winter. By which method was victory secured?
A. Six-round stoppage.
B. Eight-round count out.
C. Ten-round points decision.

49. Joe Calzaghe retained his WBO and IBF world super-middleweight titles on 14 October 2006 when he outpointed Sakio Bika over 12 rounds. At this stage of his professional career, Calzaghe was undefeated in how many professional contests?
A. 42.   B. 43.   C. 44.

50. On 15 December 2006, Colin Lynes stopped Janos Petrovics in the sixth round. How many contests did Lynes participate in during 2006?
A. One.   B. Two.   C. Three.

Robin Hood Boxing and Fitness
2a Thoresby Street, Mansfield
Nottinghamshire, NG18 1QF
Tel: 01623 476397
Mobile: 07833995770 / 07757821555
Email: Robinhoodboxing@hotmail.co.uk

Robin Hood Boxing Stable

Professional and Amateur
BBB of Control
Regular Promotions
Training

Manager/Trainer
Matt Scriven
12 years Army P.T.I.
11 years Pro Boxer

NEWCOMERS VERY WELCOME

Current Fighters

Matt Scriven – L.Middleweight
Andy Bell – British S.Flyweight Champion
Mick Monaghan – Middleweight
Dennis Corpe – L.Middleweight
Charlie Chiverton – Middleweight
Matin Mohammed – S.Featherweight
Peter Jones – S.Featherweight
David Keir – L.Middleweight
Tyrone Wright – S.Middleweight. Midlands Area
L.Heavyweight Champion
Alex Spitjo – Welterweight

Robin Hood A.B.C.

Director: P. Scriven
Secretary: T. Bell
Treasurer: R. Scriven
Trainers: Dave Pearson
Rob Sharpe

REGULAR SHOWS

Directory of Ex-Boxers' Associations

by Ray Caulfield

BOURNEMOUTH Founded 1980. HQ: The Cricketers, Windham Road, off Ashley Road, Bournemouth. Dai Dower MBE (P); Dave Fry (C); Peter Judge (T & VC); Jack Streek (S), 38 St Leonard's Farm, Ringwood Road, Ferndown, Dorset BH22 0AG (0120 289 4647)

BRIGHTON Formed 2007. HQ: Southwick Football Club, Old Barn Way, off Manor Hall Way, Southwick, Sussex. Alan Minter (P); Ernie Price (C); Barry Noonan (VC); Mick Smith (PRO); Karen Knight (T & S), 1 Tall Trees, Penstone Park, Lancing, West Sussex BN15 9AG (0190 376 6893). E-mail: kazzie.knight@homecall.co.uk

CORK Founded 1973. HQ: Glen Boxing Club, Blackpool, Cork. William O'Leary (P & C); Phil Murray (VC); John Martin (S); John Donovan (T)

CORNWALL Founded 1989. HQ: Upper Tolcarne House, Burras, Wendron, Helston. Salvo Nucciforo (VC); Eric Bradshaw (T); Stan Cullis (P & PRO), Upper Tolcarne House, Burras, Wendron, Helston, Cornwall TR13 0JD (0120 983 1463). E-mail: stan@cullis1.freeserve.co.uk

CROYDON Founded 1982. HQ: Ivy House Club, Campbell Road, West Croydon. Gilbert Allnutt (P); Frank Giles (T); Barry Penny (C); vacant (VC); Simon Euan-Smith (S & PRO), 151 Upper Selsdon Road, Sanderstead, Surrey CR2 0DO (0208 407 0785)

EASTERN AREA Founded 1973. HQ: Coach & Horses, Union Street, Norwich. Brian Fitzmaurice (P); Ron Springall (S & T); Clive Campling (C), 54 Robson Road, Norwich, Norfolk NR5 8NZ

HOME COUNTIES Founded 2005. HQ: Golden Lion Public House, High Street, London Colney, Herts. Terry Downes (P); Bob Williams (C); Ann Ayles (T); Dave Ayles (S), 3 Burgess Close, Dunstable, Beds LU6 3EU (01582 864274). E-mail: d.ayles@ntlworld.com

HULL & EAST YORKSHIRE Founded 1993. HQ: Crooked Billett, Holdens Road, Hull or Kings Arms, King Street, Bridlington. Charles McGhee (C); Johnny Borrill (P); Len Storey (T); Bert Smith (S), 54 St Aidan Road, Bridlington, E. Yorks (01262 672 573)

IPSWICH Founded 1970. HQ: Loco Club, Station Street, Stoke, Ipswich. Alby Kingham (P); Chris Collins (PRO); Vic Thurlow (C & T); Eric Roper (S); contact number (01473 712684)

IRISH Founded 1973. HQ: National Boxing Stadium, South Circular Road, Dublin. Val Harris (P); Martin Gannon (C); Tommy Butler (T); Paddy O'Reilly (VC); Willie Duggan (S), 175 Kimmage Road West, Dublin 6W

KENT Founded 1967. HQ: RAFA Club, Dock Road, Chatham. Harry Doherty (P); Bill Quinton (C); Paul Nihill MBE (S, PRO & T), 24 Walderslade Road, Chatham, Kent ME4 6NZ (0163 440 4240)

LEEDS Founded 1952. HQ: North Leeds WMC, Lincoln Green Road, Leeds. Alan Richardson (P); Kevin Cunningham (C); Peter Selby (S); Alan Alster (T); Frank Johnson (PRO), 82 Windmill Chase, Rothwell, Leeds, Yorks LS26 0XB (0113 288 7753)

LEICESTER Founded 1972. HQ: The Jungle Club, Checketts Road, Leicester. Mick Greaves (P & C); Fred Roberts (T), Alan Parr (S & PRO), 22 Hewes Close, Glen Parva, Leicester LE2 9NU (0116 277 9327/0791 332 3950). E-mail: alan.parr3@btinternet.com

LONDON Founded 1971. HQ; The Queen Mary College, Bancroft Road, Mile End, London E1. Stephen Powell (P); Micky O'Sullivan (C); Charlie Wright (VC); Ray Caulfield (T); Mrs Mary Powell (S), 36 St Peters Street, Islington, London N1 8JT (0207 226 9032). E-mail: marypowell@btconnect.com

MANCHESTER Founded 1968. HQ: Lord Nelson Public House, N'r Piccadilly Station, Manchester. Tommy Proffitt (LP); Jack Edwards (P); Neville Tetlow (VC); Kenny Baker (T); John Redfern (PRO); Jimmy Lewis (C); Eddie Copeland (S), 9 Lakeside, Hadfield, Glossop, Derbys SK13 1HW (0145 786 8142). E-mail: edwin@edwin8.wanadoo.co.uk

MERSEYSIDE Founded 1973. HQ: Arriva Club, Hockenhall Alley, Liverpool. Harry Scott (P); Terry Carson (C & PRO); Jim Boyd (VC); Jim Jenkinson (S & T), 13 Brooklands Avenue, Waterloo, Liverpool, Merseyside L22 3XY (0151 928 0301). E-mail: mersey-wirralformerboxers@hotmail.com. Website: www.mfba.org.uk

MIDLANDS Founded 2002. HQ: The Portland Pavilion, Portland Road, Edgbaston, Birmingham. Bunny Johnson (P); Martin Florey (C); Paul Rowson (VC); Stephen Florey (T); Jerry Hjelter (S & PRO), 67 Abberley Avenue, Stourport on Severn, Warwicks DY13 0LY (0129 987 9907). E-mail: jerryhjboxing@hotmail.com. Website: www.midlandexboxersassociation.fortunecity.com/index.html

NORTHAMPTONSHIRE Founded 1981. HQ: Park Inn, Silver Street, Northampton. Dick Rogers (P); Gil Wilson (C); Brian Thomas (VC); George Ward (PRO); Mrs Pam Ward (S & T), 6 Derwent Close, Kings Heath, Northampton NN5 7JS (0160 458 3057)

NORTHERN FEDERATION Founded 1974. Several member EBAs. Annual Gala. Dick McTaggart, MBE (P); Terry Carson (C); John Redfern (PRO); Eddie Copeland (S & T), 9 Lakeside, Hadfield, Glossop, Derbys SK13 1HW

NORTHERN IRELAND Founded 1970. HQ: Ulster Sports Club, High Street, Belfast. Gerry Hassett (P); Cecil Martin (C); S.Thompson (T); Terry Milligan (S), 32 Rockdale Street, Belfast BT12 7PA

NORTH STAFFS & SOUTH CHESHIRE Founded 1969. HQ: The Roe Buck, Wedgwood Place, Burslem, Stoke on Trent. Roy

Simms (C); Larry Parkes (VC); John Greatbach (T); Billy Tudor (P). Les Dean (S & PRO), Trees, Pinewood Drive, Ashley Heath, Market Drayton, Shropshire TF4 4PA (01630 672 484)

NORWICH Founded 1990. HQ: Wymondham Snooker Club, Town Green, Wymondham, Norfolk. Les King (P & C); Len Jarvis (T); Reg Harris (S), contact number (0195 360 3997)

NOTTINGHAM Founded 1979. HQ: The Wheatsheaf, Sneinton Road, Nottingham. Len Chorley (P); Walter Spencer (C); Mick Smith (VC); Gary Rooksby (T); John Kinsella (PRO); Graham Rooksby (S), 42 Spinney Road, Keyworth, Notts NG12 5LN (0115 937 5242). E-mail: nebsa@rooksby.com

PLYMOUTH Founded 1982. HQ: Stoke Social Club, Devonport Road, Plymouth. Tom Pryce-Davies (P); Jimmy Ryan (C); Jimmy Bevel (VC); Arthur Willis (T); Pat Crago (S & PRO), 8 Hawkinge Gardens, Ernsettle, Plymouth, Devon PL5 2RJ (0175 236 6339). E-mail: crago@blueyonder.co.uk

PRESTON Founded 1973. HQ: Barney's Piano Bar, Church Street, Preston. John Allen (C & S); Eddie Monahan (P); Bobby Rhodes (T), 1 Norris Street, Preston, Lancs PR1 7PX

ST HELENS Founded 1983. HQ: Royal Naval Association, Volunteer Street, St Helens. Ray Britch (C); Tommy McNamara (T); Paul Britch (S), 16 Oxley Street, Sutton, St Helens, Merseyside WA9 3PE

SCOTTISH Founded 1997. HQ: Iron Horse Public House, West Nile Street, Glasgow. John McCluskey (P); Frank O'Donnell (LP); Phil McIntyre (C); Robert Craig (VC); Peter Baines (T); Liam McColgan (S), 25 Dalton Avenue, Linnvale, Clydebank, West Dunbartonshire G81 2SH (0141 562 5575). E-mail: p.baines20@ntlworld.com

SHEFFIELD & SOUTH YORKSHIRE Founded 1974. Reformed 2002. HQ: Handsworth Social Club, 13 Hall Road, Handsworth, Sheffield (0114 269 3019). Billy Calvert (P & T); Harry Carnell (C); Eric Goodlad (VC); John Redfern (S & PRO), 33 Birch Avenue, Chapeltown, Sheffield, South Yorks S35 1RQ (0114 257 8326)

SQUARE RING (TORBAY) Founded 1978. HQ: Snooty Fox Hotel, St Marychurch. Ken Wittey (C); Johnny Mudge (S); Jim Banks (T); Paul King (P & VC), 8 Winchester Avenue, Torquay, Devon TQ2 8AR

SUNDERLAND Founded 1959. HQ: Railway Club, Holmeside, Sunderland, Tyne & Wear. George Martin (P); Ted Lynn (C); Gordon (Pedro) Phillips (VC); Geoff Rushworth (PRO); Les Simm (T & S), 21 Orchard Street, Pallion, Sunderland, Tyne & Wear SR4 6QL (0191 514 1809)

SUSSEX Founded 1974. Reformed 2003. HQ: Hove Conservative Club, 102 Blatchington Road, Hove BN3 3DL. Tommy Mellis (P); Mick Smith (PRO); Steve Wood (C); Dennis Smith (VC); Rob Benson (S & T); contact number (077799 740 213). E-mail: peter.benson@730ntlworld.com. Website: www.sussexexboxers.com

TYNESIDE Founded 1970. HQ: The Pelaw Social Club, Heworth House, Kirkstone Road, Pelaw, Gateshead. Maxie Walsh (P, PRO & C); Dave McCormick (VC); Malcolm Dinning (T); Maxie Walsh (P, C & S), c/o 9 Prendwick Court, Hebburn, Tyne & Wear NE31 2NQ (0191 483 4267)

WELSH Founded 1976. HQ: Rhydyfelin Labour Club, Pontypridd. Patron: Lord Brooks of Tremorfa. Wynford Jones (P); John Floyd (C); Danny Davies (VC); Mark Warner (T); Don James (S), 5 Aeron Terrace, Twynyroyn, Merthyr Tydfil, South Wales C47 0LN

WIRRAL Founded 1973. Reformed 2003. HQ: RNA Club, Thornbury Park Road East, Birkenhead. Frank Johnson (P); Pat Garry (T); Terry Carson (C); Pat McAteer (VC); Alan Crowther (S), 15 Scythia Close, New Ferry, Wirral, Merseyside CH62 1HH (0151 645 0466). E-mail: alancrowther@hotmail.co.uk Website: www. lmu.livjm.ac.uk/inmylife/channels/sport/1116.htm

The above information is set at the time of going to press and no responsibility can be taken for any changes in officers or addresses of HQs that may happen between then and publication or changes that have not been notified to me.

ABBREVIATIONS

P - President. HP - Honorary President. LP - Life President. AP - Acting President. C - Chairman. VC - Vice Chairman. T - Treasurer. S - Secretary. PRO - Public Relations Officer and/or Press Officer.

London Ex-Boxers' Association Treasurer, Ray Caulfield (right), seen presenting the 'Al Phillips' Trophy' to Enzo Calzaghe at the famous Newbridge Gym. The trophy is awarded annually by LEBA members to a member of the boxing fraternity for their contribution to the sport over many years

Obituaries
by Derek O'Dell

It is impossible to list everyone, but I have again done my best to include final tributes for as many of the well-known boxers and other familiar names within the sport who have passed away since the 2007 Yearbook was published. We honour them and remember them.

ABBOTT Jackie *From* Meltham. *Died* 29 May 2008, aged 72. Middleweight Jackie is remembered more for being Randolph Turpin's sparring partner than for his own achievements in the ring. On its own, his record, which began in 1952, reveals some well-known names such as Joe Somerville, Sid Cain, Johnny Williamson, Freddie Kaye and Owen Feathers. The only time Jackie fought over eight rounds was in November 1953 when he travelled to Belfast to lose on points to Jackie Mitchell. He beat Harry Harvey twice out of their three meetings, stopped Wigan's John Hunt at the old Liverpool Stadium and beat Somerville in 1960 at Shoreditch Town Hall before quitting boxing after two losses to Feathers. With his wife Sue he ran boxing gyms in Slaithwaite, Yorkshire, bringing many children off the streets to instil in them discipline and good manners.

ALLEN Vernon *From* Sydney, Australia. *Died* April 2008, aged 63. In a career that began in England in 1965, Vernon had 37 contests of which he won a third. Those cold statistics are misleading. He was a respected heavyweight, perhaps without championship aspirations but one who, with 12 wins in total, could look after himself. He had that stick-to-it quality that saw him overcome a poor first year in the game to beat Shaun Dolan and Dave Barber. Vernon lost his first five starts then stopped Tommy Woods and Tommy Wright. He fought Johnny Ould and Jimmy Tibbs but lost both times. When Dave Hawkes beat him for the third time, he upped sticks and went to Australia where he twice beat Nino Pellizzaro. He got a shot at the New South Wales heavyweight championship after stopping Ted McKenzie but was outpointed by Sentiki Qata. A draw and two losses followed then he quit the ring. After his fighting days were over, he decided to settle in Australia where he spent the last 40 years of his life.

ARAGON Art *From* Los Angeles, California, USA. *Died* 25 March 2008, aged 80. In the 1950s, Californian boxing enjoyed two or more pages of coverage in the *Ring* magazine when world-class fighters plied their trade in Los Angeles, Hollywood and San Francisco. One of them was this Mexican-American. He was box-office magic, never in a dull fight and a man whose appearance would guarantee the 'All Seats Sold' placard outside any state arena he fought in. Born in Belon, New Mexico, he kicked off his career as a brash 16-year-old. Even then he was far from modest and had the knack of needling the fans. They packed the place out, many to see him beaten, but he seldom obliged. He could hit (60 of his 89 wins came early) and he was an entertainer who fully earned his moniker 'Golden Boy'. If you ignore his last fight the only man to

beat him inside the scheduled distance was Carmen Basilio. That was in 1958 when Art was showing signs of slowing down after 14 years participation in gloved combat. He got a hiding that night but the thought of quitting never entered his head. When the time came to take his lumps, he did so uncomplainingly and earned respect from his detractors. There was a crowd of 20,000, most of whom forgave him after he had been accused the previous year of fixing some of his fights. The case was dismissed on appeal, but mud sticks. Going out on his shield against Basilio seemed to exonerate him from the ugly whispers. Art's story is not one of defeat but of resounding victories. He beat top fighters like Don Jordan, Chico Vejar, Mario Trigo, Johnny Gonsalves, Enrique Bolanos, Teddy Red Top Davis, Richie Shinn and Lauro Salas. In 1951, with a win over world lightweight champion Jimmy Carter on his record, he got a return with Carter's title at stake. Carter beat him, but Art did not lose many. He could not get past Joe Miceli, Billy Graham, Luther Rawlings and Ramon Fuentes but never became a 'trial-horse'. His career retained its momentum throughout and when he did hang 'em up, Californian boxing was never as exciting again. Art died of a stroke.

Art Aragon

BEAN Willie *From* Los Angeles, California, USA. *Died* 19 December 2007, aged 81. Joe Louis reigned supreme as heavyweight champion when Willie first laced on a glove for pay. It was only after Louis announced his retirement following his second win over Jersey Joe Walcott that he and Willie met in the ring. It was an exhibition fight, one of 120 that Louis made in his post-prime years. Willie took his opportunity and performed well. Having struggled to get into the ratings at that stage, he never rose to world class but took on some good men in his ten-year career and is still remembered by students of boxing who were around between 1946 to 1956. It is interesting to note that Willie was one of the men beaten by Archie Moore when the 'Old Mongoose' was lined up to challenge Floyd Patterson for the then vacant title. It was at the tail-end of Willie's career at a time when he was heavyweight champion of California by virtue of a victory over Young Jack Johnson. Some of his best wins came against Dave Whitlock, Turkey Thompson, Dale Hall, Pat Comiskey, Al Hooseman and Ted Lowry, who had just taken Rocky Marciano the full ten rounds. He never could get past Jimmy Bivins, who outpointed him three times, but the latter was recognised as one of the best heavyweights never to win a title. Outstanding names on Willie's record are Rex Layne, Duke Sabedong, John Holman, Clarence Henry, Howard King, Leonard Morrow and Frankie Daniels. He never chose an opponent and was always a solid, reliable and genuine fighter.

BEATTIE Tommy *From* Scotland. *Died* 11 February 2008, aged 74. When Peter Keenan, one of our outstanding post-war bantamweights, was a simon-pure and in training for a place in Britain's 1948 Olympic team, he used the services of Tommy Beattie as a sparring partner. Tommy was hardly out of junior school at the time, yet his incipient boxing talent became obvious as soon as he stepped into a gym. A distinguished amateur career followed in which he represented Scotland in international matches. Also, he grabbed several championship titles at flyweight and bantamweight level. When his boxing days were over he became a referee and judge. So adept was he in this role that he qualified to referee in the Edinburgh Commonwealth Games. He was destined to have a long experience as a referee, even continuing when the early signs of Parkinson's disease became apparent. Later, he was diagnosed as being afflicted with Alzheimer's and died in hospital. He is survived by a wife and three children.

BEAU Jimmy *From* Bridgeport, Connecticut, USA. *Died* 9 January 2008, aged 77. This tough middleweight was a former holder of the New England championship and at one time rated number five in the world by *The Ring* magazine. At that time, *The Ring* ratings were considered to be official. Jimmy started boxing in 1947 and had 23 wins in 24 outings before dropping a decision to Tommy Yarosz. Good victories followed over Jose Basora, Charlie Anglee, Henry Brimm and a notable one over Paul Pender, who never got past the fifth round. Burl Charity, later to fight in England, was beaten in 1949. Jimmy crossed gloves with

some of the top men: Irish Bob Murphy, Ronnie Delaney, Robert Villemain, Carl Bobo Olson, Nick Barone, Pierre Langlois and Eduardo Lausse. After he stopped Milton Epps he went on trial for attempted murder, for which he served a term in jail. He never fought again.

BECKETT Joe *From* Hempnall. *Died* 17 August 2007, aged 85. There were eight Allen (Beckett being Joe's ring name) boys, all of them farmers apart from Joe who turned his attention to a boxing career after leaving the army in 1946. He had joined the Norfolk Regiment in 1941 and later served with the First Airborne Division in North Africa, Greece and Italy before being taken as a POW in Arnhem. Joe made rapid strides in the paid ranks, winning the Eastern Counties middleweight championship from Ginger Sadd in 1949. In doing this he gained revenge for a decision that Sadd had scored over him in 1948. Prior to his loss to Sadd, Joe had stopped ten men in 16 outings with a solitary defeat at the hands of Hackney's Joe Rood. In his first year of combat there were drawn bouts against Rex Whitney and Jackie Brown, and creditable wins against more experienced men in Ivor Thomas, Chris Adcock, Roy Peterson, Don Smith, Bert Buxton, Harry Davis, Rees Moore, Johnny Nutall and Billy Coloulias. He held Ron Pudney to a draw but lost to Piet van Staden and to future British champions, Henry Hall and Albert Finch. In retirement he went into business on his own until reaching 65 and becoming eligible for the State Pension.

BLANCO Daniel *From* Sucre, Colombia. *Died* 4 November 2007, aged 47. Hard-punching featherweight Daniel won the vacant Central-American title in his 13th fight and, according to my records, he never lost it. Nearly all his wins came inside the distance. He was a damaging puncher who seldom needed to bother about the points' score. Daniel started as a bantamweight in 1981, losing his first fight to Jose Sandoval. Six years passed before he lost again, stopping 29 of his first 33 opponents with a draw in 1988 against Wilson Palacios. Impressive statistics. He stepped outside of his native Colombia twice, stopping Edgar Muniz in Miami and losing to Adelberto Acevedo in Panama. Other than the Sandoval loss, four defeats came at the end of his career. Two of them came in Cartagena where Luis Mendoza and Miguel Maturano beat him. The Acevedo fight followed and that was his finale.

BOYD Jack *From* New Zealand. *Died* 23 September 2007, aged 82. My contact in Australasia, Johnny Hanks, informed me of Jack's death. Jack was born in Ireland in 1925 and brought to New Zealand by his parents when he was one year old. When he reached his school years, Jack went to a boarding school in New Plymouth and it was there that he was introduced to the sport of boxing. At 21, he won the New Zealand amateur heavyweight championship when beating Maurice McHugh. He won it again two years later after taking a year out because of a broken thumb. Circumstances prevented him from accepting the role as his country's representative in the 1950 Empire Games. He was 25 then and wanted to box professionally. A man he had beaten, Frank Creagh, took his place and won the gold medal. His pro career was successful, as he was durable and never took the full count either as an amateur or a professional. Big Don Mullett outpointed him in a hard contest but Jack had good wins against the Fijian champion and against some of Australia's best heavyweights. In retirement, he did the occasional stint of refereeing but most of his energy was directed at running a farm that he and his father bought. Having married Olive Hann in 1959, they had two daughters and two sons, all of whom survive him.

BROOKES Scott *From* Mexborough. *Died* 1 April 2008, aged 20. The short life and promising boxing career of Mexborough cruiserweight Scott, came to a tragic end following a traffic accident. He was one of three boxing brothers and was unbeaten in four pro contests, outscoring Nicki Taylor, David Ingleby, Hastings Rasani and Carl Wild. A measure of his popularity could be measured by the number of boxing personalities who attended his funeral on 16 April in his hometown.

Dan Bucceroni

BUCCERONI Dan *From* Philadelphia, USA. *Died* 16 April 2008, aged 81. A heart attack did to Dan what few of his opponents could not. His name remains in the annals of boxing as one of the good, fringe-contenders in the early '50s before rising to number three in the world in 1953. He was then at his best and had lost only three fights out of 42. That run continued unchecked until the following year when he lost three consecutive fights and decided to quit. Dan was tough and he could punch. Up to 1950 only six of his wins came via points decisions. By then he had risen to top-of-the-bill status, James J. Parker, Jimmy Rouse, Dick

Wagner, Earl Sabotin, Aaron Wilson and the celebrated Roland LaStarza being among his victims. LaStarza reversed a points decision in 1952, but from that moment and up until his loss of form in 1954 he hit a purple-patch, stopping Freddie Beshore, Wes Bascom, Dave Davey and trimming Tommy Hurricane Jackson, Hein Ten Hoff, Jimmy Slade and Rocky Jones over the scheduled distance. Dan did not stay around for long after dropping a ten-round decision to Heinz Neuhaus in Germany and got out when he was still a force to be reckoned with. His amateur pedigree was impressive: National Golden Gloves champion in 1947 and Olympic representative in 1948. To his friends he was called 'Butcher Boy', but there is no record of him having used that sobriquet on fight bills. Only the best heavyweights beat him and they were few in number: Cesar Brion, Bob Murphy and, in return matches, Wagner and Jackson.

CARROLL Jimmy *From* Stockport. *Died* 22 September 2007, aged 84. Sandy-haired Jimmy, a bricklayer by trade, was a good football player before turning to boxing. He played at centre-half for Stockport County FC yet never regretted swapping one sport for another. He was a tall light-heavyweight, rated highly in his day with the scalps on his belt of Don Cockell, to whom he won and lost, Allan Cooke, Reg Spring, Ben Valentine, Dennis Powell and Gene Fowler. Jimmy was managed by George Dingley, who twice steered him to shots at the Northern Central Area cruiserweight title, only to be frustrated by his opponent crying off at the last moment. There were credible draws with Willie Schagen and Mac Joachim in 1950 but he never achieved much after Johnny McGowan beat him for the second time. Carroll went in with some of the iron of the division, men like Ernie Woodman, future heavyweight champion Johnny Williams, Tony Lord, Jock Taylor, whom he stopped in three rounds, Joe Hyman, Trevor Burt, Jack Lewis, Koffi Kiteman, Croydon's Mark Hart and Terry McDonald of Cudworth. He was one of my favourite boxers of the immediate post-war period. Jimmy boxed from 1946 to 1953, had 44 contests, winning 19, drawing five and losing 20. On paper his won/lost record does no justice to a man who met the best we had at his weight and never had an easy fight.

CASWELL Tommy *From* Mitcham. *Died* 30 August 2007, aged 83. There were three Caswell brothers - Tommy, Ray and Bill – and they all came from fighting stock, their father having fought on London undercards under the name of Bill Bowley. He knew what a hard game boxing was, so he sternly forbade his boys to participate. Only after the onset of war, when Caswell senior went in the army, did the opportunity arise for the three brothers to compete in fistic combat. They were evacuated to Leeds, well out of father's range, and it was there that Tommy, with three amateur contests to his name, turned pro under Billy Melia's management. He beat Johnny Summers in an eight-rounder and fought twice at Newcastle's St James' Hall, where he beat Bob McCardle. My records begin with his fight against experienced Karel Baert, who was knocked out in two rounds. By 1948, Johnny had beaten Ronnie Croad, Vic Brookes (twice) and Johnny McGowan, being London-based at that time and under the management of Jack Webster. Here are some of the men who Johnny beat as he rose up in the ratings; Johnny Barton, Dave Davis, Johnny Blake, Dave Edwards, Ted Raine, Billy Mawson, and Sidcup's Jock Taylor. That crafty veteran Allan Cooke sneaked an unpopular verdict to blot Tommy's record after a run of six wins but the best was yet to come. Tommy was outstanding in beating Jimmy Davis and got off the deck to stop Tony Lord, who was on a winning streak. A great fight with Pat Stribling came next. Surprisingly, Pat won on points. The two men became friends for life. Tommy was a frequent visitor to Pat's bedside before the Croydon man died and read the eulogy at his funeral. Bruce Woodcock, Johnny Williams, Tommy Yarosz and Lee Savold all used Tommy's services as a sparring partner. From there, Tommy learned the finer points of his trade. It took a good man to get the better of him, men like George Walker and Mac Joachim for instance. He never wanted me to publish his record yet I suspect he was quietly proud of it. In later years, severe back problems stopped him from working. He'd had many jobs, even one as prison warder, but in his later years he established himself as a faith healer. He is survived by his wife, Shirley, three children, and brother Bill.

CELESTINE Jerry *From* New Orleans, USA. *Died* 17 May 2008, aged 59. A succession of wins got Jerry a shot at Michael Spinks' WBA light-heavyweight title in 1982. Spinks, a technically gifted boxer, proved to be too good. Jerry had mixed with the best of his weight division. An early-career streak of 15 consecutive wins was snapped by Marvin Johnson. There followed losses to Mustafa Wassaja in Denmark and to James Scott in Rahway State Prison, where the latter was an inmate. Richie Kates also beat Jerry but was knocked out in a return. There followed a succession of wins over men like Pablo Ramus, Jesse Avila and Willie Goodman that got him into the challenger's role against Spinks. After that, he posted only three victories in nine fights but was opposing good men in Oscar Rivendeneyra, Eddie Mustafa Muhammad, Fulgencio Obelmejias and Chisanda Mutti. He closed his career with a kayo victory over Charles Henderson, which gave him statistics of 42 fights, 28 wins, 13 losses and a draw against Chick Coleman on his debut.

CHITEULE Charm *From* Zambia. *Died* 6 May 2008, aged 54. I have tried without success to trace Charm's boxing history prior to 1978, the year he turned professional. A glance at his progress in England indicates that he arrived here as a boxer of sound capability, winning his first two fights easily enough before losing to future British champion Najib Daho in Glasgow. It was its only defeat leading up to a clash with Azumah Nelson two years later. Nelson, one of the division's great fighters, stopped Charm in a match for the Commonwealth featherweight championship. To qualify for that challenge, Charm had impressively stopped Dave Needham in 1980. He returned

home to win the Zambian title from Titus Sangwape in 15 rounds. Charm could well be termed a peripatetic fighter. His career was fought out in Germany, Ireland, Zambia, Scotland, USA, Nigeria and England. There were four fights in America where he won twice, ten in Germany with nine wins, and three out of five in Great Britain. Barry McGuigan beat him in ten rounds in Belfast, but he was too good for Sammy Meck, Jarvis Greenidge, Terry McKeown, Cecilio Lastra, Ray Akwaye and Robert Mullins. He retired to his home in Zambia, where he eventually became president of the Zambian Boxing Federation.

CHOI Yo-Sam *From* Seoul, South Korea. *Died* 2 January 2008, aged 35. On Christmas Day 2007, Yo-Sam successfully defended his WBO Inter-Continental flyweight title, beating Jeri Amol on points. It was a hard-earned victory in which he sustained brain injuries that caused his collapse, dying eight days later when medics switched off his ventilator. Yo-Sam won the WBC world light-flyweight title from Saman Sorjaturong in 1999 and defended it three times before being beaten by Jorge Arce. He later challenged unsuccessfully for the WBA light-flyweight title but found Lorenzo Parra too good for him.

CORONA Rudy *From* Obregon, Mexico. *Died* 31 May 2007, aged 69. Mexican bantamweight Rudy came to Britain's shores to fight Alan Rudkin in 1968. He was a battle-worn veteran of 77 fights with his best days behind him. Unsurprisingly, he lost as he usually did when up against men from the top drawer. Although beating some good men in his prime, such as Kid Irapuato, Gil Cadilli, Karmara Diop and Manny Elias, he had no luck against men destined to be world champions, such as Eder Jofre, Davey Moore, Lonel Rose and two near champions in Joe Medel and Eloy Sanchez. Defeats against such notable greats add shine to his 77-fight record. He won two thirds of his fights which is a respectable account, but would have been far better had he been more choosey about who was in the opposite corner.

CUMMINGS Ryan *From* Wigan. *Died* 17 March 2008, aged 35. The Lancastrian light-heavyweight had a brief career of five fights with one loss before he quit the game in 1996 aged 23. He had three stoppage victories, one points win over Terry Duffus and one loss to Mark Lee Dawson at the G-Mex Leisure Centre, Manchester. His last fight, which he won in four rounds, was against Steve Osborne from Wally Swift's stable. Ryan came to London twice and scored two inside-the-distance wins at the York Hall, Bethnal Green. His demise came about in tragic circumstances.

DAVIS Danny *From* Minneapolis, Minnesota, USA. *Died* 27 December 2007, aged 78. Looking at Danny's record reminds me that the quality of a boxer's opponent is a better guideline to his ability than cold statistics. Danny won 27 and lost 13 of his recorded 43 fights. I strongly suspect that he was active beyond 1958 when the last contest I can find for him is recorded. Danny was on a seven-fight winning streak then, but even so his best days were long past and all seven opponents were fistic novices. That was not always the case. He lost twice to Auburn Copeland, twice to Kenny Lane, once to Ike Vaughn and Solomon Boysaw, with a couple of notable wins against more quality opponents in Ralph Alvarez and Glen Flanagan, who had previously beaten him. There is also a ten-round draw with Jackie Graves on his record. This American lightweight was able to hold his own with some of the best fistic talent around, yet fought mostly on the undercards of Minneapolis and St Paul promotions.

Jimmy Davis

DAVIS Jimmy *From* Bethnal Green. *Died* 13 January 2008, aged 82. Back in 1945, I thought that Jimmy was being over-ambitious in taking on Bolton coalminer Billy Walker in his pro debut. Billy was an established pro and no soft touch. Jimmy was a 1944 ABA finalist at welterweight and a firm favourite to get his career off with a win. An impartial glance at Walker's record should have sounded a warning. In the event, Jimmy did well but faded after three rounds and lost on points. He was back in action a month later when stopping Pat Cubis at the Seymour Hall and did not lose again until 1947. It is notable that he stopped seven of his 11 opponents at that stage and that the quality of them was good. They were not 'unknowns'. Jimmy was a fully-fledged middleweight at the time his first knockout defeat occurred. The man who did this was Randolph Turpin, who was on his way to enduring fame. He was back in action a week later, beating Des Jones on points. In the following month he badly injured his hand in beating Alby Hollister and from that point on he relied on boxing skills and not punching power. That he went on another seven years and 74 fights is a tribute to his cleverness. He was rather like a man trying to hold off a tank with a peashooter, that was how bad his hand injury was, yet he beat Empire champion Bos Murphy, Arthur Howard and Henry Hall, a British champion. Hard-punching Alex Buxton was too strong for our man,

beating him twice, and late in Jimmy's career middleweight champion Albert Finch edged him out over eight rounds. It took a good man to beat Jimmy. Bobby Dawson (USA), Luc van Dam (Holland), George Angelo (South Africa) all came out on top but a few defeats are inevitable if you mix in that sort of company and have bad hands. It was light-heavyweight Ron Barton who rang down the curtain on Jimmy's career. Jimmy lost in four rounds and never fought again, having crossed gloves with men like Tony Lord, Fred Jackson, Bert Sanders, Al Allotey, Richard Armagh, Ron Crookes, Tommy Caswell, Wally Beckett, Joe Hyman, Dick Langley, Michael Stack, Ken Rowland, Reg Hoblyn, Bert Hyland, Bob Cleaver, Geoff Heath, Chris Adcock and Johnny Best. All these men went the distance and all of them were losers. There are five stoppage wins from 1947 onwards and with two good hands that number would have been vastly increased. Jimmy became a trainer and was instrumental in guiding Terry Spinks to a British title. He left three children, a wife Vera, and a host of friends to mourn at his funeral in Bethnal Green.

DAVIS Paul *From* West Ham. *Died* April 2008, aged 57. Paul's ring career was brief. Beginning in 1974 and ending two years later, he had 13 contests with two losses, one to Roy Commosioung and the other to Achille Speedy Mitchell. He was offered a return with the latter and forced a draw. One month later he stopped Belfast's Derek McCarthy at Manor Place Baths and surprisingly, at 26, decided to fight no more. He drifted into acting, once appearing in a televised film with a boxing theme, before turning his attention to training boxers at his local amateur club. Paul had three wins over Les Wint and two over Mickey Morse, while his best performance was in beating Zambia's Yothum Kunda in one round.

DeJOHN Joey *From* Syracuse, New York, USA. *Died* 9 May 2008, aged 81. Middleweight crowd-pleaser Joey was the eldest of four boxing brothers – all under the same management as Carmen Basilio. He started boxing four years before Basilio came on the scene. That was in 1944 and such was his effective, free-swinging style that he had 44 fights with a sole defeat before losing to Pete Mead in a slugfest. Joey won 18 more, got another shot at Mead, and gained his revenge in 1949 by stopping his old nemesis in seven rounds. All three fights were what our American cousins term 'Pier-six brawls'. There were more of that nature in store. Fights against Jake LaMotta, Ernie The Rock Durando and Lee Sala were up there as being contenders for 'The Fight of the Year' tag. Sala broke his jaw and stopped him but took a beating in the return. There was a hard fight against Frenchman Robert Villemain in 1952, Joey losing in nine rounds, and there were signs that his career was reaching its end. There were wins, usually hard-gained, against Bob Murphy, Vinnie Cidone, Reuben Jones, Don Lee and Herbie Kronowitz, but losses to Norman Hayes, Dick Wagner and Joe Rindone cancelled out his gains. Joey's lifestyle of booze and clubbing prevented him from getting right to the top but what a colourful scrapper he was!

DE PERSIO Mario *From* Rome, Italy. *Died* 30 June 2008, aged 76. In a short four-year career, comprising 16 fights with one loss, Mario achieved what he had set out to do then walked away from the game once he had won the Italian heavyweight championship. He began boxing in 1955, won three minor fights on points before rapidly proceeding through the European ranks by scoring all his following wins inside the distance. The winning streak started with a knockout over Idrissa Diop and culminated with his second stoppage victory over Uber Bacilieri with the Italian title up for grabs. With wins over Robert Eugene, Lucien Touzard, Werner Wiegand and Gianni Luise, who knows what he might have achieved had he set his sites at higher levels.

DIGBY Phil *From* Edmonton. *Died* October 2007, aged 98. By his own admission, Phil – a modest man – was strictly a prelim fighter but he gained fame and admiration through his longevity. You won't find his name in the record books because he was known as Phil Watts during his fighting days, which were usually as a stand-in at arenas like Blackfriars Ring and the Alcazar, Edmonton. There is not another living fighter who boxed at The Ring, which was bombed in the early part of the war, or the now demolished Alcazar. Phil and his wife Peggy moved to Bishops Stortford in later life. They had family ties there but distance meant little to them. They were both regulars at the monthly LEBA meetings – a lovely couple, so polite and friendly. We say goodbye to a link with the old boxing days and to a much respected man.

DUPAS Ralph *From* New Orleans, Louisiana, USA. *Died* 27 January 2008, aged 72. Ralph was one of those talented boxers who, blessed with natural skills, began his career at an early age – 14 to be precise. He was not a big hitter but relied on his speed and excellent reflexes. Late in his career he lost a heart-breaker to Sugar Ray Robinson. The points decision against him drew criticism but Ralph came straight back to take the WBA junior-middleweight title from Denny Moyer. He defended against Moyer in a return but lost the crown in Milan to Sandro Mazzinghi. Years were catching up with Ralph at that stage and there were only eight more fights before he retired in 1966. His first fight had ended in a draw and having got a taste of fighting for pay he ran up 29 fights with just two losses before graduating to ten-rounders. It was steady progress to 1958, with good wins coming over Joe Miceli, Vince Martinez, Paddy DeMarco, Frankie Ryff, Kenny Lane, Ramon Fuentes, Armand Savoie and Diego Sosa before getting a shot at Joe Brown's lightweight title. Brown was still at his peak then and overcame Ralph's slick boxing skills to force an eight-round stoppage. Ralph fought his way back into contention and four years later challenged Emile Griffith for the welterweight title, only to lose by a narrow points margin. He came to England soon after but was disappointing when losing on a foul to Brian Curvis. Ralph campaigned twice in Australia. The first time in 1960 when he was unbeaten in four fights, George Barnes and Ruddell Stitch being two of his victims. His second tour, at a time when his long career was reaching its end, saw him beat Gary Cowburn but lose to Mazzinghi and Griffith again. A further loss to South Africa's Willie Luddick forced him to announce his retirement. He came back briefly in 1966 but failed to regain his old form, beating three little-known fighters before losing to Joe Clark. That was his swansong. His last 15 years were sad, being bedridden for many of them and admitted to a nursing home where he died. His record ran to 133 fights.

Ralph Dupas

DYNEVOR Jeff *From* Cherbourg, Queensland, Australia. *Died* in August 2008, aged 70. Jeff made his name as being the first aboriginal Australian to win a gold medal in the Empire Games when becoming the bantamweight champion at Perth in 1962. The gold medal was his after beating M. Soong Sisiu (Papua New Guinea), J. Setongo (Uganda) and Ghana's Sammy Abbey, who later fought as a professional in British rings. Jeff, who never went pro, suffered a stroke several years earlier and never fully recovered.

FATTA Carmine *From* NYC, New York, USA. *Died* 25 May 2008, aged 89. Carmine - aka Lou Paris and in some quarters Lou Muratore - was one of the dozens of Italian-American lightweights boxing out of New York between 1939 and 1947. He was a busy fighter who had a fight a fortnight in his first boxing year and had it not been for service in the US army he would have extended his ledger well beyond its 93 fights. In December 1941 he chalked up five fights with but one loss to Tippy Larkin, who was destined to outpoint him twice. In his first year, Carmine forced Maxie Shapiro to a draw, then beat Lew Feldman, Lefty LaChance and Chester Rico. There was a draw with Bobby Ruffin, a loss to Beau Jack and a win over Cleo Shans, his only victory against the same man in three outings. Sal Bartola beat him, as did quality fighter Enrique Bolanos, but there were wins over Sonny Williams and Richie Lemos. He was 29 when he hung up his gloves, having lost only 18 of his near 100 fights, and was inducted into the New Jersey Boxing Hall of Fame in 1991.

FAY Peter *From* Bournemouth. *Died* 10 December 2007, aged 79. Perhaps in the passing of Peter we have seen the last British boxer of note to wear overt signs of his profession by courtesy of a cauliflower ear. His was a beauty, more like a cauliflower on top of a cauliflower. He seemed glad to have a 'badge' to commemorate his days in the ring and what busy days they were in that 1948-1955 period. Peter's first love was the booths. He first drew on a boxing glove for pay at Sam McKeowan's travelling fight emporium in the early 1940s. As a registered professional he was at first steered by Jack Turner, who started him out in a six rounder against Don Hoole at Plymouth, Peter winning clearly. It was the start of an 80 plus fight-career and although he had his share of losses he took them in his stride. There were some notable wins too, especially against Vic Herman, Jimmy Webster, Willie Myles, Ronnie Burr, Billy Daniels and Johnny Kent. Peter never refused a scrap. He went in against Terry Allen, Charlie Hill, Hogan Kid Bassey, Teddy Odus, Ron Johnson, Arthur Gould and Jackie Fairclough. The 'never give up' spirit he displayed in the ring helped to turn his life around after a tragic injury disabled him. Peter, like his old opponent Mickey O'Sullivan, started a window-cleaning business. A fall from a ladder caused spinal injuries that forced him into a wheelchair-bound life. Never one to sink into self-pity, he became an active member of the Bournemouth EBA, an organisation of which he later became chairman. In those years he seldom if ever missed an important event. The ex-boxers' movement and ex-boxers in general will miss Peter, who died just short of his 80th birthday.

Peter Fay

FERDINAND Esau *From* San Francisco, California, USA. *Died* 25 June 2008, aged 78. One of Floyd Patterson's opponents, he started boxing as a middleweight in 1948 and won the Californian title in 1953, when beating Charley Green in Hollywood. He and Green fought six times in all and split the series at three wins each. Going up in weight, Esau annexed the state light-heavyweight title in 1954, which was the year that a young and rising star, Patterson, scored the first of two victories over him. Esau beat Neal Rivers, Buddy Turman and Harvey Taylor. His record is an unusual one of multiple fights with the same opponent, the most notable being eight with Grover Jackson and six apiece with Cordell Jones and Green.

Mickey Forrester

FORRESTER Mickey *From* West Ham. *Died* 23 May 2008, aged 81. Friends who saw Mickey box tell me that he had a good straight left. I saw him a couple of times later on and he never had to rely on 'educated' boxing. Against lesser opponents, he fought like a threshing machine. That is what a 'thinking' fighter does. He uses a style that is suitable for the occasion. Mickey knew the rudiments of the game and was all-action. Slight of build with the heart of a lion, as a featherweight he came out of London's East End and boxed for pay from 1948 to 1952. In 1950 he beat Jackie Lucraft in a South-East Area title eliminator but lost a final eliminator when Teddy Peckham outpointed him at Oxford. Mickey's best wins came over Billy Daniels, Jock Bonas, Ray Fitton and Ivor Davies. A draw against Gene Caffrey was also a good performance. After losing to Peckham he beat Tommy Jones but then suffered a heavy defeat at the hands of Dai Davies, which saw his dreams of fighting for a British title fade. Back injuries were hampering him and he was in a good deal of pain whenever he boxed. In retirement he trained amateurs and took up banking as a profession that, as a career job, is far removed from the rigours of professional sports. Mickey is survived by his wife, Lilian, and their two sons.

FRANKHAM Eli *From* Wisbech. *Died* 2 September 2007, aged 43. From a boxing family, his father, also named Eli, boxed as a pro in the early 1950s and later became the president of the National Romany Rights Association. Eli turned to amateur boxing in 1980, becoming the Eastern Counties super-heavyweight champion that year, and was extremely proud of his son Eli, who had already won two Golden Gloves titles before becoming the European schoolboy champion at 68kg just six days after his dad died from a heart attack.

GALLOWAY Bob *From* Bethnal Green. *Died* 16 June 2008, aged 87. In more recent times Bob is remembered in boxing for being a BBBoC inspector, but I remembered him better for his amateur career in which he represented his club, West Ham ABC, against an Eire select and later won the London junior bantamweight final. A thumb injury precluded further progress but he returned with a vengeance to represent England successfully in international matches. He was a London champion in 1948 at senior level but a cut eye saw him lose his chance to represent his country in the Olympics. This problem was compounded by a nose injury and a falling-out with the ABA officials. As a simon-pure he fought Sammy McCarthy, Jim Dwyer, Claude Dennington and Jimmy Webster. Injuries sustained in working on the docks kept him sidelined for nearly a year. In desperation he offered his services as a sparring partner to Al Phillips and Danny O'Sullivan and brought some cash into the household as a result. He had a short pro career, being unbeaten in five fights, with two wins coming over Cliff Giles. Bob returned to the docks and took up a trainer's position with his old West Ham club. In 1969, he took out a referees licence. Life as an inspector followed on from them and he also worked tirelessly for children's charities. Bob leaves a wife, Lillian, and two children, one of whom also boxed for West Ham ABC with fair success. In compiling this obituary I referred frequently to an article written by Bob Lonkhurst in Vol 4 No 1 issue of *Southern Ex-Boxer*, a magazine of which I was editor.

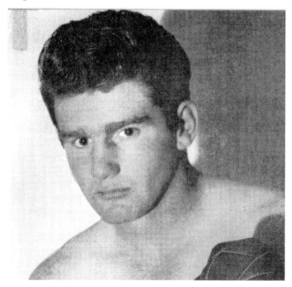

Johnny Gamble

GAMBLE Johnny *From* Merthyr. *Died* July 2008, aged 65. Johnny, a southpaw middleweight and a former ABA champion, had a brief professional career: 16 fights with 13 wins. Gordon White, Joe Somerville, Steve Richards, Ronnie Vale and Joe Bell were some of his victims. Although he lost on a foul to Dave George and was stopped by Fitzroy Lindo due to cuts, it was a bad knockout loss to hard-hitting Teddy Haynes that curtailed his career. After his licence was withdrawn, he re-surfaced in Australia in 1965 where I saw him beat Hans Waschlewski. That was his final contest.

Des Garrod

GARROD Des, MM *From* Paddington. *Died* April 2008, aged 82. One of Mickey Duff's old opponents has passed on. Des beat Duff over six rounds at Mile End Arena in 1947. Despite his self-effacing humour when reviewing his fistic skills, Mickey was never an easy man to beat. That Des did so in his fourth pro outing showed that he had promise, but although never top-rated he graduated to the ten-round class by 1950. At that level, he was less successful than he had been in his apprenticeship days. He got a meritorious draw with Bert Hornby but lost to Johnny Barnham, Ivor Kid Germain, Tommy McGovern and in his sole excursion into foreign rings, he lost to Pierre Montane in Paris. There were plenty of good nights, especially when beating Kenny Green, Ralph Moss, Johnny Carrington, Ben Duffy, George Thresher, Roy Coote, Ricky McCullough, Claude Dennington and Teddy Softly. There were draws with Johnny Russell and Ron Cooper against losses to Jock Bonas and Jim Keery. As a wartime serviceman, Des was awarded the Military Medal for bravery in the field. He boxed from 1947 to 1954 with one year off in 1953, following losses to Gordon Goodman and Johnny Hudson. When old foe Roy Coote, whom he had previously beaten, reversed the loss in a return match, Des decided enough was enough. He had participated in 41 fights over an eight-year career.

GIDMAN Alf *From* Liverpool. *Died* June 2008, aged 93. Alf's boxing activities were confined to war years. The record I have of his fights is sketchy and incomplete, but I am on firm ground when stating that his career began in August 1941 at the rather late age of 24. He boxed a draw with Paddy Nolan at the Liverpool Stadium. Nolan, an old amateur opponent, beat him in a return. In 1942 Alf was thrown in with Frank Duffy and suffered a knockout loss in two rounds. Duffy was a prospect who went on to become a force as a welter-cum-middleweight. At that stage of his career, a challenge from Alf was an over-ambitious move by the latter's management. Fights were so infrequent in the war years and boxers often had to accept an offer or go hungry. Alf stopped Bob McArdle, who later fought in the heavyweight division, and followed up with a good win over Joe Samuels. There were losses to name fighters like

Bert Hyland, Billy Cottrell and George Dilkes, another good 'un, twice beat Alf inside scheduled six-rounders. Although there are more losses than wins on the scoresheet, when you evaluate the quality of the opposition it is clear that Alf was no pushover.

GINE Jaime *From* Argentina. *Died* 11 February 2008, aged 74. When researching a good-quality South-American boxer's record from 1954 to 1963, it is a safe bet that you will come across a list of star names. Such is the case with Argentinian lightweight Jaime. Although I have traced 93 fights for him I suspect that my record is not complete. The 1950s and 1960s were vintage years for Argentinian boxing, with weekly promotions in Cordoba and Buenos Aires and more across the border in Uruguay. How times have changed. In a few months travelling throughout the continent in recent times, I have come across one gymnasium and have seen no promotions of note. This, in places where boxing once thrived and fighters were jostling for a shot at the big prizes. One who succeeded was Jaime, who boxed for seven years without defeat and that came against a great champion in Nicolino Loche. Jaime was champion of his country at the time and had previously held Loche to a draw. Other draws came against Spain's Fred Galiana – twice in sixth months, followed by stoppage wins against Nestor Savino, Italo Coluccini, Edgardo Nazrala and Raul Monzon. Those are names that meant something to close followers of boxing at that time. Also, there are 73 fights without defeat to consider when assessing his status as a world-class fighter and world class he was, with victories over Mando Garcia, Orlando Zulueta and Vicente Derado. Unfortunately, he boxed during those years when Jimmy Carter, Carlos Ortiz and Joe Brown were at their peaks. He never got world exposure because he never needed to step outside of South America, where there were always fights for him. He made a living by fighting in his own backyard and by the highest standard he was a very good fighter.

GLENCROSS Tommy *From* Glasgow. *Died* 29 February 2008, aged 60. In a career that began in Cardiff and ended 11 years later in Marylebone, London, Tommy fought only four times in his native Glasgow. It was not one of his best locations: he won two and lost two. Tommy was a southpaw and a handy one, who by 1972 had progressed far enough to challenge Jose Legra for the European featherweight championship. Legra, a former world titleholder, stayed European champion via a 15- round decision against the Scot. In his next fight, Tommy beat Evan Armstrong and usurped him as British titleholder. It went the full 15 rounds in London but the championship remained in Scottish hands. Another shot at the European crown saw him lose to Gitano Jiminez in Spain just before surrendering his hard-won British title to Armstrong. Returning to ring warfare at the higher poundage brought him a run of victories, culminating in a points win over Tommy Wright for the Scottish lightweight title. He retained it against John Gillen and held on to it for another 20 months until Willie Booth became the new champion

after ten hard-fought rounds. Tommy began boxing as a pro in 1967 and had his last fight in 1978, having been unbeaten for three years before tasting his first defeat at the hands of Ghana's Bob Allotey in distant Barcelona. He gained his championship spurs with fine wins over Billy Hardacre, Sammy Lockhart, Tony Cunningham, Gerry McBride, Kenny Cooper and Pat Pain. Later, at the lightweight limit he was in there with Vernon Sollas, Barton McAllister, Cornelius Boza-Edwards, Colin Power, Charlie Nash and Martyn Galleozzie. When Joey Singleton beat him in the Seymour Hall, Tommy knew it was time to get out of the game, leaving behind him a record of 48 fights, with 31 wins, one draw and 16 losses.

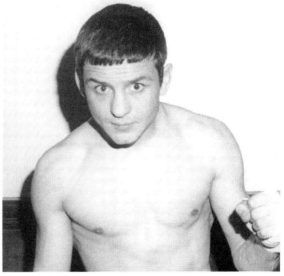

Tommy Glencross

GOROSITO Reinaldo *From* Argentina. *Died* November 2007, aged 57. In 1971 the New York Golden Gloves heavyweight championship was won by Argentina's Reinaldo and he chose the occasion to announce that he was turning pro. His paid career was to stretch ten years, during which he had varying success but lost most of the big opportunities. Les Stevens beat him over here before the Argentinian scored one of his best wins, beating Rodney Bobick in New York. Unfortunately he could not maintain the momentum, losing the return match one year later. Rodney's brother Duane also outpointed him in 1974. Reinaldo showed determination when knocking out Pablo Noe Castellino and taking world-rated Oscar Bonavena the distance in Buenos Aires. He did not lose another for a couple of years, picking up the Argentine heavyweight title, which he defended three times. He drew with power-punching Ngozika Ekwelum then went to South Africa where Kallie Knoetze outpointed him. Randy Neuman was one man who was always too good for the South American. In three fights, Reinaldo failed to register a win and when John Tate knocked him out in two rounds in 1978 it signalled the sun down to a career that ended with a win two years later against Jose Heredia in San Luis.

GOSTOLO Lee *From* Sheffield. *Died* 10 September 2007, aged 42. Cancer of the pancreas cut short the life of Lee, the ubiquitous boxing whip from Sheffield. Lee was a busy man, his boxing interests taking him far and wide. He worked for Sky TV when he was not on official boxing duty. In his brief life, his contribution to boxing was immense and his popularity was reflected in the huge turnout for his funeral. Lee leaves a wife and one son.

GRUNDLER Joe *From* Northampton, via Kufstein, Austria. *Died* December 2007, aged 83. Sid Green of Northampton reported the death of Joe, who as an amateur was three times a holder of Austrian titles at lightweight and welterweight. He represented his country in international meetings during which he beat two Swiss champions. His was an adventurous, albeit hard life. World War Two came when he was 15 so a stint in the Austrian army was inevitable. He served with a mine-clearing section and was later captured by Russians and interred in a POW camp. Joe's life changed for the better on English soil after winning a considerable sum of money on the football pools in 1957. He bought a house, invested the surplus wisely and lived comfortably until his recent death. Joe, who boxed with distinction for Northampton ABC, leaves a wife, Frances, to whom he was married for 53 years.

HARPER Maurice *From* Oakland, California, USA. *Died* 14 June 2008, aged 76. Born in Dallas, this former National AAU champion and 1948 Golden Gloves champion had a 33-fight career in the paid ranks in which he excelled himself against some of the best welterweights of his day. What puzzles me is his sparse activity. Apart from his first year as a pro, he averaged a paltry three fights a year at a time when boxers could get plenty of work. Picking a name at random from the record books I found 89 fights for Chico Vejar, who started boxing one year later than did our man. Maurice's record up to 1957, when he lost the last two fights of his career to what once were lesser mortals, shows that his was an exceptional talent. Apart from an early career loss to Milo Savage, which was due to cuts and was twice reversed, only Bobby Jones beat him up to the tail end of his career. There are wins against Charley Salas, Willie Vaughn, Del Flanagan, Joe Miceli, Livio Minelli, Italo Scortichini, Frankie Fernandez, Nick Moran and Lester Felton. Had he taken the game seriously, Maurice would almost certainly been hammering on the welterweight champion's door.

HASSETT Chuck *From* California, USA. *Died* December 2007, aged 72. A former amateur star, Chuck earned himself a reputation as a judge and a referee following retirement from the ring. Originating from Philadelphia before moving west to California, he was involved in over 100 world title bouts in one capacity or another.

HAYNES Teddy *From* Wolverhampton. *Died* 27 December 2007, aged 71. The now defunct 'Uppercut Club', under the chairmanship of Terry Downes, used to meet once a month at the Henry Cooper pub in the Old Kent Road. The landlord was Teddy, a former middleweight contender and a southpaw with a big punch. Back in the 1960s he beat Wally Swift for the Midlands Area middleweight title. He was a genial host who kept us well nourished during our meetings. Good-hearted, quietly spoken and never given to bragging about his boxing achievements, he was a hard man once within the ropes. A southpaw with a punch, dangerous and game, sums up Teddy. He came from a large family, being one of 16 children, and started boxing in 1958. Significantly, he knocked out Stan Perry in one round in his debut. When Teddy retired in 1965 only five of his fights had gone the distance. Two of those were against hard-man Johnny Berry, who conceded the points on both occasions. Others were Maxie Beech, Freddie Collins and Peter Anderson. In between those fights he stopped Maxie Smith also in one round. Those who never lasted the full course were Joe Bell, Johnny Gamble, Julius Caesar, Jimmy Assani, Orlando Paso, Roy Thomas and Scottish champion Ian McKenzie. Teddy twice lost to Willie Fisher and was also beaten by Gert van Heerden in Capetown. In 1960, after losing to future British champion George Aldridge in an area title fight, he based himself in London. It was a wise move. Teddy's career took off from that point. He went straight into the eight-round class and within two years had moved into the top-ten of British boxing ratings. In later years he moved back to the Midlands, where he died after a long illness.

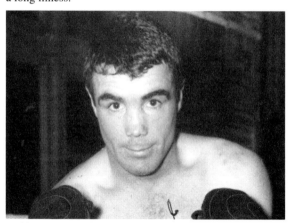

Teddy Haynes

HEALY Pat *From* Tipperary. *Died* March 2008, aged 76. Irish-born Pat was a genial, much-liked boxers' manager who based himself in London. His biggest success came when he steered Sam Soliman to the Commonwealth middleweight championship. The acquisition of that title was doubly sweet for Pat because he had offered accommodation to the Aussie when his British campaign started. Since then, Solimon has gone on to establish himself as a force at world level. Pat lost his wife Pearl just a few months before he was found dead in his London flat. He had an association, for years, as a coach and committee member for the Times ABC, but gave up these posts in 1980 to turn his attention to the paid side of the game.

HEINZ WC *From* Mount Vernon, New York, USA. *Died* 27 February 2008, aged 93. Only one fictional book on boxing is in my library. Having collected boxing literature for 64 years and maintaining a strong interest in fistic matters, I have no space to clutter my shelves with books other than those of historic nature. There are two exceptions: *Rodney Stone* by Arthur Conan Doyle and WC Heinz's *The Professional*. Heinz, a man steeped in boxing history, died this year. In his long life his contribution to boxing literature stands out like a beacon of light. I often wondered if he had ever fought himself because his fictional work reveals his deep understanding of the game. He was to those who enjoyed good writing, the Charles Dickens of his day. He edited *The Fireside Book Of Boxing* in 1961 and his selection of what is an anthology cannot be faulted. His own contribution in it, titled *Fighters Wife*, is a gem. Heinz had a public school education and graduated from college in 1937. He started work for the *New York Sun* that year and quickly showed his writing talent, going on to become a feature-writer and war correspondent during the 1939-45 conflict. He could turn his hand to most subjects but boxing remained his abiding passion. As a freelance his work has been repeated in over 20 anthologies. He won the EP Dutton award for 'Best Magazine Sports Story of the Year' five times and was elected to the International Hall of Fame. Wilfred Charles Heinz was a one-off, whose like we may never see again.

HENRY John *From* Brooklyn, NYC, New York, USA. *Died* 9 September 2007. A heavyweight, John began boxing for pay in 1956, having moderate success on his home turf (6-4-3) before moving to Sweden in 1962. There, he won all but one contest, beating Federico Friso, Ulli Ritter, Rupert Bentley and Paul Kraus. In German and British rings he was not so lucky. Jim Cooper beat him in Nottingham and Karl Mildenberger and Albert Westphal both outpointed him in Germany. John got plenty of work as sparring partner to both Floyd Patterson and Ingemar Johansson at the tail end of the Swede's career. His career petered out with just three fights between 1963-4.

HICKEY Bob *From* Edgware. *Died* July 2008, aged 95. Harold Alderman has supplied me with Bob's record (verified by Miles Templeton) that shows he boxed from 1932 to 1950, initially being billed out of Islington, and had 24 wins, five draws and 42 losses from 71 fights. Not a great record on paper, but Bob knocked out Bert Middleton and Alf Phillips and beat Idris Pickens, Jim Parsons and Tommy Davies on points. He also drew with Harry Ruff and Hackney's Bill Handley - all familiar names to those who followed the game at that time. In his post-war career only Johnny Toohig and Mias Johnson beat him inside the distance. Others he fought included the future European lightweight champion Aldo Spoldi, Hecky Holdsworth, Walter Redit, Teddy Larkham, Johnny Carrington, Dave Haydock, Billy Dixon, Harry Legge, Jack Watkins (Muswell Hill) and Freddie Sorrell.

HOLT Mike *From* Pretoria, South Africa. *Died* 19 July 2008, aged 76. In his pro debut Mike knocked out Billy Wells and got three Rand for his efforts. He also broke his hand and had to pay his corner men. It took months to convince him that it would be worthwhile, but continue he did and eventually rose up from being a domestic force at the middleweight limit to getting in the world ratings at light-heavyweight. It took only nine fights for him to become the South African middleweight champion, when beating Eddie Thomas, and the pair had three fights that ranked among the most brutal in that nation's history. A duo with ill-fated Jimmy Elliott were just as bloody and violent. They shared a win apiece before Britain's Pat McAteer defended his Empire title against Mike and won an untypically dull fight on points. There were wins over America's Garth Panter, Australia's George Barnes, Martin Hansen of Denmark, and four victories by knockout in an Australian campaign, prior to moving up a weight division and winning the South African 175lbs title. He beat Gordon Wallace, Arthur Howard and Yolande Pompey before being stopped by Yvon Durelle for the Empire title. The rock-hard Canadian described the fight as his toughest of his career. Mike never could get the Empire belt around his waist, drawing with Johnny Halafihi for the vacant title in 1960 when both had seen better days. Gustav Scholz was too classy for him and Carl Bobo Olson too ringwise. Although losses to Eddie Cotton and George Mahoni in New Zealand were followed by a good win on his home turf against Gawie de Klerk, two defeats at the hands of Gert van Heerden and a second unsuccessful return to New Zealand preceeded a run of eight victories before losing to Willie Pastrano. When van Heerden beat him for the third time, Mike announced his retirement and returned to his old trade of panel-beating. Antoine Michale Holtzhausen, as he was baptized, died in hospital weeks after undergoing surgery on his shoulder.

Mike Holt

HORSEMAN Jackie *From* Hartlepool. *Died* 23 February 2008, aged 85. Jackie always disputed the record book's version of his career, claiming that he'd had far more fights than those stated. He was right. That diligent researcher Miles Templeton put together a list of Jackie's fights going back to 1938, which was published the day after Jackie died, so he never saw it. This was tragic for him and a big disappointment to Miles. The Hartlepool man would fight at the drop of a hat and was often used as a late substitute. Matchmakers knew that he would be ready and available if asked. Jackie got few favours, winning 37 against 75 losses, but that never bothered him. He was happy just to fight and went in with Jackie Turpin, Teddy Gardner, Freddie King (Walworth), Billy Kelly, Sammy McCarthy, Teddy Peckham, Johnny Miller and Denny Dawson. Do not be fooled by his win/loss percentages, as he was good enough to win the Northern Area featherweight title back in a time when area championships meant something. He outpointed Don Scott for that title, so his name is a permanent fixture in the record books. One year after his last fight, when Jackie was working on the docks, he won the football pools and was presented with a cheque for over £200,000. He never looked back after that and lived comfortably until a stroke cut him down. He died in hospital, leaving two daughters and the boxing community to mourn his passing.

HUMPHREY John *From* Newmarket. *Died* 17 November, 2007, aged 47. The driving force behind his son John, the former Southern Area light-middle and middleweight champion, and Rocky Dean, who held the Southern Area featherweight title, John passed away after a four-year fight against cancer. John junior has not boxed since. His father was an inspiration to all those he trained, first at Soham ABC and then at New Astley ABC, and guided young John and another son, Thomas, to several national amateur titles. He also coached England teams and will be sorely missed by all those who trained under him.

IANNOTTI Joey *From* NYC, New York, USA. *Died* 13 January 2008, aged 87. An Italian-American, Joey started boxing in 1939. My records have him finishing his career in 1946 but I suspect it is incomplete. He was a featherweight who did the bulk of his fighting in New York, going through his first year of fighting unbeaten in 16 fights with 13 stoppages and three points wins. Through to 1942, he was still doing well, although incurring three losses in a further 24 outings. Lulu Constantino twice outpointed him and he conceded an eight-round decision to Al Reid, but he was now fighting in good company. From 1942 onwards his record becomes spotty but some names on it were those of good-class boxers, none other than Willie Pep for example. And there is also Eddie Compo, followed by Aaron Seltzer and Harry Jeffra. Service in the US Army from Sept 1942 put his career on hold and it was not until February 1946 that he donned the gloves again. He never regained his best form, losing six of his last 11 fights. No boxing activity is recorded for him after he lost to Dino Bleta late in the year.

JACKSON Ayree *From* Ghana. *Died* March 2008, aged 74. It surprised me that Ayree's death received such scant coverage in the trade papers. At British level, his record is outstanding with wins over George Bowes, Ken Lawrence, Oliver Paul, Ernie Fossey, Con Mount-Bassie, Matt Fulton, Phil Jones, Denny Dawson and Tommy Icke. There are no patsies in that list. Unfortunately, his early record is obscure. In Ghana, where he learned the basic skills of boxing, I know of only three contests – all ten rounders against 'name' opponents in Andrew Martey, who he outpointed, and Sugar Gibiliru, against whom he split a couple of decisions. Gibiliru is the father of Sugar Gibiliru (junior) who fought here in the 1980s. Ayree fought Percy Lewis twice, performing well enough in the first encounter to warrant a return, but both fights ended in points defeats, as did his tussle with Howard Winstone in 1961. Apart from those two notable champions only three men beat him on British soil. Good featherweights were never quick to pitch in against the man from Ghana, who could box and punch hard. Johnny Howard outpointed him in 1958, Jimmy Revie stopped him in 1967 and when Kenny Cooper outscored him the following year he drifted away from the scene. Ayree fought in Australia in 1958 and was unbeaten in that country, a stoppage win over Max Murphy being his best result. In those days he was approaching his prime and it is conceivable that he had a long pro schooling in Ghana before reaching these shores.

JACKYMELON Gary *From* Derby. *Died* 29 June 2008, aged 45. As one of Britain's greatest-ever junior boxers, Gary was expected to go on to great things as a senior but it never happened, whatever the reason. With great belief and tremendous ability, he won eight national titles - four Schools, two NABC and two Junior ABA. He consistently won 'Best Boxer of the Tournament' awards and left the sport with 93 wins from 97 contests. A family man, who leaves a wife and two children, Gary died following a massive heart attack.

JONES Fred 'Rocky' *From* Akron, Ohio, USA. *Died* February 2008, aged 86. Rocky's main claim to fame is his points win over Roland LaStarza in 1952. LaStarza was then two fights away from a crack at the world heavyweight championship. Although he beat Rocky in the return match, he did not have an easy passage, being pushed all the way. Rocky was a light-heavyweight who frequently fought men in the higher weight division. He didn't pick his opponents, which is the main reason for him winning only half his fights. Rocky stepped in with rated fighters like Charlie Powell, Dan Bucceroni (three times), Freddie Beshore, Danny Nardico, Polly Smith and Jimmy Slade. Just before beating LaStarza, he drew with Art Swiden and licked Tommy Harrison. An early victory over Jimmy Rouse in Chicago raised him to main-event status but it was all downhill after he lost the return with LaStarza. Five fights followed without a victory, but he made them sweat for their money. Rocky quit the ring in 1954 after losing to Powell. His win/loss record gives a false impression of one who was a solid, genuine pro. In his post-boxing days he worked for Scott Paper Company.

JORGENSEN Paul *From* Port Arthur, Texas, USA. *Died* 5 August 2008, aged 73. Paul's management got him plenty of work. In an eight-year career he had 94 fights and lost only eight of them. He came very close to beating Harold Gomes for the NBA junior-lightweight championship in 1959, putting his man down four times but still losing the decision. He fought from 1953 to 1960 and beat Tony Dupas, Harold Dade, Henry Pappy Gault, Lauro Salas, Teddy Red Top Davis, Lulu Perez, Carmelo Costa, Gil Cadilli, Sonny Leon and drew with Joey Lopes. Those wins show his class, and further examination of his record reveals that he was never beaten inside the distance. Paul was a durable, orthodox stylist with a strong punch, who claimed the Texas featherweight championship after beating Joe Boland in 1955. When rising star Battling Torres beat him in 1960 Paul did not carry on until he became a trial-horse for the younger generation of lightweights, despite having a few good fights left in him, and wisely decided to retire.

Hank Kaplan   Les Clark

KAPLAN Hank *From* Kendall, Florida, USA. *Died* 14 December 2007, aged 88. Back in 1960, when my friendship with Hank Kaplan had been firmly established, he wrote to me about the forthcoming return match between Ingemar Johansson and Floyd Patterson. "If the Swede is good", said Hank, "how come he never laid a glove on Cassius Clay, a novice who has yet to have his first pro fight, when they sparred in the gym"? Hank's observations gave me an insight into the probable course of the heavyweight championship. He was then a regular attendee at the Fifth Street gym in Miami and was forming a friendship with Angelo and Chris Dundee. He and I were exchanging press-cuttings, photos, books and programmes at that time. Soon, he became the press-agent for the Dundee brothers and boxing virtually took over his life, especially when he retired from his job with the US Public Health Service. Hank had a surfeit of energy. He produced his own boxing magazine, worked for *Sports Illustrated* and a radio station where he dealt with listeners' queries

on the fight game. While building up his collection of boxing literature and ephemera he helped to set up the International Hall of Fame. We first became acquainted through our membership of a collector's club run by Harry Winkler, *The Ring* magazine's Californian correspondent. Hank was later to take over the running of the club, which he re-named *The World Boxing Historians' Association*. His guidance and influence built up a strong membership force. Some of them have gone on to subscribe to the present-day *International Boxing Research Organisation* that flourished thanks to Hank's considerable input. In his 88 years on earth, Hank's contribution to the noble art is immense and enduring. Fortunately, his archives survive, as will his reputation and the fond memories of him.

KNOWLES Freddie *From* London. *Died* 16 April 2008, aged 61. A star amateur, Freddie was the victim of a heart-attack and missed reaching the three score and ten lifespan allotted by the bible. The pinnacle of his boxing career was when he reached the London ABA finals in 1971. Alan Minter edged him out of the championship, even though in a previous meeting Freddie had been victorious. Freddie, who represented England at middleweight in international bouts against Denmark, Ireland, Wales and Poland and also fought for London against Rome, was an experienced boxer with a long, successful record.

LACK Alfie *From* Kent. *Died* October 2007. Harold Alderman reports Alfie's death. During his long association with Kent boxing and the county's ex-boxers, Harold got to know Alf as well as anyone else involved with boxing. He was in the RAF during the war, boxing in services uniform, and maintained his interest in boxing when back in civvy street. When the Kent EBA was formed back in the 1960s, he was a founder member and became its chairman in its boom years. He owned a brick-laying business and his funeral was attended by dozens of his employees. He leaves a wife, son and daughters.

LANE Kenny *From* Muskegon, Michigan, USA. *Died* 5 August 2008, aged 76. Kenny had three unsuccessful shots at the world lightweight championship, losing to Joe Brown and Carlos Ortiz, whom he had previously beaten. In 1963 he gained recognition as Michigan State's champion when beating Paul Armstead, but then lost to Ortiz eight months later. Lane was one of those consistent fighters of the 1950s and '60s who stayed world-rated for most of his career. His opponents included Hoacine Khalfi, Ralph Dupas, Carlos Hernandez, Armand Savoie, Aissa Hashas, Larry Boardman, Paddy DeMarco, Isaac Vaughn, Glen Flanagan, Ludwig Lightburn, Frankie Ryff, Orlando Zulueta, Teddy Red Top Davis, Johnny Gonsalves, Lahouari Godih, Virgil Akins, Len Matthews, Jose Stable, Curtis Cokes, Tommy Tibbs, Eddie Perkins, Luis Molina and Johnny Bizzarro. He really did fight in the top class and for so long. After his unsuccessful challenge to Ortiz in 1964, he was beaten by fellow-southpaw Dave Charnley in London and that was his last performance at world-class level. He fought just once in 1964 then devoted his time to training youngsters.

At the grand age of 50 he came back to win another four fights. Two years later, in 1984, his desire to claim 100 fights saw him in action for the last time and that was it. Golf then became his sport and he died suddenly on the green.

Kenny Lane

LATKA George *From* San Jose, California, USA. *Died* 26 December 2007, aged 93. Czech-born George's promising career was interrupted when he joined the US Service in 1942. He had just beaten Petey Scalzo and Richie Lemos, which put him up there with the very best in the division. Lemos and Scalzo had previously fought each other for the NBA version of the world featherweight title. Still in his 20s, the future looked rosy for the California-based Czech but it appears that his ambition faded once his service days were over. He re-incarnated as a manager-trainer and dabbled in matchmaking. For the younger generation of fight followers he is best remembered as a top referee, a post he held for over 30 years. Those whose memories go back further, to the late 30s and 40s, will recall his fights with Ray Lunny, Juan Zurita, Baby Arizmendi, Sammy Angott, Al Citrino and that good Hawaiian-Chinese scrapper, David Kui Kong Young. George, who boxed between 1937 and 1942, had 53 contests with only seven defeats. His proud boast was that he was never beaten inside the distance. He may have been either 90 or 93 when he died, there being uncertainty about his birth year. Either way, he had a remarkable life in boxing.

LICATA Tony *From* New Orleans, Louisiana, USA. *Died* 25 May 2008, aged 56. When Tony fought Alan Minter in 1976 he was getting past his prime years but was still one of the world's best middleweights. His career had reached its apex a year earlier when he challenged Carlos Monzon for the world title. Monzon, who had a genuine claim to greatness, became the second man to beat Tony, being too strong and persistent. The American had an outstanding

record of 51 fights without a loss prior to fighting Ramon Mendez (quickly avenged), winning the vacant NABF championship on the way when beating a fading Emile Griffith. He defended the NABF title five times and was never beaten for it. A defeat by Jean Mateo in Paris followed the Monzon loss and signalled the beginning of a slide. Tony's early-career progress was steady. He beat Mike Pusateri, Danny McAloon, Luis Vinales (three times), Jose Chirino and Denny Moyer on the way to crashing into the world ratings in 1973. Wins followed over Cubby Top Cat Jackson, Vinnie Curto and Mike Rossman. His activity, once regular, dropped off after being beaten by Minter. He averaged under three fights per year up to 1980, losing to Tony Chiaverini in his final bout. His ability can be judged by his impressive 61-7-4 record, in which he met four world champions; Griffith, Minter, Monzon and Rossman. A sudden heart attack brought about his death.

LINCA Nicolae *From* Romania. *Died* 30 June 2008, aged 79. In the 1956 Melbourne Olympics, Romania's Nicolae became his country's hero by winning the only boxing gold in the nation's sporting history. Alas, his achievement was marred by two dubious decisions: one in the semi-finals against Britain's Nicky Gargano and in the final against Ireland's Freddie Teidt. Both verdicts caused an uproar. Veteran scribe Nat Fleischer said that the decision against Teidt was the worst he had seen and Gargano, a veteran of fights against the world's best welterweights and a multiple medal winner, was so disgusted that, as far as I can recall, he never fought on for much longer. Boxers do the fighting not the judging and no blame can fall on Linca for something that was not his fault. He was a good boxer at European level and deserves his place in history.

LOI Duilio *From* Trieste, Italy. *Died* 20 January 2008, aged 78. The first time Duilio stepped outside of his own country to fight, he outpointed Tommy Barnham at the Empress Hall, Earls Court. The verdict was hotly disputed and I wondered if the veracity of some of the Italian's home wins was questionable. The next time he journeyed abroad, he lost to Denmark's Jorgen Johansen when challenging for the Dane's European lightweight title. It was a disputed decision again in a rather dull fight. He later beat Johansen for the title in Milan and went on to defend it ten times. In between he had defended his Italian title twice and my doubts about his ability were fading fast. It was when I saw him at his peak in a televised recording of his win over Carlos Ortiz for the world title that I realised how good he had become. He gave Ortiz a chance to regain the crown but was again too good, too persistent and on top of matters. Duilio, who had been boxing for 13 years before he got his big chance, had come on steadily against a diet of good fighters such as Ray Famechon, Glen Flanagan, Boswell St Louis, Joe Lucy, Allan Tanner, Luigi Male, Idrissa Dione, Felix Chiocca and Eddie Perkins. It was Perkins who beat Duilio when the world junior-welterweight title was at stake. Duilio came back to take the title in a return three months later and with that victory, he wiped out the last remaining defeat on his record. There were eight draws, all against class fighters. In all, the Italian hero had 126 fights. Alzheimer's disease took a hold of him in later years and it was this that caused his death. Duilio was an aggressive fighter with a sound chin, who made up for his lack of a big punch with skills that brought adulation from Italian fans. He was one of the most popular fighters to come out of that country.

Duilio Loi

McCANN Peter *From* Birkenhead. *Died* 24 August 2008, aged 61. At the middleweight limit, Peter won the ABA championship in 1968 and represented his country in international tournaments. He was also named as a reserve for the 1968 Olympic squad. After achieving his ambition as an amateur he turned pro and boxed as a light-heavyweight. He had a sensational start. Through to the end of 1969 he had won all of five fights inside the scheduled distance, Fred Powney and Dervan Airey being two of his victims. He was inactive from 1970 to 1972 due to personal problems, coupled with prospective fights falling through, but came back in 1973 to stop Barry Clough and George Lewis. When he was himself stopped by Sid Falconer after suffering serious shoulder damage during the contest he walked away from professional boxing and went back to his trade as a pipe-fitter. Having started out with Willaston ABC, before moving on to The Star ABC and then Birkenhead ABC, he eventually returned to his first club in a training capacity. He also became an enthusiastic supporter of the Ex-Boxers' movement.

McGARRITY Charles *From* Rahway, New Jersey, USA. *Died* 18 February 2008, aged 84. Known in boxing circles as 'Kid Chocolate', this featherweight boxed from 1950 to 1956, either in the eastern part of the USA or in Canada. He was popular in Madison Square Garden, where he often supported the main event. In 1952 he appeared there six times. It was on one of those appearances that he beat Ike Chestnut, who was a featherweight contender in the 1950s. In Quebec he twice beat the vastly more experienced Fernando Gagnon, who is remembered in this country for his fights with Teddy Gardner, Bobby Boland and Tommy Proffitt. Most of Charles' fights were over six or eight rounds. Apart from the Gagnon fights only those against Harold Gomes and Bobby Courchesne were ten-rounders. He went in against Chico Velez, Carmelo Costa, Pat Marcune and Jesus Compos. All of those were 'known' fighters of the 1950s. I have 44 fights on his record, but surprisingly he never fought in his home State of New Mexico where he died. Cancer was given as the cause of his death.

McGILL Jackie *From* Glasgow. *Died* 25 May 2008, aged 52. In a brief career of 11 fights, Jackie fought some highly-rated British boxers. He started out in 1976 and finished in 1978, meeting Pat Cowdell, Alan Buchanan, Ray Cattouse, Jeff Pritchard and Tommy Wright amongst other lesser-known opponents. His first outing was against Dave Tuohey, an experienced 42-fight stylist. Jackie got there on points after an impressive display of box-fighting. Wright was the fifth man forced to lower his colours to McGill then along came Pritchard to spoil an unbeaten run. He put a blot on Jackie's record but, unwisely, agreed to a return and was beaten over eight fierce rounds. That was Jackie's last win. Future British title-holder Cattouse stopped him in three rounds and Ken Buchanan's brother, Alan, added to the misery. A further loss came against Damien McDermott and the finale came against a really good man in Cowdell. Jackie did well – well enough to show that he was still a force but his ambition had evaporated and retirement was a wise decision. Later, Jackie worked the corner of his nephew, Scott Harrison.

MAILER Norman *From* New Jersey, USA. *Died* 10 November 2007, aged 84. English-language newspapers all carried detailed obituaries of Norman Mailer. Some were rather damning of his violent temper and his private lifestyle. He was a controversial, prickly character and an unconscionable womaniser, no doubt, but I never met him so I will not give judgement. What I have done is to read many of his books and boxing articles so I can safely state that, in front of a typewriter or with pen in hand, he was a genius. As a boxing journalist he was in a class of his own. His book *The Fight*, which has for a subject the championship clash between George Foreman and Muhammed Ali, is regarded as the classic summary of that contest. Mailer produced best-sellers in *The Naked And The Dead*, *The Executioner's Song*, *The Castle in the Forest* and much more. He was prolific in his output of the written word. Nothing I have read or heard disputes his mastership as a writer and he was twice Pulitzer Prize winner. Later, he dabbled in film-making and appeared in the documentary on the Foreman-Ali fight. Norman Mailer was married six times, four coming before his 40th birthday. The first to Bea Silverman and the last to Barbara Jean Norris, whom he married at the age of 52 when she was 25. Despite alcoholic, drug-fuelled tantrums he and Barbara stuck together, albeit tenuously, until his death from acute renal failure whilst in New York's Mount Sinai hospital.

MARTIN Eric *From* California, USA. *Died* 23 December 2007, aged 49. Eric's most important fight occurred in 1987 when, after six years of campaigning, he lost to John Montes with the Californian light-welterweight title as the prize. He'd had a reasonable run up until then with just six losses in 29 fights. On the way, he had beaten Reggie Miller and in a fight in South Africa had lost to Brian Baronet after a good display. Losing to Montes seems to have discouraged him. Losses became more frequent, nine of them coming in his last 16 fights. There was a brief but unsuccessful campaign in France and a credible performance against Eric Lucas in Canada but nothing more was heard of him after he dropped an eight-round points decision to Ed Dalton in 1995.

MELTZER Hy *From* NYC, New York, USA. *Died* 1 July 2008, aged 79. In a six-year career Hy had 52 fights of which he lost just seven. He was a welterweight whose best win was over Tony LaBua in 1949. He also beat Norman Hayes and Willie Beltram, but aimed too high when encountering hard-to-beat Tippy Larkin, who stopped him in two rounds in 1949. Hy learned his boxing in the small fight clubs of New York, such as Ridgewood Grove, Eastern Parkway Arena, Coney Island Velodrome, Thompson Stadium, St Nicholas Arena and Sunnyside Gardens. These were all venues where he trod the canvas and on one occasion he boxed at the Mecca of the sport, Madison Square Garden where, in a preliminary contest, he beat debutant Tony Baldoni. Other main-event fighters whom he fought were Johnny Marino (twice a loser), Chaforo Martinez (a ten-round points loser), Baby Vasquez (who outpointed him), Walter Haines (who stopped him) and Joey Carkido with whom he drew in Miami.

MICELI Joe *From* Brooklyn, NYC, New York, USA. *Died* 18 July 2008, aged 79. When all of Joe's contemporary boxers have passed on, an era of men, the likes of whom we will never see again, will have become just a memory for those of us fortunate to have lived through his times. Consider the fact that he fought no fewer than 12 world champions - Virgil Akins, Johnny Bratton, Curtis Cokes, Ralph Dupas, Gene Fullmer, Kid Gavilan, Joey Giardello, Don Jordan, Luis Rodriguez, Johnny Saxton, Wallace Bud Smith, Ike Williams - and a list of challengers like Arthur King, Tony Pellone, Pierre Langlois, Gil Turner, Art Aragon and Bobby Dykes etc, etc, and beat most of them. He won two out of three fights with Williams, drew with Giardello and was considered unlucky to lose to Gavilan. Although a contender for years, Joe never got a title shot. He was a notoriously in-and-out fighter, beating champions like Atkins, Saxton and Smith, then losing to the likes of Maurice Harper and Dave Johnson. Perhaps it is my highest compliment to him when I say, that in the limited space I have, I cannot adequately do justice to him. 110 fights in a 13-year career is some record! Joe was a dying breed of fighter who lost his last big fight last July when a heart attack killed him.

Ricardo Moreno (left) seen here with the legendary Sugar Ray Robinson

MORENO Ricardo *From* Zocatecas, Mexico. *Died* 24 June 2008, aged 71. Ricardo was rather fortunate to get two shots at the world featherweight championship. He lost the first to Hogan Kid Bassey and the second to an even better champion, Davey Moore. There's little on the Mexican's record to say he deserved those title challenges, his first seven fights being against debutants and the next ten were little better. Then Memo Diez, with 19 fights under his belt, beat Ricardo in ten rounds. On paper his results look good: 22 fights, 20 wins. Gradually the quality of opposition increased. He beat 52-fight-veteran Oscar Suarez and had a notable win over Henry Pappy Gault, who was stopped in the third. Four more wins followed, then came a good victory over Gaetano Annaloro followed by a loss to Jose Luis Cotero. A stoppage win against Ike Chestnut (no mean performer) catapulted him into the Bassey fight. The Nigerian, on top form, knocked out his man in three rounds but one year and two wins later, the Mexican was challenging Davey Moore who dispatched him in ten rounds. From then on, Ricardo fought in good company until 1964 when he reverted to fighting novices to pad his record out with seven more wins. Prior to that he had lost to Kid Irapuato, Jose Adaine and Kid Anahuac and posted wins against tough and orthodox Pat McCoy, Hector Garcia, Luis Sanchez, Al Wilcher and Teddy Rand. Beating Danny Kid, Fernando Sota and Tony Vasquez gained Ricardo considerable credibility before two hard fights against Raul Rojas added to his loss ledger and took a lot out of him. He fought only three times more, beating Joey Aguilar and losing back-to-back fights against Alex Benitez and Silverio Ortiz.

MSOPHI Samora *From* East London, South Africa. *Died* 30 June 2008, aged 24. In a fight for the light-heavyweight championship of his country, Samora was stopped in four rounds by the defending champion, Mfundo Gwayana, and died later in hospital from a cerebral haemorrhage. This championship challenge was his tenth pro outing. Having won the first seven before Johnny Oliphant stopped him in two rounds, he came back to beat Simphiwe Mabona to qualify for a title shot. The Gwayana encounter was a punishing affair and Samora took two counts early on yet kept rallying and offering stubborn resistance. He was still on his feet and shipping heavy punishment when the referee intervened.

NEALE Ronnie *From* Bow. *Died* March 2008. Featherweight Ronnie had a brief career in which his explosive punching terminated many of his fights well inside the scheduled distance. His debut lasted under a round, Denny Lambert being the unfortunate loser. Ron Colverson fared better, lasting until the fourth round before being rescued by the referee. Joe Odus was the next victim, also in four rounds, but Denny Dennis put a stop to this run of successes when he outpointed Ronnie. They met twice more and Ronnie won them both. It was Belfast's Jimmy Brown who really spoiled his record, when stopping Ronnie in the third round. Out of the ring for a couple of years, he returned in 1958 to sensationally knockout Derek Jack in the first round before, surprisingly, deciding to hang up his gloves on that winning note.

NEILL Leonard *From* Durban, South Africa. *Died* 23 November 2007, aged 75. Boxing journalist Leonard Neill lived through a time when international fighters plied their trade in the big arenas that were used to promote the game before the days of television. He began at 17 and saw them all from Johnny Ralph to present times. Neill became the *Natal Witness's* youngest ever sports editor and later contributed to many South African and American fight journals. Interspersed with his journalistic output were spells as a commentator and matchmaker – the latter, as always, a job for a man with steel nerves. Because of the comparatively late arrival of television in South Africa, his services as a commentator lasted many years. He died in hospital, having spent his youth and mature years in service to the game he loved.

Tommy O'Neill

O'NEILL Tommy *From* Salford. *Died* May 2008, aged 75. Most travelling fairgrounds were complemented by a boxing booth in the early 1950s and it was there where Tommy got his early boxing experience after he had left the amateur scene. He was a licensed professional from 1949 and he went through to his peak years with very few, one in fact, defeats. He lost 12 in all but 11 of them came in his last 12 fights. Those who could beat him were all boxers of substance – Al Brown, Pat Gutteridge, Gordon Goodman, Boswell St Louis, Jimmy Croll and Albert Carroll. Tommy was usually there at the end, losing just once by a knockout. He twice beat Jackie Braddock by knockout, Jimmy O'Connell by a stoppage, Selwyn Evans, Tommy Robinson, Harry Legge, Bernie Newcombe and Ronnie Taylor on points and drew with Al Brown. The loss to St Louis came via a disqualification. His last fight was against Dennis Read, who beat him on points.

PALLENT Albert, MBE *From* Penge. *Died* August 2008. Albert devoted most of his adult life to training amateur boxers, first with South Norwood and then Downham Community Centre. It was he who brought on Brian Brazier, Dave Proud and Dennis Read and so many others, including Tony Stannard who gave me the sad news, while shunning personal publicity and quietly getting on with what was a labour of love. Al was one of those cornermen whose inter-round advice was sound and based on a clear understanding of a second's role. Considering the deplorable standard of corner-work in some world title fights these days, it is good to acknowledge the expertise of some of those amateur trainers like Albert, who were especially efficient. He did box professionally back in the early 1950s, but a disastrous start made him think again. After taking a five-year break he turned up at the NSC to beat Terry Russell of Poplar. Following on from that, he beat Battersea's Albert Stokes, who afterwards emigrated to New Zealand. Terry Toole, later to become a leading matchmaker, forced Albert to retire after two rounds and a further loss came against Peter Sexton. The last fight I have for him is a four-round points win over Dennis Saunders, against whom he had previously boxed a draw. In later years, Albert was a member of the Croydon EBA.

PARLOV Mate *From* Croatia. *Died* 29 July 2008, aged 60. Mate turned pro in 1975 after winning two European titles (1971 and 1973), the Olympics (1972), and World Championships (1974), all at light-heavyweight. A southpaw, he went through 12 winning fights before coming up against Matt Franklin, also known as Matt Saad Muhammad, who beat him in Milan. They drew over ten rounds seven months later, then in his next fight Mate won the European light-heavyweight title from Domenico Adinolfi and defended it three times before returning his belt. A knockout win over Miguel Angel Cuello gained him the WBC title, which Cuello had won when the WBC withdrew recognition from John Conteh. Mate then beat Conteh in his first title defence but lost his crown to Marvin Johnson in Sicily. There was one more world title challenge. He beat Tony Mundine in an eliminator for the

WBC cruiserweight diadem, drew with Marvin Camel for the championship, but was outpointed over 15 rounds in the return. It was his last fight. Until he came along, Yugoslavia as it was then known, had a limited boxing history. The advent of Mate opened new doors and established the sport in his country.

RAMOS Mando *From* Long Beach, California, USA. *Died* 6 July 2008, aged 59. Mando, a great natural fighter who was gifted with superb reflexes and punching ability, served his fistic apprenticeship in Californian rings. From the start it became clear that he was destined for high honours. By the time he was 19 he challenged Carlos Teo Cruz for the world lightweight championship. He failed in the first attempt, got a return a year later and became the youngest holder of the title for a century. At 20, with the world in front of him, his drugs and alcohol life-style was soon to impair his career. He lost his title to Ismael Laguna, won it back in 1970, held it briefly, and could have beaten all at his weight had he trained hard. He beat Spain's Pedro Carrasco for his second world title and repeated the win in Madrid. Having relied on his natural ability to win fights against good men, even though he was untrained and drinking too much, could not continue indefinitely and Chango Carmona relieved him of his world title. His career then took a downward turn. A European campaign was only moderately successful, Wayne Beale beat him back home in an American ring and that was it. Ramos had beaten Frankie Crawford, Hiroshi Kobayashi, Pete Gonzalez and namesake Sugar Ramos on the way up and at his peak mixed it with Ruben Navarro and Raul Rojas. Showing the same brand of courage that he exhibited within the ropes, Mando fought against his addictions and won. Clear of his demons, he devoted his life to lecturing on the danger of drugs to the younger and vulnerable generation. In doing so he regained the high esteem that he had once held as a superb 20-year-old boxing marvel.

REECE Len 'Luggie' *From* Cardiff. *Died* March 2008, aged 75. There were not many flyweights active in Britain in Len's day, which was why he was pushed into national title contention in his first year as a pro. He had more than just average boxing ability so he held his own with men who were heavier. In his first year, which was 1954, he went unbeaten, only Malcolm McLeod and Eric Brett going the distance with him. His reward was to start off 1957 with a match against Scotland's Frankie Jones. Len was on his way to victory when a cut eye forced the referee to intervene. A return was inevitable and this time the vacant British and Empire flyweight titles were at stake. Jones took quite a pounding from a fired-up Len, who put his man down for three counts and was way ahead on points when another cut – a very bad one – forced the referee to send him to his corner. The disappointment knocked out much of his pre-championship enthusiasm and this was reflected in subsequent form when he lost three out of four fights. Len regrouped and came back to beat Henri Schmid, then went through 1959 with only one loss. That was to Billy Rafferty who twice outpointed our man in fights two

years apart. In between there were good wins over Eddie O'Connor, Terry Toole and the excellent George Bowes. Alas, the old cut-eye bogey appeared against Alex Ambrose and Len was forced to haul down his flag after six rounds. He came back to beat Hugh Riley and George O'Neill but knew his boxing days were over when he lost to Terry Crimmins in Cardiff. In 26 fights he won 17, drew one and lost nine in a career stretching over six years. His real name was Leonard Gilbert Reece and he died of Parkinson's disease in St David's Hospital, Cardiff, leaving behind his wife Thelma and a son and daughter. As an amateur, Len won two British schoolboy titles, a youth title and was the Welsh senior champion. His brother Gil was a Welsh international footballer, who played for Sheffield United and Cardiff City and was capped 29 times.

Len Reece

RENARD Jean-Marc *From* Liege, Belgium. *Died* 27 August 2008, aged 52. The tragic suicide of former WBA featherweight challenger, Jean-Marc Renard, brings about a sad finale to the fighting lives of a fine boxing family. Jean's father, who fought from 1953 to 1964 and was a bantamweight and featherweight champion of Belgium, had 69 fights in which he opposed Floyd Robertson, Howard Winstone (twice), Alphonse Halimi (twice), Rafiu King, Mario D'Agata and Pierre Cossemyns, yet he never got a shot at the European title. His son, who fought from 1980 to 1989, won the EBU featherweight title from Alfred Raininger, lost it to Pat Cowdell and regained it when it became vacant. He was also EBU, Belgium and Benelux champion at super-featherweight. Jean-Marc inherited many of his father's boxing skills. His four losses in 45 fights were all at the hands of men who won championships: Barry McGuigan, Steve Sims,

Cowdell and Antonio Esparragoza, who beat him for the WBA featherweight championship. He beat Najib Daho and a future Commonwealth lightweight champion in Pat Doherty, but suffered terribly from brittle hands and it was that rather than the loss to Esparragoza that forced him to retire.

Luis Romero

ROMERO Luis *From* Arcila, Spain. *Died* May 2008, aged 87. One of his country's best-ever professional boxers, Luis Perez Romero, a stocky southpaw, was amateur bantamweight champion of Spain in 1941. He turned professional later in the same year. His early career record is fragmented and poorly chronicled due to Europe being embroiled in war, but my records show him the winner of 90 fights with seven losses prior to his incursion into British rings in 1950. He was European champion at that time, having knocked out Guido Ferracin for the title in August 1949. Subsequently, he beat two good British fighters in Ray Fitton and Bobby Boland. Both fights went the distance, which prompted promoter Stan Baker to match him with rising star Ronnie Draper. Romero waded straight in and punched Draper from pillar to post, forcing the Southampton man to quit on his stool after six rounds. Luis became the scourge of British bantamweights, beating Eddie Carson, Jackie Fairclough, George Stewart and Teddy Peckham, all on their own turf before losing his title to Peter Keenan. Prior to that he had defended against Danny O'Sullivan, who was one of this country's best-ever small men. Romero handed out a beating before stopping his man in round 13. Danny was never the same again. Romero, marginally past his prime, got a shot at Vic Toweel's world championship but saw the decision go against him. He won another 12 fights before Hogan Kid

Bassey beat him and put the Spaniard out of world-title contention. There were still five years of fighting ahead until he retired at 37. In an 18-year career he lost only 16 of 157 fights. Among his other opponents were Robert Tartari, Theo Medina, Bobby Ros, Fred Galiano, Rudi Langer, Tony Lombard, Roy Ankrah, Luis de Santiago, Amleto Falcinelli, Tino Cardinale, Georges Mousse, Jean Machterlink, Enzo Correggioli and Luis Fernandez. I rate him as being the hardest-punching, European bantamweight champion of my day. He was tough too, a solitary knockout defeat by de Santiago spoiling his long record, but Luis knocked him out quickly when they met again.

RYAN Jackie *From* Queensland, Australia. *Died* 28 June 2008, aged 80. Australian lightweight Jackie boxed from 1947 to 1957. He was born Kevin Blow in Rockhampton and for his boxing career he adopted the moniker of Jackie Ryan and based himself in Brisbane, where he had the majority of his fights. He could punch and started off with a series of quick wins. Jackie's first shot at the Queensland title came in 1949 when he lost to Brian Brady for the vacant championship, but he was luckier a year later when he outpointed Arthur McKillop and defended against the same foe five months later. Both were title fights. The next challenges were Dave Landers and Brady, both of whom were stopped in seven rounds. There had been a previous win over Brady, which put the series 2-1 in Jackie's favour. He and Landers also played ping-pong with the championship. That series ended 6-1 with Jackie still champion. He also defended his title against McKillop before losing it to Pat Ford in 1953. At his best he was in there with Frankie Flannery, Sigi Tennenbaum, Ray Fitton, Agustin Argote, Lahouari Godhi and Charlie Dunn. From 1949, he was a bill-topper and with his punching ability was always in with a chance. His overall record was 52 fights with 32 wins, three draws and 17 losses.

SABEDONG Duke *From* Honolulu, Hawaii. *Died* 11 August 2008, aged 78. Those of us who remember Duke Sabedong do so because he was an early opponent of Muhammad Ali, then known as Cassius Clay. Clay was in his second year of pro fighting and was on a run of five consecutive stoppage wins. Duke, in contrast, was in the eighth year of his career and had won only two of his previous seven fights. Maybe it looked like an easy night for Clay but he encountered stiff opposition and had to go ten rounds for the first time. The man from Honolulu was a difficult opponent with a deceptively spotty record, who fought and usually lost to the top men of his time. He started off well, beating Howard King and Willie Bean, but could never get the decision over Amos Lincoln. He lost all three of their fights on points before Lincoln, like Clay, went on to bigger things. When Zora Folley stopped him in 1957 Duke took a year's rest. Only Lincoln, Young Jack Johnson and Folley had beaten him at that point. The Folley fight was his 20th. Coming back and up to the 1961 meeting with Clay, his loss account increased in fights with Paul Andrews, Mike DeJohn, Willie Ray Richardson, Jim McCarter and Alejandro Lavorante. Despite a later loss to Tom McNeeley, Duke was far better than his record suggests, having forced a draw with tough Willie Besmanoff and knocking out Polly Smith. He was inactive in 1961 and retired the following year when losing to yet another contender in Eddie Machen.

SAUNDERS Donald *From* London. *Died* 29 April 2008, aged 85. There were reporters employed solely as boxing correspondents in those halcyon days of the 1950s. Donald Yeoman Saunders covered boxing for the *Daily Telegraph* from 1954 after learning his trade on the *Cardiff Western Mail*. He first became interested in boxing after listening to radio commentaries of British title bouts between Jack Petersen and Len Harvey. Saunders, himself a Welshman, followed Petersen's career closely. His style of reporting was of the 'no frills' variety. When you read his column, you got an in-depth review of the previous night's fight and it was never dull, although he never leaned toward the sensationalist style of the tabloids. Just before retiring, he predicted that satellite television would play a role in the survival of boxing as a major spectator sport. He served in the Suffolk regiment during the war and was posted to India. Saunders named the first Ali and Frazier contest as the best he had ever seen and Dave Charnley as his favourite British boxer.

SCANNELL Vernon *From* Spilsbury and Aylesbury. *Died* 16 November 2007, aged 85. "Between the ages of 14 and 17, I was painfully being torn apart by what seemed the irreconcilable passions for boxing and literature". So wrote Vernon Scannell in one of his memoirs, which he produced in 1975. He continued later: "A quarter of a century ago I hung up the gloves. I knew I'd had enough of taking it and trying to dish it out, foxing them, or slugging toe-to-toe". He was a British Schoolboys' finalist in the national championships when the standard of school's boxing was at its peak. Later, in Leeds University, he became captain of the boxing team. It was there that he won the Northern Universities' welter, middle, and cruiserweight championships. Scannell was a prolific writer and poet. Perhaps not as widely celebrated as WC Heinz or Norman Mailer but still a literary giant with a passion for boxing. Always adventurous, he boxed on fairgrounds whenever a booth was present. In the army, he was court-martialled for desertion, sentenced and incarcerated for what should have been a period of three years. The army released him to serve in the Normandy landings, during which he was wounded. He deserted again and lived under the pseudonym of Vernon Scannell. His birth name was John Vernon Bain, being born in Lincolnshire in 1922 and spending his school years in Aylesbury. A violent father and unhappy childhood brought him few fond memories, apart from when he escaped for a few moments into the Chiltern Hills. Those moments he recalled thus: "Lovely summer, never smeared or chilled". Boxing, war and music were themes that ran throughout his huge output of literary work and radio-broadcasting. His first marriage in 1954 was dissolved. In later years, when suffering from the cancer that eventually killed him, he was looked after by Jo Peters, his companion. He died in Otley, West Yorkshire.

SCHUTTE Mike *From* Johannesburg, South Africa. *Died* 14 July 2008, aged 57. After a long period of ill-health, South African heavyweight Mike passed away in Vanderbijlpark. In build he was a modern-day Tony Galento – like a barrel, short, and with thick thighs. Despite what could be termed as being 'these handicaps', he was quick on his feet even though a brawler by style. His career started with a series of quick wins that made him a favourite with boxing crowds, but he faltered when the opposition became tougher. In his prime years of 1975 to '76 he stopped Obie English, Pat Duncan, Jose Roman and Rudi Lubbers, outpointed Chuck Wepner, Rodney Bobick and Giuseppe Ros but then was himself knocked out by one punch from Dawie du Preez. He had five brutal fights with Jimmy Richards, who beat him twice, but lost the rest which included an important one for the South African title. Mike was on a winning streak of 14 when Gerrie Coetzee beat him on a foul in a really dirty fight more suited to backstreet brawling. There was a return and Coetzee was too good, winning on points. Kallie Knoetze knocked Mike out to show that he was not invulnerable. There was not much after that. He lost to Duane Bobick and had three more fights, retiring with a win over Neil Malpass. Other notable names he had beaten throughout his career were Conny Velensek, Peter Boddington, Dave Hallinan and Miguel Angel Paez. He turned to wrestling, to which sport his physique was better suited, supplemented by a career as an entertainer that enabled him to enjoy a steady income. Nicknamed 'The Tank' by boxing scribes, he was a rough, tough rumbustious character in the ring but quiet, well mannered and likeable in private life.

SECOVIK Edip *From* Vienna, Austria. *Died* 26 August 2008, aged 50. Former EBU light-middleweight champion, Edip, based in Vienna and of Serbian birth, died of stab wounds following a fracas outside a tavern. He began boxing in 1981, drawing his first fight then impressively scoring five straight knockouts before meeting Georg Steinherr, also a future EBU light-middleweight champion, who was the first to beat him. Edip, who was christened Sekowitsch, twice challenged unsuccessfully for the Austrian middleweight title, then dropped down in weight to light-middle and stopped Esperno Postl for the national title. With the belt to his name he lost only one of his next 17 fights, during which time he added the EBU title to his list of honours. He lost that crown to Guiseppe Leto and went on to fight for a variety of minor championships without achieving another major title. He was getting on in years but was still a dangerous fighter and his wins were usually within the scheduled distance. After several periods of inactivity he came back at the age of 50 to score a first-round knockout win over Steve Klockow, before his demise two months later.

SEKI Mitsunori *From* Tokyo, Japan. *Died* 6 June 2008, aged 66. Japanese southpaw Mitsunori carried his country's hopes of winning a world title on five occasions but was never lucky. He was unfortunate in challenging Vicente Saldivar, Sugar Ramos and Pone Kingpetch when they were at their best. The flyweight title was on the line against Thailand's Kingpetch when Seki was only 19 and still growing. When Saldivar retired from boxing, Howard Winstone was paired with the Japanese to contest the vacant title. The fight was just beginning to open up when a cut forced referee to call a halt and declare Winstone the winner. There was little in it at the finish. From 1962 Seki was Oriental featherweight champion. It was a title he defended 11 times and never lost. He had started out at 16 in 1958 and established himself as a force when beating Dommy Ursua, Leo Espinosa and Chartchai Chionoi, en route to his first world title bid against Kingpetch. A disastrous match followed when dangerous Mexican Joe Medel stopped him in three rounds. Mitsunori was quickly putting on weight and he won the Orient featherweight title before rising up the ratings' ladder following wins over Ronnie Jones, Tanny Campo, Jet Bally, Gene Aragon and Kang-Il Suh. In 1964 he made his first attempt to win the world featherweight championship but Sugar Ramos beat him. Mitsunori, who had been jumping between weight divisions settled down at the nine-stone limit and had a series of good wins that brought about a challenge to Saldivar. He dropped the tough Mexican only to lose a close decision. He had earned a return but was beaten decisively. The Winstone fight was his last big opportunity. Bitterly disappointed at losing a fight he could have won, Mitsunori brought down the curtain on a fine career. He was world-class in three weight divisions but lacked the essential ingredient of luck in his quest for championship honours.

SHARKEY Dave *From* Aldgate. *Died* 18 September 2007, aged 79. Dave was Al Phillip's protégé. They were active during the same period but whereas Phillips was champion, Dave was used in the capacity of sparring-partner. Al was so impressed with Dave that he took him under his wing and taught him the finer points of the game. The army called in 1948, with Dave's unit, the Fusiliers, being based in Germany. He was a non-smoker, so he traded in his ration of issued cigarettes for cash and bought a Leica camera. Later, when he was advancing his boxing career, he combined fighting with photography. His regular pitch was Trafalgar Square where he took and sold photos of tourists feeding the pigeons. Eventually, he opened up premises in Oxford Street. It was on the booths that he met Mickey Duff. He approached Mickey after the Army had demobbed him in 1949 and asked if anything could be done to resume his career. He and Mickey went to Mile End to see the Bodinetz brothers who were running shows in the local arena. There was a long discussion about suitable opponents, and Duff's expertise so impressed Morrie Bodinetz that he offered him a position as matchmaker. From that point, Mickey rose to worldwide fistic prominence, carving out a lucrative career as a boxing entrepreneur. Dave was 18 when he made his debut in 1945, boxing a draw with Southampton's Ronnie Draper, who went on to be a pretty good fighter. For his second outing, Dave got exposure at the Albert Hall where he was on the undercard of the Woodcock v Jock Porter

bill. He impressed by beating Gerald Evans and his name was then entered in an open featherweight competition. Ron Kitchen was too experienced for him, and handed Dave his first loss. From then on it was steady progress until he got his first ten-rounder against Teddy Peckham. It was described in the press as being a grand bout. It went on in Bournemouth, with local boy Peckham getting the verdict. Far from being a setback, his performance showed that Dave was on the way up. He mixed it with men like Morty Kelleher, who gave him one of his hardest fights, Des Garrod, Tony Brazil, Jock Bonas, Arthur Gould and Cliff Morris. An indication of how times have changed is that in 1947 Dave had three fights in January and four in November. His old friend Al Phillips had to withdraw from a fight with Jackie Turpin so Dave willingly substituted. He boxed well and took Turpin the full course at very short notice. Later he substituted for Turpin against Hecky Holdsworth and won the eight-round verdict. Some of his best wins came against Jackie Lucraft, Harry Legge and Teddy Larkham. His last fight was in 1950 when he retired with a cut eye against Stan Gossip. Dave was very wary of eye injuries so he got out while still on top of his game. His photography business earned him an income in post-boxing years and the business is now being run by his son, Philip, a contributor to this book.

Dave Sharkey

SPINK Dr John *From* Marlow. *Died* 17 September 2007, aged 75. A man well represented in his local community and remembered by his neighbours as 'a pillar of the town', died in his Marlow home. Locally, John Spink was medical officer for the Marlow Amateur Boxing Club and he was also a member of the BBB of C's medical panel when pro boxing was last held at High Wycombe. Dr Spink was a firm advocate of the benefits of boxing to the community and gave his services free of charge. He supported all sports and understood the social values instilled by one-on-one physical activity. He made a great contribution to boxing, to his patients and to sport in general. His funeral was attended by hundreds of friends.

STACK Michael *From* Leamington. *Died* February 2008, aged 79. By British standards, Michael was a decent middleweight who was capable of looking after himself midst the top-ten fighters of his division. He was Irish by birth and also brother-in-law to Randolph Turpin. Being in the same stable as Turpin tended to put him in a shadow. As an amateur he won the Midland Counties' championship in 1949 and turned professional at the end of the year. 1950 was a good year in which he beat Sam Burgoyne, Sammy Wilde, Billy Coloulias and Jimmy Ridgewell. South Africa's Duggie Miller beat him in his first ten rounder but he had by then made a name for himself and boxed on until 1954, mixing it with Gordon Hazell, Ron Pudney, Ron Grogan, Dick Langley, Jimmy Davis, George Dilkes, Eric McQuade, Wally Beckett, Bert Sanders, Tom Meli, Johnny Wright, Roy Agland, Les Allen, Terence Murphy, Johnny Sullivan, Larry Parkes and Fred Balio. What a fine bevy of boxing names! Michael did not win them all, of course; a breakdown of his record reveals a 50-50 win/loss ratio. In that company he established himself as a genuine fighter.

FRANZ SZUZINA *From* Bremen, Germany. *Died* 29 June 2008, aged 77. Franz's story is one of a talented boxer whose career progress brought him a national middleweight championship challenge in 1951 when he'd had only a year's professional experience. Peter Muller was too good for him on that occasion, as was Hans Stretz the following year, but between those two title fights he got some notable wins. Eduardo Lopez, Jan de Bruin, Charlie Anglee and Giovanni Manca were all licked and there was also a draw against Don Ellis, while Jimmy King, whom he was later to beat, outpointed him. Franz had matured into a rated middleweight with the prospect of better things ahead. Over the next few years he outpointed Martin Hansen, drew with Ivano Fontana, Al Mobley and Terry Moore, before losing an important one to Gustav Scholz. There was a draw and a loss to Willie Besmanoff, a win over Karl Ameisbichler, followed by losses to Pat McAteer, Charles Humez and Leen Jansen. Not satisfied with his luck in Europe, Franz campaigned in American rings where he matured into a world-class boxer, going in with Charlie Cotton, Virgil Akins, Randy Sandy, Joey Giardello, Lino Rendon, Bobby Boyd and Spider Webb. He returned briefly to Germany in 1961, beating Germinal Ballerin and drawing with an on-form Alex Buxton. His last three outings were in the USA, where he beat Jerry Luedee before bowing out with losses to Henry Hank and Rory Calhoun.

TOWEEL Vic *From* Benoni, Gauteng, South Africa. *Died* 15 August 2008, aged 80. South Africa reveres Victor Anthony Toweel as its best-ever sportsman. His professional career was brief, his achievements remarkable. After only 14 fights and aged 22, he won the world bantamweight championship from Manuel Ortiz, one of the division's greats. In his fourth fight he won the national bantamweight title and in the same year he beat the vastly more experienced Tony Lombard for the South African featherweight crown. A challenge to Ronnie Clayton for the Empire featherweight title fell through so he sweated off the pounds to beat Stan Rowan, whose Empire bantamweight championship was at stake. To round off his first year of paid boxing, he battered former world flyweight title-holder, Jackie Paterson. Five months into 1950 he beat Ortiz. Vic made such fast strides because of his vast amateur experience and it was claimed that he lost only two of 300 fights as a simon-pure. I do not have the means to cross-check that claim and while the 300 fight figure looks too 'good' there is no doubt that Vic was oozing with talent. He was one of a great fighting family and of Lebanese extraction. What abbreviated his career can be in part explained by negotiations breaking down when he challenged Ronnie Clayton at the nine-stone limit. That was the division in which he really belonged and his career became a torturous battle with the scales. A nose injury and vision problems added to his difficulties but he had so much talent that he beat three good men in Luis Romero, Danny O'Sullivan and Peter Keenan in defence of his title. He also defeated Kalla Persson, Georges Mousse, Jim Kenny, Fernando Gagnon, Theo Medina and Bobby Boland. It all caught up with him when he lost his world title to Jimmy Carruthers and failed to win it back in a return. He beat Ronnie Clayton at the heavier poundage then, disenchanted with boxing and its concomitant problems, he took a holiday in New York where he dropped a ten-round decision to rising star, Carmelo Costa. There was just one more fight and that was at the welterweight poundage four months after the New York debacle. At 27, Vic had fought for the last time and passed the torch to his brothers, all of whom did their country proud. The last 20 years of Vic's life were spent in Sydney, Australia and that is where he died.

URSUA Dommy *From* Cordova, Cebu, Philippines. *Died* 25 May 2008, aged 72. Boxing's lighter weight divisions were crammed with good, and in many cases great, fighters back in the 1950s. Dommy was active at that time. He came out of the Philippines to fight the best bantamweights of his time, with honour and distinction, performing all over the Orient and Americas, never refusing a scrap. With his all-action, power-thumping style, he brought the customers to the box-office and packed arenas to the rafters. He was under five feet in height and fought like a wildcat. Dommy won just over a half of his 59 fights but was always in there with a puncher's chance. He dropped Raul (Raton) Macias, world bantamweight champion at the time, but could not keep him down. The fans loved him and his hard punching often brought victories against the odds. Dommy started boxing in 1954 and such was his progress that he fought for the Filipino title after a handful of fights. He lost that one on points but was destined for big things. It was Tanny Campo, an outstanding glove-artist, who beat him but Tanny knew he had been in a fight. Before throwing his hat into American rings Dommy got a good win when outpointing Leo Zulueta. In 1957 he got his chance against Macias and nearly won it, with the world championship at stake. Back home again, Dommy had seven important fights in which he knocked out Johnny Jarrett, Muzakazu Osuka and Toshiro Tanaka, and lost to Al Asuncion before opposing the great Pascual Perez for the Argentinian's world flyweight championship. It took knockout specialist Perez the full 15 rounds to subdue his man, who had previously been unluckily disqualified against Pone Kingpetch in Bangkok. Back again in California, Dommy returned to winning form before travelling to Honolulu to twice beat Ray Perez. He was unluckier in Japan where he lost to Haruo Sakamoto and the top-rated Mitsunori Seki, who put the only kayo defeat on his record, dropping him for the full count in round five. The Filipino never did much after that. He was only 25 but had been in some wars that shortened his career. Two more points losses back home and a losing ten-rounder down in Santiago brought about his retirement. Unfortunately, his final years were eked out in dire poverty, dying a pauper in Cebu City with only his memories recalling better days when his name on Californian fight bills would sell-out the stadiums.

Pat Valentino

VALENTINO Pat *From* San Francisco, California, USA. *Died* 25 July 2008, aged 88. A 1940s heavyweight contender, Pat produced his best performance for his last contest when challenging Ezzard Charles for the NBA title in 1949. Charles, at the peak of his career, had a tough fight on his hands from the inspired underdog from California before his experience saw him come from behind to stop Pat in eight rounds. Two of the judges had the challenger two points ahead after seven rounds. The attendance of 19,590 was a record for California. Two draws with Joey Maxim and a win over Freddie Beshore had pushed Pat into the limelight, but a loss in 1948 to Jimmy Bivins showed that Charles was picking his challengers carefully. Pat had begun boxing in 1940, winning his first seven fights inside the distance, before outpointing Bob Nestell and stopping Ralph DeJohn. Melio Bettina beat Pat on points, then a fight with Turkey Thompson saw him victorious and becoming California State champion. He never saw his money for the Charles fight and had to sue his manager for what was due. It soured Pat's dedication to the game. He never fought a serious fight again but did meet come-backing Joe Louis in an exhibition match that strangely enough was scheduled for ten rounds. Pat never got past the eighth. During the last world war he served in the US Coastguards and in his post-boxing days he became a maitre d'hotel in a San Francisco restaurant. His birthname was Valentino Guglielmi.

VAN KLAVEREN Piet *From* Rotterdam, Holland. *Died* 28 April 2009, aged 77. The van Klaveren brothers are perhaps the best known of Dutch boxing families. Bep, the old 'Dutch Windmill', was half brother to Piet who was one of twins and considerably younger than his illustrious elder. They shared the same mother, Bep being born as Lambertus Steenhorst and later adopting the name of his stepfather. It was 1953 before Piet turned pro. He had represented Holland in the Helsinki Olympics and as a light-welterweight had reached the quarter-finals before being ousted by Ireland's Terry Milligan. In his earlier years – back in 1947 – Piet boxed his brother Wim in the South Holland championships. Two extra rounds were ordered due to the closeness of the fight in which Piet eventually emerged victorious. When he donned gloves for pay, Bep, who was 23 years his senior, had been boxing for 25 years. Piet placed himself in the hands of Theo Huizenaar, who handled most of the top Dutch boxers, including, of course, Bep, who fought on to 1956. Quickly establishing himself as a talented but light-punching lightweight, Piet became Dutch champion by default in April 1954. The Netherlands' Boxing Board handed him the title based on his good record. He had made progress by beating Britain's Johnny Mann, Syd Greb and winning then drawing against Alan Tanner. Piet had fought 27 times without loss against increasingly better opposition – Henk Klok, Louis van Hoeck, Morlay Kamara, Jacques Bataille and Karl Heinz Friedrich before being forced to retire against the European champion, Duilio Loi, in Milan. Loi was one of the best post-war Italian boxers and was destined for a long career, which saw him win a world title and retire having beaten every man he had fought. Piet got a return but lost in six rounds. The following year Piet drew with Fernand Nollet before suffering his first knockout loss at the hands of Mario Vecchiatto in Milan. In 1958, he lost a challenge for the Dutch welterweight championship, being disqualified against Theo Baars. Of his seven defeats, none came on points. He had two losses by disqualification (Baars and Leif Hansen), two defeats by Loi, the one to Vecchiatto, one to Henri Cabelduc, and his final fight against Ahmed Sebane. In 44 fights there were 34 wins and three draws. Quality wins came over Omar le Noir, Bob Stevens, Ziyaris Taki, Jo Woussem and Raymond Souply. In later years he suffered a stroke and was moved into a nursing home when his sad situation was compounded by the onset of dementia. Through all this, his twin brother Wim spent most of his days at his bedside caring for Piet right up to his death.

VAN VUUREN Piet *From* Johannesburg, South Africa. *Died* August 2008, aged 77. Piet was one of South Africa's outstanding amateurs, good enough to beat Australia's Tony Madigan at light-heavyweight in the final of the 1954 Empire Games held in Vancouver. Madigan later lost to the then Cassius Clay in the Rome Olympics. An Olympic title was one of the few championships that eluded the South African. He represented his country in Melbourne but was unfortunate to be beaten in the prelims by the eventual silver medal winner, Zbigniew Pietrzykowski of Poland. Piet won the South African championship four times at the light-heavyweight limit, preceded by a successful attempt at the middleweight title in 1951, and was a dominant force in South African amateur boxing throughout the 1950s. He could box well but often his hard punching made the scoring of points unnecessary. Despite his clean-living lifestyle, he was in bad health for the past few years.

VASQUEZ Bernabe 'Baby' *From* San Miguel, Mexico. *Died* 2 August 2008, aged 77. The competitive nature of boxing in Mexico during the 1950s and '60s can be gauged by this man's record that occupies over a page in *The Ring Record Book*. It took him five years and 40 fights before he won the Mexican lightweight title and another four years before he defended it. A defeat by Al Urbina in 1959 cost him his hard-earned diadem and then it took three years to get Urbina back in the ring. Vasquez regained his crown in decisive style but it was a short reign. Within a year, he had lost his title to Jorge Gutierrez, a man whom he had previously beaten in a title defence. Vasquez, or to give him his full name of Jose Bernabe Vasquez Rodriguez, was 18 when he started boxing. On the way to his first title he beat Diego Sosa and Baby Ortiz and won one out of three outings against Ralph Dupas. Frankie Ryff beat him in New York when he had stepped up in class but he followed up with consecutive wins against Jimmy Soo, Teddy Red Top Davis and Paolo Rossi. Some of his fights were rife with controversy. In 1958 Willie Morton beat him, but the decision was later reversed by the Mexican Commission. He got the verdict in a return then that too was cancelled out. Vasquez had 147 fights, in which he won 102 and drew four. He crossed gloves with the cream of his weight division: Jose Napoles, Sugar Ramos (twice), Eddie Perkins, Carlos Hernandez, Paul Armstead, Rip Randall and Noel Humphries. In 1974, at the age of 43, he

knocked out Juan Elizondo and then retired from boxing having lost only one of his previous 21 fights. The details of his demise are sad. Like so many Mexican stars of the past, his end came in a road-traffic accident but unlike the majority of others he had seen out his allocation of three score years and ten.

VITHICHAI Kunoi *From* Thailand. *Died* January 2008, aged 75. Some details of Thai boxers' achievements are very difficult put together, with so many of them taking the name of the gymnasium or boxing stable to which they belong. I can find nothing on Kunoi Vithichai, who was born Kuna Matthapong, until he beat Saeng Jomthong for the Thailand flyweight championship in 1954. His record beyond that is unexceptional in terms of contests won (seven) and lost (nine), until the quality of opponents are revealed, among them being Tanny Campo, Mitsunori Seki and Pone Kingpetch. He had three encounters with Kingpetch, winning the first, which reveals him as being a flyweight of substance. Kunoi beat Takeshi Yamaguchi, Leo Zulueta and Shichiro Kamura and also twice fought for the Orient title, losing both times to other good fighters in Sadao Yaoita and Danny Kid. A knockout loss to Seki was his last fight.

WAKEMAN Billy *From* Bethnal Green. *Died* 22 March 2008. Ace record compiler and colleague Miles Templeton has forwarded news of Billy's death. Billy was, indeed, an old-timer, with his earliest recorded fight being a win over Ernie Ward of Kingston in 1937. Ward turned the tables in 1938, by which time Billy had won ten out of 11 contests. He fought the ubiquitous old campaigner, Arnold Kid Sheppard, twice but each time returned home as loser. Wins followed over Islington's Dick Johnson, Rory O'Connor and Jock McGowan. He bowed out in 1939 with a win over Arthur Long. Miles has found 39 fights for Billy, with 19 wins.

WALKER Billy *From* Boldon. *Died* October 2007. Billy is remembered by London fight followers as the man who spoiled Jimmy Davis' pro debut. An odds-on outsider, Billy overcame a slow start to get his nose in front. By then, he had established himself as a man who could test the best in his division by virtue of fights against Charlie Curry of Wheatley Hill, Bob Bates (Coxhoe), Owen Hughes, Lynemouth's Sexton O'Keefe whom he beat twice, Johnny Russell (Covent Garden) who was the first to beat him, Claude Dennington, Harry Lazar, Sam Darkie Sullivan, Jimmy Molloy, Alf Danahar and former British champions, Henry Hall and Eddie Thomas. A miner by profession, after retiring from the ring following a win over Jimmy Prior, he trained amateur boxers.

WATANABE Makoto *From* Japan. *Died* 1 September 2007, aged 69. Crack Japanese welterweight, Makoto was twice champion of his country and, in late career, holder of the Oriental light-welterweight title. Beginning boxing in 1957, his career petered out following an unsuccessful bid to regain the national crown from Hisao Minami in 1966.

He first became champion in 1961 when beating old foe Jiro Sawada over ten rounds, which is the championship course in Japan. Sawada got a return but the result was the same. Makoto lost his hard-gained crown to Hachiro Ito one year later but regained it quickly before losing to Yoshinori Takahashi with the Oriental welterweight title at stake. He was successful in an effort to regain the Japanese title, then dropped down a division to claim the Oriental diadem by stopping Rocky Montante in two rounds. In over 60 fights, nine were title contests.

Billy Wells

WELLS Billy *From* South London. *Died* September 2007, aged 70. Starting out as a young amateur in 1951, Billy was nearing the veteran stage when winning an ABA heavyweight title in 1965 when boxing for Wandsworth ABC. Working as an electrician's mate for one of the leading Fleet Street newspapers he again won the ABA heavyweight title in 1968, boxing for the Lynn club, and was chosen to represent England in the Mexico City Olympics that year, going out to the eventual runner-up. Having retired on coming home, he made a comeback three years later and proceeded to win a South-East London divisional title before hanging his gloves up for good. Some 13 years later, he proudly watched his son Bobby win the ABA super-heavyweight title and go on to take a bronze in the 1984 Olympics. A great character who ultimately died in tragic circumstances, Billy will not be forgotten by those who saw him perform.

WELLS Rhoshii *From* Austin, Texas. *Died* August 2008, aged 31. The American Olympic boxing team expected much from its middleweight hopeful Rhoshii in the 1996 Games. He was 19 and gifted with fine boxing skills,

getting through three fights in style before coming unstuck against the eventual gold-medal winner. Roshii never got the exposure as a professional that he would have had he brought home the Olympic championship, yet he lost to only one man in a 22 fight career. Alejandro Garcia, then unbeaten, stopped him for the WBA middleweight title then beat him again. They were Roshii's last fights. He had transferred to Las Vegas to continue his career and it was there that he met a violent end after what appears to have been a street fight. Wells, a father of six, died later in hospital. "He was a friend to everybody", remembered former WBO heavyweight champion Lamon Brewster, who went on to say that: "He never got the credit that he should have got. He was a much better fighter than people knew he was. He was like a shining star that never got to shine". Roshii was expected to take part in 'The Contender Season Three', but never competed after failing a reaction test on the first episode.

WILLIAMS Ernie 'Sonny Boy' *From* Washington DC, USA. *Died* 1 November 2007, aged 72. Like so many men who go on to become genuine fighters, Ernie began his career with a loss. After one Johnny Gwynn outpointed him in July 1954, Ernie continued for another five years, boxing first as a lightweight then as a welterweight. He lost to world champion Joe Brown as a lightweight before going up one weight division. Wins came over Jimmy Evans, Georgie Justine and Brown Lee. At world-class level he just failed to make the grade, losing to JD Ellis, Stefan Redl and Jethro Cason, but took all of them the full course without being disgraced.

WILLIAMS John 'The Fish' *From* Wales. *Died* 2 September 2007, aged 84. Geraint Richards, on whom I rely to keep me informed on Welsh boxing matters, has supplied details of John's death. He had been a fishmonger all his working life apart from the two years when he was in uniform. I will let Geraint tell the story. "John had a lifelong interest in boxing, having boxed before and during his army service where he won the Northamptonshire Regiment welterweight championship in 1941. After being transferred to the Parachute Regiment he represented his unit regularly. The regiment was then based in Italy. Once demobbed he married his girlfriend Lillian and took up professional boxing under the banner of 'West Wales Promotions'. The Drill Hall, Aberystwyth, was always sold out when Johnny was on the bill. He was a 'banger', a Billy Walker-type of fighter, a promoter's dream. Alas, his ring career was cut short due to an aggravated war-wound. Among his opponents were Tommy Fox of Liverpool, Tommy Jones (Llanelli), Idris Hubbard, Tommy Williams, who John knocked out in two rounds, and Hywel Phillips. John was a good football player, turning out for his local YMCA, the Liberal club and Trefechan in the junior league. In 1953 I was invited to box on a bill at Aberystwyth Drill Hall and John became my trainer. We stayed together for six years until I retired. He always called in to see my mother after I had fought. If I lost it was never my fault according to John, it was due to bad judging or bad refereeing. There was no warning of his death. He and Lillian went out to lunch, came home for a couple of drinks and settled down to watch television. John nodded off and when Lillian went to wake him she discovered that he had gone. It was a terrible shock for her. He was a life-member of the Welsh EBA and immensely popular. A packed hall rose for a minute's silence in respect for their dear friend".

WOLFINDALE Fred *From* Smethwick. *Died* March 2008, aged 92. Well-known as the former trainer of Pat Cowdell and Pat's father Howard, Fred's interest in boxing, first sparked in the 1930s, brought him in contact with most Midlands' fighters of his time. In a life lasting 92 years, Fred was one of our longest-living followers of boxing. His prime achievement was in taking Pat Cowdell to a world-title shot against Salvador Sanchez in 1981. It went to a split decision much to the surprise of the bookmakers who had established the Mexican as a firm favourite. Nigel Rafferty, the Edwards brothers Harry and Terry, Peter Till and Paul Chance, all got their tuition from Fred, whose uncle Albert was also a trainer. You could safely say that he was born into boxing.

WRIGHT Michael *From* Chatham. *Died* 27 August 2007, aged 33. An illness that curtailed his boxing career after only four pro fights claimed the life of Michael at a young age. In his brief paid career, he lost just once but emphatically avenged the reverse two months later. He then beat Wayne Jones and India's Venkatesan Deverajan. Michael's amateur pedigree was sound, being an England representative against America in 1994. His pro debut, under the management of Barry Hearn, came one year later. As a simon-pure, boxing for St Mary's ABC, Chatham, he chalked up over 100 contests.

ZADELL Rudy *From* Pittsburgh, Pennsylvania, USA. *Died* 7 March 2008, aged 80. Rudy's record of 17 wins in 59 fights does not, at a glance, indicate that he was a fighter of some ability. His stature increases with closer examination. Another case of 'Look at the quality of the men he fought and not at the number of his victories'. He was a middleweight, active from 1945 to 1952, who fought some of the best men of his era such as Sammy Mastrean, George Angelo, Sammy Angott, Gene Fullmer, Fitzie Pruden, Chuck Taylor, Virgil Akins, Gil Turner and Jimmy King, who campaigned with distinction in Europe in the early 1950s. Note that Rudy was a ten-round fighter and you do not get top billing if you cannot box. I never saw him fight but know that he was a respected and useful welter-cum-middleweight.

Other pro boxers who have also passed away during the period, include **Jorge Javier Acuna** 29 (Argentinian light-welter 2004 to 2007 – 7 contests); **Alex Aroy** (Philippines light-fly 2003 to 2008 – 20 contests); **Nev Ashe** (Australian light 1954 to 1957 – 12 contests); **Joe Aurillo** 85 (USA middle 1947 to 1954 – 35 contests); **Jake Betz** (USA heavy 2007 to 2008 – 5 contests);

Larissa Brates 23 (USA Brazilian female feather 2007 – 3 contests); **Jim Stump Buffo** 46 (USA heavy 1996 to 1998 – 3 contests); **Jackson Bussell** 30 (USA light-welter 2007 – 4 contests); **Brian Bwantu** (Zambian heavy 1999 to 2003 – 4 contests); **Jorge Canovas** (Cuban welter 1945 to 1948 – 11 contests); **George Carroll** (Australian middle 1963 to 1965 – 11 contests); **Hiram Castaneda** (Mexican light-heavy 2006 to 2007 – 6 contests); **Antonio Cervino** 60 (Italian bantam 1970 to 1976 – 9 contests); **Zwelakhi Chisane** (South African light 2001 to 2004 – 9 contests); **Jesse Corona** 35 (USA cruiser 1997 to 2007 – 25 contests); **Israel Crespo** 21 (Puerto Rican fly 2005 to 2007 – 2 contests); **Willie Cruz** 35 (Puerto Rican light-middle 1993 to 2007 – 8 contests); **Jody Edwards** (South African light-welter 1996 to 2000 – 14 contests); **Sid Ellis** 91 (Australian light-heavy 1940 – 5 contests); **Justin English** 25 (USA super-middle 2003 – 3 contests); **Clem Florio** (USA middle 1950 to 1964 – 14 contests); **Ted Garcia** 90 (USA light 1935 to 1938 – 71 contests); **Gino Gelormino** 47 (USA feather 1981 to 1990 – 34 contests); **Richie Gonzalez** 66 (USA feather 1963 to 1970 – 38 contests); **Eloy Henry** 64 (Panamanian light 1959 to 1969 – 27 contests); **Jonas Hernandez** 25 (Puerto Rican super-bantam 2005 to 2008 – 10 contests); **Cho Hi** 22 (Japanese light-welter 2005 to 2008 – 11 contests); **Sam Hughes** (USA light-heavy 1942 to 1947 – 40 contests); **Don Jasper** 79 (USA heavy 1949 to 1959 – 37 contests); **Frank Jennings** (USA welter 1956 to 1958 – 44 contests); **Peter Karpau** 34 (Indonesian light-welter 2001 to 2004 – 12 contests); **Mike Keresztes** (Australian light-welter 1951 to 1952 – 16 contests); **Gordon Lott** 67 (USA middle 1964 to 1974 – 42 contests); **Luis Lugo** 28 (Mexican feather 2008 – 1 contest); **Valentine Luna** (USA welter 1949 to 1957 – 14 contests); **Amanda Lyons** (USA female super-fly 2007 – 4 contests); **Vittorio Mancini** 71 (Italian welter 1957 to 1961 – 21 contests); **Louise Miller** (USA female super-fly 2006 to 2007 – 2 contests); **Roque Montoya** 46 (USA light-middle 1979 to 1992 – 38 contests); **Godfrey Nkate** (South African light-fly 1976 to 1983 – 34 contests); **Shane Norford** 35 (Australian heavy 1995 to 2004 – 21 contests); **Adriano Offreda** 38 (German welter 1992 to 2003 – 17 contests); **Rafael Ortiz** 30 (USA light-middle – 30 contests); **Alton Rice** 44 (USA super-middle 1990 to 2005 – 8 contests); **Olivier Schaeffer** (French welter 2007 – 2 contests); **Johnny Shields** 89 (Australian light 1943 to 1946 – 19 contests); **Vitaly Shkraba** 38 (Belarusian heavy 1997 to 2007 – 28 contests); **Chris Smith** 30 (Australian super-feather – 3 contests); **Merv Smith** 81 (Australian welter 1947 to 1949 – 8 contests); **Robin Smith** 51 (USA middle 1982 to 1992 – 10 contests); **Hope Sole** (South African light 1988 to 1995 – 18 contests); **Arnold Tarr** 92 (USA middle 1936 to 1939 – 2 contests); **Bashiru Thompson** (Nigerian fly 1992 to 2008 – 22 contests); **Eddie Van Kirk** 45 (USA light-middle 1982 to 1995 – 38 contests); **Mannie Van Tonder** (South African heavy 1975 – 1 contest); **Ronny Vargas** (USA middle 2007 to 2008 – 8 contests); **Pete Zaduk** (Canadian middle 1947 to 1950 – 27 contests).

A Boxing Quiz with a Few Below the Belt: Part 13

Compiled by Les Clark

QUESTIONS

1. This former heavyweight champion was the only one to fight both Jack Dempsey and Joe Louis. Can you name him?

2. Who was the first world champion produced by the Kronk Gym in Detroit?

3. Sugar Ray Robinson's first loss was against Jake LaMotta. Name the man who inflicted his first defeat in a championship bout?

4. What was the outcome of the third bout between Rocky Graziano and Tony Zale?

5. Who was the 1986 BBBof C Yearbook's award winner for 'Sportsman of the Year'?

6. Who did Brian Anderson defeat in Belfast to win the vacant British middleweight title?

7. How many bouts did Mark Kaylor rake up before his first loss?

8. Can you name a Sheffield-born former world champion who lost his first three fights?

9. Who was the last man Muhammad Ali beat by a kayo?

10. Ernie Schaaf, an up-and-coming heavyweight contender, entered into a bout with an undisclosed injury received in a previous fight with Max Baer. He was knocked out and subsequently died following this bout in February 1933. Name his opponent?

11. How many fights did Muhammad Ali have as an amateur and what was his record?

12. In which year did Prince Naseem Hamed leave his manager/promoter?

13. Which middleweight champion challenged Jack Johnson for his heavyweight belt and even floored him before being stopped in the 12th round?

14. Can you recall the surname of Michael Gerard?

15. Can you remember the nickname of Iran Barkley?

16. Who was the first Englishman to twice fight for a world title?

17. Who knocked out Sonny Liston in Las Vegas in 1969?

18. Which former heavyweight champion once signed for Liverpool FC?

19. Who did Vicente Saldivar defeat in Rome to regain the featherweight belt?

20. Reg Gutteridge once said: "He's like a baby in a playpen". Who was he describing?

21. Do you know who was South Korea's first world champion?

22. Jesus Salud was born in the Philippines and fought out of the USA between 1983 and 2002. What was his nickname?

23. What is Clay Hodges claim to fame?

24. Which fighter had the longest unbeaten run at the start of his career, with 98 bouts?

25. Wilfred Benitez won three world titles. Who did he defeat to win his third belt?

26. When Prince Naseem Hamed left Frank Warren, who took over the duties of manager?

27. Where was Wilfred Benitez born?

28. Who was the first man to go past four rounds with Mike Tyson?

29. What was the result of the Andrew Golota v Mike Tyson bout?

30. Who was the last challenger for either version of the heavyweight title in the '60s?

31. At which venue did Prince Naseem Hamed lose to Marco Antonio Barrera?

32. After Muhammad Ali was stripped of his world titles, Jimmy Ellis was recognised by the WBA as champion, while Joe Frazier was recognised by another group. Name the body in question?

33. Muhammad Ali's first defence after stopping George Foreman was against an opponent who had him on the canvas early into the fight and lasted until stopped with only one minute left of the 15th round. Name him?

34. Which fighter equalled Jack Dempsey's record of seven knockdowns in one round of a title bout?

35. Who was the last man Muhammad Ali beat by a knockout?

36. Can you remember the name of the fighter Nigel Benn beat to win the Commonwealth belt?

37. Did Muhammad Ali ever go to jail?

38. What was the result of Marvin Hagler's first attempt to win a world title?

39. Former WBA bantamweight champion Alfonso Zamora had 38 bouts, with 33 wins and five losses. On how many occasions did one of his fights last the full distance?

40. What did Ken Norton do before he turned to professional boxing?

41. "I wrestled an alligator, chewed a brick, I'm so bad I make medicine feel sick". This was a quote by Muhammad Ali before one of his contests. Who was the opponent?

42. Do you know the name of Nigel Benn's father?

43. Who did Floyd Patterson defeat on points in Stockholm in 1965?

44. Do you recall which referee controlled Muhammad Ali's bouts against Ernie Terrell and Cleveland Williams?

45. Who was known as the Fighting Fisherman?

46. How many notches on the Lonsdale Belt did Clinton McKenzie gain?

47. Who did Les McAteer stop inside 11 rounds for the Commonwealth middleweight title?

48. Who did Joe Bygraves defeat for the Commonwealth belt and successfully it defend against before losing to Joe Erskine?

49. In 1956 six foreign fighters came to these shores to face Dick Richardson. How did he get on?

50. Who was the first recipient of the 'Best Young Boxer of the Year' award in 1951 by the British Boxing Writers' Club?

Leading BBBoC License Holders: Names and Addresses

Licensed Promoters

A Force Promotions
1539 Briarglen Avenue
Westlake Village
PO Box 577
California
USA 91361
0199 262 3062

Bruce Baker
Unit 2,Six Acres
Stoddards Lane
Beckley, Nr Rye
East Sussex
01797 260616

Mark Bateson
33 Springfield Road
Guisley
Leeds LS20 9AN
0777 860 1427

Jack Bishop
76 Gordon Road
Fareham
Hants PO16 7SS
0132 928 4708

Paul Boyce
79 Church Street
Briton Ferry
Neath SA11 2JG
0163 981 3723

(Braveheart Promotions)
Barry Hughes
5 Royal Exchange
Square
Glasgow G1 3AH
0141 248 8899

**Tony Burns
(TBS Promotions)**
67 Peel Place
Woodford Green
Essex IG5 0PT
0208 550 8911

Scott Calow
18 Farnworth Grove
Huthwaite
Notts
NG17 2NL
0787 664 1055

George Carman
5 Mansion Lane
Mobile Home Site
Iver
Bucks S10 9RQ
0175 365 3096

**Michael Carney
(Impact Boxing
Promotions)**
Bradley Arms Farm
Alton Road
Cheadle
Staffs ST10 4RA
0797 049 5597

**Paul Carpenter
(Leicester Sporting
Club)**
42 The Willows
Bedworth
Warwickshire
CV12 0NX
0787 846 7401

Miranda Carter
86 Keslake Road
London NW6 6DG
07979 494950

**Dave Coldwell
(Koncrete Promotions)**
5 Penwood Walk
Bramley
Rotherham
Yorks S66 3XS
01709 701911

Patrick Connaughton
5th Floor, Harlech Court
Bute Terrace
Cardiff CF10 2FR

**Annette Conroy
(North-East Sporting
Club)**
144 High Street East
Sunderland
Tyne and Wear SR1 2BL
0191 567 6871

**Coventry Sporting
Club**
85 Lentons Lane
Aldermans Green
Coventry CV2 1NY
02476 614114

Pat Cowdell
129a Moat Road
Oldbury, Warley
West Midlands
0121 552 8082

Dennis Cross
8 Tumbling Bank
Blackley
Manchester M9 6AU
0161 720 9371

David Currivan
15 Northolt Avenue
South Ruislip
Middlesex HA4 6SS
0208 841 9933

Jim Curry
Ring Square
57 London Road
High Wycombe
Bucks HP11 1BS
07977 410648

Wally Dixon
Littlemoss House
1 Wayne Close
Littlemoss
Droylsden
Manchester M43 7LQ
0161 223 8855

**Jack Doughty
(Tara Promotions)**
Lane End Cottage
Golden Street
Off Buckstone Road
Shaw
Oldham OL1 8LY
01706 845753

Carl Dunn
20 Fennel Grove
South Shields
Tyne & Wear
NE34 8TH
0787 299 7258

**Jim Evans
(Evans-Waterman
Promotions)**
Abgah
88 Windsor Road
Bray
Berks SL6 2DJ
0162 862 3640

Spencer Fearon
4 Curtain Road
Liverpool Street
London EC2A NQE
07957 921235

**Jonathan Feld
(World Sports
Organisation)**
c/o Angel Media Group
Ltd
The Office Islington
338 City Road
London
EC1V 2PT
0207 183 0631

Joe Frater
The Cottage
Main Road
Grainthorpe
Louth
Lincs
0147 234 3194

**Stephen Garber
(Premier SC)**
PO Box 704
Bradford
West Yorks
BD3 7WU
0870 350 5525

Dave Garside
33 Lowthian Road
Hartlepool
Cleveland
TS26 8AL
0142 929 1611
07973 792588

Christopher Gilmour
Platinum House
120 Carnegie Road
Hillington Park
Glasgow
G52 4JZ
0773 041 5036

**Tommy Gilmour MBE
(St Andrew's Sporting
Club)**
Platinum House
120 Carnegie Road
Hillington Park
Glasgow G52 4JZ
0141 810 5700

Carl Greaves
62 Nelson Road
Balderton
Newark
Notts NG24 3EL
01636 612320

Johnny Griffin
0798 921 5287
0116 262 9287

**Richard Hatton MBE
(Punch Promotions)**
47-49 Rock Street
Gee Cross
Cheshire SK14 5JX
07919 523859

Tony Hay
Romilly House
201 First Avenue
Central Park
Petherton Road
Hengrove
Bristol
BS14 9BZ
0797 466 2968

**Barry Hearn
(Matchroom)**
'Mascalls'
Mascalls Lane
Great Warley
Essex CM14 5LJ
0127 735 9900

**Michael Helliet
(Mayfair Sporting
Club)**
Flat 1
102 Whitfield Street
London W1T 5EB
0207 388 5999
0784 363 6920

**Mick Hennessy
(Hennessy Sports)**
Ravensbourne
Westerham Road
Keston
Kent BR2 6HE
0844 800 7138

**Dennis Hobson
(Fight Academy)**
130 Handsworth Road
Sheffield
South Yorkshire
S9 4AE
0114 256 0555
07836 252429

**Dennis Hobson Snr
(DVSA Promotions)**
73 Darnall Road
Don Valley
Sheffield S9 5AH
0114 243 4700

Nicholas Hodges
Llys Y Deryn
Cilcennin
Lampeter
Ceredigion
SA48 8RR
0157 047 0452

**Jayson Hollier
(Shakespeare
Promotions)**
21 Hillmorton Road
Rugby CV22 5DF
07766 640829

Alma Ingle
26 Newman Road
Wincobank
Sheffield S9 1LP
0114 281 1277

**Philip Jeffries
(Bulldog Sports
Management Ltd)**
Silkworth Cottage
Warden Low Lane
Sunderland
SR3 2PD
0191 564 0202

**Errol Johnson
(EJKO Promotions)**
36 Newton Street
West Bromwich
B71 3RQ
0121 532 6118

**Thomas Jones
(Sports Management,
Hale, Ltd)**
13 Planetree Road
Hale
Cheshire WA15 9JL
0161 980 2661

Paul McCausland
1 Prospect Heights
Carrickfergus
Northern Ireland
BT38 8QY
0289 336 5942

M & J Promotions
Jane Couch & Sandra
Rowe
Spaniorum Farm Gym
Berwick Lane
Bristol
BS35 5RX
0772 504 5405

Malcolm McKillop
14 Springfield Road
Mangotsfield
Bristol
0117 957 3567

Patrick Magee
35 Deramore Park South
Belfast BT9 5BY
02890 748588

Frank Maloney
(Maloney Promotions)
33b High Street
Chiselhurst
Kent BR7 5AE
0208 467 7647

Rebecca Margel
10 Bentcliffe Lane
Leeds
LS17 6QF
0113 268 0681

John Merton
(John Merton
Promotions)
Merton Technologies
Ltd
38 Delaune Street
London SE17 3UR
0207 582 5200

Clifton Mitchell
Newton House
1 Broadway Park Close
Derby DE22 1BU
01332 367453

Alex Morrison
197 Swanston Street
Laird Business Park
Dalmarnock
Glasgow
G40 4HW
0141 554 7777

Katherine Morrison
197 Swanston Street
Laird Business Park
Dalmarnock
Glasgow
G40 4HW
0141 554 7777

Jonathan Pegg
(Pugilist Promotions)
9 Finchmead Road
Tile Cross
Birmingham
0121 770 2214

Brian Peters
The County Club
Dunshaughlin
Co.Meath
Ireland
00353 1824 0724

Ken Purchase
(Ringside Promotions)
Allscott Mill
Allscott
Telford TF6 5EE
0195 225 0950

Carlo Rea
15 Sandpiper Crescent
Coatbridge
ML5 4UW
07766 667660

Glyn Rhodes
166 Oldfield Road
Stannington
Sheffield S6 6DY
0114 232 6513

Gus Robinson MBE
Stranton House
West View Road
Hartlepool
Cleveland TS24 0BB
0142 923 4221

Ian Robinson
(Anglo American
Sporting Club)
Tollbar House
1 Manchester Road
Droylsden
Manchester M49 6ET
0161 301 3799

Paul Rowson
(PJ Promotions)
Roughstones
75 Catholic Lane
Sedgley
West Midlands
DY3 3YE
0190 267 0007

John Rushton
20 Alverley Lane
Balby, Doncaster
Yorks DN4 9AS
0130 231 0919

Chris Sanigar
Bristol Boxing Gym
40 Thomas Street
St Agnes
Bristol
Avon BS2 9LL
0117 949 6699

Jamie Sanigar
Bristol Boxing Gym
40 Thomas Street
St Agnes
Bristol
Avon BS2 9LL
0117 949 6699

Matt Scriven
(The Robin Hood
Executive Sporting
Club)
The Old One, Two
Fitness & Boxing Studio
2a Thoresby Street
Mansfield
Notts NG18 1QF
0783 399 5770

Kevin Spratt
8 Springfield Road
Guisley
Leeds LS20 8AL
0194 387 6229

Keith Walker
(Walkers Boxing
Promotions)
Headlands House
Business Centre
Suite 21-35
Spawd Bone Lane
Knottingley
West Yorks WF11 0HY
0197 766 2616

Frank Warren
(Sports Network)
Centurion House
Bircherley Green
Hertford
Herts SG14 1AP
0199 250 5550

Derek V. Williams
65 Virginia Road
Thornton Heath
Surrey CR7 8EN
0208 765 0492

Jane Wilton
(Belfast Boxing
Promotions)
The Bridge
42 Derryboy Road
Crossgar
Northern Ireland
BT30 9LH
0289 754 2195
0160 386 8606

Stephen Wood
(C/O Viking
Promotions)
Edward Street
Cambridge Industrial
Area
Salford
Manchester M7 1RL
0161 834 9496

Note: Hull & District Sporting Club and Ian Pauly, who promoted last season, no longer hold current promoter's licenses.

Licensed Managers

Babatunde Ajayi
2 Granville Square
Blakes Road
Peckham
London SE15 6DU
0207 732 1235

Michael Alldis
77 Buckswood Drive
Gossops Green
Crawley
West Sussex RH11 8HU
0773 435 1966

Chris Aston
54/56 May Street
Crosland Moor
Huddersfield
West Yorks HD4 5DG
0148 432 9112

Andy Ayling
Centurion House
Bircherley Green
Hertford
Herts SG14 1AP
0199250 5550

Bruce Baker
Unit 2 Six Acres
Stoddards Lane
Beckley, Nr Rye
East Sussex TN31 6UG
0207 592 0102

Robert Bannan
1c Thornton Street
Townhead, Coatbridge
North Lanarkshire
ML5 2NZ
0123 660 6736

Wayne Barker
1 Manchester Road
Droylsden
Manchester M43 6EP
0161 301 3799

Steven Barrett
22 Drake Crescent
North Thamesmead
London SE28 8PZ
0208 473 0655

Mark Bateson
33 Springfield Road
Guiseley
Leeds LS20 9AN
0777 860 1427

Jack Bishop
76 Gordon Road
Fareham
Hants
PO16 7SS
0132 928 4708

Adam Booth
57 Jackson Road
Bromley
Kent BR2 8NT
07932 952666

Peter Bowen
50 Newman Avenue
Lanesfield
Wolverhampton
West Midlands
WV4 6BZ
0190 282 8159

Jackie Bowers
36 Drew Road
Silvertown
London E16
0796 188 3654

Paul Boyce
Lodge Garage
Shelone Road
Briton Ferry
Neath
SA11 2NJ
0783 637 72702

David Bradley
The Dovecote
Aston Hall
Claverley
WV5 7DZ
0174 671 0287

John Branch
44 Hill Way
Holly Lodge Estate
London NE6 4EP

John Breen
Cedar Lodge
589 Antrim Road
Belfast BT15
0289 077 0238

Steve Butler
107 Cambridge Street
Normanton
West Yorks
WF6 1ES
0192 489 1097

Roy Callaghan
158 Harwich Road
Little Clacton
Essex
CO16 9NL
0793 994 7807

Scott Calow
18 Farnsworth Grove
Huthwaite
Notts
NG17 2NL
0787 664 1055

Enzo Calzaghe
51 Caerbryn
Pentwynmawr
Newbridge
Gwent
0149 524 8988

George Carman
5 Mansion Lane
Mobile Home Site
Iver
Bucks
S10 9RQ
0175 365 3096

Michael Carney
Bradley Elms Farm
Alton Road
Threapwood
Cheadle
Stoke on Trent
Staffs
ST10 4RA
0797 049 5597

Paul Carpenter
42 The Willows
Woodlands Park
Bedworth
07828 595309

Nigel Christian
22 Spire Court
Efford
Plymouth
PL3 6HP
0175 225 1136

Richard Clark
15 St John's Avenue
Sittingbourne
Kent ME10 4NE
01795 471662

Azumah Cofie
Suite 130
Dorset House
Duke Street
Chelmsford
Essex
CM1 1TB
0786 797 7406

David Coldwell
5 Penwood Park
Bramley
Rotherham
Yorks S66 3XS
0779 945 6400

Brian Coleman
31 Gwernifor Street
Mountain Ash
Mid Glamorgan
CF45 3NA
0785 906 1911

Tommy Conroy
144 High Street East
Sunderland
Tyne and Wear
0191 567 6871

David Cowland
3 Linkfield Court
78 Auckland Road
London SE19 2DQ
0208 771 5974

John Cox
68 Chilton Way
Duston
Northants NN5 6AR
0781 499 2249

Dave Currivan
15 Northolt Avenue
South Ruislip
Middlesex
0208 841 9933

David Davies
10 Bryngelli
Carmel
Llanelli
Dyfed SA14 7TL
0126 984 3204

John Davies
5 Ash Lane
Mancot
Deeside
Flintshire CH5 2BR
0776 550 8683

Ronnie Davies
3 Vallensdean Cottages
Hangleton Lane
Portslade
Sussex
0127 341 6497

Gary De Roux
68 Lynton Road
Peterborough
PE1 3DU
0173 334 2975

Walter Dixon
Littlemoss House
1 Wayne Close
Littlemoss
Droylsden M43 7LQ
0793 170 0478

Jack Doughty
Lane End Cottage
Golden Street
Off Buckstones Road
Shaw
Oldham OL2 8LY
0170 684 5753

Mickey Duff
40 Bilton Towers
Great Cumberland Place
London
W1H 7LD
0207 724 8494

Paul Dykes
7 Hadderidge
Burslem
Stoke on Trent
ST6 3ER
0783 177 7310

John Eames
83 Stokes Road
East Ham
London E6 3SF
0207 473 3173

Graham Earl
28 Talbot Road
Luton
Beds
LU2 7RW
0158 245 1117

Jim Evans
88 Windsor Road
Maidenhead
Berks SL6 2DJ
0162 862 3640

Graham Everett
7 Laud Close
Norwich NR7 0TN
0160 370 1484

Spencer Fearon
4 Curtain Road
Liverpool Street
London EC2A NQE
07957 921235

Jonathan Feld
c/o Angel Media Group
Ltd
555, White Hart Lane
London N17 3RN
0207 183 0631

Chris Firth
14 Fisher Avenue
Whiston
Prescot
Merseyside
L35 3PF
0151 289 3579

Tania Follett
123 Calfridus Way
Bracknell
Berks
RG12 3HD
07930 904303

Philippe Fondu
1b Nursery Gardens
Birch Cottage
Chislehurst
Kent
BR7 5BW
0208 295 3598

Ali Forbes
196 Brampton Road
Bexleyheath
London DA7 4SY
0208 855 5292

Steve Foster
62 Overdale
Swinton
M27 3DL
0784 250 8193

Winston Fuller
271 Cavendish Road
Balham
London
SW12 0PH
0793 917 7929

Joseph Gallagher
0161 374 1683

Dai Gardiner
13 Hengoed Hall Drive
Cefn Hengoed
Mid Glamorgan
CF8 7JW
0144 381 2971

Dave Garside
33 Lowthian Road
Hartlepool
Cleveland
TS26 8AL
0142 929 1611

Malcolm Gates
78 Cedar Drive
Jarrow
Tyne &Wear
NE32 4BG
0191 537 2574

Jimmy Gill
13 Thompson Close
Chilwell
Notts
NG9 5GF
0115 913 5482

Tommy Gilmour
Platinum House
120 Carnegie Road
Hillington Park
Glasgow
G52 4NY
0141 810 5700

Stephen Goodwin
Unit W1
Chester Enterprise
Centre
Hoole Bridge
Chester
0124 434 2012

Lee Graham
28 Smeaton Court
50 Rockingham Street
London SE1 6PF
0207 357 6648

Carl Greaves
62 Nelson Road
Balderton
Newark
Notts NG24 3EL
0163 661 2320

Carl Gunns
151e Goscote Hall Road
Birstall
Leicester LE4 3AZ
0116 267 1494

Christopher Hall
38 Fairley Way
Cheshunt
Herts
EN7 6LG
0783 813 2091

Jess Harding
c/o UK Industrial Pallets
Ltd
Travellers Lane
Industrial Estate
Travellers Lane
Welham Green
Hatfield
Herts
AL9 7HF
0170 727 0440

Tony Harris
237 Stapleford Road
Trowell
Notts
NG9 3QE
0115 932 3252

Oliver Harrison
Farrington House
Auckland Drive
Salford
M6 6FW
0781 882 2522

Richard Hatton
25 Queens Drive
Gee Cross
Hyde
Cheshire
SK14 5LQ
0161 366 8133

Barry Hearn
'Mascalls'
Mascalls Lane
Great Warley
Brentwood
Essex CM14 5LJ
0127 735 9900

Michael Helliet
Flat 1
Lower Ground Floor
102 Whitfield Street
London W1T 5EB
0207 388 5999

Martin Herdman
24a Crown Road
St Margarets
Twickenham
Middlesex TW1 3EE
0208 891 6040

Dennis Hobson
130 Handsworth Road
Sheffield S9 4AE
0114 256 0555

Dennis Hobson Snr
73 Darnall Road
Sheffield S9 5AH
0114 243 4700

Nicholas Hodges
Llys-y-Deryn
Cilcennin
Lampeter
Ceredigion
West Wales
SA48 8RR
0157 047 0452

Frank Maloney

Philip Sharkey

Frank Maloney
33b High Street
Chislehurst
Kent BR7 5AE
0208 467 7647

Lee Maloney
4 St Pauls Cottages
Wentlock Court
Halewood Village
Liverpool
L26 0TA
0797 102 4704

Nick Manners
5 Foundry Avenue
Harehills
Leeds LS9 6BY
0793 296 5863

Rebecca Margel
10 Bentcliffe Lane
Leeds
LS17 6QF
0113 268 0681

Michael Marsden
1 North View
Roydes Lane
Rothwell
Leeds
LS26 0BQ
0113 282 5565

Terry Marsh
60 Gaynesford
Basildon
Essex SS16 5SG
0207 0152207

Clifton Mitchell
Newton House
1 Broadway Park Close
Derby DE22 1BU
01332 367453

Alex Morrison
197 Swanston Street
Laird Business Park
Dalmarnock
Glasgow G40 4HW
0141 554 7777

Bert Myers
8 Thornhill Street
Burnley
Lancs BB12 6LU
0781 696 6742

Trevor Nerwal
Wayside Cottage
64 Vicarage Lane
Water Orton
Birmingham
B46 1RU
0121 730 1546

Frankie O'Connor
48 Belhaven Terrace
Wishaw
North Lanarkshire
ML2 7AY
0169 884 1813

Ian Pauly
1202 Lincoln Road
Peterborough
PE4 6LA
0173 331 1266

Alek Penarski
4 Vale Coppice
Horwich
Bolton BL 6 5RP
0120 446 9692

Joseph Pennington
215 North Road
Clayton
Manchester
M11 4WQ
0161 223 4463

Jimmy Phelan
5 Farrington Close
Bilton Grange
Hull HU9 4AT
01482 789 959

Brian Powell
138 Laurel Road
Bassaleg
Newport
Gwent NP10 8PT
0163 389 2165

Dean Powell
Sports Network
Centurion House
Bircherley Green
Herts
07956 905741

Glyn Rhodes
166 Oldfield Road
Stannington
Sheffield S6 6DY
0114 232 6513

Gus Robinson MBE
Stranton House
Westview Road
Hartlepool
TS24 0BB
0142 923 4221

Mark Roe
48 Westbrooke Road
Sidcup
Kent DA15 7PH
0208 309 9396

Harry Holland
12 Kendall Close
Feltham
Middlesex
0208 867 0435

Jayson Hollier
21 Hillmorton Road
Rugby CV22 5DF
0779 089 6635

Lloyd Honeyghan
PO Box 17216
London SE17 1ZU
07956 405007

Barry Hughes
5 Royal Exchange
Square
Glasgow G1 3AH
0777 188 8844

Brian Hughes MBE
41 Fold Green
Chadderton
Lancs OL9 9DX
0161 620 2916

Geoff Hunter
6 Hawkshead Way
Winsford
Cheshire CW7 2SZ
0160 686 2162

Dominic Ingle
5 Eccles Street
Sheffield
S9 1LN
0114 281 1277

John Ingle
20 Rockmount Road
Wincobank
Sheffield S9
0114 261 7934

Errol Johnson
36 Newton Street
West Bromwich
West Midlands
B71 3RQ
0121 532 6118

Thomas Jones
13 Planetree Road
Hale
Cheshire
WA15 9JL
0161 980 2661

Frank Joseph
29 Arlington Road
Ealing
London W13 8PF
0777 963 5783

Brian Lawrence
218 Millfields Road
London E5 0AR
0208 561 6736

Daniel Lutaaya
c/o Zaina Bukenya
41 Cresset House
Retreat Place
London E9 6RW
0795 162 7066

Pat Lynch
80 Broad Oaks Road
Solihull
West Midlands
B91 1HZ
01676 33374

Danny McAlinden
Flat 8, Beechey House
Watts Street
London E1W 2QF
07904 163258

Paul McCausland
1 Prospect Heights
Carrickfergus
Northern Ireland
BT38 8QY
0289 336 5942

Robert McCracken
Ravensbourne
Westerham Road
Keston
Kent BR2 6HE
0190 579 8976

Jim McDonnell
2 Meadway
Hillside Avenue
Woodford Green
Essex IG8 7RF
07860 770006

John McIntyre
123 Newton Avenue
Barrhead G78 2PS
0141 571 4393

Angel McKenzie
85e Herne Hill
London SE24 9NE
0207 737 2338

Owen McMahon
3 Atlantic Avenue
Belfast BT15
0289 074 3535

Colin McMillan
60 Billet Road
Chadwell Heath
Romford
Essex RM6 5SU
0208 597 4464

Patrick Magee
35 Deramore Park South
Belfast BT9 5JY
0289 043 8743

John Rooney
11 Cedar House
Erlanger Road
London
SE14 5TB
0788 407 7024

Paul Rowson
75 Catholic Lane
Sedgley
Dudley DY3 3YE
07976 283157

John Rushton
20 Alverley Lane
Balby
Doncaster
DN4 9AS
0130 231 0919

Chris Sanigar
Bristol Boxing Gym
40 Thomas Street
St Agnes
Bristol BS2 9LL
0117 949 6699

Trevor Schofield
234 Doncaster Road
Barnsley
South Yorks
S70 1UQ
0122 629 7376

Matthew Scriven
The Old One, Two
Fitness &Boxing Studio
2a Thoresby Street
Mansfield
Notts NG18 1QF
0783 399 5770

Mike Shinfield
126 Birchwood Lane
Somercotes
Derbys DE55 4NE
0177 360 3124

Tony Sims
67 Peel Place
Clayhall
Ilford
Essex IG5 0PT
0208 550 8911

Gurchuran Singh
Pro Gymnasium
Rear of 661 Foleshill
Road
Coventry
CV6 5JQ
0777 576 7815

Les Southey
Oakhouse
Park Way
Hillingdon
Middlesex
0189 525 4719

Glenroy Taylor
73 Aspen Lane
Northolt
Middlesex
U35 6XH
0795 645 3787

John Tiftik
2 Nuffield Lodge
Carlton Gate
Admiral Walk
London W9 3TP
0795 151 8117

Jack Trickett
Blossom Barn
Blossom Lane
Woodford
Cheshire
SK7 1RE
0161 439 8943

James Tugby
5 Burnside Close
Kirby in Ashfield
Notts
NG17 8NX
0777 022 6656

Louis Veitch
80 Sherborne Road
North Shore
Blackpool
FY1 2PQ
0125 362 8943

Keith Walker
Walkers Boxing
Promotions
Headland House
Suite 21-35
Spawd Bone Lane
Knottingley
West Yorks
WF11 0HY
0197 760 7888

Frank Warren
Centurion House
Bircherley Green
Hertford
Herts
SG14 1AP
0199 250 5550

Robert Watt
32 Dowanhill Street
Glasgow
G11
0141 334 7465

Delroy Waul
35 Gair Road
Reddich
Stockport
SK5 7LH
07796 271968

Derek V. Williams
65 Virginia Road
Surrey
CR7 8EN
0208 765 0492

Derek Williams
Pendeen
Bodiniel Road
Bodmin
Cornwall
PL31 2PE
0777 633 0516

John Williams
3a Langham Road
Tottenham
London
N15 3QX
0778 782 2245

Alan Wilton
The Bridge
42 Derryboy Road
Crossgar
BT30 9LH
0289 754 2195

Stephen Wood
Edward Street
Cambridge Industrial
Area
Salford
Manchester
M7 1RL
0161 834 9496

Richie Woodhall
3 Leasowe Green
Lightmoor
Telford
Shropshire
TF4 3QX
0195 259 3886

Tex Woodward
Spanorium Farm
Compton Greenfield
Bristol
BS12 3RX
0145 463 2448

Licensed Matchmakers

Neil Bowers
59 Carson Road
Canning Town
London
E16 4BD
0207 473 5631

Nigel Christian
22 Spire Court
Efford
Plymouth
PL3 6HP
0175 225 1136

Jim Evans
88 Windsor Road
Bray
Maidenhead
Berks SL6 2DJ
0162 862 3640

Jimmy Gill
13 Thompson Close
Chilwell
Notts NG9 5GF
0115 913 5482

Tommy Gilmour MBE
Platinum House
120 Carnegie Road
Hillington Park
Glasgow
G52 4NY
0141 810 5700

Roy Hilder
2 Farrington Place
Chislehurst
Kent BR7 6BE
0208 325 6156

John Ingle
20 Rockmount Road
Wincobank
Sheffield S9 1LP
0114 261 7934

Errol Johnson
36 Newton Street
West Bromwich
Birmingham
B71 3RQ
0121 532 6118

Michael Marsden
1 North View
Roydes Lane
Rothwell
Leeds LS26 0BQ
0113 282 2210

Ken Morton
3 St Quintin Mount
'Bradway'
Sheffield S17 4PQ
0114 262 1829

Jonathan Pegg
9 Finchmead Road
Tile Cross
Birmingham
B33 0LP
07973 635135

Dean Powell
Sports Network
Centurion House
Bircherley Green
Herts SG14 1AP
0199 250 5550

Richard Poxon
148 Cliffefield Road
Sheffield S8 9BS
0114 225 7856

Chris Sanigar
Bristol Boxing Gym
40 Thomas Street
St Agnes
Bristol
BS2 9LL
0117 949 6699

John Wilson
1 Shenley Hill
Radlett
Herts
WD7 3AS
01923 857874

Paul Rowson is one of boxing's new breed of manager/promoters   **Philip Sharkey**

Licensed BBBoC Referees, Timekeepers, Ringwhips and Inspectors

Licensed Referees

Class 'B'
Michael Alexander	Central Area
Nigel Gill	Midlands Area
Paul McCullagh	Northern Ireland
Kenneth Pringle	Scottish Area
Gary Williams	Northern Area

Class 'A'
Mark Curry	Northern Area
Kenneth Curtis	Southern Area
Keith Garner	Central Area
Paul Graham	Scottish Area
Stephen Gray	Central Area
Jeff Hinds	Southern Area
David Irving	Northern Ireland
Wynford Jones	Welsh Area
Shaun Messer	Midlands Area
Sean Russell	Northern Ireland
Grant Wallis	Western Area
Bob Williams	Southern Area
Andrew Wright	Northern Area

Class 'A' Star
Richie Davies	Southern Area
Phil Edwards	Central Area
Howard Foster	Central Area
Mark Green	Southern Area
Ian John-Lewis	Southern Area
John Keane	Midlands Area
Victor Loughlin	Scottish Area
Marcus McDonnell	Southern Area
Terry O'Connor	Midlands Area
Dave Parris	Southern Area
Mickey Vann	Central Area

Licensed Timekeepers

Arnold Bryson	Northern Area
Neil Burder	Welsh Area
Anthony Dunkerley	Midlands Area
Andrew East	Central Area
Robert Edgeworth	Southern Area
Dale Elliott	Northern Ireland
Martin Fallon	Midlands Area
Harry Foxall	Midlands Area
Eric Gilmour	Scottish Area
Gary Grennan	Central Area
Brian Heath	Midlands Area
James Kirkwood	Scottish Area
Jon Lee	Western Area
Roddy McAllister	Scottish Area
Michael McCann	Southern Area
Peter McCann	Southern Area
Barry Pinder	Central Area
Raymond Rice	Southern Area
Colin Roberts	Central Area
David Walters	Welsh Area

Kevin Walters	Northern Area
Nick White	Southern Area

Licensed Ringwhips

Jeremy Brown	Scottish Area
Michael Burke	Scottish Area
Steve Butler	Central Area
Ernie Draper	Southern Area
Mark Elkin	Midlands Area
Simon Goodall	Midlands Area
Mark Currivan	Southern Area
David Hall	Central Area
Mervyn Lewis	Welsh Area
Stuart Lithgo	Northern Area
Tommy Miller (Jnr)	Central Area
Sandy Risley	Southern Area
Tony Sarullo	Western Area
Stephen Sidebottom	Central Area
Gary Stanford	Southern Area

Inspectors

Herold Adams	Southern Area
Alan Alster	Central Area
William Ball	Southern Area
Richard Barber	Southern Area
Don Bartlett	Midlands Area
Gary Bevin	Central Area
David Boulter	Central Area
Geoff Boulter	Midlands Area
Fred Breyer	Southern Area
Walter Campbell	Northern Ireland
Edward Cassidy	Northern Ireland
Michael Collier	Southern Area
Dai Corp	Welsh Area
Julian Courtney	Welsh Area
Maurice Cunningham	Northern Ireland
Robert Curry	Northern Area
Mark Davidson	Central Area
Jaswinder Dhaliwal	Midlands Area
Christopher Dolman	Midlands Area
Will Downie	Scottish Area
Gordon Foulds	Scottish Area
Kevin Fulthorpe	Welsh Area
James Gamble	Northern Ireland
Paul Gooding	Welsh Area
Michael Hills	Northern Area
Alan Honnibal	Western Area
Wayne Hutton	Northern Ireland
James Ivory	Central Area
Philip Jones	Midlands Area
Nicholas Laidman	Southern Area
John Latham	Central Area
Kevin Leafe	Central Area
Denzil Lewis	Central Area
Eddie Lillis	Central Area
Reginald Long	Northern Area

Bob Lonkhurst	Southern Area
Sam McAughtry	Northern Ireland
Dave McAuley	Northern Ireland
Liam McColgan	Scottish Area
Billy McCrory	Northern Ireland
Keith MacFarlane	Scottish Area
Gerry McGinley	Scottish Area
Paul McKeown	Northern Ireland
Neil McLean	Scottish Area
Michael Madden	Northern Ireland
Paddy Maguire	Northern Ireland
Andy Morris	Central Area
Daryl Neatis	Northern Area
Thomas Nichol	Northern Ireland
Phil O'Hare	Central Area
Richard Parsons	Western Area
Ron Pavett	Welsh Area
Richard Peers	Central Area
Dave Porter	Southern Area
Fred Potter	Northern Area
Suzanne Potts	Midlands Area
Martin Quinn	Northern Ireland
Steve Ray	Central Area
Hugh Russell	Northern Ireland
Charlie Sexton	Scottish Area
Neil Sinclair	Southern Area
Glyn Thomas	Welsh Area
Nigel Underwood	Midlands Area
Richard Vaughan	Midlands Area
David Venn	Northern Area
Phil Waites	Midlands Area
Ron Warburton	Central Area
Mark Warner	Welsh Area
Danny Wells	Southern Area
Craig Williams	Northern Area
Robert Wilson	Scottish Area
Fred Wright	Central Area

Mark Green, Class 'A' Star referee

Philip Sharkey

VIP Promotions Ltd.

TAKING BOXING FORWARD

C/o Edward Street, Cambridge Industrial Area, Salford 7, Gtr Manchester M7 1RL
Tel: 0161-834 9496   Fax: 0161-832 8099   Email: swood@vip-ltd.co.uk

Manager & Promoter: Stephen Wood
Matchmaker: Ken Morton

Current List of VIP Boxers

Scott Mitchell – Heavyweight
Paul Keir – Cruiserweight
Alistair Morrison – L.Heavyweight
Carl Dilks – S.Middleweight
Tony Quigley – S.Middleweight
Martin Murray – Middleweight
Jamie Moore – L.Middleweight
Alex Matvienko – L.Middleweight
Brian Rose – L.Middleweight
Jack Arnfield – L.Middleweight
Shaun Horsfall – Welterweight
Chris Johnson – Welterweight
Mark Thompson – Welterweight
Chris O'Brian – Welterweight
Rick Godding – L.Welterweight
Tyrone Nurse – Lightweight
Lee Jennings – Lightweight
Tamao Dwyer – Lightweight
Michael Gomez – S.Featherweight
Gary Sykes – S.Featherweight
Anthony McCormack – S.Featherweight
Jon Kays – Featherweight
Mike Robinson – S.Bantamweight
Mark Moran – S.Bantamweight
Stuart McFadyen – Bantamweight
Gary Davies – Bantamweight

NB All Above Fighters Are Managed By Ourselves. Other Boxers Are Available Through Our Associate Connections

Regular Promotions / Good Management / Top-Class Training
Any unattached boxer should contact us direct to discuss their future
Website: www.vipboxing.com

Fully Licensed by the British Boxing Board of Control

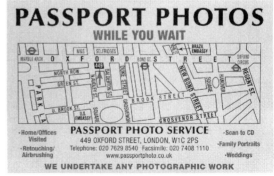

Boxers' Record Index

Advertisers